THE AVARS

THE AVARS

A Steppe Empire in
Central Europe, 567–822

Walter Pohl

CORNELL UNIVERSITY PRESS ITHACA AND LONDON

Original German-language edition, *Die Awaren: Ein Steppenvolk im Mitteleuropa, 567–822 n. Chr.* (3rd ed. 2015) by Walter Pohl, © Verlag C.H. Beck oHG, München 2015.

First published 2018 by Cornell University Press

Printed in the United States of America

Library of Congress Cataloging-in-Publication Data

Names: Pohl, Walter, 1953– author.
Title: The Avars : a steppe empire in Europe, 567–822 / Walter Pohl.
Other titles: Awaren. English
Description: Ithaca [New York] : Cornell University Press, 2018. |
    Includes bibliographical references and index.
Identifiers: LCCN 2018007698 (print) | LCCN 2018008080 (ebook) |
    ISBN 9781501729409 (pdf) | ISBN 9781501729416 (epub/mobi) |
    ISBN 9780801442100 | ISBN 9780801442100 (cloth ; alk. paper)
Subjects: LCSH: Avars—Europe, Central. | Europe, Central—History.
Classification: LCC DJK46.3 (ebook) | LCC DJK46.3.P6413 2018 (print) |
    DDC 943.0009/021—dc23
LC record available at https://lccn.loc.gov/2018007698

To my mother
Edith Pohl
1921–2016

Contents

Maps

Timeline

ca. 463	First mention of central Asian Avars in Byzantine sources (Priscus) in connection with westward migration of Sabirs, Ogurs, Saragurs, and Onogurs
527–565	Emperor Justinian I
552–555	The Turks under Bumin destroy the central Asian empire of the Rouran
Dec. 558/Jan. 559	First Avar embassy under Kandikh in Constantinople; Avars north of the Caucasus
559	Invasion by Cutrigurs under Zabergan stopped outside Constantinople by Belisarius
ca. 558–562	Western Turks under Istemi in alliance with the Persians subdue Hephthalite Empire
559–561	Avars advance north of the Black Sea and defeat Sabirs, Utigurs, and Antes
ca. 560–582/83	Baian, khagan of the Avars
560/61–572	Alboin, king of the Lombards
562/63	First Turkish embassy in Constantinople warns against alliance with the Avars
562	Sigibert I, king of the Franks, repels an Avar attack near the Elbe
563	Avars at the Lower Danube; negotiations about a settlement on Roman territory fail
565–578	Emperor Justin II
Nov. 565	The Avar envoy Targitius arrives shortly after Justin II's coronation; the emperor refuses to pay further subsidies
566	A second Avar expedition against the Franks under Sigibert I is victorious; he buys off the Avars with foodstuffs and concludes an alliance with them
566	The Gepids defeat the Lombards with Byzantine support, but do not hand over Sirmium to the Byzantines as promised
Winter 566/67	A Lombard embassy concludes an alliance against the Gepids with Khagan Baian, but only under great concessions

Fall 584	After the Byzantines have refused to raise the subsidies, the Avars capture Singidunum, Viminacium, and Augusta and march as far as Anchialus; failed mission of Comentiolus to the khagan
Spring 585	A second Byzantine embassy under Elpidius concludes a treaty with the Avars that raises the subsidies to 100,000 solidi
Fall 586	On the instigation of the fugitive Avar high priest Bookolabras, Maurice interns the Avar ambassador Targitius; the khagan renews his attacks and plunders Aquis, Bononia, Ratiaria, Apiaria, Durostorum, Zaldapa, Pannasa, Tropaeum Traiani, and Marcianopolis
Sept. 586	Avar-led Slavic siege of Thessalonica fails
587	War in Thrace, fighting at Tomis and at Sabulente Canalis; Avar attacks on Mesembria and unsuccessful sieges of Beroe, Diocletianopolis, and Philippopolis; successful intervention of John Mystacon at Adrianople
587/88	Avars and Slavs take Patras and other Greek cities and begin to settle in Greece
591–616	Lombard king Agilulf
591	Peace treaty between Byzantium and the new Persian king Chosroes
592	Slavs attack Singidunum; Avar war, fighting at the Procliana Pass; siege of Drizipera; Avar victory at Heraclea; General Priscus besieged in Tzurullon; renewal of the treaty
592	Bavarian campaign under Tassilo I against Slavs
593	Campaign of Priscus against Slavs north of the lower Danube; victories over the groups under Ardagast and Musucius
594	Slavic raids against Zaldapa, Aquis, and Scopi; Petrus leads a campaign against Slavs, victory over the Peiragast group, and defeat at the Helibacius
595	Campaign of Priscus against the Avars, confrontation at Singidunum; Avar raid on inland Dalmatia
595	Bavarian attack on Slavs; counterattack by the khagan, Bavarian army routed
596–597	Eighteen months of peace along the Danube
596	Avars attack Thuringia; the Frankish queen Brunhild buys them off
Fall 597	Avar campaign along the Danube; Avar army hibernates near Tomi

598	Fighting in Thrace, Comentiolus defeated at Iatrus; Avars capture Drizipera; their army decimated by the plague; Roman envoy Harmaton negotiates a rise of subsidies to 120,000 solidi
599	Offensive of Priscus on Avar territory: victories opposite Viminacium, and over the khagan's army at the Tisza
ca. 600	Avar peace treaties with Lombards and Franks
601/2	Avars, Slavs, and Lombards raid Byzantine Istria
601	Avar army under Apsikh and Roman army under Petrus face each other at the Iron Gate
602	Avars under Apsikh defeat the Antes; Roman units under Guduin attack Slavs north of the lower Danube, but rebel against the order to hibernate in Slavic lands
Nov. 602	Rebels under Phocas overthrow and kill Emperor Maurice
602–610	Emperor Phocas; new war against the Persians
Aug. 603	A Slavic contingent sent by the Avars helps the Lombard king Agilulf to take Cremona
ca. 604	Avar-Byzantine treaty; subsidies probably rise to 140,000 solidi
ca. 602/10–626/30	Another son of Baian reigns as khagan
604	Slavic surprise attack on Thessalonica
609/10	Avar-Slav raids in Illyricum
Fall 610	Civil war in Byzantium; Phocas overthrown
610–641	Emperor Heraclius
ca. 611	Avar victory over the Lombard dux of Friuli, Gisulf II; capture of Forum Iulii/Cividale and deportation of the captives to Pannonia
ca. 611	Bavarians under Garibald defeated by Slavs at Aguntum; Brunhild's enemies suspect her of plotting with the Avars
ca. 615	Avars and Slavs capture Naissus and Serdica
ca. 615	Siege of Thessalonica by Slavs under Chatzon
617 or 618	33-day siege of Thessalonica by Avars and Slavs under the command of the khagan
ca. 618	Avar expedition to Thrace
618/19	Avar-Byzantine treaty (180,000 solidi?)
June 623	Failed Avar ambush against Emperor Heraclius near Heraclea; raids inside the Long Walls
623	New treaty with subsidies of 200,000 solidi
623–638	Dagobert I, king of the Franks
623/24	Beginning of the successful rebellion of Slavs in Bohemia/Moravia under Samo

ca. 625–640	Salona abandoned because of Slavic pressure, population moves to Split
Summer 626	Great Avar siege of Constantinople with Persian support fails after ten days
Winter 627/28	The Persian war ends with Byzantine victory; Heraclius in Ctesiphon
630	Frankish embassy in Constantinople
630/31	Throne conflicts in the Avar Empire between an Avar and a Bulgar contender; flight of the defeated Bulgars to Bavaria, where a large part is massacred; survivors under Alciocus flee to the "March of the Vinedi" to Duke Walluc
ca. 631	Large-scale Frankish attack on Samo's kingdom repelled at Wogastisburc; Lombard victory over Slavs in the Alps
630/35	Bulgar Empire north of the Black Sea under Khan Kuvrat expands against Avars and Turks
636–642	Arab/Islamic expansion to Palestine, Syria, and Egypt
642–668	Emperor Constans II
650s/660s	Death of Khan Kuvrat; dissolution of his empire and rise of the Khazar khaganate
ca. 660	Death of Samo and dissolution of his kingdom
662–671	Grimoald, king of the Lombards
662	The dethroned Lombard king Perctarit, an exile at the Avar court, has to continue his flight because of diplomatic pressures by King Grimoald
663	Emperor Constans II fights the Lombards in southern Italy
663	Duke Lupus of Friuli rebels against King Grimoald; on Grimoald's invitation, the Avars invade Friuli, and Lupus falls in battle; the Avars leave only when Grimoald arrives with his army
ca. 663	Alzeco comes to Italy with his Bulgars and settles with Lombard consent in the duchy of Benevento
668–685	Emperor Constantine IV
July 677	A conflict with the Slavic prince Perbund leads to a Slavic siege of Thessalonica
678	An Arabic fleet is defeated at Constantinople
678/79	The last attested Avar embassy in Constantinople congratulates the emperor on his victory
680	Bulgars under Asparukh defeat the Byzantines near the Danube delta; Bulgar khanate established in Moesia

ca. 680	Kuver and his mixed group of Sermesianoi break free from Avar Pannonia and settle in the Keramesian Plain; failed plot of Mavros against Thessalonica
685–695, 705–711	Emperor Justinian II
712–744	Liutprand, king of the Lombards
ca. 713/14	Destruction of Lorch by the Avars
742	The Carantanians under Boruth repel an Avar attack with the support of the Bavarian duke Odilo; beginning of Bavarian overlordship and Christian mission in Carantania
748–788	Tassilo III, duke of the Bavarians
768–814	Charlemagne, king of the Franks
774	Charlemagne defeats the Lombard king Desiderius and becomes king of the Lombards
782	Avar embassy meets Charlemagne at Lippspringe; an Avar army appears at the Enns
788	Tassilo III dethroned and confined
788	Frankish-Avar War; Avars defeated near the Italian and Bavarian borders
790	Avar embassy in Worms; no consensus on the boundary
Aug. 791	A Frankish-Lombard army takes an Avar fortification at the Italian border
Fall 791	Great Avar campaign led by Charlemagne, departing from Lorch in September and proceeding to the Rába without much resistance; horse pestilence, return via Savaria
791–end of 793	Charlemagne in Regensburg; preparations for an Avar war, works for Danube-Main canal
793–795	Saxon uprising
794/95	Inner conflict in the Avar Empire; death of the khagan and the *iugurrus*
795	Envoys of the tudun meet Charlemagne at Hliune at the Elbe and offer submission
Fall 795	A Frankish-Slav army under Woynimir advances to the "ring" of the khagans and sacks it
796	The tudun comes to Charlemagne, submits, and is baptized; an army under Pippin of Italy and Duke Eric of Friuli sacks the ring again; the khagan submits; a synod at the Danube deals with the conversion of the Avars
797	Campaign of Eric of Friuli in Pannonia; fights against Slavs
End of 797	Avar embassy meets Charlemagne at Herstelle

798	Bishop Arn of Salzburg is raised to archbishop with a view to the eastern missions
799–803	Great Avar uprising against the Franks
799	Eric of Friuli is killed by the residents of Tarsatica; Prefect Gerold I is murdered during a campaign against the Avars
802	The counts Chadaloh and Goteram fall in a fight against Avars near the castellum Guntionis
802/03–814	Bulgar khan Krum
803	The Franks finally put down the Avar revolt; the tudun comes to Charlemagne at Regensburg and submits
ca. 804	Campaign of the Bulgar khan Krum against the Avars
Early 805	The Christian kapkhan Theodore visits Charlemagne in Aachen and asks for land because of Slavic attacks; he obtains the region between Carnuntum and Savaria, but dies soon
Sept. 805	The Avar khagan asks Charlemagne to reestablish his supreme rule; on September 21, he is baptized with the name Abraham in the Fischa river
805	The capitulary of Thionville institutes Lorch as a toll post toward Slavs and Avars
811	A Frankish army mediates in fights between Avars and Slavs in Pannonia; the *canizauci*, the tudun, and other Avar and Slavic princes are summoned to Aachen
811	Emperor Nicephorus invades Bulgaria and falls in battle; in the Bulgar army, Avars are also attested
814	Khan Krum plans to attack Constantinople; his army is said to have included Avar mercenaries; Krum dies before putting the plan into action
822	Last attested Avar embassy at the Frankish court
828	The administrative reform of the eastern territories of Bavaria removes the Avar tributary principality

Preface

The Avars dominated much of eastern central Europe from the late sixth to the end of the eighth century and were one of the big powers of the period: as powerful as Attila's empire, and as time-resistant as Mongol rule in eastern Europe. Still, historians have mostly neglected the Avar khaganate. The only longer study available in the English language is a ninety-page article by H. H. Howorth in the *Journal of the Royal Asiatic Society* published in 1889.[1]

The present book therefore fills a gap. It was first published in German in 1988 and is now in its third edition.[2] I am grateful to Cornell University Press for accepting to publish an English translation. Preparing it was not an easy task and has taken a number of years to complete. I first cut some sections dealing with outdated debates or regional problems. Then the text was translated into English. I continued working on the basis of the translation and ended up introducing major revisions and updates. The basic approach, set out in the first chapter, remains the same. Fortunately, relatively little had to be changed in the historical narrative. Caution in reconstructing events on the basis of patchy or doubtful sources had been part of the initial approach; in some respects I have become even more cautious over the years. Still, my aim remained to provide a historical narrative where feasible, even though sometimes alternative reconstructions would be possible. The bottom line of a six-hundred-page book should not be that ultimately we cannot tell what happened.

In some fields, new evidence and lively debates have made substantial revisions necessary. Much has happened in research on the central Eurasian steppes, which was relevant both for the Eurasian background of Avar history and for structural comparison. There is also much recent research and debate about the early Slavs that I had to take on board; readers may notice that I have further developed my own position on the subject, already sketched in the German version. Even more has changed in archaeology, where an enormous amount of new evidence has emerged in the last thirty years. Some of the paradigms current when I wrote the German book were also transformed. Therefore, thanks to the advice of a number of eminent archaeological colleagues, I have completely rewritten the archaeological sections of this book. On the whole, I cannot claim to have done full justice to all the new works on different aspects of the topic that have appeared in thirty years. In the course of revising the manuscript, I frequently had to refrain from going deeper into many issues that are somehow connected to the topic of the book, but not central to it. Unfortunately, I have not been able to consult two books still in the making while I finished mine: Georgios Kardaras was preparing an English version of his Greek book on the Avars and Byzantium; and Csanád Bálint will present a larger, more archaeologically oriented synthesis of the same subject.[3] On the whole, I am confident that my book provides an overview of Avar history that, as far as possible, corresponds to the state of the art in the various disciplines involved and offers a number of new ideas, also as compared with the German version.

This book, which already has a history in itself, owes a lot to more people than I can possibly acknowledge here. Before and all the more since it appeared in German I had many opportunities to exchange ideas with numerous scholars who know much more about aspects of the topic than I would ever be able to master. The first thanks go to my academic teacher, Herwig Wolfram, who suggested to me to work on the Avars early in my career. Falko Daim provided the opportunity (and the funding) to concentrate on the Avar book in his part of a large project in the 1980s. C. H. Beck publishers accepted the book for publication and have kept it on the market since it appeared. A number of eminent British and American colleagues then sought a publisher for an English translation but were told that both the Avars and the author were too little known to promise relevant sales. Therefore, I am particularly grateful to Florin Curta for having raised interest in the book at Cornell University Press, and of course to Cornell for having accepted it. Will Sayers has swiftly translated it. Since that time, I have taxed the patience of John Ackerman, Peter Potter, and Mahinder S. Kingra, under whose guidance the book has finally gone to press. Thanks are also due to the scholarly institutions that I could rely on during my work: the University of Vienna, with its Institut für Österreichische Geschichtsforschung; the Institute for Medieval Research of the Austrian Academy of Sciences, which has offered me a generous research environment during the time when I worked on the English version; and not least, the Austrian Research Fund FWF and the European Research Council, which at different stages supported my research with grants and projects.[4]

Among the colleagues and scholars who have read sections of the English version and/or helped me with advice, material, and bibliography, my special thanks go to Csanád Bálint, Francesco Borri, Florin Curta, Falko Daim, Nicola Di Cosmo, Max Diesenberger, Stefan Eichert, Andreas Fischer, Herwig Friesinger, Matthias Hardt, Wolfgang Haubrichs, Georg Holzer, Michael Maas, Johannes Preiser-Kapeller, Helmut Reimitz, Philipp von Rummel, Pavlína Rychterová, Peter Stadler, Tsvetelin Stepanov, Peter Štih, Erik Szameit, Tivadar Vida, Herwig Wolfram, and Jozef Zábojník. Over the years, I have also profited much from exchanges with Alexander Avenarius (†), Volker Bierbrauer, Sebastian Brather, Rajko Bratož, Neven Budak, Evangelos Chrysos, Slavko Ciglenečki, Uwe

Fiedler, Éva Garam, Patrick J. Geary, Franz Glaser, Peter B. Golden, John Haldon, Guy Halsall, Orsolya Heinrich-Tamáska, Joachim Henning, Hajnalka Herold, David Kalhous, Radoslav Katičić, Attila Kiss (†), Gábor Kiss, Johannes Koder, Sabine Ladstätter, Mihailo Milinković, Róbert Müller, Leena Mari Peltomaa, Andrew Poulter, András Róna-Tás, Alexander Sarantis, Michael Schmauder, Peter Schreiner, Andreas Schwarcz, Sören Stark, Béla Miklós Szőke, Jaroslav Tejral, Frans Theuws, Péter Tomka, Przemysław Urbańczyk, István Vásáry, Ian Wood, and Daniel Ziemann. Christina Pössel corrected the English in some chapters. Finally, Nicola Edelmann helped me with footnotes, bibliography, and copy editing throughout the long phase of preparation of this book.

THE AVARS

APPROACHING THE AVARS

The first chapter of this book addresses the question of why and how we can write a history of the Avars. Why are the Avars significant for European history, and why have they remained a marginal concern in its study? At a point where Eurocentric history is being criticized as seeing the world from a hegemonic but rather particular historiographic perspective, it seems promising to turn to a neglected Eurasian element in the European past: the steppe peoples. The history of contemporary perceptions, and of scholarly study of this alternative form of life in premodern Europe, is interesting in itself and exposes the deep ambiguity of European attitudes to its both threatening and fascinating eastern neighbors.

1.1 Marginal Europeans?

Few of the peoples who determined the fate of Europe during the transition from Antiquity to the Middle Ages have remained so poorly known as the Avars. For almost a quarter millennium, from 558 to 796, they ruled vast stretches of central and eastern Europe from their power base on the middle Danube. At the height of its power the Avar khaganate put the Byzantines and the Franks on the defensive, maintained relations with peoples as distant as the Persian Sassanians and the Turks of central Asia, and put a decisive stamp on Slavic expansion between the Baltic and the Aegean. After the fall of the Avar Empire, the court of

Charlemagne was astonished at the treasures that had been amassed in the "ring" of the khagans between the Danube and the Tisza.

Nevertheless the Avars have remained alien to European history. Attila's Huns, who maintained their rule for only a few decades, are much more present in the consciousness of posterity. *The Song of the Nibelungs* (*Das Nibelungenlied*) and frescoes in the Vatican tell of Attila, and European schoolchildren learn his name. The khagan Baian, who established the Avars as a great power, is hardly mentioned in reference works. This may also be due to the fact that he and his successors gave his western neighbors, Franks and Lombards, little cause for complaint. While the Huns and the Magyars made their way from the Carpathian Basin across half of western Europe, the Avars directed their attacks almost exclusively against Byzantium.

The Avars themselves have remained mute for us. Whereas the rulers of the Bulgars and the Turks in this same era had lengthy inscriptions chiseled in stone, we know of only a few brief runic texts from the Avar domain. As a consequence, the history of the Avars was written by their enemies. For contemporary observers the opponent was almost anonymous. Baian is the only Avar ruler whose name has been transmitted; all the others are designated in the sources by their title, khagan. A handful of other exotic titles, such as *iugurrus, kapkhan, canizauci*, and a scant dozen names are all that has been preserved. Does this anonymity reflect a conscious program or does it express the chroniclers' sense of Avar foreignness?

For them this "ugly nation of hairy barbarians" appeared faithless, brutal, greedy, and unpredictable.[1] At the same time the Byzantines were not reluctant to adopt the military accomplishments of the "barbarians" such as the stirrup, which Avar horsemen from the steppe were the first to introduce into Europe. The armies of the Christian empire and the "ugly" central Asian horsemen had more in common than could be accounted for by the ideology of the times. The modern historical sciences have long fed on the prejudices of their informants. A "deadly storm tide" that drew "prosperous states and peoples into the maelstrom of a common annihilation" is how the Avars are viewed by one of their most distinguished modern historians.[2]

That the Avar military campaigns often spread death and destruction across the provinces of the Byzantine Empire cannot be denied. The army of the khagans resembled a highly specialized war machine,[3] which only war itself could keep running. Yet what appeared to the enemy as blind rage was a carefully managed economy of force, a skillful alternation of threats, attacks, and negotiations that sustained the outpouring of riches from the empire. The khaganate made it possible for warriors to acquire in regulated fashion the prestige and goods through which they expressed their status and power. For the empire in turn, war and peace, inside and outside, became rather calculable. The highly militarized late Roman state and the barbarian rulers competed for the distribution of the wealth still produced by the Mediterranean economy. In the west the post-Roman kingdoms of the Goths, Franks, and Lombards successfully mastered the apparatus of the state. The Avars did not aim for similar integration. When they made the attempt, like the later Bulgars and Hungarians, of founding a Christian state on the Roman model, it was too late to give their empire a durable foundation. The Christian khaganate, which the last Avars tried to establish east of Lake Neusiedl, was a belated caricature of the lost opportunity of integration in Christian Europe.

This failure was clearly the outcome of a centuries-long process and not its precondition, as a cliché-driven historiography of these nomads might easily lead us to believe. It was not because of the Avars' savagery and foreignness that they remained barbarians and as such disappeared again from history. The conditions for this failure at the same time led to the making of Europe as we know it, and thus are a part of the early history of the West. Medievalists should therefore not assume that a Frank, a Roman, or a Byzantine in the sixth, seventh, or eighth century was "one of us" and that an Avar on the other hand was a foreigner. For a long time, the "Germanic" peoples were seen as the direct ancestors of the Germans and thus as subjects of history, while the eastern barbarians were a matter for ethnography. An ethnocentric world view could establish the superiority of the Christian West (or even worse, the Nordic race) by drawing on prejudices that were already well known to Antiquity. For his war of conquest against the godless Avars Charlemagne was able to draw on a whole register of conventional resentment.[4] In the modern age similar propaganda has accompanied the colonial subjugation of "savages" overseas. From the nineteenth century on, nationalism sought its justification to no little extent in a misconceived view of the peoples of the early Middle Ages.

Our painfully slow emergence from nationalism and ethnocentricity gives research on the barbarians a new relevance. After a century that reached the pinnacle of civilization but also the pinnacle of barbarity (in its pejorative sense), we need to account for the origins of our culture's double face anew. The way in which the Other was fixed in prejudice and eventually repressed in the course of a process of civilization has become an issue. The nomad, the nonsedentary is discovered as the quintessential Other. For instance, a postmodern "treatise on nomadology" set out to explore ways to a "nomadic thinking" that would transcend the dualistic logic of the West.[5] Ethnology, once a discipline that reaffirmed the superiority of occidental culture, is now expected to provide information on alternative forms of life and material for the critique of civilization. Cultural transfers, acculturation, and the formation of identities become preferred areas of interdisciplinary research.

As long as such an interest does not fall back into the cliché of the noble savage, which from the time of Tacitus was the obverse of the barbarian stereotype, early medieval studies will have to take it seriously. An impressive array of research over the last decades has revealed the diversity of lifestyles in early medieval Europe and their complementarity. Even in the east-central European domain of the Avars a whole series of cultural patterns abutted one another. Where written sources are silent, archaeology is eloquent; some sixty thousand Avar graves have been excavated so far.[6] The possibilities and limitations of historical interpretation of such finds are certainly not uncontested, and the dialogue between archaeology and historical research suffers from occasional misunderstandings. Yet results to date have clarified a great deal. Ethnic diversity and flexibility, cultural exchange, often over great distances, wide-ranging political activity, and regional differentiation emerge with increasing clarity from current investigations into the empires of the steppe.[7] Early medieval peoples consisted of diverse groups that had found a common political frame and soon felt that they belonged; this simple model is quite useful to understand ethnicity on the steppe.[8] The unusually rapid course of such ethnic processes in steppe environments permits new perspectives on the dynamics in the formation of ethnic identities.

Writing a history of the Avars presents two very different challenges. On the one hand it must address the many questions of detail that have arisen from recent advances in our understanding. Given the paucity of historical information, nuances in the interpretation of the sources may lead to a significantly different overall picture. An overview of the basic sources and of discussions among specialists is therefore necessary. The present work consciously runs the risk of interdisciplinarity and from the medievalist's side seeks a dialogue with the numerous disciplines involved: archaeology and ancient history, ethnology, classical, Byzantine, Slavic, and Oriental studies, in addition to an array of other philologies, whose research findings will enrich our knowledge of the Avars. Since the author has not mastered the methodology of all these disciplines, he must often limit himself to reporting their results and assess them from a historian's perspective. Nevertheless, in the case of the Avars such a synopsis is all the more necessary. It is to be hoped that the overview thus obtained may compensate for deficiencies in matters of detail. If this history of the Avars can serve as a tool for a diversity of future investigations that go far beyond its own possibilities, it will have attained its goal. Several new aspects and questions that are here raised will hopefully be of use.

On the other hand, it is not enough to recount the many ramifications of specialist studies and, to that end, advance a collection of material plus respective historical critique. The objective of this book, whatever the difficulties, is a view of the whole. If the confrontation between barbarian and imperial policies, the encounters between various patterns of culture and social organization are described here, it is in order to contribute toward an understanding of a process from which, ultimately, the European Middle Ages would emerge. Perhaps a neglected part of the picture of European history can thereby be made more evident. The present history of the Avars is also directed to those readers for whom the fate of this—and other—early peoples has hitherto been less than familiar and who, like the author, are prepared to accept the challenge of this alterity.

1.2 Sources and Prejudices

Historical accounts of the Avars come from their neighbors, who were often also their enemies, peoples who by virtue of religion and culture felt superior to them. This does not invalidate such sources. Partisan historical representations are seldom completely pulled from thin air. A millennium of classical ethnography had turned prejudice, as topos, into a method.[9] The cultivated Byzantine and his often somewhat less cultivated contemporary in the West long saw the "Scythians," as they were still occasionally called, through the eyes of Herodotus, Strabo, and Justin. Synesius of Cyrene stated in about the year 400, when new peoples were crossing the borders of the empire almost yearly: "There are no new barbarians; the old Scythians are always thinking up new names to deceive the Romans."[10] The view he expressed remained a reference point until the Carolingian era and beyond. The Huns were often called Scythians, and the Avars and Bulgars, in their turn, Huns. The Hungarians were variously named Scythians, Huns, Avars, or Turks. Goths and after them occasionally even Slavs were identified as *Getae*. Most of them were linked with the apocalyptic peoples Gog and Magog of the Bible, who were still entered on maps of the High Middle Ages.[11]

In the first centuries A.D., most authors distinguished crudely between "Scythians," armed horsemen who came from the steppe, and "Germans," who lived in the West. In late Antiquity, the Goths were consistently counted among the eastern "Scythians." Judgments were often schematic, as made by Procopius when he alluded to the "Hunnic" lifestyle of the Slavs. The passage is nevertheless a good example of how the use of the topos still permitted the communication of reliable information.[12] A manual on warfare written about 600, called the *Strategicon* of Maurice, divides the barbarians into four groups according to their ways of life and war: the Persians; the "blond peoples," among whom the Franks and Lombards (the collective term *German* was not used any more at the time); the "Scythians," that is, the Avars and Turks and the other Hunnic peoples; and the Slavs and Antes.[13] For military purposes this was evidently adequate.

In the sixth or seventh century it was not difficult to acquire information about the barbarians. Even the distant Turks, soon after their first embassy, maintained a colony counting more than a hundred residents in Constantinople.[14] Byzantine diplomats regularly gathered information on all the peoples who could be of interest to imperial diplomacy. In wartime it was often of decisive importance to be up-to-date on the political structure, modes of warfare, or internal tensions among the barbarians. This was the case not only for the imperial court but to a degree also for the residents of every province that had to reckon with barbarian incursions. The way in which clerics of Thessalonica describe the various attacks on their city in the *Miracula Sancti Demetrii* shows a relatively sound knowledge of the enemy.

Even the sober accounts of well-informed contemporaries are stamped with often unstated value judgments. To a cultivated Byzantine (and to a pious cleric in the West) nomadic life must have appeared coarse, brutal, and uncivilized. A summary of the barbarian topoi in Ammianus Marcellinus (fourth century) offers, inter alia, the following characteristics typical of barbarians: savagery, lack of restraint, rage, excessive courage, arrogance, cunning, boldness, inconstancy, greed.[15] Even the names, coincidentally or not, were eloquent: *Avari* could be understood in Latin as "the greedy," *Bulgares* as "the vulgar," and the name of the Slavs apparently gave reason to replace the ancient *servus* with the modern word "slave." With such a negative perspective it made no difference that barbarian society was occasionally described for culture-critical purposes as a positive antithesis to the writer's own world, as Tacitus in his *Germania* or Salvian of Marseille illustrate. Even though the Avars found no Tacitus of their own, there are individual examples of this attitude. The ecclesiastical historian John of Ephesus describes how the Avar conquerors in 582 generously gave food to the half-starved inhabitants of Sirmium: "People also speak of the compassion shown by the barbarians to the inhabitants, on seeing the pitiable condition to which they were reduced by famine, and which well deserves the admiration of Christians, whose conduct too frequently it condemns; because they do not show kindness to their fellow-servants, nor pity those of their own flesh."[16] Something similar happened later in the midst of war when the khagan gave the opposing Roman army some wagonloads of food, so that they might celebrate Easter in proper fashion.[17] That the simple life among the "Scythians" could offer an attractive alternative to many disaffected Greeks is illustrated in Priscus's account of a Greek merchant he met at the court of Attila who had advanced to the status of Hun warrior. To the harsh criticism of the Roman-turned-barbarian who wished to "enjoy undisturbed the fruits of his bravery" the author opposes an apology for the Roman world.[18]

The Romans' sense of superiority over the savages could not be shaken by such traces of noble innocence in the portrait of the barbarians. The atrocities that were ascribed to "Scythians" of all kinds served as illustrations of the fact that a life with human dignity was impossible outside the Roman-Christian ecumene. For many, this perception rose to the intensity of a blind hate, as exhibited in the tirades of Theodore Syncellus after the siege of Constantinople in 626. He viewed the khagan as the "pernicious offspring of the eternally evil spirit; he has shown himself to be the devil's son, not by the necessity of nature, but by his own decision, and all devilish turpitude is incarnated in him. Like an anti-god who strives for dominance over land and sea, he stretches his mouth up toward heaven and with his tongue reaches down to earth in order to annihilate the people of God like abandoned eggs."[19] Such depictions most of all served as a moralistic summons to desist from sin, because of which God had sent such punishments. The notion that barbarian incursions befell Christianity as divine retribution had become self-evident for contemporaries. The Frankish author of the seventh-century *Chronicle of Fredegar* put this thought in the mouth of Samo, king of the Wends, when he is vilified as a "heathen dog" by a Frankish ambassador: "Then if you are God's servants, and we his hounds, and since you persist in offending Him, we are within our rights to tear you to pieces!"[20] Christian Byzantine state ideology could only regard the existence of pagan, hostile barbarian kingdoms on its borders as a passing trial or punishment in the context of the divine plan of salvation. Baptism and subjugation by the emperor remained the ultimate objectives of Byzantine (and later also Frankish) policy.

Being savage, faithless, cruel, and perfidious was the very modality of the existence of Avars and other "Huns," quite independent of how they might comport themselves. It is to the credit of many Byzantine authors that these ascriptions, with which they are lavish, do not fully obscure the reality behind the accounts. The course of the battles between the Byzantines and the Avars, as they are depicted in Menander, Theophylact Simocatta, and others, reveals that neither side had much for which to condemn the other. Yet one has the impression that senseless cruelties rather belonged in the repertory of the Christian empire. The rare forays into enemy territory were regularly exploited for the massacre of sleeping noncombatants.[21] A captive Persian emissary, during the siege of 626, was sent back to the khagan demonstratively mutilated, with the severed head of another fastened around his neck.[22] Only exceptionally did the khagan have his prisoners massacred.[23]

Breaches of treaties occurred on both sides. The Byzantines were the first to detain Avar envoys.[24] But clearly the khagan did not balk at swearing false oaths of various kinds and violating diplomatic rules.[25] The *Strategicon* of Maurice draws from this the usual conclusions: "They are very superstitious, treacherous, foul, faithless, possessed by an insatiate desire for riches. They scorn their oath, do not observe agreements, and are not satisfied by gifts. Even before they accept the gift, they are making plans for treachery and betrayal of their agreements."[26] The same manual repeatedly counsels Roman commanders to miss no opportunity to deceive the opponent and take him by surprise.[27] The policies of both the empire and the barbarians operated with similar methods, and the inhabitants of the Roman provinces had good reason to fear imperial forces almost as much as the barbarians.[28] The *pax Romana* was no less an expansive program than the hegemonic aspirations of the khagan. When Menander has the Emperor Justin say to Avar emissaries, "A war would do the Romans more good than a peace,"[29] this was no mere bluff. Byzantine armies initiated hostilities just as often as did the Avars. When boundaries threatened to become blurred in this way, language had to establish clear distinctions. The rhetoric provided a basis for dealing with the barbarians.

Rigorous criticism of the texts is therefore necessary. Even though the sources for the history of the Avars should not be summarily dismissed as "literary constructs" or "opaque barriers," text and context have to be considered critically, especially since many of them were written down at some temporal distance from events and were often transmitted in much later manuscripts.[30] Sources have all too often been exploited as mere mines of information in research on the Avars; the validity of isolated pieces of information has been accepted or rejected on the basis of sometimes quite arduous reconstructions of the events. Despite all the distortions, the contemporary accounts of the barbarians represent the traces of a tempestuous encounter of cultures, a dialogue that had consequences for both sides.

We owe a substantial part of the information on the European Avars to Byzantine authors. The newcomers from the East arrived in the 550s in one of the most productive periods of Byzantine historiography. Few periods of Roman history are so well documented as the reign of Justinian. Procopius's eight-volume history of Justinian's wars goes up to 552 and gives a rather detailed if sometimes polemical description of the empire and its barbarians prior to the arrival of the Avars.[31] Agathias, who wrote during the reign of Justin II, picked up the thread of his work and continued it to the year 559.[32] But of the Avars he mentions only their hairstyle. Menander Protector successively wrote a history of the years 558 to 582, our primary source for the first Avar wars. Unfortunately the work itself is lost. But its numerous accounts of embassies, based on excellent sources of information, were fortunately still judged so instructive in the tenth century that many were incorporated in the *Excerpta de legationibus*.[33] The last of the literarily versed and historically interested jurists who has left us a work of early Byzantine history is Theophylact Simocatta. Under the emperor Heraclius he continued the work of Menander and described the reign of Maurice (582–602).[34] This Egyptian, who was long judged by classical philologists a "paragon of the grotesque" because of his luxuriant rhetoric, is our chief witness for Avar history.[35] It may well be that in this mimetic homage to classical models he no longer reaches the level of his predecessors. Moreover, he seems to have misunderstood and arbitrarily arranged some of his at times excellent sources. Nonetheless, the extensive descriptions offer on the whole a valuable picture of the battles and thus also of the policies of the khaganate.

The experiences of Byzantine generals in the Avar and Slav wars under Maurice informed a source of a different kind: a manual on warfare that was compiled around 600 by an anonymous author, known as the *Strategicon* of Maurice.[36] Whoever the author was, it is a handbook based on praxis that illustrates how pragmatic and flexible the Byzantines could be in their relations with their opponents and how seriously they took the conduct of psychological warfare.

Not only the military but also the church was challenged by the barbarian incursions. One of the most interesting but also most debated sources for the early Avar period is the *Ecclesiastical History* of John of Ephesus, preserved in a Syrian compilation from the time of the Crusades, the work of Michael the Syrian. A Monophysite bishop, John spent the last years of his life around 580 cloistered near Constantinople, where, well on in years, he still incorporated a considerable amount of current information.[37] He wrote under the fresh impression of the first great Avar-Slav invasion of 584 on the basis of indirect information, so he reflects perceptions in Constantinople rather than actual events. Some material about the Avars is also found in the *Ecclesiastical History* of Evagrius Scholasticus, probably composed in 593 in Syria.[38]

Firsthand information assembled with hagiographic intentions is found in the *Miracula Sancti Demetrii*, a collection of accounts of the miraculous interventions of the patron saint in the manifold crises that befell his city, Thessalonica. The first part, written during the reign of Heraclius, recounts among other things the first great Avar-Slav siege of the city. Further attacks are described in a continuation compiled toward the end of the seventh century.[39] The supernatural actions of Demetrius are swiftly woven into a surprisingly sober account, rich in detail and for the most part quite plausible—after all, the audience of the text, the citizens of Thessalonica, had also witnessed the sieges.[40]

Similar intentions to reinforce the cohesion of the community during difficult times guided the composition of Theodore Syncellus's sermon on the liberation of Constantinople from the hardships of the Avar siege in the year 626. Composed on the heels of these events, it expostulates on the moral, salvific, and eschatological dimension of the rescue of the imperial city by the Mother of God.[41] The same events are treated in two further contemporary sources: One is a poem composed for the occasion by George of Pisidia, which, despite all its rhetorical effects, offers some valuable pieces of information.[42] The other is the less high-blown, unfortunately incomplete but still relatively extensive account of the Easter Chronicle (*Chronicon Paschale*).[43]

After 626 the Avars more or less disappear from the field of vision of Byzantine historiography. The seventh and eighth centuries are, to a degree, the dark ages of the writing of history in Byzantium.[44] After Theophylact Simocatta the chronicle tradition breaks off. It is not until the late eighth century that we again find a historical work on a grander scale. The patriarch Nicephorus, in his *Breviarium*, gives some relevant information about the Avars and Bulgars.[45] More extensive is the *Chronography* of Theophanes the Confessor, composed soon after 810 by a well-connected monk. The years between 285 and 813 are dealt with in annalistic fashion, with, however, some chronological uncertainties. For the period of the Avar wars the chronicler draws mostly on the work of Theophylact; for the seventh century, he relies on the same set of information as Nicephorus.[46]

Finally, a considerable enrichment to our knowledge of the Avars is offered by two later works. In the tenth century the learned emperor Constantine Porphyrogenitus compiled the celebrated treatise *De administrando imperio* in the framework of a vast encyclopedic undertaking. Particularly for the history of the western Balkans and for the early Croats and Serbs this work offers unique material, albeit often with a tendency toward the legendary.[47] The *Suda Lexicon*, compiled at the close of the tenth century, also contains some otherwise unknown passages about the Avars, among which some fragments from Menander.[48]

In the Latin West less notice was initially taken of the Avars. Very sketchy statements are found in some contemporary chronicles, as for example in Victor of Tunnuna, John of Biclaro, and Isidore of Seville. The lost work of Secundus of Trento, who died in 612, is only known from extensive excerpts found in Paul the Deacon's Lombard history.[49] His contemporary Pope Gregory the Great was above all interested in the ecclesiastical disputes of the time. But his letters do provide valuable clues for understanding the displacements of the Slavs and Avars in the direction of the Adriatic.[50] The khaganate plays a similarly peripheral role in the work of Gregory of Tours.[51] The *Chronicle of Fredegar* in the mid-seventh century provides patchy but valuable information on events east of the Frankish frontier.[52] The principal source for relations between the Avars and the West from the beginning is the Lombard history that Paul the Deacon, connected to both Lombard and Carolingian courts, committed to vellum toward the end of the eighth century. Since his origins were in Friuli, he also had family traditions about experiences with the Avars.[53] The conflicts between the Franks and the

Avars on the one hand and the Bavarians and the Slavs on the other up to the year 610, the Lombard-Avar entente, and the two raids on Friuli are for the most part known only from his record.

When Paul composed his history of the Lombards, the Avars were again on Charlemagne's political agenda for the Franks. The *Royal Frankish Annals* and a series of other annalistic works register precisely, if often scantily, the various stages of the conflict with the eastern neighbor.[54] The collapse of the khaganate for the first time revealed, as if on an operating table, its inner structure to Frankish observers. Now, since everyone seemed to be driving his own foreign policy, the various dignitaries with their oriental titles could be recorded in the annals, albeit not without some phonetic difficulty.

The heroes of the wars against the Avars were celebrated before the Carolingian public. A poem on the victory of King Pippin over the Avars in 796 and an obituary of Eric of Friuli by Paulinus of Aquileia have been preserved.[55] An episcopal synod that was held in enemy territory in 796 expressed concern for the conversion of the subjugated, and this was also a topic in the correspondence between Alcuin and Arn, the archbishop of Salzburg.[56] Even a letter from Charlemagne to his wife Fastrada about the Avar war of 791 has been preserved.[57] Charlemagne's biographer Einhard, in his summary, identifies the subjugation of the Avars as the emperor's greatest military accomplishment.[58] Lastly, the Carolingian efforts to organize the newly conquered eastern territories conserved, well into the ninth century, traces of the vanishing Avar elite.[59]

1.3 Steppe Research and Its Methodological Problems

"L'histoire des Avares reste à écrire." With this statement Denis Sinor (1963) outlined an undertaking that, despite intensive research, remained unrealized at the time.[60] In 1983 Omeljan Pritsak characterized the Avars as "stepchildren in historical studies."[61] Admittedly, there have been several efforts at a historical synthesis. Arnulf Kollautz, in collaboration with Hisayuki Miyakawa, portrayed the "history and culture of a nomadic people from the age of migrations" (as the title might read in translation), departing from a straightforward identification of the Rouran of central Asia with the European Avars.[62] Rich in material, this work threw into relief a fundamental problem of research on the Avars: the patchy evidence and the wide range of regional particularities hardly allows a coherent narrative. The "histoire des Avares" is often obscured by the focus on detail.

In more coherent fashion, Alexander Avenarius attempted to delineate the fate of "the Avars in Europe."[63] The work was written under the difficult conditions of repression after the "Prague Spring" of 1968 and could not deal equitably with the current state of research in all areas. In point of fact, for few other questions of the European Middle Ages is the historian more obliged to turn to the help offered by a number of more or less exotic disciplines. The historian of the Avars should not only gain a mastery over the Latin and Greek sources with all their nuances but must in addition deal in critical fashion with Iranian, Armenian, Syriac, Arabic, and Chinese texts, should be at home with Slavic, Hungarian, Turkic, and Mongolic linguistics and onomastics, be competent to interpret with caution the published and, to the greatest degree possible, unpublished findings of archaeologists, master the approaches and models of social anthropology, and, lastly, offer new insights into old problems discussed by colleagues in his own field.

It is no coincidence that one of the classics of steppe research is entitled *Osteuropäische und ostasiatische Streifzüge* (Rambles in eastern Europe and eastern Asia). It was not least the unsystematic and often excursive form of the work that enabled the author, Josef Marquart, at the turn of the twentieth century, to draw connecting lines between disciplines that may still be fruitfully pursued today. It was precisely these interdisciplinary ramblers who provided the decisive stimulus for the exploration of the nomadic peoples. In the second half of the nineteenth century the German Wilhelm Radloff made his way through the "Wild East" in the service of the Russian tsar. He collected an immense body of ethnographical and linguistic data, excavated caves from the Ice Age and kurgans or mounds from the Iron Age, undertook metallurgical investigations, and published his material in the form of a memoir "from Siberia." Long before "interdisciplinary" became a vogue word in the humanities, frontier crossers such as Radloff and Marquart laid the foundations for research into the medieval steppes, combining archaeology and ethnography, linguistics and history.[64]

In the constricted circumstances of the redrawn national boundaries of eastern Europe after 1918, this panoramic view could hardly be sustained. Rigid nationalistic thinking, which drew from Germanic, Slavic, or Hunnic antiquity justifications for chauvinistic politics, did not hinder serious research but ensnarled it in a vicious circle of fierce discussions about wrongly formulated questions. Were the Slavs the slaves of the Avars or the Avars merely the rulers of an alliance of Slavic tribes? Are the Romanians direct descendants of the Daco-Romans or the late results of a reversal of ethnic processes in the mountain regions between the Hungarians and the Slavs? How Carantanian are the Carinthians and the Slovenes, how Slavic the Serbs and Croats? A protracted dispute arose over eighth-century graves in Slovakia as to whether the long-departed were Avars or Slavs, Avaro-Slavs or proto-Great-Moravians, until scholars settled on the neutral term "Avar-period" (*awarenzeitlich*). Just how explosive historical research into remote periods could be when fed into political disputes was evidenced in the stir that arose in Romania over a history of Transylvania that was published in Hungary in 1986.[65] The multifaceted historical contexts for research into the early Middle Ages in central and eastern Europe must be taken into account.[66] After 1989 the search for national origins gained a new and often tragic topicality.

The multiple, changeable identities of the steppe peoples could in fact have undermined the retrospective disputes over nationality. We know from inscriptions in Old Turkic and from Chinese and Byzantine chronicles how rapidly the "peoples" of the horsemen and their followers took shape and then fell apart again. Sources attest that the Goths qualified as Scythians and that Gothic was spoken at the court of Attila the Hun. The "Hun" and "Avar" names that have come down to us are of extremely varied provenance. Germanic warriors, and even the rebellious sixth-century youth of Constantinople, assumed "Hunnic" dress; the Byzantines, Avar weaponry; the Slavs, Avar and German titles.[67] The efforts of highly qualified historians to identify peoples with the same name but widely separated locations in time and space as "one and the same" has therefore led to many dead ends.[68] Migrations, which continuously moved new groups of nomad warriors from one end of the Eurasian steppe zone to the other, are a fascinating object of study. Yet *the* Avars, ("Proto")-Bulgars, or Magyars are not to be found in some fanciful original homeland somewhere between Manchuria and the Ural, even if we find similar ethnonyms there.

Soon after the apocalypse of nationalism in Nazi Germany 1933–45, the biological definition of ethnicity began to be abandoned in early medieval studies; a subjective sense of belonging came to be seen as the decisive feature of ethnic identity. Reinhard Wenskus maintained that early medieval peoples were not of common origin but rather held together by common myths and norms.[69] Concepts of ethnicity and identity have been further developed since. One problem with the post-1945 approaches was that in many cases, the early medieval sense of belonging is hard to trace in the sources. It is more productive to conceptualize ethnic identities as the results of a process of communication and interaction in which self-identification of individuals with a group, identification of the group as such by its representatives and in rituals, and the perceptions of the group by outsiders all play a part.[70] In any case, ethnic identities cannot be assumed as fixed categories; rather, ethnic processes are a part of the historical development under investigation.

While archaeologists excavate hundreds of new Avar graves annually between the Moravian and Serbian Morava Rivers, the historian is not favored with such an increase in source material. Nevertheless, work on the written evidence has made significant progress. The Hungarian Byzantinist Samuel Szádeczky-Kardoss presented a compilation of the sources for the history of the Avars with a short description of contents in 1972.[71] A lexicon of the early medieval names and their occurrences from eastern Europe, the *Glossar zur frühmittelalterlichen Geschichte im östlichen Europa*, was unfortunately discontinued after the first fascicule, but at least the lemma "Avars" has been published.[72] Over the years, decisive improvements were made in the editing and publication of important sources. Most of the essential authors for the history of the Avars are now available in new critical editions and/or translations (see section 1.2). In many cases the new editions proved a stimulus to numerous new studies.[73]

The archaeological legacy of the Avar period is richer than for almost all other early medieval peoples and cultures, a fact that makes its exploration of particular methodological interest. Some time ago, Falko Daim presented a reliable summary of the present state of research in English.[74] It is not easy to keep track of all the new finds, since they come from almost a dozen countries, are studied in many different languages, and remain for the most part unpublished, while the body of available data is immense. The historian can barely call a dozen Avars by name, while the archaeologist knows not the name but many typical and individual characteristics of thousands of individuals of the Avar period. According to recent assessments more than two thousand Avar-period sites and approximately sixty thousand graves have been identified so far. Yet relatively few cemeteries have been fully excavated and published. Even though this flood of evidence occasionally lures the excavator into making hasty historical judgments, the historian, on the other hand, cannot simply ignore this mass of contemporary evidence.

For the nonspecialist who studies the excavation reports it may seem that the Avars come alive for us only in death. Relatively few settlements from the Avar period have been excavated so far. The Avar cult of the dead, on the other hand, has left striking traces. Prominent warriors were often buried in richly decorated costume and with magnificent weapons, sometimes with their horses. Their wives bore equally rich jewelry and decorations. A particularly rich example is a grave discovered in a sandpit in Kunbábony in 1971 and initially ascribed to a khagan.[75] The extensive burial ground of Zamárdi in southwestern Hungary, excavated in the 1990s, with its thousands of graves, produced much new information on the first period of Avar rule and its impressive cultural diversity.[76] The symbolic significance of grave goods as markers of status, their style, provenance, and distribution, the technologies used, the burial rites and organization of the cemeteries, the information on food and tools, the traces of illness and wounds, and much, much more make it possible to draw a host of conclusions. A strength of the school of Gyula László and István Bóna in Hungary was the great attention paid to social and economic questions.[77]

"The finds, however, will give no answers without a prior question from the researcher,"[78] and these questions are connected to the inquirer's historical understanding and interests. Many methodological questions are being debated: To what extent can an archaeologically based relative chronology provide a basis for historical datings? What is the relationship between archaeological culture and the ethnic and political entity? Can archaeological finds be interpreted ethnically at all?[79] These and similar questions call for further discussion in collaboration among the disciplines. It is, however, clear that each discipline must first begin with its own methodology to try to draw tenable conclusions, before results from neighboring disciplines are called on in support. A mixed argumentation can lead to circular reasoning and results. The same is true for the collaboration between history and onomastics.

A more attentive epistemological discussion and insight into fundamental methodological differences among the disciplines could further their collaboration. Both archaeology and historical linguistics seek to classify their material. But fundamental errors occur when the resultant schemata are equated with historical categories. An archaeological culture or a language group cannot, without further ado, be equated with a people or with a polity.[80] This is all the more true for early medieval ways of life, which, on the level of larger entities such as the Avar Empire, were much less homogeneous than modern nation-states. Archaeological cultures are abstractions based on certain features regarded as distinctive, not natural units. Furthermore, even an archaeological (or linguistic) chronology based on a broad range of material must presuppose the contemporaneity of the noncontemporaneous. While the historian can often date more precisely, the written sources only rarely permit spatial delimitation. Thus, the integration of data from all disciplines can offer a complex picture of life under Avar rule, and with the massive evidence at hand it seems plausible to describe the dominant cultural forms to be found in the Carpathian Basin from the late sixth to the end of the eighth century as "Avar."

The German version of this book came out first in 1988; it is now available in the third edition.[81] Surprisingly, relatively little has been published about the Avars since 1988 that would transform the picture drawn almost thirty years ago. However, significant progress has been made in several fields. Archaeology has advanced in a spectacular way, both on the methodological and conceptual levels and in the sheer mass of new material available. Already in the 1980s, a few tens of thousands of graves had been excavated; now this number has almost doubled, making the material evidence from the Avar khaganate easily the best-researched of all early medieval polities in Europe. Whereas in the late 1980s, scholars could rely on just a handful of complete publications of Avar-period cemeteries, many more, and some settlements, have now been made available, mostly in German or English. An impressive variety of further evidence is now accessible through interim reports or particular studies. Although I could not hope to do justice to this enormous body of material and to all the new insights into life under Avar rule that it provides, I have thoroughly revised the archaeological sections in this book.[82]

An area of research that has also seen a very dynamic development is the study of central Asian steppe empires.[83] This is also due to the fact that new texts and inscriptions have become available, which have provided some missing links in our understanding of the period.[84] New approaches to the character of steppe polities were developed, in particular, building on the relatively copious Chinese sources. In 1989, only a year after my book on *Die Awaren*, Thomas Barfield's work on *The Perilous Frontier* came out, offering a wide-ranging comparative study of relations between China and nomadic empires.[85] The chronological and thematic range of his study was of course much broader than that of mine; but in retrospect, some approaches and results of the two books seem interestingly related. Barfield's central hypothesis, the distinction between Mongol raiders and Manchurian conquerors, has justly been criticized. However, the attempt to study nomadic empires and sedentary polities as essentially linked and to concentrate on the impact of their exchanges has proved more fruitful than the traditional insistence on the fundamental alterity of nomadic societies.

In this respect, we have learned much about China-steppe relations, not least, from fundamental work by Nicola Di Cosmo.[86] This is also highly relevant for the relationship between late Rome and the Huns, or between Byzantium and the Avars. Two opposing attitudes should be avoided: On the one hand, romantic or nationalistic identification with past barbarians was current in German nationalism, which instilled pride in the Germanic forefathers. In a similar way, Hungarian national historiography promoted direct identification with Huns, Avars, and ancient Hungarians, underlined their Otherness, and tended to explain their culture as far as possible by Eastern influences.[87] On the other hand, steppe peoples have traditionally been regarded as devoid of a creative culture of their own, and whatever features of civilization they had was supposed to have come from sedentary neighbors. This was particularly characteristic of Chinese research on the Eurasian steppes, which derived steppe culture from Chinese influences. Only recently have Chinese scholars taken their distance from such Sinocentric attitudes.[88] It is ironic that this departure from Sinocentrism in China comes at a time when the late antique barbarians are often being seen more in a Roman cultural matrix than ever before in the West.

One important aspect to be taken into account is the language in which we speak about steppe peoples. To talk about the Avars as nomads may be misleading, because they seem to have become more or less sedentary at some point. Theirs was not the only form of pastoralism practiced in the region at that time; the romance-speaking Vlachs in the Balkans survived for many centuries as transhumant (seasonally migrating) herdsmen. Thus, "steppe empire" or "mounted warriors" are more adequate labels. Ethnic terminology is a particularly problematic field. Notions such as "people," "tribe," "nation," "race," and the like have been stamped and colored in multiple ways by recent history. However concrete and realistic these notions may sound, their scholarly use is burdened with a series of assumptions and overtones and may get in the way of a differentiated understanding. A "people," like a "class" or "layer," is not a natural given but an abstraction. All these collective terms can serve to organize our knowledge about certain aspects of early medieval life but cannot adequately encompass the multiplicity of forms of existence. They are more valuable not as classificatory but rather as operational concepts. "This concept does not describe a logical class of similar individuals but rather a phenomenon, which in its reality must be continuously re-established." The "typological concepts" that thereby emerge "are blurred in definition, because the various factors and characteristics cannot always unambiguously indicate whether a given individual falls within the contours of this concept."[89]

That they do not have the same concepts in mind when dealing with the Avars, Slavs, or Romans is a first difficulty in the communication among historians and is all the more true for interdisciplinary cooperation: a person who is a Slav for a linguist, because he/she spoke Slavonic or had a Slavic name, may have seen himself/herself as thoroughly Avar and may also have been buried in Avar attire. On the other hand, people buried in what for the archaeologist is an Avar grave may have regarded themselves as Slavs or Gepids, or may even have been members of the Byzantine army. This is particularly true when an ethnic classification is based on only a few criteria. There are some Avars who are more Avar than others. In any case, a history of the Avars must simultaneously be a history of the non-Avars, a history of the (territorial and social) space in which Avars became politically active.

The historian has no other recourse than to employ historically grown concepts with their charge of both contemporary and modern shadings. Where possible, the use of early medieval terminology can help to avoid modern overtones. The early medieval shades of meaning that one still has to reckon with at least have the advantage of being more or less part of the object of study. The matter is further complicated by the fact that many Byzantine historians prefer laborious, antiquarian circumlocutions to current terminology. Political semantics are then an important component of all historical research into the early Middle Ages.

By way of clarification, I would like to offer a brief commentary on the choice of terms employed. For the modern notion of a "people" or "ethnic group" medieval

Latin mostly employed the terms *gens, populus*, and *natio*. Their meanings overlap, and they were sometimes used interchangeably. *Natio* mostly emphasizes
individual origin in a particular country, city, or people and is relatively rarely
applied to a collective. *Populus* emphasizes a political or Christian community
as constituted by law, shared political responsibility, or religious commitment—
above all, the people of Rome.[90] *Gens*, by contrast, was supposed to be constituted
by birth and common origin and could refer to a people, tribe, or even dynasty.
In the early Middle Ages, the distinction, never quite clear-cut, was blurred further.
This was also due to political change: among the Goths, Franks, or Lombards the
two forms of organization, *populus* and *gens*, gradually merged. In any case, the
gradual distinctions between the three terms, *populus, gens*, and *natio*, are impossible to render in English. The old-fashioned translations using "race" for *gens*
and "nation" for *natio* can still be found today but are misleading at best. It does
not make sense to call the Avars a "race" or a "nation," and contemporaries certainly did not have anything like these concepts in mind when they called the
Avars *gens* or *natio*.

The concept of "tribe" that is associated with supposed primitiveness will only
sparingly be used here. The Avars were a vertically organized macrofederation
that controlled vast territories. Like many premodern peoples, they may have
comprised a number of tribes or tribal bands. Such tribes are, however, scarcely
known, and their political field of play was slight. The situation of the early
Slavs was different, and emerging regional groups could perhaps be regarded as
"tribes." I will mostly resort to relatively neutral terms such as "group" or "polity."

Substantially more expressive is the concept of "barbarian." The term
is problematic because it is charged with prejudices, but so far has proved
indispensable in order to identify the multiform host of non-Romans on both
sides of the old frontiers of the empire. On the other side we have the "Romans."[91]
If the Greek-speaking Byzantines are often called "Romans" in these pages, this is
in accord with their conception of themselves. They saw themselves as *Rhomaioi*
or Romans and their Greek language as the Roman language in distinction to
Latin. Their political organization was the empire (*imperium*), and on the other
side of the frontier stretched the barbarian lands (*barbaricum*), in which the *gentes*
(or in Greek, *ethnē*) lived. Roman provincials who no longer (or only nominally)
lived under imperial rule (as in the Alps) are also called Romans, although
contemporary usage of the term had become fuzzy. Unlike the German language,
which allows a differentiation between *Römer* (the citizens of the empire) and
Romanen (a population preserving some Roman culture and perhaps their Latin
language, under barbarian rule), this English translation calls both "Romans."

Generally speaking, conventional designations as found in the sources are
usually used for the names of peoples and tribes. It is self-evident that the Croats,

Bulgars, and Turks of the early Middle Ages are not identical to the present-day nations with these same names. For this reason, artificial terms such as "Proto-Bulgars" will be avoided, just as no one would consider identifying Socrates or Pericles as "Proto-Greeks." The same is true of the central Asian Turks of the sixth and seventh centuries. The Moravians of the ninth century are often called "Great Moravians" in modern historiography. For the Franks, they simply were *Marahenses* or similar. Only the tenth-century Byzantine author Constantine Porphyrogenitus, according to the usual terminology (*Scythia minor* on Roman territory, *Scythia maior/Megalē Scythia* beyond it) calls their country *Megalē Moravia* as distinct from the land along the Serbian Morava River, which once belonged to imperial territory. The translation "Great Moravia" adds no greater precision but rather invites misunderstandings. But in the case of the "Megalē Bulgaria" of Kuvrat, this same qualifier will be allowed to stand, albeit in quotation marks, because (unlike in the Moravian case) it does assist in establishing a distinction with other politically relevant Bulgarian realms of the period.

In geographical references the use of modern political terminology often cannot be avoided, especially where they do not clearly correspond to a delimited natural landscape or ancient entity. This may call up undesirable national associations but facilitates the easy location of the region in question on a modern map, even though Austria and Hungary, Slovakia and Transylvania, Croatia, Serbia, and Romania did not exist in the period. The same applies to the use of modern place-names, where an English translation is not available, though with a few exceptions. The "treasure of Nagyszentmiklós" has found a home in scholarly literature under its Hungarian designation and will be so named in what follows, even though the place of discovery presently lies in Romania (called Sânnicolau Mare), and the treasure itself in Vienna. The Russian name Malaja Pereščepina for the rich burial site associated with Khan Kuvrat now in the Ukraine (called Mala Pereščepino in Ukrainian) is also still often used in scholarship.

Barbarian organizational forms are difficult to grasp. I will call the Avar Empire, after the title of its ruler, a khaganate. The "khagan" (never, in the contemporary sources, called "khan") when employed without an attribute (as is common in the sources) always stands for the ruler of the Avars. Turkish and other khagans will be designated as such. Much less clear is the terminology in our sources for Slavic rulers. The leaders of small Slavic communities are often described in rather vague fashion. In Greek sources, the Latin loan word *reges* or *archontes* or *phylarchoi* are used. In the Latin sources, on the other hand, the title *rex* is first used for Samo; Slavic princes are otherwise called *duces*. In this book reference will generally be to princes or leaders, unless the terminology of the sources is used.

What has been said of ethnic names applies even more to personal names. With barbarian names, the Latinized or Grecized version of the sources will be preferred to hypothetical Slavic, Turkic, or Germanic forms, although Greek or Latin endings will generally be dropped. Many spellings are still disputed. Whether Greek *chaganos* and Latin *caganus* are best rendered with *khagan*, *chagan*, *qagan*, or even *qayan* is a matter of philological debate. In such cases the most established spellings (in this case, khagan) will usually be preferred. The same goes for the reproduction of Greek names; in most cases, English-style Latinization of Greek names is used here. As with all other non-Latin scripts, I have transcribed Greek terms or short quotes in Latin. Transcriptions of Byzantine Greek are, however, deceptive as concerns phonetic valence; the emperor Heraclius was spelled in the classical manner as Herakleios, but pronounced as *Iraklios*. A phonetic rendering of Greek is, however, used for barbarian names: otherwise we would have to call the Avars Abars and the Slavs Sklab(ene)s. For transcriptions of Chinese names, I have had to switch from the old Wade-Giles system to simple Pinyin, without diacritic signs. Still, spelling and choosing the right name form always implies controversial choices. The same goes for many aspects of writing a book, and I hope for the readers' understanding wherever they would have decided differently.

THE AVAR MIGRATION

Avar history in Europe began with an embassy sent to Constantinople from the steppes north of the Caucasus in the winter of 557/58. The emperor Justinian, who had successfully governed the Roman Empire for more than thirty years, gave them a friendly reception. They arrived in a situation in which the Balkan provinces had come under pressure from a number of barbarian peoples living beyond the northern frontiers, so that the Avars were regarded as a valuable ally. This chapter discusses where they had come from and under which circumstances; and it recounts the story of their advance in eastern Europe until their final settlement in the Carpathian Basin.

2.1 Constantinople 558

The first thing that struck the Greeks about the Avars was their long pigtails, dirty and braided *à la chinoise*. In the metropolis of Constantinople, where foreigners from every country came and went, the appearance of the first Avar delegation drew a crowd. "The whole city ran up to see them, since they had never seen such a people before. For they wore their hair very long in the back, tied with ribbons and braided, while their other clothing was similar to that of the other Huns," reports Theophanes. This occurred in or around January 558.[1]

Their hairstyle is also the only feature that the contemporary Agathias communicates about the Avars in his detailed history of the years 552–59. The

Frankish kings, he states, let their hair grow long. "It is not, however, like that of the Turks and Avars, unkempt, dry and dirty, and tied up in an unsightly knot."[2] From this limited interest one almost gets the impression that the arrival of the newcomers from the east was an occasion for gossip rather than for high-level politics. Initially the Byzantines probably underestimated the significance of these exotic strangers, who "in flight from their country" had come to the frontiers of the empire, as Theophanes mentions. The political background of the entry of the Avars on the scene is explained by Menander. "After many wanderings they came to the Alans and begged Sarosius, the leader of the Alans, that he bring them to the attention of the Romans. Sarosius informed Germanus's son Justin, who at that time was general of the forces in Lazica, about the Avars, Justin told Justinian, and the Emperor ordered the general to send the embassy of the tribe to Byzantium."[3] The Avars were then encamped in the steppes north of the Caucasus and established contact through the Alans who lived in the Caucasus region. After some bureaucratic delay, the ambassadors under Kandikh could set out for Constantinople.

If we may trust the account of the chronicler, the ambassador then boasted before the emperor as coming from "the bravest of all peoples." He made no mention of the fact that his army had crossed half the Asian continent in flight and offered the emperor an alliance with the "unconquered" Avars. They could exterminate all the enemies of the empire, but obviously only on the condition that they receive "the most valuable gifts, yearly payments and very fertile land to inhabit."[4] The emperor, after consultation with his privy council, accepted the offer. "He immediately sent the gifts: cords worked with gold, couches, silken garments and a great many other objects which would mollify the arrogant sprits of the Avars." With final agreement on the alliance, Justinian sent a certain *spatharius* Valentinus to the Avars, who was to incite them "to war against the enemies of the Romans."[5]

This procedure was in no way exceptional. Almost all barbarian peoples were associated with the Roman Empire in similar fashion. Annual payments from Byzantium permitted both lesser and greater "Scythian" military leaders to consolidate their authority in return for military support or a suspension of plundering. Thus, imperial diplomacy was able to create a complex system of power groups in competition with one another on the northern frontier. This did not prevent recurrent raids into the empire. Yet, since the fall of Attila's empire roughly a century earlier, none of the barbarian kingdoms had been able to establish hegemony over the northern barbarians and pose a real threat to Byzantium. The sons of Attila, Goths, Bulgars, Cutrigurs, Utigurs, Antes, and Slavs had succeeded one another in incursions into Roman territory. But when one of the adversaries threatened to become too dangerous, imperial diplomacy always succeeded in stirring up other groups against it.

With this low-profile policy on the northern frontier it proved possible for Justinian to free up money and troops for his ambitious plans for the west. While Roman armies conquered Vandal North Africa, Ostrogothic Italy, as well as portions of Spain, and in the east fought against the Persians, the Balkan Peninsula remained the preferred target of barbarian depredation: in 540 and 544 by the Bulgarian "Huns," in 545 by Slavs, who again made incursions in 548 and 550–52, at one occasion with the aid of the Gepids. In 551 the Cutrigurs invaded.[6] The emperor reacted to this with the construction of fortifications at a forced pace. In particular, the frontier forts along the Danube were reinforced. Here, excavations reveal that barbarian federates were often responsible for the defense of the provinces. The composition of the garrisons reflects two centuries of shifting history.[7] Between Singidunum/Belgrade and the mouth of the Danube lay, according to Procopius, over a hundred towns and fortresses, a previously unmatched concentration, with a distance of four to six miles between posts. Even toward the close of the sixth century Theophylact mentions the names of twenty-four such fortified sites in the course of recounting events of the war.[8]

The outcome of this kind of defense was a stalemate. The barbarians scarcely succeeded in occupying fortresses along the frontier (*limes*), let alone important towns in the interior of the provinces. On the other hand, Roman life in the Balkan Peninsula was under pressure because of the frequent incursions. Thrace, once one of the most important areas for imperial troop recruitment, lost significantly in population and economic power. "Illyria and all of Thrace, that is, from the Ionian Gulf to the suburbs of Constantinople, including Greece and the Chersonese, were overrun by the Huns, Slavs and Antes, almost every year, from the time when Justinian took over the Roman Empire; and intolerable things they did to the inhabitants. For in each of these incursions, I should say, more than two hundred thousand Romans were slain or enslaved, so that all this country became a desert like that of Scythia." So wrote Procopius in his *Secret History*.[9] Even if hatred of "the prince of demons" prompts the author to gross exaggeration, the hinterland of the imperial capital had indeed become the target of repeated barbarian attacks.

At the end of his reign, when Justinian had realized almost all his foreign policy objectives, the price of his success became ever more apparent. Procopius's devastating account in the *Secret History* is only one expression of the growing criticism, which also left traces in other historians. Agathias deplores the decay and dispersion of the Roman army that the aging emperor had permitted. Instead of more than six hundred thousand men, only some 150,000 were then under arms, neglected and malcontent, because the emperor preferred to pacify the barbarians with diplomacy and gifts. Jordanes concludes his *Roman History* with a reference to the everyday incursions of the "Bulgars, Antes and Slavs" and with a resigned recollection of past glories.[10] In similar fashion, although with more respect, Menander accounts for the alliance with the Avars: "Now he [Justinian] was an old man, and his bold and warlike spirit had become feeble, and he sought ways other than war to ward off the power of the barbarians."[11]

However, the reasons for the decline of the Balkan provinces lay deeper. The age of Justinian had indeed brought a certain prosperity. Not only fortified walls but also huge churches and other buildings were erected. The cities suffered less from the barbarian assaults than the hinterland. Still, the weakening of the rural regions had economic consequences. The small farmers had to struggle desperately for their survival. Justinian's legislation sought to protect them against the great demesnes, which still threatened their existence in many regions. In the Danube provinces the villa organization of late Antiquity was already in the process of dissolution.[12] The great property-holders were affected by an increasing shortage of labor. These troubled times favored the flight of slaves and colons, and social tensions became more acute. Runaway slaves, dispossessed peasants, poverty-stricken townspeople, rebellious soldiers, and scattered barbarians formed bands of *scamarae*, armed robbers.[13] This *ataktos bios*, unregulated life, against which military measures were to be mounted through a decree of 569, undermined Roman order and furthered the gradual barbarization of the countryside.

Since the middle of the sixth century there had also been the plague, which visited the empire in cycles: a demographic shock that spurred depopulation.[14] In this situation the late Roman apparatus of state tended to become counter-productive. The decimated populace, struggling with economic difficulties, was exposed to increased pressure of taxation. Military expenses grew as the empire sought to keep things under control. Occasional tax and debt relief after devastating invasions could not check this cataclysmic downward spiral.

That a barbarian incursion may have been seen by many as more tolerable than the appearance of a tax official is a point made by John the Lydian.[15] Procopius worried that Roman citizens would sooner cross over to the barbarians than pay their taxes. Pope Gregory would later make the same observation.[16] During Maurice's Balkan wars the residents of Asemus expelled the emperor's brother from the city, when he tried to raise troops there.[17] Obviously it should not be concluded from such cautionary examples that the inhabitants of the Balkan provinces in general would have preferred barbarian rule.[18] Yet for many under these circumstances there may have been little motivation to defend Roman order on the Danube at all costs.

The weakness of the Roman position in the Balkans became evident in events of the year 559, when the Avars were still encamped on the steppes beyond the Caucasus. For seven years relative peace had reigned in the Balkan provinces; at least no information has come down on any larger barbarian incursion during this period. In the winter of 558–59 the Cutrigur Huns under Zabergan and some Slavic bands crossed the Danube. While part of the invaders turned toward Greece, Zabergan's army marched on Constantinople and established itself on the outskirts of the capital. The emperor did not have a sufficient number of troops at his disposal to drive off the pillaging barbarians. Finally Belisarius, the aged victor over the Vandals and Goths, had to march out against the barbarian horsemen with a small elite troop and a host of peasants. But neither his victory nor some further successful skirmishes were sufficient to drive the Cutrigurs off. Justinian finally had to secure their withdrawal with gold.[19]

The emperor now turned to the neighbors of the Cutrigurs, the Utigurs under Sandilkh, likewise a Hunnic people, and tried to incite them to an attack on Zabergan.

> Justinian added to his messages to Sandilkh that if he destroyed the Cutrigurs the Emperor would transfer to him all the yearly tribute-monies that were paid by the Roman Empire to Zabergan. Therefore, Sandilkh, who wished to be on friendly terms with the Romans, replied that utterly to destroy one's fellow tribesmen was unholy and altogether improper, "for they not only speak our language, dwell in tents like us, dress like us and live like us, but they are our kin, even if they follow other leaders. Nevertheless, we shall deprive the Cutrigurs of their horses and take possession of them ourselves, so that without their mounts they will be unable to pillage the Romans." This Justinian had asked them to do.[20]

In Agathias's account Sandilkh has less compunction in attacking his Cutrigur neighbors. "And so from that time onwards both peoples continued to make war against each other for a very long period of time and they became increasingly hostile as a result. On some occasions they would confine themselves to predatory incursions, on others they would resort to open warfare, until they have so weakened themselves and their numbers have become so seriously depleted that they have lost their ethnic identity. The scattered remnant of these Hunnic tribes has in fact been reduced to servitude in the lands of other peoples whose names they have assumed."[21] The time had come for the Avars, who in 559 apparently did not yet figure in the calculations of the besieged emperor.

2.2 The Empire and the Steppe Peoples

The realms of the Scythians, which Herodotus had described, had long since disappeared from the steppes on the northern shores of the Black Sea. Yet a millennium after the classical geographer the Byzantines still viewed the inhabitants of the lands beyond the *Pontos Euxeinos* as Scythians, which had become an ethnographic umbrella term. Sarmatians, Goths, and Huns had succeeded one another in ruling over parts of the vast steppes of present-day southern Russia and Ukraine. They had rarely managed to unify the European steppes in one empire; in that respect, Attila's empire had been the exception, not the rule. After its fall in 453–54, no power succeeded in winning a position of preeminence on the northern Roman frontier. While conditions were stabilizing farther west with the rise of the Frankish kingdom, a multitude of short-lived barbarian kingdoms competed north of the lower Danube.

It appeared even to Roman observers that the "Scythians" were in reality a host of different peoples that contended with each other for the best launching point for raids into imperial territory.

> All these peoples were referred to by the general name of Scythians or Huns, whereas individual tribes had their own particular names, rooted in ancestral tradition, such as Cutrigurs, Utigurs, Ultizurs, Burugundi and so on and so forth. . . . But their stay was destined to be a brief one, and at the end of it they vanished without leaving a trace of themselves. This fact is illustrated by the case of the Ultizurs and the Burugundi who were well-known right up to the time of Emperor Leo [457–74] . . . but whom in our day and age we neither know nor, I imagine, are likely to, since they have either perished or migrated to the ends of the earth.[22]

Procopius, the historian of Justinian's wars, concludes his depiction of the Black Sea peoples with the statement that he had not been able to indicate exact distances. Beyond the Black Sea lived great hosts of barbarians, of whom only a few were known to the Romans as a result of embassies. Neither was more precise information to be found in the older geographers.[23] Yet in Justinian's time there flourished ethnographical digressions that attempted to label the multiplicity of barbarian peoples for the readers of historical works. More or less extensive ethnographical descriptions are preserved in Jordanes, Procopius, Agathias, Evagrius, and the so-called *Ecclesiastical History of Zacharias Rhetor*, written in Syriac in the 560s. Much of this is based on information that had been obtained through diplomatic exchanges. From a remark by Procopius we may assume that the names of the Cutrigurs and Utigurs were first heard in Constantinople in 547–48, and this via an embassy from the Crimean

Goths.[24] Some information came from the accounts of eyewitnesses. An artisan from Anatolian Amida, who had been bought by north Caucasian "Huns" after the conquest of his town by the Persians, supplied the author of the *Ecclesiastical History* with material for one such ethnographical digression. Additional material was drawn by this author from unknown written sources, in particular, a list of sixteen peoples on the far side of the Caucasus: "And beyond the [Caspian] Gates are the Burgar, a pagan and barbarian people with their own language, and they have cities. There are the Alans, who have five cities. There are the people of the region of Dadu, who live in the mountains and have fortresses. There are the Onogur, a tent-dwelling people, the Ogur, the Sabir, the Burgar, the Khorthrigor, the Avar, the Khasir, the Dirmar, the Sarurgur, the Bagarsik, the Khulas, the Abdel, the Ephthalite: these thirteen peoples are tent-dwellers, living on the meat of cattle, fish and wild animals and by weapons." Beyond them, the text enumerates the tribes of the pigmies, of the dog-men, and the Amazons.[25] This disputed catalog of peoples illustrates the difficulties with which any historical ethnography of the steppe zone must contend. The passage is preserved in the Syriac translation of a Greek chronicle compilation going up to the end of the 560s, which in turn built on the fifth-century *Ecclesiastical History* by Zacharias Rhetor. It was even hypothesized that the Greek original goes back to the Middle Persian version of an even older Greek text. If we reflect on how many variants of Hunnic or Turkic names even relatively well-transmitted Greek texts offer, we will use this valuable source with caution. Much material is Justinianic, and the list of peoples certainly reflects the situation in the mid-sixth century.[26]

Modern research strives meticulously to reconcile the often contradictory statements of individual authors. Even a critical review of the dispersed source material that has been preserved in a dozen languages has required enormous scholarly effort.[27] Yet until now scholars have not fully succeeded in clarifying the identity, relationships, and distinctiveness of the peoples whose names are known; debates continue. This difficulty becomes evident in a consideration of those Huns whom the Avars encountered on the Black Sea. Most of them bore similarly constructed names; along with the previously mentioned Cutrigurs and Utigurs we know of Onogurs, Saragurs, and Ogurs, and to these are added some similar names that are not unambiguously classifiable.[28] In addition there are the Bulgars, whose close association with the "Ogur" peoples is known from a series of texts. According to Theophanes, Khan Kuvrat ruled in Pontic "Great Bulgaria" over the Onogur-Bulgars and the related tribe of the Cutrigurs.[29] Soon, of all these names only that of the Bulgars would remain in the European consciousness.

From a later perspective, the -*gur* peoples on the Black Sea thus have been considered as part of the early history of the Bulgarians. When at the end of the fifth century the Byzantines first had to deal with the Bulgars, the latter by no means had a comparable significance. They caused Theoderic some difficulties before he became known as "the Great," and their bands crisscrossed the Balkans as affiliates of the Roman army or, more often, as pillagers.[30] It is curious that it is above all the Latin sources that frequently employ the name of the Bulgars for this period, among them, Ennodius in his panegyric for Theoderic, Jordanes in his *Getica*, and the *Chronicles* of Cassiodorus and of Marcellinus Comes. In the Ostrogothic kingdom, people seem to have been well informed about their former opponents. On the other hand, the Greek chroniclers usually speak generally of "Huns." Only John Malalas and John of Antioch, and a few later Greek histories, mention the name of the Bulgars in the sixth century, while Priscus, Procopius, Evagrius, and Agathias do not employ it.[31] When the last-named authors look for greater precision than that offered by the collective term "Huns," they speak of Cutrigurs, Utigurs, and similar peoples.

After the fall of Attila's empire and the withdrawal of the Goths toward the West, the name "Huns" became increasingly synonymous with the older "Scythians" as a general designation for the steppe peoples. In fact, there is probably no more accurate term for the Pontic steppe warriors in the age of Justinian than simply to call them "Huns." In Ostrogothic Italy matters were simpler, since the Bulgars were clearly the only group from the steppe apart from Attila's Huns with which the Goths had come into closer contact. The well-informed historians of the East knew that they were dealing with a variety of shifting groupings.

Behind all this, there was a relatively homogeneous stratum of warriors, who were the agents in the formation of the various powers. They had coalesced in the second half of the fifth century from three groups. The first was those Huns of Attila who had turned back from the Carpathian Basin to the Black Sea, initially under the leadership of the sons of the great king of the Huns. Jordanes knew of such a return migration. The later Bulgarian tradition counted Attila's son Irnik/ Ernak among the first Bulgarian princes.[32] Secondly, newcomers arrived from the east in the 460s. A fragment of Priscus recounts: "About that time the Saragurs, Ogurs, and Onogurs sent envoys to the eastern Romans. These peoples had been driven from their homeland after a battle with the Sabirs, who in turn had been displaced by the Avars." In the forest belt of southern Russia the Saragurs encountered the Hunnic Akatzirs, erstwhile subjects of Attila, and subjugated them after lengthy battles.[33] All the peoples implicated in these migrations appear in Priscus for the first time and are not named again for quite some time. We will return to the question of the Avars, most probably understood here as the central Asian Rouran.

Thirdly, Procopius emphasizes the continuity of "Hun" settlement on the Maeotis, the Sea of Azov, so that it cannot have been only migrants from the east

who had an impact on the new ethnic landscape in the region. This corresponds
to the archaeological evidence, at least west of the Maeotis, as summarized by
Florin Curta: "The archaeological evidence suggests that the sixth- and early
seventh-century burials in the Black Sea lowlands were not of nomads coming
from afar, but of members of the communities that occupied the settlements at
the interface between the steppe and the forest-belts."[34] The -*gur* groups from the
east were, however, the name-giving element, even though it would not be until
the middle of the sixth century that the bearers of such names became politically
active on a large scale. Those Huns who contributed to the instability of the
Balkan provinces into the third decade of the sixth century were called Bulgars.
Sometime before 547–48 the Cutrigurs assumed the initiative. At about the same
time, before 552, the Onogurs made their presence felt by a raid on the Caucasus
region. Somewhat later, in 568, a Byzantine envoy encountered Ogurs on the
lower course of the Volga who were subjects of the Turkish khagan.[35] Conversely,
we hear little of Bulgars in this region.

The three lists of peoples that were compiled after the middle of the
sixth century supplement this picture, albeit in quite contradictory fashion.
Among the "numerous Hunnic peoples" north of the Caucasus near the
Sabirs, Procopius mentions only the Utigurs, who lived east of the Sea of
Azov, and the Cutrigurs who had crossed to settle on the other side.[36] Besides
these, he knows of the Antes in the northwest and the "Tetraxitic" Goths who
lived in the Crimea and on the Kerch Peninsula. Substantially more detailed
is Jordanes. Between the Dniester and the Dnieper, he writes, live the Antes,
north of them the Akatzirs already known from Attila's time.[37] Beyond these,
north of the Black Sea, are the Bulgars. In the region around the Crimean port
of Cherson are the Hunnic Altziagirs; on the Sea of Azov, the Hunugurs, of
whom Jordanes has a bit to say, above all that they once dwelled in the Balkan
provinces. However, this may also refer to the (Crimean) Goths named in the
same context. The Sabirs complement this rather hard-to-follow digression in
Jordanes's Gothic history.[38] The list by the so-called Zacharias Rhetor is little
more than a directory of steppe peoples. The Bwrgr/Bulgars are mentioned
twice north of the Caucasus, both among town dwellers and among nomads.
Also to be counted among the latter are the Onogurs, Ogurs, Sabirs, Cutrigurs,
and Saragurs.[39] The Utigurs seem to have been left out.

The three lists are not easy to harmonize. For example, the identification of
the Hunugurs in Jordanes with the Onogurs is debatable. By the Sea of Azov
one would actually expect Cutrigurs and Utigurs. Or are these hidden behind
the Bulgars of Jordanes? It is customary to resolve this puzzle by viewing the
Onogurs and usually also the Cutrigurs and Utigurs as Bulgars or at least Bulgar tribes. On the other hand, some scholars have classified the Bulgars as a

tribe in the Onogur federation.[40] The catch in all these identifications is that they project the conditions of the seventh century back onto the sixth. What Theophanes wrote in the ninth century about the Bulgars of the seventh reflects a change in circumstances. The second Bulgar ethnogenesis, after the end of Avar and Turkish hegemony in the seventh century, united some of the barbarian groups that had remained north of the Black Sea under Khan Kuvrat's rule. In Justinian's time neither "Bulgar" nor "Onogur" is attested as an umbrella term. Jordanes names the Bulgars and Onogurs as next to each other; Zacharias adds the Cutrigurs and others. All these peoples were commonly regarded as Huns. While in the course of the seventh century the multiplicity of similar names in the Black Sea steppes disappeared again, it persisted in the central Asian steppe. Over time Toquz-Oguz, Oguzes, Uyghurs, Ghuzz, and others appeared on the scene.

It is evident that these peoples drew on a common set of traditions. For the Cutrigurs and Utigurs there is evidence that they saw themselves as allied and speaking the same language, and believed they had been separated from a greater alliance to which they had once belonged.[41] Most striking is the shared system of denomination and the often regular construction of -*gur* names. The first part of the compound is often a number or color word. The Onogurs were then the "ten Ogurs," Utur-gur could be understood as "thirty," Kutur-gur and Toquz-Oguz as "nine Ogurs," Saragurs as "white Ogurs."[42] The collective suffix -*gur*, or rather -*ghur*, is very frequent among ancient Turks.[43] The alternative endings, -*gur* and -*guz*, correspond to two linguistic groups of the Turkic language, Oguric and Common Turkic. Most scholars agree that *ogur* meant something like "tribe." Sometimes the word is connected to Turkic *oq*, "arrow," which seems to be confirmed by the Chinese *Tang shu*: "The khagan divides his realm into ten tribes; each tribe has a leader to whom he sends an arrow. The name [of these ten men] was 'the ten shê'; they were also called 'the ten arrows.'"[44] Archaeological observations have been interpreted to indicate that the arrow served as a symbol of rank among the Avars.[45]

What explains these striking commonalities of -*gur* peoples? The identity or nonidentity of all these peoples (and others, for instance Hungarians and Ugrians) was affirmed in ever new combinations and as promptly rejected by others.[46] These various attempts cannot be treated here in detail. Yet even peoples with similar or corresponding names can often hardly be associated, for instance, the Onogurs of the Greek sources and the On oq of Turkic inscriptions. The former, who played a secondary role in the Caucasian foothills in the sixth century, became part of the Bulgar realm during the reign of Kuvrat. The On oq appear in the Orkhon inscriptions as enemies of the west Turkish khaganate, were conquered, "settled and organized," and thereafter passed as part of the "united Turkish peoples," as one of the Turkish khagan's "own peoples."[47] The Oguz and Toquz-Oguz in the north were also defeated but continued to be distinctive entities. This multitude of similar names could be interpreted as pointing to a consistent tribal grouping. However, "Ogur" does not usually appear as a common denominator for all these peoples; the Ogurs are rather mentioned as one people among others, for instance, in Priscus and Menander.[48] Rather, the -gur peoples belonged to different empires, federations, or loose groupings; Peter Golden has described them as "stateless nomads," with little propensity for constructing strong realms of their own. They may well have emerged from the loose grouping called Tiele (T'ie-leh) in Chinese sources.[49] In eastern Europe, they were regarded as "Huns" in the sixth century, and sometimes as "Bulgars" in the seventh. They also appeared in the Common Turkic form (-guz) in Turkish realms; with the Uyghurs, their onomastic principle finally became imperial.

This spread of a narrow set of ethnic names in ever-new but similar variants, often under foreign leadership, is remarkable. The name "Hun" was diffused through several powerful states or empires that bore that name between Mongolia, the northern periphery of Persia, and the eastern European steppes.[50] "Ogur" groupings, on the other hand, are attested in all the known steppe empires of the period, usually without assuming supreme power. Rather, they represented a looser form of cohesion typically organized in regional polities. They could also relatively easily be integrated into emerging empires. The spread of "Ogur" names can thus be explained by the success of a flexible mode of organization and identification that was compatible with various political contexts, much better than by some common ethnic origin. North of the Black Sea, it seems that like so many other steppe peoples in that region, the -gur peoples had arrived as fugitives from central Asia, and they certainly did not constitute a politically active tribal confederation. As we will see, perhaps untypically, their traces disappear rather quickly in the Avar Empire.

The question of identification of people with similar names in different regions or periods is, in any case, often unsolvable. When are similar-sounding names variants of the same name? When do they denote different tribes? The problem lies in establishing analogies between Turkic names and their representation in texts in many languages that adapt them to their phonetic system, in particular, Chinese. To take just one example: the Romans were generally called rōm or rūm by their Eastern neighbors, which turned to hrōm or frōm in Middle Persian, and was then taken over as purum by the Turks and as fulin by the Chinese. Additionally, the Chinese often sought to translate names into their language, or replaced them with a similarly sounding Chinese word that seemed to fit: for instance, the Rouran were also called Ruanruan, "wriggling worms." Besides, these Chinese name forms may also differ widely between different texts.[51] And if we can establish an equation, when does the same name also signal political or ethnic continuity? Static models of classification or ethnic genealogies cannot describe such a dynamic and often ambiguous reality. Thus, the historian cannot assume that a given name always designates the same people. Even more than with single tribes or peoples, the umbrella terms employed in Greek and Byzantine literature, such as "Huns," represent an abstraction: "The names of alliances of a higher order (Galatians, Thracians, Scythians, etc.) emanate from reality but at the same time serve more frequently than those of individual tribes as typological concepts in the service of classificatory order. For that reason they more easily distance themselves from reality and their use also becomes a basis for speculation," as Dieter Timpe describes the methods of ancient ethnography. One and the same name can now serve as the proper name of a people, now be employed to identify an ethnographic ideal type.[52] Still, this rather flexible and often disorderly matrix of social identity and difference did serve to distinguish between collective actors, both in self-definitions and outside perceptions. This was what I would call ethnicity: a system of establishing cognitive distinctions between collective social actors understood as natural communities. Ethnic identities were then created by a series of self- and outside identifications in a circuit of interaction and communication.[53] There is no "real" ethnicity behind ethnonyms in our sources that could be objectively defined by modern categories of common blood, genes, or language.

Of the Black Sea peoples we can thus only say this: In the sixth century the Onogurs were just as little a Bulgar tribe as the Bulgars an Onogur tribe. Which peoples considered themselves related, or at least were considered as such, can be determined in only a few cases (Cutrigurs and Utigurs in the sixth century, Bulgars, Onogurs/Hunnogundurs, and Cutrigurs in the seventh century). It is possible that this was an expression of a parallel descent from "ogur"-organized groups, but we have no proof for that. In any case, they represent a common model of midrange political organization and often appear as subject groups of a more powerful empire. They could keep their identity in foreign empires; however, in the long run many of these names disappeared under Avar and Turkish rule. Agathias says about Utigurs and Cutrigurs, weakened by their conflict, that "the scattered remnant of these Hunnic tribes has in fact been reduced to servitude in the lands of other peoples whose names they have assumed."[54] The multiplicity of names of the sixth century gradually disappeared north of the Black Sea. In the seventh century the name "Bulgars" became common among them, or at least that is the retrospective impression we gather from the mostly later sources.[55]

2.3 Fugitives from the East

Who were the pigtailed aliens from the steppe who wanted to do business with the aging emperor Justinian? The Byzantines did not fail to gather information about where they had come from. At that time contacts with the east were quite intense. Constantinople had long sought dependable allies behind the back of its archenemy, the Persians. Long-distance trade also mattered. The Persians controlled a stretch of the Silk Road, and by the first half of the sixth century, they had succeeded in driving up the price of the precious fabric considerably. This is one reason why the central Eurasian steppes became so important for the Byzantines, and we have much more information about them in the historiography of the sixth century than in most classical centuries; the Byzantines also sought direct contacts with India, to which the geographical work by Cosmas Indicopleustes attests.[56]

For some time in the fifth and sixth centuries, the dominating power in central Asia were the Rouran (spelt Juan-juan in older literature), known from Chinese sources. After the dissolution of the Han Empire in China, they ruled the steppes of Mongolia and the region around the Tian Shan and Altai Mountains, and thus controlled the trade routes of the Tarim Basin, much as the Xiongnu (Hsiung-nu) had done before them. They confronted the Chinese Empire of the Northern Wei, itself founded by steppe warriors, the Tuoba branch of the Xianbei (Hsien-pi). From the Xianbei, the Rouran rulers had adopted the sublime title khagan, which soon became a mark of distinction in the steppe. It is very likely that they called themselves, or at least were called, Avars, but this is not consensual.[57]

The legend about the origin of the Rouran transmitted in the Chinese *Wei shu*, the official history of the Northern Wei dynasty, is derogatory to say the least and probably goes back to Tuoba contempt for them.[58] A former slave, called Mugulü because of his bald head, was to be decapitated and fled into the desert. "He assembled more than a hundred fugitive slaves and they attached themselves to the tribe of Hetulin. After Mugulü died, his son, Cheluhui, who was a rugged man, began to acquire his own tribal horde who called themselves Rouran, but they were subject to the Tuoba Xianbei. Later Emperor Shizu [of Northern Wei, 424–51] considered that they were ignorant and shaped like worms, and so changed their name into Ruru." They were "mixed barbarians from outside the barrier," as the *Nan Qi shu* (History of the Southern Qi Dynasty) states.[59] As Peter Golden argues, "the Rouran were undoubtedly polyglot and their 'empire' contained a variety of peoples." Their name "was not an ethnonym but a sobriquet . . . that the ruling house took and which was picked up and used as an ethnonym."[60]

After times of inner conflict, Anagui Khagan, undisputed ruler from 521, restored Rouran power. A legend tells how he arrogantly refused a marriage

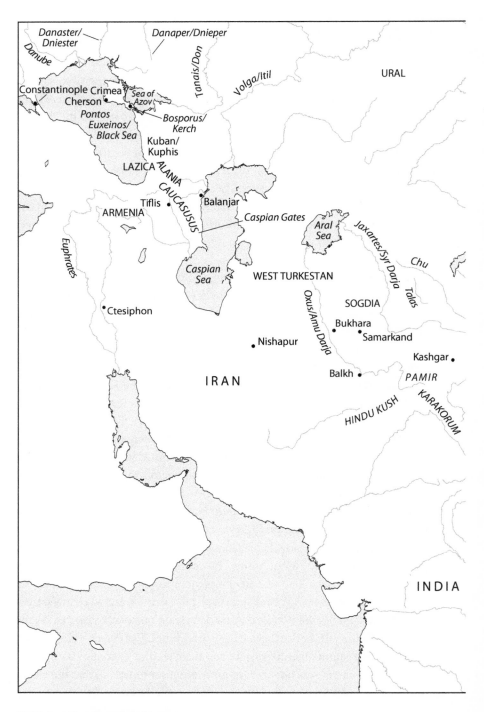

MAP 1. The Eurasian Steppes

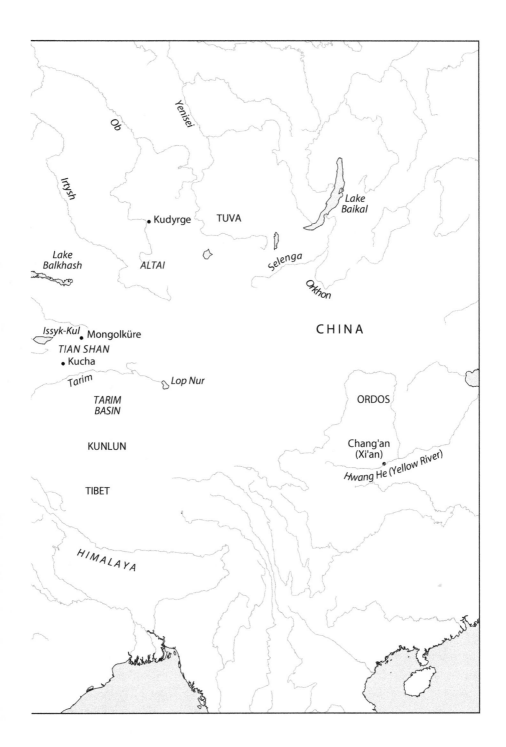

Ob

Yenisei

Irtysh

Kudyrge

TUVA

Lake
Baikal

Lake
Balkhash

ALTAI

Selenga

Orkhon

Issyk-Kul ● Mongolküre

CHINA

TIAN SHAN

● Kucha

Tarim

Lop Nur

TARIM
BASIN

ORDOS

KUNLUN

Chang'an
(Xi'an)
●

Hwang He (Yellow River)

TIBET

HIMALAYA

alliance with his Turkish subjects, who consequently rose against him; the khaganate of the Rouran fell in 552–55, after crushing defeats against the Turks. Their empire, and their elites, disintegrated into various groups who opted for different strategies of survival; but most of them met a violent end. The account found in the *Bei shi* (History of the Northern Dynasties) provides an instructive example for the demise of a steppe empire. In 552, "Anagui was destroyed by the Tujue (T'u-küe)/Turks and killed himself. Having the support of the horde, the crown-prince, Anluochen, together with Dengzhu, Sili, Anagui's younger male cousin, and Kuti, the son of Dengzhu, fled to the Northern Qi dynasty. The remnant forces established Tiefa, the second son of Dengzhu, as lord."[61] In 553, the Qi emperor sent Kuti back, and Tiefa was killed by the Khitan, who installed Dengzhu as the ruler. He was killed in turn by the aristocratic opposition and succeeded by his son Kuti. In the same year, the Turks attacked again, and Kuti flew once more to China "with his entire people." The Northern Qi emperor sent an army northwards to push back the Turks, dethroned Kuti, and put Anluochen in his place. He promptly rebelled against the Chinese but was defeated: "Anluochen, with his wives, sons, and over thirty thousand followers were captured alive," and the Chinese also defeated further remaining Rouran groups. In the meantime, Anagui's uncle Dengshuzi had been raised by yet another part of the Rouran, was defeated by the Tujue, and fled to the Western Wei; but the Turks required them to be killed, whereupon three thousand men including Dengshuzi were slaughtered.[62] The last resistance was quelled in 555; a small group of Rouran remained under Turkish rule. The rather tedious narrative of inner conflict, desperate resistance, military disasters, and cruel massacres makes it clear that *the* Rouran/Avars cannot have migrated to Europe in any sufficient strength to establish themselves there. Their hordes were scattered, and most prominent members of the ruling dynasty were dead. The title khagan passed to the Ashina clan, rulers of the Tujue. What is remarkable is that unlike other steppe peoples, the name quickly disappeared after the fall of the Rouran empire, just as it happened after the dissolution of the Avar realm a quarter of a millennium later.

The new Turkish power quickly outdid their previous masters, swept to the southwest, and around 560 also destroyed the kingdom of the Hephthalites, a "Hunnic" dynasty that ruled over the Sogdian lands between the rivers Oxus/Amu Darja and Jaxartes/Syr Darja. Thus, they had controlled a number of flourishing trading cities at the hub between China, India, Persia, and the West, and lived in a succession of conflicts and alliances with the Sassanian rulers of Iran. Whatever the origin of this people, they "made use of the old imperial name of Huns" and were generally regarded as such by contemporary authors; Procopius called them "White Huns."[63]

Byzantium had hopes for an alliance with the new Turk Empire against the Persians, and diplomatic contacts were close. "In this way the Turkish people became friends of the Romans and established these relations with our state," as Menander summarizes.[64] The Turks also informed the Byzantines about their views on the Avar migration. For decades the Turkish khagans were to consider the Avars, whom they called Varchonites, as their rightful subjects. As late as the 570s Turxanthus accused a Roman envoy of having signed a pact with his runaway slaves, the Varchonites.[65] In 568 Justin II asked the Turkish envoy, the Sogdian Maniakh, how many Avars had absconded and how many remained under Turkish rule. "There are some who still adhere to us; those who fled number, I think, around twenty thousand," he replied.[66] Unlike many fantastic numbers in our sources from the period, the Sogdian's information seems rather plausible. That the Avars were not quite so unconquered as Kandikh asserted before Justinian was widely known in Byzantium and was repeatedly thrown back at them. The envoy Comentiolus told the khagan to his face in 584 that his Avars had initially been accommodated by the Romans as refugees, "when your part split off and separated from the original eastern tribe."[67] The khagan became so enraged over this awkward truth that he almost had the envoy executed. At the end of the century, the military commander Priscus still seized on this old accusation. In Theophylact we find an explanatory digression at this point, which will be dealt with below.[68] Evagrius Scholasticus, whose *Ecclesiastical History* was finished in ca. 592, also states: "The Avars are a Scythian people, one of the wagon-dwellers who range across the planes over there beyond the Caucasus; they had fled en masse from their neighbours, the Turks, after being ill-treated by them, and had come to the Bosporus."[69] Theodore Syncellus also wrote in 626 that the Avars under Baian had come to Europe as fugitives.[70]

There can be no doubt that the "Avars" who were encamped in the Caucasus region in 558 had fled from the Turkish expansion in central Asia. In so doing, they had split their group, which was called *Uarkhonitai* by the Turks, and many had remained behind under Turkish rule. There is also evidence that shortly after 580 more Varchonite tribes left the east for Europe and joined the Avar khaganate.[71] The circumstances of the Avar migration are described in a little-noted fragment from Menander in the *Excerpta de sententiis*. "When Sizabulus, the leader of the Turks, learned of the flight of the Avars and the damage they had caused to Turkish possessions at their departure," he declared that the Avars would not escape the Turkish swords. "When I have ended the war with the Hephthalites, I shall attack the Avars and they shall not escape my might."[72]

The refugees had thus used the war of the Turks against the Hephthalites to escape from the sphere of Turkish power. This means that even before the destruction of the Hephthalite polity they had been Turkish tributaries. Whether they defected from the Turkish army or broke out from the hinterland in the latter's absence cannot be determined. The Turks were clearly resentful that the Varchonite tributaries had made off at such a decisive moment. Turxanthus threatened to crush them like ants beneath the hooves of the Turkish horses, and the Avars themselves were apparently not comfortable with thoughts of their former masters.[73]

The flight from the Turks was not, however, the first that the West had heard about "Avars." Nearly a century earlier Priscus mentions them as a link in the chain that had pushed the Ogurs and other peoples toward the Black Sea. Two variants complicate this account. In the *Excerpta de legationibus* we learn only that the Avars, driven off by the peoples by the ocean, came up against the Sabirs.[74] The entry for the "Avars" in the *Suda Lexicon* that was compiled about the year 1000 contains another version of Priscus's text, which gives the story a mythological turn: The peoples that lived by the ocean shore were driven off by a multitude of man-eating griffins and by the fog that rose from the ocean, and as a consequence occupied the land of the Avars.[75] This story of remote mythical horror picks up elements from an ancient Scythian tale that Herodotus had already told of the Hyperboreans who lived by the northern sea.[76]

2.4 Avars or Pseudo-Avars?

If we only had the above cited sources on the migration of the Avars, we would still know more about their origins than is the case for many other peoples that suddenly appeared on the frontiers of the empire out of unfathomable Scythia. Yet Theophylact, who wrote more than two generations later with the aid of excellent sources (although he was often unsure of their correct order), has passed along substantially more information. His "Scythian digression," in which he seeks to explain the flight of the Avars from the east, is as rich in detail as it is in obscurities and is consequently much debated. The red thread in the digression, more confused than clarified by the author's interpolations, is a letter that a Turkish khagan (unnamed in the text) sent to Emperor Maurice to report his victory in a civil war. Theophylact inserts the letter into his narrative of 595, "when summer had arrived in this particular year." Scholars have tried to connect the events referred to in the text to what we know about the Turks from Chinese sources. But an inscription on the memorial statue of the Turkish khagan Niri (Nili in Chinese sources) at Xiao Hongnahai/Mongolküre, near the modern Chinese-Kasakh border, has made a more plausible interpretation possible, proposed by Étienne de la Vaissière: Niri had written the letter after a victory over his rival Dulan, called Turum in the letter, when the latter had proclaimed himself grand khagan of the Turks, the event mentioned in the inscription.[77] The letter also contained a brief narrative of the victories of the Turkish khagans over their enemies, which Theophylact erroneously ascribes to the one who had dispatched the letter. It presents no chronological account but supplies the rationale for the fact that the grand khagan could now call himself "ruler over seven peoples and lord of the seven zones of the earth." Similar but more extensive lists of subjugated peoples are found in two Orkhon inscriptions from the second Turkish khaganate.[78]

In the sequence reproduced in Theophylact the victory dispatch of the otherwise unnamed Turkish khagan reads as follows: First the Hephthalites (or *Abdeloi*) were conquered, then the Avars, of which a part fled toward *Tabgast* and another to the *Mukri* in the same region. Then are listed the Ogurs settled on the "black river" Til, some tribes of which are called *Var* and *Chunni*. Lastly, the *Kolch* are conquered in a bloody war.

Identifying these names still poses problems, despite a series of attempts undertaken with great erudition. The *Tabgast* to which a portion of the defeated Avars fled certainly refers to the empire of the Tuoba Wei in northern China; China is still called Tabghach in the Orkhon inscriptions, which refer to Chinese emperors as "khagan of the Tabghach." Theophylact probably confuses it with an otherwise unknown Bactrian city, allegedly founded by Alexander the Great. The people called Avars must be the Rouran, and according to this account the greater part fled eastward, to China and to the neighboring (Korean or perhaps Manchurian) *Mukri*.[79] The "black river" could be the Volga, Menander's "Atil." The *Kolch* were probably the *Choliatai* among whom the companions of the ambassador Zemarchus were waiting for his return from the Turkish war against the Persians in 570.[80] Because Theophylact, on the basis of the letter, believed that all these triumphs had been Niri's achievement, he dates them to the reign of Maurice. Of the victory over the Avars he therefore explains: "But no-one should believe that we have given a false account of the events, if he knows that the barbarians who have settled in Europe and Pannonia are Avars, whose arrival dates to before the time of Maurice. The barbarians in the Danube region are wrongly designated Avars."[81]

This is the core statement in Theophylact's digression on the origin of the Avars: It is not the Avars whom the Turkish khagan defeated who are the ancestors of the European Avars, but those Ogurs who were named—"supposedly after two mythical kings"—*Var* and *Chunni*.

> During the imperial rule of Justinian a small portion of the original tribe withdrew from these *Var* and *Chunni* and invaded Europe. These people called themselves Avars and designated their leaders with the

title *khagan*. How their name came to be changed we shall now tell. . . . When the *Barselt* and Onogurs and Sabirs and other Hunnic peoples of the region saw that a part of the *Var* and *Chunni* had fled into their districts, they became greatly afraid, since they assumed that the invaders were Avars. They honored the refugees with fine presents and believed that they would remain unharmed in return. When the *Var* and *Chunni* saw how successfully their flight had begun they made their own the error of those who had been sent to them and called themselves Avars. Among the Scythian peoples it is in fact said that the Avars are a people of great skill.[82]

Theophylact's bold assertion that the European Avars were in reality false Avars, *Pseudabaroi*, has been variously interpreted. That the true Avars of his account represent the Rouran is plausible. The list of victories of the Turkish khagan would be incomplete without a mention of the Rouran, with whose defeat Turkish dominion began.[83]

The name Avars, or similar, appears in the steppe zone in several variants. As early as in Herodotus we find a Scythian Abaris myth recounted. Its hero was the Hyperborean Abaris who traversed the world on an arrow.[84] "Aparnoi" are mentioned in Dagestan in Strabo's *Geography*. The city of Nishapur, or another city in Khorassan, was sometimes called Abar-šahr.[85] Yet the name really spread only in the late sixth century. Chinese sources repeatedly mention a people by the name of Aba (A-pa). In the year 585 they rebelled against the Turkish khagan Shabolüe.[86] Shortly after 600 they again took part in an insurrection by the Tiele federation against Turkish rule.[87] Perhaps the name "Apar" in the Kültegin inscription is a reference to them, if the traditional reading is correct.[88] The Avars occur in the list of peoples beyond the Caucasus in the *Chronicle* of Pseudo-Zacharias Rhetor, compiled in 568/69.[89] Theophylact apparently thought the Avars had been former neighbors of the Persians, when he writes of the flight of the chief shaman Bookolabras (around 580) to "his" Huns, "whom many also call Turks, nearby to the Persians."[90] Flavius Corippus also alludes to Persian–Avar relations. The Persians had initially feared the Avar khagan and had to treat for peace.[91] The fact that even today there are Avars in the Caucasus, who were already documented there in the Middle Ages, is part of this west Asian name tradition. An Ossete epic recounts that one could make one's fortune in the land of the Avars.[92] Yet as proofs of a consistent tradition of Avars north of Persia, these references are too scattered spatially and chronologically.[93]

Etymological interpretations of the name *Avar* are so speculative that they can scarcely be used as arguments for the origin of the European Avars. This is also true of the derivation from Mongolic *abarga*, "worm, snake," which may be linked to the derogatory Chinese variant of the name Rouran: Ruanruan, "worms coiled about themselves."[94] Like the Turkish etymology of *avar* as "rebellious, disobedient," it would not explain the name's Scythian past.[95] The success of the name *Avar* may be connected with the fact that it resonated in so many languages. As opaque as the name Avar itself are the two components of the name of the Varchonites. *Chunni* and *Ch(i)onites* are variants of the ethnonym Hun, whose extremely varied use precludes any more exact ethnic classification.[96] *Uar*, which according to Theophylact was the name of one of the Avar tribal ancestors, could simply be a variant of the name *Avar*. But clearly contemporaries did not view the two names as identical. In the Iranian languages, the word means "broad, wide" and was frequently used in the names of great rivers. The Huns took over *Var* as the name for the Dnieper.[97] Perhaps this is reflected in the information in the *Suda Lexicon* that the Avars initially set out from the banks of the Dnieper.[98] Half a millennium later there was a Mongol tribe called the *Varguni*.[99] Even if this name should be analogous to the Varchonites, it tells us nothing about the bearers of the name in the sixth century.

Due to this complicated evidence, the theories about the origins of the European Avars are multifarious. As early as the eighteenth century, Joseph de Guignes conjectured that despite Theophylact's assertion, Baian's Avars were descended from the Rouran, and this thesis became generally accepted, even though critical voices were raised against it here and there. The chronology seemed to support this proposition. Of both peoples it was known that they braided their hair in pigtails.[100] Theophylact's history of the Pseudo-Avars was frequently interpreted as a topos.[101] Michael Whitby dismissed it in rather wholesale fashion: "Theophylact's personal speculations about Avar origins are historically worthless."[102] And Peter Golden concludes: "The Pseudo-Avars may be safely removed from historical analysis. What remains are the Rouran (and variants) and the Abar/Avar/Awar. These are clearly one and the same people in Central Eurasia."[103]

Theophylact may have made many mistakes in his digression, but he had good information at his fingertips, and the central point he made was by no means his "personal speculation": the contention that the European Avars were not really Avars was the official diplomatic position of the Turks in their contacts with Byzantium, as incontrovertibly emerges from Menander's reports. One might still argue that the Turks lied, although they certainly knew better. But dismissing Theophylact's explanation altogether would be the wrong start.[104] A detailed critique of the identification of Rouran and European Avars was published by Yu Taishan in the 1980s, but hardly noticed in the West.[105] He argued that it would have been hard for remnants of the Rouran to escape westward where not only the Turks but also other former enemies blocked the way. Rather, he maintains, the Avars should be identified with the Yueban (Yueh-pan): "'Yueban' can assuredly be regarded as another transliteration of Avar or Apar."[106] They lived west of the Rouran and were defeated by them around 450, and then some of them moved westward, where Priscus took note of them. However, this would not explain why the Turks were so angry about the flight of the Avars a hundred years later.

H. W. Haussig, who also suggested that the Avars, whom he identified as part of the *Hua* of Chinese sources (along with the Hephthalites), had already lived near the Caucasus for a century when they established contact with the Byzantines, runs into the same problem.[107] Other researchers have traced the Avars back to the Ogurs of the Altai region.[108] But Priscus mentioned the two peoples as adjacent and hostile to one another.[109] The Hephthalite kingdom has also been considered a point of departure for the Avar migration, because of the occurrence of *Avar* and *Var* names in this region. However, its destruction by the Turks cannot have been the reason for the Avar migration, for at that time the Avar envoys had already reached Constantinople.[110] Haussig has also suggested that the name *Avar* was a traditional Sogdian designation for aliens such as the nomad peoples and thus had no ethnic specificity.[111] This would account for the rather diffuse evidence for the name in central Asia. However, it cannot explain why Sogdian envoys of Turkish khagans argued so forcefully that the European Avars were not "real" Avars, because then there could be no real Avars.

Károly Czeglédy proposed a very detailed hypothesis: he regards "Varchonites" as a broad umbrella term, which applied not only to the Hua (and their leading dynasty, the Hephthalites), but to the Rouran as well. From the latter were descended, as he seeks to prove, the European Avars as well. He makes a clear distinction between them and the Ogurs, whom he identifies with the Tiele of the Chinese sources.[112] Yet this contradicts Theophylact's contention that the Varchonites were in fact Ogurs; and if the Rouran were also Varchonites, why should the Turks argue that the fugitives were not Avars but Varchonites? As it would seem, neither Rouran nor Tiele or Yueban, dissident Turks nor scattered Hephthalites, Hungarian nor Uyghur Ogurs can simply be identified with the Avars who were encamped near the Caucasus in 558. It is a widespread misunderstanding to attempt an unequivocal identification of the European Avars with a central Asian people. So far, that has been the goal of most efforts to unravel the inconsistencies in Theophylact's many-layered text.

Obviously, for their contemporaries, the Avars (as they were known in the West) or Varchonites (as the Turks called them) were a clearly circumscribed group, a part of which remained under Turkish rule.[113] But their origin was diffuse, as was customary in the steppe. "They consist of thousands, even tens of thousands of tribes," wrote a Chinese emperor around 600 of the Turks.[114] The empires of the steppe horsemen were imperial federations with carefully hier-archized but very unstable relationships among the various groups. The most closely related could be the bitterest enemies; new entities could arise from the most diverse elements. "If Elteriš Khagan had not ruled, and if I myself, fol-lowing him, had not acted, there would be neither a realm (*el*) nor a people (*budun*)," we read in the Tonyukuk inscription of the eighth century.[115] The Orkhon inscriptions repeatedly emphasize how a successful ruler creates a great people from a small group: "Having become khagan, I gathered the whole mis-erable people; I have made the poor people rich, a people few [in number] have I made numerous."[116] The members of subjugated peoples affiliate themselves, are organized, and can promptly participate in the next military campaign.[117] This organizing of tribes and peoples through a mythically authorized constitu-tion was regarded as fundamental for the rise of the second Turkish khaganate at the close of the seventh century: "Over such an extent did they [the Turkish khagans] rule that they reordered the 'blue Turks,' who were without rulers and tribal organization."[118] The foundation of steppe empires led to recurrent shifts in the ethnic landscape of the steppe, and thus, eventually, the same name des-ignated more than one people or tribe, as Wilhelm Radloff already showed for the Kara-Kirghiz.[119] The mention of an ethnonym "in the context of the ethno-genesis of a central Asian people tells us nothing about who the bearers of this name really were."[120]

Conditions in Attila's empire illustrate that the peoples of the steppe were not fixed, stable entities: a Hun nobleman who soon appears as a Germanic king (Edica); a grandson of Attila who, according to circumstance, appears as a Hun or a Gepid (Mundo); a Greek merchant who emerges as a Hun warrior; and, after the collapse of the empire, a series of polyethnic groups that seek refuge in the Roman Empire.[121] If our sources were more limited than they are, we might easily draw the erroneous conclusion that Theoderic's Gothic "Scythians" were the descendants of Attila's Hunnic "Scythians," among whom Theoderic's uncle had assumed a leading position.

In such circumstances, origin myths were used for orientation, not only for those affected but also for learned ethnographers, who added their own timeworn concepts. "Above all, the sphere of migration, war for booty, and raiding parties could not be plausibly grasped by the ethnographers of Antiquity." The conceptual world of Antiquity had "at its disposal above all a model of origin and growth; as a consequence, the topos of *origo* was everywhere addressed."[122] What was transmitted in the guise of this topos is not necessarily limited to learned constructs but often contains contemporary information. Nonetheless, origin stories have a truth of their own; they do not reflect empirical data but mythical facts (in the sense of *factum*, "made"). In our sources, the myths of the peoples and those of the ethnographers are entangled. Usually they tell us more about the time when they were composed than about the past they address. If one were to transfer their information into modern scholarly language, it would automatically be falsified.[123]

Taking the oft-disparaged passage by Theophylact seriously as a source does not entail simply accepting or refuting his assertions. Clad in topical dress, his "Scythian digression," along with all its confusions, contains a considerable amount of knowledge about ethnic processes in the steppe zone. What emerges is that the equation "one people, one name" is inappropriate. Apart from shifts in ethnic identities that were always possible in the steppe, we have to take into account that the names that occur in Theophylact's account may be relevant on different levels. This emerges from Christopher Atwood's recent reflections on "ethnonyms, dynastonyms, and lineage names in Inner Asian dynasties."[124] Atwood distinguishes between four levels of names found in the sources to describe a steppe empire: First, the name of the ruling lineage, for instance the Ashina clan of the Turks or the Oqor clan of the Rouran, often derived from an eponymous ancestor. Second, a "dynastic name" that defined the entire empire, among which Atwood counts Xiongnu, Turk, or Rouran. Third, an ethnonym distinguishing a wider ruling group, such as "Avar" under the Rouran. And fourth, in some cases a further, possibly less prestigious ethnonym. Atwood's term "dynastonym" makes sense from the Chinese perspective, where successive empires were always distinguished by the name of their dynasties. It is less appropriate for the history of western Eurasia, where we should not forget that names such as the Merovingian, Carolingian, or Sassanian dynasty/empire are modern historical constructs, which are not prominently represented in contemporary sources. It would be more adequate to speak of political rather than dynastic identities.

The names used in Theophylact and elsewhere for the Avars are not easy to bring in line with Atwood's model. Yet it may be worth reflecting on it. Was "Avars" the imperial, political identity of the new power (Atwood's "dynastonym"), underlining that a core group of the Rouran Empire continued the rule of the khagans? Were "Var" and "Chunni" "genealogies of rulers," as Theophylact says, or alternative ethnonyms, blended into a shared "Varchonite" identity? Was "Ogur" an "alternative ethnonym" in the build-up of the Avar Empire, perhaps even conflated with the Oqor lineage of the Rouran? What exactly all these names meant could obviously shift with political fortune and the ethnic composition of a steppe polity. Theophylact may have translated a more complex structure of identification (in line with Atwood's model) into an ethnic origin narrative that was more attuned to the Roman ethnographic tradition. Over time, the political identity of the

Avars prevailed, whereas the composite ethnic identification as Varchonites faded out.

However that may be, if we take the contradictions and inconsistencies of the sources seriously, it is more or less the following picture that emerges:

1. That the European Avars were also called Varchonites is already attested to in Menander (see section 2.3); and, Theophylact adds, "down until our times," the seventh century, the European Avars "were divided according to genealogies of the rulers, and the one was called Var in time-honored fashion, and the other Chunni."[125] This observation by the chronicler is one of the few in which we come upon the trace of an actual Avar self-identification. All the rest comes from the accounts of their Turkish or Sogdian enemies, who also considered Baian's Avars to be Varchonites, as Menander asserts. However, this name does not help in tracing the European Avars to any particular central Asian people/s. It attests that they were considered a mixed population, and that the mixture included the very general label "Huns."

2. It is quite likely that the Rouran of Chinese sources were called, or called themselves Avars. Yet they do not seem to have been the sole bearers of this name. That should not surprise us. Recourse to such tradition was customary when names were given among the steppe peoples. "In order to invest them with religious and magic powers, these names [i.e., the title of the ruler and the name of the realm] would be selected from an ancient list of words transmitted especially for these occasions."[126] Theophylact describes such a practice quite accurately: the choice of a name for a new and ambitious group in a dialectic of external perceptions and self-designation. The *Oguz-Namē* later ascribes a similar appropriation of a prestigious origin to the Seljuks, in that case by affirming descent from the Turkish Ashina dynasty, which enjoyed the greatest prestige.[127] Whether the composite group that emerged from the ruins of the Rouran realm could legitimately be called Avars or could be ridiculed as Pseudo-Avars was a political issue but is unhelpful as a scholarly question.

3. The Avars of the West therefore cannot simply be identified with any "Avars" of the east. In their formation, no fewer than four names played a role, and all deserve to be taken seriously, quite independently of the context in which Theophylact mentions them: Avars, Var, Chunni, and Ogurs. This list resembles the enumeration of peoples subdued by the khagans of the Turks in the letter mentioned by Theophylact. This authorizes conclusions about the political program of the new "Avars":

they chose a name that enjoyed particular prestige among the steppe peoples; at the same time they were open to almost all ambitious victims of Turkish expansion. It became clear shortly after 552 that the mounted warriors between the Volga and the Great Wall of China had only the choices of living under Turkish rule or of migrating. While the core of the Rouran population between the Turks and China was destroyed, the future Avars prepared for an orderly withdrawal, for which the war against the Hephthalites gave the occasion. The bulk of the newly formed army was probably constituted by subordinate military groupings of the "ogur" model (see section 2.2). Yet they did not carry a name of that type and aimed higher. The newly formed group appropriated the prestigious name Avars. This was first of all their political identity, the name of the polity (rather than the dynasty)—they were Avars by decision. During the Hephthalite war, groups of those attacked by the Turks and additional west Asian-Caucasian groups quite possibly joined the movement westward.

4. It is doubtful whether the Rouran core group, compromised by the total defeat, could achieve this. Chinese sources relate that the nucleus of the Rouran was exterminated by the Turks with Chinese support in an uncustomarily brutal annihilation. Individual members of the ruling clan may have survived the Turkish and Chinese attacks and legitimized the appropriation of the title khagan by the new Avars. In this way, they could attract a growing following of people from the former Rouran realm and beyond it. Given the numbers many steppe dynasties acquired in the course of generations, it is not unlikely that the Avar khagan Baian could claim descent from the ruling clan of the Rouran.[128] Whatever his origin, what mattered was the title "khagan"; it remained so central to the legitimacy of the Avar polity that except for Baian, no other khagan's name appears in the sources. No doubt it was this presumption that enraged the Turkish khagans so much against their "fugitive slaves."

That the Avars who reached Europe did not originate in one single region is also suggested by the archaeological record in the Carpathian Basin. There is no trace of a homogeneous archaeological culture imported into the Carpathian Basin from anywhere else. Relatively insignificant reminiscences of central and inner Asia are found along with others from the region of the Caucasus.[129] The problem is that there is very little archaeological evidence from the realm of the Rouran, but they seem to have been more Sinicized in the sixth century than any evidence later found in the Carpathian Basin would suggest. For contemporary Byzantine observers, right up to Theophylact, the heterogeneous origin of the Avars was clearly apparent. But the Baian dynasty succeeded in monopolizing the name *Avars*; divergent names and identities were soon obliterated.

2.5 The Advance of the Avars

Some twenty thousand Avar warriors were encamped on the steppes north of the Caucasus in the year 558 and awaited the return of their envoys from Constantinople. This figure, which a Turkish emissary later communicated to the Romans, may be slightly exaggerated but is quite credible in contrast to the often fantastic numbers of barbarians given in the sources of the period. Arabic authors of the ninth century also put the strength of the Hungarians at twenty thousand men.[130] For the conditions of the time this was a considerable military force; a strong army in the age of migrations consisted of about fifteen to twenty thousand warriors. The Roman armies that defeated the Vandals in Africa and the Ostrogoths in Italy were in most cases no stronger than twelve to eighteen thousand soldiers. Although the total strength of imperial forces has been put at two hundred thousand to three hundred thousand, on only three occasions in the course of the sixth century was there an imperial army of about thirty thousand men in the field.[131] The pretentious words of the envoy Kandikh before Justinian then had a clear basis. Such high-flying statements as those with which Menander ornaments his accounts belonged to the repertory of the European Avars from the beginning. The sources establish how the ambassadors from the steppe could draw on many different registers. From the departure from central Asia onward the Avar khagan was prepared to play for higher stakes than his competitors from the Hun/Ogur milieu. He quickly succeeded in giving his followers a new self-confidence.

Deliberately or not, the Avars seem to have stirred up reminiscences of ancient Scythia among their Byzantine counterparts: the Avar name that caused fear and terror among opponents; the name (or title) of the envoy Targitius, who was named after a legendary Scythian king; perhaps even the tale of the griffins played a role here. According to Priscus, the Avars had initially been driven off by griffins on the shore of the ocean.[132] Herodotus had recounted a similar Scythian tale after Aristeas. He repeatedly mentions the gold-hoarding griffins by the ocean as the dangerous neighbors of the Hyperboreans of the far north and of the one-eyed Arimasps, and also bears witness to the Scythian veneration of griffins.[133] This motif was repeated for over a millennium in Greek ethnography and appears in the sixth century in the work of Stephen of Byzantium.[134] Priscus's account was taken over by the *Suda Lexicon* of the High

Middle Ages in the entry "Avar."[135] In the eighth century, the griffin became the most frequent motif in Avar art.[136] This creates a fascinating chain of associations that spans a millennium of steppe history. The mention in Priscus basically shows the mythological associations that the name *Avar* prompted among the Greeks. But both worlds were in constant exchange, especially with regard to symbols of power and prestige. Cultural traditions of the steppe and ethnographic constructions may not have been so remote from each other. The Byzantine image of the Scythians was not limited to ancient literary fiction, and the self-representation of the "Scythian" Avars was far from authentic—both influenced each other in the course of cultural exchange.

It is not improbable that the name *Avars* and the images related to it produced similar mythological associations among both friends and foes, as Theophylact indicates.[137] The Avars had a reputation for "politics of the supernatural." According to Gregory of Tours, they defeated the Franks by magical means. "Skilled in the arts of magic, they [the Avars] displayed various illusions and drew a great victory from it."[138] This constitutes a striking parallel to the Chinese perception of the Rouran, which included instances of weather magic in war.[139] The Avars played on the awe that their unfamiliar appearance, mythical associations, and sudden attacks could evoke. Their diplomacy frequently relied on arrogant appearances and the intimidation of the opponent. The envoys' inflated words could thus become a self-fulfilling prophecy. The high claims staked with the appropriation of the name "Avars" were reconfirmed with each victory and could thus become the common denominator of a heterogeneous people.

The progress of the Avar army through the steppe belt north of the Black Sea was hardly as swift as Menander's account suggests. The Cutrigurs attacked Constantinople in 558/59 without any documented Avar involvement, and Agathias, who wrote in these years, did not mention them as a political player. The exact course of their victorious advance cannot be accurately reconstructed. Menander names as subjugated peoples the "Unigurs" (probably the Onogurs), the Hunnic Zali, the Sabirs, and finally the Antes, in this sequence.[140] The *Suda Lexicon* preserves information, probably also going back to Menander, that the Avars originally set out from the area where the Danaper/Dnieper flows.[141] In any case, the first victims of the Avar attack were probably, like a century earlier, the Sabirs. In the sixth century they were located north of the Caucasus, had invaded Armenia in 515 and 548, and subsequently played a certain role in varying alliances with Byzantium and the Persians.[142] They are not mentioned as being part of the Avar army after their defeat. Their kingdom in the Caucasus region continued to exist, however, and from there they pursued their seesaw politics between the Romans and the Persians.[143] The year 559 in no way marked the fall of the Sabir kingdom; the victory over the Sabirs was just one episode in the Avar migration.

Similarly not too much importance should be attached to the defeat of the otherwise scarcely known Zali.[144]

It is remarkable that Menander mentions a victory over the Onogurs, but no confrontation with the Utigurs and Cutrigurs. The latter two had been weakened by fratricidal strife. Khagan Baian later claimed the yearly payments that both peoples had received from the emperor on the grounds that he had subdued them.[145] The Cutrigurs are mentioned once in 568 as an autonomous but none too respected unit in the Avar army.[146] The *Histories* of Agathias end with the fall of Utigurs and Cutrigurs; as a result of their conflict, both peoples lose their "identity": "The scattered remnant of these Hunnic tribes has in fact been reduced to servitude in the lands of other peoples whose names they have assumed. . . . But the complete annihilation of these two peoples occurred at a later date, so that I shall do my best to preserve a strict chronological order and provide a detailed account of this event in its proper place." This promise, unfortunately, was left unfulfilled.[147]

These examples show that the "annihilation" of a steppe kingdom, despite all the rhetorical assertions, is not always to be understood literally. The Utigurs preserved their kingdom by the Sea of Azov after the Avar horsemen had moved on. About 575 the Roman envoy Valentinus on his way to the Turks encountered the followers of the Utigur prince Anagaius, who as a Turkish vassal shortly thereafter took part in the campaign against the city of Bosporus. Now the Turks could boast in turn of having subjugated the peoples of the Black Sea. "Today they serve as our slaves," crowed Turxanthus before a Roman embassy.[148] A few decades later the Cutrigurs again show up on the Pontic steppe and play a substantial role in the "Great Bulgaria" of Khan Kuvrat.[149] Under Avar rule, warriors from the Black Sea steppes came to be subsumed under the label "Bulgars," a name that is not even mentioned among the peoples they encountered on their march westward.

Menander treats the Avar attack on the Antes, who probably lived northeast of the Carpathians, in somewhat more extensive fashion.[150] After the first defeats they sent one of their most prominent representatives to the khagan. He had the Slavic name Mezamir and was the brother of Kelagast, perhaps their leader or king. Instead of negotiating about the release of prisoners, as had been agreed, he made the mistake of addressing the Avars in the Avar way: "When he came to the Avars he spoke arrogantly and very rashly." The khagan was apparently advised in this matter by a Cutrigur familiar with the area. He had unflattering words to say about the Antes. He pointed out that the arrogant envoy was the most powerful man of his people and counseled his assassination. Dispatching the "rash fool" was not following the rules of diplomacy, but it produced results. The resistance of the Antes fell apart.

The interest of the Avars in the Antes seems to have been limited to pillaging and submission. This is the fashion in which sedentary peoples were dealt with. In conflict among nomads it was subordination that counted. Yet the Antes were not "annihilated" in this way. In 602 an Avar army still had to set off against these allies of the Byzantines who once again posed a threat.[151] Within a few years, the Avars had successfully completed their military campaign through the Pontic steppe zone. But it would be erroneous to assert that they had extended their rule "from the Elbe to the Caucasus" or even as far as the Dnieper.[152] No direct exercise of influence is further attested in this region (apart from the preemptive strike against the Antes). The interest of the Avars was henceforth concentrated on southeastern and eastern central Europe. In 562 or more likely 563 the Avars were on the Danube. The only threat that they still had at their backs was the Turkish khaganate.

2.6 Byzantium and the Turks

While the Avars were on the Danube, the first envoys from the new great power in the east appeared in Constantinople. At the imperial court there was still some uncertainty about the newcomers. Theophanes of Byzantium recounts: "East of the Tanais [the Don] dwell the Turks, earlier called Massagetes, whom the Persians call Kermichions in their language. These then sent gifts and envoys to the Emperor Justin, with the request that he not receive the Avars. . . . When the Avars came later, to request Pannonia as an area to settle and to plead for peace, he concluded no agreement with them because of the accords and treaties with the Turks."[153] A similar piece of information is also found in Theophanes the Confessor. According to him, "envoys arrived from Askel, king of the Hermichions, who dwell inland from the barbarian nation near the ocean."[154] He dates the event to the thirty-sixth year of Justinian, 562–63. The question whether the two passages refer to the same or to two embassies is less relevant than the unusual names used by both. Some scholars identified the Hermichions in the second passage with the Avars, but that is incompatible with the first one.[155] The demand not to support the Avars is consistent with Turkish diplomacy. A Turkish delegation may have come after the victory over the Hephthalites. But why do the Turks appear here as "Kermichions"? Clearly, it was an Iranian-speaking interpreter who presented the gentlemen from far-off central Asia at the imperial court, probably a Sogdian as some years later. *Xyōn* was a Persian form of "Huns," and Kermichions may mean "Red Huns," from Persian *karmir*, "red," in contrast to the "White Huns," as the Hephthalites had been called.[156]

It is more difficult to identify "king" Askel. No Turkish ruler at the time had a matching name. At that time two khagans ruled over the Turks: One, according to Chinese sources, was named Sse-kin, called himself Muqan Khagan, and ruled from about 553 to 572. The other one, who reigned until 575, was called Istemi in the Turkish inscriptions, and Stembischadas or Stembiskhagan by Theophylact. His title was Syr Yabgu, which was understood as a name by the Byzantines and rendered as Sizabulos by Menander.[157] Theophylact ascribes the overthrow of the Hephthalites and Avars to Istemi, together with a second, unnamed leader. This agrees with Turkish tradition, which in the Kültegin inscription credits the founders of the realm, Bumin and Istemi, with victory over all their enemies.[158] In fact, after the early death of Bumin it was his younger son Muqan who led the Turks to the final obliteration of the Rouran and in the war against the Hephthalites. There is little to gain by identifying Askel with the even more obscure Scultor mentioned in Corippus's panegyric to Justin II.[159] Many scholars have identified either or both of them with Istemi, who established an increasingly autonomous west Turkish realm and later cultivated diplomatic relations with Byzantium.[160] That is possible, although Askel may also have been a subordinate Turkish leader conducting operations in the west of the expanding Turkish realm. The many variants of a single ruler's name are generally difficult to handle. What problems a foreigner must have had with the titles and names of the khagans is illustrated by a Chinese notice on the ascension to the throne of Shetu: according to the *Sui shu* he was elected under the title "I-li-kü-lu Shad Mo-ho-shi-po-lo" and thereafter called himself Shabolüe.[161]

Within a few years the khaganate of the Turks had attained a position of power unusual even for the Eurasian steppe. Its policies were principally oriented toward the east. The Turks knew how to exploit the contention among the divided Chinese realms; Turkish armies drove deep into the core of Chinese lands and compelled the emperors to costly gifts, which were preferably paid out in the form of silk. Westward, the Turks controlled the silk trade up to the Persian frontier, which, according to the Orkhon inscriptions, mostly ran along the Tämir-qapiq, the Iron Gate, a pass between the present-day cities of Samarkand and Balkh.[162] Because of silk, the new rulers of the steppe soon came into conflict with the Sassanian rulers of Persia.

Menander recounts that the Sogdians lobbied the Persian court for trading privileges with the approbation of the Turkish khagan Sizabulos. King Chosroes I, "who was little pleased that the Turks should freely enter Persia," answered with a provocation: he bought up the Sogdian silk and had it burned before the eyes of the envoys. At this point the trade conflict became a matter of state. When Sizabulos, with a second delegation, pressed for a treaty, the Persian king brusquely dismissed his former allies. Some members of the delegation were even poisoned, the Turks asserted. The Persians maintained that they had fallen victim to the torrid climate.[163] Chosroes I clearly feared losing control over the lucrative silk trade. In the West, the price of a pound of silk (about 330 grams) under Justinian was fifteen solidi, that is, about sixty-five grams of gold.[164] At some point, the Byzantines succeeded in getting a silkworm culture into their own hands from the Sogdians. However, this politically momentous smuggling business, in which two Indian monks played a principal role, did not make the West independent of silk imports, and Chinese silk remained in high demand.[165] The Sassanian ruler was not prepared to drop this card from his hand. In 567 a Persian delegation appeared in China, obviously in order to propose an alliance to contain Turkish power.[166]

On this geopolitical chessboard the Turks now made the logical move. They turned toward Byzantium. We are well informed of the subsequent exchange of embassies by Menander. Again, the well-connected Sogdians had taken the initiative, and their prince Maniakh was entrusted by Sizabulos with the leadership of the mission to Constantinople. The delegation appeared at the close of the year 568 in the imperial city, bringing silk of considerable value as gifts, and proposed a friendship treaty. One of the issues was excluding the Persian middlemen from the silk trade. This may not have been accomplished, but the alliance was sealed with ceremonial oaths.[167] The emperor informed himself carefully of the circumstances of his new allies. The extensive realm was then ruled by four princes, while supreme rule was exercised by Sizabulos, as he claimed.[168] As usual the Turks enumerated their tributary peoples. The Byzantines were particularly interested in the Avars, who were about to settle in the Carpathian Basin.

To confirm the treaty, in the late summer of 569 Justin sent one of his highest military officers on the long journey to the Turkish ruler. This was the *magister militum* of the east, Zemarchus, who would be the commander-in-chief in an eventual war against the Persians.[169] This shows that the Byzantines expected very tangible military support from the Turks. Accompanied by Maniakh, the general reached Sogdiana, where the Turks had readied a memorable reception. First, he was offered iron to purchase: the Turks were widely known as smiths, and blacksmithing had an important sacral signification. Then some shamans sought to exorcize a spirit from him by means of fire. Finally (according to John of Ephesus, after one year), they reached the Ektag, the Golden Mountain, in the vicinity of which lay the khagan's residence.[170]

Sizabulos/Istemi took the occasion to show off his treasure before the eyes of the Romans. Zemarchus would also accompany the ruler on a campaign against the Persians, well attended by a Kirghiz slave woman and twenty servants. In the end, once he was on his way back, Istemi gave him an envoy of his own, whose title was *tagma-tarkhan*. Menander describes the difficult route of the delegation to the Caspian Sea, then along its northern shore and across the Volga, where they encountered Ogurs, and finally across the Kuban through enemy territory to the land of the Alans and the Black Sea.[171] For part of the way, the party probably traveled along the route so vividly described by Ibn Fadlan more than three hundred years later. Zemarchus's two-year journey greatly excited the imagination of the Byzantines. The capital soon swarmed with rumors and fantastic accounts of the land of the Turks, some of which were preserved by John of Ephesus.[172] For instance, he recounts that the envoys had found the king in tears, since an ancient prophecy held that a Roman embassy to that distant region meant the end of the world.

These contacts with inner Asia triggered great fear and hope in Constantinople. But both tellers of tall tales and exponents of realpolitik were to be disappointed. The alliance with the Turks, despite a series of adventure-ridden journeys by envoys, had few noticeable results. Emperor Justin II clearly seems to have betted on the Turkish card for a considerable time. The powerful ally in the east gave him the confidence to risk a war against the Persians and induced him into a dangerous underestimation of the Avars.[173] Trusting the dismissive words of the Turks about the Avar "ants," Justin delayed any treaty with Baian for years.

2.7 The Discovery of Europe

On the northern frontier of the empire the situation had become increasingly unstable. Hostile competition between the barbarian peoples was fueled by Byzantine diplomacy with all means possible. In 559 the Utigurs were incited against the pillaging Cutrigurs, who, after their defeat, were then supported against the former. At the same time Byzantium was allied with the Avars against both of these, while having a pact with the Turks against the same Avars. In this strife, where each party was incited against the other, the emperor could not hope for lasting security. More quickly than anticipated, the Avars asserted themselves. The khagan had hardly brought the entire Pontic zone under actual control, but he had achieved his goal: to emerge as the victor over his competitors on the frontier of the empire and from this position of strength to be able to continue negotiations with the empire. All prior experience would have told the emperor to now view his former allies as enemies. He had to count on a recurrence of the threatening situation experienced with Zabergan's incursion a few years earlier. Yet to deal openly with the khagan as an opponent, the military forces were as inadequate as they had been during the Cutrigur campaign. With all means possible the emperor sought to delay an impending Avar attack.[174]

In 561/62, an Avar delegation to Constantinople demanded the land promised for settlement on imperial territory. The tug-of-war that then ensued recalls the lengthy negotiations that earlier emperors had pursued with various Gothic kings. Then, the fundamental issue had been incorporation in the Roman military economy. The new settlers had been de jure imperial troops, who regularly received allocations from the Roman military budget and were supplied with foodstuffs by the inhabitants of the provinces. At the same time they had gained an operational basis from which to exert further pressure on the imperial administration. This precarious system of settled federates still had an advantage for the Romans in that barbarians within the Roman system were more calculable, and it drove a wedge between the "internal" and "external" barbarians. But the risk was that barbarian rulers based on Roman infrastructure would become independent, as had the barbarian kingdoms of the West. Combat against them had been the primary goal of Justinian's policies.[175] The emperor therefore sought to avoid an Avar settlement in a Roman province but had little else to offer.

The Avar envoys, who wished to inspect the lands for settlement, were received with little enthusiasm. On the advice of the general Justin, the emperor offered the Avars that part of the province of Pannonia II in which the Heruls had once lived.[176] Pannonia II comprised a none too extensive area between the Sava, Danube, and Fruška Gora, in which the ancient metropolis of Sirmium lay. This city was the residence of the Gepid king; only a strip of land along the route to Singidunum/Belgrade, around the ruins of Bassianae/Petrovci, still lay in the Roman sphere of influence. About 512, Emperor Anastasius had settled the displaced Heruls here on the Gothic frontier, who in the 540s numbered only a few thousand men, the greater part of whom then joined the Gepids.[177] This exposed front of the Roman line of defense lay right in the conflict zone between the Gepids and Lombards, which had already determined the fate of the Heruls. Little wonder that the Avars declined; they did not wish, according to Menander, to live outside "Scythia," whether that meant, according to Byzantine usage, the province of Scythia minor that the Avars demanded or the Black Sea steppe where the Avar power base lay.

While negotiations dragged on without results, the general won an Avar envoy over to his side, "Kunimon [who] had told him confidentially that their intent was different from what they professed. Their demands were very modest, and by asserting their goodwill towards the Romans they were using their reasonableness as a mask for their treachery until by this means they had crossed the Danube. Their intent, however, was otherwise, and, if they managed to cross the Danube, they planned to launch an attack with their whole army."[178] The Avar Kunimon bore the name of the Gepid king

Cunimund. It cannot be excluded that Menander misunderstood his original and that in reality it was an envoy of the Gepid king who warned of the new neighbors. But it may also have been a Goth or Gepid who had joined the Avar army and had been sent along with the delegation because of his knowledge of conditions on the Danube.

Again, the general Justin played for time. He sent the Avar envoys back again to Constantinople and secretly advised the emperor to detain them there as long as possible. They were in fact held there under all possible pretexts without any concessions being made to their demands. They used the time to buy weapons and clothes. The emperor ordered his general Justin to appropriate the weapons from the envoys on their way home. "Thereafter the hostility between the Romans and the Avars, which had already been smoldering, broke out."[179] Meanwhile, Justinian had entrusted the organization of defense to his *maiordomus* Bonus.[180] What then occurred remains unclear, since the fragment of Menander breaks off at this point. Sometimes information from the so-called *Chronicle of Monemvasia* (from about 900) that Justinian had allowed the Avars to take up residence in the city of Durostorum/Silistra in Moesia is used to fill the gap.[181] Had the emperor ended up by accommodating the Avars? Rather, this is an error in the *Chronicle*, in which the distinction between the Avars and the Slavs has been lost. For when Justin II assumed the emperorship in 565, the Avars were still on the other side of the Danube.

However, we hear nothing of hostilities either, so the Avars did not react with full force. The aged Belisarius did not have to help out once again. On the contrary, the Avar army made itself felt elsewhere. It took the route north of the Carpathians and moved against the Franks. Shortly after the death of King Chlothar I (December 5, 561), his son Sigibert of Austrasia won a victory "in Thuringia iuxta Albim fluvium" over the forces of the khagan.[182] The date of Chlothar's death is the only point of reference for the chronology of Avar moves in the years 558–65. It is customary to date the confrontation on the Danube to the years 561–62, and the Frankish campaign to 562. In any case, the reverse sequence is also plausible. This would make it easier to understand why the Avars turned against the enemies of the empire, who primarily threatened Byzantine rule in northern Italy. In 561 the Frankish *dux* Amingus engaged in a bloody battle with the troops of Narses on the Adige river in Italy.[183] East Roman diplomacy is often assumed as instigating the Avar campaign on the Elbe.[184] But this cannot be the complete explanation. For, a few years later, the khagan repeated his attack on the remote northeast of the Frankish kingdom. This was the year after the new emperor Justin had denied the Avar emissary Targitius any form of tributary payment with harsh words.[185] In this campaign in 566 the Frankish forces suffered a serious defeat. The Avars, as Gregory of Tours noted, were allied with magical forces and crippled the Frankish resistance with all sorts of illusions. King Sigibert himself fell into Avar captivity. But he quickly freed himself from this awkward situation: "although he could not beat them in battle, he managed to suborn them later by bribery."[186] From the Romans the Franks had learned not only to propitiate victorious enemies with "gifts," but also to cloak these embarrassing facts in fine words.

In a surprise move the khagan sealed a treaty with the Frankish king and agreed to withdraw within three days in return for supplies for his apparently badly provisioned army. This requires an explanation: Why mount a large-scale campaign against the kingdom of the Franks if, after a brilliant victory, one could be bought off with "flour, lentils, sheep and beef"?[187] Once again many historians see Byzantine diplomacy at work or believe that in his treaty with Sigibert Baian had obtained support against the Gepids. Some even speculated that with this treaty, Sigibert had ceded the "Germanic east" to the Avars and saw in this the beginnings of the Slavic settlement on the Elbe and Oder.[188]

Why did Baian twice in a row prefer expeditions into regions where nothing was to be gained except supply problems, over an attack on the still rich Balkan provinces? The transparent interests of imperial politics can give historians no adequate explanation for the khagan's motives. The argument that the Avars were too weak for an assault on the empire cannot explain the equally risky venture on the Elbe, when we bear in mind how common barbarian raids on the Balkans had become. That "the shadows of Narses and Belisarius spread anxiety and fear in the Avar camps" is scarcely plausible.[189] If we explain Avar undertakings in those years simply with reference to their anxiety or their "pro-Byzantine policy,"[190] we imply that they had no strategy of their own. However, barbarian peoples were not simple pawns of imperial politics. As Ernst Stein noted, "Avar diplomacy exhibits a breadth of vision and logic that stand in no relation to the cultural level of this people and are equal to those of the Romans."[191] Avar policy is obviously more difficult to grasp, since it can be assessed only from the testimony of opponents. Even today the historian is more at home with imperial reasons of state than with the strategies of a nomad ruler.

Still, we should not give up explaining barbarian policy altogether. If we inquire as to its conditions, an internal coherence can be established, even if this picture remains hypothetical. Such an attempt at explanation should not be steered simply by our perception of political utility, a criterion that Baian's two Frankish campaigns scarcely satisfy. Equally determinative of action were notions of legitimacy, prestige, and symbolic dominion. They were decisive for the cohesion of a barbarian polity and for the success of its ruler. The khagan's art of leadership consisted of adapting these symbolic forms of legitimization to the realities of power politics and, conversely, of interpreting current realities in a traditional sense. The Old Turkic inscriptions and the letter of the Turkish khagan that is preserved in Theophylact's digression exhibit such formalized self-representation of a steppe ruler. An essential component in this is the catalog of subjugated peoples, mostly arranged by the quarters of the compass. The basic constituent of a steppe empire was to have conquered the neighboring peoples on every side.

This required no factual control over these peoples. Just as the Turks decades later still considered the Pannonian Avars as their vassals and made this matter the crucial point in their relations with Byzantium, Baian, from the Carpathian Basin, laid claim to the annual tribute of the Cutrigurs and Utigurs living by the Sea of Azov, "since today Baian is the master of all these tribes."[192] The khagan's victory over all opponents within his reach founded and legitimized a new order of rulership. It is no coincidence that the first Avar delegation boasted before Justinian of being capable of defeating "all" enemies and that later the Avar khagan asserted before the envoy Theodore that he was the lord of all peoples. Corippus has Avar envoys boast that their khagan had waged war at the ends of the world and overcome famous tyrants.[193] We get even more of this rhetoric from the Turks. Turxanthus assured that "the whole world is subject to me from the farthest East to the very western edge."[194]

In fact, Baian did succeed within a few years in establishing symbolic supremacy over all his competitors. In the case of the Franks it is evident that it was not a matter of conquering even portions of the Frankish kingdom. The decisive factor was that the defeat of 562 was not a matter to let rest; a ranking had to be established, if the khagan actually wished to legitimize himself as world ruler in the eyes of his warriors. The clause in the pact in 566–67 with the Lombards, according to which the latter had to surrender a tenth of their livestock to the Avars, may have had a similar significance.[195] In both cases, a tribute of food may have been endowed with symbolic meanings by the Avars, apart from its practical value.

The chief objective of the first decade of Avar policy was the establishment of hegemony in the barbarian lands and thereby confirmation of the position of the khagan in a fast-growing polyethnic confederation of warriors. Too hasty a major attack on the empire would have threatened this strategy. Experience had shown that pillaging barbarian armies often split apart once on imperial soil, as also occurred in 558–59 with Zabergan's army.[196] A failure early on may have cost Baian his position. He thus initially limited himself to large-scale demands and small-scale skirmishes. Through this cautious strategy the khagan laid the foundation for the power politics of the following years.

2.8 Decisive Years

During the night of November 14, 565, the seventy-eight-year old Justinian died; on the next day his nephew and successor, Justin II, assumed the rulership. From the very beginning he made it clear that he would pursue a different foreign policy. Unlike his predecessor, he assumed the epithet *pacificus*. This in no way meant that he intended to live in peace with his neighbors. Quite the contrary, this was a conscious regress to the ancient Roman virtue of defending the *pax Romana* by all means possible. The often-criticized appeasement policy of Justinian toward the northern barbarians would be abandoned.[197] Decisive for this step was not so much the constrained financial situation—wars were generally more expensive than a bought peace—as the need to improve the battered prestige of the empire. In this sense it is perhaps suitable that Michael the Syrian, the chronicler of the crusader age, characterizes Justin as the "last Frank," that is, the last Latin Roman on the imperial throne.[198]

The new emperor had his accession to the throne celebrated in ancient Roman fashion with a panegyric in Latin. Corippus's poem has been preserved, save for its first lines. The remaining part of the preface begins with an enumeration of foreign embassies: "That famed people, the Avars, dreadful with their snaky hair, horrible to look upon and fierce in bloody warfare, begs for peace in the middle of your palace."[199] A long section then celebrates Justin's handling of an Avar embassy: That Baian's envoys humbled themselves before the emperor was the case only in the sense of court ceremonial. Nonetheless, the description that the poet gives of the entrance of the envoys is illuminating: the display of imperial grandeur on the "Mount Olympus" of the empire, which Corippus describes at great length, as well as the self-assurance of the barbarians, who were not shy in making their demands.[200]

No later than the seventh day after his accession, the Avar embassy, which had already been staying in Constantinople, was given an audience with the emperor.[201] The leader of the delegation was Targitius,[202] one of the few Avar dignitaries known by name. Justin mobilized all his resources to impress the barbarians. In the great hall of audiences, he had taken his seat on the huge, elaborately decorated throne, flanked by winged goddesses of victory, who held a golden laurel wreath above his head. He wore a brilliant white and purple robe, a golden cloak, and golden belt, as well as purple boots of Parthian leather. The entire room was lavishly decorated with gold, precious stones, and costly carpets and draperies. About the emperor the senate had taken seats in long rows, while at the entry stood guards in splendid uniforms. "Indeed, as the veil was drawn back and the inner doors opened, and the gold-covered halls shone, the Avar Tergazis beheld from below how the imperial head blazed under the holy diadem, and genuflecting three times he adored him, and remained prostrate and cast to the floor." The elaborate imperial presentation could not fail to have its effect on the barbarians, who were now led in. "They believed that the Roman palace was a second heaven." In spite of all the rhetorical indulgence of the panegyrist this assertion is scarcely exaggerated. Generations of barbarian warriors had given their lives in order to win a reflection of the luxurious displays of the "New Rome." The *imitatio imperii* was the foundation of barbarian rule. It bound the empire and the barbarians together in contradictory but indissoluble fashion. Archaeological evidence shows that representation of status predominantly followed Byzantine models in the Avar khaganate. Targitius then transmitted the khagan's message. Corippus has these exotic aliens from the north speak principally of snow and ice, which reflects the geographical conceptions of the author rather than the words of the envoys. In this context the observation that the Persian Empire had to buy peace from the Avars is less meaningful than the student of Avar history might wish. An Avar host had hardly crossed the (frozen!) Euphrates, as is here asserted. Notwithstanding, pertinent information can be extracted from Targitius's speech. According to him, Baian's army had put up its tents on the Danube. The emissary boasted, as usual, of having subjugated a host of peoples and kingdoms. And he demanded the customary tribute that Baian had received during Justinian's reign. The treaty from 558 had thus apparently continued to be honored despite the turbulence of the year 563. But now Justin rebuffed the Avars. He emphasized that Justinian's gifts had been freely given and that the Avars had no real claim to them. He did not fail to mention the flight of the Avars from their homeland in the east. And he stated that in the event of an Avar attack the Romans would know how to defend themselves.

Both the Avars' demands and Justinian's refusal are confirmed in Menander's account of these same events.[203] The two speeches, which he too cites, are reproduced in somewhat different fashion. In this version Targitius is appreciably more affable. Yet the Avars demanded, according to Menander, even more gifts than previously. According to Menander it was above all gold chains, decorated couches, and other luxury goods that were desired. Justin responded that the best gift would be to instill a proper anxiety in the Avars, so that they would not dare to attack the Romans, which would cost them their lives.

The emperor is seen at his most hostile in the version of John of Ephesus.[204] Here he insults the Avar envoys as dead curs and threatens to have their hair cut off. Then he has them, some three hundred men in all, interned in Chalcedon and finally orders them never to be seen in the capital again. The forced detention by the Sea of Marmara definitively cures the barbarians of their lust to attack. The place that the embassy of 565 occupies in different accounts and the various elaborations that it is subjected to show that Justin's performance impressed the Byzantines. It represented a policy of strength that flattered the Roman self-image, although most of the authors knew how subsequent history unfolded when they wrote. In any case, Justin's gesture initially had the desired effect. The threatened attack was deferred, and Baian, as Menander writes, first turned against the Franks.[205]

It is improbable that it was actually fear of Roman weapons that dissuaded the khagan from an attack against imperial lands. Perhaps the Turkish threat played a role. The provisioning of the army must, in any case, have caused difficulties. The winter of 566 was unusually severe. Marius of Avenches recounts that the snow lay in his Burgundian homeland for five months.[206] After their defeat that year, the Franks were obliged to supply the Avars with foodstuffs. In the following year, as part of an agreement, the Lombards had to give up a portion of their livestock. For the moment this was more important than any gold chains and couches that might be had from Byzantium. The basis for an attack against the empire had first to be secured.

The turn toward the west was surely connected to the escalating conflict between the Lombards and the Gepids, into which the Avars would soon be drawn. After 453 the Gepids had won the core areas of Attila's fallen empire. Their kingdom comprised the eastern half of the Carpathian Basin and Transylvania. Their king, Cunimund, now had his residence in Sirmium, close to lands under Roman control—and not far from those of the Lombards. In 508 the Lombards had conquered the kingdom of the Heruls in southern Moravia and Lower Austria. With time they had advanced toward the southeast. The center of their zone of power now lay in Pannonia, which they controlled except for the area around Sirmium. The power struggle between the two peoples that had initiated in the 540s, fueled by the Romans, flamed up again in 565. Initially beaten, the Gepids secured Byzantine support with the promise of the return of Sirmium but did not keep this promise after the victory of 566.[207]

The Lombard king Alboin would not let the matter of the defeat rest. Years ago the Gepids had summoned the Cutrigurs into the country against his father. Now he sent an embassy to Baian. The delegates had first to convince the khagan of the desirability of a pact. They pointed to the Roman support of the Gepids. The destruction of the Gepid kingdom would also strike a blow against Emperor Justin, who was so hostile toward the Avars. After the occupation of the Gepid lands, the Avars and Lombards could march together into Scythia (minor) and Thrace and even attack Constantinople. "The envoys of the Lombards declared that it would be to the advantage of the Avars to launch a war against the Romans. Otherwise, the Romans would act first and use every means to destroy the power of the Avars, wherever in the world they happened to be."[208]

"When Baian received the envoys of the Lombards, he decided to toy with them since he wished to make an alliance with them that was more to his advantage. Now he claimed that he could not join them, now that he could but was unwilling. When, in short, he had used every trick upon his petitioners, he gave the appearance of agreeing reluctantly and only on condition that the Avars received immediately one tenth of all the livestock that the Lombards possessed and that, if they prevailed, they should have half the booty and all the land of the Gepids."[209] The negotiating skill of the khagan had its effect. Alboin was clearly ready to pay a high price to bring about a decision to move against his archenemies, the Gepids.

Cunimund now understood what a predicament he was in; once again he promised the surrender of Sirmium to the Romans. At the same time, a Lombard embassy also tried to induce the emperor into an accord. The emperor decided to let the tragedy run its course and dismissed the Gepids with vague promises. Now the fate of the Gepid kingdom, attacked in 567 from both sides, was inexorably set. Cunimund decided to move against the Lombards first. On the battlefield he lost both his kingdom and his life, reputedly at the hand of Alboin himself. The Gepid army was shattered. Alboin took a great deal of booty, among which Cunimund's daughter, Rosamund, whom he forced into a marriage. "The people [genus] of the Gepidae were so diminished that from that time on they had no king. But all who were able to survive the war were either subjected to the Lombards or groan even up to the present time in bondage to a grievous mastery since the Huns possess their country [patria]."[210] The Avars were able, without any major battles, to take possession of the Gepid lands on the Tisza. A Roman army under Bonus seized Sirmium and a number of illustrious Gepid refugees.[211]

The other half of the Carpathian Basin was also to fall into the hands of the Avars without a fight. On April 2, 568, Easter Monday, a mass migration toward Italy was set in motion by Alboin. Gepids, Sarmatians, Suebi, Pannonians, Noricans, possibly Bulgars, and even Saxons joined the Lombard army.[212] A ninth-century chronicle claims that Alboin had left Pannonia to the Avars under the condition that his people could retain the right to return for two centuries.[213] This information, written down after the fall of the Lombard kingdom in Italy, may not be accurate, but it shows that the memory of the Pannonian homeland was preserved in Italy. Likewise, the Italian Ostrogoths considered Pannonia their home, and Heruls and Vandals, long after their emigration, are said to have maintained contacts with the regions of their origin. In a very few years the political geography of east central Europe had been fundamentally altered. The dramatic events of 565–68 appealed to the imagination. When, after 590 and during the Avar war under Maurice, a Gepid robber and murderer was seized, the young man asserted that he had captured his precious booty from one of Alboin's sons in Cunimund's last battle.[214] He thus reinterpreted Gepid ethnic tradition—which no longer corresponded to a coherent ethnic entity—as his own personal history. The *origo gentis Langobardorum*, and later Paul the Deacon, passed down the events in Italy, and Alboin's figure was soon woven about with legend.[215] Even contemporaries perceived the events as a fundamental change, as the numerous, often very laconic entries in the chronicles attest. The political background to these events can hardly be made out from the source material; here the historian's analysis is required.

2.9 568: A Turning Point

In many textbooks, the Avar occupation of the Carpathian Basin and the emigration of the Lombards mark the end of the age of migrations, often also of Antiquity, and the dawn of the Middle Ages.[216] The events of 567–68 are seen as decisive for the later fate of east central Europe. The historian's stand on the larger issues is reflected in his interpretation of these events. Few political decisions of the early Middle Ages have been so frequently analyzed and criticized by modern historians—and from such differing perspectives.

"While the Suebi abandoned the oldest seats of the Germans between the Elbe and the Oder, the Gepids fell into dissolution, Alboin and his followers departed for Italy, and the Avars assumed their position on the Danube; the entire East, as far as the Germans had ruled it, was relinquished to the Avars and their followers, the Slavs." Thus K. Müllenhof summarized the outcome of that year.[217] It is not coincidental that disapprobation resonates in many older representations of events by German historians. At a time when the "German East" was seen as a vital issue for the nation, Alboin's course of action must have appeared difficult to grasp.

The events are a lesson in late antique politics: the "Germanic" king Alboin had neither Germanic nor territorial issues on his mind. What for later historians such as Ludwig Schmidt was "a serious political mistake,"[218] the destruction of the Gepid kingdom and the evacuation of the Carpathian Basin, was the very source of Alboin's success. It was also chalked up to Justin II as an error to have abandoned the Gepid kingdom on the Danube. Yet this was in line with a traditional principle of late antique diplomacy: to support the hungry opponent against the sated one and not to allow barbarian kingdoms to rest in peace, just as had been practiced earlier in the cases of Odoacer, the Vandals, and the Ostrogoths. This strategy seems counterproductive at first glance, since it involved exchanging a less threatening enemy for a more dangerous one: instead of a predictable Gepid king, who lived in the old imperial city of Sirmium with his bishop, an aggressive Avar khagan. The imperial strategists could hardly, as Avenarius assumes,[219] have counted on constructing a "dependable relationship of alliance" with Baian instead of the "too costly" policy of equilibrium. But was a stable barbarian *cordon sanitaire* in the interests of the empire at all? The Gepids increasingly availed themselves of the artifices of imperial politics and dispatched Cutrigurs and Slavs on plundering raids into the empire, without themselves getting their hands dirty.[220] Sirmium, in ruins after the death of Attila, must have enjoyed a revival under Gepid rule. Under Cunimund it was the royal residence, the episcopal see, and site of a mint. The fortifications were sufficiently strong in 567, immediately after the entry of the Byzantines, to stand off an Avar siege. There was reason in Constantinople to fear the competitor more than the opponent, not least because a functioning barbarian community could easily seem a preferable alternative to Roman townsmen disgruntled over high taxes and bureaucracy. The often-quoted conversation between Priscus and a Greek merchant turned Hun at Attila's court is an indication of discontent among well-to-do citizens in the Balkan provinces.[221] If Procopius's lament in his *Secret History* only reflects to a degree the mood of the provincials, the population of the Balkan provinces no longer had many grounds to prefer the empire, often represented by barbarian soldiers, over barbarian rule. To some extent Alboin's success in Italy depended on the unpopularity of imperial administration.

Against the Avars, recently irrupted from the steppes of central Asia, imperial propaganda could close the ranks more easily than against the familiar Gepids. It is not by chance that Corippus, in his inaugural poem for Justin, uses the Avar envoys as a barbarian foil to the glory of the emperor. The population of Sirmium that had borne Gothic and Gepid rule fell into anguish and fear before the Avars, as a graffito on a brick recounts.[222] "Deus adiuta Romanis" was the emergency slogan that Heraclius had struck on coins before the Avar offensive of 626. Significantly this was to be the last Latin numismatic inscription in the east.[223] Justin's policy therefore tolerated what so rankled Western historians, who saw themselves rooted in the opposing tradition: by sacrificing the post-Roman kingdoms on the Danube, the remains of Roman civilization were abandoned in the region. But in this way Byzantium was spared the fate of the West, which was to be sapped from within by the creation of barbarian kingdoms on Roman foundations. This policy, which also corresponded to the *reconquista* of Justinian, doubtless had far-reaching consequences for the Danube and Balkan regions. We do not do it justice if we only lament Justin's "wrong decision" of 567.

Many historians show even less understanding for Alboin's policies. Why did the Lombard king concede such favorable conditions to the Avars? To his allies, who did not even have to engage in battle, he handed over all of the Gepid lands along with complementary gifts. These questions are usually given a psychological answer: Baian's diabolical negotiating skill, when he detained the Lombard envoys for weeks in the dead of winter.[224] Bóna also explains the Lombard generosity by growing Slavic pressure; but this can hardly have been decisive. The sources offer no hint of a Slavic role in the events of these years. Why did the Lombards withdraw from the long-disputed area only one year after their victory? Scholars have often asserted that it was out of fear of the Avars. Hence "for Alboin, after his Pyrrhic victory, there remained only the withdrawal to Italy, unless he wished to share with his people the cruel fate of the Gepids, hard drudgery under the Avars."[225] Other historians are of the opinion that the Lombards withdrew voluntarily. Thus, Goubert sees Alboin as a "great statesman," who had always had Italy in sight.[226] This is more plausible, but it does not explain why he still had to fight with the Gepids.

The Avars are hardly credited with an independent strategy. "The Avars really enter large-scale politics only on the heels of the Lombards," avers Goubert.[227] Many historians refer their penetration into the Carpathian Basin to the threatening Byzantine-Turkish alliance, which would have forced them to surrender the Black Sea area, or to Justin's rebuff in 565, which left them to seize the next best opportunity.[228]

Baian as an object of Byzantine or Lombard diplomacy, Alboin as the victim of Avar diplomacy, Justin as the victim of his own diplomacy, and, lastly, Cunimund as the victim of all three. These are the variations proposed in scholarly literature. The sources, which tell us nothing of the motives of the actors, permit all these hypotheses. Yet the turn of events in 567–68 had roots in the distant past. If we pursue the changing conditions of barbarian politics in the Carpathian Basin, the drama surrounding Alboin seems rather less abruptly staged.

Herwig Wolfram has described the Carpathian Basin of the late fourth and fifth centuries as a zone where barbarian leaders could build up a critical mass for further exploits in the heartlands of the empire.[229] Most of the great invasions of the Western and Eastern Empires had their point of departure here. However, these were not accomplished peoples who were waiting on the banks of the Danube for a favorable moment. In the frontier zone of the Roman Empire a barbarian military aristocracy had formed, to a degree rooted in its ethnic traditions but striving for the opportunities of life that the empire offered: power, prestige, riches, such as tribal society had never known. The late Roman state controlled its growing inner tensions through increasing militarization. This offered a highly specialized barbarian warrior caste, which initially belonged to none of the factions surrounding the imperial throne, room for development. Many surrendered their tribal ties in order to become Roman soldiers. The Roman armies that fought Alaric or Attila were often no different in composition from those of their opponents. Since 378 prospects had evolved to be assumed en bloc into imperial service as barbarian units and thereby to combine a traditional affiliation with new possibilities of making one's fortune. Such a band of federates had the advantage over a regular army that its cohesion did not depend simply on regular pay; thus, Gothic or Vandal armies on the move did not dissolve even after crushing defeats. Their sense of belonging was deepened by common exploits in an often-hostile Roman environment. The new ethnic identities that developed in successful federate armies relied on old and prestigious names and perhaps tribal traditions but were open for warriors who wanted to belong. The strength of their inner solidarity and their military success determined the fate of the new peoples that came to dominate power politics in many regions of the empire.

After the death of Attila in 453, the course of just a few decades was marked by the rise and fall of Scirian, Swabian, Sarmatian, Rugian, and Herul kingdoms on the middle Danube, and by the competition of two Theoderics and their armies for Gothic kingship and the Roman title of *patricius*. All these groupings were dominated by an ethnically varied but culturally quite homogeneous warrior aristocracy and its followers. Its most prominent representatives combined illustrious ancestors with far-reaching contacts and an instinct for seizing the opportune moment. Many, like the Hun-Gepid Mundo, successfully changed sides more than once. Others, like the Scirian Odoacer, had the capacity after losing one kingdom to win yet another. Barbarian king, bandit, or Roman officer: it was only a question of scale and the credibility of one's aspirations to leadership.[230] The barbarian aristocracy of the Carpathian Basin reached its apogee in the fifth century. Its success should not hide the fact that its lifestyle continuously undermined the tenuous equilibrium it was based on. The growing social imparity destroyed the old tribal order on which the cohesion of the *gens* was based. And the constant conflicts among the warrior elite destroyed the remains of the Roman infrastructure, which alone could satisfy the aspirations of the barbarian warriors, accustomed as they were to success. Rivalry among the *gentes* increased, and Roman diplomacy contributed further to prevent the stabilization of barbarian powers. Because of repeated depredations, the provision of food supplies in the Danube provinces was eventually threatened, and this played a role in the departure of the Goths and Heruls. After the Ostrogothic strikes against the neighboring kingdoms of 468–73 and their departure into the Balkan Peninsula, no stable power could be established in Pannonia. The dissolution of the Western Roman Empire and the shrinking sphere of action of the Eastern Roman Empire turned the once geopolitically critical Carpathian Basin into an outback. The Gepid kingdom, which had asserted itself on the Tisza and in Transylvania, lost in importance. But this peripheral position permitted its further existence, despite repeated defeats at the hands of the Ostrogoths. After the latter had conquered Sirmium in 504 and the Lombards had succeeded in 508 to the kingdom of the Heruls in Moravia and Lower Austria, relative peace ruled in the Carpathian Basin for a few decades. Those who had not emigrated into the empire had to lower their aspirations, and the peasant population, a mixture of Romans, Suebi, Gepids, and others, seems to have been able to recover.

In parallel with these developments the regions within the imperial boundaries slowly consolidated. In the west Theoderic's rule and his system of alliances assured a certain equilibrium, and in the east, after the financial recovery under Anastasius, Justinian could go on the offensive. The grandly conceived *renovatio imperii* also renewed and enhanced the prospects of the barbarian warriors on the periphery. The far-reaching system of subsidies and Justinian's great need for soldiers produced an upturn for barbarian politics on the Danube.[231] Huns, Bulgars, Lombards, Gepids, Heruls fought in the Roman armies that sought to suppress the Italian Ostrogoths. The efforts of reconstruction in the Balkan provinces reestablished profitable targets for pillaging raids, despite all the fortifications. In Pannonia, long a political vacuum, expansionist powers began to grab their opportunities. The Gepids took Sirmium and for the first time menaced the regions to the south. Bulgars raided as far as the Long Wall and intervened on the middle Danube in Roman service. The remains of the Heruls in Pannonia II fought successively on the Roman, Gepid, and Lombard side, but also against each other. The Frankish kingdom expanded its sphere of interest up to the borders of Pannonia. King Theudebert allegedly even thought of initiating a joint march on Constantinople. On the northern edge of the Carpathian Basin, as in Wallachia, Slavic groups pressed forward, politically identifiable around 550 as supporters of Hildigis, the pretender to the Lombard throne.[232]

The most expansive power on the middle Danube were the Lombards. Around 500 they were still Herul vassals in the former Rugian lands in today's Lower Austria, but they quickly expanded their rule over Pannonia, where Justinian in 548 confirmed their settlement in what had earlier been Ostrogothic Savia and in the southeastern corner of Noricum.[233] Herul, Suebian, and Gothic groups joined the successful *exercitus Langobardorum*, an integration that the Lombard kings consciously fostered.

About 550 conflict erupted with the Gepid neighbors. It is customary to see the city of Sirmium as the bone of contention between the two powers. But if that was the case, why did the Lombards, after their victory in 567, display no further interest in Sirmium; and why did the Gepids promise their capital to the Romans in order to receive their support in the war against the Lombards? From the very beginning, much more was at stake: not matters of territory but claims to leadership of the entire warrior aristocracy of the Carpathian Basin. Already in the first wars, each side operated with a pretender to the throne of the other. A provisional peace was reached only when both parties agreed to have their pretenders killed, so greatly did they fear a legitimate competitor in the service of their opponent.

Although this first round resulted in a stalemate, the flexible Lombard policy won clear advantages in the following years. The Gepid kingdom, focused on defense, had never understood how to encourage other groups to join it. In 512 the Heruls were left to their own devices, the ambitious Mundo had to try his luck on his own hand, and even the greater part of the Sirmian Gepids, after the defeat of 504, joined the Ostrogoths without delay.[234] The Lombard king Alboin, who had come to power about 560, attempted to profile himself from the beginning as the "better" king of the Gepids. This is the best way in which the legendary account of his wars against the Gepids can be understood, which occupies a great deal of space in Paul the Deacon.[235] In a battle, Prince Alboin killed the Gepid crown prince Thurismod. On the orders of his father Audoin he then rode to the Gepid king Thurisind in order to be adopted as his son in arms. He almost fell victim to the vengeance of the enraged Gepids, but the plan succeeded because of the wise Thurisind's call to moderation. In Paul's text the idea is advanced that he thus assumed the place of the slain prince. According to another legend Alboin started the next war by abducting the Gepid princess Rosamund.[236] In any case he took her as wife after the victory. He killed her father Cunimund in battle and had a goblet made of his skull,[237] an ancient magical practice, in order to absorb into himself the powers of the deceased.

It is pointless to discuss the historicity of all these legendary elements. Whether all this happened or not, its very form permits insight into how Alboin's deeds were perceived, and quite possibly how he represented himself. A series of symbolic actions served the purpose of undermining the loyalty of Gepid warriors to their royal house and of transferring it to Alboin. This policy was successful. The credibility of Gepid kingship declined, and after the death of Cunimund his heirs set off for Constantinople. "The people of the Gepids were so diminished that from that time on they had no king."[238] The most active part of the warriors joined Alboin. While Scirians, Rugians, and Heruls had tried to restore their kingdoms decades after their fall, if under different names (for instance, the Scirian Odoacer became king in Italy, the Rugian Eraric king of the Goths, and the Herul Sinduald *rex Brentorum* in Trento), the Gepids henceforth appear only as nameless subjects of Lombard, Avar, or Roman rulers.

It is an irony of history that Alboin's masterly policy led to his personal tragedy. When, so a widely known legend runs, he tried to force his wife to drink from her father's skull, she had him murdered and fled to the Romans.[239] Alboin had exploited a symbolic language of kinship and ethnic affiliation in order to legitimize his position as king and to extend his rule to new groups. When he thought that he mastered them so fully that he could toy with them, it resulted in his downfall. Despite a ten-year leadership crisis that ensued, the Italian kingdom that Alboin had founded survived.

The events of 567–68 are easier to understand against this background. The kingdom of the Gepids succumbed because it had lost its attraction for its own and foreign followers and offered no better prospects for the future. The heightened rivalry between the *gentes* and the repeated devastation of the Balkan provinces in Justinian's later years had the effect that successful barbarian policies could now be undertaken only on an ever greater scale. As had occurred a century earlier, the smaller *gentes* were eliminated one after another. In this situation, similar to that around 470 for the Ostrogoths, Alboin's concern was no longer territorial gains on the Danube. As in the time of the young Theoderic, all competitors had to be defeated before leaving Pannonia with sufficient forces. The objective was to integrate the warrior aristocracy of the Danubian lands under the Lombard crown. Only in this fashion could Alboin, as the Ostrogothic Amals before him, hope to accumulate the force to assert himself in the ancient heartland of the empire.

It is possible that Alboin actually planned, as his envoys to Baian asserted, to make an immediate attack on Constantinople together with the Avars.[240] But he seems to have quickly decided to leave the east to the Avars, just as the Ostrogoths had divided their areas of operation in 473. The alliance with Baian offered an advantage. If it were assured that the Avars would move into the just emptied lands, then Alboin's subjects, if they remained in Pannonia, would lose all chance of becoming their own masters again. On the other hand, if indeed this late piece of information is correct, a contractual right of return could help dispel possible reservations about the risk of an emigration.

It is evident that Alboin was not able to achieve his goal completely. As in all migratory movements a portion of the population remained behind and ended up under Avar rule. Yet in the army that set out for Italy at Easter 568, all the important ethnic groupings of the Carpathian Basin were represented. The surrender of their position on the middle Danube, which this implied, was perhaps accelerated by Alboin's policy. But the Lombard king is not to be held responsible for the fact that those who followed him saw no future for themselves in the Carpathian Basin. Here, a new ruling elite established itself.

THE NEW POWER, 567–90

The Avar Empire in Europe took considerable time to build. The ambitious new power needed about ten years of wars and negotiations to find a secure basis to establish its empire: the lands along the middle Danube in the Carpathian Basin. It would take another fifteen years until this process of consolidation was concluded with the conquest of the city of Sirmium in 582. Only then could the Avars start to launch major attacks on the Byzantine Empire, which were to have devastating effects in the course of the 580s.

3.1 The First Attack on Sirmium

The Avar entry into the Carpathian Basin in 567 becomes apparent in our sources only when their army reached the walls of the old metropolis Sirmium. After the defeat of Cunimund, the Gepid garrison had folded without resistance before Roman forces. Its commander, Usdibad, together with Reptila, the nephew of Cunimund, and the Arian bishop, Thrasaric, had turned the Gepid royal treasure over to the Romans and had gone into exile.[1] Now a Roman military force under Bonus was in possession of Sirmium. "After 125 years the city was again Roman."[2] Urban life had prospered during the last period of Gepid rule. King Cunimund had his residence there, and the Christian Gepids had their own Arian bishop. Now, during the first Avar siege, the Orthodox bishop played a significant role.[3] The reputation of the Gepids reached as far

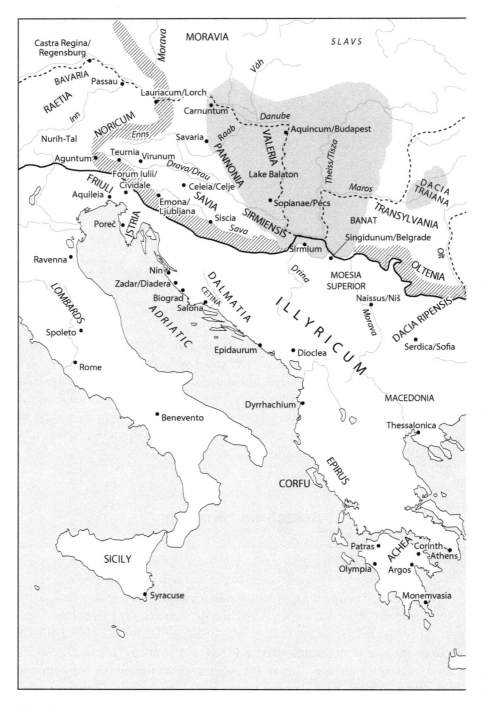

MAP 2. The Avar Empire and Its Political Environment around 600

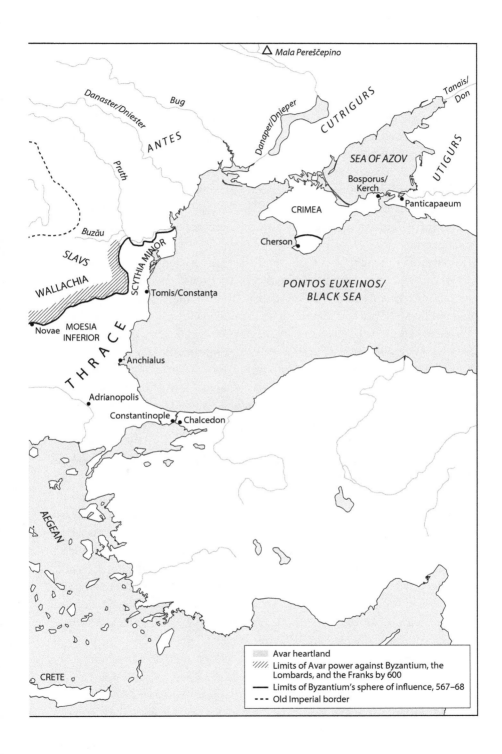

as England, and their name was included in the extensive catalog of peoples in the poem *Widsith*.[4]

The first confrontation between the new Avar power and the old empire was accompanied by threatening gestures. Before the siege of Sirmium the Avars raised their terrible battle cry and beat drums in order to intimidate their opponents, but Bonus had warned his soldiers and they responded to the barbarian "cacophony" by hammering out just as deafening a noise on their shields and canteens.[5] The inhabitants of the city were less cold-blooded. From the roofs of the baths they saw Avar negotiators approaching after the battle but thought it was a renewed attack and raised the alarm. The public baths had then survived the Gepid period, and as late as the fourteenth century the imposing ruins could still be seen.[6]

Menander's account of the course of the battle has unfortunately not been preserved, and the transmitted fragments deal merely with the subsequent complicated negotiations. We know only that the master of soldiers Bonus was wounded. In order to give no sign of weakness to the Avar envoys, the old warhorse had himself patched up by the physician Theodore. Despite the great pain he was in, he personally led negotiations outside the city. Apparently the Romans had earlier succeeded in repulsing the Avars. Baian's army had withdrawn some distance from the city, and there was no longer a question of capitulation. Before the battle the khagan had thrown both the emperor's envoys, Vitalian and Comita, into chains.[7] Now he himself sought to negotiate with the Romans.

The envoys with whom the wounded Bonus dealt before the city walls set out the themes that would stamp the tough negotiations of the following years. The Avars had taken possession of the land of the Gepids by right of conquest. The occupation of Sirmium by imperial troops was then an act of war, as was the asylum given Usdibad by the Romans. On this point the conceptions of justice of the nomadic peoples were stricter than Roman international law.[8] As a consequence of the victory over the Gepids, Usdibad had become Baian's subject. If the Romans harbored the refugee, this was just as grave as the occupation of a territory, in the context of the personal bonds on which the barbarian polity was founded. Contention over the extradition of Usdibad remained a central issue of all negotiations for years. It is interesting that it is only Usdibad who is mentioned, and not Reptila or Thrasaric.

Bonus rejected the accusations. The Avars had attacked Roman territory. The barbarians complained that Justin had repeatedly insulted Baian and had not fulfilled his obligations, which probably dated from the accord with Justinian. Bonus made excuses. The emperor, he claimed, had already given the money for the Avars to his envoys. But when he learned of the khagan's arrogance, unusual even for a barbarian, and his threats, he suspended the payment. Despite all the accusations the Avars were quite prepared to treat for peace. Apparently Baian did not wish to be drawn into a lengthy war. He pressed for immediate negotiations. Now it was Bonus who hesitated. He proposed that a delegation be sent to the emperor, since he himself could not make decisions concerning the conditions for a peace.

The khagan's reaction to this offer was one of surprising candor. "I would be ashamed and dishonored before the tribes who follow me in alliance, if I should withdraw from this place having achieved nothing at all and having brought myself no profit. In order that I should not appear to have made the assault to no purpose and benefit, send me some small gifts. For when I passed through Scythia I brought nothing, and it is impossible for me to leave here too without some gain."[9] This request from a successful military commander who had just conquered a great kingdom seems odd. It permits some conclusions as concerns the situation of the Avar army. The man of the hour was Alboin: he had beaten Cunimund and won great spoils, among which the princess Rosamund. John of Biclaro, for instance, speaks only of the Lombards, who had finished off the Gepid kingdom.[10] Alboin's victory, and the booty that had been won, was so great that it became the stuff of legend.[11] The Avars had arrived too late. The defeated Gepid nobility had already joined up with Alboin or the Romans. The Avars could now occupy a country settled by peasants, but the army wanted more visible results.

The reference to the passage through Scythia indicates that Baian's army came out of the region to the east of the Carpathians. In 566–67 the Avars had probably wintered, as they did the year before, on the "Scythian" section of the lower Danube.[12] According to Menander, the occupation of the Gepid lands only started after the siege of Sirmium. That Baian, for his withdrawal, wanted from Bonus "no more than a silver plate, a small amount of gold, and a Scythian tunic" is a valuable indication that the conquest of the Carpathian Basin did not begin as a triumphal entry. The defenders of the city found these requests moderate, but they were not in agreement with the emperor's new barbarian policy, and Bonus did not dare to set a precedent on his own authority. He contended that, aside from weapons and equipment, they possessed nothing of value. This statement threw Baian into a rage. He threatened to send an army to pillage imperial lands. "'I shall send against the Roman lands those who, if they happen to be destroyed, shall cause me no pain.' He ordered ten thousand of the so-called Cutrigur Huns to cross the river Sava and devastate the land toward Dalmatia."[13]

This statement is often cited in order to characterize the relationship of the khagan to conquered peoples. Clearly the Cutrigur auxiliaries could operate relatively independently but did not enjoy the same status as the Avar units. The khagan used them, in the slow-moving negotiations, to put pressure on the

Romans and thereby at the same time to accommodate the Cutrigur desire for booty. After that, we hear no more of the Cutrigurs. Most of them probably came to be viewed as Bulgars.[14]

In any case negotiations collapsed for the time being. Without a formal accord both sides had a moment to catch their breath, a respite they badly needed. Baian and his army crossed the Danube and began the systematic occupation of Gepid lands. This undertaking left no forces free for a subsequent attack on Sirmium. After the Lombards cleared out of Pannonia in 568, this area also had to be organized. Meanwhile Emperor Justin could be convinced of the success of his policy of strength. At little military cost and without paying subsidies he had gained an important strategic position. In the winter of 567–68 he ruled over the most extensive Roman realm since the great Theodosius. The success stiffened the emperor's attitude. In negotiations with the khagan's envoys, which drew out over the following years, he always presented himself as triumphant. But the imperial display increasingly lost its justification. The Lombards were conquering the ancient heartland of the empire, piece by piece. And on the Danube Baian's host was step by step building up an Avar power, proceeding much more circumspectly than the emperor on the Bosporus.

3.2 Between Peace and War

The negotiations that had been broken off before the walls of Sirmium dragged on for years.[15] What lay between the efforts at peace recorded in Menander's preserved fragments *de legationibus* can only be guessed at. Apparently it did not come to significant military engagements until 570 and 571, and then a peace was concluded.[16]

Without a coherent narrative, the context of the negotiations remains blurred. The alliance that, according to Menander, was concluded with the Turks in 568–69 strengthened the Roman position but must have generated exaggerated hopes of intervention against both Avars and Persians.[17] When the Turkish khagan boasted of trampling the Avars under his hooves like ants,[18] it could lead Justin to a dangerous underestimation of the Avars. Meanwhile Alboin relieved the emperor of the fruits of the twenty-year war against the Goths. In 569 Milan was captured without much resistance, and it was not until 572 that the assassination of the Lombard king gave the imperial troops in Italy a respite.[19] The Persian war, expected in 569, was again postponed and tribute paid until 572. Only then did Justin provoke the next twenty-year war. He may have hoped to have finished with the Avars by 572. On many occasions his impatience with the generals on the Danube is apparent. For example, he lavished reproaches on Bonus on the occasion of the first Avar delegation, which he received in 567, for having negotiated with the Avars at all. The hesitation of the commander-in-chief during the discussions before Sirmium is understandable: not equipped for war and not empowered for peace, he could only try to win time. The emperor's horizon is apparent in Corippus's poem, in which barbarians are envisaged in the ancient Roman, Caesarian way as decorative supernumeraries in the imperial pageantry.

Initially a treaty indeed meant more to the khagan than it did to the Romans. Bonus declined to pay the khagan for his readiness to conclude a peace. Baian got his small presents after all. Vitalian, the envoy detained by the khagan, had been broken by his imprisonment. He had himself sent to the *hyparch* of Illyricum and on his own account raised eight hundred solidi: no great sum but more than the symbolic gifts that Baian had demanded of Bonus.

Then Targitius, accompanied by Vitalian, went to Constantinople in order to submit the Avars' demands. The catalog remained the same: first, the surrender of Sirmium; then, the annual payments that Justinian had made to the Cutrigurs and Utigurs; lastly, the extradition of Usdibad and his following.[20] No one could deny that the Gepids were now Baian's "slaves," Targitius told the emperor. Elsewhere, he invoked the laws of war in this regard. According to this logic, the subjugation of a people established not only the rule over land and people, but also a legal claim to the annual payments that the subdued peoples had previously received.

Furthermore, Targitius argued, according to Menander, that Baian was a son of the emperor, who has a claim to maintenance, a claim that would not prejudice imperial prerogatives.[21] This surprising assertion is hardly just a rhetorical flourish on the part of Menander and perhaps more than a diplomatic ploy by Targitius. It follows the logic under which barbarian federates had occupied imperial lands since the late fourth century, and their rule over Roman provinces had been legitimized by treaties, imperial titles, and formal recognition of the superiority of the emperor. At this point, the Avars still seem to have negotiated on the basis of this model. In this sense, Sirmium was more than a strategic site. It represented legitimate possession of a portion of imperial land.[22] However, in none of the negotiations between 567 and 571 was the obvious demand that Targitius had brought up after the accession of Justin ever mentioned: the subsidies that Justinian had paid the Avars themselves. Did Menander pass this over because it seemed self-evident to him?

In any case, a sum was never specified, unlike in later peace negotiations. The Avar envoys still argued about what was due to them and did not simply demand what they wished. Such behavior is characteristic of Baian's politics. In his view, it was not simply about stipulated annual payments but about the practical recognition of well-won rights. Later Avar rulers modified their claims according to their military situation. The catalog of demands from 567 was not altered as a consequence of defeats or victories. Later, territorial demands were no longer made. Perhaps a less stubborn ruler than Justin II would have been able to negotiate better with Baian; whether that would have made any difference in the long run is, however, doubtful. Justin's answer to the envoys boiled down to a simple maxim: "It is more painful to be the friends of the Avars—nomads and foreigners—than their enemies."[23]

Thus, the emperor met the requests of the Avars with threats, insults, and a counterdemand for the release of the Gepids under Avar rule. He knew that this meant war and informed Bonus by letter to prepare for it. In addition, the general received serious reproaches from the emperor for having sent him such negotiators in the first place. What happened then we do not know; in any case, no larger battles are attested. If we date Targitius's first mission to the winter of 567–68, the withdrawal of the Lombards and the new challenges in Pannonia could have prevented the outbreak of war.

Shortly thereafter, perhaps the following winter, Targitius returned to Constantinople. He repeated Baian's demands to the emperor. Since the annual payments to the Utigur "Huns" for the foregoing years had not been made, he demanded retrospective payment as well. Justin replied just as arrogantly as the previous time: "like an emperor," as Menander writes approvingly. After Targitius had pursued these negotiations through several audiences, Justin became impatient. He dismissed Targitius and charged his general Tiberius, then *Comes Excubitorum*, with further negotiations with the Avars.[24]

After a further Avar delegation had been flatly turned away, finally Apsikh appeared in Constantinople. For his mission to the imperial city he apparently had wide-ranging authority. This resulted in a kind of peace conference between Tiberius and Apsikh, and their followers, in the course of which a peace plan was worked out. The Roman negotiators declared themselves ready to formally hand over not Sirmium but land for the Avars to settle. Whether this actually referred to territory under imperial control (for example, the remainder of Pannonia Sirmiensis, which included the Bassianae area that had already once been offered to the Avars) is doubtful.[25] More probably it meant allotting to the Avars those parts of Pannonia on which the Lombards had been acknowledged as federates in 547/48. Roman terminology was very consistent on this point and spoke of a permission to settle on imperial territory even if barbarians already lived there.

The second condition of the draft treaty provided for the status of Avar hostages, who according to established Roman practice were to guarantee the agreement. This led to a very instructive controversy between Tiberius and the emperor. The general had agreed with Apsikh that "the Byzantines would receive the sons of their [the Avars'] leading men as hostages." Justin insisted on getting the sons of the khagan himself into his hands. "Tiberius disagreed, for he argued that, if they took the sons of the leading men amongst the Scythians, it was likely that, should the Khagan wish to break the agreements, the fathers of the hostages would object."[26] In the end, the emperor entirely rejected the peace plan. He appealed by letter to the battle lust of his troops. For Tiberius there was nothing else to be done than to recommend a close watch on the fords by Bonus, who was still in Sirmium. Unfortunately, the historical context of Apsikh's failed mission is not evident in the Menander fragments. The stipulations of the peace proposal were clearly more favorable for the Romans than Targitius's earlier conditions (which could, however, be comprised in them, without being explicitly mentioned). For 570 the Spanish chronicler John of Biclaro laconically informs us of a victory of Tiberius over the Avars.[27] Apsikh's embassy can more plausibly be dated after that.[28]

The emperor had overestimated the potential of his Balkan army. After the beginning of the war against the Persians in 572, he had only a modest number of troops at his disposal in the west. Tiberius, who apparently marched against the Avars again, was defeated. Menander gives no detail. It is possible that another fragment belongs to this account, in which it is stated that small bands of Avars had penetrated into imperial lands, at which the Roman generals attacked them.[29] In any case it eventually came to one of the few large-scale pitched battles between Romans and Avars. Theophanes and Evagrius give accounts of this for the year 574.[30] Tiberius, who advanced against the barbarians, was surprised by them and had to retreat with great losses. According to Evagrius he marched out with a large, hastily drummed up army; but "the soldiers did not endure even the sight of the barbarians." Tiberius just barely escaped capture. According to a fragment from Menander preserved in the Excerpta de sententiis, after the defeat of the Romans the Avar leader sent an emissary to Tiberius to ask him why he, with such inferior numbers, had dared to go to battle against "the Avars and the Scythians." "Do you not have writings and records from which you can read and learn that the tribes of the Scythians are impossible to defeat and conquer?"[31]

The debacle led to a change in policy. Along with the Avar mission traveling to Constantinople for the peace negotiations Tiberius sent a tribune who gave a detailed account of the situation to Justin. The failure of his policy toward the Avars could have played a role in the decision of the sick emperor to withdraw from affairs of state. Apart from that, he was increasingly afflicted by his "plague of demons," apparently a pathological paranoia.[32] In December 574 Tiberius was elevated to Caesar and thereby to coruler.[33] Now the relationship with the Avars improved; that same winter the new coemperor signed a treaty with the Avars.[34] It is unfortunate that we know little about the conditions of this treaty, the first that was reached between Byzantium and the Avar khaganate in the Carpathian Basin.[35] Yet, as Menander states later in the context of other negotiations, an annual payment of eighty thousand gold solidi was agreed on.[36]

Once again complications arose. On the way home, the Avar delegation was ambushed by *scamarae*, as organized bandits were then called. The brigands took horses, silver, and other objects of value, which set the diplomatic carousel into motion again. Tiberius finally succeeded in tracking down the perpetrators and having the stolen goods returned.[37] The affair is characteristic of conditions in the Balkan provinces. If bandits did not hesitate to attack a party of mounted Avar warriors, normal travelers can hardly have had an easy life.

The victory of 574 and the involvement of the Romans in the war against the Persians could have facilitated further Avar incursions. Still, the Byzantines got off rather lightly in the course of the 570s. Baian had confronted the army of Tiberius but appears to have left the Balkan provinces and their cities largely untouched. This cautious policy can hardly be explained with reference to the weakness of the Avars. The recent victory over Tiberius and the start of the Persian war should have dispelled all the khagan's reservations. The Slavs too exploited this opportunity. But Baian clearly had other objectives. "At that time he was not hostile toward the Romans, and, indeed, from the very beginning of Tiberius' reign had wished to be friendly with our state."[38] That was hardly because of the khagan's peaceful attitudes. Obviously, he sought to achieve his objectives without a major confrontation with the Romans. Just the opposite. In order to impose his hegemony over barbarian lands collaboration with the empire suited his purposes well.

3.3 Baian's Alliance with Byzantium

For some years, common interests bound the two great powers on the Danube. Baian's friendship with his old opponent Tiberius, as Menander emphasizes, was stamped by realpolitik. The hegemony of the khagan north of the Danube was threatened from two sides. Allied groups of Turks had advanced on the Pontic steppes, and Turxanthus/Türk Shad, the son of Sizabulos, waved his horsewhip in wild threats against his "Avar" slaves.[39] On the lower Danube the initiative passed more and more to Slavic groups who showed no awe of the Avar khagan. At least with these he tried to set an example, with Byzantium covering his rear. The Slavs were hardly dangerous opponents but rather unpleasant competitors.

The role of the Turks in the political calculations of Baian is difficult to evaluate. We know better than he that the threats of Turxanthus were followed by no action. Yet the panic that the rumor of a Turkish attack unleashed in the Avar army, even later under Baian's son, shows how seriously this danger was taken.[40] The role that the Avars played in Turkish politics could not be illustrated more clearly than in the disagreeable surprise experienced at this time by a Roman embassy to the Turkish court.[41]

In the year 576 Tiberius sent his trusted Valentinus, who had already twice made this journey, to the Turks. Evidence of the close relationship with the central Asian ally is found in the presence of more than one hundred Turks, who had come to the imperial city on one mission or another and who now set out with Valentinus. Starting from the Crimea the envoys crossed the land of the Utigurs, who now lived under Turkish rule. Baian's assertion that he had subjected all the Utigurs was now—if ever it were true—overtaken by events.

Sizabulos/Istemi, a Roman ally since 567, had just died. Menander claims that the Turks had divided their realm into eight parts, under a senior leader called Arsilas. The westernmost Turkish leader was now Turxanthus, as the Byzantines called him by his title (Türk Shad).[42] After Valentinus had presented the greetings of the new emperor with all forms of politeness and slowly got to the matter at hand, the Persian war, Turxanthus reproached him harshly. He accused the Romans of lies and deceit, because they had concluded a treaty with the Avars/Varchonites. "And your Emperor shall pay me due penalty, for he has spoken words of friendship with me while making a treaty with the Warkhonitai, our slaves (he meant the Avars) who have fled their masters. When I wish it, the Warkhonitai shall come to me as subjects of the Turks. If they as much as see my horsewhip sent to them, they will flee to the lowest reaches of the earth." After further threats against the Avars he reproached the Romans that they guided his ambassadors only through the Caucasus so that the difficult route would dissuade them from attack. "But I know very well where the river Danapris [Dnieper] flows, and the Danube and the Hebrus [Maritza], and from where our slaves, the Warkhonitai, crossed into Roman territory."[43]

Just like the refuge given Usdibad for Baian, the treaty with the Avars was a hostile act for Turxanthus. The issue was important enough for him that he was ready to threaten the Roman envoys with death because of it. Valentinus and companions got off lightly in this tense situation; they only had to follow Turkish custom at the funeral celebrations for Sizabulos and lacerate their cheeks with their daggers, a custom also reported from the burial of Attila. After the funeral, the atmosphere brightened a bit, and negotiations were continued. Then the envoys were sent on eastward to Turxanthus's brother Tardu at the Ektel, the "Golden Mountain," where Zemarchus had met Sizabulos. Tardu (575–602) had thus inherited his father's preferred residence, probably also his title yabgu, before he assumed the title khagan at some point. Tardu/Tatou is more prominent in the Chinese sources, where Turxanthus cannot be identified. He clearly was the senior brother, as also expressed by the lower grade of *shad* for Turxanthus, and by the fact that Valentinus was sent on to meet him. Why Turxanthus staged Sizabulos/Istemi's funeral without Tardu's presence is unclear; probably Sizabulos had taken part in the preparations for the following offensive in the west and died in their course.[44] Menander's report of the presence of a Roman envoy at Istemi's funeral finds a striking confirmation in the inscription of the Turkish khagan Bilge in the seventh century, where Istemi is hailed as founder of the empire. When he died, "the ambassadors from Boklii Cholii, China (*tabyač*), Tibet, Avar (*apar*), Rome (*purum*), Kyrgiz, Uch-Kurykan, Otuz-Tatars, Kytans, Tatabs came to the funerals, so many people came to mourn over the great khagan. He was a famous khagan!"[45] If we believe this late and certainly stylized account, Avar envoys were also present at Istemi's funeral.

Soon, Turxanthus dispatched an army to the coast of the Black Sea, where together with Anagai's Utigurs they conquered the Byzantine city of Bosporus/Kerch. The shad's diatribe against the Byzantines had clearly served as pretext for this attack. Some years later the Turks appeared before Cherson, on the southern coast of the Crimea—unless Tiberius had simply made up this bit of news in order to intimidate the Avars.[46] It is perfectly possible that Baian was biding his time during the first years of the reign of the unpredictable Turxanthus to see whether the storm clouds would draw closer. Unlike at most other times, the Romans and the Avars had the same concerns in the years after 576. Both camps had Turkish attacks to fear. A second thing in common was even more immediate. The peace accord of 574 had given the Slavs on the lower Danube an opportunity to go to war on their own account. This suited neither the emperor nor the khagan.

In 578, the fourth year of Tiberius's reign as Caesar, an alleged hundred thousand Slavs devastated Thrace and other regions of the empire. John of Biclaro may be referring to the same event when he gives an account of a Slav incursion in Thrace and the destruction of many cities among the events of the tenth year of Justin II's reign.[47] The Iberian chronicler also speaks of Avar attacks in this same context. In Justin's tenth year Avars are reported to have "deceitfully blockaded" the Thracian coast. In the first year of Tiberius's reign as emperor, 578/79, they are claimed to have advanced as far as the Long Wall in a fresh attack on Thrace.[48] This contradicts Menander's observation that the Avars had a friendly relationship with Tiberius since he became Caesar.[49] This problem can be resolved if we refer these attacks to Slavs. It is difficult to conceive of the Avar horsemen in naval attacks. The problems in the Black Sea could very well have been connected with the Turkish assaults on Black Sea ports.

Drawing up an exact chronology of Slavic pillaging campaigns would be an undertaking with very poor prospects. The Avar khagan concluded peace treaties and then broke them. Depending on the reliability of the sources the wars that he fought are all more or less datable. The Slavic incursions, unless it was the khagan who had prompted them, were not centrally directed. One Slavic group heard of the departure or of the victory of another; through messengers neighbors encouraged each other to come along; groups united and then separated again.[50] A historical narrative can offer only a rough graph of intensity. Years of relative peace alternated with frequent raids. Slavic activity reached a first apogee in the year 578. The concerted action by the Romans and Avars that follows shows that the majority of the plunderers had left family and belongings at home.

Despite the victory at Melitene in 575 most of the imperial troops were tied down in the Persian theater. In this situation the emperor asked the khagan for help. He convinced him "to make war on the Slavs, so that all of those who were laying waste Roman territory would be drawn back by the troubles at home, choosing rather to defend their own lands."[51] Baian quickly readied himself to attack the Slavs north of the lower Danube, since he had his own reasons for doing so.

> For the leader of the Avars had sent to Daurentius and the chiefs of his people ordering them to obey the commands of the Avars and to be numbered amongst their tributaries. Dauritas and his fellow chiefs replied, "What man has been born, what man is warmed by the rays of the sun who shall make our might his subject? Others do not conquer our land, we conquer theirs. And so it shall always be for us, as long as there are wars and weapons." Thus boasted the Slavs, and the Avars replied with a like arrogance. After this came abuse and insults, and because they were barbarians with their haughty and stubborn spirits, a shouting match developed. The Slavs were so unable to restrain their rage that they slew the envoys who had come to them, and Baian received a report of these doings from others. As a result he nursed his grievance for a long time and kept his hatred concealed, angered that they had not become his subjects, not to mention that he had suffered an irreparable wrong at their hands.[52]

The performance of the self-confident Slavic prince, however Menander may have enhanced it, contributes to an understanding of the Avar-Slav relationship. Since 567 the khaganate had lost control over the region north and west of the delta of the Danube. The luckless mission shows that the khagan regarded the Slavs of the lower Danube as his tributaries. How he understood this relationship is explicitly stated here: to obey Avar orders and pay tribute. The matter of military support is clearer in other sources than here.[53] The "refusal to submit to him" angered the khagan and was in contradiction to the Avar conception of rulership. Actual Avar control over subjugated tribes at such a distance from the center of the realm cannot have been very intensive. The khagan even needed Byzantine help to avenge the murder of the envoys. The recognition in principle of Avar dominion was more important than the direct exploitation of it. Above all the khagan could not tolerate that the Slavs would mount profitable raids on imperial territory without him having a say in it. As the lord of all barbarian warriors he claimed a monopoly over such ventures. This was in all likelihood the sore point in the contention with the proud Slavs of Dauritas.

The Slavic pillagers must already have accumulated a certain amount of riches in their homeland. The khagan counted on their country being "full of gold, since the Roman Empire had long been plundered by the Slavs whose own land had never been raided by any other people at all."[54] Later the khagan boasted of having "freed several thousand Romans who languished in Slavic captivity."[55] The Slav warriors on the lower Danube increasingly evolved as competitors of the khaganate.

Baian then needed little urging to mount a war against the Slavs. Immediately the Roman military machine went into action. John, the praetorian prefect of Illyricum,[56] was entrusted with its organization. He had the Avar horsemen ferried across the Danube in heavy cargo ships, reputedly sixty thousand men (surely an exaggeration). With a Roman protective escort the barbarians were led along the Danube corridor to the province of Scythia. If Menander's information is accurate, Dauritas's Slavs must have been living in the area where Priscus in 593 crossed the Danube at Durostorum in pursuit of the Ardagast group.[57] There or somewhat farther downstream the heavily armed Avar horsemen were again ferried over the river.

Despite the well-organized advance the khagan's army scarcely met a Slavic opponent face to face. They drew back into the thick forests, as they would do later when faced with Maurice's armies, or they were away on pillaging raids. The Avars were not equipped for war in wooded areas. So they contented themselves, as usual, with devastating the Slav villages. Whether this large-scale undertaking had any effect at all apart from a modest amount of plunder is not explicit in the sources. It did not stop subsequent Slavic raids. However, it can be conjectured that the Slavs had learned a lesson. It was better not to give the khagan direct cause for anger. The Slavs could also be sent by their Avar rulers on raids that they would have undertaken in any case, a practice that became increasingly common. The relationship between the khagan and the Slavs in Wallachia remained problematic, as the events of the 590s would show.

3.4 The Conquest of Sirmium

If Baian wished to regain the political initiative, he could not be content with this blow against the Danube Slavs. As the leader of a barbarian army hungry for success and booty he had to do more than simply carry out actions in the Roman interest against Slavic plunderers. Pressure from his warriors was already apparent at the first siege of Sirmium. It is understandable that ten years later they would be even less content to watch the Slavs pillage the Balkan provinces unimpeded. A lasting peace with Byzantium, no matter how well paid, was something the khagan could not afford.

Tiberius knew from his own experience just how dangerous the Avar army was. But the political caution that Baian had thus far displayed seems to have led him into illusions. With the exception of two or three brief wars, nothing had happened in almost twenty years. No matter how much the khagan had threatened, demands for the surrender of Sirmium had until then been above all a diplomatic problem, and Baian had finally allowed himself to be bought off. When in 579 the familiar Targitius appeared punctually in Constantinople to pick up the annual payment, everything appeared to be in order. The garrisons in the two advanced posts of Sirmium and Singidunum were not prepared for war, and the new emperor had thrown all available forces into the war in the east, where Maurice led them across the Tigris into Mesopotamia.

Lulling the emperor into complacency was part of Baian's plan. It is almost as if he took pleasure in playing out this comedy to the final act. Scarcely had Targitius returned from Byzantium with the customary treasures than the khagan and his army pushed to the Sava between Sirmium and Singidunum. There he began the construction of a bridge.[58]

Contemporaries were intrigued by barbarians crossing major rivers; barbarians building bridges created particular interest. Menander, who had already described the double crossing of the Danube the previous year in considerable detail, devotes several pages to the bridge over the Sava. His elderly contemporary, John of Ephesus, who had no official sources at his disposal, repeats what had reached his monastery cell on the Isle of Princes. A version of the bridge-building story takes up considerable space.[59] Theophylact also has an extensive account of a later bridging of the Sava.[60] Even in the *Suda Lexicon*, information on the khagan's bridge-building venture has been preserved.[61] In reality, it must have entailed considerable difficulty to transport a mounted army across a great river. In almost all migration legends, crossing the Danube plays a key role as a "primordial deed," for example in the accounts of the Bulgars, Croats, Serbs, and Kuver's *Sermesianoi*.[62] For the Byzantines, crossing the Danube was also trespassing across the imperial frontier.

At the time of the death of the emperor Justin, 578, John of Ephesus in fact relates two bridge-building efforts by the "long-haired" Avars.[63] The first, for him the more consequential venture, is the bridge across the Danube. Justin, he recounts, at the friendly request of the Avars had sent architects and engineers who were to construct a palace and baths for the khagan. Such a technology transfer was not unusual for the times, but in the preserved accounts such ventures usually end in tragedy. An architect from Sirmium, who had once constructed baths for Attila's counselor Onegesios, had been retained as bath slave, rather than being released as he had hoped.[64] A sad fate also befell that Busas who reputedly taught the Avars the construction of siege machines.[65] Baian's architects landed in a predicament, when the khagan tried to coerce them into constructing a bridge for him over the Danube. At first they refused to bridge "the river that is like a sea." When the khagan threatened them with a drawn sword, they retorted that the emperor too would have them killed, if they allowed themselves to be forced into completing the assignment. But in the end they gave in all the same. Their hope that the barbarians would be unable to procure timber of sufficiently good quality for construction was dashed. When the bridge was completed, the Avar ruler again demanded that Emperor Tiberius surrender Sirmium. When he refused, war broke out. Then the architects had to build a second bridge.

Menander also provides an account on the technical problems that the Avars encountered in getting across the river. However, he does not say that the problem was solved with Roman know-how. Furthermore, the khagan had to fear his project being disrupted by the Roman fleet on the Danube and by the garrison at Singidunum. "Therefore he brought together on the Danube in Upper Pannonia many huge ships and he built large troop-transports not according to shipwrights' standards but from what was available on the spot. He loaded them with many soldiers and oarsmen, who rowed not in rhythm but in a barbarously uncoordinated manner, and sent the vessels *en masse* down the river, while he with the whole of his army marched by way of the island of Sirmium and reached the River Save."[66] The bridge across the Danube that John describes would not have been necessary to reach Sirmium; it was, as Menander says, the Sava that had to be bridged in order to close in the city and cut it off from the Roman supply route.

While "the entire Avar host" worked under high pressure at the completion of the bridge, the Romans in Sirmium and Singidunum began to have suspicions. The highest-ranking Roman officer in the region was then Sethos in Singidunum. He protested against the construction work and inquired as to the reasons for it. Now the khagan began his obfuscations. He asserted that he again wished to march on the Slavs, retold the story of the murdered envoys, and announced that because of it he would be sending a mission to Constantinople. If he were hampered in the construction of the bridge, he would have to consider it a violation of the treaty.

The garrison at Singidunum was not deceived but intimidated. They knew that with such weak forces very little resistance could be mounted against the Avar army. Baian added a final act to his comedy. He offered to swear that he had nothing up his sleeve as far as the Romans were concerned, and with grand gestures took one oath in the Avar fashion with his sword and another on the Bible.[67] The khagan's tactic, to win time by all means possible, worked. As envoy he pointedly sent the leader of the "hawks" at his court, "the major advocate continually urging war with the Romans," to Constantinople.[68] This officer served up to the emperor the story of the planned campaign against the Slavs. Tiberius didn't believe a word of it. But with the troop shortage he had to play along with the shell game. He advised that they delay this undertaking, since the Turks were already encamped at Cherson in the Crimea. This the Avar in turn probably saw through. But he pretended to go along with it and allowed himself to be loaded down with gifts, the final expedient of weaponless Byzantine politics. This would prove fatal to him. The weak Roman escort could not prevent him being murdered by pillaging Slavs on his way through Illyricum. If the story is true, this was the second Avar embassy in recent years to pay for the dissolution of Roman order in the Balkans with their lives. Even Baian's show of power the previous year had won the Avars no respect from the Slavic warriors.[69] Or was the story just to cover up that the Romans had rid themselves of an unwelcome ambassador?

A little later the khagan let drop his mask. Soon after his unfortunate colleague, the envoy Solachus entered the imperial city.[70] He spoke bluntly to the emperor: "Since in the future food or any other assistance cannot be brought to the city of Sirmium by river, there is no strategy that will protect the Romans there unless a Roman army comes large enough to drive the Avar army away by force and break the bridge." Scornfully he said that the emperor of the Romans should not risk a war "for one worthless city (or rather 'a jar,' which is the expression he used)."[71] He demanded the surrender of the city and guaranteed the inhabitants free departure with all their goods and chattels. The justification offered by the khagan is interesting:

> The khagan fears that at present the Romans are pretending to adhere to the peace treaty only until they settle the war with the Persians. When they have settled that, then they will throw their whole army against the Avars, having Sirmium as a very valuable bridgehead against them and being separated by no river or any other obstacle. For it is clear and most obvious that, at a time when there was a secure peace between the

Emperor and the Avars, he did not surround the city of Sirmium with such strong walls for their benefit. . . . The khagan was satisfied with the gifts sent to him each year by the emperor; for gold, silver and silken clothes were valuable commodities. However, since life was the more valuable and desirable than all of these, he had been worrying about this and reflecting that many of the people that beforetimes had come to this land had first been enticed with such gifts by the Romans, who in the end had attacked and destroyed them utterly.[72]

Of course, Baian knew the strengths and weaknesses of his opponent too well to feel seriously threatened. Perhaps more pragmatically, there was a point that the khagan would address in his negotiations with the Roman commander Theognis. "He added a plausible reason for his desire to control the city, in order to prevent deserters from the Avar army coming over to the Romans."[73] "Glorious Sirmium" had to cease to be a source of attraction for warriors in the Avar sphere of power. Then followed the familiar argument that by virtue of the victory over the Gepids the city belonged to the Avars.[74]

Scholars have often considered Sirmium as the key to the Balkan Peninsula, and the fall of the city is judged the "turning point in the history of the peninsula."[75] Possession of the city may have facilitated further raids on the Balkan provinces. Yet the Avars had already penetrated as far as Thrace before, and occasionally made the effort of building a boat-bridge over the Danube after taking it.[76] More important than the strategic significance of the city for either party must have been its symbolic worth. Tiberius says in Menander that "I should rather betroth to him one of my two daughters than willingly surrender the city of Sirmium."[77] It is in this sense that Stein judges that in the battle for the city "its moral significance by far exceeded its strategic worth."[78] At the end of the 570s, the Roman Balkans as a whole were under pressure. Roman order in the provinces relied ever more on a system of fortifications, to which Justinian had given definitive form. Holding the ancient city on the Sava was decisive for the morale of the defenders in other places. It symbolized the emperor's readiness to defend a fortress on the border. For the same reason the battle over the prestige of possessing Sirmium was inescapable for the khagan. He had too often insisted on the surrender of the city and reaffirmed his right to it. If he vacillated further, he would appear the loser in the eyes of his army.

After Solachus's demands had been rejected, Tiberius tried as best he could to organize the defense of the city. As a consequence of the Avar bridge, the normal supply route up the Sava was cut off. The principal road from Singidunum was in Avar hands too. But it proved possible to send reinforcements to the beleaguered city "some through Illyricum, some through Dalmatia."[79] We may assume that this took place on the Drina road. According to John of Ephesus the emperor meanwhile tried to persuade the Lombards and other peoples to intervene. Feelers were also put out to the Turks and the steppe peoples subject to them. With great ostentation the *protospatharios* Narses, once Justin's favorite, set off on this mission. But this diplomatic offensive was plagued with bad luck. The ship loaded with gold for those barbarians who were prepared to commit themselves sank near the mouth of the Danube. Narses was so affected by this that he fell sick and soon died.[80] Whether it was because of the loss of the ship or not, this time proven Byzantine strategy could bring no relief to the besieged city.

Nevertheless the Avars were unable to make any headway against the city fortifications, which had been repaired since 567. The siege of Sirmium lasted almost three years.[81] By means of a second bridge, probably upstream of the city, the ring around the city was closed. An Avar contingent under Apsikh, one of the most prominent of the Avar leaders, guarded the bridge on the road toward Dalmatia. But the Romans did not show themselves. Apsikh then thought that the site might be left unguarded and joined his forces with those of the main army, which had taken a stand by the downstream bridge.[82]

Already prior to this move, negotiations had once again resumed. On the river islets of Casia and Carbonaria, the Roman commander-in-chief Theognis met the khagan. Baian staged a grand show. From a golden throne under a canopy and covered by shields, he negotiated with the Romans.[83] Again the khagan demanded that Sirmium be surrendered. Theognis countered by demanding the withdrawal of the Avar army. Finally, the negotiations were broken off without results.

In the course of time, difficulties in securing supplies became noticeable. Grain convoys were no longer able to pass through the Avar blockade. Famine broke out; horses and cats had to be eaten. The city commander Salomon was not up to the task that had befallen him. Complaints and grievances on the part of the townspeople were the result. The desperate situation of the inhabitants is documented by an inscription scratched onto a brick, which was found at the close of the nineteenth century: "Oh Lord, help the town and halt the Avar and protect the Romanía and the scribe. Amen."[84] Otherwise excavations at Sremska Mitrovica have so far provided no information on the siege.[85]

Avar tactics suggested that no interruption in the siege was to be expected. It was news of the desperate situation of the inhabitants, perhaps also their direct intervention, that finally convinced the emperor that the city could not be held. Concurrently the Slav incursions had reached a new apogee in 581. John of Ephesus recounts that in the third year after the death of Justin the Slavs pillaged all of Hellas, the region of Thessalonica, and all of Thrace up to the Long Wall.[86] Although the dating and interpretation are debated, this indicates the difficult strategic situation for Byzantium. The war against the Persians had been going on for a decade with no prospect of a decisive outcome. The diplomatic efforts to contain the Lombards with Frankish help had at best only partial results. Thus, there were scarcely troops at hand for deployment in the Balkan provinces. As a result of his predecessor's policies, with which he had long ago broken, Tiberius was now in a corner. It is under these circumstances that we must view his decision finally to surrender Sirmium.

In 582, he charged Theognis by letter to arrange for the transfer of the city in return for safe conduct.[87] Baian assured the inhabitants of the city that they might leave, but without goods and chattels. He said that he was satisfied with the eighty thousand solidi per year that had been agreed on in 574, but demanded a catch-up payment of the outstanding amounts. The Bookolabras affair also caused complications. The Avar chief shaman had seduced one of the khagan's wives and had fled to the Romans.[88] Baian now demanded his extradition and was almost ready to let negotiations break down over the matter. Finally he gave in, satisfied with the promise that the defector would be hunted down. With this the fall of the city was assured.

At this point Menander's work ends. If we are to believe the account of John of Ephesus, the city's ordeal did not end with its surrender.[89] The tragic irony was that the unexpected humanity of the barbarians actually cost many city residents their lives. The Avars brought bread and wine into the city in order to assuage the hunger of the besieged. The starved inhabitants of Sirmium threw themselves with such ravenousness over the food that many ate themselves to death. The survivors withdrew, some to Salona, where Sirmian immigrants are named on inscriptions.[90] The Avars settled down in Sirmium, as John explicitly observes. The tragedy of Sirmium was completed the following year, when the city was destroyed in a great fire.[91] The barbarians, who had no experience in urban firefighting, escaped with their bare lives. The Syrian's account sounds like a parable. Still, it is remarkable for running contrary to barbarian stereotypes. The Avars do not massacre the inhabitants, but kill some by feeding them; they do not burn the city, but are hit by a fire as inhabitants. Whether we can believe any of this is unclear. There is no other record of Avars settling in a city. The graves of Avar horsemen, situated in ruined houses, confirm some Avar residence but also the decay of Sirmium.[92]

The conquest of Sirmium was widely recorded. In distant Spain John of Biclaro mentions the Avar conquests in Pannonia in one breath along with the (probably Slavic) incursions in Thrace and Greece.[93] Theophylact, Theophanes, and Evagrius recount the fall of Sirmium, without giving any details.[94] The event marks a turning point in Avar–Byzantine relations. Both rulers, Baian and Tiberius, died soon thereafter. The new emperor, Maurice, who mounted the throne in August 582, had little faith in peaceful coexistence on the Danube. And Baian's son as the new khagan pursued an appreciably more offensive policy than his father, who left to him a consolidated realm and unchallenged rule.[95]

3.5 583/84: Avar Raids and Symbolic Politics

Tiberius survived the collapse of his defense efforts by only a few months and died in August 582. The treaty that his successor Maurice inherited cost eighty thousand gold solidi per year, delivered "in the form of merchandise of silver and of embroidered cloth."[96] This indicates that the subsidies were not necessarily paid in cash. Theophylact goes into the usual verbal contortions to explain these "most disgraceful terms": "Like a panel of judges in session, they gave the barbarians glorious gifts, as if a prize for excellence."[97]

Among the Avars too there was a new leader in charge, whom the imperial envoy Comentiolus could remind somewhat later of the friendly reception that had been accorded his ancestors.[98] Baian must then have died shortly after the taking of Sirmium, and one of his sons had succeeded him. This may have occurred in the winter of 582–83, shortly before the embassy that Theophanes puts in May 583.[99] Events that followed would accord well with a change of ruler. Baian, the practitioner of realpolitik, had gone; the heir to his victories sought to reconfirm his position vis-à-vis the emperor.

Peace reigned for scarcely two years, Theophylact recounts, when the khagan began to make further demands.[100] It had come to his ears that the emperor possessed giant animals, and he wished to have one of them. And the emperor did in fact send him an Indian elephant. This was a favorite gift in diplomatic intercourse. Justin II, for example, once received "elephant tusks and a giraffe," as John of Biclaro remarked. The Spanish chronicler, who had spent his youth on the Golden Horn, also remembered the thirty-five elephants from the Persian war that had been paraded triumphantly through the city.[101] Perhaps the khagan's elephant came from this booty. The fabulous animal did not long remain a guest in the Carpathian Basin.

> But when the khagan saw the elephant, the Indian creature, he at once terminated the display, and commanded that the beast return to the emperor, whether in terror or scorn of the marvel, I cannot say. . . .
> He pestered the emperor to fashion a gold couch and send that to him as well, for the peak of his current good fortune had raised him so high; the emperor had the gift made and royally conveyed it. But he arrogantly assumed even haughtier airs, as if he had been besmirched

by the unworthiness of the gift, and he sent back to the emperor the ostentatious gold couch as though it were something cheap and common. Furthermore he demanded that, in addition to the 80,000 gold coins, he be paid by the Romans a further 20,000 each year.[102]

Arrogance, greed, and exorbitance: the author of the account omits none of the customary attributes of a barbarian ruler. However, when we consider the significance of gifts in barbarian society (and beyond), the khagan's gestures can be understood. The khagan wishes to push gift-giving to the emperor's limit; he thereby displays to his army the respect that he enjoys. By refusing reception of the gifts, he tries to invalidate the hierarchy that awards the giver precedence. The best that the emperor can give is, for the khagan, not good enough. This is the symbolic content of the story.[103] It appears to have been well received by readers; even the twelfth-century chronicler Zonaras took up the anecdote of the hapless journey of the elephant to Pannonia.[104] Maurice decided to refuse any increase in subsidies, even though he was poorly prepared for the war that was to follow from this refusal. However, in the course of 584, he could only observe how the khagan tried to grab what he had not been given.[105]

The Avars' first goal was Singidunum/Belgrade. Justinian had once heavily fortified the city at the mouth of the Sava and made it into a "glistening, very important city."[106] That the city, from which the siege of Sirmium had shortly before been suspiciously observed, should now be "ungarrisoned and bereft of military equipment," as Theophylact would have it, seems exaggerated. Anyone could work out what the Avars' next objective would be. Nevertheless, the khagan succeeded in taking the city with a surprise attack, when a portion of the townspeople were outside the walls, occupied with the harvest. Serious fighting occurred only at the gates, with the Avars gaining a "Cadmean" victory.

Once again speed had proven the Avars' best weapon. "Easily and without effort," the khagan took two further cities. The first of these was Viminacium/Kostolac near the mouth of the Morava. The settlement on the plain had decayed since the time of Attila, but Justinian moved it to higher ground and had it fortified.[107] A good piece downstream lay Augusta at the mouth of the river that today still bears the name Ogost.[108] That this less significant fortress should be mentioned as captured shows that the khagan had bypassed more important cities such as Bononia/Vidin and Ratiaria/Arčer. Perhaps the advanced season also forced him to hurry.

Soon the Avars were encamped before the Thracian harbor of Anchialus/Anhialo on the Black Sea. They did not stop to mount a siege but were content to lay waste the surrounding area. The barbarians were particularly pleased with the spa near the city. Justinian had once had it surrounded with walls, "and thus made the cure free of danger."[109] Now the wives of the khagan bathed here, and the pleasure they took may have spared the spa from destruction.

A strange scene was played out in the baths of Anchialus, according to John of Ephesus.[110] During the capture of the baths of Anchialus, the "Slavs" (as he often calls the Avars) found the purple robe of Anastasia, the consort of Tiberius, who had earlier donated it to a church when she was visiting the spa. The khagan put on the robe and said, "Whether the emperor of the Romans wishes it or not, the realm has now been given to me!" The translation of the phrase from Syriac is debatable, as is the original meaning in Greek, and whether any of this ever happened remains obscure. It certainly was not the intention of the clerical author to document the khagan's self-representation but rather to emphasize his sacrilegious barbarian arrogance. All we can say is that his supposed performance is plausible as a Byzantine perception of barbarian rulership and captures some of the logic of its representation. The Avar elite made ample use of Byzantine symbols in displays of their status, and at the same time, the khagan had to demonstrate that he had won everything on his own merits. With the victor's rights, he put on a splendid Roman robe and so through Roman state symbolism demonstrated his barbarian right to rule.[111] The khagan had recently ascended the throne, and his first military campaign in imperial territory offered an opportunity for the demonstration of his qualifications as a leader.

John of Ephesus tells the story of the war that culminated in the scene at Anchialus somewhat differently. He mentions joint attacks with subject Slavs and with Lombards. In this venture two cities and additional fortresses were captured, the inhabitants were invited to get on with their lives in peace—and to pay the Avars tribute.[112] Could that refer to Singidunum—whose inhabitants had been attacked during the harvest season—and Viminacium? The order to continue with harvesting and to deliver a portion of it was perhaps to enhance the army's food supplies. In the longer term, this makes sense only if the affected cities lay near the region of Avar settlement.

In what follows John describes the concern in Constantinople and the defensive measures that were undertaken. Even clerics put on uniforms in order to guard the Long Wall. Churches suffered much from the enemy. The Slavs (and here it is probably the actual Slavs who are meant) pillaged church treasures. Their king used the ciborium from the church of Corinth as a marquee. John of Ephesus evidently kept up-to-date on events until his death, although he was more or less sequestered because of his Monophysite tendencies. His sources were not official war reports or court journals but rather what people were saying in the capital. The almost octogenarian cleric had some difficulty in distinguishing between Avars and Slavs. But when, immediately after the desecration of the ciborium, he mentions the Antes, he can scarcely have made this up.[113]

As he tells it, during the campaign the Antes, abetted by Roman money, had made an incursion into the land of the Slavs "west of the river that is called the Danube." The pillaging of their homeland only magnified the anger of the Slavs, and since they could not seize the well-fortified capital, they turned toward Anchialus. We do, in fact, hear of a treaty between the Romans and the Antes in the year 600, when an Avar host marched against its old enemy on the other side of the Carpathians.[114] The plan to attack the unprotected homeland during an Avar attack could well have been drawn from the repertory of Byzantine diplomacy. That the Antes really dared to make a raid into the Carpathian Basin is, however, very implausible.

Soon after the khagan's triumphant self-staging in the baths, the mood in the Avar camp swung about. "And the khagan was terrified by rumors that the people of the Turks was pursuing him. And they went to Sirmium, since they feared that the Turks would capture the palace that belonged to the khagan as well as all its possessions. However, when the Avars sent the Turks eight *kentenaria* of gold, the Turks turned away from them. At this time three brothers had come from inner Scythia, bringing with them 30,000 Scythians."[115]

That the retreat from Anchialus in the fall of 584 was the consequence of fear of the Turks is not improbable. Even though the season was well advanced, the Avars could, as in the following year, have wintered in their target area. The envoy Comentiolus also seems to have held the Turkish card in his hand. In his high-flying speech before the khagan he does not fail to mention the earlier flight of the Avars from the east.[116] The envoy's rude handling could well be explained if the khagan suspected the Romans of inciting the Turks against him.

The Avar khagan's successful offensive may well be due to reinforcements from the east. Even though Theophylact's elaborate rhetorical constructs must be taken with more than a pinch of salt, a clear hint occurs in Comentiolus's speech. The land of the Avars is big enough, he said, "so that the inhabitants are never overcrowded and incomers never lack a subdivision."[117] Theophylact's Scythian digression gives more precise information and could be matched with John's account about the three brothers: three further Varchonite tribes had arrived in Europe, the Tarniakh, Kotzagir, and Zabender. Altogether about ten thousand men, these newcomers were fleeing from the Turks into the Carpathian Basin.[118] Just as a generation earlier, the second Varchonite migration seems to have been a consequence of extensive warfare in central Asia, this time among the Turks. It is not easy to date the new wave of migrants; Theophylact only mentions it in the context of a letter sent by a Turkish khagan in the 590s. His information can be matched to accounts from Chinese sources and to the names from the Mongolküre inscription, but different options remain for the reasons that may have pushed further groups of Varchonites to leave the Turkish realm.[119] It is not unlikely that it happened in the mid-580s. According to the *Sui shu*, during an attack on China in 582 several western subject peoples, among them Yida (Hephthalites), rebelled but were defeated. A revolt of the Aba (Avars?) seems to have happened in 585; they are reported to have fled when the Turks received Chinese support. As in the 550s, this would again point to dissonant perceptions as Varchonites (by Turks and Byzantines) and Avars. Protracted internal conflicts in the Turkish khaganate may also offer an explanation. Theophylact's text, based on Khagan Niri's letter, refers to one episode, the rise and fall of Khagan Turum/Dulan, in the 590s.[120]

In 584, negotiations with the Avars were only resumed three months after the beginning of the war. Maurice now sent an uneven pair to the khagan: the senator Elpidius, who had earlier been *praetor* of Sicily, and Comentiolus, an officer of the guard. The former cautiously reminded the Avar leader of the treaty from 582. The khagan calmly replied that no treaty would prevent him from overrunning the Long Wall in the near future. Into the senator's embarrassed silence jumped Comentiolus, who could no longer contain himself, with a string of accusations. Theophylact reproduces the alleged speech of the ill-restrained envoy at some length.[121] Along with the usual commonplaces there is one that is characteristic of attitudes toward the barbarians. The annual payments are explained as gifts, because "the Romans are generous people, and they treasure liberality and generosity." Earlier, "after your splintered segment had broken away from its ancestral tribe in the east," the Avars had been received as refugees—a favorite argument. But now they lived in sufficiency in a vast and thinly populated land and still found it necessary to attack the Romans.

The khagan was not pleased with the presumptuous imperial rhetoric. Trembling with anger and with flashing eyes he ordered Comentiolus thrown into chains. "According to the customs of the country," the latter learned, a sentence of death threatened him. But the next day, the "most powerful men" among the Avars succeeded in appeasing their lord.[122] This is not the only reference to a more prudent policy advanced by the Avar *logades*. The envoys would return to the emperor unharmed. Their mission had clearly failed.

A peace treaty was reached only in the following year, 585.[123] Elpidius had again traveled to the khagan, who had apparently drawn back to the region around Sirmium for the winter. In the meantime the "doves" at the Avar court had prevailed. Their most eminent representative, the experienced negotiator Targitius, went with Elpidius to the imperial city in order to put the finishing touches to the peace. The Romans finally had to put up the additional twenty thousand solidi that had been demanded since Baian's son took over. The annual payment now amounted to a hundred thousand pieces of gold, still appreciably less than the sum that Attila had extorted in his heyday. Events that follow show that negotiations were successfully concluded in the spring of 585. But the treaty would not survive the summer.

3.6 585/86: Slavic Raids and the Bookolabras Affair

The peace between the khagan and the emperor did not end the war in the Balkans. The Avar ruler returned home, and Slavic bands extended their plundering campaigns over the greater part of the peninsula. Byzantine observers saw the hand of the khagan behind this. We may assume that such Slavic actions had the approval of the Avar leader; his initiative would hardly have been necessary.

These were the years when John of Ephesus composed his church history. "See, until the present day, in the year 895, they occupy and dwell in the Roman provinces, with no care or fear, plundering, murdering, and burning, having become rich and possessed of gold and silver, herds of horses and many weapons, and have learned better than the Romans how to wage war."[124] This hardly marks the beginning of Slavic settlement in the Balkan Peninsula; John does not speak of land-starved farmers in search of new fields but of pillagers, who "have learned . . . to wage war" and who could be mistaken for Avars. Even when they remained for years, most of them one day went back to their place of departure, as did Ardagast, who set up camp at Adrianople in 585 and then many years later was tracked down in his homeland north of the Danube.[125]

The peace with the Avars made the Slavic incursions all the more visible. In the summer of 585 they advanced to the Long Wall. Maurice personally took charge of defense measures; he had the fortifications watched by his guard and then ordered Comentiolus to take the offensive against the plunderers.[126] The officer, whatever his failings as a diplomat, was fortunate. On the Erginus/Ergene he surprised and defeated a rather large troop of Slavs. At the close of summer he marched on the emperor's orders in the direction of Adrianople. There the Roman army ran into a Slav column heavily loaded with booty. Exceptionally, the name of the leader has been preserved, Ardagast, although he is here introduced without any title. At the otherwise unknown fortress of Ensinon Roman arms defeated the Slav warriors, prisoners were freed, and Astikē, the area on the other side of Adrianople, was cleared of enemies. While Ardagast's bands withdrew across the Danube, Comentiolus erected a victory monument on the battlefield.

Meanwhile the Bookolabras scandal at the Avar court had turned into a political issue again; only Theophylact gives a relatively detailed account of what had happened.[127] The high priest, whose title was Bookolabras, had flown to the Romans after a love affair with one of Baian's wives. That must have taken place during the siege of Sirmium, since there was already talk of it during negotiations for a surrender. Menander mentions it but without giving any names.[128] Yet it seems obvious that the "member of the khagan's following" who had come together "in amorous congress" with a wife of the khagan was none other than the shaman. Negotiations about the surrender of Sirmium had almost failed because of the khagan's demand for the extradition of the transgressor. Clearly, the ruler's honor was at stake. The Roman negotiator Theognis made excuses; in such a vast empire it would be impossible to locate a wandering fugitive. Finally, the khagan insisted that the Roman general pledge to have the fugitive hunted down and immediately turned over to him or at least that he be informed of his death. Theophylact recounts that Bookolabras had convinced seven subject Gepids to accompany him; he wanted to return to the people from which he was descended. "These are Huns, who dwell in the east as neighbours of the Persians and whom it is more familiar for many to call Turks." This hardly means that the high priest was an exiled Turk. The Varchonites, who called themselves Avars, had once come from what was now the land of the Turks, and this was where the fugitive wished to return. Soon after he had crossed the Danube the high priest was seized by a Roman border patrol. It is an almost Freudian irony that this Avar sexual transgressor was seized in the town of Libidina. Bookolabras described his origins, his earlier activities, and the reason that had brought him there. The soldiers believed him (or feared his magical arts) and sent him on to Constantinople. The shaman was welcomed in Constantinople and kept there like so many members of barbarian elites who might still become useful one day.

It was only after Baian's death that the affair caused serious complications. In the spring of 586, according to the peace treaty concluded in 585, Targitius came to collect the one hundred thousand solidi. But as Theophylact indicates, the fact that Bookolabras stayed as a guest of state in Constantinople constituted a breach of the treaty. The shaman may also have let on that the khagan had incited Slavic plunderers and was already preparing for the next war. This suspicion was perhaps not unfounded (something similar had occurred in 579), but the emperor's reaction was nonetheless unreflected. He had Targitius arrested and held prisoner for half a year on the Isle of Princes. Maurice was surely thinking of the poor treatment of his protégé Comentiolus at the khagan's court. But while reason had prevailed in that instance, the emperor remained stubborn.

Maurice thus made two mistakes at one stroke. First, he himself offended against international law on which Roman envoys were accustomed to call and gave the khagan an unimpeachable cause for war. Second, he locked up and estranged the most influential of the doves at the Avar court. Very likely it had been none other than the old diplomat Targitius who had argued for the release of Comentiolus. It would take almost ten years before his moderating influence was again traceable. The emperor had even considered having the Avar envoys executed. The runaway shaman seems to have made a great impression on him.

The khagan used the rest of the year 586 to deliver a major blow to Justinian's Danube *limes*. Never before had the Avar army taken so many fortresses in such a short time. The Avars' victorious campaign began below the Iron Gate with the capture of Akys/Prahovo near Negotin, Bononia/Vidin, and Ratiaria/Arčer. A series of cities also fell in the border region of Moesia and Scythia minor: Durostorum/Silistra, Zaldapa, Tropaeum Traiani, Marcianopolis/Devnja, and Pannasa on the river Panysus/Kamčaja. Perhaps the capture of Apiaria also belongs here, although it is related as occurring in the following year. Theophylact wrote that the capture of these cities had occurred "with considerable labour."[129] Many of these places continued to be of importance, so they were not completely destroyed. Still, once again some important fortresses restored in the Justinianic period had fallen.

3.7 587: The War in Thrace

The khagan's campaign of conquest on the Danube in the fall of 586 had been only a prelude; this much was clear to the Romans. Maurice now appointed Comentiolus, the victor over the Slavs, as commander for the European war. Although Philippicus was involved in the exhausting war on the frontier with Persia at the same time, it proved possible to assemble an army of ten thousand men in Anchialus. When Comentiolus mustered his troops, he had to admit that four thousand of them were as good as unfit to fight. He entrusted them with guarding the camp and equipment. The remainder he divided into three detachments, lead by Castus, Martinus, and himself.[130] We unfortunately do not know whether the Avars wintered on imperial soil, as in 597–98 outside Tomis/Constanţa. It is quite likely that this time too they encamped somewhere near the Black Sea coast, for operations began where they had stopped the previous year. The barbarian host had been divided into smaller units to facilitate supplying the troops. This dispersal gave the Romans a short-term strategic advantage.

Castus turned with his soldiers toward the devastated city of Zaldapa, on the road from Marcianopolis/Devnja to the Danube, where he routed out a band of barbarians, probably no greater a force than the at most two thousand men that he himself led. He succeeded in chasing the surprised enemy from their booty. This he entrusted to one of his bodyguards who promptly lost it again to the barbarians.

Near Tomis Martinus almost succeeded in an appreciably more important surprise attack. That this occurred near Tomis/Constanța and not the Dacian Tomis is evident from the course of the battle. As scouts had informed the general, the khagan himself was then in the region. The Romans set an ambush. Death staring him in the face, the Avar ruler managed to escape with his closest followers to an island. The Constanța region is rich in lagoons. The division of the army had left the Avars vulnerable. A bit later the khagan eluded a second ambush. The episodes show that the Avars were best beaten with their own weapons: cunning and speed.

Quickly the two army groups withdrew to Marcianopolis, where Comentiolus had spent the whole time in inactivity. Finally, the none-too-venturesome commander ordered the Haemus pass to be occupied. The whole army then withdrew to Sabulente Canalis, which lay on the road to Anchialus. Theophylact draws on Aelian's description of the Tempe Valley to provide a setting for the subsequent bucolic battle scene. The khagan had meanwhile reassembled his army. Martinus and Castus were ordered to observe their opponent's moves. Castus succeeded in wiping out the Avar vanguard on the bank of the Panysus/Kamčaja. Overconfident as a result of his success, he did not, as ordered, promptly turn back to the main body of the army. While he spent the night on the river bank, an enemy detachment crossed the wooden bridge and cut off his rear. Thus hemmed in, Castus ordered his soldiers to scatter into the woods. "Like hares or deer," the Romans stayed hidden in the undergrowth. The Avars succeeded in laying their hands on some of the enemy. Threatened with a terrible death, they betrayed the place of refuge of the commander and the game of hide-and-seek ended with the capture of Castus, who had perched in the middle of the woods "like an unpicked bunch of grapes."[131]

While Comentiolus guarded the pleasant valley of Sabulente, the Avars took another route and crossed the foothills of the Balkan Mountains. A large host now moved toward the south. Five hundred Roman soldiers, who were to defend the area of Mesembria/Nesebăr, met their deaths. It is not expressly stated that the city also fell; accounts tell only of the fate of the garrison. Ansimuth, the commander of the Thracian foot-soldiers, tried to save what could be saved and to lead the remaining units safely to the Long Wall. But in so doing he himself fell into the hands of the Avar vanguard.

As news of one misadventure after another piled up, Comentiolus held a council of war in his now worthless position in the Haemus forests. He still had four thousand soldiers fit for battle and just as many unfit. Theophylact has two speakers appear in the discussion, one of whom counsels withdrawal while the other evokes the old Roman virtues in flaming words. Contrary to this rhetoric, the *Strategicon* advised, in the event of an enemy incursion, preserving the army unharmed as much as possible and avoiding battle. This would leave the opponent less maneuvering room to mount a siege. The manual of warfare also considered troop psychology: "For a person operating in his own country is less inclined to fight; he has many ways of saving himself and does not want to take unnecessary risks."[132] Comentiolus's hesitation is then not simply to be ascribed to his cowardice; indeed, this is one of the passages where the polemical intent of Theophylact's source becomes most obvious.

The handbook also recommended harassing the enemy. Chance once again helped Comentiolus out. When he had withdrawn with his army, he heard that the khagan had set up his headquarters nearby but that his army was still scattered and engaged in plundering. This was a fresh opportunity for a surprise attack against the enemy leader. But once again, the effort failed. Someone noted that a pack animal was poorly loaded and called out to the driver to turn around. This command in Late Latin, "torna, torna," instead spread through the ranks and was misunderstood as a signal to flee.[133] Panic broke out. Warned by the tumult, the khagan made off in haste. Once again the reckless Avar leader had luck on his side at the last minute.

The further course of the war is not wholly clear. Theophylact has the fall of Apiaria follow as an unfortunate consequence of the carelessness of the pack train driver, which he localizes to the vicinity of Libidurgus near Mesembria.[134] Then follow one after another the sieges of Beroe, Diocletianopolis, and Philippopolis. If the Avar army was thus in movement on the Anchialus–Philippopolis/Plovdiv road, the story about the siege of the insignificant Danube fortress Apiaria/Rahovo (near Ruse) must have happened in the previous year and is only misplaced here.[135]

Still, in the context in which it is recounted, the fable about the fall of Apiaria is not entirely out of place. For after the khagan had luckily survived the various harassments of the Roman army, he resumed his war against the cities. Apiaria then marks the acquisition of Byzantine siege technique by the Avars. To blame for the barbarians' success in breaching so many fortresses was, in the final analysis, a woman, the historian tells us. The woman was the wife of a soldier by name of Busas and, prompted by the many absences of her spouse, she had taken a young man as lover. One day, while he was out hunting, Busas was caught by the Avars: "The hunter fell into the snare."[136]

As usual the Avars wanted to make a profitable deal with the prisoner. They dragged him before the city walls to give him an opportunity to raise the ransom sum. Otherwise, they threatened to kill him on the spot. In tears Busas detailed his military services and as proof laid bare his old war wounds. Yet his wife and her lover sensed an opportunity to be quit of the man at the foot of the walls and prevented his ransoming. The tragedy ran its course. As much for revenge as to save his skin, the veteran promised to help the Avars in their capture of the city. He instructed them, "since they had as yet no knowledge of such implements," in the construction of a siege machine for long-range assault, probably the *helepolis*, a catapult.[137] Soon thereafter the betrayed traitor was witness to the destruction of his native city. Encapsulated in this story is the fact that the Avars became only gradually familiar with siege technology. It also illustrates a topos rejected by Deleuze and Guattari: "The idea that the nomads received their technical weapons and political counseling from renegades from an imperial state is highly improbable."[138]

Not until before Beroe/Stara Zagora did the khagan's army meet serious opposition.[139] The khagan was finally forced to leave the well-defended city in peace in return for a little money. And on the walls of Diocletianopolis/Hisaya (between Plovdiv and Kalowo) catapults and other machines were hoisted when the Avars pulled up. "After experiencing the proverbial fate of the wolf," the khagan stood there with his dashed hopes.[140] The same happened before Philippopolis/Plovdiv and Adrianopolis/Edirne. The forts along the Danube had been easier to take, while larger cities could hardly be cracked.

Meanwhile news had reached Constantinople of Castus's and Ansimuth's mishaps, and the officers' failures made the emperor the butt of popular mockery. Nothing was left for him to do but to ransom Castus, as some aged contemporaries of Theophylact still remembered.[141] In place of the luckless Comentiolus Maurice appointed John Mystacon, "the Moustached," as *strategos*. Only some years before, he had relieved him of his command in the Persian war for his lack of success.[142] Mystacon, with his adjutant Drocto, a Lombard, set out for Adrianople.[143] This barbarian in Roman uniform succeeded in beating the Avars with their own methods. He feigned flight during the battle, then swung suddenly about and fell on his pursuers who had broken ranks. The *Strategicon* calls this ploy "the Scythian attack."[144] The barbarians were forced to give up the siege of the city and retreat.

Like Comentiolus the year before, Mystacon did not pursue the defeated, a decision that Theophylact expressly welcomes. Adrianople clearly represented a kind of threshold. Here began the sensitive zone, in proximity to the capital city, in which military involvement was higher. Beyond that, the enemy army was left more room to maneuver. It does not appear that the war ended with Drocto's bit of bravura. There is no talk of a peace treaty; the Avars simply disappear from Theophylact's account for some years. Theophanes fades out his account of them even earlier, after the Busas story, with a vague reference to the capture of many cities. Whatever may have happened during these years in the western part of the Balkan Peninsula, it did not come to the attention of the chroniclers in the capital city. In Thrace, everyday life returned, but without lasting peace. Soon the Slav incursions reached a new high point, events that Theophylact recounts in a single sentence.[145]

3.8 The Carpathian Basin in the Later Sixth Century: The Archaeological Evidence

In 567 the Avars occupied the kingdom of the Gepids, and a year later the former Lombard territory that largely corresponded to the old province of Pannonia. In Byzantine perception, this was "a vast, mostly unpopulated region. It is settled only here and there by barbarians who lead an almost bestial life, shut off from other human beings, for the most part it is altogether barren." This is at least how Procopius describes the Carpathian Basin in the middle of the sixth century.[146] Of course, he had never been there. By the standards of the Byzantine core areas, Pannonia with its towns in decay and its rudimentary infrastructure must have seemed barbaric; after all, most of it had been controlled by diverse barbarians for more than a century. Textual and archaeological evidence shows that late antique Christian communities still lived there under Lombard rule before 568. However at least part of these "Pannonians" moved to Italy with the Lombards in 568.[147]

For the Avars, the organization and settlement of this huge area seem to have taken some time. This was by no means a small achievement; as Tivadar Vida has remarked, apart from the short-lived empire of the Huns, no other power had ever been "capable of integrating the motley of ethnic groups with widely differing cultural backgrounds" in the entire Carpathian Basin.[148] We have no written account of these efforts. Archaeologists have long attempted to arrive at a clearer picture of the first decades of Avar rule.[149] Object types such as reflex bows and three-edged arrowheads, stirrups, and multiple belts with mountings were dated to the last third of the sixth century and described as the archaeological remains of the first generation of Avars in the region. In the 1950s the characteristics of the early Avar period, the first of three chronological groups of finds from the Avar era, were first defined: stirrups with long foot-rings and round foot-plates; leaf-shaped iron lance heads; pieces of lamellar armor; straight, two-edged swords, often attached to a P-shaped ring; an item of clothing particularly characteristic of the Avars, the belt sets with ancillary straps, decorated with strap-ends and metal fittings pressed in a mold or chased from sheet metal; the horse harnesses may have similar decoration. Some of these early datings, for instance of the belt sets, have since been revised.[150] The early Avar period was successively divided into two or three phases: a first phase until ca. 600 and a second until about 630, sometimes also taken together as a first phase, and a second (or third) up to ca. 650–70, although the exact dating remains controversial.[151]

As it turned out, there was no easy answer to the question of where the new archaeological culture had come from. Obviously, the Avars did not impose a consistent material culture on central Europe. A multitude of influences and parallels was detected in the burials and funeral customs of the early Avar period in the Carpathian Basin. Objects and customs from the central Asian steppe do not constitute the bulk of the early Avar-period material. Some scholars pointed to features from eastern central Asia, the steppes north of the Chinese Empire and the Altai region, where the Rouran had ruled, but the archaeological record from this region in the period is limited, and what is known is quite different from what we know about the Avars. Others discussed possible parallels with west central Asia and the steppe zone north of the Sassanian Empire that had been dominated by the Hephthalites, for instance the swords with P-shaped belt-rings, plate armor, silver pseudo-buckles, and spherical earrings. Sassanian-Persian influence was also proposed, such as the representations of lions that decorated the belt of a warrior from the early period who was buried in Csengele. Features from the south Russian steppe, such as the fastenings of the Martinovka (Martinyvka) type, and from the Caucasus region were also noted and sometimes interpreted as traces of Cutrigur or Bulgar followers in the khagan's host.[152] It seemed clear that in order to understand Avar culture and identity, one had to look to the central Eurasian steppes where they had come from. The steppe was regarded as a basically autonomous cultural zone, which was of course open to external influences, but essentially followed ancient nomadic traditions.

No doubt such steppe characteristics could be found in the Avar settlement area, especially if one looked for them. The impression of a self-contained steppe culture was created by rich grave finds that seemed typical for the Avars. However, this impression was distorted because in Byzantium, where grave goods were not common, only chance survivals could attest to the use of objects that could be found in considerable quantities in Avar graves. Byzantine parallels were detected only by systematically looking for them. Then, they would suddenly appear—on mosaics, in hoard finds, or described in written sources. It emerged that the same type of object north of the Caucasus and in the Carpathian Basin was not necessarily proof that the Avars had brought it from the east; it could also have arrived in both cases from Constantinople. As Tivadar Vida put it, "a better understanding of the Avars' integration into the contemporary European world . . . called for a paradigm shift: the earlier focus on the eastern traditions in Avar studies obscured all local cultural phenomena, social displays, lifeways, identities and symbols."[153] The pilot studies that established this new paradigm dealt with the Avar multipartite belts, which came to be fundamental for the status and cultural identity of the Avar warriors, but were in fact already attested in the Mediterranean before the Avars came.[154]

Archaeological research on the Avars in the late twentieth and early twenty-first centuries has therefore learned to frame questions differently. For a long time, Avar archaeology had mainly aimed for "attribution" of objects: if an object or a practice could be attributed to an ethnic or cultural group, a social stratum or a religious creed, the archaeologist's work was done, because he had made his evidence available under the right heading for other archaeologists, but also for historians or linguists, and then the results of the different disciplines could be synchronized. The vexed question of "ethnic attribution" of archaeological evidence just addresses one of these mechanisms of attribution.[155] The search for "attribution" is not necessarily a wrong approach, but it is limited and, as an ultimate research goal, misleading.

The wide currency of "Byzantine" objects in the early Avar period is a good example for these limits. A critical review of early Avar object types showed that many of them were not particular to the steppe zone, but much rather represented crafts also current in Byzantium.[156] This observation is also valid for the steppes north of the Black Sea and the Caucasus regions. As in earlier centuries, the eastern European steppes and the Carpathian Basin formed an interrelated cultural zone in which multiethnic barbarian warrior cultures developed in a field of Roman/Byzantine attraction. The archaeological culture/s in the Avar Empire could therefore also be described as a "Byzantine peripheral culture." The question of Byzantine influence in Avar archaeological material is of course very complex. Objects produced in the Byzantine world, such as silver ware, glass vessels, and amphorae (as containers for wine and oil), came to the Carpathian Basin as gifts, trade goods, and war booty. In the early Avar period, many goods also seem to have been produced by Byzantine artisans for Avar tastes. Late antique artisanal traditions were to an extent continued in Pannonia. Classical/Byzantine motifs and techniques were also taken over, adapted, and transformed. In any case, the late antique/Byzantine components, often difficult to distinguish, were an important factor in the development of Avar craftsmanship.[157] Why did the Avars adopt so many cultural traits from their principal enemies? Perhaps Colin Renfrew's concept of "competitive emulation" used "to describe the propensity of political elites to adopt culture from rival 'peer polities'" can help to frame the question. Jonathan Skaff has employed it in his analysis of the relations between Tang China and the Turks.[158]

While Avar warriors gradually adopted tokens of Byzantine culture, groups with a different cultural background were integrated in the Avar realm. A good example of this process is the huge cemetery of Zamárdi on Lake Balaton, with thousands of graves, some of them very rich. So far, more than two thousand graves have been excavated, and four thousand more are expected. Despite extensive grave-robbing, the finds show that a large and prosperous group, a rather hybrid population, lived in Zamárdi in the early Avar period. "The finds represent the material culture of half of Europe and the Near East. There are bronze vessels from Byzantium, silver-inlaid iron folding chairs of Italo-Lombard provenance, glass vessels from East Rome and Italy, and even late Sassanian horse harness from Iran. . . . On the one hand horse and rider burials and pagan Avar symbolic objects bear witness to the conceptual world of the Avars; on the other numerous crucifixes in silver-lead and objects decorated with crosses are proof of the influence of Christianity."[159] The settlement expanded and became increasingly more mainstream Avar in the seventh century.

Gradual cultural integration can also be traced at Csákberény-Ormondpuszta, between Budapest and Lake Balaton, where in the 1930s Gyula László excavated 451 Avar-period graves. Inhumations started, obviously soon after 568, with a loose structure of dispersed family groups, grouped around "founder graves." Grave goods are culturally rather heterogeneous among these groups, which in part seem to represent an indigenous population. In the warrior graves (some including horse burials), however, we do not find Merovingian-style weapons, unlike around Lake Balaton; quite probably these are traces of the steppe riders who now controlled Pannonia. From ca. 600 onward, both the layout of the cemetery and the cultural profile of the burials gradually become more homogeneous and follow the mainstream of the khaganate.[160]

The first Avar khagans ruled over a culturally very heterogeneous population, and also over a good number of prosperous subjects who forged a vital and manifold late antique culture, especially in Pannonia, which appears to have been more vigorous than before, under Lombard rule. By comparison, finds from the late sixth century that can clearly be attributed to first-generation Avar immigrants are relatively rare. This is a currently debated issue. It depends on the dating of specific traits of Avar steppe culture (for instance stirrups or braid clasps), which seem to emerge more clearly in the seventh century.[161] Without the written sources, it would not be easy to interpret the demographic and cultural change in the Carpathian Basin in the last third of the sixth century. One could hypothesize the arrival of a new ruling elite that had come from central Asia east of the Tisza. However, one would rather assume a new prosperous kingdom established by Romano-barbarian elites in Pannonia. The dominance of European objects in graves is not unlike the archaeological evidence for the Hun period in the Carpathian Basin, in which the steppe heritage is even more limited.[162] Still, it is a question that has puzzled Avar archaeology for some time. Who were these wealthy Pannonians under Avar rule, and how can we explain their cultural habitus? To what extent did the "Avar" core group of steppe warriors partake in this particular mix of traditional late antique, contemporary Byzantine, western Romano-barbarian ("Germanic"), and local provincial cultural idioms, and what were their own inalienable traditions and preferences? It may be convenient to keep these two questions apart: Avars (and their hybrid self-representation in funerary ritual) and their subjects, some of whom had the means to stage rather different displays of status at a funeral. Both lines of enquiry have been aptly summed up in two recent publications by Tivadar Vida.[163]

According to Vida, "the Avars arrived in the Carpathian Basin with puritanical trappings: their costume and their belts were fitted with simple functional elements such as buckles, hooks and rivets made from bone, iron and bronze or, more rarely, from precious metals." Only around the turn of the century did they adopt Byzantine-style jewelry and accessories, for instance, belts decorated with golden pseudo-buckles.[164] An early and functional element is the stirrup, which the Avars arguably brought from central Asia.[165] It has, however, been argued that from early on, high-quality metal stirrups were actually the products of Byzantine workshops, like other types of cavalry armor.[166] However that may be, mounted combat with bow and lance was the mark of Avar military superiority, and certainly a sign of identity when put in the grave. Burials with a horse, sometimes also partial horse burial, is a very diffused habit in the steppe and, even though it was not unknown in Europe (most famously, in the burial of Clovis's father, Childeric, perhaps following Thuringian precedent), was very probably part of the Avar cultural baggage.[167] Relations to the eastern European steppes may become evident in Martinovka-style metal objects, although these are not distinctive and are also found in Keszthely culture assemblages.[168] What seems fairly characteristic for early Avar warriors are single burials, sometimes in groups with a distance between ten and one hundred meters.[169] However, some of the larger Avar cemeteries, such as Tiszafüred, also seem to have started fairly early. A funerary ritual that is already attested in the Hunnic period is the sacrificial assemblage (*Totenopfer*): a shallow votive deposit pit some distance from the grave, or without a grave, in which weapons and horse harness were deposited.[170] There is still some debate as to the exact dating of some of these "puritanical trappings."

All these characteristics and more may serve to reconstruct a cultural model of the first generation of Avars in the Carpathian Basin, although we must be aware that it is a construct. Clusters of object assemblages and burial practices denote statistical probability, with differing significance, and the distribution of some of these characteristics is uneven: sacrificial assemblages are concentrated along the Danube, particularly in northeastern Pannonia and between the Danube and the Tisza, while partial animal burials occur exclusively east of the Tisza.[171] Furthermore, the situation in which Baian's army moved into the Carpathian

Basin was already very dynamic. Some of the mounted warriors who had joined the Avars in the steppes north of the Black Sea may have adopted some of the Avar habitus, while the Avar core group came in touch with Byzantine cultural idioms, which some of them may have adopted sooner than others. This process of mutual acculturation surely continued in the new homeland. As always, we can never be sure whether a warrior buried with his horse, horse gear, simple belt, and weapons in a solitary grave was of Avar origin and/or regarded himself as one. However, we can assume that whoever buried him wanted to stress his Avar affiliation, at least posthumously. General cultural models constructed by archaeologists should be used with caution; yet in this case, it is quite likely that this was how you could recognize an Avar mounted warrior.[172]

On the other hand, it is not unlikely that some members of the Avar elite may have followed some of the "Germanic" or "Roman" styles described below, at least as concerns grave goods. What is exclusively Hunnic in the archaeological record from Attila's empire is also relatively limited—bronze cauldrons, funerary offerings, perhaps skull deformation and diadems—and has few parallels in regions of "Hun" domination before their arrival. The bulk of Hun-period finds is not at all dissimilar from the barbarian warrior elite in other parts of Europe.[173] Jordanes writes that at Attila's funeral, what they put in his grave were "arms acquired by the slaughter of enemies, metal discs worn on the chest adorned with shining precious stones, and different types of insignia that serve as adornment of the court."[174] Whether by Priscus (cited twice in that chapter) or by Jordanes, that may be the Roman view of barbarian funerals; but clearly the Roman perception was not that only typically Hunnic objects were used as grave goods at a Hun funeral. Objects taken from defeated enemies might confer more prestige than the arms that the defunct had used for a lifetime. Therefore, we should not take for granted that the first-generation Avar warriors were always buried with their own weapons.

In the first decades of the Avar period, the late Roman/barbarian culture in the Carpathian Basin is well linked and not at all dissimilar to that of its European neighbors, most of all, that of Lombard Italy.[175] It also shows numerous features that early medieval archaeology defines as "Germanic" and that were used in the contemporary Mediterranean and/or western Europe. For instance, Germanic "Animal Style II" finds close parallels in the Carpathian Basin, related to material from Lombard Italy but also from the Merovingian area; however, there are specific variants particular to Pannonia, for instance, in the "toothcut" (*Zahnschnitt*) ornament.[176] A lot of finds have close Merovingian parallels, for instance the three- or four-piece belt sets current in phase Early Merovingian II between 570/80 and 620/30; such belts are almost exclusively attested in Pannonia and in the Transylvanian Basin.[177] From 590 onward, they were gradually replaced by the multipiece Civezzano type belt sets current in Italy; this transition to multipartite belts happened at the same time as in Italy and the Merovingian realm.[178] Western elements are generally stronger in female costume. One feature are the Merovingian long straps hanging from the hip; what is specific to the Carpathian Basin is that the belt-fittings were placed between the legs, and amulets were often attached. This is a Merovingian characteristic that seems to go back to Byzantine models, as becomes apparent in the mosaics of the basilicas of Poreč or San Vitale in Ravenna. However, the amulets in Avar lands were usually different from the Western ones.[179]

These and other Merovingian and Italian objects often appear consistently in certain cemeteries, especially in Pannonia, where they seem to be related to particular groups of the population. What appears to be the cemetery of a "Germanic" village from the Avar period was brought to light at Kölked near Mohács.[180] This settlement, in which an average of thirty families lived from about 570 to 750, lay on the old road along the *limes*. As in other early cemeteries (Budakalász, Szekszárd), a separate cluster of men inhumed with weapons and horses seems to indicate a small "Avar" military unit in the service of the khagan.[181] The excavator, Attila Kiss, had regarded this as evidence for a village of Gepids resettled from their old homes in the Tisza region. He interpreted the many Western-style objects in early Avar graves as signs of continuity of a Germanic and particularly Gepid population that had lived in the Carpathian Basin before 568.[182] However, as Tivadar Vida has argued, the most conspicuous parallels of these and other "Germanic" finds are not the pre-568 population in Pannonia, whether Lombards or Gepids; the closest analogies can rather be found in the contemporary furnished burials of Lombard Italy. The early Avar-period Pannonians were not simply isolated survivors of a previous population; above all, the female burials show "the quick adoption of almost everything that was in fashion across the European continent."[183] The finds attest to much livelier relations of Avar Pannonia with the Western kingdoms than we would otherwise assume. On the other hand, some more archaic motifs seem to indicate a slight sense of distance from contemporary styles.

This is puzzling evidence. We have solid information that numerous Gepids continued to live in separate villages in their old settlement areas under Avar rule, where the army under Priscus encountered and massacred some in 599; they also fought in Avar armies in sizable contingents.[184] However, there are as yet no substantial archaeological traces of them: "the spectacular disappearance of Gepidic material culture," in the words of Tivadar Vida.[185] We can only assume that their cemeteries, which have usually been dated to before 567, were at first continued under Avar rule, without any notable adaptations to their new cultural environment; recently, material that supports this hypothesis has begun to emerge.

On the other hand, a huge, multiethnic army of Western barbarians left Lombard Pannonia in 568, and suddenly the archaeological evidence for a flourishing late Roman- and Western-style population emerges in more conspicuous ways than in the Lombard kingdom previously. Direct written evidence to interpret this situation is lacking; only further archaeological investigation will add precision to this picture. At this point, the historian can only consider a few possible scenarios that might contribute to our understanding.

First, we should take into consideration that the Lombard kingdom in Pannonia was, by the standards of the time, a poor polity. Huns, Goths, Gepids, Heruls, and others had already depleted the riches of the province for over a century before the Lombards came. Apart from their bitter wars against the Gepids, the Lombards did not launch any major raids on Roman provinces. Unlike many other *gentes*, Lombards, who were regarded as unruly and hard to control, rarely fought in Roman armies. Their involvement in the Gothic wars seems to have been limited to a contingent in the battle of the Busta Gallorum in 552, after which they were quickly dispatched back home because "they kept setting fire to whatever buildings they chanced upon and violating by force the women who had taken refuge in the sanctuaries."[186] Justinian gave them permission to settle in Pannonia under a treaty in 547, but the Gepids remained more important as Byzantine allies; neither of the two kingdoms seems to have received substantial subsidies.[187] This relative poverty was the reason why the Lombard and Gepid kingdoms had no future in the Carpathian Basin, and a great number of them left "the poor lands of Pannonia" for more profitable exploits in Italy.[188] The Avar khaganate soon procured much more wealth, which obviously was not monopolized by a core group of steppe riders but trickled down to some of those who supported their rule.

Second, one distinctive feature of the Avar polity obviously was the readiness to invest rather heavily in funerary ritual, soon after their settlement in Pannonia. This attitude corresponded to an extent with that of their western neighbors. Yet while Avar exuberance in furnished burials reached its peak in the seventh century, Lombards, Franks, Bavarians, and Alamans gradually gave up grand grave goods. Most of them were already Christians in the late sixth century, and although that did not automatically imply renouncing grave apparel, it helps to explain why the grave-good habit had been rather patchy in the "barbarian" kingdoms in Italy, Gaul, and Hispania from the start.[189] Certainly furnished burials did not spread among the late Roman population of these countries, while, as we shall see, quite un-Roman Roman-style funerary displays became fashionable under Avar rule. Obviously, many of the wealthy non-Avar subjects of the khagan took up the challenge to compete for prestigious self-representation alongside the Avar warriors. This change in the attitudes toward death may also go some way toward explaining the virtual explosion in rich Western-/Byzantine-style burials in Pannonia in the late sixth century.

Third, who were all these people who followed the latest Lombard, Merovingian, and Byzantine fashion in Avar Pannonia (or even Transylvania)? They certainly were a rather mixed population of different groups who had made their fortune in the ascending khaganate. We will address the question of the Avar "Romans" below and start with possible "barbarian" elements. The closest stylistic parallels seem to be with Lombard Italy, and these may involve several groups. One, which has been in the discussion for a long time, are Lombards who had stayed in Pannonia when Alboin's army left, in spite of his pressure on them to follow him.[190] As we have seen, the problem is that there is little continuity between the Lombard and Avar periods; most cemeteries break off around (not necessarily in) 568, and the material changes. Of course, on the basis of the archaeological evidence we can now safely assume that these Pannonian Lombards kept in touch with the migrants, as in the phenomenon of "transnationalism" well-known in modern migration studies.[191] This means that migration routes remained open in both directions.

It is not unlikely that some groups of Lombards came back from Italy in the years after 568. Alboin's army quickly broke up in Italy, and only part of it remained loyal to the king. The Saxons who had joined him returned home; one group repeatedly attacked Frankish Burgundy; others went south and founded the quasi-independent duchies of Spoleto and Benevento. Many joined the Byzantine army and sometimes changed their allegiance repeatedly. After Alboin and his successor Cleph had both been murdered, a ten-year interregnum ensued in 574–84, and only after that was the Lombard kingdom gradually consolidated. In the meantime, Lombard warriors had many options, and one of them may have been to return to Pannonia and join the expanding Avar power. In fact, that was the only alternative to being integrated into a profitable but rather tight late antique system in which the maintenance and provisioning of warriors depended on regular pay and eventually on legitimate access to land, with all the problems that this might create.[192] It is perfectly conceivable that to some Lombards, Pannonia now seemed more attractive than Italy: the early Avar system meant more liberty, less control, and no taxes for mobile warriors from the west. As well, peasants most likely had to face lower rents than in the post-Roman kingdoms, or none at all. Even warriors from the Merovingian sphere may have been attracted. For a time in the mid-sixth century, Merovingian dominion stretched to the borders of Pannonia and included parts of Noricum Mediterraneum (mainly modern Carinthia). Since Narses had pushed the Franks out of Italy in the late 550s and early 560s, however, Merovingian expansion had quickly lost momentum, and further expeditions into Italy until 590 had only limited success. After the death of Chlothar I in 561, inner conflicts between his heirs became endemic. The Avar khaganate was hardly too alien and despotic for noble Germanic warriors to join. The archaeological evidence creates the overwhelming impression that Lombards or Franks could have felt at home in many places in early Avar Pannonia. We have no written evidence that they did; but such movements were normally beneath the attention of our sources.

3.9 Cultures around Keszthely

The most distinctive traces of non-Avar groups that lived under the rule of the Baian dynasty in the Carpathian Basin become apparent in the so-called Keszthely culture. In the old Roman fortress at Keszthely-Fenékpuszta (identifications with Roman names, such as Valcum, are contested; the present name Keszthely is derived from the Latin word *castellum*), where the Zala River flows into Lake Balaton, a dynamic demographic and cultural development is obvious after the Avar occupation.[193] The walls of the fortress still seem to have been standing, and in the early Avar period it was inhabited by groups with a late antique Christian habitus. A large basilica with three apses was still in use, perhaps was even (re)constructed in the second half of the sixth century at Keszthely. It contains some graves without grave goods, and others that had been plundered. Burying the dead in the church was an emerging Christian custom that is otherwise rarely found in late antique churches in Pannonia.[194] What remains indicates "Germanic" connections.[195] Close to the basilica, and near the *horreum*, the old Roman storehouse, lay an elite cemetery with thirty-nine graves with grave goods, rich and poor, among them glass tumblers and Roman ceramic mugs, but also stylus needles and pyramid earrings, which later were distinctive for the Keszthely culture of the seventh and eighth centuries, when it had lost touch with the outside world. The most elaborate silver needle carries the inscription BONOSA, probably the name of the woman with whom it was buried.[196] The postholes nearby have often been interpreted as a wooden church.[197] Outside the south walls, following classical habits, lay another cemetery, where apart from a few well-equipped graves some of the less wealthy inhabitants of the fortress were buried.[198] Other cemeteries lay at a greater distance.

The whole area seems to have been densely populated. Several major and smaller cemeteries were excavated since Vilmos Lipp first dug here in the 1880s; unsurprisingly, he had decided that these must be fourth- to fifth-century sites.[199] Most of these cemeteries, however, are now assumed to have been started only in the seventh century, perhaps after the fort had been destroyed: for instance Keszthely-Dobogó on a hill northwest of the town, which comprises approximately 4,000 graves of the seventh and eighth century; Alsópáhok counts 1,500; and there are more distant ones at Lesencetomaj, Szigliget-Várhegy, and Gyenesdiás.[200] Over time, a particular set of characteristic objects, above all female adornments, emerged, which gradually became isolated and were found in the area up to the early ninth century: earrings in the form of small baskets, disc fibulae, snake-shaped bracelets, and stylus needles in the tradition of late Antiquity. In the period around 600, the cultural ensemble was much more varied and lively. There are also cemeteries where "Germanic" elements prevail. One rich grave of a Western-style warrior on a hilltop site contained a golden belt buckle with the inscription *Antikos*—that may mean he had, as a leader of auxiliary troops in the Avar army, defeated the Antes, perhaps in the 602 campaign.[201] In central Asia, there are also cases in which the owner's name was inscribed on the belt buckle.[202]

The existence of an affluent population following late Roman models under Avar rule was so unexpected that it provoked a variety of attempts to explain it. Some scholars even tried to revise political history to make room for this island of Romanness: they assumed that in the middle of a country ruled by barbarians a Byzantine garrison was in service from 546 to 582.[203] Or did the Keszthely culture represent the remains of a native Roman population that had preserved its traditions into the Avar period? A Romanized provincial population had surely survived in Pannonia.[204] There are some traces of continuous settlement, mainly in the "poor" graves south of the castle wall, but perhaps also those without grave goods in the *horreum* cemetery. Some of the better-furnished graves could also easily be dated to the Lombard period.[205] It also seems that some cemeteries start with unfurnished graves, and only eventually do grave goods begin to appear.[206] First results of strontium isotope analyses in the *horreum* and southern wall cemeteries indicate that only about one fourth of the deceased seem to be immigrants from outside of Pannonia, and they had arrived from different areas. A small number of C14 datings suggest that some burials may go back to the mid-sixth century or even earlier.[207] Generally, it has to be noted that the date 568 for the beginning of the cemeteries in and around Keszthely is historical and is only roughly supported by intrinsically archaeological datings.[208]

Assessing the impact of this continuity of course depends on the dating of the archaeological remains, which leaves a lot of leeway because an important feature in late Roman burials is the lack of grave goods, with the exception of a few female ornamental types, such as stylus needles, polyhedric or basket earrings, and iron bracelets. Volker Bierbrauer has argued that we should limit the term "Keszthely culture" to describing this late to post-Roman cluster.[209] However, what has increasingly emerged in recent studies is the manifold and partly hybrid character of the population around Keszthely; this is how the label generally seems to be understood. A different historical explanation was offered by István Bóna: these were captives from Byzantine provinces in the Balkans that the Avars settled in Pannonia.[210] However, the prosperity of the inhabitants of Keszthely, and their weapons (in part, from the West) contradict this interpretation. In the later seventh century, the *Miracula S. Demetrii* do confirm the upward social mobility of Roman prisoners, but that took generations, whereas the wealthy population of the *castellum* at Fenékpuszta seems to have appeared out of the blue.[211] Again, the hypothesis cannot explain the multiplicity and the dynamic changes of the archaeological evidence. Florin Curta argued that the fortress may already have flourished in the 550s, when the Lombards under Alboin had wide-ranging contacts with Byzantium and the West.[212] That is possible, although one might wonder whether Alboin would not have forced members of a Roman elite in such a strategic position to leave with him.

Overall, these explanations (apart from the Byzantine garrison) do not exclude each other, although each of them seems insufficient. However we date the possibly pre-Avar traces in and around Keszthely, they do not add up to a continuous development of the early Avar Keszthely phenomenon throughout the sixth century. What made this funerary culture so conspicuous in the early Avar period? It would be hard to explain without migrations to the Roman fort and its surroundings at the beginning of the Avar period. Rather than one single, massive immigration, several groups seem to have arrived from different regions. What also mattered was increasing wealth (easy to explain in the early Avar context) and an extension of the grave-good custom. In and around Fenékpuszta, at least seven, mostly new cemeteries existed contemporaneously, but each with a somewhat different cultural profile. These were neither exclusively the traces of an autochthonous population nor of a single wave of migrants. The population of the region had different backgrounds, and their specific lifestyles were respected to a considerable degree. The Keszthely region must have been an attractive place for people with a wide horizon; that can hardly have happened without the khagan's initiative. That may have included forced resettlement but also benefits for groups who came of their own accord.

Models of cohabitation between steppe riders and differentiated sedentary societies were more ambitious in central Asia; the Keszthely culture, and overall Pannonian prosperity, was as far as the Avars could emulate these models. A relatively stable coexistence of steppe warriors with more or less prosperous cities was the rule in central Asia. "In the vicinity of political centers in Mongolia there were often small agricultural areas manned by Chinese and other prisoners of war," in which specialized craftsmen also had their place, as Attila Kiss remarked long ago.[213] In fact, relations between nomadic polities and sedentary populations were not simply a matter of enclaves of unfree labor and forced production. Successful examples in the period are the cooperation of Sogdian traders and producers in Sogdiana with Hephthalite and Turkish rule, or Turkish control of the Ordos region and the Turfan oasis.[214] The Avars never got that far because, inter alia, there was neither a transcontinental trade network (the "Silk Route") to exploit nor an intensive and differentiated oasis economy as in Bukhara. Still, the late antique contact zone around Lake Balaton may have filled similar functions on a smaller scale. Not by coincidence, the late antique fortress of Keszthely-Fenékpuszta lay on a long-distance road from the Baltic to the Adriatic; it was the khaganate's window on Italy, a region where they carefully guarded their friendship with the Lombard kings.

The conflicts and inner migrations of the seventh century took the bloom off this region. The fortress of Keszthely was destroyed, probably after a siege (a beam had been used to reinforce one of the gates), most likely in the civil wars around 630. It was not rebuilt.[215] Late Roman and Western cultural features gradually gave way to different types of evidence, although some built directly on the earlier material. The cultural multiplicity of the expansive period did not stop after 626. New cemeteries were established. Some representatives of the Roman-style elite in the ancient fortress seem to have met a violent end, while others continued to live in the area. In parallel, the less spectacular but almost equally hybrid cultural world of early Avar Pannonia gradually became part of the increasingly homogeneous cultural idioms of the middle and late Avar periods.[216]

Further discoveries and studies will surely advance our knowledge of this bustling center of non-Avars in the early khaganate. Yet a question of methodology should be raised here. Not all lines of interpretation of the rich and puzzling material of the Keszthely culture have proved equally productive. It is unhelpful to pose the question in terms of late antique continuity versus the "end of antiquity" in Pannonia. As has become increasingly clear, the Keszthely phenomenon was not simply a recovery of battered Pannonian Romanness, but an up-to-date participation in the emblems of postimperial cultural multiplicity. Nor does an attempt to disentangle origins and ethnic identities behind the various clusters of grave assemblages seem adequate. Trying to classify elements of the hybrid culture of early Avar Pannonia by ethnonyms will not help us much in understanding this unexpected flowering of Western civilization under an Eastern regime. Who among the late sixth-century inhabitants of the Balaton region were Byzantine, Pannonian, Norican, or "Roman" Romans, Gepids, Suebi, Lombards, or other "Germans"? Paul the Deacon's catalog of the ethnic groups that had come to Italy with Alboin also indicates who may have stayed behind: apart from Lombards, he lists "*Gepidos, Vulgares, Sarmatas, Pannonios, Suavos, Noricos,* and others," who now lived in separate villages in Lombard Italy.[217] It is not impossible that the groups buried in the different cemeteries around Keszthely were also distinguished by these or other ethnic labels at the time, but we cannot tell by archaeological means. As mentioned above, the local leader in grave A at Keszthely-Fenékpuszta Pusztaszentegyháza-Dűlő (perhaps the most challenging name of any Hungarian dig) even had an ethnonym, *Antikos*, proudly inscribed on his golden belt buckle, but that does not mean he belonged to the Antes. If the inhabitants of Pannonia in the period were distinguished by ethnonyms at all, these had only local or regional significance, like the Italian villages of Paul's time. None of the archaeologically viable ethnic affiliations in Pannonia is mentioned as fighting in Avar armies by Byzantine chroniclers: they speak of Cutrigurs, Bulgars, Slavs, and Gepids.[218] Additionally, the *Miracula S. Demetrii* mention Roman captives from the Balkan provinces as inhabitants of Pannonia, and Paul the Deacon, Lombards from Cividale.[219]

The mixed group that inhabited early Avar Pannonia does not seem to have developed a shared identity or sense of common purpose.[220] They may also have been competitors. Gábor Kiss has suggested that the two Christian elite groups who buried some of their dead in the two neighboring cemeteries at the basilica and the *horreum* might have been rivals or belonged to different confessions. When the fortress was stormed in the seventh century, the graves in the basilica were systematically robbed and the basilica destroyed but the *horreum* cemetery was left intact.[221] It is in fact unlikely that these people conceived of themselves as "Romans." The Romance-speaking population under barbarian rule that we quite confidently call "Romans" rather rarely appears under that name in contemporary sources; rather, old provincial or new regional names were used, as was the case with Paul's *Pannonii*.[222] However, the geographical range of the ancient provincial designations along the Danube changed in the course of the early Middle Ages, so that Isidore in the seventh century locates Pannonia between the Sava and Drava rivers, adjacent to Italy. This follows the usage in the Ostrogothic kingdom.[223] In what ways that may have had a bearing on identifications of the Pannonians is unclear. In the late seventh century, the author of the *Miracula S. Demetrii* calls the similarly hybrid following of Kuver *Sermesianoi*, the "Sirmians," after the ancient metropolis of the province.[224] This rather improvised external identifier indicates that there was no strong, generally accepted identity that the "Pannonians" of the early Avar period shared. Another thing that the archaeological record does not show is whether and when any of these late antique/Western Pannonians may have begun to identify themselves as Avars. We can assume that this developed in parallel with the homogenization of their cultural expressions, but that surely was a fuzzy process.

Generally, the categories used in much of the archaeological literature—
"Avar," "Roman," "Germanic," "Lombard," "Gepid," "Frank"—roughly distinguish
clusters in the archaeological evidence and do not indicate fixed ethnic identities.
This is a delicate point because the rather straightforward use of ethnic categories
in early medieval archaeology has been justly criticized.[225] Attempts to break
distinctions in the material of the early Avar period down to the level of single
peoples living in the Carpathian Basin and to produce ethnic maps specifying
their settlement areas certainly overestimate to what extent types of grave
apparel can serve as ethnic markers.[226] Where we have generally accepted neutral
designations such as "Keszthely culture," it may in many cases be preferable to
use them. But that leaves the problem of distinguishing between its "Pannonian,"
"Byzantine," or "Germanic" components. Therefore, to start speaking of a
"Kölked culture" instead of "Germanic" would not solve the problem. Avoiding
any ethnic categories altogether, as has variously been suggested, would eliminate
a basic way in which contemporaries distinguished between broad collectives
and navigated the social world.[227] Premodern ethnic distinctions follow a rather
fuzzy logic, and that necessarily has an impact on our use of ethnic categories.
In my view, the only realistic way out of the dilemma is to be aware of what
the ethnonyms that we employ mean in context. The six names listed at the
beginning of this paragraph are a good example, for they have very different
shades of meaning.

What they have in common is that in the archaeological debate they are
used to distinguish between different styles of being dressed for burial. For
instance, typical "Germanic" female costume, following Tivadar Vida, would
consist of "hair-pins, disc brooches, ornamental pendants, amulet pendants,
amulet capsules and shoe mounts."[228] In this definition, individuals and
cemeteries can obviously be more or less "Germanic"; it does not allow us to
clearly delineate who belongs and who does not. This is in fact more or less the
case for all workable definitions of premodern ethnicity.[229] However, the name
"Germanic" for the late sixth century is synthetic; it does not correspond to
any contemporary usage. It is only used in an antiquarian sense in the period.
The *Strategicon*, written in ca. 600, uses the circumscription *xantha ethnē*, the
blond peoples, "such as the Franks, the Lombards and the others with the same
way of life"; no mention of "Germans."[230] This is an interesting concept, similar
to the archaeological definition of "Germanic" in the early Avar period, apart
from the blond hair that we can hardly ascertain. "Franks" or "Merovingians"
as used by historians mostly refers to the Merovingian kingdom(s) as a political
actor, corresponding to contemporary usage in which not the state but the
people is endowed with agency; in this sense, the term may include Alamans
and Bavarians. Only sometimes does "Franks" actually distinguish the ruling

Frankish minority from its various subjects.[231] "Merovingian" style finds in the Carpathian Basin thus do not necessarily represent ethnic Franks or even former subjects of Merovingian kings. Rather, they express the cultural hegemony that the Merovingian kingdoms had established over wide parts of western and central Europe in the sixth century.

"Roman" is even more complex; in early medieval sources, it may indicate the Roman Empire of the Greek *Rhomaioi*, the inhabitants of Rome, a Roman population under barbarian rule, those who confess Roman law or Roman Catholic religion, those who have been educated according to a traditional canon, and finally the Carolingian empire of the Franks.[232] In the communication between archaeologists and historians, then, there is a problem in defining a population as "Roman" or "Germanic." At best, this is a way of avoiding specificity where we cannot be more precise, but it may also imply a unity of cultural affiliation that had in fact become very loose. In the course of the early Middle Ages, "Christian" and "Roman" cultural models eventually converged, and "Byzantine" and (diverse) "Roman" forms of expression, although remaining within a shared cultural matrix, became distinct. It is possible that many of these "Romans" (in archaeological parlance) would have identified themselves as "Romans," although they may have denied this name to other self-styled "Romans"—in particular, the Byzantine "Greeks." With the "Germans," on the other hand, we can be pretty sure that none of the archaeologically defined "Germanic" groups in the Carpathian Basin or elsewhere would have named themselves in that way. That does not necessarily mean that the term should be avoided at all costs in archaeology, but we have to be aware that it does not indicate a self-aware "people" but a "population" that scholars define by certain traits.

The alternative to these broad designations is to use more specific categories. In the case of "Roman," a term frequently employed in the written sources, these are to an extent synthetic: provincial, Italian/Latin, Byzantine Romans. Conversely, while the term "German(ic)" is not used for contemporary distinctions in the texts, "Gepids" and "Lombards" constitute unproblematic ethnic markers in the written sources. Quite paradoxically, that makes misunderstandings more likely in archaeological usage, because the terms sound more precise but do not correspond to any clear cultural ensemble. Therefore, many archaeologists nowadays tend to avoid speaking of "Gepid" or "Lombard" cemeteries under Avar rule. As shown above, it also makes sense to differentiate between Pannonian and Italian "Lombard" styles. "Merovingian" or "Western" is more neutral but not always easy to delineate. "Avars" is a somehow different problem again. It works on two levels, first, as a general denominator of the "early Avar period" to designate the material culture of the core areas of the khaganate, and second, to identify its "eastern" ruling group of steppe warriors. The two meanings should be clearly distinguished. In any case, the archaeological evidence makes it clear that the Avar empire of Baian and his successors was no uniform, self-contained ethnic and cultural block. Both internally and externally, it was open to the multiplicity of lifestyles that existed in eastern central Europe and beyond it.

4

AVARS AND SLAVS

The 580s marked the massive emergence of the Avars as a military power that could challenge Byzantine control over most of the Balkan Peninsula. Yet repeated raids on Roman provinces also demonstrated that Slavs could continue to act as independent players who had maintained their offensive capacity. Relations between the Avar khaganate and decentralized Slavic groups were quite varied, from brutal submission of Slavs or Avar support of their expansion to temporary alliances and independent Slavic raids. A complementary social and political structure established itself in the lands along the Danube, much to the detriment of the Roman side. Slavic raids feature quite prominently in our written sources. However, much of their context remains rather obscure. Who were these Slavs, and to what extent was their expansive dynamic different from so many other barbarian groups that southern Europe had seen in the past? This chapter, therefore, addresses not only Slavic operations in the Balkan provinces, and the ways in which Avars were involved in them (section 4.2–3), but also some fundamental questions about Slavic origins and expansion (section 4.1 and 4.6), and about Avar–Slav relations (section 4.4–5).[1]

4.1 Slavs before the Avars:
Perceptions and Origins

"The obscure advance of the Slavs"—so Lucien Musset characterizes Slavic expansion as distinguished from the "Germanic waves."[2] Other favored images for this phenomenon correspond to the terminology of modern guerilla warfare: "infiltration," "percolation," "trickling in." It is difficult to deal with the emergence of the Slavs because late antique historiography was oriented toward large groups organized under leaders. Other forms of social organization were noted only exceptionally, even though they were presumably the rule among the neighbors of the Romans and not the exception. No Alaric, Geiseric, or Alboin incarnates the migration of the Slavs. In this respect, the Slavicization of eastern Europe is indeed an "obscure" process. Ever since the Polish count Potocki presented his program of Slavic prehistory to the enlightened French public more than two hundred years ago, research on the early Slavs has wrestled with the elucidation of this picture.[3]

Slavs are first mentioned in the sources shortly before the Avars appeared. Substantial evidence occurs in two works written in Constantinople in the early 550s, the histories of Procopius and Jordanes. Procopius, in his accounts of Justinian's wars, almost regularly mentions Slavic raids on the lower Danube from the fourth decade of the sixth century onward.[4] His ethnographic information about the Slavs is more extensive than about most other peoples. The earliest date in his *Wars* at which Slavs are mentioned is shortly after the destruction of the kingdom of the Heruli on the Norican Danube (ca. 508), when this people settled on Roman land in Pannonia. There, one faction established contact with the ancient homeland on the island of Thule to invite a prince from the ancient dynasty, touching "all the tribes of the *Sclaveni*" in the course of their journey northward.[5] However, that may rather be an ethnographic perception from Procopius's day. The first time Slavs are actually mentioned in the narrative is in a very untypical way, during the Gothic siege of Rome in 537, when Byzantine reinforcements arrived. These were "sixteen hundred horsemen, the most of whom were Huns and *Sclaveni* and Antes." As we hear later, some of these Slavs were expert in ambushes; "in fact, they are constantly practising this in their native haunts along the river Danube, both on the Romans and on the barbarians as well."[6] Slavic cavalry, as far as we know, had no future in the Byzantine army; but it may have been an option along the way. Slavic ambushes, on the other hand, are repeatedly mentioned later.

Another important piece of information is dated to just before 550, when the Lombards and Gepids in the Carpathian Basin had closer contacts with the Slavs. During the war of 547–48, Hildigis, the pretender to the Lombard throne, came to the Gepids with a following of Slavs, among whom he had clearly lived in exile for some time. He was soon obliged to withdraw with his followers after a peace settlement had been reached. The frustrated Lombard prince was just as unsatisfied among the Slavs as in Italy or Byzantium, where he later appeared with his followers. He paid with his life for this second involvement in a Gepid-Lombard conflict.[7] Whence Hildigis came with his Slavs cannot exactly be determined. According to Procopius it was in any case north of the Danube, most likely north of the Lombard and Gepid settlement area, and probably also north of the Carpathians, beyond the range of Lombard and Gepid power. This also seems to have been where those Slavs came from who after a raid through Illyricum in 551 sought help from the Gepids in order to recross the Danube. The Gepids charged a piece of gold per head in passage money.[8] These Slavic plunderers were by no means poor.

Procopius also relates some particularly unedifying details about tortures of Roman prisoners by Slavic raiders.[9] On the occasion of a strange affair in which a man from the Antes was passed off as the deceased Roman commander Chilbudios, he gives a fuller account of the Slavs and their neighbors, the Antes:

> They live in pitiful hovels which they set far apart from one another, but, as a general thing, every man is constantly changing his place of abode. When they enter battle, the majority of them go against their enemy on foot, carrying little shields and javelins in their hands, but they never wear corselets. Indeed some of them do not wear even a shirt or a cloak but gathering their trousers up as far as their private parts they enter into battle with their opponents. And both the two peoples have also the same language, an utterly barbarous tongue. Nay further, they do not differ at all from one another in appearance.... And they live a hard life, giving no heed to bodily comforts, just as the Massagetae do, and, like them, they are continually and at all times covered with filth; however, they are in no respect base or evil-doers, but they preserve the Hunnic character in all its simplicity.[10]

Sclaveni and Antes were, according to Procopius, "both called Sporoi in olden times," an enigmatic reference that has not yet been explained convincingly.[11]

In Jordanes's *Getica*, Sclaveni (or Sclavini) occur four times; his description differs from that of Procopius on several accounts.[12] In his ethnographic digression, he locates the populous people of the Venethi or Venethae north of the Carpathians, stretching far and wide from the source of the Vistula River. Their "names vary now by family and place"; they are mainly called Sclaveni and Antes. These Sclaveni, he says, settle "from the city of Novietunum and the lake called Mursianus to the Dniestr and in the north the Vistula." This cryptic localization most likely uses the wetlands near the city of Mursa in Southern Pannonia and Noviodunum at the Delta of the Danube as terminal points of the area where Slavic raiders might be expected to cross the Danube—quite an apt description. The Antes, "who are the strongest of them," live "where the Black Sea bends, from the Dniestr to the Dniepr." Then the text moves on to the peoples living in the Baltic regions.[13] This would mean that Venethi is the umbrella term, among whom Sclaveni and Antes can be subsumed. A slightly different model occurs elsewhere in Jordanes, where he says that in the fourth century the Gothic king Ermanaric subdued the Venethi, from whom three peoples have sprung in his day, Venethi, Antes, and Sclaveni—three related peoples, all derived from the fourth-century Venethi.[14]

Jordanes was the first to use the name Venethi for the Slavs, an outside designation that later became current in Latin texts (mostly in the form *Winedi*).[15] Greek sources, among them, Procopius, do not use the name Venethi at all. For Greek speakers, *Venetioi* were one of the Circus factions, and *Venet(i)oi*, the inhabitants of the province of Venetia.[16] *Sclaven(o)i* was obviously derived from the Slavic name *slověnin/slověne*. The etymology of the name is difficult because there are several Slavic words that could explain it, among them such onomastic favorites as "glory" or "word." The latter meaning, interpreted as "those who speak," could be understood in contrast to the *němъci*, the "mute" (the Slavic word for the Germans), an attractive hypothesis, which has the weakness that *němъci* is only attested almost half a millennium after the Sclaveni.[17] *Wenedi* (as Wends, Wendish in English, *Wenden* and *Windische* in German) was originally the name used by Germanic-speakers for their eastern neighbors and was derived from the name of the Venethi of the Roman period. It forms a binary opposite with the alliterating name Welsh, Welsche, Walchen, Vlach, etc., which came from the Gallic Volcae and was used by the early Germans for their western neighbors, mainly Latin speakers. This means that Jordanes, who certainly spoke Gothic, introduced the Germanic outside designation Winedi for the Slavs. He draws the obvious connection between these Wends and ancient Venethi found in his sources, but also appropriately uses it as an umbrella term, which corresponds to the rather indistinct Germanic usage. However, this creates contradictions that he resolves differently in the two relevant passages: How were the Slavs of his day related to the Venethi? One solution is a genealogical model, in which the Slavs are descended from the ancient Venethi and are now related to the remaining Venethi of his day. In the other passage, Slavs, Antes, and others (obviously very local names, *per familias et loca*) are subsumed under the general label Venethi, which does not designate any specific group. Sclaveni and Antes thus figure as the principal groups in a very mixed population. This seems to be adequate for a fluid ethnic situation dominated by local identities but characterized by emerging general designations. It is important to note what Jordanes does not say. He does not speak of Slavs in the fourth century, but only of Venethi. And, unlike later Latin authors, Jordanes does not simply identify Venethi and Slavs. As is usual with contemporary descriptions of dynamic ethnic situations, any attempt to interpret what he really meant is bound to go wrong from the start. Nothing proves that the Venethi of the first centuries are identical or directly related to the Slavs of the sixth century, just as the Welsh, the *Welsche*, and the Vlachs have little to do with the Volcae from whom their name is derived.[18]

It is also important to note that Jordanes does not say that the Antes were Slavs; he subsumes them under the more general label of Venethi and calls them the strongest of them. Procopius also considers them as closely related to the Slavs and mentions "Sclaveni and Antes" next to each other. Procopius notes that both Slavs and Antes were "not ruled by one man, but they have lived from old under a democracy."[19] It is often assumed that the Antes were more capable of centrally organized political activity than the Slavs proper, a difference that has been explained by a core of Sarmatian origins that overlay the Slavic peasantry, or by the challenges and influences from the neighboring steppe zone.[20] However that may be, the patchy information about them should not be used as direct evidence for early Slavic social structure. Only some of the names of Antes seem to be Slavic; others can be derived from Germanic or Iranian roots, which points to a rather mixed population.[21] According to the written sources, the Antes settled the middle Dniester and Dnieper areas. The precise location is, however, debated.[22] They disappeared from the written record soon after 600.

The entry of the Slavs into history shows some unusual features. They were numerous but had become apparent only very recently; they did not fit into the classical ethnographic typology of Scythians, Germans, and Celts; and they were badly organized but rather successful. It is not surprising that, initially, authors were unsure where they had come from and tried to link them with peoples more or less known from ancient ethnography: Venethi, Massagetae, Huns, or *Sporoi*. In Byzantine perceptions, they were first subsumed among the Scythians and steppe peoples and were incorporated into the Roman army as cavalry. Most of all, they are already supposed to be numerous, or at least to inhabit vast territories, although settled in small groups far apart: "living one man apart from another, they inhabit the country in very sporadic fashion."[23] How was it possible that such a wide-ranging people had not been noticed before? The phenomenon of Slavic expansion was difficult to grasp for contemporaries and continues to be difficult to describe with our historical categories. Between the late fifth and the seventh century a quiet revolution occurred in vast areas of eastern and central Europe that did not follow established historiographical models, then and now.

Where did these people come from, and what made them succeed? In ancient as in modern historiography, the "topos origo" was employed to grasp the emergence and the characteristics of a people; distant national origins were supposed to reveal the true character of a nation.[24] Slavic national histories, from the day when František Palacky and Pavel Šafařík first inspired the enthusiasm for Slavic antiquities up to the later twentieth century, therefore sought to trace the Slavs back to an *Urheimat*, a primeval abode.[25] Many modern scholars took Jordanes's information for granted and built arduous reconstructions on it. This link between Slavs and Venethi was key to projecting early Slavic history far into the past. After 1945, the continuation of this line of research was somehow veiled behind Marxist rhetoric but basically went on unbroken. An extreme example is the book on the early Slavs by Pavel Dolukhanov that appeared in 1996 in the *Longmans General Education Series* in Britain.[26] The bulk of his book deals with the period before Slavs are even mentioned in the sources, right back to the Neolithic. A further identification of the Venethi also had ideological consequences: in Slovenia, they were also connected with the pre-Roman Veneti in northern Italy, which made the Slavs the forefathers of present Italian populations.[27]

The obscure origin of the Slavs in a hypothetical homeland was sometimes called "ethnogenesis." "Ethnogenesis" meaning a remote origin by which, once and forever, a new people was created is a very different concept from the usage in Vienna, which entailed a more open sense and special attention to continuing ethnic change.[28] More modestly, in Michel Kazanski's *Les Slaves* (1999), the first chapter deals with "Les Slaves avant les Slaves, Ier–IVème siècle."[29] However, archaeological research can contribute little to tracing "Slavs" back beyond the time when they are attested in the written sources.[30] For some time, the combination of "Prague type" pottery, sunken huts, and cremation burials has been regarded as distinctive for the Slavs, a combination that appears north of the Carpathians in ca. 500, as Kazimierz Godłowski has argued, which would fit the historiographic evidence.[31] However, this formula is not applicable everywhere, and the simple pottery is not always distinctive.

The core discipline in the search for the original homeland of the Slavs was therefore Slavic philology. Several acknowledged methods were used to detect where the Slavic language might have come from: looking for zones of concentration of old Slavic hydronymy and toponymy, or excluding those where it could not be found; assessing the oldest Slavic terminology of plants, animals, food, and other environmental markers for regions where all this could have been present; or analyzing traces of language contact and early loanwords for possible relations with neighboring languages.[32] It can indeed be made plausible that a Paleoslavic language existed; Slavicists point to a surprisingly uniform

Slavic language that still existed around 600 and that is at the basis of later Slavic languages.[33] Yet in spite of an impressive number of linguistic studies, no consensus could be reached, although the majority of scholars opted for the Pripjet region as the ancestral home of "the Slavs."[34] It has been concluded that "the linguistic search for a Slav homeland seems so far to have proved abortive."[35] The linguistic homogeneity of sixth-century Slavic means that divergences and convergences of single Slavic languages cannot be used to extrapolate further back into a period before Slavs appear in our written sources.

The main point, however, is that Slavic language did not necessarily imply Slavic identity or outside perception as Slavs. If the etymology that explains the name *slověne as "those who speak" in contrast to *němьci, "the mute," is correct, the language may of course have had some bearing on identity.[36] Yet even so, Slav identity would be logically posterior to the language, and it is hard to tell when exactly it appeared as a self-designation. It is not unlikely that in seventh-/ eighth-century central Europe, Slavic may have served as a lingua franca of rather inhomogeneous populations.[37] This would help to explain its homogeneity over long distances and would imply that the language was initially not the key feature of Slavic identity.

In any case, if we have no proof that the name "Slavs" was used by anybody before the middle of the sixth century, it makes no sense to speak of Slavs prior to the sixth century. That was the beginning of Slavic history; all else is speculation. Although we can assume that Paleoslavic was spoken earlier than that, this does not necessarily mean that those people considered themselves Slavs; the name may not even have existed. Whoever spoke this language did not have much impact on the history of the period and was most likely not perceived as a "Slav." Hundreds of names of barbarian peoples and tribes came to the notice of ancient ethnographers, and the works of Ptolemy, Tacitus, or the Tabula Peutingeriana contain a wealth of ethnonyms far beyond the Roman *limes*. Slavs of the earlier imperial period would have had to hide deep in the Pripjet marshes to escape the searching eyes of Roman officers, slave traders, and scholars. This does not mean that the Slavs of the sixth century appeared in eastern Europe out of the blue. Their ancestors may have lived in a particular area for a long time and even built square sunken-floor huts with internal hearths since the third century AD. But nothing suggests that these forefathers called themselves Slavs, and from what point they spoke a Slavic language is still in debate. Later, speakers of this language seem to roughly correspond to the population called "Slavs" or "Wends" in our sources. Despite this near-overlap, the image of a Slavic people or of a Slavic family of peoples in the early Middle Ages that seems to emerge from this observation is already an abstraction. However useful it has proven, it can prompt misleading conclusions and falsely formulated questions.

On the basis of the evidence on the early Slavs, the model of ethnogenesis developed with reference to the migratory Germanic peoples is of only limited use.[38] We know little about Slavic identity formation and any traditions that might have contributed to it. Where leaders emerge, they are often imported; even today, the terminology of rule in Slavic languages mostly consists of loanwords from different languages. Attempts to reconstruct an original, common Slavic social system can at best be applied only beneath this level, in segmented social formations.[39] Perhaps the "obscure advance" of the Slavs is best characterized as follows: it became common to be a Slav, to speak Slavic, and to live in decentralized rural communities even where a more hierarchical social order had existed before. The model for this process cannot be philogenetic and genealogical, the unificatory family tree, but rather the rhizome, the multicentered network of roots.[40] This is what I argued in the German version of this book.[41]

In 2001, Florin Curta's book about *The Making of the Slavs* moved the debate about the origin of the Slavs to another plane.[42] He argued that the use of the ethnonym "Slavs" became common only in the contact zone between Byzantines and Slavs along the lower Danube. As I had done, he criticized the model of Slavic expansion from an original *Urheimat* and insisted on their appearance in the Justinianic period. However, he went one step further and maintained that the Slavs had essentially been created by Byzantine perceptions: "The making of the Slavs was less a matter of ethnogenesis and more one of invention, imagining and labeling by Byzantine authors." Thus, "in the shadow of Justinian's forts" along the *limes* on the lower Danube, some sort of Slavic group identity could emerge.[43] Danijel Dzino then "postmodernized" Curta's approach in his book about the early Croats, *Becoming Slav, Becoming Croat*, in which he understood the early Slavs as a process rather than an entity.[44]

Curta's work, since then supplemented by his numerous regional studies,[45] has the great merit of liberating the sixth- and seventh-century evidence from the retrospective self-assuredness in which often inconclusive evidence had always been fed into a coherent vision of Slavic expansion, whose Slavic character had never been in doubt. Predictably, his work was met by some severe criticism in general and in detail. I included a very favorable discussion of it in my paper about "Non-Roman Europe" at the Harvard Medieval Seminar in 2001, and it was not very well received by some of the senior scholars in the audience. The book may have its weaknesses, and I do not agree with all of its propositions, but its groundbreaking role should in any case be acknowledged.

Curta based his discussion on those Slavs who, in the sixth century, featured prominently in Byzantine historiography, of which we are lucky to have a fair amount at our disposal. This is very reasonable, for this is more or less all we know about Slavs in the sixth century. On the other hand, the warlike Slavs along the lower Danube who increasingly threatened the Balkan provinces are, as we will see, quite unusual among the scattered sixth- to eighth-century populations usually classed as Slavs. The considerable riches accumulated in their recurrent raids on Roman territory triggered a process of elite formation and social differentiation in the territories north of the lower Danube. The Byzantines could identify Slavic *archontes*, leaders, by name (such as Dauritas or Musucius) and knew about their whereabouts. The archaeological remains from the sixth and seventh centuries north of the Danube, whether we unproblematically class them as Slavic or not, to an extent express this process of social differentiation and elite representation, although it is still more than modest in comparison with what was found north of the Danube from previous centuries. Curta makes much of the brooches and "bow-fibulae" as tokens of elite identity and supraregional exchanges.[46] It makes sense to contextualize such finds in the process of the "making of the Slavs."

However, if that was *the* Slavic model that made the Slavs, it did not really come off. The emerging Slavic principalities on the lower Danube had no future of their own in the conflict zone between Byzantines, Avars, and later Bulgars. Only a small number of them attained some prosperity and social differentiation in the *Sklaviniai* on the fringes of the Byzantine Empire, in the course of the seventh century. Otherwise, the Roman infrastructure that could have conferred social status and provided luxury goods collapsed in most parts of the Balkan Peninsula. There is no attested direct continuation of established war-leaders in most areas later settled by Slavs, and neither in the relatively rich archaeological evidence of the later sixth and earlier seventh century. The question that we will have to pursue in the following, therefore, is in fact a double one: Why were the Slavs so resilient? And why didn't they continue the fairly successful precedent of the sixth-century warrior elites beyond the Danube *limes*? Perhaps the failure to establish stable Slavic powers enabled, in a paradoxical way, the enduring success of Slavic expansion, as I have argued in the German version of this book. It seems that the decentralized forms of organization, perceived as "more primitive" by contemporary and modern authors alike, were better suited to the conditions of the period.[47]

To assess the particularity of early Slavic identity formation, it is useful to compare their emergence with that of the Germans.[48] The Germani whom Julius Caesar met in northeastern Gaul were a regional people who most likely spoke a Celtic, not a Germanic, language and had a material culture that resembled that of the Celtic Gauls, although they were reputed to have come from east of the Rhine. Julius Caesar, however, used the name *Germani* as an umbrella term for the many larger and smaller tribes who lived east of the Rhine. Most of them probably did not think of themselves as *Germani* but identified with their tribe. The majority of them spoke Germanic, and some shared a material culture (the Jastorf culture) that in turn would develop without fundamental breaks into the distinctive regional cultures of the Germania of the imperial age. The term "Germanic" as used by historians, archaeologists, and philologists never quite converges, although it overlaps. More remarkably, we have little evidence of anyone calling themselves "Germans," apart from a few Roman soldiers of Germanic origins. What, by comparison, is striking among the early Slavs is the lack of known particular tribal or ethnic names (if we discount the Antes). Even regional units that the Byzantines learned to spot and identify in protracted conflict, such as the Dauritas group north of the lower Danube, could only be labeled after their leader. Later, Slavs often adopted regional designations from their area of immigration, such as Carantani, Maravani, or Dukljane, or even used the common name Slavs for regional distinction, like the Slovenes and Slovaks of today. This is very unlike Roman relations with the early Germans, who were perceived in a rich web of particular denominations. Thus, the umbrella terms *Germani* and *Sclavi* were similarly broad, but differently from the Germanic case, with the Slavs we have no clue what was beneath it—perhaps the names "varied by family and place," as Jordanes claims? This has obvious consequences for Slavic identity; whereas early Germans always had more specific and stronger identities in their single tribes or peoples, and therefore the name *Germani* stopped being used in the fifth century, Slavs may have been more motivated to identify with the umbrella term; and indeed, unlike the name "Germans," it continued to be used for self-identification.[49]

A brief account of the Slavicization of large parts of central and eastern Europe, as I will try to sketch it in the following, must of necessity simplify, although at the current state of research the differentiation, the detailed picture, seems more adequate.[50] When the Avars arrived, Slavic groups were already settled north of the Carpathians and of the lower Danube. Yet the situation was relatively unstable; with the exception of the Antes, no large-scale power centers and specific identities had formed. But on the other hand, several Slavic groups did not limit themselves to tranquil agriculturalism. When Slavs appear in the sources before 568, they do so as warriors and raiders, for whom the formation of bands with a leader and his following (as under Hildigis) was not foreign, despite the fact that these associations remained unstable.

4.2 The Saint and the Barbarians

If we possessed only secular chronicles, composed from the perspective of the administration of the empire, such as those of Menander, Theophylact, or Theophanes, we would know nothing about the barbarian attacks on Thessalonica, the most important provincial metropolis in the Balkans. Fortunately, a source of another kind has been preserved there: the account of the miraculous intervention of the patron saint in the life of the city, the *Miracula S. Demetrii*. Despite the supernatural subject matter, the text does not focus on pious legends. These are detailed accounts by well-informed contemporaries, who were for the most part eyewitnesses of the events. To describe how the saint influenced the destiny of his city they present a remarkably sober and precise narrative. As firsthand sources about otherwise unknown events, the *Miracles* are comparable to the *Vita Severini* that deals with the end of Roman Noricum in the late fifth century. If the latter depicts the acts of a living holy man in a time of constant barbarian attacks, the former extols the interventions of a dead saint. The first book of miracle stories was composed by Archbishop John soon after 610, in the first years of the reign of Heraclius. He describes the events of the last two decades of the sixth century, which he had himself experienced. The second book contains events from the later seventh century and was obviously compiled before its end. In both books, the saint repeatedly had to save his city from the great affliction of the barbarians.[51] The text presents Avar and Slav attacks viewed from the perspective of those affected. Thus it offers a valuable complement to the chronicles in which such events are viewed more or less from the perspective of the Byzantine bureaucracy.

For the chronicles of the capital, all roads lead to Constantinople; what occurs beyond them, they for the most part disregard. This reticence reflects the strategic interests at the center of the empire: when the Avars attacked, Sirmium or Novae were more problematic than Thessalonica or the Greek peninsula. Great armies were deployed along the Danube or in the passes of the Balkan mountains; in the south and west only the regional militias were there to confront the invaders. In the Greek peninsula, the fort of Isthmia, which controlled traffic across the isthmus of Corinth, may have been the only one controlled by a regular army unit in the sixth century.[52] That the *Miracles* are our best source for the events in the western part of the Balkans is then no coincidence. Thanks for saving Thessalonica would not go to the emperor and his generals, but to St. Demetrius and his clerics.

It is a strange irony that John, the author of the first book, explicitly ascribes the first great siege of the city (which most likely took place in 586) to the circumstance that it was particularly close to the emperor's heart. According to his account, the leader of the Avars—the title khagan is not mentioned here—was so enraged over the dismissal of an embassy to Maurice that he sought the means "to inflict on him the greatest possible suffering." Since he knew that Thessalonica was more important to the emperor than all the other cities of Thrace and Illyricum, "he called together the whole untamed tribe of Slavs (this people was then wholly subject to him), placed barbarians of other tribes at their side, and ordered them all to march against Thessalonica. It was the greatest army that has been seen in our times, estimated to have been more than 100,000 men."[53]

The barbarian army, which on its course "turned the country into a desert," appeared before the city on Sunday, September 22. The element of surprise played an important role. The besiegers succeeded in appearing before the walls almost at the same moment as the news of their arrival. The timing was well chosen. Well into the month of July the plague had raged, and the city had lost half its population. Of the remaining residents, a share had stayed out in the country for the harvest, and their return was now cut off. The best Byzantine troops were engaged in the province of Hellas under the command of the eparch, while the most prominent townspeople had set off for Constantinople with their retinue in order to lodge complaints about this very commander.[54]

The enemies, "as numerous as the sands of the sea," then found the city almost entirely bereft of defenders. Although the author exaggerates the hopelessness of the situation, he gives the valuable detail that people had felt safe in the city so far. The attack "brought unspeakable anguish to the city and they were forced to contemplate an enemy's battle array for the first time." Only those who had done their military service far from home recognized the terrifying spectacle. Since the great Cutrigur and Slavic attacks in the time of Justinian no barbarian host had appeared beneath the walls of the city.[55]

The besiegers also proved to be inexperienced. When they reached Thessalonica during the night of September 22–23, they erroneously made camp before the fortified sanctuary of the Holy Matron, which they took to be the city. Only in the morning did they try to mount the walls of the real city with ladders that they had brought along. Meanwhile, the defenders had in all haste stationed themselves along the tops of these walls. Reputedly, it was the uniformed saint himself who threw the first enemy from the wall. The unexpected opposition spread panic among the besiegers, and they withdrew. The surprise tactic had failed, which the townsfolk ascribed to the protection of their well-armed patron.

Now the barbarians made arrangements for a long siege. The city was surrounded and closed off. Because of the large numbers of warriors, who formed a living barricade, it was not even judged necessary to erect palisades. On the outskirts of the city barbarian bands plundered and collected supplies to provision the army. Archbishop Eusebius, whom we know from the letters of Pope Gregory, meanwhile concerned himself with the spiritual defense of the city.[56] He had already been warned of the attack in a dream. His efforts bore fruit as phantom soldiers appeared, ready for battle, on the walls.

Meanwhile, in the barbarian camp difficulties were accumulating. A considerable number of the attackers passed to the Byzantine side. With the aid of an interpreter it was learned from them that the khagan had known of the situation of Thessalonica after the epidemic. He had firmly counted on his troops being able to take the city on the very first day.[57] Despite all their efforts the besiegers could not solve their supply problems. The provisions that they had been able to round up in the vicinity of the city were used up after breakfast on the second day, although the barbarians were not squeamish about their food: they ate fruit, twigs, roots, herbs, thistles, and other wild plants, eventually even dust. But even this barbarian menu was not sufficient to nourish the besieging army: "the earth could not bear their weight."[58]

The unexpected failure of the first attack unleashed feverish activity beneath the walls. By the first evening the townspeople were offered an eerie spectacle. Around the city huge fires were lit, like a river of flames, and from this were heard the battle cries of the barbarians as if from a single throat, "even more terrifying than the fire." After this psychological warfare with its *son et lumière* effects, a huge number of siege machines were built during the night and the following day. The battle-tried archbishop makes mention of the whole arsenal of Roman war technology: the *helepolis*, a catapult, the *testudo* or tortoise, the ram, as well as other catapults, which—after some experimenting—were protected against fire by the hides of freshly slaughtered animals. He counted fifty such machines along the eastern length of the wall alone.[59]

Starting on the third day of the siege, the barbarians attacked the walls of the city with the aid of the siege machines. Yet the accuracy of the improvised machines left much to be desired, and only a few of the huge blocks of stone that were cast against the walls ever reached their target. On the other hand, the defenders succeeded in disabling many of the siege machines with well-aimed stones and fire-arrows. Targeted sorties foiled the sapping of the walls under the cover of testudos. Even when the gate to the city once got stuck and could no longer be closed, the protection of the patron saint prevented the worst from happening.

Slowly, the morale of the defenders rose, while the unused city baths filled with interned barbarian defectors. On Sunday, the seventh day of the siege, began the all-out attack of the barbarians, an expected move of which the defectors had already warned. Yet instead of the anticipated life-or-death battle, the defenders witnessed a strange spectacle. Suddenly the attackers rushed off, shouting, to the hills surrounding the city. As later became evident, they thought they had witnessed a huge, hidden army attacking from all the gates of the city, the same vision that once led the khagan to abandon the siege of Drizipera in Theophylact's account.[60] In the general panic the besiegers began to fight among themselves.

From the walls the Byzantines could observe clashes among the enemy troops on their way back to their tents.

During the night the greater part of the besiegers withdrew. The next morning the remainder of the barbarians before the gates of the city asked for admittance. At first, the defenders thought it a battle feint, yet the defectors were simply driven by hunger to join the victors. Their statements made it possible to recognize in the leader of the phantom army, who had borne the uniform of a cavalry officer, St. Demetrius himself. The mounted scouts who were now sent out confirmed that the barbarians had withdrawn in great disorder, since the road was strewn with pieces of their clothing and their possessions.

When did this memorable Slav–Avar siege take place? During the reign of Maurice, September 22 twice fell on a Sunday, in 586 and 597. Bishop Eusebius is attested in the letters of Pope Gregory from 597 to 603 but may also have led the church in Thessalonica in 586.[61] The dating can then be derived only from assessments of the general political situation.[62] As Lemerle rightly emphasizes, the khagan was not personally present at the siege. The chief burden of the battles was borne by the Slavs; the remaining barbarians that the khagan assigned to them may have been Avars and Bulgars, perhaps also Gepids. The thwarted embassy to the emperor, which so enraged the khagan according to the *Miracles*, fits in well with the cause of the war in 586: the mission of Targitius, which ended with his internment on the Isle of Princes. The khagan, who must have received word of the plague in the city, had sent Slavic plunderers, the same motif that Theophylact assumed behind the Slav incursions of these years. The khagan hoped that the large, but ill-prepared siege army would succeed through speed. The attack may as much have been in the interest of the participating Slavs as of the khagan. However, only the Avar ruler could coordinate the march of such a large army, even though he could not prevent internal conflict and secession, as the course of the siege makes evident.

The failure of this undertaking reveals how difficult the leadership of a huge barbarian army must have been. The supply problems of the besiegers are not once attributed by the hagiographer to the provident intervention of the saint. Once beyond a certain size, an army could no longer live off the land through which it passed. Even Roman armies experienced similar problems on imperial lands.[63] At that time the barbarians were not yet well versed in siege tactics, even if they had learned from the Romans in this respect. Psychological factors must have weighed even more heavily. From the perspective of the modern urbanite, the city of antiquity was a center of civilization threatened by the "pernicious flood of barbarians." We should, however, not forget that to the Slavic peasant warriors, in whose world construction in stone scarcely existed, the massive fortifications they faced in Roman lands must have seemed threatening. Behind the towering walls anything might lie hidden: the anxieties and visions to which the sources allude are then less strange than the city dwellers may have presumed. The barbarian art of leadership therefore was not least a matter of psychology. The charisma of the ruler and the supernatural power that he ascribed to himself stood against Roman self-assurance, which also had a religious basis. The miracle of Thessalonica was that the besiegers had too little to put up against the saint's reassuring effect on the defenders. Neither the familiar battle cries nor the order of the distant khagan could prevent the small anxieties right up to the mass panic, the inner conflicts, and ultimately, the army's dissolution.

The Avar strategy, which entailed the concentration of great forces in order to achieve spectacular successes, was scarcely viable without the participation of the khagan and his entourage. For the most part, the Slavs employed a different tactic. They operated in smaller bands of a few hundred or thousand warriors. Smaller Slavic groups also appeared repeatedly before Thessalonica; one of them tried to take the city by surprise on the feast day of its patron saint.[64]

What conclusions for the situation in the parts of the Balkan Peninsula that Byzantine chronographers hardly mention can we draw from these observations about Thessalonica? One thing seems obvious: if the most important city in the western Balkans did not see an Avar army at its gates during those years, it is difficult to imagine a specifically targeted Avar invasion of the Greek peninsula. On the other hand, the *Miracles* indicate that without the consent of the Avars nothing decisive could be undertaken in the region. The author expressly notes that about 586 "all" the Slavs were subject to the Avars, as distinct from the time of the composition, the first years of Heraclius's reign. This must have been the situation on the Greek peninsula as well. Wherever the Slavs were active in these years, Byzantine observers saw the khagan behind them. On this Menander, Theophylact, John of Ephesus, and the *Miracles* are in agreement. Evagrius and the *Chronicle of Monemvasia* see only the Avars at work. We may be sure that the Slavic raids on the Peloponnesus also had the khagan's blessing. Assent was not given out of disinterestedness. It was certainly intended to increase pressure on the Romans and thus to improve the khagan's own bargaining position. This is in fact the reason the *Miracles* adduce for the attack on Thessalonica. In addition, the Slav fighters had to be kept in the right mood, if their loyalty were not to be lost.

4.3 Slavic Campaigns and Memories of Avars on the Greek Peninsula

When around the year 900 Arethas of Caesarea composed a report for the emperor Leo VI about the stubborn conflict of the metropolitan of Patras with the Slavs of his diocese, he sought to reconstruct the history of Slavic immigration into Greece.

The result of his efforts has been preserved under the misleading title *Chronicle of Monemvasia* and has stimulated a long suite of academic discussions.[65]

One thing is remarkable: the author explains the Slavic presence in Greece as a consequence of Avar incursions in the first years of Maurice's reign. In his studies, he had found material on the origin of the Avars and on their conquests from 582 to 586. These are the well-known bits of information: the conquests of Sirmium, Singidunum, Viminacium, Augusta, Anchialus; Elpidius's embassy; and the advance to the Long Walls. They came from the same sources that we have to rely on: Menander, Evagrius, Theophylact, Theophanes.[66] The wars from 580 to 586 had really made history. Hundreds of years later accounts of them were still being handed down from chronicle to chronicle, and they were regarded as a rupture in the development of the Balkan Peninsula. In ecclesiastical documents from the Peloponnesus, in Syrian transmissions (Michael the Syrian, Bar Hebraeus), and in Byzantine chronicles of the High Middle Ages (George the Monk, Zonaras) many a detail from the Avar campaigns can be retrieved.

What the author of the *Chronicle of Monemvasia* learned, on the other hand, about his own subject, the Slavic appropriation of great parts of the Peloponnesus, is comparatively scant. He gives one exact date—the sixth year of the reign of Maurice, AM 6096 (587–88)[67]—and enumerates the regions of Greece in which the Avars/Slavs settled. This is remarkable. More than a millennium ago, no more could be found out about the Slavic immigration in Greece than we know today. "In the course of another invasion, they [the Avars] took possession of all Thessaly and all Hellas, Old Epirus, Attica and Euboea. Those who pressed into the Peloponnesus seized it by force of arms. They pursued and annihilated the native and Hellene population, and established themselves firmly. Those who escaped their murderous hands scattered, each in his own direction," states the *Chronicle*. Then follows an enumeration of the inhabitants' various places of refuge, on islands, in Sicily, and in newly founded Monemvasia on the east coast of the peninsula. "After the Avars had thus occupied the Peloponnesus and had established themselves there, they remained there for 218 years, subject to neither the emperor of the Romans nor anyone else, that is, from the 6096th year from the creation of the world, the sixth year of the rule of Maurice, until the year 6313, the fourth in the reign of Nicephorus, the elder, whose son was Stauracius."[68]

The terse account in the *Chronicle of Monemvasia* is one of the most heavily commented on in the literature of the early medieval history of southeastern Europe. When exactly it was composed, whether before, around, or after 900, is not decisive for its value as a source for Slavic immigration. But how the scant information can be integrated into a big picture of the Slavicization of Greece is something on which views still diverge, although extreme positions have lost their impact. At the beginning of the nineteenth century, the German scholar Jakob Philipp Fallmerayer had provoked heated debates with his thesis that the modern Greeks were in fact Albanians and Slavs.[69] He thereby created an enduring challenge for the historians of the newly independent Greek state. Is the account of the Hellenic diaspora in the *Chronicle* credible? Only gradually have meticulous studies, revealing new sources, created the basis for a more nuanced debate.[70]

Two points are of primary interest for the historian of the Avars. First, the author of the *Chronicle* has the Avars immigrate and live there for two hundred years, yet when the Byzantine state again imposed its rule at the beginning of the ninth century, it is Slavs who are subjugated. What was the relationship between the Slavs in Greece and the Avar khaganate? Second, how can the Avar–Slav advance into the extreme south of the peninsula be seen in the context of events in the remainder of the Balkans? It is highly unlikely that substantial groups of Avars settled in Greece on a permanent basis (for which archaeological evidence is lacking). The question remains as to how active their participation was in the Slavic raids of the 580s; the answer hinges on our reconstruction of the events from some brief and rather doubtful accounts.

On the basis of the *Miracula S. Demetrii* one could assume that the storm first broke in 586, after the invaders had in vain attacked the city of Thessalonica. That is the date given in the *Chronicle of Monemvasia*: 587–88. However, the remark in the *Miracula* that a large part of the troops stationed in the city were in Hellas during the siege contradicts this interpretation.[71] The "matters of state" that necessitated their absence are surely to be associated with Slavic raids. A somewhat earlier date for the Slavic invasions of Greece is given in another late source, a seventeenth-century note on a manuscript at Mount Athos that dates the founding of Monemvasia to AM 6075, probably 583.[72]

Contemporary testimony is found in Evagrius, a lawyer from Antiocheia, whose *Ecclesiastical History* was concluded in 593/94.[73] "The Avars twice penetrated as far as the so-called Long Wall, captured by siege and enslaved Singidunum, and Anchialus, and the whole of Hellas and other cities and forts, destroying and burning everything." Most likely, this rare piece of information about events in the European part of Byzantium in the *History* is the result of Evagrius's visit to Constantinople in 588.[74] Evagrius has contracted the events of several years, during which the Avars and Slavs reached the periphery of the capital at least twice, in 584 (when Singidunum fell and the Avars bathed in Anchialus) and 585 (when Slav raiders reached the Long Walls). His Avars move on to Hellas after plundering in Illyricum and Thrace; he does not mention the Slavs. John of Ephesus tells the opposite story; Slavs capture Corinth, where their leader sets up a ciborium like a tent, and then move on to Anchialus.[75]

That Corinth was abandoned and that the inhabitants withdrew to the island of Aegina is also mentioned in the *Chronicle of Monemvasia*.[76] But that cannot have been a direct consequence of the events in the 580s, when Corinth clearly continued to play a role. When Pope Gregory sent his legate Boniface with a set of important letters to Constantinople in February 591, the latter's route went through Corinth. The covering letter from Gregory to Archbishop Anastasius of Corinth has been preserved. The pope requests, "since the unreliability of the times puts the greatest obstacles in the path of a journey," that his envoy be given support by all for "whatever he may need on the way in the form of provisions or the procuring of a ship."[77] These were uncertain times, yet a bishop resided in Corinth (most likely in the fortress of Acrocorinth) who could help the papal legate along on his journey. Probably only the unfortified lower city had fallen into the hands of the barbarians at that time, and the inhabitants withdrew to Acrocorinth, protected by imposing walls of rock. Or at least the city was quickly reconquered, a task that may have been assumed by the contingent from Thessalonica mentioned in the *Miracula S. Demetrii*.[78] Excavations on the site confirm that Corinth had already been in decline since the fifth century but was not abandoned during the reign of Maurice. Numerous later coins have been found there, going up to the reign of Constans II (642–58).[79] There are, however, traces of siege and destruction at the fortress of Isthmia and the eastern Corinthian port of Kenchreai.[80] The church of Patras had been subject to the metropolitan of Corinth. When the *Chronicle of Monemvasia* emphasizes the fall of Corinth, this clearly is in defense of the position of the bishop of Patras.[81]

Athens also remained under Byzantine control for most of the seventh century, in spite of two layers of destruction. During the rule of Constans II, who resided in the city in 662–63, a great deal of reconstruction was carried out. At about the same time Western clerics visited the "most eminent of Greek cities." In the eighth century the bishop of Athens appears to have obtained the rights of a metropolitan and is mentioned repeatedly in the *Chronographia* of Theophanes.[82] Some Byzantine control also seems to have been maintained in the western half of the Peloponnesus, although Slavs clearly settled in Olympia and at other places.[83]

However, eventually most of the Greek peninsula was settled by Slavs.[84] Constantine Porphyrogenitus dates a further Slavicization of the Peleponnesus to no earlier than the mid-eighth century, when an epidemic decimated the native population.[85] The eighth-century Anglo-Saxon pilgrim Willibald located Monemvasia "in Slawinia terra."[86] An epitome of Strabo claims that by the seventh century the "Scythian Slavs" had occupied almost the entirety of Greece and the Peleponnesus.[87]

Many historians have connected Slavic settlement with the conquests of 580.[88] Others do not assume large-scale Slavic immigration before the beginning of the seventh century.[89] On the whole, the picture of the Slavic conquest and settlement of Greece has become differentiated in the course of the long debate. It cannot be a question of a single invasion leading to the appropriation of territory but rather of a long interplay between armed conflict and peaceful coexistence. The rural population was already in decline, which facilitated the installation of newcomers.[90] New conflicts followed phases of Byzantine restoration. Indigenous farmers and herdsmen, who had nothing to hide or to defend, withdrew into the mountains in the face of the immigrants. This movement to retreats is also mentioned in the *Chronicle of Monemvasia*.[91] Country towns on valley floors were deserted, and the Slavs showed a preference for mountainsides, where many smaller villages sprang up, as shown, for example, by the findings in the Dropulli Valley in Epirus.[92] A series of small refugee settlements on islands near the coast has been excavated.[93] Archaeology begins to fill the gaps in the written evidence. The excavations at Olympia have rendered important traces of Slavic settlement with some relationship to the material culture of the Avar realm.[94] The so-called wandering soldier from Corinth was inhumated with belt buckles, a two-edged sword with crossbar, Byzantine rings, and rough handmade pottery also used in the Carpathian Basin. Ethnic attributions such as "Avar" or "Bulgar" have been discussed but also refuted.[95] Such evidence may reflect the barbarization of the late antique world, or the "byzantinization" of barbarians. If this was indeed an "Avar" invader, he was only a poor cousin of the warriors of the early Avar period whose graves were found in the Carpathian Basin. Rather, he was a mercenary called to the defense of an already impoverished Greek city.

Were the Slavic farmers who settled in the Greek peninsula the successors to the warriors who attacked the walls of Thessalonica in 586 and in that same year conquered a series of Greek cities? From conquest to settlement is still a great step. Already during the reign of Justinian, Slavs and Cutrigurs had pushed into Greece, without staying there. The first siege of Thessalonica shows how quickly plunderers could stand between the alternatives of "eating dust" and withdrawing or staying in the country and growing food. When the raids in an impoverished country ceased to feed them, Slavic warriors apparently found no difficulty in cultivating the fields again—in distinction to the warrior aristocracy of the steppe horsemen. This explains their long-term success. Although the preserved sources emphasize the violent character of the Avar–Slav thrusts, the Slavic settlers of Greece were above all farmers. Not the spectacular single events mentioned in the sources but long-term processes were determining for changes in settlement.

After all these considerations the course of the Slavic advance into Greece could be sketched as follows: Macedonia and Greece were relatively little affected by the

Slavic invasions in the last years of Tiberius's rule. More numerous contingents were already reaching the Aegean from 584, while the Avars were marching into Thrace. Soon after that John of Ephesus must have heard of the plundering of Corinth's lower city. The invaders had initially bypassed Thessalonica. Only two years later did the offensive expand to include Macedonia. The high point of these raids was the siege of Thessalonica in the year 586. The Avar khagan had taken the initiative in this but did not take part. After the failure of the attack on Thessalonica, the raids continued in the Greek peninsula, where Patras was conquered, perhaps in 587–88. The bishop and many inhabitants saw no other possibility than to flee to Sicily. Limited urban life went on until at least 600.[96] Yet in the following years the situation did not improve to the point where the emigrants could think of returning. It is then plausible that a number of Slavs had already stayed behind in the Peloponnesus, most likely in the central mountainous regions toward Arcadia. According to the testimony of place-names the later Slavic settlement was also concentrated on this mountainous area.[97] In these lightly populated open areas they met little resistance. At least the cities of Corinth, Athens, Argos, and Monemvasia could still maintain themselves on the mainland. This did not prevent the peninsula from being struck by a new wave of immigrants between the years 616 and 626, which appreciably strengthened the Slavic settlement.

It is difficult to determine to what extent Avars participated in these Slavic raids. The texts on these events do not really distinguish between Avars and Slavs. John of Ephesus differentiates between Avars and Slavs in general but mixes them up in the course of events. In the story of the profanation of the ciborium of Corinth, however, he only speaks of Slavs, and of their king.[98] And the *Miracula S. Demetrii*, the second part of which gives such a clear description of Slav–Avar relations, on the occasion of the first siege speak most often in sweeping terms of "barbarians."[99] The *Chronicle of Monemvasia* could not resolve these contradictions. The author turned invading Avars into settled Slavs without any explanation. This is all the more remarkable given the clear, almost schematic differentiation in the other Byzantine sources, most detailed in the *Strategicon*.

Informed contemporaries largely distinguished Avars from Slavs according to their military function, as the *Strategicon* shows. Yet this demarcation could easily become blurred, for instance when successful Slavic raiders began to fight on horseback. Avar military attire and weapons established models for ambitious soldiers—even in the army of the emperor.[100] The learned clerics who wrote about Avar attacks were even less precise in their ethnic distinctions. The account of the miraculous intervention of St. Demetrius during the first barbarian attack on Thessalonica remains the best illustration of the Avar–Slav conquest of Greece that we have. The author of the miracle stories of 586 expressly notes that with the exception of a few veterans in the city, no one was familiar with the appearance of a barbarian horde. It was only through the defectors that they learned that they were dealing with Slavs whom the khagan had sent.

Those who translated the khagan's orders (or suggestions) into deeds with greater success in the Greek peninsula perhaps had more reason to proudly present themselves as Avars, even though most of them were of Slavic descent. "The Avars are coming!" Who in the distant Peloponnesus could have judged how appropriate such a cry of terror actually was? The Slavs who invaded the Greek peninsula were hardly looking for new land for settlement, as romantic historians once imagined. Farmers seeking land do not set out at harvest time for a distant region in order to attack a great city situated there. Many of them had already been raiding regularly for years. To arrive before Thessalonica at almost the same time as news of their presence in the region could hardly have been accomplished on foot. The lessons of mounted warfare were still best learned from the Avars. With what success Slavic raiders modeled themselves on their masters would have differed from troop to troop. Those who settled there obviously ceased to identify themselves as Avars soon. Only rarely does the name appear for barbarian inhabitants of Greece; the *Vita sancti Pancratii* seems to support the notion that in the vicinity of Athens the name "Avar" was used for Slavic groups.[101] The residue of Greek life and culture could not sustain high-status warriors any more. The new settlers needed to live off the land, and the Avar mask dropped. The townspeople of Patras took with them into exile the certainty of having been driven off by the Avars. Those among the conquerors who identified themselves as Avars moved on. Those who stayed settled down as Slavs.

Therefore, the Avars had something to do with the Slavicization of Greece, although indirectly. We have no evidence that the core of the Avar cavalry participated directly in the conquest. Yet the Slavs of the first wave in the 580s most likely considered themselves subjects of the khagan, as the defectors in Thessalonica recounted. Those who settled the Peloponnesus were no longer subject to the rule of the Avar leader. This may explain why here, at the greatest distance from the Avar power center, Slavs settled relatively early. The Greek hinterland was also of minor strategic interest for the empire. Justinian had fortified the isthmus, but to the south had not improved the defenses.[102] In the mountainous regions off the major military routes, smaller bands of settlers could relatively easily establish themselves, "subject to no-one" as the *Chronicle* recounts. Long after the reconquest the Byzantine state had constant problems with the fractious Slavs of the Peloponnesus.[103] The explanation for their presence was sought in the Avar raids of the 580s. In retrospect, this was perhaps when it all began. Yet the main role of the Avars in the process was to keep the Byzantines busy on other fronts.

4.4 The *Obor* and His Slavs

Academic passions have long run high over the question of Avar–Slav relations. Behind the learned discussion were both Slavic self-esteem and a German or Hungarian sense of superiority. At the end of the nineteenth century, the Germanized Czech historian Jan Peisker excluded any possibility of independent Slavic evolution under the "Avar yoke." According to him, only the Avars and later the Franks had brought the Slavs into the fold of culture.[104] As late as the 1950s Helmut Preidel viewed the Slavs as the slaves of the East Germans who had stayed behind, among whom it was the Frank Samo who first laid the ground for an "aristocracy."[105] On the same tangent is Pritsak's theory of the formation of the Slavs in the service of nomadic overlords; an independent development is practically excluded.[106]

On the other hand, Avar lordship of the Slavs outside the Carpathian Basin has often been discounted, and the Avar Empire was understood as a kind of Slavic tribal confederacy under Avar ascendancy.[107] Notable Slav scholars attempted to reconstruct an original common Slavic culture on the basis of later evidence.[108] Yet an uninterrupted, organic development of an authentic Slavic culture can hardly be presumed.[109]

Today it is agreed that the Avar–Slav relationship cannot be subsumed in a simple formula.[110] On the one hand there were certainly autogenous factors in the Slav expansion, not just the pressure of the nomad horsemen. Even at the height of Avar power the Slavs left traces of their own and had some political impact. On the other hand the confrontation with the superior military power of the mounted warriors did not pass without leaving traces on the Slavs. Similar influences on early Slavic society came from the Byzantines and Franks.

Among the Slavs themselves the Avars remained for the most part a bad memory. The *obor* became a terror-inspiring giant in later stories and fairy tales— or a swearword.[111] Closer in time is what came to the attention of the author of the seventh-century *Chronicle of Fredegar* on the occasion of the insurgency of Samo and the Bohemian Slavs. "Every year the Huns wintered with the Slavs, sleeping with their wives and daughters, and in addition the Slavs paid tribute and endured many other burdens."[112] A similar story of Slav oppression was told in the twelfth century in the *Russian Primary Chronicle*: "They made war upon the Slavs, and harassed the Dulebians, who were themselves Slavs. They even did violence to the Dulebian women. When an Avar made a journey, he did not cause either a horse or a steer to be harnessed, but gave command instead that three or four or five women should be yoked to his cart and be made to draw him."[113] Similarities between these two accounts have been used to posit a general model or explained by literary borrowings.[114] The common element is above all that Slavic women are represented in both cases as the victims of Avar violence. This is not surprising. After the conquest of Cividale, as was usual in the period, the women were led away as slaves.[115] The *Primary Chronicle* and Fredegar to an extent stylize a general experience with steppe peoples. Along with their role in production and reproduction the Slavs were also, according to Fredegar, used as auxiliary troops in the Avar army. "The Wends had long since been subjected to the Huns, who used them as *befulci*. Whenever the Huns took the field against another people, they stayed encamped in battle array while the Wends did the fighting. If the Wends won, the Huns advanced to pillage, but if they lost the Huns backed them up and they resumed the fight. The Wends were called *befulci* by the Huns because at the beginning of a battle they formed a second battle-line and advanced into battle before the Huns."[116] The term *befulci* has been discussed a great deal. It seems inconsequential whether it is explained as a Slavic word for buffalo-driver, an Umbrian pronunciation of "herdsmen," a Frankish term for "ancillary people" (*by-folk*) or a bilingual *bis-folc*, or even the root of modern Hungarian *mufurc*, "recruit, greenhorn."[117] Again, the description corresponds to some degree with what we read in other sources; but we should not simply take Fredegar's account as a general formula of Avar–Slav relations under the early khaganate.

It is often attested that Slavs formed large contingents in the Avar army. The prisoner numbers from the battle on the Tisza that Theophylact transmits show the Slavs to be in a majority.[118] In the Avar army, the Slavs played different roles.[119] In the front rank of the Slavic ring of besiegers in 626 fought "naked," at least unprotected, warriors, while the second rank consisted of armored foot soldiers.[120] Many must have done sapper duty, for example, in the construction of bridges and ships.[121] The Slavs who in 593 built a bridge over the Sava for the khagan "provided shipping in accordance with his order; for such are the things which fear of appointed officers [taxiarchs] can accomplish."[122] Repeatedly the Slavs appear as amphibian troops and as oarsmen in their dugouts, as in 626 during the siege of Constantinople, when more than a thousand boats were brought from the Danube to the Golden Horn.[123]

It was noted in Constantinople in 626 that the Slavs followed the khagan only through coercion.[124] In other contexts, Slavs often fought independently, albeit at the khagan's command.[125] Slavic contingents could be "seconded to the Lombard king."[126] Others could only be invited to fight alongside the Avars or be persuaded through gifts and gentle pressure to collaborate. An anecdote from

Theophylact is typical in this respect.[127] During Maurice's unfortunate campaign of 592, he writes, three Slavs were captured, without weapons but bearing only a cithara. When questioned, "they replied that they were Sklavenes by origin and that they lived at the boundary of the western ocean; the khagan had dispatched ambassadors to their parts to levy a military force and had lavished many gifts on their people's rulers; and so they accepted the gifts but refused him the alliance, asserting that the length of the journey daunted them, while they sent back to the khagan for the purpose of making a defence these same men who had been captured; they had completed the journey in fifteen months; but the khagan had forgotten the law of ambassadors and had decreed a ban on their return." Thereafter they had slipped off to the Romans. Finally, the three noble savages affirmed that iron was unknown in their lands and that they had also "never heard of war" and were only interested in playing the lyre and in musical competitions.

As Marcin Wołoszyn has demonstrated, the anecdote is rich in stereotypes from ancient ethnography; it occurs in a context of omens and fantastic events during Maurice's expedition against the Avars.[128] Still, the well-built narrative offers some insights into the dynamics of Avar–Slav relations: the khagan's efforts to recruit Slavic warriors from distant regions; his two-part strategy of gifts and hidden threats; how Slavs preferred to evade his demands with pretexts and feigned harmlessness rather than through open refusal; lastly, the incapacity of the Avars to react with more than a symbolic reprisal. The last point, however, is clearly a consequence of the distance and the political situation. Whether the Slavs from the ocean came from the Baltic Sea, as has often been maintained,[129] is hard to ascertain among the lofty Hyperborean images.

Scholarly literature usually distinguishes between the khagan's "internal" and "external" Slavs.[130] This was, however, no clear-cut distinction. As concerns the political aspirations of the khaganate there could be no "external Slavs." Realpolitik had to weigh military expenditure against political gain in each case. Just how difficult it was to handle this double reality is illustrated by the diplomatic tug-of-war with Byzantium over the Danube Slavs.[131] On the Slavic side even greater caution was required. Before Samo's rebellion only the Antes and the Danube Slavs of Dauritas had dared an open confrontation.[132] In both cases, the superiority of the khaganate became clearly evident. In 626 the angry khagan did not hesitate to have the Slavic survivors of the fiasco at the Golden Horn put to death.[133] Yet where they were not exposed to a sufficient concentration of Avar power, small groups of Slavs could acquire more and more room to move.

Making common cause with the khaganate was often enough in the interests of the Slavs. After the failed siege of Thessalonica about 615, Chatzon's Slavs tried to make amends: "For this purpose they collected imposing gifts and had them brought to the khagan; they also promised him a huge amount of money and booty from the capture of Thessalonica, if only he would assist the Slavs in the conquest of the city." They found further arguments to make the entire proposition attractive to the khagan. The khagan then mobilized his army, including the "internal" Slavs, as the *Miracula* explicitly state.[134] Thenceforth the Macedonian Slavs, who had set the ball rolling, also had to bow to his command for the duration of the campaign.

Undertakings on a certain scale, it would appear, required the agreement and support of the khagan. Slavic warriors seldom constituted major invasion armies, nor permanent large forces. They fought mostly in groups of a few hundred warriors or even fewer. Contemporary observers could distinguish between Avars and Slavs based on their styles of life and warfare, and on their various forms of organization. Most extensively, Maurice's *Strategicon* describes the difference between Avar despotism and small Slavic communities. According to this source, the Slavs are "without rulers and hate one another; they know nothing of tactics and do not attempt to fight in organized units." They live in "wooded and marshy areas of difficult access," raise livestock and cultivate millet, are hospitable and allow themselves "to be neither subjugated nor ruled." They are armed only with small javelins and wooden bows with small poisoned arrows. "Since there are many kings among them, always at odds with one another, it is not difficult to win over some of them by persuasion or by gifts ... and then to attack the others," recommends the treatise on warfare.[135]

This information surely goes back to the Roman offensives of the 590s against the Slavs on the lower Danube and is confirmed by Theophylact's accounts of these wars. The Slavs seldom faced a Roman army in pitched battle. They were masters at exploiting the terrain, and their numerous ambushes claimed a large number of victims. The Avars, too, came to know the dogged resistance of these "anarchic" Slavs.[136] After successful plundering they generally withdrew to their settlements, where they continued to live off their agrarian economy. Yet along the lower Danube the frequent wars and successful plundering raids had created the basis for the emergence of regional lordships. Dauritas, Ardagast, Peiragast, and others excelled as military leaders, even if their power was limited by tribal rights of participation, as Procopius and Menander point out.[137] At the height of their success, these Slavic leaders came close to the position of the military kings in the migration period, yet they lacked the Roman institutional context that had bolstered the position of Germanic warlords in previous centuries. Florin Curta has compared the development of the Gothic Tervingi north of the lower Danube in the fourth century with that of the Slavs in the sixth, in response to an active imperial frontier policy, and noticed important parallels.[138] However, these two stories continued very differently: Visigothic leaders and their armies made splendid careers in the imperial system and then carved out their realms within the Empire; Slavic groups uprooted it where they gained the upper hand.

The differentiation that better-informed Byzantines could establish between Avars and Slavs did not represent an ethnic boundary in the modern sense. John of Ephesus's lament over Slavs who had become rich and powerful, who now fought from horseback and had appropriated all the state-of-the-art techniques of war, shows that military success could change the traditional Slavic way of life.[139] It is likely that many Slav warriors made their careers in the Avar khaganate: "A Slav aristocrat, who had entered the Avar empire and had his status confirmed there, soon felt himself an Avar."[140] Through this Avarization of Slavic mounted warriors the old distinction between "Avar" cavalry and "Slavic" infantry was reconfirmed. The fuzziness that resulted from this continuous movement could make less well-informed contemporaries confound Avars and Slavs or lump them all together. Caution is also necessary in the "ethnic" interpretation of archaeological evidence. Not all Slavs traveled with a pot of the Prague type under their arm, and not every warrior with Avar equipment had assumed an Avar identity along with his arms and armor.[141]

Both the Byzantines and the Germanic-speaking neighbors perceived the Avars and Slavs above all as their enemies. For this reason they were primarily interested in the military aspect of the Avar–Slav relationship. The economic and cultural dimensions of life were not taken into consideration. Still, we hear twice of Avar demands for Slavs for tribute. In one instance it became a casus belli, when in the late 570s the Slavs of Dauritas killed an Avar envoy, who had come with a demand for tribute.[142] Fredegar also has something to say about Slavs paying tribute.[143] Modern researchers, schooled in legal history, have advanced numerous conjectures about the character of this tributary relationship.[144] Such speculations can only be based on general assumptions. Too little noted is the fact that two very different kinds of tribute obligations are in play. One form were symbolic contributions, through which the khagan would be recognized as supreme ruler. In this sense, the demand for tribute was a matter of prestige, and as such, it led to the contention with Dauritas's group. In that instance, the conflict was most likely over shares in the booty from the raids of the Danube Slavs. Symbolic levies of this kind repeatedly appear in negotiations between Avars and Byzantines.[145]

Another form of tribute was necessary in order to satisfy the basic needs of the Avar warrior elite: livestock or food supplies, everyday artisanal products, and the like. This chiefly concerned the agrarian groups that had settled in the vicinity of the Avars and those Slavs with whom Avar units were billeted over the winter, as Fredegar describes it. Our sources are almost entirely silent about the organization of this accommodation. Even archaeologists can only determine the traces of a population with an agrarian economy, whose work could complement the nomadic stock-raising economy, with which it would blend in the course of time.[146] In which kinds of social organization the Slavs and other sedentary groups provided the economic base for the Avar warrior society can scarcely be elucidated from the sources. But it may be assumed that the Slavic settlement became strategically important to the Avar military campaigns. Early ventures had repeatedly been compromised by supply difficulties, for instance in the war against the Franks in 566 and during the first siege of Thessalonica.[147] During later attacks on this city both the besiegers and the besieged could be provisioned by the local Slavic tribes.[148]

4.5 Avar Rule and Slavic Expansion

The old question of whether the Slavs advanced to most parts of eastern Europe on Avar orders, in flight before the Avars, or on their own initiative hardly makes sense. The sources do not even allow being more precise about the character and chronology of this expansion; its motivation cannot be established. Slavic expansion began before the Avar incursion and changed in the new political situation after 568. It is, however, striking how neatly the sphere of Avar activity coincides with the region into which the Slavs expanded. Nowhere did the khagan's troops go beyond the western boundary of Slavic migration. Unlike the Huns and Magyars, they left Bavaria and northern Italy almost untouched. Istria and Cividale, Aguntum and Lorch, Thuringia and the Elbe were the farthest goals of Avar armies as well as of Slavic settlers. Within these limits the decentralized Slavic advances into relatively closely delineated areas and the more massive Avar interventions were complementary. In the Balkans, Avar invasions and Slavic expansion also coincided to a considerable degree, with the possible exception of the Greek peninsula where the direct participation of the Avar army is questionable.

The politics of the khaganate in the west clearly promoted the advance of the Slavs. When Slavs were attacked, the Avar army intervened. The Bavarian host that marched into Noricum against the Slavs unexpectedly had to face the khagan's troops, and about two thousand Bavarians were reported dead.[149] At about the same time, around 596, the Avars again made their presence felt in distant Thuringia. The advance of Slavic settlement provided a welcome infrastructure to Avar rule and secured distant boundaries, particularly in mountainous areas. The khagan had acquired a monopoly as the protector of the Slavic settlers of central Europe. Therefore, Avar military presence had to be demonstrated not only to neighbors but above all to the Slavs who had expanded into frontier zones.

While the Slavs on the lower Danube advanced far into Byzantine territories, independently and in the wake of Avar military expeditions, the Slavs in the West only moved into some peripheral areas of the western kingdoms, mainly along the Elbe and in modern Carinthia and Slovenia, and did not engage much in raiding beyond that.[150] It was not until well after 626 that some minor expeditions into Friuli and some activities of Samo's Wends and of the Sorbs are traceable.[151] This corresponds to the khagan's policy of peace with regard to the great Western powers. The double objective, to keep the Slavs under control and to have free hand for the struggle against Byzantium, was achieved until 626. For this reason the Avars largely abstained from any offensive policy in the west and accommodated themselves to the gradual, small-scale Slavic activities.

The extent of actual control exerted over the Slavs in the periphery of the Avar Empire seems to have varied. North of the Carpathians Avar influence seems to have been relatively weak.[152] Further to the south, in Moravia and Bohemia, Slavic groups seem to have been drawn more closely into the magnetism of the Avar khaganate.[153] The same can be assumed for present-day Carinthia and Slovenia. In these regions a flourishing late antique civilization of the sixth century disappears from the written and archaeological record in the seventh; an impressive number of hillforts with stone churches were abandoned.[154] In Carinthia, direct Avar rule was to be replaced by the seventh-century *marca Vinedorum* and by eighth-century Carantania, the only emerging Slavic regional power in central Europe traceable in our sources at the time.[155] In the archaeological record, there are hardly any remains that could be ascribed to Avar warriors in the region. The traces of seventh-century Slavs in the Eastern Alps and in Slovenia are still rare, but that may in part be due to lacunas in research.[156] The material heritage of the Carantanians in the eighth century is relatively well documented. In Slovenia, sunken huts ascribed to the early Slavic period begin to appear in considerable numbers; dating still remains a problem with many of these early Slavic finds, and they may well be from the eighth century.[157] It is striking how completely many of the features of an established sixth-century Christian culture disappear in the seventh century in this region, as they do in many parts of the Balkan Peninsula. However, there are traces of some continuity in population: placenames derived from the name "Vlah," the Slavic form of the Germanic term for the Romans, indicate surviving indigenous groups, like elsewhere in the Eastern Alps. A Slovene word for "maid," *krščenica*, is derived from "Christian woman," which seems to indicate that surviving Christians had lower social status. It is unlikely that the previous population was "wiped out" by expanding Slavs.[158]

A somewhat similar picture emerges for western Illyricum, essentially the ancient Roman province of Dalmatia. The coastal cities of modern Dalmatia (a much narrower strip of land along the Adriatic coast than the ancient province) are a specific case, because in some of them urban life was maintained.[159] "The cultural habitus of the South Slavs reveals signs of continuity of the cultural habitus of the pre-Slavic population," as Danijel Dzino maintains, and more so in Dalmatia.[160] There is, again, a debate about dating. Cemeteries with relatively substantial grave goods along the Dalmatian coast and in some of the inland river valleys were traditionally defined as "Old Croat" and dated from the later seventh century onward.[161] However, Vladimir Sokol has challenged this view and argues for a beginning of this horizon as late as ca. 800, which seems too neatly tailored to the theory of late immigration of the Croats after the fall of the Avar Empire, implying an ethnic identification of these finds.[162] It is remarkable how rare the traces of cremation burials in large areas in southern Pannonia along the Sava and Drava rivers still are.[163] The relative lack of traces of the early Slavic population in many regions constitutes a major methodological problem. It can be partially explained by gaps in our research to which the often scant material remains of the Slavs have led, and occasionally even by a lack of interest in finding early Slavs. Clearly Slavs took the path to the afterlife less well equipped than was customarily the case among the Avars. North of the Danube Slavic cemeteries have often been identified by funerary urns of the "Prague type." Scholars such as Gabriel Fusek and Michał Parczewski have proposed highly sophisticated typologies of very simple handmade pottery.[164] However, the differences between coarse, locally made pottery can hardly be used as a supraregional ethnic indicator. The fact remains that in many regions, a "poor" culture appears in the sixth/seventh century, variously characterized by cremation, very simple pots, lack of foreign or more sophisticated finds, and/or sunken huts.[165] However, we can only attribute it to Slavs with reference to written sources that attest their presence in the regions in question. It is risky to date the archaeological evidence on the basis of the written record, because that could lead to circular arguments. Yet the very patchy material in most cases does not easily render chronological clues.[166] Gabriel Fusek has developed a sophisticated chronology for the early Slavic finds in modern Slovakia on the basis of the pottery, distinguishing between a first phase in the sixth century and a second phase in the first half of the seventh.[167] This is not readily transferable, though. In the core area of the khaganate, Slavs may also have used Avar-style inhumation. Beyond that area, Avar cultural influences are only slow to appear. The Carantanian elite in the eighth century used Avar and Byzantine prestige objects, among others, to enhance their status in burials.[168]

Western observers perceived the Avars and the Slavs as separate but mostly cooperating peoples. Clearly, more than in the case of the Balkan Slavs, much might be undertaken with the khagan, some things without him, but nothing against him. Where the Slavs appeared up to 626, the Avars were not far behind, be it in the Pustertal, at Cividale, in Istria, or (as it seems) in the conquest of Salona.

Only in the eighth century would the mountainous areas between Dalmatia and the Alps become defensive positions for the Slavs striving for secession from the Avar khaganate.

On the eastern fringes of Avar domination the opportunities and risks of raids into the empire exacerbated the Avar–Slav relationship. Avar power over the Slavs in present-day Wallachia was never overwhelming. Even Baian's grandly conceived expedition of 578 did not prevent the Ardagast group and others from further operating on their own account. The khagan clearly saw them all as subjects: he could order them to undertake attacks on imperial lands and help them when they were in trouble[169] or demand retribution when the Romans fought back. The discussion of whether the Slavs on the lower Danube were free or Avar subjects is a debate over words that are meaningless in the context of this flexible relationship.

In archaeological terms the predominantly Slavic population of present-day Wallachia in the sixth and seventh centuries is quite readily conceived, as illustrated by the great cemetery of Sărata Monteoru with about 1,500 urn graves, or the neighboring site of Pietroasele.[170] Romanian research has long taken pains to demonstrate Daco-Roman/Romanian continuity here, but apart from a few traces of Romans and Gepids in written sources, ethnic attributions hardly emerge from the archaeological evidence. Cultural goods similar to the Avar heartlands can be found in excavations along the lower Danube.[171] Many archaeological remains in the area can certainly be connected with the Slavs, although there is debate just how a Slavic identity is to be determined in archaeological terms. North of the lower Danube, the type of bow fibulae appears that Joachim Werner classed as "Slavic."[172] The generally modest remains, the predominance of cremation, and the dearth of grave goods obviously make an ethnic interpretation of the archaeological finds in Slavic settlement areas particularly difficult. What is striking is the absence of well-furnished warrior burials otherwise fairly common among early medieval barbarians, not least the Avars. The bow fibulae, however modest, could be regarded as a principal sign of status in graves.

The riches of the Slavic chieftains along the lower Danube only find expression in written sources. Toward 600 regional rulers and warlords had appeared who clearly were more prosperous than in other Slavic settlement areas. Presumably, the most active elements among the Slavs on the lower Danube were also the first to leave their homeland in order to seek their fortune in the Roman provinces. But successful raids in Roman provinces did not lead to the creation of stable centers of power, whether that was due to Avar and Byzantine repression or to inner resistance. In the seventh century there was not much more to be gained by the Slavs north of the Danube. The warrior aristocracy that had emerged under leaders such as Dauritas or Ardagast did not develop further. Asparukh's

Bulgars were the first to fully integrate the Slavs in the lower Danube region into a power that threatened the empire.

Slavic raids in the Balkan provinces are attested since the mid-sixth century; when Slavs began to settle there is still debated.[173] But there still is ample leeway for interpretation on the basis of the sources, as can be illustrated by one of the most important points of contention. The *Ecclesiastical History* of John of Ephesus, preserved in Michael the Syrian's text from the High Middle Ages, recounts the massive Slavic incursion at the time of the work's composition in the 580s, under which the Balkan provinces had to suffer for years.[174] Whether the invaders remained "until God drove them off," "as long as God will tolerate them," or whether they "withdrew by God's will" serves, according to the translation, as proof for or against a settlement about 580. John died in monastic confinement in the late 580s, that is, before the Slavic plunderers would have had the opportunity to put down firm roots. He is then little qualified to serve as chief witness for the question of permanent Slavic settlement.

As the recent discussion illustrates, the search for a precise date is fundamentally flawed. The Slavicization of great parts of Thrace and Illyria must be seen as a process, the stages of which can be arranged in only a rough chronology. Basically, we can only state which forms of the Slavic presence may have been plausible at a given time. The Roman *limes* on the Danube had never been an impenetrable defense line that could prevent greater or lesser groups of barbarians from crossing the river. Settling barbarian federates in thinly populated areas had been standard practice for the Roman authorities since 378. In the fifth century, Gothic and Hunnic raids, especially Attila's large-scale expeditions, led to demographic decline and loss of prosperity.[175] As the archaeological evidence suggests, the picture did not remain as bleak throughout, and there are clear signs of recovery in many regions in the sixth century. Barbarian immigrants surely contributed to resettlement.

For a long time the Roman provinces on the Danube displayed a rather variegated picture of half- or little-Romanized barbarians of every conceivable origin. Barbarians could live in Roman provinces as frontier troops or as farmers, like the peaceful *Gothi minores*. The barbarization of the *limes* zone was accentuated in the Justinianic period as a result of the increased need for troops of barbarian origin, who, as archaeological finds establish, were the dominant presence in the extensive system of forts on the frontier.[176] The Danube *limes* was indeed "a complex interface," as Florin Curta argues; it is no wonder that the Byzantines usually employed the word *mesitēs*, literally "intermediary," to designate this boundary.[177] Barbarian warriors sometimes also fought on their own account, alongside adventurous outsiders among the provincial population. Transitions were surely fluid among Roman soldiers, *scamarae* outlaws, and the plundering and invading barbarians of Slavic and other origin, of which the chroniclers write—"soldier and barbarian became identical notions in popular speech."[178] Skillful adventurers could in the course of their lives make their way under all three names.[179] From the mid-sixth century onward, the Justinianic plague sparked off another downward spiral in population numbers. In many remote and depopulated regions, farmers and herdsmen could move and settle down without encountering resistance. The chroniclers were not interested in such immigrants as long as they did not cause problems.

Therefore, it is possible that smaller Slavic groups already entered the empire as auxiliary soldiers or farmers since the mid-sixth century. A distinction should, however, be made: between large-scale plunderers and settlers. Those who settled down in depopulated regions were not necessarily the successful raiders. These often remained for years at a time in the target area and knew how to divest the flat lands systematically of their resources.[180] But, like Ardagast and his followers, the majority always crossed back over the Danube.[181] The Byzantine army was not always capable of preventing widespread plundering. Only occasionally was it in a position to deprive its opponents of their booty or undertake reprisal campaigns against the Slavic settlements north of the Danube.

Until 602 or even 610 it is, however, hard to imagine that a large armed Slavic group would settle permanently in imperial territory with its spoils and prisoners after a successful campaign. Otherwise, as the opponents of early Slavicization rightly argue, Maurice would scarcely have launched his preemptive attacks against the Slavs on the far side of the Danube. For Slavic warriors, after devastating a section of the country, immediately turning their swords into plowshares and peaceably going about their customary tasks would at least have required the Romans' agreement as long as the latter disposed of an intact army. Unlike with Goths and others in the late fourth and fifth centuries, we hear nothing of any en-bloc settlement of Slavic soldiers or farmers as organized groups under a treaty. On the other hand, it would hardly be surprising if Slavs settled in depopulated areas over the course of time. Increasing pressure on the provincials, the abandonment of Roman settlements, and the establishment of Slavic groups took effect more slowly than a direct expulsion but led to similar outcomes.

Evidence for the eventual withdrawal of the Romans from the interior of the peninsula increases toward the end of the sixth century, as in the adjacent areas of the Eastern Alps. In May 591 Pope Gregory I enjoined all Illyrian bishops still resident in their cities to receive their colleagues who had fled before the raging of war and sustain them. He thereby confirmed a *iussio* of the emperor communicated by the Illyrian prefect.[182] The administration still worked, and this was clearly conceived as a temporary measure. The insecure future of Illyricum posed some unusual problems. After the conquest of his city by enemies the bishop of Lissus/Lesh in present-day Albania had flown to Squillace in Calabria where the episcopal see was vacant. In July 592, Gregory permitted him to fulfill some pastoral duties. However, he reminded him that if, as was to be hoped, the situation at Lissus would return to normal, he would have to return to his old see; if the city remained "captive," he was to stay in his new diocese.[183] Most large cities, however, held out into the seventh century, as coin finds in Caričin Grad (Justiniana Prima) and Naissus/Niš illustrate.

Toward the end of the sixth century in Serdica/Sofia the aqueducts were still being extended. Excavations in Caričin Grad moreover show that the barbarization and decline of the city was a lengthy process: three-edged arrowheads and other pieces of steppe warrior equipment found among Byzantine pots, installation in decrepit buildings, the remains of settlement above fired layers, traces of stock keeping within the city, and other evidence of ruralization.[184] Much has been achieved, but archaeological research into the final phase of Byzantine culture and into the Slavic transformation in the Balkans does not yet project a clear picture. Dates given in publications are frequently based on interpretations of written sources and may lead to circular arguments.[185]

A kind of negative picture of the territorial space open to the Slavs can be drawn from Byzantine military operations and the resistance that they met. Until 602 the imperial field army fought repeatedly in Thrace and along the Danube frontier. The coastal cities could obtain reinforcements by sea. Centers such as Thessalonica and Salona disposed of troop contingents that were also capable of carrying out offensive operations (which, as became clear in the siege of Thessalonica in 586, could put the defense of these cities at risk).[186] In the Dalmatian interior in 595 the Romans had to limit themselves to following the khagan's army by roundabout ways and attacking his transport column. During that campaign, the Avars destroyed forty forts, which the Slavs had not accomplished so far.[187] In the previous year a Roman army had encountered six hundred Slavs who, after the conquest of three smaller cities, had carried off their plunder and prisoners with them in their carts. The decision to march on southward after the conquest of Scopi sealed the fate of these Slavic "Getes," as Theophylact calls them in historicizing terms.[188]

Archaeological evidence indicates that after the damages in the 580s, many of the *limes* forts were repaired. Even 602–3, when the Persian war started up again, and the civil war between Phocas and Heraclius in 610 did not mark the end of Byzantine presence in the Balkans. However, after the Persian occupation of many oriental provinces, Byzantine troops were increasingly moved to the eastern front, and the defense system in the Balkans crumbled. Now Slavic raiders could settle down, and settlers start to conquer. The Slavs who laid siege to Thessalonica in 615 brought their families and possessions with them, presumably with the intention of settling.[189] Without a Roman army having been able to protect them, the last fortresses on the Danube *limes* fell.[190] There are hardly traces of Slavs settling in conquered Roman forts; in some cases, remains of a Roman population seem to have stayed on for a while.[191] At around the same time, the great inland cities of Serdica and Naissus fell. Roman armies ceased to operate outside the environs of the coastal centers Constantinople and Thessalonica.

In the course of the seventh century Slavic settlers in some areas gradually became affiliated with the Roman social and legal organization. A regional Slavic entity under the leadership of its prince at least theoretically accountable to the emperor is called a *sklavinía* in the sources.[192] In the course of the seventh century, new regional Slavic entities formed, whose names are quite characteristically derived from territorial and rarely from tribal designations.[193] By 670, Perbund, the king of the Strymones, was thoroughly Hellenized. He dressed in the Byzantine manner and spoke excellent Greek. Not until this order of things was established did the unmanageable "masses of Slavs" become susceptible to naming and differentiation by the Byzantine observers. Avars and Byzantines, later also the Danube Bulgars, competed to organize the Slavs in their own best interests, as far as they could. The wide-ranging expansion of Slavic settlement was reached without constructing large-scale polities.

4.6 Becoming Slavs

How can the success of the Slavs be explained? Slavic expansion followed rather different patterns from previous "barbarians" who had won control over Roman provinces. Before their migrations the Germans had been at the focal point of Roman foreign policy and under the influence of ancient civilization for hundreds of years. Their subsequent spectacular successes are explained by highly specialized warfare and centralization under powerful kings and military leaders. However, eventually most of their kingdoms collapsed. The long-term shifts in population that resulted from the migrations to western Europe and some Mediterranean regions were limited: speakers of Germanic languages extended their settlement areas a few hundred kilometers south of the upper Danube and east of the Rhine and to England, while they gave up the lands east of the Elbe. The Slavs hardly possessed comparable forms of organization that could be adapted to the needs and opportunities of late Roman society. They were only perceived by authors in Constantinople in the middle of the sixth century. Yet, in the course of a few generations, they spread over most of eastern

Europe, from the Baltic to the Aegean and from the Eastern Alps to the forests of Russia. And they were there to stay.

Slavic expansion has been one of the most heavily ideologized topics since the nineteenth century, given that it concerns the national origins of about a dozen modern nations. Yet a conventional model of a migration of peoples and a purely ethnic perspective can scarcely explain how half of Europe was Slavicized in a relatively brief period. The decline of the Roman order and the retreat or dispersion of groups that were oriented toward it created space not only for immigrants but also for new social and economic developments. Much of this would not be considered progress in the modern sense, for example, the obvious decrease in the social division of labor and cultural production. Yet this was not a simple relapse into barbarism. For example, in southeastern Europe the lighter earth-turning plow, which permitted the effective exploitation of smaller lots, established itself only in the centuries after the collapse of Byzantine rule.[194]

Sixth-century authors already emphasized the great numbers that assured the success of the Slavs, or rather, underlined the vast thinly populated countries that they possessed.[195] Procopius stressed the unusual cruelty of Slavic raiders, who not only killed the men and took women and children into slavery, but slew all their prisoners, and sometimes with particularly unpleasant methods.[196] However, later sources mention that Slavs sold back all their captives, or even let them live among them in freedom,[197] so their success can hardly be explained by the ruthless extermination of previous settlers. As we have seen above (section 4.1), the different explanations of their origin by Procopius and Jordanes are not tailored to explaining their large numbers either.

A different explanation for the spread of the Slavs was proposed in a paper published at the end of 2016: a rare genetic defect that is mostly confined to Slavic populations was used to hypothesize that a "genetic reproductive edge may have boosted Slavic expansions."[198] Twenty-four samples from the Czech Republic of patients with the NBS syndrome, which carries an increased cancer risk but higher fertility, were at the basis of this theory. It is likely that with the swift progress of genetics, more and perhaps also more substantial hypotheses of this type will emerge. That is an uncomfortable perspective if one considers the circumstances and the political impact of nineteenth- to twentieth-century biological definitions of national and racial affiliations and should be met with well-informed critique.[199] We should be skeptical against such offhand assumptions of a distant biological origin of "the Slavs." Ancient DNA from early Slavic milieus will, of course, be hard to get because of the diffused practice of cremation.

To assess how far Slavs had actually spread before the arrival of the Avars, and how far they got in the last third of the sixth century, we first need to be aware of how fast the perceptions of Slavic presence spread. As shown above, information about the Slavs was first written down in Constantinople, mainly by Procopius and Jordanes around 550. They regarded Slavic attacks on the Balkan provinces from north of the lower Danube. Slavs north of the Carpathians also emerge relatively clearly several times, especially as neighbors of the Gepids whose land they had to cross after a raid in imperial territory.[200] About a decade later, the *Erotapokriseis* by the so-called Pseudo-Caesarius locates the savage Slavs close to the peaceful inhabitants along the Danube in the context of a discussion of the theory of climates.[201] Otherwise, not much appears in Byzantine sources in the 560s and 570s: Agathias only refers to one Slavic soldier in the Byzantine army during the siege of a fort in Lazica.[202] Malalas, unlike Agathias, mentions their participation in the great Cutrigur attack on the periphery of Constantinople in 558/59.[203] Both Agathias and Malalas use the shorter name form *Sklaboi*, which may well have been a Constantinopolitan simplification of *Sklabēnoi*, which was closer to the Slavic name form.[204] Slavs are not mentioned in the panegyric by Corippus. Yet in the course of the later sixth century, they returned very much on the agenda and are featured prominently in the fragments of Menander, in the final chapters of John of Ephesus, in the *Strategicon* of Maurice, in the *Miracula S. Demetrii*, and, of course, in the *Chronicle* of Theophylact Simocatta. By now, the concern was more and more with Slavs as enemies in the Balkan provinces, who could come from their autonomous settlements north of the lower Danube or march along in Avar armies. The impression is that under Avar rule, large groups had been settled in the Carpathian Basin.[205]

In the Latin West, it took much longer to take notice of the Slavs. Most sixth-century authors do not mention them, most notably Gregory of Tours in his *Histories*, written in the 590s. As we have seen, Pope Gregory I refers to them in his letters. However, initially he only speaks of "enemies" or "barbarians"; only in 599 and 600, after receiving the information from the exarch, does he call them Slavs.[206] In fact, the earliest Western reference to Slavs is found in the epitaph of Archbishop Martin of Bracara (modern-day Braga in Portugal) composed in about 570, which lists the Slavs along with Rugians, Pannonians, and Dacians as peoples of his old homeland, Pannonia. Martin had not necessarily picked up the name in his childhood in Pannonia, but rather in Constantinople on his pilgrimage to Jerusalem.[207] The earliest historian in the West who speaks of Slavs is John of Biclaro in Spain, who wrote in 590; he had spent many years in Constantinople, probably from 559 to 576.[208] Isidore of Seville later mentions them once in his *Chronicle*, but not among the many peoples listed in his *Etymologies*.[209] So far, these are hardly Western perceptions, but Byzantine ones; curiously, Slavs are mentioned most consistently in distant Spain. An indirect Italian attestation of early seventh-century perceptions of Slavs is found in Paul the Deacon's late eighth-century history of the Lombards. For the time around 600, he relied on the lost *Historiola* by Secundus of Trento, Queen Theodelinda's adviser. The two earliest mentions regard conflicts between Bavarians and Slavs, one that can be dated to ca. 592, and the other to ca. 595.[210] Theodelinda came from Bavaria and was surely well informed about its fortunes; Slavs were getting close, a fact surely also noticed at Trento. A later passage that can be traced to Secundus refers to a joint attack on Istria by Avars, Slavs, and Lombards in ca. 602.[211] For traces of Slavs in Frankish sources, we have to wait for seventh-century missionary hagiography. In the first book of the *Life of Saint Columbanus*, written in ca. 640, Jonas of Bobbio recounts how the saint planned to travel to the lands of the *Venetii* "who are also Slavs" to evangelize them. Then an angel appeared to him with a map, showing him that this whole part of the world had to remain deserted, because the people was not yet ready for the faith.[212]

What we get in the sixth-century Greek and Latin sources on the Slavs is thus very much a view from Constantinople. They obviously rely on good information and on recently established identifications for a type of enemy that was very unfamiliar, did not correspond with established stereotypes, and was therefore hard to come to terms with. Western observers initially got their patchy information on the Slavs, if at all, from Byzantium. They had noticed the Avar presence in Pannonia and mostly labeled them with the familiar name "Huns," being content as long as they did not constitute much of a threat. They did not class the Slavs as an analogous ethnic-political group. They were either subsumed under the Avars or vaguely described as barbarians. Only in the so-called *Chronicle of Fredegar*, compiled in the last third of the seventh century, do we get a fully developed perception of the Winedi, as he calls the Slavs. This is the first time that the Germanic name appears in the West. Two explanations for the slow perception of Slavs in the West are possible: either the low-threshold displays of Slavic power did not make their ethnic identity immediately obvious, or Slavic identity was slow to emerge in the western fringes of the Avar Empire, and one first had to learn from the Byzantines how the new neighbors and enemies were to be called.

Both options are equally plausible and not necessarily alternatives, and may rather have formed a continuum of emerging identifications. However, they indicate that we should not take the label "Slavs" for granted in the sixth and even early seventh century in those contexts where the sources do not use it routinely. The methodological principle to be maintained in research about early Slavs therefore is this: historical, archaeological, and philological data should be interpreted on their own terms and not used to fill the gaps in the evidence in the other disciplines. It may also be useful to distinguish between several uses of the ethnonym "Slavs." First, in literary sources it served as a Byzantine classification of a type of enemy that could be distinguished by its rudimentary social organization, way of fighting largely on foot and without sophisticated equipment, and stubborn resistance to subjugation and integration; this "ideal type" of Slavs is best expressed in the *Strategicon* of Maurice.[213] In fact, behind this "ideal type" there are quite a number of ways in which Slavs can be represented in the sources: anarchic or ruled by a king, expert warriors or peasants who hide in endless forests when they are attacked. Second, linguists conceive of Slavs as speakers of the Common Slavic language, as far as that can be reconstructed in the earliest period. Third, a simple lifestyle can be grasped by archaeologists in many regions through coarse pottery, cremation burials, and sunken huts, or sometimes not at all. The people who lived more or less according to this model in a vast, thinly populated zone in eastern Europe were only gradually perceived by their neighbors as "Slavs" (or "Wends"). Fourth are self-identified Slavs, a category that takes us deep into the realms of hypothesis and speculation. And fifth, there are generalizing assessments by modern scholars. Researchers have long become accustomed to labeling the entire population from the Baltic to the Aegean, as far as it did not belong to any of the more obvious peoples, "Slavs." That was the result of amalgamating the other levels and of trying hard to fill the gaps with hypotheses.

Basically, the methodological caveats are the same as with other barbarians of late Antiquity or the early Middle Ages. I have proposed to assess ethnic identities as the result of circuits of identification, which consisted of acts of identification of individuals with an (ethnic) group, of the symbolic identification of the group as such, and of outside perceptions. If there is sufficient interaction on these levels, and an overlap in these modes of identification, the existence of an ethnic identity can be assumed.[214] With Goths, Franks, or Lombards in Roman lands there are good reasons to believe that they were to an extent self-defined groups. We have some evidence for all three modes of identification and can roughly delineate the ethnic and the political boundaries between these groups. With the earliest Slavs, at least with those beyond the limelight of sixth- and seventh-century Byzantine texts, there is hardly any evidence to make even an informed guess. What is striking is the almost complete absence of any trace of collective self-identification or of the representation of Slavic rulership until the eighth century or, in many regions, even later. Only eventually do the written record, language, and archaeological evidence converge, and the first traces of self-identification appear. For tenth- to early twelfth-century texts such as the *Chronicle of Monemvasia*, Constantine Porphyrogenitus's *De administrando imperio*, the *Russian Primary Chronicle*, or the *Chronicle* of Cosmas of Prague, there was no question who the Slavs were. Looking back from a world of Slavs around the turn of the millennium to their beginnings, it must have seemed quite likely that these people had always been Slavs, lived like Slavs, and spoken the Slavic language. For us, it is hard to tell what the rhythms of their outward and inward Slavicization were.

All we can safely say is that in our early sources, the names "Slavs" and "Wends" spread as outside designations. Our earliest witnesses from the west, John of Biclaro and Pope Gregory the Great, may never have seen a Slav; Gregory knew the name of these obscure enemies from a letter of the exarch. Western observers were surprisingly late in defining the new and puzzling reality in eastern Europe with ethnic terms, given that this was the cognitive principle in which they habitually established broad distinctions in their political world. Even the wholesale Germanic outside designation "Wends" was slow to catch on; it was only clearly established at the time of Fredegar, in the later seventh century. We may still use "Slavs" as a general label for the agricultural population in all the countries that the Avars had once laid their hands on, and a bit beyond that. However, we need to be aware that these were not necessarily full-fledged Slavs in the sixth or seventh centuries. It was rather a matter of "becoming Slavs," as Danijel Dzino has put it. In the seventh century, he argues, "they shared a common cultural habitus but had no sense of a common identity."[215] At the same time, we need to be aware of the regional differences in this cultural habitus: the emerging Slavic world may be united by the relative simplicity of the material remains, but not always by particular types of simple cultural manifestations.

Why did they become Slavs in so many regions with widely different conditions and contexts? What I argued in the 1988 edition of this book was that their simple lifestyle may have been one secret of their success. A people can become numerous only when its ways of life and its social organization correspond well to external conditions. That was obviously the case with the Slavs. A simple but very adaptable mixed rural economy made it possible to settle ravaged or uncultivated swathes of land between the Baltic and the Aegean.[216] "Hi paludes silvasque pro civitatibus habent," as settlements they have the marshes and forests, as Jordanes describes their preference for remote settlement areas, which led to the opening up of new spaces for cultivation.[217] Production in the rural economy of vast parts of eastern Europe had declined severely, and the population had also dwindled in many regions because of the Justinianic plague. The basic agricultural population that had for centuries endured and provisioned armies of all kinds was greatly reduced in numbers. The high degree of centralization and militarization of the Gothic peoples had come as a direct challenge to the power of Byzantium, but in the long run prevented their lasting establishment in eastern Roman provinces. The provisioning problems of numerous warriors and the strong competition among the invading peoples had made most of these highly specialized economies of plunder hard to sustain.

Early Slavic communities, on the other hand, were self-sufficient and did not permit a permanent centralization or the consolidation of military kingship. "They are . . . independent, absolutely refusing to be enslaved or governed, least of all in their own lands," as the *Strategicon* describes this form of organization. "Owing to their lack of government and their ill feeling toward one another they are not acquainted with an order of battle."[218] And the so-called Pseudo-Caesarius claims that the Slavs often killed their leaders, "sometimes on feasts, sometimes on travels."[219] These statements have been regarded as a "well-worn topos."[220] Yet it is a phenomenon well known in anthropology. The French ethnologist Pierre Clastres has called this principle "societies against the state," describing the sophisticated mechanisms that in various tribal societies could hinder the consolidation of rulership.[221] And James C. Scott has taken the example of Zomia, the highlands between Southeast Asia and China, as an example of "the art of not being governed."[222] In fact, the topos about the early Slavs was well chosen. Although Slavs had to succumb to Avars and later to Bulgars, it took centuries until something like a Slavic state could develop. Until the ninth century, few Slavic "peoples" (with the exception of the Antes) or major tribes emerged.

The decentralized organization, the dispersed style of life, and the preference for less accessible, forested and marshy areas made enemy attacks difficult, as the *Strategicon* and Theophylact's battle accounts illustrate.[223] In addition, Slavic communities could react flexibly to every threat to its members. The Byzantine manual on warfare warns that with attacks on a village or a tribe, one always had to reckon with the intervention of neighbors.[224] This reaction is shown to good effect in the course of the Perbund affair, when the poor treatment of a tribal leader mobilized a broad Slavic coalition against Thessalonica.[225] Slavic armies also received reinforcements during successful plundering but could just as easily split up again.[226] All of this shows that local Slavic groups did communicate with each other when necessity arose. However, joint actions of Slavic warriors were temporary. During the first siege of Thessalonica serious internal conflicts arose after the first week.[227] The *Strategicon* counsels playing Slavic princes off against one another.[228]

That does not mean that early Slavic society was necessarily static. The Slavic principalities that emerged on the lower Danube in the last third of the sixth century could regularly mobilize considerable military potential and became players in the difficult political field of tension between Byzantium and the Avars. Some recognizable leaders emerged, such as Dauritas, Ardagast, Peiragast, or Musucius. Still, the Byzantines had to hope for defectors to gather intelligence about them, such as the Christian Gepid who informed them about Musucius. It was obviously difficult to extract relevant information from the

Slavs: "Alexander enquired by interrogation what was the captives' race; but the barbarians ... declared that they welcomed tortures, disposing the agonies of the lash about the body as if it were another's. But the Gepid described everything and revealed events in detail."[229] This Gepid was also the informant who disclosed that Musucius "was called *rex* in the barbarian tongue." Gothic **rik* was related to Latin *rex* and meant "prince," "king." Therefore, we should not put too much weight on Gepid's use of the title *rex* for a Slav leader, rather unusual at the time.[230] In fact, the Byzantine sources use a great variety of terms to describe Slavic leaders: *phylarchos, archon, exarchos, ēgemōn, taxiarchos, ethnarchos.*[231] Only in the seventh century did *reges* appear in the Byzantine *sclavinias* of Macedonia and became stable partners of the empire. The Franks called Slavic leaders beyond their borders *duces*. Samo's Frankish-inspired overlordship was the first to comprise a larger unit, but his royal position remained an episode.[232] Florin Curta has drawn on anthropological models by Marshall Sahlins and Maurice Godelier to distinguish between "great men," "big men," and chiefs among the Slavs.[233] As far as this is based on observations of their actions and of their room to move, this can be useful; unfortunately, the Greek titles do not help much, for we cannot assume a clear conception of Slavic hierarchy behind them. The Romans had soon learned the title of the Avar khagan, and they could translate Gothic *rik, reiks* into Greek and Latin, but they did not know which titles the early Slavs used. We have a similar problem, because written Slavic languages mostly used loanwords for their leaders. Among the earliest Germanic loanwords, there is **kuningu/knjez*, prince, from *kuninc*, king (already available at the time of Ardagast and Musucius), which was later supplemented by *kral*, king, derived from Charlemagne's name. Gothic *rik* was not adopted in Slavic, unlike some basic terms such as bread, kettle, donkey, and "to buy."[234] In the seventh to eleventh centuries, Turco-Bulgaric words for lord, nobleman, strong man, and dignity/rank came into Old Russian and/or Old Church Slavonic.[235] Only *wladyka*, the elder, has a Slavic root. The largely imported terms for offices and hierarchy fit in well with all the stories we hear about imported leaders: Chilbudios, Hildigis, Samo, and others.[236]

There may have been a similar logic at work behind social differentiation in the frontier societies of the north-Danubian Tervingi/Visigoths in the fourth century and the sixth-century Slavs in the same area, but there are also important differences.[237] The fifth-century history of the Visigoths differed fundamentally from that of the Slavs in the seventh. Visigothic kings with their armies marched through Roman provinces until they reached a negotiated settlement, which guaranteed their privileged position in the Roman system and their maintenance by taxes and rents. Nothing of the sort happened to Slavic settlers between Thrace and Noricum; they contributed to destroying the Roman infrastructure that they might otherwise have exploited. How can we explain this difference?

A number of distinguishable factors were already at work in the sixth century. Some were due to the changes in the Balkan provinces, which made integration more difficult. The Roman *limes* and the military units deployed there had always depended on massive transfers from the imperial budget; these transfers had often also created considerable prosperity in the region where they were spent. It seems that Justinian's fortification program could not achieve a similar balance between the centrally subsidized building program and regional productivity. In many regions in the Balkan Peninsula, the thinly populated countryside could not carry the weight of the expenses of the state apparatus and the costs of defense.[238] Another important element was the changed political landscape of the sixth century. It was hard for emerging Slavic principalities to stand their own in the tension field between the Avar and the Byzantine Empires. The Avars tolerated and to an extent even encouraged the rise of manageable Slavic units and regional power centers, but they struck hard at possible competitors (such as Dauritas or the Antes). Their military expeditions impoverished the provinces in which Slavs were about to settle. The Byzantines treated the Slavs rather differently from the way they had dealt with Goths and other Germanic peoples. Military conflict, even early in the fourth century, was usually ended by negotiations and treaties, which does not seem to have been the usual practice with Slavs. As a next step, Gothic groups and even Gothic units under their own leaders were integrated into the Roman army as regular troops or federates. We have repeated attestations of Slavic soldiers in Byzantine armies in Procopius or Agathias, but no evidence for careers of Slavic officers, in contrast to the spectacular rise of Gothic commanders in the Roman army of the fourth and fifth centuries.[239] This was not only the Slavs' fault but may also have resulted from the experience of the dissolution of the Western Empire, which sixth-century Byzantine policy strove to avoid in the hinterland of the capital. The most successful Slavic leaders, such as Ardagast, were the priority targets of Byzantine counterattacks; no attempt was made to win them over, as was done with Lombard dukes almost immediately after the Lombard conquest of parts of Italy.

Yet there was a Slavic side to this history of failed integration; it does not seem that the Slavs sought the type of privileged (but, in the day of Justinian, also precarious) warrior status in a late Roman society that Goths or Lombards had achieved. There were Slavs along the sixth-century Danube who could have profited from such an arrangement. The Slavic princes on the lower Danube did have a certain retinue. Even the insubordinate Dauritas did not respond to the Avar envoys on his own, but together with the *hegemones* of his tribe.[240] Yet there was no specialized warrior caste that as among other migratory peoples, lived off the production of others. There are signs of long-distance exchange, as with the bow fibulae and a few amphorae found north of the lower Danube.[241] By comparison with contemporary cemeteries in many other barbarian regions in Europe, the evidence is poor, and all the more if we compare it with sixth- to seventh-century graves from the Avar realm, some of which are strikingly rich.[242] Early Slavic society did not invest much in objects that would accompany the deceased to the netherworld; mostly a simple pot for the ash was considered enough. Neither did the early Slavs seem to care to appease the gods by lasting signs of their devotion, or to safeguard the memories of their leaders and their communities by signs that remained visible. Slavic communities also proved surprisingly immune to the temptations and luxuries of the Roman world that other barbarians strove hard to achieve and that the Avar khagan so liberally allowed his envoys to explore. As our written sources narrow down to a trickle after 602, we do not know what happened to the social differentiation that was under way among the Slavic raiders of the late sixth century. Could it have kept its momentum? At the present state of the evidence, it is at least safe to say that it did not spread with Slavic expansion. A more than rudimentary material culture is only found in some fringe areas of Slavic settlement, for instance in Dalmatia and Albania, and in parts of Greece, but often of insecure date and interpretation.[243]

Marked differences in social status are not only relatively rare and unstable among the leading groups in Slavic society; low-status groups also hardly become apparent in the late sixth century. Unlike under Avar rule, it does not seem to have been customary to enslave prisoners. The human spoils were either killed immediately or, preferably, sold.[244] They were hardly settled on land as subjects, as among the Avars and Bulgars. "They do not keep those who are among them in perpetual slavery, as do other nations. But they set a definite period of time for them and then give them the chance either, if they so desire, to return to their own homes with a small recompense or to remain there as free men and friends," the *Strategicon* maintains.[245] This was scarcely a question of hospitality, as Beševliev would have it.[246] "The need to turn prisoners of war into servants hardly occurs under simple economic conditions." This is how Wenskus interpreted the recommendations of the treatise on warfare.[247]

The information in the *Strategicon* contains a valuable clue to explaining the rapid Slavicization of large stretches of land. Whereas courage in war was the only way to social advancement among the Hunnic and Gothic peoples, among the Slavs a farmer could live as a free man. This openness made it attractive for many modest Romans and barbarians to live as Slavs. This is illustrated by a warning in the manual on warfare: "The so-called refugees who are ordered to point out the roads and furnish certain information must be very closely watched. Even some Romans have given in to the times, forget their own people, and prefer to gain the good will of the enemy. Those who remain loyal ought to be rewarded, and the evildoers punished."[248] In a time when wide segments of the population no longer had many reasons to defend their Romanness, the Slavicization of the Balkan provinces was not simply the replacement of one people by another. Many provincials who had worked the land under unfavorable conditions may have "forgotten" their Roman identity to become free Slavs, without obligation to pay taxes or rents.

To underline the relatively low degree of social differentiation among early Slavs risks affirming the old stereotype of ancient Slavic democracy, or primitivity, and lock the perception of the early Slavs in images of Otherness as they were already proposed by Herder. Pristine Slavic democracy was praised by the founding fathers of Slavic national history in the nineteenth century, Palacký and Šafařík, to distinguish them from the autocratic Germans.[249] In the twentieth century, Marxist historiography developed the model of military democracy, which should help to gloss over the apparent problems to construct a direct transition from ancient slave-holding societies to feudalism.[250] The problem was that this could not be consistently argued as a mode of production within the parameters of historical materialism. My explanation for Slavic expansion in the 1988 book was sometimes criticized as just another adaptation of the democracy model.[251] However, "democracy" and "egalitarianism" are not the point; it is just that a conceptual difference needs to be made from the much more hierarchical post-Roman societies in the West, let alone Byzantium. Florin Curta has also objected to my use of the term "segmentary society" by polemicizing against the anthropological model of "segmentary lineage" and arguing that our sources cannot prove the existence of any lineage structure among the early Slavs; I had not claimed that at all.[252]

Whether early Slavic societies were technically segmentary or not, and regardless of the Slavic great men, big men, chiefs, or kings that emerged somewhere at some point, the puzzling fact is that the Slavicization of much of eastern and central Europe can in no way be explained by the success of Slavic leaders and by the expansion of Slavic polities, as was the case in the post-Roman West. My argument is that the habitus of being Slavs did not spread in spite of their simple material culture and relatively undifferentiated society, but because of it. Perhaps that did not happen because the Slavs were so different from others, but because whoever lived differently from the hegemonial cultural models of late Antiquity became a Slav in the course of time. The way of life that Byzantine and later also Western sources described as Slavic offered an alternative to the hierarchic late Roman societies, where to produce also meant paying heavy taxes and dues. This explanation has the advantage of reducing the weight of the ethnic and of the military factors in the expansion of the Slavs, which are often exaggerated, and of providing space for an economic and a cultural dimension of the process. As I see it, ethnicity was not the precondition or the driving force of the "obscure progression" of the Slavs; rather (and here I agree with Florin Curta), it was the result.

Slavic expansion was boosted by a series of opportunities. First, the ambitious warrior elites that lived north of the Carpathians until the fourth century (for instance, the Vandals) all moved south and created space for other types of communities. Groups of Slavic speakers must have been instrumental for that change; it is fruitless to debate whether these were Slavs, Slaves-avant-les-Slaves, Proto-Slavs, or no Slavs at all. Second, Justinian's policy to concentrate his considerable military potential in the wars in the West and against the Persians, and to rely on fortifications in the Balkan provinces, meant that relatively small Slavic units, from a few hundred upward, had a chance to plunder the countryside and attack small forts. The self-awareness of being Slavs may have been stimulated by the confrontation with the Byzantine Empire.[253] Third, the Slavs were very useful to the Avars by providing basic food and commodities, labor and services, and on top of that, specialized military support when necessary. As a low-status group that was locally rooted but widely connected, they had the opportunity of incorporating other low-status groups. And fourth, the eventual collapse of the Roman order removed the pressure that had kept a very hierarchical system in place that was based on the sophisticated exploitation of agricultural labor. Massive Avar attacks and insistent Slavic raids had precipitated its fall but could not have had that result without an inner dynamic that successively made the Roman order ever harder to maintain. Extensive social spaces emerged that could accommodate a very different lifestyle. The neighbors learned, sooner or later, that these were the Slavs, and variously projected images of savagery or bucolic simplicity on them. At what points which of these unsophisticated settlers learned that they were "Slavs," and whether they learned it from these neighbors or from each other, is hard to tell. In any case, it was a label that stuck, and it stuck much better than the label "Germani" for the new military elites in the West, a label that largely disappeared in the fifth century.[254]

Politics on the grand scale, as conducted by the Goths, Lombards, or Avars, impressed contemporaries as it does modern historians. Yet the very success of these highly specialized warrior castes, and the social polarization that their policy entailed, over time consumed their own foundations. The Slavs of the sixth or seventh centuries produced no Theoderic, but they were also spared a Teja. The many small entities that they formed were inferior to both their barbarian and imperial competitors in a direct confrontation, yet they were more resilient and had a good chance of outliving them all.

THE BALKAN WARS OF
MAURICE, 591–602

The 580s had brought a number of devastating Avar attacks that the Byzantines, engaged in the Persian war, were hardly able to control. The wars went on in the 590s on an almost yearly basis, but victory and defeat were now more evenly distributed. Again, Theophylact's often detailed narrative provides us with some valuable information on the ways in which the Avars organized their raids into the Balkan provinces.

5.1 Maurice's Campaign and the Date of the Wars

"At this time the Avars, who fought against the Romans, were turned away more by gold than by iron." This laconic assessment of Maurice's rule was penned in distant Spain in the *Chronicle* of Isidore of Seville.[1] The chronicler's judgment perhaps reflects the outcome and not the emperor's efforts. The Balkan front seldom stood so squarely at the center of interest as during the last decade of his reign. Since the end of the Persian war of 591–92, the greater part of the Roman army was concentrated here.[2] In the history of Theophylact Simocatta, which depicts Maurice's rule in eight books, the Balkan wars dominate the stage.

The Egyptian Theophylact, who wrote after 628, about one generation after the events, hardly possessed the knowledge and overview of his model, Menander. Book 6 about the Balkan wars of the 590s in particular has been called "a welter of mismatched material from different sources."[3] However, Theophylact

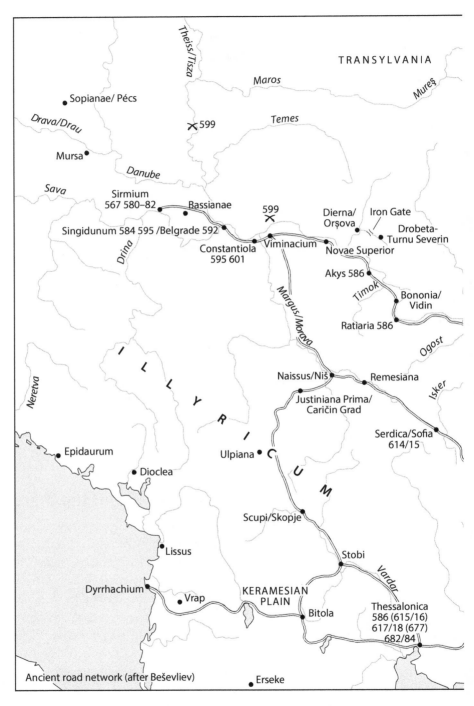

MAP 3. The Avar-Byzantine Wars on the Balkan Peninsula

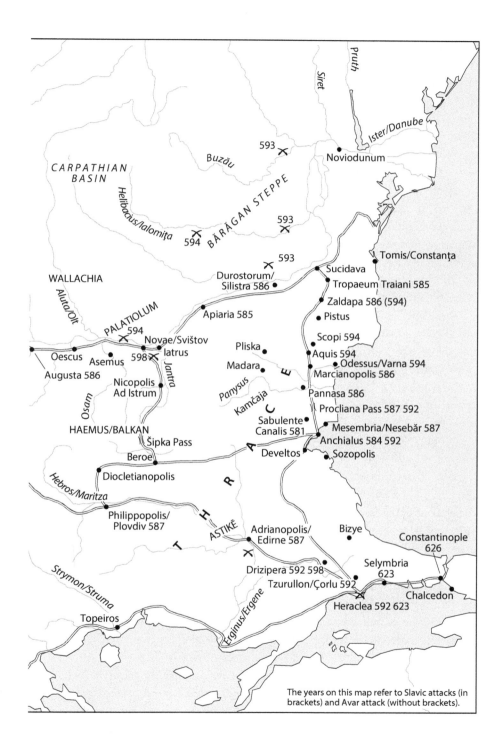

The years on this map refer to Slavic attacks (in brackets) and Avar attack (without brackets).

Labels on the map:

pruth

Siret

Ister/Danube

593

Noviodunum

CARPATHIAN BASIN

Buzău

BĂRĂGAN STEPPE

Helibacus/Ialomiţa

594

593

593

Tomis/Constanţa

WALLACHIA

Durostorum/Silistra 586

Sucidava

Tropaeum Traiani 585

Zaldapa 586 (594)

Aluta/Olt

Apiaria 585

Pistus

PALATIOLUM

594

Novae/Svištov

Iatrus

Pliska

Scopi 594

Aquis 594

Odessus/Varna 594

Oescus

Asemus

598

Madara

Marcianopolis 586

Augusta 586

Osam

Nicopolis Ad Istrum

Jantra

Panysus

Pannasa 586

Kamčaja

Procliana Pass 587 592

HAEMUS/BALKAN

Sabulente Canalis 581

Mesembria/Nesebăr 587

Šipka Pass

Anchialus 584 592

Beroe

Develtos

Sozopolis

Diocletianopolis

Hebros/Maritza

Philippopolis/Plovdiv 587

ASTIKĒ

Bizye

Constantinople 626

Adrianopolis/Edirne 587

Strymon/Struma

Drizipera 592 598

Selymbria 623

Chalcedon

Tzurullon/Çorlu 592

Erginus/Ergene

Topeiros

Heraclea 592 623

THRACE

had excellent sources at his disposal, and in the rare cases where we can check the information it seems accurate. For the 590s, he most likely relied on some kind of campaign log reworked under Phocas to underline the achievements of those generals who had shifted their allegiance to the usurper, and the faults of those who had not, such as Comentiolus or the emperor's brother Peter. The often minute narratives are mostly summarized in a few sentences in modern accounts.[4] However, few chroniclers of late Antiquity have depicted the barbarian wars of their time with so few illusions as Theophylact. The miserliness of the emperor, the cowardice of his commanders, the rebelliousness of the troops, and the distrust of the population all contributed, as he shows, to finally bringing the years-long efforts of the Byzantines to naught. Opponents became increasingly similar to one another. "Barbarians" fought on both sides; the khagan at times reacted more humanely than the Christian emperor and his generals. A sense of futility emerges from the narrative; in spite of all the efforts of the Byzantine army, the future of the Balkan provinces was not decided on the battlefield.

There are further grounds for historians' difficulties with Theophylact. The individual campaigns are difficult to date. The author himself probably did not always know the precise dates when he was organizing his material. In the ninth century Theophanes divided the events recounted by Theophylact fairly arbitrarily among separate years.[5] The modern historian is little wiser. The one incontrovertible fact is that with the fall of Maurice in November 602 the war was over. Theophylact also states when the emperor's offensives began. But his chronological references contradict one another. He writes that at the end of the Persian War, the emperor deployed his troops to the Balkans in order to drive back the Avars and Slavs. The peace with Chosroes II was most likely struck in the fall of 591.[6] This is contradicted by another of Theophylact's statements, to the effect that the transfer of troops occurred in the ninth year of the emperor's rule, that is, between August 590 and August 591. Another fixed point of reference is offered by the solar eclipse that the emperor is supposed to have observed after his departure from the capital to Thrace in Theophylact's narrative. Unfortunately, the sun was darkened twice during the period in question, on October 4, 590, and on March 19, 592.[7] Lastly, an embassy from the Frankish king Theuderic (II) is mentioned as having been received during Maurice's campaign. Theuderic, however, acceded to the throne in the spring of 596, after the death of Childebert II, under the guardianship of the powerful queen Brunhild.[8]

Particularly in older scholarly literature the beginning of the war is frequently dated to the year 591.[9] A later beginning for the war, around or after 595, has also been discussed.[10] Nonetheless, however they are twisted and turned, the events of the war can hardly be fitted into the time between the accession of Theuderic II and the revolt of Phocas. After the detailed studies of Haussig,

Nystazopoulou-Pelekidou, and Whitby and Whitby, the start of the war is now generally assigned to the years 592–93.[11] For the dramatic course of events on the Danube, it makes little difference whether individual events occurred one year earlier or later.

Procopius had earlier accused the emperor Justinian of having stripped the Balkan provinces of troops for the sake of his ambitious policies and thereby having ruined them.[12] With the Persian war Justin II had been forced to defend the Danube frontier just as ineffectively. Tiberius and Maurice inherited from him the two-front war on the Danube and on the Tigris, and many of the defeats at the hands of the Avars are ascribed by chroniclers to the lack of troops. It would then be understandable for the emperor, after the advantageous peace accord with the new Persian king, to hope that he could fundamentally alter the strategic situation in the Balkans with the bulk of his army.

Theophylact's story of the emperor's ambitious expedition against the Avars, however, is more of a political satire that stands at the beginning of his account of the Balkan wars of the 590s, a grotesque account of Maurice's inefficiency and failure probably produced under Phocas. Unfortunately, we hear nothing of the events of the preceding years nor of the emperor's appreciation of the strategic situation. The whole account of his Anchialus venture does not give the impression that he faced an immediate threat. Except as a pretext for a display of power, the Avars are not involved. The emperor's difficulties were of another kind. First, his counselors, the patriarch, and the empress all tried to discourage him from personally going on the campaign. At Hebdomon, one of the first stops on the march, a solar eclipse occurred. The emperor turned back and then received Persian envoys at court. The second attempt was no less overshadowed by dire omens, despite the army reputedly carrying a sliver of the Cross in the vanguard. A giant wild boar charged the emperor, and his horse was close to throwing him.[13] Maurice continued by ship and was overtaken by a terrible tempest. And soon after landing, a marvel was brought to him, a child with a fish's tail and without eyes, to which a local woman had just given birth.[14] They were still not too distant from the capital, but the region had recently been devastated by the Avars. In Heraclea/Eregli on the Sea of Marmara they had burned the Glyceria church. Michael Whitby has concluded from this and similar chronological inconsistencies that Maurice's campaign would fit much better to the situation of 598.[15] Probably it never happened at all.

More ominous events accompanied the further advance. The emperor's horse collapsed under the weight of its gold ornaments. The rich equine trappings, as found in Avar graves, were then not an exclusively barbarian custom. Theophylact's taste for fantastic tales introduces a detective story at this point in his narrative. The Gepid robber who here appears with suspiciously rich gold ornaments is not exposed until many chapters later.[16] As a contrast, we meet the unarmed Slavs from the "ocean" who, with their lyre, wanted to convince the khagan of the unsuitability of their tribe for war.[17] After the army had toiled through the Xerogypsos marshes, it arrived in Anchialus. The war had not even begun yet, but the emperor turned back. Once again a Persian delegation served as excuse. Two days later, the Franks Boso and Betto also appeared, according to Theophylact, as the envoys of Theuderic II.[18] Diplomatic ties with the Franks were close. For years Byzantium had sought their help against the Lombards. Five embassies from Maurice to Childebert II are known.[19] The last, in 590 or 591, had settled the sensitive matter of the killing of Frankish envoys in Carthage.[20] For a war against the Avars, the Franks now demanded money of the Romans, just as they had done several times for an intervention in Italy against the Lombards. In Maurice's opinion the Franks could just as well fight without payment. These negotiations may be connected with the war that Brunhild's forces fought with the Avars in Thuringia in 596.[21] Theophylact probably combined details on two distinct Frankish embassies: Childebert's in 592, like Theuderic's in 596, was intended to provide information about the new ruler on the throne, and both must have been interested in a pact against the Avars. In 592 Tassilo, imposed as Bavarian *dux* by Childebert, was engaged in battle with the Slavs in the Alps.[22]

5.2 The Avars on the Offensive

After the legends from the emperor's campaign, Theophylact follows with a much more sober description of an Avar attack. The khagan had demanded an increase in the annual tribute, which Maurice had refused. Then the Avars prepared for war, and Priscus was appointed commander in Europe. This may have happened between 588, when Priscus lost his command in the east, and 592, the year before his Slavic campaign. Michael Whitby has offered an attractive argument for dating it to 588.[23] In any case, a considerable Roman force had reoccupied the city of Singidunum, ravaged in 584. They observed a troop of Slavs who were building boats in accord with the khagan's orders. The Romans crossed over and burned the Slavic flotilla. The khagan, who had ordered the boats to be built, retorted with an attack on Singidunum. After a siege of about one week, the khagan withdrew his barbarians, demanding payment for this from the defenders. The defenders could, without delay, produce two thousand gold coins, a table inset with gold, and a costly tapestry; this shows that this hotly contested city still was a pivot of the Roman defense lines.[24]

At the time, the khagan and the bulk of his army were encamped near Sirmium, where they waited for the boats to be built in order to be ferried across

the Sava. The extensive description of the final Avar preparations for war is surprising. For example, the army's distance by march from Sirmium is given as five
parasangae, as if it were being set down in the logbook of a Roman army.[25] The
whole story of the river crossing seems like an echo of Menander's account of
the preparations for the conquest of Sirmium.[26] Whether we can conclude from
the sources that Sirmium was the khagan's capital at this time, as it had once been
for the king of the Gepids, is open to question.[27] We only hear that the Avar army
was assembled in this region. The former imperial city, burned shortly after its
capture in 582–83, was still of strategic importance.

The excellent organization of the khagan's army in this account is striking. The
difficulties involved in crossing a river with a mounted army are clearly apparent
in Menander's account. Now the Avars had Slavic specialists commanded by their
own taxiarchs. Forays on individual initiative, as at Singidunum, were abandoned
in favor of an orderly advance. While the khagan was crossing the Sava, the
emperor appointed Priscus field commander for Europe. Priscus, whom the
army had chased out of Anatolia some years earlier, when he tried to ram through
a decrease in pay,[28] is the only one of the rapidly changing commanders-in-chief
of whom Theophylact paints a positive portrait, for he later supported Phocas.
Yet in this instance he was no match for the well-prepared Avar attack. The
khagan sent a small mounted detachment on ahead, to create anxiety among
the Romans. Allegedly, the Avar vanguard reached Bononia/Vidin in five days, a
good 185 miles away, on the present-day Bulgarian section of the Danube road.[29]
Priscus in turn dispatched a thousand-man cavalry unit under Salvian, to defend
the passage across the Balkan Mountains at least.

Salvian in fact succeeded in reaching the Procliana Pass on the route between
Anchialus and Marcianopolis five days before the Avar vanguard and to throw
it back in a one-day battle. The khagan then sent eight thousand troops who
were to open the way for the passage of the main army. Exceptionally, we hear
the name of their leader: Samur. The Romans stood firm before this augmented
force as well. The mountainous terrain did not favor the Avar fighting style.
When finally the khagan arrived with the rest of his forces, the defenders made
off under cover of night. It was not until the fourth day that observers in the
Avar army noticed that the pass was now open. In the early dawn of the next
day the army hurried through the most dangerous defiles. Three days' march
from there they reached the valley of Sabulente Canalis that had been disputed
some years earlier. Soon the Avars stood before Anchialus, in the vicinity of present-
day Nesebăr. Priscus's army had withdrawn without engaging. Only a few
Roman spies were seized by the Avars, but despite rough treatment, they could
not be forced to speak. In, apparently, five days the Avars put behind them about
125 miles to Drizipera/Kariştiran (near Lüle-Burgaz) and were then less than

100 miles distant from the capital. It was probably here (and not in Anchialus) that the Avars burned the church of St. Alexander. Apparently the invaders met fewer obstacles in their path than did the emperor on his march in the opposite direction recounted above.

The Avars set about besieging Drizipera but ran up against unexpectedly strong resistance. After a week the now impatient khagan had siege machines built. Yet God helps him who helps himself, as Theophylact comments; the defenders opened the gates and threatened to attack the enemy. The khagan imagined that he saw a giant army advancing on him in full daylight and sounded the retreat.[30] Obviously this "flight" was in the right direction, that is, forward. Soon the Avars were before Heraclea/Eregli, the ancient Perinth on the Sea of Marmara, whose inhabitants—in Theophylact's garbled chronology—had shortly before been so lavishly compensated by the emperor for the ravages of the Avars.

Only here did the Roman army again engage. After an imaginary army had turned back the khagan at Drizipera, Priscus believed that he would be able to drive off the Avars definitively with a surprise attack. Yet it was the Romans who were surprised. For it was probably on this occasion that the night attack of the Avars was carried out, an attack that would be entered in the manual on war as an example. "Others have drawn up in combat formation for several days near their own camp as if for a pitched battle. They pretended to be frightened by the enemy and on this account would not stray beyond the area of their own camp. Then while the enemy were relaxing, they would attack them at night. This is what the khagan of the Avars did to the Roman cavalry at Heraclea, for it did not stay safely inside the fortifications with the infantry, but was outside unprotected."[31] The Romans were defeated without a major field battle; without a cavalry, infantry troops can hardly face an army of steppe riders. They withdrew inland to Tzurullon/ Çorlu, where they were surrounded by the Avar forces. Priscus was caught in the trap. Then the emperor helped his hard-pressed field commander out of the pinch with a deceptive maneuver. He sent a messenger with a sham letter to Priscus with the order to allow himself to be caught by the enemy at Tzurullon. In the letter he informed his commander-in-chief of his intention to send a fleet to Pannonia, where it would attack the Avars' families. The presumed letter is reproduced in Theophylact,[32] and it does not spare the "wicked" and "accursed" Avars of insults.

The trick worked. The khagan apparently withdrew to his realm in return for a small sum in gold. This facile conclusion to the great Avar invasion leaves the historian unsatisfied. For, even if the cunning emperor had successfully deceived the barbarian ruler, it does not explain how, at the beginning of the following year of Theophylact's account, the two camps apparently enjoyed contractually regulated peaceful relations.[33] This is another reason to assume that this year's events are misplaced in Theophylact's narrative. How the peace with the Avars that continued, or was renewed after the victory in the Persian war, had come about does not emerge from Theophylact's narrative. In any case, in the following years, despite some diplomatic confrontations, no battles ensued. The Romans now had a free hand against the Slavs on the lower Danube.

5.3 593: Attacks on the Slavs North of the Danube

With this year's events, we are on chronologically more solid ground, for from now on Theophylact's narrative evolves with less chronological inconsistencies. Maurice wished to exploit the breathing space in the Avar war, on which the Romans seemed to rely, in order to confront a less spectacular but almost equally unpleasant opponent: the Slavs on the farther bank of the lower Danube. His instructions to Priscus, again in command, illustrate the strategic credo to which he held until his fall: Thrace could be protected only if the Slavic raiders on the other side of the river were not left in peace. This conception was not unreasonable. The events of the preceding years had shown that Justinian's purely defensive strategy—reinforcement of the *limes* against the barbarian incursions by means of a deeply staggered system of forts—was not sufficient. The Avars, who had already taken a series of important fortresses after the fall of Sirmium, had made progress in siege technique. Moreover, the still intact fortresses of the *limes* did not prevent Avars and Slavs from pushing forward to the immediate vicinity of the capital city. Even the Slavs were no longer intimidated by the more important cities, as the attack on Singidunum in the narrative for the preceding year illustrates. The emperor's strategy was now to sever the Slavic threat at the root. This would also deprive the khagan of an ally, even if an uncertain one, and of a trump in negotiations. Not since the fourth century had the Roman troops operated in such great numbers on the far side of the Danube. Then, the Goths north of the Danube had also been difficult to pin down, hard to beat, and not to be wiped out.[34] Like the Goths before them, the Slavs were now designated with the old name of Getes. This time the conditions for a cleansing operation in the approaches to the *limes* were even less favorable. That the Slavs living outside imperial territory should become the object of an attack at all illustrates one thing: there were no larger Slavic groups established on imperial territory yet who would have been considered a plausible target. Slavic enemies who could be attacked still lived on the other side of the frontier, and among them Ardagast, who in 585, the year of the great Slav invasion, had been cornered at Adrianople.[35] He was now, eight years later, the first target of the attacks.

In early 593 Priscus, along with Gentzon/Gento, the commander of the foot soldiers, gathered his fighting forces in Heraclea and Drizipera.[36] From there, he reached Durostorum/Silistra on the Danube in twenty days' march. The Avars had closely observed the Roman troop movements. An Avar embassy soon arrived in Durostorum, demanding an explanation of the Romans' intentions. The leader of the embassy was a certain Kokh, whose presumed speech Theophylact quotes at length, according to the rhetorical tastes of the times. He emphatically addresses the peace and the accords that the Romans had now broken. Even Priscus, "who recently escorted the peaceful marriage between Avars and Romans," was drawn up, heavily equipped, on the Danube.[37] "You have administered baseness to the barbarians: we should not have known about treaty-breaking, if we had not found you as teachers of deceit." Thus the Avar accuses the Roman general. For a moment, behind the stereotype of the untrustworthy barbarian, appears the opposing image of the noble savage. The soldiers are impressed, but Priscus keeps a cool head. He explains to the khagan's envoy that through the "agreement and truce with the Avars" the war against the Getes (the Slavs) had not ended. For the time being, the eloquent barbarian had to take this lesson in Roman international law away with him.

Priscus now had boats built and crossed the Danube. The Roman intelligence had worked well. The attackers succeeded in taking Ardagast by surprise at night when his warriors were in part off on raids. The Slav leader, startled from his sleep, leaped on his horse and galloped off. His pursuers soon caught up with him. He defended himself against the superior force and continued his flight on foot. In the impassable terrain he had almost shaken the Romans off when he stumbled over a fallen log. Ardagast, who seemed lost, managed with his last strength to submerge himself in the nearby river Argeş and thus disappear. Most of his people were less fortunate; they were meanwhile being cut down by the imperial army. In addition, the Romans devastated the Slavic lands, destroyed fields, felled trees, and took all the surviving inhabitants as slaves to Byzantium. They also took considerable booty, over which contention immediately arose. At this point, the Slavs on the imperial frontier were not simply poor farmers. The goods accumulated on numerous raids were attractive enough, and the Roman soldiers, not exactly accustomed to booty in the Balkan wars, were not prepared to renounce their claim to it. Priscus, recently back in imperial favor and thus far with little to show for his efforts, wanted to give a good part of it to the emperor. When unrest and tumult broke out in the army at this, Priscus summoned his officers before the sun came up, assured himself of their support, and then delivered a "Themistoclean speech" to his soldiers in Latin. Theophylact cites the rhetorical exploit as an example of the power of the word; the commander's call to fight for glory and honor and not out of greed calmed the troops for the moment. In the longer term this measure certainly contributed to damping enthusiasm for the arduous war against the Slavs.[38]

The transfer of the Slavic booty proved no less difficult. Priscus dispatched Tatimer with three hundred men. On the sixth day the troop was attacked by Slavs. Although Tatimer was wounded in this battle, the attackers could be repulsed and the treasure transported to Constantinople intact. This event shows that at this time, far inside the borders of the empire, bellicose Slavs were to be found. That they had already been settled there is not a necessary conclusion. For the emperor this highly visible success came at just the right time. Tatimer was hailed by the people of the city; the emperor celebrated a service of gratitude in Hagia Sophia.

In the meantime the Slavic war north of the Danube continued. The main problem now was to find the opponent. On Priscus's orders the taxiarch Alexander crossed the river Helibacius/Ialomiṭa and cornered a nearby troop of Slavs. These withdrew into marshes and thickets, where they almost overcame the confused Romans. The Roman attempt to burn down the forest, in order to deprive the Slavs of their cover, failed because the terrain was too wet. The few prisoners that were taken refused, even under torture, to reveal the hiding spots of the other Slavs.[39]

The Roman troops, moving awkwardly in this terrain, finally had a bit of luck. A defector put himself at the disposal of the taxiarch Alexander. The man was a Gepid and had once been Christian but lived among the Slavs. What we learn about him provides a spotlight on the complex ethnic and social processes, which are otherwise seldom noted in the sources. He spoke Slavic, could sing Avar songs, knew his way around his environment, and was so respected by the Slavs that their king Musucius entrusted 150 boats and their crews to him on the strength of his word. The Romans repeatedly met informants like him, former residents of the provinces or Christians, and had learned that they could not always trust them; rarely was their help so precious. The Slavic troop with which the Romans had clashed in the Helibacius wetlands came, according to the informant, from Musucius, "who was called *rex* in the barbarian tongue" (probably *reiks* in the Gepid's Gothic).[40] He was encamped about thirty *parasangae* away (about a hundred miles). They were reconnoitering the situation after the attack on Ardagast and were scouting out the Romans' movements, another indication of emerging Slavic military organization. The Gepid volunteered to set a trap for Musucius, for which a great reward was promised.

While Priscus had the Slav prisoners killed, the Gepid hurried to Musucius and asked him for boats and rowers in order to bring Ardagast's fleeing subjects across the river Paspirion. During the night he then fetched Alexander along with two hundred soldiers. Those Slavs who had not already fallen into wine-induced sleep the Gepid purportedly lulled with melancholy Avar songs, which was also to be the signal for the Romans. Alexander's people fell on the boat crews and "provided the mortal penalty for sleep."[41]

On the captured boats, Priscus and three thousand men crossed the river that same night. The unfortunate Musucius was sleeping off a drinking bout after having buried a brother and was taken alive, while the remainder of his subjects were slaughtered. The Romans "reveled in a night of bloodshed." In the morning after this gory venture, Priscus had the rest of the army ferried across the Paspirion. The successful blitzkrieg had cheered the troops, and now it was their turn to be taken in drunken surprise after a night of carousing. Only the alert Gentzon, commander of the infantry, prevented the Slavs, thirsty for revenge, from carrying out a massacre among the imperial troops similar to that of the day before. Priscus had the officer in charge of the watch impaled and a number of soldiers flogged.[42]

Even more was to be expected of the army. Maurice, whose hopes to deal a decisive blow to the Slavs in the north had been strengthened by the success thus far, wanted to extend the cleansing action. He sent Tatimer back to Priscus with the order to pass the winter in enemy territory.[43] Behind this was a strategy recommended by the *Strategicon* for war against the Slavs:[44] in the winter, when the rivers and marshes were frozen and the trees were bare, it was easier to combat the Slavs. Yet the theory was not easily put into practice, and the soldiers had a different view of things. They feared the fierce cold and constant enemy attacks, and only Priscus's art of persuasion could forestall a mutiny. Soon afterward, and against the emperor's orders, he withdrew across the Danube.[45]

5.4 594: The Limits of the Slavic War

Since the protest of his envoy Kokh, the khagan had tolerated the Roman adventure in the Slavic lands. Perhaps he had also hoped to see the glorious Roman army sink into the marshes. Now, in the winter of 593–94, he could no longer stay on the sidelines. When Priscus had returned across the Danube, an Avar embassy demanded an explanation of his plans. This section in Theophylact reads like a failed attempt to stitch two different sources together. In any case, the fine words of the field commander seem not to have mollified the khagan in the least. Soon Priscus had intelligence that the khagan was planning a new invasion. He had already ordered Slavic troops to cross the Danube.

The khagan's situation was not a simple one. Exceptionally, Theophylact's account permits insight into the difficult position of a barbarian ruler. He had not protected the Slavs, who were enraged at Priscus's brutality and success. What the khagan had ordered—an invasion of imperial territory—they would also do for their own reasons. The khagan could, however, not tolerate that the Slavic princes took the initiative on the Danube of their own accord. Besides, he "was annoyed by the extensive successes of Roman forces."[46]

On the other hand, chastising the unruly Slavs in the periphery of his empire could also be in his own interest. Dissent among the Avars ensued, and this information from Theophylact is of particular value. There was a peace party at the khagan's court: "Targitius and the barbarian elite urged the khagan to put an end to the war, for they said that his indignation against the Romans was unjustified."[47] The doves got their way in the end, and the khagan pronounced himself ready to receive an ambassador from Priscus.

Theophylact recounts the audience of Theodore, a doctor and polished speaker, with the khagan as a further lesson of the power of the word.[48] Once again, the khagan boasted that he was "the master of every people, and that there existed no one, even as far as the sun extended his gaze, who would be able to confront him." Theodore reacted with the wheel parable about the Pharaoh Sesostris and the captured king, who recognizes the course of destiny in the turning of the wheel; this moved the heart of the "pompous" khagan. The discreet reference to the "gold-inlaid carriage" of the Pharaoh, "wreathed with precious stones," appears to have appealed to the Avar ruler's taste. Topical as the account of this exchange is, it surely relies on long-standing experience with what diplomats and steppe rulers said on these occasions, which was probably as topical as Theophylact's rhetorical embellishments. What a classicizing Greek writer presented as hubris and barbarian arrogance was probably not too different from expressions of Avar ideology of rulership. To confirm it in front of the emperor's envoy was part of the balancing act that was necessary for the khagan to stay in power. The addressees of his high-flown words were above all his own people. But for them to be effective, a tangible outcome from the negotiations was also necessary. The khagan then demanded a share of the spoils, for, as he said, "Priscus has attacked my land and wrought injury on my subjects. Let the results of success be shared."[49]

What appeared to the Byzantines as the khagan's unexpected mildness was a small diplomatic victory for the Avar ruler, since by the surrender of a portion of the booty the Romans acknowledged that the Slavic region north of the Danube was a sphere of Avar influence. Priscus had, de facto, retracted his answer to Kokh that the Romans' Slavic campaign did not affect Avar interests. On the other hand, the khagan retroactively accepted Priscus's actions by receiving the transfer of a share of the plunder. He profited from the successful attack on the very people whose ruler he claimed to be.

The contradictory situation in the region of present-day Wallachia has led to differences of opinion among historians. Were the Slavs north of the lower

Danube under Avar rule or not?[50] Obviously, there were differences between claims and reality as concerned the power of the khagan. But the reality of the matter was continuously subject to change. Every attempt to define the Avar ruler's actual sphere of power over a longer period is condemned to failure. Not even at a given moment could the khagan's realm simply be pinned down on a map. The spheres of influence and maneuvering room of Avar politics were too variable. Fixed borders arose only when they were contractually agreed upon with the Byzantines. Beyond that, there were certain security zones in which the arrival of a Roman army would be interpreted as a hostile act. Otherwise Kokh would not, already at Durostorum, have been in a position to decry the rupture of the peace by Priscus. Between Avars and other barbarians, there were areas of dominance of various grades, right up to the all-encompassing sphere of a symbolic claim to lordship. Every step in Avar politics was in response to a concrete disruption in, or threat to, this construction of rulership. What seems contradictory to us arises from the continuous balancing act of a great power without an apparatus of a state. The khagan's actions had to be pragmatic and symbolic at the same time.

The treaty from the winter of 593–94 is a good example. A mutually acceptable solution was found to prevent the threatening war. Priscus's surrender of a part of the war spoils to the khagan was not simple compensation—a share of the booty would not have been sufficient for that. Priscus laid his victory at the feet of the Avar ruler and let him participate in it through a share of the spoils, just as he had done the previous year with his own emperor. The khagan expressed this in his answer to Theodore: in return for allowing his "friend" Priscus to raid in his territory, he expected to become "a partner in the spoils."[51] The khagan was no head of state who felt responsible for the protection of his subjects. He was the leader of a barbarian army that considered all who were not part of it potential booty. This was not the only time the Slavs on the lower Danube fell victim to the complicity between the empire and the Avar ruler. A line of common interests against the unruly Slavs runs from the Avars' Slavic war of 578 to the treaty of 598.[52]

The prospect of having to turn a portion of the plunder over to the enemy led to fresh discord in the Roman army. It required all Priscus's powers of persuasion to calm the soldiers. They finally agreed to return all the prisoners to the khagan and to keep the rest of the booty. According to Theophylact there were five thousand barbarians who had to be freed. This, of course, obliterated much of the military effect of the operation. Then the army set out on the return march to Drizipera.

While Priscus was working his way out of a tricky situation, his days as commander-in-chief were already numbered. Maurice was angered by the general's compromise with the Avars, and particularly by the surrender of the prisoners of war, which he considered stupid. His objectives for the European wars had no room for such pragmatic solutions. Priscus was replaced by the emperor's brother Peter. Perhaps Maurice wished the future successes that he anticipated to accrue to the credit of his own family.

War in the year 594 would show that the emperor's great hopes were ill-founded. Neither Priscus's raids in Slavic lands nor the precarious peace with the khagan prevented the Slavs from fresh incursions. The emperor's brother was obliged to start his operation deep inside his own country. He set up his headquarters in Odessus/Varna on the Black Sea.[53] The small-scale war that he waged on the Danube took place under the watchful eyes of the Avars. The khagan tolerated the expeditions against the Danube Slavs more or less until he decided to oppose them. And the mood of the Roman soldiers grew ever worse and gave the impression of a latent mutiny.

The emperor and his brother made little effort to improve army morale. Peter introduced himself as commander with an imperial decree that only one third of the soldiers' pay would henceforth be paid out in money, with the rest in the form of weapons and clothing.[54] Immediately, rebellious feelings and cursing of the emperor boiled over again in the camp. Only concessions that disabled veterans would be cared for and that the children of the fallen might assume their positions on the muster roll could calm the storm.

Already at the first stage of the march the army encountered Slavs; and as was often the case, the raiders were already loaded with plunder when they were apprehended. They had ravaged Zaldapa, Aquis, and Scopi. The latter of these was not Scupi/Skopje;[55] they were, rather, small fortresses in lower Moesia and Scythia minor, between Odessus/Varna and Durostorum/Silistra. Peter had ordered on ahead one thousand men under the experienced officer Alexander, but they had little taste for an attack. The Slavs barricaded themselves in a circle of wagons, with the women and children in the center. Alexander had to hector his soldiers in their mother tongue—one of the references to the colloquial Latin of the lower ranks—in order to prod them into an attack. The battle proceeded along the predictable lines of an American western: the Romans had to dismount, suffered heavy losses, and finally stormed the wagons, at which point the defenders hacked down their Roman prisoners before themselves falling. Peter celebrated the victory, of which he had had no part, with a hunt, during which he was injured. Maurice insisted nonetheless that the campaign continue and wrote his brother a number of unfriendly letters. He finally charged him not to leave Thrace, because he had heard of an imminent attack by the Slavs on the capital city. Peter then took the route by which the Slavs had come, and by way of Pistus/Ruse, the devastated Zaldapa/Abrit, and Iatrus/Krivina, reached the city Novae/Svištov on the Danube. This must have been on August 22, since the townspeople insisted that he celebrate the feast of the martyr Lupus with them the next day.[56]

Less enjoyable events were waiting for Peter in nearby Asemus, whose name is today preserved in that of the river Osam. He was received by the strong garrison of the city with great honor. Peter was so impressed by the warlike men of the city guard that he immediately wanted to take them with him. The residents of the city appealed this with reference to the emperor Justin, who had conceded to them such strong protection because of the numerous barbarian raids. When the field commander insisted on stripping the city of its defenders, the latter took refuge in the church. Peter ordered Gento, who still had the command of the infantry, to bring the city guard out of their place of refuge, but this officer of barbarian descent was more in awe of the holy place than the emperor's brother. The next day Peter tried to have the bishop arrested, but the townsfolk of Asemus threw out his soldiers and barred the gates. Up on the walls they sang songs of praise for the distant emperor and execrated his field commander. The latter had to abandon his agenda. We may assume that this disgrace is but one example of the tense relationship between the provincials and imperial power.[57]

The next, almost more consequential, error was made by the field commander one week later. Peter had one thousand men ferried over the Danube to conduct reconnaissance, where they unexpectedly ran into a troop of a thousand Bulgars. The barbarians, confident of the state of peace between the emperor and the khagan, went peacefully on their way. The Roman troop leader had them attacked, at which they urged him, through an envoy, to respect the peace treaty. The officer sent them to Peter. Peter rebuffed the call for peace and announced boastfully that they would all soon be put to the sword. At this, the Bulgars attacked the Roman troop and drove it off in flight. Peter now recognized his error, for which the officer had to atone.

The incident led to diplomatic complications. The khagan had his ambassadors protest in the sharpest terms against the breach of the treaty. Peter feigned ignorance and succeeded in placating the Avars with showy gifts and the payment of a fine.[58] The story is important evidence for the presence and role of Bulgars in the Avar Empire. They were counted a part of the Avar army but could operate relatively independently. Perhaps they were charged with observing Roman troop movements for the khagan or with demonstrating an Avar presence in the territory of the Slavs.

After all these embarrassments Peter wanted to be able to boast of some success. He had twenty hand-picked soldiers put across the Danube to scout out the enemy. The careful scouts moved, as was customary, only by night, which would seal their fate. They were discovered fast asleep in the daytime by some passing Slavs and were taken prisoner. Under torture they revealed Peter's plans. The leader, *phylarchos*, of the Slavs, Peiragast, could now set a trap for the Romans. When Peter, who still did not know the enemy's disposition, had the first thousand men transported across the Danube, they were all cut down by the Slavs hidden in the forest.

With his superior forces and by firing on the Slavs from the boats, Peter then finally succeeded in forcing his way across the river. Peiragast was also hit by an arrow and died. At any event the Romans had still not moved any horses to the opposite shore, and many of the defeated made their escape at this point. Continuing its march the imperial army entered a region without fresh water, most likely the Bărăgan steppe,[59] and the soldiers had to suffer terrible thirst. "Since the army could no longer stand the lack of water, they quenched their thirst with wine." A terrible confusion ensued. At last, a Slav prisoner betrayed the fact that they were only four *parasangae* (about fourteen miles) distant from the Helibacius/Ialomiţa. But the army promptly fell into another ambush by the "amphibian" Slavs. While the Romans pressed greedily forward to the water, Slavs who had hidden on the opposite shore broke out and cut down a great number of Roman troops. The attempt to get to the other bank with improvised rafts ended in a further debacle.[60]

As a consequence of his misfortunes, Peter was again replaced by Priscus, who had shown greater skill and probably had had better luck in his bush war. His rival's failures had in any case shown that the victories of the previous year had in no way depleted the fighting ability of the Danube Slavs. That no permanent results could be achieved was likely due to more than the incompetence of this or that commander.

5.5 595: The Illyrian War

The 580s had been a period of successive and devastating Avar attacks. The 590s were in general a quieter period in the Balkan provinces. It seems obvious that the peace with Persia and the availability of a stronger Byzantine army in the Balkan provinces had an effect on the offensive efforts of the khagan. It would not be until 598 that the Avar army again advanced into the European core areas of the Roman Empire. Theophylact's history of the wars clearly shows the strategic limits of both powers. In case of a massive Avar attack, the Romans mainly attempted to save their own army, and to outmaneuver the enemy by ambushes, skirmishes, and siege warfare. Likewise, the Avars never sought a single decisive battle; it was not their objective to destroy an opposing army. The reasons why the khagan started a war, and what targets he would choose, are rarely quite clear. A casus belli, as the Roman offensive on the Danube might have been, was not necessarily a sufficient reason for actually going to war.

Around 595 further reasons arose for refraining from an offensive against Byzantium. The situation on the western flank of the Avar kingdom had become volatile. It was then not necessarily to the credit of the Roman generals that Thrace enjoyed some years of quiet. On the contrary. The imperial army itself was rather battered from the Slavic wars. When Priscus, back at his post since the spring of 595, mustered his troops in the city, he realized that they had suffered considerable losses. He made up for them as well as he could and pressed forward to the Danube in a two-week march.[61] He crossed the river and set up his camp in Novae superior, upstream from the Iron Gate.[62] The Byzantine army was then appreciably closer to the center of the Avar khaganate than in preceding years. What the strategic objectives were is unclear. This was not the place to start an offensive into the Avar heartlands (such as the one that Priscus undertook a few years later). At best, it was a mountainous area that would make it difficult to deploy a full-scale Avar army. Did the Byzantines seek to provoke the Avars to attack? In any case, it was obvious that the aim was not another expedition against the Slavs in the lowlands north of the lower Danube.

Soon the familiar diplomatic game got under way again. Through his envoys, the khagan inquired as to the reasons for the military campaign. The Roman field commander put him off with excuses. He pointed out that the area was particularly well suited to hunting and rich in water. However, this time the Avar was more stubborn. He reiterated that the Romans had entered foreign territory and had thereby broken the peace agreement. This was a reasonable argument; Roman units had undeniably crossed the Danube. To these accusations the Roman commander replied, as the Romans often did, by disputing the barbarians' claim to the land in question, advancing the Roman claim instead. Even on the northern bank of the Danube, Priscus could imagine himself in Roman territory, more exactly, in Trajan's old Dacia, which at least the bridgeheads north of the river recalled.[63] The khagan had every reason to protest. Roman troops had crossed the river at quite a distance upstream from previous years, closer to the region that the Avars directly controlled. The Avar envoy observed that in any case war would decide on whose territory they were, and withdrew.[64]

This is the place where Theophylact introduces his digression about the origin of the "Pseudo-Avars": "they say that Priscus reproached the khagan with his flight from the east."[65] This may be another indication that Priscus was out to provoke the Avars. He had not only insisted on the humble beginnings of the Avar khaganate but had also pointed to an actual threat. The Romans' diplomatic contacts with the Turkish khaganate had always been directed against the Avars. The letter from Niri Khagan, from which much of the information in the digression was derived, seems to have arrived in this very year, 595, after Niri's victory over his rival Dulan Khagan.[66] Did the Byzantines hope for Turkish support, or at least try to frighten the Avars? This did not keep the khagan from following his threats by a careful dose of real action. On the tenth day after the meeting, messengers brought information that the barbarians were taking down the walls of Singidunum (Theophylact does not mention their taking the city) and planned to drag the inhabitants off to enemy territory. Without hesitation Priscus marched upstream along the Danube and set up his camp on the island Singa in the vicinity of Constantiola, about thirty miles downstream from Singidunum.[67]

This set the stage for a memorable meeting between the Roman general and the Avar khagan. The Avar ruler had taken up a position on the shore; Priscus's boat was anchored in the Danube at hailing distance. Arrangements for the summit conference on the Danube show the mistrust that ruled between the two powers. Theophylact reproduces the speeches of the protagonists, rather unadorned in light of his usual rhetorical taste.[68] It was the khagan who insisted that Priscus should respect the treaties. He demanded the withdrawal of the Roman army from the river as a condition for peace. "What are you doing, Romans, in the land which is mine? Why have you extended your steps beyond what is proper? The Ister is foreign to you, its swell hostile. This we have won with arms, this we have enslaved by the spear."

This did not necessarily mean an Avar claim to the right bank of the Danube; rather, it was a reference to the river itself, against the crossing of which the Romans had been warned. In fact, Priscus sat at this moment in his boat on the river, and his fleet lay at anchor off the island of Singa. The khagan regarded the constant presence of Roman armies on the river as harmful to Avar interests. The Slavic war on the lower reaches of the river had just barely been tolerable. Now Priscus was standing at the edge of the Carpathian Basin. The khagan had to reckon with an extension of the Roman offensive into the zone of Avar settlement. He demanded the immediate withdrawal of the Roman army. The declaration of an "Ister Avaricus" was intended to buttress this point. Whenever, in the following years, a Roman army advanced to this point, in that neuralgic zone between Singidunum and the Iron Gate, it resulted in a confrontation. It would be wrong to draw too far-reaching conclusions from this rhetoric. It was just a political move in the strategic poker game of the two great powers. In the peace of 598, after the triumphal Avar advance through Thrace, the Danube was established as a nominal boundary, so that crossing it against the Slavs could still be countenanced. When about 600 the Avars were hard-pressed, the 595 interpretation was put forward again (cf. sections 5.7–9). This alone illustrates its predominantly defensive character. When the Avars set out on a major raid, they did not limit themselves to scarcely profitable frontier garrisons on the upper *limes*.

In any case, Priscus did not let himself be drawn into a discussion of the Danube frontier. He demanded the return of Singidunum. At this the furious khagan threatened to take many more cities and withdrew from the riverbank to his tent. It has sometimes been assumed that this year's Avar operations led to the abandonment of the Illyrian *limes*.[69] Yet even Singidunum was immediately retaken by a Roman force under Guduin. When the Avar garrison saw the Roman fleet approaching, they tried to erect a barricade of wagons before the city. As soon as the Romans had overrun the line of defense, the barbarians took to their heels, not least for fear that they would also be attacked by the inhabitants of the city.[70] The next day the damaged walls of the city were repaired. Singidunum served as a basis of operations for the Byzantine attacks against the Avars a few years later.

With this, the khagan officially "publicly dissolved the treaties" through a messenger to Priscus. Yet he did not proceed on the usual route along the Danube. This time he turned toward the "Ionian Gulf," that is, the Adriatic, and marched into Dalmatia.[71] Obviously, he did not want to face the army led by Priscus, and perhaps the Turks, by going east. Regrettably, nothing more precise about the objectives of the Avar army can be said. According to Theophylact, after a few days' march it attacked the otherwise unknown city of *Bonkeis* and eventually conquered it.[72] This city and forty additional fortresses fell into barbarian hands.

Priscus did not move his entire army to shield the Dalmatians from Avar plundering; that might have been too risky. However, he sent the experienced Guduin with two thousand men, to keep an eye on the enemy. The Roman detachment, unlike the invading army, did not dare to use the main road. Instead, it had to move through pathless, unknown country. The undertaking had unanticipated success. One day Guduin's troops spotted a barbarian detachment from an elevation. Roman scouts succeeded in making their way forward undetected at night and took a barbarian prisoner. Guduin extracted from him the information that their division consisted of two thousand men and had been entrusted by the khagan with guarding spoils. As was always the case under such circumstances, the enemy was dazed with drink at night. The Romans had an easy time of it with the unsuspecting barbarians. The recovered plunder was immediately sent back to Priscus. At little expense the Byzantines had succeeded in divesting the khagan of the fruits of his conquests. Theophylact ascribes to his depressed state that nothing memorable occurred between the Avars and the Romans "for eighteen months and more." During this time both armies were camped on the Danube.[73]

Which part of Dalmatia was ravaged is difficult to determine. The inhabitants of the coast had other worries at this time, for instance, the years-long conflict between Pope Gregory the Great and the archbishop of Salona, which stimulated an active correspondence.[74] As shown in the next section, in the same year 595 the Avars annihilated a troop of Bavarians who had attacked the Slavs, somewhere in the Eastern Alps. That would have meant that they advanced westward along the Sava or the Drava. Guduin's actions show that fighting occurred in mountainous territory. Some plundering may have also occurred in northern Dalmatia, roughly present-day Bosnia.[75] The khagan's engagement in such a relatively profitless undertaking in the mountains must be connected with the situation in the west of his realm. An advance to the southwest led, as he had threatened, onto imperial territory. At the same time it demonstrated the Avar presence in a region in which the encroachment of the Slavs began to make itself felt. Perhaps the khagan had originally planned to push forward to the Dalmatian coast and on the way learned of the conflicts between Slavs and Bavarians. In any case, events in the west in that year must have been sufficiently important that the war against Byzantium could, for the time being, be allowed to subside.

5.6 The Avars' Western Policy and the Slavs

While Byzantine commanders fought with shifting success in the Slav lands along the lower Danube, similar conflicts were beginning on the western edge of the Avar sphere of power. And they brought the khagan similar problems. Here as there, the Slavs, whose leadership he claimed, fought on their own initiative and thereby provoked counterattacks by the affected neighbors. These retaliatory strikes in turn required an Avar response. In the long run the khagan could not afford to leave the initiative to the Slavs alone, no more than he could let their defeats go unanswered. As with Byzantium, he succeeded in limiting the inevitable confrontation in the west. The fact that a carefully mixed dose of intervention, threat, and diplomacy could prevent a longer war once again illustrates the khagan's skill.

Toward the end of the sixth century, Slavic groups, perhaps with Avar support, succeeded in Carinthia as in Carniola (in modern Slovenia) in eliminating the remains of the Roman order that had subsisted in southern Noricum and south-western Pannonia under Frankish and Lombard rule, respectively.[76] This process is documented in some written sources, but it occurred without the chroniclers taking much notice of the change and therefore is hard to date exactly. We must thank the unending squabbles of church politics in the patriarchate of Aquileia for information that at least allows us to reconstruct the end of episcopal organization in the non-Italian parts of the patriarchate.

As a consequence of the Lombard conquest of 568 a large part of the Aquileian metropolitan district had become, from a Roman point of view, *ecclesia in gentibus*, a church under barbarian rule.[77] In the tension zone between the empire and the Lombards, between the pope and the exarchate, the church of Aquileia took a schismatic stand in the Three-Chapter Controversy. A letter from this conflict bears the signatures of bishops under Lombard rule, who complained to Maurice in 591 about the pope.[78] In the previous year at the synod of Marano a conflict over a forced reconciliation with Rome had been smoothed over. Paul the Deacon enumerates the exponents of the two points of view.[79]

At the beginning of the seventh century, there was a momentous split between the Byzantine see of Grado, to which the patriarch had withdrawn in 568 in the face of the Lombards, and the reestablished patriarchal see in Lombard Aquileia. When in 827 a decision was sought between the two rival patriarchs at the Council of Mantua, both churches were able to present evidentiary material from about 600. Included there was a list of signatures from a synod held in Grado between 572 and 577, which was thus preserved in the protocol from 827.[80] In the continuing conflict over the patriarchate the parties descended to falsifying such documentary evidence. Most likely the list of signatories from a synod in 579, widely cited in earlier scholarly literature, is a forgery from Grado.[81]

The successive lists of bishops illustrate the decline of the *ecclesia in gentibus*. In the 570s the bishops of Celeia/Celje and of Emona/Ljubljana, of Teurnia near Spittal/Drau and of Aguntum/Lienz, along with their colleagues from northeastern Italy, had taken part in the synod held in Grado. Soon thereafter the Christian strongholds in the frontier area between the Avars, Franks, and Lombards seem to have fallen into Slavic hands. In the ecclesiastical conflicts from about 590 none of the bishops from the Carinthian Alps participated. Bishop John of Celeia is attested somewhat longer. After 587, according to Paul the Deacon, he belonged to the compromise faction and in 590 was probably still in his diocese.[82] Shortly thereafter he fled *de Pannoniis* to Istria, where he established a bishopric in Civitas Nova. Schismatics finally forced him to continue his flight to Sicily, as we learn from a letter of Pope Gregory from 599.[83] This means that a Pannonian bishop had followed the creed of Constantinople and not that of Aquileia in the Three-Chapter Controversy.

A puzzle is constituted by bishop *Vindemius Cessensis*, present at the Grado synod, whose diocese has often been identified with Siscia on the Sava River.[84] Italian research would place him, on the other hand, on the island of Cissa in the Bay of Rovinj. The fate of this Istrian Atlantis is mysterious. Presumably it disappeared in the floods that followed an earthquake in about 700.[85] Whatever the case, a bishopric in Siscia during the Avar era cannot be reconstructed with reference to this Vindemius Cessensis.

None of these sources blame Avars or Slavs for the displacement of bishops, and of the population in general; all that we know is that the bishops flew, and there is no hint of martyrdom. It is not unreasonable to suspect that barbarian raids prompted this widespread emigration. As we have seen in chapter 4, contemporary sources (such as the letters of Pope Gregory the Great) were surprisingly vague about who exactly these enemies were. That only became clear in retrospect. Paul the Deacon, although with hindsight, is unambiguous. It was already a *provincia Sclaborum*, into which the newly installed Bavarian duke Tassilo penetrated in about 592. The information is derived from the *Historiola* by Secundus of Trento written in ca. 610, who was aware of his Slavic neighbors; but the name of the province might be Paul's addition.[86] In any case, Tassilo already attempted a rollback against Slavs operating in eastern Tyrol and Carinthia. Like his Byzantine colleague Priscus, the Bavarian *dux* won *maxima praeda*, very rich spoils, from the Slavs. In this way he gained a share of what once had belonged to the last of the Noricans. Excavations at the late Roman hillforts of the sixth century—Hemmaberg, Grazerkogel, Laubendorf, or the Kirchbichl at Lavant—show that the Norican church disposed of substantial means before the Slavic incursions.[87] On the Hoischhügel near Maglern, on the present-day Italian border, one of the defenders buried his treasure of about twenty gold solidi, among which coins from the reign of Justin II (565–78) and Lombard imitations.[88] An impressive number of late antique hillforts were also found in Slovenia.[89] That Tassilo's opponents were the Slavs in *Noricum ripense* is suggested by the parallel with the Bavarian advance around 610. On this occasion the fight was over Aguntum/Lienz. The battles of the 590s probably took place along the Drau/Drava River too; rich spoils would have been much harder to get north of the Alps.[90]

The attackers were in both cases the Bavarians. In 589, the Bavarian princess Theodelinda had married the Lombard king Authari, and Tassilo's move was surely coordinated with the Lombards. The peace accord with the Lombards in 591 gave the Merovingian king Childebert II the opportunity to install Tassilo as duke over the unruly Bavarians, probably in 592.[91] The attack on the Slavs in Noricum seems to have been a way for Tassilo to legitimize his position. At about the same time, the new Lombard king Agilulf concluded the first of a series of peace agreements with the Avars.[92] Perhaps this entailed recognition of the new Slavic settlement areas in former Lombard territories in modern Slovenia and Carinthia.

The bishops who met in Grado in 591 had probably also come to terms with the loss of the Norican dioceses. In their petition to the emperor Maurice, the old Alpine bishops' sees are still mentioned, but their signatures are lacking. The Slavic threat was not on the agenda. The chief concern in the patriarchate of Aquileia was the Three-Chapter Controversy and the ensuing problems with the exarch and with Pope Gregory.[93] The letter recalled that Frankish bishops had once ordained priests in Noricum and blatantly threatened that something similar could happen again if the emperor did not lend them his support. This implied that they would turn to the Lombard side, where King Agilulf and Queen Theodelinda openly supported the schismatic side in the controversy.

The Bavarians had now established themselves south of the Brenner Pass; Norican refugees found a new home in the Raetian Pustertal, which is later attested as Nurih-Tal, the "valley of Noricum."[94] Tassilo tried to advance along the Drava with Frankish cover and Lombard consent. While the three great powers, Franks, Lombards, and Avars, had pledged themselves to nonbelligerence in 591/92, the Bavarians and Slavs waged a proxy war in the Alps. Sooner or later that had to have consequences on the balance of power. Perhaps the Byzantine movements prevented the Avars from immediately responding to the Bavarian offensive. The confused situation in upper Italy did not allow any intervention from that side. Agilulf had to deal with the rebellious *duces*; the exarch Romanus was eager to exploit these difficulties but was again at odds with Pope Gregory. And the latter could not effect a reconciliation with the schismatic bishops in the patriarchate of Aquileia, who were squabbling among themselves. Even the reception of and care for the refugees, which was Gregory's concern, was thwarted by the schism, as in the case of Bishop John of Celeia. Nonetheless, the Slavic expansion came to a halt at the Italian frontier. The Avar–Lombard axis spared Lombard Italy the fate of the Balkan provinces. Apparently, the Slavs in the Alps respected the khagan's policy to avoid confrontation with the Lombards. On the other hand, the years after 592 saw the reestablishment of a Byzantine-Frankish commonality of interests. In the south as in the east, the kings of Frankish Austrasia bordered on the enemies of the emperor, Lombards and Avars.

In Bavaria the events in the Avar khaganate seem to have been monitored. Probably it was in 595, when the khagan's army was engaged in the battles over Singidunum, that the Bavarians felt secure enough for a new raid on the Slavs on the Drava.[95] But they were disappointed. This time the khagan came to the aid of the Slavs, and the two thousand Bavarians were all killed. The exact dating of the events that Paul the Deacon drew from the contemporary *Historiola* of Secundus of Trento is, however, hypothetical. If the chronicler of the Lombards has the events in their correct sequence, the Bavarian fiasco occurred just before the death of Childebert II in the spring of 596. Shortly thereafter the Franks had to deal with the khagan's army themselves. The Avars penetrated Thuringia, and Queen Brunhild, who held the regency for Theuderic II and Theudebert II, had to pay them to withdraw.[96] As earlier in 562 and 565, the Avars did not exploit their victory over the Franks to advance to the Rhine. It was merely a demonstration of power, and intended to dissuade the Franks from interfering in Slavic territories or from coming to the aid of the Byzantines.

Soon after the wars against Bavarians and Franks, the khagan sent a new embassy to King Agilulf to reinforce the Lombard–Avar relationship.[97] Agilulf, in turn, sought to safeguard himself by signing a treaty with Theuderic II.[98] By his victories, the khagan had reestablished his supremacy over the Slavs in the west and had marked off their settlement area as an Avar sphere of interest. He had no further plans of expansion along the western frontier. To Franks and Lombards, continuing war in the Alps or along the Elbe offered too little to be considered worthwhile. The reestablishment of the mutual nonaggression pact was therefore in the interest of all three barbarian powers. Thus, peace returned in the west of the Avar realm.

The problems of the 590s in the west may make the prudent behavior of the Avars in the east more understandable. In 593 and 594, the khagan had hesitated to risk a full-fledged war with the Byzantines; in 595, he declared it, but then turned to peripheral areas in northwest Illyricum. In 596, the Avars were engaged with the Franks. Probably the Avars intended to reinforce the Slavic position in the west by pushing in the direction of the Adriatic, and by dissuading any Frankish intervention. The ensuing eight-month break in fighting on the Danube was exploited by the khagan in order definitively to settle the situation in the west.

5.7 598: Only the Plague Can Stop the Avars

Theophylact's account resumes after the eighteen months of standoff on the Danube. If this chronology is correct, an Avar campaign began late in 597, but nothing decisive happened that year; the two armies still followed each other at some distance, and neither risked a major battle. The military situation only became more dynamic in 598.[99] The khagan had moved his army on the old invasion route into the Roman Empire: along the Danube through Moesia to Thrace. In the autumn of 597, the Avars appeared before Tomis/Constanţa on the Black Sea. Priscus came to the aid of the besieged city. While the two armies remained encamped facing each other before Tomis, winter arrived. Once, far from Rome, Ovid had spent the melancholy years of his exile in this city. Now, not too distant from each other, Romans and barbarians set up their winter camps here.

What happened at the end of the winter is an illustrative example of barbarian psychology. When spring finally came to the region, the Romans were suffering from hunger. After a series of barbarian incursions, the province of Scythia minor apparently could not support two armies for an extended time, although the Avars seem to have secured themselves better provisions in enemy country than the Byzantines in their own. Easter, which in 598 fell on March 30, brought an unexpected turn of events. The khagan made it known through envoys that he would gladly alleviate the hunger of the Romans, if they would permit it. "This novel offering" immediately raised Priscus's suspicions. Yet in the end he conceded to swear to a five-day cease-fire. The khagan kept his word. He provisioned the enemy's suffering soldiers with many cartloads of food. This barbarian emergency aid permitted the Romans to celebrate a worthy Easter. Until his own day, says Theophylact, this incredible example of "barbarian philanthropy" was highly prized.

On the fourth day the khagan's messenger again appeared and requested as a countergift Indian spices. Priscus, whose kitchen was apparently well supplied with such condiments, sent the ruler of the Avars "pepper, the Indian leaf, cassia and the thing called saussurea." The khagan was "scented with spices." As a result, "the opposing armies camped together, and there was no fear in either force."[100] Perhaps such fraternization had already been initiated during the long winter; even the wars of the twentieth century, stamped with inflamed nationalistic hate, experienced "Christmas at the front."

The khagan's behavior contradicts all the clichés of the cruel pillagers that have been propagated down to our contemporaries. Probably it was not just noble-mindedness that lay behind this. Spectacular generosity is a basic characteristic of every successful barbarian ruler. The Romans mostly saw only the obverse of this trait, namely, the skill by which he acquired the means for his gifts. For this reason, the barbarians were considered greedy. The means collected in this way were mostly directed to other members of the barbarian community. High rank carried an obligation to great gifts. When the Romans accepted such gifts for the Easter celebration in Tomis, it augmented the prestige of the giver. But it was not a calculated move by the khagan when he flattered his sense of self in this fashion. Just as with the request for spices, something of the spontaneous feeling for life of an Avar ruler comes to light here through all the cultural filters.

It was the khagan himself who ended the Easter peace with a command. At the conclusion of the feast days, about which he was well informed, he demanded the disengagement of the two military forces. "And so in this way the barbarian was parted from the Romans." For both parties the year would turn out to be one of the most onerous in terms of losses. On the sixth day the khagan learned that a Roman army had entered Nicopolis under Comentiolus. He marched via Sucidava upstream along the Danube to Iatrus/Krivina, where he established his camp.[101] The Avars moved against Comentiolus at once, sure that they would be able to prevent his joining up with Priscus. Again, it seems that Theophylact has patched up his sources somehow.

The description of the battle that ensued clearly comes from the propagandistic version of the account of Maurice's wars produced under Phocas, which also makes Comentiolus appear as a traitor who does everything to confuse the Roman army on the day of the fight. Yet the decimated army hung on until the evening. Comentiolus stole away in the night but not before he had urged his best units to flee. The next day the remaining Romans drew back across the river Iatrus/Jantra. Here they again fell into an Avar ambush, but with great losses the meager remains of the army fought their way through the defiles.[102] Comentio-lus fled to Drizipera where he requested admittance. Yet the gates did not open. From the city walls stones and curses rained down on the treacherous general. He was obliged to continue his flight to Constantinople. Here he was at once formally charged with treason. Maurice appointed arbitrators, who eventually acquitted the field commander. The next summer Comentiolus was back at his post. Shortly after his assumption of power Phocas had him killed.[103]

John of Antioch gives a rather different version of events.[104] According to him it was the emperor himself who was behind the plot because he hated the army. But his letter instructing Comentiolus to turn the rebellious army over to the Avars was discovered, and he had to shift the blame to the commander. While Comentiolus was facing charges by the military, Philippicus, the emperor's son-in-law, assumed command in Thrace. Theophylact knows nothing about Philippicus's activity in the Avar war, but his information does not rule it out. It is confirmed by a fragment from Michael the Syrian.[105] According to this source, the "Bulgars" had ravaged Thrace until the Romans under Philippicus marched against them. This does not mean that Bulgars constituted a majority in the khagan's army. As a contemporary of the Bulgars but not of the Avars, Michael rather identified the Avars in his sources with the Bulgars. But it seems quite plausible that Philippicus conducted ineffective defensive actions in the vicinity of the capital until the next summer, when he was again replaced by Comentiolus.

While Comentiolus was making his way to the capital after abandoning his army, the Avars were on his heels. Shortly after he arrived in Drizipera, they showed up and conquered the city. There they burned the church of St. Alexander, destroyed the silver-adorned grave of the martyr, and scattered his bones. This is the second time in just a few years that we hear of the destruction of a church dedicated to Alexander.[106] Theophylact attributes to the desecration of the martyr the disaster that now befell the barbarians. Soon after the victory celebration in Drizipera, an epidemic broke out in the barbarian camp. The khagan was seriously affected: seven of his sons are reported to have fallen victim to the incurable disease on the same day. Meanwhile, Comentiolus brought the news of the defeat to the capital, which caused some panic. People are reported to have thought of giving up Europe entirely and of moving to Chalcedon on the other side of the Bosporus. But the emperor mobilized the last reserves, had the city's citizens armed, and garrisoned the Long Walls. After a week he sent an embassy to the khagan upon request by the senate.

When the emperor's envoy, Harmaton, arrived in Drizipera, the khagan let him wait for ten days. Not even the rich gifts that he brought impressed the grieving Avar ruler. When Harmaton was admitted to the khagan's tent on the twelfth day, the latter refused to accept the emperor's gifts. The ambassador needed to deploy all his eloquence to have the gifts accepted. Yet the following day the khagan could finally be persuaded to agree to a peace pact. The khagan accused the emperor of having broken the peace, and again, as he had done before Priscus on the bank of the Danube, he called on God to serve as arbiter between Maurice and himself—an almost defiant gesture after he had been struck such a blow by fate.[107]

Although hammered out under adverse conditions, the peace agreement offered an advantage to both parties. The khagan was able to increase his annual tribute by an additional twenty thousand solidi and now received one hundred twenty thousand. The Romans succeeded in having the Danube explicitly designated as the boundary. They renounced the bridgeheads north of the river that had been disputed in 595. However, it was expressly agreed that the Danube frontier could be crossed to fight the Slavs. With this, another cause of disagreement from earlier years was disposed of according to Roman wishes. For it is evident that the Byzantines were greatly interested in this provision, even if it was certainly formulated in neutral fashion. This signified no less than that "the Slavs living in the two countries were not recognized as subjects of international law."[108]

The treaty shows that the emperor was prepared to make some concessions to the Avars in return for having a free hand to deal with the Slavs north of the Danube. It also shows that the fate of these subjects did not lie too close to the khagan's heart, who, despite his decimated army, still had a strong negotiating position. Occupying land south of the Danube was not an objective for the khagan either. The vulnerability of the Roman defense system had again been made evident, and the khagan clearly believed that he could do without direct control of the Illyrian bank of the Danube.

Exceptionally, Theophanes has more to say about the negotiations in Drizipera than does his source Theophylact.[109] Before the peace was concluded, he recounts, the khagan wanted to return prisoners for a ransom of one *nomisma* per head. Maurice declined this offer, at which point the barbarian dropped the price by half. The parsimonious emperor, however, would not even offer one *siliquia* per head. Then the angered barbarian had all the prisoners killed. Surely these stories about Maurice were circulated after his fall; but they may also be expressions of widespread opposition during his last years on the throne. Their historical core cannot be more precisely established. But they do show what could be expected from the barbarians and what was not. The execution of prisoners was seen as an exception; otherwise there was a very profitable trade in ransoming.

The position of the two adversaries had become more difficult with the events of 598. Maurice lost further credit in his army, and dissatisfaction with his rule spread. Whatever exactly had happened at Iatrus, the conduct of Comentiolus, and his successive reappointment, had damaged the reputation of the military leadership. The frequent changes at the head of the European army prevented the employment of a coherent strategy and subverted the loyalty of the troops. On the other hand, the khagan could draw no further profit from his victory and from the intrigues in the camp of his opponent. Even though the plague appears to our understanding an unmotivated stroke of fate, a charismatic barbarian leader would be held as responsible for it as for a lost war.

In the meantime, Priscus had, at any event, sought to maintain his army intact, quite in line with the instructions of the *Strategicon*.[110] The setbacks that the Romans suffered, along with other factors, then make an immediate offensive little plausible. "Nobody makes a habit of immediately retrieving a defeat, except the Scythians, and it is particularly foreign to the Romans," observes the manual on warfare.[111] The peace accord would scarcely have been described in such detail if it did not at least remain in force until the next year.

5.8 599: The Khagan under Pressure

When the plague-afflicted barbarian army withdrew across the Danube, Priscus moved forward. He established his winter quarters in Singidunum, which had become a cornerstone of the Roman defense. At the same time Comentiolus's trial was proceeding in Constantinople, although it would end with his acquittal and reinstatement as *strategos*. This gives the impression that he was Priscus's superior. When the warm season arrived, he joined the army to assume his command. On the orders of the emperor, the peace agreement with the Avars was publicly rescinded.[112]

The army now moved down the Danube to the island of Viminacium/Kostolac, to which, apparently, the name of the city destroyed in 584 had been transferred. Here, below the mouth of the Morava where the Danube divides into several courses, an attempt was made to cross the river. That the army did not simply take the old imperial road to Sirmium is a sure sign that the former Illyrian metropolis was not the seat of the khagan's residence at this time. The khagan remained north of the Danube, from where he delegated a part of the army to four of his sons, in order to prevent the enemy from crossing the river.

Still, a Roman division, which had thrown a boat-bridge across the river, was able to force a landing and established a bridgehead on the Avar shore. During this time Comentiolus sat sick in Viminacium and had little taste to undertake a risky maneuver in Avar land. Priscus in turn was unwilling to risk a battle without his colleague. Not until the soldiers, besieged in their camp, sent an urgent request for reinforcement was Priscus obliged to enter battle. The first attack by the khagan's sons was successfully turned back. The next day Priscus had all the boats and rafts brought back to the island in order to cut off the path of retreat for his soldiers.

When the Avars renewed their attack on the fourth day, Priscus drew up his army in three blocks before the barricades. The Avars, well armed, had divided their army into fifteen units, which attacked from all sides. Yet again the Romans defended the camp with success. As the sun began to set over the battlefield, the Romans had lost three hundred fighters, the barbarians reportedly four thousand.

Three days later, when the next Avar attack came, Priscus ordered his troops to draw up in three divisions and surrounded his opponents. Theophylact reports that nine thousand Avars were left lying on the battlefield. Ten days passed before the khagan's sons were again ready to fight. Priscus engaged the enemy and chose his ground with care. He succeeded in taking the Avars in a pincer movement and to force them onto moorland.[113] The Romans had learned their lesson in the Slavic marshes. Along with their army the Avar princes met defeat in the morass. In this battle alone fifteen thousand are reputed to have lost their lives; the numbers are surely exaggerated.[114]

The khagan, who this time appears to have participated in the battle, barely succeeded in fleeing to the Tisza. After the loss of seven sons and a portion of his army to the plague, fate had dealt another heavy blow to the Avar ruler. According to the guidelines for successful command in the field, Priscus exploited the momentum of his victory.[115] He advanced into a region where no Roman army had been for centuries, that is, through the Banat to the lower course of the Tisza. Here, in the heart of Avar territory, a new battle took place one month after the encounters near Viminacium. The day for the battle was, with unusual courtesy, agreed between the two parties. The khagan organized his army into twelve massed groups, for "in combat they do not, as do the Romans and Persians, form their battle line in three parts, but in several units of irregular size, all joined closely together."[116] Priscus confused his opponent with a daring move by arranging his army on the battlefield in inverse order and could continue his series of victories. It was one of the largest battles that were fought during the entire Avar war.

Yet the Roman field commander did not dare to march into the land between the Danube and Tisza rivers, the center of his opponent's territory. It became apparent that the war against the steppe dwellers was not to be won in conventional fashion. A Persian war could be decided, as by Heraclius, by a march on the opposing capital city. The Avars could be defeated only if they showed up for a battle in the first place. Even then, victory remained without consequences. All that Priscus could do was to set a division of four thousand men across the Tisza, in order to scout out events on the opponent's side. First off, the Romans found three Gepid villages in their path. Unaffected by the bustle of war about them, the inhabitants had celebrated a great feast the night before and were now sleeping off their intoxication. Shortly before dawn the Romans carried out a gruesome massacre among the sleeping barbarians. If we are to credit Theophylact's account of the war, this was the greatest victory of all; he speaks of no fewer than thirty thousand dead Gepids and great spoils.

The example is instructive in several respects. First, it shows how information from the theater of war was grossly exaggerated. Maurice badly needed military success and so even a massacre of drunken villagers could be hyperbolically re-cast as a major event. Second, the existence of Gepid villages in the old settlement area on the Tisza shows that the descendants of the Gepids vanquished in 567 now had a sufficient life under Avar rule. Third, the behavior of the Roman military in enemy territory shows how little grounds the empire had for accusing its "barbarian" opponents of inhuman behavior. The khagan had let the inhabitants of Singidunum or Drizipera live, although he had not found them in bed but had met them weapons in hand. The Romans had no scruples about slaughtering sleeping civilians in thorough fashion. The accusation of the Avar ambassador Kokh that the barbarians had learned all their evil ways from the Romans finds some justification in the light of these events.[117]

The khagan needed three weeks to mobilize his reserves, among whom there were many Slavs. Priscus during this time remained stationed on the Tisza. The final battle of the campaign was no less bitter than the foregoing. Again the Romans were successful in forcing their opponents into the river, in which many, especially Slavs, died. The Romans also succeeded in taking a great quantity of prisoners, whose number has come down to us. Even if we take into account the inevitable exaggerations, it is evident that on this occasion Slavs had had to bear the chief burden of the battle.

In their exact numbers Theophylact and Theophanes differ.[118] Theophylact mentions 3,000 Avars, 6,200 "other barbarians," and 8,000 Slavs. According to Theophanes there were likewise 3,000 Avars, 3,200 Gepids, 2,000 additional bar-barians, and only 800 Slavs. Theophylact's reckoning is surely to be preferred, especially as concerns the number of Slavs. Yet the reference to Gepids in the later author is valuable, and we may understand Bulgars and Gepids to be referenced in the "other barbarians," both with a contingent that roughly matched the cor-responding Avar unit in size.

The proportions of prisoners are, however, hardly characteristic for the composition of an Avar army. The subject peoples were surely drawn by the khagan's summons to defend their homeland and had less part in profit-able raiding expeditions. The events of the two years had entailed consider-able bloodletting of the core of Avar forces. Moreover, Slavic foot soldiers, who probably also fought in the first rank, were easier to capture alive than a mounted Avar warrior. Lastly, a prisoner of war would be more likely to identify himself to the Romans as "another barbarian," even if he normally counted himself among the Avars. Whether the captured Slavs were from the Carpathian Basin or its bordering regions, belonged to the regular Avar army or not, are questions that can scarcely be decided in light of the above. After his victory Priscus had the prisoners taken to Tomis. The khagan had lost an army but not his composure. He succeeded in sending envoys to the emperor before the latter had any precise notion of the military situation. There the barbarians demanded, under threat, the release of the prisoners. The emperor was taken in by the ploy and had the khagan's warriors in Tomis sent back promptly.[119]

Meanwhile, the season of poor weather had arrived. Priscus could not further exploit his victory. Comentiolus, who apparently had no hand in these successes, wanted to take the fastest route back to Constantinople. Arriving in Novae/Svištov, he announced that he would take the old Via Traiana over the Balkan Mountains.[120] It was pointed out to him that there was only one man, more than one hundred years old, who still knew the way, which, he said, had not been used in ninety years. Despite all the warnings, the impatient field commander set out. In the mountains he was taken by surprise by the arrival of winter, and a goodly portion of his followers fell victim to the cold and winter storms. Comentiolus then decided to winter in Philippopolis/Plovdiv. He did not return to the capital until the spring but found that he still had Maurice's support despite all the adversities.[121]

Priscus's victories show what the Byzantine military was still capable of at the very end of the sixth century. Yet the extraordinary success in the land of the Avars also illustrates the fact that the Avar war could not be definitively won. Theophylact's account highlights the volatility of military success. The bravery of Roman soldiers is often eclipsed by the incompetence and arrogance of the emperor and his commanders, and by recurrent opposition in the army. The enemies, the Avars and Slavs, almost seem of secondary interest in his narrative. That reflects the situation of an army that was chiefly concerned with itself.

5.9 600–602: The End of Imperial Politics on the Danube

Priscus's spectacular success bought the emperor a little time. In the nineteenth year of Maurice's reign, in the period from September 600 to August 601, there was no fighting on the Danube. In the following year, the emperor's brother Peter was reappointed commander in Europe.[122] During this time the khagan was not inactive. He tried to compensate for the setback with a diplomatic offensive. Since contacts with the Lombards had already been quite close, he concluded an eternal peace with envoys of King Agilulf.[123] On the envoys' way back to Italy he sent his own ambassador along, "who then traveled on to Gaul and requested that the kings of the Franks keep the peace with the Avars as well as with the Lombards." The purpose of the Avar peace mission was above all to counteract a Byzantine-Frankish alliance like that of 596.

In addition, the pact with the Lombards had an offensive signification. Earlier Agilulf had sent the khagan "artisans for the construction of boats," with which he then "conquered an island in Thrace."[124] Presumably the strategic importance of the Danube in the last battles and the successful strike by the Roman flotilla against Singidunum may have stimulated a desire on the khagan's part for Danube ships of his own. The Slavic *monoxyla* or dugouts, which were sufficient only for crossing rivers, could not compete with the Byzantine *dromones*. The shipbuilders from Italy may have helped in this respect. Appreciably more comprehensible is another point in the Avar–Lombard agreement. While the Avar ambassador was still on his goodwill tour of European royal courts, Avars, Slavs, and Lombards together attacked Byzantine Istria.[125] This concerted action nullified the defensive actions taken by the exarch, for which Pope Gregory had sent his congratulations in May 599.[126] The cease-fire between Agilulf and the exarch had run out in March 601, and the Lombards also took Padua in the same year. In gratitude for Lombard support at a difficult time, the khagan, when the crisis had passed, helped the Lombard king out with a Slavic contingent for the conquest of Cremona in August 603.[127]

Maurice, who had to face riots in Constantinople because of a famine, decided in 601 once again to polish his image through successes on the inhospitable Danube. The reinstallment of his brother Peter as field commander should assure that this time events would reflect more to the credit of the imperial family. The successful Priscus was quietly moved off the stage.[128] According to Theophylact, this happened in the twentieth year of the emperor's rule after the marriage of Prince Theodosius (November 601). Yet events under the command of the emperor's brother cannot be comprised in a single year, so Peter's appointment must have happened earlier in 601.

After he was called up, the new commander-in-chief let the summer elapse without activity, while he remained in Palastolum on the Danube.[129] At the beginning of autumn he learned that Apsikh, the Avar commander, had concentrated his army by the "cataracts" at the Iron Gate.[130] Peter sought to resolve the situation through negotiations. The commander of the Avars demanded a surrender of the position at the Iron Gate, but Peter countered that such an abandonment would be incompatible with the peace treaty. Still preoccupied by

Priscus's offensives, the Avars were probably aiming at a revision of the peace of Drizipera. Probably they sought to bring the Roman base of operations between Singidunum and the cataracts under closer control. The words were not followed by deeds, and both parties withdrew to their winter quarters.

The khagan's army had established its headquarters in Constantiola, where the memorable encounter with Priscus had taken place. The khagan left the direction of operations and the negotiations to Apsikh. This is unusual. Certainly his position had been weakened, and those *logades* that had already once shown their opposition may have curtailed his functions. The khagan's hesitation was also noted in Constantinople, where the emperor reckoned with a surprise attack in 602. Yet while the khagan needed a victory, he risked no direct attack on the empire in the following year. Instead, in the summer of 602 he dispatched Apsikh against the Antes, who were allies of the Romans.[131] A Roman alliance with the Antes is already attested by John of Ephesus in the 580s.[132] The Avar strike seems to have been successful; this is the last mention of the Antes, living northeast of the Carpathians.

Then something extraordinary happened in this year to reveal the weakness of the Avar position: large numbers defected from the Avars and joined the Byzantine side.[133] If we reflect on the emphasis with which Baian's envoys had repeatedly demanded the return of deserters of every kind, we can assess the significance of this event. Theophylact would have attached no special weight to it if it had been an everyday occurrence, as was the enrollment of other barbarians in the imperial army. He continues: "So the khagan was thrown into confusion at the news; he became greatly terrified, imploring and devising many schemes to win back the force which had defected." The Avar dissidents were clearly confident that their khagan no longer had the power to demand their extradition by the emperor.

Maurice had become impatient. He wanted to see his opponent's weakness exploited. He ordered Peter, who had wintered safely in Adrianople, to cross the Danube. The latter came only to the decision to send his *hypostrategos* Guduin into the land of the Slavs. The raid by the deputy commander, who later became *dux* of Naples under Phocas (and is therefore another positive figure in Theophylact's account),[134] took its usual course. The Romans killed everyone they could catch and covered themselves in "glory and spoils." Yet Guduin, who took his assignment seriously, prevented his soldiers from recrossing the Danube.

What followed is history on a large scale. The events that then evolved on the Danube with fatal logic have often been regarded as decisive. Without the fall of Maurice, the almost thirty-year war with the Persians would not have broken out, and without the weakening of the two archenemies, the Arabs would not have conquered the entire Middle East. But the rebellion of the Balkan army against

Maurice was only the drop that caused the cup to spill over. The emperor's far-reaching political conception and its military feasibility were increasingly divergent. The Byzantine successes against the Avars had above all strengthened the position of the Slavs. The empire was thrust back into a war that could never be made profitable, least of all in terms of the emperor's policies, which, true to his epithet *pacificus*, were designed to create peace at home through military successes abroad.

The emperor's command to pass the winter in the land of the Slavs again, despite previous protests and failures, made Maurice's regime collapse. The troops immediately raised more or less reasonable objections: little hope of booty, exhaustion of the horses, and the great numbers of the enemy. The field commander shifted responsibility to his brother, and Maurice held all the more firmly to his plan. The troops, already distressed over the long wait, mutinied and crossed the Danube toward Palastolum, then farther past Asemus to Curisca, at which point yet another crossing of the Danube was planned.[135] Yet Maurice aggravated the prevailing mood with an incautious letter, which reputedly said that they would have to provision themselves to "provide for the treasury an interruption of public maintenance."[136] Now the army went out of control and marched on Constantinople. As had been the ancient practice with the military emperors, the *exercitus Romanus* voiced its claim to be able to "make" its own emperor and proclaimed the centurion Phocas. In the capital city, the rebels met less resistance than expected, the fleeing Maurice was seized, and on November 27, 602, was executed along with his family. The fall of Maurice ends Theophylact's account of the Balkan war, and from this point on the historical record becomes very patchy.

LIFE AND ORGANIZATION
IN THE AVAR EMPIRE

The period between 559 and 602 is the only one for which a fairly continuous narrative of Avar history is possible, thanks to, most of all, the works of Menander and Theophylact. What we know (or can assume) about the seventh and eighth centuries will be outlined in chapters 7 and 8. The present chapter is devoted to ways of life and organization in the Avar Empire. Again, much of the information offered in written sources about the structures of Avar rule comes in accounts about the sixth century. Therefore, I have placed this chapter here, at a juncture not so much of Avar history, but of what we know about it.

6.1 Nomads, Warriors, Steppe Peoples

Arguably, after 568 central Asia extended to the Vienna Woods. Even if only a minority of the European Avars had their origins on the vast steppes beyond the Caspian Sea, a zone of intense cultural exchange with similar organizational structures and forms of life extended from the Great Wall of China to the Eastern Alps. Events in the Far East directly affected the plains of the middle Danube. The term "central Eurasia," which has recently come to be used, is very appropriate to describe this differentiated but entangled cultural and political landscape.[1] In order to understand the particularity of the Avar realm both in the central Eurasian and in the European context, comparing it with roughly contemporary polities in central Asia is instructive.[2] On the other hand, conclusions based on analogy require caution.[3] Simply subsuming our evidence under broad concepts is rather unproductive. Even the concept of nomadism is too multifaceted to be conveniently applied to the European Avars. This first section will therefore sketch some basic conditions of existence in the steppe, in order to better assess similarities to and differences from the structures of the Avar Empire. Seen in terms of the steppe empires of central Eurasia, the khaganate on the Danube was an exception, defined by specific ecological, geopolitical, and cultural conditions.

The civilized observer, then as now, is inclined to consider sedentary agriculturalism as on a higher cultural level than the rough life of itinerant herdsmen.[4] This is not justified. Pastoral nomadism is one of the most specialized forms of economic activity and makes possible the exploitation of vast areas of dry land that could not otherwise be inhabited.[5] This way of life did not evolve until thousands of years after farming, roughly around the beginning of the first millennium BCE. The organization of life on the steppe, on closer consideration, proves rather diverse. Since the Eurasian steppe zone offers very disparate conditions, from mountain regions through deserts, dry steppes, grass steppes, to forest steppes on the northern edge, there arose over time a whole bundle of nonsedentary economic forms: "primitive" pastoralism, near- and far-ranging camel and horse nomadism, transhumance, mountain pastoralism, and others.[6] Nikolay Kradin observes: "In Mongolia, there is no sole scheme of migrating even at the present time. Not less than ten different variants of seasonal roaming are known."[7]

"Unlike agrarian societies, nomadism is not labor-intensive and does not require large populations for production purposes," as Peter Golden has argued.[8] Still, life in these ecological niches was harsh and required, for the optimal exploitation of pasture and water, "a notable degree of collective discipline, integrated task-performance and technical expertise."[9] Hard winters, droughts, and epidemics could suddenly deprive pastoralists of a great part of their herds. Foraging and raiding other groups of pastoralists was also common practice, which could destroy the means of survival of one group and build the fortune of another—this is the way in which Temujin, later Genghis Khan, started his career.[10]

Hunting and the defense of the herds required the superior speed and fighting ability of the practiced rider, and organizational skills and discipline were needed for the coordination of movements over wide spaces. As a consequence, the steppe warriors developed advanced military abilities. Only the great empires of the ancient world were a match for them. Contacts with China, Iran, and the Roman Empire proved important challenges for nomad polities. Military confrontation forced both sides to learn from one another and furthered the perfection of their fighting styles. The riches of the great states created incentives for the consolidation of ever greater bands of mounted warriors.[11] Long-distance trade between urban cultures offered the steppe peoples new economic possibilities.

This complex and sometimes elusive way of life presents a challenge to social models and historical grand narratives mostly generated on the basis of sedentary societies. As Nikolay N. Kradin has remarked, "the reconstructions of social systems in nomadic archaeology are based more often on free interpretations than on strict facts."[12] Often, ethnic or social distinctions were treated as invariables exposed to historical and political contingencies. Life in the steppe has been regarded as almost immutable, evolving within a very limited range of strategies for survival in a hostile environment, and consequently governed by a virtually unchanging social order. In particular, many scholars assumed that ancient ties of kinship and clan solidarities shaped nomadic life in unchanging ways; David Sneath has recently argued convincingly against such ahistorical views.[13] "Kinetic empires" should not be assessed in static categories.[14]

Much research on steppe peoples conducted in the twentieth century in the Soviet Union and elsewhere was framed by Marxist paradigms. However, Marxism faced a fundamental difficulty in accommodating nomadic societies in its five-stage scheme of modes of production. Were they slave-holding, feudal, or something else again? They could either be subsumed under the stages reached at the same time by sedentary states, so that the Xiongnu were slave-holding, the Turks early feudal, and the Mongols mature feudal, although there was little in the evidence to support such attributions.[15] Or one could construct alternative types complementary to the European stage scheme. Nomads could be included in the model of "Asiatic mode of production" or as a special type of "nomadic feudalism."[16] Labels such as "military democracy," elaborated by Morgan and seized on by Marx and Engels, or "patriarchal feudalism," current for a while in Soviet research, or "barbarian state," or "rudimentary class society," also occurred in the debate.[17] In fact, they are not quite Marxist, since they do not describe modes of production but rather those of political organization.

Since the 1990s, Marxist models have quietly faded out in research about the steppes. Indeed, debating labels brought little progress; however, the question of the economic basis of empires should not be discarded together with the straightjacket of linear theories of progress. All the empires of the steppes were based on their specific mix of modes of production. First, pastoralism was practiced in extended families and tribes, and these relatively self-sufficient economies produced essential food supplies and objects of daily use.[18] Probably "individual possession of livestock" was combined "with collective occupancy of the land"; the power to dispose of pasture resources was the decisive element.[19] Second, along with the pastoral economy, predatory expansion played a decisive role. By means of the tributary transfer of goods or by a partial integration in the military bureaucracy of a sedentary state, the warrior elite profited from and to an extent participated in the particular conditions for exploitation in these class societies. Third, the mounted warriors also siphoned off the production of the sedentary farmer populations in the regions they ruled.[20] It is obvious that there was a considerable potential for antagonism between these three forms of political economy. This tension could express itself in a disdain for sedentary work, in destructive raids on agricultural or urban productive zones, or also in a successive marginalization of pastoralists once a nomadic elite had appropriated a thriving sedentary economy. Still, there was also a lot of potential in uniting the three spheres within a sole political system, and steppe peoples were capable of achieving that.

Anthropological and sociological model building has had an increasing influence on recent research on central Eurasia. In the 1970s, the theory of the "Early State" by Claessen and Skalník began to have an impact.[21] Later, theories of chiefdom or models based on the distinction between "great men," "big men," etc. had some influence.[22] The key question here was labeling political organization: Were nomadic polities states, empires, tribal or imperial confederations, or just precarious aggregations of smaller units? That led to a further question. Was large-scale political organization in the steppe structurally dependent on sedentary societies, or did nomadic polities have an autonomous social basis?[23] Beyond such large-scale dichotomies, research on the relationship between sedentary empires and their steppe neighbors has made considerable progress, in particular on the *histoire croisée* of China and the nomad empires.[24] I would like to mention three monographs that have all appeared after the German version of the present book and have pushed the agenda forward in remarkable ways.

The first book was Thomas Barfield's *The Perilous Frontier: Nomadic Empires and China, 221 BC to AD 1757*, which appeared in 1989. No steppe empire emerged in the steppes north of China, he argued, in periods of weakness of the Chinese Empire; to the contrary, they throve on the resources of strong neighbors. They usually did not attempt to conquer Chinese heartlands: "In essence my contention is that the steppe tribes of Mongolia played a key role in frontier politics without becoming conquerors of China, and that Manchuria, for political and ecological reasons, was the breeding ground for foreign dynasties when native dynasties collapsed."[25] As Barfield acknowledges, his model does not always work (the Mongols are a strong case against it).[26] However, it raises a point that is also important for the Huns, Avars, and Hungarians in Europe: they never sought to conquer the heartlands of the empires that they raided but remained in a peripheral area, the Carpathian Basin. This is very much unlike Goths, Vandals, or Franks who occupied core provinces of the Roman Empire in the fifth and sixth centuries, or later Arabs and Berbers in the seventh and eighth, Normans in the tenth and eleventh, and Islamic Turks from the twelfth century onward. Whatever the reason, this difference points to a first-rate structural feature of the polities in question.

The second and very influential book was Nicola Di Cosmo's *Ancient China and Its Enemies: The Rise of Nomadic Power in East Asia*, which came out in 2004. It looked at the rise of the Xiongnu Empire both through the lens of Chinese perceptions and through its structural conditions. The achievement lay in its differentiated critique of misleading narratives of relationships between the Chinese and the nomads. Traditional views had relied both on an uncritical reading of ancient Chinese historiography, and often also on a Sinocentric perspective. This implied the notion of a clearly delineated frontier between China and the steppe that is the product of ecological conditions and completely different lifestyles, the notion of a "timeless frontier relationship" between a culturally superior China and northern "barbarians," and the notion that social differentiation and the rise of nomadic states necessarily responded to Chinese stimuli. Rather, in the case of the Xiongnu, "the probable cause for the emergence of a statelike structure lay in a political mechanism already in existence within the tribal society of the nomads, which allowed for the centralization of political and military power at times of crisis."[27] "All large steppe formations about which we have sufficient information . . . arise from a period of intense struggle between various nomadic groups, not by going to war with sedentary states."[28] The same could surely be said about Attila's Hun Empire and that of the Avars. Steppe empires may have needed intense raiding and bargaining with sedentary powers to fuel their prestige economies, but they were not simply creations of China or Rome and followed their own logic in these exchanges. Di Cosmo's critique of grand narratives comes close to the concerns of the present book: we should read the sources critically as (usually) intentional outside accounts of foreign societies.[29] We should focus as much as possible on the inner dynamic and contradictions of steppe polities and historicize the relations between the steppe and the sedentary empires without aiming at the construction of a one-size-fits-all model. A cyclical concept of the rise and fall of steppe empires is certainly attractive, but it should not impede the view of the changing contexts and the gradual structural changes that frame central Eurasian history.

The third book is Jonathan Skaff's *Sui-Tang China and Its Turko-Mongol Neighbors: Culture, Power and Connections, 580–800*, published in 2012.[30] It offers an outline of "overlapping and entangled webs of culture that shared many strands" and "foundational conceptual structures" between China and the steppe empires.[31] This shared basis of political culture included the claim of "universal kingship, which was heaven-mandated in east Asia, and competed symbolically with diplomacy involving elaborate displays of pageantry, status ranking, obeisance, gift exchanges, and feasting." As a mechanism of conflict resolution, diplomacy offered the forging of honorable and "reciprocally amenable patron–client relationships." It revolved around a mutual acceptance of status ranking and of the many ways in which status could be symbolically displayed. There was a basic agreement about the forms in which political relations alternated between the "soft power" of diplomacy and the "hard power" of warfare. "Diplomatic relationships and rituals were acted out within the framework of these widely shared conceptual parameters."[32] Both China and the steppe empires were most successful when they managed to dominate the middle ground (in particular, the Ordos region) by offering to local nomadic and sedentary groups protection, prosperity, and a degree of cultural autonomy. This seems to be where both the Byzantine Empire and the Avars had problems. Many of the elements of the shared conceptual parameters that Skaff lists for eastern Eurasia can also be detected in the exchanges between the Avars and Byzantium. Others are conspicuously absent: for instance, there is no evidence of marriage contracts between the Avars and Byzantium (due not least to the unacceptability of Christian–pagan marriages) and of other cultural concessions, which the Sui and Tang emperors were prepared to make.

Generally, the formation and collapse of realms and peoples occurred at a quicker pace than among the sedentary peoples.[33] The "Account of the Western Regions" in the Chinese *Bei shi* (*Pei-shih*), written in the mid-seventh century, observes: "Since ancient times many generations have passed, followed by annexations and conflicts between the countries, their rise and fall. As a consequence, the earlier designations were changed and another people, that had newly established itself, was designated with the old name. Over and above this, the members of tribes intermixed, and their territories were called after the literary, that is, the earlier, names."[34] This has encouraged cyclical models of the rise and fall of steppe empires. However, as Nicola Di Cosmo has rightly maintained, a single model is not sufficient to explain the succession of steppe empires. There even were fundamental differences between the establishment and structure of different empires founded by people known as "Huns": the Xiongnu, the *Hwn* states in the Iranian periphery, and Attila's empire, created about sixty years after the Huns had arrived in Europe.[35] Thus, we should not look for similarities that could warrant the use of a set model for the organization of the Avar Empire, which could then allow us to complement the patchy information in our sources with central Asian parallels. Rather, some of the better-documented contemporary cases may help us to understand the range of options that a nomadic polity might have in certain situations, and the different dynamic that empire building might acquire in various contexts, even if the challenges faced may have been similar.

Turkish khagans left behind stylized accounts of the foundation of their empires in their inscriptions. It was no cause for reproach to have started small. On the contrary, rulers gloried in having broken free of foreign rule with only a handful of faithful followers, as in the Kültegin inscription in the Orkhon Valley:

> My father, the khagan, went off with seventeen men. Having heard the news that [he] was marching off, those who were in the towns went up mountains and those who were on mountains came down (from there); thus they gathered and numbered to seventy men. Due to the fact that heaven granted strength, the soldiers of my father, the khagan, were like wolves, and his enemies were like sheep. Having gone on campaigns eastward and westward, he gathered together and collected people; they all numbered seven hundred men. After they had numbered seven hundred men [he] organized and ordered the people . . . in accordance with the rules of the ancestors.[36]

The inscriptions focus much more on victories over other steppe peoples than on conflicts with China.

The first Turkish khagans had imposed order on the "state and institutions of the Turkish peoples," as the inscription states: "[All the peoples living in] the four quarters of the world were hostile [to them]. Having marched with the armies, they conquered all the peoples in the four quarters of the world and subjugated them. They made the proud enemies bow and the powerful ones kneel."[37] Those who joined the victorious army were similarly "organized" and could then take part in the next campaign.[38] This alternation between military success and the reorganization of newly attracted adherents is referenced throughout the Old Turkic inscriptions. Seldom in the sources of the early Middle Ages does the direct connection between the formation of a people and the organization of power find so clear an expression.[39]

Theodore Syncellus, in the seventh century, presented Avar history in similar fashion.[40] Baian "flew from distant lands like a plague sent from God to where his people (*ethnos*) now lives. . . . [Baian and his sons] soon seized power through plundering and the massacre of the neighboring peoples and enslaved them; they grew and increased and covered this land with their multitudes." He emphasizes the connection between success and increase that is also addressed in the Orkhon inscriptions. The "order" that the khagans, according to their own statements, imposed on their peoples seems to Theodore, as their opponent, slavery. Noble origins are also among the attributes of successful rulers. These may be realized through biological descent or through a process of grafting. The Turkish Ashina dynasty, which traced its descent back to a she-wolf, would be used to lend legitimacy to almost all emerging dynasties of the following centuries. Even the Seljuks were accused of wrongly tracing their ascent back to a branch of this lineage of khagans.[41] After Genghis Khan his dynasty was the most eminent, and later steppe rulers derived their own lineages from it.

This conservatism in the legitimization and representation of rulership corresponds to the rapid decline to which it was in reality exposed. When Theophylact once has an ambassador recount to the Avar khagan the old wheel of fortune parable about the transitoriness of power, the image is well chosen.[42] The Orkhon inscriptions explain that the first Turkish khaganate was able to retain its power only so long as the khagan himself was brave and astute and had wise councilors and the begs, the nobles, and his people were united. Yet the sons of the founders of the realm did not inherit the same virtues. Their dissension was exploited by the "cunning and deceit" of the Chinese, and the empire crumbled. The Chinese sources, not without some satisfaction, also emphasize the constant inner conflict among their Turkish neighbors. For many Turkish warriors, service in the Chinese Empire finally seemed to offer greater chances for advancement. "The Turkish lords abandoned their Turkish titles. Those lords who were in China held the Chinese titles and obeyed the Chinese emperor." The people complained. "We used to be a people who had its own realm. Where is our realm now? . . . Where is our own khagan? To which khagan are we giving our services?"[43] The people needed a just and warlike khagan, who worked hard for their well-being, and only he could really make them into a people.[44]

It goes without saying that the happy ending of the inscriptions was only a provisional one. Soon the second Turkish khaganate of the seventh century was succeeded by the Uyghurs, then by the Karluks, and these in turn by the Oguz. This constant rise and fall of powers made for an ongoing redistribution of chances and new formations of peoples and polities. This is still evident in the description of conditions among the Kara-Kirghiz that Radloff offered in the nineteenth century. This people was divided into right and left halves, which each comprised about six "tribes," which were in turn composed of a number of "clans," in Radloff's terminology.[45] Like in the Orkhon inscriptions, the names of these subunits testified the eventful history to which they owed their momentary confederation. Many of them corresponded to the names of other peoples or their constituent tribes. Ethnonyms could come to be applied to designate small groups of other peoples, not only when the formerly prestigious holders of an empire had to submit to others but also through very different groups taking over these prestige-laden names.[46] The ethnic language was used to situate more or less prestigious, reliable, or potentially dangerous groups of subjects within the shifting architecture of power of a steppe empire. Almost every year, new campaigns could change the hierarchy of steppe communities under a khagan's rule. Grasping the dynamic of this constant transformation, which was realized in consciously conservative forms and with a restricted repertoire of possibilities, has been a basic problem for research.

Many scholars have argued that a ritual order, strong clan ties, and solidarities formed a counterweight to the extraordinary mobility of the nomads and the instability of their political order.[47] The military organization was built upon the decimal system, a practice later taken over by the Gothic and other "Scythian" peoples of late Antiquity.[48] In the spatial organization and deployment of the army cosmological representations played an important role. The points of the compass, colors, and numbers served as symbols in the creation of order. The Kültegin inscription resumes Bilge Khagan's exploits by the four corners of the earth: "Forward, to the sunrise; from the right in the land of midday (the south); back toward the sunset; from the left in the land of midnight (the north)—everywhere where people live, they are all subordinated to me."[49] Prominent warriors occupied various ranks in a hierarchy based on prestige and dignity. This ranking found expression in a complicated drinking ceremonial[50] and in accession to offices and honors. According to Chinese sources, there were twenty-eight classes of hereditary dignitaries among the Turks of the sixth century.[51]

Omeljan Pritsak's model of the early medieval steppe empires is based on the political semantics of the Old Turkic inscriptions; he acknowledges that the translation into modern concepts is far from straightforward.[52] The steppe empire (el) relies on traditional law (törü) and the legitimacy of the ruler (kut-ülüg), which in turn rests on the charisma of the dynasty (kut) and on the heavenly mandate of rulership (ülüg). It consists of bodun/budun, tribal groups or confederations, who are divided both into military units (tümän/tens of thousands, oq/arrows, etc.) and into tribes and clans. Each tribe/military unit (oq) has its own chieftain, the beg, and often their own military contingent. Along with and above this is the central administration, with its dignitaries, often members of the ruling dynasty, and its military entourage (buyruq). The settlement unit is the tent and the el-kün, the "unit of peace," also called aul, which on average comprises about three hundred people in fifty tents. Similar conclusions were reached by Ildikó Ecsedy from the investigation of Chinese terminology for the Turks of the sixth century. She understood the Turkic Empire as the union of three organizational principles: a network of exogamous, patrilinear kinship groups, the clans (tsu or hsing; in the last concept suppressed matrilinear traditions also reverberate); a grouping of economic-territorial unions, the tribes (pu-lo); and the central politico-military organization (kuo/state), which is administered by a few dominant tribes.[53]

However, as David Sneath has argued, the translation of community terms from Turkish, Chinese, or Mongol texts is not without problems; "tribe" or "clan" implies a consistent principle of organization according to real or putative kinship that is not present in all the terms translated that way. Yet we should be careful not to smuggle our assumptions on the nature of tribes, clans, or ethnic groups into reconstructions of steppe societies. Sneath suggests "house," in the European medieval sense, instead of "clan," as a more neutral term, which may or may not imply distinctions by kinship.[54] However, Latin and Greek texts do perceive of the Avars as organized in ethnic subgroups: for instance, the *Strategicon* states that before battle, the armies of Avars and Turks are scattered in "tribes and clans," *kata genē kai phylas*.[55] Whether that reflects an actual sense of kinship is hard to ascertain, but not unlikely, as long as we do not assume actual "common blood."[56] The basic unit in the Eurasian steppe, here called *phylē*, was the house, clan, or camp, sometimes called *aul* in research literature about the Avars, and seems to have included several families, with their slaves and dependents.[57] The association of a number of families, related or not, and their yurts was required for the defense of the livestock. These wandering/settlement units also constituted the basic elements from which armies were drawn. Their necessities of reproduction were in a tension with the requirements of imperial military organization, but perhaps less so than in the more labor-intensive agrarian societies. On the other hand, the herds could only exist decentralized in small groups, in order not to exhaust the pasture resources. The "house," *aul*, or however it may have been called, was a very fluid entity of fluctuating size. Unions through marriage, the vagaries of herding, conflict, or growth could lead to changes much more easily than in a sedentary village community. Therefore, the basic unit was not simply constituted by kinship.

This corresponds to a fundamental contradiction in steppe empires. For military purposes, they rely on a great concentration of forces; but feeding the herds requires a dispersal in space, even on military campaigns (as attested repeatedly on Avar campaigns in the late sixth century). Another centrifugal element is the ongoing competition among regional/tribal leaders and the ruler's attempts not to allow them to become too strong. All this prevented the establishment of a stable inner order. Shifting alliances and constellations, the contingency of war and the death of leaders, the formation of new warrior bands and retinues constantly disrupted the structure of the subgroups. As long as the khagan had the power, he continuously created new units through the reorganization of the army, distributed tasks and offices to the (often rival) members of his dynasty and other prominent men, and tried to balance the prestige and eminence of the great families through increasingly complicated ranking systems. This required complex "strategies of cohesion and control," as Michael Drompp has called it.[58] On the other hand, households, ethnic, regional, and status groups tend continuously to consolidate themselves as autonomous communities, and weakness on the part of the central authority soon erodes its options for interfering in such communities.

Splitting off from foreign rule, if we are to credit the sources, was also the main reason for larger and smaller migrations, which often covered thousands of miles and generated new peoples and powers. Sometimes such secessions were prompted by scarcity resulting from climate shifts. Powerful steppe empires generally reacted with a heightened push toward expansion to keep such movements under control. It was disadvantaged members of a dynasty or conquered clans who formed the core groups for these wide-ranging migrations. The sources generally state a desire for independence and inner rivalries as the reasons for migrations and subdivisions. As a rule, we hear of these ventures only if they are extraordinarily successful. On a smaller scale, similar migrations were clearly common in the steppe realms and contributed to their inner dynamic. These processes can be observed only on the highest levels in the Turkish realm and even less so among the Avars. Compared to the success both of the Chinese in recruiting steppe warriors and of the Romans in attracting Western barbarians, the defections from the Avar khaganate seem to have been rare, and if they happened, the defectors were not called Avars anymore.

Despite their wide-ranging military organization nomadic societies were not always capable of developing differentiated forms of rule over sedentary populations. Only in some areas did the integration of steppe warriors into differentiated urban and agricultural societies seem to have had good chances of success: mostly in dry lands with prosperous oases along important trade routes, for example in Bactria and Sogdiana, in the Tarim Basin, or in the Ordos region in north China. Nicola Di Cosmo has argued that "experiences such as that of the Tuoba Wei polity in Northern China were extremely important in several respects: the incorporation of foreign religions in the ruling ideology, a certain degree of urbanization, and the development of hybrid administrative structures."[59] A city as a capital of the western Turkic khaganate was only an episode, located at Ak-Beshim, in the Chu River valley on the northern frontier of Kyrghyzia, where the impressive remains of the Sogdian city of Suyab have been excavated. Here, Buddhist temples and Nestorian churches were found, and Sogdian coins were minted in the name of Turkish rulers.[60] However, in the eighth century the Uyghurs built a large city, Karabalghasun (Ordu-Baliq), which served as a supply center and probably also as a capital.[61]

In the European steppes, such conditions rarely existed, with the partial exception of the northern coast of the Black Sea and the lower Volga. The early medieval Carpathian Basin and lower Danube area offered different options for integration by the coexistence with an agricultural population, part of whose produce was siphoned off for the maintenance of the steppe warriors. This happened at the expense of the cities that were deprived of their share in tribute. Eventually, European steppe empires (Bulgars, Hungarians), at the price of their ruralization, a restriction on their pastoral economy, and the cessation of plundering, reached an accommodation with the sedentary culture of neighboring regions. The steppe peoples could also leave nomadic life behind them and construct a durable state apparatus as a warrior caste. The completely different outcomes of this process between Huns, Avars, Bulgars, and Magyars shows that the relative significance of the three forms of economy in the various steppe empires differed considerably.

6.2 "Their Life Is War"

"Savage peoples, whose life is war." This is how a contemporary author characterizes those who attacked Constantinople in 626 under Avar leadership. "After a war," as Priscus quotes a Roman who had become a Hun, "men amongst the Scythians live at ease, each enjoying his own possessions and troubling others or being troubled not at all or very little."[62] This corresponds well to what the *Strategicon* said of the Turks: "They are not engaged in most human endeavors, nor have they trained themselves for anything else except to conduct themselves bravely against their enemies."[63] The impact of the Avar attacks has often been explained by their warlike disposition and life-long training. Furthermore, it was attributed to the military and strategic advances in the Eurasian steppes. The most conspicuous weapon of the Huns had been the composite reflex bow. The Avars introduced the iron stirrup; it offered a solid hold for mounted archers and lance-bearing riders. Wittfogel has called this the "second cavalry revolution"; the third revolution was an improvement in military organization, which likewise began with the Turks in the sixth century. Both achievements, in a centuries-long process, strengthened the striking power of the armies of horsemen and eventually established the superiority of the Mongols.[64] "In open or moderately hilly terrain, no single opponent in contemporary Europe—the Byzantine army not excepted—was capable of successfully resisting the armored Avar horsemen and their armor-piercing lances." So István Bóna characterizes the superiority of the Avar army.[65] Recent research has put less weight on the superiority of nomadic military technology and organization, which should not be regarded as an intrinsic feature of steppe empires.[66] The invincibility of the Avars should not be exaggerated. In the relatively few major battles about which we have information, the Byzantines often fought quite successfully. Furthermore, they were always eager to copy their opponent's achievements. Informed contemporaries were aware that the Avar army had certain advantages in military technology. Still, the military strength of the Avars should not be undervalued either. Maurice's *Strategicon* values the Avars, "well versed in war," very highly.[67]

The Avars had a state-of-the-art fighting technique that combined several elements of nomad warcraft, as the *Strategicon* indicates: "They are armed with mail, swords, bows, and lances. In combat most of them attack doubly armed; lances (*kontaria*, the Latin *contus*) slung over their shoulders and holding bows in their hands, they make use of both as need requires. Not only do they wear armor themselves, but in addition the horses of their illustrious men are covered in front with iron or felt. They give special attention to training in archery on horseback."[68] At about the same time the Chinese *Zhou shu* depicts the Turkish warriors in comparable fashion. "By way of weapons they possessed bows, arrows, shrieking arrowheads, coats of mail, long cavalry lances, and swords; decorating their belts they also carry daggers."[69] Archaeological evidence largely confirms the picture of the written sources. Early Avar horse burials often also contain lances, stirrups, the bone-plates of reflex bows, and three-sided arrowheads, and sometimes swords.[70] Two armored archers are shown on the cloak clasp from Grave 144 in Mödling.[71]

These "doubly-armed" horsemen combined the advantages of two traditional types of cavalry: On the one hand was the *cataphractarius*, a heavily armored lance-bearing horseman, as he is represented in stylized ancient fashion, without bow, stirrups, and saddle, on a gold vessel found in the treasure of Nagyszentmiklós.[72] On the other hand, there was the more mobile mounted archer who relied mostly on his bow.[73] The reflex bow was an ancient weapon, not particular to the steppe peoples. The knocks reinforced with bones were a Xiongnu innovation that had soon spread westward, to the Sarmatians and elsewhere, as it seems not by export but by emulation.[74] The Avars also used this rigid reflex composite bow. It was made up of several layers of wood, sinew, and horn and was reinforced with plates of bone, which considerably heightened its penetrating power. A very well conserved bow from the eighth century CE was found in the Žargalant Chajrchan Mountains in western Mongolia, which could be reconstructed in detail.[75] This composite bow was the long-range weapon par excellence. The heavy arrows with their three-edged heads had a range up to hundreds of yards. The bow was shorter than most simplex bows, which facilitated its handling from the saddle, an exercise in which the Huns and Avars possessed an extraordinary proficiency. At full gallop they could shoot up to twenty arrows a minute, facing forward or turned backward.[76]

The Avars brought an important innovation in cavalry technique to Europe: the iron stirrup, which improved the stability of the mounted archers. Stirrups first appeared in China and the northern part of Korea in the fourth century CE.[77] In the central Asian steppes they spread around the same time as in the Carpathian Basin and reach a wide currency in the Turkish khaganate and beyond it very quickly.[78] It is still not clear how exactly they were diffused. Lynn White Jr.

has highlighted the stirrup as a decisive element in the development of European knighthood and an instance of the influence of technology on the evolution of society.[79] This is surely exaggerated, for the stirrup was rather slowly taken up in the West.[80] Florin Curta has returned to this old debate and shown that the Avars certainly used the stirrup in mounted shock combat, especially in their expansive period; out of sixty-nine early Avar burial assemblages containing stirrups, forty-four contained lances as the only weapons, usually high quality.[81] Interestingly, in the passages in which the *Strategicon* describes the Avar horsemen, the stirrup is not mentioned. However, it testifies that the Byzantines had already introduced it into the standard equipment of cavalry soldiers by the year 600.[82]

The Roman army also appropriated other innovations from the Avar warriors. According to the *Strategicon*, they sought to prepare their cavalry for the same multiple cavalry tactics that the Avars used. The very first chapter establishes that Roman soldiers had to be trained in using bow and lance in turn on horseback, although the author of the handbook was aware that many Roman soldiers were not very good shots with the bow; still, they had to be forced to use it. The equipment of Roman cavalry should include full armor from the knuckles to the hood, quiver for thirty to forty arrows with extra room for the bow, cavalry lances "of Avar type," and sword.[83] This focus on cavalry represented a sixth-century innovation in the Byzantine army, which to an extent replaced the traditional Roman battle tactics that relied mostly on the formidable infantry lines. Infantry, however, proved vulnerable to fast and repeated cavalry attacks by Huns or Avars; the best they could do was withstand, but hardly strike back.[84] The extent to which the emperor's soldiers had been forced to adapt to their "hideous" opponents reveals something about the arms race of the sixth century and about the advantages that the Avars initially had.

In addition to the stirrup and the already familiar reflex bow, the standard equipment of the Byzantine cavalryman also included further pieces of Avar equipment:[85] the horseman's lance, with a thong in the middle; a fringed neckguard or gorget made of felt and wool; the horse's breastplate of iron or felt, which protected the chest and neck of the animal; and lastly the long tunic with mail on quilting, "worked in the fashion of the Avars," which reached below the knee when the warrior was mounted. This Avar-style clothing permitted the horseman to appear "splendid." According to the *Suda Lexicon* it later also so appealed to the Bulgars that they adopted it, probably a retrospective explanation for the similarity in the clothing.[86] An army newly assembled by Tiberius in 574 was so intimidated by the mere sight of the Avar army that it fled the field.[87] "Both sumptuous and practical" were the Avar tents in Roman eyes, and they copied them for the cavalry. These were round tents, perhaps also the later well-known yurts with their lattice framework. Lastly, even the Byzantine military technicians could learn something from the Avars: the construction of boat-bridges "in the Scythian manner."[88]

Avar tactics were to prove exemplary for the Romans in many respects. The Turks and Avars were credited with being the only Scythians who reflected on tactics.[89] The handbook recommends that the cavalry draw up in companies according to the role they would play in the battle, "just as the Avars and Turks line up today keeping themselves in that formation, and so they can quickly be called to support any unit that may give way in battle."[90] It was the Avar custom to keep a strategic force in reserve, which could make a surprise intervention.[91] The Byzantines sought to copy this "Scythian assault."[92]

These and similar surprises and ambushes made up the preferred strategy of the Avars. "They prefer battles fought at long range, ambushes, encircling their adversary, simulated retreats and sudden returns. . . . They are clever at estimating suitable opportunities to do this and taking prompt advantage of them. They prefer to prevail over their enemies not so much by force as by deceit, surprise attacks, and cutting off supplies."[93] The "mock flight" of the Huns and Avars was also recounted in the West in the seventh century. In the updated version of the Theoderic legend that Fredegar reproduces, the Avar Xerxer, whose name is probably loaned from the Alexander romance, overcomes his Gothic opponents with this ploy.[94] Other steppe peoples employed similar tricks, such as the Magyars in their first incursion into Italy.[95] Part of the psychological warfare were the war cries that the Avars (like the Slavs and other barbarians) uttered at the beginning of battle.[96] In the tenth century, Liudprand of Cremona noticed the "devilish hui hui" of the Hungarians.[97] For the Byzantines this "wolfish howling" was a trademark of the steppe peoples.[98]

Unlike other barbarians, the Avars were also credited with great tenacity. "When they make their enemies take to flight, they put everything else aside, and are not content, as the Persians, the Romans, and other peoples, with pursuing them at a reasonable distance and plundering their goods, but they do not let up at all until they have achieved the complete destruction of their enemies, and they employ every means to this end."[99] "This people does not, as do the others, give up the struggle when worsted in the first battle. But until their strength gives out, they try all sorts of ways to assail their enemies."[100] This is repeatedly confirmed in Theophylact's account of the wars. The bridgehead that Priscus established across from Viminacium was attacked again and again despite repeated failures.[101] Presumably the prestige of the Avar ruler demanded that he did not remain inactive in adversity. That serious defeats could threaten the position and even the life of a khagan is repeatedly attested among the steppe peoples.

The Avar fighting style also had its weak points. As much as possible the Avars sought to avoid fighting at close quarters and hand-to-hand, tactics at which Germanic peoples were specialists. Nor was fighting on foot to their taste. The *Strategicon* establishes this by reference to the old topos about the steppe horsemen: "They have been brought up on horseback, and owing to their lack of exercise they simply cannot walk about on their own feet."[102] Appearances could probably support such a judgment. Wilhelm Radloff noted in the nineteenth century: "Altai man does not know how to go on foot. His walk is shuffling, shaky, and very slow. He also has especially inappropriate footwear. . . . But as soon as the Altai man mounts up, his whole bearing changes. Here he feels in his rightful place. . . . Horse and rider merge into a single whole."[103] "Native centaur dignity" was Peter Fleming's characterization of the appearance of the Mongols on horseback, while on foot they rather seem Shakespeare's "poor monster Caliban."[104]

In battle, in any case, the Avars were dependent on their horses. "Lack of pasture" hurt them greatly.[105] They usually brought along more horses than were needed for battle. The surplus was kept under light watch during the fighting. Many sudden turns during the Avar wars can be explained by the fact that the herds were suffering shortages. The great need for pasture necessitated the army spreading out even in enemy territory: "They do not stay in camp like Romans and Persians, but remain scattered in tribes and clans until the day of battle, constantly letting their horses graze in summer and winter."[106] The strategic disadvantage here is evident, and the Byzantines repeatedly came close to overcoming the khagan when he was accompanied by only a small retinue.[107]

The Avars had difficulties with siege craft but were quick learners.[108] Sirmium had to be starved out in 580–82, as they had no means of dealing with the city walls. The situation changed in the following years when a long row of forts on the *limes* fell, often, however, taken by surprise. Theophylact credits Avar progress in siege craft to a captured Roman soldier from Apiaria.[109] In 586 the inhabitants of Thessalonica could observe from their walls how the barbarians built siege machines, although these did not always function as desired.[110] At any rate the Avars proved avid pupils in the old Greek art of *poliorkia*, the siege of cities. In the end, only the walls of Constantinople and a few other major cities resisted their attacks. The accounts of the siege of Constantinople 626 show that the chief burden of the siege was put on the Slavs and other supporting peoples. Slav dugouts were brought into action from the water side. For amphibian operations against coastal cities the khagan on one occasion had Lombard specialists brought in.[111] The khagan also required assistance in the construction of a bridge over the Sava, where, according to John of Ephesus, Roman architects were obliged to help. Clearly the Avars themselves scarcely used city walls for their own defense. The barbarian conquerors at Singidunum barricaded themselves before the city behind their carts.[112] Such wagon forts are also known from the Slavs and other peoples.[113] Only the Avars of a later period are known to have erected palisades and other fortifications against their enemies.[114]

Findings from graves confirm the general picture of the manual on warfare.[115] Since Avar warriors were often buried with their weapons, their equipment can be quite well reconstructed, even if complete sets of military equipment have seldom been preserved in graves. In this respect, the considerable value of the various pieces of equipment must be taken into consideration. Not every warrior's family could afford everything, and only a selection of objects was put into the grave; other pieces were surely passed on as inheritance. And there are clearly also men in prominent positions who were buried without weapons or with decorative arms that were not intended for battle.[116] From the coat of mail, often only symbolic pieces are included.[117] This said, fragments of armor, iron lance-heads, iron stirrups, three-edged arrowheads, and pieces of bow reinforcements are all standard constituents in grave goods.[118] Swords are also very common. Typical of the early Avars are relatively long, single-edged cavalry sabers.[119] Gergely Csiky has recently published a minute study of Avar-Age short-range weapons, sabers, swords, and also spears.[120] Some, but not all, eminent warrior horsemen were buried with their horses fully harnessed.[121]

The weapon finds show that the Avars also appreciated Byzantine craftsmanship or took Byzantine weapons as models. The interchanges between nomadic and Byzantine weaponsmiths have not yet been adequately investigated. According to a fragment from Menander, the Avars of the early period purchased arms in Constantinople.[122] Charlemagne later banned but could not stop Frankish arms exports.[123] The technology transfer between the Carolingian Empire and the barbarians worked very well in both directions, as scattered evidence indicates.

We have some clues about the numbers of Avar armies; however, many of them are probably exaggerated.[124] Inflated numbers of opponents to explain defeat or to magnify victories belong to the standard repertoire of the historiography of all ages. Additionally, Roman scouts were easily deceived by the large number of horses when they were assessing the strength of an Avar army. "Most people are incapable of forming a good estimate if an army numbers twenty or thirty thousand, especially with the Scythians because of their many horses."[125] That the Avars lost four thousand, nine thousand, and then fifteen thousand warriors in three successive days of battle and thirty thousand soon after on Priscus's expedition into Avar territory in 599 clearly belongs to the genre of triumphal exaggerations.[126] The number of sixty thousand Avar horsemen ferried across the Danube in 578 is also hardly credible, although these could have been easily counted; Menander distances himself with a cautious "it is said that . . ." from this information.[127] It was also easier to count prisoners of war. After the victory at the Tisza in 599, Theophylact enumerates 3,000 Avars, 6,200 "other barbarians," and 8,000 Slavs.[128] The proportions between the components of the Avar army are plausible, but a number of over seventeen thousand captives who would then be taken as far as Tomi at the Black Sea seems unconvincing, given the other exaggerated numbers from the same campaign (in particular, the thirty thousand inhabitants of three Gepid villages slaughtered in their sleep).[129] After all, this part of the report comes from a source underlining the exploits of the general Priscus. By contrast, the numbers of immigrating Avars supplied by the Turks are realistic. Twenty thousand Varchonites had left central Asia in 558; in the 580s, they were joined by an "additional force" of a further ten thousand from the Tarniakh, Zabender, and Kotzagir.[130] Steppe peoples calculated armed forces by divisions of one thousand and of ten thousand men (the Turkish *tümen*).[131] A total Avar force of thirty thousand, plus Bulgar and Slav auxiliary troops, is realistic; of course, it grew with success. Large armies in the period numbered about twenty to thirty thousand.[132] Agathias, in the later sixth century, puts the required strength of Justinian's army at 645,000 men, while the actual strength was only 150,000, stationed between Spain and Egypt.[133]

We know little about the internal organization of the Avar army. In the battle on the Tisza, the khagan "deployed for battle in twelve companies." Byzantine observers noted that the Avars and Turks fought "more strongly in formations than other Scythians" and were centrally organized. In most cases, the khagan personally led the army into battle. Among the steppe peoples, army organization and strong rulership were supposed to be closely associated; the *Strategicon* attributes the Avars' success not least to the despotic rule to which they were subject.[134] As shown above, this corresponds to the close link between a khagan's unquestioned rule, his rightful ordering of the people, constant campaigns, and military success that the Orkhon inscriptions underline.

6.3 The Early Avar Khaganate

"They steadfastly bear labors and hardships because they obey a ruler, and their commanders subject them to cruel punishments for their misdeeds. They are governed not by love but by fear. They endure heat and cold, and the want of many necessities, since they are nomads." With this ancient topos, the *Strategicon* describes Avar despotism and thereby explains the superiority of the Avars (and Turks) over other Scythian peoples, and even more over the "anarchic" Slavs.[135] A later medieval European observer, John of Plano Carpini, shares this mixture of aversion and admiration for the despotic rule of the steppe peoples. "They are more obedient to their lords and masters than any other clergy or lay-people in the whole world."[136]

There were obviously also other assessments about contemporary steppe empires. A Chinese general of the sixth century said of the Turks, "the soldiers of the Tujue abhor honors and rewards, and disregard their superiors. They are indeed many in number but they have no concern for laws or orders."[137] The Buddhist pilgrim Xuanzang (Hsuan-Tsang) met a troop of Turkic horsemen in the Tian Shan Mountains who had just plundered a caravan and "as usual" disputed the booty by recourse to armed force.[138] The last Avars reputedly told the Bulgar khagan that discord and rebelliousness wrecked their empire. A similar complaint appears in the Old Turkic inscriptions.[139] A successful and circumspect ruler could bring the many nuclei of nomad society under control; but his very success spurred the ambition of many competitors in the second and third generation. The centrifugal tendency eventually won out over a center that was hardly shored up by established institutions, and a new empire could begin. Seen from this perspective the relative stability of the Avar Empire is remarkable. The khaganate on the Danube withstood its defeats at the hands of Priscus around 600, the catastrophe at Constantinople around 626, the wave of defections that this favored, the Kuver rebellion and the success of Asparukh and his Bulgars in 680, and the defeat by the Bavarians in 740. The cohesion of the Avar elite was essentially maintained despite all these setbacks. Such coherence is unusual. Desertions, divisions, and the emergence of rival ruling centers were common in all the steppe empires. Huns and Goths repeatedly abandoned their kings in order to make their way in Roman service or act on their own. For generations the ranks of Roman officers were dominated by barbarian defectors. As early as Justinian's rule, Bulgar units were fighting in Italy.[140] In the seventh century Bulgars lived and fought under various rulers on the Volga, Don, and Danube, in Byzantium, Bavaria, Carinthia, and Italy, in the Avar and Khazar Empires, in Thrace and Macedonia. Turkish generals in the service of the Tang dynasty conquered formerly Turkish areas in central Asia for the Chinese. At the same time, as far as we know, Avars fought almost exclusively for the khagan.

Theophylact describes as an exception what happened after the defeats of 600: "Large numbers defected from the Avars and hastened to desert to the emperor. So the khagan was thrown into confusion at the news; he became greatly terrified, imploring and devising many schemes to win back the forces that had defected."[141] The *Strategicon* makes evident (perhaps in reference to the same events) that such defections could present a real threat to the Avars: "They are seriously hurt by defections and desertion. They are very fickle, avaricious and, composed of so many clans (*phylai*) as they are, they have no sense of kinship (*syngenē*) or unity with one another. If a few begin to desert and are well received, many more will follow."[142]

Such defectors have, however, left no traces in the Byzantine record. Presumably they lost the name "Avar" even faster than the conquered Avars after the defeat of the khaganate. Even if the "Hun" Apsikh, who fought for Byzantium toward the end of the sixth century, may have come from the Avar Empire like his more important contemporary of the same name, in the emperor's army he was not viewed as an Avar.[143] The Avar chief shaman Bookolabras, who feared the vengeance of the deceived khagan because of his arts of seduction, wanted to flee with Gepid servants to "his" Turks.[144] The larger-scale defections of the seventh century, the flight of the Alciocus group around 630 and of Kuver's people around 680, occurred under Bulgar names. In their adventures outside the khaganate none is any longer called an Avar.[145] Clearly the Avar khagans in Europe did not have to deal with outside competitors claiming the same title or with lasting divisions of the rulership that were so common among the Turks.

We do not know how this successful monopolization of the Avar name was achieved. Baian owed his position as a successful ruler, like his Hunnic and Gothic predecessors, above all to his military success and the loyalty of the army that he led. We have only a few hints how his rule was legitimized. Moreover, what the Byzantines perceived in the sixth and seventh centuries differed significantly from the situation that the Frankish conquerors encountered toward the year 800. There is no evidence that before 700 a *iugurrus* or *tudun* played a role in Avar politics. At that time, the one unambiguously identifiable title is that of the ruler: the khagan. The Avar rulers were the first in Europe to bear this title, which had so far denoted a position of exceptional prestige in the Far East.[146] In Europe, their use of it was uncontested until the Khazars (whose leaders may have been descended from the Turkish Ashina dynasty) adopted it in the second half of the seventh century.[147] The title became the Avar hallmark to such a degree that it replaced the ruler's name and was even frequently taken to be a name itself. Fredegar's *rex Gaganus* is not an isolated error.[148]

Baian remains the only ruler whose name has come down to us, and he disappears from the sources after the conquest of Sirmium in 582. The name is also known from other peoples. A son of the Bulgar khan Kuvrat bore this name in the seventh century; a predecessor of Genghis Khan called himself Torholjin *baiyan*; and a General Bayan took part in the conquest of China under Kublai Khan.[149] In Mongolian and in many Turkic languages the word for "rich" is derived from the root *baj*, and this is the usual explanation of the name.[150] Baian himself remains rather featureless in the sources. Qualities such as deceptiveness, cruelty, greed, faithlessness, ostentation, impulsiveness, but also courage, tenacity, and prudence could be ascribed to every barbarian prince of importance on the basis of the Byzantine accounts. They would probably be just as suitable for most of the Roman emperors.

It is only from a passing remark by Theodore Syncellus that we know that two sons succeeded Baian, the younger of whom was still leading the Avars in the defeat of 626.[151] The father of the khagan, so we are told in 626, had come from distant regions to seek refuge among the Romans. "The rule of this father was passed down to his son, the successor, the elder brother of the dog of today." It has been concluded that the younger brother acceded to the throne just before 610, based on information in Paul the Deacon about the conquest of Cividale by a young Avar prince, who won the heart of the wife of the just fallen Lombard *dux*.[152] This account is legendary. It is plausible that after the problems around 600 the older brother had not been able to maintain his rule for long. His reign had begun in ca. 583, as Thérèse Olajos concluded from the remark of a Byzantine envoy shortly thereafter.[153] In support of this interpretation is the fact that, although Baian was well known to Menander whose work he continued, Theophylact does not mention his name any more. This would suggest a rule of just a bit more than twenty years for each of the three rulers: Baian from before 562 (whether or not he led the migration from central Asia is unknown) until about 583; the elder son until sometime after 602; and the younger until 626, at the very latest 630. The fact that the first son of Baian was not succeeded by one of his own grown sons but rather by a brother may be due to the fact that these sons had not proved themselves as military leaders (and some had died in the plague of 598); or it may be a sign of a tanistry system of succession, by which the oldest surviving offspring of Baian would have the right to rule.[154] Among the Turks and Bulgars, too, the brothers of a ruler were often preferred over his sons in the succession.[155] How decisions were made in these matters, we do not know; in the change of ruler that seems to have occurred after 602 we may assume some influence on the part of the Avar notables, under the leadership of Apsikh.

After 626 the dynasty quite likely had gambled away its prestige, since such failures usually weaken the position of a steppe ruler considerably. A few years later an Avar and a Bulgar pretender to the dignity of the Avar leadership fought against each other.[156] The status of the khagan per se was apparently not diminished. In what followed, he still appears as solely responsible for Avar policy. Not until the last stages of the Avar khaganate is a double rulership attested.

Like many military kings of the age of migrations, Baian and his successors almost always lead the Avar army in person. On only one occasion did Baian's successor delegate this assignment to his sons. After their failures, the khagan kept to the background in the following years. When an Avar army marched up to the Danube "cataracts" in 601, the Romans negotiated with Apsikh, who presented himself as the deputy field commander (*hypostrategos*). The next year the khagan sent Apsikh against the Antes.[157] The Byzantine sources give the impression that decisions as to peace and war lay in the hands of the khagan. He dispatched and received embassies and personally led negotiations, the delay in which imperial envoys sometimes ascribed entirely to his moods.[158] He bound his entire people with contracts and oaths or at least, as before the siege of Sirmium, committed perjury in the name of "the whole people of the Avars" (Menander in this connection uses both *ethnos* and *phylon*).[159]

In this sense Kollautz is not entirely wrong when he pointedly states: "The history of all nomadic peoples is the history of their khagans."[160] This conception corresponds both to the self-representation of the steppe rulers (as preserved in the Old Turkic and Bulgar inscriptions) and to Byzantine perceptions of "Scythian" despotism.[161] A people that "has lost its order and its khagan" also loses its identity and cohesion. The Bilge Khagan inscription puts it like this: "The common people said then: 'I had a state, where is it now? Which country do I serve? I had a khagan, where is he now? Which khagan do I serve?' They could not continue their generation. The Turkic people began to degenerate."[162] Yet Avar history was not a one-man show, as attested by accounts about the limits of the khagan's power and his capacity to implement his decisions. Clearly he was to some degree dependent on the consensus of at least the preeminent chiefs and warriors.

When, in the long negotiations between Baian and Justin II, the leaders of the talks, Tiberius and Apsikh, finally agreed on a peace plan, an indicative difference of opinion arose between the emperor Justin and Caesar Tiberius. It had been agreed that some of the sons of eminent Avars would be given as hostages; now the emperor insisted on getting the khagan's own sons in his hands. Tiberius, who was certainly better informed about conditions among the Avars, calculated that the Avar *archontes* would "never tolerate that the khagan decided to break the treaties."[163] This consideration was realistic, as proven more than once. There were influential lobbies at the Avar court. Before the war over Sirmium an envoy came to Constantinople in 579, from whom the Romans knew that he had always urged the khagan to war against the Romans. He was murdered by raiding Slavs on his return journey, but this no longer had any effect on the outbreak of war, which had long been decided.[164] It is perhaps reflective of the more aggressive policies of Baian's son that it was above all the doves at court who tried to exert pressure on him. In 584 the khagan became enraged during negotiations with the Romans over the envoy Comentiolus, whom he wanted to put to death. "On the following day his passion became calm, and the most powerful of the Avars soothed their leader with persuasive arguments, gradually convincing him not to pronounce the death penalty against Comentiolus."[165] Some ten years later the most powerful men among the Avars succeeded in preventing the outbreak of hostilities. The khagan viewed Priscus's actions in Slav territory as a casus belli. "Now Targitius and the barbarian elite urged the Chagan to put an end to the war, for they said that his indignation against the Romans was unjustified."[166] Perhaps it was no coincidence that just a bit later the khagan emphasized to the envoy that he was "the master of every people" and that there was no one able to confront him.[167]

With all his power the khagan's position did not permit arbitrary decisions; it was bound by tradition and the organization of the polity. We do not know in which ways the assembly of the army or the counsel of the *logades* was institutionalized. It was in the nature of steppe rulership that the ruler was ultimately accountable to such, formal or informal, collective organs.[168] The ruler's self-representation, which both the Byzantine chroniclers and modern historians dismiss as the usual vaingloriousness, was also addressed to the Avar leadership elite. This was not merely a barbarian custom. The court ceremonial with which the Christian emperor of the East Romans managed to impress ambassadors worked with the same means: pomp, demonstrations of power, gifts, ritualized pronouncements about his office, boasts and threats, even calculated bluffing.[169] Kingdoms without a state apparatus, whose cohesion could scarcely be enforced but rested on their people's readiness to follow, had to strive all the harder to create a strong impression. The few accounts of the self-imaging and self-staging of the Avar khagan and their eastern parallels permit some insight into the methods whereby rule was exercised and to what extent it relied on relations with the Byzantines.

6.4 The Avars and Byzantium

Scarcely had they arrived on the doorstep of the empire, when the Avars despite all difficulties sent their first embassy to Constantinople.[170] Such haste to contact Byzantium was characteristic of the politics of the Baian dynasty. It corresponded with the strategy to which the Turkish Ashina dynasty, according to the *Zhou shu*, owed its rise to empire: "the wish to communicate with China."[171] The position of the first khagans relied on Byzantium and on the prestige goods produced in the Mediterranean economy. Toward the center of the Byzantine Empire flowed vast riches, which a complicated bureaucracy extracted from producers by means of a rather oppressive tax system. The barbarian peoples, with their direct but short-term appropriation of the wealth generated in Roman provinces, were the competitors and beneficiaries of this bureaucracy at one and the same time. Mere rule over Slavic farmers or impoverished Pannonians would not have been able to generate comparable wealth.[172] This distinguishes the Avar Empire from contemporary Slavic societies and recalls the Germanic armies of the age of migrations.

How much the khagans needed a continuous influx of prestige goods can be illustrated by Baian's behavior after the failure of the first siege of Sirmium (567). Quite openly he explained his demand for "small gifts" in return for his departure on the fact that he had to take into consideration the peoples who followed him and who could not possibly be led away without some token of success.[173] After all, this modest supplicant had just brought the whole kingdom of the Gepids in his possession almost without a fight. The khagan only asked for "a silver basin, some gold, in addition to a cloak of the kind that the noble Scythians wear." His motives were scarcely *amour-propre blessé* and *avidité*, as Lemerle interpreted a similar demand after the great siege of Thessalonica (around 616).[174] Not weakness of character but rather the equilibrium of barbarian society is the driving force behind the desire for at least symbolic "gifts." The reference to pressure from his army is not mere rhetoric but points to the necessity of success as the precondition under which he operated. Mere territorial gain could not satisfy Baian's followers, although Gepid farmers remained to till the land. If victory on the battlefield had not been realized, then the superiority of the Avar ruler at least had to be expressed in appropriate symbolic fashion.

For earlier generations of barbarian military leaders it had been somewhat easier to secure their positions through plundering or the occupation of thriving Roman provinces. Although the Balkans had gradually recovered in the course of the sixth century, the wealth of imperial lands had generally decreased since the fourth century. Repeated barbarian raids in the Balkans under Justinian had depleted the booty that was available. In the later sixth century, Baian and his sons faced increasingly difficult conditions. From the very beginning they played for higher stakes than most other barbarian leaders; but from this no special "barbarity" or "greed" should be concluded, because it required very differentiated policies. More than studies thus far have shown, Baian's policies initially followed the models of the age of migrations. The agreement with Justinian was the kind of treaty (*foedus*) under which barbarian armies under their own leaders inside, but sometimes also outside the empire had been nominally attached as allies to the Roman army, even if the terminology had changed in the meantime.[175] Baian took the logical second step when a few years later he demanded the right to settle on the lands of the empire. But, since the bad experiences with the gradual appropriation of the Western Roman Empire by Gothic, Vandal, and Frankish leaders, the imperial authorities were cautious. Justinian's offer was too unattractive, and the negotiated Avar settlement came to nothing.

When Justin II, breaking with Justinian's policy of securing the balance of power among the northern barbarians with subsidies, stopped payments to the

Avars in 565, they did not put the new policy to the test at once.[176] They were obviously pursuing other goals: overcome their barbarian neighbors in order to establish their hegemony north of the Byzantine borders. In 568, they occupied imperial land at least indirectly, although Pannonia (with the exception of Sirmium) had seen no imperial functionaries for a long time. The Avar demands at that stage appear quite modest, but Justin kept refusing a new treaty. The concern of the Avars to conclude an alliance with Byzantium is evident in the many delegations that were sent to the imperial court to this end. Incursions into imperial territory were limited undertakings, intended to maintain pressure on the negotiations. The need to organize the new settlement areas may explain why Baian was then concerned to "live in good understanding" with the Romans.[177] His prudent policies show that aggression did not always represent the best strategy for the construction of a steppe empire. In order to prevail over barbarian competitors, provisional cooperation with the neighboring Roman Empire could be more favorable. After 375, the Huns took even longer to establish a stable hegemony before they started their massive attacks on Rome.[178] Steppe empires in eastern central Eurasia sometimes followed the same strategy. In 545 when the first Chinese embassy came to the Turks, "they wished each other good fortune and said, 'Our state will flourish for today an ambassador from a great empire has come to us.'"[179] Close relations with the Chinese imperial family were always a trump card for Turkish khagans in their dealings with competitors. Similarly, Baian secured the establishment of his central European empire through alliances with Byzantium—until he had established control over all relevant forces north of the Byzantine frontier.

In the 580s, about twenty years after the Avar arrival in Europe, the Balkan provinces became frequent targets of their incursions. In the negotiations territorial demands now disappear. The khagans did not even demand a buffer zone south of the Danube as Attila had once done. At the center of negotiations was now an increase in the annual tribute. Soon after the capture of Sirmium (582), which resolved the last territorial issue raised by the Avars, Baian's son made the first move in the game.[180] During the rule of the emperor Maurice (582–602), the Avar army marched at least four times to the vicinity of Constantinople (584–85, 586, 592, 598). Still, the treaty of 598 reaffirmed the Danube as border.[181] The events of these years reveal a seemingly paradoxical situation: when the Avars feel strong, they are not interested in control of the southern bank of the Danube. Only when Roman armies march up to the sensitive Illyrian bank of the Danube do the khagan's protests regularly follow.[182] After the collapse of frontier defenses the Balkan provinces apparently had even worse to suffer until 626. But these were not random plundering campaigns. The participating warrior groups had to remain under control. The khagan was therefore always ready to conclude a peace, especially when he had the military advantage. Of course the Avars were after spoils and wished to improve their negotiating position. But a collapse of imperial resistance would have threatened Avar control over the various *gentes*, because it would have made central coordination of attacks superfluous. In a sense, the khagans needed their Byzantine opponents. They hesitated to deal the enemy a decisive blow until 626.

But on the other side as well, after Priscus's spectacular successes, there was no attempt to deliver further blows to the stricken khaganate. Instead of continuing the offensive that had begun so successfully, the Byzantines returned to policing the Slavs north of the lower Danube. The Avar Empire was a powerful and dangerous enemy, but its policies were calculable. No improvement of the situation could be expected from its collapse, but rather an expansion of the unmanageable activities of the Slavs. For these reasons Byzantium twice made an alliance with the khagan that was explicitly directed against the Slavs.[183] It is no coincidence that most of the Byzantine offensive efforts in the 590s fizzled out in the Slavic marshes. On the other hand imperial troops were much easier to motivate for a war against the Avars. It is not by chance that a mutiny always arose in the army when it was marching against the Slavs.[184] Little honor and booty were to be won in the dirty war against the Slavs on the Danube. First they had to be tracked down. Then the fighting was in difficult terrain, always threatened by ambushes. And when once the army was triumphant, little had been won. We get the impression that despite all the protests, the khagan followed the war of attrition in Wallachia with satisfaction. The Avars themselves had experienced difficulties enough there.

For the empire, the Avar war offered a second advantage. It was clearly easier to mount a front against the horsemen with their long braids. The cooperation between the Roman population and peoples of Germanic origin, Christianized generations back, had sapped the Western Empire. The "hideous," heathen Avars were obviously perceived as more alien. Many provincials preferred to leave the Balkan provinces for an Italy threatened by the Lombards. The open frontier to the barbarian lands was not so much threatened by massive attacks as by a general fading of imperial power. The embarrassing event of Asemus when the emperor's brother at the head of an imperial army was simply thrown out of the city by residents when he tried to recruit them provides a spotlight on the weakness of imperial authority among the inhabitants of the provinces.[185] Only with regulated, centrally directed warfare could the imperial state apparatus preserve a certain credibility. The Slavs, with whom one could scarcely negotiate and conclude a peace, made a systematic defense policy impossible. The endless skirmishes on both sides of the imperial border reveal the helplessness of the emperor's army against the Slavic hosts.

Symptomatic of this state of affairs is the revolt during the Slavic war that led to Maurice's fall and eventually to the collapse of the Danube frontier. For the khagan this was a victory without taking up arms, yet in the longer term it also threatened his unchallenged position among the barbarians. Eventually, he would have to initiate ever greater and riskier undertakings in order to be able to show his continuing success. In the end he risked a decisive confrontation with Byzantium when he besieged Constantinople in 626. This step tipped the precarious balance between the empire and the khaganate. The stream of gold from Byzantium dried up. The khagans could nonetheless maintain themselves for almost two more centuries; none of the neighboring powers had the means to exploit their setbacks. The treasures that had been built up over two generations still assured the khagans of an advantage over all their barbarian competitors.

On the whole, the confrontation between the Avars and Byzantium was neither the heroic defensive struggle of a threatened civilization against a "fatal flood" from the east, nor the bold charge of noble savages against a decadent autocracy. Relations between the emperor and the khagan largely followed the forms of international law, or were at least perceived that way by contemporary authors. War and peace were clearly distinguishable; agreements binding for both parties were worked out and concluded (even if repeatedly broken, by both parties); diplomatic forms were observed (although occasionally violated, again also by Byzantium); and legal arguments were employed, even by Avar diplomats, if we believe our sources. Yet the legal forms also reveal substantial ambivalence, as usual when power politics are expressed in legal discourse. Imperial space meant something different to the Romans and Avars, which made debates about boundary issues somehow opaque. The ambivalence becomes best visible in the regular payments that gave the barbarians the means to their rule and helped the Romans bridge the fatal difference between political pretensions and actual military power. In these payments the dependence of one side on the other became very apparent, and everything was done to gloss over this connection. For the Romans the annual monetary obligations toward practically all their neighbors were not only a drain on the state treasury but also a challenge to their hegemony.

Menander, the most penetrating observer of the diplomacy of his time, seeks with all kinds of justifications to have us forget that these payments had long become indispensable. "What Justinian earlier gave to the Huns, out of pity not fear, because he did not wish to shed blood," thus he has Justin II explain to Targitius the policy of his predecessor.[186] By Justinian's advanced age Menander explains the fact that the Avars were not immediately driven away by force of arms.[187] At the same time he praises the old emperor for having incited the barbarians against one another through gifts. "This, in my view, was a very wise move, since whether the Avars prevailed or were defeated, both eventualities would be to the Romans' advantage."[188] Other authors were harsher in their judgment of Justinian's policy of subsidies. Procopius delivers a devastating condemnation in his *Secret History*.[189] Agathias bemoaned the decline of the Roman army. According to him, with advancing age the emperor had increasingly avoided the risk of a war and had held off the enemy with gifts rather than with attacks.[190] John of Ephesus has a telling story of Zemarchus's mission to the Turkish court (568–69). There the khagan asked him, "Is what the Persians told me true, that 'the king of the Romans is our subject since he pays us tribute as would a subject'?" The Roman could get out of this predicament only by referring to Trajan's monuments in the Persian Empire, which recalled the Romans' superiority. In the following, John mentions the *murmuratio* in Constantinople against the sale of the empire to the barbarians.[191] The Franks landed in a similar quandary between pretensions and reality after the Avar attack of 566, when Sigibert *arte donandi*, "through the art of giving," was able to conclude an expensive peace with the victors. "This was greatly to his credit, rather than something for him to be ashamed of," Gregory of Tours hastens to assure his readers.[192]

A similar rhetoric was used in the same period in China. The early seventh-century emperor Gaozu (Kao-tsu) criticized previous imperial policy: "They believed that the fate of their state depended on the intentions of the barbarians. . . . Because of this they exhausted the entire fortune of their people in currying friendship with the Tujue (T'u-küe). They drew all their wealth from their treasuries and cast it away into the desert. It is my opinion that one . . . repudiates the path of the ruler when one exacts onerous levies from the people and gives the proceeds to the evil wolves (i.e., the Tujue), who not only have never shown China any gratitude but have even become bandits."[193] As early as the Han dynasty the Chinese had already implemented a policy against the Xiongnu similar to that of the later Byzantines. The *heqin* (*ho-ch'in*) policy, first implemented in 198 BCE, was essentially "a means of buying peace in exchange for goods." In several respects, it went beyond the late Roman strategy with the same aim: it included marriage alliances between the Chinese emperor and the Xiongnu; it formally established equal rank between the two rulers; and it went along with attempts to civilize the Xiongnu elite, for instance by sending rhetoricians who explained the rules of proper conduct.[194] The Chinese sent silk, cloth, grain, wine, and other goods rather than money; it was therefore easier to present them as magnanimous gifts. As in Byzantium, the payments could also be considered as rewards for services rendered.[195] The expression "tribute" was also carefully avoided in reference to the payments that a millennium later the Song Empire would make to the Liao.[196]

When Justin II suspended the subsidies to the Avars, this gave Byzantine authors a welcome occasion to indulge in reassuring rhetoric. Menander has the Avar ambassadors argue,

> "It is right, O Emperor, that, inheriting your father's sovereignty, you should bring benefits to his friends just as your father did. . . . When your father lavished gifts upon us, we paid him back both by not invading Roman territory, though we are able to do so, and by performing still more. For we destroyed wholesale the neighboring barbarians who were continually ravaging Thrace, and none at all of those who survive overrun the borders of the Thracians. . . . You must be aware that our leader cannot be a good friend of yours and of the Roman state unless he first receives that for which he forbore to attack the Romans." The Avar envoys made this ambiguous speech, now pleading, now threatening, because they thought that by this means they would frighten and intimidate the Emperor, and as a result the Romans would be compelled to pay tribute to the Avars.[197]

Justin retorted unambiguously: "I shall never need an alliance with you, nor shall you receive from us anything other than what we wish to give, and that as a free gift for your service, not, as you expect, a tribute (*forologia*) upon us."[198]

Menander's two simulated speeches reflect quite well the problem the two parties had with the annual tribute. The term *chrēma*, "money," was so generally chosen that it allowed no inferences to be drawn as to the legal situation. The interpretation as a favor for service (*eranos douleias*), as Justin phrased it, fit in best with imperial Byzantine self-perception. Apart from that, the payments could be understood as the emperor's gifts to favored rulers. *Dōra*, "gifts," is the most frequent circumlocution in the histories. Often the attribute "customary" (in Latin, *consueta dona*) is added, whereby the contractual claims of the barbarians are glossed over. This could be sustained only so long as the recipients did not take up their arms against Byzantium and thereby tried to coerce further payments. These could easily be conceived of as tribute (*forologia*, says Justin; Menander speaks of *hypoforoi*, tributaries). Therefore, it was preferable to buy off the enemy with a single sum. If regular payments were part of the conditions for peace, as was often the case with the Avars, the fiction of payments for military service was maintained as far as possible.

The mixture of flattering requests and scarcely veiled threats that Menander replicates seems quite plausible. However, the Byzantine payments could also create ideological problems for the khagan. In barbarian societies to give was to display superiority.[199] The khagan needed goods from Byzantium. By accepting gifts that he did not reciprocate in similar fashion he recognized the higher rank of the emperor. The dispute over the character of the gifts was played out on the symbolic level. The best example is the story of the elephant and the golden couch that Baian's son sent back immediately after receiving them.[200] By refusing to receive these gifts with an expression of disdain, he attempted to withdraw from the ritual ranking. In this sense, war also had a symbolic dimension. Regardless of whether it led to an increase in the annual tribute or not, a victory demonstrated that it was not simply a matter of gifts. Yet this could change nothing in the fundamental ambivalence of the payments.

Before the capture of Sirmium Baian refused to accept gold and gifts, with, according to Menander, this justification: "The Khagan was satisfied with the gifts sent each year to him by the emperor; for gold, silver and silken clothes were valuable commodities. However, since life was more valuable and desirable than all of these, he had been worrying about this and reflecting that many of the peoples who had come to this land before had first been enticed with such gifts by the Romans, who in the end had attacked and destroyed them entirely."[201] This sounds like Byzantine self-flattery, but the reign of Justinian had shown that Byzantium could quickly turn against long-term allies, or let them perish.

The recipients were aware that the Byzantines used gifts to incite the barbarians against each other. The envoy Valentinus was obliged to hear this from the Turkish khagan Turxanthus: "'Are you not those very Romans who use ten tongues and lie with all of them?' As he spoke he placed his ten fingers in his mouth. Then he continued, 'As now there are ten fingers in my mouth, so you Romans have used many tongues. Sometimes you deceive me, sometimes my slaves, the *Uarkhonitai*. In a word, having flattered and deluded all the tribes with your various speeches and with your treacherous designs, when harm descends upon their heads you abandon them and take all the benefits for yourselves.'"[202] This was not simply a Greek rhetorical exercise: in similar fashion a Turkish khagan complains about the Chinese in his Orkhon inscription. "The Chinese people give us gold, silver and silk in abundance. The words of the Chinese people have always been sweet and the materials of the Chinese peoples have always been soft. Deceiving by means of their sweet words and soft materials, the Chinese are said to cause the remote peoples to come close in this manner. After such people have settled close to them, they have come to feel their ill will there. . . . Being deceived by their sweet words and soft silk, you, Turkic people, were dying."[203] "The cunning and deceptions of the Chinese people and their propensity to intrigue" had promoted discord and thus led to the downfall of the first Turkish khaganate.[204] This critique of the Chinese is somehow ironic: the memorial complexes of Bilge Khagan and Kültegin at Khöshöö Tsaidam were, as Bilge Khagan proudly states in his inscription, made by artists sent from the Chinese court, which is confirmed by its décor and by a Chinese inscription on one side of the stele containing a condolence message from the Chinese emperor.[205] Two Turkish elite graves excavated in 2011 in Shoroon Bumbagar in central Mongolia, following the patterns of Chinese funerary architecture and adorned with Chinese-style wall paintings, show clearly how Sinicized the eastern Turkish nobles had become in the second half of the seventh century.[206] The ambivalent message of the Turkic inscriptions becomes quite clear: the longing for the "luxurious necessities" that came from China had caused the downfall of the first Turkish khaganate; a good khagan could provide the same luxuries, but the Turkish people needed to stand united behind him, otherwise the Chinese would overwhelm them again.

Among the barbarians as well as among the imperial functionaries serious reservations against this system for the transfer of goods arose. The Romans and Chinese complained that the barbarians received lavish gifts from the inflated levies and still kept robbing and plundering. The Avars, as the Turks, probably knew that their dependency on a transfer of riches could be exploited by imperial diplomacy at the first opportunity in order to destroy them. However, Avar–Byzantine relations also differ from contemporary dealings between Turks and Chinese. Between China and the northern barbarians an exchange system had been established that relied more on reciprocity. Tribute and gifts were only a part of this exchange. Chinese sources repeatedly mention goods coming from the Turks, which consisted above all in livestock and "products of the land."[207]

This balance was naturally often disrupted and had to be reestablished. Yet it does appear that in the Far East the openness between the two societies, despite all the prejudices, was greater than between Byzantium and the Avars. One of the first Turkish khagans, Taspar (T'a-po, ca. 572–81), converted to Buddhism and is reported "to have taken only vegetable nourishment . . . and regretted keenly that he had not been born in China."[208] On the other hand, the Turks influenced the lives of the Chinese upper classes. The famous poet Bai Juyi (Po Chü-I, about 800) celebrated in two songs the blue felt tent in which he lived in nomad fashion in the winter and to which no palace could compare.[209] This was, of course, a minority opinion of a critical voice in Tang China; for many, the nomads were still despicable barbarians. Still, shared cultural idioms gave both Turks and Chinese considerable possibilities to exert influence on each other. Successful emperors received the homage of many "external vassals." The Turks could have an impact on Chinese policy, although the success of the Liao or the Mongols remained out of reach. Several Turkish khagans brought Chinese princesses home as brides. In the year before the attack on the Rouran, Bumin (T'u-men) married the princess "Eternal Joy." The khagan Shabolüe married Princess "Thousand Gold," whose tragic fate is extensively treated in the sources.[210] In 568 a daughter of the khagan married Emperor Wudi.[211] A marriage alliance with the Turks was also considered in Byzantium. In the Persian war, Heraclius sought to win the support of the Turks and promised their khagan his daughter Eudocia, whose portrait he brought along.[212]

The Avars did not obtain such connections with the Byzantine imperial house. Soon after 567 Targitius contented himself, in order to legitimize Avar demands, with arguing that Baian was in fact a son of the emperor.[213] Baian's younger son also called the Emperor Heraclius his "father and benefactor" sometime before 626.[214] The expression of international relationships through the use of kinship terminology was a Roman tradition as well as barbarian custom. For example, Emperor Zeno adopted Theoderic as his son-in-arms, and he, in turn, the Herul king Rodulf; the Lombard prince Alboin was adopted by a Gepid king whose son he had just killed in battle.[215] Chinese emperors repeatedly adopted barbarian rulers as their sons.[216] In the case of the Avar khagan no formal act of adoption is reported. Baian and Justin had in fact not even concluded a treaty. It was more a question of diplomatic rhetoric, such as Heraclius used in a difficult situation, when in a letter he called the khagan the "protector of his son" during the period of his absence.[217] The example of the Turks shows how kinship metaphors could be modified according to political realities. At the zenith of their power in about 570 Taspar Khagan (T'a-po) could boast before his followers, "Need I have any concern that I might lack anything at all if only my two sons remain pious and obedient?" By this he meant the two Chinese emperors of Northern Zhou and Northern Qi.[218] Two generations later a Turkish khagan is called a son of the emperor.[219]

Obviously the Byzantine court was very sparing in its use of titles and dignities for the Avar khagans. Many earlier barbarian rulers, such as Attila, Clovis, or Theoderic, had borne the title of *patricius* or *magister militum*, which corresponded to one of the highest command positions in the Roman army.[220] The title *patricius* was accorded to one Hunnic prince who in about 620 came to Constantinople to be baptized, as well as to the Bulgar khan Kuvrat around 635.[221] Justinian II, as a reward for the help of the Bulgar khan Tervel in regaining his throne, raised him to the rank of Caesar as the first barbarian prince—the origin of Bulgar tsardom.[222] Nothing of this kind is reported of the Avars. An international Roman-barbarian aristocracy, as in the time of the Huns, could no longer emerge. Perhaps the experience of the fall of the Western Empire had led to a hardening of positions in the Byzantium of the sixth century and prevented stronger social interpenetration. This reaction constrained the possibilities of Avar politics and did not permit a more thorough integration into the Roman world. But the Avars themselves seem to have been less ready for integration than many other barbarian peoples.

6.5 Avar Gold: Prestige, Gifts, Representation

Extensive eyewitness accounts, such as those of Priscus at Attila's court or Menander from his reception by a Turkish khagan, are not available for the Avar Empire.[223] A few brief entries in the sources, mostly on the occasion of peace negotiations, are all that we hear about the self-representation of the Avar khagans. The accounts are embellished with the rhetorical exercises of classicizing chroniclers but sometimes contain plausible details. "Baian arrived, dismounted and took his seat on a golden throne which had been set up for him with two sheets of linen erected above it like a tent. Before his chest and face they held up shields like a defensive wall to prevent the Romans suddenly shooting arrows at him." Thus appeared the khagan before the Roman general Theognis for the negotiations over Sirmium in 580.[224] A few years later, if we believe John of Ephesus, occurred the bizarre scene in the baths of Anchialus in which the new khagan appeared in the robe of the empress Anastasia.[225] Theophylact's account of diplomatic encounters is particularly poor in context. The physical settings of his extensive battles of words are hardly mentioned at all. The only scenery that Theophylact sketches with a few words is the khagan sitting on the bank of the Danube while negotiating with the general Priscus, whose boat kept to some distance.[226]

Byzantine sources also provide no information on the residence of the khagan. The fact that he sometimes camped in the area of Sirmium and that once, reputedly, he barricaded himself there for fear of the Turks cannot be taken as evidence that he had his capital in the city.[227] The "Avar ring" east of the Danube that the Franks conquered in 796 is not yet mentioned in the Greek sources (see sections 8.2 and 8.4). The rich graves from the seventh century between the Danube and the Tisza suggest that the geographical center of Avar rule may have lain there.[228]

Despite all the newly won riches, the Avar court in the sixth century probably did not measure up to the residences of the Turkish khagans. Of this Zemarchus's embassy in 569–71 brought back an impressive account, on which Menander drew. The khagan "was in a tent, sitting upon a golden throne with two wheels, which could be drawn when necessary by one horse." The banquets took place in three different tents made of silken cloth. "Sizabul sat there on a couch made completely of gold. In the middle of the building were golden urns, water-sprinklers and also golden pitchers." The third day, however, they met in another tent, this time with gilded wooden pillars. The couch was also gilded and was borne up by four golden peacocks. "In front of this dwelling were drawn up over a wide area wagons containing many silver objects, dishes and bowls, and a large number of statues of animals, also of silver and in no way inferior to those which we make;

so wealthy is the ruler of the Turks."[229] Thrones supported by bird figures seem to be represented on Turkish bronze coins from the area of Tashkent and are not unknown in the Iranian world.[230]

Chinese sources describe the splendor of Turkish courts in similar fashion. The khagan Shabolüe (Sha-po-lüe) stationed soldiers to receive the Chinese envoys and "put his treasures on show."[231] One of his successors received a Chinese guest as follows: "The khagan wore a coat of green satin and had his hair quite free; only his forehead was bound round several times with a strip of silk ten feet long, the rest of it trailing behind him. . . . The khagan lived in a great tent adorned with flowers of gold so bright that they were blinding to look upon." Thus the celebrated Buddhist pilgrim of the seventh century, Xuanzang, described the khagan of the West Turks.[232] The residence of the Hephthalites in the year 518 is pictured by Songyun (Sung-yün): "The king had a great felt tent forty feet square erected; all around its inner walls are wool carpets. He wears clothes of decorated silk; he sits on a golden couch, for which four golden phoenixes form the feet."[233] In contrast, Attila's wooden palace and the banquet given there as described by Priscus seem quite modest.[234]

In the case of the first Avar khagans, we know that many of the treasures similar to those that the guests admired at the Turkish court were gifts from the emperor. The first Avar embassy in 558 already received "cords worked with gold, couches, silken garments and a great many other objects."[235] "Cords worked with gold as if made to confine what was escaping, and likewise couches and other luxury goods" became customary gifts in the following years.[236] "Gold and silver and dresses and girdles and saddles ornamented with gold" had been distributed by Justinian to Avar envoys and for their princes, so that more and more Avar ambassadors appeared in Constantinople under every conceivable pretext, as John of Ephesus recounts.[237] It is interesting that "girdles and saddles," key objects of nomad life, appear on this list. After the accession of Justin II the demands at first became more modest: "a silver plate, a small amount of gold and a Scythian tunic" were in vain demanded by Baian before Sirmium in 567.[238] Later negotiations shift increasingly to address a fixed sum of money, which was obviously paid partly in gold coin, partly in silver and silk cloth, and used to purchase goods in Constantinople upon delivery.[239] The *Suda Lexicon* recalls Avar demands for gold, silver, and precious stones.[240] Emperors also sent diplomatic gifts, for example the "ostentatious gold couch" that the khagan returned to Maurice shortly after 582.[241] Indian spices were also in demand.[242] More detailed are the lists by the Chinese of the goods that their emperor gave to the Turks: carriages, horses, drums, wind instruments, banners, golden vases, dresses, cloth, bedding, each item according to the rank of the recipient.[243]

Peace agreements express in solidi the current exchange rate for Avar power. A solidus was nominally 4.55 grams of gold, and seventy-two solidi made up one pound. A year's pay for a Roman soldier in the sixth century amounted to about four solidi. This amount sufficed for a daily ration of three pounds of bread, one pound of meat, a half-liter of wine, and a pint of beer.[244] The salary of higher officers (prefects, *duces*) amounted to four hundred solidi and more. The African *praefectus praetorio* received 7,200 solidi, other chief officers up to 45,000 solidi, sufficient to maintain a sizable private army.[245] It is hardly surprising to learn that Roman military expenses amounted—according to Stein's estimation—to about six million solidi in the sixth century and thereby encumbered the greater part of the budget.[246]

Compared to this, Avar demands for tribute were relatively modest. From 574–75 on, Baian received eighty thousand solidi annually, and this amount did not immediately change after the fall of Sirmium.[247] In 585 Baian's son, after initially fruitless negotiations, obtained an increase to one hundred thousand solidi. In 598 the sum rose to 120,000 solidi.[248] Since the interruption in tribute payments during war years was generally made up by retroactive payments later, Baian and his son had, by 602, cashed in almost three million solidi. Comparatively speaking, they did very well. Attila managed to get the tribute raised from about 25,000 to more than 150,000 solidi within a short period, but he only received this amount for a few years.[249] During the years of peace around 565 the Persians had to content themselves with thirty thousand solidi. The Turks demanded not pieces of gold from the Chinese emperor but mainly silk. About the year 570 they were receiving annually one hundred thousand lengths of four different kinds of silk; in 607 the figure was two hundred thousand pieces.[250] Nonetheless, the Turkish khagans often made substantial countergifts, at times taking the form of several thousand horses.[251]

After 602 the Avars probably continued to receive their usual tribute, which was increased in 604 when the Persian war started.[252] In 623–24, before Heraclius marched off against the Persians, they received the record sum of two hundred thousand solidi.[253] After the defeat in 626, the sum must have dropped drastically, if anything was paid at all, and after the founding of the Bulgar khanate on the Danube around 680 the Avars more or less receded from Byzantine sight. In addition to the roughly six million solidi in gold and valuables that had streamed to the khagan up until this time, there were also sums for ransomed prisoners and the spoils of battle.[254] These enormous sums spawned a golden age in the Carpathian Basin, traces of which are found in grave goods. "Before the year 626 we know hardly any grave of an Avar freeman without gold jewelry."[255] Byzantine solidi themselves were more rarely buried with the deceased, although new finds could quickly increase the number of known cases. Imitations of Roman solidi found in seven graves, from a time when these coins were not available any more, show that Roman coins possessed a certain prestige value.[256] A great part of the gold would, however, have been melted down, received in the form of ingots, or paid in silver and other goods.

Great amounts of gold have been found in rich graves from the seventh century. The grave goods of an Avar nobleman were found in 1971 by workers in a sandpit in Kunbábony and recovered only in part. About 3.4 kilograms of gold, over seven pounds, are still extant. The grave goods give an impression of the representation of the Avar elite. The grave was initially believed to be that of a khagan, but the relatively small grave-pit and the absence of any clearly identifiable insignia of rulership contradict such an interpretation. By way of parade weapons, the deceased had a sword in a sheath with gold fittings, a saber with a gold-decorated grip, a ceremonial bow with gold tips and quiver with gold fittings, and six knives and daggers, all richly decorated with gold. Two belt-sets are adorned with gold, in particular, with pseudo-buckles, which have no function. In addition, the grave was furnished with a drinking set, consisting of golden drinking horns and cups, and with a pitcher of solid gold.[257] Almost as lavish are the graves in Bócsa, Tépe, and Kunágota; somewhat more modest those of Ozora, Kunmadaras, Kecel, and others.[258] Perhaps from the hoard of an Avar khagan of the eighth century is the Albanian treasure from Vrap (its counterpart from Erseke could be a forgery), whose vessels and belt buckles weigh a total of almost twenty pounds of gold and over fifteen pounds of silver. The solid gold belt end and a buckle alone each weigh about eight ounces.[259]

In 795/96, the Franks captured the treasure of the Avar khagans; this *thesaurus inestimabilis*, "inestimable treasure," "that had been accumulated over many centuries," struck them as unique.[260] For Charlemagne's biographer Einhard it was the greatest treasure that the Franks had ever captured, who could thus give back to Christendom what the Avars had once taken in plunder.[261] The Northumbrian annals knew of "fifteen wagons, each pulled by four oxen, filled with gold and silver and costly silken clothing."[262] The emperor divided this among bishoprics, abbeys, and the secular elite, used it for diplomatic presents, decorated his palace with it, and gave a share to the pope.[263] "A belt, a Hunnic sword, and two silk garments" went to the Anglo-Saxon king Offa. A Lombard history composed about 810 refers to "many holy vessels that these cruel sinners have stolen."[264] So far, the only trace of these gifts distributed all over Europe is the cover of a small silver box found in Sorpe, in Catalonia, for which an Avar coat clasp had been used; it shows the image of a Byzantine emperor.[265] A Byzantine emperor on an Avar dress accessory captured by the Franks and then donated to a Catalonian church: a remarkable case of object migration. Reflexes of the "Hunnic" treasure are also found in later German legends. The thirteenth-century Saxon World Chronicle, the first work in German of its kind, knew of the "groten schat van golde unde van silvere, den de koninc Ezzele unde sine nakomelinge lange gesament haben" (the great treasure of gold and silver that King Etzel and his successors had gathered over time).[266]

A more substantial trace of the Avar treasures is probably the gold hoard that came to light in 1799 in Nagyszentmiklós, present-day Sânnicolau Mare in Romania.[267] It consists of twenty-three gold vessels, mostly jugs, cups, and bowls, including a drinking horn, with a total weight of about twenty-two pounds.[268] Most celebrated is the representation of the "victorious prince" on jug no. 2; on the other side, a rider hunting with the bow on a winged lion with a crowned and bearded human face is pictured.[269] An extraordinary motif, with a few parallels in central Asian art, is the so-called "rape in the sky," with a giant eagle grabbing a human figure, which occurs twice.[270] Animal combat scenes, fantastic animals (among them, griffins), and "drinking boats" decorated with bulls' heads complete what could have been used as a luxury drinking set making a rather coherent impression. Only at the second glance do stylistic differences emerge, which point to Avar, Byzantine, Iranian, or central Eurasian parallels and may be dated to a bracket of two centuries, largely coinciding with the period of Avar rule.[271] For instance, the drinking horn finds its closest parallels in the Avar princely graves of the seventh century at Kunbábony, Bócsa, which contain comparable, if much smaller table-sets, and at Malaja Pereščepina.[272] There is an unusual number of inscriptions on the vessels; one is in Greek, one is in a Turkish dialect and refers to a *Boila Zoapan*, combining the Bulgar rank of *boilas* with title *župan* in an unusual spelling.[273] Furthermore, there are fourteen short runic inscriptions, with a total of seventy-seven letters, showing twenty-four different characters.[274] Not all of them are coeval to the production of the vessels, but on the whole, they contribute to the unity of the treasure.

The signification and dating of the find were long disputed. Initially it was thought to be Attila's treasure but was later associated with the Bulgars of the ninth century or with the Hungarians of the tenth. Like many extraordinary treasures it contains pieces from different periods, but most are unique and thus are hard to date precisely. Comparable pieces are scarcely known from the Danube Bulgars, whereas the parallels to Avar finds are by far the most substantial.[275] The runic characters are very similar to the Avar bone inscription from Szarvas from the first half of the eighth century.[276] Typological, epigraphic, iconographic, and artisanal arguments therefore clearly point toward an Avar origin of the treasure, assembled in the course of almost two centuries. It is tempting to conclude that this rich hoard of gold from the Carpathian Basin once belonged to the Avar khagans and was buried during the turbulent times around the year 800. Yet it could also have belonged to a noble Avar family in the eastern half of the Carpathian

Basin, as Csanád Bálint has argued.[277] However the treasure found its way into the earth, the exclusive golden table service gives a good impression of how the khagan's hoard might have appeared in the eighth century.

The gold that reached the barbarians rarely served as currency for payment. The Arabs were astounded to see the women of rich Volga Bulgars carrying huge numbers of dirhems (Arabic coins) around their necks, with the male elite similarly festooning their arms.[278] But the *Strategicon* also recommends for Roman soldiers: "The more splendid a soldier is in his armament, the more confidence he gains in himself and the more fear he inspires in the enemy."[279] The purpose of wealth was above all that, here or in the beyond, it should be displayed; splendor and prestige were closely connected. This was especially true of the ruler's treasure. The role that the royal treasure played in the rise and fall of Roman-barbarian kingdoms is well known. Byzantine historians each time identify it as the triumph of imperial policy when they succeeded in getting their hands on the royal treasure of an enemy, something that happened within a relatively short time with the Ostrogoths, Gepids, and Lombards.[280]

The prestige value turned the ruler's treasure into means of exercising power. Through carefully allocated gifts, the prince could assure himself of the loyalty of his followers. The *Suda Lexicon* describes the scene of how the Bulgar khan Tervel, who had just successfully helped Justinian II to return to power, rewarded his army. "The Bulgar ruler placed the horsewhip and the war-shield with its boss on the ground and put so much money over them that they were entirely covered. Then he drove his lance into the earth and piled silken clothes high and wide. Lastly, he distributed to his soldiers gold with his right hand and silver with his left hand from chests that he continuously had refilled."[281] When a group of warriors joined forces with the young Genghis Khan they justified their decision as follows, according to Rashid ad-Din: "He put off his clothing and made a gift of it; he alighted from his horse in order to give it away. He possessed a land, maintained an army, and maintained the *ulus* (state) with magnanimity."[282] Imperial largesse, "nourishing the people," was what most of all created acceptance for a ruler.[283]

Anthropological research into the exchange of gifts has had a great impact on medieval research. In his classic study, *The Gift*, Marcel Mauss affirms: "Between chiefs and their vassals, between vassals and their tenants, through such gifts a hierarchy is established. To give is to show one's superiority, to be more, to be higher in rank, *magister*. To accept without giving in return, or without giving back more, is to become client and servant."[284] Charlemagne did not act otherwise when he received the Avar spoils. The less a polity is reinforced by the organizational forms of a state, the more important this kind of exchange becomes. A continuous circulation of gifts held barbarian society together. An important nexus for this circulation of prestige goods was the court of the king or khagan. "They hoard but in order to spend, to place under an obligation."[285] However, such transactions did not follow any universal, transhistorical logic; and they were not necessarily successful in creating social cohesion. They could also express competition, be contradictory, change their meanings, lead to misunderstandings, or be judged inadequate.[286]

The practical usefulness of the gift was not its central feature. The ornamental weapons of princes and nobles, like those found in Kunbábony, were not made for battle and perhaps were only intended for the burial. "In these societies ... it is indeed something other than utility that circulates ... riches are from every view point as much a means of retaining prestige as something useful."[287] The barbarian "greed" and "avarice" denounced by contemporaries is then not so much a striving for luxury as for prestige, which is highlighted through the display of splendor. In order to satisfy this need, a complex *économie ostentatoire* developed,[288] the traces of which have been preserved for us in the graves of noble Avars. However, it needs to be noted that the graves contain only those objects that had been withdrawn from circulation as gifts and had become the "inalienable possessions" of their owners in death.[289] To an extent, they indicated the social rank of the owner and would preserve it for eternity.[290] The multiplicity of stylistic influences met by the archaeologist can thus be explained: the very alienness of the spoils may bear witness to the success and rank of the bearer. The habitus or social appearance of the barbarian warrior is situated in a tension field between adaptation and accentuation, between extravagance and conformity. The semantics of prestige also denote both incorporation in the reference or peer group and the exceptionality that the bearer claims for himself.

When the *Strategicon*, like so many other "civilized" contemporaries, characterizes the Avars by their "insatiability for gold," something quite different lies behind.[291] The overriding goal of the warrior life was the acquisition of glory and prestige. The anthropologist Mario Erdheim has characterized the importance of prestige in Aztec warrior society as follows: "The prestige of an individual consists in the knowledge that the members of his reference or peer group have of his exemplarity."[292] Success in this sense is to be understood as the realization of traditional values. "Striving for prestige, the individual realized the transmitted myths, the knowledge from his past, and thus contributed to continuity, that is, to the preservation and further development of his culture."[293]

As is still partly the case today, prestige found expression in status symbols and in external appearance, in the style of clothing, the richness of personal decoration, and the quality of arms. The belt can serve as an example here, because it is instructive in many respects. It was a dress accessory used every day, by men or also by women. It could be used as a marker of individual distinction and of identification with a group, and for indicating a person's rank within a community. It could be specific for a group or current across many groups, within the steppe and outside it. It could serve as a diplomatic gift, which is repeatedly attested between the Turks and the Tang.[294] It was a functional object that could be decorated with a rich variety of symbolic objects and images. The belt plaques and other elements could follow rather standardized patterns or allow for a wider variety of forms. Its message could be modulated according to political constellations or social needs. Belt fashions changed rather quickly and are therefore used for dating in archaeology. We have some information on the symbolic character of the belt from eastern central Asia. "Turkic epitaphs from southern Siberia indicate that gold belts had approximately the same high prestige value as battle standards. . . . One warrior received golden plaques from a qaghan because of his valor. Another boasted of possessing a belt with forty-two gold plaques."[295] In the central Asian steppe, the investiture with belt and riding coat established patron–client relations, both within a realm and in external relations.[296]

The question of origins of the Avar belts is complex.[297] It has several aspects. The belts of the seventh and eighth centuries in the Avar realm were multipartite, with side-straps hanging down from the main belt. They were mostly adorned with metal belt fittings, which were often decorated with elaborate ornaments or animal motifs. These fittings could be of different materials and produced in different techniques. Variously, we can infer from their uses and from the context of finds or pictorial representations that they may have indicated status, social function, or affiliation.[298] It seems that the Avars adopted these belts only sometime after arriving in the Carpathian Basin. This corresponds to the observation that in China and the adjacent steppes, single belts were worn at the time, such as the Chinese-type ceremonial belt worn by a seated statue, probably the khagan himself, in the seventh-century memorial complex of Bilge Khagan at Khöshöö Tsaidam.[299] Side-straps only appear in Turkish contexts in the later seventh century, cast silver and bronze mounts occur, if relatively rarely, in the eighth century.[300]

The belt-set found in kurgan 11 at Balyk-Sook I has several short side-straps, but its simple silver mounts look very unlike Avar belt-sets.[301] Stronger similarities with Avar belts are in fact found in the east much earlier: the early Xiongnu in the second/first century BCE produced belt plaques, often with animal combat scenes, which can be found in almost identical types in distant regions of their realm and beyond it.[302] This is strikingly similar to the wide currency of almost stereotypical belt plaques in the Avar realm in the eighth century, adorned with griffins, plant ornaments, and again animal combat scenes.[303] As often in the steppe, these conspicuous parallels, however, are not linked by any detectable chain of transmission.

In sixth-century Iran, there is no evidence for multipartite belts; but in the later sixth century, both in Iran and in the steppes north of the Black Sea, belts with cast mask fittings appear.[304] This type of fittings is also attested in Lombard Italy; but in the Carpathian Basin, only a few used pieces decorated with masks appear, not entire sets. Multipartite belts seem to appear first in Byzantium and the Mediterranean. Even though they are not attested as grave goods there, their wide diffusion can be inferred from a few hoards and from a number of pictorial representations. There is substantial evidence that multipartite, often ornate belts were used in the Byzantine world since the later sixth century, with a few earlier examples. They are often depicted on military persons, possibly of barbarian origin, and in hunting scenes.[305] Some belt fittings were found in Byzantine fortresses in the Balkan provinces, where they were obviously used by soldiers.[306] They do not represent, as it seems, the standard uniform of the soldiers, but a particular mark of distinction, perhaps connected with officers of barbarian origin.[307] Therefore, they are not mentioned in the *Strategicon*, where the soldiers are only said to wear "narrow belts."[308]

The earliest belt-sets found in graves in the Avar realm seem to date after 600. They were used as funerary apparel for two hundred years, until the end of the khaganate. However, materials, forms, and motifs used on the belt change. In the beginning, the fittings consist of strap ends on the main belt and on the side-straps. Soon, quadrangular plaques are added on the main belt. In the second quarter of the seventh century, the so-called pseudo-buckles, purely decorative elements from sheet metal, appear.[309] They are probably derived from the Black Sea steppes and may indicate Bulgar influence. The golden belts with lavish pseudo-buckles in the rich graves of Kunbábony and Bócsa represent luxury versions of these simpler types, again as in the eastern European steppes.[310] In the second half of the seventh century, different forms of decoration appear on the belt fittings: wickerwork, geometric decoration, and for the first time, animals appear on Byzantine buckles.[311] The structure of the fittings also evolves, from the Byzantine models to a particular set of more or less functional metal parts.[312] The late Avar period, in the eighth century, represents the peak of rich belt ornaments, now cast in bronze: almost a "bronze industry," as it has been called.[313] In the first half of the century, the griffin motif and lattice ornaments dominate the belt plaques in almost stereotypical ways. These belt-sets are widely diffused in the Avar realm, and there is a clear attempt at uniformity of expression behind them. In the last third of the eighth century, new motifs replace the griffin: finer lattice decoration, fish-scale ornaments, or boars' heads.

In the seventh and eighth centuries, multipartite belts were widely used.[314] In the Merovingian east, they appear early in the seventh century and are used until late in that century. They are probably derived from Lombard Italy.[315] In an early eighth-century fresco in the Church of S. Maria Antiqua in Rome, even a young male relative of the pope wears one.[316] Byzantine belts still occasionally came into the Carpathian Basin, more frequently in the seventh century, and just a few in the eighth; they were also used by Carantanian Slavs.[317] The decoration of the Avar belt plaques is culturally hybrid: some types show clear Byzantine derivation (for instance, representations of emperors); others are, perhaps deliberately, more linked to the steppes, and even have parallels in Tang art, which in turn could also go back to previous Western influence.[318] It is only in the Tang period, in the course of the seventh century, that multipartite belts are attested in China.

Unlike in the East, there is no written indication of the prestige value of the belt in the West. In Byzantine pictorial representations, uses of the belt as status symbols can in some cases be assumed.[319] We can also infer that the belt-sets were a symbol of status among the Avars, which could be indicated by form, fittings, kind and number of additional straps, and richness of decoration. The wide currency of the belt fittings in Avar graves and their basic uniformity, particularly in the eighth century, point to a significance for the group identity of the deceased. The semantics of prestige are, however, not all that easy for us to decipher. Only rarely have the written sources transmitted any instructions for use. For instance, the number of stones that were laid on the grave of a Turkish warrior showed the number of enemies that he had killed, as a Chinese chronicle reveals: "The number of stones often ran into the hundreds or thousands," it laconically adds.[320] The success of later grave robbers suggests that Avar graves were also marked. The depth and proportions of the burial pit corresponded to social status. Belt-wearers also generally lay in larger graves.[321]

How did a warrior acquire prestige? It is self-evident that performance in battle, or perhaps on the hunt, outweighed all other merits. A Roman architect at Attila's court, who constructed a fabulous bathhouse for an eminent Hun and as reward was demoted to the lowest level of the social hierarchy as a bathhouse slave, made this discovery the hard way, while a Roman captive made his career and acquired his freedom as a "Hun" warrior.[322] Yet personal bravado was not sufficient. Only the peer group could impart knowledge of the excellence of an individual.

In steppe empires, the khagan strove to channel the competition between nobles and warriors by gifts and gestures of favor. As long as the differentiated distinctions in status remained in approximate balance across the empire, the ruler could also retain his authority, and vice versa. When a ruler was no longer successful in maintaining order over the acquisition of prestige, it resulted in "envy and mutual recriminations," as the Avar prisoners supposedly complained to the Bulgar khan after the downfall of their khaganate.[323] The status of the khagan and the traditional order had been compromised. The Avar Empire thus sustained its cohesion above all by regulating the acquisition of prestige. Just as the khagan was the model for the warrior, the goods that he distributed were exemplary. A court workshop, as a nexus for "prestige artifacts," has, despite many attempts, not yet been demonstrated.[324] In the case of many objects, regional sets of workshops can rather be assumed. However, it cannot be denied that many artifacts had a rather uniform style throughout the Avar Empire. This is the artistic outcome of the Avar *économie ostentatoire*, a political system tailored to regulate the acquisition of prestige for its members: a system that could be reproduced as long as these members felt that they had better opportunities to acquire prestige and rewards inside it than without it.

6.6 *Logades* and Warriors

"The begs and the people," according to the Old Turkic inscriptions, were, along with the khagan and his dynasty, the basis of an empire; its fate depended on their unity.[325] A further distinction can be recognized among the Uyghurs in the Terkhin inscription from the eighth century. Three electoral bodies participated in the choice of a khagan: the nine great *buyruqs* (*toquz-buyruq*); a thousand military leaders; and the *qara bodun*, the people (arms-bearing, and thus entitled to participation).[326] Among the Danube Bulgars, according to the inscriptions, the khan was followed by two ranks of nobles, for which the terms were *boila* and *bagain*, as well as the *bulgars*, which plausibly points to the members of the army.[327]

A similar stratification may be assumed for the Avars, although it is not attested in writing.[328] When Avar dignitaries (except the khagan) appear in Menander, their status is paraphrased as *archontes*, that is, "those who govern."[329] In Theophylact the terms are *dynotatoi* ("the most powerful") and *logades* ("the elect").[330] The untechnical title *archontes* could designate both higher Roman functionaries and the leaders of peoples during the age of migrations.[331] Once the title *rex* had become established for monarchic rulers, *archōn* acquired a more oligarchic meaning. Yet in official documents, it continued to be used as a title for barbarian rulers. As late as the tenth century the Bulgar khan would be addressed by the Byzantines as *archōn Boulgarias*.[332] In distinction to *logades* the term does suggest a somehow autonomous position.

The term *logades* is also used in our sources for Attila's Huns. Otto Maenchen-Helfen's investigations into Priscus's usage have shown that this expression is not to be understood literally as the "elect" here. "There is no proof that these prominent men among the Huns had anything in common except their prominence."[333] Preeminent among the *logades* were the *epitēdeioi*, the "friends" with whom Attila surrounded himself. Bound to him by personal loyalty, they formed a counterweight to the tribal structure, the *kata phyla kai genē archontes*.[334] The personally selected "companions of the ruler" played a similar role among the Mongols.[335] Among the Huns some of these "elect" acquire a personal profile in Priscus's eyewitness account.[336] In the case of the Avars we know only a handful of names. In particular, it is unclear whether the Avar *logades* were tribal leaders or the personal appointments of the khagan and to what extent they were obliged to him for their positions. The khagan would appear to have chosen the emissaries. And it was also he who determined who would lead the army as his deputy. We also know of a case in which the khagan appointed a person as a kind of governor—that Kuver who showed so little appreciation of it.[337]

Names are almost exclusively preserved for the Avar envoys. Of the first, named Kandikh, we know nothing further.[338] Somewhat better known is Targitius, who is first named as ambassador in the fall of 565 and then appears several times more.[339] On the occasion of the mission of 567–68, he is introduced as an Avar leader (*ho tōn Abarōn hegoumenos*), and in the following years he often appears at the imperial court.[340] "A very eminent man among the people of the Avars," Theophylact calls him, when he negotiated a short-lived peace agreement in tense circumstances at Constantinople in 585.[341] During the subsequent mission he was interned for a time on the Isle of Princes.[342] Just how much political influence he had was shown in the winter of 593–94, when he, together with the *logades*, prevented the khagan from declaring war on the Romans.[343] The phrasing leaves open whether he himself belonged to this group of *logades*. That he is singled out by name may be a consequence of the fact that the Romans knew him well, although in such a case we might have looked for the phrase "and the other *logades*."

We know only one other Avar from the sixth century who may have been Targitius's equivalent in rank. His name, office, or title was Apsikh. He too had to prove his worth as envoy to the imperial court. After the failure of the negotiations that Targitius had been conducting with Justin II since 567, new representatives from both sides came to the task: Apsikh and Tiberius. The two parties agreed that sons of prominent Avars would be given as hostages, something that Justin blocked.[344] Tiberius's argument that the khagan could thus be better kept under control than by having his own sons as hostages may owe something to Apsikh's negotiating tactics. Whatever the case, Apsikh then displayed his military skill. During the siege of Sirmium (580–82) he commanded an Avar unit that was charged with turning back the Roman replacement troops on the bridge to Dalmatia. Yet no Romans appeared, upon which Apsikh's troops joined Baian's main army, which was engaged at another bridge in a three-day battle.[345] Then we hear nothing of Apsikh for a considerable time. Not until 601 is an Avar *hypostrategos* mentioned by this name. In these years, when the khagan's position was under pressure, he played a decisive role. In the summer of 601 he led the Avar army to the Iron Gate and negotiated with the Romans. At this time the khagan was staying at the field camp in Constantiola but did not take an active part in events. The following summer Apsikh marched on the khagan's orders against the Antes.[346]

Thus, Apsikh, like Targitius, appears in the sources over a thirty-year period. At the end of this time he is still capable of a difficult ride into the land of the Antes. Were these names in reality titles of rank?[347] Yet there are no parallels of such titles in the rich nomenclature of the steppe peoples at the time. A thirty-year period of service is not unusual for a diplomat. Narses and Belisarius were no longer young when they won their major victories. It is, however, striking that Targitius bore the same name as an archaic Scythian king.[348] Among titles, honorific names, and personal names, boundaries appear to have been fluid; it is also conceivable that sons were given their fathers' names.

We know a few more names from among the most powerful Avars of the time. Solachus was the name of the envoy who in 580 delivered Baian's declaration of war.[349] In charge of an advance party of eight thousand warriors, who were to free a mountain pass in 592, was a certain Samur.[350] In the following year a "barbarian" by the name of Kokh appeared in Priscus's camp in Durostorum and in the khagan's name protested against the attacks on the Slavs.[351] An Avar "exarch" by the name of Hermitzis stood out for his execration of the defenders during the great siege of 626.[352] Bookolabras is the name of a priest and magician, presumably of Turkish origin, from about 580.[353] All the others in the Avar kingdom who are known by name were, in the opinion of the sources, Bulgars, or their name suggested a foreign origin. "That Cotragerus" who in 562 urged war on the Antes was likely a Cutrigur of unknown name. In any case, his counsel was heard.[354] Kunimon, a member of an Avar delegation, who bore the same name as a Gepid king, acted against Avar interests and was perhaps only a Gepid guide accompanying the first known Avar embassy in Europe.[355] From the seventh century we know of several illustrious Avar dissidents who (at least after their flight) were considered Bulgars: Alciocus, Kuver, and his polyglot follower Mavros.[356] Also of questionable loyalty was Unguimeri, the bearer of a Germanic name, and, moreover, the only "Avar" of the eighth century who is known by name.[357] Although the small number means that a consideration of the names can have no statistical significance, they do attest to the fact that the polyethnicity of the Avars extended into the highest reaches of society.

The scant written evidence can be completed on certain points by archaeological finds. For the upper social stratum during the seventh century, rich graves such as those found at Kunágota, Szentendre, and Ozora may serve as examples. Warriors were buried along with their richly harnessed horses and had long swords in sheaths with gold fittings.[358] Well-to-do warriors were quite numerous, and they lived in small settlements whose cemeteries usually did not have more than a dozen graves. Horse burials were similarly very common. Belts, straps, and weapons were ornamented with gold and silver in keeping with wealth and rank.[359] The exceptionally large and rich cemetery of Zamárdi south of Lake Balaton, which started in the late sixth century, is conspicuous because of its predominantly Western material.[360] Sometimes the arrangement of the graves in the necropolis seems to reflect social relationships. In Alattyán, next to a man with a rich belt but no weapons is the more modest grave of an armed man, with rich women's and children's graves round about, and poorer graves just beyond these.[361] A similar division of a cemetery among several families, whose leaders lay in the center, can often be noted.[362]

6.7 Forms of Production and Distribution

Traditional accounts of the history of steppe peoples often concentrate on rulers and mounted warriors. In Beševliev's classic work on the "proto-Bulgars," with its nearly two hundred pages on life and culture, just two of these are devoted to a chapter on agriculture, stock raising, crafts, and trade.[363] This is entirely in proportion to the written evidence that allows little more than the conclusion that agriculture and stock raising were indeed practiced, which is hardly surprising; only archaeological sources allow us to go beyond that. Other accounts limit themselves to portraying the steppe peoples as essentially parasitic: the Avars attacked other peoples in order to rob them. The bill was paid above all by the Romans and by Slavic farmers.[364] This corresponds to Roman perceptions. Yet to reduce the Avar economy to their exploitation of sedentary populations would be a gross simplification, for two reasons. First, the society of late Antiquity relied as much on exploitation and military domination as its barbarian counterpart. The legal forms in which this appropriation was realized and the large-scale cultural achievements that were thereby made possible should not divert attention from the fact that a great many inhabitants of the empire had little more to fear from barbarian rule than from the agents of the Roman state. Second, Avar society was itself internally differentiated. It satisfied essential production needs on its own. Plunder and tribute did bring enormous riches to the Carpathian Basin but contributed very little to the survival of the Avar warriors.

Avar warrior society depended on a double acquisition. Externally, it acquired prestige goods, or the materials for their production, above all in the wars against the Romans. Internally, it relied on the foodstuffs and goods produced, usually in small units, by the clans themselves and by dependent farmers. These two economic circuits certainly did not operate completely independently of each other but can still be distinguished in our scant information. They satisfied two distinct claims of the ruling warrior elite: to assure survival and, beyond this, to enable a life appropriate to one's status.

The economic sphere that the Avars occupied provided all the fundamentals for the creation of their empire. The steppe zones on the middle Danube permitted the raising of their herds. Slavic and indigenous farmers provided complements to the food supply. And the strategic position on the border of the Roman Empire facilitated access to the vast riches that it managed. How these elements complemented one another can be described only approximately. The existence of an extensive steppe in the Carpathian Basin in the first millennium CE has been a matter of debate. Today's wide steppes of the Puszta are to an extent man-made, and more extensive than in previous periods. However, recent bioarchaeological research seems to show that the previous forest steppe had already been transformed into grass steppes about three thousand years ago in parts of the Carpathian Basin.[365] If no sufficient open land had been available, it would be hard to explain that Huns, Avars, and Hungarians successively established their realms there. Unlike most central Asian steppe regions, however, these steppes were more closely linked with agrarian lands and forests. In general, how the land could be used depended on its previous uses, so that these were "cultural steppes."

So far, we have only limited information on nomadic stock raising for the first century of the khaganate. The *Strategicon* mentions the huge herds of horses that the Avars took along on military campaigns.[366] A trace of differentiated animal husbandry are the meat deposits in graves, which were more or less common during the entire Avar period. But they do not permit much in the way of further conclusions. Wealthy warriors certainly disposed of large herds, but whether they were collective or individual property and who tended these herds cannot be determined from the grave finds.

In most cemeteries there are a number of poorer graves, even some without grave goods, which indicates that a group of dependents were part of the local communities. Whatever their legal status, the poor, male and female, probably had to do household work and helped with the care of the livestock.[367] What is striking, especially in the early cemeteries, is their relatively modest number. In Alattyán, men without knives and women without grave goods account for only about 10 percent of all graves. In addition to these are very modest graves in which men are accompanied by knives, an iron buckle, and occasionally fire kits or whetstones.[368] Among the steppe peoples the need for slaves was generally slight. Wealthy horsemen possessed only a few household slaves.[369]

It is not yet clear to what extent Avar warriors and their households participated in production and the domestic economy. Well-to-do women of the early Avar period had a great deal of jewelry in their graves but no domestic objects, and few tools.[370] Nonetheless organizing supplies, raising horses, training and war, the organization of the empire, and social obligations certainly made heavy demands on the Avar warrior (and on his wife). The importance of the hunt is suggested by hunting scenes of belt fittings and other objects. In the graves there are joints of meat from deer and other game, although in appreciably smaller quantities than meat from domestic animals.[371] At any event successful early Avar warriors were dependent on the proper functioning of a pastoral economy in their immediate vicinity, one increasingly complemented by other forms of agrarian production. Provisioning through the Roman *annona* and the supraregional trade in food stuffs, to which the migrant armies of earlier centuries could aspire, was no longer possible.

Many Avar villages that have been excavated in the last decades show that permanent settlements and mixed agriculture need not point to a non-Avar subject population. It was not until the 1960s that the first Avar settlement in Dunaújváros was studied; since then, there have been numerous further excavations.[372] The finds reveal that relatively quickly villages with wooden houses of the "eastern European house type" were built, whose cemeteries largely contain "Avar" material. In Dunaújváros on the old *limes* road thirty-four sunken huts (*Grubenhäuser*) from the seventh century were found. A number of sunken huts and a free-standing oven from the late Avar period were excavated at Eperjes.[373]

A fundamental ecological difference from the greater part of the Eurasian steppe belt was the fact that the Avars founded their khaganate on arable land. Wide areas were under agricultural cultivation or were susceptible to such cultivation. This advantage was exploited from the outset. Whether or not Avar warriors regularly took winter quarters among Slavic farmers at the periphery of the empire, as Fredegar claims, is hard to ascertain.[374] In any case, particular traditions of sedentary life continued, or even unfolded under Avar rule. Gepid villages continued functioning after 567 and could celebrate their own festivals, as Theophylact reports.[375] The excavator Attila Kiss had also attributed the wealthy Avar-period village at Kölked near Mohács, with its two cemeteries (A and B), to the Gepids, an ethnic attribution that is hardly tenable; in any case, the villagers continued many "Germanic" and non-Avar ways of life over generations.[376] Such villages had their own elite, which is expressed in rich burials. The differences only disappear in the second third of the seventh century.[377]

The hybrid, but distinctively Romano-barbarian Keszthely culture in the vicinity of Lake Balaton, but also populations elsewhere in Pannonia, adopted late antique models and forms of artisanal production from the barbarian *regna* in the west.[378] With the discovery of the large cemetery—about six thousand graves!—of Zamárdi and its rich burials, a circle of wealthy Avars that profited from the economic activities of the region, but also non-Avar elites, has become visible.[379] Whether the Keszthely culture existed continuously since late Antiquity or whether it was the result of Avar settlement policies has been debated, and the dominant opinion has changed from continuity to interruption and back again.[380] The relative shares of displaced Byzantines, native Pannonians, Germanic retainers, Italian exchanges, or Avar warriors are open to debate. Here, the significance of the thriving late Roman population for the economy and culture of the Avar Empire needs to be underlined.

The Avars' interest in a functioning agrarian economy is illustrated in a rather imprecise bit of information from John of Ephesus from the 580s. The Avars conquered two Roman cities and other forts. "They said to the inhabitants, 'Go out, sow and reap, and we will take half of the tribute from you.'"[381] Presumably this refers to Singidunum, and perhaps Viminacium, and other forts in the region that fell in 584. We know from Theophylact that the inhabitants of Singidunum were just harvesting their fields when the Avars attacked. John is certainly not a very reliable source of information, and the translation and meaning of the passage are debated.[382] Yet the later destiny of Singidunum, which in the course of the war would change hands several times, shows that the city was not destroyed and depopulated.[383] John of Ephesus also relates that the Avars spared the city of Sirmium, whose starved residents were immediately given food supplies by the Avars after they had taken it. It was not until a year later that the city was destroyed by fire.[384] It is possible that the Avars attempted to preserve the economic life of conquered cities in their vicinity and to construct stable tribute relationships (as, for the most part, the Rugians and Goths, Gepids and Lombards along the middle Danube had done).

Mostly, however, the Avars resorted to relocating Roman prisoners of war and other productive groups to their own hinterland, at a safe distance from the Roman frontier. This is attested for the great military campaigns in the first years of the rule of Heraclius (after 610): "The entire population was deported to that region of Pannonia whose capital had once been Sirmium, on the Danube; the khagan settled them here as his subjects."[385] After the second conquest of Singidunum (595), the khagan appears to have forced the inhabitants "to give up their homes" and made them "homeless in the lands of the enemy."[386] This plan was, however, scuttled by the rapid counterattack of the Roman army, and the barbarian garrison was caught between the new attackers and the townspeople. In 623 "men, women, children, and the aged" were carried off from the surroundings of Constantinople across the Danube into enemy territory.[387] The khagan promised the Lombards of the conquered city of Cividale that they would be resettled in Pannonia. Yet all the arms-bearing men were immediately executed, and only the women and children experienced the "misery of captivity" in the *patria Avarorum*.[388] Like the *Miracula S. Demetrii*, Paul the Deacon writes of attempts to fly after many years of captivity. It was his great-grandfather, Lopichis, who, once an adult, risked escaping on his own, while his four brothers remained with the Avars. He had acquired bow and arrow in the Avar manner and was reportedly guided by a wolf in his flight, which is a motif particularly widespread among the steppe peoples.[389]

A longer account of the fates of Roman captives and of their offspring in Pannonia is found in the *Miracles of Saint Demetrius*.[390] The value of the account is debated; many scholars have built far-reaching hypotheses on it; others have seen it as a biblical exodus narrative that contains little actual information.[391] The story presumes that even Christians, Romans, and prisoners of war could make a career in barbarian society This invites some conclusions about the status of the productive classes in the Avar Empire. They were not permitted to leave the Avar realm, but this also applied to the free warriors; unlike those, as we may assume, they had to pay tribute. In return, their way of life and their communities were respected. They were not divided up as slaves among the Avar settlements. In the event of need, they could (or had to) perform military service. If they proved themselves, they might win their freedom. The descendants of the Roman prisoners led by Kuver had acquired sufficient fighting skills to beat the khagan's army in several battles. It is conceivable that economic success was the springboard to social advancement among the Pannonian Romans. They could then acquire good military equipment. As among the Huns, success in war was probably the precondition for freedom.[392] To all appearances, subject status was no obstacle to marriage unions with warrior families. This picture is generally substantiated by the finds from the Keszthely culture.

The archaeological material provides rich evidence about handicrafts of the Avar period, although it is often hard to tell whether they can be regarded as 'Avar' handicrafts. When artisanal objects do not correspond to those consistently found elsewhere, we tend to associate "typical" products with the Avars: Avar belts, weapons, fibulae, or pottery. But how "Avar" were early Avar handicrafts? Apart from the methodological problems of ethnic identification of object types, who was it who produced the "typically Avar" belt fittings, weapons, and jewelry? Despite the sheer size of the available material, the answer is not an easy one. Unlike twenty-five years ago, considerable Byzantine influence on Avar culture is now readily acknowledged by most scholars. This is also due to the progress of technical analyses of Avar jewelry.[393] Many that were placed with noble Avars as grave goods betray the traditions of Byzantine craftsmanship. This does not mean that Avar craftsmen were incapable of producing high quality.

Relatively few pieces can be shown to be direct Byzantine imports. In a recent article, Csanád Bálint has argued that much Avar goldwork follows Byzantine techniques, but not on the level that a workshop in Constantinople could have produced, at least up to the end of the seventh century. On the other hand, the quality of goldwork in the Avar realm was superior to the golden objects found elsewhere in eastern Europe. The treasure of Nagyszentmiklós, assembled over a period of 150 years, unites pieces of exceptional quality (superior to the equally rich hoard of Malaja Pereščepina in present-day Ukraine, which probably represents the grave goods of the Bulgar khan Kuvrat), but as such stands quite aloof from the rest of eighth-century Avar objects.[394] It is unlikely that the Avar artisans came with their skills from central Asia, or were already found in Pannonia when the Avars arrived. The goldsmiths' craft only became conspicuous in the seventh century. Remarkably, and unlike in other contemporary cultures in eastern Europe, Avar goldsmiths were buried with their tools; we have about twenty graves with a variety of tools and forms.[395] Some goldsmiths were buried with arms and horses. The goldsmith's grave from Kunszentmárton from the first half of the seventh century contains series of press forms, molds for casting, and matrices (some of Byzantine type) for the belt fittings and jewelry that were then popular. Also included were tongs, hammers, punches, casting spoons, and bellows, as well as a precision scale with a set of Byzantine weights.[396] These goldsmiths produced to Avar tastes, but with mostly Byzantine techniques. Avar culture had an ample capacity for the assimilation of foreign influences.[397] The analysis of Avar-age metalworking technologies, particularly bronze casting, has also shown that sophisticated craftsmen were available in the Avar realm: "The combined stylistic and technological analysis suggests a consistent association of sophisticated stylistic messages and application of complicated or 'high-tech' procedures," as Orsolya Heinrich-Tamáska concludes.[398] Other crafts, such as works in glass and stone, also produced remarkable pieces.[399]

What was most important in the world of the warrior, that is, arms, belt fittings, horse harness, jewelry, and the like, is also what makes the Avar style most apparent to us. For the Avar warrior, the origin of the craftsman who produced these objects to his taste probably was a matter of secondary importance. Some high-level pieces may also have been made by itinerant craftsmen. Two Byzantine sources mention that the khagan had foreign specialists brought in. Byzantine *mechanici et architecti* were apparently meant to construct a palace and baths for Baian, when he forced them to build a bridge across the Danube instead.[400] From the Lombard king Agilulf, with whom he was on friendly terms, the khagan obtained *artefices* for the construction of ships.[401] Such technical help was quite common as a token of friendship between rulers. But it could also occur that expert artisans were held captive at court, as by the Rugian queen Giso in the late fifth century.[402]

The status of the smith was conspicuous but also ambivalent in steppe societies. As early as Herodotus we learn that from among the sons of the king Targitaos it was only the youngest who could handle molten gold; and it was he who inherited the throne. The descent of the Turks was traced back to smiths. But ambivalence in the smith's status is shown when the khagan of the Rouran rejected a Turkish marriage proposal on the grounds of such origins. After this insult, the Turks seized their weapons and destroyed the empire of the Rouran.[403] The Turks received the Byzantine envoys of Zemarchus by proffering iron, which they symbolically offered for sale, and this may be related to the legends of their origins.[404] Even Genghis Khan drew legitimacy from the myth of a smith ancestor. The title *tarkhan*, attested among the late Avars, is reminiscent of the smith Tarkhan of an old legend.[405] Such important roles in formative myths derive from the role that the development of metallurgy played in the military superiority and economic independence of the nomads. However, what that means for the social status of smiths is subject to a controversial debate.[406] Craftsmen, including smiths, were considered inferior to warriors who did not have to do hard work in many early medieval societies. Martin Ježek has even argued that many smiths' tools in wealthy graves only have a symbolical function, hinting, for instance, at the transformative power of the deceased.[407] This, however, can hardly be the case with the grave assemblage of the goldsmith from Kunszentmárton "with the most extensive collection of metal-smith's tools and other accessories, as well as half-products and other materials, so far known from early medieval Europe."[408] The position of the high-status warrior-smith seems to have been an option in Avar societies, as some of the goldsmiths' graves indicate.

Many object types, for instance belt fittings, are distributed across the Carpathian Basin. Whether this wide distribution points to the mobility of the owners of the pieces, of itinerant artisans, or to trade cannot easily be resolved from the archaeological perspective. For the Avars we are probably best advised to reckon with customized production rather than with manufacture for a larger market, but this does not exclude the possibility of interregional exchange.[409] Metallurgical analyses have shown that multiple casting techniques were employed for the late Avar bronze belt fittings.[410]

The source of the metals remains unclear. Where, for instance, did the bronze for the massive belt fittings of the late Avar period come from? The metal mounts and fittings for a single belt-set weighed on average almost ten ounces.[411] The opinion that the Roman bronze statues in Pannonia were systematically smelted down seems now superseded; however, it must have been common to reuse old metal.[412] Perhaps there was a trade in half-finished alloys, something that may be clarified by workshop and materials analyses.[413] The late Avar bronze-casting "industry" in any case presupposes a certain supraregional division of labor.

However, there were also local workshops. In the village of Eperjes the remains of smelting ovens and iron slag were found.[414] In all likelihood the larger settlements had their own foundry pits, as is confirmed by the finds in Moravian Mikulčice from the late Avar period.[415] A good number of late seventh- to eighth-century "Avar-type" iron furnaces have so far been uncovered, especially in Pannonia; metallurgical analyses led to the conclusion that the Carpathian Basin always had to import iron.[416] In the Slavic area north of the Carpathians, the mining of bog iron is well documented.[417] We have no direct evidence for mining in the Avar era. But salt was certainly mined in Transylvania. Kurt Horedt assumed Gepid "salt lords" in Transylvania until the middle of the seventh century. Toward 700 the number of Avar graves in the Mureş Valley increases, which could indicate that the Avars themselves had taken control of the salt trade.[418] When King Arnulf wanted to cut the Moravians off from salt coming from the Bulgar kingdom at the end of the ninth century, it was most likely a question of salt from central Transylvania.[419]

6.8 Exchanges and Their Limits

We know little about Avar trade. It is characteristic that a handbook on trade relations in the early Middle Ages notes the Avars only in the margin and even then, surprisingly, as pirates.[420] Trade between the empire and steppe peoples was a political matter, regulated by treaties. In 468–69 Attila's sons sent an embassy to Emperor Leo that "a peace treaty should be made and that in the old manner they should meet with the Romans at the Danube, establish a market and exchange whatever they required." The emperor, however, decided that the Huns should not have access to Roman trade.[421] A very similar request, "to be able to establish markets along the frontier in order to conduct trade with China," was presented in 584 by a Turkish delegation to the Chinese emperor.[422] The Bulgar khan Krum proposed very far-reaching trade regulations in 812.[423] Restrictions on trade and the expulsion of Bulgar traders led to war between the Bulgars and Byzantium in 894.[424] In our sources about the Avars' treaties with Byzantium, no such formal trade agreement is mentioned.

A great number of Byzantine objects must have arrived in the Carpathian Basin as tribute and plunder. Theophylact specifies that under the treaty of 583, "80,000 gold coins in the form of merchandise of silver and embroidered cloth" were supposed to be sent from Byzantium.[425] Objects in gold and silver, especially jewelry, glass vessels and amphorae, silk clothing, probably also spices, which so delighted the khagan before Tomis in 598, are all attested in the written sources.[426] Given that steady stream of a variety of objects, it is surprising how relatively little can be found in Avar graves.[427] For instance, there is relatively little evidence for amphorae as containers of wine and oil, although excessive consumption of wine would later be made partly responsible for the fall of the khaganate.[428] It is hard, then, to assume intensive trade relations on top of the tribute. In the early Avar period, especially in Pannonia, we find a lot of object types in common with the Merovingian sphere, and in particular, with Italy. The question whether these shared cultural traits are an indicator of people living in a Western cultural continuum under Avar rule, or of influences and exchanges, still is not settled.[429]

The sources are silent as to what the Avars may have exported. We have written testimony for only one kind of business, which in any case generated considerable revenues: trade in people. It was common to put prisoners of war from the Roman provinces up for ransom afterward. After the great siege of Thessalonica (around 616) had failed and a peace agreement had been reached, "the barbarians came fearlessly up to the walls in order to sell their prisoners for paltry sums and to trade in various goods."[430] We hear about ransom sums for prisoners, although in a context of slander against the emperor. In 598 the khagan allegedly offered the prisoners at one solidus per head. When the emperor would not agree, he cut the price by half. But Maurice would not accept even this bargain, at which point the khagan had the prisoners killed. The avaricious emperor became widely hated for this.[431] In the time of Attila the ransom for prisoners was set between eight and twelve solidi.[432] It was clearly an exception when such transactions did not take place. In 640 the pope sent a delegate to Dalmatia in order to recover relics and buy the freedom of prisoners.[433] The fate of this human booty in times that were unfavorable for women is described melodramatically by Paul the Deacon. After the capture of Cividale around 610 the women were raped, the men killed. The *ducissa* Romilda, who had opened the gates to the khagan, was given by him, after one night, to twelve Avars, "who abused her through the whole night with their lust, succeeding each other by turns." Her daughters made themselves so revolting with the smell of rotting chicken meat that these "stinking Lombard women" are reputed to have saved their virginity. "They were afterwards sold throughout various regions and secured worthy marriages on account of their noble birth."[434] The tale allows the speculation that prominent Bavarians and Alamans had no objections to acquiring slave women from the Avars and, if they were from good families, to marrying them. We may assume a steady demand for young female slaves in a warrior society. In the steppe, it was part of the customary honorable reception given guests to provide them with a female slave for the duration of their stay. This honor was offered to Priscus's embassy on its way to Attila: "The Scythians are accustomed to honor their guests in this way." The emperor's ambassadors, however, reported to have declined these pleasures.[435] Zemarchus, envoy to the Turks, also received a slave girl taken in war.[436]

There is, however, no trace of an Avar involvement in commercial slave trade, which had been the fuel of ancient civilizations and continued to be important in long-distance exchanges in the early Middle Ages.[437] That Latin *servus* for slave was replaced in the West by a word derived from the name *Slav* is not the Avars' fault. Something similar occurred among the Arabs.[438] Extensive finds of dirhems and of iron shackles and fetters in the lands between the Black Sea and the Baltic allow us to reconstruct this profitable trade.[439] Of course, the peak of this massive export of (mostly) Slavic slaves to the Islamic world was only reached after the Avar Empire had fallen, but in its beginnings it had passed the Carpathian Basin by. Only isolated finds of dirhems in the Avar sphere of power from the second half of the eighth century point to trade relations with the Arab world, as in Petrovci, near the old Bassianae, west of Belgrade, where eight newly minted dirhems (from between 762 and 794–99) came to light.[440] In the ninth century, as Ivo Štefan has argued, the large Moravian settlements such as Mikulčice and Pohansko were centers of the slave trade, and shackles were found along the "amber route" that connected it with the Adriatic.[441]

Neither do we have any hint of regular exports of animals and animal products from the Avar realm. Such commerce is only attested for the Black Sea region. Jordanes reports that in the sixth century the Onogurs on the Black Sea transmitted ermine skins from the Kama region.[442] The Khazars of the ninth century exported pelts, especially beaver skins, fish and fish glue, wax, and honey to Constantinople.[443] For the Chinese, horses were the most prized products of the "northern peoples." We have extensive information about the horse markets at the border in the Tang period, about their regulations and prices.[444] In contrast to the steppe peoples farther to the east the Avars could not profit from the lucrative transit trade on the Silk Road. From Cherson, "whither Asia's greedy merchant brings his wares,"[445] the produce of the East was transported by ship to Constantinople, and from there, if at all, moved on to the West. Grave finds do attest to a certain exchange between the Carpathian Basin and the south Russian steppe, above all in luxury handicrafts. Objects from the Far East also reached the Avars, although we cannot determine whether they were brought by immigrants, acquired from the Byzantines, or bought from traders.[446] There is evidence that at least in the early Avar period exchanges continued on the Amber Road.[447]

We can scarcely expect to find traces of an evolved Avar monetary economy, as a fragment from Pseudo-Masudi ascribes to the Bulgars.[448] The solidi paid out by the Byzantines were used in part for purchases, but in the main they were melted down to meet the demands for gold in Avar handicrafts. Clearly the prestige value stood in the foreground. In the graves gold coins served as *oboli* for the dead, placed in the mouth of the deceased, a custom that was practiced from China to the Roman world. Others were worn as ornaments, partly with holes drilled in them.[449] Only a limited number of small copper coins, which were used in daily business in the Byzantine economic sphere, were found so far among the Avars; they virtually disappear after Heraclius.[450] After 626, gold coins still reached the Avar realm, but become very rare after 680. At this time it was not only the political situation that was changing with the establishment of the Bulgar khanate at the lower Danube, but the circulation also declined in Byzantium. Nonetheless, Wolfgang Hahn's tabulations demonstrate that in the eastern Alpine area, even during the "darkest" centuries, some coins seem to have circulated. In the region of present-day Lower Austria and Burgenland stray finds have included five smallish coins from the reign of Justin II, two from Maurice, two from Phocas, four from Heraclius, and two from Constans II, plus one from the eighth century. In the wider Avar sphere of power, coins from the times of these emperors have been recovered from the Carantanian centers in the Zollfeld and Aichfeld (Knittelfeld) as well as from the area of Poetovio/Ptuj and Celeia/ Celje. The coin hoard from Hellmonsödt near Linz may point to a Bavarian trade with the East. It comprised in all eighty coins struck during the reigns of Maurice, Constans II, and even Justinian II (685–95).[451]

Overall, it seems that the fundamental economic circuits of the Avar Empire were little commercialized. The subsistence economy, the supply of life's necessities, left little room for exchange. Avar villages must have been relatively self-sufficient.[452] Where warriors had to be provisioned, this occurred directly (as in Fredegar's example) or by means of levies on farmers, who were settled in the ambit of their lords and had to provision them. Other goods were acquired as tribute from populations settled farther away. Avar envoys demanded tribute from the Slavs north of the lower Danube in the 570s, although we do not hear what they required.[453] Slavic tribes had to pay the Hungarians tribute in the form of marten pelts.[454] According to the early twelfth-century *Russian Primary Chronicle*, the Khazars "fell on the Polyanians and said, 'Pay us tribute!'" For each chimney, the Slavic tribes delivered, according to their means, a white squirrel or a coin.[455] For the Avars, the Romans were the main source of prestige goods.

European steppe rulers may have had an interest in limiting or curbing trades. The peace proposal made by Khan Krum in 812 contained a restrictive clause "that those who traded in both countries should be certified by means of diplomas and seals," otherwise their assets would be confiscated by the treasury.[456] Perhaps a reason is that if everything could be acquired through purchase, it threatened the difficult ranking by prestige and the role that the ruler played in all this. In this sense, as the *Suda Lexicon* claims, the captured Avars explained to the Bulgar khan the fall of their empire: "They all became merchants and cheated each other."[457] Reportedly, their statement prompted Krum to his protectionist measures. We know from central Asia that the mounted warriors could coexist with a developed commodities economy and exploit it. But it is possible that like Krum, the Avar khagans sought to establish a tight control of international exchanges in their realm.

Through the well-rehearsed prestige economy the Avars' loyalty to their khaganate could be maintained past the period of triumphs. If it had been a question only of winning gold, prisoners, or spoils, Avar warriors could have acted on their own initiative, as common raiders, *scamarae*, or by a career in the imperial army. Yet a barbarian empire was not just a union of people with a common material purpose. The warrior participated in a higher entity. Neither was the sense of belonging that bound him to it a purely psychological phenomenon. The "economy of violence" and the warriors' world view, prestige and its forms of expression, gifts and their symbolic meaning, the legitimation of rulership and its political exercise—all these show the close intertwining of the symbolic and material foundations of the steppe empires.

6.9 Religion and Ritual

Around the middle of the twentieth century, myths and rites of the steppe people, their shamanistic practices, cosmology, gods, and beliefs, were considered a fascinating subject. Scholars treated it in highly knowledgeable and imaginative ways, often framed by wide-reaching intercultural comparison.[458] These were generations of scholars who had been intellectually formed in the irrationalist and often right-wing cultural climate of the first half of the twentieth century. They filled the spaces left obscure by our patchy evidence on early medieval steppe religion/s with sources from other periods (for instance, Herodotus's lively accounts of Scythian religious practices) or with material from modern ethnography. In their writings, one can still feel the excitement of the search for parallels and analogies across time and space. However, this approach presumes a basically immutable steppe culture, in which encounters with the supernatural follow the same models across the ages. That is a paradigm that has now, more or less tacitly, been abandoned. Perhaps steppe cultures are not quite as malleable, hybrid, and dynamic as a postmodern drift of ideas would have it. Yet, methodological caution is necessary. We cannot reconstruct Avar religion on the basis of Herodotus, Ibn Fadlan, or the *Secret History of the Mongols*. Perhaps it is possible to hypothesize similarities to contemporary ancient Turkic or Khazar beliefs and practices, especially if there is comparable archaeological evidence. Still, differences between the Avars and both successive neighboring empires are obvious enough. Due to such difficulties, indigenous medieval religion among the steppe peoples has not been among the hot topics in recent research.[459] Most contributions dealt with their conversions to one of the confessions current among the sedentary peoples: Buddhism, Judaism, Manichaeism, Islam, or Christianity.[460] Therefore, the comparative material sketched below is not intended to shed additional light on what the Avars believed, but just to provide a wider context of options that they had.

Not surprisingly, the religious practices of the steppe peoples seemed alien to the Christian Byzantines. Ambassador Zemarchus had an extraordinary experience when he entered the land of the Turks, recounted by Menander.

> Certain others of their own tribe appeared, who, they said, were exorcisers of ill-omened things, and they came up to Zemarchus and his companions. They took all the baggage that they were carrying and placed it on the ground. Then they set fire to branches of the frankincense tree, chanted some barbarous words in their Scythian tongue, making noise with bells and drums, waved about the baggage the frankincense boughs as they were crackling with the flames, and, falling into a frenzy and acting like madmen, supposed that they were driving away evil spirits. For in this way some men were thought to be averters of and guardians against evil. When they had chased away the evil beings, as they supposed, and had led Zemarchus himself through the fire, they thought that by this means they had purified themselves also.[461]

One need know only a little about shamanism to recognize some typical elements in the description: possession, purification, incantation formulas, exorcism, liminal rituals, fire rites.[462] Whether this passage can be interpreted as a sign of a consistent and specific role of shamans among the Turks is, however, unclear.[463] Theophylact, in his digression about the origin of the Avars, also mentions that "the Turks honor fire to a quite extraordinary degree."[464] Magic was certainly part of the image of the steppe peoples in general. In the year 566 the Avar victory over the Franks was attributed to such practices: "Adept in the magical arts, they displayed various illusions to them."[465] The *Suda Lexicon* informs that the Avars had once tricked Roman scouts with the creation of artificial downpours and darkness, and could thus approach undetected.[466] A similar story is reported about the Rouran in a Chinese source, who "are able to make sacrifices to heaven and cause wind and snow to occur. . . . So when they are defeated in battle no one can catch up with them."[467]

We owe our knowledge about an Avar high priest and his title to an affair he had with one of the khagan's wives, and his consequent flight. This Bookolabras and his crime were important enough to Baian that in the moment of triumph after the conquest of Sirmium he would have been ready to allow negotiations to founder over his demand to have the fugitive returned to his hands dead or alive.[468] When the khagan later learned that the Romans had received the fugitive with honor, this was seen as a cause for a fresh war. Theophylact translates the title, *bookolabras*, as "magician, priest."[469] A very similar title is known from Bulgar inscriptions: (*boila*) *kolobros*.[470] This corresponds to the Old Turkic *qolobur* (also *qolaguz* or *qulavuz*, "guide, leader"); *böqü-qulavuz* could be the "high priest."[471] Theophylact's short passage about the religious practices of the Turks is rather unspecific about spiritual leaders: "They have priests who, in their opinion, even expound the prophecy for the future."[472]

The other instance in which Avar religion became a political matter and thus found a place in the histories occurred a few years earlier. Baian had a bridge built in order to prepare for the siege of Sirmium. To lull the Romans into a false security, before the inhabitants of Singidunum,

> he immediately drew his sword and swore the oaths of the Avars, invoking against himself and the whole Avar nation the sanction that, if he planned to build the bridges over the Save out of any design against the Romans, he and the whole Avar tribe should be destroyed by the sword, heaven above and God in his heavens should send fire against them, the mountains and the forests around them fall upon them and the river Save overflow its banks and drown them. Thus were the barbarian oaths sworn by the Khagan. "Now," he said, "I wish to swear the Roman oaths."

He stood up from his throne, pretended to receive the books with great fear and reverence, and threw himself on the ground.[473] Shortly thereafter it became apparent that he had never intended to honor his oaths. Oath-taking by damning oneself was a barbarian custom, as was the absence of a feeling that one was bound by such an oath in dealings with one's enemies.[474] It was a different matter in the case of guests. An Avar khagan's punctilious honoring of his oath was praised, from his later English exile, by the expelled Lombard king Perctarit, who had once found refuge among the Avars.[475] When a Lombard delegation offered gold for his rendition, the khagan felt himself bound toward his protégée Perctarit by the oath that he had made "before an idol." But to preclude diplomatic complications he suggested the fugitive continue his flight.

The oath on the sword that Baian pronounced was also customary among the Bulgars, although they did not brandish it but put it in the middle to swear upon it.[476] It was said of the Bulgars that during peace negotiations oaths were taken according to the customs of both parties. For instance, the emperor Leo V in 815–16 had to pour water onto the earth, reverse horses' saddles, and slaughter dogs. The drastic self-damning according to pagan rites promptly led to a state crisis in Byzantium.[477] Similar problems faced the Salzburg archbishop Theotmar in about 900. In a letter to the pope he defends himself against accusations that he had sealed a treaty with the Hungarians through oaths on "the dog, the wolf, and other extremely sacrilegious and heathen things (*ethnicas res*)."[478] Perhaps this was the rite of cutting a dog in two at oath-taking, attested for Hungarians, Mongols, and, specifically, Cumans; it implicitly meant wishing the dog's fate on the one who violated the oath.[479] A treaty between the Chinese and the Tibetans in 737 was sealed by the sacrifice of a white dog.[480] That the heavens might crash to the earth, as Baian swore, recalls a Turkish creation myth that Radloff recounted.[481] According to the myth, the first human being, Erlik, wanted to construct a heaven on the model of the highest god. The latter, however, destroyed it and the ruins fell to earth, and "where it had been smooth and level, it was ruined"; mountains, gorges, and forests arose.

The information that the khagan swore by the god in heaven is valuable. Among most of the pagan steppe peoples the sky god Tängri was accounted the highest being.[482] Theophylact writes that the Turks "only worship and call god him who made the heaven and earth. To him they sacrifice horses, cattle and sheep."[483] The Orkhon inscriptions establish that the khagan was sent or invested by Tängri, that he had to execute Tängri's will, and that he could maintain his mandate as long as the cosmic order was preserved.[484] They also show that this heavenly mandate could be conceptualized in various ways. Tonyukuk, the senior adviser of Ilteriş Khagan, speaks of a rather indirect influence of the god of heaven: "Tängri gave me intelligence, and I raised the khagan."[485] The inscription of Bilge Khagan recounts his own ascension to the throne: "I, Tängri-like and Tängri-born as Turkic Kagan, mounted the throne."[486] The same process (and the same title) were framed differently in the inscription of Bilge's younger brother and adviser Kültegin: "Then Turkish Tängri (heaven) above, Turkish Yer (earth) and Sub (water) spoke as follows: 'In order that the Turkish people (*bodun*) would not be ruined and in order that it should be a people again, they raised my father Ilteriş Kagan and my mother Ilbilga Katun up and sat them upon the throne.'"[487] Here, reference is made to all three Turkish elemental gods.[488] Theophylact also notes that the Turks "revere air and water, and they praise the earth."[489] Similar lists occur again and again in the steppe and elsewhere. The *Vita* of Pancratius of Taormina, written in the ninth century, claims that the Avars venerated swords, as well as images of animals, fire, and water. Yet the information, unless it is a mere topos, is actually in reference to Slavs in Greece, at Athens and Dyrrhachium.[490]

The way in which the Turks derived the authority of their khagans from a god in heaven created an interesting tension with the Chinese "Son of Heaven"; it is not unlikely that as an exceptionally strong statement of heavenly rulership it was influenced by Chinese notions.[491] When the Bulgar khans attribute themselves the title *ek theou archōn* in their inscriptions, this is perhaps not merely an imitation of the Greek title of *basileus* (*ek theou basileus*) but a convergence of Christian and pagan legitimations of rulership.[492] In the inscription of the Bulgar khan Omurtag at Madara from the 820s, he mentions that he "made sacrifice to god Tangra."[493] Unfortunately, we have no direct trace of Avar rulership ideology. However, as between the Turks and China, it is clear that the language of divinely sanctioned rulership was mutually comprehensible between Byzantium and the Avars. It must have appeared familiar to the Christians when the Avar khagan repeatedly called on god to arbitrate between him and the emperor. On one occasion, "the barbarian said this, word for word: May God judge between the khagan and between Maurice the emperor. May the recompense that is from God at some time demand an account."[494] Does the rare insistence that this was a word-for-word quote reckon with the reader's incredulity that an Avar would have used such familiar Christian phrases? God as the defender of the truth is also mentioned in a Bulgar inscription.[495]

István Bóna has suggested that an image scratched on a bone jar from Mokrin may be a trace of the world view of Tängrism in an Avar context.[496] A tree with nine branches that grows from a column on a double hill reaches up to the sun and moon, and below it cattle graze. A later Turkish creation myth tells of a heavenly tree that grows from the navel of the world through seventeen heavenly spheres.[497] Representations of trees are repeatedly found in Avar art. It is, however, more likely that they were influenced by the iconography of the tree of life of late Antiquity.

Archaeology offers rich evidence of the burial customs of the Avars.[498] As Falko Daim has argued, grave finds do not assist in determining personal representations of religious belief, but rather the unifying traditions and customs of the community, with their local variations and spheres of influence. Within this frame, competition for status and right behavior could be channeled. Usually, only the "underground" dimension of burial customs is accessible to us. If the Byzantine envoy Valentinus had to lacerate his cheeks with a dagger along with a Turkish congregation in mourning, such a custom cannot be confirmed through archaeology.[499] However, it is attested in a number of independent sources from central Asia.[500]

The custom of inhumation was common to the European Avars.[501] The Slavs in the neighborhood mostly cremated their dead, and not all steppe peoples of central Asia were inhumed either. According to the information of Chinese sources the Turks of the sixth century cremated their dead, although this has not been fully corroborated by archaeology.[502] The orientation of Avar graves varies between and even within periods.[503] The deceased were frequently placed in coffins, made of planks or hollowed out tree trunks. In individual cases we get "the impression of a lovingly laid-out living space as the final resting place."[504] The custom of meat as grave good was widespread, and the quality and preservation of the cuts of meat vary considerably from one cemetery to another.[505] Some conclusions about burial customs can be reached indirectly. The graves may have carried signs, since apparently later grave robbers easily found what they were looking for.[506]

Horses burials were a common feature in the steppe, and they are also fairly common among the Avars.[507] There could be a whole horse or parts of it in the grave; sometimes a horse was cremated at the grave and the remains buried along with the deceased, traceable in the burn marks on the horse harness.[508] Attested in writing for both the Turks and the Bulgars is the practice of having women or slaves follow a nobleman into the grave. According to Menander, this was done so that in the beyond they could inform the deceased of his appropriate burial.[509] Something similar has not been established so far for the Avars.

The Avars invested heavily in grave goods, and noble burials may contain impressive quantities of gold and silver. However, by comparison to the central Asian steppe, it is also striking what they did not include. Since the time of the Scythians, kurgans, grave mounds with subterranean chambers, had been the predominant burial architecture of a prince of the steppe.[510] Leading representatives of the Xiongnu and of other powerful neighbors of the Chinese Empire were often buried in Chinese-style subterranean burial chambers decorated with colorful paintings.[511] Turkish rulers were honored with extensive memorial complexes such as the ones in the Orkhon Valley, sometimes including stone monuments with long inscriptions relating the deeds of the deceased.[512] One inscription found there attests that this lavish funerary architecture was executed by Chinese artisans: When Kültegin had died in 731, "Čan Seŋün, the nephew of the Chinese Emperor, came in order to build the mausoleum, to make sculptures, to paint and to prepare stone inscriptions."[513] High-status Bulgars were buried in decorated aristocratic graves, and at least from the ninth century, several funerary inscriptions have been preserved.[514] No extensive kurgans, lavish grave architecture, grave chambers with paintings, stone statues, or funerary inscriptions are as yet attested among the Avars. From this point of view, their memorial culture was rather modest. A document from 808 mentions *tumuli*, "grave mounds," by the *loca Avarorum* near Lake Neusiedl, but archaeologists find nothing like the numerous and often extensive kurgans elsewhere in the same period, for instance, in the Caucasus region.[515]

Little can be said of Avar Christianity or Christian Avars. Turkish khagans accepted Buddhism, Khazars converted to Judaism, Uyghurs embraced Manichaeism, the Bulgars and Hungarians opted for various forms of Christianity, and Islam established itself among many Turkic and Mongol peoples.[516] This was, however, a slow process that mostly started in the eighth century or later.

Sometimes only the leaders of a steppe empire converted to a sedentary confession; Ibn Rusta and other Islamic sources insist that only the Khazar elites had become Jewish, which must have happened sometime in the mid-eighth century.[517] While this was a surprisingly idiosyncratic choice, many conversions of steppe rulers were more due to expedience. The diplomatic mission of Ibn Fadlan in 921/22, known through his lively report that has been transmitted, was triggered by the invitation of the ruler of the Volga Bulgars to be instructed in the teachings of Islam; characteristically, he asked for both a mosque and a fortress to be built in his capital, in order to protect him against his enemies.[518] Some more or less contemporary authors regarded such conversions as a sign of decadence, such as an anonymous and undated Zoroastrian text from Iran: "Like the faith of Jesus from Byzantium, and the faith of Moses from the Khazars, and the faith of Mani from the Uigurs took away the strength and vigor that they had previously possessed, threw them into vileness and decadence among their rivals."[519] In other cases, conversion or, rather, syncretism could be a useful tool for the legitimation of a steppe ruler: for instance, in 714 the Turkish khagan Qapaghan devised the flowery title "Supernatural, Harmonious, and Eternally Pure Father of the Imperial Princess; Man of Heaven, Obtainer of Karmic Reward in Heaven; Sage in Heaven, Qutlugh Khagan of the Turks"; this, of course, expressed his direct competition with the equally exuberant rulership ideology of the Chinese empress Wu, including a strong Buddhist flavor.[520] In the later tenth century, the Hungarian king Geza converted to Christianity but kept sacrificing to "various illusory gods"; when the bishop reproached him, he simply stated that he was rich and powerful enough for that.[521] His son, St. Stephen, tried to enforce Christian exclusivity and had to face serious opposition. The same had already happened to the Bulgar khans after they had been converted in the later ninth century.[522] Over time, however, Christianity helped to stabilize the Bulgar and the Hungarian state. The Avar khagans did not reach that stage.

The Avar elite only became Christian under Frankish rule (see section 8.4). When Baian was to swear on the Bible, the signification of the book had first to be explained to him.[523] The fact that they were pagans was underlined by Carolingian propagandists and missionaries before and after the war in the 790s. "This people is, however, stupid, unreasonable, certainly ignorant and illiterate," notes the synod held during the campaign on the Danube in 796.[524] Several missionaries in the course of the seventh and eighth centuries had considered traveling to Slavs and Avars to convert them, but then decided not even to risk trying. The first was St. Columbanus in about 610. An angel appeared to him, "and showed him in a little circle the outline of the earth, just as the circle of the world is usually drawn with a pen in a book: 'You see,' the angel said, 'that the entire circle remains empty. Go to the right or the left where you will that you may enjoy the fruits of your labors.' Columbanus then realized that progress in faith for this people was not ready to hand."[525] His pupil Amandus later actually crossed the Danube and preached to the Slavs, and hoped to reach at least the palm of martyrdom; but having achieved neither that nor any success, he returned.[526] Around 700, St. Emmeram quickly abandoned his plans to cross the Enns on his missionary journeys to the Avars once he had been warned by the Bavarian authorities, and neither did St. Rupert proceed beyond Lauriacum/Lorch.[527]

Like most other steppe empires the Avars did accept religious difference among their subject peoples, as becomes obvious in the "Keszthely culture" (see section 3.9). Members of such Christian communities had for the most part already been Christians before they came under Avar rule in one way or another. The most obvious trace of such communities is the basilica in the fortress of Fenékpuszta.[528] In the heyday of the Christians on the shores of Lake Balaton around 600, they were well connected with the Mediterranean Christian world. The so-called disc-fibulae with Christian motifs that were found in the graves of Keszthely-Fenékpuszta were common pilgrim mementos from Palestine.[529] Even though these connections faded out in the course of the seventh century, many residents of the region were still buried with folded hands and without grave goods until the eighth century.[530] Traces of a Christian population are not only found around Keszthely but also in other localities right to the end of the Avar period, for example, in Savaria/Szombathely or in the vicinity of Sopianae/Pécs.[531] The question of Christianity in the Avar period is linked, but not identical, with that of the survival of provincial populations in the Roman tradition.[532]

Beyond such recognizable Christian communities, there were networks that distributed "artifacts with explicit Christian symbolism"—disc-fibulae, ampullae, lamps—in the Avar sphere of power. However, Christian symbols in Avar-period graves cannot be taken as proof of Christianity; they may also have been cherished as exotic or magical objects.[533] Even the frequent crucifixes or cruciform decorations that were unearthed in Zamárdi do not prove that the bearers saw themselves as Christians, no more than do the liturgical objects or inscriptions in the treasures of Malaja Pereščepina or Nagyszentmiklós, even if they may illustrate the readiness of the barbarians to adopt Christian symbols.[534] To the degree that the owners were aware at all of the meaning of this symbolism, it could be incorporated in their world view without difficulty. There was no canonical paganism that would have excluded the assumption of diverse Christian attributes. Provided no organized church existed on the other side that fought against pagan forms of expression (for which the pope's exacting responses to the Bulgars are illustrative),[535] at best a syncretism with Christian features could emerge.

An impact of this "insular Christianity" on the Avar elite can hardly be assumed. Its cultural effects were probably greatest in the first decades, when certain supraregional connections were still in place. In the following centuries Christian communities maintained themselves, but their practices came to deviate from orthodoxy. Baptism was administered with water, but the necessary accompanying Latin formulae were forgotten. Thus, the synod of 796 had to debate whether baptisms performed *ab clericis illiteratis*, by illiterate clerics, were valid and came to the conclusion that at least an appeal to the Holy Spirit was indispensable: water was not enough (*sola aqua nihil valet*).[536] The protocol from the synod, however, states emphatically that baptisms *a sacerdotibus terrae istius*, by the priests of this country, of whatever denomination, were basically valid as long as they were performed in the name of the Trinity.

The Avar mission was initiated after the Frankish conquest with great ambition, yet results were meager. This was not only because of the disinclination of Archbishop Arn to spend time in the "wild east." Avar notables had to allow themselves to be baptized, change their names to Abraham or Theodore, and attempt to hold the rest of the khaganate together with Frankish tolerance. Yet the new religion brought them no luck. Pagan Slavs vitiated the results of missionary policy. Perhaps the loss of their sacral political traditions contributed to the swift disappearance of the Avars from history. It was only around the middle of the ninth century that the Franks succeeded in creating a more or less functional ecclesiastical center for Pannonia in Mosapurc/Zalavár—not by coincidence, that was very close to Keszthely.

6.10 The Development of Identities in the Avar Empire

Who Were the Avars?

In the German version of this book that came out in 1988, this chapter was entitled "Avar Ethnogenesis" and offered a rather extensive summary of my approach to the study of ethnic identities in the Avar sphere of power.[537] I maintained that "who was an Avar and who was not can no longer be taken for granted." Ethnic affiliation depended on a dynamic process, and was certainly not determined by common blood. I argued that different criteria commonly used to define ethnic groups, such as common origin, language, territory, culture, habitus, sense of belonging, or political institutions, did not allow the delineation of coherent ethnic groups on the basis of our evidence. Speakers of the same language, people inhabiting a common territory, those distinguishable by a similar cultural habitus or subject to the same polity did not coincide in early medieval Europe. None of these criteria allows a clear prediction that those who met them understood themselves, for instance, as Avars. Ethnic boundaries were permeable, but that did not mean that they did not matter—I should have cited Fredrik Barth in this context.[538] A point that I made that I still find fundamental is that in Avar-period eastern central Europe, ethnic distinctions tended to correlate with social status and function, so the Avars were essentially the ruling elite of high-status mounted warriors with their (extended) families. Less prestigious, but still privileged groups of horsemen who were prepared to live under foreign rule tended to be called Bulgars; and Slavs were a peasant population of lower status with specific military skills (for instance, in amphibious warfare).

Some of these arguments need not be repeated here; that ethnicity is not determined by blood or race, or that archaeological evidence can rarely be used as direct proof for the ethnic identity of the deceased have become mainstream positions. I have therefore cut or omitted some lengthy arguments in such matters and sparingly inserted more recent perspectives on ethnicity. I have kept the references to the relatively meager sources about identities in the Avar realm to make it clear how far the evidence can take us. The Avars are not an easy example to demonstrate early medieval constructions of identity. As far as steppe peoples go, the Turkish inscriptions provide far better material to trace identity formation; for the Avars, we have to rely on outside perceptions alone, and on the clues for negotiations of identity that they give.[539]

Something that I did not feel I had to explain in 1988 is why I used the concept of ethnicity at all. Its usefulness has meanwhile been doubted. For instance, in a posthumously published paper, Timothy Reuter argued: "We don't know when or how Avar identity ceased to be meaningful to Avars, though it clearly must have done at some point, since there aren't any now. It's far from clear that Avars thought they were Avars when they still were Avars, if you see what I mean."[540] This is a valid observation. It points to a methodological problem raised by the subjective definition of ethnicity proposed by Reinhard Wenskus, which I still used in *Die Awaren*.[541] I have meanwhile proposed ways out of the problem. One is a model of identity formation and maintenance in a circuit of identifications. I conceive of social identities as the dynamic result of a process of communication and interaction in which individuals identify with a group (which accepts their allegiance or not); the group expresses its identity in joint action, collective rituals, or through its representatives; and outsiders acknowledge the existence of the group on the basis of their perceptions and interactions.[542] Consistent outside identification can increase the plausibility that it reacted to perceptible acts of self-identification and joint action. A further way is to distinguish between "ethnic identity," which requires some level of self-identification, and ethnicity. In this minimal sense, I would define ethnicity as a principle of distinction between social groups by ethnonyms and by the employment of ethnic terminology (*gens, genus, ethnos*, etc.).[543] This allows grasping the overwhelming use of ethnic language in the historiography of the period to describe collective agency. We can let the "Avar khaganate" or "the Merovingians" act in our historical narratives. Early medieval authors did not. It was either "the khagan" or "the Avars" who had agency. A less distinctive terminology, in particular "the barbarians," was only used for stylistic variation or if the precise ethnonym was unclear. In particular cases, this may not always be proof that these "Avars thought they were Avars," as Reuter argued. However, it represents the mental map according to which collective action was perceived and social spaces were delineated. On the whole, it is very likely that self-identifications more or less followed this model.

Not all collective identifications are ethnic, of course; they can also express allegiance to a city, to a territory, to a polity, or to a religion. These distinctive features exist outside the group and its members. Group allegiances can then be changed by migration or conversion. The point of reference of ethnicity, on the other hand, is thought to lie in the people themselves, in their common origin or inner predisposition. In many languages, this attitude is expressed in an ethnic terminology built on metaphors of procreation, such as *gens*, *genus*, and *natio* in Latin. However, most identities are mixed, and in different ways combine notions of common origin, shared territory, political unity, and veneration of the same god/s. Therefore, it makes little sense to debate whether an identity was ethnic, territorial, *or* political. It is more productive to study which modes of identification matter more or less in which communicative acts or perceptions. Uncertain terminology, contradictions, misunderstandings, and disagreements can often be interpreted as traces of unstable or shifting identities.

In the case of the early Avars, some fluctuation in the name is obvious. First, the Romans often called them Huns or Scythians according to the usual scheme of ethnographic classification. Similar things happened with many peoples, and that does not necessarily point to controversial identifications: the Hellenes have been called Greeks by many of their neighbors for over 2,500 years, but the terms remained easily translatable. What does point to a lack of consensus about the correct identification of the Avars as an ethnic group, however, is that the Turks and to an extent the Byzantines refused to call them Avars. Rather, they were identified as Varchonites or, as Theophylact insists, as Pseudo-Avars. "In point of fact even up to our present times the Pseudo-Avars (for it is more correct to refer to them thus) are divided in their ancestry, some bearing the time-honoured name of Var while others are called Chunni."[544] According to Theophylact, part of the Ogurs called themselves *Var* and another *Chunni*, and together they formed the Varchonites (see sec 2.4). The three groups of Tarniakh, Kotzagir, and Zabender who reinforced the Avars after 580 were also regarded as Varchonites by Theophylact.[545] This is a rather complicated account of an ethnic process: two smaller parts of a larger group (the Ogurs) merge, and split again as some of these Varchonites move westward, later followed by other Varchonite groups. At least, this demonstrates that a Byzantine historian was aware how complicated ethnic processes in the steppe could be. However, much of his story relies on information that came from the Turks. Thus, this narrative of Avar origins hardly goes back to the author's confusion, but rather to debates about political legitimacy in the power centers of the steppe. The very insistence with which Turkish envoys and Byzantine authors maintained that the European Avars were not the real Avars attests that this is in fact what the Avars claimed: to be *the* Avars. This was of high political relevance, because it implied that as direct successor of the Rouran khaganate the Avar ruler was the rightful khagan, and therefore at least on a par with the Turkish khagans. It was an ethnic argument about political legitimacy.

We have no idea whether any European Avars would have regarded themselves as Varchonites and subscribed to Theophylact's bipartite ethnic origin story for them: according to that, both groups, Var and Chunni, traced their names back to mythical rulers with these names—which is a frequent ethnographic topos.[546] Could the Avar core group have consisted of two clans who derived their names from a pair of mythical ancestors? Such bipartite mythologies or divisions were not uncommon among the steppe peoples. A parallel case is the Hungarian origin legend of the two brothers Hunor and Magor as ancestors of the Magyars.[547] Again, one bears the name of the Huns, the other of the Magyars. Wilhelm Radloff was able to observe a bipartite structure among the Kara-Kirghiz in the nineteenth century. The Mongols were at times ruled by two rival clans, and the Xiongnu were also divided into two wings, while the ruler occupied the center ground.[548] Among the Mongols the two wings of the army were named *barangar* and *juangar*—two terms somehow assonant with Var and Chunni.[549] However, in the case of the Avars, no such division becomes visible in the sources, although the Byzantines observed Avar strategy closely and were only too ready to exploit the internal rivalries of their opponents.

In the late sixth century, the name Varchonites disappears from the sources, and from then on the Avars are simply called Avars. Unfortunately, we have no clue whether the glorious past of the Rouran/Avars in central Asia was actively remembered or actually used for political legitimation in Europe. We would expect some such set of foundational memories, because a sense of belonging is usually derived from a shared past and (often invented) common origins. A strong statement of this is found in Rashid ad-Din's account of the Mongols: "Since they have neither religion nor faith, in which they might raise their children as others do, the father and mother explain to each new child their origin and describe the clan to it."[550] Interestingly, the role of the mother in passing on narratives of identity is highlighted here, unlike in the passage from the *Miracula S. Demetrii* cited below.

What exactly is the implication when Avars are mentioned in the sources? The use of the name is relatively fuzzy, or sometimes situational. In the early period, the implication is that these are the ones who have arrived from Asia. The Romans repeatedly reminded the Avars that they were a "splintered segment [that] had broken away from its ancestral tribe in the east."[551] In outside perceptions, the name may distinguish a group characterized by an unusual hairstyle (braids) and by its costume and arms; this becomes visible in the *Strategicon*, where certain "Avar" items are appropriated into the equipment of the Byzantine army, for instance Avar tunics, cavalry lances, and elements of armor or tents.[552] In political terms it references representatives of the Avar Empire, which can mean members of the army, court circles, or envoys. In the narrow sense, the "Avars" represented only a minority in their own army until 626. The numbers for the prisoners that Priscus took in the battle on the Tisza in 599 at least point in this direction: three thousand Avars, a roughly equal contingent of other barbarians, and eight thousand Slavs.[553] These were, however, the khagan's defensive forces; moreover, foot soldiers were more easily taken prisoner than Avar horsemen, who probably were also better motivated to fight. One wonders how the Byzantines arrived at these numbers: Did they ask, or rely on appearances? In negotiations with the khagan, such numbers could surely matter.

Hardly any encounters with lower-status Avars are recorded in the texts. Low-status groups in the Avar Empire are represented as Gepid villagers, Roman captives, or Slavic boatmen. In the full sense, then, ideal-type Avars were those who fought for the Avar Empire on horseback and participated in its public life, subscribed to the traditional ways of life, and expressed this affiliation in their clothing and customs. Initially this must have been quite a limited group of people. Eventually, the success of the khaganate must have made the name, the habitus, and the lifestyle of the leading clans very attractive.[554] This trickle-down effect led to the creation of a relatively homogeneous late Avar culture, as we can see in the archaeological record (see section 8.1). Presumably, this process also spread the Avar name, although we cannot directly conclude that from the archaeological evidence.

Steppe empires were deliberately polyethnic and used ethnic/status differences for their internal organization. As already mentioned (section 6.3), the *Strategicon* claims that the Avars "are composed of so many clans (*phylai*) . . . [that] they have no sense of kinship (*syngenē*) or unity with one another."[555] The khaganate apparently did maintain some sense of unity until long after the *Strategicon* was written, but it was hardly based on the ethnic allegiance of its subjects. Like Attila, the Avar khagans tolerated or even encouraged the existence of ethnically circumscribed warrior groups within their sphere of power. We have attestations of independent operations undertaken by a ten-thousand-man troop of Cutrigurs and by a thousand-man contingent of Bulgars.[556] Their standing was lower than that of the core of the Avar army, as shown by the khagan's derogatory words about the Cutrigurs, who would be "no loss" if they were defeated. "The peoples that follow me in alliance," this is how Baian called his army in 567, to which he owed his victory.[557] At the end of the Avar Empire in 796, Charlemagne's councilor Alcuin wrote in a letter to the emperor of the *gentes populique Hunorum*, who had now been overcome.[558] Likewise, the Byzantine ambassador Zemarchus assured the Turkish khagan of the emperor's friendship for "those belonging to the Turks and for the tribes subject to the Turks."[559] The treatment of subdued peoples in the steppe was carefully nuanced. Depending on circumstances, they could be killed, enslaved, put to flight, or integrated on different levels of status; this could lead to mixed marriages and shifts in identity.[560] Coerced integration figures prominently in Old Turkic inscriptions and in Mongolian epics. After a victory the Mongols killed "the best men, those who could speak" of the enemy, and the "ill-minded." The "well-minded," the "good people," became "our own people," were taken "into the homeland," where "the subjects of the two khagans were brought and bound together."[561] The Orkhon inscriptions repeatedly speak of similar processes. The enemy khagan and his higher functionaries are killed; "the begs and the people" join the victors and are "gathered and organized."[562] "Those who gave up joined me, became my people (*budun*)," says the Bilge Khagan inscription about a defeated people.[563] On the other hand, the secession of a small group, gathered for example around a prince excluded from succession, could quickly lead to the formation of a new people.[564] Ethnic processes of this kind probably transformed the structure of the Avar Empire over the course of time. On the other hand, this was no linear process in which a heterogeneous population could be transformed into Avars. According to political conditions it might either lead to Avarization or to the formation of new regional entities.

The most elaborate account of ethnic processes within the Avar Empire is the story about Kuver in the *Miracula S. Demetrii*.[565] The intention of the story is demonstrating the miraculous power of St. Demetrius, but the contemporary author had good access to firsthand information by those of Kuver's followers who had found refuge in Thessalonica, and used a lot of circumstantial details to enhance the credibility of his account. A long time ago, he begins, many inhabitants of the Balkan provinces had been dragged off to Pannonia.

> Thereafter they mixed with Bulgars, Avars and other heathen peoples (*ethnikoi*), had children with one another, and became a populous nation (*laos*). Each son, however, assumed from his father the traditions

and attitudes of his kin (*genos*) toward the customs of the Romans. . . .
Sixty years and more after the barbarians had subjected their forefathers, a new and different people (*laos*) had developed. With time, however, most of them became freemen. The khagan of the Avars, who now
considered them as a people (*ethnos*) of their own, according to the
constitution of his people (*kathōs to genei ethos*) appointed a leader
(*archōn*) over them by the name of Kuver.[566]

What makes the story plausible is a rare perception of the dynamic character of
ethnic identity, and of the role of social memory in its preservation. According
to this account, there were Avars, Bulgars, and other *ethnikoi* in the Carpathian Basin. The descendants of Roman prisoners merged with them and thereby
became a *laos* (this term underlines their great number and can designate both
a people and a military host). The khagan considered the new "people" to be an
ethnos of its own and sanctioned the fact with the grant of a certain political
autonomy in that he appointed an *archōn* according to the *ethos* or customary
principles of his people (*genos*).

Early medieval writers often employed various terms almost as synonyms
according to stylistic criteria; but ethnic terms could also be used for distinction
to a certain degree. In its New Testament usage, *ethnikoi* designated paganism
and also referenced origin. The Avars and Bulgars, who were integrated into
Kuver's *ethnos*, continue to be described as *ethnikoi*, which also points to their
paganism.[567] *Laos* refers to a new people that has emerged by the choice of its
members.[568] *Ethnos* is used for a distinctive ethnic unit with some political
organization, recognized by the khagan or another superior power.[569] In this
sense, an earlier chapter described the Slavic *ethnē* around Thessalonica, who
were incorporated under their own kings in the Byzantine state organization.[570]
Elsewhere, the Avars, but also the Bulgars under Avar rule,[571] can be described
as *ethnē*. The anonymous author of the *Miracula* thus distinguishes between the
ethnikoi of the Avars and Bulgars as (pagan) ethnic groups, from which a *laos*
(which has connotations of great number) or an *ethnos* (which emphasizes the
element of political organization) could emerge. In this new entity the *ethnikoi*
initially remained distinguishable. In the course of the account, however, a new
ethnonym establishes itself: *Sermesianoi*, the people from (the area of) Sirmium.
Not untypically, this is a territorial (and paradoxically, civic) name—this was the
(very recent) common origin of the migrant group, and the place-name thus
acquired an ethnic meaning.

How could different peoples within and beyond the Avar realm be distinguished?[572] Early medieval observers mostly judged according to clothing,
customs, and ways of fighting. Maurice's *Strategicon* categorizes according to

equipment and tactics, lifestyle, and internal organization. This, however, only makes it possible to distinguish broadly between Persians, "Scythians" (Avars, Turks, and other Hunnic peoples), "blonde peoples, such as Franks, Lombards and the other peoples with the same lifestyle," and "Slavs."[573] Ancient ethnographic knowledge and recent observations are carefully blended in the respective chapters. One valuable piece of information about the Avars is that on a military expedition, they remain separated "according to kin and tribes," *kata genē kai phylas*.[574] The *Strategicon* has little to say about outward appearance, which features more prominently in other sources. Initially the Avars could be recognized by their hairstyle: "They wore their hair very long at the back, tied with ribbons and plaited," according to Theophanes.[575] The picture may have become more blurred as both the Roman army and the Bulgars imitated the weapons and clothing of the Avar warriors, and vice versa. Avar habitus would have appealed to others for the respect it inspired, although they did not necessarily regard themselves as Avars. This "ethnic mimicry" may in some cases have furthered an actual upward social mobility and assimilation; in other cases it was a mere pseudo-morphosis.[576] For outside observers, the difference between adequate perceptions, identification of partly assimilated groups, cultural prejudice, and simple mistakes may have been rather fluid.[577] We have the same problem in the interpretation of archaeological evidence. Here, at best, ethnic identifications may have some statistical probability. There are no object types or find circumstances that unambiguously attest to a precise ethnic identity.[578]

In this sense our question is not so much who was an Avar or Slav as who became Avar or Slav through specific practice and was then recognized as such. This might presuppose a certain lifestyle and adaptation to surroundings, social status, and styles of interaction and identification. Socio-ethnic divisions surely played a role between Avars and Slavs, and also explain the striking disappearance of the Avars once their military and political role had played itself out (see section 8.5). The Avars were a political ethnos. Unlike most other early medieval peoples, Avars are rarely attested as such outside the khaganate and its sphere of power. In particular, the comparison with the Huns is telling. Starting with the Xiongnu, Hunnic peoples spread all over central Eurasia in the fourth and fifth centuries. Whether directly related or not, they could be recognized by the same ethnonym, which gradually turned into a generic term. Hunnic rulers adopted the most varied titles, such as *chanyu, shah, rex, devaraja,* or *huangdi*; they used Chinese, Sogdian, Bactrian, Middle Persian, Brahmi, or Latin, perhaps also Gothic for their self-representation; and Huns served in Chinese, Sasanian, or Roman armies.[579] The Avars also used an awe-inspiring name, but its use was more contested and ambivalent, so that the Chinese knew them as Rouran, and Turks and Byzantines believed that those in Europe were only Pseudo-Avars. Once upon a time, the Rouran themselves had been despised as "mixed barbarians from outside the barrier," fugitive slaves from the Xianbei, by the Chinese.[580] Later, the Turks despised the Avars as their fugitive slaves, a mixed horde of "Pseudo-Avars," a judgment that Menander and Theophylact gladly reported.[581] What defined both the Rouran and the European Avar realms was the title khagan. This, however, does not mean that Avar identity was not ethnic but only political. Agency is attributed as much to the Avars as to their khagans in our sources. Avar imperial ethnicity constituted a particular blend of ethnic and political identification in which only sovereign rule could guarantee the survival of the *gens*.

Avar Language/s

Many scholars who worked on the Eurasian steppe in the nineteenth and twentieth centuries realized that steppe peoples came and went, their composition changed, and their fates depended much on shifting political constellations. In an age that regarded nations and their interaction as the fundamental constituents of history, this did not seem to provide a sufficient basis for a valid historical metanarrative. Linguistic groups appeared to offer an alternative, and to allow constructing larger and more time-resistant ethnic units. In this perspective, the history of central Eurasia had been shaped by Iranians (or "Aryans"), Turks, Mongols, and perhaps a few others. The challenge was to subsume the ethnic groups attested in the sources under these categories. It was relatively easy to argue that Iranians—Scythians, Sarmatians, and Alans—had dominated the European steppes in Antiquity, that Turks (Bulgars, Khazars) had taken over in the seventh century, before Mongols replaced them in the thirteenth. However, many peoples attested in the sources were not so easily subsumed. Huns and Avars posed a particular problem, because the limited number of transmitted names did not allow a clear linguistic categorization. There were several very erudite hypotheses on the language the Avars spoke. Pelliot, and after him Menges, tried to establish that the Avars spoke Mongolic, a view that was shared by many researchers. It is mostly based on the identification of the Rouran with the European Avars.[582] The problem here is that the first substantial evidence for the Mongolian language dates from the fourteenth century.[583] Other scholars take the Avars to be a Turkic-speaking people.[584] In more recent discussions, differentiated positions are beginning to be staked out. More room is given to multilingualism or language replacement.[585] One could, of course, also follow the hypothesis Doerfer had put forward on the language of the Huns: it could have been an unknown language that has long since died out.[586]

The attempts to class the Avar language as Turkic, Mongolic, or something completely different still continue, against all odds. From a historical point of view, we should clearly distinguish between the "pseudo-peoples" of linguistics, that is the number of native speakers of a philologically reconstructed language or language family, and peoples in the historical sense.[587] Speakers of related dialects or languages did not necessarily feel particularly related, especially when dialectal differences sufficed to create a sense of foreignness. The early Middle Ages provide a number of good examples for a change of native language that did not imply a change of identity: Bulgars did not feel less Bulgar when they started speaking a Slavic language, just as no contemporary author took notice that Franks and Lombards had switched to the Romance language of their subjects.[588] Therefore, no linguistic argument can tell us who the Avars really were, however much we would like to know which language or languages they spoke.

The traces of Avar language that we have are disappointingly brief and interestingly hybrid.[589] The very names "Avar" and "Varchonite" (Var and Chunni) clearly cross linguistic boundaries. The evidence falls in three categories: early Avar personal names, late Avar titles, and a few short runic inscriptions. About a dozen Avar names are transmitted in Greek sources and seem to come from different languages.[590] *Baian* has been linked with Mongolic or Chuwash-Turkic and also occurs among the Bulgars (Kuvrat's oldest son). *Targitius* is already attested among the Scythians (Targitaos) and resembles a common name in contemporary central Asia, Targüt.[591] The envoy *Kunimon* has a Gepidic name, like the contemporary king of the Gepids.[592] *Kandikh* corresponds to the Alanic name Candac.[593] *Apsikh* is also the name of a Hun in the Byzantine army around 580.[594] *Kokh* is best explained as Turkic (*kök*, blue),[595] as is the name of the Bulgar refugee *Alciocus* (six arrows, see section 7.6). *Bookolabras*, the name/title of the fugitive Avar high priest, corresponds to a Turkic title used by the Bulgars; it probably corresponds to *böqü-qolavuz* (high priest) or similar in Turkic languages.[596] *Solakhos*, *Samur*, and *Hermitzis* can be variously interpreted.[597]

Even though the etymologies could surely be tweaked to provide a somehow more consistent picture, the evidence does not seem to lend itself easily to a clear linguistic classification. Furthermore, a difference should be made between the symbolic language used for names, titles, or perhaps also cultic purposes, which may include antiquated or foreign names and words, and the language(s) of communication. Names easily crossed linguistic frontiers. For example, Genghis Khan was called Temujin after a Tatar prince whom his father had conquered at the time of his birth.[598] All the more were titles often prized for their foreignness. The title *khagan* is mostly understood as Mongolic, sometimes also as Persian in origin.[599] It soon spread to the Turks and the Khazars, and even the Tang emperor Taizong was acclaimed as "Heavenly Khagan" after subduing the eastern Turkish khaganate in 630.[600] The late Avar titles such as *tudun*, *kapkhan*, or *iugurrus* mostly reflect Bulgar and Khazar usage. Their linguistic origin is not consistent; their diffusion is probably due to the Turkic khaganate.[601]

The third type of evidence are short runic inscriptions. The most conspicuous of these inscriptions are the fourteen short texts on the gold vessel from Nagyszentmiklós.[602] Furthermore, there are about a dozen bone objects from Avar graves with short inscriptions in runic characters. The longest of these, on the needle case of an elderly lady of the eighth century, was discovered in Szarvas in the 1980s and consists of fifty-eight characters.[603] Some runic signs are also found on metal belt plaques.[604] They correspond to a great extent to the set of letters in the runic inscription of the Nagyszentmiklós treasure. However, as we do not know in which language these runic inscriptions were written, any attempt to decipher them remains hypothetical. András Róna-Tas has proposed a Turkic reading, while István Vásáry assumes a Mongolic text. Other eastern European runic inscriptions hardly offer better clues.[605] There is not even a consensus on the exact reading of the inscription in Greek characters found on vessel 21, apart from the fact that it is probably Turkish and mentions the Bulgar rank *boila* and the Slavic title of possible steppe origin, *župan*. The conclusion by Róna-Tas that "the inscription is an unmistakable imprint of the presence of a Slavicized Turkic ruling class" seems quite arduous on the basis of a single inscription, although it seems to indicate that at the courts of the Avar aristocracy, someone understood Turkish and could read the Greek alphabet.[606] A knowledge of Slavic can hardly be deduced from the use of the title *zoapan*. Runes were more diffused, although it would appear that Avar runic literacy was a rather marginal phenomenon, confined to a sphere of ritual and representation. It could reflect outdated linguistic conditions and thus would permit few conclusions about everyday language use. Perhaps the anonymous eighth-century author of *Aethicus Ister*, who presents himself as an Istrian "Scythian," had been inspired by similar runic signs to develop his fantasy alphabet. He also featured the Turks rather prominently, although in an unpleasant way.[607]

Only one source names languages that were spoken or understood in the Avar Empire. One of Kuver's commanders, who had the Greek (or grecized) name Mavros ("the dark"), spoke, as the *Miracula S. Demetrii* report, "our language, as well as those of the Romans, the Slavs and the Bulgars." Lemerle has translated *glōssa tēn Rōmaiōn* as "language of the Greeks," and "Romans" always are the Byzantines; but that leaves the question of what "our language" means. Perhaps the "language of the Romans" was here understood as Latin.[608] As Johannes Koder has shown, the Greek expression *romaistē* "always refers to the Latin language," and that may help to explain an exceptional use of "Romans" here.[609] No language of the Avars is mentioned here, although Mavros had lived in Avar Pannonia as a member of the elite. In any case, the information in the *Miracula* points to multilingualism in the sphere of Kuver's mixed following but probably also in the whole Avar Empire. This corresponds to information in

Priscus about polyglossia at Attila's court, where at a banquet Zercon the jester "caused all to burst into uncontrollable laughter" by "the words which he spoke all jumbled together (for he mixed Latin, Hunnic, and Gothic)."[610] A few Sogdian inscriptions on Avar objects do not necessarily indicate that Sogdian was spoken among them, although it was used as a lingua franca in central Asia in the fifth and sixth centuries.[611]

Many Slavic philologists assume that Slavic may have been the lingua franca of the late Avar period. The striking uniformity of the Slavonic language at that time can only be explained if there was a language continuum in which the Avar realm was a central node.[612] A similar thing happened in the Bulgar khanate in the course of the eighth and ninth centuries.[613] Of course, a Slavonic linguistic continuum does not exclude the use of their own language by the Avar elite. Such a white spot on the early medieval linguistic map may disturb the linguist. The historian can be consoled by the fact that the white spot probably was a rather colorful one.

Bulgars

The Bulgars of the sixth and seventh centuries are a compelling example of the manifold ruptures, new inceptions, and regroupings that are concealed behind the name of a people. It cannot be taken for granted that all the groups mentioned under that name were actually related; in the century between Baian and Asparukh, it seems to have been applied rather generically to mobile groups of steppe riders who fought under the Avars but then emancipated themselves.[614] To what extent the ethnonym was used for self-identification or rather for outside classification is unclear; we only know that in the long run, Bulgars used it for themselves. The seal of the Byzantine patrician Mavros, "prince of the *Sermesianoi* and Bulgars," is the first case where the ethnonym is attested in a self-definition. The fragmented Tervel inscription at Madara from the early eighth century mentions Bulgars; the khan Omurtag in 821/22 names them as his subjects; but only Khan Persian in an inscription of 837 includes them formally in his title.[615]

Bulgars had the capacity to remain recognizable under foreign rule for considerable time, whether they fought in Roman, Avar, or Lombard armies. The Bulgars, who from the end of the fifth century operated under that name in the Black Sea steppes and in the Balkan provinces, had lost much of their significance when the Avars arrived. Considerable contingents fought in Roman armies.[616] On the Black Sea the initiative had passed to Cutrigurs and Utigurs. Their realms presumably comprised about the same groups as the polities of the Bulgars before and after them. Bulgars are named neither in the context of the triumphant Avar campaign of 559–62 nor in the Avar army of 567. Instead, a large and relatively autonomous Cutrigur group appears on that occasion.[617] This first mention of Avar Cutrigurs is also the last. As often, the name did not maintain itself much longer than the kingdom that it had designated.

Toward the end of the sixth century, groups defined as Bulgars resurface under Avar rule. The first indication is Theophylact's notice from 594, when a Roman vanguard chanced upon a thousand Bulgars near the mouth of the Olt. Attacking them occasioned not only military disgrace but also a furious protest from the khagan.[618] The mission of the Bulgars appears to have been to follow the movements of the Roman army and perhaps to demonstrate the presence of the khagan in Slavic territory. This corresponded to the usual strategy of steppe empires: to protect the periphery by subject peoples.[619] Events prove that these Bulgars were in close contact with Avar headquarters. In 599, Bulgars are not mentioned among the Roman captives from the army that defended the Avar heartland in the battle at the Tisza River.[620]

We have evidence for the participation of Bulgars in the great sieges of Thessalonica around 618 and Constantinople (626).[621] Yet they played no prominent role in the battles. We have no information where these Bulgars came from, and whether they lived under direct control of the khaganate or had only been mobilized for the two major campaigns. One thing is clear: the defeat of the Avar khaganate in 626 and its subsequent period of weakness gave the Bulgars a decisive push. Within a short time, the disciplined comrades-in-arms had become dangerous competitors, who challenged the Avar khaganate on several fronts.[622]

Gepids and Lombards

The Gepids split after the decisive defeat against the Lombards in 567. Members of the elite joined the Byzantines: the dead king Cunimund's nephew Reptila and Bishop Thrasaric, who brought the royal treasure with them; Usdibad with his followers, whose extradition the khagan would subsequently and repeatedly demand.[623] Others left the Carpathian Basin with Alboin in 568, and according to Paul the Deacon Gepids still settled in separate villages in eighth-century Italy.[624] Those who remained had to live under Avar rule. Mobile warriors probably left, while well-entrenched farmers had good reasons for staying put.

The movement of refugees into the empire did not break off after 567. Seven Gepids were the only ones who were ready to follow the shaman Bookolabras into exile.[625] Occasionally, Gepids are still featured in historiography. A young Gepid serving in the Byzantine army in the early 590s who had killed and robbed an imperial bodyguard at a hunt gets extensive coverage in Theophylact, including a sequel of the story.[626] At court, he argued that he had won his precious belt in the battle that King Cunimund fought against the Lombards, almost thirty years earlier. The story gives Theophylact an occasion to recount these events at some length and make the implicit point that some knowledge of history had been helpful to unmask the murderer's excuses. It also implies that the young Gepid could still tap into some of the social memory of his people, which had lost its community-building power but remained useful for individual narratives of identification. In 593, another Gepid who had left his homeland helped the Romans to a considerable victory over the Slavs north of the lower Danube. He had enjoyed a respected position under the Slavic *archōn* Musucius, could sing Avar songs, preserved his Gepid-Christian traditions, and betrayed his new homeland to the Byzantines at the decisive moment.[627]

Gepids in Avar lands figure in Theophylact's account of Priscus's offensive in 599. After the Byzantine victory at the Tisza River, a detachment from Priscus's army massacred the peaceful Gepid inhabitants of three villages on the west bank of the river.[628] These villages obviously had not been involved in the events of war nearby. "They sat together at a banquet and celebrated a local feast. They were fully absorbed in their drinking and spent the entire night at the feast." Theophylact gives a grossly exaggerated number of thirty thousand dead, perhaps intended to gloss over the fact that Priscus had not followed up on his victory. These Gepids did not live under severe repression. They had the means to celebrate their festivals and were worth plundering. Gepids are also mentioned in one late source among the prisoners taken by Priscus in that campaign.[629] The only mention of Gepid participation in one of the khagan's military campaigns comes in Theophanes's report of the siege of 626.[630] However, contemporary observers such as Theophylact, the *Miracula S. Demetrii*, the *Chronicon Paschale*, or George of Pisidia do not take note of them.

Archaeologists have long tried to substantiate the Gepid presence in the Avar realm, which is attested in the written sources, in the archaeological evidence. Continued Gepid settlement in Transylvania seems to emerge from Avar influence in later phases of Gepid cemeteries, for instance, at Noşlac and at Bratei.[631] This is less marked along the Tisza, which was the main Gepid settlement area before the fall of the kingdom. Furthermore, Attila Kiss, the excavator, assumed that the large and prosperous village at Kölked on the west bank of the Danube had been settled by Gepids, an attribution that has now been abandoned; western connections are much more prominent in the material.[632] The hybrid archaeological record of the early Avar period hardly favors ethnic attributions. Furthermore, Gepids who simply continued using objects and practices they were familiar with under Avar rule after 567 may not emerge very clearly in the archaeological record, which cannot be used to make clear chronological distinctions between pre-567 and post-567.

The new Frankish overlords of the Carolingian period still encountered people who called themselves Gepids. Paul the Deacon emphasizes that *usque ad hodie*, that is, toward the end of the eighth century, Gepids lived under Avar rule.[633] The poet Theodulf, bishop of Orléans, mentions the *Pannonicus Gipes* along with the *deformis Abar*—the latter name shows that he updated his ancient models at least partly.[634] And it is certainly no literary reminiscence when the *Conversio Bagoariorum et Carantanorum*, composed in 871, writes of *Pannonia inferior*: "Some of the Gepids settle here until now."[635] If these authors knew about Gepids in the Carpathian Basin, this makes it likely that the name must have been passed down from generation to generation for more than two hundred years. The final mention of Pannonian Gepids is in any case later than the last mention of the Avars, who had destroyed their kingdom three hundred years earlier.

Far less can be said about Lombard groups under Avar rule. The sources know nothing of Lombards who stayed behind. Marius of Avenches remarks that in the exodus of 568 the old dwelling places were committed to the flames.[636] Yet, as we know, migrations of the period hardly included entire peoples, even though the sources may emphasize just this point. John of Ephesus remarks that the Lombards along with the Slavs were under Avar rule, but that is more likely a misconception than precise knowledge.[637] Since the fall of Cividale in ca. 610, Lombard prisoners of war (and their descendants) lived in Pannonia.[638] Later the khagan's court was the goal of prominent Lombard refugees. The substantial archaeological evidence of close connections to Lombard Italy and of other Western/"Germanic" elements from the early Avar period makes it likely that Lombards who had stayed behind or returned lived in late sixth- and early seventh-century Pannonia; but they cannot be pinned down more precisely. The same applies to (post-)Roman provincials or captives (see section 3.8).

Romans and Provincial Populations

No written source provides substantial information on the autochthonous population of Pannonia or the adjacent former Roman provinces under Avar rule. There are two indications that many of them left with Alboin to go to Italy in 568. Paul the Deacon mentions *Norici* and *Pannonii* among the peoples that had come to Italy.[639] A bishop Vigilius of Scarabantia (modern Sopron) occurs in the list of signatories at a synod of Grado between 572 and 577; it is very likely that he had resided in his see until 568 and then left with the Lombards.[640] This isolated piece of information makes it likely that Christian life and some elements of church organization were still intact in some Pannonian towns under Lombard rule. This impression is basically confirmed by archaeological evidence (for instance, in Savaria), although much of it is hard to date.[641] It is also clear from the archaeological record that not all of this ended in 568, although in many places the exact dates when "Roman" life faded out are hard to ascertain. The most striking example of a consolidated Christian community that continued late antique traditions after 568 is found in the fortress of Keszthely-Fenékpuszta at Lake Balaton (see section. 3.9). This late or post-Roman Pannonian population is not mentioned in written sources. For a while, it could still relate to Christian centers in modern Slovenia and Carinthia, which were again linked to the patriarchate of Aquileia. The Christian landscape that had been preserved in the Eastern Alps, however, was destroyed in the late sixth century by the expansion of Slavs and Avars (see section 5.6). It is not unlikely that parts of that Christian population were then transferred to Pannonia.

We have relatively good evidence that Avar captives from Byzantine towns were resettled in Pannonia. The most extensive account of their fate is given in the Kuver story in the *Miracula S. Demetrii* (see above and section 7.7). The implication is that such (Latin- or Greek-speaking) Romans preserved their identity for generations under Roman rule and maintained their Christian creed. They do not appear very clearly in the archaeological evidence; the older theory that the "Keszthely culture" was not least their achievement has lost much of its attraction (see section 3.9). It seems that the Roman identity of these Pannonian groups faded out before their Christianity: when the Franks arrived, they encountered Christians but did not report any Roman presence in the former Avar khaganate (see section 6.9). The heated debate about "Daco-Roman" continuity in Transylvania that was led between Romanian and Hungarian scholars in the 1980s and 1990s now seems to have subsided.[642] The survival of the Vlachs, largely as Romance-speaking transhumant herdsmen, seems to have been a more complex process and cannot simply be explained by Roman continuity in a given territory.[643] "Vlachs," and "Walchen" in the Eastern Alps, go back to the Germanic term for "Romans" (which is also preserved in the name "Welsh").[644] It was only gradually and in some places transformed from an outside designation to a name that expressed self-identification.

On the whole, naming post-Roman Romans is often problematic. The term had already had many meanings in Antiquity, which were, however, all attached somehow to the Roman Empire: the inhabitants of the Byzantine Empire remained "*Rhomaioi*," Romans, whereas beyond the shrinking imperial frontiers the use of "Roman" became patchy and acquired rather varied significance, legal, cultural, religious, or social.[645] Roman identities tended to become regionalized and attach themselves to former Roman territories, as with the (Hi)spani, the Aquitanians, or the *Sermesianoi*. If we use the term "Romans" for an Avar-period population, we have to be aware that we may mean rather different groups: descendants of Roman provincials, Romanized barbarians, Christians, Latin or

Greek speakers, or prisoners of war and their offspring. Whether they regarded themselves as "Romans" can hardly be determined.

Slavs

Among all the peoples living under Avar rule, the Slavs are by far most frequently mentioned, both in military encounters along the Danube and the Save close to the Avar core areas, and in the periphery of Avar power, where their relationship with the Avars varied considerably (see chapter 4). Slavs participated on a regular basis in Avar military campaigns. In this context they are frequently mentioned on the southern fringes of the Carpathian Basin.[646] We may assume that they cannot have come from any great distance to have been deployed there with their boats. A passage in John of Ephesus that around 584 the Antes attacked the Slavs "west of the Danube" has been taken as indicating a Slavic presence in Pannonia; but given this author's vague notions of the barbarian world this cannot be taken as proof.[647] More cannot be extracted from the written sources about Slavic settlement in the central regions of the Avar realm. Only after 796 would Slavic groups become a political factor on the middle Danube.

Distribution maps of early Slavic cultural features, so far as they can be drawn at all, show mostly blank areas for the Carpathian Basin. This does not unequivocally mean that there were no Slavs under Avar rule; traces of early Slavs are also lacking in seventh-century Carinthia where their presence emerges more clearly in the literary sources. Slavs mostly practiced cremation of their dead and did not use funerary rituals that leave many lasting traces. Their settlements, mostly in sunken huts, were similarly evanescent. At best, such finds pose grave problems of dating and attribution.[648] Only a systematic archaeological interest can detect them, and that interest has long been lacking in non-Slavic countries in eastern central Europe.

From among the great mass of find material from the Avar period and from the core of the Avar Empire few traces have been found that can be interpreted as Slavic, and they have mostly remained controversial.[649] It is conceivable that in poor graves in Avar cemeteries people of Slavic origin were also buried. But the question must be asked whether it is meaningful to speak of "Slavs" when all we have is a lack of tangible evidence. It remains possible that Slavs, like Gepids, may have lived in their own settlements, substantial traces of which have yet to be found. This would be probable, not only because of their military commitment (of which there are no more traces after 626). Avar and Slav economic practices were initially complementary. Slavic (and other) farmers supplemented the Avar pastoral and raiding economy. Only if Slavs lived in the vicinity of the Avar settlement area could their products be regularly transported there.

The archaeological evidence is better in the periphery of the Avar Empire. In particular, a lot of research has been done on the fringes of the Carpathian Basin in modern Slovakia, a region close to the Avar heartlands. In the flat lands north of the Danube, Avar cemeteries and settlements are found.[650] In the 1970s and 1980s, there was some controversial debate whether these were Avars, Avaro-Slavs, or perhaps Avarized Slavs, which has meanwhile subsided.[651] North of that zone, in the foothills of the Carpathians, Slavs are attested before the Avars arrived, and they live on continuously after that. Their main archaeological feature is simple pottery, usually called the "Prague type." Its minute study by Gabriel Fusek has yielded a relative chronology that can in some cases be validated by Merovingian and Avar links. On that basis, a first phase has been dated until ca. 600, and the second phase until the late seventh century.[652] In the eighth century, when the archaeological traces of Slavic settlement become more nuanced in the Carpathian countries, Avar influence can also be detected in Moravia and Bohemia; for instance, at Mikulčice, a future center of the Moravian duchy of the ninth century.[653]

In Austria, Slavic settlement only becomes tangible in the eighth century, when the cremation habit begins to subside. Some higher-status graves are found in the Eastern Alps, in the former duchy of Carantania, for instance at Grabelsdorf and Krungl; much more moderate burials also appear.[654] This area stretches into the south of Lower Austria (the Pitten region), which seems to have formed a contact zone with the Avar settlements a bit farther north and east. The beginnings of Slavic settlements in western Lower Austria are hard to date but might also predate the fall of the khaganate.[655] Similar problems of dating concern the presence of Slavs along the Save in Croatia and Slovenia.[656]

All these "Slavic" regions display rather varied types of evidence, chronologies, and states of the art in their excavation and interpretation. In any case, they cannot provide any coherent Slavic cultural model that would find correspondence in the core areas of the khaganate. To date, we can just assume that a portion of the population of the Carpathian Basin must have been of Slavic origin, just as Slavs, along with Avars, made up the most important contingents in the Avar army.[657] However, there was no cohesive and articulate Slavic social stratum that could have smoothly succeeded the khaganate in the Carpathian Basin after its fall. After 800 the bulk of the late Avar population must relatively quickly have been Slavicized. Ethnic processes are reversible; it is not unlikely that while many Slavs had become Avars until the eighth century, a countermovement set in after the end of the khaganate.

THE SEVENTH CENTURY

Priscus's success in 599/600 had shaken the prestige of the khaganate. In Italy, too, the Byzantine victories were noticed. Paul the Deacon recorded this as Maurice's most significant accomplishment.[1] Despite some internal conflicts the momentary threat to the Avars quickly passed. The imperial generals did not have the capacity to renew the offensive, and with Maurice's fall in the late autumn of 602 the danger had passed. To say that the Avar Empire had been "on the verge of dissolution" is certainly exaggerated.[2] We know that it eventually regained the initiative. However, after the end of Theophylact's narrative, information about events in the Balkans becomes very patchy indeed.

7.1 Consolidation and New Offensives

The Avars after 602

In the history of the Balkan countries the year 602 is often considered the date on which the dams burst. From this time onward, it is claimed, both Avars and Slavs could more or less do as they pleased in the Roman provinces. The collapse of Maurice's active defense strategy certainly left a mark. Yet the mutiny of the army in Europe and Phocas's usurpation only made visible what had long been foreshadowed. Earlier Avar and Slavic raids had already caused heavy destruction. The basis for Roman organization on the Danube had begun to falter. It was no palace intrigue that gave the death blow to Maurice's barbarian war. It was the fight on the frontier that decided the emperor's fall.

Thereafter it took some time for the new situation to display any consequences. The course of events is difficult to follow in its detail. From a remark in the *Armenian History* by Sebeos it seems that after the overthrow of Maurice, the army returned to Thrace.[3] No major Avar raids seem to have ensued. Theophanes notes that the Avars ravaged Thrace but has nothing specific to add. Still, he makes Phocas responsible for undermining Byzantine defenses. He picks up Theophylact's notice that on his accession Heraclius came across no more than two soldiers from the "tyrant" Phocas's army.[4] Besides the laconic information by Theophanes, only an Egyptian and a Spanish source note Avar and Slav attacks until about 615. John of Nikiu knew of "barbarian" raids on Illyricum in Phocas's reign, against which only Thessalonica was able to hold out.[5] Isidore of Seville notes for the year 614 the Slavic conquest of "Graecia," which may refer to all of Illyricum but also to Greece proper.[6]

Posterity has excoriated the usurper Phocas.[7] Yet not all his contemporaries saw him in this light. He was the last emperor to whom a monument was erected on the Forum Romanum. Indeed, the course of destiny was a gradual one. The Persian war escalated after 604, the frontier fort at Dara fell in 606, Edessa in 609. The following winter the Byzantine defense system disintegrated, and a Persian army for the first time could advance to Chalcedon on the Bosporus.[8] In the interior, Phocas quickly brought the rebellions of 604–5 under control, and it was not until the failed harvest and cold of 609 that the growing discontent passed into general insurrection, in which Heraclius, the son of the exarch of Africa, finally made his way to power in the fall of 610.[9]

To the acute threat on the eastern front Phocas reacted in a fashion similar to that of most of his predecessors. He withdrew troops from Europe and bought peace on the now inadequately protected Danube frontier. Likely in 604 he made a new pact with the Avars, "increasing the tribute to the khagan in the belief that the Avar nation was at rest." This may have brought the annual tribute from 120,000 to 140,000 solidi.[10] Theophanes's phrasing seems to indicate that the treaty did not follow a major Avar campaign but was intended to compensate in some way for the weakening of imperial defenses. The treaty hardly prevented the further erosion of the *limes* and the Slavicization of broad reaches of the countryside, yet it still seems to have protected the remaining larger inland cities from concentrated Avar attacks.

There is no written indication as to what happened to the forts along the Danube that had recently served the armies of Priscus and Peter as staging points, such as Singidunum, Novae, Durostorum, Tomis, or Asemus. We have to rely on archaeological clues, although these may not always provide reliable dates; where available, coins or coin hoards offer a chronological frame.[11] Some important towns seem to have been destroyed in the Avar wars of the 580s, such as Ratiaria or Oescus; others seem to have operated until the reign of Phocas, such as Nicopolis ad Istrum or Novae (which was consecutively used as a simple rural settlement in the seventh and eighth centuries), or that of Heraclius, as Odessos and Marcianopolis. The late antique Byzantine fort on the Tsarevets Hill near Nicopolis was destroyed by fire in the mid-seventh century. Coins in the fortress of Durostorum end after Phocas, but later ones up to Constantine IV appeared as stray finds on the banks of the Danube; on the ruins of the Roman bath, houses and pottery attributed to Slavs were excavated.[12] Whether destruction layers can be dated to the early seventh century or to the conquest by Asparukh is in debate. Generally, then, the strongholds along the *limes* seem to have been given up from west to east. In Scythia minor, building activities in some places continued into the early seventh century, and coins still kept arriving. There is evidence for a gradual ruralization of towns along the *limes* rather than their systematic destruction.[13] The so-called *Notitia of Epiphanius*, a bishops' list usually dated to the seventh century, either to the reign of Heraclius or even later, still mentions the bishoprics of Novae, Transmarisca, Durostorum, and Sucidava.[14] However, as is attested in the Adriatic regions, bishops may have maintained the denomination of their sees in exile for considerable time. On the whole, we may assume that the resumption of the large-scale Avar campaigns in the Balkan Peninsula did not occur until the first years of Heraclius's reign.[15]

During Phocas's reign, there would appear to have been a change of ruler among the Avars. A younger son of the empire's founder, Baian, succeeded his elder brother.[16] The succession of brothers instead of sons of the ruling khagan also occurred among the Turks.[17] Baian's grandsons had not been very fortunate. Some had died in the plague of 598; in the following year others were responsible for a series of Avar defeats. As had been the case in 582–84 no source directly noted the change in rule or the name of the new ruler. The exact point in time is thus unsure. But we may assume that the new khagan took the throne shortly before 610 and soon thereafter initiated fresh offensives.

Western Policy and the Conquest of Cividale

Whether the khagan exploited the disorder in Byzantium in 609–10 for a renewed attack, as John of Nikiu seems to suggest, is unsure. Clearly he intervened in the internal conflicts of his western neighbors shortly thereafter—a clear change of policy from the sixth century. In the Frankish sphere, the tension grew between the Austrasian king Theudebert II and his brother Theuderic II, with whom Brunhild ruled the kingdom in Burgundy. The quarrel determined the play of diplomacy in the West. In 604 the Lombard king Agilulf had engaged his son Adaloald to one of Theudebert's daughters. Conversely, Theuderic was to marry a daughter of the Visigothic king Witteric. Yet at the urging of Brunhild, he duped the Goths by sending the bride back but retaining the dowry. Burgundy was then ringed round by enemies, whose alliance, however, was none too effective. In February 610 Gundemar seized the Gothic throne. He stayed in the alliance against Brunhild and supported her opponent Theudebert, even with money.[18]

Responsible for this move was the count of Septimania, the exposed region around Narbonne, which was most affected by conditions among the Franks. His name was Bulgar. The letter in which he informs his Frankish partner of the payment has been preserved. He speaks in it of rumors that Brunhild had called on the Avars for help against Theudebert and asks for more information, in particular whether Theudebert had already defeated the Avars.[19] It is not known whether this, as in 596, really led to a direct conflict between the Avars and the Franks. Yet some kind of proxy war seems to have been waged in the East Tyrolian Alps. The Bavarian *dux* Garibald, son of the recently deceased Tassilo II, was defeated at Aguntum/Lienz by Slavs who went on to ravage the Bavarian borderland, probably in the Pustertal. However, the Bavarians succeeded in driving off their enemies and in recovering their booty.[20]

The Avars themselves were active elsewhere at this time. Paul the Deacon gives a rather legendary account of their attacks on Gisulf II, the Lombard *dux* of Friuli. After Gisulf and many of his followers had died on the battlefield, his wife Romilda, their sons (among whom the future king Grimoald), and the rest of the army barricaded themselves in Forum Iulii/Cividale. It was reportedly Romilda herself, enchanted by the beauty of the young khagan, who opened the gates to him, after which the men were slaughtered and the women and children taken captive. Only Gisulf's sons succeeded in getting away.[21]

No one had hurried to the help of the besieged Friulians. Nonetheless, the khagan did not exploit his victory for a further advance. This may suggest that an agreement with King Agilulf, who had considerable difficulties with Gisulf, had made the Avar campaign possible. Grimoald did the same thing when he later became king.[22] The question of whether such an intrigue is conceivable is linked to the confusing diplomatic situation of the times. The mosaic cannot be pieced together easily. The Lombard royal house was connected through Agilulf's wife Theudelinde with the Bavarian Agilolfings, and through Adaloald's wife with Theudebert II. The pact with the Austrasians was renewed in 612 shortly before the death of the latter. In the event that the rumors have some basis, that the Avars were actually allied with Brunhild, they would have been on the other side. Consonant with this would be the Slavic-Bavarian conflict, regardless of whether a Bavarian advance provoked it or whether it should be interpreted as the Avars taking sides in domestic Frankish struggles. But the Avar campaign against Friuli was hardly based on any kind of pact with Brunhild. In any case, the Lombard king stayed out of the matter, and the fall of Cividale had no traceable consequences in other theaters of conflict. The traditional good relations between the Avars and Lombards seem, in any case, not to have appreciably worsened.

Activities on the western frontier of the Avar sphere of power may have been prompted by conflicts in the Western kingdoms but were hardly channeled into their fault lines; they mainly served Avar and Slavic ends. The young khagan, who needed to prove himself as a military leader, had delivered a notable victory to his army. The Slavs followed suit by plundering in Istria.[23] The strike against the rebellious Gisulf suited Agilulf, even if he had not incited it. In far-off Spain, where Frankish quarrels mattered more, the interpretation of events in the east appears to have been that the godless Avars had taken the side of the hated Brunhild. In any case, the Avars did not allow themselves to be drawn further into the conflict among the Western powers. Nor did they seek to profit from the tense political situation by further attacks. The neighbors, especially Friulians and Bavarians who often followed their own goals in the borderlands, had been warned.

The Great Offensive of 615

Instead of a Balkan policy at any price, which had cost Maurice his throne and his life, the Byzantines now seemed to have no policy for the Balkans at all. Heraclius, who had marched into Constantinople as its savior, staggered from one defeat to another in his first years of rule. The army and state finances were shattered by the civil wars and by the societal tensions in which these were grounded. The richest provinces of the empire fell one after another to the Persians: in 611–14 Syria was conquered, Jerusalem fell in 614, and in the years up to 619 Egypt.[24] Clearly, in this situation, the Romans could do little for the impoverished Balkan provinces. It was not until 619–20 that Heraclius succeeded in acquiring the means for a more active foreign policy through a financial and military reform.[25]

Afterward, Byzantines would not willingly recall these unpleasant times. Our sources do not become more extensive again until 620. For events in the Balkans we are almost completely limited to speculations. It is only through the *Miracula S. Demetrii* that we are somewhat better informed about the repeated sieges of Thessalonica. This account does permit some conclusions to be drawn about the larger situation.

The initiative had passed to the Slavs. On none other than the night of the feast of the city's patron saint Demetrius on a Monday, October 26, a modest but experienced military troop of Slavs approached the city unobserved. As if by a miracle the roughly five thousand enemy soldiers were discovered before they could launch an attack at dawn, and they were repulsed on the open field of battle.[26] The inhabitants of the city had nearly been taken by surprise because a "deep peace" ruled everywhere. This encourages the assumption that this event occurred in 604, when Phocas had just concluded a peace accord with the Avars.[27] Clearly at this time people in Thessalonica could still count on a pact with the khagan to deter the Slavs from attacking. Yet they were wrong. Slavic groups obviously no longer needed the khagan's assent to attempt a well-organized surprise attack against the metropolis of Illyricum.

The next siege of Thessalonica, which occurred some ten years later, reveals further progress in the independent organization of the Slavs.[28] For the first time in this account (which was, however, composed two generations later) the names of Slavic tribes are given: Drogubites, Sagudates, Belezegites, Baiunetes, Berzetes. "They devastated all Thessaly and all the islands that lay about it and Hellas, further the Cyclades and the whole of Achaia, Epirus and the greater part of Illyricum and a part of Asia and left, as said above, very many cities and provinces depopulated."[29] Even though the list does not permit any precise geographical conclusions, it reveals the difference in the political situation from that of 604, when the city wrongly imagined itself safely at peace. It is noteworthy that the initiative for all this plundering is ascribed to the Slavs alone.

The military leader (*archōn*) of this obviously well-organized barbarian army was a certain Chatzon. The Slavs had readied a large number of their dugouts in order to be able to attack the city from the sea, and they also had siege engines at their disposal. They had brought along their women and belongings in order to be able to settle in the area after the capture of the city. If this information is accurate, it would signify three things. First, the attackers had not yet taken up any kind of permanent residence in proximity to the city. Second, the Slavic military campaigns of these years had the conquest of settlement areas as their goal. The fact that the attack on the city was repeated two years later also points to the wish to stay. Third, the list of tribal names probably anticipates a later period when they had already become familiar to the inhabitants of Thessalonica. Most of them would be mentioned again a half century later during the Perbund affair.[30]

Despite their initial fears, the city residents, reinforced by fugitives, succeeded in defending themselves. When the Slavs attacked the harbor in their boats, the defenders risked a sortie and repelled the attack.[31] They also captured Chatzon, the Slavic leader, and hid him in a private house as a pawn for further negotiations. But, as the account of the *Miracula* reports with explicit approval, some women dragged him out and through the city, and finally stoned him. A number of the Slavs' captives seized the opportunity to seek refuge in Thessalonica. This in turn further strengthened the Slavs' resolve to conquer the city by whatever means possible.

> They gathered impressive gifts and had them brought before the khagan of the Avars. They promised him that in this undertaking he would take a huge amount of treasure as spoils, which he, as they promised, could obtain from our city, in the event he should lend them help in arms. They assured him that the city would be easy to take. For they had already made the cities and eparchies round about uninhabitable; only this city had held out in their midst. And the city had received all the fugitives from the regions of the Danube, from Pannonia and Dacia and Dardania and the other eparchies and cities.[32]

Among these refugees, as is later noted, were also inhabitants of the principal inland cities of Naissus/Niš and Serdica/Sofia, who had already experienced the effectiveness of barbarian siege machines.

The grim situation in the region described by the *Miracula* corresponds with the meager information provided by John of Nikiu and Isidore of Seville.[33] In the first years of Heraclius's rule most remaining Roman bastions in the interior of the Balkan Peninsula fell. Only a few fortified places on the coasts and the cities in the vicinity of Constantinople could hold out.[34] Attempts have been made to establish the chronology of the conquests with the aid of coin finds. In Caričin Grad the sequence of coins ends in 606–7; in Naissus a *follis* from 613 in a Byzantine grave and a solidus minted between 613 and 616 are the most recent coins.[35] The fall of Naissus can then be dated to ca. 614–15, before Chatzon's siege. What role the Avars may have had there, the *Miracula* do not say, yet the text suggests that the region from which the refugees had come was considered the khagan's turf. Isidore mentions only Slavs as aggressors. John of Nikiu, on the other hand, names only the Avars (in the form *Alwarikon*) among the various barbarian peoples.[36]

The "Khagan's War" against Thessalonica

The relationship between the Avars and Slavs in that period can be reconstructed with some probability with the help of the *Miracula S. Demetrii*. The Slavs who joined forces to attack Thessalonica under Chatzon could operate independently and could demand *symmachia*, military alliance, from the khagan. In their contacts with him, however, they rather appear as suppliants (even though the khagan occasionally buttressed the call for military cooperation with gifts too).[37] In battle the Slavs had to subordinate themselves to the khagan's leadership. Other Slavs who lived in closer proximity to the center of Avar power were, like the

Bulgars, directly subject to the khagan's commands and belonged to the military force that he mobilized for the attack on Thessalonica. Preparations apparently took some time, but two years after the siege of Chatzon, most likely in 617 or 618, the besieging army marched up to the city.[38]

The "khagan's war," as the *Miracula* call it, was probably the most severe siege of all those that the holy Demetrius helped the inhabitants to withstand.[39] First, select horsemen dashed forward before the city dwellers were aware of it and overcame all those who were outside the city walls. After a few days, the mass of the army arrived under the khagan's leadership, accompanied by siege machines. Clearly the attack came as a surprise for the emperor too. It was accounted a miracle that a series of supply ships had been able to reach the city in time. The barbarians were better equipped with siege machines than in 586. This time they even had siege towers at their disposal. They were higher than the city walls, and on their platforms there was room for heavily armored fighters. Ladders on wheels and fire catapults completed the siege equipment. Yet not all the machinery functioned satisfactorily. One tower collapsed and buried its crew beneath it. The testudos that were brought up against the walls proved to be unreliable. In addition, the hail of arrows that was showered on the defenders resulted in little injury. The siege lasted thirty-three days. It was appreciably better organized than all previous efforts, which had to be broken off after a few days because of the demoralization of the attackers and supply difficulties.

After a month of fruitless attacks the khagan succeeded in saving face. He entered into negotiations with the defenders, demanded gold in return for a withdrawal, and threatened fresh attacks. An accord was reached, the Avars pulled back, but not without burning down the churches in the surroundings. Other barbarians began trading with the city folk and offered their prisoners for ransom. This was perhaps the beginning of a more peaceful coexistence between Thessalonica and its Slavic neighbors, and the city was now spared further attacks for more than a generation.

Dalmatia

Around the turn of the seventh century Pope Gregory had corresponded with Salona in a drawn-out ecclesiastical dispute.[40] This unedifying contention was one of the city's last signs of life in our sources. No contemporary text has information on the fall of Salona, once the metropolis of Dalmatia, and on the withdrawal of its population to Spalato/Split, the ancient palace of Diocletian. Only a legendary account has been preserved in Constantine Porphyrogenitus. In chapters 29 and 30 of his *De administrando imperio*, compiled three centuries after the event, two versions of this legend are given.[41] The Danube, we are told, once marked the border of Dalmatia. On the far side lived the Avars, and the garrison in Salona had to stand guard on the river. According to the version in chapter 30, the Dalmatians once fell upon the women and children of the Avars when the latter were off on a military campaign. When they attempted to repeat this raid again the following year, they fell into Avar captivity. The Avars put on the Roman uniforms, gained access to the city of Salona on Holy Saturday, and in this way were able to take it. From this base they conquered the greater part of Dalmatia and settled there.

This story has often been used as a basis for modern reconstructions of the events, in spite of its obvious contradictions. That troops from Salona did actually cross the Danube, in order to ravage the lands of the Avars, seems inconceivable for the time after 602. The story may express a retrospective feeling in Byzantium that Priscus's campaigns north of the Danube around 600 had precipitated the fatal blows by Avars and Slavs against the Balkan provinces that were to follow. What is striking is that here, as in Greece, the name of the Avars is preserved as the attackers, although the Dalmatian coast clearly fell into Slavic hands.

Constantine's alternative version in chapter 29 contains an even more puzzling phrase in this respect, identifying the enemies as the "unarmed Slavs who are called Avars." It seems to indicate that the distinction that had mattered much to contemporaries had long lost its significance.[42] Chapter 29 also shifts the topographic focus to the *clisura* at the Kleisa pass, only four miles distant from the city, where the Salonitans guarded the approaches to the city, and where they were fooled (as in the other version) by the Roman uniforms that the barbarians wore. Although the name of the Danube also features here, the narrative does not give the impression that the river could have been so far away. Croat scholars have put forward the attractive hypothesis that the story must initially have been about the Cetina, only to be replaced with the name of the better-known Danube in Constantinople.[43] Thus, the version in chapter 30, which at first glance appears to be more plausible, in fact seems to be the result of a revision intended to harmonize the story with what was known about the period from other sources. The awkward "unarmed Slavs who are called Avars" were made to look more like the Avars known from historiography, whose border was known to have been the Danube. What seemed puzzling to Constantine (or a previous redactor) very likely comes from a Dalmatian source; but how reliable its basic narrative is remains a matter of speculation.

Dating the events is even more problematic. Chapter 31 about the origin of the Croats states that the Romans had been chased away by the Avars in the reign of Heraclius (610–41), which is plausible although the passage anachronistically links the beginnings of the Croat state and church organization to the same period.[44] Chapter 29 dates the flight of Salonitans from the Slavs to Raousi/

Dubrovnik to five hundred years before the composition of the text in 948/49; even if we assume that the number is corrupt (perhaps for three hundred years?), it does not allow more than speculation.

Other sources have been adduced to clarify the chronology. The weathered gravestone of an abbess that was found in Salona played a large role in the discussion. The pious woman, a fugitive from Sirmium (which fell in 582), died on May 4 of a fifth indiction, which could have been in 587, 602, or perhaps even 617 (but not in 612, as has been maintained)—not a very reliable terminus post quem for the fall of the city.[45] The date that Isidore gives for the conquest of "Graecia," 614, was often taken as a likely date for the fall of Salona and figures in most reference works.[46]

A later date, 625, is given in the thirteenth-century chronicle by the archdeacon Thomas of Spalato, who calls the conquerors "Goths," an erudite identification that provided a basis for twentieth-century Ustaša ideology that saw the Croats as descended from the Goths.[47] More reliable is the terminus ante quem for major Slavic raids in Dalmatia provided by the *Liber Pontificalis*. According to this work, Pope John IV (640–42), himself a Dalmatian, "sent much money by the holy and trustworthy abbot Martin throughout Dalmatia and Histria to redeem captives who had been despoiled by the barbarians"; the abbot also brought many Dalmatian relics to Rome, among them the remains of St. Anastasius, a martyr in the prosecution of Diocletian, who had been venerated at Salona.[48] This indicates that the city had more or less been abandoned at that time; and most likely, not too long before that date. Whether it had been captured at all cannot be taken for granted on the basis of the late legends of its fall.

Excavations in Salona have reinvigorated the discussion. It was previously assumed that here too the series of coins broke off in 613–14, but a find of fifty-one copper coins has entailed a correction: the last coin of the hoard was minted between 625 and 630, and a further two are from 614–15.[49] There are traces of reinforcement of the walls, but so far no signs of destruction have come to light.[50] Archaeological evidence also allows us to conclude that life in Salona did not end with a single stroke. The resettlement in Spalato, in the old palace of Diocletian, only seems to have gained momentum in the mid-seventh century.[51] But it is remarkable that no Dalmatian bishops are mentioned as participating in any of the councils before Nicaea 787 (unlike those from Istria). The further coexistence of Romans with Slavs in Dalmatia seems to have been relatively peaceful; in the hinterland, Dalmatians were "becoming Slavs," and later, Croats.[52] In the long run, several Roman cities maintained themselves: along with Spalato/Split were Diadera/Zara/Zadar and Ragusa/Raousion/ Dubrovnik, which absorbed the population of the destroyed Epidamnus.[53] As in other parts of the empire that came under increasing barbarian pressure, shrinking cities may also have been abandoned for sites that could more easily be defended.[54]

The apparent paradox of the "Slavs who are called Avars" recalls the situation in Greece, where later sources similarly tried to bridge over the contradiction between memories of Avar attacks and the evident settlement by Slavs.[55] The basis for the confusion may be a similarly complex Avar–Slav relationship as is evident in the *Miracula S. Demetrii*. In the first quarter of the seventh century Slavic groups may be assumed to have settled gradually in the vicinity of the Dalmatian coast. Initially, no dangerous attack was anticipated on their part. It is possible that Slavic groups assembled for a surprise strike against the city and that they sought help from the Avars. A further parallel to the account of the siege of Thessalonica in ca. 615 is the choice of a prominent feast day for the attack, here the Easter weekend, when the Salonitans were less watchful. Is this a literary motif intended to explain the lack of preparations on the Byzantine side, or does it point to the familiarity of the attackers with Christian customs? In any case, there is no indication of a great array of forces under the leadership of the khagan attacking Dalmatia as was the case at Thessalonica in 617 or 618. It is possible that smaller Avar groups, whose great prestige attached their name to the events, joined the Slavic raids. But it may also be that only retrospective perceptions connected the gradual Slavic expansion in Dalmatia with the more formidable name of the Avars. Later generations may have condensed the gradual abandonment of the city into the fable of the hubris, deception, and fall of Roman Salona. Thus, the fall of Salona became emblematic for the decline of the once-thriving ancient cityscape of the Dalmatian coast.

7.2 The Surprise Attack on the Emperor

Sunday, June 5, 623. An extraordinary summit conference had been arranged for this day. In the vicinity of the Long Walls, between Selymbria/Silivri and Heraclea/Eregli on the Sea of Marmara, about forty miles west of Constantinople, emperor and khagan were to negotiate the conditions of peace.[56] After the campaign of 622, Heraclius had left the greater part of his army on the Persian frontier and had returned to the capital in order to terminate an Avar attack by diplomatic means. The patrician Athanasius, accompanied by Cosmas, was sent to the khagan to work out the conditions for peace. The Avar ruler stated that he was amicably disposed toward the Romans and wished to arrange the conditions of the treaty in person with the emperor.[57] Heraclius agreed, and the meeting was organized.

Three days after the Roman delegation had arrived in Selymbria, the Avars appeared at Heraclea. The emperor had mobilized everything with a view to impressing the khagan. He left Selymbria with all the regalia of his office, a diadem on his head, and with a great entourage of senators and clerics, dignitaries and representatives of the citizenry, with musicians and the palace choir. Rich gifts and sumptuous clothes had been brought for the Avars, and a horse race had even been planned. Many citizens had come out after rumors about the events had spread.[58] Then the emperor was informed that Avar horsemen had concealed themselves in the wooded areas by the Long Walls. They clearly had a mission to cut off the return route of the magnificent but ill defensible procession.

It is no longer possible to determine whether this was a long elaborated plan to seize the person of the emperor or whether the khagan intended only to exert additional pressure during negotiations. Both Byzantine and modern historians take the first possibility as a given, and the further course of events speaks for this interpretation. The emperor reacted quickly. He exchanged his imperial vestments for inconspicuous clothing, hid the diadem under his arm, and took the return route to the capital city at a gallop. The Avar horsemen were on his heels. For a first time they thereby succeeded in forcing their way into the area enclosed by the Long Walls. Finally, Heraclius and his retinue reached the Golden Gate of the Theodosian Walls. He alerted the garrison, while the Avars set up their camp a few miles from the city walls next to the Hebdomon Palace (present-day Bakirköy). The imperial vestments, gifts, musical instruments, and everything that the fleeing Romans had left behind fell into Avar hands. They plundered the surroundings of the capital and some churches.[59] They also took a great number of captives. It is reported that they took seventy thousand Byzantines prisoner, men, women, young, and old, and carried them off across the Danube.[60]

When this happened has long been debated. The *Chronicon Paschale* dates the events to 623 (in this year June 5 actually did fall on a Sunday), while Theophanes puts them in 619. The reason why many historians have preferred the earlier date is that Heraclius's Persian campaign began in 622.[61] Yet in a thorough analysis Stratos has dispelled the reservations against the year 623, showing this contemporary dating to be preferable and without inconsistencies. June 5 is additionally confirmed by the fact that processions of thanks for being saved from the barbarian threat were long held on this day.[62] News of these events reached as far afield as Spain and was there mentioned in a supplement to Isidore's chronicle. "The Huns broke through the Long Walls, pressed forward to the ramparts of Constantinople, and negotiated with aforesaid emperor (Heraclius), who stood on the wall; when they received a sum of money from him for a peace, they withdrew for a time." The event is here situated in the fourteenth year of Heraclius's rule (October 623–24) and in the fortieth year of the Frankish king Chlothar (623–24). This constitutes a weighty argument for the dating of 623.[63] The brief entry focuses on the fact that the barbarians broke through the Long Walls and on the emperor's personal involvement in negotiations.

The emperor's efforts to strike a peace did not come to an end with the collapse of the summit conference. He had no choice, if he wished to go on the offensive against the Persians. The *Easter Chronicle* provides no information on a pact having been concluded. Theophanes does, and situates it in the year after the surprise attack at Heraclea, according to his chronology in 620.[64]

Theodore Syncellus dates the events "a few years" before the siege of 626. The peace negotiations were not easy; according to Theodore's account, the khagan first threatened to destroy Constantinople, if he did not obtain half of all the goods and treasures to be found in the city. Still, the emperor "did not leave this proud and boastful man without making peace with him" before going to the east again.[65] The khagan received the usual subsidies, if we follow Theodore's account: "He received all that in consequence of the earlier peace treaty, and he reinforced the terms of the treaty also with an ancient formula on oath, given by his emissary." On top of his booty, the khagan thus acquired a huge amount of money and goods, but "payment of treasure became the stimulant to still greater faithlessness."[66] Nicephorus, who gives no date (before the army's departure against the Persians, he simply writes), knows of "gifts" of two hundred thousand solidi, an amount never previously paid to barbarians.[67] In addition, the emperor had to give a bastard son, John Athalaricus (perhaps born from a Gothic concubine), his nephew Stephanus, son of his sister Maria, and John, a son of the patrician Bonus, to the Avars as hostages. It was not until years later, conceivably as late as 636, that Maria succeeded in ransoming her son and the other remaining hostages from the khagan.[68]

This pacification of the Avars seems to have retained Heraclius in the capital until the following spring. In March 624 he returned to the Persian theater.[69] The conclusion of the peace accord is then probably to be dated to the winter of 623–24. Was this peace treaty the first to have been concluded since the time of Phocas? That is unlikely. Under Maurice, a formal peace agreement had always been reached after each of the Avar campaigns. The chronology of war and peace in the first years of Heraclius's rule can hardly be reconstructed. The conquest of the inland cities and the attack against Thessalonica repeatedly disrupted the conditions that the treaties were meant to secure, but the khagan must also have been interested in having the regular payments from Byzantium continue. With the accession of a new emperor it was customary to renew treaties, and this must have happened in 610/11 as well, especially as a new khagan had also taken over; at this point, the Avars may have achieved another raise (160,000?).

Another peace agreement was most probably concluded after the siege of Thessalonica in 618/19, for which "the amount of the tribute" had to be agreed upon (and most likely, raised).[70] One hundred eighty thousand gold coins is a conceivable figure; the two hundred thousand of 623 would be the logical next step. Peace had to be reestablished before Heraclius could launch his offensive in the east. It is hardly conceivable that the emperor planned the advance against the Persians without having at least formally secured his back. About this time and by requisitioning ecclesiastical assets the emperor again had the means at hand for a more active foreign policy. He exploited them to assemble an army and clearly developed a long-term strategy that was also diplomatically secured.[71] The considerable increase in Byzantine payments in these years is also reflected in the archaeological evidence; the number of gold coins preserved on Avar territory reaches an all-time high for emissions of the years 616–25.[72] Before Heraclius set out against the Persians (Theophanes seems to have the correct date here, 622), he wrote a letter to the khagan, in which he called him the guardian of his son and reminded him of the obligations of his alliance. In this letter he also entrusted to the khagan the general protection of the city and its affairs. The khagan in turn called him his father and benefactor.[73] The treaty to which the emperor referred must have been the one concluded in 618/19.[74]

As long as Heraclius was preparing his army, the peace accord held. But it was perhaps broken as early as 622 when the army set out for Persia, otherwise the emperor would not have returned to the capital the following winter.[75] In any case we should reckon with an attack in 623, which culminated in the dramatic events near the capital. During these two years many Slavic groups also took advantage of the opportunity for new raids. A Syrian source reports that their boats even reached Crete.[76] The emperor had no alternative but to swallow the indignity of the attack against his person. He pursued his bold plan in the east and relied on the strong defenses of the capital city.

The khagan too had come under pressure. Slavs were taking the initiative in every corner of the Balkan Peninsula. Even though they occasionally required Avar help, they could no longer be effectively controlled. The khagan could only hope that under his leadership they would have the opportunity for even greater successes than they could achieve on their own. The events of 616–18 demonstrate that laying siege to large, well-fortified cities was generally beyond the means of the Slavic confederacies. Baian's younger son, under the pressure of circumstances, had to develop competence as a *poliorkeutes*, a specialist in siege craft. This ran counter to the fighting style of the horsemen from the steppes, who were not accustomed to attack walls. Thus, Cividale fell through betrayal, Salona (if it did) by surprise, while Thessalonica held out. Yet the khagan had no other choice. With ever more ambitious military campaigns he had to take the attack to the center of the empire, which alone would be worth the outlay. For unrest was also growing among the Slavic groups within his direct sphere of power. If we follow Fredegar, the Samo rebellion already began in 623–24, perhaps while the khagan was engaged far away in the periphery of Constantinople.[77] The attack on the emperor arose more likely from this pressing need for success than from anger over the intrigues of imperial diplomacy.[78] The course of this venture, extraordinary as it may have been, shows how limited the range of success of the Avar army actually was unless they undertook concerted sieges. Even though the sources state that huge numbers of prisoners were taken in 623, the two churches that were plundered are given special mention. Such successes could not assure the khagan's supremacy in the longer run. As a consequence, he now bet everything on one card.

7.3 626: The Siege of Constantinople

"In 626, [Illig Khagan's] deepest incursion ever brought his Türk armies to the north bank of the Wei River near Chang'an. . . . [The emperor] Taizong rode with six horsemen to the Bian Bridge to personally accuse Illig Khagan of shamelessly breaking their covenant, which allegedly involved marriage relations and Tang payments of large quantities of gold and silk. On this occasion Taizong and Illig sealed another covenant on the bridge by sacrificing a white horse."[79] It was the last great military expedition against China of the first Turkish khaganate, before it would have to subject itself to the Chinese a few years later. The Turkish Empire in central Asia had emerged around the time when the Avars, who had fled from the Turks, had established theirs in Europe. The parallels with the troubled negotiations between Heraclius and the khagan and with the Avar siege of Constantinople in 626 may seem fortuitous. Yet they reveal something of the rhythm that informed the steppe empires. Both empires launched one more spectacular expedition at a moment when their expansive dynamic was about to exhaust itself. Both seemed at the apogee of their power; both negotiated on a par with the emperor in the vicinity of the capital; and both had to be cajoled by a rhetoric of kinship and bought off by immense gifts (like the Avars in 623). It is likely that the Turkish offensive and the ensuing troubles of their empire were prompted by unusually cold years; and it is possible that this also affected the Avars.[80] However, there are also obvious differences: the Turks did not actually besiege Chang'an, and they could not profit from the massive attacks of another power on the Chinese realm. Furthermore, the renewed Chinese Empire turned out to be in the ascent again under the newly established Tang dynasty (618–907), after a long period of disunity, and soon defeated the eastern Turkish khaganate;[81] whereas the Byzantines were about to lose the bulk of their territories. Both processes would of course only become obvious in retrospect.

Regardless of its long-term consequences, the Avar-Persian siege of Constantinople in 626 made a dramatic impression on contemporaries. It has occasionally
been doubted that events were as dramatic as the sources, quite intentionally,
make them appear.[82] There is a point to that observation. However, it was the
Baian dynasty's most ambitious undertaking by far, and clearly not intended to
simply achieve a further rise in tributes. And it was the first full-fledged barbarian
siege that the New Rome had experienced so far. Barbarian armies had of course
often threatened the imperial city. It was in the periphery of Constantinople that
Theoderic had put Emperor Zeno under pressure.[83] Belisarius had been forced
to drive the Cutrigurs from the suburbs in his old age.[84] Theudebert, king of
the Franks, boasted that he would march against Constantinople together with
Lombards and Gepids.[85] But none of these barbarians had actually attempted a
siege of the city on the Bosporus.

Several sources in the otherwise "dark" seventh century provide extensive
accounts, which attests to the significance of the event.[86] The *Chronicon Paschale*
gives a detailed account of the course of the siege, but the text has a lacuna in
its last three days.[87] A homily ascribed to Theodore Syncellus, a deacon of the
Hagia Sophia and member of a delegation to the khagan, glorifies the salvation
of the city and puts it into a closely knit biblical and exegetical context.[88] Another
eyewitness, George of Pisidia, also a close collaborator of the patriarch Sergius,
wrote a poem on the miraculous delivery of the city known under the title *Bellum Avaricum*.[89] Among the later chroniclers the patriarch Nicephorus is more
detailed than Theophanes, who treats the siege as little more than a footnote
of operations in the Persian war, of which he gives a "confused and confusing"
account.[90]

Unfortunately, the diplomatic run-up to the great siege of the city is poorly
known. We know that Heraclius attempted to secure his offensive in the east
through money and exquisite rhetoric addressed to the khagan, but we have no
detailed information about other missions exchanged on the occasion.[91] Certainly the Persians and Avars had coordinated their attacks, just as, at the same
time, Heraclius was in contact with the Turks. After Heraclius's successes in the
preceding years on the northern frontier of Persia, King Chosroes II had come
under pressure. He hoped to deliver a decisive blow to his opponent by a direct
attack on Constantinople. A newly assembled army under Shahrbaraz marched
from Syria to Chalcedon on the Asian shore of the Bosporus. Heraclius decided
not to abandon the strategic advantages that he had won on the Persian frontier
and to stay with his troops, also in order to block the advance of a second army
under Shahin.[92] The command in Constantinople was entrusted to the *Magister
militum praesentalis*, Bonus. The young Caesar Constantine and the patriarch
Sergius were also in the city. The danger had become obvious fairly soon, and

there was time for extensive preparations, so that the city was well equipped and provisioned to withstand a siege.[93] By letter the emperor gave instructions for the provisions that were to be made in the face of the expected siege.[94] In addition, he dispatched a portion of the army to the capital. The *Easter Chronicle* mentions twelve thousand cavalrymen present in the city at the beginning of the siege; these had hardly all been sent back by Heraclius.[95] An embassy under the experienced patrician Athanasius went to the khagan in order to dissuade him, at the last minute, from his plans. But the Avar ruler declined all offers. When his army had reached Adrianople, he sent the ambassador on ahead. With biting irony, he told him that the Byzantines should see with which gifts they could still deter him from the conquest of the city. When the patrician once more appeared before the khagan, the latter responded to all offers with a demand for the surrender of the city.[96]

On June 29, the Avar vanguard, about thirty thousand horsemen according to the rather exaggerated numbers given in the sources, reached the environs of the city. They established their camp at Melantias on the Sea of Marmara, at some distance from the city walls. From time to time small detachments pushed forward up to the fortifications. Since scarcely an enemy was to be seen, groups of city dwellers risked going out to the tenth milestone ten days later under military protection in order to bring in the harvest. But skirmishes erupted in which some Byzantines were killed or taken captive.[97] The same day (likely July 8) about a thousand Avars rode to Sycae/Galata on the shore of the Bosporus, near the Church of the Maccabees, and showed up to the Persians on the other shore.[98] Exactly one month after the vanguard, on Tuesday, July 29, the khagan appeared at the head of the rest of his troops. George of Pisidia puts the number of the besiegers at eighty thousand. This is probably exaggerated but is no fantastic number.[99] According to the standards of the time thirty thousand was already a very large army. In order to storm the capital, at least as many were surely needed. If the khagan summoned all "the savage peoples whose life is war,"[100] his army might well have exceeded this figure.

Before the actual military action a war of nerves began. The khagan drew up before the Philoxenon Gate (a less important gate in the middle section of the Theodosian Walls) for a display of power. In the morning sun the armor and shields of the barbarians sparkled, a terrifying view for the city folk assembled on the wall.[101] Patriarch Sergius tried to raise morale by carrying a wonder-working icon, believed to be painted not by human hand, along the wall.[102] Icons of the Virgin Mary were placed above the city gates.[103] The Mother of God (*theotokos*) would protect her city, as St. Demetrius had protected Thessalonica.

The next day, in all calm, the khagan prepared to unleash the storm. He did not balk at demanding that livestock be delivered by the city residents. In a gesture of magnanimity and perhaps to demonstrate that the city was well stocked, the emperor's son acceded to this demand.[104] At dawn on July 31 the attack on the city walls began. The Avars concentrated their attack on a section about a half-mile long between the Pemptu and Polyandriu Gates. Slavs had been stationed along the other sections. In the front rank fought unprotected Slavic warriors, behind them armored infantrymen.[105] The attackers rained a hail of arrows down on the bulwarks. The fighting continued until the eleventh hour. Not until evening were the first siege machines ready for action. By now, the barbarians had clearly become expert in the construction of these engines.[106]

On August 1 the first general attack was undertaken with the aid of the machines. The sources enumerate the usual siege engines, stone and fire catapults, rams, and testudos.[107] Along the section between the Polyandriu and Hagiu Romanu Gates twelve giant siege towers were pulled up to the walls, the platforms of which projected over their top. By means of a sailor's ingenious, crane-like construction, the besieged Byzantines succeeded in setting several of these towers on fire.[108] In the Golden Horn the Slavic dugouts were let into the water. They had been brought from the Danube in the baggage train.[109] The Slavic rowers already had a great deal of experience with this kind of fighting from their numerous raids. The boats were assembled by the Kalliniku bridge, where the larger Byzantine ships could not maneuver because of the shoals.

During the fighting the commander Bonus had a further plea to negotiate sent to the khagan. The only offer that came as a reply was: "Withdraw from the city, leave me your property and save yourselves and your families."[110] The next day, August 2, a high-ranking delegation with rich gifts made its way out of the city toward the Avar ruler. Along with the chief negotiator Athanasius and the patricians Georgius and Theodosius, there was also Theodore Syncellus, who later composed the sermon on the siege. In his account, he replaced the names of the envoys with those of Hezekiah's embassy to Babylon and said he would "overlook the fourth delegate, because Hezekiah . . . sent only three men," a clear indication that he had been that fourth man. The khagan received the Byzantines at the same time as three silk-clad Persians. While the latter were allowed to sit, the former had to remain standing. A Turkish khagan had once savored a similar meeting with Byzantine and Persian delegations, albeit with reversed roles.[111] Triumphantly the Avar ruler informed the Romans that Shahrbaraz would be sending him reinforcements. Regardless of whether three thousand or only one thousand Persians were to be involved,[112] the symbolic value of such support was far greater than the actual help offered. Quite freely in the presence of the Romans it was agreed that the Slavic oarsmen would transport the Persian *symmachoi* across the Bosporus. The khagan stated that the city should have no hopes of being spared. Neither had the emperor succeeded in advancing into

Persia nor was he now present with his army in order to defend his capital. The Romans did not let themselves be rattled by this, and they had probably already heard of the emperor's victory over the army of Shahin.[113]

The khagan repeated more or less the conditions for capitulation uttered before. The eyewitness Theodore recalled that the barbarian wished to leave the city depopulated. It was to be evacuated and along with all its treasures be turned over to the Avars. The inhabitants, only with their clothes and without any possessions, were to surrender to the Persians, and the khagan promised that Shahrbaraz would not harm a hair of their heads.[114] This presumably corresponded to the agreement that had just been negotiated between Avars and Persians. The price for Persian support was the delivery of the inhabitants. No doubt the population of the capital was more useful for resettlement in distant Persian towns than for mainly agricultural work in Avar Pannonia.[115] The offer clarifies the khagan's military objectives. It has often been maintained that the Avars wanted to establish control over Constantinople and thus over the European part of the empire.[116] There is no indication whatsoever that he intended to do that. The Balkan provinces would have looked pretty different in the seventh century had the khagans attempted to attach them to their realm. It is obvious that the Avars were not interested in maintaining the Byzantine infrastructure and administration in order to rule over Roman territories, as Goths or Franks had done. Baian's son wanted the city without people, just as after his raids in 447 Attila required that a broad strip of land south of the Danube, as far as Naissus, should not be cultivated by Romans any more. Indeed, that city was deserted when Priscus passed through it on a diplomatic mission a few years later.[117] Yet for permanent domination, an empty city would have been worthless. Theodore states quite clearly what the khagan's intention was: "The goal of war is in general the hope of booty, the removal of men, the seizure of goods; this is why barbarian peoples begin a war."[118] No word about conquering territories. The Avar khagans had no vision of an Avarized Roman Empire, or of governing urbanized lands.

The Byzantines' attempts to seek a negotiated solution seem to indicate that they were by no means sure that they could entrust themselves to the city's fortifications. But at the same time it was consonant with experience and tactics to date in dealing with the Avars. It had always proved possible, at difficult moments, to buy peace from the khagan. His hesitancies and threats always turned out to be negotiating tactics. But this time the proven negotiating strategy did not work. The khagan knew that he could no longer turn back. Possibly he actually believed that the Byzantines' prospects were hopeless and willingly let this view be strengthened by the Persians. The Avars may not have realized that from Chalcedon Shahrbaraz could do relatively little as long as the Roman fleet controlled the straits.

After some heated verbal exchanges the illustrious delegation departed from the camp of the enemy, with whom they nonetheless left the ineffectual gifts. The mood in Constantinople that Saturday evening was depressed. Yet it was decided to prevent the Avar and Persian armies from joining up under any circumstances. Watchfulness on the Bosporus that night was turned to good account. When the three Persian emissaries wanted to cross at one of the narrowest places on the Bosporus in the vicinity of Chalae/Bebek, they were intercepted by Roman ships and overpowered. This symbolic victory was exploited for one of those spectacles of demonstrative cruelty in which the Byzantines have always taken pleasure. One of the captives was sent to the khagan with his hands hacked off. The hands, along with the severed head of another envoy who had been killed during capture, were tied around his neck. He was forced to march through the gate that was watched over by an icon of the Virgin Mary. The third envoy was decapitated on a ship in view of the Persians. His head and a mocking letter were slung ashore.[119] In the course of this Sunday, August 3, one of the Avar leaders, Hermitzis (the *Easter Chronicle* calls him an *exarchos*), came up to the walls and accused the Romans of having murdered the very persons who had eaten the day before in the company of the khagan. The khagan, too, let himself be seen near the walls. In accord with the bizarre etiquette of this battle of life and death, food and wine were sent to him from the city.[120]

All these apparently secondary happenings were moments in an intensive symbolic communication that would be continued during the entire siege. Here too the bloody struggle between besiegers and besieged was being decided. It was more than psychological warfare that was being waged with the aid of gifts, severed heads, threats, and peace overtures. Conflicts are times of intensified symbolic communication, intended to motivate and legitimate one's own side and to discourage the enemy.[121] These signs are not easy for us to decipher. At issue was to give the extreme (and often enough fatal) efforts of individuals meaning and convince them that success was feasible. For this reason, our sources often devote more space to such circumstantial information than to the military activity. On this level, the Virgin Mary was a very real factor in the conflict. That she was subsequently celebrated as having saved the city must have seemed fully justified in the minds of many of those involved.

The battle on the city walls continued all Sunday, then Monday and Tuesday. Theodore Syncellus has nothing much to report about these three days, the sixth to eighth of the siege. In the *Chronicon Paschale*, one folio recounting the events of Monday, August 4, to Wednesday, August 6, is missing.[122] It was presumably Monday night when a flotilla of Slavic dugouts at Chalae attempted to effect the marine transport of the Persian contingent. The Byzantine ships were initially hampered by unfavorable winds, and the Slavic rowers were able to reach the

Asian shore. Yet the superiority of the Roman navy finally determined the outcome. Most of the crews of the dugouts and their Persian passengers met their deaths on the attempted return crossing.[123]

This effort to cross the Bosporus was the only direct Persian contribution to the siege. Theodore recounts that the Avars had their heavy cavalry drawn up on the shore of the Bosporus. This gesture was answered in kind on the other side. Thus, writes the Syncellus, enemies attacked the city from both Europe and Asia. But this parade was no more than a mere show of power.[124] The Persians do not appear to have had ships at their disposal. Their strategic goal was above all to weaken the Byzantines and to induce Heraclius to abandon his plans for an offensive.

From Wednesday, August 6, onward, the barbarian attacks increased in strength on all sides. The khagan wanted to force a showdown. Fighting continued that night as well.[125] On Thursday Patriarch Sergius was once again on the city walls in the midst of the fighting with the miraculously painted image of Christ.[126] The battle was concentrated in the Blachernae quarter of the city, where one end of the city wall meets the Golden Horn. On land the Avar army had taken up a position near the Church of Mary, outside the Theodosian Walls.[127] Fire, trumpets, war cries, and the din of battle accompanied a major onslaught on the fortifications.[128]

Yet this was not the decisive battle. The khagan's troops attacked the bulwarks stubbornly yet without success. The attackers' hopes were now concentrated on a mass landing of dugouts on the poorly protected shore of the Golden Horn. Accompanying the Slavic rowers were heavily armed foot soldiers, in particular Bulgars.[129] Reportedly Slavic women were also among the rowers, whose corpses were found floating in the water after the battle.[130] The Slavic boats covered the Golden Horn like a net, almost turning it into dry land, people would later remember.[131] The attack on the water was also concentrated on the Blachernae quarter, the northwestern corner of the city.

Against the Slavic boats the Byzantines engaged biremes and triremes, while the larger ships remained out in the Bosporus. Accounts of the course of the battle are not in full agreement. George of Pisidia and Theodore Syncellus describe a bitterly fought battle at sea, in which the Roman ships first turned in flight but later carried the day.[132] Other sources have a stratagem at their focal point. Nicephorus relates that at Bonus's command the Slavs were sent fire signals that they thought were the khagan's orders to attack.[133] The *Chronicon Paschale* mentions a similar ploy toward the end of the battle: Armenian sailors who made a sortie lit a fire near Hagios Nikolaos, which the Slavs erroneously took to be a sign from the Avars that they could find refuge there. Many Slavs then crossed the bay and fell into the ambush prepared by the Armenians, who cut everyone down. In this way the Romans were able to pull the dugouts up on land.[134]

Modern accounts usually follow Nicephorus's version of a premature Slav attack due to Byzantine trickery.[135] In any case, all sources agree that the fate of the city was determined—as would be the case repeatedly later—at sea. The Slavic boatmen were defeated, as they had already been a few years before in the port of Thessalonica. From a hill and on horseback, surrounded by armed men, the khagan had closely followed the battle on the waters of the Golden Horn. After the battle, as the *Easter Chronicle* tells it, the enraged khagan had the last survivors from the massacre on the Golden Horn cut down to a man.[136] This was a basically impotent reaction by the all-powerful barbarian prince to the fact that the failure of the "naked Slavs" was inevitably tied to his own. Many of the boat crews had not fought with the utmost determination. They jumped into the water, hid themselves under their overturned boats, or tried to save themselves by diving away. Many succeeded in making it to the other shore and in disappearing into the surrounding hills.[137]

When defeat was certain, the khagan rode back to his camp before the city walls and struck himself on the breast and cheeks.[138] He made arrangements for an orderly withdrawal. Throughout the night the barbarians burned their siege machines so that the next day thick clouds of smoke lay over the city. Some church buildings were also burned down, among which the Church of Cosmas and Damien, which had already been plundered in 623. Miraculously, as was reported, the Church of Mary in Blachernae remained unharmed. When the Persians saw the fires, they believed that the city had been taken. As Theodore Syncellus assumed, they followed the spectacle with mixed feelings, taking great pleasure in the fall of the enemy capital but at the same time begrudging the khagan this success.[139] They hardly imagined that only a few years later, Heraclius would enter their own capital.

Rarely do the potential and the limits of the Avar Empire become so decipherable as in the accounts of the siege of 626. Over the years, the khaganate had achieved an impressive diversification of its forces. Apart from Avar and Bulgar cavalry, the siege army comprised Slavic infantry and boatmen, Gepid fighters, and siege engineers. These forces were well fed and coordinated; steppe empires had always been expert in logistics and in the organization of movements. The siege of Constantinople was the most ambitious enterprise, and the ultimate test of this multitask army. However, the military and political integration of these multiethnic and hierarchically ordered forces had remained precarious. That created a clear military disadvantage. The Avars' greatest asset, the armored horsemen, do not seem to have contributed much to the siege. Every once in a while, Avar cavalry units were allowed to parade back and forth outside the Land Wall or on the shore of Sycae. The deadly rain of arrows, which had decided so many battles in the open field, could have little impact on the bastions of the imperial city, though. The khagan could hardly put his core troops at risk in the carnage at the walls. The main role of the Avar cavalry, then, seems to have been to supervise the assault troops in the first lines and to prevent them from turning back. Cutting down desperate Slavs fleeing from the death trap in the Golden Horn was hardly an act of frustration about the lost battle, but must have been the set task of the Avar horsemen, in order to keep the fighting going on. The relationship of the khagan and the Slavs, who were supposed to rake the chestnuts out of the fire for him, was strained. The misunderstanding about the fire signal symbolizes the difficult communications.

There were a few further shortcomings in the awe-inspiring array of the siege army. The Avar siege machines were, despite considerable progress in decades of siege warfare, not in the same class as the superior Byzantine military technology. Furthermore, the Persians' commitment to the cause seems to have been limited too. Shahrbaraz had not made any provisions that would have put the Persians in a position to contribute to the siege. Like the khagan, he apparently had reservations about risking too many casualties in his army.

The "dog," as the Byzantines called the khagan, was then obliged to take the road home. But before he left he sent another delegation to the Byzantines. He was not drawing back out of fear, he informed them, but because of a lack of food supplies. He now had to assure the victualing of his troops, and he would soon be back.[140] Feeding the gigantic army was surely a problem and had contributed to the need for a quick decision. The siege of Thessalonica in 586 had failed within a week because of supply problems. The Byzantines knew that the emperor's brother Theodore was approaching with a relief army. Bonus informed the khagan that he had been authorized to treat for peace up to this point; from now on the imperial army would accompany the Avars on their retreat, and a peace accord could be negotiated in their own homeland.[141] In fact, we do not know whether a peace treaty was concluded after the siege at all; the hostages were only ransomed by Maria, the emperor's sister, years later.[142]

The course of the withdrawal in 626 corresponded almost exactly to the events after the siege of Thessalonica some years earlier: the burning of siege engines and of some churches and buildings outside the walls, threats of new attacks, and at the same time a resumption of negotiations. On Friday, August 8, only a few horsemen from the rearguard were to be seen before the walls. Some claimed that the withdrawal of the Slavs had forced the khagan to abandon the siege.[143] This is not unlikely; without them, the siege could not go on. He still had the power to hold his army together to some degree for an orderly retreat. Yet the signs of disintegration were all too visible, even to the Byzantines. Bonus had to prevent the city dwellers from going out from the walls to chase barbarians on their own initiative. Even women and children were participating in devil-may-care sorties.

As the rearguard drew off in the course of Friday, Patriarch Sergius arranged a first procession of gratitude to the Golden Gate, from which one could observe the clouds of smoke that roiled over the battlefield.[144]

Even before the siege, Patriarch Sergius had started to promote his narrative of the events, if we are to believe the retrospective accounts: pleas for divine protection of the city, for instance, by prayers, by processions, and by putting up icons of the virgin above the city gates. In the absence of the emperor and his army, that seemed all the more necessary to boost the morale of the defenders. After victory, this allowed developing a coherent narrative of divine intervention. Most of the surviving sources come, in fact, from the patriarch's inner circle. In these texts, the Avars assume the usual role allotted to pagan steppe peoples in a drama of salvation history much larger than their attacks. The siege of 626, unlike many other events in the period, did not only strike the note of divine punishment, but also allowed the highlighting of God's grace and Mary's benevolent intervention. In spite of their heavily didactic and apologetic bias, these accounts contain enough circumstantial detail to inspire some confidence in their factual basis. The year 626 was a shared memory of the citizens, and in their joint recollection the events could not simply be reinvented. The shaping of social memory in the patriarch's interest had to be more sophisticated.

Soon after the events, the patriarch's close collaborator, Theodore Syncellus, presented this argument in elaborate form in his *Homily on the Siege of Constantinople*.[145] On a basic level, there is a good dose of antibarbarian/antipagan rhetoric against "the dog," "the leech," "a demon in human form," "the child of the devil" (the khagan), and "the devil" (Chosroes), and a plot building up extreme danger and final deliverance. Unsurprisingly, Theodore explains the siege as a punishment for the sins of the citizens, who were then saved by the direct intervention of the Virgin.[146] More subtly, his narrative of events consequently ascribes agency to Mary, and ultimately to God, but achieves this without a hint of *Kaiserkritik*: the emperor and his son, the patriarch Sergius and the master of soldiers Bonus, and the defenders altogether, armed with prayers, are credited with their commitment to the cause and with their circumspect actions.

However, there is also a more sophisticated exegetical agenda in Theodore's text. His account is full of Old Testament prophecies and parallels, which he fashions to fit the argument. The two main passages used as prefigurations for the events of 626 are Isaiah's warnings to King Ahaz of Judah, surrounded by enemies (Isa. 7), and Ezekiel's prophecy of the raid of Gog and his riders on Israel (Eze. 38–39). The apocalyptic prophesies about Gog and Magog were often used to explain the appearance of mounted warriors from the north in late Antiquity, and likened, for instance, to Goths and Huns; these identifications were often quite controversial. Around the time of the siege, in ca. 620, Isidore of Seville identified the Goths with Gog on etymological grounds in his *History of the Goths*.[147] The implication here was that even apocalyptic foes could be harnessed to the cause of Catholic Christendom. No such perspectives exist for the Avars in Theodore's account. One of his arguments, and a quite unusual one, for connecting Gog and the Avars was that both were "a multitude of peoples."[148] His concern was with arguing that both Isaiah's and Ezekiel's prophecies actually foreshadowed the siege of Constantinople. Although he never expresses that explicitly, by implication the capital was the New Jerusalem. After the Persian capture of Jerusalem in 614, arguing that "Old Jerusalem" could not be the object of Old Testament prophecies any more must have seemed a pressing agenda, and it came with a clear subtext of anti-Jewish polemic.[149] Even though the Jews in Palestine were now supported by the Sasanians at the expense of the Christians, Old Testament Israel was irretrievably gone; the future of biblical Israel lay in Christian history. Therefore, God had saved the Christian "navel of the Earth," Constantinople.[150] Theodore proposed nothing less than a Christian imperial ideology for an empire under pressure, which would later be useful for "an empire that would not die."[151] Even centuries later the Byzantines still remembered August 7 as the day the city had been freed from barbarian oppression, an event that was celebrated with the famous Akathist Hymn, one of the best-known liturgical hymns in the orthodox world.[152]

The Avars also appear in one of the most successful texts of the period, the so-called Apocalypse of Pseudo-Methodius, written in Syriac in ca. 690; it was soon translated into Greek and Latin and became widely diffused. The text pretends to be a brief history of the world written in the fourth century and continued with extensive prophecies, some of which were in fact retrospective; among others, predicting the final defeat of the "Ishmaelites," the Arabs. In a list of earthly kingdoms that had come to an end—Hebrews, Babylonians, Egyptians, Macedonians—it also states: "The kingdom of the barbarians, that is the Avars and the Turks, armed itself against the Romans, <and> the latter were swallowed up by it."[153] This is followed by the demise of the Persian kingdom and the rise of the Ishmaelites. Thus, in Syria at the end of the seventh century the Avars could still be regarded as an apocalyptic enemy of the Romans, surely a vague memory of the siege of 626.

Byzantine authors fade out the further fate of the defeated Avars in 626 and the following years; with the withdrawal from Constantinople, they more or less disappear from the picture. The decisive stage in the war against the Persians commanded the attention of contemporaries. The inner conflicts that crippled the Avar Empire would only be noted in the margins. In the spring of 629 George of Pisidia speaks in his poem concerning the recovery of Jerusalem of the bloody disputes between the "Scythians" and the Slavs that had made it impossible for them to fight on the same side.[154] It is debatable to what extent the Byzantines could have exploited this strategic advantage better.[155] But the narrow window of opportunity of five years[156] would hardly have sufficed to reestablish Byzantine rule in the Balkans. From 634, the Arab expansion constituted an even greater threat to the empire. They severely limited the long-term possibilities of Byzantium's Balkan policy. Not least among the consequences was that the stricken khaganate could survive the defeat of 626 and the difficult conflicts that followed it. While the first Turkish khaganate succumbed to Chinese offensives in 630, its "Varchonite" enemies maintained a less conspicuous but resilient presence in central Europe for almost two more centuries.

7.4 Samo

In 623 Chlothar II, king of the Franks, who had outlived all his Merovingian rivals, put his son Dagobert on the throne of a diminished Austrasia east of the Ardennes and Vosges Mountains.[157] Cut off from the core of Frankish territory, Dagobert became involved with the eastern fringe of his kingdom. The duchies east of the Rhine, especially Bavaria and Thuringia, were drifting away from Frankish rule; engaging them in joint projects on their Slavic frontier may have been one way to reestablish common ground. It is surely not by chance that in Fredegar the first mention of the new king is in the account of Samo's rebellion, which is treated extensively.[158] The so-called *Fredegar Chronicle* is the only text (apart from others that depend on it) that mentions Samo, the Slavic rebellion against the Avars, and Samo's later victory against Dagobert.[159] This narrative has important functions in the fourth book of the *Chronicle*. The successful rebellion represents the great hopes put into Dagobert when he became king in Austrasia; the bad handling of the Frankish conflict with Samo exemplifies the disappointment with him when he ruled the entire Frankish realm; and Samo's death in 659 (if we follow the chronological indications in the text) seems to be the latest dateable addition to the *Chronicle*.[160] For the author, these events in the distant lands of the Wends were not just peripheral affairs.

However, the narrative of Samo's rise to kingship leaves the Frankish political context aside, and Samo is presented as a simple traveling merchant. "In the fortieth year of Chlothar's reign, a certain Frank named Samo joined with other merchants in order to go and do business with those Slavs who are known as Wends."[161] Few statements in the chronicle have been so exhaustively discussed. To the extent that Samo's Frankish origins were not simply dismissed, the surprisingly precise localization of Samo's origins, *de pago Senonago*, was variously interpreted as Soignies in modern Belgium or as Sens in Burgundy.

The lower Franconian Saal(e)gau has also been proposed.[162] An origin for Samo in the Frankish-Slavic border zone is quite an attractive hypothesis, although bound to remain speculative.

Opinions are divided as to Samo's intentions on his journey to the Slavs, who at that time were already in open revolt against the Avar Empire. Only some scholars have taken Samo's *neguciantes* to have been simple merchants. Others speculated that they had been sent by Dagobert to support a rebellion against the Avars.[163] The terminology is clear: it was not an official embassy, which Fredegar would have called *legatio* or similar. Of course, the dividing lines between merchants, adventurers, and political envoys may have been fuzzy under the circumstances. Trade with the barbarian world was a political issue, especially when arms and slaves were involved. Some years later, it was precisely the murder of Frankish *neguciantes* that was seen as a casus belli between Dagobert and Samo.[164] In the other passage of the fourth book of Fredegar where *neguciatores* is used, Queen Brunhild buys a slave girl from them, who eventually becomes the wife of Theudebert II, Brunhild's grandson.[165] It is not unlikely that in the conflicts around Samo, the control of a profitable slave trade was at stake. Traders' bases *in terra Sclavorum* could turn into centers for political aggregation and were of some strategic importance; as Jiří Macháček has argued, the Moravian state of the ninth century was based on a much more extensive trade network.[166] In any case, Samo and his associates must already have had good contacts in the lands of the Slavs. Without further ado they joined the battle on the side of their trading partners.

Fredegar gives an extensive account of the repression of the Slavs by Avars spending their winter in Slavic settlements. The sons of Avar warriors with Slavic women had now grown up. These *filii Chunorum* were also the first to rise up in arms against the empire of their fathers. Whatever the sources for this story were, it does not sound implausible, given that poor treatment of Slavs and their growing resistance also feature in Byzantine accounts of 626. The *Chronicle* dates the rebellion and Samo's involvement in it to the fortieth year of Chlothar's reign, 623–24. This dating would mean that already before the great siege of Constantinople a secessionist movement was under way in the far western reaches of the Avar Empire. The year 623, when the Avar army first marched on Constantinople, could have provided an opportunity. Yet the rather legendary and chronologically error-ridden account of events in the Lombard kingdom that Fredegar also dates to Chlothar's fortieth year treats above all of the fall of King Adaloald in 626. It is perfectly possible that Samo's revolt happened only after news about the failed siege had reached the country. In 626, the political constellation in the Frankish kingdoms was still the same: Dagobert governed Austrasia, while his father Chlothar II ruled the rest of the Frankish realm.[167]

In the battle against the Avars Samo proved his great *utilitas*, so that the Wends (as Fredegar calls the Slavs) were finally able to prevail. "Recognizing his utility, the Wends made Samo their king."[168] The concept of *utilitas* unites military competence with other leadership qualities. The choice of Samo is certainly also an expression of the Wends' Frankish option. Dagobert could provide rear cover against the Avars, which was at first indispensable. In addition, appointing Samo made it easier to balance interests among the various tribal and regional entities. A Wendish king with his roots in one of these groups would hardly have been able to maintain his supremacy so long, once the solidarization effect caused by the Avar war had worn off. Samo's rule initially entailed a certain dependence on the king of the Franks. Samo did not contest this fact, even when some years later he came into open conflict with Dagobert.[169]

Samo quickly understood how to enhance his position among the Wends. In a series of battles against the Avars the new kingdom established itself against its former rulers. Internally, Samo confirmed his position through a series of political marriages. His twelve Wendish spouses that Fredegar mentions may mean that he wished to gain support by marrying into the leading clans. Rulers of steppe kingdoms also frequently had several wives. In any case, Samo succeeded in maintaining his rule for thirty-five years. His kingdom has been regarded as "the first Slavic state," and it surely represents an important step in the emergence of more complex Slavic societies.[170] After his death, the kingdom collapsed, lacking an uncontested successor among Samo's many sons and an institutional tradition on which to draw.[171]

When Dagobert succeeded his father to the throne in the rest of the kingdom in 629/30, expectations were high: "Even the people who lived on the Slav-Avar frontier earnestly desired him to come to them. They confidently promised that he should dominate the Avars and the Slavs and all the other peoples, up to the frontier of the Roman Empire (*usque ad manum publicam*)."[172] The spectacular victories of Heraclius in the years before, and the crisis in the Avar khaganate, seem to have spurred imperial ambitions at Dagobert's court. Fredegar implies that the initiative had come from the eastern duchies, but the agency was surely Dagobert's.

Frankish *neguciantes* had been robbed and killed in the lands of the Slavs, which could serve as a pretext for war. Dagobert sent his envoy Sycharius to demand satisfaction of Samo. Fredegar has Sycharius enter a verbal duel with the Slavic king, which amounts to an exemplary case of early medieval international relations. However reliable the information in this account might be, the dialogue shows that when Fredegar wrote, different ways of dealing with the unruly neighbors in the east had become an issue in the kingdom of the Franks. Samo initially refused to receive the envoy, at which the latter dressed as a Slav and thus appeared before the king. In the name of Dagobert he demanded compensation for the murder. With "heathen vainglory" Samo refused such restitution but instead proposed *placita* (an assembly to negotiate a formal settlement) between the two parties.[173] In so doing he wanted to clarify other matters of contention at the same time. Such negotiations must clearly have implied parity between the two parties. Sycharius became angry at this and reminded Samo in the sharpest words that he owed the king of the Franks *servicium*, service.

Samo was offended, which did not prevent him from giving a diplomatic answer: "The land we occupy is Dagobert's and we are his, on condition that he chooses to maintain his friendly relations with us."[174] Sycharius, "sicut stultus legatus" (like a foolhardy envoy), reacted with insults. "It is impossible for Christians and servants of the Lord to live on terms of friendship with dogs." At this the king of the Wends threw the ambassador out with the announcement that the dogs could rend the flesh of God's disobedient servants with their teeth. Sycharius did not follow up on the ambiguity that lay in Samo's words. Samo did not at all deny the tie to the Frankish king, which, however, he formulated in quite general fashion without the use of technical terminology. His call for *amicitia* did not contradict this. As understood in the early Middle Ages an *amicitia* was conceivable between parties who were not peers.[175] The double assertion that both the land and the people were Dagobert's was not completely devoid of content, as long as the interests of the Wends were protected and as far as possible furthered. Just like the annual payments of the Byzantines to the Avars, the diplomatic traffic between the Franks and Samo was eased by the elasticity of the late Roman terminology in which they communicated. This normally permitted both sides to save face. It was not until one of the parties took the claims that derived from its own view of the legal situation too seriously that matters escalated into conflict.

It is interesting that Fredegar qualifies Sycharius's behavior in extremely critical fashion. For him, he was a "foolhardy envoy" because he got into questions of interpretation with Samo, which could only lead to contention. To an extent, the author tries to exculpate Dagobert: the peoples on the frontier were pushing him to an offensive, and his envoy made war inevitable by his arrogant stance. The implication is that Dagobert was about to lose control, and that had fatal consequences on his foreign policy.

However, the ensuing attack on Samo was not an undesired consequence of failed negotiations but part of a well-prepared major offensive. Dagobert had safeguarded his eastern policy by international diplomacy. In 630 a Frankish embassy returned home after the conclusion of an "eternal" alliance with Constantinople, the first in the seventh century about which we have concrete information.[176] It may have been a routine mission announcing Dagobert's succession to his father in the entire kingdom, but it was remarkable enough to be mentioned in the *Chronicle*. Dagobert had also gained Lombards as his allies. The partner in this policy was apparently not the Lombard king—the royal administration in Pavia had never cared much about conditions on the Slavic frontier—but rather the *dux* of Friuli, where one had always pursued external affairs quite independently.

When war broke out in Dagobert's ninth year, 631 or 632, three armies marched into Slavic lands.[177] Fredegar's account is not quite clear on that point; he mentions the main Austrasian army and the Alamanni under Duke Chrodobert. In addition, there were the Lombards, who moved against the Slavs.[178] According to an account in Paul the Deacon, two sons of Duke Gisulf II occupied "the region called Zellia up to the place that is called Meclaria."[179] Localization and chronology are contentious. The most accepted interpretation identifies *Meclaria* with Maglern in the Gail Valley (*Gailtal*), near the border between Austria and Italy, where a fort with an unknown name lay in late Antiquity. The *regio Zellia*, probably the (lower?) Gailtal, has been associated with the river name *Gail*.[180] The tribute obligations of the Slavs of Zellia were maintained into the time of *dux* Ratchis about 740. The end of this relationship is best explained by the beginnings of Bavarian supremacy over the Carantanians.[181] No more exact dating of the Lombard advance to *Zellia* can be given. Taso and Cacco followed their father Gisulf II in about 611. By 625 they seem to have fallen victims to an intrigue of the Byzantine exarch, if Paul the Deacon's vague chronology of those years is to be trusted.[182] On the other hand, a successful Lombard attack on the Slavs in their neighborhood is more likely to have taken place in the troubled years after 626; on that premise, it would be tempting to identify the occupation of *Zellia* with the Lombard support for Dagobert in 631/32.

Like the Alemannic force under Chrodobert, the Lombards conquered their Slavic opponents and took a great number of captives. Less fortunate was Dagobert's main army, which besieged the Wends in the *castrum* of *Wogastisburc* for three days in vain and was finally beaten off into flight. This otherwise unknown fort was often sought in the vicinity of Kadeň/Kaaden in northern Bohemia, but its localization remains hypothetical.[183] Fredegar makes the lack of commitment on the part of the Frankish army and the Austrasian notables responsible for this defeat; the latter were to enforce a fresh division of the Frankish kingdom two years later.[184] The lost war led to a decisive weakening of the Frankish position on the Slavic frontier. Dervan, *dux* of the Sorbs, until now a Frankish vassal, attached himself to the successful Wendish king.[185] Thuringia and some regions under Frankish control became targets of Slavic raids. The king of the Franks had to renounce the tribute from the Saxons, and Thuringia began to push for independence.[186]

The high hopes for Frankish expansion in the east had come to nothing, and within a few years, the eastern duchies were on the defensive and drifting away from the Frankish kings. The *Fredegar Chronicle* presents these as crucial years for a deplorable loss of cohesion in the Merovingian kingdoms: the failure of the formerly good king Dagobert to deliver on his promises, and his increasing neglect of Austrasian concerns. The Samo stories are emblematic in that respect. Still, the *Chronicle* seems to downplay the role of Dagobert in these events: he has no part in Samo's rebellion, he is under pressure from the eastern duchies to launch an offensive, and the war on Samo is provoked by the murder of traders and by an intemperate envoy. We may wonder whether there was a more coherent policy behind all that. Can stirring rebellion against the Avars in the precarious period after 623 have something to do with Byzantine incentives to Dagobert, after all? Could the intention in 631/32 initially have been to attack the Avars with Samo's support, *servicium*? Was the "stupidity" of the envoy Sycharius in failing to negotiate the modalities of such an alliance? Were the nine thousand Bulgars accommodated in Bavaria (see section 6.5) part of an ambitious plan to attack the Avar heartlands, and were they murdered after the plan had to be called off? If Dagobert had such a grand strategy, Fredegar has successfully obscured it, and we can only regard this option as a highly speculative alternative narrative. All we know for sure is that things went wrong for the Franks, and that Samo's position was greatly enhanced.

The location and extent of Samo's kingdom continue to be debated. The center of the kingdom is generally sought in Bohemia or Moravia, but sometimes also in Lower Austria or western Slovakia.[187] The extension of Samo's power, before and after 631, is also a matter of discussion. Frequently, what was soon to become Carantania (modern Carinthia and Styria) is regarded as a part of his realm, which could be deduced from the Lombard participation in Dagobert's war.[188] Did Samo's domain really extend from the Elbe to the Karawanken range, or was it a more regional formation on the Frankish frontier? Samo's successful self-assertion against the two neighboring great powers was scarcely a local event. Revolt against the Avars involved a wide-reaching area between the Carpathians and the Alps, and Dagobert's campaign required widespread mobilization, something a recalcitrant princeling on the Frankish border could scarcely have provoked. Samo's royal title, in Fredegar's perception, signifies that his rule was accorded a higher rank than the *dux* of the Sorbs or of the *marca Vinedorum* (Wendish march) possessed.

On the other hand, Samo's capacity to establish stable supraregional control was limited. To the extent that his policy represented a shared interest to curb Avar and Frankish influence in Slavic lands or coordinate raids into neighboring regions, he could surely put into the field a considerable military force for the occasion. Marriage alliances helped to align a number of autonomous units to the king of the Wends. However, the position of the "first Slavic king" had no institutional foundation, and his supremacy can scarcely have been much more than a certain preeminence. With the death of the ruler about 660 his kingdom collapsed.

In the current state of research, it seems most likely that the core of Samo's kingdom was in Bohemia or Moravia. The embroilment with the Franks, the alignment with the Sorbs, and the frequent plundering raids into Thuringia and Saxony make it seem unlikely that Samo's kingdom was situated on the middle Danube. Other regions seem to have been more or less loosely attached. The "*dux* of the Wends" Valluc, who most probably ruled over what would be called Carantania in the eighth century, and Dervan, duke of the Sorbs, may have subjected themselves to Samo at some point. Such an alliance could go back to the common struggles against the Avars and must have proved advantageous against the continuing Avar menace. As was the case elsewhere in Slavic settlement areas, local and regional polities remained fundamental for further developments. Still, Samo's victories on the western flank of the Avar Empire had created room for the emergence of independent Slavic groups, a space that lasted far longer than his kingdom. In the wide areas where neither the Avar nor the Frankish power could assert themselves for the rest of the seventh and most of the eighth century, a more or less self-contained development of bigger and smaller Slavic communities could now take place. Similar spaces opened up in much of the Balkan Peninsula, where both Byzantium and the Avars had lost control. Strikingly, in the early seventh century, all three hegemonial powers in Europe, Byzantium, the Franks, and the Avars, lost control over large areas they had so far dominated, almost at the same time.

7.5 Croat Migrations?

In many eastern European nations, ancient and medieval origin stories were used to elaborate modern national myths; results of scholarship were incorporated into these myths in eclectic ways. Few European countries, though, developed such a variety of national origin myths as Croatia: migration or autochthony; prehistoric, ancient, or early medieval immigration; Illyrian, Gothic, Iranian, or Slavic origins. Predictably, the creation of an independent Croat state and the war in Yugoslavia led to a resurgence of pseudo-scientific narratives of national origin. They often relied on similarity of names, exploring a range of identifications going far back beyond the scope of this book (for instance, with the Hurrians of the second millennium BCE).[189] This makes the topic of this chapter uncomfortable; any argument for or against an early medieval Croat migration, or on the meaning of the ethnonym, may encourage fantastic reconstructions of a deep past of the Croats that contradict the main contention of this chapter: that no Croat people is discernible in the region before the later ninth century.[190]

Still, this section is placed here because an important source offers an account of Croat settlement in the seventh century. In the tenth century, Constantine Porphyrogenitus dated the arrival of Croats and Serbs in the Balkans to the reign of Heraclius; therefore, modern historical narratives of Croat origins have often dated the arrival, or the secession, of the Croats in the years of turmoil in the khaganate around 630. However, there is no evidence of Croats in the region for more than two centuries after that. The German version of this book thus rejected the model of a Croat migration in the seventh century, which also met with the skepticism of other scholars in the 1980s. In the 1988 book, and in some publications that followed, I put forth the hypothesis that "Croats" might originally have been the name of a regional Slavic elite that like Samo's followers, revolted against the Avars in the seventh century, but only gave rise to a "Croat" people and duchy in the middle of the ninth century. I still think that this would be a viable interpretation but have become more skeptical about possibilities to substantiate it.

However that may be, the gradual emergence of a Croat people has meanwhile become widely accepted. Still, a brief overview of the evidence and the debate may be helpful at this point. Nothing very consequential may have happened in the region in the 620s and 630s, and no contemporary source sheds any light on these events. Like elsewhere, Roman urban life in the coastal strip of Dalmatia came to be reduced to a few residual places in the first half of the seventh century, although the exact chronology and the role of Slavs in the process is uncertain (see section 7.1). We only hear of frontier battles between the Friulian Lombards and their Slavic neighbors, and eventually of minor Slavic raids across the Adriatic. We may, furthermore, assume that the rebellions against the Avar khaganate also involved the lands along the Save, but again have no information.

These gaps in our knowledge seem to be filled by what Constantine Porphyrogenitus compiled in the middle of the tenth century, an account of the entry of the Croats and Serbs into their later homelands. The origins of the Croats are treated in two somewhat divergent versions.[191] *De administrando imperio*, chapter 30, recounts that after the capture of Salona the Avars settled in Dalmatia. "But the Croats at that time were dwelling beyond Bavaria, where the Belocroats are now. From them split off a family (*genea*) of five brothers, Klukas and Lobelos and Kosentzis and Muchlo and Chrobatos, and two sisters, Tuga and Buga, who came with their folk (*laos*) to Dalmatia and found the Avars in possession of that land. After they had fought one another for some years, the Croats prevailed and killed some of the Avars and the remainder they compelled to be subject to them."[192] Thus the Croats took possession of Dalmatia, while some split off to settle in Illyricum and Pannonia. In the time of Constantine, there were still some among them who were considered Avars. The Belocroats (or White Croats as the author translates) remained in the vicinity of the Franks, to whose king, Otto I, they were subject. Then follow detailed accounts about the fate of the Dalmatian Croats during the Carolingian period, when they were dominated by the Franks for some time. Yet after the victory over Kotzilis the Croats remained independent and, under the archon Porinos, received baptism from the pope.

The second version in chapter 31 also recounts that the Dalmatian Croats are descended from the White Croats, living beyond the Hungarians, near the Franks. At the time when the Avars had subjugated the Dalmatian Romans, the Croats, like somewhat later the Serbs, turned to Emperor Heraclius, under whose authority they drove the Avars out of Dalmatia (a dating element absent in chap. 30). This led to their being Christianized and receiving bishops from Rome, which occurred under Porgas. Since that time they were subject to the emperor.[193] Here too the first fairly concrete details of the historical narrative are from the second half of the ninth century.

This double account of the migration has led to spirited controversy. In the wake of Dümmler, Slavic archaeology frequently rejected it entirely and presumed the emergence of the south Slavic Croats and Serbs in situ.[194] But many scholars also took Constantine's migration story at face value. In fact, several tenth-century sources confirm the existence of ("White") Croats north of the Carpathians. At that time, similar names are also attested elsewhere. For instance, Constantine's *De ceremoniis* knows of "*Krevatades*" and "*Sarban*" in the Caucasus region. Many historians have thus assumed an Iranian-Sarmatian origin for the tribal core of the Croats. That would also account for the difficulties in explaining the names of the seven brothers and sisters as Slavonic.[195] According to this theory warriors of Iranian descent had subjugated the Slavic population northeast of the Carpathians. A portion of these Croats would then around the year 626 have moved into Dalmatia, where they succeeded the Avars as rulers of the Slavs.

Another option is to discard the dating given in chapter 31 and date a migration of Croats to the northwestern Balkans to the late eighth century, during the war between the Avars and the Franks. Porinos/Porgas can then be identified with the *dux* Borna known from Carolingian sources.[196] Both migration theories face the problem that there is no contemporary trace of long-range population movements in the sources. What we know is that the region between the middle Danube and the Adriatic had become Slavicized from the late sixth century onward; but it is rather unlikely that these Slavs came from north of the Carpathians. The name

Croat, which is hardly Slavic, has been variously interpreted.[197] But etymology will hardly answer the question of the origin of the Croats.

A fundamental problem that all reconstructions have to face is that the name "Croats" is not attested at all in the area until the second half of the ninth century. Before that, the generic terms *gentes* or "Slavs" are used for the inhabitants of the region. In 641 Abbot Martin is en route in Dalmatia and Istria on the orders of the Dalmatian pope John IV "to redeem captives who had been despoiled by the *gentes*." Pope Agathon complains in 680 that many bishops must serve among pagan peoples, both Lombards and Slavs ("in medio gentium, tam Langobardorum quamque Sclavorum").[198] Friuli, in the second half of the seventh century, had to be defended against Slavic incursions, and already in the 640s Slavs who had crossed the Adriatic landed in the duchy of Benevento. Raduald, grown up in Friuli, could speak to them *propria illorum lingua*.[199] The Romans on the Adriatic coast were facing Slavs, but these were not called Croats. There is no trace of a unified (Croatian or Slavic) principality either: there may have been small groups that formed under the leadership of *župans*, as Constantine Porphyrogenitus writes.[200] And there is no trace of a migration from north of the Carpathians at any time in the seventh or eighth centuries in the sources, written or archaeological.[201]

The Carolingian expansion encountered Slavic peoples in this zone, who were mostly named by the Franks after the administrative units of late Antiquity. Borna, the *dux Guduscanorum*, was also called *dux Dalmatiae atque Liburniae*; nowhere is he entitled *dux Chroatorum*.[202] Croats and their dukes only appear in the later ninth century (the exact chronology can be debated).[203]

At about the same time similar names appear in the sources north of the Carpathians, although the name forms in very diverse sources are often far from conclusive and may have nothing to do with the Croats in the Adriatic hinterland. According to King Alfred's Old English translation of Orosius the Daleminzi lived northeast of the Moravians, east of them were the *Horigti*, and to the north the *Surpe*.[204] The *Geography* of Ibn Rusta, who wrote in the tenth century but whose textual transmission is complicated, gives a name for the seat of the Slavic king *Swet malik* (Svatopluk?) that has often been interpreted as *Chrwat*. However, the name forms found in the manuscripts range from *Ǧ.rwāb* to *H.zrāt*.[205] The early twelfth-century *Primary Chronicle* (or *Nestor Chronicle*) of the Rus' lists the *Chorwates* among other Slavic tribes north of the Carpathians.[206] In the eleventh century we hear of Bohemian Croats south of the Carpathians, as in Henry IV's foundation document from 1086 for the bishopric of Prague, where there is a mention of "Chrouati et altera Chrowati."[207]

Traces of a forgotten empire between the Neisse and the Dniester, as Dvornik would have it?[208] The name *Croat*, or similar, also occurs elsewhere. In Carinthia a

Croat district is mentioned in the second half of the tenth century.[209] Place-names attributed to Croats have been found in Carinthia, eastern Germany, Bohemia, Moravia, Slovenia, and Greece, although some of these might be otherwise interpreted.[210] These findings are complicated by the discovery of the similarly widespread occurrence of the name *Dulebi* (northeast of the Carpathians, in southern Bohemia, in Styria) and of the name of the Serbs. Some further Slavic ethnonyms (for instance, Abodrites) are met both north and south of the Carpathians.[211]

All of these names can be found on the periphery of the Avar Empire and of the later Hungarian kingdom. In some cases they may go back to population displacements from the time of the foundation of the Hungarian kingdom in the Carpathian Basin in about 900. Yet some of these traces (like those of the Croats) seem to lead farther back into the ninth century. And as in other instances of identical or similar ethnonyms in eastern Europe and central Asia, they are not necessarily proof of the dispersal of a once-united tribe or people. In the case of the Croats, the ethnonym is not attested in the Balkans or north of the Carpathians before the ninth century, so it is unlikely that a once-united Slavic people was scattered across the periphery of the Avar or Hungarian realm at any one time.

It may, however, be noted that personal names of some similarity are attested in the seventh century in conflicts in which Avars were involved. Interestingly, they occur in similar stories of migration and/or revolt against the Avars. One of them is the Bulgar khan Kuvrat who, according to the eighth-century account of the patriarch Nicephorus, rebelled against the Avars in about 635 and thereby became the founder of "Great Bulgaria" north of the Black Sea.[212] Kuver was the name of a regional leader who revolted against the khagan along with the descendants of Roman captives in Pannonia around 680 and withdrew to Macedonia.[213] These cases, and possible common traits, will be discussed in the following chapters (and we shall return to the question of the Croats toward the end of section 7.7).

In any case, a Croatian migration under Heraclius cannot be regarded as a historical fact any longer.[214] But Constantine's narrative allows us to detect some traces of an origin myth that sought to establish a prestigious position for the Croats by their migration and victory over the Avars. Other peoples and tribes seem to have claimed similar origin stories; Constantine provides information on a number of parallel migrations from lands north of the Carpathians to the western Balkans. These regard Serbs, Zachlumi, Terbuniotes, and Pagani.[215] Again he sets out what was important for Byzantium: The new settlement areas were originally Roman provinces. They were depopulated by the Avar attacks. During the reign of Heraclius groups split off from the unbaptized Serbs beyond the Hungarians (or, in the case of the Zachlumi, from the "Litziki" on the Vistula river) and sought the protection of the Emperor Heraclius. The Serbs were then settled with the help of the *strategos* of Belegradon (probably Belgrade, although that surely is an anachronism). In the case of the Serbs, the origin story has no details. The two brothers under whom the Serbs divided up are without names, and their successors up to Boieslav also go unnamed.[216] Probably the Serbian origin story was only constructed in Byzantium in analogy to that of the Croats. As in the Croatian chapter, a more detailed historical narrative does not go back any earlier than to the middle of the ninth century, when Blastimer, Boieslav's grandson, waged war against the Bulgar khan Persian (who likely died in 852). In western sources the *Sorabi*, "a people said to occupy a large part of Dalmatia," are first mentioned in the *Royal Frankish Annals* for 822; the term Dalmatia is surely intended in the sense of the ancient province here.[217]

The degree to which this complicated story has been taken seriously varies considerably. Jireček rejects it out of hand; Dvornik and Stratos accept it almost entirely.[218] An origin for the Serbs of the seventh century in the northern Carpathian foothills could be supported by the fact that Sorbs are attested along the middle Elbe at that time.[219] Equally conceivable is that the equation of Serbs and Sorbs originated at a much later time.[220] The stereotypical emphasis on the origin of the Balkan Slavs in the pagan regions of the north first of all corresponds to the Byzantine world view that each settled *ethnos* possessed a double homeland: one on the far side of the imperial frontier, where heathen peoples dwelled—"Greater" (*megalē*/*maior*) Scythia, Bulgaria, Moravia, etc.— and one on imperial territory, where they became part of the Christian ecumene (the *Scythia, Gothia minor,* the Sklavinias, etc.).[221]

This ideological interpretation of the settlement of the Croats, Serbs, and others on imperial territory stands in the foreground of Constantine's description. It helped the Byzantines to couch the deplorable fact that former Roman provinces had long been lost to foreign peoples in a Christian teleology (these people had arrived to be baptized) and in an insistence on Byzantine agency (Heraclius had settled the barbarians on Roman territory). Thus, it allowed maintaining the pretense that all these territories rightfully belonged to the empire. *De administrando imperio* is thus not just a chronicle that arose out of a love of antiquarian lore but has above all a practical, political dimension. The core of the account is that Heraclius, through his legalization of the Croatian and Serbian settlement on imperial lands, created a new legal status for them within a Christian Byzantine commonwealth.

Compared to this, the enumeration of the places of origin, just like the fanciful etymologies of ethnonyms, are secondary matters. In addition, a careful and categorical distinction is being made between Avar plunderers and the new, legitimate inhabitants.[222] Perhaps locating the original homelands of the Croats and Serbs at such a great distance should help to maintain this distinction and avoid the impression that the settlement of raiders had been retroactively legitimated. The fact that the smaller peoples were also counted among the Serbs does not quite correspond to reality, even for the tenth century, as Neven Budak has shown. For the ninth century the sources display a multiplicity of regional ethnic groups between the Adriatic and the valley of the Morava and in no sense two large and uniform Croat and Serbian states.[223]

The population history of the northwestern Balkans, and the ethnic processes involved, can thus be reconstructed in several rough stages. Danijel Dzino has underlined that there were two separate processes: in the seventh and eighth century, "the process of acculturation between the indigenous population and the immigrant groups, 'becoming Slavs,' which resulted in the transformation of the cultural habitus that was perceived by outsiders as 'Slav,'" and, in the ninth century, "the development of complex political entities, 'becoming Croats.'"[224] In the sixth century, the western part of the Balkan Peninsula had been quite densely populated with hundreds of mostly smaller fortified hilltop settlements, although these decreased from Macedonia northward.[225] In a first stage, from the late sixth century onward, Slavs immigrated in the wake of Avar armies and began to settle in the country. Gradually, they pushed Roman control back to a few coastal strongholds, and the ancient infrastructure collapsed, whereas a ruralized population remained, which displays elements of regional continuity.[226] The capture of major urban centers may have required some Avar support (a direct involvement of the Avar army in—inland—Dalmatia is attested in 595, see section 5.5). Avar control surely was strongest in the Save Valley and faded out toward the coast.

In a second stage, after 626, the Slavic population in the former province of Dalmatia, and perhaps also some of the Avar warriors operating in the region, more or less freed themselves from Avar domination. But in the process, no larger units (such as Samo's kingdom or the principality of Carantania) became prominent here. To a degree, the Avars seem to have retained or reestablished their hegemony along the Save and remained the only power to reckon with in the area. The remaining post-Roman population was gradually Slavicized, although we have no clue at which point they began to regard themselves as Slavs.[227]

The third stage was precipitated by the fall of the Avar Empire at the end of the eighth century, in which some of the Slavs of the region were involved. In the course of these events, some degree of migration may have added to the ethnic quilt in the northwestern Balkans, but large-scale movements are unlikely. The Franks were interested in the establishment of stable and dependent regional Slavic units along their periphery. This led to the development of principalities more or less under Frankish control, some of which the Franks simply knew by the name of the duke or his main stronghold (Liudevit at Siscia), while others were defined by reference to regional/ethnic groups (Borna, duke of the *Guduscani* and *Timociani*).[228] The duchy of the Croats emerged somewhat later, when Frankish control was already eroding, which allowed gradually establishing a less ephemeral polity.

On the whole, consolidated Slavic regional powers and their ethnic designations were later to appear between the middle Danube and the Adriatic than elsewhere (for instance, the Carantanians or the Moravians). It also needs to be said that the name "Croats" did not enter the political language of the (Eastern) Frankish state until the twelfth century. The name is not mentioned in the Carolingian annals or in Ottonian historiography. Otto von Freising's *Gesta Friderici* is the first relevant work of Frankish/German historiography that speaks of "Croatia" (though not of "Croats").[229] Croats are mentioned in the *History of the Venetians* by John the Deacon, written around 1000 (the first time in an entry for the year 912), although Venetian historiography usually speaks more generally about Slavs or "Dalmatian peoples."[230] This evidence contradicts any notion of a "Croat" state established in the seventh century, whether by immigration or on a local basis. Croat ethnogenesis seems to postdate the establishment of the political unit in ancient Dalmatia. The name may go back to the period of the crisis of the Avar Empire after 626 as a term designating social status. This possibility will be discussed at the end of section 7.7, after presenting the cases of Kuvrat and Kuver.

7.6 Alciocus and Kuvrat

The situation in the Avar Empire after the defeat before the walls of Constantinople is rather reminiscent of the struggles after Attila's death. In both cases the issue was hardly, as long believed, a quasi-nationalistic uprising of oppressed tribes against a nomadic ruling people.[231] In 454 the rupture seems to have cut right across the ruling elite of mounted warriors, including Attila's sons. If the dissension could subsequently be interpreted in ethnic terms, this was rather because some of the resulting fracture lines developed over time into ethnic differences. In the case of the Hunnic Empire the composition of the various entities is relatively easy to reconstruct on the basis of Jordanes's account.[232] After the battle at the Nedao, Gothic and Gepid kings succeeded relatively quickly in reestablishing clearly delineated political units, while rather mixed dissident groups withdrew to Roman territory. Our information on the power struggles after 626 is much patchier, but attractive alternative centers of power, led by their own kings, did not emerge in the Avar Empire. The Avar khaganate was not replaced as the central political organization even when it had greatly lost in prestige.

This is the background to Fredegar's account of the internal conflicts in the empire of the Avars. He situates the following events in the ninth year of Dagobert's rule (631–32), after the war on Samo. This dating may not be precise, yet the repeatedly proposed shift to the years 635–36 presumes an unlikely identification of this conflict with Kuvrat's Avar war, which is narrated rather differently in Nicephorus.[233] "In this year a violent quarrel broke out in the Pannonian kingdom of the Avars or Huns. The matter in dispute was the succession to the throne (*de regnum*): one of the Avars and another from the Bulgars collected a numerous army and fought each other."[234] As the text is phrased, the objective of the Bulgar contender was not to replace the Avar khaganate by a Bulgar one, but to succeed to its throne. We know nothing of any form of organization that would have gathered all the Bulgars under Avar rule (like the Gepid or Gothic kings under the rule of Attila had done). Still, in Fredegar's view it was an ethnic conflict, and "the Avars overcame the Bulgars" and expelled them from Pannonia. The Bulgar warriors, reportedly nine thousand strong, fled with women and children to the Bavarians. The Frankish king Dagobert, contacted by the fugitives, initially provided for the Bulgars to be accommodated in winter quarters, distributed across Bavaria. But then he ordered them all to be wiped out. Only Alciocus with seven hundred men, women, and children succeeded in fleeing to the *marca Vinedorum*, where he spent many years under the protection of Walluc, the *dux* of the Wends. The *marca Vinedorum* was very likely the region later called Carantania; the Slavs to the northeast of Bavaria were ruled by Samo, while a *dux* Walluc could have easily ruled over the Alpine lands to the southwest.[235]

Many historians consider the Bavarian version of the St. Bartholomew's night massacre simply a legend.[236] It is quite possible that the mass killing has been exaggerated, and it is difficult to conceive that more than eight thousand warriors and their families could have been wiped out in one night. Yet otherwise the story fits well into the political world of about 630. The inner conflicts in the Avar Empire at this time are attested to by several sources. We also know of Dagobert's interest in the eastern borderlands. The unfriendly treatment of the asylum-seekers may reflect a modified strategy of the Frankish king. Instead of supporting, as previously, the secessionist movements in the Avar khaganate, he attacked his earlier protégé Samo in the year when the Avar war of succession ended. He may have wished not to anger the Avars, and it is not unlikely that the new khagan had sent an embassy protesting against the reception of his Bulgar enemies. The Bulgar refugees may then have fallen victim to the improved relationship with the khaganate in a deal in which Dagobert sought to gain support against Samo.

More than thirty years later, according to Paul the Deacon, a *Vulgarum dux* with the quite similar name Alzeco came to Italy with his army and offered his services to King Grimoald (662–71). As a consequence the Bulgars were settled near Sepino, Boiano, and Isernia in the duchy of Benevento, which at the time was ruled by Grimoald's son Romuald.[237] Alzeco had to renounce his title of *dux* and was integrated into the Lombard nobility with the rank of *gastald*. Alzeco's dukedom has often been understood as a Byzantine title, and from this it has been concluded that the Bulgars were deserters from the imperial army.[238] Yet Alzeco's status "with the whole army of his dukedom," *cum omni sui ducatus exercitu*, corresponded to that of a *dux gentis*, an autonomous, nonroyal barbarian leader. With his subordination to a Lombard duke he had to forfeit this autonomous position of power.[239] The descendants of Alzeco's Bulgars were apparently still speaking their own language, as well as Latin, at the end of the eighth century. Paul the Deacon also enumerated Bulgars, in an unusual context, among the subjects of the Duke of Benevento, Arichis II (758–87), in a panegyric poem: *Apulus et Calaber, Vulgar, Campanus et Umber*.[240]

Recently, unusual archaeological evidence has come to light in a cluster of three cemeteries at Campochiaro, some forty miles north of Benevento: Vicenne, Morrione, and Tratturo. From the beginning, it has been connected with Alzeco's Bulgars. At Vicenne, in a cemetery otherwise rather typical of Lombard Italy, twelve horse burials (out of 167 graves) with harness and metal stirrups were found; the percentage of horse burials in the other cemeteries is lower.[241] Stirrups and horse burials occur elsewhere outside the steppe realms, but the layout corresponds in many respects to Avar practice. The apparel buried with the riders is mixed: traces of bows and arrows that are rare in Italian cemeteries of the period, and there are several further parallels to objects found in early Avar cemeteries such as Zamárdi, Hegykő, or Bócsa.[242] The material has been dated to the seventh century; coin finds are from the second half of that century. Even though an ethnic identification is always problematic, these very particular horse burials in southern Italy could hardly be explained without assuming that this group of riders had arrived from the Carpathian Basin or around it (the archaeological evidence alone does not allow an ethnic identification). Parallels with the Black Sea steppes are less significant, and the evidence does not suggest the following of one of Kuvrat's sons. It is remarkable that the cemetery is very close to Boiano, a place where Alzeco's group was settled according to Paul the Deacon's report. It is rare that written reports and archaeological sources correspond so closely in the early Middle Ages.

The similarity in names is a strong argument for identifying the Italian immigrant Alzeco with the refugee of 631, or with his son or successor. Perhaps the name is also to be understood as a title of rank or office. Alciocus could easily be explained by Turkic *alti-oq*, "six arrows." Alternatively, as Margetić has suggested, the Alzeco story may have been inserted into Paul the Deacon's *History* in the wrong place, and he may have joined Grimoald and Raduald earlier, when the younger sons of Gisulf II of Friuli won the duchy of Benevento in the early 640s.[243]

While Alciocus and his Bulgars were residing with the Slavs of the Alps, far to the east, the rise and fall of a Bulgar empire was taking place, the *megalē Bulgaria*, "Great Bulgaria" on the steppes of the Black Sea, over which Kuvrat ruled.[244] The history of Kuvrat's empire, which is sometimes mentioned together with the Avars in the sources, is a puzzle, the chief pieces of which will be reviewed in the following.

1. The patriarch Nicephorus writes in his *Brevarium* (in the late eighth century) that Kuvrat, the nephew of Organa, ruler of the Onogundurs, rose in revolt against the khagan of the Avars and drove all the members of this people from the country. He then concluded a peace accord with Heraclius, which both observed throughout the rest of their lives, and he was named *patricius* by the emperor.[245]

2. John of Nikiu has an account of the troubled times after the deaths of Heraclius (February 11, 641) and his successor Constantine III (May 24, 641), during which the imperial widow Martina and her son Heracleonas opposed Constantine's son Constans. A rumor in Constantinople had it that "*Ketdrates*, the ruler of the *Muntanes*, the nephew of *Kuernake*," who had been baptized in Constantinople and grown up there (presumably as a hostage), supported Martina and her sons. For he had grown up in Constantinople and had been baptized, had overcome all the heathen peoples, and had always been on friendly terms with Heraclius. The somewhat garbled name is usually referred to Kuvrat, the nephew of Organa.[246]

3. Clearly drawing on a common source, Nicephorus and Theophanes write of the origins of the Bulgars. The *palaia Bulgaria hē megalē*, old Great Bulgaria, was situated on the Sea of Azov and along the *Kuphis*, where the *Kotragēs*, a people related to the Bulgars, also dwelled. Theophanes goes on: "In the days of Constantine, who dwelt in the West, Krobatos, the chieftain of the aforesaid Bulgaria and of the Kotragoi, died leaving five sons." In what follows he gives an account of the fate of the five sons, who against the express wish of their father go their separate ways with their followers. The first, Batbaian (according to Theophanes) or Baian (Nicephorus) remains "until the present day" in the land of his father. The phrasing suggests that the source for the two ninth-century chronicles lies in the late seventh century. The second son, Kotragos,

crosses the Tanais/Don and settles down opposite the former. The fourth and fifth sons, who remain nameless, go to Pannonia and Ravenna, respectively, and the third, Asparukh, crosses the Danaper/Dnieper and Danaster/Dniester and reaches the Danube.[247]

4. At an earlier point in his chronicle Nicephorus tells how the ruler and *archontes* of an unnamed Hunnic entity were baptized in Constantinople, and the prince received the title *patrikios*.[248]

5. A Bulgarian list of rulers, preserved in a late medieval chronicle but perhaps drawn from an older tradition, contains quite different information about the Bulgar rulers. After the mythical rulers Avitohol and Irnik, in whom we likely have reminiscences of Attila and his son Ernak, follows Gostun, the "viceroy" from the Ermi clan, who ruled for only two years. Thereafter followed Kurt for sixty years, Bezmer for three years, and Esperih for sixty-one years, with whom the series of Danube Bulgar princes begins. All three were from the Dulo clan.[249]

6. A very rich grave was found at Mala Pereshchepino (Malaja Pereščepina) near Poltava, in northern Ukraine. The monogram on the ring has been deciphered by Werner Seibt as "*Chobratou patrikiou.*" The coins of Emperor Constans minted between 642 and 647 and the chronological parallels of the finds support this identification, although it has sometimes been doubted.[250] The hoard contains, among others, Sassanid silver bowls from the fourth century and the silver chalice of Paternus, a bishop in Tomis around 520; Byzantine and Persian silver tableware; and a golden drinking horn and pseudo-buckles that have close parallels in Avar graves (see section 7.8). The richness and nature of the grave goods point to an influential ruler who was in close relations with Byzantium.

The pieces of the Kuvrat puzzle can be put together in various ways. We can use them to reconstruct a "maximal" Kuvrat, who was baptized in Constantinople in about 620 (or who grew up there as a hostage), then succeeded his uncle Organa, rebelled against the Avars, after which in an alliance with Heraclius and as a Roman *patricius* he built up his Pontic kingdom, dying sometime after the death of the emperor. The "Hunnic" ruler appointed *patricius* around 620 could also have been his uncle Organa.[251] Some of this reconstruction is hypothetical and has been doubted.[252] However, the parallels between the accounts in Nicephorus and in John of Nikiu (in spite of the garbled Ethiopic names) are too close to be easily discarded. Of the "minimal" Kuvrat we can at least say with some certainty that he was Organa's nephew, that he ruled over the northeastern shore of the Black Sea during the last years of Heraclius and the first of Constans II, and that he was well-linked with Constantinople. Organa must have been his predecessor and already enjoyed good relations with Byzantium; probably Kuvrat had acceded to the throne not very long before the rebellion in about 635. It is well attested that he died during the rule of Constans II (642–68). An early death during the 640s seems unlikely, given the lasting reputation that Kuvrat acquired; a death date in the 660s would link up more smoothly with the fates of his sons.[253]

The location of Kuvrat's realm has been debated on the basis of the information given in Theophanes, who circumscribes the location of Old Bulgaria by a confusing mix of topographic features, most prominently, the *Kuphis* river and the Maeotic Sea, but also the Volga, the Don, the "Cimmerian Bosporus" (the Strait of Kerch), the "Ram's head" (the southern promontory of the Crimean Peninsula), and *Necropela* (the gulf at the mouth of the Dnieper). The *Kuphis* has often been identified with the Kuban, an eastern tributary of the Sea of Azov, but now most scholars would rather identify it with the lower Bug River, which runs west of the Dnieper.[254] The location of Kuvrat's grave at Malaja Perščepina is surprisingly distant from the landmarks given by Theophanes. The site lay on the edge of the steppe zone, in the northwestern periphery of Kuvrat's lands. Perhaps he had been forced to withdraw before his death by the expansion of the Khazars.[255] Given his fame in the sources, Kuvrat's empire probably extended across the whole northern coast of the Black Sea.

At any rate, Kuvrat's empire did not long survive its great ruler. It soon came under pressure by the Khazars. In 652 they had been attacked by the Arabs in their city Balanjar on the river Sulak near the Caspian Sea and then removed their capital northward to the Volga. In 659 the remains of the western Turkish khaganate fell victim to a Chinese attack, which must have enhanced the power of the Khazars substantially. Perhaps they were also reinforced by refugees from central Asia. Successively, the Khazars went on the offensive. In the beginning of the 660s they invaded Armenia. Soon after that we may assume the subjugation of Great Bulgaria.[256]

Kuvrat (and before him, his uncle Organa) had succeeded in the first half of the seventh century in uniting the rest of the Onogurs, Cutrigurs, and Bulgars, who had remained on the Black Sea coast, into a Bulgar empire. This was a process of the seventh century, continuing the merging of different steppe peoples subject to the Avar khaganate in the later sixth century. The problems of the previous identity or affinity of the Onogurs/Onogundurs, Cutrigurs, and Bulgars, on which so much acuity has been spent (see section 2.2), contributes little to a better understanding. The Onogurs, Cutrigurs, and Bulgars of the sixth century were not identical with one another, while in the seventh century, after their merging, the name Bulgars dominated, sometimes still in the compound Onogur-Bulgars.

The power politics that framed this process are not quite clear. If we credit Nicephorus, Kuvrat freed himself from Avar rule around 635. If we assume that the region around the Sea of Azov had been the core of Kuvrat's Magna Bulgaria, that piece of information does not seem to fit. It would be surprising if the area had remained under Avar control until 635. After Baian's migration from the Caucasus to the Danube there is little indication of Avar influence north of the Black Sea. The khaganate had difficulties with the Slavs on the lower Danube and with the Antes northeast of the Carpathians.[257] The steppes north of the Black Sea were controlled by the western Turkish khaganate, to which the Utigurs and Ogurs were subjected. About 576 Turxanthus captured the city of Bosporus/Kerch.[258] It is conceivable that with the decline in Turkish power the Avars could have increased their influence on the Pontic steppe after 602, but hardly as far as the Sea of Azov. After 626 their role as a hegemonial power was over. In the same period, Turkish control is documented over the routes to the Caucasus. The Turks crossed the Caspian Gates in 627 and 628 into Persarmenia, where they supported Heraclius in the siege of Tiflis.[259] Thus, it has often been assumed that Kuvrat freed himself not from Avar but from Turkish rule, and that Nicephorus made a mistake.[260]

However, just as the Avars and the eastern Turks, the western Turkish khaganate descended into a deep crisis in ca. 630. In Étienne de la Vaissière's reconstruction, the leader of the Turkish army who came to the aid of Heraclius, Ziebel, was Sipi, the brother of the supreme western Turkish ruler, Tong (T'ung) Yabghu Khagan, and second in rank after him. After his raids on Sassanid territories, Sipi murdered Tong in 628. In the following year, he was in turn overthrown by Tong's son, and the western Turkish khaganate lapsed into a period of internal strife. It was now divided into five clans of the Duolu (T'u-lu) and five of the Nushibi (Nu-shi-pi), which together made up the ten shads, or, in Turkic, the On oq.[261] Turkish presence north of the Caspian Sea and the Caucasus continued, and blended in some way into the ascendance of the Khazar khaganate.[262]

What does that mean for the rise of Kuvrat and his Bulgars? It is remarkable that the Bulgarian list of rulers assigns Kurt/Kuvrat to the Dulo dynasty. Is that a chance parallel in widely different sources, or could Organa and Kuvrat have been Turkish leaders left to their own resources north of the Black Sea when the western khaganate crumbled, who managed to secure a new power base by unifying the "Bulgar" groups in the Pontic steppes? However that may be, a Bulgar liberation struggle against the Turkish khaganate in ca. 635 seems unlikely in the periphery of an empire in the process of dissolution. The assumption that Nicephorus was after all correct and the establishment of a large-scale Bulgar realm provoked a conflict with the Avars is, on the other hand, not implausible after all. What is unlikely is that the theater of such a struggle could have been somewhere east of the Dnieper. However, the issue could have been hegemony.

The Avar claimant to the throne of the khagan in 630 had defeated a strong Bulgar faction inside the khaganate. Many of them may have found refuge with Organa and Kuvrat. Just as Baian, in the years around 560, had systematically sought to establish his superiority by defeating all surrounding barbarian powers, including the Franks, Kuvrat must have had a vital interest in challenging the unsurpassed prestige of the Avar khagans. Yet the Avar ruler also had a few reasons to risk a war: legitimize his rule after the initial succession conflict, regain the initiative, reassure his own following, and stop an emerging competitor; perhaps he was also worried about strong contingents of Bulgar refugees, as in the case of the Franks. A war would not have been about the possession of territories, but about precedence and hegemony. In that sense, the Avar defeat was as consequential as the failed siege of Constantinople. It established the Bulgars as the superior power in the European steppe zone. It is surely no coincidence that at that point, the latter phase of the early Avar period brought a growing influence of styles current in the Pontic steppes, and that even Byzantine material now reached the Carpathian Basin via the Black Sea region.[263]

The account in the *Chronicle of Nicephorus* is therefore perhaps not quite exact, but it describes a logical development: the passing of symbolic hegemony in the steppe from the Avars to the Bulgars. Immediately preceding this passage the text speaks of Maria, the sister of the emperor, exchanging envoys and gifts with the Avars in order to ransom her son Stephanus, who had been given as a hostage in 623. "Pleased with such gifts, the Avar [chief] urged Anianos the magister that he, too, should send gifts and ransom the other hostages he was holding; which, indeed, was done."[264] Diplomatic contacts between Byzantium and the Avars were still going on, and in spite of all turmoil, the hostages had been kept safe at the khagan's court. The information on the fight between Kuvrat and the Avars may go back to the these hostages. This Avar perspective might explain an ongoing claim of Avar supremacy, and the strange phrase that Kuvrat had been "abusing the army that he had from the latter [the khagan of the Avars]."[265] It also means that the war had perhaps happened before 635. However, it was hardly the same conflict that Fredegar mentioned. Except for the fact that both cases deal with Bulgars fighting against Avars, the brief accounts of Fredegar and Nicephorus have little in common. In Fredegar the issue is the succession in the Avar khaganate; in Nicephorus it is driving off the Avars. Fredegar locates the fighting in Pannonia, Nicephorus in Bulgar lands at the Black Sea coast. Fredegar has the Avars victorious and the Bulgars in flight, while for Nicephorus it is the Avars who are chased off.[266] The long-term effect of the two conflicts was also different: in the Carpathian Basin, the Avars maintained their rule for almost two centuries; but at the Black Sea coast and in the vicinity of Byzantium, the Bulgars prevailed. That the Byzantines around 800 associated the rise of the Bulgars with the fall of the Avar Empire was thus thoroughly justified. The Bulgars in the steppes of eastern Europe were thenceforth the main northern partner and enemy of Byzantium.

7.7 Kuver and Asparukh

With the severe internal conflicts after 626 the khaganate lost its hegemony over the central-eastern European barbarian world. On the lower Danube and in the Balkan provinces local and regional Slavic groups and principalities strengthened their positions; eventually, some entered into contractual relations with Byzantium. Regional Slavic areas in Macedonia are mentioned in the *Miracula S. Demetrii*, and the "Seven Tribes," among them the Severians, appear in Moesia when the Bulgars subdued them at the end of the seventh century.[267] Along the western Avar frontier regional power centers began to form in the Eastern Alps (the *marca Vinedorum* and later Carantania) and in Bohemia/Moravia (Samo's kingdom). The relatively large-scale political organization of the Slavs between the Elbe and the Alps, which expanded rapidly under Samo around 630, could not be consolidated. Still, the "Wends," as they are now often called in Latin texts, had become familiar. Fredegar employs Frankish political terminology when he writes of *reges, duces,* and the *marca* of the Wends.

In the Carpathian Basin itself, the khaganate held on to power despite internal conflicts. One reason for this resilience was the weakness of the other great powers. Far from being able to initiate a consistent Balkan policy again, the Byzantine Empire fell into new difficulties from 634 on, a few years after the end of the thirty-year Persian war, because of the Arab advance. The Frankish kings, after the renewed divisions of 633 and 639, no longer pursued an active eastern policy and had to recognize the practical independence of the eastern duchies, Alamannia, Bavaria, and Thuringia. There is an almost complete absence of information on Bavaria in the seventh century. The Lombard kings after Rothari (636–52) gained some ground against the powerful *duces* and the exarchate but continued to be tied down on both fronts. Like Bavaria, Friuli was too weak for a policy of expansion and was still threatened by occasional maneuvers of the king. Overall, the seventh century in Latin Europe was a peaceful age with few major interstate wars, in spite of frequent inner conflict.

In a regionalized Europe, the Pannonian region had lost much of its geo-political importance. The devastated city of Sirmium was no longer the key to Italy or the Balkans, as in the time of Theoderic. For Constantinople the pacification of the Slavs on its own doorstep was now more important than the events on the middle Danube. The Carpathian Basin had changed from a zone for ethnic agglomeration to a steppe enclave. It was perhaps a catalyst for a series of decentralized ethnogeneses in eastern central Europe but was no longer at the focal point of the power balance between the barbarian world and the provinces of the empire. The tension between the rich lands of the south and west and the ambitious and specialized warlords on their northern and eastern borders had almost subsided, and with it, the strategic role of Pannonia. The vital nexus between the Avars and the empire was broken in 626, not so much by the defensive success of the Romans as by the near complete leveling out of the differences between former Roman and barbarian territories. The urban economy was now restricted to a few staging points on the coast; the rest had become loosely settled farmland. Supraregional connections had lost much of their significance.[268]

This shrinking of the horizon had undermined the position of the Avar Empire as a great power. Yet it also prevented its collapse. The changed conditions made the growth of a new power even more difficult than the continuation of the old one, which could draw on the wealth of the khagans, accumulated in more prosperous times. The ruralization of vast regions was both a basis for and result of Slavic expansion. War ceased to be a full-time profession; without regular booty, gifts, and subsidies, many Avar warriors had to become farmers, a process documented in the archaeological evidence.[269] In this way the economic basis of the Avar Empire could be assured, but its offensive power declined. Information about the Avars in the admittedly sparse sources of the time is then a rarity.

After 630/35 we scarcely hear of the khagans for thirty years. Not until the 660s do they start to make news again. As repeatedly before, the Avar Empire was drawn into internal Lombard politics. Like under Agilulf, a peace accord was concluded with the Lombards, to which the khagan ascribed some importance. In 662, when the overthrown king Perctarit fled to the Avars after the usurpation of Grimoald, the Lombard king needed only to call on this agreement and the refugee was asked to leave, although not actually extradited.[270] A mere threat to revoke the pact was sufficient for the khagan to back down. Paul the Deacon even speaks of an "order" from Grimoald (*cacano . . . per legatos mandavit*). By contrast, the Franks, among whom the fugitive finally landed, would exploit the opportunity to invade northern Italy with military force.[271] Still, Perctarit remained grateful to the khagan for granting him temporary asylum. Almost thirty years later, when he had reconquered the throne, he told the visiting English bishop Wilfrid of the hospitality of the Avars. In his account, the khagan had sworn by his pagan gods that he would never hand over the fugitive. When the envoys from Perctarit's enemies arrived and offered a bushel full of gold coins (*aureorum solidorum modium plenum*), the pagan ruler refused to extradite him, claiming that the gods would destroy him if he broke his oath.[272]

Grimoald, who continued to have all kinds of difficulties to contend with, soon decided to put the khagan's observance of the treaty to a further test. Lupus, *dux* of Friuli, who had already plundered Byzantine Grado, had taken advantage of Grimoald's expedition against Emperor Constans in southern Italy (663) to rise in revolt against the king. Grimoald now adopted a tactic that had cost his father, Gisulf II, his life. He invited the Avars to march against Lupus. Again, Paul uses the verb *mandare*, "to order," in this context.[273] It would seem that the Avars were not considered very dangerous at this time. The Avar army did in fact mobilize; Lupus engaged it near Flovius (probably on the Vipava), and in a three-day battle was beaten and fell.[274] Paul had allegedly heard from eyewitnesses of the heroic exploits of the *dux*, who now, like so many of his predecessors, paid for his ambitions with his life.

As half a century earlier, the Avars devastated the open land, while the Lombards retreated into their forts and castles. After some days, Grimoald's envoys ordered their allies, who had now done their duty, to leave Friuli again. The latter now insisted that they had taken possession of the land by right of conquest. But in Paul's narrative, a bluff on the part of the king was all that was needed to make the khagan withdraw. Grimoald had his small army repeatedly parade in front of the Avar delegates and voiced some unmistakable threats. Whether this story is drawn from the author's store of anecdotes or not, the Avars did not let matters come to a confrontation and soon retreated from Friuli.[275] The transitory occupation of Friuli did not then spring from any well-reflected expansion policy but only from an attempt to exploit a favorable moment. Perhaps envoys from Emperor Constans had encouraged an Avar engagement against the Lombards. In any case the activities of Constans II in the west seem to have temporarily reinforced the interest of Byzantine politics in the Avars, for Byzantine coins of the 660s and 670s are more frequent than before and after.[276]

The remaining acts of the Friulian drama were played out without Avar participation. Lupus's son Arnefrit fled in the face of Grimoald "ad Sclavorum gentem in Carnuntum, quod corrupte vocitant Carantanum" (to the people of the Slavs in Carnuntum, which they erroneously call Carantanum). Paul is taking his bearings from the geography of Antiquity, as befits an intellectual of the Carolingian period. It is uncertain whether the name of the Carantanians comes from a seventh-century source or whether it has been added by Paul.[277] At any event, the passage is evidence that the alpine Slavs had more or less defended their independence from the Avars, while the contact zone with the Lombard kingdom on the upper Save was probably under some sort of control of the khagan. Arnefrit attempted to win back the paternal duchy with Slavic support but fell in battle near Nemas/Nimis, north of Cividale. The location of the battle points to Arnefrit's troop having come from Carinthia through the Valcanale.

The new *dux*, Wechtari, who knew how to rule *suaviter*, "gently," quickly won the sympathies of the Friulians to his side. He is reported to have repelled a further Slavic attack with just twenty-five men on one of the bridges over the Natisone.[278] The account shows that the unruly neighbors to the north now preoccupied the imagination of the Lombards along the frontier, but they were not accounted equals as opponents. Shortly thereafter, if we follow the order of Paul's narrative, Alzeco entered Italy with his followers.[279]

In the following chapter, Paul reports the accession of Emperor Constantine IV in 668. Under his rule, the last diplomatic contact between emperor and khagan is documented. In 678 an Arabic fleet was defeated before Constantinople. "When the inhabitants of the West had learned this, namely the Khagan of the Avars as well as the kings, chieftains, and *gastaldi* who lived beyond them, and the princes of the western nations, they sent ambassadors and gifts to the emperor, requesting that peace and friendship should be confirmed with them."[280] Even if part of the intentions of the source were to emphasize the great number of dignitaries that were to be found at the court, the passage is nonetheless characteristic for the transformed conditions on the Danube and Adriatic. The khagan was clearly the most prominent figure and the only one to be mentioned with his people's name. Yet there existed as well a multitude of bigger and smaller groups with a variety of forms of organization, which maintained independent relations with the empire. The title *gastald* points to a Lombard embassy. In addition there would have been Slavic *gentes* who had in the meantime become autonomous political players. This Avar mission surely brought solidi of the emperor home as a countergift.

However, these diplomatic contacts had little practical significance. Those Slavic groups that lived within range of the Byzantine army would perhaps want to preclude any intervention on the conclusion of the Arab war. For good or ill, the Avars had little to expect from the Romans. There is no trace of an alliance against the Bulgars, which would have been an obvious Roman concern. Yet the emperor only confirmed his "imperial peace."

In the meantime, eastern Europe went through another wave of political reshuffling that had been triggered by the fall of the west Turkish khaganate in 658/59. The Khazar khaganate came to dominate the steppes north of the Caucasus, and the Bulgar Empire north of the Black Sea disappeared. The story of its dissolution is framed in the sources as the separation of five brothers, each of whom moved elsewhere.[281] Batbaian, Kuvrat's oldest son, was soon subjugated by the Khazars, who extended their empire across the entire northern coast of the Black Sea. Kotragos crossed the Don and settled on the other side (from the following, it would appear that this was east of the Don). Perhaps it was mainly this group who migrated north along the Volga. Asparukh went over the Dnieper and the Dniester and eventually into Byzantine territory. The two further brothers remain nameless; one is said to have become subject of the Avar khagan in Pannonia, the other of the empire in the Pentapolis of Ravenna. Tsvetelin Stepanov has recently argued that Asparukh, who obviously inherited the title of khan and the main part of the army, must have been Kuvrat's youngest son and that the fourth and fifth brothers were an addition in the text.[282] In a late adaption of the motif of the migration of Kuvrat's sons in Michael the Syrian, there are in fact only three brothers.[283] In any case, the most tangible and durable effect was the establishment of Asparukh's Bulgars on the lower Danube. According to Nicephorus and Theophanes, they first stopped in the *Onglos*, a marshy area surrounded by rivers, which has been located in southern Moldavia, in Wallachia, or in the Dobrudja.[284]

More distant sources connect the Bulgar advance with the decline of Avar power in the area. According to the *Armenian Geography*, Asparukh, fleeing the Khazars, reached the island of Peuke in the Danube delta and pushed the Avars to the west.[285] This hardly refers to an actual conflict between Avars and Bulgars but can be understood in the same terms as the general observation in Michael the Syrian that the Bulgars had occupied districts once frequented by the Avars.[286] From the Byzantine perspective the Bulgars were the successors to the Avars as enemies on the Danube. The Armenian and Syrian sources hardly disposed of otherwise unpreserved information about Bulgar-Avar clashes but used the reference to the Avars as a means to organize the ethnogeographic dimension of events, as was customary in the ethnography of Antiquity.

It is likely that some Bulgars had already settled in the area near the delta of the Danube, whether to the south or to the north of the river, for quite some time before Asparukh emerged as their successful leader—after all, the victory of the Khazars had already happened around 660.[287] Whether Asparukh had actually led a Bulgar army directly from the area of Khazar expansion to the Danube is hard to ascertain, although this would conform to established practice in steppe empires. The chronology is difficult to reconstruct. In any case, Asparukh's Bulgars began raids into the peripheral regions of the empire. Constantine IV, after his victory over the Arabs, marched against them in 680. Yet the Bulgars hid in the marshy areas of the Danube delta, and the imperial offensive evaporated. The emperor, suffering from gout, withdrew to Mesembria to convalesce, at which point the abandoned army began to break up. Bulgar attacks turned the retreat into panicked flight, and Asparukh's army took a firm hold south of the Danube.[288]

In the following years, the Bulgars organized their new khanate in the former provinces of Moesia inferior and Scythia minor. Archaeological evidence allows us to circumscribe their initial settlement area quite precisely; it is a relatively small region north of the Balkan Mountains, stretching from Varna to both sides of the Danube between Svištov and Silistra.[289] It is quite probable that they could also rely on Bulgars already present in the area since the time of the Avar raids. But most of all, the region had been settled by Slavs. Six of the Slavic "Seven Tribes" were resettled in the south and west of the Bulgar realm, "as far as the Avaria." Nothing is said here about the location and extent of the "Avaria" but it is generally held that the defenders of the Bulgar borders were settled between the rivers Timok and Isker.[290] If this were the case, "Avaria" would have begun west of the Iron Gate and would also have included the old *limes* forts in the region of Viminacium and Singidunum. But perhaps the geographic notions of the Avar realm had already become vague. Or, consistent with the former use of such ethnogeographic terms, the name Avaria, otherwise never used in Byzantine sources of the entire Avar Empire, only designated a small stretch of former imperial territory around Sirmium and Singidunum later controlled by the Avars.

While the great ecumenical synod was being held in Constantinople in 681, Emperor Constantine was forced to conclude a peace with the Bulgars. The establishment of the Bulgars between the Danube and the Balkan Mountains is often held responsible for the rupture in relations between the Avars and Byzantium. In any case solidi of Constantine IV are the last Byzantine gold coins to be found in Avar graves.[291] Still, we should not simply explain the winding down of Avar–Byzantine relations by the formation of the Bulgarian Empire. This constellation could also have been a reason for forming an alliance against the new neighbors. But the means for such a strategy were lacking in Byzantium, and the khagans could content themselves with maintaining the status quo—more or less. Power politics on the grand scale were no longer being played out on the Danube and the Tisza.

Furthermore, in the years around 680, as it seems, the khagan again had to face internal difficulties, at least if we believe the extensive account of another miracle worked by St. Demetrius at Thessalonica.[292] In spite of the hagiographic stylization, this report is very detailed and on the whole plausible. A Roman-barbarian *ethnos* that lived in Pannonia revolted. According to the *Miracula*, it had formed under Avar rule from the descendants of Roman captives, Bulgars, and Avars, and Kuver had been placed at their head by the khagan.[293] Now, the rebels wanted to find their fortune in Byzantium and marched south. The khagan pursued them but, over five or six battles, was defeated and had to draw back with the remainder of his army to the north. The victorious Kuver crossed the Danube (or the Save) with his followers, continued moving south, and set up on the Keramesian Plain, between Bitola and Monastir.[294] From here, many of the Christians planned to go back to the cities of their forefathers.

Kuver, on the other hand, wanted to remain the "leader and khagan" of his army and pursue his own power politics. He did what many barbarian military leaders had done before him once on imperial territory: he sent an embassy to the emperor that requested a grant of the area now taken in possession. The emperor agreed, and the Slavic Drogubites in the vicinity were instructed to provide Kuver's army with food supplies. This shows that Slavic farmers now had to maintain the system for provisioning an army operating in formerly Roman provinces. However, many of Kuver's Christian followers now began to move to Thessalonica. He then decided secretly to take control of the city and on that basis to construct a substantial kingdom. To this end, he tried a stratagem. One of his *archontes* by the name of Mavros, a multilingual man who spoke Greek, Slavonic, Bulgarian, and Latin, was to appear to defect from him, settle with his followers in Thessalonica, and then at the most favorable moment turn the city over to Kuver.[295]

The structure of the *Sermesianoi*, as the newcomers were called after their origins around the city of Sirmium, reflects conditions in the Avar Empire. At the head was Kuver, whom the Greeks defined as *archōn*, leader, and who wished to establish himself as khagan by extending his power (the sources employ the Avar title *khagan*, not the Bulgar *khan*). He obviously shared his power with other *archontes*, among whom Mavros. Decisions were reached in common consultation. An *archōn* such as Mavros had his own retinue, estates, and several wives.[296] He was later regarded as a Bulgar but bore a Greek name (or one translated into Greek). His prominent position among the barbarians also guaranteed, as was customary, a high rank in the Byzantine army, where he was appointed by imperial command *strategos* over the army of the *Sermesianoi*.[297]

Once again the intervention of St. Demetrius was needed to protect the city from the machinations of such a powerful man. In fact, the intentions of Mavros to deliver the city to Kuver are the most doubtful element in the story; this plan was never carried out. Instead, Mavros made a splendid career in imperial service. The *Miracles* recount that on imperial orders he and his retinue of *Sermesianoi* were taken by ship to Constantinople, where he received a military command (perhaps in Thrace). It was Mavros's son who later revealed the plot to seize Thessalonica to the emperor, at which point the would-be or presumed traitor was relieved of his command. His son probably succeeded him. The report about Mavros's career is confirmed by independent evidence. The seal of a Patrikios Mavros, "*archōn* of the *Sermesianoi* Bulgars," has been preserved. A *patricius* of this name again played a role in affairs at Cherson in the last phase of the reign of Justinian II in 710–11, but it is not clear whether he was the same man. He was apparently called Bessos, the Thracian, perhaps because there were two patricians called Mavros.[298] In any case, the agile Mavros had outwitted his accomplice Kuver, of whom we hear nothing more. The *Sermesianoi* were likely settled in the vicinity of the capital, and those who remained with Kuver clearly no longer posed a threat to Thessalonica.

In scholarly literature, Kuver is repeatedly associated with the unnamed fourth son of Kuvrat, who, according to Theophanes, went with his followers to Pannonia.[299] As proof for this hypothesis Beševliev advanced a weathered and hardly readable inscription at Madara, which he attributed to Asparukh's successor Tervel and read as follows: "My uncles at Thessalonica did not trust the emperor with the cut-off nose and went back to Kisiniie."[300] The disfigured *basileus* is Justinian II, who had his nose cut off when he was deposed in 698 but returned to power in 705 with the aid of Tervel. Beševliev believed that Tervel's uncles were Kuver and Mavros, who had declined a similar request for help from the deposed emperor and gave no credence to his promises. But even if Beševliev's reading of the fragment should be correct, his interpretation is very doubtful indeed. It requires a circular argument: identifying Kuvrat's unnamed son with Kuver in order to prove that Kuver was in fact Kuvrat's son. Even if we accept this premise, it runs into a number of contradictions. Why should the Bulgar khan praise his uncles in his inscription for doing the exact opposite of what he himself had done? He had supported and not distrusted Justinian II in his bid for a return to power. Besides, the Mavros who was involved in the throne conflicts around Justinian also staunchly supported him. The inscription also mentions several uncles, not just one, and there is no hint in the *Miracula* (or in Theophanes) that Mavros was Kuver's brother.[301] The Madara inscription, thus, does not help to prove that Kuver was Kuvrat's son. That is an assumption perhaps suggested by the similar name. However, the stories of Kuver and of Kuvrat's son do not match at all. Kuvrat's fourth son is said to have gone to Pannonia, whereas Kuver left the Avar Empire at around the same time. If Kuver was Asparukh's brother, it would have been in the intention of the *Miracula* to highlight that, in order to make the danger from which the saint had delivered the city seem even bigger. In fact, the text does not even state that Kuver was a Bulgar. This is only mentioned in a heading added to the manuscript in the twelfth century.[302]

In spite of these weaknesses in the hypothesis, Hungarian archaeologists have attempted to associate fundamental changes in Avar archaeological culture with the immigration of the son of Kuvrat.[303] This hypothesis clearly has nothing to do with the account in the *Miracula*; the name Kuver has just been borrowed as a tag for an assumed wave of immigration from the east to the Carpathian Basin, which the Kuver story can neither confirm nor disprove. The assumption that Kuver as the son of Kuvrat could have brought a new archaeological culture that remained current in the Carpathian Basin, while Kuver himself rebelled and left after a short while, is highly implausible. Closer to the *Miracula* account was the hypothesis by Joachim Werner that the treasure from Vrap in Albania was a khagan's treasure stolen by Kuver, but it has mostly been refuted on archaeological grounds.[304]

Only two Bulgar groups that emerged from the collapse of the Kuvrat empire are more or less historically verifiable: Those Bulgars who remained on the Black Sea and were in part absorbed in the Khazar Empire, in part escaped to the north and there can be traced from the ninth century on the Volga and in the *mavrē Bulgaria* ("Black Bulgaria") mentioned by Constantine Porphyrogenitus.[305] The other group were the Bulgars who settled on the Danube with Asparukh. Beyond this and already in the time of Kuvrat, there were Bulgars in the Avar Empire, the Alciocus group in Carantania and later in Italy, and Bulgars in the Byzantine Empire (among them, the *Sermesianoi*). No cooperation or communication between them is attested. It may well be that new Bulgar groups arrived in the Carpathian Basin after the fall of Kuvrat's empire, but the Kuver story adds nothing to the archaeological debate about the reasons for cultural change in the Carpathian Basin around that time, apart from providing a potentially deceptive narrative.

It is perhaps more productive to assume that the story of the five brothers served as a retrospective explanation for the existence of Bulgar groups in several countries, whether for the Byzantines or the Bulgars themselves. With this approach, the Kuver account, the story of Khan Kuvrat and his sons, and the Croatian migration legend in Constantine Porphyrogenitus (see section 6.5) can be analyzed as ethnic origin stories; the parallels between them are remarkable. The surprising similarity in the names Kuver, Kuvrat (transmitted as Krobatos in Theophanes),[306] and Chrobatos, has tempted many historians into postulating a single identity or a family relationship, which is hardly tenable.[307] Apart from the similar names, all these accounts contain the following characteristic elements, albeit in varying sequence:

1. Division of an existing entity and departure of one group from the old homeland
2. Crossing of the Danube
3. Battles with the Avars and shaking off their rule
4. Subjugation of local (Slavic) groups

Furthermore, both the Croat and the Bulgar origin stories contain the motif of the five brothers. One of the brothers occupies the center. In the story of the Bulgars it is the eldest son of Kuvrat, (Bat)baian, whose name is in turn similar to that of a later Croatian princely title, *ban*. Among the Croats it is the last-named (youngest?) brother who bears the name of his people. This structure may be a reflection of a cosmological model found among many steppe peoples: a center and four cardinal points.[308]

If we understand Constantine's account and the story of the five brothers as fragments of an origin story told from a Byzantine perspective, we avoid the historian's alternative of having to judge the information as true or false. Origin legends have their own truth, which does not consist of a correct rendering of erstwhile events.[309] They represent some sort of communication between members of the group concerned and outside observers, and imply some sense of belonging and historical legitimation. That such legends were not completely malleable is indicated by their lacunas: Unlike for the five sons of Kuvrat, a common ancestor for the five brothers is lacking in the Croatian account.

In all three accounts the victory over the Avars was the decisive step toward the formation of a new ethnic group and its autonomous rule in a former Roman province. The course of such a rebellion can be reconstructed from the Kuver story but also from that of Samo. Both show that it was not a matter of consolidated peoples that rose against the khagan. The leaders of the revolt were the leaders of regional warrior groups once in Avar service. Although this is pure speculation, the name "Croat" in the seventh century was not yet an ethnonym; it may have designated a rank or social status.[310] Eventually it may have become the name for warrior groups on the periphery of the Avar Empire who took control there, such as the *praetoriani* who made possible the restoration of duke Borna's rule in the early ninth century.[311] In the course of time, the name could be used as an ethnonym.[312] We need not even assume actual continuity between successful rebels or regional warlords of the seventh century and "Croat" elites of the ninth; as with the title *ban* that was adopted by the Croats, the retrospective adoption of prestigious names from the Avar past could serve for the legitimation of a recently established political entity. This might also be the sense of Constantine's remark that there were still some who were regarded as Avars among the Croats.[313]

In any case, soon after 626, the history of the Avar khaganate slips into obscurity, and the rare spotlights on isolated events have brought more controversy than reliable knowledge. Slavic and Bulgar groups emerged as alternative political players on the periphery of the khaganate. We know little about their development. Only Asparukh's Bulgarian kingdom became an important partner and rival of the Byzantines in the former Balkan provinces and grabbed most of the limelight in the scant sources about the period. But there is a type of evidence that can give a wealth of information about life in the Avar Empire, which is almost unparalleled in seventh-century Europe: the rich archaeological evidence from the Carpathian Basin.

7.8 Continuity and Cultural Change

The written sources for the seventh century are scant, but they repeatedly mention wars and internal conflicts in the Avar khaganate. In the past scholars used this fragmentary information to date transformations in the material culture; more recently, many have become more cautious. Textual and archaeological evidence cannot simply be joined together like pieces of a puzzle. Rather, they offer different perspectives on a complex reality. Whereas the Avars almost disappear from historiographic accounts after 626 but for a few isolated glimpses, the bulk of the archaeological evidence only sets in around 600. The defeat at Constantinople in 626 marked the end of Avar offensive policy and triggered internal struggles. However, this did not cause a sudden break in the forms of cultural expression. The archaeological evidence paints a very differentiated picture of how the khaganate coped with the challenges posed by the consequences of its defeat.

For the period up to 626, we have detailed written information on the large amounts of gold that arrived in the Carpathian Basin from Constantinople; but the influx seems to have ceased after that. This change is confirmed by coin finds on Avar territory: no less than twenty-five solidi from Heraclius's last issue before 625 have been found, but only five issued between 625 and 641, and none so far from the period between 641 and 651.[314] After the middle of the century, a trickle of solidi sets in again, until it virtually stops after the foundation of Asparukh's khanate in 681.[315] Remarkably, the archaeological golden age in the Avar realm reached its peak after 626, with a substantial number of golden objects in very rich graves from the middle of the seventh century (see below).

Archaeologists distinguish between an early, middle, and late Avar period. A detailed relative chronology of many types of finds is well established, but indications connecting these to an absolute chronology decrease as coins gradually disappear from graves during the seventh century. Nor is the interpretation of coins found in graves and their significance for the dating of the rest of the assemblages uncontroversial.[316] Different archaeologists ascribe particular groups of objects to one or the other period. The dates attributed by scholars to the three periods therefore vary by a number of decades. Many archaeologists have dated the second phase of the early Avar period from ca. 626 to about 670, and the middle Avar period from ca. 670 to ca. 700/10, lasting only about a generation.[317] There is general agreement that the middle Avar period came to an end around 700.[318] This relatively short duration of the middle Avar period is problematic, however, as a considerable number of graves and cemeteries that correspond to the characteristics of the middle Avar period have been discovered. Dating all of these to within a period of only thirty or forty years would imply a sudden substantial growth in population.[319] Falko Daim and other scholars have therefore argued for an earlier beginning of the middle Avar period around 650.[320] An even earlier date can be reached if one includes the horizon of Bócsa-Kunbábony (see below), otherwise regarded as belonging to the early Avar period.[321] As Csanád Bálint has argued, the debates about the onset of the middle Avar period are a methodological example for the impact of historical framing of archaeological interpretation.[322]

What emerges from the archaeological record is that the upheavals around 626 did not cause any major breaks in Avar material culture and is hard to link with the chronology of the phases of the Avar period.[323] Long-term developments in the first half of the seventh century included a continuous trend toward more permanent settlements. An increasing number of larger cemeteries were laid out and continued in use for longer periods of time.[324] Whereas much of the earliest material from the Avar realm shows close links with late antique, Byzantine, and Western (Merovingian or Italian) cultural spheres, in the first half of the seventh century common traits of a particular "Avar" material culture emerge more clearly. In the second third of the seventh century, a closer relationship with the steppe zone north of the Black Sea becomes evident. One of the characteristic elements of this turn to the steppe are the so-called pseudo-buckles, whose purpose is purely ornamental.[325]

The most spectacular Avar graves discovered thus far can be dated roughly to the middle of the seventh century—the only period from which we have evidence of highest-level inhumations so far.[326] The richest grave was found at Kunbábony in 1971, initially believed to be that of a khagan: it was furnished with two gold-trimmed belts, swords, drinking horns, a gold vessel, and a gold-decorated quiver with two dozen arrows.[327] Quite remarkably, it also contained a crescent-shaped golden pectoral similar to pieces found in burials of the Rouran period in central Asia, such as Bikeqi, Galuut Sum, Yihe Nao'er or Khermen-tal.[328] The "princely" burial at Bócsa was almost as rich as Kunbábony and is also located in the northern half of the area between the rivers Danube and Tisza. These gold-rich burials reflect the self-fashioning of an Avar ruling elite that in a time of political stagnation around the mid-seventh century, adopted new forms of representation also current in the steppes north of the Black Sea, now dominated by the Bulgar khanate. The golden pseudo-buckles, as found in Bócsa or Tépe but also at Malaja Perščepina in today's Ukraine, were one of the key characteristics of the rich graves in the Carpathian Basin and in the steppes north of the Black Sea.[329] From an eastern European perspective, Igor Gavrituchin speaks of a "Bócsa-Pereshchepino circle."[330]

Unlike contemporary rich Avar burials in the Carpathian Basin, Malaja Perščepina also contains a fair number of Byzantine objects—such as an entire set of silver tableware and sixty-nine Byzantine gold coins, most of them worked into a golden necklace—but also Sasanian vessels, and a drinking horn like the one found in Kunbábony.[331] It was much richer than Kunbábony or Bócsa, containing about 55 pounds of gold and 110 pounds of silver. This wealth can easily be explained by the identification of the find as the grave of the Bulgar khan Kuvrat; the Greek monograms on two seal rings have been read as his name. The composition of the treasure shows that political momentum now lay with the

Bulgar khans, whose forms of representation in turn influenced the self-styling of the Avar elite. This may indicate that Kuvrat exercised some kind of political hegemony over the Avars. In any case, his success changed the idioms of power and prestige in and beyond Kuvrat's sphere of domination north of the Black Sea.[332]

Whereas the archaeological evidence of the decades after 626 can still be seen in a continuum with the initial period of Avar settlement in the Carpathian Basin, the picture changes around or after the middle of the seventh century. The impression is of a consolidation of the Avar khaganate: different population groups and their varied forms of expression that are distinctive in the early Avar material are now fused into a more homogeneous burial culture. The characteristics of the middle Avar period were initially established by Ilona Kovrig and further refined by subsequent research, even if the absolute chronology still remains an object of debate.[333] Its characteristics include pressed belt fittings, often decorated with engraved braid patterns, sometimes also with glass inlay. The clasps for braided hair have a rectangular shape. Sabers with cambered edges and broader bows appear; occasionally, battle axes were also buried. In place of the Byzantine coins that now disappear from Avar burials, discs of gold leaf were occasionally placed as obols in the mouths of the dead.[334] The rich graves of Igar, Ozora-Tótipuszta, Gyenesdiás, and others contain predominantly objects of Byzantine provenance, demonstrating that the Avars had not become altogether isolated.[335] They were still quite well connected with Byzantium, from where objects continued to arrive, if in lesser numbers than before. The evidence of contacts with the West points to selective adoption of material: three types (out of many) of Italian/Bavarian belt-sets have been found in Pannonian graves, and each of them several times—as if they had been sold from a vendor's tray.[336]

Middle and late Avar cemeteries are more regularly laid out than the often randomly placed burials of the early period. Some cemeteries break off during the transition to the middle Avar period or display a rupture in the chronology of burials, and many new cemeteries came into existence. In the past, scholars regarded the more uniform orientation of grave pits as a feature introduced at the beginning of the middle Avar period; recent research, however, has shown that while the variety found in the early Avar period decreased, exceptions nevertheless remained.[337] The divergent cultural complexes of the graves of the early Avar period increasingly converged in the course of the second half of the seventh century. In comparison with the early Avar period the area of settlement had grown and the density of settlement in southern Slovakia and the Vienna Basin increased. Nevertheless, here too some early Avar cemeteries continued in use.[338]

Archaeologists regard the middle Avar period as a time of transition, which may have comprised only one or two generations.[339] Many have attributed these changes to a mass immigration around 670/80. This interpretation is based on a combination of Theophanes's mention of a nameless fourth son of Khan Kuvrat who migrated to Pannonia, and the account in the *Miracula S. Demetrii* of a group of Bulgars and Romans led by Kuver breaking out of the Avar realm and attacking Thessalonica.[340] The success of this theory can be explained by its seeming explanatory power concerning several of the parameters for dating cultural changes in the Carpathian Basin: it could account for the consolidation of the Avar khaganate, the appearance of new types of material, and the reemergence of Byzantine objects. A mass immigration would also explain the sudden rise in population suggested by the establishment of many new cemeteries. Of course, the demographic increase only seems so dramatic if the beginning of the middle Avar period is dated to ca. 670, and not earlier.[341] The Kuver theory also catered to the widespread belief that only an influx of newcomers could have caused profound changes in the archaeological evidence.[342] Until the 1990s, many Hungarian scholars also believed that these late seventh century newcomers were Onogurs, that is, Hungarians—the theory of the so-called "double land-taking" of the Hungarians.[343] The later Avars would thus be revealed as proto-Hungarians, which would have moved the beginnings of Hungarian dominance in the Carpathian Basin forward by almost a quarter millennium.[344] This theory has since receded into the background; but a migration from the steppes in the 670s is still in discussion.

Amongst archaeologists there were always alternative opinions about dating the change, for instance, to the middle of the seventh century.[345] Slovak archaeologists criticized the migration hypothesis by pointing to the strong evidence for continuity.[346] The German version of the present book strongly argued against the uncritical use of fragmentary and ambiguous historiographical accounts for the interpretation of the archaeological finds, but had only limited impact on Hungarian research.[347] As already argued in section 7.7, the Kuver of the *Miracula S. Demetrii* is quite unsuited for the role of causing a cultural revolution in the Carpathian Basin; the source describes his withdrawal, not his immigration. Furthermore, in the text he is only a regional leader, *archōn*, in the area of Sirmium. If we leave out Kuver and simply consider what Theophanes writes about Kuvrat's legendary fourth son, the relevant piece of information is that he came to Pannonia "and became subject of the Avar khagan in Avar Pannonia and remained there with his army."[348] Playing a clearly subordinate role, he would thus not have been in a position to spread a new archaeological culture throughout the khaganate. Identifying this fourth son with Kuver is unlikely in itself, given that Kuver did not "remain with his army" but left with it. There is no indication that middle Avar culture originated in Pannonia or more precisely in the area around Sirmium. The Avar Empire remained just that, the empire of the Avars.

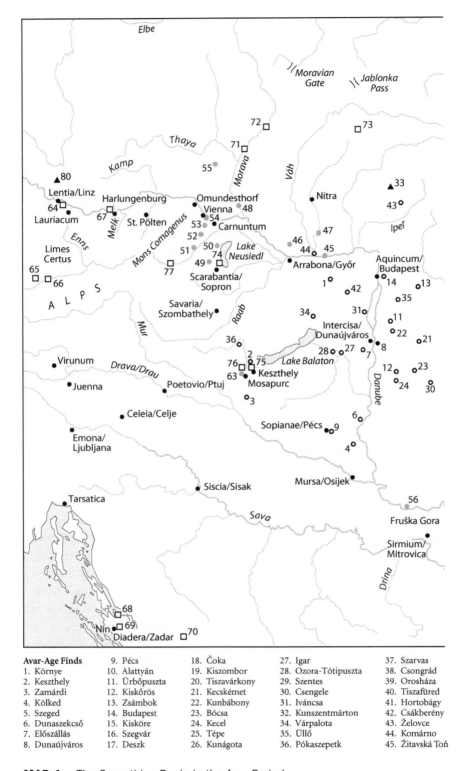

MAP 4. The Carpathian Basin in the Avar Period

Avar-Age Finds

1. Környe	9. Pécs	18. Čoka	27. Igar	37. Szarvas
2. Keszthely	10. Alattyán	19. Kiszombor	28. Ozora-Tótipuszta	38. Csongrád
3. Zamárdi	11. Ürbőpuszta	20. Tiszavárkony	29. Szentes	39. Orosháza
4. Kölked	12. Kiskőrös	21. Kecskemét	30. Csengele	40. Tiszafüred
5. Szeged	13. Zsámbok	22. Kunbábony	31. Iváncsa	41. Hortobágy
6. Dunaszekcső	14. Budapest	23. Bócsa	32. Kunszentmárton	42. Csákberény
7. Előszállás	15. Kisköre	24. Kecel	33. Várpalota	43. Želovce
8. Dunaújváros	16. Szegvár	25. Tépe	34. Üllő	44. Komárno
	17. Deszk	26. Kunágota	35. Pókaszepetk	45. Žitavská Toň
			36. Pókaszepetk	

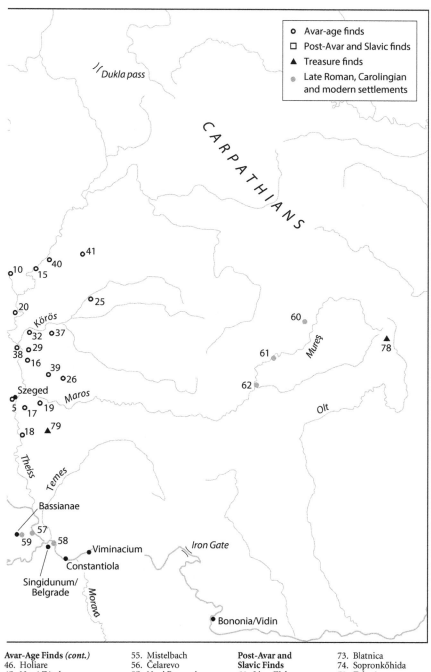

Avar-age finds
Post-Avar and Slavic finds
Treasure finds
Late Roman, Carolingian and modern settlements

Dukla pass

C A R P A T H I A N S

o 41
o 40
10 o   o 15
20
o 25
Körös
o 32   o 37
o 29
38   o 16
o 39
o 26
Szeged
Maros
5   o 17   o 19
o 18   ▲ 79

60
61
62
Mureş
Olt
78 ▲

Theiss
Temes
Bassianae
57
59   58
Viminacium
Constantiola
Singidunum/
Belgrade
Morava
Iron Gate
Bononia/Vidin

Avar-Age Finds *(cont.)*
46. Holiare
47. Nové Zámky
48. Devínska Nová Ves
49. Zillingtal
50. Sommerein
51. Leobersdorf
52. Mödling
53. Zwölfaxing
54. Vienna

55. Mistelbach
56. Čelarevo
57. Novi Banovci
58. Pančevo
59. Vojka
60. Band
61. Noşlac
62. Teiuş
63. Zalakomár

**Post-Avar and
Slavic Finds**
64. Linz-Zizlau
65. Krungl
66. Hohenberg
67. Wimm
68. Nin
69. Kašić
70. Cetina
71. Mikulčice
72. Staré Město

73. Blatnica
74. Sopronkőhida
75. Zalavár
76. Borjuállás
77. Köttlach

Treasure Finds
33. Zemiansky Vrbovok
78. Firtoşu
79. Nagyszentmiklós
80. Hellmonsödt

This does not preclude that some migration from the east took place in this period. In the steppes small-scale migrations and cultural exchanges were constantly occurring. In times of crisis—as in 670/80—these migratory movements could reach points of heightened activity. Large, consistent migrations of armies identifiable by the names of peoples and their leaders, such as the Bulgars under Asparukh, were the exception and tended to leave behind at least some traces in the written sources. In fact, the methodological problem is not to explain how certain phenomena from north of the Black Sea could find their way into the Carpathian Basin. What needs to be explained is how and why new cultural elements actually spread there and became standard in Avar graves. The ethnic hypothesis of a new people overlaying or even driving off an older population would require more substantial historical and archaeological arguments to make it plausible.

However, the migration theory sits as uneasily with the archaeological evidence as it does with the written sources.[349] Crucially, the characteristics of the middle Avar period have not been found in any consistent way in the steppes north of the Black Sea, or indeed anywhere else in central Eurasia.[350] Lively contacts between the Avar realm and the steppes north of the Black Sea, most conspicuously between the Mala Pereshchepino group and that of Bócsa, are attested before the emergence of the middle Avar period. These contacts seem to have declined in the middle Avar period. There is little that links the archaeological heritage of Asparukh's Bulgars and the Avars; as Uwe Fiedler has emphasized, "so far there are no typically middle Avar products known from Bulgaria." Objects of late Avar type probably arrived in the Bulgar khanate as booty or through the resettlement of defeated Avars after the end of their rule.[351] All this argues against a Bulgar origin of middle Avar culture. In addition, the archaeological evidence in the Carpathian Basin suggests not so much a sudden change of cultural habitus as a gradual process of transformation.[352] Large cemeteries in use since the early Avar period, such as Tiszafüred, Kölked-Feketekapu A, Vác-Kavicsbánya, or Zamárdi continued to be used.[353] Many middle Avar types of artifacts, such as earrings with bobbles, seem to have derived from earlier Avar forms. In the case of other objects, such as stirrups, the development seems to have taken place over a longer period of time, spanning both early and middle Avar periods, as presently conceived.[354]

In the period after the defeat of the Avars at the siege of Constantinople in 626, their empire underwent gradual but fundamental changes and repeated internal crises. The three known episodes of fierce fighting around 630 and 680 randomly reported in our sources may not have been the only internal conflicts of this kind. The political superstructure of the Avar Empire had to adapt to substantially transformed conditions, because the prestige economy that had satisfied the demands of the warriors had relied on military success and the resulting steady stream of goods from the Byzantine empire, which was interrupted after 626. This not only led to increased competition between members of the elite; more fundamentally, it also contributed to the growing ruralization of Avar society, which now formed the economic underpinning of the empire.[355] The steep rise in the quantity of material remains and the considerable number of new cemeteries begun in the middle Avar period may be evidence of an increasingly sedentary lifestyle of the warriors on horseback, of an increase in population, and of the spread of the practice of furnished burial in stable cemeteries. Paleoclimatic data suggest more favorable ecological conditions and an expansion of agriculture in the seventh-century Carpathian Basin.[356] According to the archaeological material, the influence from the eastern steppes decreased in the late seventh century. As the flow of tribute and booty ceased, the numbers of the privileged warrior elite that could be sustained most likely declined. Instead of the very rich single elite graves of the preceding period, we now find small elite cemeteries with more modest graves.[357] A considerable number of warriors probably found themselves forced to turn to agriculture themselves, something that cannot have been effected without conflict among the steppe horsemen so accustomed to military success. At the same time, the exploitation of the subordinate local population seems to have intensified.[358] Gradually, however, inner stability seems to have returned to the Avar polity.[359]

The troubled seventh century changed the organization of life in the Avar Empire. In the eighth century the economic practices and social structure, the political system and the material culture had changed significantly from those of the early Avar period. The pacified Avars almost vanish from the written record until the end of the eighth century when Frankish armies began to penetrate into the Carpathian Basin. By contrast, the archaeological evidence becomes extraordinarily plentiful: there is hardly any region and period in early medieval Europe that matches the eighth-century Carpathian Basin in this respect. The culture of the late Avar period became surprisingly homogeneous throughout the Avar core area stretching from the Vienna Woods to the Iron Gate.

THE CENTURY OF THE GRIFFIN

Life under Avar rule in the eighth century was, in many respects, different from that in previous periods. The difference emerges most clearly in two types of sources, to which the first two subchapters are devoted: first, the extensive and rather homogeneous archaeological evidence; and second, the Avar titles of rank that only emerge in late eighth-century Frankish historiography. A narrative of events only becomes possible in the latter parts of the century, which will be addressed in the closing sections of this chapter. Only the history of the fall of the khaganate in the 790s allows some glimpses of the situation in the Carpathian Basin, at a moment when Avar glory was about to fade forever.

8.1 Ways of Life in Archaeological Evidence

The finds from many thousand excavated graves from the eighth-century Carpathian Basin do not represent an elite culture, as in many other archaeological contexts of the early medieval period. We have no "princely" burials, only a few relatively high-status ones, and gold is rarely found in graves. The influx from Byzantium had almost completely dried up; in the Avar core area, no Byzantine coins are found.[1] However, the enormous Avar treasure captured by the Franks in 795/96 and the Nagyszentmiklós/Sânnicolau Mare hoard demonstrate that considerable riches were still available in the eighth century.[2] We may yet discover rich graves of the late Avar period; but at present, the Nagyszentmiklós treasure stands out almost unconnected from the eighth-century archaeological record. It seems logical that after new supplies of prestige goods had been reduced to a trickle, families kept what they had rather than lavishing it on a magnificent funeral. A similar phenomenon can be observed northwest of the Black Sea: "No elite nomadic assemblages of the 8th century . . . are known in the Dnieper region."[3] This was only partly due to the contraction of the Byzantine Empire, which had to fight hard for its survival at this time and was therefore less concerned with the northern steppes. The topography of power in the steppe had also changed. The Khazar Empire had its core area north of the Caucasus; it faced the Caliphate rather than Byzantium and kept mostly friendly relations with the latter.[4] A smaller realm ruled by steppe riders and oriented toward Constantinople had emerged on the lower Danube, the Bulgar khanate. Its territorial range was relatively modest, which corresponded somehow to the limited possibilities of the Byzantines.

Apart from the geopolitical conditions of the Avar polity, what we find in graves is also a matter of cultural habitus. Grave goods represent a massive social investment. From the beginning, the Avar realm is extraordinary for the amount of funerary apparel left in graves, especially if we compare it to the Rouran lands (with very few furnished graves discovered so far), with many regions settled by early Slavs (where we find cremation burials almost without any grave goods), or with the Bulgar khanate on the Danube, where eighth-century graves are rather poorer than those in the Avar sphere of power.[5] In the course of the seventh century, the grave-good habit had been largely abandoned in the Lombard and Merovingian kingdoms. Nevertheless, high esteem for well-furnished graves was hardly an ethnic characteristic of "the Avars"; particularly in the early Avar period, quite distinctive cultural groups shared this readiness to display the status of the deceased both in this world and in the afterlife. That had quickly become an important part of the prestige economy of the Avar Empire. The practice of richly furnished graves continued throughout the duration of the khaganate, though it changed over time. In the eighth century, it involved a much broader population than before: even hard-working farmers in peripheral areas had some quantities of bronze and other metals put into their graves. Only toward the end of the eighth century (and of the khaganate) did this habit begin to fade out in some places.[6] On the whole, massive investments into funerary ritual were a distinctive feature of the Avar khaganate, and this practice included wider groups of the population than in most other contemporary polities where burials included grave goods.

This is an element that reflects the integrative power of the Avar khaganate, which managed to channel social competition both between and within the different groups into a cohesive set of ritual practices and symbolic objects.[7] By the eighth century, in spite of some persistent regional differences, it had also achieved a considerable degree of cultural uniformity. Again, the belt is the key item for archaeologists; it allows them to distinguish not only between burials of the middle and those of the late Avar periods, but also enables the identification of three separate phases for the eighth century (late Avar I, II, and IIIa and IIIb).[8] The multiple belt-set worn by men was a primary place for decoration. The multiple belt was long supposed to be an Avar characteristic because of its extensive presence in the archaeological record of the Carpathian Basin. However, as shown above, it had probably spread from Byzantium into the steppes and to other regions in the late sixth century.[9] The combination of the belt-set, the techniques of production, and the ornamental motifs changed repeatedly in the course of the Avar era, and were transformed again at the beginning of the late Avar period. What remained was that men were regularly buried with their belts, or at least with some of their fittings. As Peter Stadler has calculated, more than three thousand of about thirty thousand male graves contained a full belt-set, that is, about 10 percent of men and boys; the percentage is roughly similar throughout the Avar settlement area.[10] Obviously, these belts helped to display the identity of the deceased at the burial, and to translate it into the afterlife. The make and decoration of the belts probably reflected the rank, descent, and affinities of their bearers, even if the language of these signs can no longer be deciphered.

What had in the seventh century been pressed sheet metal was now cast in bronze (or more specifically, in copper alloy). Bronze casting was used for the belt-buckles, but also for the ends of several side straps that hung from the main belt, and for further fittings. The same technique was used for harness mounts and other objects. As Gergely Szenthe has recently argued, bronze casting, "a characteristic trait of late Avar material culture, can also be noted across the entire northern periphery of the Mediterranean, from Western Europe to Central Asia." It "was not particularly sophisticated and was vertically less articulated, while being quite extensive horizontally." Late antique metalwork had applied a wide range of techniques; most of these skills had obviously been lost in the eighth-century Carpathian Basin, a "striking difference" from the quality of seventh-century Avar artifacts. The prestige value of these rather simple artifacts was achieved "through the increasing amount of aesthetic work invested."[11] This was not an isolated development; cast bronze objects can be found north of the Caucasus and the Black Sea as well as in the Frankish world and the Mediterranean heartlands from the late seventh century onward.[12] Specific to the Avar cultural sphere, however, were the objects' mass production "according to uniform formal principles" and the ornamental canon.

Elsewhere, some of the motifs current on the bronze plaques in the Carpathian Basin were combined with precious metals, most notably in the Vrap treasure, where griffins and lattice ornaments similar to the late Avar bronze casts occur. This treasure, found in Albania and dated to ca. 700, contains an extraordinary amount of gold but includes a limited range of object types produced without much sophistication. Was it produced in the Carpathian Basin, as Werner believed, in Byzantium, as Daim argued, or in Bulgar workshops, as Stanilov maintained?[13] A few close parallels have indeed been found in Bulgaria, for instance the belt plaques with griffin and lattice ornaments from Velino, near Pliska.[14] Nevertheless, the evidence is insufficient to prove a Bulgar origin for late Avar bronze casts. Even if, as Werner and Stanilov have argued, Kuver had been the owner of the Vrap treasure, he had brought it from the Carpathian Basin and not from Bulgaria (see section 7.7). Wherever the objects from Vrap had been made, what is striking is that even the elite in the Carpathian Basin do not seem to have invested in a similar splendor for their funerary apparel; at most, the bronze casts were gilded.

In spite of its technological simplicity, the casting technique permitted much greater variation in the forms of ornamentation.[15] Eighth-century belt-sets show a variety of new motifs and decorative elements. In the first half of the eighth century, griffin and lattice ornaments dominate the belt plaques. The late Avar griffin is a near-universal symbol; however, when, why, and from whom it was adopted is open to discussion. It represents over a millennium of art history in the interplay between the iconography of the steppe horsemen and the artisanal traditions of the sedentary populations. Scythian ornamentation, Iranian representation of power, and Hellenic-Roman influences could have provided models for late Avar artifacts in now scarcely distinguishable ways.[16] Many of the dynamic scenes of fighting animals, griffins, and other zoomorphic representations recall the Scythian animal scenes or those of the Xiongnu; but no direct lines connect these manifestations of steppe culture. Griffins and battling beasts were also well known in Roman and Byzantine art. The artistic production of the Mediterranean world had a decisive role in the development and transmission of this style.[17]

The production and distribution of ornamental belts combined considerable formal and aesthetic unity with local variation. Many of the more frequent motifs, above all, the griffin, must have been recognizable across the Carpathian Basin. Still, craft production seems to have been decentralized, as in the seventh century.[18] A belt that was put together the wrong way round but otherwise manufactured according to established practice shows that it must have been mounted locally and symbolizes the scope for local particularities within a unifying tradition.[19] In the bronze-casting "industry," shared technological skills and aesthetic visions seem to have complemented an essentially local production. We know little about how this worked, but it implies a shared sense of purpose and allegiance that we could call identity. The question of the origins of the bronze industry and its motifs is perhaps secondary; nowhere in the early Middle Ages were cast bronze belt fittings with figures of griffins of this kind so widespread as in the late Avar Carpathian Basin. A few pieces were found in Bulgarian graves, east of the Carpathians or north of the Avar heartlands, but they only show a certain diffusion of the Avar belt habitus, whether by emulation or contingency.[20]

In many respects, older Avar traditions continued in the eighth century. Avar men still wore braids like the envoys of 558 had, although the clasps had changed: they were now cast and prism-shaped. Similar hairstyles were common among the Rouran and the Oguz, later also among the Mongols and Seljuks, while the Turks, Bulgars, and Khazars wore their hair long and loose.[21] The weaponry, reflex bows, sabers, and occasional battle-axes of the eighth century remained similar to that of the earlier periods, though the reinforcing pieces on the bows became broader, whilst the three-edged arrowheads became rather narrow. Cloak fasteners used by women were often ornamented with glass inlay. In the middle of the century, melon-seed-shaped beads and other new jewelry forms appear.[22] Bronze casting permitted the prestige economy to be sustained.

Fewer weapons have been found in eighth-century graves than in earlier ones; only in some peripheral regions did the number of warrior graves increase.[23] An unusually high number of horsemen's graves have been found in the large cemeteries of southwestern Slovakia (Devínska Nová Vés, Holiare, Nové Zámky, Žitavská Toň, Komárno).[24] A relatively high percentage of burials with weapons and/or belts (17 percent) has been discovered at Edelstal, in the north of today's Burgenland (Austria). In other cemeteries in the western periphery, for instance at Leobersdorf, weapons are rare.[25] A number of graves with arms have been found in cemeteries on the Avar Empire's southern flank, such as Pančevo at the mouth of the Temes, or Vojka on the route between Singidunum and Bassianae.[26] In the northeast of the Carpathian Basin lies the cemetery of Hortobágy-Arkus, where unusually wealthy warriors were buried with gilded bronze belt fittings. Most likely there was a regional administrative center in this area that was sur-rounded by relatively large settlements (as in Tiszafüred).[27] The unusual depth of the graves at Hortobágy was likely also a status symbol. Perhaps it is due to their depth that relatively few wealthy graves from the eighth century have been found. In some cemeteries it can be observed that weapons are no longer placed in the graves of men wearing rich belts but do occur in otherwise modest graves.[28] In the interior regions of the Carpathian Basin, weapons are rarely found in eighth-century graves.[29]

These findings should not be interpreted to suggest that Avar men no longer owned weapons. Yet the decreasing role of weapons in the inhumation ritual shows that war had lost its role as the community's most important constitutive factor. It is perhaps not coincidental that the central agonistic metaphors in late Avar art are battling beasts, predators, or hunting scenes. They appear in many variations on bronze strap ends, belt buckles, decorative discs, and horse harnesses. Mythical creatures fight against hoofed animals or people; hunters with bows on galloping horses pursue their prey; eagle, boar, dragon, and horse heads are entwined in conflict with each other. In the mythology of the steppe such representations of fighting animals may symbolize the cycle of death and rebirth.[30] Perhaps these expressive means enabled the Avar warrior, in a largely agricultural environment, to preserve his identity and his pride.

The majority of the population were farmers.[31] In many graves tools such as sickles, adzes, buckets, or even knives for pruning fruit trees and vines have been found.[32] Agricultural instruments, such as sickles, are sometimes found in hoards; in graves, several of them may appear.[33] Ceramics, usually "yellow" pottery, are found more frequently than in earlier Avar graves.[34] Anthropological investigations in Leobersdorf have revealed signs of abrasion or traces of other illnesses on many skeletons, likely due to heavy physical work, while no war injuries were identified.[35] This recalls Ibn Fadlan's judgment on the Volga Bulgars: "I saw no-one in good health. Most of them are sickly, and the majority regularly die from the colic."[36] The widespread evidence of meat deposits in graves proves that horses, cattle, sheep, goats, pigs, chickens, and probably also geese were raised. Cheese or other milk products were also occasionally placed in graves.[37]

The majority of the late Avar population obviously lived in permanent settlements, and cemeteries were in continuous use, often over several generations. A sedentary lifestyle had become predominant, though seasonal migration of a portion of the population with the herds cannot be excluded.[38] Avar settlements have only relatively recently received much scholarly attention, with a number of publications already available.[39] As in the whole of eastern central Europe (and not only there), sunken huts (Grubenhäuser) are a recurrent feature. We still do not understand how these settlements worked, and it is possible that households used more than one of these usually small buildings. A similar layout need not indicate similar function, and the presence or absence of a hearth or stove is significant.[40] Postholes indicative of the existence of wooden houses also occur, sometimes in the same settlement as sunken huts. A house of considerable proportions, around twenty square meters, obviously constructed in blockhouse technique without posts and with a big fireplace was discovered at Sighişoara-Dealul Viilor in Transylvania; it was dated to the eighth century on the basis of pottery finds.[41]

In many regions, quite dense settlement can be established, for instance, along the lower Körös River and in the Vienna Basin.[42] In all, over one thousand sites from the middle and late Avar periods are currently known. Some Avar settlements must have been relatively large, as some cemeteries comprise more than a thousand graves. In Tiszafüred, for example, 1,300 graves spanning several generations have been found, the majority from the middle and late Avar periods.[43] Most settlements uncovered so far, however, were used for several generations but were rather small, so that they could hardly be called villages. At Zillingtal in eastern Austria, for instance, an agricultural settlement inhabited in five phases from the middle through late Avar periods has been excavated; it was situated at a distance of almost one mile from (but in sight of) the hilltop cemetery. The settlement occupied the site of a Roman villa, although no substantial remains of that building remained; what mattered was rather the favorable position. In the ruins of the villa, postholes for rectangular posts and traces of a smelting furnace were excavated. Outside it, a number of pits and the postholes of a further building were found; there were no traces of sunken huts.[44] An interesting feature of some Avar settlements are the ditches between the houses.[45] Perhaps they had the same function as the ditches used both for water supply and canalization in many central Asian villages even today.

One question has been frequently discussed in late Avar studies, despite the fact that there is very little evidence to address it. This is the ethnic categorization and delimitation of the eighth-century "Avars." The period's relatively uniform culture scarcely allows for ethnic differentiation. Even where a century earlier a rather distinctive cultural habitus prevailed, as in Kölked-Feketekapu, the finds for the eighth century fit into the late Avar mainstream.[46] The survival of distinctively non-Avar cultural features is attested only in the region of Keszthely, even though "typical" Avar material had also gained ground here in the course of the seventh century. The post-Roman culture at the western end of Lake Balaton, particularly in the marshy areas at the mouth of the Zala, had become isolated but preserved some typical decorative styles, though only in the female graves. Gold and silver disappeared, and an impoverishment of form was sometimes compensated for by increasing size. Gigantic basket earrings that would have hung down almost to their wearers' shoulders were fabricated in bronze.[47] However, it cannot be taken for granted that these are the traces of a surviving "Roman" population; it may also be the survival of a regional style.

Another question that can hardly be answered is the relationship between Avars and Slavs in the eighth-century Avar sphere of power. It is debatable whether Slavs constituted a significant portion of the late Avar population. Some finds from the cemeteries of the seventh and eighth centuries, such as cremated remains and individual decorative objects in Pókaszepetk, have been interpreted as Slavic, but such evidence is not particularly widespread.[48] Peter Stadler has attempted to detect a Slavic element in the population of the northwestern regions of the khaganate through particular decorations of pottery.[49] However, this would not be a very strong criterion for an ethnic boundary, even if we assumed that object types could be regarded as ethnically distinctive. The debate over "Slavic" or "Avar" attribution of cemeteries from the Avar period in present-day Slovakia has subsided. The cultural boundary in the north of the Avar settlement zone probably lay on the northern edge of the lowlands. To the south lay "Avar" inhumation graves, to the north "Slavic" cremation graves; biritual cemeteries are found in the marginal zone. Slavs may of course have followed the cultural patterns current in the whole Avar Empire.[50] Yet this was not usually the case in peripheral areas. In some cemeteries in Lower Austria that originated in the eighth century but continued in a clearly Slavic context in the ninth, such as Pitten, funerary habits differ considerably from "Avar" ones.[51] On the other hand, certain emerging Slavic centers at some distance from Avar settlement areas used an Avar language of representation, and even produced Avar-style cast bronze plaques, for instance Mikulčice in Moravia.[52]

A fundamental methodological principle is that archaeological classification, ethnic identification, and political affiliation do not necessarily correspond to each other. Even if we can determine one of these elements for a given population, we cannot take the others for granted. It is possible that people of Slavic extraction or language were buried in "Avar"-style graves. It is also conceivable, as has often been asserted, that Slavic was the (or a) lingua franca of the late Avar Empire.[53] The old discussion of just how Slavic the Avar Empire of the eighth century was is hardly meaningful given the present state of research; so far, we can only work with general assumptions. According to all the available written sources, the inhabitants of the khaganate in the eighth century were viewed as Avars. The texts are silent about the role of Slavs in the central settlement area of the eighth-century khaganate. The complementary archaeological evidence shows a relatively uniform archaeological culture that can quite legitimately be connected with the Avars.[54] This allows us to draw some general conclusions about how Avars lived in this period, but not necessarily about the subjective identity of any individual or community. One is tempted to conclude that many Avars of this period were descended from Slavs of the sixth century and that their descendants in the ninth century were once again Slavs. Yet they may have seen themselves as thoroughly Avar in the late Avar khaganate (or may have been perceived as such).

The frontier zones of the Avar Empire were in part rather thinly populated. At the Enns River in 791, Charlemagne's army crossed the *limes certus*, demarcating the zones of power, but did not meet Avar fortifications until the Vienna Woods.[55] Here began the Avar settlement area. Its archaeological traces are richly represented in the Vienna Basin but only sporadically in western and northern Lower Austria.[56] On the middle and upper stretches of the Save as well, few remains that can be defined as "Avar" have thus far come to light.[57] There are, however, traces of Avar groups guarding the road toward the Adriatic.[58] In both regions, Slavic finds have usually been dated to the period after the fall of the Avar Empire, but some of them may also go back to an earlier period.[59] In any case, the extension of the archaeologically determinable Avar settlement has little to say about where the political border ran.

What can be said about the social history of the Avar khaganate in the eighth century on the basis of the archaeological evidence? In spite of all regional variation, there is a strong sense of unity in the cultural manifestations of the Carpathian Basin. The griffin can serve as an emblem of this shared cultural idiom. In archaeological terms, one can legitimately speak of an archaeological culture of the (late) "Avar period." Unlike in earlier centuries, this "Avar" culture seems to have been related to a political and perhaps ethnic identity. Several features contribute to that impression. First, there is the sheer mass of available burials, which provides a solid body of evidence. Even if the particularity of the Avar material may be overestimated due to the much smaller number of furnished graves in many neighboring regions, we do not have to rely on defining a few object types as "typically Avar," but can argue on the basis of a representative sample. Second, much of the material is conspicuously similar and must have been recognizable to contemporaries, such as the Avar belt-sets. Third, there was a relatively flat hierarchy between ordinary and elite graves; we are thus not dealing simply with forms of elite representation. The variability of decorated metal casts on belts and elsewhere allowed for differentiation according to regional particularity and social status, but it is a sustained idiom, and we understand little of it. It rather seems that identification more than distinction was the main purpose of the eighth-century belts. Of course, it distinguished those who wore a complete belt-set at burial, and perhaps also in life, from those who had none or just a very reduced one. Yet both the belt and bronze casts were available to unusually broad social groups.[60] Elite groups did not, and perhaps did not have the means to, invest heavily in funerary displays; but an unusually wide section of the population invested something in a furnished burial. To them we owe a fairly representative, if unspectacular picture of eighth-century Avar society.

8.2 The Hierarchy of the Late Avar State

Until the late seventh century the chroniclers ascribe Avar policy-making exclusively to the khagan. He alone—or, rather, his office—appeared as the representative of the Avar polity, as an aggressor or the guarantor of treaties. Even if the actual division of powers did not entirely correspond to this view, he represented the Avar realm.[61] It was not until the Carolingian Empire, at the apogee of its power, attacked its still awe-inspiring neighbor that quite a different system of Avar governance became evident. Almost before the eyes of the Frankish chroniclers, the khaganate dissolved into its constituent parts (see section 8.4). Scrupulously but surely with little understanding, the alien titles of the alternating partners in negotiations were recorded by Carolingian diplomats: *khagan, iugurrus, tudun, kapkhan, tarkhan, canizauci*. It was no longer enough to fight against the khagan or to negotiate with him; it became necessary to know who else mattered. Every holder of high office now pursued his own strategies in order to save what could be saved.

Caution is then advised in the interpretation of this evidence. We know only of the dissolution of the late Avar state organization, and little about its prior normal functioning. While the Avar steppe aristocracy was losing its last bastions, the recorded titles point once again, more clearly than ever, to the east. All known late Avar titles are also attested in other steppe empires: especially among the central Asian Turks of the sixth and seventh centuries and among the Danube Bulgars and the Khazars of the eighth and ninth centuries. The spread of these titles is presumed to go back to the Turks, who had for some decades ruled over the steppes from the Chinese to the Roman frontier. According to Chinese sources, they had twenty-eight different hereditary titles.[62] This elaborate terminology by and large continued in use in succeeding empires, including that of the late Avars.

Thus nothing in the late Avar political system was unique, but the elements were arranged in a specific combination. There is no indication as to when the new titles were introduced; though we can safely say that it must have been after 626, because otherwise the Byzantine sources would have mentioned them. We should not regard the ranks and titles recorded by the Carolingian authors as a static system: we have to reckon with shifts in dynasties, with the rise of new groups, and with changes in the political language according to transformations in the internal power balance. Similar phenomena are observable during the decline of the Turkish khaganate. The new titles and forms of representation could help to maintain a ruralized steppe aristocracy's sense of cultural superiority. They probably also represent an institutionalization of Avar rule that was modeled after the recent accomplishments of the central Asian khaganates.

The similarities between late Avar titles and those in other roughly contemporary steppe realms have been emphasized by many historians, who sought to develop an overarching central Eurasian system, something like an original blueprint of nomad society.[63] Yet we should not take an archetype as our point of departure, but rather each specific historical situation. Only by analyzing who is shown as acting in the sources can the actual political organization be assessed. Closer analysis shows that neither the political conditions nor the titles were the same across the various steppe empires. There was no universal model; the same titles may even hide quite divergent functions. Conclusions based on analogy, therefore, can easily mislead. We know the building blocks of late Avar forms of organization, but we should not, without further reflection, assemble them according to models that originate elsewhere. Nevertheless, the following comparison of the Avar hierarchy with those of other steppe empires will enable us to identify certain commonalities in political language and organization.

The Avar "Dual Kingship": Khagan and Iugurrus

The sources never expressly mention a dual kingship among the Avars. Yet there are indications that point in this direction. The well-informed *Annals of Lorsch* describe the recently conquered Avar "ring" in 796: "Where the kings (*reges*) of the Avars were accustomed to reside with their nobles (*cum principibus suis*)."[64] What may be meant by these *reges* is made clearer on two other occasions. In 782 the "caganus et iugurrus, principes Hunorum" sent an embassy to Charlemagne.[65] In 796 both rulers were killed "by their own people" in internal conflicts.[66] Then both titles disappear from the accounts until 805, when the baptized khagan Abraham seeks to reestablish his "honor antiquus" with the approval of the emperor, without there being any mention of a second ruler.[67] Already in the little scene described in the panegyric poem on King Pippin of Italy at the court of the khagan, the latter appears—with his wife, "catuna mulier"—as the sole representative of the foundering empire.[68]

From this it would seem justified to conclude that in the years up to 796 there were two rulers who generally acted in unison—or remained inactive in unison, as in 791. Nothing is known of the division of powers between the two. The Carolingian terminology is imprecise; at one point, the two were distinguished as *reges* from the *principes*,[69] at another, they are called *principes* themselves.[70] We may assume that the khagan, always named first, was the more senior of the two.

Modern historiography has relied on the theory of nomadic dual kingship to bridge the gaps in the evidence. In fact, in almost all the steppe empires of the early Middle Ages two rulers are at least periodically attested, from the Hunnic kings Attila and Bleda and the Turks, Khazars, and early Magyars up to later Islamic dynasties such as the Karachanids. Arabic travelers and writers of the ninth and tenth centuries have left detailed descriptions as to how the Khazar state organization of the time functioned. According to Ibn Rusta, the khagan was only the nominal supreme ruler, while the *iša* was the military commander-in-chief and actual regent.[71] The further texts in this Arabic geographical line of transmission give very similar accounts; Gardīzī states quite directly: "The Khazar khagan only disposes of the name [of a king] and nothing more."[72] A more detailed description is found in Ibn Fadlan who traveled to the Volga

Bulgars in 922: "The king of the Khazars, whose title is *khāqān*, only appears in public once every four months. He is called the Great Khāqān, whereas his deputy is called *khāqān beg*. It is he who leads the armies, directs the affairs of the kingdom, appears in public and receives the allegiance of the neighboring kings."[73] Constantine Porphyrogenitus also mentions the khagan and *pech* (*beg*) of the Khazars as acting in unison; elsewhere, the *khagan-archōn* is the sole actor.[74] According to al-Masudi (ca. 943), the khagan was not even allowed to show himself to the courtiers. "Despite this, the authority of the ruler would not be accepted without the presence of a khāqān in his palace in the capital."[75] The khagan, he says, was from ancient times always chosen from the same family. The model that emerges from these reports is clear; the khagan has a purely symbolical role, embodying the ancient prestige of his dynasty, while his deputy pursues all government activities. Presumably, the khagan's duty was sacral, preserving the harmony between heaven and earth. According to al-Masudi, the khagan was held responsible for famine, disaster, or reversals in war; people would then require him to be killed, as in Al-Istakhri's account.[76]

It was above all András Alföldi who, in the 1930s, constructed a general theory of nomadic double kingship on the basis of these descriptions.[77] He argued that this institution derived from the cosmology of the steppe peoples, above all from the ceremonial division of the army into a left and right wing, which supposedly led to the bipartite division of the rulership.[78] In this view dual kingship was an archaic institution. Alföldi's theory was generally accepted, and most significant works on Avar history have since assumed a double kingship of the Khazar type.[79]

But the situation is not as clear as the Arabic travel accounts might have us believe, even in the Khazar case. In the Caucasian wars of the eighth century, the khagan alone is named as ruler; various *tarkhans* appear as military leaders alongside him.[80] When the deposed Justinian II found asylum among the Khazars in 704, his host was the khagan alone.[81] It is not until 833 that the khagan and beg together send an embassy to Constantinople, if Constantine Porphyrogenitus's information is correct.[82] The exceptional letter of the Jewish Khazar khagan Joseph to a Jewish courtier in Umayyad al-Andalus dating to the mid-tenth century gives an extensive list of the Khazar rulers but without mentioning dual kingship.[83] The so-called Cambridge Document from the Cairo Genizah, however, which contains a similar letter, speaks of the introduction of dual rulership: after their conversion to Judaism, the Khazars introduced a khagan-judge and a king-general.[84]

The difference in titles for the second ruler is also striking. In some sources he is called *iša*, in others *beg*, which may represent a change in the tenth century.[85] The first title could be derived from the Turkish *shad*, who is repeatedly attested as a son (on occasion, nephew) of a *(sir-)yabgu*. This was a member of the ruling dynasty who could exercise rule over a portion of the realm.[86] *Beg* is the general designation in the Orkhon inscriptions for a member of the steppe aristocracy.[87] In fact, Ibn Fadlan described the Khazar system of rule as a tetrarchy. Along with the great khagan and the beg, he names, on the next hierarchical level, the *kündür khagan* as deputy to the khagan beg (the title corresponds to *kende*, the early Magyar supreme ruler) and the *jawshīghīr* as his lieutenant (probably to be interpreted as the "Head of the Royal Falcon Hunting").[88]

Artamonov concluded that the Khazar double kingship had arisen from the factual disempowerment of the khagan's dynasty.[89] This could be compared to the relationship between the late Merovingians and their Carolingian "begs," who for a long period did not dare remove the powerless members of the ancient royal family. In any case the "Khazar model" was subject to historical change. Even if there should have been a beg in the eighth century, which is not documented,[90] the khagan was hardly ousted from active politics before the ninth century. Moreover, there is no indication that Khazar dual kingship derived from an originally bipartite structure of the Khazars. Neither two wings of the army with independent commanders nor an origin for the Khazar people from two ethnic units (like the Var and Chunni among the Avars) is reported.

The situation among the Turks was even more complicated. In Turkish origin legends, the motifs of four or ten brothers occur, but there is no clear indication of a binary division.[91] At an early date, the khaganate was divided into an eastern and a western realm.[92] No doubt the extensive conquests of the first khagans made such a division necessary. Only members of the Ashina dynasty were eligible for rulership.[93] In later Turkish memory, Bumin and Istemi were both credited with the foundation of the khaganate: "Having become masters of the Türk people, they installed and ruled its empire and fixed the law of the country."[94] This may be a trace of a mental map that allowed conceptualizing a binary familial and territorial structure in the Turkish khaganate. However, it differed completely from the Khazar model, which was according to function, not territory, and in which only the Great Khagan came from the Ashina dynasty.

The identification of the names and titles of Turkish rulers in Chinese, western Asian, and European sources is not straightforward, and consequently, the exact history of partitions is hard to reconstruct (see section 2.6). Accounts in Chinese sources give the impression that there was no established system, and on the whole divisions and subdivisions were decided on a situational basis.[95] In political practice, since the 570s the Turkish Empire was divided into a western and an eastern realm; in both of these, two or more hierarchically distinguished rulers were in charge.[96] Theophylact, based on the khagan's letter, mentions four "great" khagans in the context of the Turum revolt, each of whom ruled over his own district.[97] Menander states in the context of the embassy of Valentinus to Turxanthus that "the ruler of the Turkish people had divided all the land into eight parts. The senior ruler of the Turks was called Arsilas."[98]

Invaluable background to the succession of rulers is provided by one of the few contemporary Turkish sources, the Bugut inscription, a rather fragmentary epitaph in Sogdian with some Turkish terms, which was erected "by the Turks" under Nivar Khagan (ca. 581–87). It is part of a memorial complex of Mahan-Tegin, younger brother and coruler of the eastern khagan Muhan (ca. 553–72), who subsequently became his successor for six years. He probably picked his younger brother and eventually successor Taspar (Tapo, ca. 572–81) to share in his rule. The inscription says that "Mahan-Tegin rose to the position of khagan" while Muhan was still in office, and "after [that they] were saviors for the whole world during a long period."[99] Fragmentary as it is, the Bugut inscription indicates the way in which changes of rulership or other important matters were negotiated and legitimized. After Muhan's death, Mahan-Tegin "asks the gods," and the officeholders (among them tarkhans and tuduns) address him and ask him to "distribute the money" and "feed the people" as Muhan had done. The same procedure is recited for Taspar Khagan; he asks the officeholders and his kinsmen for approval. The spirit of the ancestor Bumin (who had died in 552) "orders" Taspar to establish a *samgha*, a Buddhist community, on that occasion; it is unclear whether the ancestor is directly invoked in the accession ritual.[100] Until Taspar, Bumin's sons seem to have succeeded one another in the eastern khaganate, with a younger brother as second khagan, while Istemi's branch of the family ruled in the west.

The structure of Turkish rule is complicated by the titles of individual rulers and corulers, which, according to Chinese informants, were hierarchically ranked. In addition to the khagan, the titles of *yehu/yabgu, she/shad, tele/tegin, tutunfa/tudun(beg)*, and additional lesser ranks—all hereditary—are known.[101] Such a title of rank would not automatically be set aside when its bearer advanced in his career; rather he assumed one or more additional titles. Mahan-Tegin obviously kept the title *tegin* when he became khagan. The custom of making members of a dynasty corulers, deputies, or regents could generate conflict and divisions. Yet all title-bearers effectively seem to have ruled. Only Taspar may have withdrawn from the exercise of power toward the end of his reign under the influence of Buddhism.[102] In contrast to Khazar custom, positions in the Turkish khaganates could be exchanged. The title of khagan was borne not only by the supreme ruler but sometimes also by other ruling members of the dynasty. The divisions of rulership, initially undertaken ad hoc, gradually led to the establishment of stable component parts of the empire. The Old Turkic inscriptions show that the titles of *yabgu* or *shad* could also denote regional rulers. Kutluq, who restored Turkish power toward the end of the seventh century, named one brother *shad* of the Tardush, and another *yabgu* of the Tölös; in turn, the yabgu could become khagan.[103]

Many of the titles attested among the Turks were also used by the Danube Bulgars. There is no mention of a dual kingship, though it was inferred to have existed by Beševliev, who argued that the kapkhan was the Bulgars' second ruler.[104] Some pieces of evidence, however, seem to contradict this. Under Krum at the beginning of the ninth century the *boilas kapkhan* was the commander of the right wing of the army, with the *ičirgu boilas* leading the left wing.[105] Both must have belonged to the six great *boilades* whom Constantine Porphyrogenitus mentions as the highest dignitaries after the khan.[106] From Kuvrat through Asparukh to the Christian khans and czars, the rulers held the political reins in their hands; there is no trace here of the Khazar model. The Byzantines observed the ranking and power relationships of their neighbors so carefully that a division of the rulership would not have escaped them.

A sacral supreme prince is, however, attested among the Hungarians at the end of the ninth century. His title, *kende*, corresponds to the third in the Khazar hierarchy, the *kündür*, in whose area of control the Magyars had probably lived.[107] The second ruler and leader of the army was the *gyula*, until Gyula Árpád concentrated all power in his own person after the assassination of the *kende* Cussan/Kurszán about 903.[108] The title *gyula* was, however, retained, and Constantine Porphyrogenitus knew of a hierarchy of three dignitaries at the head of the Hungarian "Turks." Below the supreme ruler from the family of Árpád stood the *gylas* and the *karchas*, "who have the rank of judge."[109] The evolution of the Hungarian hierarchy shows the dynamic development in the division of rulership among the steppe peoples.

In the polities that succeeded the Turkish Empire various forms of divided rule evolved. Among the Toquz-Oguz/Uyghurs the khagan was from time to time excluded from the exercise of power, as among the Khazars, but here, several deputies shared in the business of ruling.[110] Among the Oguz (Ghuzz), as Ibn Fadlan recounts, the *yabgu* was the supreme ruler, while his deputy had the title of *kudarkin*. The army was commanded by the ruler's son; the most eminent general serving under him had the title *tarkhan*.[111] The political structure of the Karachanids is of particular interest. This was an Islamicized steppe dynasty that ruled parts of central Asia from the tenth to the twelfth century. Among them the title *yugruš* is attested. One of the principal works of early Turkic literature, the *Kutadgu Bilig*, composed in ca. 1070 as a mirror of princes for the Karachanid ruler, contains extensive discussions on the art of governance; it describes the Karachanid hierarchy, if in idealized form.[112] Several authors have drawn an analogy between the *yugruš* and the Avar *iugurrus*.[113]

This parallel is valuable, yet caution is required. The *Kutadgu Bilig* mentions a whole series of titles, as do contemporary Islamic sources. The titles of the two Karachanid rulers are usually represented as *arslan-khan* and *bughra-khan*. Their names refer to the heraldic animals of the two halves of the empire, the lion and the camel. In addition, there were four sub-khagans, whose names are composed of the elements *arslan* and *bugra* and the denominators of rank *ilig/elik* (prince) and *tigin/tegin*. Then follow six deputies, who are also drawn from the ruling dynasty.[114] Many of these dignitaries appear in the accounts of Islamic historians as army commanders, often also as princes over various parts of the empire. Just as in the case of the Turks of the sixth century, advancement was possible. Occasionally there were wars between brothers, which proves that the various partial rulers disposed of their own armed forces.

The *yugruš*, on the other hand, like the *yabgu* and some additional functionaries, did not come from the ruling dynasty but from the people. He wishes, so the idealizing *Kutadgu Bilig* recounts, to serve the khagan or the *elik*, quits the people, and goes to the court, where he is carefully tested and instructed in the duties of a vizier.[115] Al-Kashgari has a similar account. The *yugruš* comes from the people, becomes the vizier of the khagan, and in rank is only one level below him.[116] In the later period of the Karachanid Empire the office of *yugruš* evolved into a simple honorary title. The office of the Karachanid *yugruš* had more in common with the Abbasid vizierate than with a nomadic double kingship.

This sketchy comparison shows that the divisions of rule could take quite different forms in the steppe empires. Ultimately, they responded to several structural problems. First, the huge spaces over which many empires spanned could hardly be controlled. An effective organization of government required a division of armed power and leadership. Subunits were instituted, mostly ruled by members of the ruling dynasties. Second, this tendency was accentuated by problems of succession. When a khagan might have twenty-five wives,[117] there would be a great number of potentially legitimate sons entitled to inherit; the Karachanids, for instances, equipped many of them with apanages.[118] Several strategies were possible to avoid succession conflicts in the family. In the short term, attempting to integrate the entire offspring of a founding ruler made sense. Divisions of power could serve as a means to preclude conflict.[119] A tanistry system, which privileged brothers of the deceased rulers over his sons, tendentially limited contenders and could postpone conflict among the next generation (see section 6.2). The Xianbei also practiced fraternal succession.[120] In the first Turkish khaganate, the rule also repeatedly passed from uncle to nephew, although sons would have been available, as it seems.[121] The Turkish model of a pair of brothers as senior and junior ruler was at times reminiscent of the Diocletian tetrarchy. Investing junior princes with dynastic subunits could also have helped to maintain the coherence of the state. However, in the long run, such divisions of empire tended toward independence, and, as Jack Goody has observed, "with each successive generation, the problem of determining seniority [becomes] more complex."[122] "In comparison with the Hsiung-nu, the Turks were much more prone to civil war. This was due both to the large number of potential heirs and to their inability to eliminate collateral claims except by force," as Thomas Barfield has argued.[123] The Khazar model may constitute a radical solution: make the office of khagan as unattractive as possible.

A third problem lay in the fact that steppe empires often overlay preexisting ethnic and political communities, whose internal structure was preserved and integrated into the system of rule. A deputy of the central ruler was sometimes placed alongside the formerly independent rulers. Such subaltern dual rule is attested in Khazar Cherson about 710. The tudun, appointed *archōn* of the city by the khagan, was flanked by the *zoilos* or *protopolitēs* (city governor), who was drawn from one of the resident families.[124] If such a regional entity freed itself again from the central power, a dual kingship could arise.[125] From one segment in the constitution of an empire a new system could thus emerge.

One strategy to avoid excessive intradynastic conflict was to appoint lower-born persons or even slaves to influential executive positions, so that they would not have the legitimacy to seize power in an aristocratic society. This solution was especially current in the Islamic world. This, however, could create a fourth structural problem, which was the seizure of power by those who had it at their hands. Typically, the outcome was the reduction of the old ruler to a merely symbolic function. This is what happened to the Abbasids and the Khazar Ashinas in the ninth century; the Carolingian *maior domus*, the Japanese *shogun*, the Turkish emirs of the caliphate enjoyed a similar fortune as the Khazar begs.[126] Many rulers attempted to introduce safeguards against such a gradual usurpation, as can be deduced from the *Kutadgu Bilig*. The decline of a ruling dynasty could thus lead to the emergence of dual kingship as a power-sharing compromise. Yet, this was relatively uncommon in steppe empires. What the various forms of dual kingship in steppe empires had in common is that they arose only over the course of time, after the victorious phase that followed the successful founding of the empire, when the prestige of the dynasty was on the wane. It was not ancestral but functional.

The multiplicity of causes and forms finds a correspondence in the multiplicity of titles. While the ruler almost invariably called himself khagan or khan, the title of the second ruler was different almost everywhere: *Beg* and *iša* among the Khazars, *bughra khagan* among the Karachanids, *gyula* among the Hungarians, *kapkhan* (if at all) among the Bulgars; among the Turks, *yabgu*, *shad*, or *tegin* could occupy the second position, and they could use the title khagan or not. It is apparent that most of these designations are drawn from a limited vocabulary through which the steppe peoples expressed dignity, rank, and function. Almost all the titles are attested among more than one people, where they do not necessarily mean the same thing. Only the *iugurrus* of the Avars is otherwise unknown at the time. The nomad dual rulership can thus be described as a limited repertory of forms of political organization that was flexible enough for the expression of specific power relationships.

What the position of the *iugurrus* might have been among the Avars therefore cannot be derived from either the Khazar or Karachanid analogies. But it is evident that in the Avar khaganate, too, the emergence of a pair of rulers is the consequence of a weakening of rulership. We cannot determine whether it emerged along with the introduction of the other titles. Developments after 796 show how dependent the division of power between the different dignitaries was on short-lived political circumstances. Obviously, the office was not filled again after the death of the *iugurrus* in 796. Other dignitaries were now the khagan's rivals for power in the crumbling Avar Empire.

Only two pieces of information shed some light on the roles of khagan and iugurrus up to 796. They jointly sent envoys to the Franks.[127] And both, in the course of inner strife in 795–96, were killed *a suis*, by their own people.[128] The texts seem to indicate that they had fought against one another, each supported by his own retinue. All the rest remains speculation. There is no evidence to suggest that the khagan was as remote from political affairs as was reported of the Khazar ruler of the tenth century. Nor is there any hint that the territory of the khaganate or the functions of governance were divided between the two princes. The annals expressly state that the two rulers and the *principes* were accustomed to live in the Avar ring.[129] They acted together in matters of foreign policy. Most likely, we can assume a form of dual governance in which the power of the khagan was restricted but not fully eclipsed. The iugurrus is never reported to have acted on his own initiative. But even their joint power was limited. It is evident that already before 796 the khagan and iugurrus had both lost control over the other high dignitaries, especially the tudun.

Tudun

The most frequently mentioned late Avar title of rank is the tudun. The annals first take notice of him in 795, when the holder of this office submitted to the Franks. This treason paid off. In the following years the tudun played the leading role among the Avar princes, until in 803 his initially successful revolt collapsed. The name has been transmitted in a series of variant forms, of which *zotan(us)* is the most widespread.[130] The change from *tudun* to *zotan* can be explained by two consecutive Old High German sound shifts. The first is the tenuis shift [t] > [ts], which explains the initial z; it generally took place in the sixth and perhaps the seventh century. The second shift happened in the eighth century and transformed the voiced medial [d] into a voiceless [t]. This clearly indicates that the title had been familiar for long enough to undergo the sound shift.[131] The distribution of the forms among the different annals is no coincidence: the Salzburg annals, the Alamannic annals (probably from Murbach and Reichenau), and the Guelferbytani (written in Regensburg) use the form Zotan (or similar), whereas those close to the court (*Annales regni Francorum*, *Lorsch*, and *Metz*) mostly employ the actual title tudun. In Bavaria, it seems, one must have regularly been in touch with the tudun since the seventh century.

References to the status of the tudun before 796 are rather varied: "Unus ex primoribus Hunorum,"[132] "qui in gente et regno Avarorum magnam potestatem habebat,"[133] "dux de Pannonia,"[134] "princeps Pannoniae,"[135] "de terra Avarorum regulus."[136] He submitted "cum terra et populo suo" to the Franks,[137] handed over his "patria" to Charlemagne,[138] and received baptism along with his "populus" (one source adds "comites").[139] His rule quite clearly comprised a specific area of the Avar Empire where he ruled over his own "populus," chiefly the armed following that accompanied him to the emperor in 796—a "magna pars Avarorum" as the *Royal Frankish Annals* note.[140] It is tempting to conclude that the tudun was the governor of the western part of the empire, which would explain why his name had been familiar in Bavaria and why he could pursue an independent western policy. But caution is required in the interpretation of "princeps Pannoniae."[141] By 803, when he is presented under that title, the tudun could have attained a higher status than before 796. Moreover, in the parlance of the Carolingians, "Pannonia" was not restricted to the old Roman province.[142]

Soon after his submission the tudun defected again, this time from the Franks. Einhard's annals note this for the year 796, along with the just punishment meted out to him.[143] This may be a reference to the revolt of 799. Not before 803 did a Frankish army bring the tudun's region definitively under control. The defeated "princeps Pannoniae" was brought along on the return march, and submitted to the emperor in Regensburg.[144] This princely title could mean that by 803 the tudun was no longer subservient to any khagan. At any event, by this time he was the chief adversary in the Franks' Pannonian affairs. This did not change until 805 when the kapkhan group appeared and the khaganate was restored. For this reason the tudun was only the second man, after the *canizauci*, in 811 when the entire Avar leadership was ordered to Aachen to attend upon the emperor.[145] These two were the last Avar functionaries of whom the annals take note. A later learned tradition took the tudun to be *the* ruler of the Avars. When almost two hundred years later Bishop Pilgrim of Passau forged a letter from Pope Eugene from 824, he addressed it to "simul etiam Tudundo necnon Moimaro ducibus et optimatibus exercitibusque plebis Hunie, qui et Auaria dicitur, atque Marauie."[146]

The title of tudun is one of the most widespread among the steppe peoples. Whether it comes from China, where *tutun* or *tu dong* could designate a provincial governor or commander, or from the steppe is as yet unclear.[147] In the Turkish khaganate, the late sixth-century Bugut inscription already mentions the title tudun (in the plural) among several types of officials who approved of a new khagan.[148] Chinese sources indicate that *tudun (beg)* was a title used for Turkish governors of subjugated regions.[149] For instance, in the 580s the Turkish khagan Shabolüe sent a *tutun* to govern the Khitan, their eastern neighbors, who promptly assassinated him.[150] When Justinian II's fleets captured the city of Cherson in 710, a Khazar tudun was in residence as governor.[151] Among the Danubian Bulgars of the time the title played no role.[152]

On the eastern steppes the title tudun was not restricted to a single officeholder. For the Avars this cannot be excluded either, although the sources do give the impression that there was only one tudun. He was presumably third in the Avar hierarchy before 796. The fact that he disposed of his own *terra/patria* and own *populus* or *comites* accelerated the collapse of the Avar Empire as soon as the organization of the khaganate had lost its internal cohesion. His defection to the Franks left the Avar Empire unprotected at a decisive moment.

Tarkhan

The title and rank of tarkhan has been transmitted in only a single poem that celebrates King Pippin's victory in 796 over the Avars.[153] Here the khagan appears "cum tarcan primatibus," with the noble tarkhans in his retinue. The annals do not expressly name the tarkhans, and their dignity is likely hidden behind the "primates" or "alii primores" who are occasionally mentioned. The name is possibly derived from the archaic steppe myth of the smith Tarkhan.[154] It already designated a dignitary among Tuoba Wei and the Rouran. A brother of Khagan Anagui bore this title around the middle of the sixth century.[155] The Turkish khagan Sizabulos, around 570, sent the *tagma-tarkhan* to accompany the Byzantine Zemarchus as ambassador on his return journey. Menander expressly notes that tarkhan was his *axiōma*, his honorific title, while Tagma was his name.[156] An early epigraphic occurrence is in the Bugut inscription.[157] Many Turkish tarkhans appear in the Orkhon inscriptions. The title is at times further specified by means of an accompanying epithet.[158] Tonjukuk, the "Bismarck of the steppe" (Pritsak), calls himself "Boila Baga Tarqan" in his inscription, whereas in the Terkhin inscription the title is El-etmiš Bilgä Qutluq-tarqan-säŋün.[159] The title tarkhan was also borne by one of the last Hephthalite princes in present-day Afghanistan, who fell in about 700 in a revolt against the Arabs.[160] Among the Khazars, tarkhans frequently led armies against the Armenians and Arabs.[161] They are mentioned by Ibn Fadlan as generals second to the commander-in-chief among the Oguz.[162] Yet in the Turkish sphere of influence the tarkhans often also had civil duties.[163] A later oriental source, Juvaini, recounts that the tarkhans needed to pay no taxes, were first to receive their share of the spoils, and might enter into the khagan's presence at any time.[164] Tarkhans appear among the Bulgars as a "special class of the aristocracy."[165] In Bulgaria, the honorific *tarkhan* was generally defined more precisely through the addition of a title relating to function and office. One of Khan Omurtag's inscriptions (815–32) mentions a *zoupan tarkanos*.[166] Another source states that during an expedition against the Franks a *zera tarkhan* by the name of Negavonais was drowned in the Tisza.[167] These two dignitaries, but also a few others mentioned in Omurtag's memorial inscriptions, are qualified by the phrase "he ate at my table" and by the name of their respective clans.[168]

Everywhere, Tarkhan seems to be an honorific that designated status but not a specific office. Al-Khwarizmi generally mentions the Turkish tarkhans as members of the nobility.[169] With such origins, they were predestined for the assumption of various offices, which could then be made explicit in the title. Just like *tüyün/tudun*, tarkhan still appears in the seventeenth century as an honorary title of the Bashkir princes.[170] Elsewhere, as among the Hungarians, the title could become a tribal name.[171] Among the Mongols and Kirghiz it took the special meaning "exempt from taxes."[172] Even a personal name could be derived from the title.[173]

Kapkhan

There has been a lengthy debate as to whether the title *kapkhan* was ever in use among the Avars. A "princeps Hunorum" by this name or title occurs only once in the annals. In 805 he came personally before the emperor "propter necessitatem populi sui," because of the plight of his people, and successfully pleaded to be granted the land between Carnuntum and Savaria. He had already been baptized and bore a Christian name, Theodore.[174] But he died soon after his return to his people. Still in the same year, the khagan, by the name of Abraham, sent an envoy. The delegate pled for the "old honor that the khagan had always enjoyed among the Huns."[175]

The conflicts between Avar dignitaries caused confusion among the Carolingian annalists. The designation *capcanus* in the *Royal Frankish Annals* soon blurred into *captanus*, *cap(p)anus*, *cabuanus*, and finally fell together with *caganus*,[176] so that the *Annales Mettenses* call Abraham the "alter caganus."[177] Thus, it has often been assumed that Abraham simply was Theodore's successor, who had lobbied Charlemagne about his confirmation as a ruler and of his preeminence in relation to other princes.[178]

However, the title kapkhan cannot be a mere error on the part of the *Royal Frankish Annals*, since it is attested among other steppe peoples. Among the Danube Bulgars the kapkhan (*kavchanos*) Isbul seems to have played such a prominent role in the first half of the ninth century that Beševliev saw him as a second prince next to the khagan.[179] In the eleventh century the title had become the name of a clan, *tōn kopkhanōn*.[180] In the Turkic Tonjukuk inscription there is a much-discussed mention of a *kap(a)khan khagan*; the sense of the text seems to be that in the absence of the khagan, Tonjukuk would assume the rule, and in his absence, the *kapakhan khagan* would be responsible.[181]

Problematic as some of this evidence is, one conclusion can be drawn: kapkhan and khagan is not simply the same title, even if an analogy has also been suggested for some central Asian cases.[182] The title kapkhan mostly defines a position of considerable power, but in the Bulgar case it becomes clear that it is subordinate to the khan. It occurs less frequently than other titles. The Frankish scribes clearly were not familiar with it. From the range of their spellings, *capcanus* represents the *lectio difficilior* and has to be accepted, especially as it comes from the *Royal Frankish Annals*. Had Theodore been khagan, the annals would have certainly used this by now familiar term. But it would seem that in 796, no khagan had been raised, and that the Avar Empire had disintegrated into regional principalities. Only under this assumption does Abraham's attempt at restoration in 805 have any meaning. The "honor antiquus, quem Caganus apud Hunos habere solebat" was not the title that kapkhan Theodore had held. Otherwise the annals would not have needed to emphasize that Abraham now obtained the totality of the kingdom according to their prior custom, "summam totius regni iuxta priscum eorum ritum."[183] The restoration of the khaganate was intended to re-establish the pre-796 hierarchy of dignitaries. Perhaps Abraham was Theodore's successor and strove for something higher. It is also conceivable that he governed a different group of people and wished to exploit the death of his rival in order to impose himself as supreme ruler.

Little can be deduced about the position of the kapkhan. It is possible that (like the *canizauci* in 811) he may have sought a prestigious new title on the Bulgar model, one not fraught with the memories of the Avar power struggles. The kapkhan title would have been very suitable for this purpose. It resonated with khagan and yet was distinct. It is equally conceivable that a kapkhan already existed before 796 and, for instance, ruled the eastern half of the empire. This view could find support in the fact that just around 804 the Bulgar khan Krum had marched up there, creating a *necessitas* that could very well have prompted the kapkhan's people to request new territory as far in the west as possible.

For the kapkhan himself, at least, the journey to Aachen did not pay off. His death nullified any prospect of creating a "kapkhanate" around Lake Neusiedl, and the title disappeared from the sources. In 811 the annals once again name another title.

Canizauci

The new order of 805 brought no lasting peace to troubled Pannonia. Six years later a Frankish army had yet again to march to Avar country "ad controversias Hunorum et Sclavorum finiendas," in order to put an end to the conflicts of the Huns and Slavs. The emperor's delegates summoned the quarreling parties to Aachen, where they met the emperor in November: "Canizauci princeps Avarum et tudun et alii primores," along with the *duces* of the Slavs.[184] Was the *canizauci* the khagan of the Avars or just a tribal prince along with the others?[185]

The *Royal Frankish Annals* call the *canizauci* "princeps Avarum." The terminology of the annals is not unambiguous, but the khagan is generally called *princeps* too. In 782 the khagan and the iugurrus are called "principes Hunorum,"[186] and similarly in 796.[187] The *Annals of Lorsch* on the other hand call the two rulers "reges," who reside in the ring with their "principes."[188] This is, however, the only place where demonstrably subordinate dignitaries are styled as "principes." The tudun is called "princeps Pannoniorum" for the first time in 803, when he faces up to the Franks as an autonomous prince, analogous to the "princeps Hunorum" used for the kapkhan in 805.[189] Now, in 811, the *canizauci* is the "princeps," and the tudun only preeminent among the "primores." The same sentence also calls the emperor "princeps." The switch in terminology can be from no earlier than 805. The *canizauci* must have claimed the "honor antiquus," the restored, at least nominally supreme rulership over the entire Avar realm.

The Bulgar khan had a similar title. He is several times called κανα συβιγη in the inscriptions.[190] The attribute presumably served to lift the great khan, in his capacity as supreme military commander, above the tribal princes who apparently could also lay a claim to the title of khan.[191] The title has also been read as *kanas ybige*.[192] Yet *sybige* has a parallel in the Oghuz *sübaši/sübeki*, the military commander,[193] and the form *kana* without the *s* is documented several times.[194]

For the conditions of the time it was no terrible distortion for the Frankish scribe to have written the alien title as *canizauci*. The Avar use of the Bulgar nomenclature of lordship is significant for the last acts of the Avar khaganate. The Bulgar khan Krum won his historic victory over Emperor Nicephorus, who fell on the battlefield, at the end of July 811, only a few months before the *canizauci* appeared at Aachen. The imitation of the successful Bulgar ruler was intended to make some of his radiance fall on the Avar khaganate, threatened on all sides.

The *canizauci*'s objective was to confirm his preeminence over both the Avar and the Slavic *primores* and *duces*. For this, the strained *honor antiquus* was no longer sufficient. In addition, in the event of any claims by the victorious Bulgars who had already once marched in as far as the Tisza River, the khagan's parity in rank with his superior rival could be emphasized. In the Frankish annals at least he was successful. In the account there the *canizauci* is the first in rank. This also suggests that the order established in 805 was still intact and that it was the khagan himself who enhanced his image with the new attribute. As so often, the splendid new varnish did not prevent the collapse into total insignificance.

Župan

The only indication that the title *župan*, later very diffused among the Slavs, was in use among the late Avars are the *boila zoapan* and the *butaul zoapan* in a non-Greek text inscribed in Greek letters on bowl 21 of the Nagyszentmiklós treasure.[195] *Boila* is a class of nobles in the Bulgar khanate, and otherwise not attested among the Avars.[196] Butaul may be the name of a *župan*. If Csanád Bálint's contention that the treasure was assembled by a regional family of Avar nobles is accurate, this could very well have been a hereditary title; the *zoapan*/župan to whom the massive gold bowl (more than two hundred grams of twenty-two carat gold) belonged must have been a top-level aristocrat.[197] Of course, the bowl may also have come to the Carpathian Basin as booty or present. In any case, the early steppe use of the title points to rather high status that it expressed. The term probably originated with the Turks, among whom the title *xhouban* (*ch'u-pan*) is attested in the seventh century; only later did *čupan* designate a village head.[198] The title is well attested in the ninth-century Bulgar khanate where župans are mentioned among the dignitaries at Khan Omurtag's table; composite titles such as *zoupan tarkanos* and *zoupanos megas* (great župan) also appear in the inscriptions.[199] A fragment of a Bulgar military inventory lists a certain Toruna pile zhupan with twenty coats of mail and forty helmets he could lead into the field, a modest number in comparison with some of the boilades mentioned.[200] The Croat principality of the tenth century was divided up in eleven *zupanias*, according to Constantine Porphyrogenitus.[201] The earliest mention of the title among the central Europe Slavs is from the region of Kremsmünster in Upper Austria, not too far from the Avar western boundary. At the foundation of the monastery in 777 a *jopan* by the name of Physso was among the local leaders who paced off the future limits; most likely, a village elder.[202] The status that the title conferred among the Slavs was obviously rather modest, mostly designating a local chieftain. Therefore, it is very unlikely that Bulgars or Avars adopted a modest Slavic title for distinguished members of their nobility; rather, it worked the other way around. The spread of the title *župan* among the Croats and Slavs is best explained by seeing the Avars as intermediaries.

Katun: Avar Queens and Avar Women

The poem on Pippin's victory over the Avars contains the only reference to the title of the (main) spouse of the khagan. As the Frankish army approached, the treacherous Unguimeri not only wished for the fall of the khagan, but also for that of "catunae mulieri, maledictae coniugi."[203] This female ruler's title, too, is widely attested on the steppes. It may originate in Sogdian.[204] It was already the title of the wife of the khagan of the Rouran.[205] In the Old Turkic inscriptions there is firsthand documentation for its use among the Turks and Uyghurs; the Terkhin (or Tariat) inscription, written in ca. 751, begins: "I, the Heavenly-born El-etmiš bilgä-qagan (together with) El-bilgä qatun, having taken the title of qagan and qatun. . . ."[206] It is remarkable that both the khagan and his queen figure here in the *intitulatio*. An Armenian source also uses the title for the wife of the khagan of the Turks of the sixth century.[207] Katun was used not only for wives of rulers, but in some cases also for daughters or sisters; for instance, a daughter of the Khazar khagan who was married to an Arab governor in about 760.[208] It adorned the sister of a Khazar beg who provided relief during a famine.[209] Modern Turkish *kadın*, "woman," is probably derived from this title.[210]

The Avar *katun* then bore a very common title. But it is significant, and not only for Avar male society, that the only mention of a queen should call her "maledicta coniunx." The sources of the period similarly depicted Irene, the Byzantine empress, Fastrada, Charlemagne's spouse, and Liutberga, the wife of Tassilo III, as evil queens. The latter was even accused of having made a pact with the Avars.[211] Very little about the role of women in Avar society can be read from these sources. The katun's influence was probably quite limited as a rule. The khagans were accustomed to have a number of wives.[212] According to Theophylact Simocatta, the Avar khagan took his wives on military campaigns, and at one point their pleasure at bathing in the baths at Anchialus is described.[213] Some archaeological finds indicate that elite males, not only the khagan, could have several wives.[214]

It was a sacrilege deserving of death to become involved with one of the khagan's wives, as the fate of Bookolabras amply demonstrates.[215] Among the Ghuzz/ Oghurs Ibn Fadlan learned that adultery in particular was followed by horrible punishments: the adulterer is tied to the branches of two trees and thus ripped apart.[216] Capital punishment for adultery was also practiced among the Turks, according to Chinese sources.[217] Gardīzī reports that a man committing adultery with a virgin receives three hundred blows with a stick.[218] Among the steppe peoples women were frequently separated from their men for long periods. The severe punishments were intended to preclude any disagreeable surprises resulting from the long absences of the men. On the other hand, the very mobility of the men must have entailed a certain independence for women. Nevertheless, the Mongols' women, as the *Secret History* recounts, were called "the inferiors," and young women were much desired spoils of war.[219]

The status of women among the Avars can only be guessed at on the basis of archaeological evidence. There is nothing like the striking case of rich grave goods including belts in women's graves known from Newolino in the Kama region.[220] In the Carpathian Basin, the finds of belt sets in four female graves at Želovce may be due to a sexing error.[221] There are, however, a number of strap ends in many women's graves in Tiszafüred and surroundings.[222] What we have are women buried with horses, an inhumation practice otherwise only attested for men. So far, twenty-seven cases excavated in southern Slovakia are known, for instance, in some of the graves at Komárno.[223] Among the working population we may assume a gender-specific division of labor from the higher incidence of arthritis among men.[224]

The "Ring" and Avar Defensive Works

In 796 Pippin's army succeeded in capturing the khagan's residence, which had already been plundered by his shock troops under Woynimir. "Locum, ubi reges Avarorum cum principibus suis sedere consueti erant, quem in nostra lingua Hringe nominant" (The place where the kings of the Avars used to reside with their princes, which they call hring in our language);[225] "hringum gentis Avarorum longis retro temporibus quietum";[226] "Hunorum regia, Hringum quam vocitant";[227] "eorum regia quae, ut dictum est, hringus, a Langobardis autem campus vocatur" (their residence that, as is said, is called hring, but by the Lombards, field).[228] Here lay the gigantic treasure that so amazed contemporaries. Stories soon accumulated around the legendary center of the Avar Empire. Almost a century later Notker of St. Gall wrote down what a veteran of the Avar war had purportedly told him when he was a boy. The whole land of the Huns was enclosed by nine circular walls or enclosures, the informant said, between which the distance was similar to that between Zurich and Constance. The ramparts were twenty feet wide and high, made of wood and filled with stone, and within the innermost ring were stored the treasures that had earlier been accumulated by the Goths and Vandals.[229]

These legends were taken up again by the antiquarians and folklorists of the nineteenth century. The fundamental error consisted in identifying several prehistoric circular enclosures as Avar rings. Today it is incontrovertible that the word referred only to the residence of the khagan.[230] Was it a ringlike fortification or just a nomad encampment on open ground, which could, for that reason, also be called a *campus*? The term *campus* as used by the Lombards may be explained by a reference in the *History of the Lombards* that Paul the Deacon had written just years before. It recounts how during their migration the Lombards had settled "in wide fields, which are called in the barbarian language *feld*."[231] It was known that the home of the Lombards once lay on the plains of Pannonia, where the Avars later settled. Pippin's Lombards must have been particularly motivated by the prospect of reconquering their old homeland, the *feld* or *campus* of their migration legend.

There is, however, another striking parallel in a building inscription by the Bulgar khan Omurtag from ca. 822 in which he is presented as residing in his camp, *kampos*, Pliska, and deciding to build a palace there. *Kampos* seems to have referred to a nonpermanent but probably fortified military camp.[232] Archaeologically, the various remains of fortified residences and of long walls, dikes, and enclosures at Pliska cannot securely be dated to before or after the inscription.[233] The outer enclosure was rectangular. In any case, the word *campus* does not mean that there were no fixed residences in this central area of the Avar Empire. Einhard recounts that Pippin's army plundered and destroyed the ring.[234]

The ambivalence of a fixed residence and a zone with special legal status that surrounded it is also characteristic of accounts from central Asia. The concept of *ordu* could cover them both. This term was later transferred to the troops under the direct command of the ruler, from which the English word *horde* is derived.[235] Among the Khitan, the *ordu* was both "the camp or residence of the barbarian king and the territory directly subject to him, that served to protect him."[236] How such a residence might look is noted by an Arabic traveler to the Toquz-Oguz/ Uyghurs. He described the circular arrangement of the camp. Around the khagan's tent city, twelve thousand men, his immediate subjects, stood guard. At a distance of four days' march, tribal leaders and dignitaries with their followers formed a farther ring.[237] The ruler of the Uyghurs crisscrossed the pasturelands with his twenty thousand horses and his mobile residence. In the case of the Avars of the eighth century we should rather assume that the khagans already had a fixed site of residence, even if they did not hold court in a regular capital city like the Khazars and Bulgars.[238]

The ring of the Avars was then most likely a fixed palace settlement, laid out in a circle, with tents or wooden structures. The sources do not say that it was fortified. And clearly it could not be defended in 795 and 796. Yet it is probable that the legend of the huge, fortified site that the monk of St. Gall wrote down may have had some kind of historical core, and defenses were in place somewhere.[239] Around the ring probably an area with particular legal status extended, the center of the empire in a wider sense. In 2017, new archaeological evidence began to emerge near Kecskemét, between the Danube and the Tisza: remains of a rectangular rampart that may enclose an area of several square kilometers, similar to the outer demarcation of the residential zone at Pliska. Further excavations may confirm the initial hypothesis that this was the site of the eighth-century Avar residence.[240]

A further spectacular piece of archaeological evidence for defensive works probably constructed by the Avars still awaits further analysis: extensive dikes and ditches that surround the core area of the Carpathian Basin. Their main part stretches from the Serbian Danube northward along the foothills of the Transylvanian Carpathians up to the upper stretches of the Tisza River, and then turns west along the northern edge of the Great Hungarian Plain to the knee of the Danube near Budapest. Often several dikes run in roughly parallel lines, some of which may also have been built by the early Hungarians. Smaller stretches of earthen walls can be found in the south, roughly between the mouth of the Tisza and Lake Balaton. The total distance covered is over eight hundred miles, an enormous workload to be covered only by forced labor, perhaps by slaves and prisoners of war. These dikes have usually been regarded as Roman advance defense lines or as Sarmatian works.[241] However, there is increasing evidence that the dikes cut through Sarmatian settlements and cemeteries, so they should be posterior. Recently, they have therefore been attributed to the Avars, in particular by Uwe Fiedler.[242] As yet, we lack any precise archaeological dates for the walls, and they could also have been built before or after the Avar period. The Avar hypothesis, however, has some plausibility, not only because it needed stable and powerful rulers to achieve such massive building projects; the walls also coincide rather well with the extension of early Avar cemeteries in eastern Hungary. Pannonia remained largely unprotected.

If these dikes were built by the Avars, what was their function? They are in fact just one example of a striking number of extensive early medieval earthworks in many parts of Europe, including Offa's Dyke between England and Wales and the Danewerk on the southern boundary of the Danish kingdom, both probably built in the eighth century and mentioned in contemporary sources.[243] Closer to the Carpathian Basin, extensive dikes were also constructed under the Bulgar khans.[244] Their defensive function is not always obvious; the large and complicated earthworks in the Dobrudja do not follow any likely borders or defensible lines, and the function of the about twenty miles of defensive constructions around Pliska is also unclear. Squatriti concluded that their use was perhaps symbolic rather than military: "The Bulgar dikes radiated the khans' glories across the cultural landscape they fashioned."[245] This may help to explain why the Avars should have built such massive earthworks (if the attribution can be upheld).

The dikes would not have helped against Byzantine attacks (the expedition by Priscus was the only Byzantine offensive operation and did not encounter any relevant defensive structures). And they did not protect the western boundaries against Lombards and Franks, where Charlemagne's army encountered some fortifications on both sides of the Danube in 791 (see section 8.4). They could have had some function against an attack from the northeast, and might express preoccupations with real or imagined threats from Turks before the 620s, Bulgars after 630, and Khazars in the eighth century. If the Avars conserved any memories from central Asia, they certainly knew that most steppe empires had been overwhelmed by competitors from the steppe; not least, that of the Rouran. Long dikes may not have been very efficient defenses, but they could suggest to friend and foe that one was prepared for an attack. As in the case of the Bulgars, though, they hardly marked an outer frontier. Frankish legends about Avar bulwarks thus had at least some factual basis.

8.3 *Limes Certus*: The Avars and the West

When Frankish armies under the command of Charlemagne set out against the Avars in 791, they stopped at the Enns River in order to pray and fast for three days. "For this river, which flows through the middle of the border area between the Bavarians and the Huns, serves as a sure frontier for the two realms."[246] Between the Avars and the Bavarians there had been relations regulated by treaty; the frontier, the *limes certus*, was fixed. Decades later the alpine foothills of Lower Austria were still called *terra Avarorum* or *provincia Avarorum*, and the Diedenhofen capitulary in 805 established Lorch as the customs station toward the *partes Sclavorum et Avarorum*.[247] It may be assumed that as early as 700 the border had been here at the lower Enns. Two saints' lives, written down in the second half of the eighth century, have clear references to this effect. Around the year 696 on a trip down the Danube Bishop Rupert turned back at Lorch and redirected his steps toward Salzburg.[248] When St. Emmeram intended to undertake a mission "ad robustam gentem Avarorum," he did not even get this far. Duke Theodo counseled him against the journey. "At that time a conflict had broken out between the Huns and the people of the Bavarians, so that the towns along the Enns, which formed the border, were devastated.... For, even if someone were obligated to another by oaths, he still thought more of subterfuge than of the professed friendship."[249] This attack, which most likely took place in 715, broke earlier treaties.[250] These were relevant issues when Arbeo wrote, in the 760s/770s; but he could assume that things had not been all that different at the beginning of the century.

For the messengers of the faith of the seventh century nothing was to be achieved east of Bavaria. Around 610 Columbanus dreamed in good time of the lack of prospects of a journey to the Avars, and some thirty years later Amandus suffered the missionary's worst possible fate among the Slavs of the lands along the Danube: he was not even judged worthy of martyrdom.[251] In the eighth century, the "Hunni" on Bede's mission list were at least notionally counted among the people of the Germania when it came to spreading the faith.[252]

In the earlier eighth century, missions and the establishment of ecclesiastical organization among the Bavarians and other peoples east of the Rhine remained far preferable to attempts at conversion among Avars and Slavs. The missionary center that Rupert built up in Salzburg would later be of decisive importance for the Christianization of the lands on the middle Danube and in the Eastern Alps. In Rupert's time, around 700, the range of missionary activities only stretched to nearby Bischofshofen where a church was built in the neighborhood of unruly Slavs. Corbinian's fantastic journey to "Valeria," the old eastern part of Pannonia, was pasted together later by his biographer on the basis of ancient texts.[253]

The Slavic neighbors were still judged as potentially dangerous. Another, even more legendary hagiographical text claims that "Vandals" (Wends) at the time of Emperor Leontius (695–98) attacked the area around the Chiemsee and martyred two hermits at Irschenberg in Bavaria; the dating by the years of a minor Byzantine emperor is remarkable.[254] The *Annales Mettenses Priores* maintain that toward the end of the seventh century, at the court of the Carolingian major of the palace, Pippin II, embassies of the "Greeks, Romans, Lombards, Huns (Avars), Slavs and Saracens, poured in to him." This part of the annals was, however, written shortly after 800 as eulogy of the Carolingian forefathers.[255]

All these legendary records contribute little to a narrative of Avar history in the later seventh and earlier eighth centuries. The Avars of the eighth century were generally peaceful neighbors. The Lombard king Liutprand (712–44) had no problems with them.[256] In a law promulgated by his successor Ratchis in 746 *Avaria* is named along with the Lombard duchies, Francia, Bavaria, and Alemannia: without the king's permission no one was allowed to send envoys to these powers.[257] What is also interesting here is that this is the first mention in Latin of the term *Avaria*.[258] The Avar name had, after almost two centuries, attached itself to their homeland; a usage that only recurs for the Frankish Avaria after 800 (see section 8.5). A good example of this terminology is the confirmation of Charlemagne's Aio charter from 799, which Louis the Pious issued in 816.[259] In 799 the region was called *partes Avariae*, but in 816 the terms *regnum Abarorum* and *Abaria* are used. It was not until its incorporation into the organization of the Frankish kingdom that the Avar region finally became an Avaria in the terminology of Latin writers. At any event, a memory continued of the Avars having once occupied a part of the territories of the East Roman Empire. The Ravenna geographer around 700 uses the terms "Dacia" and "Gepidia" for the lands "ubi modo Uni, qui et Avari, inhabitant."[260] That he should indicate Dacia and not Pannonia as the homeland of the Avars is probably based on Jordanes who located the Gepids in Dacia; and in the land of the Gepids the Avars now lived. The term *Avaria* does not occur here.

It is only in 741 or more likely 742 that we hear of conflict on the western Avar border. Then "the Huns in inimical unrest began to press the Carantanians hard. Their prince was then Boruth, who informed the Bavarians that the host of the Huns might move against them and asked that they come to his aid. These appeared at once, drove off the Huns, secured the Carantanians' allegiance," and began missionary work in the country.[261] The dating relies on the fact that in 743 Duke Odilo already led a Carantanian contingent against the Carolingians.[262] The decision of the alpine Slavs to side with the Bavarians changed the political geography of the Eastern Alps. The Avars obviously suffered a defeat. The conversion of Carantania began at a slow pace, and even the account of the *Conversio Bagoariorum et Carantanorum*, written from the perspective of Salzburg, had to admit setbacks, pagan resistance, and revolts.[263] The khaganate was not involved in these conflicts anymore and was obviously unable to profit by such opportunities. Close cooperation between the Bavarian dukes, the Carantanian princes, and the Church of Salzburg gradually achieved the Christianization of Carantania. A series of monastic foundations in the vicinity of Slavic settlement areas in Upper Austria (Mondsee, Kremsmünster, Mattsee) and in south Tyrol (Innichen), above all under Tassilo III (748–88), provided the infrastructure for further missionary activities. An active Bavarian policy in the frontier zones to the east laid the ground for the further expansion of the Carolingian period.

Under Avar rule the territory to the east of the Enns was thinly settled, presumably above all by Slavs. Only indistinct traces point to German-speaking population groups and traditions dating from the age of migrations. A few Germanic names occur in the last phase of Avar presence, such as Unguimeri who accompanied the khagan at the submission to the Franks in 796, or the brothers Wirut, Gisalmar, and Wentilmar who donated land in the Avar country in 808.[264] The Carolingian conquerors also used a few German-language place-names in the new territories, among them Herilungoburg near Pöchlarn and Omundesthorf, which Charlemagne passed on the Pannonian frontier in 791.[265] The preservation of pre-Avar river names does not prove that there were Germanic or Roman settlements on their banks. People in Lorch certainly had some information on the way to their Avar neighbors. We know from many early medieval sources that such itineraries in particular contained information on the rivers to be crossed.[266]

Only after the Carolingian conquest of the Avaria could an ecclesiastical organization and structures of landholding be built up east of the Enns River. Yet soon the beginnings of Bavarian and Frankish presence in the region came to be dated to the period before 791, an interpretation that many modern historians gladly made their own. For instance, the foundation charter of the monastery at Kremsmünster in 777 contains an interpolated grant of land in *Grunzwitigau* in the Lower Austrian Dunkelsteiner Wald.[267] According to the second *Passio s. Quirini* of the High Middle Ages the founders of Tegernsee, Adalbert and Otakar, were also the founders of the monastery dedicated to St. Hippolytus in St. Pölten, which would point to a time shortly after the foundation of Tegernsee in ca. 760. More likely the founder was a later member of the family, perhaps the Audaccrus/Otakar who had fought against the Avars on the Ybbsfeld in 788.[268]

The Danubian region of Lower Austria can be seen as a contact zone between the Avar realm and the west; these exchanges have left sparse traces in the historical, archaeological, and onomastic evidence. Excavations demonstrate that with the entry of the Avars no iron curtain fell along the Enns. The cemetery of Linz-Zizlau is exemplary for the seventh century in showing that the areas around Lorch and Linz were cultural nodes. Warrior grave 74 is particularly characteristic. The man was buried in Western costume. Next to the body lay an Avar lance and eleven three-edged arrowheads. Avar imports were also found in other graves, where it is often difficult to distinguish among trade goods, booty, and the possessions of immigrants from the Avar sphere.[269] Objects from Bavaria have been identified in Lower Austrian Avar graves from the end of the seventh century, such as the belts from Sommerein (grave 16) and Mödling (grave 240), a sword in Wien-Liesing, weapons in Zwölfaxing, or a vessel in Wien-Unter St. Veit.[270] These are surely not the remains of Bavarian colonists but traces of cultural contacts (which need not always have been peaceful). Late Avar and Byzantine materials, combined in a particular manner, are above all found in the Slavic environment of the Eastern Alps, such as the impressive gilded belt-set from Hohenberg in the valley of the Enns or the bronze belt fittings from Krungl in the Styrian Salzkammergut, both from the second half of the eighth century.[271] The Slavs who settled around 800 in Wimm near Maria Taferl on the Lower Austrian stretch of the Danube used individual parts of late Avar belt fittings.[272] Avar traces are also to be found in the Slavic cemetery in Micheldorf from the ninth century.[273] However, Avar weapons and accessories did not normally travel far and wide.[274] Exchanges with Western peoples were far greater in the early Avar period, when Avar horse harness in particular but also laminated armor and armor-piercing lances served as models.[275] The reflex bow was occasionally used by the Lombards, Alamans, and Franks.[276] But it never became firmly established and was always a prestige object. Over time the West adopted the stirrup.[277] It is certainly exaggerated to speak of a

total encapsulation of the Avar Empire in the eighth century. Supraregional connections had declined, but this was not simply due to a splendid isolation on the
part of the Avars but to the general regionalization that had begun in the seventh
century. There were still exchanges on a small scale, traces of which can be identified on both sides of the *limes certus*, the Enns.[278] The Avars, at any event, missed
the opportunity for a new expansive policy that emerged around the middle of the
eighth century, a trend that favored the rise of the Carolingians. When in 788 the
expanding Frankish power reached the Enns, the khaganate had little more than
the memories of its former greatness to oppose it.

8.4 The Collapse of Avar Power

"Charlemagne's greatest war, apart from that against the Saxons, was the Avar
war (*contra Avaros vel Hunos*); it was conducted with more fervor and greater
force of arms than all the others." Einhard's judgment in his biography of the
emperor surely reflects the perceptions of the Carolingian court.[279] The war
ended after eight years with a complete victory, Einhard continues: following
this great bloodshed, Pannonia was emptied of people, the khagan's residence
had been devastated, the Avar nobility had perished, and all the treasures had
been taken as spoils: "and human memory cannot remember any war that had
been waged against the Franks in which these were more enriched and their
resources were increased more."[280] Even taking into account the possibility of
propagandistic exaggeration, this was surely the Carolingians' most profitable
victory. Yet Einhard's account also hints at the contradictions of this unusual
war. The war was pursued by the Franks with almost no loss of life. The two most
prominent victims named by Einhard, Eric of Friuli and Gerold, did not actually
die fighting against Avars.

"Abares, Arabes Nomadesque" bowed their heads to Charlemagne, as the poet
Theodulf presents the Carolingian's triumph in a world-encompassing play on
words.[281] Corippus had been the last poet to celebrate a ruler, Justin II, in Latin
in similar fashion. Charlemagne, in a certain sense, achieved what Justin had
only boasted of. Even the image of the pig-tailed Avars crops up again. "Textis
crinibus," with plaited hair, the Hun turns to Christ, and "he who once was savage
is now humble before the faith."[282] The fine words betray the great importance
attached to the Avar war at Charlemagne's court. The victory, which also delivered the remains of the old imperial city of Sirmium into the hands of the Franks,
was a milestone on the way from *regnum Francorum* to empire.

Josef Deér has shown in detail how Carolingian propaganda prepared the
offensive in Pannonia, using the timeless stereotype of the menace from the East.

The "Avarorum malitia" was, by the end of the eighth century, little more than a distant historical memory, even though it plays a role in some historiographical works of the period.[283] The casus belli was certainly not a threatened "German outpost" near the Vienna Woods, as nationalistic historians believed.[284] The war was a matter of expansion, not of defense. Yet the symbolic significance of the war against the pagans on the Danube should not be underestimated. More than any other opponents, the Avars embodied the heritage of the age of migrations. "So many precious objects were taken in this war, that it might be fairly said that the Franks had justly seized from the Huns what the Huns had unjustly seized from the other peoples," as Einhard justified the expropriation of the expropriators.[285] The Avar "Huns" were the successors of Huns, Goths, Vandals, and all the other savage peoples who over the course of more than two centuries had plundered their Western Roman neighbors' riches from their bases in Pannonia.[286] For the Carolingian age, they represented the pagan par excellence. Sometime after 820, the artist of the Utrecht Psalter illustrated the passage of Psalm 43, "Judge me, O God, and distinguish my cause from the nation that is not holy: deliver me from the unjust and deceitful man," with Avar horsemen with stirrups and short reflex bows.[287] Charlemagne acted in the name of the Christian West that had long suffered from barbarian depredations. The Franks' own past as one of these *gentes* could in this new confrontation finally be forgotten. The victory over the Avars symbolized a line drawn under the dark centuries during which the West had suffered from barbarian incursions. The pieces of the spoils that the emperor distributed across Europe, from England to Rome, were meant to emphasize this, and the mission to the Avars begun with high hopes was intended to consolidate the new conditions.

Compared to the symbolic significance of the victory, the territorial gains mattered little. However, neither the Bavarian and Frankish "colonization" of the east nor the Christian mission matched the high hopes. Still, new opportunities were being created. In the course of the eighth century, the Bavarian dukes and aristocracy, as well as the church, had established bases for expansion along the duchy's eastern border.[288] In 788, the Carolingians succeeded in deposing the autonomous Bavarian duke Tassilo III. The loyalty of the Bavarians could best be won by opening up new opportunities for them.[289] Charlemagne not only continued the expansionist policies of the Bavarian dukes, but advanced them on a substantially greater scale. The ambitious if uneventful campaign of 791 was in this sense also a demonstration of power and ambition. The Frankish king had not anticipated how easy it would be to challenge Avar power. After the defeat of the Avars, the Franks succeeded only partly in exploiting this victory and never gained full control over the former khaganate. The Avar war nevertheless had decisive consequences for the settlement history of the middle Danube region.

"Avaria" east of the Enns became a Bavarian-Slavic frontier area under Frankish rule, the "Wild East" of the eastern Frankish kingdom.

Since the 770s, the Avars closely followed the threatening developments on their western border and, within the limits of their possibilities, tried to defend the status quo. In 774 the Lombards, long-time Avar allies, succumbed to the Franks, who thereby became the sole neighbors of the Avars to the west.[290] Two years later a Lombard rebellion against the new rulers failed, and it was probably no coincidence that at least one of the noblemen involved, Aio, fled to the Avars. Only in 799 was Aio pardoned and regained his properties near Cividale.[291] A short time later Charlemagne's superior force also made itself felt in Bavaria. In 781 Tassilo III had to renew his oath of allegiance in Worms and hand over hostages.[292] The Avars reacted promptly. In July 782 Avar envoys appeared at Lippspringe "for the sake of peace"; the annals reveal only that Charlemagne "heard and dismissed them."[293] At the same time a considerable Avar army drew up on the Enns but left after a mere show of power. "Nocuerunt nihil," they did no damage, the Bavarian annals note with relief.[294] The Avars' gestures combined a peace offer with a threat. It was certainly intended to signify that the *limes certus* would be defended in case of need. It is uncertain whether the Avars' actions were the result of an agreement with Tassilo; they might have been meant to strengthen the duke's position.[295] The Avar army, however, did not exploit the fact that Charlemagne's military focus that year lay to the north, in the war against Saxons and Sorbs.[296]

Yet the Avars were not spared from being drawn into the conflict between Tassilo and Charlemagne. In 788 the Bavarian duke was accused before an imperial assembly in Ingelheim of having made a pact with the Avars and was deposed.[297] The Franks above all blamed Tassilo's Lombard wife Liutberga for having stirred up "the Huns."[298] Even though the sources reflect Frankish propaganda, it is possible that a Bavarian-Lombard coalition of the defeated sought, with Avar help and Byzantine backing, to check Charlemagne's triumphal advance. But Tassilo's fall could not be prevented, and opposition to Charlemagne remained isolated. In 788 only the Avars took to the field on two fronts.

The principal attack apparently occurred in Friuli. Alcuin notes in a letter from 790 that the Avars had pillaged in Italy but had been driven off, and a number of annals mention the same events.[299] A charter from Verona claiming that the Avars had advanced as far as the city and severely damaged the walls near the Church of St. Zeno when King Pippin of Italy was young has, however, been proven a forgery.[300] In the northern theater of war the Franks went on the offensive. They engaged the Avars on the Ybbsfeld near the Danube, some forty miles east of the Enns border, and won a victory under the leadership of the two royal *missi* Grahamannus and Audaccrus. That same year the defeated Avars tried to retaliate with an incursion into Bavaria, but Charlemagne's commanders were again victorious.[301]

It was a predominantly Bavarian army "with some Franks" that won this victory. Even Charlemagne's two representatives were drawn from the Bavarian aristocracy. Grahamannus/Graman held lands, significantly, near the border in Traungau, and belonged to a group of nobles who, in close association with Bishop Arn of Salzburg, "strongly influenced political developments across the hiatus of 788."[302] Audaccrus/Otakar was from a very prominent family whose many members of the same name are difficult to distinguish from one another. Their involvement illustrates the backing that Charlemagne's offensives in the east had in Bavaria.[303] Toward the end of his reign, Tassilo's anti-Carolingian policies no longer coincided with the wide-ranging interests of the Bavarian aristocracy, who saw the opportunities that the other side of the *limes certus* offered. Tassilo's alliance of despair with the Avars stood in the way of such expansive ambitions. Many Bavarian noblemen were therefore ready enough to extend their sphere of influence eastward in the service of the successful Carolingian ruler. After the fall of the khaganate, royal mandates, monastic foundations, and land grants soon gave them new positions of power east of the Enns.[304]

The "weak intervention"[305] of 788 damaged the position of the khaganate, and the Avars were unwilling to mount further attacks. For the Franks, on the other hand, the Avar problem was now high on the agenda. In mid-789 Alcuin enquired by letter what Charlemagne was thinking of doing "de Hunorum hoste."[306] Avar envoys appeared at an assembly at Worms in 790. The *Royal Frankish Annals'* revised version, written shortly after 800, notes that the negotiations concerned "the borders of the kingdoms and where they ought to be."[307] This question was left unresolved, and the annals saw this as the *casus belli* for the Avar campaign of 791. The Franks had obviously demanded the surrender of considerable lands east of the Enns, while the Avar delegates wanted to maintain the old *limes certus*.

791: Charlemagne's Campaign into the Land of the Avars

The Avar war that Charlemagne initiated in 791 was an impressive performance, in more than one sense. Franks and Saxons, Frisians, Thuringians, Bavarians, even Slavs gathered that summer at Regensburg.[308] Before this assembly of armies, the Avars were ceremoniously accused of insufferable "malitia" that had to be punished by a military campaign.[309] The army was then divided: One division was to move along the northern bank of the Danube under the command of the *comes* Theoderic and the chamberlain Meginfred. The main army kept to the south of the river. In addition, a fleet was built for the Danube, manned mostly by Bavarians.[310] Meginfred is named as a witness in two charters from Freising drawn up at the field camp at Lorch.[311] Both armies followed the Danube as far as possible, allowing them to maintain contact with the fleet.[312] In order to be able to provision the army, Charlemagne had waited for the harvest to be brought in, which explains that the war began relatively late in the year: "At the time when the kings customarily set out for war."[313]

At the beginning of September, the Carolingian armies pitched camp at Lorch near the mouth of the Enns. On Monday, September 5, three days of fasting and prayers, accompanied by solemn masses, were begun in order to win heavenly blessing for the great undertaking.[314] More detail is offered in a letter sent by Charlemagne to his spouse Fastrada.[315] The priests, the king wrote, had banned the consumption of wine and meat, excepting only those suffering from "infirmitas" due to their advanced age or their youth. It was permissible to buy oneself free of the ban on wine, the "potentiores," at the cost of one solidus a day, the poorer soldiers "each according to his own good will and in proportion to his means." The number of fighters who were prepared to pay for the privilege of wine has not come down to us; Charlemagne himself, as Einhard recounts, was rather disinclined to fast.[316] During this time each priest had to say a mass and the clerics had to sing psalms and recite litanies, "as our priests considered proper." This liturgical spectacle says a great deal about early medieval religious beliefs. The rituals united warriors and noncombatants before the actual campaign to enhance their commitment and seek divine aid for its success.[317]

The camp at Lorch also provided an opportunity for the expedition's participants to resolve their various conflicts within a fitting context. At a great court, presided over by Bishop Arn, the Bavarian prefect Gerold, and the chamberlain Meginfred, the inheritance conflict of the Huosi, one of the five most prominent families of Bavaria, was deliberated. Three days of negotiation were needed to reach an agreement.[318] The resulting document testifies to the considerable participation of the Bavarian nobility in Charlemagne's Avar war. Among the many witnesses of the document who prepared to take part in the military expedition a certain *Nibulunc* is named, bracing for the march along the Danube into the land of the Huns, just as the knights in the Song of the Nibelungs. Just how significant contemporaries considered the 791 campaign is demonstrated by the fact that some Freising charters take its year as their chronological point of reference.[319]

The charter evidence indicates that the army only set out from Lorch after a week or two. Meanwhile, the first victory was reported from the south, where the *scara*, the troop of young Pippin of Italy under the leadership of the *duces* of Istria (presumably Duke John) and Friuli, had already crossed the border into the "partes Avariae" in mid-August.[320] Battle was joined at an Avar fort, and the "uualum" was captured, several Avars killed, and 150 of them captured.[321] After the victory the *scara* from Italy obviously withdrew.[322] Charlemagne seems to have waited at Lorch for the announcement of victory from Italy before he himself broke camp and set off.[323]

The two armies met no resistance as they marched downstream along the Danube. It was not until they were deep in Avar territory that they encountered the first Avar fortifications. Meginfred's army captured and destroyed a fort on the Kamp river.[324] South of the Danube Avar border defenses were first met at the Vienna Woods, "iuxta Comagenos civitatem in monte Cumeoberg." Here too the Avar garrison fled. It may seem unusual for a people of mounted warriors to barricade themselves behind fortifications, yet the information of the sources is clear. It shows how far the Avar warriors had moved away from a nomadic way of life.[325]

At the "Chuneberg," the Hun mountain, as some interpreted the name Cumeoberg, the roughly thirteen-year-old Louis, the future emperor, had to turn back. His father had girded him with his sword for the first time for this expedition.[326] Charlemagne does not seem to have considered the march up to here particularly unsafe for his son. Louis's impressions seem to have been unfavorable, as he never again returned to the region.[327] Another illustrious companion left the Frankish army forever in the Hunnic "hag" at "Chunisberg." This was Angilram, bishop of Metz, who died here later on his return journey on October 26.[328] The strain of the campaign also cost the lives of several of his colleagues.[329] They were, however, only indirectly victims of the war, as the Avars offered little resistance.

Beyond the Vienna Wood, the army not only entered Avar settlement areas, it also crossed the ancient boundary into the former Roman province of Pannonia. The *Annales Maximiani* mention a place called Omundesthorf, past which Charlemagne marched into Pannonia. That has often been regarded as a surviving Germanic settlement near Vienna; but rather, Omundesthorf may have been at the Enns, for Pannonia was supposed to extend to the Enns in the Carolingian period.[330] The Avars offered no resistance to the advancing Frankish armies. It must have been the middle of October when Charlemagne's army reached the river Rába. The armies encamped at the mouth of the river, near modern Győr, for a few days. Here the Franks were hampered not only by the advanced season but above all by a pestilence, "so that hardly one tenth of all the horses for the troops were said to have remained."[331] It is very likely that the disease had already affected the Avar horses, which may explain why the Franks encountered no resistance.[332] Charlemagne decided to return home via ancient Savaria, which was known as the birthplace of Saint Martin, while he commanded the northern army to take the route across "Bohemia."[333] In all, the Frankish army spent fifty-two days in enemy territory, unless this number is symbolic.[334] In any case, we can assume a duration for the campaign of about two months, from early/mid-September to the first half of November, during which the army covered about four hundred miles in Avar territory.[335]

The concrete results of the campaign were meager. The decisive blow against the Avars had not been delivered. The annals recount only the devastation, plundering, and the many prisoners who were carried off. Carolingian propaganda hailed this as a victory, even a triumph.[336] The attackers did indeed enter densely settled territory east of the Vienna Woods. Excavations in the Vienna Basin and the Little Hungarian Plain give some idea of what might have been taken as spoils here. It was mainly an area of small agrarian settlements.[337] The Avar horsemen and other warriors, like the garrisons from the forts on the Kamp and in the Vienna Woods before, seem to have made off in timely fashion. Gold and treasures as they were later plundered in the "ring" were presumably not available in this region. That the Avar territories were "for the greater part devastated" in 791, as the *Annales Mosellani* would have it,[338] was surely a rather egregious exaggeration; the Frankish campaign affected only a small part of the Avar Empire.

On the other hand, the success lay exactly in the way in which two Frankish armies had been able to devastate the Avar realm for weeks undisturbed, "absque bello,"[339] without anyone being able to hinder them. Such an event must have done permanent damage to the prestige of the khaganate and the credibility of its ruler. The internal conflicts and divisions that would become evident some years later had their root not least in the impotence revealed by Charlemagne's large-scale campaign. It would therefore not be justified to see the campaign of 791 as a failure, even if the Franks knew that no decisive victory had been achieved. Charlemagne's intensive buildup of arms in the following years showed that he was determined to force this decisive moment as soon as possible.

792 to 796

The Avar war remained on the agenda and was one of the reasons Charlemagne stayed in Regensburg until the end of the year 793.[340] Perseverance in the war against the pagans and the massive preparations also provided a distraction from domestic political matters at a troubled time.[341] The potential of the Danube fleet, in particular, was to be improved. "On river boats a bridge was built, which was so connected with anchors and ropes that it could be brought together and then separated again."[342] All *comites* were charged with ensuring good bridges and providing good ships.[343] Assembling the Danube fleet more easily was also a main aim of one of the most ambitious projects of the time, the construction of a canal between Altmühl and Rednitz in order to create a navigable link between the Rhine and the Danube.[344] In the autumn of 793 the emperor encamped at the construction site; however, despite the huge investment of labor, this prestige project eventually had to be abandoned and left to the rulers of a much later age.[345]

Charlemagne's ambitious activities in the southeast alerted his enemies. The recently subjugated Saxons hoped for an Avar counterattack and sent envoys to the Avars to incite them to an alliance.[346] In July 792 a Frankish flotilla was attacked on the Elbe; in 793, a general rebellion broke out, also joined by Slavs and part of the Frisians.[347] Even in far-off Spain, the emir of Cordoba put his trust in the power of the Avars to tie down the Frankish army in distant Pannonia.[348] On top of these external threats, a family quarrel erupted in the autumn of 792, when Charles's eldest son, the illegitimate Pippin "the Hunchback" (not to be confused with the Italian king of the same name), rose in revolt; the "cruelty" of Queen Fastrada was blamed for this embarrassing affair.[349] This multitude of difficulties obliged Charles to postpone the great Avar war; in 794 the Franks waged war on the Saxons and Saracens, and the Saxon war lasted well into the year 795.[350]

The hopes of Charles's enemies in the power of the Avars, however, proved illusory. The unsatisfactory campaign of 791, which had encouraged the Franks' opponents, turned into a great Frankish victory through its aftereffects. Many of the Avars had clearly been convinced of the superiority of Frankish arms. With the ruling elite discredited by its defenselessness, rivalries erupted amongst the Avar princes. We do not know exactly when the civil war, "intestina clades," first mentioned in the *Royal Frankish Annals* of 796, broke out, but it seems to have reached its apogee in 795.[351]

While the Saxon war was still under way, ambassadors from the tudun in Pannonia appeared in Hliune on the Elbe, where Charlemagne had set up camp, and offered the king the subjection of their lord with his land and people.[352] He also wished to accept the Christian faith. In this the tudun was following an old behavior pattern of the steppe horsemen who might abandon a failed leader relatively quickly in order to associate themselves with the victor. The strong cohesion that had distinguished the Avar Empire was disintegrating, sealing the fate of the khaganate even before it had suffered a decisive defeat.

Still in 795, the Franks exploited the weakening of their opponent for an audacious surprise attack. The idea for this tactic was probably not the king's, who preferred to think in imperial terms, but likely came from Eric, the duke of Friuli. Perhaps experience with the huge and cumbersome army of 791 made a rapid strike on a lesser scale seem a viable alternative. Eric equipped a troop that was to make a thrust into the center of the Avar Empire. This commando operation was led by the Slav Woynimir, who was probably more familiar with circumstances in the Avar kingdom. Speed and sudden appearances had always been the Avars' trump card; now they were beaten with their own tactics. By the autumn of 795 Woynimir's troops had reached the "ring" and had taken part of the fabulous Avar treasure as booty.[353] Eric did not personally participate in the risky venture. Who exactly Woynimir was is hard to tell, but Eric must have known him well enough to entrust him with such an enterprise. It is quite likely that Woynimir had made a career among the Franks and was not simply a Slavic leader from the Avar borderlands.

Large campaigns were now no longer needed. In 796 victory fell to the Franks all by itself. The tudun appeared, as he had promised, before Charles with a great following, took his oath of allegiance, and accepted baptism, at which point he was richly rewarded.[354] While Charlemagne went on campaign against the Saxons, King Pippin of Italy and Duke Eric of Friuli repeated Woyni-mir's operation by assembling a larger army in which Bavarians and Alamans also took part.[355] This expedition seemed more like an act of state than a military operation. On the march from Friuli to the Danube it met no resistance. When the Franks encamped on the Danube, the new khagan, who had risen to power after the civil war, appeared with a retinue including his spouse, the katun, tarkhans, and other dignitaries. What led to his submission is depicted in dramatized form in the panegyric poem to King Pippin. Unguimeri, "Avarorum genere," scornfully reproached the khagan, stating that his empire was destroyed and his rule ended: nothing was left for him but to submit.[356] Pippin immediately sent messengers with the good news to his father, who was campaigning with his army in Saxony. The *Royal Frankish Annals*, clearly relying on the reports that Charlemagne received, confirm that the khagan met Pippin in order to surrender.[357]

However, not all Avars felt bound by the submission of their khagan; some of them withdrew across the Tisza in order to wait there for further developments.[358] Pippin's army now crossed the Danube and occupied the abandoned "ring," which was again thoroughly plundered and finally destroyed. From here he again sent envoys to Charlemagne.[359] The most pressing matter was now considered to be the Avars' Christianization. The eminent clerics who had accompanied the army held a synod in the camp on the Danube under the direction of the patriarch Paulinus of Aquileia in order to discuss questions relating to the mission. The synodal acts sum up debates about the obligation to undertake the pagan mission but also about the concrete challenges posed by the conversion of an irrational people without script and scripture, "gens bruta et irrationabilis vel certe idiotae et sine litteris."[360]

Bishop Arn of Salzburg was probably among the participants. In a letter written shortly after Easter 796 Alcuin sent him on his way with comforting advice: "The military force that accompanies you is intended for your security and defense. . . . The (Avar) realm was long stable and powerful. Yet stronger is he who has conquered it." He also urged Arn not to repeat in the Avar mission the mistakes that had been made in Saxony.[361] Alcuin's correspondence from that period combines congratulations for the victory over the "gentes populosque Hunorum" with hopes of their conversion. It shows that the task of Christianization was being undertaken with a host of good intentions. Paulinus of Aquileia and Arn of Salzburg, the responsible bishops, were, however, less enthusiastic, as Alcuin's admonitions show.[362] Yet for contemporaries the "subiectio pacifica" could not be separated from the "christianitatis fidei promissio."[363] Both were appreciably harder to achieve than the rapid victory had suggested: only gradually was an infrastructure established in conquered Pannonia that enabled these two objectives to be pursued.[364]

Debate continues on whether the year 796 already sealed the fate of the Avar Empire. Some scholars believe that it was only the Bulgar attack in 804–5 that led to the collapse of the khaganate.[365] The years 799–803 proved that the Avar force had not been completely broken. The Franks had won no single, decisive victory. Yet the uncontested submission shows how far advanced the decline of the Avar realm was. This process accelerated after 796, so that the Franks actually became interested in preserving the dependent Avar principalities.[366] After 796 we can no longer assume a unified Avar Empire; there is no mention in the sources of a khagan for a considerable period. In Pannonia west of the Danube the tudun ruled as Charlemagne's vassal, and it was he who in the revolt of 799–803 became the Franks' principal opponent. Those Avars who wanted to avoid Frankish rule had sought refuge east of the Tisza, and their leader may have been the kapkhan. The Franks, however, were content with the nominal subjugation of the entire khaganate and did not involve themselves in the affairs of the Tisza Avars, who in turn gave the Franks no occasion to concern themselves further with the regions east of the Danube.

797 to 811

In the years after 796 other problems came to the fore for the Carolingian public. More attention is devoted in the annals to the war against the Saxons or the conflicts in Spain than to conditions in the land of the Avars. In 797 a Lombard-Bavarian army under Eric of Friuli was probably once again active in Pannonia; the Alemannic annals also mention King Pippin's struggles with Slavs.[367] At the end of the same year an Avar embassy with rich gifts attended Charles at Herstelle.[368] Unfortunately we do not know which of the Avar princes had sent it. In 798, Arn, bishop of Salzburg, was promoted to archbishop, not least in the context of the Avar mission. In January 799 Alcuin inquired of him by letter "what Avaria does and believes."[369] Yet progress was clearly slight. When rebellion broke out in the east in 799, Alcuin observed critically: "The loss of the Huns, as you say, is due to our negligence."[370]

Frankish policies in the southeast did, in fact, suffer a serious reverse in 799. As the Avars revolted, the two responsible commanders of Carolingian forces, Duke Eric of Friuli and Gerold, prefect of the eastern territories, were both killed in the same year, though neither died in battle with the Avars.[371] Eric "fell victim to an attack by the residents of the city of Tarsatica in Liburnia."[372] Tarsatica/Trsat, on a hilltop in present-day Rijeka, belonged to the coastal strip of Liburnia that had remained under Byzantine rule in the seventh century. Apparently the Franks now claimed sovereignty over the city, as they did over the Istrian Peninsula. That the populations of these old Roman cities were dissatisfied with the Frankish functionaries is demonstrated by the grievances voiced in the so-called Placitum of Risano held a few years later near Koper in Istria.[373] The attack on Eric by the townsfolk of Tarsatica suggests that they had Byzantine backing.[374] The Byzantines may also have encouraged the revolt of Avar groups. Paulinus, patriarch of Aquileia and a skilled poet, honored the fallen Eric with a poem that reveals the tension between dreams and realities of Frankish expansion.[375] Among the cities that grieve for him, first named is Sirmium, desolate but still linked to imperial traditions; then follow the urban centers of Istria and Friuli. The poem then culminates in a vision in which Scythia, the marshes of the Sea of Azov, and the Caspian Gates appear as potential targets for imperial expansion. The victory over the "Scythians" of the Carpathian Basin extended the Carolingian horizon to include the vast spaces of the ancient geographers.

However, the death of the Carolingian commander Gerold, on September 1, 799, also fell short of these new vistas opened up by the Avar war. Einhard recounts that Charlemagne's brother-in-law was killed with two companions, "uncertain by whom," while inspecting the troops before the battle against the Avars.[376] The *Royal Frankish Annals* are silent about this murder mystery and have him die an honorable death in battle.[377] The double loss of Eric and Gerold deprived the Franks' Avar policy of its principal leaders, and it is unclear whether the revolt was put down that year.[378] A few years later, in 802, unrest in Pannonia again claimed the lives of two high-ranking individuals. The counts Chadaloh and Goteram died during an Avar attack at "castellum Guntionis," together with many others.[379] This locality is probably not identical, as was once assumed, with present-day Köszeg/Güns. Excavations in the church of Traismauer have revealed the skeleton of a man with a three-edged Avar arrowhead stuck in his ribcage, and it is possible that the deceased, certainly of high rank, was one of the two fallen counts.[380] After several indirect victims of the Avar wars here we have the first prominent individuals actually killed at Avar hands. Retribution in the form of a counterattack did not occur until the following year, 803, when Charlemagne himself came to Bavaria and sent an army on to Pannonia, awaiting its return in Regensburg. For the first time in years the annals could again record a success in the southeast. With the victorious army returned the tudun, who pledged allegiance to the emperor. Among his followers were "multi Sclavi et Hunni." Pannonian affairs could then be considered as settled.[381]

With the last great Avar revolt at an end, however, the "Pannonian problem" became reversed, as the remaining Avars increasingly came under Slavic pressure. Now protective Frankish intervention was required to assure the continuing existence of the Avar principalities. A Bulgar attack probably also played a role in this. A fragment preserved in the *Suda Lexicon* recounts that Khan Krum (before 803–14) "annihilated" the Avars and asked the Avar prisoners about the reasons "for the ruin of your leader and your entire people."[382] It is tempting to date this event to 804, and to associate it with the flight of the kapkhan and his followers to the Franks,[383] although the *Royal Frankish Annals* give Slavic "infestationes" as the reason.[384]

At the beginning of 805 the Christian kapkhan Theodore appeared in person before the emperor Charles at Aachen, "and requested that he grant him a place to settle between Savaria and Carnuntum, since he could no longer remain in his present place of residence because of the incursions of the Slavs."[385] This was the year of the Bohemian war, as grandly conceived as it was unsuccessful, and the Avar received a sympathetic hearing. The emperor granted the kapkhan's request and gave the Avar prince rich gifts on his return journey. But scarcely back at home, Theodore died.

The Avar "reservation" between Carnuntum/Petronell on the Danube and Savaria/Szombathely, stretching a good sixty miles along the ancient Roman road to Italy, has become an accepted fact in modern research.[386] Yet we do not know what became of it in the following years, after Theodore's sudden death. In any case, in the region around Lake Neusiedl the Avars could expect more Frankish support in the face of Slavic and Bulgar attacks than farther afield in the Carpathian Basin. The recognition of the kapkhanate east of the foothills of the Alps obviously did not affect the sphere of power of the tudun, who had submitted in 803. The extent and location of the territory was likely determined by the Franks, who may have used Roman maps or itineraries for this purpose.[387]

Immediately after the kapkhan's death, another Avar prince took advantage of the favorable mood in Aachen and sent a delegation to Charlemagne. After nine years, this is the first time that we hear of a khagan again. He asked the emperor for the restoration of his supreme rule, the "summa totius regni."[388] The modest progress of the Avar mission is evident in the fact that the khagan was still a pagan. This defect was now rectified. On September 21, 805, he was baptized in the Fischa River, not far from the ruins of Carnuntum, and took the name Abraham.[389] Abraham's rule was surely meant to include the kapkhan group in western Pannonia, not far away from the Fischa. The tudun, too, now had to recognize the preeminence of this new partner in Frankish politics.

Only a few years later, in 808, most likely in the same region, three brothers donated land bordering "loca Avarorum" to St. Emmeram in Regensburg.[390] The document offers a snapshot of a region in transition. Three brothers, Wirut, Gisalmar, and Wentilmar, had inherited land from their father Elis, and thus were apparently not newcomers to the area. Their names are German; only Wirut might have been Slavic. Georg Holzer has offered two possible explanations: either *Vyrutъ in the sense of "expelled," "outcast," or a name constructed with the suffix utъ/-uta, attested in several personal names in the former Slavic regions of Austria (for instance, the Carantanian duke Borutъ).[391] Alternatively, it could be read as Wirunt (a name well attested in Old High German). The servant who was part of the donation also had a German name, Gereloh. It is remarkable that the area donated is clearly delineated, mainly by streams with German names (*Vuisaha, Eolvespah, Wintarpah*).[392] The *Vuisaha* has been identified with the Fischa, or with the Wiesbach in today's Wiesen; etymologically, it does point to a Wiesach, a "meadow stream."[393] *Eolvespah* has been read as a misspelling of "Wolf's Brook," later Slavicized as Wulka (from *vlk*—wolf). That would locate the donated property in a stretch of about twenty miles to the west of modern Mattersburg, where indeed Regensburg seems to have had possessions in the eleventh century.[394]

The names of the streams sound a bit like recent colonizers' denominations. Rather than the kapkhan's wide stretch of land allotted in 805, "loca Avarorum" indicates specific Avar settlements: apparently, "Avars' places" were sufficiently rare in the area only twelve years after the fall of the khaganate to serve as a means of localization. It would of course be tempting to interpret the donors as remains of the local Avar/Slavic elites, who had been quick to embrace Christianity and Germanic naming customs. Could this be a rare trace of a hybrid late Avar population? However, the personal names rather point to richly endowed colonists of the first hour, who already gave up after the recent troubles, or at least sought protection by the superior resources of an episcopal church. The charter contains two sets of witnesses: the first probably from the original act of donation that may have taken place in the region, and the second at Regensburg in the presence of the count and the bishop; both contain almost exclusively more or less standard German names.

As Max Diesenberger has shown, Regensburg seems to have been genuinely interested in the new territories in Pannonia at the time. This is indicated by a liturgical text, a reworking of the *Life of St. Emmeram* for the night office, produced in the early ninth century. Unlike in Arbeo's *Life* written a generation earlier, Emmeram's missionary efforts in Pannonia are now highlighted: the saint "had come to the land of the Vandals with the intention of daily converting the gentes of the Huns, who knew not the God of heaven, to Christianity."[395] This account of the patron saint was no doubt intended to encourage the clerics of the early ninth century to follow his example. The Avar khaganate had become a land of the Vandals/Wends, where Huns/Avars had to be converted. The ethnonym Vandali, or similar, was now sometimes used for the Slavs, and the Avars were increasingly reduced to the generic name "Huns," as in a ninth-century Bavarian glossary, where *Sclavus et Avarus* is translated into Old High German as *Uuinida* and *Huni*.[396]

In all these sources, the region east of Vienna appears as the transitional zone to the Avar settlement region and to the ambit of the newly established tributary khaganate. Nonetheless the area to the west up to the Enns also continued to be viewed as the "provincia Avarorum."[397] In Lorch, on the old *limes certus*, was the customs post for border trade. The Diedenhofen capitulary of 805 established precise conditions for trade with the Avars and Slavs to the east and banned the export of arms across this border.[398] This was, of course, a Frankish Avaria and not a sovereign state, just as there could be a "*Gothia*" or "*Sclavinia*" on the territory of the Roman Empire. This is also illustrated by a pious donation in 811 "in Avaria" at the mouth of the Pielach, near modern Melk, some fifty miles east of the Enns River.[399]

"Avaria" was soon to be a land without Avars. The regained "ancient honor" did not assure the new khagan's position in the long term. Even the assumption of the Bulgar khan's title, *khana sybige*, could not save this khaganate by Frankish dispensation from its Slavic enemies. In 811 a Frankish army had to march into Pannonia to put an end to conflicts there and summon the princes involved to Aachen. These were the khagan/*canizauci*, the tudun, and the Slavic *duces* from the regions on the Danube.[400] The emperor once again set things right in Pannonia, where the Avar princes were less and less able to maintain themselves without Frankish backing. This is the last appearance of Avar dignitaries in the sources. In 822 Avar envoys are mentioned one more time. The new order of 828, at the latest, abolished the tributary Avar principality in western Pannonia, one generation after the fall of the khaganate.[401]

8.5 Why Did the Avars Disappear?

Why had the Avar realm fallen after almost 250 years of its unchallenged existence? Of course, this is a rather long period as compared to other steppe empires. The contemporary Turks did not enjoy a similar period of relatively stable rule; their first empire collapsed in ca. 630, and the second one ended in ca. 740 and was replaced by the Uyghurs.[402] We may as well ask why the Avar khaganate had persisted for so long. On the other hand, Bulgars and later Hungarians would maintain their rule in spite of serious setbacks, at least up to the Ottoman conquest, so it is not unreasonable to wonder why the Avar realm disappeared. The moment when that happened coincided with an apogee of Frankish power under Charlemagne and with the resurgence of the Bulgar khanate under Krum (803–14).[403] None of the two powers, however, managed to establish a firm control over the Avar heartlands, where an emerging Slavic warrior elite became dominant.

Recent paleoclimatic research may offer some additional clues to the decline of Avar rule in the second half of the eighth century. A group of Hungarian authors even pointedly asked in the title of a paper published in 2016: "Did an extremely dry climate lead actually to the collapse of the Avar Empire in the Carpathian Basin?"[404] Their discussion was based on intensive research in the wetlands of Lake Baláta (not identical with the much larger Lake Balaton) in southwestern Hungary; it did not confirm the initial hypothesis. A recent and very valuable overview by Johannes Preiser-Kapeller, which also takes into account results from further sites and from written sources, also indicates that the climate in the Carpathian Basin was not, as sometimes supposed, extremely dry toward the end of the eighth century.[405] Rather, climatic extremes, such as droughts and flooding and cold winters, are reported more frequently. Of course, it has to be taken into account that in the period around 800 we are much better served by Carolingian annals written more or less contemporaneously to the events, so that extreme weather conditions are also featured more extensively in the written record than before. However, another remarkable observation emerged from the data collected at Lake Baláta. This area had been grassland characterized by stock breeding since the late Roman period, when the traces of agricultural cultivation had faded out. In the middle of the eighth century, however, a period of reforestation set in, which points to a considerable decrease in animal husbandry. If the evidence from Lake Baláta can be shown to be representative, the contraction of open grassland would also mean that horse breeding was in decline, and that must have affected the military capacity of the Avar cavalry. Toward the end of the eighth century, a horse pestilence accelerated the process, which decisively weakened the main military asset of the Avars.[406] Thus, it was hardly a climatic shock that made the khaganate so vulnerable to Frankish attacks. Rather, the horse-breeding steppe economy that had so far supported the wealth of the Avar elite and its military force seems to have been in decline for about half a century. This erosion of the power base of the khagans was made worse by the contingency of an incipient panzootic. At that point, the pretenses of a leading caste of steppe lords with exotic titles could not be maintained anymore.

"The Avars were great of body and proud of mind, and God destroyed them and they have perished, and not a single Avar remains. And there is a proverb in Russia until this day: they disappeared like the *obor*, from whom there are neither descendants nor heirs."[407] The judgment of the *Russian Primary Chronicle* (or *Nestor Chronicle*), composed in the early twelfth century, is often cited as an epilogue to Avar history. Even the fourteenth-century copyist of manuscript L had forgotten the Avars so thoroughly that he misread Obri, the Avars, for *dobrie*, "good": "the good waged war against the Slavs."[408] It is possible that the chronicler had drawn the supposed proverb from a letter of Nicholas I Mysticus, which the patriarch wrote at the beginning of the tenth century to the Bulgar czar Symeon. He spoke of the Avars in comparable terms: "They too disappeared and no trace of this people any longer remains."[409] Wherever the Avars' disappearance became proverbial, there was good reason for it. It would not occur again in central European history that so powerful an empire and its leading people would disappear from history without a trace.

Where did the Avars disappear to? The Franks boasted of having annihilated "the entire Hunnic nobility" and of having completely depopulated Pannonia.[410] The poem on Pippin's victory over the Avars formulates this military objective as the khagan's fear when the Frankish army advanced: "depopulare populum."[411] The account in the annals shows that from 803 onward Frankish policy had quite the opposite objective. Historical research has long undervalued this difference between rhetoric and reality. The disappearance of the Avars did not seem to require an explanation.

On the other hand, efforts have been made, especially in Hungary, to demonstrate an Avar survival in the ninth century, until the last Avars were integrated around 900 into the Magyar kingdom. This national myth could build on the ancient topos of the continuity of steppe peoples: Scythians, Huns, and later Avars and Magyars. This could entail calling the later people by the names of the earlier ones. Regino of Prüm in the tenth century, Godfrey of Viterbo and others in the twelfth and thirteenth centuries call the Hungarians the "new" Scythians, like the "old" Avars.[412] Alternatively, one people could be supposed to have directly replaced the other. In this sense, Andrea Dandolo writes that the Hungarians had taken possession of Pannonia after ousting the Avars, "eiectis inde Avaribus."[413] Medieval Hungarian chroniclers identified the Széklers (Székely) as remnants of the Huns among the Hungarians.[414] All this is, of course, no proof of Avar-Hungarian continuity. The Avars, despite being so often called Huns, had no direct connection to Attila either, although Carolingian propaganda exploited this notion. In order to establish such continuity a gap of at least two generations in the sources would need to be bridged over. For the last Avar embassy to Emperor Louis the Pious is mentioned as occurring in 822, and this at the end of a long list of Slavic *gentes*, just before the plunge into insignificance.[415] What follows are reminiscences. "Avaria" or "provincia Avarorum," even "regnum Avarorum" remain common designations for the lands east of the Enns for a good part of the ninth century.[416] On various occasions Avar khagans or tuduns of the past are recalled.[417] No actual Avar agency is attested.

For a long time, Hungarian scholars have looked for evidence of Avar survivals.[418] The mention of "Huns" in Carolingian annals in 863 is actually a reference to the Bulgars who supported Louis the German in that year against his rebellious son Karlmann and the Moravians. Their khan Boris met Ludwig on the Lower Austrian Danube and even declared himself ready to receive baptism.[419] The "Pannoniorum et Avarum solitudines," in which according to Regino the Hungarians began to roam from 889 onward, refers to former populations, not to the actual existence of free Avars or ancient Pannonians.[420] Much weightier is the observation that the Franks of the ninth century had to engage in numerous battles in this region with Moravians and other Slavs, Bulgars and Hungarians, conflicts that are often amply documented. No Avars were involved.

Therefore, we cannot assume an Avar continuity in the ninth century. The events of the time attest to the fact that the Avars disappeared as an organized people. This by no means signifies that they were fully exterminated at the beginning of the century. The Frankish conquest, Slavic pressure, and the advance of the Bulgars led to great shifts both in population and ethnic identity. The name "Avar" lost its cachet and disappeared; the people remained. "People were Avars as long as they remained their own masters."[421] When the name "Avar" no longer designated a political entity that could boast a connection with the "honor antiquus" of the khaganate, it quickly lost its power of attraction. How long there were still regional or local groups who called themselves Avars cannot be determined from the sources. By 830 there was no longer a politically effective entity that operated under this name. The descendants of the Avars merged with Slavs and others to form new local and regional entities that remained mostly vague for outside observers. "The people that remained of the Huns and Slavs," thus the *Conversio Bagoariorum et Carantanorum* calls these inhabitants of Pannonia in about 870.[422] For ethnic processes with an open outcome, as they occurred in the Carpathian Basin, this is a very adequate definition. It shows that people in Salzburg were unable at that time to assign a more explicit name. It makes no sense to designate this mixed population, or a hypothetical element in them, with the old name "Avars." At the end of the ninth century, Notker of St. Gall, in his description of Charlemagne's wars, counts the Avars among the "Winidi," Slavs.[423] This illustrates the shifts in identity that had occurred. On the other hand it is significant that in the Carpathian Basin coherent Slavic peoples with definite names did not emerge as was the case elsewhere in eastern Europe at that time. For future research, as Ágnes Sós writes, "the principal challenge [remains] to investigate the settlement history of smaller territorial units, while taking into account that the Slav-Avar assimilation depended on geographical, ethnic, and other factors, which could have very different effects on small areas, and thus followed its own varied course."[424] Such differentiations may above all be expected from the results of archaeological research.

The focus of power had shifted away from the former Avar heartland. Apart from the Franks and the Bulgars, the most conspicuous power center in the wider region in the ninth century was Moravia. Quite symbolically, the last mention of Avar envoys to the Franks at Frankfurt in 822 is also the first of the Moravians.[425] Moravian *duces* controlled the region north of the Danube, roughly modern Moravia and Slovakia, with centers in Mikulčice, Staré Město, and Pohansko in southern Moravia and in Nitra in Slovakia.[426] Mikulčice is an impressive site, a settlement of about ten hectares with the remains of ten churches. It had grown fast since its beginnings in the eighth century, when Avar influences were still quite substantial.[427] Recent research has made it very plausible that the site, and the Moravian duchy altogether, owed its fortune to the slave trade.[428] The traders operating via Moravia obviously controlled the southern route on which Slavic slaves were sent to Venice for shipping to the Islamic world. They were thus interested in unimpeded transit along the old Roman road through Pannonia.

These trade interests and the Frankish attempts to establish control over the Moravian centers created conflictual relations with the Frankish kings and their representatives in the eastern fringe areas, enacted in the changing fortune of battles and treaties. Toward the end of the ninth century, the Moravians became serious contenders of the Franks for the control of Pannonia—just before the Hungarians ousted both powers from the Carpathian Basin.[429] In a certain sense what is often misleadingly called "Great Moravia" succeeded the Avars as a regional power east of the Franks. The name "Great Moravia" in Constantine Porphyrogenitus, however, does not refer to the size or importance of the principality, but to the fact that it was outside the ancient Roman border, similar to the "Great Bulgaria" of the seventh century. It is not unlikely that some groups of Avar warriors had found a Slavic future there. However, they did not continue the Avar forms of representation. Traces of Avar heritage are relatively sparse in the ninth-century archaeological record.[430] This was a rather different world of Slavic hillforts and strongholds, linked in many respects with the Carolingian cultural sphere, but not without its particularities, especially in the female ornaments.[431]

In the western half of the Carpathian Basin no one was initially powerful enough to impose himself as a reliable partner for the Carolingian administration. It was not until the appointment of the Moravian dissident Privina in Mosapurc/Zalavár at the western end of Lake Balaton in 840 that some stability was introduced. Frankish counts and the Bavarian church made slow progress in the organization of this territory. Just how loosely knit the Frankish network was in the area is illustrated during the conflict over Methodius around 870.[432]

The eastern half of the Carpathian Basin and the descendants of the Avars who lived there slowly fell under Bulgar influence. A Bulgar army seems to have appeared here for the first time in ca. 804. The "Hungarian Anonymous" reports that after the death of Attila, the "keanus magnus, dux Bulgariae" occupied the territory between the Danube and the Tisza, up to the border with the Poles and Ruthenians.[433] But this account confuses several temporal strata, and no attempt should be made link it to any specific events. We should not conclude that Krum shifted the Bulgar border to the Tisza.[434] At least in theory the Franks claimed to rule, along with Pannonia, "adpositam in altera Danubii ripa Daciam," the trans-Danubian Great Hungarian Plain, which had come to be called Dacia.[435] The first tangles between the Franks and Bulgars occurred in the 820s. In 818 the Timociani, who lived on the Timok, east of the Iron Gate, freed themselves from the *societas* of the Bulgars and asked to be taken under Frankish rule.[436] And in 824 envoys appeared in Aachen from the Abodrites/Praedencenti who lived "as neighbors of the Bulgars on the Danube in Dacia" and asked for support against the Bulgars, at which Louis the Pious snubbed the Bulgar ambassadors.[437] As a consequence a determination of the border between the Bulgars and the Franks became necessary.[438] After this date the Bulgars posed a threat to Frankish Pannonia. In 827 followed the first Bulgar attack, along the Drava/Drau.[439] At this point the eastern part of the Carpathian Basin can be considered, with some plausibility, as part of the Bulgar sphere of power.[440] The association of the Avars and Slavs living east of the Tisza with the Bulgars was probably no more intensive than the *societas* of the Timok Slavs or that of the Abodrite *contermini* with the Franks.[441]

On the other hand, there are some attestations that Avar groups were fighting in the Bulgar army in these years. In 811, when Emperor Nicephorus had Krum's capital Pliska plundered, the threatened khan took on Avars and Slavs as mercenary soldiers. In 814, after Krum's victory, Avars and Slavs were part of the army with which the khan hoped to capture Constantinople. But the Bulgar attack failed even before the start of the campaign because of the khan's death.[442] Thereafter traces of the Bulgarian Avars are lost, much more quickly than the earlier Avar Bulgars disappeared from the sources. A story transmitted much later in the *Suda Lexicon* claims that Krum had asked the Avars for the reasons why their khaganate had fallen and then introduced legislation to avoid them: he had all the grapevines cut down and restricted trade.[443]

The population of the Avar period in the Carpathian Basin did not only stop being called by that name relatively soon. The archaeological traces of the rather consistent forms of cultural expression of the eighth century also fade, not without hesitation in some parts. Quite remarkably, what seems to vanish first is the production of new objects following the old patterns, or their modification. Old objects often continue to be employed, mended, sometimes also put to rather different uses. The material culture that came to dominate the Carpathian Basin in the ninth century cannot be described as an organic development of the late Avar era. In spite of several elements of continuity, which had regional effects in varying degrees, it was subject to all kinds of new influences. In many respects, it was also impoverished. The agents of these changes were in part the descendants of the late Avar population of the eighth century but also immigrants.

On the Tisza, many Avar cemeteries continued to be used. About one hundred graves in the great necropolis of Tiszafüred can be dated to the ninth century. The graves become poorer, parts of belt fittings are used contrary to their original purpose as simple pieces of jewelry, and the craft of bronze casting disappears.[444] East of the Danube there are also traces of influence from the south Russian steppe in the ninth century, and parallels to contemporary material from the Saltovo-Mayaki culture appear. Yet the mixed culture of this period does not have fixed and sharp contours.[445]

West of the Danube Frankish influence can be detected. Frankish weapons such as the long sax, fluted lance-heads, arrowheads with sockets, as well as new types of women's jewelry (wire earrings, amphora beads) are found along with elements of older styles of dress.[446] Particularly visible are the gradual changes in the first half of the ninth century at the western end of Lake Balaton, where Mosapurc became a center of Slavic rule over a peripheral area of the Carolingian Empire.[447] In the marshy areas at the mouth of the Zala the remains of a series of island settlements have been revealed, such as in Zalakomár or Borjuállás. Avar traditions were displaced by Slavic influences, some of which are reminiscent of Moravia, and by Frankish imports. Not until the middle of the century do pagan customs begin to retreat. Churches are built, and Frankish influence becomes more pronounced.[448] Farther to the north is the cemetery of Sopronkőhida, approximately in the area that was intended for the kapkhan's followers in 805. A mixed culture of the ninth century can be distinguished here.[449] In all, and admitting for some chronological uncertainty, the late Avar material that can be dated with some certainty to the ninth century is surprisingly meager compared to the great mass of finds from the eighth century.

In the "Avaria" of eastern Austria a break around 800 emerges more clearly, although it is often not precisely datable. Here the consequences of the Frankish military campaigns were more serious, and the new Carolingian order was imposed more quickly. Many Avar cemeteries were abandoned, and new ones with predominantly Slavic characteristics were laid out. Frankish and Christian influences made themselves felt only gradually in this environment. The latest Avar and earliest Slavic cemeteries have a great deal in common. Older elements of Avar ornamentation were reused as individual pieces.[450]

Politically and culturally, the Carpathian Basin remained a frontier area during the entire ninth century, not completely in the grasp of any of the neighboring powers. On the other hand, the regional Slavic princes were not powerful enough to free themselves from their domination. Only with the entry of the Hungarians on the scene did the heterogeneous population on the middle Danube come together in a single kingdom that in a sense continued the interrupted history of the Huns and Avars. Occasionally, it was also designated with these traditional names. But medieval Hungarians felt much more attached to the episode of Attila's rule than to the quarter millennium of Avar rule. Grafting onto the Avars, which might have been a readily available ideological tactic, was not pursued. The Avars were quite irrelevant for the Hungarian historiographers of the Middle Ages. Neither the Anonymous nor Simon of Kéza even mention their name.

Memories of the Avars were more actively maintained in Byzantium than in the West.[451] But even there, the Huns were more conspicuous; their name remained generic for all later steppe peoples and was used for Hungarians, Cumans, Seljuks, and Ottomans, among others, while that of the Avars was hardly employed.[452] In the West, Attila was also transformed into the legendary Hunnic king Etzel in the *Nibelungenlied*, who remained a figure of popular tradition, while the Avars played a secondary role. Perhaps it was the continued interest in the literature of late Antiquity that bestowed such posthumous prestige on the Huns of Attila, similar to the contemporary Vandals, Burgundians, and Goths and their short-lived kingdoms. For a while, some interest in the Avars was revived by the appearance of the Hungarians, with whom they could be identified. In the tenth century, Widukind described the Avars as "those whom we now call Hungarians" and as "the remains of the Huns." Charlemagne had defeated them and enclosed them behind a huge wall (a motif from the Alexander legend also connected with the apocalyptic peoples Gog and Magog); but a hundred years later, under King Arnulf, they had broken free and returned as Hungarians.[453] Later chronicles sometimes mention Charlemagne's victory over the Avars.[454] A more extensive, but completely fantastic account of an Avar rule over Austria is found in the late medieval Austrian *Chronik von den 95 Herrschaften*, in which a Roman count named Amman is sent to Austria, which he names *Avara*.[455] The text is exceptional for integrating the eastern barbarians into an imaginary Austrian prehistory, but only in name.

The restrained Avar activity toward the West probably contributed to their limited attraction to later authors. Their weak resistance to the Frankish conquerors may also have led to a depreciation in their posthumous reputation. Notker of St. Gall, toward the end of the ninth century, turned the formerly awesome barbarians into inferior enemies.[456] The legendary warrior Eishere, whom Notker claims to have known personally, tells of his battles in Charlemagne's army "in regione Winidum" against "Bohemians, Wilzes, and Avars" and expresses his scorn for these opponents. "What do I care for those little frogs? I used to carry seven, eight, or even nine of them around spitted on my lance, while they mumbled incomprehensible rubbish." The braggart ranks the once so feared Avars lower than the Wendish "frogs" and in last place. Nothing similar would have been written about Attila's Huns even after the fall of their empire. And thus, after only a few generations, the Avars disappeared almost completely from history.

8.6 Conclusion

A mixed group of steppe warriors and their families in flight adopts a prestigious name, victoriously moves across thousands of miles and founds an empire, and can thus consolidate itself as a people. When, after a quarter millennium, its identity and institutions lose their motivating force, this people disappears, apparently without leaving a trace. This is the history of the Avars in a nutshell. It should be understood as a process, not as the exploits of a people that essentially remained unchanged from beginning to end. What to contemporaries and even more to posterity seemed a people defined by common descent was initially a heterogeneous group drawn together by an established model of organization, by the political culture of steppe warriors, and by a shared history of success. More than other steppe peoples, the Avars were a political ethnos, perhaps similar to the Rouran in that respect, combining pretensions of supreme authority (the "ancient honor" of the khagans) with a rather opaque ethnic background, which already contemporaries disagreed about. Only those who followed the khagan could remain Avars. No one outside the empire made their fortune under this name. Personal names increasingly blended into designations of rank and office, and soon even the khagans, after the founder Baian, remained nameless for outsiders (sections 2.4 and 6.10).

The difference from other European steppe realms brings out the particularity of the Avar khaganate. Hunnic rulers from the Xiongnu to Attila's Huns bore very different titles and adapted their political systems smoothly to their respective environment. What distinguished them was their ethnonym, which in the fourth and fifth centuries spread almost everywhere in the Eurasian steppe, faster than those who could have descended from the Xiongnu, and was soon used as a generic term for steppe warriors and their peoples. The diffusion of Bulgars from the Caucasus to southern Italy in the sixth and seventh centuries was similarly wide-ranging, although it seems to have followed a different logic: whereas Hun leaders sought to compete with the highest-ranking emperors and kings of the political landscape they had entered, Bulgar groups spread under the rule of Avars, Byzantines, or Lombards, until, occasionally, they found a chance to grab power themselves. Eventually, that led to the consolidation of a Bulgar khanate at the lower Danube, which acquired many traits of a steppe empire, two centuries after Bulgars had first appeared in the region. Bulgar groups were distinguished by the name of their leaders, no matter which office he might occupy: a Byzantine *strategos*, a Lombard *gastald*, or Avar khagan; they could still remain Bulgars under foreign rule, sometimes for centuries (sections 2.2 and 6.10). Whenever major warrior groups broke away from the Avar Empire, they did not identify themselves as Avars but as Bulgars (sections 7.6–7.7).

Wherever "Avars" are reported to have driven the Roman population from their lands and settled there, these settlers became known as Slavs, as in Greece or Dalmatia (sections 4.4 and 7.1). Alongside Avars and Bulgars, "Slav" was the third model of barbarian life in post-Roman eastern Europe. As has been argued here, Slavs did not insert themselves as privileged warriors into the late Roman system, as Goths or Lombards had done. Neither did they seek to profit from the systematic exploitation of Roman resources through large-scale attacks, negotiations, and tribute relations, like Huns and Avars. Slavic leaders on the lower Danube built up some military force and embarked on repeated raids from the middle of the sixth to the early seventh century, and could muster considerable military power when they joined forces; but this dynamic remained ephemeral. No professional warrior caste, division of labor, and stable supraregional rulership emerged among the Slavs before the ninth century, and the Roman infrastructure that had alimented the privileged lifestyles of warriors elsewhere was largely destroyed.

Slavic life unfolded in local agrarian communities, which often succumbed to foreign rule but in the long term proved more resilient than the polities of their rulers. It was a simple life, with minimal investments in buildings, lasting forms of representation, or the cult of the dead, but without systematic taxation and rents, and without steep hierarchies. The resultant lacunae in the archaeological record make it hard to trace the progress of the Slavs. It took a while until all neighbors consistently used the ethnonyms "Slavs" or "Wends" for an agrarian population with a simple lifestyle that spread far and wide between the Baltic and the Mediterranean. This belated perception of Slavs in the Latin West probably corresponded to an only gradual process of Slavicization of the many groups that roughly conformed to this form of existence. However, among the many different options open to the inhabitants of eastern Europe during the dramatic process of contraction of the late Roman imperial system, arguably this was the most successful one (sections 4.1 and 4.6).

These three distinct models of organization and identification permitted the emergence of three distinct peoples along the middle and lower Danube: Avars, Bulgars, and Slavs. Occupation and behavior determined ethnic identities at least as much as vice versa. However, this should not be understood in purely functionalist terms. Traditions and breaks in tradition, resilience and idiosyncrasy, myth and illusion, ambition and acculturation could all influence the continuity or transformation of "ethnic practice." Inherited skills and a sense of belonging, persistent social boundaries, and historical contingencies shaped the organization of life just as much as the other way around. These changes were open-ended, as the example of the Avars illustrates: ethnic processes are reversible (section 6.10). The very concept of "people" or "ethnic group" may designate very different realities. The observation in the *Strategicon* that the Avars "have no sense of kinship . . . with one another" may be exaggerated; but apparently, the Avars were a "political ethnos," and it was mostly their central organization that provided an identity (section 6.3). The far-flung "Slavic multitudes" lacked just that; they were highly decentralized and yet surprisingly uniform in language and in the modesty of cultural representation (section 4.1).

The success of a polity and a people is determined by how well practice and politics are able to respond to changing conditions. The history of the Avars, however sparse the sources, offers an instructive example. It was not arrogance, greed, and random plundering that allowed the Avars to become a hegemonic power, but a calculated policy. From a coalition of the defeated that withdrew in 558 from the newly constructed empire of the Turks (see sections 2.3–4), an ambitious program of expansion that exploited prestigious traditions of the steppes quickly created a formidable power on the northern frontier of Byzantium. While various Hunnic and other peoples in the last years of Justinian's reign plundered the Balkan provinces in sharp competition with each other, Baian's Avars purposefully turned toward the emperor as allies against their barbarian rivals, while the empire was initially spared (sections 2.5–9 and 3.3). Thus, for some decades the Avar Empire succeeded in aligning the overwhelming majority of barbarian warriors in a wide territory north of the Danube and the Black Sea. In time, this enabled the first khagans to challenge the Byzantine Empire as few other enemies had done before the Islamic conquests.

Baian and his sons almost had a monopoly position on the northern frontier of Byzantium. This gave them the possibility, in a calculated interplay of war and peace (chapters 3 and 5), of giving their growing number of followers optimal opportunities to win prestige and access to enormous treasures (sections 6.5–6). Over time, however, this led to a fatal dependency on the Byzantine Empire and its riches: precious objects can be plundered only once (sections 6.4–5). The increasing claims of the khagan's warriors and the progressive devastation of the Balkan provinces forced the Avar ruler to ever greater ventures, until the failure of the ambitious attack on Constantinople in 626 led to the collapse of this policy of calculated aggression (sections 7.1–3). As in almost all steppe empires, after two or three generations the limits of expansion led to irreconcilable internal contradictions and interrupted the expansive dynamics.

Yet even after severe inner battles the Avar khaganate was still able to maintain itself on a more modest scale in the Carpathian Basin. The resilience of the khaganate was partly due to the fact that there was no opponent powerful enough to subject or replace it, perhaps also to the contingency of a victory over a Bulgar rebellion in ca. 630. The regionalization of the seventh century, the decline of royal power in the Frankish kingdoms, the fragmentation of the Bulgar khanate north of the Black Sea, and the Arab attacks on Byzantium all made it relatively easy for the nameless successors to the Baianids to defend their empire, shored up by the treasures accumulated in better times. The groups that had formed in the peripheral zones of the Avar Empire, and since 626 had broken away from the khaganate, such as Samo's Wends, the Carantanians, or the Slavs in the northwestern Balkans, did not develop into dangerous competitors but adopted Slavic lifestyles and forms of organization and pursued no supraregional power politics (sections 7.4–5).

After 626 we hear little of Avar attacks, and the khagans cease to play a conspicuous role in international power politics (sections 7.6–7 and 8.3). The Avars were increasingly forced to accommodate themselves to Slavic ways of life. Grave finds from the eighth century show that war was no longer the chief constitutive factor in personal identities and that most of the Avar population lived in modest agricultural settlements (see sections 7.8 and 8.1). Conspicuous consumption in costumes and funerary rites involved relatively large parts of the population, but left little room for elite distinction (for instance, by grave goods of precious metal). However, the Slavicization of the economic base, which assured the survival of the Avar Empire, did not effect any perceptible Slavicization of culture or of the organization of the state. Quite the contrary. Traditions from the steppe were continued and new ones were imported. Avars still wore their hair long and

braided and were buried with their characteristic multipartite belts. The introduction of the technology of bronze casting around 700 made possible the mass
production of representative belt fittings, on which griffin motifs often served as
emblem, reverberating of a millennial tradition of cultural exchange between the
symbolic repertory of the steppes and the craftsmanship of Greeks and Persians.
Unlike in the earlier periods, contemporary Byzantine and Western cultural
influences now subsided.

In the political sphere, an elaborate hierarchy of various titles roughly following the Turkish model, and in parallel with Bulgar usage, emerged. The khagan had to share his power with a iugurrus as second ruler, with the tudun and
kapkhan who commanded their own armies, and with tarkhans and other holders of high office. The Eastern influences in culture and state organization have
often been explained by the invasion of a new steppe people that would have
overlaid the Avars in the later seventh century. In fact, the Avar Empire was always
open to the east, for immigration as well as for cultural exchange. Yet it should
be noted that middle and late Avar culture and the hierarchy of ranks and titles
combined Eastern and other elements in quite specific fashions (see sections 7.8
and 8.2). The Avar political system of the eighth century was not simply a dual
kingship of the "Khazar" or "nomad" type. A comparison of the forms of government of various steppe empires from the period shows that, according to circumstances, very different political systems could arise from a limited repertory of
titles and forms of organization. Similar titles could designate different offices,
while analogous positions could be differently named (section 8.2).

The preservation of traditions from the steppes long assisted in maintaining
the prestige of the once so powerful khaganate among its followers and its
neighbors. From the middle of the eighth century, there are signs of decline, both
economically (reforestation and the diminution of pastures) and politically (the
Bavarian expansion into Carantania). However, it took Charlemagne's armies to
expose the fragile reality behind the great name "Avars." Not so much Frankish
victories as the inability to mount an effective defense of the khaganate led to its
fall, without any decisive battles. Various high officeholders began to pursue their
own policies, and the "ancient honor" of the khagans could not be maintained,
even with Frankish support (sections 8.4–5). The ruralized steppe empire was
no longer a match for the ambitious power politics that the Carolingian Empire
pursued.

Unlike other heirs of the migration age in Europe the khaganate had not
learned how to avail itself of a simplified Roman administration and of an
ecclesiastical organization. Only the Bulgars and Hungarians of the following
centuries would be capable of adapting to a Christian environment and thereby of
putting their rule on a new basis. For learned contemporaries and witnesses of its

fall, the Avar Empire seemed like a foreign body, the relic of a finally vanquished barbarian age. For us this alienness constitutes the Avars' attraction as a topic of study. The failed attempt to impose the ways of life of the Eurasian steppe in central Europe represents a tradition that gradually came to be exorcized from the European legacy, locked in the defamatory image of the "enemy from the east." By comparison, the ultimate failure of the Avars illuminates what made the success of the Western model in a critical phase of its development possible. Yet this perspective is built on hindsight. On its own terms, we may consider the quarter millennium of Avar rule in central Europe as the story of a successful synthesis that lasted longer than most other barbarian polities of the period. The Avar Empire should be acknowledged as a relevant part of European history.

AMOUNT OF SUBSIDIES PAID BY BYZANTIUM TO THE AVARS

YEAR	SUM IN SOLIDI	SOURCE
558–565	"Yearly payments" and "accustomed gifts"	Menander 5.1, 5.4
565–574	No treaty	Menander 8, 12.5–7
574/75–579	80,000	Menander 15.5, 27.3
582–584	80,000 plus arrears for three years	Menander 27.3
585–597	100,000	Theophylact 1.3, 1.6
598–603	120,000	Theophylact 7.15
604–?	Phocas increases the tribute (140,000?)	Theophanes 6096
611?	Heraclius may have increased it further	—
618/19–622/23	180,000?	Theophanes 6111; cf. 6112, 6113
623/24–626	Raised to 200,000	Nicephorus 13

Abbreviations

Acta Arch. Hung.	*Acta Archaeologica Academiae Scientiarum Hungaricae*
Acta Orient. Hung.	*Acta Orientalia Academiae Scientiarum Hungaricae*
AW	Akademie der Wissenschaften
CFHB	Corpus fontium historiae Byzantinae
CSCO	Corpus scriptorum Christianorum Orientalium
CSHB	Corpus scriptorum historiae Byzantinae
DAI	*De administrando imperii*
DsÖAW	Denkschriften der Österreichische Akademie der Wissenschaften, Philosophisch-Historische Klasse
Kollautz and Miyakawa	Arnulf Kollautz and Hisayuki Miyakawa, *Geschichte und Kultur eines völkerwanderungszeitlichen Nomadenvolkes: Die Jou-Jan der Mongolei und die Awaren in Mitteleuropa*, 2 vols. (Klagenfurt, 1970)
MGH	Monumenta Germaniae Historica
AA	Auctores antiquissimi
Capit.	Capitularia regum Francorum
DD	Diplomata
DD H IV	Diplomata of Henry IV
DD Kar.	Diplomata of Charlemagne
DD LD	Diplomata of Louis the German
DD O I	Diplomata of Otto I
Dt. Chron.	Deutsche Chroniken
Epp.	Epistolae
SS	Scriptores (in Folio)
SS rer. Germ.	Scriptores rerum Germanicarum
SS rer. Langob.	Scriptores rerum Langobardicarum et Italicarum
SS rer. Merov.	Scriptores rerum Merovingicarum
MIÖG	*Mitteilungen des Instituts für Österreichische Geschichtsforschung*
PLRE	J. R. Martindale, *The Prosopography of the Later Roman Empire*, vol. 3A–B (Cambridge, 1992)

RE	*Paulys Realencyclopädie der classischen Altertumswissenschaft*, 24 vols. (Stuttgart, 1893–1963); 2nd ser., 10 vols. (Stuttgart, 1914–72); *Supplements*, 15 vols. (Stuttgart, 1903–78)
RGA	*Reallexikon der Germanischen Altertumskunde*, ed. Heinrich Beck, Dieter Geuenich, and Heiko Steuer, 2nd ed., 35 vols (Berlin, 1972–2008)
Slov. Arch.	*Slovenská Archeológia*
SSCI	Settimana di studio del Centro italiano di studi sull'alto Medioevo
UAJB	*Ural-Altaische Jahrbücher*
VIÖG	Veröffentlichungen des Instituts für Österreichische Geschichtsforschung

Notes

PREFACE

1. Henry H. Howorth, "The Avars," *Journal of Royal Asiatic Society of Great Britain and Ireland* 21 (1889): 721–810.

2. Walter Pohl, *Die Awaren: Ein Steppenvolk in Mitteleuropa, 567–822 n. Chr.* (Munich, 1988; 3rd ed., 2015).

3. Georgios Kardaras, To Byzantio kai hoi Abaroi (6.–9. ai.): politikes, diplōmatikes kai politismikes scheseis, EIE/IBE, Monographs 15 (Athens, 2010); English version: *Byzantium and the Avars, 6th–9th c. A. D.: Political, Diplomatic and Cultural Relations* (Leiden, forthcoming); Csanád Bálint, *The Avars, Byzantium and Italy* (forthcoming).

4. In particular, by the SFB (Spezialforschungsbereich) F42-G18 "Visions of Community: Comparative Approaches to Ethnicity, Region and Empire in Christianity, Islam and Buddhism, 400–1600 CE (VISCOM)" funded by the FWF (2011–19), and by the ERC Advanced Grant project "Social Cohesion, Identity and Religion in Europe, 400–1200 (SCIRE)" in the Seventh Framework Programme (FP7/2007–13) under the ERC grant agreement no. 269591.

1. APPROACHING THE AVARS

1. John of Ephesus, *Historiae Ecclesiasticae pars tertia* 6.45, ed. Ernest W. Brooks, CSCO 106, Scriptores Syri 55 (Louvain, 1964), 260; English translation: John of Ephesus, *The Third Part of the Ecclesiastical History of John, Bishop of Ephesus*, trans. Robert Payne-Smith (Oxford, 1860).

2. Arnulf Kollautz, "Die Awaren: Die Schichtung in einer Nomadenherrschaft," *Saeculum* 5 (1954): 129.

3. On this concept, see Gilles Deleuze and Félix Guattari, *Mille plateaux: Capitalisme et schizophrenie* (Paris, 1980); Gilles Deleuze and Félix Guattari, *A Thousand Plateaus: Capitalism and Schizophrenia*, trans. Brian Massumi (Minneapolis, 1987), also at http://projectlamar.com/media/A-Thousand-Plateaus.pdf.

4. Josef Deér, "Karl der Grosse und der Untergang des Awarenreiches," in *Karl der Grosse: Lebenswerk und Nachleben*, vol. 1, *Persönlichkeit und Geschichte*, ed. Helmut Beumann (Düsseldorf, 1967), 719–91.

5. Deleuze and Guattari, *A Thousand Plateaus*, 1–25, 351–423.

6. Falko Daim, "The Avars: Steppe People of Central Europe," *Archaeology* 37 (1984): 33–39, and Daim, "Avars and Avar Archaeology: An Introduction," in *Regna and Gentes: The Relationship between Late Antique and Early Medieval Peoples and Kingdoms in the Transformation of the Roman World*, ed. Hans-Werner Goetz, Jörg Jarnut, and Walter Pohl, The Transformation of the Roman World 13 (Leiden, 2003), 463–570. See also Bálint, *The Avars, Byzantium and Italy*.

7. Jürgen Bemmann and Michael Schmauder, eds., *The Complexity of Interaction along the Eurasian Steppe Zone in the First Millennium CE* (Bonn, 2015); Michael Maas and Nicola Di Cosmo, eds., *Eurasian Empires in Late Antiquity* (forthcoming).

8. Fundamental studies are Reinhard Wenskus, *Stammesbildung und Verfassung: Das Werden der frühmittelalterlichen Gentes*, 2nd ed. (Graz, 1977), and Herwig Wolfram, *Die Goten: Von den Anfängen bis zur Mitte des sechsten Jahrhunderts; Versuch einer historischen*

Ethnographie, 5th ed. (Munich, 2009); Wolfram, *History of the Goths*, trans. Thomas J. Dunlap (Berkeley, 1988); more recently, Walter Pohl, "Ethnicity, Theory and Tradition: A Response," in *On Barbarian Identity: Critical Approaches to Ethnogenesis Theory*, ed. Andrew Gillett (Turnhout, 2002), 221–40; Pohl, "Archaeology of Identity: Introduction," in *Archaeology of Identity/Archäologie der Identität*, ed. Walter Pohl and Mathias Mehofer, Forschungen zur Geschichte des Mittelalters 17 (Vienna, 2010), 9–24.

9. On Roman ethnography, see Klaus E. Müller, *Geschichte der antiken Ethnographie und ethnologischen Theoriebildung*, vol. 2 (Wiesbaden, 1980), and Michael Maas, *The Conqueror's Gift: Ethnography, Identity and Roman Imperial Power at the End of Antiquity*, forthcoming. Assuming an end of the classical ethnographic tradition in the seventh century: Anthony Kaldellis, *Ethnography after Antiquity: Foreign Lands and Peoples in Byzantine Literature; Empire and After* (Philadelphia, 2013).

10. Synesius of Cyrene, *Oratio de regno ad Arcadium imperatorem* 11, ed. and trans. Augustine Fitzgerald, *The Essays and Hymns of Synesius of Cyrene*, 2 vols. (London, 1930), 1:27. Agathias, on the other hand, is of the opinion that new peoples might very well appear and then disappear; *Agathiae Myrinaei Historiarum libri V*, ed. Rudolf Keydell, CFHB 2 (Berlin, 1967); Agathias, *The Histories* 5.11.4, trans. Joseph D. Frendo, CFHB 2B (Berlin, 1975), 146 (hereafter cited after Frendo's translation). Similarly, Orosius, *Seven Books of History against the Pagans* 7.32.11, trans. A. T. Fear, Translated Texts for Historians 54 (Liverpool, 2010), 380.

11. A fine example is the so-called Cotton Tiberius *mappa mundi*, on which they appear as neighbors of the "Turci griphorum" between the Sea of Azov (the ancient Maeotis) and the Caspian Sea; see David Hill, *An Atlas of Anglo-Saxon England* (Toronto, 1981), 2–3. See also Walter Pohl, "The Role of Steppe Peoples in Eastern and Central Europe in the First Millennium A.D.," in *Origins of Central Europe*, ed. Przemysław Urbańczyk (Warsaw, 1997), 65–78.

12. Procopius, *Bella* 7.14, ed. and trans. Henry B. Dewing, *Procopius in Seven Volumes*, vols. 1–5 (Cambridge, MA, 1914–28), 4:272–73. See also the partial edition and translation *History of the Wars, Secret History, and Buildings*, ed. and trans. Averil Cameron (New York, 1967).

13. Maurice, *Strategicon* 11.2–4, ed. George T. Dennis and Ernst Gamillscheg, CFHB 17 (Vienna, 1981), 360–89; *Maurice's Strategikon: Handbook of Byzantine Military Strategy*, trans. George T. Dennis (Philadelphia, 1984), henceforth abbreviated as *Strategicon*.

14. Menander, frag. 19.1, ed. and trans. Roger C. Blockley, *The History of Menander the Guardsman* (Liverpool, 1985), 170.

15. Ursula-Barbara Dittrich, *Die Beziehungen Roms zu den Sarmaten und Quaden im 4. Jahrhundert n. Chr. nach der Darstellung des Ammianus Marcellinus* (Bonn, 1984); Yves Albert Dauge, *Le barbare: Recherches sur la conception romaine de la barbarie et de la civilisation* (Brussels, 1981); Müller, *Geschichte der antiken Ethnographie*, 427–29; François Hartog, *Le miroir d'Hérodote* (Paris, 1991).

16. John of Ephesus 5.32, 256 (cf. section 3.4).

17. Cf. section 5.7.

18. Priscus, frag. 11.2, ed. and trans. Roger C. Blockley, *The Fragmentary Classicising Historians of the Later Roman Empire*, vol. 2 (Cambridge, 1983), 266–73.

19. Theodore Syncellus, *Homilia de Obsidione Avarica Constantinopolis*, ed. Leo Sternbach, Analecta Avarica (Cracow, 1900), 4–5; French translation: *Traduction et commentaire de l'homélie écrite probablement par Théodore le Syncelle sur le siège de Constantinople en 626*, ed. and trans. Ferenc Makk, Acta Universitatis de Attila József Nominatae, Acta Antiqua et Archaeologica 19 (Szeged, 1975), 13–14; an English translation by Roger Pearse (Ipswich, 2007) is available at http://www.tertullian.org/fathers/theodore_syncellus_01_homily.htm, although the translation here is my own.

20. Fredegar, *Chronicae* 4.68, ed. Bruno Krusch, MGH SS rer. Merov. 2 (Hanover, 1888), 154–55; unless otherwise noted, the page numbers cited refer to *The Fourth Book of the Chronicles of Fredegar*, trans. John Michael Wallace-Hadrill (London, 1960), 56–58.

21. *Theophylacti Simocattae Historiae* 6.9.12–13, ed. Karl de Boor (Leipzig, 1887), 238 and 8.3.12, 288; cf. sections 5.3 and 5.8; *The History of Theophylact Simocatta: An English Translation with Introduction and Notes*, trans. Michael Whitby and Mary Whitby (Oxford, 1986), 173 and 213. Unless otherwise noted, the English translation is cited throughout this book. Walter Pohl, "Perceptions of Barbarian Violence," in *Violence in Late Antiquity: Perceptions and Practices*, ed. Harold A. Drake (Aldershot, 2006), 15–26.

22. Cf. section 7.3; *Chronicon Paschale*, ed. Ludwig Dindorf, CSHB, 2 vols. (Bonn, 1832), 1:723, 5–15; *Chronicon Paschale, 284–628 AD*, a. 626, trans. Michael Whitby and Mary Whitby, Translated Texts for Historians 7 (Liverpool, 1989), 177. Unless otherwise noted, the page numbers cited refer to the English translation by Whitby and Whitby.

23. Theophanes Confessor, *Chronographia* 6092, ed. Karl de Boor (Leipzig, 1883), 280; *The Chronicle of Theophanes Confessor: Byzantine and Near Eastern History, AD 284–813*, trans. Cyril Mango and Roger Scott (Oxford, 1997), 404. However, this information is not found in Theophylact. Theophanes also ascribes the massacre to the obduracy of the emperor, who did not want to pay the ransom money; cf. section 5.7. After the conquest of Cividale, the men capable of bearing arms were presumably all killed by the Avars; Paul the Deacon, *Historia Langobardorum* 4.37, ed. Georg Waitz, MGH SS rer. Germ. 48 (Hanover, 1878), 163. Cf. section 7.1.

24. Menander, frag. 5.4, ed. and trans. Blockley, 52.

25. Menander, frag. 25.1, ed. and trans. Blockley, 220; Theophanes, *Chronographia* 6110, trans. Mango and Scott, 433–34; cf. sections 3.4 and 7.2.

26. *Strategicon* 11.2, 361–62.

27. *Strategicon* 4.2, 195; 9.2, 307.

28. Cf. section 2.1.

29. Menander, frag. 12.6, ed. and trans. Blockley, 140.

30. On sources as literary constructs, see Walter A. Goffart, *The Narrators of Barbarian History (A.D. 550–800): Jordanes, Gregory of Tours, Bede, and Paul the Deacon* (Princeton, NJ, 1988); but see Walter Pohl, "History in Fragments: Montecassino's Politics of Memory," *Early Medieval Europe* 10, no. 3 (2001): 343–74.

31. Survey of the Byzantine sources of the time in Gyula Moravcsik, *Byzantinoturcica*, 2nd ed., 2 vols. (Berlin, 1958), 1:302–4; Herbert Hunger, *Die hochsprachliche profane Literatur der Byzantiner*, 2 vols., Handbuch der Altertumswissenschaft 12.5 (Munich, 1978), vol. 1, especially 1:292–93; Johannes Karayannopoulos and Günter Weiss, *Quellenkunde zur Geschichte von Byzanz (324–1453)*, 2 vols., Schriften zur Geistesgeschichte des östlichen Europa 14 (Wiesbaden, 1982), vol. 2; Warren Treadgold, *The Early Byzantine Historians* (New York, 2010). See also Averil Cameron, *Procopius and the Sixth Century* (Berkeley, 1985).

32. Agathias 5.11.4, 146.

33. Menander, ed. and trans. Blockley; Treadgold, *The Early Byzantine Historians*, 293–99.

34. *The History of Theophylact Simocatta*, trans. Whitby and Whitby; see Michael Whitby, *The Emperor Maurice and His Historian: Theophylact Simocatta on Persian and Balkan Warfare* (Oxford, 1988). German translation: Theophylaktos Simokates, *Geschichte*, trans. Peter Schreiner (Stuttgart, 1985). According to Schreiner, the author's name was Simokates, with one "t." On the chronological problems of the text, see section 5.1.

35. "Ausbund an Fratzenhaftigkeit": The quotation is from Ulrich von Wilamowitz (1905), cited in Schreiner's "Einleitung," in Theophylaktos Simokates, *Geschichte*, 15; see

also his own balanced judgment on the author (ibid., 8–10), and Whitby, *The Emperor Maurice and His Historian.*

36. New edition 1981 by Dennis and Gamillscheg. Its information on the Avars and Slavs is extensively reviewed in John Earl Wiita, "The Ethnika in Byzantine Military Treatises" (PhD diss., University of Florida, 1977).

37. Translations of Michael the Syrian are in John of Ephesus, *The Third Part of the Ecclesiastical History*, trans. Payne-Smith (cited in the following); *Chronique de Michel le Syrien: Patriarche jacobite d'Antioche (1166–1199)*, ed. and trans. Jean Baptiste Chabot (Paris, 1899–1910; repr. Brussels, 1963). See, further, Ernest Honigmann, "L'histoire ecclésiastique de Jean d'Éphèse," *Byzantion* 14 (1939): 623–24; Dorothea Weltecke, *Die "Beschreibung der Zeiten" von Mōr Michael dem Großen (1126–1199): Eine Studie zu ihrem historischen und historiographiegeschichtlichen Kontext*, CSCO 594, Subsidia 110 (Louvain, 2003).

38. *The Ecclesiastical History of Evagrius Scholasticus*, trans. Michael Whitby, Translated Texts for Historians 33 (Liverpool, 2000). Pauline Allen, *Evagrius Scholasticus, the Church Historian* (Louvain, 1981).

39. Paul Lemerle published a Greek-French edition of the *Miracula Sancti Demetrii*, with a second volume of extensive commentary: *Les Plus Anciens Recueils des miracles de Saint Démétrius et la pénétration des Slaves dans les Balkans*, 2 vols. (Paris, 1979–81); citations in the following are from the first volume.

40. Johannes Koder, "Byzanz, die Griechen und die Romaiosynē—eine 'Ethnogenese' der Römer?," in *Typen der Ethnogenese unter besonderer Berücksichtigung der Bayern*, vol. 1, ed. Herwig Wolfram and Walter Pohl, DsÖAW 201 (Vienna, 1990), 103–12; Johannes Koder, "Anmerkungen zu den Miracula Sancti Demetrii," in *Byzantium: Tribute to Andreas N. Stratos*, ed. Nia A. Stratos (Athens, 1986), 2:523–25. Koder calls attention to the mixed character of the *Miracula*, with a hagiographical purpose and a chronicle-like description, which expertly employs the terminology of the imperial administration.

41. Theodore Syncellus, *Homilia de Obsidione Avarica Constantinopolis*, trans. Pearse.

42. George of Pisidia (Georgios Pisides); for an edition in Greek and Italian, see *Bellum Avaricum*, ed. and trans. Agostino Pertusi, in *Giorgio Piside, Poemi*, vol. 1, *Panegirici epici*, Studia Patristica et Byzantina 7 (Ettal, 1959), 176–200. On George's historical poems, see Mary Whitby, "Defender of the Cross: George of Pisidia on the Emperor Heraclius and His Deputies," in *The Propaganda of Power: The Role of Panegyric in Late Antiquity*, ed. Mary Whitby (Leiden, 1998), 247–76.

43. *Chronicon Paschale* a. 626, 168–81; Treadgold, *The Early Byzantine Historians*, 340–49. For the year 626 and relevant sources, see section 7.3.

44. Leslie Brubaker and John Haldon, eds., *Byzantium in the Iconoclast Era (ca. 680–850): The Sources. An Annotated Survey* (Aldershot, 2001); Hunger, *Die hochsprachliche profane Literatur der Byzantiner*, 1:334–39 (Theophanes); Karayannopoulos and Weiss, *Quellenkunde zur Geschichte von Byzanz*, 2:338–39.

45. Nicephorus, *Short History*, ed. and trans. Cyril Mango (Washington, DC, 1990). See also Cyril Mango, "The Brevarium of the Patriarch Nikephoros," in N. Stratos, *Byzantium*, 2:539–52, who characterizes the work as more a "rhetorical exercise than a work of history"; more appreciative view in Karayannopoulos and Weiss, *Quellenkunde zur Geschichte von Byzanz*, 2:33–34.

46. Theophanes Confessor, *Chronographia*, trans. Mango and Scott.

47. Greek-English edition: Constantine Porphyrogenitus, *De administrando imperio*, ed. Gyula Moravcsik and trans. Romilly James Heald Jenkins, 2nd ed., vol. 1 (Budapest, 1963); Romilly James Heald Jenkins, ed., *Constantine Porphyrogenitus, De administrando imperio*, vol. 2, *Commentary* (London, 1963), with commentary by Francis Dvornik et al.

48. Moravcsik, *Byzantinoturcica*, 2:312–15.

49. Walter Pohl, "Paulus Diaconus und die 'Historia Langobardorum': Text und Tradition," in *Historiographie im frühen Mittelalter*, ed. Anton Scharer and Georg Scheibelreiter, VIÖG 32 (Vienna, 1994), 375–405.

50. Gregory the Great, *Registrum epistolarum*, ed. Dag Norberg, 2 vols., Corpus Christianorum: Series Latina 140–140a (Turnhout, 1982). See Carole Ellen Straw, *Gregory the Great* (Aldershot, 1996); Robert A. Markus, *Gregory the Great and His World* (Cambridge, 1997).

51. Gregory of Tours, *Decem libri historiarum*, ed. Bruno Krusch and Wilhelm Levison, MGH SS rer. Merov. 1.1 (1937; repr., Hanover, 1965); Gregory of Tours, *The History of the Franks*, trans. Lewis Thorpe (1974; repr. London, 1986). See Ian N. Wood, *Gregory of Tours* (Bangor, 1994); Martin Heinzelmann, *Gregory of Tours: History and Society in the Sixth Century* (Cambridge, 2001); Helmut Reimitz, *History, Frankish Identity and the Framing of Western Ethnicity, 550–850* (Cambridge, 2015), 25–124.

52. *The Fourth Book of the Chronicles of Fredegar*, ed. and trans. Wallace-Hadrill; see Roger Collins, *Fredegar* (Aldershot, 1996); Reimitz, *History, Frankish Identity and the Framing of Western Ethnicity*, 166–239.

53. Walter Pohl, "Paul the Deacon—between Sacci and Marsuppia," in *Ego Trouble: Authors and Their Identities in the Early Middle Ages*, ed. Richard Corradini et al., Forschungen zur Geschichte des Mittelalters 15 (Vienna, 2010), 111–24; Goffart, *Narrators of Barbarian History*, 329–431, for a skeptical view of his value as a source.

54. For an English translation of selected annals, see *Carolingian Chronicles: Royal Frankish Annals, and Nithard's Histories*, trans. Bernhard Walter Scholz, with Barbara Rogers (Ann Arbor, 1970). See Rosamond McKitterick, *History and Memory in the Carolingian World* (Cambridge, 2004). In the case of the Frankish annals as in other cases, I have often cited the MGH edition, which is available online and open access (http://www.dmgh.de), rather than more recent but less accessible editions.

55. *De Pippini regis victoria Avarica*, ed. Ernst Dümmler, MGH Poetae 1 (Berlin, 1881), 116–17; Paulinus of Aquileia, *Versus Paulini de Herico duce*, ed. Ernst Dümmler, MHG Poetae 1 (Berlin, 1881), 131–33.

56. *Conventus episcoporum ad ripas Danuvii*, ed. Albert Werminghoff, MGH LL, Concilia 2.1 (Berlin, 1906), 172–76; cf. Helmut Reimitz, "Grenzen und Grenzüberschreitungen im karolingischen Mitteleuropa," in *Grenze und Differenz im frühen Mittelalter*, ed. Walter Pohl and Helmut Reimitz, Forschungen zur Geschichte des Mittelalters 1 (Vienna, 2000), 156–58; Maximilian Diesenberger and Herwig Wolfram, "Arn und Alkuin: Zwei Freunde und ihre Schriften," in *Erzbischof Arn von Salzburg*, ed. Meta Niederkorn-Bruck and Anton Scharer, VIÖG 40 (Vienna, 2004), 81–106.

57. Charlemagne, *Epistula* 20, ed. Ernst Dümmler, MGH Epp. Karolini aevi 2 (Berlin, 1895), 528–29.

58. Einhard, *Vita Karoli Magni* 13, ed. Oswald Holder-Egger, MGH SS rer. Germ. 25 (Berlin, 1911), 15; *The Life of Charlemagne*, in *Charlemagne's Courtier: The Complete Einhard*, ed. and trans. Paul Edward Dutton (Peterborough, 1998), 24.

59. Herwig Wolfram, *Grenzen und Räume: Geschichte Österreichs vor seiner Entstehung, 378–907*, Österreichische Geschichte 1 (Vienna, 1995), 211–74.

60. Denis Sinor, *Introduction à l'étude de l'Eurasie centrale* (Wiesbaden, 1963), 265.

61. Omeljan Pritsak, "The Slavs and the Avars," in *Gli slavi occidentali e meridionali nell'alto medioevo*, 2 vols., SSCI 30 (Spoleto, 1983), 1:353.

62. Arnulf Kollautz and Hisayuki Miyakawa, *Geschichte und Kultur eines völkerwanderungszeitlichen Nomadenvolkes: Die Jou-Jan der Mongolei und die Awaren in Mitteleuropa*, 2 vols. (Klagenfurt, 1970), henceforth abbreviated as Kollautz and Miyakawa. On the problem of the identification with the Rouran, see section 2.3–4.

63. Alexander Avenarius, *Die Awaren in Europa* (Amsterdam, 1974); other histories of the Avars by Slavic scholars: Jovan Kovačević, *Avarski Kaganat* (Belgrad, 1977)

(in Serbian); Wojciech Szymánsky and Elzbieta Dabrowska, *Awarzy—Węgrzy* (Warsaw, 1979) (in Polish).

64. Josef Marquart, *Osteuropäische und ostasiatische Streifzüge* (Leipzig, 1903); Wilhelm Radloff, *Aus Sibirien*, 2 vols. (Leipzig, 1884). See also Ádám Bollók, "Excavating Early Medieval Material Culture and Writing History in Late Nineteenth- and Early Twentieth-Century Hungarian Archaeology," *Hungarian Historical Review* 5, no. 2 (2016): 277–304.

65. Béla Köpeczi, ed., *Erdély Története három kötetben* [History of Transylvania in three volumes] (Budapest, 1986); see László Péter, ed., *Historians and the History of Transylvania* (New York, 1992).

66. See, for instance, Florin Curta, "From Kossinna to Bromlej: Ethnogenesis in Slavic Archaeology," in Gillett, *On Barbarian Identity*, 201–18.

67. On Hunnic dress, see Procopius, *Anecdota* 7.11–14, ed. and trans. Henry B. Dewing, *Procopius in Seven Volumes*, vol. 6 (Cambridge, MA, 1935), 80–81, and Walter Pohl, "Telling the Difference: Signs of Ethnic Identity," in *Strategies of Distinction: The Construction of Ethnic Communities, 300–800*, ed. Walter Pohl and Helmut Reimitz, The Transformation of the Roman World 2 (Leiden, 1998), 48.

68. As in Kollautz and Miyakawa's identification of the Avars and Rouran; explicitly stated by Károly Czeglédy, "From East to West: The Age of Nomadic Migrations in Eurasia," *Archivum Eurasiae Medii Aevi* 3 (1983): 26: "Indeed, it is a breathtaking task to try to pry out of the written remains evidence pertaining to one and the same people, one and the same tribal union"; cf. section 2.2–4.

69. Wenskus, *Stammesbildung und Verfassung*. Further comment in Wolfram, *Die Goten*, 40–41; Wolfram, *History of the Goths*, 28–29; Walter Pohl, "Tradition, Ethnogenese und literarische Gestaltung: eine Zwischenbilanz," in *Ethnogenese und Überlieferung: Angewandte Methoden der Frühmittelalterforschung*, ed. Karl Brunner and Brigitte Merta, VIÖG 31 (Vienna, 1994), 9–26; Pohl, "Ethnicity, Theory and Tradition," with an assessment of the strengths and weaknesses of Wenskus's model. For a fierce and, to my mind, unfair criticism of Wenskus, see Alexander C. Murray, "Reinhard Wenskus on Ethnogenesis, Ethnicity, and the Origin of the Franks," in Gillett, *On Barbarian Identity*, 39–68. Approaches similar to Wenskus were used in studies of early medieval eastern Europe by František Graus, "Die Entwicklung Mitteleuropas im 8. Jahrhundert und die Vorbedingungen der Staatenentwicklung in diesem Gebiet," in *I problemi dell'occidente nel secolo VIII*, SSCI 20 (Spoleto, 1973), 1:451–54; Manfred Hellmann, "Grundlagen slawischer Verfassungsgeschichte des frühen Mittelalters," *Jahrbücher für Geschichte Osteuropas*, n.s., 2 (1954): 387–404; and Wolfgang Fritze, "Zur Bedeutung der Awaren für die slawische Ausdehnungsbewegung im frühen Mittelalter," in *Studien zur Völkerwanderungszeit im östlichen Mitteleuropa*, ed. Gerhard Mildenberger (Marburg, 1980), 498–545.

70. Walter Pohl, "Introduction. Strategies of Identification: A Methodological Profile," in *Strategies of Identification: Ethnicity and Religion in Early Medieval Europe*, ed. Walter Pohl and Gerda Heydemann (Turnhout, 2013), 1–64.

71. Samuel Szádeczky-Kardoss, *Ein Versuch zur Sammlung und chronologischen Anordnung der griechischen Quellen der Awarengeschichte*, Acta Universitatis de Attila József Nominatae, Acta Antiqua et Archaeologica 16, Opuscula Byzantina 1 (Szeged, 1972).

72. Christian Lübke and Andrzej Wędzki, eds., *Glossar zur frühmittelalterlichen Geschichte im östlichen Europa: Enzyklopädie zur Geschichte des östlichen Europa, 6.–13. Jahrhundert, Heft A: Aalborg–Awdańce* (Greifswald, 1998).

73. See, for instance, numerous studies by Evangelos Chrysos, as well as Andreas N. Stratos, *Byzantium in the Seventh Century*, 3 vols. (Amsterdam, 1968–71), and John Haldon, *Byzantium in the Seventh Century* (Cambridge, 1990).

74. Daim, "Avars and Avar Archaeology."

75. Elvira H. Tóth and Attila Horváth, *Kunbábony: Das Grab eines Awarenkhagans* (Kecskémet, 1992).

76. Edit Bárdos and Éva Garam, *Das awarenzeitliche Gräberfeld in Zamárdi-Rétiföldek*, 2 vols. (Budapest, 2009–14).

77. The fundamental studies were Gyula László, *Études archéologiques sur l'histoire de la société des Avars*, Archaeologica Hungarica 24 (Budapest, 1954), and Ilona Kovrig, *Das awarenzeitliche Gräberfeld von Alattyán*, Archaeologica Hungarica 40 (Budapest, 1963). Many of László's methods would not stand up to present-day criticism; their lasting value lies in the questions they stimulated. See also the numerous publications of the late István Bóna, as well as, inter alia, those of C. Bálint, E. Garam, A. Kiss, A. Sós, R. Müller, P. Tomka, and T. Vida.

78. Falko Daim, "Gedanken zum Ethnosbegriff," *Mitteilungen der Anthropologischen Gesellschaft in Wien* 112 (1982): 69.

79. See, for instance, Sebastian Brather, *Ethnische Interpretationen in der frühgeschichtlichen Archäologie: Geschichte, Grundlagen und Alternativen*, RGA Erg. Bd. 42 (Berlin, 2004); Volker Bierbrauer, *Ethnos und Mobilität im 5. Jahrhundert aus archäologischer Sicht: Vom Kaukasus bis Niederösterreich*, Bayerische Akademie der Wissenschaften, phil.-hist. Kl., n.s., 131 (Munich, 2008); Pohl, "Archaeology of Identity: Introduction"; Florin Curta, "Medieval Archaeology and Ethnicity: Where Are We?," *History Compass* 9, no. 7 (2011): 537–48.

80. See, for instance, Brather, *Ethnische Interpretationen in der frühgeschichtlichen Archäologie*; Bierbrauer, *Ethnos und Mobilität im 5. Jahrhundert aus archäologischer Sicht*; Florin Curta, "Some Remarks on Ethnicity in Medieval Archaeology," *Early Medieval Europe* 15, no. 2 (2007): 159–85; Pohl and Mehofer, *Archaeology of Identity/Archäologie der Identität*.

81. Pohl, *Die Awaren*.

82. See sections 3.8, 7.8, and 8.1. I am grateful to many archaeologist colleagues for their help and generosity; among them, Csanád Bálint, Falko Daim, Peter Stadler, Tivadar Vida, and Jozef Zábojník.

83. Very well documented in two recent collaborative volumes: Bemmann and Schmauder, *Complexity of Interaction*; Maas and Di Cosmo, *Eurasian Empires in Late Antiquity*. I have tried to incorporate some of the new results and models in sections 2 and 6, without being able to do them full justice in the revision of a translated book.

84. See Sören Stark, *Die Alttürkenzeit in Mittel- und Zentralasien: Archäologische und historische Studien* (Wiesbaden, 2008), 71–79; and especially the Xiao Hongnahai/Mongolküre inscription, ibid., 73–75.

85. Thomas J. Barfield, *The Perilous Frontier: Nomadic Empires and China, 221 BC to AD 1757* (Cambridge, MA, 1989).

86. A fundamental study is Nicola Di Cosmo, *Ancient China and Its Enemies: The Rise of Nomadic Power in East Asia* (Cambridge, 2004). See also Nicola Di Cosmo, "China-Steppe Relations in Historical Perspective," in Bemmann and Schmauder, *Complexity of Interaction*, 49–72; and Jonathan Skaff, *Sui-Tang China and Its Turko-Mongol Neighbors: Culture, Power and Connections, 580–800* (Oxford, 2012).

87. Csanád Bálint, "On 'Orient Preference' in the Archaeology of the Avars, Protobulgars and Ancient Hungarians," in *Post-Roman Towns, Trade and Settlement in Europe and Byzantium*, vol. 1, *The Heirs of the Roman West*, ed. Joachim Henning, Millennium-Studies 5.1 (Berlin, 2007), 545–67.

88. Luo Xin, "Chinese and Inner Asian Perspectives on the History of the Northern Dynasties (386–589) in Chinese Historiography," in *Empires and Exchanges in Eurasian Late Antiquity: Rome, China, Iran, and the Steppe, ca. 250–750*, ed. Nicola Di Cosmo and Michael Maas (Cambridge, 2018), 166–75.

89. Wolfgang Oeser, "Methodologische Bemerkungen," in *Entstehung von Sprachen und Völkern*, ed. Per Sture Ureland, Linguistische Arbeiten 162 (Tübingen, 1985), 3.

90. See Patrick. J. Geary, *The Myth of Nations: The Medieval Origins of Europe* (Princeton, NJ, 2001), and František Graus, *Die Nationenbildung der Westslawen im Mittelalter* (Sigmaringen, 1980).

91. See Clemens Gantner et al., eds., *Transformations of Romanness in the Early Middle Ages: Regions and Identities* (Berlin, 2018).

2. THE AVAR MIGRATION

1. Theophanes, *Chronographia* 6050, 339–40. John Malalas, *Chronographia*, ed. Ludwig Dindorf, CSHB (Bonn, 1831), 489. On these events, see also Victor of Tunnuna, *Chronica* a. 563.2, ed. Antonio Placanica, *Vittore da Tunnuna, Chronica: Chiesa e impero nell'età di Giustiniano* (Florence, 1997), 58. Szádeczky-Kardoss, *Ein Versuch*, 62, dates the arrival of the envoys to the end of 557 or the beginning of 558. Ernst Stein, *Histoire du Bas-Empire*, 2 vols. (Paris, 1949), 2:542 (January 558). Blockley in Menander, ed. and trans. Blockley, 253, prefers 559–60, but does not explain why.

2. Agathias 1.3.4, 11. On perceptions of Avar hairstyle, see Pohl, "Telling the Difference," 56.

3. Menander, frag. 5.1, ed. and trans. Blockley, 48.

4. Menander, frag. 5.1, ed. and trans. Blockley, 48.

5. Menander, frag. 5.2, ed. and trans. Blockley, 50.

6. Stein, *Histoire du Bas-Empire*, 2:521–35; Alexander Sarantis, *Justinian's Balkan Wars: Campaigning, Diplomacy and Development in Illyricum, Thrace and the Northern World, A.D 527–65* (Prenton, 2016), 227–324. See also Walter Pohl, "Justinian and the Barbarian Kingdoms," in *The Age of Justinian*, ed. Michael Maas (Cambridge, 2005), 448–76.

7. Procopius's *De aedificiis*, ed. and trans. Henry B. Dewing, *Procopius in Seven Volumes*, vol. 7 (Cambridge, MA, 1940), contains a precise, if likely too optimistic, presentation of Justinian's fort construction program; cf. Velizar Velkov, *Cities in Thrace and Dacia in Late Antiquity* (Amsterdam, 1977); Cameron, *Procopius and the Sixth Century*, 84–112; Florin Curta, *The Making of the Slavs: History and Archaeology of the Lower Danube Region, c. 500–700* (Cambridge, 2001), 120–89; Sarantis, *Justinian's Balkan Wars*, 161–97.

8. Velizar Velkov, "Der Donaulimes in Bulgarien und das Vordringen der Slawen," in *Die Völker Südosteuropas vom 6.–8. Jahrhundert: Symposion Tutzing, 1985*, ed. Bernhard Hänsel, Südosteuropäisches Jahrbuch 17 (Munich, 1987), 154.

9. Procopius, *Anecdota* 18.21, ed. and trans. Dewing, 216–19.

10. Agathias 5.14, 180; Jordanes, *Historia Romana* 388, ed. Theodor Mommsen, MGH AA 5.1 (Berlin, 1882), 52.

11. Menander, frag. 5.1, ed. and trans. Blockley, 48; cf. section 6.10.

12. Velizar Velkov, "Les campagnes et la population rurale en Thrace au IVe–VIe siècle," *Byzantinobulgarica* 1 (1962): 31–60; Joachim Henning, *Südosteuropa zwischen Antike und Mittelalter: Archäologische Beiträge zur Landwirtschaft des 1. Jahrtausend u. Z.*, Schriften zur Ur- und Frühgeschichte 42 (Berlin, 1987), 35 and 108–10; Curta, *Making of the Slavs*, 120–69.

13. Samuel Szádeczky-Kardoss, "Scamarae," in *RE Suppl.* 11 (1968), 1239–42.

14. See, among other sources, Procopius, *Bella* 2.22–23, ed. and trans. Dewing, 1:450–73; Agathias 5.10, 145–46; *Miracula Demetrii* 1.3, 75–78; see Lester K. Little, ed., *Plague and the End of Antiquity: The Pandemic of 541–750* (Cambridge, 2007).

15. John the Lydian, *De magistratibus populi Romani*, ed. Richard Wuensch (1903; repr., Stuttgart, 1967), 162.

16. Procopius, *Anecdota* 11, ed. and trans. Dewing, 129–43; Gregory the Great, *Registrum epistolarum* 5.38, ed. Norberg, 1:312–13.

17. Theophylact Simocatta 7.3, 249–50; cf. section 5.4.

18. Emphasized by Hans Ditten, "Zur Bedeutung der Einwanderung der Slawen," in *Byzanz im 7. Jahrhundert: Untersuchungen zur Herausbildung des Feudalismus*, ed. Friedhelm Winkelmann et al., Berliner Byzantinische Arbeiten 48 (Berlin, 1978), 94; cf. John Moorhead, "Italian Loyalties during Justinian's Gothic War," *Byzantion* 53 (1983): 575–96.

19. Agathias 5.11–25, 146–62. Sarantis, *Justinian's Balkan Wars*, 336–49.

20. Menander, frag. 2, ed. and trans. Blockley, 42–45.

21. Agathias 5.25.3–4, 161. I have replaced Frendo's "national identity" with "ethnic identity."

22. Agathias 5.11, 146; cf. Moravcsik, *Byzantinoturcica*, 1:29.

23. Procopius, *Bella* 8.5.31–33, ed. and trans. Dewing, 5:99.

24. Procopius, *Bella* 8.4.12–13, ed. and trans. Dewing, 5:87; cf. Moravcsik, *Byzantinoturcica*, 1:307.

25. *The Chronicle of Pseudo-Zachariah Rhetor: Church and War in Late Antiquity* 12.7, trans. Geoffrey Greatrex, Robert R. Phenix, and Cornelia B. Horn, Translated Texts for Historians 55 (Liverpool, 2011), 448–50.

26. Károly Czeglédy, "Pseudo-Zacharias Rhetor on the Nomads," in *Studia Turcica*, ed. Louis Ligeti (Budapest, 1971), 133–48; Klaus Wegenast, "Zacharias Scholastikos," in *RE*, 2nd ser., 9.2 (1967), 2212–16; Josef Rist, "Die sogenannte Kirchengeschichte des Zacharias Rhetor: Überlieferung, Inhalt und theologische Bedeutung," in *Syriaca*, vol. 1, *Zur Geschichte, Theologie, Liturgie und Gegenwartslage der syrischen Kirchen*, ed. Martin Tamcke, Studien zur orientalischen Kirchengeschichte 17 (Münster, 2002), 77–99; Geoffrey Greatrex, "Introduction," in *The Chronicle of Pseudo-Zachariah Rhetor*, trans. Greatrex, 1–94.

27. Basic studies until the present day are those by Marquart, in particular his *Osteuropäische und ostasiatische Streifzüge*, as well as Moravcsik's two-volume *Byzantinoturcica*, which offers a bibliography of sources and a list of all attestations of Turkic-language names in Greek texts. After 1945, scholars such as Altheim, Czeglédy, Haussig, Pritsak, Klyashtornyi, Sinor, Szádeczky-Kardoss, Golden, Vásáry, and Róna-Tas have worked with the sources for the history of the steppe peoples of the sixth century. For recent perspectives, see Peter B. Golden, *Central Asia in World History* (Oxford, 2011); Di Cosmo, "China-Steppe Relations in Historical Perspective"; Étienne de la Vaissière, "The Steppe World and the Rise of the Huns," in *The Cambridge Companion to the Age of Attila*, ed. Michael Maas (Cambridge, 2014), 175–92; Walter Pohl, "Ethnicity and Empire in the Western Eurasian Steppes," in Maas and Di Cosmo, *Eurasian Empires in Late Antiquity* (forthcoming).

28. On some early names of this type, see Otto J. Maenchen-Helfen, *The World of the Huns: Studies in Their History and Culture* (Berkeley, 1973), 298–99.

29. Theophanes, *Chronographia* 6171, 357; see section 7.6, below.

30. Summary in Veselin Beševliev, *Die protobulgarische Periode der bulgarischen Geschichte* (Amsterdam, 1981), 76–90, with a list of sources; Daniel Ziemann, *Vom Wandervolk zur Großmacht: die Entstehung Bulgariens im frühen Mittelalter (7.–9. Jahrhundert)*, Kölner historische Abhandlungen 43 (Cologne, 2007), 31–39 and 44–50.

31. Ennodius, *Panegyricus dictus Theoderici* 5.19 and 12.60–69, ed. Christian Rohr, *Der Theoderich-Panegyricus des Ennodius*, MGH Studien und Texte 12 (Hanover, 1995), 209 and 239–47; Marcellinus Comes, *Chronicon* a. 499, a. 502, a. 530, a. 535, a. 540, ed. Theodor Mommsen, MGH AA 11 (Berlin, 1894), 95–96, 102–4, 108; Cassiodorus, *Chronicon* a. 504 (1344), ed. Theodor Mommsen, MGH AA 11 (Berlin, 1894), 160; Jordanes, *Historia Romana* 363 and 388, ed. Mommsen, 47, 52; Jordanes, *Getica* 37, ed. Theodor Mommsen, MGH AA 5.1 (Berlin, 1882), 63; Malalas, *Chronographia*, ed. Dindorf, 451; John of Antioch, *Fragmenta ex historia chronica*, frag. 303.74, ed. Umberto Roberto (Berlin, 2005), 516.

32. Jordanes, *Getica*, at 5.38, ed. Mommsen, 63–64, and 50.264, 126. The list of Bulgarian rulers is translated in Kiril Petkov, *The Voices of Medieval Bulgaria, Seventh–Fifteenth Century: The Records of a Bygone Culture* (Leiden, 2008), 3–5; cf. Moravcsik, *Byzantinoturcica*, 2:296–97; cf. section 7.6.

33. Priscus, frag. 40, ed. and trans. Blockley, 344. The name of the Ogurs has been transmitted in the form *Ourogoi*. General information in András Mohay, "Priskos' Fragment über die Wanderungen der Steppenvölker," *Acta Antiqua Academiae Scientiarum Hungaricae* 24 (1976): 125–40; Peter B. Golden, "The Migration of the Oguz," *Archivum Ottomanicum* 4 (1972): 41–84; Golden, "Nomads of the Western Eurasian Steppes: Oγurs, Onoγurs and Khazars," in *Studies on the Peoples and Cultures of the Eurasian Steppes*, ed. Peter B. Golden and Catalin Hriban (Bucaresti, 2011), 135–62. On the Akatzirs, cf. Priscus, frag. 11.2, ed. and trans. Blockley, 258, 269, 275; frag. 40.2, 345; frag. 47, 353; Otto Maenchen-Helfen, "Akatir," *Central Asiatic Journal* 11 (1966): 275–86; Walter B. Henning, "A Farewell to the Khagan of the Aq-Aqatärän," *Bulletin of the School of Oriental and African Studies* 14, no. 3 (1952): 506–7; Czeglédy, "From East to West," 98.

34. Procopius, *Bella* 8.4, ed. and trans. Dewing, 5:82–99, esp. 84–85; Florin Curta, "The North-Western Region of the Black Sea during the 6th and Early 7th Century AD," *Ancient West & East* 7 (2008): 176.

35. Menander, frag. 10.4, ed. and trans. Blockley, 124; Samuel Szádeczky-Kardoss, "Onoguroi," in *RE Suppl.* 12 (1970), 902–6; Szádeczky-Kardoss, "Kutriguroi," in *RE Suppl.* 12 (1970), 517; Szádeczky-Kardoss, "Ugoroi," in *RE Suppl.* 14 (1974), 848, each with information on sources.

36. Procopius, *Bella* 8.4.8, ed. and trans. Dewing, 5:84, and 8.5.2–4, 5:88–89.

37. Jordanes may have known about the Akatzirs, who are otherwise no longer named in his time, from Priscus. Jordanes, in turn, served as a model for the Anonymous of Ravenna, author of a *Cosmography*, who in ca. 700 identified the Akatzirs with the Khazars of his own period; Anonymus Ravennatis, *Cosmographia* 4.1, ed. Joseph Schnetz, *Itineraria Romana*, vol. 2, *Ravennatis Anonymi cosmographia et Guidonis geographica* (Leipzig, 1940), 44. This does not mean that the two peoples were actually related.

38. Jordanes, *Getica* 5.35–37, ed. Mommsen, 63. See Andrew H. Merrills, *History and Geography in Late Antiquity* (Cambridge, 2005), 115–31.

39. See above, notes 25–26, and Marquart, *Osteuropäische und ostasiatische Streifzüge*, 356; Czeglédy, "Pseudo-Zacharias Rhetor on the Nomads," 137.

40. Sinor, *Introduction à l'étude de l'Eurasie centrale*, 268; Gyula Moravcsik, "Zur Geschichte der Onoguren," *Ungarische Jahrbücher* 10 (1930): 89; Beševliev, *Die protobulgarische Periode*, 148; Czeglédy, "From East to West," 103; Franz Altheim, ed., *Geschichte der Hunnen*, 5 vols. (Baden-Baden, 1959–62), 1:255; Hans Ditten, "Protobulgaren und Germanen im 5.–7. Jahrhundert (vor der Gründung des ersten bulgarischen Reiches)," *Bulgarian Historical Review* 8 (1980): 64–65; András Róna-Tas, *Hungarians and Europe in the Early Middle Ages: An Introduction to Early Hungarian History* (Budapest, 1999), 209–12; Golden, "Nomads of the Western Eurasian Steppes."

41. Menander, frag. 2, ed. and trans. Blockley, 42; Procopius, *Bella* 8.5.2–4, ed. and trans. Dewing, 5:88–89.

42. Omeljan Pritsak, "Tribal Names and Titles among the Altaic Peoples," in *The Turks in the Early Islamic World*, ed. C. Edmund Bosworth (Aldershot, 2007), 64 and 72–74; English translation of Pritsak, "Stammesnamen und Titulaturen der altaischen Völker," *UAJB* 24 (1952): 49–104; Károly Czeglédy, "On the Numerical Composition of the Ancient Turkish Tribal Confederations," *Acta Orient. Hung.* 25 (1972): 275–81; Peter B. Golden, "The Stateless Nomads of Central Eurasia," in Di Cosmo and Maas, *Empires and Exchanges in Eurasian Late Antiquity*, 317–32.

43. Pritsak, "Tribal Names," 95. Peter B. Golden, "Oq and Oğur-Oğuz," *Turkic Languages* 16 (2012): 155–99.

44. Edouard Chavannes, *Documents sur les Tou-kiue (Turcs) occidentaux* (St. Petersburg, 1907); Peter B. Golden, *Khazar Studies: An Historico-Philological Inquiry into the Origins of the Khazars*, 2 vols. (Budapest, 1980), 1:29; Sinor, *Introduction à l'étude de l'Eurasie centrale*, 267–68.

45. László, *Études archéologiques*, 291; István Bóna, "Ein Vierteljahrhundert Völkerwanderungszeitforschung in Ungarn," *Acta Arch. Hung.* 23 (1971): 291.

46. Marquart, *Osteuropäische und ostasiatische Streifzüge*, 27–30; Moravcsik, *Byzantinoturcica*, 1:65–67; Hans W. Haussig, "Theophylakts Exkurs über die skythischen Völker," *Byzantion* 23 (1953): 275–436; Szádeczky-Kardoss, "Onoguroi," 902–4; Wilhelm Barthold, *Histoire des turcs de l'Asie centrale* (Paris, 1945), 25; Edwin G. Pulleyblank, "Some Remarks on the Toquz Oghuz Problem," *UAJB* 28 (1956): 35–42; James Hamilton, "Toquz-Oguz et On-Uygur," *Journal Asiatique* 250 (1962): 33–54; Golden, "The Migration of the Oguz"; István Vásáry, *Geschichte des frühen Innerasiens* (Herne, 1999), 140–46; Róna-Tas, *Hungarians and Europe in the Early Middle Ages*, 209–11.

47. Kültegin inscription, 19, http://bitig.org/?lang=e&mod=1&tid=1&oid=15&m=1; see also Vilhelm Thomsen, "Alttürkische Inschriften in der Mongolei," *Zeitschrift der Deutschen Morgenländischen Gesellschaft* 78 (1924–25): 140, 150, 154, 170.

48. Priscus, frag. 40, ed. and trans. Blockley, 344 (if *Urogi* can be regarded as a misspelling of *Oguri*); Menander, frag. 10.4, ed. and trans. Blockley, 124.

49. Golden, "Stateless Nomads." Czeglédy, "From East to West," 36–40 and 97–102, 109–12, identifies the "Ogur" tribe/s with the Tiele federation, which spread far and wide since the fourth century. A different view in Hans W. Haussig, "Über die Bedeutung der Namen Hunnen und Awaren," *UAJB* 47 (1975): 97: "Ogur/Oguz" was a general foreign designation for the nomadic Turkic tribes of central and northern Asia. Overview of the debate: Cheng Fangyi, "The Research on the Identification between Tiele (鐵勒) and the Oγuric Tribes," *Archivum Eurasiae Medii Aevi* 19 (2012): 81–113. See also Golden, "Nomads of the Western Eurasian Steppes," 135–45, and Golden, "Oq and Oğur-Oğuz."

50. Étienne de la Vaissière, "Huns et Xiongnu," *Central Asiatic Journal* 49 (2005): 3–26.

51. Vásáry, *Geschichte des frühen Innerasiens*, 69. For diverse Chinese name forms, see the appendix in Golden, "Stateless Nomads."

52. Dieter Timpe, "Ethnologische Begriffsbildung in der Antike," in *Germanenprobleme in heutiger Sicht*, ed. Heinrich Beck, RGA Erg. Bd. 1 (Berlin, 1986), 33.

53. Pohl, "Introduction. Strategies of Identification"; Pohl, "Ethnicity and Empire."

54. Agathias 5.25, 196–97; cf. section 2.1.

55. See section 7.6.

56. See, among others, Nicolas Oikonomides, "Silk Trade and Production in Byzantium from the Sixth to the Ninth Century: The Seals of Kommerkiarioi," *Dumbarton Oaks Papers* 40 (1986): 33–53; Valerie Hansen, *Silk Road: A New History* (Oxford, 2012); Victor H. Mair and Jane Hickman, eds., *Reconfiguring the Silk Road: New Research on East–West Exchange in Antiquity* (Philadelphia, 2014); and section 2.6.

57. For recent overviews of the Rouran, see Nikolay N. Kradin, "From Tribal Confederation to Empire: The Evolution of the Rouran Society," *Acta Orient. Hung.* 58 (2005): 149–69; Peter B. Golden, "Some Notes on the Avars and Rouran," in *The Steppe Lands and the World Beyond Them: Studies in Honor of Victor Spinei on His 70th Birthday*, ed. Florin Curta and Bogdan-Petru Maleon (Iași, 2013), 43–66. See also Leonid R. Kyzlasov, "Northern Nomads," in *History of Civilizations of Central Asia*, vol. 3, *The Crossroads of Civilizations: A.D. 250 to 750*, ed. Boris A. Litvinsky, Zhang Guang-da, and Reza Shabani Samghabadi (Paris, 1996), 315–26. For an identification with the Avars, see Kollautz and Miyakawa; see also the detailed account of the fall of the Rouran Empire, ibid., 1:133–37;

Peter B. Golden, "Ethnogenesis in the Tribal Zone: The Shaping of the Turks," in Golden and Hriban, *Studies on the Peoples*, 50–51; Étienne de la Vaissière, "Theophylact's Turkish Exkurs Revisited," in *De Samarcande à Istanbul: Étapes orientales. Hommages à Pierre Chuvin II*, ed. Véronique Schiltz (Paris, 2015), 91–102. Against an identification, see Denis Sinor, "The Establishment and Dissolution of the Türk Empire," in *The Cambridge History of Early Inner Asia*, ed. Denis Sinor (Cambridge, 2000), 291–97; Yu Taishan, "Doubts about the Theory of Rouran-Avar Identity and the Hypothesis about Avar-Yueban Identity," in Yu Taishan, *China and the Mediterranean World in Ancient Times*, ed. Victor Spinei (Bucharest, 2014), 297–326.

58. Golden, "Some Notes on the Avars and Rouran," 53.

59. *Wei shu*, 103; *Nan Qi shu*, 59, both trans. in Yu, "Doubts," 317.

60. Golden, "Some Notes on the Avars and Rouran," 51 and 66.

61. *Bei shi*, 98, trans. in Yu, "Doubts," 312.

62. *Bei shi*, 99, trans. in Yu, "Doubts," 313–14; see also *Sui shu*, 84, and *Zhou shu*, 50, in Liu Mau-Tsai, *Die chinesischen Nachrichten zur Geschichte der Ost-Türken (T'u-küe)*, 2 vols., Göttinger Asiatische Forschungen 10 (Wiesbaden, 1958), 1:10; cf. Hisayuki Miyakawa and Arnulf Kollautz, "Die Mongolei in der Epoche der Jou-jan (5. und 6. Jh. n. Chr.)," *Central Asiatic Journal* 12 (1968–69): 208.

63. Procopius, *Bella* 1.3.1, ed. and trans. Dewing, 1:13. Étienne de la Vaissière, "Is There a 'Nationality of the Hephthalites'?," *Bulletin of the Asia Institute* 17 (2007): 124 (proposing an Ogur origin of the Hephthalites); Roman Ghirshman, *Les Chionites-Hephthalites* (Cairo, 1948); Arnulf Kollautz and Hisayuki Miyakawa, "Abdelai," in *Reallexikon der Byzantinistik* 1.2 (Amsterdam, 1969), 88–126; János Harmatta, ed., *From Hecateus to al-Huwarizmi: Bactrian, Pahlavi, Sogdian, Persian, Sanskrit, Syriac, Arabic, Chinese, Greek and Latin Sources for the History of Pre-Islamic Central Asia*, Collection of the Sources for the History of Pre-Islamic Asia, ser. 1, 3 (Budapest, 1984); Róna-Tas, *Hungarians and Europe in the Early Middle Ages*, 213–15; Boris A. Litvinsky, "The Hephthalite Empire," in Litvinsky, Guang-da, and Samghabadi, *History of Civilizations of Central Asia*, 135–76; Frantz Grenet, "Regional Interaction in Central Asia and North-West India in the Kidarite and Hephthalite Period," in *Indo-Iranian Languages and Peoples*, ed. Nicholas Sims-Williams, Proceedings of the British Academy 116 (Oxford, 2002), 203–34; Aydogdy Kurbanov, "The Hephthalites: Archaeological and Historical Analysis" (PhD diss., Freie Universität Berlin, 2010), http://www.diss.fu-berlin.de/diss/servlets/MCRFileNodeServlet/FUDISS_derivate_000000007165/01_Text.pdf. When exactly the empire of the Hephthalites fell is uncertain. Chavannes, *Documents sur les Tou-kiue*, puts the end of the war between 563 and 567; Knud Hannestad, "Les relations de Byzance avec la Transcaucasie et l'Asie centrale aux 5e et 6e siècles," *Byzantion* 25–27 (1955–57): 445, on the contrary, in 561 at the latest. The last embassy of the Ye-ta/Hephthalites to China was in 558; *Pei shi*, in Liu Mau-Tsai, *Die chinesischen Nachrichten*, 1:97; Otto Franke, *Geschichte des chinesischen Reiches*, 3 vols. (Leipzig, 1936), 2:233–34. For an early dating of the fall, see Mario Grignaschi, "La chute de l'empire hephthalite dans les sources byzantines et le problème des Avares," in Harmatta, *From Hecateus to al-Huwarizmi*, 219–48 (for two campaigns, 555 and 556–57); Czeglédy, "From East to West," 38, for the year 557; an earlier, similar opinion in Adolf Lippold, "Hephthalitai," in *RE Suppl.* 14 (1974), 137. At any event, the Persians also fought in an alliance with the Turks and may only have won their victory over the Hephthalites after the peace accord with Byzantium (at the end of 561): Geo Widengren, "Xosrau Anōšurvān, les Hephthalites et les peuples turcs," *Orientalia Suecana* 1 (1952): 72–73. The end of the war could reasonably be dated to 562–63, which would fit well with the subsequent Turkish embassy of 562–63 (see section 2.6). General treatment of these events also in Bertold Spuler, "Geschichte Mittelasiens seit dem Auftreten der Türken," in *Geschichte Mittelasiens*, ed. Bertold Spuler, Handbuch der Orientalistik 1.5.5 (Leiden, 1966), 123–310;

René Grousset, *The Empire of the Steppes: A History of Central Asia*, trans. Naomi Walford (New Brunswick, 1970), 67–71; Ehsan Yarshater, ed., *The Cambridge History of Iran*, vol. 3, *The Seleucid, Parthian and Sasanid Periods*, bk. 1 (Cambridge, 1983); Klaus Schippmann, *Grundzüge der Geschichte des sasanidischen Reiches* (Darmstadt, 1990), 57–59; Vásáry, *Geschichte des frühen Innerasiens*, 64–70; Denis Sinor and Sergei G. D. Klyashtorny, "The Türk Empire," in Litvinsky, Guang-da, and Samghabadi, *History of Civilizations of Central Asia*, 327–47; Sinor, "The Establishment and Dissolution of the Türk Empire," 291–300; Golden, "Ethnogenesis in the Tribal Zone."

64. Menander, frag. 10.1, ed. and trans. Blockley, 116.

65. Menander, frag. 19.1, ed. and trans. Blockley, 174.

66. Menander, frag. 10.1, ed. and trans. Blockley, 114–16. As a tributary prince of the Turks, Maniakh governed the formerly Hephthalite Sogdians, who had a reputation for far-reaching trade connections and diplomatic skills.

67. Theophylact Simocatta 1.5, 50.

68. Theophylact Simocatta 7.7, 256.

69. Evagrius 5.1, trans. Whitby, 255. I have replaced Whitby's "race" for *ethnos* by "people."

70. Theodore Syncellus 5.15–16, ed. and trans. Makk, 14.

71. See section 3.5.

72. Menander, frag. 4.2, ed. and trans. Blockley, 44–46.

73. Menander, frag. 19.1, ed. and trans. Blockley, 174. See section 3.5.

74. Priscus, frag. 40.1, ed. and trans. Blockley, 344.

75. Priscus, frag. 40.1, ed. and trans. Blockley, 344; *Suidae Lexicon*, ed. Ada Adler, 5 vols., Lexicographi Graeci 1.1–5 (Leipzig, 1925–38; repr. 1967–71), 1:312, *s.v. Abaris*.

76. Herodotus, *Historiae* 4.27, ed. A. D. Godley, Loeb Classical Series, vol. 2 (Cambridge, MA, 1982), 227.

77. Theophylact Simocatta, 7.7–9, 188. Étienne de la Vaissière, "Maurice et le qaghan: À propos de la digression de Théophylacte Simocatta sur les Turcs," *Revue des Études Byzantines* 68 (2010): 219–24; de la Vaissière, "Theophylact's Turkish Exkurs Revisited"; de la Vaissière, "Away from the Ötüken: A Geopolitical Approach to the Seventh Century Eastern Turks," in Bemmann and Schmauder, *Complexity of Interaction*, 453–62. See also Whitby, *The Emperor Maurice and His Historian*, 188–93. Some authors believed that the khagan—usually identified as Tardu—had referred to events of the 580s. Others maintained that Theophylact had inserted a letter only composed in 600 (Haussig, "Theophylakts Exkurs," 384) or 598 (Czeglédy, "From East to West," 107). Both solutions are not very plausible. See also Pohl, "Ethnicity and Empire."

78. Sergey G. Klyashtorny, "The Terkhin Inscription," *Acta Orient. Hung.* 36 (1982): 335–66; Haussig, "Theophylacts Exkurs," 330.

79. Franke, *Geschichte des chinesischen Reiches*, 3:292–94; Haussig, "Theophylakts Exkurs," 389–91; Czeglédy, "From East to West," 107. For the Tabghach khagan in the Kültegin and Bilge khagan inscriptions, see Sören Stark, "Luxurious Necessities: Some Observations on Foreign Commodities and Nomadic Polities in Central Asia in the Sixth to Ninth Centuries," in Bemmann and Schmauder, *Complexity of Interaction*, 488.

80. Menander, frag. 10.4, ed. and trans. Blockley, 124. On the localization of the Choliates to the north of the Syr Darja, see Czeglédy, "From East to West," 115.

81. Theophylact Simocatta 7.7, 257.

82. Theophylact Simocatta 7.8, 259.

83. It should not be surprising that the Avars only come second in the list. The two lists of peoples of the Orkhon inscriptions also follow a geographical order; cf. Haussig, "Theophylakts Exkurs," 330 and 372. The Byzantines understood the Atil/Til to be the Volga, where they also knew of Ogurs (Menander, frag. 10.4, ed. and trans. Blockley, 124).

Czeglédy, "From East to West," 118, supports this identification. Hans W. Haussig, "Die Quellen über die zentralasiatische Herkunft der europäischen Awaren," *Central Asiatic Journal* 2 (1956): 34, and Whitby and Whitby, in Theophylact Simocatta, 189, n. 38, opt for the Tarim River. This was rejected by William Samolin, in a review of Haussig, "Theophylakts Exkurs," in *Central Asiatic Journal* 2 (1956): 315. Haussig later proposed the Don: "Über die Bedeutung," 96. Quite likely the information "on the Til" is an addition by Theophylact, who knew from Menander that Ogurs lived on the Volga.

84. Herodotus 4.36, ed. Godley, 235. The name of the Avar envoy Targitius (cf. section 6.5) is also linked to Scythian history.

85. Aparnoi: Strabo 11.9.2–3 (if the conjecture is correct). Abar-šahr: Altheim, *Geschichte der Hunnen*, 1:28; Mehrdad Kia, *The Persian Empire: A Historical Encyclopedia* (Santa Barbara, 2016), 52–53.

86. *Sui shu*, German trans. in Liu Mau-Tsai, *Die chinesischen Nachrichten*, 1:51; Yu, "Doubts," 310–11.

87. Liu Mau-Tsai, *Die chinesischen Nachrichten*, 1:108 and 2:558, n. 555.

88. Kültegin inscription, side 1, http://bitig.org/?lang=e&mod=1&tid=1&oid=15&m=1. Haussig, "Theophylakts Exkurs," 330–31; Yu, "Doubts," 320. They could of course also be European Avars. Regarded as remains of the Rouran: Franke, *Geschichte des chinesischen Reiches*, 3:291–92; Liu Mau-Tsai, *Die chinesischen Nachrichten*, 2:527, n. 273. For a different emendation as *par* (Tibet), based on the Turkish edition of the Orkhon inscriptions by Erhan Aydın, *Orhon Yazıtları* (Konya, 2012), 45 and 79, see Golden, "Some Notes on the Avars and Rouran," 61.

89. *The Chronicle of Pseudo-Zachariah Rhetor* 12.7, ed. Greatrex, Phenix, and Horn, 449.

90. Theophylact Simocatta 1.8, 54.

91. Flavius Corippus, *In laudem Iustini Augusti Minoris libri IV* 3, ed. Karl Hahn, MGH AA B/I (Berlin, 1879), 277–83; alternatively, ed. and trans. Averil Cameron (London, 1976), 60–73 and 102–10. The passage is indeed full of topoi, as, for example, in the description of the crossing of the frozen Euphrates. The panegyricist is nonetheless dealing with current events.

92. Vladimir A. Kuznetsov, "The Avars in the Nart Epos of the Ossets," *Acta Orient. Hung.* 38 (1984): 165–69; Hans W. Haussig, *Die Geschichte Zentralasiens und der Seidenstrasse in vorislamischer Zeit* (Darmstadt, 1983), 162; Emanuel Sarkisyanz, *Geschichte der orientalischen Völker Russlands bis 1917* (Munich, 1961), 128–30. In 1955, 240,000 Avars were still living in Caucasian Daghestan; cf. Hélène Carrère-d'Encausse and Alexandre Benningsen, "Avars," in *The Encyclopaedia of Islam*, new ed. (Leiden, 1960), 755.

93. Making much of Western Asian Avars: Altheim, *Geschichte der Hunnen*, 2:27; Haussig, *Die Geschichte Zentralasiens*, 160–63.

94. *Wei shu*, Liu Mau-Tsai, *Die chinesischen Nachrichten*, 1:103; Franke, *Geschichte des chinesischen Reiches*, 3:291; Grousset, *Empire of the Steppes*, 172; Kollautz and Miyakawa, 1:145.

95. Gyula Németh, *A honfoglaló magyarság kialakulása* (Budapest, 1930), 105; subsequently, Carlile A. Macartney, "On the Greek Sources for the History of the Turks," *Bulletin of the School of Oriental and African Studies* 11, no. 2 (1944): 270; A. Zeki Validi Togan, *Ibn Fadlans Reisebericht*, Abhandlungen für die Kunde des Morgenlandes 24.3 (Leipzig, 1939), 225; Togan is critical of attempts at etymological interpretations. See also Howorth, "The Avars," 722–23.

96. See, most recently, Christopher Atwood, "The Qai, the Khongai, and the Names of the Xiōngnú," *International Journal of Eurasian Studies* 2 (2015): 35–63.

97. Maenchen-Helfen, *The World of the Huns*, 424.

98. *Suidae Lexicon*, ed. Adler, 2:634, *s.v. himonia*.

99. Andreas Alföldi, "Zur historischen Bestimmung der Awarenfunde," *Eurasia Septentrionalis Antiqua* 9 (1934): 292.

100. On the identification of the European Avars with the Rouran, see Joseph de Guignes, *Histoire générale des Huns, des Turcs, des Mongols et des autres Tartares occidentaux*, 4 vols. (Paris, 1756–58), 1:352; Kollautz and Miyakawa, 1:13–15; Czeglédy, "From East to West," 107–10; Chavannes, *Documents sur les Tou-kiue*, 229–31; Stein, *Histoire du Bas-Empire*, 2:541; Steven Runciman, *A History of the First Bulgarian Empire* (London, 1930), 10; Grousset, *Empire of the Steppes*, 172; George Vernadsky, *Ancient Russia* (New Haven, CT, 1946), 178; de la Vaissière, "Maurice et le qaghan."

101. Czeglédy, "From East to West," 108–24.

102. Whitby, *The Emperor Maurice and His Historian*, 317.

103. Golden, "Some Notes on the Avars and Rouran," 65. For a recent critical analysis of Theophylact's text, see de la Vaissière, "Theophylact's Turkish Exkurs Revisited."

104. Pohl, "Ethnicity and Empire."

105. Yu, "Doubts."

106. Yu, "Doubts," 320. Also for an identification of the Avars with the Yueban: Edward H. Parker, "China, the Avars and the Franks," *Asiatic Quarterly Review* 3, no. 13 (1902): 446–60; Pritsak, "The Slavs and the Avars," 364.

107. Hans W. Haussig, "Zur Lösung der Awarenfrage," *Byzantinoslavica* 34 (1973): 192.

108. Josef Marquart, "Über das Volkstum der Komanen," *Abhandlungen der Akademie der Wissenschaften in Göttingen*, n.s., 13 (1914): 74; Macartney, "On the Greek Sources."

109. Priscus, frag. 40, ed. and trans. Blockley, 344.

110. That the Avars escaped before the end of the Hephthalite war becomes clear in Menander, frag. 4.2, ed. and trans. Blockley, 44–46. Haussig, "Theophylacts Exkurs"; Haussig, "Zur Lösung der Awarenfrage"; Haussig, "Die Quellen über die zentralasiatische Herkunft"; Haussig, "Über die Bedeutung"; similarly Altheim, *Geschichte der Hunnen*, 1:85–86; William Samolin, "Some Notes on the Avar Problem," *Central Asiatic Journal* 3 (1957–58): 62–65.

111. Haussig, "Über die Bedeutung," 98.

112. Czeglédy, "From East to West," 97–100.

113. Menander, frag. 10.1, ed. and trans. Blockley, 114–16; cf. Menander, frag. 19.1, ed. and trans. Blockley, 174. See section 2.3.

114. *Sui shu*, 84, in Liu Mau-Tsai, *Die chinesischen Nachrichten*, 1:47.

115. Thomsen, "Alttürkische Inschriften in der Mongolei," 170.

116. Tonyukuk inscription, 54, http://bitig.org/?lang=e&mod=1&tid=1&oid=17&m=1; Thomsen, "Alttürkische Inschriften in der Mongolei," 142 and 147.

117. Thomsen, "Alttürkische Inschriften in der Mongolei," 168. See also the Bilge Khagan inscription, front side 14 and 24, http://bitig.org/?lang=e&mod=1&tid=1&oid=16&m=1.

118. Thomsen, "Alttürkische Inschriften in der Mongolei," 145.

119. Radloff, *Aus Sibirien*, 1:230; a list of examples for the same names in different contexts in Pritsak, "Tribal Names," 66–67.

120. Walther Heissig, "Ethnische Gruppenbildung in Zentralasien im Licht mündlicher und schriftlicher Überlieferung," in *Studien zur Ethnogenese*, Abhandlungen der Rheinisch-Westfälischen AW 72 (Opladen, 1985), 30.

121. Walter Pohl, "Die Gepiden und die Gentes an der mittleren Donau nach dem Zerfall des Attilareiches," in *Die Völker an der mittleren und unteren Donau im fünften und sechsten Jahrhundert: Berichte des Symposions der Kommission für Frühmittelalterforschung, 24. bis 27. Oktober 1978, Stift Zwettl, Niederösterreich*, ed. Herwig Wolfram and Falko Daim, DsÖAW 145 (Vienna, 1980), 240–305, especially 260–62 and 292–93; see also section 6.10.

122. Timpe, "Ethnologische Begriffsbildung in der Antike," 36–37.

123. Herwig Wolfram, "Origo gentis," in *RGA*, 22:174–78; Walter Pohl, "Origo gentis (Langobarden)," in *RGA*, 22:183–88; Pohl, "Ethnicity, Theory and Tradition."

124. This is the title of a subchapter in Atwood, "The Qai," 36–38.

125. Theophylact Simocatta, 7.8, 258–59. Such information was fundamental to Byzantine diplomacy and it dealt with well-known neighbors.

126. Pritsak, "Tribal Names," 62.

127. Togan, *Ibn Fadlans Reisebericht*, 274–75.

128. Since the German edition (Pohl, *Die Awaren*, 36–37), I have slightly modified my position to allow for some presence of Rouran, perhaps even of the ruling clan, among the Avars moving to Europe. I am grateful to Peter B. Golden and Étienne de la Vaissière for discussions about this issue. However, I would still insist on the composite character of the migrating Avars. The substantial testimony of Menander and Theophylact points in this direction and should not be brushed away.

129. Csanád Bálint, *Die Archäologie der Steppe: Steppenvölker zwischen Wolga und Donau vom 6. bis zum 9. Jahrhundert* (Vienna, 1988), 152–57.

130. Ibn Rusta 4.2, "Beschreibung der Nordvölker nach dem *Kitāb al-a'lāq an-nafīsa* des Abū 'Alī ibn 'Umar ibn Rusta," trans. Hansgerd Göckenjan and István Zimonyi, *Orientalische Berichte über die Völker Osteuropas und Zentralasiens im Mittelalter: Die Ǧayhānī-Tradition (Ibn Rusta, Gardīzī, Ḥudūd al-'Ālam, al-Bakrī und al-Marwazī* (Wiesbaden, 2001). See also Antal Bartha, *Hungarian Society in the 9th and 10th Centuries*, Studia Historica Academiae Scientiarum Hungaricae 85 (Budapest, 1975), 110; C. E. Bosworth, "Ebn Rosta," in *Encyclopaedia Iranica*, vol. 8, fasc. 1 (New York, 2003), 49–50. András Róna-Tas, "The Khazars and the Magyars," in *The World of the Khazars: New Perspectives*, ed. Peter B. Golden, Haggai Ben-Shammai, and András Róna-Tas, Handbook of Oriental Studies 17 (Leiden, 2007), 275.

131. On the number of Avars, see Menander, frag. 10.1, ed. and trans. Blockley, 114; for those of Gothic armies, Wolfram, *History of the Goths*, 7. For the size of Roman armies, Agathias 5.13, 148; Arnold M. H. Jones, *The Later Roman Empire (284–602): A Social, Economic and Administrative Survey*, 3 vols. (Oxford, 1964), 2:679–86; Ernst Stein, *Studien zur Geschichte des byzantinischen Reiches vornehmlich unter den Kaisern Justinus II und Tiberius Constantinus* (Stuttgart, 1919), 80, n. 4. Concerning the numbers of fleeing Avars, neither the Turks nor the East Romans had any reason to exaggerate.

132. Priscus, frag. 40, ed. and trans. Blockley, 344.

133. Herodotus 4.13, ed. Godley, 213–14; 4.27, 227; 4.79, 279.

134. Stephanos Byzantios, *Ethnika*, ed. Margarethe Billerbeck and Arlette Neumann-Hartmann, Corpus Fontium Historiae Byzantinae 42, 5 vols. (Berlin, 2006–17), vol. 4, 263, *s.v. tarkynia*.

135. *Suidae Lexicon*, ed. Adler, 1:3–4, *s.v. Abaris*.

136. Cf. section 8.1.

137. Theophylact Simocatta 7.8, 258–59.

138. "Isti magias artibus instructi, diversas eis fantasias ostenderunt et eos valde superant": Gregory of Tours, *Decem libri historiarum* 4.29, ed. Krusch and Levison, 161; cf. sections 2.7 and 6.8.

139. Ádám Molnár, *Weather Magic in Inner Asia* (Bloomington, IN, 1994); Golden, *Central Asia in World History*, 36.

140. Menander, frag. 5.2–3, ed. and trans. Blockley, 48–51.

141. *Suidae Lexicon*, ed. Adler, 2:634, *s.v. himonia*.

142. Priscus, frag. 40, ed. and trans. Blockley, 344; Theophanes, *Chronographia* 6013, 167. On the Sabirs, see Sinor, *Introduction à l'étude de l'Eurasie centrale*, 267; Haussig, "Theophylakts Exkurs," 364; Golden, "Nomads of the Western Eurasian Steppes," 146–47. The information in Victor of Tunnuna, *Chronica* a. 559.2, ed. Placanica, 56, about "Ugni" (Huns) attacking Armenia probably refers to the Sabirs, not to the Avars.

143. Menander, frag. 18.6, ed. and trans. Blockley, 164.

144. On the Zali and their possible identification with the Barselt (Theophylact Simocatta 7.8, 258), see Haussig, "Theophylacts Exkurs," 362; Golden, *Khazar Studies*, 1:143–47; Maenchen-Helfen, *Die Welt der Hunnen*, 300, who also makes reference to the "Saloi" of Ptolemy.

145. See section 3.2.

146. Menander, frag. 12.5, ed. and trans. Blockley, 136. See section 3.1.

147. Agathias 5.25, 162.

148. Menander, frag. 19.1, ed. and trans. Blockley, 172–75. This regarded the Alans and the Onogurs who had obviously chosen to resist the Turks. Two manuscripts have *Uniguroi* here, two *Ouiguroi*, one *Utiguroi*. Dindorf prefers the latter reading: Menander, ed. Ludwig August Dindorf, *Historici Graeci minores* (Bonn, 1871), 2:87, de Boor and Blockley the first. Considering the position of Anagaius it is more likely that the Utigurs had joined the Turks of their own accord.

149. See sections 6.10 and 7.6.

150. Menander, frag. 5.3, ed. and trans. Blockley, 50. It is hardly credible that the Antes governed an empire from the Neisse to the Don, as Francis Dvornik, *The Making of Central and Eastern Europe* (London, 1949), 278, would have it. For their localization between the Dniester and Dnieper, see section 4.1.

151. Theophylact Simocatta 8.5.13, 217. See section 5.9.

152. For instance, in Beševliev, *Die protobulgarische Periode*, 102; Stratos, *Byzantium in the Seventh Century*, 1:31. Samuel Szádeczky-Kardoss, "Über die Wandlungen der Ostgrenze der awarischen Machtsphäre," in his *Avarica: Über die Awarengeschichte und ihre Quellen*, Acta Universitatis de Attila József Nominatae, Opuscula Byzantina 8 (Szeged, 1986), 159, would extend the Avar frontier beyond the Don.

153. Theophanes Byzantios, *Fragmentum*, ed. Karl Müller, Fragmenta historicorum graecorum 4 (Paris, 1885), 4.270b. Cf. Kollautz and Miyakawa, "Abdelai," 94–95. On Theophanes Byzantios, see Karayannopoulos and Weiss, *Quellenkunde zur Geschichte von Byzanz*, 2:285. In general about the early medieval Turks and their language, see Barthold, *Histoire des Turcs*; Grousset, *Empire*, 80–115; Karl H. Menges, *The Turkic Languages and Peoples: An Introduction to Turkic Studies* (Wiesbaden, 1968); Talât Tekin, *A Grammar of Orkhon Turkic* (Bloomington, 1968); Sinor, "The Establishment and Dissolution of the Türk Empire," 288–316; Wolfgang-Ekkehard Scharlipp, *Die frühen Türken in Zentralasien: Eine Einführung in ihre Geschichte und Kultur* (Darmstadt, 1992); Sinor and Klyashtorny, "The Türk Empire"; Michael Drompp, "Strategies of Cohesion and Control in the Türk and Uyghur Empires," in Bemmann and Schmauder, *Complexity of Interaction*, 437–52; Golden, *Central Asia in World History*, 35–44.

154. Theophanes, *Chronographia* 6055, 351.

155. Stein, *Histoire du Bas-Empire*, 2:545; Altheim, *Geschichte der Hunnen*, 1:26.

156. Sinor, "The Establishment and Dissolution of the Türk Empire," 301. White Huns: Procopius, *Bella* 1.3.1, ed. and trans. Dewing, 1:13.

157. *Zhou shu*, 50, in Liu Mau-Tsai, *Die chinesischen Nachrichten*, 1:7–8; Franke, *Geschichte des chinesischen Reiches*, 2:241; Thomsen, "Alttürkische Inschriften in der Mongolei," 122–24 and 145; Menander, frag. 10.3, ed. and trans. Blockley, 119–21; see the commentary, ibid. 262, n. 112; Theophylact Simocatta 7.7, 257, and trans. Schreiner, 186 (who reads "Stembischadas"). Haussig, "Theophylakts Exkurs," 282, opts for "Stembischagan"; see, further, his "Die Quellen über die zentralasiatische Herkunft," 27. Depending on the reading the title could be either "khagan" or "shad." On the interpretation of "Sizabulos" as the title "Syr Yabgu," see Haussig, "Theophylakts Exkurs," 374; Moravcsik, *Byzantinoturcica*, 2:275–76. For the identification of Istemi with Sizabulos, see Macartney, "On the Greek Sources," 270; Czeglédy, "From East to West," 107; against an identification, see

Haussig, "Die Quellen über die zentralasiatische Herkunft," 29; Sinor, "The Establishment and Dissolution of the Türk Empire," 305, who sees Sizabulos (and his son Turxanthos) as a "minor potentate." Yet it is hard to see why Byzantine envoys should travel so far to meet minor Turkish leaders.

158. Thomsen, "Alttürkische Inschriften in der Mongolei," 145.

159. Corippus, *In laudem Iustini* 3, 390, ed. and trans. Cameron, 72 and 110; ed. Serge Antès (Paris, 1981), 70 (Scultor); see also the comment, ibid., 122–24. However, the text does not say that Scultor was a Turk, just that he sent an embassy with many presents. The name is mentioned in the speech to the Avar envoys as an example of a ruler "ready to serve us at court," an example that the Avars should follow.

160. Askel and Scultor as names for Istemi: Togan, *Ibn Fadlans Reisebericht*, 194 and 223; Stein, *Histoire du Bas-Empire*, 2:545; Czeglédy, "From East to West," 77. Askel as the name of a western Turkish tribe: Sinor, "The Establishment and Dissolution of the Türk Empire," 302.

161. *Sui shu*, 84, in Liu Mau-Tsai, *Die chinesischen Nachrichten*, 1:44. The transcription used here follows the old style. The discovery of the Xiao Hongnahai/Mongolküre inscription has added to our knowledge about the Ashina dynasty and its Turkic names. For the inscription and its site, see Stark, *Die Alttürkenzeit in Mittel- und Zentralasien*, 73–75. For an updated genealogy, see Étienne de la Vaissière, "Oncles et frères: Les qaghans Ashinas et le vocabulaire turc de la parenté," *Turcica* 42 (2010): 273.

162. Thomsen, "Alttürkische Inschriften in der Mongolei," 124; Franke, *Geschichte des chinesischen Reiches*, 2:241 and 245–46; Liu Mau-Tsai, *Die chinesischen Nachrichten*, 1:11–13, with a list of the embassies and military campaigns, 1:402–4.

163. Menander, frag. 10.1, ed. and trans. Blockley, 110–17. Stein, *Studien zur Geschichte*, 18–19, remains skeptical of the tendentiousness of this anecdote.

164. Hisayuki Miyakawa and Arnulf Kollautz, "Ein Dokument zum Fernhandel zwischen Byzanz und China zur Zeit Theophylakts," *Byzantinische Zeitschrift* 77 (1984): 19. For the silk trade in general, see Angelika Muthesius, *Studies in Byzantine and Islamic Silk Weaving* (London, 1995).

165. Procopius, *Bella* 8.17, ed. and trans. Dewing, 5:226–31; Theophanes Byzantios, ed. Müller, 270; Stein, *Histoire du Bas-Empire*, 2:769–71; Hannestad, "Les relations," 432–34; Haussig, *Die Geschichte Zentralasiens*, 151–52 and 180–82. Silk clothing was still found in the Avar spoils from 796; cf. section 6.4.

166. Hannestad, "Les relations," 453.

167. Menander, frag. 10.1, ed. and trans. Blockley, 114–17. In general, see Mark Whittow, "Byzantium's Eurasian Policy in the Age of the Türk Empire," in Di Cosmo and Maas, *Empires and Exchanges in Eurasian Late Antiquity*, 271–86.

168. In reality, the eastern Turkish khagan Muqan held supreme power, while Istemi was only second, and carried the title *yabgu*. For the Chinese sources, see Liu Mau-Tsai, *Die chinesischen Nachrichten*, 1:19 and 41–42.

169. Menander, frag. 10.3, ed. and trans. Blockley, 118. On the dating, see ibid., 263, n. 126. Menander's dating is more reliable than that of John of Ephesus (6.23, 344) to the seventh year of Justin's rule, which doubtless takes its cue from the return of the envoys in 571.

170. Menander, frag. 10.3, ed. and trans. Blockley, 119; John of Ephesus 6.23, 344. The identification of the Ektag is debated, but it is supposed to have lain in the Tienshan; Haussig, "Theophylakts Exkurs," 345; Blockley, in Menander, ed. and trans. Blockley, 264, n.129. On the shamans, see section 6.9.

171. Menander, frag. 10.3–4, ed. and trans. Blockley, 118–27. On the title *tagmatarkhan*, see section 8.2.

172. John of Ephesus 6.23, 344–46; Michael the Syrian 10.10, 315.

173. This is confirmed by Menander, frag. 13.5, ed. and trans. Blockley, 146.

174. The following events are described by Menander, frag. 5.4, ed. and trans. Blockley, 50–53.

175. Cf. Herwig Wolfram, *The Roman Empire and Its Germanic Peoples* (Berkeley, 1997); Walter Pohl, ed., *Kingdoms of the Empire: The Integration of Barbarians in Late Antiquity*, The Transformation of the Roman World 1 (Leiden, 1997).

176. Sarantis, *Justinian's Balkan Wars*, 351–52; Iustinus 4, in J. R. Martindale, *The Prosopography of the Later Roman Empire*, vol. 3A–B (Cambridge, 1992), 750–54 (henceforth abbreviated as *PLRE*).

177. Procopius, *Bella* 6.14–15, ed. and trans. Dewing, 3:408–25; Wolfram, *History of the Goths*, 323.

178. Menander, frag. 5.4, ed. and trans. Blockley, 52; Stein, *Histoire du Bas-Empire*, 2:543.

179. Menander, frag. 5.4, ed. and trans. Blockley, 52. Victor of Tunnuna puts the "first" Avar embassy, which Justinian dismissed "cum donis maximis," in the year 563. This does not quite fit with the events recounted by Menander and must represent a compression of several such embassies. For this period Victor is usually off by two years, which would bring us to 561. See Antonio Placanica, "Introduzione," in *Vittore de Tunnuna, Chronica*, ed. Placanica, xxix.

180. Bonus 4, *PLRE*, 3A:241–42. On the title, see Stein, *Studien zur Geschichte*, 33, n. 12.

181. Paul Lemerle, "La chronique improprement dite de Monemvasie: Le contexte historique et légendaire," *Revue des Études Byzantines* 21 (1963): 5–49; *Cronaca di Monemvasia*, ed. Ivan Dujčev, Istituto Siciliano di Studi Bizantini e Neoellenici, Testi e monumenti, Testi 12 (Palermo, 1976), 4. See also section 4.4.

182. Gregory of Tours, *Decem libri historiarum* 4.23, ed. Krusch and Levison, 155–56; Paul the Deacon, *Historia Langobardorum* 2.10, ed. Waitz, 92–93; Fredegar 3.55, ed. Krusch, 107–8. Fritze, "Zur Bedeutung der Awaren," 524–26.

183. Menander, frag. 3.1, ed. and trans. Blockley, 44; Jones, *The Later Roman Empire*, 1:426–27; *PLRE*, 3A:55.

184. Fritze, "Zur Bedeutung der Awaren," 527.

185. Corippus, *In laudem Iustini* 3.258, ed. and trans. Cameron, 68 and 3.311–98, 70–72.

186. "Quos non potuit superare virtute proelii, superavit arte donandi": Gregory of Tours, *Decem libri historiarum* 4.29, ed. Krusch and Levison, 162.

187. Menander, frag. 11, ed. and trans. Blockley, 128.

188. Cf. Fritze, "Zur Bedeutung der Awaren," 522–30; Kollautz and Miyakawa, 1:166–67.

189. As in Paul Goubert, "Les Avares d'après les sources grecques du VIe siècle," in *Akten des 24. internationalen Orientalisten-Kongresses* (Wiesbaden, 1959), 214.

190. Avenarius, *Die Awaren in Europa*, 59. Similar view in Kollautz, "Die Awaren," 133; Mircea Rusu, "Les populations du groupe turc, les Slaves et les autochthones du bassin carpato-danubien aux VIe–IXe siècles," *Revue Roumaine d'Histoire* 19 (1980): 21.

191. Stein, *Studien zur Geschichte*, 10.

192. Menander, frag. 12.6, ed. and trans. Blockley, 140.

193. Menander, frag. 5.1, ed. and trans. Blockley, 48; Corippus, *In laudem Iustini* 3.271–78, ed. and trans. Cameron, 69; Theophylact Simocatta 6.11, 243.

194. Menander, frag. 19.1, ed. and trans. Blockley, 174; Blockley in his edition translates Menander's *hypokeklitai* rather weakly as "is open to me."

195. Menander, frag. 12.2, ed. and trans. Blockley, 130.

196. Agathias 5.11, 146.

197. For a recent general view on Roman barbarian policy, see Alexander Sarantis, "Eastern Roman Management of Barbarian States in the Lower-Middle Danube Frontier

Zones, AD 332–610," in *Grenzübergänge: Spätrömisch, frühchristlich, frühbyzantinisch als Kategorien der historisch-archäologischen Forschung an der mittleren Donau*, ed. Ivan Bugarski et al., Akten des 27. internationalen Symposiums der Grundprobleme der frühgeschichtlichen Entwicklung im mittleren Donauraum, Ruma, 4.–7.11.2015 (Remshalden, 2016), 41–66.

198. Michael the Syrian 10.11, 316.

199. Corippus, *In laudem Iustini*, Praefatio 5, ed. and trans. Cameron, 33. See Ulrich Justus Stache, *Flavius Cresconius Corippus: In laudem Iustini Minoris; Ein Kommentar* (Berlin, 1976), 431; Stein, *Studien zur Geschichte*, 4–5; Jones, *The Later Roman Empire*, 1:306; Averil Cameron, "The Early Religious Practices of Justin II," *Church History* 13 (1976): 51–67; Haldon, *Byzantium in the Seventh Century*, 32; Walter Pohl, "Ritualized Encounters: Late Roman Diplomats and Barbarians, Fifth–Sixth Century," in *Court Ceremonies and Rituals of Power in the Medieval Mediterranean*, ed. Alexander Beihammer, Stavroula Constantinou, and Maria Parani (Leiden, 2013), 67–86.

200. Corippus, *In laudem Iustini* 3.231–401, ed. and trans. Cameron, 67–72.

201. On the reception of barbarian embassies by the emperor in the orb or "eyeball" of the world, see Herbert Hunger, "Der Kaiserpalast zu Konstantinopel: Seine Funktion in der byzantinischen Außenpolitik," *Jahrbuch der Österreichischen Byzantinistik* 36 (1986): 1–11. It was during the rule of Justin II that construction was begun on the Chrysotriklinios, a domed, octagonal throne room, among whose decorations were a golden tree and an organ studded with precious stones. For the reception of foreign delegations the Magnaura Palace was generally used. See also Robin Cormack, "But Is It Art?," in *Byzantine Diplomacy: Papers from the Twenty-Fourth Spring Symposium of Byzantine Studies, Cambridge, March 1990*, ed. Jonathan Shepard and Simon Franklin (Aldershot, 1992), 223–24; Michael McCormick, "Analyzing Imperial Ceremonies," *Jahrbuch der Österreichischen Byzantinistik* 35 (1985): 1–20; Ekaterina Nechaeva, *Embassies-Negotiations-Gifts: Systems of East Roman Diplomacy in Late Antiquity* (Stuttgart, 2014).

202. Rendered here as *Tergazis*; Stache, *Flavius Cresconius Corippus*, 442–43, prefers the likewise transmitted form *Targites*. On this topic, see *PLRE*, 3B:1217, and section 6.5. The following quotes are from Corippus, *In laudem Iustini* 3.255–59, ed. and trans. Cameron, 68; 3.244, 68.

203. Menander, frag. 8, ed. and trans. Blockley, 92.

204. John of Ephesus 6.24, 247.

205. Menander, frag. 8, ed. and trans. Blockley, 96; cf. section 2.7.

206. Marius of Avenches, *Chronica* a. 566, ed. Theodor Mommsen, MGH AA 11 (Berlin, 1894), 238.

207. Paul the Deacon, *Historia Langobardorum* 1.27, ed. Waitz, 80; Theophylact Simocatta, 6.10.7–13, 174–75. Frank E. Wozniak, "Byzantine Diplomacy and the Lombard-Gepidic Wars," *Balkan Studies* 20 (1979): 139–58; Stein, *Studien zur Geschichte*, 8; István Bóna, *Der Anbruch des Mittelalters: Gepiden und Langobarden im Karpatenbecken* (Budapest, 1976), 97–100; Pohl, "Die Gepiden und die Gentes," 299; Walter Pohl, "The Empire and the Lombards: Treaties and Negotiations in the Sixth Century," in Pohl, *Kingdoms of the Empire*, 88–98.

208. Menander, frag. 12.1, ed. and trans. Blockley, 128.

209. Menander, frag. 12.2, ed. and trans. Blockley, 130.

210. Paul the Deacon, *Historia Langobardorum* 1.27, ed. Waitz, 81.

211. See section 3.1.

212. Paul the Deacon, *Historia Langobardorum* 2.26, ed. Waitz, 103.

213. *Historia Langobardorum Codicis Gothani*, ed. Georg Waitz, MGH SS rer. Langob. (Hanover, 1878), 9.

214. Theophylact Simocatta 6.10, 173–76.

215. Walter Pohl, *Le origini etniche dell'Europa: Barbari e Romani tra antichità e medioevo* (Rome, 2000), 149–66; Francesco Borri, *Alboino: Frammenti di un racconto (secoli VI–XI)* (Rome, 2017).

216. See, for instance, the German title of the book by István Bóna, *Anbruch des Mittelalters*; the English title is *The Dawn of the Dark Ages: The Gepids and the Lombards in the Carpathian Basin* (Budapest, 1976).

217. Karl Müllenhof, *Deutsche Altertumskunde*, vol. 2 (Berlin, 1887), 103. Similarly, Kollautz and Miyakawa, 1:167.

218. Ludwig Schmidt, *Die Ostgermanen*, 2nd ed. (Munich, 1941), 545.

219. Avenarius, *Die Awaren in Europa*, 85.

220. Procopius, *Bella* 8.18.17, ed. and trans. Dewing, 5:238, and 8.25.5, 5:316.

221. Priscus, frag. 11.2, ed. and trans. Blockley, 266–73. The Greek had transformed himself into an Avar warrior and in a speech justifies his decision by a scathing critique of life in the Eastern Roman Empire.

222. Cf. section 3.4.

223. Stratos, *Byzantium in the Seventh Century*, 1:126.

224. Bóna, *Der Anbruch des Mittelalters*, 99–102; Kollautz and Miyakawa, 1:168–71; Avenarius, *Die Awaren in Europa*, 75.

225. Arnulf Kollautz, "Awaren, Langobarden und Slawen in Noricum und Istrien," *Carinthia I* 155 (1965): 619; similarly Avenarius, *Die Awaren in Europa*, 77; Bóna, *Anbruch des Mittelalters*, 102 ("the destruction of the Gepid kingdom proved to be a fatal error"); similar, if more cautious, view in Stein, *Studien zur Geschichte*, 11 and 32.

226. Goubert, "Les Avares d'après les sources grecques," 215; Ludmil Hauptmann, "Les rapports des Byzantins avec les Slaves et les Avares pendant la seconde moitié du VIe siècle," *Byzantion* 4 (1927–28): 154.

227. Goubert, "Les Avares d'après les sources grecques," 214.

228. Avenarius, *Die Awaren in Europa*, 63; Bóna, *Anbruch des Mittelalters*, 99; John Bagnell Bury, *A History of the Later Roman Empire: From Arcadius to Irene (395–800)*, 2 vols. (London, 1889), 2:115.

229. Wolfram, *History of the Goths*, 321. On the following, see Pohl, "Die Gepiden und die Gentes"; Walter Pohl, *Die Völkerwanderung: Eroberung und Integration*, 2nd ed. (Stuttgart, 2005), especially 195–98.

230. See also Geoffrey Greatrex, "Roman Identity in the Sixth Century," in *Ethnicity and Culture in Late Antiquity*, ed. Stephen Mitchell and Geoffrey Greatrex (Oakville, CT, 2000), 267–92.

231. Pohl, "Justinian and the Barbarian Kingdoms."

232. Procopius, *Bella* 7.35.12–22, ed. and trans. Dewing, 4:462–65. On the Slavic advance, see section 4.1.

233. Procopius, *Bella* 7.33.10, ed. and trans. Dewing, 4:440; Pohl, "The Empire and the Lombards," 88–90. See also Stein, *Histoire du Bas-Empire*, 2:531; Joachim Werner, *Die Langobarden in Pannonien: Beiträge zur Kenntnis der langobardischen Bodenfunde vor 568*, Abhandlungen der Bayerischen Akademie der Wissenschaften, n.s., 55 (Munich, 1962); Jörg Jarnut, *Geschichte der Langobarden* (Stuttgart, 1982), 23–26; Konstantinos P. Christou, *Byzanz und die Langobarden: Von der Ansiedlung in Pannonien bis zur endgültigen Anerkennung 500–680*, Historical Monographs 11 (Athens, 1991), 90–91.

234. Procopius, *Bella* 6.14, ed. and trans. Dewing, 3:402–13; Jordanes, *Getica* 301, ed. Mommsen, 135; Cassiodorus, *Variae epistulae* 5.10, ed. Theodor Mommsen, MGH AA 12 (Berlin, 1894), 145; Pohl, "Die Gepiden und die Gentes," 292–98.

235. Paul the Deacon, *Historia Langobardorum* 1.23–27, ed. Waitz, 70–81; Pohl, *Le origini etniche dell'Europa*, 149–66.

236. Theophylact Simocatta, 6.10, 174–76.

237. Paul the Deacon, *Historia Langobardorum* 2.28, ed. Waitz, 87.

238. Paul the Deacon, *Historia Langobardorum* 1.27, ed. Waitz, 81.

239. Paul the Deacon, *Historia Langobardorum* 2.28–30, ed. Waitz, 87–90. Cf. Otto Gschwantler, "Die Heldensage von Alboin und Rosimund," in *Festgabe für Otto Höfler zum 75. Geburtstag*, ed. Helmut Birkhan (Vienna, 1976), 214–54; Walter Pohl, "Alboin und der Langobardenzug nach Italien: Aufstieg und Fall eines Barbarenkönigs," in *Sie schufen Europa: Historische Portraits von Konstantin bis Karl dem Großen*, ed. Mischa Meier (Munich, 2007), 216–27.

240. Menander, frag. 12.1, ed. and trans. Blockley, 128.

3. THE NEW POWER, 567–90

1. Menander, frag. 12.5, ed. and trans. Blockley, 134; John of Biclaro, *Chronica* 19, ed. Theodor Mommsen, MGH AA 11 (Berlin, 1894; repr. Munich, 1981), 212–13; cited hereafter after the English translation in *Conquerors and Chroniclers of Early Medieval Spain*, trans. Kenneth Baxter Wolf, Translated Texts for Historians 9, 2nd ed. (Liverpool, 1999), 61–62; Pohl, "Die Gepiden und die Gentes," 300; Stein, *Studien zur Geschichte*, 10–11; Bury, *History of the Later Roman Empire*, 2:116–17; Miroslava Mirković, "Sirmium, Its History from the 1st Century AD to 582 AD," in *Sirmium*, vol. 1, *Archaeological Investigation in Syrmian Pannonia* (Belgrade, 1977), 52.

2. Bóna, *Der Anbruch des Mittelalters*, 101.

3. Menander, frag. 12.5, ed. and trans. Blockley, 136; Vladislav Popović, "Le dernier évêque de Sirmium," *Revue des Études Augustiniennes* 21 (1975): 91–111; Popović, "Les témoins archéologiques des invasions avaro-slaves dans l'Illyricum byzantin," *Mélanges de l'École Française de Rome* 87 (1985): 447. Friedrich Stefan, *Die Münzstätte Sirmium unter den Ostgoten und Gepiden: ein Beitrag zur Geschichte des germanischen Münzwesens in der Zeit der Völkerwanderung* (Munich, 1925), assumes a separate minting of coins with Cunimund's monogram. Johannes Hartner, Vienna, plans a publication on the Gepid coins.

4. "Mid Geþþum": *Widsith* 60, ed. Kemp Malone (Copenhagen, 1962), 24.

5. Menander, frag. 12.3, ed. and trans. Blockley, 130–32.

6. Menander, frag. 12.5, ed. and trans. Blockley, 132; Mirković, "Sirmium," 58.

7. Menander, frag. 12.4, ed. and trans. Blockley, 132.

8. Walter Pohl, "Konfliktverlauf und Konfliktbewältigung: Römer und Barbaren im frühen Mittelalter," *Frühmittelalterliche Studien* 26 (1992): 165–207.

9. Menander, frag. 12.5, ed. and trans. Blockley, 134; cf. section 6.10.

10. John of Biclaro, *Chronica* 19, 61.

11. Theophylact Simocatta, 6.10, 174–76.

12. Cf. Corippus, *In laudem Iustini* 3.300, ed. and trans. Cameron, 70.

13. Menander, frag. 12.5, ed. and trans. Blockley, 136.

14. Cf. section 6.10.

15. Menander, frags. 12.6–15.6, ed. and trans. Blockley, 138–51.

16. Stein, *Studien zur Geschichte*, 12–13.

17. Menander, frag. 10.1, ed. and trans. Blockley, 110; see section 2.6.

18. Menander, frag. 19.1, ed. and trans. Blockley, 174.

19. Pohl, "The Empire and the Lombards."

20. Menander, frag. 12.6, ed. and trans. Blockley, 138.

21. Menander, frag. 12.6, ed. and trans. Blockley, 138; see section 6.10.

22. An actual *adoptio per arma*, the recognition of its khagan as the emperor's "son in arms," is, however, improbable, contrary to Dietrich Claude, "Zur Begründung familiärer Beziehungen zwischen dem Kaiser und barbarischen Herrschern," in *Das Reich und die Barbaren*, ed. Evangelos Chrysos and Andreas Schwarcz, VIÖG 29 (Vienna, 1989), 25–56.

23. Menander, frag. 12.6, ed. and trans. Blockley, 140.

24. Menander, frag. 12.7, ed. and trans. Blockley, 142.

25. Menander, frag. 15.1, ed. and trans. Blockley, 148.

26. Menander, frag. 15.1, ed. and trans. Blockley, 148; cf. section 6.6.

27. John of Biclaro, *Chronica* 13, 60. John had spent years in Constantinople; still, his chronology is garbled. For instance, his account of the collapse of the Gepid kingdom is dated two years too late.

28. Stein, *Studien zur Geschichte*, 13; Arnulf Kollautz, "Völkerbewegungen an der unteren und mittleren Donau im Zeitraum von 558/62 bis 582," in Mildenberger, *Studien zur Völkerwanderungszeit im östlichen Mitteleuropa*, 475.

29. Menander, frag. 15.2, ed. and trans. Blockley, 148.

30. Theophanes, *Chronographia* 6066, 365–66; Evagrius 5.11, trans. Whitby, 270.

31. Menander, frag. 15.3, ed. and trans. Blockley, 148–51.

32. "Some thought his infirmity to be a movement of the brain, others, a vexation by demons": John of Biclaro, *Chronica* 25 (573), 63.

33. The title Caesar meant coregency and entitlement to the throne but not sovereign rule, for which the sources employ the terms *basileus* and *autokrator*, which Tiberius did not achieve until after the death of Justin in October 578. Dates reckoned by the years after Tiberius became Caesar refer to 574. Cf. Ljubomir Maksimović, "Chronological Notes about Slavonic Raids into Byzantine Territory at the End of the Seventies and at the Beginning of the Eighties of the 6th Century," *Zbornik Radova* 8 (1964): 263–65.

34. The exact dating of the war and of the following peace treaty has been discussed; some scholars believed that there had been more wars between 568 and 574 (see Pohl, *Die Awaren*, 356 n. 24). According to Menander, frag. 25.1, ed. and trans. Blockley, 218, peace was concluded immediately after Tiberius became Caesar in early December 574. When the ambassador Valentinus informed the Turkish khagan in 576 of the accession of Tiberius, the latter already knew where the Avars had penetrated East Roman territory and, above all, of the recently concluded treaty (Menander, frag. 19.1, ed. and trans. Blockley, 174).

35. Menander, frag. 15.5, ed. and trans. Blockley, 150.

36. Menander, frag. 25.1, ed. and trans. Blockley, 216. On the annual tribute payments, see section 6.4.

37. Menander, frag. 15.6, ed. and trans. Blockley, 50.

38. Menander, frag. 27, ed. and trans. Blockley, 192.

39. Menander, frag. 19.1, ed. and trans. Blockley, 174–79.

40. See section 3.5.

41. On the following, see Menander, frag. 19.1, ed. and trans. Blockley, 170–79. Stein, *Studien zur Geschichte*, 59.

42. Menander, frag. 19.1, ed. and trans. Blockley, 172 and 178. Haussig, *Die Geschichte Zentralasiens*, dates Valentinus's embassy to 579, after Tiberius had become emperor. However, as Menander, frag. 19.1.37, ed. and trans. Blockley, 172, writes, Valentinus's mission was to communicate his accession to the title of Caesar. Sizabulos/Istemi died in 575 (see section 2.6). Vásáry, *Geschichte des frühen Innerasiens*, 73–74. On Turxanthus/Türk Shad, see Moravcsik, *Byzantinoturcica*, 2:276; Golden, *Khazar Studies*, 1:97–100.

43. Menander, frag. 19.1, ed. and trans. Blockley, 174.

44. Menander, frag. 19.1, ed. and trans. Blockley, 178. Menander uses *hómaimos*, brother (or "close relative"?), for the relationship between Turxanthos and Tardu. Sinor, "The Establishment and Dissolution of the Türk Empire," 304–5. For the "Golden Mountain," more appropriately called Ektag in Menander, frag. 10.3, ed. and trans. Blockley, 118, see Pierre Chuvin, "Les ambassades byzantines auprès des premièrs souverains turcs de Sogdiane: Problèmes d'onomastique et de toponymie," *Cahiers d'Asie Centrale* 1, no. 2 (1996): 345–55.

45. The Bilge Khagan inscription, front side, 5, http://bitig.org/?lang=e&mod=1&tid=1&oid=16&m=1.

46. Menander, frag. 19.1–2, ed. and trans. Blockley, 178; frag. 25.2, 224.

47. Menander, frag. 20.2, ed. and trans. Blockley, 190; John of Biclaro, *Chronica* 41 (576 by the Spanish royal dating), 66. A number of scholars have sought to harmonize the information in Menander either with a Slav incursion of John of Ephesus (6.25, 248–49) in the third year of the imperial rule of Tiberius, which leads to a later date (Paul Lemerle, "Invasions et migrations dans les Balkans depuis la fin de l'époque romaine jusqu'au VIIIe siècle," *Revue Historique* 211 [1954]: 289; Beševliev, *Die protobulgarische Periode*, 103) or with John of Biclaro, which implies an earlier date: Bury, *History of the Later Roman Empire*, 2:216; Paul Goubert, "Les guerres sur le Danube à la fin du VIe siècle d'après Ménandre le Protecteur et Théophylacte Simocatta," in *Actes du XIIe Congrès des Études Byzantines* (Belgrade, 1964), 2:216; Kollautz and Miyakawa, 1:240; Avenarius, *Die Awaren in Europa*, 88. In fact, Menander offers the most reliable date, from which we should not deviate because of either the Hispanic or Syrian John.

48. John of Biclaro, *Chronica* 42 and 46, 66.

49. Menander, frag. 21, ed. and trans. Blockley, 192.

50. Summarized in Wilhelm Ensslin, "Slaveneinfälle," in *RE* 3.1 (1927), 697–706; Lemerle, "Invasions et migrations"; Curta, *Making of the Slavs*, 90–107; see section 4.6.

51. Menander, frag. 21, ed. and trans. Blockley, 192. On this and the following, see Stein, *Studien zur Geschichte*, 103 (578); Bury, *History of the Later Roman Empire*, 2:217–18 (577); Goubert, "Les Avares d'après les sources grecques," 216 (577); Avenarius, *Die Awaren in Europa*, 88–89 (578).

52. Menander, frag. 21, ed. and trans. Blockley, 195. The text gives the name as *Daurentios* and then *Dauritas*.

53. Theophylact Simocatta, 6.2.10–16, 160–61.

54. Menander, frag. 21, ed. and trans. Blockley, 194.

55. Menander, frag. 25.1, ed. and trans. Blockley, 219.

56. Cf. Jones, *The Later Roman Empire*, 1:307.

57. Theophylact Simocatta 6.6–9, 167–73.

58. On this and the following, see Menander, frag. 25.1, ed. and trans. Blockley, 216–23; Lemerle, "Invasions et migrations," 279–80; Bury, *History of the Later Roman Empire*, 2:118; Stein, *Studien zur Geschichte*, 109–11; Avenarius, *Die Awaren in Europa*, 90–91. The dating of these embassies to 579 is based on Menander's information (frag. 27.3, ed. and trans. Blockley, 240) that in the negotiations about the surrender of the city the Avars demanded the tribute payments for three years, which can only be 580–82.

59. John of Ephesus 5.24, 247–48.

60. Theophylact Simocatta 6.4.4–6, 163; cf. section 5.2.

61. *Suidae Lexicon*, ed. Adler, 3:212, *s.v. kymotomos*.

62. See section 7.5–7.

63. John of Ephesus 5.24, 247–48.

64. Priscus, frag. 11.2, ed. and trans. Blockley, 264.

65. See section 3.7.

66. Menander, frag. 25.1, ed. and trans. Blockley, 218. By Upper Pannonia we should probably understand not only the former province of *Pannonia superior* but all of Avar Pannonia. The "island of Sirmium," as it is actually called in the Greek text, was likely the whole Sirmian region between the Danube and the Sava, as Blockley, in Menander, ed. and trans. Blockley, 284, suggests.

67. Menander, frag. 25.1, ed. and trans. Blockley, 220–22; cf. section 6.9.

68. Menander, frag. 25.2, ed. and trans. Blockley, 224.

69. Menander, frag. 25.2, ed. and trans. Blockley, 222–24.

70. On the name, see Moravcsik, *Byzantinoturcica*, 2:240.

71. Menander, frag. 25.2, ed. and trans. Blockley, 224.

72. Menander, frag. 25.2, ed. and trans. Blockley, 224–26.

73. Menander, frag. 27.2, ed. and trans. Blockley, 238.

74. Menander, frag. 25.2, ed. and trans. Blockley, 224–26.

75. Bury, *History of the Later Roman Empire*, 2:118; similar view in Lemerle, "Invasions et migrations," 290; Fritze, "Zur Bedeutung der Awaren," 512.

76. Theophylact Simocatta 6.4.4–6, 173.

77. Menander, frag. 25.2, ed. and trans. Blockley, 226.

78. Stein, *Studien zur Geschichte*, 113.

79. Menander, frag. 25.2, ed. and trans. Blockley, 227.

80. John of Ephesus 5.30–31, 255–56.

81. John of Ephesus 5.32, 256, writes of two years; according to Menander, however, the war lasted from mid-579 until 582.

82. Menander, frag. 27.3, ed. and trans. Blockley, 240.

83. Menander, frag. 27.2, ed. and trans. Blockley, 238.

84. Rudolf Noll, "Ein Ziegel als sprechendes Zeugnis einer historischen Katastrophe (zum Untergang Sirmiums 582 n. Chr.)," *Anzeiger der Phil.-Hist. Klasse der Österreichischen Akademie der Wissenschaften* 126 (1990): 139–54; Johannes Koder, "Remarks on Linguistic Romanness in Byzantium," in Gantner et al., *Transformations of Romanness in the Early Middle Ages*, 111–22.

85. Popović, "Les témoins archéologiques," 464.

86. John of Ephesus, 5.25, 248–49. Lemerle, "Invasions et migrations," 290; Curta, *Making of the Slavs*, 92.

87. Menander, frag. 27.3, ed. and trans. Blockley, 240; John of Ephesus, 5.32, 256. If Menander's information (frag. 27.3, ed. and trans. Blockley, 240) that the Avars demanded the subsidies for three years is correct, the date of the negotiations for surrender can only be in 582. See Menander, ed. and trans. Blockley, 386 n. 18. Whitby, *The Emperor Maurice and His Historian*, 88, prefers a slightly earlier date (581/82). This seems irrelevant but has consequences for his dating of all the following events (ibid., 90), which he consistently places one year earlier than I would.

88. Cf. section 3.6.

89. John of Ephesus 5.32, 256.

90. Mirković, "Sirmium," 57.

91. John of Ephesus 5.23, 256.

92. Vladislav Popović, "A Survey of the Topography and Urban Organization of Sirmium in the Late Empire," in *Sirmium*, 1:131.

93. "The Avars were expelled from Thrace but they seized parts of Greece and Pannonia": John of Biclaro, *Chronica* 53, 67, dated to the third year of Tiberius.

94. Theophylact Simocatta 1.3, 24; Theophanes, *Chronographia* 6075, 375–76; Evagrius 5.12, trans. Whitby, 271–72.

95. Sinor, "The Establishment and Dissolution of the Türk Empire," 305.

96. Theophylact Simocatta 1.3.13, 24; Stein, *Studien zur Geschichte*, 113.

97. Theophylact Simocatta 1.3.7, 24; cf. section 6.10.

98. Theophylact Simocatta 1.5, 27; Thérèse Olajos, "La chronologie de la dynastie avare de Baian," *Revue des Études Byzantines* 34 (1976): 155–56.

99. Theophanes, *Chronographia* 6075, 374; see below.

100. Theophylact Simocatta 1.3, 24.

101. John of Biclaro, *Chronica* 28, 63; 35, 64–65.

102. Theophylact Simocatta 1.3, 24.

103. Cf. section 6.5.

104. John Zonaras, *Epitoma Historiarum* 13–18, ed. Theodor Büttner-Wobst, vol. 3, Corpus scriptorum historiae Byzantinae 50 (Bonn, 1897), 14.12, 291.

105. Theophylact Simocatta 1.4, 24; Theophanes, *Chronographia* 6075, 375. Theophanes's dating of these events to the year 6075, i.e., 582–83, has prompted many historians to disregard the two years' peace mentioned by Theophylact and place the Avar invasion in 583; among them, Bury, *History of the Later Roman Empire*, 1:119; Moravcsik, *Byzantinoturcica*, 1:546; Whitby, *The Emperor Maurice and His Historian*, 141–42. For 584: Howorth, "The Avars," 750; Avenarius, *Die Awaren in Europa*, 94; Olajos, "La chronologie," 155. Theophanes has taken this date from another source than the material from Theophylact that follows. The fact that he also has the beginning of the war entered under AM 6075 is no primary information. As is later often the case, he distributes information taken from Theophylact quite arbitrarily among the years 583, 584, and 587.

106. Procopius, *De aedificiis* 4.5, ed. and trans. Dewing, 269. See Wolfgang Pülhorn, "Archäologischer Kommentar zu den 'Bauten' des Prokop," in Prokop, *Bauten*, vol. 5 of *Prokop Werke*, ed. and trans. Otto Veh (Munich, 1977), 447; Andreas Mócsy, *Pannonia and Upper Moesia: A History of the Middle Danube Provinces of the Roman Empire*, The Provinces of the Roman Empire 4 (London, 1974), 126–28; Peter Schreiner, "Städte und Wegenetz in Moesien, Dakien und Thrakien nach dem Zeugnis des Theophylaktos Simokates," in his *Studia Byzantino-Bulgarica*, Miscellanea Bulgarica 2 (Vienna, 1986), 60. For the events, see Theophylact Simocatta 4.1–5, 24–25.

107. Procopius, *De aedificiis* 4.6, ed. and trans. Dewing, 269.

108. Procopius, *De aedificiis* 4.6, ed. and trans. Dewing, 277; Beševliev, *Die protobulgarische Periode*, 105.

109. Procopius, *De aedificiis* 3.7, ed. and trans. Dewing, 219.

110. John of Ephesus 6.45–49, 260 (with a Latin translation of the Syrian text). Preserved in Michael the Syrian, 10.21, 362–63. Comments in Hauptmann, "Les rapports," 157.

111. Michael McCormick has investigated a similar procedure in Clovis's *imitatio imperii*; "Clovis at Tours, Byzantine Public Ritual and the Origins of Medieval Ruler Symbolism," in Chrysos and Schwarcz, *Das Reich und die Barbaren*, 155–80. In distinction to Clovis or Mavros, an example adduced by McCormick as *comparandum*, the khagan's gesture was clearly not legitimized by the emperor but was an arrogation.

112. John of Ephesus 6.45, 259; Michael the Syrian 10.21, 361.

113. The major part of the *Ecclesiastical History* had already been composed by 581; Hunger, *Die hochsprachliche profane Literatur der Byzantiner*, 1:324. The additions were clearly composed at various different times; the conclusion, however, references events of the winter of 584–85. Also mentioned is the acquittal of Gregory of Antioch in 588. Brooks, "Praefatio," in John of Ephesus, ed. Brooks, ii, and Honigmann, "L'histoire ecclésiastique de Jean d'Éphèse," 623, put John's death in 585; Curta, *Making of the Slavs*, in 588.

114. Cf. section 5.9.

115. John of Ephesus 6.49, 260; Michael the Syrian 10.21, 363; Hauptmann, "Les rapports," 157; Altheim, *Geschichte der Hunnen*, 1:90–91, whose interpretation of this obscure passage is reproduced here.

116. Theophylact Simocatta 1.5, 27.

117. Theophylact Simocatta 1.5, 27.

118. Theophylact Simocatta 7.8.16, 191.

119. *Sui shu* 51, 54, and 84, in Liu Mau-Tsai, *Die chinesischen Nachrichten*, 1:49–51; Chavannes, *Documents sur les Tou-kiue*, 49; Yu, "Doubts," 310–11; de la Vaissière, "Oncles et frères."

120. Haussig, "Theophylakts Exkurs," 379; Sinor, "The Establishment and Dissolution of the Türk Empire," 305; de la Vaissière, "Theophylact's Turkish Exkurs Revisited,"

99–100; de la Vaissière, "Maurice et le qaghan"; Étienne de la Vaissière, "Ziebel Qaghan Identified," in *Constructing the Seventh Century*, ed. Constantine Zuckerman, Travaux et Mémoires 17 (Paris, 2013), 741.

121. Theophylact Simocatta 1.5, 26–27; Whitby, *The Emperor Maurice and His Historian*, 142; on the dating to the winter of 584–85, see Olajos, "La chronologie," 154.

122. Theophylact Simocatta 1.6, 28.

123. Theophylact Simocatta 1.6.4–6, 28. By the years given Theophylact does not mean the calendar years beginning September 1 but campaign years from winter to winter, as Martin J. Higgins, *The Persian War of the Emperor Maurice* (Washington, DC, 1939), 56, noted; cf. Whitby, *The Emperor Maurice and His Historian*, 313.

124. John of Ephesus 6.25, 248–49. The Syrian year 895 corresponds to 583–84, and the chronicler remarks that the Slav incursion began in the third year of the reign of Tiberius, 581, and that it lasted four years until the present. See Jon Nestor, "La pénétration des Slaves dans la péninsule balkanique et la Grèce continentale," *Revue des Études Sud-Est Européennes* 1 (1963): 52; Maksimović, "Chronological Notes about Slavonic Raids," 271; Curta, *Making of the Slavs*, 95; Whitby, *The Emperor Maurice and His Historian*, 111.

125. Cf. section 5.3.

126. Theophylact Simocatta 1.7, 29; Theophanes, *Chronographia* 6076, 376. There is some leeway in the dating of the attack on the Long Wall: Howorth, "The Avars," 752 (585); Bury, *History of the Later Roman Empire*, 2:119 (585); Ensslin, "Slaveneinfälle," 701 (585); Avenarius, *Die Awaren in Europa*, 95 (584); Velkov, *Cities in Thrace and Dacia*, 54 (summer 586); Whitby, *The Emperor Maurice and His Historian*, 90 and 143 (584).

127. Theophylact Simocatta 1.8, 30. On the role of the *magos* and *hiereus* Bookolabras, cf. section 6.9.

128. Menander, frag. 27.3, ed. and trans. Blockley, 240.

129. Theophylact Simocatta 1.8, 31; Theophanes, *Chronographia* 6079, 380. On the cities, see Procopius, *De aedificiis* 4.6, ed. and trans. Dewing, 273–77; 4.11, 309–15; Velkov, *Cities in Thrace and Dacia*, 87. On the events, see Howorth, "The Avars," 753; Bury, *History of the Later Roman Empire*, 2:120; Whitby, *The Emperor Maurice and His Historian*, 145–47 (dated to fall 586). In contrast to Pohl, *Die Awaren*, 85, I have accepted Whitby's dating here and in the following chapter.

130. For the events of this year: Theophylact Simocatta 2.10–17, 57–68; Theophanes, *Chronographia* 6079, 380–81 (who combines it with the autumn of the preceding year and whose account goes only up to the siege of Beroe). Howorth, "The Avars," 753–57 (586); Bury, *History of the Later Roman Empire*, 2:120–23 (587); Lemerle, "Invasions et migrations," 290 (585); Vladislav Popović, "Aux origines de la slavisation des Balkans: La constitution des premières sklavinies macédoniennes vers la fin du VIe siècle," *Comptes rendus: Académie des Inscriptions et Belles-Lettres* 1 (1980): 239 (586–87); Velkov, *Cities in Thrace and Dacia*, 54 (587); Jones, *The Later Roman Empire*, 1:310 (586); Whitby, *The Emperor Maurice and His Historian*, 148–51; ibid., 285–86, on the dating of the events of the Persian campaign that Theophylact (1.9–2.10, 31–57) inserts at great length between the accounts of the two successive years of Avar raids and that suggest dating these to fall 586 and to 587.

131. Theophylact Simocatta 2.12.4, 60.

132. Theophylact Simocatta 2.2.13–15, 61–65; *Strategicon* 10.2, 341.

133. Haralambie Mihăescu, "Torna, torna, fratre," *Byzantina* 8 (1976): 21–35.

134. Theophylact Simocatta 2.16, 65–67.

135. Howorth, "The Avars," 756; Velkov, *Cities in Thrace and Dacia*, 55; Schreiner, "Städte und Wegenetz," 68; Whitby, *The Emperor Maurice and His Historian*, 150.

136. Theophylact Simocatta 2.16, 65–66; Georgios Kardaras, "The Episode of Bousas (586/7) and the Use of Siege Engines by the Avars," *Byzantinoslavica* 63 (2005): 53–66.

137. Theophylact Simocatta 2.16.10, 66.

138. Deleuze and Guattari, *A Thousand Plateaus*, 394.

139. Velkov, *Cities in Thrace and Dacia*, 111.

140. Theophylact Simocatta 2.17.1, 67.

141. Theophylact Simocatta 2.17.5–7, 67.

142. Theophylact Simocatta 1.13.1, 38, and 2.17.8, 67; Jones, *The Later Roman Empire*, 1:310; *PLRE*, 3A:679–81 (Ioannes 101).

143. Theophylact Simocatta 2.17.10–13, 68. On Drocto or (the full name) Droctulf, see Paul the Deacon, *Historia Langobardorum* 3.18–19, ed. Waitz, 124–26; *PLRE*, 3A:425–27.

144. *Strategicon* 4.2, 195.

145. Theophylact Simocatta 3.4.7, 77. For the end of Theophylact's narrative, see Whitby, *The Emperor Maurice and His Historian*, 150–51.

146. Procopius, *De aedificiis* 4.5, ed. and trans. Dewing, 267.

147. Paul the Deacon, *Historia Langobardorum* 2.26, ed. Waitz, 103: he mentions *Pannonii* and *Norici* among the *gentes* led to Italy by Alboin. Among the Pannonian exiles in late sixth-century Italy was also a bishop of Scarabantia/Sopron, see section 6.9. Rajko Bratož, "Die Auswanderung der Bevölkerung aus den pannonischen Provinzen während des 5. und 6. Jahrhunderts," in *Römische Legionslager in den Rhein- und Donauprovinzen: Nuclei spätantik-frühmittelalterlichen Lebens?*, ed. Michaela Konrad and Christian Witschel, Abhandlungen der Bayerischen Akademie der Wissenschaften, n.s., 138 (Munich, 2011), 589–614.

148. Tivadar Vida, "'They Asked to Be Settled in Pannonia . . .': A Study on Integration and Acculturation—the Case of the Avars," in *Zwischen Byzanz und der Steppe: archäologische und historische Studien. Festschrift für Csanád Bálint zum 70. Geburtstag / Between Byzantium and the Steppe: Archaeological and Historical Studies in Honour of Csanád Bálint on the Occasion of His 70th Birthday*, ed. Ádám Bollók, Gergely Csiky, and Tivadar Vida (Budapest, 2016), 253.

149. For recent archaeological research on the Avar lands in the late sixth century, see Daim, "Avars and Avar Archaeology"; Falko Daim, ed., *Awarenforschungen*, 2 vols. (Vienna, 1992); Daim, ed., *Die Awaren am Rand der byzantinischen Welt: Studien zu Diplomatie, Handel und Technologietransfer im Frühmittelalter* (Innsbruck, 2000); Bálint, *Die Archäologie der Steppe*; Csanád Bálint, "Probleme der archäologischen Forschung zur awarischen Landnahme," in *Ausgewählte Probleme europäischer Landnahmen des Früh- und Hochmittelalter: methodische Grundlagendiskussion im Grenzbereich zwischen Archäologie und Geschichte*, ed. Michael Müller and Reinhard Schneider (Sigmaringen, 1993), 195–274; Bálint, "Byzantinisches zur Herkunftsfrage des vielteiligen Gürtels," in *Kontakte zwischen Iran, Byzanz und der Steppe im 6.–7. Jahrhundert*, ed. Csanád Bálint (Naples, 2000), 99–162; Éva Garam, *Funde byzantinischer Herkunft in der Awarenzeit vom Ende des 6. bis zum Ende des 7. Jahrhunderts* (Budapest, 2001); Attila Kiss, "Germanen im awarenzeitlichen Karpatenbecken," in Daim, *Awarenforschungen*, 1:35–134; Falko Daim et al., eds., *Hunnen + Awaren: Reitervölker aus dem Osten. Burgenländische Landesausstellung 1996, Schloss Halbturn, 26. April–31. Oktober 1996*, exhibition catalog (Eisenstadt, 1996); Péter Somogyi, *Byzantinische Fundmünzen der Awarenzeit* (Innsbruck, 1997); Somogyi, *Byzantinische Fundmünzen der Awarenzeit in ihrem europäischen Umfeld*, Dissertationes Pannonicae Ser. IV vol. 2 (Budapest, 2014); Peter Stadler, *Quantitative Studien zur Archäologie der Awaren I*, Österreichische Akademie der Wissenschaften, Philosophisch-historische Klasse, Mitteilungen der Prähistorischen Kommission 60 (Vienna, 2005); Tivadar Vida, "Conflict and Coexistence: The Local Population of the Carpathian Basin under Avar Rule (Sixth to Seventh Century)," in *The Other Europe in the Middle Ages: Avars, Bulgars, Khazars and Cumans*, ed. Florin Curta with Roman Kovalev, East Central and Eastern Europe in the Middle Ages, 450–1450, 2 (Leiden, 2007), 13–46; Florin Curta, "The Earliest Avar-Age Stirrups, or the 'Stirrup Controversy' Revisited," in Curta, *The Other Europe in the Middle Ages*, 297–326; Vida, "'They Asked to Be Settled in Pannonia.'"

150. Ilona Kovrig, "Contribution au problème de l'occupation de l'Hongrie par les Avares," *Acta Arch. Hung.* 6 (1955): 163–91; Bóna, "Ein Vierteljahrhundert," 290; extension and refinement of the typology in Éva Garam, "Der awarische Fundstoff im Karpatenbecken und seine zeitliche Gliederung," in Hänsel, *Die Völker Südosteuropas vom 6.–8. Jahrhundert*, 191–202; Garam, "Bemerkungen zum ältesten Fundmaterial der Awarenzeit," in *Typen der Ethnogenese unter besonderer Berücksichtigung der Bayern*, vol. 2, ed. Herwig Friesinger and Falko Daim, DsÖAW 204 (Vienna, 1990), 253–72; Bálint, *Die Archäologie der Steppe*, 151–59; István Bóna, "Die Geschichte der Awaren im Lichte der archäologischen Quellen," in *Popoli delle Steppe: Unni, Avari, Ungari*, 2 vols., SSCI 35 (Spoleto, 1988), 2:437–64; Daim, "Avars and Avar Archaeology," 465–87. For the development of the belt, see section 6.5.

151. The beginning of the Avar period was dated by the year 568 known from the written sources.

152. Kovrig, "Contribution au problème," 163–65; Csanád Bálint, "Über einige östliche Beziehungen der Frühawarenzeit (568–ca. 670–680)," *Mitteilungen des Archäologischen Instituts der Ungarischen Akademie der Wissenschaften* 10/11 (1980): 131–34; Bálint, *Die Archäologie der Steppe*; Garam, "Bemerkungen," 255; Péter Tomka, "Die Lehre der Bestattungsbräuche," *Antaeus* 29–30 (2008): 233–63.

153. Vida, "'They Asked to Be Settled in Pannonia,'" 252. See also Bálint, "On 'Orient Preference.'"

154. Csanád Bálint, "Kontakte zwischen Byzanz, Iran und der Steppe: Das Grab von Üč Tepe (Azerbaidžan) und der beschlagverzierte Gürtel im 6. und 7. Jahrhundert," in Daim, *Awarenforschungen*, 1:309–496; Bálint, "Byzantinisches"; Falko Daim, "'Byzantinische' Gürtelgarnituren des 8. Jahrhunderts," in Daim, *Die Awaren am Rand der byzantinischen Welt*, 77–204; Daim, "Byzantine Belts and Avar Birds: Diplomacy, Trade and Cultural Transfer in the Eighth Century," in *The Transformation of Frontiers: From Late Antiquity to the Carolingians*, ed. Walter Pohl, Ian Wood, and Helmut Reimitz, The Transformation of the Roman World 10 (Leiden, 2001), 143–88; see section 6.4.

155. For a critical view, see Brather, *Ethnische Interpretationen in der frühgeschichtlichen Archäologie*; more affirmative, Bierbrauer, *Ethnos und Mobilität im 5. Jahrhundert aus archäologischer Sicht*; Pohl and Mehofer, *Archaeology of Identity/Archäologie der Identität*.

156. Garam, *Funde byzantinischer Herkunft*; Bálint, "Byzantinisches."

157. Csanád Bálint, "Zur Frage der byzantinischen Beziehungen im Fundmaterial Ungarns: Archäologische Forschungen zwischen 1970 und 1984," *Antaeus* 14 (1985): 212–14; Daim, *Die Awaren am Rand der byzantinischen Welt*; Garam, *Funde byzantinischer Herkunft*; Daim, "'Byzantinische' Gürtelgarnituren des 8. Jahrhunderts"; see also Orsolya Heinrich-Tamáska, "Avar-Age Metalworking Technologies in the Carpathian Basin (Sixth to Eighth Century)," in Curta *The Other Europe in the Middle Ages*, 237–61.

158. Colin Renfrew, "Introduction," in *Peer Polity Interaction and Socio-Political Change*, ed. Colin Renfrew and J. F. Cherry (Cambridge, 1986), 1–8; Skaff, *Sui-Tang China and Its Turko-Mongol Neighbors*, 298.

159. István Bóna, "Gepiden in Siebenbürgen—Gepiden an der Theiss," *Acta Arch. Hung.* 31 (1979): 33–35; Elisabeth Bárdos, "La necropoli avara di Zamárdi," in *L'oro degli Avari: Popolo delle steppe in Europa*, Catalogo della mostra (Milan, 2000), 76–143; Bárdos and Garam, *Das awarenzeitliche Gräberfeld*.

160. Gyula László, *Das awarenzeitliche Gräberfeld in Csákberény-Orondpuszta*, Monumenta Avarorum Archaeologica 11 (Budapest, 2015); see in particular Tivadar Vida, "Das kulturelle Bild der Gemeinschaft von Csákberény-Ormondpuszta," ibid., 236–41.

161. Vida, "Conflict and Coexistence"; Curta, "The Earliest Avar-Age Stirrups."

162. Michel Kazanski, "Les Goths et les Huns: À propos des relations entre barbares sedentaires et nomades," *Archéologie Médiévale* 22 (1992): 191–221; Bierbrauer, *Ethnos*

und Mobilität im 5. Jahrhundert aus archäologischer Sicht; Michael Schmauder, *Die Hunnen: ein Reitervolk in Europa* (Darmstadt, 2009).

163. Vida, "Conflict and Coexistence"; Vida, "'They Asked to Be Settled in Pannonia.'"

164. Vida, "'They Asked to Be Settled in Pannonia,'" 259. See also section 7.8.

165. Curta, "The Earliest Avar-Age Stirrups"; on the early central Asian distribution, see Stark, *Die Alttürkenzeit in Mittel- und Zentralasien*, 147–49. See section 6.2.

166. Ute von Freeden, "Awarische Funde in Süddeutschland?," *Jahrbuch des Römisch-Germanischen Zentralmuseums* 38 (1991): 593–601; Mechthild Schulze-Dörrlamm, "Awarische Einflüsse auf die Bewaffnung und Kampftechnik des ostfränkischen Heeres in der Zeit um 600?," in *Arms and Armour as Indicators of Cultural Transfer: The Steppes and the Ancient World from Hellenistic Times to the Early Middle Ages*, ed. Markus Mode and Jürgen Tubach (Wiesbaden, 2006), 485–507; Vida, "'They Asked to Be Settled in Pannonia,'" 256.

167. Tomka, "Die Lehre der Bestattungsbräuche," 246–49. Both lance heads and horse burial were also diffused among the Turks: Stark, *Die Alttürkenzeit in Mittel- und Zentralasien*, 165 and 103–5. For Tournai, see Dieter Quast, ed., *Das Grab des fränkischen Königs Childerich in Tournai und die Anastasis Childerici von Jean-Jacques Chifflet aus dem Jahre 1655* (Mainz, 2015).

168. Bálint, *Die Archäologie der Steppe*, 88–92 and 182; Daim, "Avars and Avar Archaeology," 470. For the Keszthely culture, see below.

169. Tomka, "Die Lehre der Bestattungsbräuche," 236–41.

170. Daim, "Avars and Avar Archaeology," 468; Tomka, "Die Lehre der Bestattungsbräuche," 249–55.

171. See the map in Vida, "'They Asked to Be Settled in Pannonia,'" 257. See also Gábor Lőrinczy, "Frühawarenzeitliche Bestattungssitten im Gebiet der Grossen Ungarischen Tiefebene östlich der Theiss: Archäologische Angaben und Bemerkungen zur Geschichte der Region im 6. und 7. Jahrhundert," *Acta Arch. Hung.* 68 (2017): 137–70.

172. Cf. the description in *Strategicon* 11.2, 363, and section 6.2 and 6.10.

173. For a comparison, see Michael Schmauder, "Huns, Avars, Hungarians: Reflections on the Interactions between Steppe Empires in Southeast Europe and the Late Roman to Early Byzantine Empires," in Bemmann and Schmauder, *Complexity of Interaction*, 671–92.

174. Jordanes, *Getica* 49.258, ed. Mommsen, 125.

175. Cf. Adrienn Blay and Levente Samu, "Über die mediterranen Kontakte des frühawarenzeitlichen Karpatenbeckens am Beispiel ausgewählter Fundgruppen," in Bugarski et al., *GrenzÜbergänge*, 291–310.

176. Günther Haseloff, "Germanischer und östlicher Tierstil," in *Popoli delle steppe*, 2:681–707; Daim, "Avars and Avar Archaeology," 471–80; Vida, "Conflict and Coexistence," 23 (gold objects from the Jankovich collection); Orsolya Heinrich-Tamáska, "Tier- und Zahnschnittornamentik im awarenzeitlichen Karpatenbecken," *Berichte der Römisch-Germanischen Kommission* 87 (2006): 507–628; Heinrich-Tamáska, "Avar-Age Metalworking Technologies." Frankish parallels for *Zahnschnitt*: Falko Daim, "Des Kaisers ungeliebte Söhne: Die Awaren und das Byzantinische Reich," *Eurasia Antiqua* 17, 2011 (2012): 8.

177. See the distribution map in Vida, "'They Asked to Be Settled in Pannonia,'" 259.

178. Daim, "Avars and Avar Archaeology," 476–77; Vida, "Conflict and Coexistence," 18–23.

179. Vida, "Conflict and Coexistence," 25–26; see also Éva Garam, "Kugeln—Kapseln—Taschen—Scheiben in awarenzeitlichen Gräbern," in *Festschrift für Hermann Dannheimer zum 80. Geburtstag*, ed. Rupert Gebhard, Hans-Jörg Kellner, Alois Schmid, and Ludwig Wamser, special issue, *Bayerische Vorgeschichtsblätter* 75 (2010): 147–68.

180. István Bóna, "Beiträge zu den ethnischen Verhältnissen des 6.–7. Jahrhunderts in Westungarn," *Alba Regia* 2–3 (1963): 61–63; Attila Kiss, *Das awarenzeitlich-gepidische Gräberfeld von Kölked-Feketekapu A* (Innsbruck, 1996); Kiss, *Das awarenzeitliche Gräberfeld in Kölked-Feketekapu B*, 2 vols. (Budapest, 2001).

181. Gyula Rosner, *Das awarenzeitliche Gräberfeld von Szekszárd—Bogyiszlói Straße* (Budapest, 1999); Vida, "Conflict and Coexistence," 17 and 39.

182. Kiss, "Germanen im awarenzeitlichen Karpatenbecken"; Attila Kiss, "Das Weiterleben der Gepiden in der Awarenzeit," in Hänsel, *Die Völker Südosteuropas vom 6.–8. Jahrhundert*, 203–5; Kiss, *Das awarenzeitlich-gepidische Gräberfeld*.

183. "No burial assemblage produced so far artifacts, which could be treated as continuing the tradition of the early sixth-century assemblages in the Carpathian Basin attributed to either Lombards or Gepids." Vida, "Conflict and Coexistence," 16–17.

184. Theophylact 8.3, 213. See section 6.10.

185. Vida, "'They Asked to Be Settled in Pannonia,'" 253. On Gepid archaeology, see István Bóna and Margit Nagy, *Gepidische Gräberfelder am Theissgebiet*, vol. 1 (Budapest, 2002).

186. Two thousand five hundred Lombards reinforcing Narses in 552: Procopius, *Bella* 8.26.11, ed. and trans. Dewing, 5:331; unruly conduct: Procopius, *Bella* 8.33.2, ed. and trans. Dewing, 5:389.

187. Pohl, "The Empire and the Lombards."

188. "Paupertina Pannoniae rura": Paul the Deacon, *Historia Langobardorum* 2.5, ed. Waitz, 88.

189. The habit of putting precious and everyday objects into graves was at a high point in fifth-and sixth-century Europe, but with great regional differences. On the gradual impact of Christianity on funerary habits, see Frederick S. Paxton, *Christianizing Death: The Creation of a Ritual Process in Early Medieval Europe* (Ithaca, NY, 1990); Bonnie Effros, *Caring for Body and Soul: Burial and the Afterlife in the Merovingian World* (University Park, PA, 2002).

190. Paul the Deacon, *Historia Langobardorum* 2.6, ed. Waitz, 89.

191. See, for instance, Thomas Faist, *The Volume and Dynamics of International Migration and Transnational Social Spaces* (Oxford, 2000).

192. Walter Pohl, "I longobardi e la terra," in *Expropriations et confiscations dans les royaumes barbares: Une approche régionale*, ed. Pierfrancesco Porena and Yann Rivière (Rome, 2012), 279–94.

193. For this and the following, see the syntheses by Falko Daim, "Keszthely," in *RGA*, 16:468–74; Gábor Kiss, "Der Wandel im archäologischen Nachlass der Keszthely-Kultur im Laufe des 7. und 8. Jahrhunderts—Versuche zur Periodisierung," *Antaeus* 29–30 (2008): 265–77; Róbert Müller, "Spätantike Elemente in den Gräberfeldern der frühen Keszthely-Kultur," in Bollók, Csiky, and Vida, *Zwischen Byzanz und der Steppe/Between Byzantium and the Steppe*, 271–90; Orsolya Heinrich-Tamáska, ed., *Keszthely-Fenékpuszta im Kontext spätantiker Kontinuitätsforschung zwischen Noricum and Moesia* (Budapest, 2011); Daim, "Avars and Avar Archaeology," 473–76; Tivadar Vida, "Local or Foreign Romans? The Problem of the Late Antique Population of the 6th–7th Centuries in Pannonia," in *Foreigners in Early Medieval Europe: Thirteen International Studies on Early Medieval Mobility*, ed. Dieter Quast (Mainz, 2009), 233–59; see also Róbert Müller, *Die Gräberfelder vor der Südmauer der Befestigung von Keszthely-Fenékpuszta* (Budapest, 2010); Müller, *Die Gräberfelder von Keszthely-Fenékpuszta Ödenkirche-Flur* (Budapest, 2014). For a discussion of the possible name, see Orsolya Heinrich-Tamáska, "Die spätrömische Innenbefestigung von Keszthely-Fenékpuszta: Innere Chronologie und funktioneller Wandel," in Heinrich-Tamáska, *Keszthely-Fenékpuszta*, 658–61.

194. Orsolya Heinrich-Tamáska, "Sakral- oder Profanbauten? Zur Funktion und Datierung der Kirchen von Keszthely-Fenékpuszta (Komitat Zala, Ungarn)," in *Kirchenarchäologie heute: Fragestellungen—Methoden—Ergebnisse,* ed. Niklot Krohn (Darmstadt, 2010), 91–112.

195. Károly Sági, "Die zweite altchristliche Basilika von Fenékpuszta," *Acta Antiqua Academiae Scientiarum Hungaricae* 9 (1961): 397–459; Müller, "Spätantike Elemente," 282. For the supraregional connections of the Keszthely culture, see the classic study by Manfred Menke, "Zu den Fibeln der Awarenzeit aus Keszthely," *A Wosinsky Mór Múzeum Évkönyve* 15 (1990): 187–214.

196. Tivadar Vida, "Das Gräberfeld neben dem Horreum in der Innenbefestingung von Keszthely-Fenékpuszta," in Heinrich-Tamáska, *Keszthely-Fenékpuszta,* 396–455 (Bonosa needle: 404). For the later Keszthely culture, see section 8.1.

197. Against the interpretation as a church: Heinrich-Tamáska, "Sakral- oder Profanbauten?," 100. Differently: Kiss, "Der Wandel," 269.

198. Müller, *Die Gräberfelder vor der Südmauer.*

199. Kiss, "Der Wandel," 265.

200. Daim, "Avars and Avar Archaeology," 474.

201. Keszthely-Fenékpuszta Pusztaszentegyháza-Dűlő, grave A: Müller, "Spätantike Elemente," 272; Kiss, "Der Wandel," 268; Müller, *Die Gräberfelder von Keszthely-Fenékpuszta Ödenkirche-Flur.*

202. Stark, *Die Alttürkenzeit in Mittel- und Zentralasien,* 171 with n. 953.

203. László Barkóczi and Ágnes Salamon, "Remarks on the 6th Century History of Pannonia," *Acta Arch. Hung.* 23 (1971): 139–49; Ágnes Salamon, "Über die ethnischen und historischen Beziehungen des Gräberfeldes von Környe," *Acta Arch. Hung.* 21 (1969): 273–98.

204. Tivadar Vida, "Die Zeit zwischen dem 4. und 6. Jahrhundert im mittleren Donauraum aus archäologischer Sicht," in Konrad and Witschel, *Römische Legionslager in den Rhein- und Donauprovinzen,* 571–88.

205. Volker Bierbrauer, "Die Keszthely-Kultur und die romanische Kontinuität in Westungarn (5.–8. Jh.): Neue Überlegungen zu einem alten Problem," in *Von Sachsen nach Jerusalem: Menschen und Institutionen im Wandel der Zeit; Festschrift f. Wolfgang Giese zum 65. Geburtstag,* ed. Hubertus Seibert and Gertrud Thoma (Munich, 2004), 60–63; Vida, "Das Gräberfeld," 413–14; more cautious, Müller, "Spätantike Elemente," 279–81.

206. Müller, "Spätantike Elemente," 274.

207. Orsolya Heinrich-Tamáska and Mike Schweissing, "Strontiumisotopen- und Radiokarbonuntersuchungen am anthropologischen Fundmaterial von Keszthely-Fenékpuszta: ihr Aussagepotential zu Fragen der Migration und Chronologie," in Heinrich-Tamáska, *Keszthely-Fenékpuszta,* 457–74.

208. Bierbrauer, "Keszthely-Kultur," 58; István Koncz, "568—A Historical Date and Its Archaeological Consequences," *Acta Arch. Hung.* 66 (2015): 315–40.

209. Bierbrauer, "Die Keszthely-Kultur."

210. Bóna, "Gepiden in Siebenbürgen," 33–35; Bóna, "Ein Vierteljahrhundert," 296–97.

211. *Miracula Demetrii,* 2.5.284–85, 222; cf. Procopius, *Bella* 7.14, ed. and trans. Dewing, 4:262–75; see sections 6.10 and 7.7.

212. Florin Curta, "Before Cyril and Methodius: Christianity and Barbarians beyond the Sixth- and Seventh-Century Danube Frontier," in *East Central and Eastern Europe in the Middle Ages,* ed. Florin Curta (Ann Arbor, 2005), 189–91.

213. Attila Kiss, "Die Stellung der Keszthely-Kultur in der Frage der Römischen Kontinuität Pannoniens," *A Janus Pannonius Múzeum Évkönyve,* 1965, 49–59.

214. Klaus Hesse, "Der Austausch als stabilisierender Faktor der politischen Herrschaft in der Geschichte der Mongolei: Das Beispiel der Hsiung-nu," *UAJB*, n.s., 4 (1984): 150–70; Sören Stark, "Nomaden und Sesshafte in Mittel- und Zentralasien: Nomadische Adaptionsstrategien am Fallbeispiel der Alttürken," in *Grenzüberschreitende Formen des Kontakts zwischen Orient und Okzident im Altertum*, ed. Monika Schuol, Udo Hartmann, and Andreas Luther (Stuttgart, 2002), 363–404; Golden, *Central Asia in World History*, 50–55.

215. Róbert Müller, "Die spätrömische Festung Valcum am Plattensee," in *Germanen, Hunnen und Awaren: Schätze der Völkerwanderungszeit*, ed. Gerhard Bott and Walter Meier-Arendt, exhibition catalog (Nuremberg, 1987), 272; Kiss, "Der Wandel," 268. I owe to Csanád Bálint the observation that the destruction may also have happened toward the end of the seventh century.

216. See sections 7.8 and 8.1.

217. Paul the Deacon, *Historia Langobardorum* 2.26, ed. Waitz, 103.

218. See section 6.10. Earlier attempts to identify a Cutrigur group in the early Avar material seem to have failed: Csanád Bálint, "A Contribution to Research on Ethnicity: A View from and on the East," in Pohl and Mehofer, *Archaeology of Identity/Archäologie der Identität*, 160.

219. *Miracula Demetrii* 2.4.284, 222; Paul the Deacon, *Historia Langobardorum* 4.37, ed. Waitz, 162–63.

220. Tivadar Vida, "The Many Identities of the Barbarians in the Middle Danube Region in the Early Middle Ages," in *Entangled Identities and Otherness in Late Antique and Early Medieval Europe: Historical, Archaeological and Bioarchaeological Approaches*, ed. Jorge López Quiroga, Michel Kazanski, and Vujadin Ivanišević (Oxford, 2017), 120–31.

221. Kiss, "Der Wandel," 268–69.

222. Walter Pohl, "Introduction: Early Medieval Romanness—a Multiple Identity," in Gantner et al., *Transformations of Romanness in the Early Middle Ages*, 3–40.

223. Isidore of Seville, *Etymologiae* 14.4.16, ed. Wallace M. Lindsay (Oxford, 1911): "Pannonia ab Alpibus Apenninis est nuncupata, quibus ab Italia scernitur . . . duobus satis acribus fluviis, Dravo Savoque, vallata." Herwig Wolfram, *Salzburg, Bayern, Österreich: Die Conversio Bagoariorum et Carantanorum und die Quellen ihrer Zeit*, MIÖG Erg. Bd. 31 (Vienna, 1995), 68–71.

224. *Miracula Demetrii* 2.5.292, 230.

225. Brather, *Ethnische Interpretationen in der frühgeschichtlichen Archäologie*, 185–206; for a cautious discussion, see Vida, "'They Asked to Be Settled in Pannonia,'" 258; Bálint, "A Contribution to Research on Ethnicity," 160–61; see also Pohl, "Archaeology of Identity: Introduction"; see section 6.10.

226. See, for instance, Peter Stadler, "Ethnische Gruppen im Awarenreich," in Pohl and Mehofer, *Archaeology of Identity/Archäologie der Identität*, 142–43, figures 25–27. A critical overview of the problem of distinguishing between ethnic groups within the Avar realm is already found in Bálint, *Die Archäologie der Steppe*, 176–83.

227. Walter Pohl, "Christian and Barbarian Identities in the Early Medieval West: Introduction," in *Post-Roman Transitions: Christian and Barbarian Identities in the Early Medieval West*, ed. Walter Pohl and Gerda Heydemann (Turnhout, 2013), 1–46.

228. Vida, "'They Asked to Be Settled in Pannonia,'" 258.

229. Pohl, "Introduction. Strategies of Identification."

230. *Strategicon* 11.3, 369. Use of *Germani*: Walter Pohl, "Der Germanenbegriff vom 3. bis 8. Jahrhundert: Identifikationen und Abgrenzungen," in *Zur Geschichte der Gleichung "germanisch-deutsch*," ed. Heinrich Beck et al., RGA Erg. Bd. 34 (Berlin, 2004), 163–83.

231. See Reimitz, *History, Frankish Identity and the Framing of Western Ethnicity*.

232. Gantner et al., *Transformations of Romanness in the Early Middle Ages*.

4. AVARS AND SLAVS

1. This chapter reflects a particularly lively area of research; I have updated and partly rewritten it, without doing full justice to everything that has been published since the German version appeared in 1988. The general interpretation as laid out in section 4.6 follows the lines already proposed in 1988.

2. Lucien Musset, *Les invasions*, vol. 2, *Le second assaut contre l'Europe chrétienne*, Nouvelle Clio 12.1 (Paris, 1971), 83–85.

3. For the history of research, see Alexander Gieysztor, "Les antiquités slaves: Problèmes d'une historiographie bicentenaire," in *Gli slavi occidentali*, 1:15–40; Wolfgang Fritze, "Slawische Altertumswissenschaft," in Wolfgang Fritze, *Frühzeit zwischen Ostsee und Donau: Ausgewählte Beiträge zum geschichtlichen Werden im östlichen Mitteleuropa*, Berliner Historische Studien 6 (Berlin, 1982), 17–30; Curta, "From Kossinna to Bromlej"; Sebastian Brather and Christine Kratzke, eds., *Auf dem Weg zum Germanica Slavica-Konzept: Perspektiven von Geschichtswissenschaft, Archäologie, Onomastik und Kunstgeschichte seit dem 19. Jahrhundert* (Leipzig, 2005); Przemysław Urbańczyk, *Herrschaft und Politik im frühen Mittelalter: Ein historisch-anthropologischer Essay über gesellschaftlichen Wandel und Integration in Mitteleuropa*, Gesellschaften und Staaten im Epochenwandel 14 (Frankfurt am Main, 2007). Recent syntheses of early Slavic history and/or archaeology: Francis Conte, *Les Slaves: Aux origines des civilisations d'Europe* (Paris, 1986); Martin Gojda, *The Ancient Slavs: Settlement and Society* (Edinburgh, 1991); Paul M. Barford, *The Early Slavs: Culture and Society in Early Medieval Eastern Europe* (Ithaca, NY, 2001); Curta, *Making of the Slavs*; Eduard Mühle, *Die Slaven im Mittelalter*, Das mittelalterliche Jahrtausend 4 (Berlin, 2016).

4. For an overview, see Curta, *Making of the Slavs*, 74–107.

5. Procopius, *Bella* 6.15.2, ed. and trans. Dewing, 3:414. The topographic context is vague, and Procopius hardly knew whether these Heruls had crossed Moravia (Jerzy Szydłowski, "Zur Anwesenheit von Westslawen an der mittleren Donau im ausgehenden 5. und 6. Jahrhundert," in Wolfram and Daim, *Die Völker an der mittleren und unteren Donau im fünften und sechsten Jahrhundert*, 234–37), the Dukla and Jablonka passes across the Carpathians (Joachim Herrmann, "Die Slawen der Völkerwanderungszeit," in *Welt der Slawen: Geschichte, Gesellschaft, Kultur*, ed. Joachim Herrmann [Leipzig, 1986], 33), or, very unlikely, went east of the Carpathians (Schmidt, *Die Ostgermanen*, 553) or even up the Dniester (Pritsak, "The Slavs and the Avars," 407–8). In any case, the remark concerns the situation when Procopius wrote, hardly in 508.

6. Procopius, *Bella* 5.27.2, ed. and trans. Dewing, 3:252; 6.26.18, 4:88.

7. Procopius, *Bella* 7.35.19–22, ed. and trans. Dewing, 4:462–65.

8. Procopius, *Bella* 8.25.1–5, ed. and trans. Dewing, 5:31.

9. Procopius, *Bella* 7.38.6–23, ed. and trans. Dewing, 5:22–27.

10. Procopius, *Bella* 7.14.22–30, ed. and trans. Dewing, 4:270–73. The reference to the Massagetae/Huns shows that Procopius could only describe the apparent "primitivity" of the Slavs by recourse to the stereotype of steppe nomads, without considering the difference. See also Curta, *Making of the Slavs*, 75–81.

11. For the *Sporoi*, see also Dvornik, *The Making of Central and Eastern Europe*, 277–79; Barford, *The Early Slavs*, 36. An identification with Serbs, as argued in older research (see Bury, *A History of the Later Roman Empire*, 2:295), is anachronistic. Procopius clearly assumes a steppe background, perhaps the *Sparnoi* repeatedly mentioned in Strabo, 11.8.2 and 11.9.2, close to Hyrcania, south of the Caspian Sea, or the Scythian *Spali* in Jordanes, *Getica* 4.28, ed. Mommsen, 61.

12. For an elegant synthesis of the background of Procopius's and Jordanes's digressions, see Curta, *Making of the Slavs*, 36–43. Jordanes may have directly responded to Procopius with opposite views: Goffart, *Narrators of Barbarian History*, 93–96, which,

however, presumes his late dating of the *Getica*. For Procopius on the Slavs, see also Cameron, *Procopius and the Sixth Century*, 218–19; for Jordanes, Florin Curta, "Hiding Behind a Piece of Tapestry: Jordanes and the Slavic Venethi," *Jahrbücher für Geschichte Osteuropas*, n.s., 47 (1999): 321–40.

13. Jordanes, *Getica* 5.34, ed. Mommsen, 63: "Introrsus illis Dacia est, ad coronae speciem arduis Alpibus emunita, iuxta quorum sinistrum latus, qui in aquilone vergit, ab ortu Vistulae fluminis per inmensa spatia Venetharum natio populosa consedit. Quorum nomina licet nunc per varias familias et loca mutentur, principaliter tamen Sclaveni et Antes nominantur. Sclaveni a civitate Novietunense et laco qui appellatur Mursiano usque ad Danastrum et in boream Viscla tenus commorantur; hi paludes silvasque pro civitatibus habent."

14. Jordanes, *Getica* 23.119, ed. Mommsen, 88–89: "Hermanaricus in Venethos arma commovit, . . . hi, ut in initio expositionis vel catalogo gentium dicere coepimus, ab una stirpe exorti, tria nunc nomina ediderunt, id est Venethi, Antes, Sclaveni; qui quamvis nunc, ita facientibus peccatis nostris, ubique deseviunt, tamen tunc omnes Hermanarici imperiis servierunt."

15. Jutta Reisinger and Günter Sowa, *Das Ethnikon Sclavi in den lateinischen Quellen bis zum Jahr 900*, Glossar zur frühmittelalterlichen Geschichte im östlichen Europa, Beiheft Nr. 6 (Stuttgart, 1990), 35–37.

16. Procopius, *Bella* 1.24.2, ed. and trans. Dewing, 1:218 (in transcription, *Benetoi*); 5.15.25, 3:156 (*Benetioi*).

17. For the etymology of the name of the Slavs, see Max Vasmer, *Russisches etymologisches Wörterbuch*, vol. 2, *L–Ssuda* (Heidelberg, 1955), 656–57; Herrmann, "Die Slawen der Völkerwanderungszeit," 22.

18. For the outside designation of medieval Romans as *Welsch*, see Walter Pohl, Wolfgang Haubrichs, and Ingrid Hartl, eds., *Walchen, Romani und Latini: Variationen einer nachrömischen Gruppenbezeichnung zwischen Britannien und dem Balkan*, Forschungen zu Geschichte des Mittelalters (Vienna, 2017).

19. Procopius, *Bella* 7.14.22, ed. and trans. Dewing, 4:268.

20. Dvornik, *The Making of Central and Eastern Europe*, 279–81; George Vernadsky, "On the Origin of the Antae," *Journal of the American Oriental Society* 59 (1939): 56–66; Bohdan Struminskyj, "Were the Antes Eastern Slavs?," *Harvard Ukrainian Studies* 3/4 (1979–80): 786–96; Pritsak, "The Slavs and the Avars," 398; Adam Ziółkowski, "When Did the Slavs Originate? The Case of the Antes," *Palamedes* 9–10, no. 1 (2014–15): 211–36.

21. Disputed: Mezamiros, Menander, frag. 5.3, ed. and trans. Blockley, 50. Hardly Slavic: the legendary king Boz in Jordanes, *Getica* 48, ed. Mommsen, 121. See Georg Holzer, "Gli Slavi prima del loro arrivo in Occidente," in *Lo Spazio Letterario del Medioevo*, vol. 3, *Le Culture Slave*, ed. Mario Capaldo (Rome, 2006), 44–45.

22. Jordanes, *Getica* 5.35, ed. Mommsen, 63, locates the *Antae* along the middle Dniester and east of that up to the Dnieper. Procopius, *Bella* 8.4, ed. and trans. Dewing, 5:85, places the "numerous tribes of the Antes" north of the Utigurs who lived at the Maiotis. In any case, they must have lived at the margins of the steppe, and their forms of life and organization seem to have been a synthesis between Slavic and steppe culture. Their settlement area hardly touched the Danube (although Justinian offered them the fort Turris on the Danube at one point (Procopius, *Bella* 7.14.32, ed. and trans. Dewing, 4:272). In any case, they played no direct part in the numerous wars in the Balkan provinces and along the Danube in the later sixth century described in Menander and Theophylact. An overview of the problems of archaeological identification: Bálint, "Über einige östliche Beziehungen," 136; Bálint, *Die Archäologie der Steppe*, 84–88; see also Curta, "The North-Western Region of the Black Sea."

23. Procopius, *Bella* 7.14.29, ed. and trans. Dewing, 4:272.

24. Timpe, "Ethnologische Begriffsbildung in der Antike"; Walter Pohl, ed., *Die Suche nach den Ursprüngen: Von der Bedeutung des frühen Mittelalters*, Forschungen zur Geschichte des Mittelalters 8 (Vienna, 2004).

25. Some classics: Pavel Jozef Šafařík, *Slawische Altertümer*, 2 vols. (Prague, 1843–44); Lubomir Niederle, *Manuel d'antiquité slave*, vol. 1, *L'histoire* (Paris, 1923). See also Curta, *Making of the Slavs*, 6–14.

26. Pavel M. Dolukhanov, *The Early Slavs: Eastern Europe from the Initial Settlement to the Kievan Rus* (New York, 1996). For a critique of such positions, see Florin Curta, "Four Questions for Those Who Still Believe in Prehistoric Slavs and Other Fairy Tales," *Starohrvatska prosvjeta* 42 (2015): 286–303.

27. Rajko Bratož, "Il mito dei Veneti presso gil Sloveni," *Quaderni Giuliani di Storia* 26, no. 1 (2005): 17–54.

28. Herwig Wolfram, "Typen der Ethnogenese: Ein Versuch," in *Die Franken und die Alemannen bis zur "Schlacht bei Zülpich" (496/97)*, ed. Dieter Geuenich, RGA Erg. Bd. 19 (Berlin, 1998), 608–27; Walter Pohl, "Conceptions of Ethnicity in Early Medieval Studies," in *Debating the Middle Ages: Issues and Readings*, ed. Lester K. Little and Barbara Rosenwein (Oxford, 1998), 15–24; previously published in *Archaeologia Polona* 29 (1991): 39–49.

29. Michel Kazanski, *Les Slaves: Les origines, Ier–VIIe siècle après J.-C.* (Paris, 1999).

30. Barford, *The Early Slavs*, 38–44.

31. Kazimierz Godłowski, "Die Frage der slawischen Einwanderung in östliche Mitteleuropa," *Zeitschrift für Ostforschung* 28 (1979): 416–47; Barford, *The Early Slavs*, 10–12.

32. The latest authoritative overviews of these problems have appeared in the handbook Karl Gutschmidt et al., eds., *Die slavischen Sprachen: Ein internationales Handbuch zu ihrer Struktur, ihrer Geschichte und ihrer Erforschung / The Slavic Languages: An International Handbook of Their Structure, Their History and Their Investigation*, 2 vols. 1 (Berlin, 2014), in particular, Georg Holzer, "Vorhistorische Periode," 2:1117–31; and Georg Udolph, "Ethnogenese und Urheimat der Slaven," 2:1131–43. See also Radoslav Katičić, *Literatur- und Geistesgeschichte des kroatischen Frühmittelalters* (Vienna, 1999).

33. Horace Lunt, "Slavs, Common Slavic and Old Church Slavonic," in *Litterae Slavicae Medii Aevi: Francisco Venceslao Mares Sexagenario Oblatae*, ed. Johannes Reinhart (Munich, 1985), 185–204; Henrik Birnbaum, "Von ethnolinguistischer Einheit zur Vielfalt: Die Slaven im Zuge der Landnahme auf der Balkanhalbinsel," *Südost-Forschungen* 51 (1992): 1–19; Georg Holzer, "Die Einheitlichkeit des Slavischen um 600 n. Chr. und ihr Zerfall," *Wiener Slavistisches Jahrbuch* 41 (1995): 55–90; Florin Curta, "The Slavic *Lingua Franca* (Linguistic Notes of an Archaeologist Turned Historian)," *East Central Europe/ L'Europe du Centre-Est* 31, no. 1 (2004): 125–48.

34. Udolph, "Ethnogenese und Urheimat der Slaven," 1133, rejecting, among others, the hypotheses by Zbigniew Gołab, *The Origins of the Slaws: A Linguist's View* (Columbus, 1992); and Heinrich Kunstmann, *Die Slaven: Ihr Name, ihre Wanderung nach Europa und die Anfänge der russischen Geschichte in historisch-onomastischer Sicht* (Stuttgart, 1996).

35. Barford, *The Early Slavs*, 37, with reference to Hanna Popowska-Taborska, "The Slavs in the Early Middle Ages from the Viewpoint of Contemporary Linguistics," in Urbańczyk, *Origins of Central Europe*, 91–96.

36. For an overview of the debate and a different etymology, see Henning Andersen, "On SLOVĔNE and the History of Slavic Patrials," *Scando-Slavica* 63, no. 1 (2017): 3–42.

37. This hypothesis was proposed by Pritsak, "The Slavs and the Avars"; see also Curta, "The Slavic *Lingua Franca*"; Holzer, "Vorhistorische Periode."

38. Wenskus, *Stammesbildung und Verfassung*; for an overview, see Pohl, "Ethnicity, Theory and Tradition," and Walter Pohl, "Von der Ethnogenese zur Identitätsforschung,"

in *Neue Wege der Frühmittelalterforschung*, ed. Max Diesenberger, Walter Pohl, and Bernhard Zeller (Vienna, forthcoming).

39. František Graus, "Deutsche und slawische Verfassungsgeschichte?," *Historische Zeitschrift* 197, no. 1 (1963): 292 and 307; Barford, *The Early Slavs*, 124–38. See also Urbańczyk, *Herrschaft und Politik*, 130–55.

40. Cf. Deleuze and Guattari, *A Thousand Plateaus*, 3–25.

41. Pohl, *Die Awaren*, 95. See also section 4.6.

42. Curta, *Making of the Slavs*.

43. Curta, *Making of the Slavs*, 349.

44. Danijel Dzino, *Becoming Slav, Becoming Croat: Identity Transformations in Post-Roman and Early Medieval Dalmatia*, East Central and Eastern Europe in the Middle Ages, 450–1450, 12 (Leiden, 2010).

45. See, for instance, Florin Curta, "Barbarians in Dark-Age Greece: Slavs or Avars?," in *Civitas Divino-Humana: In honorem annorum LX Georgii Bakalov*, ed. Tsvetelin Stepanov and Veselina Vachkova (Sofia, 2004), 513–50; Curta, "The Early Slavs in Bohemia and Moravia: A Response to My Critics," *Archeologické rozhledy* 61 (2009): 725–54; Curta, "The Early Slavs in the Northern and Eastern Adriatic Region: A Critical Approach," *Archeologia medievale* 37 (2010): 307–29; Curta, "Were There Any Slavs in Seventh-Century Macedonia?," *Istorija* 47, no. 1 (2012): 61–75. For a synthesis of his position and the early debates, see Florin Curta, "The Making of the Slavs between Ethnogenesis, Invention, and Migration," *Studia Slavica et Balcanica Petropolitana* 6, no. 2 (2008): 155–72.

46. Curta, *Making of the Slavs*, 228–75.

47. See section 4.6.

48. For the following, see Walter Pohl, *Die Germanen*, 2nd ed. (Munich, 2004). For a similar comparison, with partly diverging conclusions, see Florin Curta, "Frontier Ethnogenesis in Late Antiquity: The Danube, the Tervingi, and the Slavs," in *Borders, Barriers, and Ethnogenesis: Frontiers in Late Antiquity and the Middle Ages*, ed. Florin Curta (Turnhout, 2005), 173–204.

49. Pohl, "Der Germanenbegriff vom 3. bis 8. Jahrhundert."

50. See, for instance, the handbook edited by Joachim Herrmann, *Die Slawen in Deutschland: Geschichte und Kultur der slawischen Stämme westlich von Oder und Neiße vom 6. bis 12. Jahrhundert. Ein Handbuch*, 2nd ed. (Berlin, 1985), which offers a wide range of regional and chronological differentiations for the western Slavs; it must, however, be used with caution, for its dates tend to be too early.

51. About the *Miracula*: Paul Lemerle, "La composition et la chronologie des deux premiers livres des Miracula S. Demetrii," *Byzantinische Zeitschrift* 46 (1953): 349–60; Koder, "Anmerkungen zu den Miracula Sancti Demetrii," 523–25. Paul Speck, "De miraculis Sancti Demetrii, qui Thessalonicam profugus venit, oder: Ketzerisches zu den Wundergeschichten des Heiligen Demetrios und zu seiner Basilika in Thessalonike," in *Varia IV*, Poikila Byzantina 12 (Bonn, 1993), 275, regarded book 1 as a much later compilation but has not found much consensus; see Florin Curta, *The Edinburgh History of the Greeks, ca. 500 to 1050* (Edinburgh, 2011), 42, n. 14.

52. Cf. Vasilka Tăpkova-Zaimova, "Sur quelques aspects de la colonisation slave en Macédoine et Grèce," in Vasilka Tăpkova-Zaimova, *Byzance et les Balkans à partir du VIe siècle: Les mouvements ethniques et les états* (London, 1979), 114; Curta, *Edinburgh History of the Greeks*, 23.

53. *Miracula Demetrii* 1.13.117, 134.

54. *Miracula Demetrii* 1.13.124–29, 136–37.

55. Lemerle, "Invasions et migrations," 285–86. On Thessalonica in the sixth century, see Jean-Michel Spieser, *Thessalonique et ses monuments du IVe au VIe siècle: Contribution à l'étude d'une ville paléochrétienne* (Athens, 1984); Curta, *Making of the Slavs*, 136–38.

56. Gregory the Great, *Registrum epistolarum* 8.10, ed. Norberg, 2:527 (from the year 597), and several further letters.

57. For this and the following events: *Miracula Demetrii* 1.14.131–60, 146–56.

58. *Miracula Demetrii* 1.14.137, 148.

59. *Miracula Demetrii* 1.14.138–39, 148–49; 151, 154; 154, 155. The description of siege machines occurs in many accounts of barbarian sieges and may be a topos.

60. Theophylact Simocatta 6.5.7, 165.

61. Gregory the Great, *Registrum epistolarum* 8.10, ed. Norberg, 2:527.

62. Lemerle, *Les Plus Anciens Recueils*, 2:49–69, prefers the date 586 after a detailed analysis of the historical context (against his own earlier opinion in Lemerle, "La composition et la chronologie," 352–53). Also for 586: Peter Charanis, "On the Slavic Settlement in the Peloponnesus," *Byzantinische Zeitschrift* 46 (1953): 101; Alexander Avenarius, "Die Awaren und die Slawen in den Miracula Sancti Demetrii," *Byzantina* 5 (1973): 18; Popović, "Aux origines de la slavisation des Balkans," 232; Whitby, *The Emperor Maurice and His Historian*, 117–18; Curta, *Making of the Slavs*, 98; for 597: Velkov, *Cities in Thrace and Dacia*, 56; Maria Nystazopoulou-Pelekidou, "Symbolē eis tēn chronologēsin tōn abarikōn kai slabikōn epidromōn epi Maurikiou (582–602)," *Symmeikta* 2 (1971): 173; Speros Vryonis, "The Evolution of Slavic Society and the Slavic Invasions in Greece: The First Major Slavic Attack on Thessaloniki, A. D. 597," *Hesperia* 50 (1981): 378–80.

63. Cf. section 5.8.

64. *Miracula Demetrii* 1.12 (probably in 604, cf. Lemerle, *Les Plus Anciens Recueils*, 2:72–73, and section 7.1).

65. About the authorship of Arethas: Johannes Koder, "Arethas von Kaisareia und die sogenannte Chronik von Monemvasia," *Jahrbuch der österreichischen Byzantinistik* 25 (1976): 75–80; Ewald Kislinger, *Regionalgeschichte als Quellenproblem: Die Chronik von Monembasia und das sizilianische Demenna* (Vienna, 2001), 13–40; see also Lemerle, *Les Plus Anciens Recueils*, 2:63. The editor Dujčev, "Introduzione," xliv–xlvi, gives a later date.

66. Lemerle, "La chronique improprement dite de Monemvasie," 8–9; Dujčev, "Introduzione," xxviii; Moravcsik, *Byzantinoturcica*, 1:237–38.

67. Lemerle, "La chronique improprement dite de Monemvasie," 10; *Cronaca di Monemvasia*, ed. Dujčev, 16.

68. *Cronaca di Monemvasia*, ed. Dujčev, 12–19; Lemerle, "La chronique improprement dite de Monemvasie," 9–10. The reading "engenē" (native) instead of "eugenē" (noble) follows Koder, "Anmerkungen zu den Miracula Sancti Demetrii," 528–30. The list of Avar–Slav conquests in Greece is most likely derived from *Miracula Demetrii* 2.1, 179, from the late seventh century.

69. On Fallmerayer, see Claudia Märtl and Peter Schreiner, eds., *Jakob Philipp Fallmerayer (1790–1861): Der Gelehrte und seine Aktualität im 21. Jahrhundert*, Abhandlungen der Bayerischen Akademie der Wissenschaften, phil.-hist. Klasse, n.s., 139 (Munich, 2013).

70. Max Vasmer, *Die Slaven in Griechenland*, Abh. Press. AW, Ph.-H. Kl. 12 (Berlin, 1941); Antoine Bon, *Le Péloponnèse byzantin jusqu'en 1204* (Paris, 1951); Lemerle, "La chronique improprement dite de Monemvasie"; Peter Charanis, "The Chronicle of Monemvasia and the Question of the Slavonic Settlements in Greece," *Dumbarton Oaks Papers* 5 (1950): 141–60; Charanis, "The Slavs, Byzantium and the Historical Significance of the First Bulgarian Kingdom," *Balkan Studies* 17 (1976): 5–24; Johannes Karayannopoulos, "Zur Frage der Slawenansiedlungen auf dem Peloponnes," *Revue des Études Sud-Est Européennes* 9 (1971): 443–60; *Cronaca di Monemvasia*, ed. Dujčev; Popović, "Aux origines de la slavisation des Balkans"; Koder, "Arethas von Kaisareia"; Otto Kresten, "Zur Echtheit des Sigillion des Kaisers Nikephoros I. für Patras," *Römische Historische Mitteilungen* 19 (1977): 15–78; Nystazopoulou-Pelekidou, "Symbolē," 146–48; Curta, *Edinburgh History of the Greeks*; Florin Curta, "Still Waiting for the Barbarians? The Making of the Slavs in

'Dark-Age' Greece," in *Neglected Barbarians*, ed. Florin Curta, Studies in the Early Middle Ages 32 (Turnhout, 2011), 403–78.

71. *Miracula Demetrii* 1.13.128, 137.

72. Peter Schreiner, "Note sur la fondation de Monemvasie en 582/583," *Travaux et Mémoires* 4 (1970): 471–75; reprinted in Schreiner, *Die byzantinischen Kleinchroniken*, vol. 1, *Einleitung und Text* (Vienna, 1975), 519–23; cf. Lemerle, *Les Plus Anciens Recueils*, 2:63–64.

73. Evagrius 6.10, trans. Whitby, 301. Kenneth Setton, "The Bulgars in the Balkans and the Occupation of Corinth in the Sixth Century," *Speculum* 25 (1950): 502–43; and Setton, "The Emperor Constans II. and the Capture of Corinth by the Onogur Bulgars," *Speculum* 27 (1952): 351–62; Peter Charanis, "On the Capture of Corinth by the Onogurs and Its Recapture by the Byzantines," *Speculum* 27 (1952): 343–50; Charanis, "On the Slavic Settlement," 94–103.

74. Evagrius, *Ecclesiastical History*, trans. Whitby, 301 n. 37.

75. John of Ephesus 6.47, 260; Michael the Syrian, ed. and trans. Chabot, 2.362. For John, see sections 1.2. and 3.5; for his death date, see Pauline Allen, "A New Date for the Last Recorded Events in John of Ephesus' Historia Ecclesiastica," *Orientalia Lovanensia Periodica* 10 (1979): 251–54.

76. Lemerle, "La chronique improprement dite de Monemvasie," 9–10; *Cronaca di Monemvasia*, ed. Dujčev, 13.

77. Gregory the Great, *Registrum epistolarum* 1.26, ed. Norberg, 1:34. Corinth mentioned in synodal acts from the seventh and eighth centuries: Popović, "Aux origines de la slavisation des Balkans," 251; Charanis, "The Slavs," 8.

78. Charanis, "On the Slavic Settlement," 103.

79. Popović, "Aux origines de la slavisation des Balkans," 233 with literature; Cécile Morrisson, "Byzance au VIIe siècle: Le témoinage de la numismatique," in N. Stratos, *Byzantium*, 1:158–59; Bon, *Le Péloponnèse byzantin*, 54; John Rosser, "The Role of the Great Isthmus Corridor in the Slavonic Invasions of Greece," *Byzantinische Forschungen* 9 (1985): 245–53; Eric A. Ivison, "Burial and Urbanism in Late Antique and Early Byzantine Corinth (c. 400–700)," in *Towns in Transition: Urban Evolution in Late Antiquity and the Early Middle Ages*, ed. Neil Christie and Simon T. Loseby (Aldershot, 1996), 99–125; Curta, *Making of the Slavs*, 141–42; John H. W. G. Liebeschuetz, *The Decline and Fall of the Ancient City* (Oxford, 2001), 188.

80. Michael Weithmann, *Die slawische Bevölkerung auf der griechischen Halbinsel: Ein Beitrag zur historischen Ethnographie Südeuropas* (Munich, 1978), 215–18 and 246–48.

81. Kresten, "Zur Echtheit des Sigillion," 68–70; Stratos, *Byzantium in the Seventh Century*. 3:166.

82. Theophanes, *Chronographia* 6260, 613; 6290, 650. Margaret Thompson, *The Athenian Agora*, vol. 2, *Coins: From the Roman through the Venetian Period* (Princeton, NJ, 1954); Popović, "Aux origines de la slavisation des Balkans," 233; Stratos, *Byzantium in the Seventh Century*, 3:170–71.

83. Anna Lambropoulou, "The Presence of Slavs in the Western Peloponnese during the 7th to 8th Centuries," in Quast, *Foreigners in Early Medieval Europe*, 197–218.

84. Fundamental: Vasmer, *Die Slaven in Griechenland*, esp. 317; see also Charanis, "On the Slavic Settlement," 99; and Johannes Koder and Friedrich Hild, *Hellas und Thessalia*, Tabula Imperii Byzantini 1 (Vienna, 1976), 331 (map); Johannes Koder, *Der Lebensraum der Byzantiner: Historisch-geographischer Abriß ihres mittelalterlichen Staates im östlichen Mittelmeerraum*, Byzantinische Geschichtsschreiber Erg. Bd. 1 (Graz, 1984), 144, with illustration 22.

85. Constantine Porphyrogenitus, *De thematibus*, ed. Agostino Pertusi, *Costantino Porfirogenito de Thematibus: Introduzione, Testo Critico, Commento*, Biblioteca Apostolica

Vaticana (Rome, 1952), 91; Stratos, *Byzantium in the Seventh Century*, 3:153; Koder, "Byzanz, die Griechen und die Romaiosynē."

86. *Vita Willibaldi*, ed. Oswald Holder-Egger, MGH SS 15.1 (Stuttgart, 1887), 93, referring to a voyage in the 720s.

87. *Geographi Graeci minores*, vol. 2, ed. and trans. Karl Müller, Scriptorum graecorum bibliotheca 54 (Paris, 1861), 574.

88. Francis Dvornik, *The Slavs: Their Early History and Civilization*, Survey of Slavic Civilizations 2 (Boston, 1959), 40; Lothar Waldmüller, *Die ersten Begegnungen der Slawen mit dem Christentum und den christlichen Völkern vom 6. bis zum 8. Jahrhundert*, Enzyclopädie der Byzantinistik 51 (Amsterdam, 1976), 167; Schreiner, "Note sur la fondation," 475; Charanis, "The Slavs," 7; Popović, "Aux origines de la slavisation des Balkans," 234; Jadran Ferluga, "Gli Slavi del sud ed altri gruppi etnici di fronte a Bisanzio," in *Gli slavi occidentali*, 1:312–13; Tăpkova-Zaimova, "Sur quelques aspects," 116; Weithmann, *Die slawische Bevölkerung*, 104–6; Florin Curta, *Southeastern Europe in the Middle Ages, 500–1250* (Cambridge, 2006); Curta, "Still Waiting for the Barbarians?" Some of these authors assume that Slavs began to inhabit the mountainous regions of Greece before they settled elsewhere in the Balkan Peninsula.

89. Stratos, *Byzantium in the Seventh Century*, 3:145–48, with extensive discussion; Lemerle, "La chronique improprement dite de Monemvasie," 48; cf. Maria Nystazopoulou-Pelekidou, "Les Slaves dans l'empire byzantin," in *The 17th International Byzantine Congress: Major Papers, Dumbarton Oaks/Georgetown University, Washington, D.C., August 3–8, 1986* (New York, 1986), 350; an even later date, the late seventh century, according to Johannes Karayannopoulos, "Byzance et les Slaves," in *Abstracts of Short Papers, the 17th International Byzantine Conference, Dumbarton Oaks/Georgetown University, Washington, D.C., August 3–8, 1986* (New York, 1986), 166.

90. Ferluga, "Gli Slavi del sud," 313: "Vuoto militare e demografico"; cf. Lemerle, "Invasions et migrations," 281; good overview with further bibliography: Curta, *Making of the Slavs*, 142–51.

91. *Cronaca di Monemvasia*, ed. Dujčev, 17; Lemerle, "La chronique improprement dite de Monemvasie," 10.

92. Koder, *Der Lebensraum der Byzantiner*, 122: about fifty small villages along the slopes replaced three larger settlements in the valley; see also Peter Soustal, *Nikopolis und Kephallinia*, Tabula Imperii Byzantini 3 (Vienna, 1981).

93. Sinclair F. Hood, "Isles of Refuge in the Early Byzantine Period," *Papers of the British School in Athens* 65 (1970): 37–44. Most of these islands were only adequate for temporary retreat and not for permanent settlement.

94. Tivadar Vida and Thomas Volling, *Das slawische Brandgräberfeld von Olympia*, Archäologie in Eurasien 9 (Rahden, 2000).

95. Avar/Cutrigur attribution: Gladys R. Davidson and Tibor Horvath, "The Avar Invasion of Corinth," *Hesperia* 6 (1937): 227–34. Popović, "Aux origines de la slavisation des Balkans," 235–36, subsumes them under the Byzantine "Syracuse type." See also Weithmann, *Die slawische Bevölkerung*, 246–48. Florin Curta, "Female Dress and Slavic Bow Fibulae in Greece," *Hesperia* 74 (2005): 101–46, argues in favor of the apparel of a steppe warrior.

96. This is demonstrated by finds of coins: Nystazopoulou-Pelekidou, "Les Slaves dans l'empire byzantin," 349.

97. Koder and Hild, *Hellas und Thessalia*, 331. See also Johannes Koder, "Zur Frage der slavischen Siedlungsgebiete im mittelalterlichen Griechenland," *Byzantinische Zeitschrift* 71 (1978): 315–31.

98. John of Ephesus 6.47, 260; Michael the Syrian 10.21, ed. and trans. Chabot, 2:362. Then, however, he has these Slavs march on to Anchialus, where their king, Khagan,

dresses in Anastasia's purple robe. Evagrius 6.10, trans. Whitby, 301, tells the story the other way around: the Avars "capture Singidunum, Anchialus, and the whole of Greece." See also Curta, "Barbarians in Dark-Age Greece," 518–19, who is inclined to believe that John of Ephesus could not tell the difference, but Evagrius could.

99. *Miracula Demetrii* 2.2, 197–98, and 1.13–15, 134–60.

100. See section 6.2.

101. Thérèse Olajos, "Quelques remarques sur une peuplade slave en Hellade," in *Abstracts of Short Papers, the 17th International Byzantine Conference*, 243.

102. Cf. Koder and Hild, *Hellas und Thessalia*, 53–54.

103. *DAI* 49 and 50, 228–46.

104. Jan Peisker, "Die älteren Beziehungen der Slaven zu Turkotataren und Germanen und ihre sozialgeschichtliche Bedeutung," *Vierteljahresschrift zur Sozial- und Wirtschaftsgeschichte* 3, no. 2–3 (Leipzig, 1905): 187–360; see also Peisker, "The Expansion of the Slavs," in *Cambridge Medieval History*, vol. 2, *The Rise of the Saracens and the Foundation of the Western Empire* (Cambridge, 1913), 418–58. Similarly Ludmil Hauptmann, "Politische Umwälzungen unter den Slowenen vom Ende des sechsten Jahrhunderts bis zur Mitte des neunten," *MIÖG* 36 (1915): 229–87, and Hauptmann, "Die Frühzeit der West- und Südslawen," in *Historia Mundi: Ein Handbuch der Weltgeschichte in zehn Bänden*, vol. 5, *Frühes Mittelalter*, ed. Franz Altheim (Bern, 1956), 301–31; Kollautz, "Die Awaren," 132–33.

105. Helmut Preidel, *Die Anfänge der slawischen Besiedlung Böhmens und Mährens*, 2 vols. (Gräfeling bei München, 1957), 1:83 and 203–6.

106. Pritsak, "The Slavs and the Avars," 353–55.

107. Josip Mal, *Probleme aus der Frühzeit der Slovenen* (Laibach, 1939), 11–13; similar, although more differentiated, Bogo Grafenauer, "Razmerje med Slovani in Obri do obleganja Carigrada (626) in njegove gospodarsko-družbene podlage," *Zgodovinski Časopis* 4 (1955): 145–48; Alexander Avenarius, "Zur Problematik der awarisch-slawischen Beziehungen an der unteren Donau im 6.–7. Jh.," *Studia Historica Slovaca* 7 (1974): 11.

108. Lubomir Niederle, *Slovanské starožitnosti*, vol. 1, bk. 1 (Prague, 1902), iii.

109. See, for instance, Manfred Hellmann, "Problematik der slawischen Frühzeit," *Jahrbücher für Geschichte Osteuropas*, n.s., 7 (1959): 196; Fritze, "Slawische Altertumswissenschaft," 19; František Graus, "Deutsche und slawische Verfassungsgeschichte?," *Historische Zeitschrift* 197, no. 1 (1963): 307; Graus, "Die Entwicklung Mitteleuropas," 462–63; Ditten, "Zur Bedeutung der Einwanderung der Slawen," 81–83.

110. See also Jozef Zábojník, "The Slavs and the Avar Khaganate," in *Great Moravia and the Beginnings of Christianity*, ed. Pavel Kouřil (Brno, 2015), 35–41.

111. Bohumila Zástěrová, "Zu den Quellen zur Geschichte Wolhyniens und der Duleben im 6. Jahrhundert," in *Byzantinistische Beiträge*, ed. Johannes Irmscher (Berlin, 1964), 231–32; Arnulf Kollautz, "Nestors Quelle über die Unterdrückung der Duleben durch die Obri (Awaren)," *Die Welt der Slaven* 27 (1982): 316–17; Avenarius, *Die Awaren in Europa*, 214.

112. Fredegar 4.48, 39–40.

113. *The Russian Primary Chronicle: Laurentian Text* 12, trans. Samuel Hazzard Cross and Olgerd P. Sherbowitz-Wetzor (Cambridge, MA, 1953), 55.

114. Vaclav Chaloupecký, "Considérations sur Samon, le premier roi des Slaves," *Byzantinoslavica* 11 (1950): 227; Kollautz and Miyakawa, 1:236; differently: Avenarius, *Die Awaren in Europa*, 191–218.

115. Paul the Deacon, *Historia Langobardorum* 4.37, ed. Waitz, 186.

116. Fredegar 4.48, 39–40; cf. Pohl, "Perceptions of Barbarian Violence."

117. Different etymologies in Theodor Mayer, "Zu Fredegars Bericht über die Slawen," in *Festschrift Oswald Redlich*, MIÖG Erg. Bd. 11 (Innsbruck, 1929), 114–20; Kollautz and Miyakawa, 1:229; Chaloupecký, "Considérations sur Samon," 227; Preidel, *Die Anfänge der*

slawischen Besiedlung, 1:86. Fredegar's own interpretation need not be more than Frankish folk-etymology.

118. Theophylact Simocatta 8.3.15, 213; see section 5.8.

119. The detailed description of Avar battle order in the *Strategicon* 11.2, 362, contains no information on a Slav battle line.

120. *Chronicon Paschale* a. 626, 173; see section 7.3.

121. Theophylact Simocatta 6.3.9, 163.

122. Theophylact Simocatta 6.4.4–5, 163.

123. *Chronicon Paschale* a. 626, 178; Slav boatmen are first mentioned in the Cutrigur invasion of 559, Agathias 5.22, 192–93; cf. section 2.1.

124. *Chronicon Paschale* a. 626, 178.

125. *Miracula Demetrii* 1.13.117, 134.

126. Paul the Deacon, *Historia Langobardorum* 4.28, ed. Waitz, 157.

127. Theophylact Simocatta 6.2.10–16, 160. See also Marcin Wołoszyn, *Theophylaktos Simokates und die Slawen am Ende des westlichen Ozeans—die erste Erwähnung der Ostseeslawen?* (Kraków, 2014). I have twice replaced Whitby's translation "nation," first with "origin" and then "people."

128. Wołoszyn, *Theophylaktos Simokates und die Slawen*, 51–69; see section 5.1.

129. Joachim Herrmann, "Byzanz und die Slawen 'am äußersten Ende des westlichen Ozeans,'" in *Les slaves et le monde mediterraneen, VIe–XIe siècles*, Symposion international de archéologie slave (Sofia, 1973), 42.

130. Avenarius, *Die Awaren in Europa*, 133.

131. See section 5.4.

132. See sections 3.3 and 5.9.

133. *Chronicon Paschale* a. 626, 178. See section 7.3.

134. *Miracula Demetrii* 1.2.198, 185: "Ta endoteron autou barbara phyla" (Lemerle translates "qui vivaient sur son territoire," 181); cf. section 7.1.

135. *Strategicon* 11.4, 372–81.

136. See section 3.3.

137. Procopius, *Bella* 7.14.21–22, ed. and trans. Dewing, 4:268; Menander, frag. 21, ed. and trans. Blockley, 194.

138. Curta, "Frontier Ethnogenesis in Late Antiquity." See also Florin Curta, "Feasting with 'Kings' in an Ancient Democracy: On the Slavic Society of the Early Middle Ages (Sixth to Seventh Century A. D.)," *Essays in Medieval Studies* 15 (1997): 19–34.

139. John of Ephesus 6.25, 249; cf. section 3.6.

140. Falko Daim, *Die Awaren in Niederösterreich*, Wissenschaftliche Schriftenreihe Niederösterreichs 28 (St. Pölten, 1977), 18.

141. Sebastian Brather, *Archäologie der westlichen Slawen* (Berlin, 2001); for a more (and perhaps too) optimistic view, see Peter Stadler, "Avar Chronology Revisited, and the Question of Ethnicity in the Avar Qaganate," in Curta, *The Other Europe in the Middle Ages*, 47–82.

142. Menander, frag. 21, ed. and trans. Blockley, 195; cf. section 3.3.

143. Fredegar 4.48, 39–40.

144. Among others, Preidel, *Die Anfänge der slawischen Besiedlung*, 1:85–88; Avenarius, *Die Awaren in Europa*, 87–89.

145. Cf. sections 5.4. and 6.10.

146. Fritze, "Zur Bedeutung der Awaren," 545; cf. section 6.7 and 6.10.

147. Frankish war of 566: Menander, frag. 11, ed. and trans. Blockley, 128. First siege of Thessalonica: *Miracula Demetrii* 1.14.137, 148. Cf. *Strategicon* 11.2, 365, and section 6.2.

148. *Miracula Demetrii* 2.5.290, 223, and 2.4.254, 203; Lemerle, *Les Plus Anciens Recueils*, 2:121.

149. Paul the Deacon, *Historia Langobardorum* 4.10, ed. Waitz, 150; cf. section 5.6.

150. Sebastian Brather, "The Beginnings of Slavic Settlement East of the River Elbe," *Antiquity* 78 (2004): 314–29; Peter Štih, "Wiped Out by Slavic Settlement? The Issue of Continuity between Antiquity and the Early Middle Ages in the Slovene Area," in Štih, *The Middle Ages between the Eastern Alps and the Northern Adriatic: Select Papers on Slovene Historiography and Medieval History* (Leiden, 1020), 87–99.

151. Paul the Deacon, *Historia Langobardorum* 5.23, ed. Waitz, 196; Fredegar 4.74 and 75, 62–63.

152. Herrmann, *Die Slawen in Deutschland*; Herrmann, "Byzanz und die Slawen," 37–40 (Slavs move to the Baltic regions to escape Avar influence); Heinrich Kunstmann, "Der Name der Abodriten," *Die Welt der Slawen* 26 (1981): 413–15, with the overall hypothesis of a Slavic migration from southeast to northwest, which was met with great skepticism.

153. Fredegar 4.68, 56–58. See Zábojník, "The Slavs and the Avar Khaganate," and section 7.4.

154. Štih, *The Middle Ages between the Eastern Alps and the Northern Adriatic*; Rajko Bratož, ed., *Slovenija in sosednje dežele med antiko in karolinško dobo: začetki slovenske etnogeneze / Slowenien und die Nachbarländer zwischen Antike und karolingischer Periode: Anfänge der slowenischen Ethnogenese*, 2 vols. (Ljubljana, 2000), with the contributions by Slavko Ciglenečki, "Archaeological Investigations of the Decline of Antiquity in Slovenia," 1:119–34; and Franz Glaser, "Der Untergang der Antike und ihr Nachleben in Noricum," 1:199–218. See also Franz Glaser, *Frühes Christentum im Alpenraum* (Graz, 1997).

155. Wolfram, *Salzburg, Bayern, Österreich*; Hans-Dietrich Kahl, *Der Staat der Karantanen: Fakten, Thesen und Fragen zu einer frühen slawischen Machtbildung im Ostalpenraum (7.–9. Jh.)* (Ljubljana, 2002); Falko Daim, "Archaeology, Ethnicity and the Structures of Identification: The Example of the Avars, Carantanians and Moravians in the Eighth Century," in Pohl and Reimitz, *Strategies of Distinction*, 71–94; Stefan Eichert, *Die frühmittelalterlichen Grabfunde Kärntens: Die materielle Kultur Karantaniens anhand der Grabfunde vom Ende der Spätantike bis ins 11. Jahrhundert* (Klagenfurt, 2010). See section 5.6.

156. Sabine Ladstätter, "Von Noricum Mediterraneum zur Provincia Sclaborum: Die Kontinuitätsfrage aus archäologischer Sicht," in Bratož, *Slovenija*, 1:219–38; Ladstätter, *Die materielle Kultur der Spätantike in den Ostalpen: Eine Fallstudie am Beispiel der westlichen Doppelkirchenanlage auf dem Hemmaberg*, Mitteilungen der Prähistorischen Kommission 35 (Vienna, 2000); Erik Szameit, "Zum archäologischen Bild der frühen Slawen in Österreich: Mit Fragen zur ethnischen Bestimmung karolingerzeitlicher Gräberfelder im Ostalpenraum," in Bratož, *Slovenija*, 1:507–44; Stefan Eichert, *Frühmittelalterliche Strukturen im Ostalpenraum: Studien zu Geschichte und Archäologie Karantaniens* (Klagenfurt, 2012), 215–18, who assumes a transitional phase between 590 and 660, before Slavic traces become clearer.

157. Curta, "The Early Slavs in the Northern and Eastern Adriatic Region"; Slavko Ciglenečki, "Tracce di un insediamento tardo (VI–IX sec.) nei siti della tarda antichita in Slovenia," in *Il territorio tra tardoantico e altomedioevo: metodi di indagine e risultati; 3° seminario sul tardoantico e l'altomedioevo nell'area alpina e padana, Monte Barro-Galbiate (Como), 9–11 settembre 1991*, ed. Gian Pietro Brogiolo and Lanfredo Casteletti (Florence, 1992), 53–59.

158. Štih, "Wiped Out by Slavic Settlement?," 95.

159. See sections 5.5. and 7.1.

160. Dzino, *Becoming Slav, Becoming Croat*, 41.

161. For an overview, see Dzino, *Becoming Slav, Becoming Croat*, 118–74.

162. Vladimir Sokol, *Medieval Jewelry and Burial Assemblages in Croatia: A Study of Graves and Gravegoods, ca. 800 to ca. 1450* (Leiden, 2016), 88–112. For a critique of Sokol's

position based on an earlier publication, see Dzino, *Becoming Slav, Becoming Croat,* 122–24. For the problem of the early Croats, see section 7.5.

163. Dzino, *Becoming Slav, Becoming Croat,* 130; Curta, "The Early Slavs in the Northern and Eastern Adriatic Region."

164. Mihał Parczewski, *Die Anfänge der frühslawischen Kultur in Polen* (Vienna, 1993), 30–62 (however, the distinctions between his twelve types of handmade pottery in tables 4–12 are only perceptible to a very expert eye); Gabriel Fusek and Jozef Zábojník, "Ausklang der Spätantike und Anfang des Frühmittelalters in der nördlichen Peripherie des Karpatenbeckens," in *Archeologia o poczatkach Słowian: Materialy z konferencji, Kraków, 19–21 listopada 2001* (Kraków, 2005), 541–66; Gabriel Fusek, "Beitrag zu Problemen der Datierung von der Besiedlung der Westslowakei in der älteren Phase des Frühmittelalters," in *The Early Slavic Settlement of Central Europe in the Light of New Dating Evidence,* Interdisciplinary Medieval Studies 3 (Wroclaw, 2013), 139–50.

165. This is how Parczewski, *Die Anfänge,* 124, defines early Slavic culture.

166. Erik Szameit, "Slawische Körpergräber des 8. Jahrhunderts im österreichischen Donauraum und ihre Beziehungen zum spätmerowingischen Kulturkreis," in *Ethnische und kulturelle Verhältnisse an der mittleren Donau vom 6. bis zum 11. Jahrhundert: Symposium, Nitra 6. bis 10. November 1994,* ed. Darina Bialeková and Jozef Zábojník (Bratislava, 1996), 215–25; Parczewski, *Die Anfänge.*

167. Gabriel Fusek, "Formanalyse vollständiger Gefäße oder ein weiterer Versuch, frühmittelalterliche Keramikgefäße aus der Slowakei zu klassifizieren," *Spisy archeologického ústavu AV ČR Brno* 4 (1995): 15–34; Fusek and Zábojník, "Ausklang der Spätantike," 552. For a critique, see Florin Curta, "The Prague Type: A Critical Approach to Pottery-Classification," *Archaeologia Bulgarica* 5 (2001): 73–106.

168. Falko Daim, "Die vielteilige Gürtelgarnitur aus Hohenberg, Steiermark," in Daim et al., *Hunnen + Awaren,* 225–27; Erik Szameit, "Das frühmittelalterliche Grab von Grabelsdorf bei St. Kanzian am Klopeinersee, Kärnten: Ein Beitrag zur Datierung und Deutung awarischer Bronzen im Ostalpenraum," *Archaeologia Austriaca* 77 (1993): 213–34; Stefan Eichert, "Grabelsdorf—villa Gabrielis: Betrachtungen zur Entwicklung einer Siedlung vom 7. bis ins 11. Jahrhundert," *Carinthia I* 200 (2010): 105–32.

169. Paul the Deacon, *Historia Langobardorum* 4.10, ed. Waitz, 150.

170. Detailed discussion with bibliography in Curta, *Making of the Slavs,* 227–310. For earlier scholarly literature, see Maria Comşa, "La pénétration des Slaves dans le territoire de la Roumanie entre le VIe et IXe siècle à la lumière des recherches archéologiques," *Slavia Antiqua* 7 (1960): 175–78; Kazanski, *Les Slaves.*

171. Views on the grave finds of Tirgşor: Rusu, "Les populations du groupe turc," 22 (sixth century); Kurt Horedt, "Das Awarenproblem in Rumänien," *Študijné zvesti* 16 (1968): 105 (seventh to eighth century, not unconditionally Avar); Bálint, *Die Archäologie der Steppe,* 126–27 (late Avar period).

172. Joachim Werner, "Slawische Bügelfibeln des 7. Jahrhunderts," in *Reinecke Festschrift* (Mainz, 1950), 150–72. Overview of the current state of research in Curta, *Making of the Slavs,* especially 247–75, who considers the bow fibulae as an indicator for the rise of Slavic warlords: "Everything points to the conclusion that 'Slavic' bow fibulae were not simply symbols of social status or gender, but badges of power" (ibid., 274). See also Curta, "Female Dress," and Florin Curta, "'Slavic' Bow Fibulae: Twenty Years of Research," *Berichte der Römisch-Germanischen Kommission* 93 (2012): 235–342.

173. Classic studies are Šafařík, *Slawische Altertümer;* Niederle, *Manuel d'antiquité slave;* Robert Roesler, "Über den Zeitpunkt der slawischen Ansiedlung an der unteren Donau," *Sitzungsberichte der kaiserlichen Akademie der Wissenschaften* 73 (1873): 77–126; further scholarly opinions in Nestor, "La pénétration des Slaves," 41–43; Beševliev, *Die protobulgarische Periode,* 134–36; Maksimović, "Chronological Notes about Slavonic

Raids," 269–71; Popović, "Les témoins archéologiques," 488–89; Lemerle, *Les Plus Anciens Recueils*, 2:179–81; Stratos, *Byzantium in the Seventh Century*, 1:33; Ditten, "Zur Bedeutung der Einwanderung der Slawen," 84–86; Koder, *Der Lebensraum der Byzantiner*, 142–43; Nystazopoulou-Pelekidou, "Les Slaves dans l'empire byzantin," 346; Curta, *Making of the Slavs*, 120–227.

174. John of Ephesus 6.25, 248–49; cf. section 3.5.

175. Andrew Poulter, ed., *The Transition to Late Antiquity, on the Danube and Beyond* (Oxford, 2008), and section 2.1.

176. Popović, "Les témoins archéologiques," 479–81; Florin Curta, "Peasants as 'Makeshift Soldiers for the Occasion': Sixth-Century Settlement Patterns in the Balkans," in *Urban Centers and Rural Contexts in Late Antiquity*, ed. Thomas S. Burns and John W. Eadie (East Lansing, 2001), 199–217; Curta, *Making of the Slavs*, 190–227; Poulter, *The Transition to Late Antiquity*; Andreas Schwarcz, Peter Soustal, and Antoaneta Tcholakova, eds., *Der Donaulimes in der Spätantike und im Frühmittelalter*, Miscellanea Bulgarica 22 (Vienna, 2016); cf. section 2.1.

177. Curta, "The Early Slavs in Bohemia and Moravia," 727; *mesitēs*: Evangelos Chrysos, "Die Nordgrenze des byzantinischen Reiches im 6. bis 8. Jahrhundert," in Hänsel, *Die Völker Südosteuropas vom 6.–8. Jahrhundert*, 29.

178. Manfred Clauss, "Heerwesen (Heeresreligion)," in *Reallexikon für Antike und Christentum: Sachwörterbuch zur Auseinandersetzung des Christentums mit der antiken Welt*, vol. 13, *Gütergemeinschaft–Heilgötter* (Stuttgart, 1986), 1104, with survey of literature.

179. Accomplished, for example, by the Hunnic Gepid Mundo, who moved from being Attila's grandson and a Gepid aristocrat to robber chieftain, then Gothic *dux*, and finally Roman general; cf. Pohl, "Die Gepiden und die Gentes," 292–93.

180. For a first time most likely from 550 to 551; Procopius, *Bella* 7.40.1–8, and 7.40.31–45, ed. and trans. Dewing, 5:36–41 and 48–53. In the 580s, the raids seem to have taken even longer: John of Ephesus 6.25, 248–49. See Sarantis, *Justinian's Balkan Wars*, 278–88 and 377.

181. Ardagast's return is confirmed in Theophylact Simocatta 1.7.6, 29, and 6.6–7, 165–69.

182. Gregory the Great, *Registrum epistolarum* 1.43, ed. Norberg, 1:57; Franz Dölger, *Regesten der Kaiserurkunden des oströmischen Reiches von 565–1453*, vol. 1 (Munich, 1924), no. 105, 13.

183. Gregory the Great, *Registrum epistolarum* 2.31, ed. Norberg, 1:117 (June 592). Somewhat later similar problems arose in Istria; cf. section 5.6. Barbarian incursions are also mentioned in letter 2.20, 1:107, to the Illyrian prefect Jobinus (March 592) and in letter 10.15, 2:842, to the bishop of Salona (July 600), where he specifically mentions Slavs already threatening Istria and Italy.

184. Popović, "Les témoins archéologiques," 491–93; Vladislav Popović, *Caričin Grad* (Belgrad, 1980).

185. See, among others, Zivka Vázarova, *Slawen und Protobulgaren* (Sofia, 1976); Täpkova-Zaimova, *Byzance et les Balkans à partir du VIe siècle*; Uwe Fiedler, *Studien zu Gräberfeldern des 6.–9. Jahrhunderts an der unteren Donau* (Bonn, 1992); Barford, *The Early Slavs*, 55–62; Curta, *Making of the Slavs*, 120–226; Curta, "Were There Any Slavs."

186. According to the *Miracula Demetrii*, the army of the eparch was en route during the first siege; see section 4.3. The legendary account in Constantine Porphyrogenitus blames the fall of Salona on a risky expedition undertaken by its defenders; see section 7.1.

187. Theophylact Simocatta, 7.12.1, 195; see section 5.5. The Avar military campaign did not simply initiate Slavic settlement of Bosnia; Slavs had probably operated in the area before, and the Avar raid opened additional spaces for Slavic operations and settlement.

188. Theophylact Simocatta, 7.2.2, 180; for the problems of identifying these cities, see ibid., n. 5; cf. section 5.4.

189. *Miracula Demetrii* 2.1.180, 175.

190. Popović, "Les témoins archéologiques," 482–84, on the basis of coin finds in the forts, which generally conclude with mintings from 592–93 or 594–95. This does not mean that the fortresses fell in the following year, as Popović concludes, but marks the beginning of the end. Cf. *Iatrus-Krivina: Spätantike Befestigung und frühmittelalterliche Siedlung an der unteren Donau*, vol. 1, *Ergebnisse der Ausgrabungen 1966–1973* (Berlin, 1979), 20; Velkov, "Der Donaulimes in Bulgarien," 163; Constantin Scorpan, *Limes Scythiae: Topographical and Stratigraphical Research on the Late Roman Fortifications on the Lower Danube* (Oxford, 1985); Curta, *Making of the Slavs*, 155–89; Poulter, *The Transition to Late Antiquity*; Andrew Poulter, *Nicopolis ad Istrum: A Roman, Late Roman and Early Byzantine City. Excavations 1985–1992*, Society for the Promotion of Roman Studies (London, 1995). Schwarcz, Soustal, and Tcholakova, *Der Donaulimes in der Spätantike*. See section 7.1.

191. Velkov, "Der Donaulimes in Bulgarien," 163–64.

192. Historical research presents the *sklavinía* generally as an original, autonomous Slavic organizational form; see, for example, Lubomir E. Havlík, "Die Byzantiner über die Verfassung der Slawen im 6. und 7. Jahrhundert," in *From Late Antiquity to Early Byzantium: Byzantine Symposium of the 16th Eirene Conference*, ed. Vladimir Vavřinek (Prague, 1985), 174–75; Lemerle, *Les Plus Anciens Recueils*, 2:300; Karayannopoulos, "Byzance et les Slaves," 165; Nystazopoulou-Pelekidou, "Les Slaves dans l'empire byzantin," 352. Evangelos Chrysos, "Settlements of Slavs and Byzantine Sovereignty in the Balkans," in *Byzantina Mediterranea: Festschrift für Johannes Koder zum 65. Geburtstag*, ed. Klaus Belke et al. (Vienna, 2007), 123–35, argued that for the Byzantines a *sklavinía* was constituted by some form of formal incorporation into the empire. In fact, the late appearance of the term is remarkable, and the early ninth-century chronicler Theophanes only begins using it for events of the second half of the seventh century. See also Florin Curta, "Sklaviniai and Ethnic Adjectives: A Clarification," *Byzantion: Nea Hellás* 30 (2011): 85–98, with minor modifications of Chrysos's views. Overview of sources in Peter Charanis, "Observations on the History of Greece during the Early Middle Ages," *Balkan Studies* 11 (1970): 14–34. Of course, the Byzantine use of the concept with its ideological implications says nothing about what must have been the internal Slavic organization of the various *Sclaviniai*.

193. This process is most apparent in the differences among the various sieges of Thessalonica; cf. Lemerle, "Invasions et migrations," 300–302; the names for the Macedonian Slavs in the *Miracula Demetrii* 2.1.179, 175. For the state of research in the late 1980s, see Ditten, "Zur Bedeutung der Einwanderung der Slawen," 99. An overview of the "Byzantine" Slavs in Michael D. Graebner, *The Role of the Slavs within the Byzantine Empire, 500–1018* (New Brunswick, NJ, 1975); Barford, *The Early Slavs*, 91–95.

194. Henning, *Südosteuropa zwischen Antike und Mittelalter*, esp. 108–11.

195. Procopius, *Bella* 7.14.30, ed. and trans. Dewing, 4:272 ("they hold a great amount of land" but "inhabit their country in a very sporadic fashion"); Jordanes, *Getica* 23.119, ed. Mommsen, 88 ("per immense spatia Venetharum natio populosa consedit"); Menander, frag. 10.2, ed. and trans. Blockley, 190.

196. Procopius, *Bella* 7.38.18–19, ed. and trans. Dewing, 5:24–27.

197. *Miracula Demetrii* 2.2.214, 183–84; *Strategicon* 11.4, 372.

198. Eva Seemanova et al., "The Slavic NBN Founder Mutation: A Role for Reproductive Fitness?," *PLoS ONE* 11 (2016), e0167984, doi: 10.1371/journal.pone.0167984, http://journals.plos.org/plosone/article?id=10.1371/journal.pone.0167984.

199. For a recent state-of-the art methodological discussion of historical interpretations of genetic evidence in early medieval studies, see Patrick J. Geary and Krishna

Veeramah, "Mapping European Population Movement through Genomic Research," *Medieval Worlds* 4 (2016): 65–78, doi: 10.1553/medievalworlds_no4_2016s65, http://www.medievalworlds.net/medieval_worlds?frames=yes.

200. See section 4.1.

201. Pseudo-Caesarius, *Erotapokriseis*, ed. Rudolf Riedinger (Munich, 1969), 302, 305–6. Curta, *Making of the Slavs*, 43–44.

202. Agathias 4.20.4, 121.

203. Malalas, *Chronographia* 18.235, ed. Dindorf, 490; English translation: *The Chronicle of John Malalas* 18.129, trans. Elizabeth Jeffreys, Michael Jeffreys, and Roger Scott, with Brian Croke (Melbourne, 1986), 421. Mischa Meier, Christine Radtki, and Fabian Schulz, eds., *Die Weltchronik des Johannes Malalas: Autor—Werk—Überlieferung*, Malalas Studien 1 (Stuttgart, 2016).

204. Curta, *Making of the Slavs*, 44.

205. See section 3 and section 5.

206. Gregory the Great, *Registrum epistolarum* 9.155.1, ed. Norberg, 2:710, with reference to a letter by the exarch Callinicus that had announced a victory over the Slavs; ibid., 10.15.5, 2:842.

207. *Versus Martini Dvmiensis episcopi in Basilica*, ed. Rudolf Peiper, MGH AA 6.2 (Berlin, 1883), 194–96. Cf. Jaroslav Šašel, "Antiqui barbari: Zur Besiedlungsgeschichte Ostnoricums und Pannoniens im 5. und 6. Jahrhundert nach den Schriftquellen," in *Von der Spätantike zum frühen Mittelalter*, ed. Eugen Ewig and Joachim Werner, Vorträge und Forschungen 25 (Sigmaringen, 1979), 125–39; Curta, *Making of the Slavs*, 46.

208. John of Biclaro, *Chronica* 41 and 60, 66 and 69.

209. Isidore of Seville, *Chronicon* 5813, ed. Theodor Mommsen, MGH AA 11 (Berlin, 1894), 479.

210. Paul the Deacon, *Historia Langobardorum* 4.7 and 4.10, ed. Waitz, 146 and 159–60. Florin Curta, "Slavs in Fredegar and Paul the Deacon: Medieval Gens or 'Scourge of God'?," *Early Medieval Europe* 6, no. 2 (1997): 141–67, esp. 155. On Paul, see Pohl, "Paulus Diaconus und die 'Historia Langobardorum.'"

211. Paul the Deacon, *Historia Langobardorum* 4.27, ed. Waitz, 156.

212. Jonas of Bobbio, *Life of Columbanus* 1.27, trans. Alexander O'Hara and Ian Wood, Translated Texts for Historians 64 (Liverpool, 2017), 162.

213. *Strategicon* 11.4, 370–87.

214. Pohl, "Introduction. Strategies of Identification." See section 6.10.

215. Dzino, *Becoming Slav, Becoming Croat*, 212.

216. Elena E. Lipsic, *Byzanz und die Slawen: Beiträge zur byzantinischen Geschichte des 6.–9. Jahrhunderts* (Weimar, 1951), 101–3; Joachim Henning, "Untersuchungen zur Entwicklung der Landwirtschaft in Südosteuropa im Übergang von der Spätantike zum frühen Mittelalter," *Ethnographisch-archäologische Zeitschrift* 25 (1984): 123–30; and Henning, *Südosteuropa zwischen Antike und Mittelalter*, especially 108–10.

217. Jordanes, *Getica* 5.35, ed. Mommsen, 63; in Greece, too, Slavic settlers showed a preference for less accessible mountainous areas; cf. Koder, *Der Lebensraum der Byzantiner*, 144.

218. *Strategicon* 11.4, 371–72. See also Curta, *Making of the Slavs*, 319.

219. Pseudo-Caesarius, *Erotapokriseis*, ed. Riedinger, 302; cf. Curta, "Frontier Ethnogenesis in Late Antiquity," 184 (who argues that at the end of the sixth century, "the picture radically changes").

220. Curta, *Making of the Slavs*, 324; see also Dzino, *Becoming Slav, Becoming Croat*.

221. Pierre Clastres, *Staatsfeinde: Studien zur politischen Anthropologie* (Frankfurt am Main, 1976). Cf. Christian Sigrist, *Regulierte Anarchie: Untersuchungen zum Fehlen und zur Entstehung politischer Herrschaft in segmentären Gesellschaften* (Freiburg, 1967).

222. James C. Scott, *The Art of Not Being Governed: An Anarchist History of Upland Southeast Asia* (New Haven, CT, 2009). This book is mainly about keeping foreign states at bay, and thus not fully adaptable to the early Slavic case, but parallels can often be noted: "Their physical dispersion in rugged terrain, their mobility . . . their pliable ethnic identities . . . serve to avoid incorporation into states and to prevent states from springing up among them." Ibid., x.

223. *Strategicon* 11.4, 372; Wiita, "The Ethnika in Byzantine Military Treatises," 332.

224. *Strategicon* 11.4, 382.

225. *Miracula Demetrii* 2.4, 198–99.

226. E.g. Procopius, *Bella* 7.40, ed. and trans. Dewing, 5:39.

227. *Miracula Demetrii* 1.14.157–60, 144–45.

228. *Strategicon* 11.4, 380.

229. Theophylact Simocatta 6.8.13–6.9.6, 171–72.

230. Ferdinand Holthausen, *Gotisches etymologisches Wörterbuch*, 2nd ed. (Heidelberg, 2002), 82. The use of the title *rex* in *Strategicon* 11.4, 128, might go back to the same source. See also Michael Whitby, "Theophylact's Knowledge of Languages," *Byzantion* 52 (1982): 425–28. *Rex* is then used in the later seventh century in the second book of the *Miracula Demetrii* 2.4.231–36.

231. A good overview in Curta, *Making of the Slavs*, 326–27.

232. See section 7.4.

233. Curta, *Making of the Slavs*, 325–32. See also Marshall D. Sahlins, "Poor man, rich man, big man, chief: political types in Melanesia and Polynesia," *Comparative Studies in Society and History* 5 (1963): 283–303; Maurice Godelier, *The Making of Great Men. Male Domination and Power among the New Guinea Baruya* (Cambridge, 1986).

234. Holzer, "Vorhistorische Periode," 1120–21.

235. Stansisław Stachowski, "Türkischer Einfluss auf den slavischen Wortschatz," in Gutschmidt et al., *Die slavischen Sprachen/The Slavic Languages*, 2:1200.

236. Przemysław Urbańczyk, "Foreign Leaders in Early Slavic Societies," in *Integration und Herrschaft: Ethnische Identitäten und kulturelle Muster im frühen Mittelalter*, ed. Walter Pohl and Max Diesenberger, Forschungen zur Geschichte des Mittelalters 3 (Vienna, 2002), 257–68.

237. Curta, "Frontier Ethnogenesis in Late Antiquity."

238. Curta, "Peasants as 'Makeshift Soldiers for the Occasion.'" However, there are examples that point to an integration of sixth-century fortresses into a productive rural hinterland, for instance, Nicopolis ad Istrum with its massive storehouses; see Poulter, *Nicopolis ad Istrum*.

239. John L. Teall, "The Barbarians in Justinian's Armies," *Speculum* 40 (1965): 294–322.

240. Dauritas: Menander, frag. 21, ed. and trans. Blockley, 194.

241. Curta, *Making of the Slavs*, 274–75; Florin Curta, "Amphorae and Seals: The 'Sub-Byzantine' Avars and the Quaestura Exercitus," in Bollók, Csiky, and Vida, *Zwischen Byzanz und der Steppe/Between Byzantium and the Steppe*, 307–34.

242. See sections 3.8 and 7.8.

243. See section 4.4. and 4.5.

244. On the killing of prisoners, see sections 5.7 and 6.7; sales of prisoners, for example, in *Miracula Demetrii* 2.2.214, 183–84.

245. *Strategicon* 11.4, 372.

246. Beševliev, *Die protobulgarische Periode*, 142.

247. Wenskus, *Stammesbildung und Verfassung*, 454; he quite rightly calls attention to the contradictory evidence. Procopius, *Bella* 7.14, ed. and trans. Dewing, 4:263–67, writes on several occasions of slaves of the Antes.

248. *Strategicon* 11.4.131–36, 381.

249. Šafařík, *Slawische Altertümer*; Sebastian Brather, "Slawenbilder: 'Slawische Alter-tumskunde' im 19. und 20. Jahrhundert," *Archeologické rozhledy* 53 (2001): 717–51; Krzysztof A. Makovski and Frank Hadler, eds., *Approaches to Slavic Unity: Austro-Slavism, Pan-Slavism, Neo-Slavism, and Solidarity among the Slavs Today* (Poznán, 2013). See also Peter Štih, "On Nationalized History, Myths and Stereotypes," in Štih, *The Middle Ages*, 9–37.

250. Anatoly Khazanov, "'Military Democracy' and the Epoch of Class Formation," in *Soviet Ethnology and Anthropology Today*, ed. Julian V. Bromlej, Studies in Anthropology 1 (The Hague, 1974), 133–46; Curta, *Making of the Slavs*, 312–19.

251. Dzino, *Becoming Slav, Becoming Croat*, 172; with reference to Curta, *Making of the Slavs*, 311–34.

252. Curta, *Making of the Slavs*, 319–25. The classical description of segmentary societ-ies, which are characterized by lack of hierarchy and the coexistence of analogous and hor-izontally related social units, is given in Émile Durkheim, *De la division du travail social*, 10th ed. (Paris, 1978), 150–52. Curta is correct that Byzantine views of the Slavs may have been topical and that some social inequality and leadership emerged in the sixth century: I certainly did not claim that Slavic society was "frozen in time," as Curta writes. However, all the evidence we have suggests that early Slavs did not form stable supraregional or even regional powers until the eighth century. We need to find ways to account for this differ-ence. See also Urbańczyk, "Foreign Leaders in Early Slavic Societies."

253. These are two of Curta's attractive key arguments: *Making of the Slavs*, 120–90.

254. Pohl, "Der Germanenbegriff vom 3. bis 8. Jahrhundert."

5. THE BALKAN WARS OF MAURICE, 591–602

1. Isidore of Seville, *Chronica* 1, 5800, 409, ed. José Carlos Martín, CCSL 112 (Turn-hout, 2003), 200.

2. Theophylact Simocatta 5.16, 155–57; Denis A. Zakythinos, *Byzantinische Geschichte, 324–1071* (Vienna, 1979), 511; Stratos, *Byzantium in the Seventh Century*, 1:32; Georg Ostrogorsky, *Geschichte des byzantinischen Staates*, 3rd ed., Handbuch der Alter-tumswissenschaften 12.1.2 (Munich, 1963), 58; Bury, *History of the Later Roman Empire*, 2:124; for the organization of the Byzantine army, see John Haldon, *Warfare and Society in the Byzantine World, 565–1204* (London, 1999), 67–71.

3. Treadgold, *The Early Byzantine Historians*, 329–40, at 336 and 339; Whitby, *The Emperor Maurice and His Historian*; Whitby and Whitby, *The History of Theophylact Simo-catta*, xvi–xxv; Hunger, *Die hochsprachliche profane Literatur der Byzantiner*, 1:313–15; Theophylact Simocatta, trans. Schreiner, 1–3 and 13; Curta, *The Making of the Slavs*, 55–59; cf. sec 1.2.

4. Relatively extensive narratives are found in Howorth, "The Avars," 758–65; Bury, *History of the Later Roman Empire*, 2:124–30; Avenarius, *Die Awaren in Europa*, 102–10; Curta, *Making of the Slavs*, 99–106; Ziemann, *Vom Wandervolk zur Großmacht*, 115–23; John H. W. G Liebeschuetz, "The Lower Danube Region under Pressure: From Valens to Heraclius," in Poulter, *The Transition to Late Antiquity*, 120–28; Sarantis, *Justinian's Balkan Wars*, 382–86.

5. Theophanes, *Chronographia* 6082–94, 390–414. On the reliability of his datings, see Georg Ostrogorsky, "Die Chronologie des Theophanes im 7. und 8. Jahrhundert," *Byz-antinisch-neugriechische Jahrbücher* 7 (1928–29): 1–3 and especially 24–25; Cyril Mango and Roger Scott, "Introduction," in *Chronicle of Theophanes Confessor*, trans. Mango and Scott, lxiii–lxxiv.

6. Theophylact Simocatta 5.15, 153; *The Armenian History attributed to Sebeos* 13, trans. R. W. Thomson, Translated Texts for Historians 31, 2 vols. (Liverpool, 1999), 1:28, with the commentary by James Howard-Johnston, 2:172–73. The general assumption in

earlier scholarly literature was the spring of this year; cf. Dölger, *Regesten der Kaiserurkunden*, no. 104, 13. Since the study by Higgins, *The Persian War*, 42–54, the autumn dating has established itself; see, for instance, Zakythinos, *Byzantinische Geschichte*, 51; Theophylact Simocatta, trans. Schreiner, 321, n. 793; trans. Whitby and Whitby, 155 n. 86; Whitby, *The Emperor Maurice and His Historian*, 302–4.

7. Friedrich Karl Ginzel, *Spezieller Kanon der Sonnen- und Mondfinsternisse für das Ländergebiet der klassischen Altertumswissenschaften und den Zeitraum von 900 vor Chr. bis 600 nach Chr.* (Berlin, 1899), 227.

8. For the embassy, see Theophylact Simocatta 6.3, 161–62; for Theuderic, see Fredegar 4.16, 11. On the date (between the end of March and July 596), see Reinhard Schneider, *Königswahl und Königserhebung im Frühmittelalter* (Stuttgart, 1972), 131; Peter Schreiner, "Eine merowingische Gesandtschaft in Konstantinopel (590?)," *Frühmittelalterliche Studien* 19 (1985): 198; Eugen Ewig, *Die Merowinger und das Imperium*, Rhein.-westfäl. AW, Vorträge G 261 (Opladen, 1983), 48.

9. Howorth, "The Avars"; John Bagnell Bury, "The Chronology of Theophylaktos Simokatta," *English Historical Review* 3 (1888): 310; Moravcsik, *Byzantinoturcica*, 1:344; Dölger, *Regesten der Kaiserurkunden*, no. 102, 12. Most of these scholars assume a break in the accounts of the wars from approximately 594 to 599, e.g., Kollautz and Miyakawa, 1:249. This results in a curious imbalance in the account of the events of the war. The first campaigns were divided up among several years, while numerous accounts of operations in the field had to be compressed to the years around 600.

10. Gerard Labuda, "Chronologie des guerres de Byzance contre les Avares et les Slaves à la fin du VIe siècle," *Byzantinoslavica* 11 (1950): 170; subsequently, Fritze, "Zur Bedeutung der Awaren," 539–40; similar view in Avenarius, *Die Awaren in Europa*, 219–20; for the war starting only in 597, see Timothy Alan Duket, *A Study in Byzantine Historiography: An Analysis of Theophanes' "Chronographia" and Its Relationship to Theophylact's "History"* (Boston, 1980), especially the table at 17–18, 23–25 and 52–55. His war year 598 is particularly eventful since he situates both Slavic campaigns of Priscus and Peter then. How Priscus could then reject the emperor's command on staying for the winter in barbarian lands, having already been recalled in the middle of the summer, remains unexplained.

11. Haussig, "Theophylakts Exkurs," 293–95 and 406–8 (593); Nystazopoulou-Pelekidou, "Symbolē," 145–47 (592); Theophylact Simocatta, ed. Whitby and Whitby, 167 n. 35; Curta, *Making of the Slavs*, 100–101 (593). An extensive discussion is also to be found in the German edition of this book: Pohl, *Die Awaren*, 128–30.

12. Procopius, *Anecdota* 18.14–21, ed. and trans. Dewing, 217.

13. Theophylact Simocatta 5.16, 155.

14. Theophylact Simocatta 6.1, 158.

15. Theophylact Simocatta 2.10–17, 56–68. During the two great campaigns of 584 and 586 the Avars apparently did not reach Heraclea, but the Slavs, at the same time, most likely did. It is tempting to turn the chronology around and to put the incursion, which in Theophylact follows Maurice's campaign—with a battle near Heraclea—earlier, as in Szádeczky-Kardoss, *Ein Versuch*, 75–77. The strange reversal in the course of events—Heraclea being battered by the Avars after the city had been compensated for that very reason—seems to betray the reworking of the account of Maurice's expedition. For dating Maurice's campaign to 598, see Whitby and Whitby, *The History of Theophylact Simocatta*, 200 n. 73.

16. Theophylact Simocatta 6.10, 56–68.

17. Theophylact Simocatta 6.2, 160. On this subject, see Herrmann, "Byzanz und die Slawen"; see section 4.5.

18. Theophylact Simocatta 6.3, 162.

19. Gregory of Tours, *Decem libri historiarum* 8.17, ed. Krusch and Levison, 384; 9.25, 444–45; 10.4, 486–87; Paul the Deacon, *Historia Langobardorum* 3.17, ed. Waitz, 123; 3.22, 127; 3.29, 133; Telemachos C. Lounghis, *Les ambassades byzantines en occident* (Athens, 1980), 466–67; Paul Goubert, *Byzance avant l'Islam*, vol. 2, *Byzance et l'occident sous les successeurs de Justinien*, bk. 1, *Byzance et les Francs* (Paris, 1956), 165–73; he situates the mission of Boso and Betto in the year 592, ibid., 90; Ewig, *Die Merowinger und das Imperium*, 44–46.

20. Lounghis, *Les ambassades byzantines en occident*, 467; Goubert, *Byzance avant l'Islam*, 2.1:82–85.

21. Paul the Deacon, *Historia Langobardorum* 4.11, ed. Waitz, 150; Fritze, "Zur Bedeutung der Awaren," 536; see section 5.6.

22. Paul the Deacon, *Historia Langobardorum* 4.7, ed. Waitz, 146; see section 5.6.

23. Theophylact Simocatta 6.3.9–6.6.1, 161–67; Theophanes, *Chronographia* 6084, 392–93. On these events, see Szádeczky-Kardoss, *Ein Versuch*, 77 (592 or 595–96); Howorth, "The Avars," 759 (592); Bury, *History of the Later Roman Empire*, 2:126 (591); Avenarius, *Die Awaren in Europa*, 103 (596); Hauptmann, "Les rapports," 160 (592); Beševliev, *Die protobulgarische Periode*, 108 (593); Popović, "Les témoins archéologiques," 476 (592 or rather 593, arguing on the basis of coin finds); Curta, *Making of the Slavs*, 100 (593). Whitby, *The Emperor Maurice and His Historian*, 152–53, argues for 588 because of similarities with accounts of an Avar attack in Evagrius 6.10, trans. Whitby, 301 (Avars penetrate twice to the Long Wall and capture Singidunum and Anchialus—however, in Theophylact 6.4.3, 163, the siege of Singidunum is abandoned) and John of Ephesus, and because of a letter by Pope Gregory I to Priscus in July 593 (Gregory the Great, *Registrum epistularum* 3.51, ed. Norberg, 1:196) congratulating him on having recuperated imperial grace, which is harder to imagine if he had been continuously in command in 592/93. Theophylact could have misunderstood that there was a pause of more than a year between the first two campaigns of Priscus. The same dating in *PLRE*, 3B s.v. Priscus 6, 1052–57. The argument is attractive, but not quite conclusive.

24. Theophylact Simocatta 6.4, 163–64. Theophylact's account invites the assumption that after the capture of the city in 584, Singidunum was soon reoccupied by the Romans. In 592, in any case, the city was and remained Roman, and in 595 fell only temporarily into Avar hands.

25. The Greek *parasang* measured about 3.6 miles.

26. Menander, frag. 25.1, ed. and trans. Blockley, 216–18; cf. section 3.4.

27. Thus, for example, Mirković, "Sirmium," 58; Hauptmann, "Les rapports," 160.

28. Theophylact Simocatta 3.1–3, 72–76; Theophanes, *Chronographia* 6079, 382.

29. On the following, see Theophylact Simocatta 6.4, 163–64; Theophanes, *Chronographia* 6084, 392–93, who explicitly assigns blame for the outbreak of war on the emperor.

30. Theophylact Simocatta 6.5, 165.

31. *Strategicon* 9.2, 307.

32. Theophylact Simocatta 6.5, 166.

33. Theophylact Simocatta 6.6.7, 167.

34. Cf. Wolfram, *History of the Goths*, 67; Peter Heather, "The Late Roman Art of Client Management: Imperial Defence in the Fourth Century West," in Pohl, Wood, and Reimitz, *Transformation of Frontiers*, 15–68; Curta, "Frontier Ethnogenesis in Late Antiquity."

35. Theophylact Simocatta 1.7.5, 29; cf. section 4.6.

36. On the following, see Theophylact Simocatta 6.6, 167–68; Theophanes, *Chronographia* 6085, 394; Howorth, "The Avars," 760 (593); Ensslin, "Slaveneinfälle," 702 (592); Kollautz and Miyakawa, 1:250 (593); Labuda, "Chronologie des guerres de Byzance," 170 (596); Nystazopoulou-Pelekidou, "Symbolē," 163 (593); Avenarius, *Die Awaren in Europa*,

104–7 (597); Whitby, *The Emperor Maurice and His Historian*, 158–60 (593); Curta, *Making of the Slavs*, 100–101 (593). On Gento, see *PLRE*, 3A:512–13.

37. Theophylact Simocatta 6.7.8, 168. What exactly this refers to is unclear; the "terms . . . for a minimal sum" negotiated by Priscus after the emperor's ruse in the preceding chapter (6.5.16, 166) are the only possible cross-reference in the text.

38. Theophylact Simocatta 6.7, 168–70; Theophanes, *Chronographia* 6085, 394.

39. Theophylact Simocatta 6.8, 170–71.

40. Theophylact Simocatta 6.9.1, 172.

41. Theophylact Simocatta 6.9.11, 173.

42. Theophylact Simocatta 6.9, 171–73; Theophanes, *Chronographia* 6085, 394.

43. Theophylact Simocatta 6.10, 173; Theophanes, *Chronographia* 6086, 395–96.

44. *Strategicon* 11.4, 376.

45. Theophylact Simocatta 6.10, 173, and 6.11, 176.

46. Theophylact Simocatta 6.11, 176.

47. Theophylact Simocatta 6.11.6, 176.

48. Roger C. Blockley, "Doctors as Diplomats in the Sixth Century A.D.," *Florilegium* 2 (1980): 89–100.

49. Theophylact Simocatta 6.11.17, 178.

50. Against Avar rule over the Slavs at the lower Danube: Lemerle, "Invasions et migrations," 291; Ferluga, "Gli Slavi del sud," 312; Ditten, "Zur Bedeutung der Einwanderung der Slawen," 90; in favor: Hauptmann, "Les rapports," 158. Differentiating between actual and potential power, Avenarius, *Die Awaren in Europa*, 104–6. "The Slavs had become a bone of contention between the Empire and the qaganate": Curta, *Making of the Slavs*, 103.

51. Theophylact Simocatta 6.11.18, 178.

52. Slavic war of 578: Menander, frag. 21, ed. and trans. Blockley, 192–95; treaty of 598: Theophylact Simocatta 7.15.14, 201.

53. For this and the following, see Theophylact Simocatta 7.1, 179–80; Theophanes, *Chronographia* 6088–89, 398–400; Howorth, "The Avars," 765–66; Whitby, *The Emperor Maurice and His Historian*, 160; Curta, *Making of the Slavs*, 103–4.

54. On the customary pay for soldiers, see Jones, *The Later Roman Empire*, 1:314: "Hitherto the soldiers had received cash allowances for their arms and uniforms, and had no doubt not always spent them for these purposes." A differing view in Theophylact Simocatta, trans. Schreiner, 335, n. 902, who, along with Robert Grosse, *Römische Militärgeschichte von Gallienus bis zum Beginn der byzantinischen Themenverfassung* (Berlin, 1920), 243, assumes that this *typos* on the emperor's part entailed no real modification.

55. Zaldapa is attested in Procopius, *De aedificiis* 4.11, ed. and trans. Dewing, 315, in the Moesian interior; it lay on the route that Petrus somewhat later took to the Danube. Cf. Velkov, *Cities in Thrace and Dacia*, 109. For Aquis/Akys and Scopi/Skopis, see Veselin Beševliev, "Bemerkungen über die antiken Heerstraßen in Ostteil der Balkanhalbinsel," *Klio* 51 (1969): 493.

56. Theophylact Simocatta 7.2, 180–82; Nystazopoulou-Pelekidou, "Symbolē," 197.

57. Theophylact Simocatta 7.3, 182–83; Theophanes, *Chronographia* 6089, 399–400. On this topic, see Dietrich Claude, *Die byzantinische Stadt im 6. Jahrhundert* (Munich, 1960), 130–31; Liebeschuetz, *Decline and Fall of the Ancient City*, 188.

58. Theophylact Simocatta 7.4, 183–84; Theophanes, *Chronographia* 6089, 275. Cf. Beševliev, *Die protobulgarische Periode*, 88; Samuel Szádeczky-Kardoss, "Eine unbeachtete Quellenstelle über die Protobulgaren am Ende des 6. Jahrhunderts," *Bulgarian Historical Review* 11, no. 2 (1983): 78; Ziemann, *Vom Wandervolk zur Großmacht*, 118–19.

59. Beševliev, *Die protobulgarische Periode*, 112.

60. Theophylact Simocatta 7.5, 184–86.

61. On the events of the year, see Theophylact Simocatta 7.7.1–5, 187–88; Theophanes, *Chronographia* 6090, 401. Bury, *History of the Later Roman Empire*, 2:136 (598); Kollautz and Miyakawa, 1:250 (596); Avenarius, *Die Awaren in Europa*, 106 (599); Whitby, *The Emperor Maurice and His Historian*, 161 (595).

62. Upper Novae is probably the Novae/Čezava above the Iron Gate, which Justinian had fortified: Procopius, *De aedificiis* 4.6, ed. and trans. Dewing, 269; Popović, "Les témoins archéologiques," 476; Mócsy, *Pannonia and Upper Moesia*; Theophylact Simocatta, trans. Schreiner, 340, n. 949. A different identification in Veselin Beševliev, *Zur Deutung der Kastellnamen in Prokops Werk "De aedificiis"* (Amsterdam, 1970), 118 (with a ruin near Bononia/Vidin). Theophylact writes that Priscus had crossed the river three days before the arrival in Upper Novae, and Čezava lay on the Roman bank of the river. Just which maneuver the general executed at the Iron Gate remains unclear; perhaps he tried to erect a bridgehead on the left bank of the Danube.

63. Chrysos, "Die Nordgrenze," 34–35.

64. Theophylact introduces an Avar envoy as Priscus's counterpart but then, as elsewhere, has the khagan himself speak in a heightening of the dramatic effect; Theophylact Simocatta 7.7.4–5, 187–88.

65. Theophylact Simocatta 7.7.6–7.9, 188–91; see section 2.3–4.

66. De la Vaissière, "Maurice et le qaghan"; de la Vaissière, "Theophylact's Turkish Exkurs Revisited," 91; see section 3.3 and 3.5.

67. Theophylact Simocatta 7.10–11, 191–94. Perhaps he camped on the island near present-day Vinca, about twenty miles from Belgrade: Fraňo Barišić, "Visantijski Singidunum," *Zbornik Radova* 3 (1955): 11; Kollautz and Miyakawa, 1:250.

68. Theophylact Simocatta 7.10–11, 193–94.

69. Popović, "Les témoins archéologiques," 477.

70. Theophylact Simocatta 7.11, 194; Theophanes, *Chronographia* 6090, 401 (adding to his account based on Theophylact, probably by mistake, that Priscus had driven the Bulgars out of Singidunum).

71. Theophylact Simocatta 7.12, 195; Theophanes, *Chronographia* 6091, 402 (placed in the following year); Howorth, "The Avars," 769 (598); Hauptmann, "Les rapports," 161 (595); Bury, *History of the Later Roman Empire*, 2:136–38 (598); Moravcsik, *Byzantinoturcica*, 1:544 (598–99); Avenarius, *Die Awaren in Europa*, 220 (spring 599); Kollautz and Miyakawa, 1:250 (spring 596); Popović, "Les témoins archéologiques," 476 (597).

72. Varying localizations in Beševliev, *Zur Deutung der Kastellnamen*, 96; Louis de Voinovitch, *Histoire de la Dalmatie*, 2 vols. (Paris, 1934), 1:238; Popović, "Les témoins archéologiques," 486. The name may simply be misspelled in the transmitted text.

73. Theophylact Simocatta 7.12, 195. After Guduin's surprise attack, Theophanes has the khagan return to his own lands but make a large-scale invasion into Thrace the next year (*Chronographia* 6091, 401, and 6092, 402). On the dating of the eighteen-month interval (autumn 595 until summer 597), see section 5.1.

74. Gregory the Great, *Registrum epistularum* 2.19, ed. Norberg, 1:18–19; 3.22, 1:167–68; 4.16, 1:234–35; 4.20, 1:238; 5.39, 1:317; 6.3, 1:371; 6.25, 1:395–97; 6.26, 1:397–98.

75. John J. Wilkes, *Dalmatia*, History of the Provinces of the Roman Empire (London, 1969), 436, connects the loss of the interior of the province of Dalmatia with the khagan's campaign. Yet this does not mean that Bosnia was now occupied by Slavs overnight; the devastation of some areas along the main routes simply facilitated the gradual settlement of the Slavs. See also Dzino, *Becoming Slav, Becoming Croat*, 88 and 97.

76. On Slavic expansion, see section 4.1 and 4.5–6.

77. Heinrich Berg, "Bischöfe und Bischofssitze im Ostalpen- und Donauraum vom 4. bis zum 8. Jahrhundert," in *Die Bayern und ihre Nachbarn*, vol. 1, ed. Herwig Wolfram and Andreas Schwarcz, DsÖAW 179 (Vienna, 1985), 82; Harald Krahwinkler, *Friaul im*

Frühmittelalter: Geschichte einer Region vom Ende des 5. bis zum Ende des 10. Jahrhunderts (Vienna, 1992), 69–76.

78. Edited in Gregory the Great, *Registrum epistularum* 1.16a, ed. Paul Ewald and Ludwig Hartmann, MGH Epp. 1 (Berlin, 1891), 17–21; new edition in *Concilium Universale Constantinopolitanum sub Iustiniano habitum, Acta Conciliorum Oecumenicorum* 4/2, ed. Eduard Schwartz (Berlin, 1959), 132–35. For the Three-Chapter Controversy, see Celia Chazelle and Catherine Cubitt, eds., *The Crisis of the Oikoumene: The Three Chapters and the Failed Quest for Unity in the Sixth-Century Mediterranean*, Studies in the Early Middle Ages 14 (Turnhout, 2007); on Aquileia's role in it, see Claire Sotinel, "The Three Chapters and the Transformations of Italy," in Chazelle and Cubitt, *Crisis of the Oikoumene*, 115–19. See also Rajko Bratož, "Der Metropolitansprengel von Aquileia vom 5. bis zum frühen 7. Jahrhundert," in *Die Ausgrabungen im spätantik-frühmittelalterlichen Bischofssitz Sabiona-Säben in Südtirol*, vol. 1, bk. 2, *Frühchristliche Kirche und Gräberfeld*, ed. Volker Bierbrauer and Hans Nothdurfter (Munich, 2015), 665–700.

79. Paul the Deacon, *Historia Langobardorum* 3.26, ed. Waitz, 129. The list may not enumerate all participants, but only the principal exponents of both camps; see Berg, "Bischöfe und Bischofssitze," 81–82.

80. *Concilium Mantuanum*, ed. Albert Werminghoff, MGH Concilia 2.2 (Hanover, 1908), 588. See Berg, "Bischöfe und Bischofssitze," 78–80; Wolfram, *Grenzen und Räume*, 97–98.

81. John the Deacon, *Istoria Veneticorum* 1.11, ed. Andrea Berto (Bologna, 1999), 62. Used in Pio Paschini, *Storia del Friuli*, vol. 1, *Dalle origini al formarsi dello stato patriarcale*, 3rd ed. (Udine, 1975), 100; seen as derived from the list of 572/77 in Berg, "Bischöfe und Bischofssitze," 79–80.

82. Paul the Deacon, *Historia Langobardorum* 3.26, ed. Waitz, 129. Berg, "Bischöfe und Bischofssitze," 85–86; Rajko Bratož, "Das Christentum in Slowenien in der Spätantike," in *Kulturhistorische und archäologische Probleme des Südostalpenraumes in der Spätantike: Symposion Klagenfurt 1981*, ed. Herbert Grassl (Vienna, 1985), 41, regards 591 as the terminal date for the bishoprics in Slovenia; see also Bratož, "Die Auswanderung der Bevölkerung aus den pannonischen Provinzen," 608–11.

83. Gregory the Great, *Registrum epistularum* 9.155, ed. Norberg, 2:110–11.

84. *Concilium Mantuanum*, ed. Werminghoff, 588, l. 17. Identification with Siscia: Jacques Zeiller, *Les origines chrétiennes dans les provinces danubiennes de l'empire romain* (Paris, 1906), 140; Popović, "Les témoins archéologiques," 465.

85. Paschini, *Storia del Friuli*, 78; Carlo de Franceschi, "Saggi e considerazioni sull'Istria nell'alto medioevo, 2. Cessensis episcopus," *Atti e Memorie della Società per la Storia dell'Istria* 18 (1970): 69–106. Also pointing to the submerged bishopric is the signature of an Ursinus on a protocol from the Roman synod of 680; according to the Greek version he was "episkopos Keisou eparchias Istrias," but in the contemporary Latin version, edited in *Sacrorum conciliorum nova et amplissima collectio* 11, ed. Joannes D. Mansi (Paris, 1901), 311, the form *Cenetensis* (for Ceneda) is found.

86. Paul the Deacon, *Historia Langobardorum* 4.7, ed. Waitz, 146.

87. Glaser, *Frühes Christentum im Alpenraum*, 96–148; Glaser, "Der Untergang der Antike"; Ladstätter, "Von Noricum Mediterraneum zur Provincia Sclaborum."

88. Glaser, *Frühes Christentum im Alpenraum*, 88–89.

89. Slavko Ciglenečki, "Castra und Höhensiedlungen vom 3. bis 6. Jahrhundert in Slowenien," in *Höhensiedlungen zwischen Antike und Mittelalter von den Ardennen bis zur Adria*, ed. Heiko Steuer and Volker Bierbrauer (Berlin, 2008), 481–532.

90. Cf. Paul the Deacon, *Historia Langobardorum* 4.39, ed. Waitz, 133 (battle between Bavarians and Slavs at Aguntum, near the *Baioariorum termini*). Fritze, "Zur Bedeutung der Awaren," 537, n.170; Herwig Wolfram, "Ethnogenesen im frühmittelalterlichen

Donau- und Ostalpenraum (6. bis 10. Jahrhundert)," in *Frühmittelalterliche Ethnogenese im Alpenraum*, ed. Helmut Beumann and Werner Schröder, Nationes 5 (Sigmaringen, 1985), 126.

91. Paul the Deacon, *Historia Langobardorum* 4.7, ed. Waitz, 146; Kurt Reindel, "Das Zeitalter der Agilolfinger: Die politische Entwicklung," in *Handbuch der bayerischen Geschichte*, vol. 1, ed. Max Spindler, 2nd ed. (Munich, 1981), 143; Hans-Dietrich Kahl, "Die Baiern und ihre Nachbarn bis zum Tode des Herzogs Theodo (717–718)," in Wolfram and Schwarcz, *Die Bayern und ihre Nachbarn*, 182–83.

92. Paul the Deacon, *Historia Langobardorum* 4.4, ed. Waitz, 145.

93. Gregory the Great, *Registrum epistularum* 1.16b, ed. Ewald and Hartmann, 20; ed. Schwartz, 134–35; Paul Goubert, *Byzance avant l'Islam*, vol. 2, *Byzance et l'occident sous les successeurs de Justinien*, bk. 2, *Rome, Byzance et Carthage* (Paris, 1965), 102; Krahwinkler, *Friaul im Frühmittelalter*, 75–76.

94. Wolfram, *Salzburg, Bayern, Österreich*, 36–38.

95. Paul the Deacon, *Historia Langobardorum* 4.10, ed. Waitz, 150; Fritze, "Zur Bedeutung der Awaren," 536–38 (595); Avenarius, *Die Awaren in Europa*, 117 (595); Krahwinkler, *Friaul im Frühmittelalter*, 36 (595); Wolfram, *Grenzen und Räume*, 78 (595); Labuda, "Chronologie des guerres de Byzance," 171 (594–95); Kollautz, "Awaren, Langobarden und Slawen in Noricum und Istrien," 633–36 (595). It is perhaps no coincidence that in 592 and 595 the Bavarians exploited Avar-Byzantine wars for their attacks on the Slavs.

96. Paul the Deacon, *Historia Langobardorum* 4.11, ed. Waitz, 150; Fritze, "Zur Bedeutung der Awaren," 536–38 ("spring 596 at the very earliest"); Avenarius, *Die Awaren in Europa*, 119 (596); Ewig, *Die Merowinger und das Imperium*, 48 (596).

97. Paul the Deacon, *Historia Langobardorum* 4.12, ed. Waitz, 150.

98. Paul the Deacon, *Historia Langobardorum* 4.13, ed. Waitz, 150.

99. Theophylact Simocatta 7.13–15, 196–201; Theophanes, *Chronographia* 6092, 403–4. On this and the following, see Szádeczky-Kardoss, *Ein Versuch*, 80 (598 or 600); Howorth, "The Avars," 770 (599); Bury, *History of the Later Roman Empire*, 2:138 (600); Avenarius, *Die Awaren in Europa*, 106 (601); Haussig, "Theophylakts Exkurs," 296 (598); Kollautz and Miyakawa, 1:253 (596); Nystazopoulou-Pelekidou, "Symbolē," 174 (598); Beševliev, *Die protobulgarische Periode*, 115 (600); Whitby, *The Emperor Maurice and His Historian*, 161–63 (598).

100. Theophylact Simocatta 7.13, 196–97.

101. Nicopolis ad Istrum/Nikjüp; cf. Procopius, *De aedificiis* 4.11, ed. and trans. Dewing, 313; Poulter, *Nicopolis ad Istrum*; Mark Whittow, "Nicopolis ad Istrum: Backward and Balkan?," *Proceedings of the British Academy* 141 (2007): 375–89. What further happened with Priscus's army we do not know. It was not until the following year that Comentiolus joined forces with him in Singidunum. Sucidava is here called Sikidiba (Beševliev, *Zur Deutung der Kastellnamen*, 141; identification doubted by Schreiner, "Städte und Wegenetz," 68).

102. Theophylact Simocatta 7.14, 198–99; Theophanes, *Chronographia* 6092, 403. Later chronicles, for instance Zonaras (14.13, ed. Büttner-Wobst, 296) and George the Monk (Georgios Monachos), *Chronicon*, ed. Karl de Boor, 2 vols. (Leipzig, 1904), 2:658, move Comentiolus's treason even further to the center of their account. It explains at one and the same time the defeat at the hands of the Avars and the fall of Maurice. See, too, the *Byzantine Chronicle* 1.13, ed. Peter Schreiner, *Die Byzantinischen Kleinchroniken*, vol. 3 (Vienna, 1979), 11–16, at 13–14.

103. Theophylact Simocatta 8.1.9–10, 210; *PLRE*, 3A:321–25. On Theophylact's bias against Comentiolus, see Whitby, *The Emperor Maurice and His Historian*, 94–104 and 210–11. But even if it was not for treachery, Comentiolus must have organized the retreat from Iatrus rather badly.

104. John of Antioch, *Fragmenta ex historia chronica* 316, ed. Roberto, 546.

105. Michael the Syrian 10.24, 374–75; Szádeczky-Kardoss, "Eine unbeachtete Quellenstelle," 77.

106. Theophylact Simocatta 7.14, 199; cf. the passage at 6.5.2, 166–67, where the church is located at Anchialus, but burned down just before an attack on Drizipera; this may also be a doublet.

107. Theophylact Simocatta 7.15, 200–201.

108. Chrysos, "Die Nordgrenze," 36–37, who extensively discusses the significance of the treaty; see, further, Avenarius, "Zur Problematik der awarisch-slawischen Beziehungen," 23.

109. Theophanes, *Chronographia* 6092, 404.

110. *Strategicon* 8.2, 297; 10.2, 341.

111. *Strategicon* 7.11, 251.

112. Theophylact Simocatta 8.1.9–8.4.2, 210–13; Theophanes, *Chronographia* 6093, 407–8; Howorth, "The Avars," 773–74 (601); Bury, *History of the Later Roman Empire*, 2:140–41 (600); Haussig, "Theophylakts Exkurs," 296 (599); Goubert, "Les guerres sur le Danube," 118 (601); Labuda, "Chronologie des guerres de Byzance," 170 (600); Kollautz and Miyakawa, 1:254 (600); Stratos, *Byzantium in the Seventh Century*, 1:44 (602); Avenarius, *Die Awaren in Europa*, 108 (601); Whitby, *The Emperor Maurice and His Historian*, 164 (599).

113. The heights on which the Romans had drawn up were perhaps the Roman entrenchments between Kubin and Alibunar, where there were once extensive marshes: Kollautz, "Abaria," in *Reallexikon der Byzantinistik*, 1.2:5.

114. Theophylact Simocatta 8.3, 288; Theophanes, *Chronographia* 6093, 282.

115. *Strategicon* 7.12, 255, counsels staying on the attack "until the decisive annihilation" of the enemy.

116. *Strategicon* 11.2, 363.

117. Theophylact Simocatta 6.6.6–12, 167–68; Pohl, "Perceptions of Barbarian Violence."

118. Theophylact Simocatta 8.3.15, 213; Theophanes, *Chronographia* 6093, 407.

119. Theophylact Simocatta 8.4.2, 213. Szádeczky-Kardoss is of the opinion that only the "real" Avars, but not prisoners from among their ancillary peoples, were freed; see "Die Hauptzüge der Sozialordnung des Awarenkhaganats im Zeitalter der regesten byzantinisch-awarischen Verbindungen," in his *Avarica*, 220. In fact, in this passage Theophylact speaks only of the captured Avars. Yet it is just as possible that by this he understands all those belonging to the Avar army.

120. On the Via Traiana, see Beševliev, "Bemerkungen über die antiken Heerstraßen," 484–85.

121. Theophylact Simocatta 8.4, 214; Theophanes, *Chronographia* 6093, 408.

122. Theophylact Simocatta 8.4.9, 214.

123. Paul the Deacon, *Historia Langobardorum* 4.24, ed. Waitz, 156. Krahwinkler, *Friaul im Frühmittelalter*, 39; Fritze, "Zur Bedeutung der Awaren," 520–23.

124. Paul the Deacon, *Historia Langobardorum* 4.20, ed. Waitz, 154. This information is difficult to incorporate. In Paul the Deacon it is found in the same chapter as the capture of Agilulf's daughter by the exarch Callinicus in the spring of 601. See Ludo Moritz Hartmann, *Geschichte Italiens im Mittelalter*, vol. 2, bk. 1, *Römer und Langobarden bis zur Theilung Italiens* (Gotha, 1900), 115; Kollautz, "Völkerbewegungen an der unteren und mittleren Donau," 480.

125. Paul the Deacon, *Historia Langobardorum* 4.24, ed. Waitz, 156. Hartmann, *Geschichte Italiens im Mittelalter*, 115–16 (601); Krahwinkler, *Friaul im Frühmittelalter*, 39 (602); Fritze, "Zur Bedeutung der Awaren," 520 and 535.

126. Gregory the Great, *Registrum epistularum* 9.155, ed. Norberg, 2:710.

127. Paul the Deacon, *Historia Langobardorum* 4.28, ed. Waitz, 128.

128. On the chronology of Maurice's last years, see Whitby, *The Emperor Maurice and His Historian*, 164–69.

129. Probably the *Palatiolum* in Procopius, *De aedificiis* 4.6, ed. and trans. Dewing, 279, in the vicinity of the mouth of the Osam. Cf. Beševliev, *Zur Deutung der Kastellnamen*, 121; Theophylact Simocatta, trans. Schreiner, 365, n. 1082.

130. Theophylact Simocatta 8.5, 216–17; Theophanes, *Chronographia* 6094, 409–10. Szádeczky-Kardoss, *Ein Versuch*, 83 (601); Howorth, "The Avars," 775–76 (602); Bury, *History of the Later Roman Empire*, 2:141 (601); Labuda, "Chronologie des guerres de Byzance," 170 (602); Goubert, "Les guerres sur le Danube," 118 (601); Stratos, *Byzantium in the Seventh Century*, 1:44 (602); Whitby, *The Emperor Maurice and His Historian*, 164; on Apsikh, see section 6.5.

131. Theophylact Simocatta 8.5.13, 217. On the events of this year, see Howorth, "The Avars," 776–77; Bury, *History of the Later Roman Empire*, 2:142; Avenarius, *Die Awaren in Europa*, 109; Stratos, *Byzantium in the Seventh Century*, 1:44–45.

132. John of Ephesus 5.47, 260.

133. Theophylact Simocatta 8.61, 217.

134. Gregory the Great, *Registrum epistularum* 14.10, ed. Norberg, 2:1079 (603); Hartmann, *Geschichte Italiens im Mittelalter*, 123; *PLRE*, 3A:561–62.

135. Theophylact Simocatta 8.6–7, 218–20.

136. The order in fact corresponds to the advice given in *Strategicon* 11.4, 381, which suggests transporting provisions from Slavic lands into the empire. Cf. Curta, "Peasants as 'Makeshift Soldiers for the Occasion,'" 212.

6. LIFE AND ORGANIZATION IN THE AVAR EMPIRE

1. The definition given by the Central Eurasian Studies program website at Harvard (http://cesww.fas.harvard.edu/ces_definition.html) excludes most European steppes, which would have to be included in the first millennium CE. See also István Zimonyi and Osman Karatay, eds., *Central Eurasia in the Middle Ages: Studies in Honour of Peter B. Golden* (Wiesbaden, 2016).

2. Overview of the subject in Sinor, *Introduction à l'étude de l'Eurasie centrale*, with annotated bibliography; Barthold, *Histoire des Turcs*; Haussig, *Die Geschichte Zentralasiens*; Grousset, *Empire of the Steppes*; Anatoly M. Khazanov, *Nomads and the Outside World*, Studies in Social Anthropology 44 (Cambridge, 1984); Peter B. Golden, *An Introduction to the History of the Turkic Peoples* (Wiesbaden, 1992); David Christian, *A History of Russia, Central Asia and Mongolia*, vol. 1, *Inner Eurasia from Prehistory to the Mongol Empire* (Oxford, 1998); Vásáry, *Geschichte des frühen Innerasiens*; Litvinsky, Guang-da, and Samghabadi, *History of Civilizations of Central Asia*; Svat Soucek, *A History of Inner Asia* (Cambridge, 2000).

3. See Di Cosmo, "China-Steppe Relations in Historical Perspective," 53–54. Generally on the problems of comparison, see Walter Pohl, "Introduction: Meanings of Community and the Uses of Terminology," in *Meanings of Community across Medieval Eurasia*, ed. Walter Pohl, Christina Lutter, and Eirik Hovden (Leiden, 2016), 1–20; Pohl, "Ethnicity and Empire."

4. Deleuze and Guattari, *A Thousand Plateaus*, 394: "Historians, bourgeois or Soviet (Grousset or Vladimirtsov), consider the nomads a pitiable segment of humanity that understands nothing"; nomads should be "defined not by ignorance but by their positive characteristics, by their specific space, by a composition all their own that broke with lineages and warded off the state-form." Gavin Hambly, *Zentralasien*, Fischer-Weltgeschichte 16 (Frankfurt am Main, 1966), 23, calls attention to the great sense of self-worth of the

central Asian nomads, who in their turn despised the sedentary peoples. Cf. also Ildikó Ecsedy, "Nomads in History and Historical Research," *Acta Orient. Hung.* 35 (1981): 201–27; Christian, *History of Russia, Central Asia and Mongolia,* 3–20. Nomadism as primitive and immutable: Vásáry, *Geschichte des frühen Innerasiens,* 19–20.

5. Hambly, *Zentralasien,* 20; Khazanov, *Nomads and the Outside World,* 19–25; Christian, *History of Russia, Central Asia and Mongolia,* 124–34; Di Cosmo, *Ancient China and Its Enemies,* 22–31.

6. Overview in Lawrence Krader, *Peoples of Central Asia* (Bloomington, 1963); Owen Lattimore, *Inner Asian Frontiers of China,* 2nd ed. (New York, 1951), 61–65; Ali Asghar Askarov, Vitali Volkov, and Namsraïn Ser-Odjav, "Pastoral and Nomadic Tribes at the Beginning of the First Millennium B.C.," in *History of Civilizations of Central Asia,* vol. 1, *The Dawn of Civilisation: Earliest Times to 700 B.C.,* ed. Ahmad Hasan Dani and Vadim Mikhaïlovich Masson (Paris, 1992), 459–75.

7. Nikolay N. Kradin, "Nomadic Empires in Inner Asia," in Bemmann and Schmauder, *Complexity of Interaction,* 21.

8. Golden, *Central Asia in World History,* 12.

9. Perry Anderson, *Passages from Antiquity to Feudalism* (London, 1975), 221.

10. Kradin, "Nomadic Empires in Inner Asia," 21.

11. Peter B. Golden, "Nomads and Their Sedentary Neighbors in Pre-Činggisid Eurasia," *Archivum Eurasiae Medii Aevi* 7 (1987–91): 41–82; Kradin, "Nomadic Empires in Inner Asia"; Ursula Brosseder, "A Study on the Complexity and Dynamics of Interaction and Exchange in Late Iron Age Eurasia," in Bemmann and Schmauder, *Complexity of Interaction,* 199–332; Di Cosmo, "China-Steppe Relations in Historical Perspective," 62.

12. Kradin, "Nomadic Empires in Inner Asia," 14.

13. David Sneath, *The Headless State: Aristocratic Orders, Kinship Society, and Misrepresentations of Nomadic Inner Asia* (New York, 2007).

14. For the term, see Pekka Hämäläinen, "What's in a Concept? The Kinetic Empire of the Comanches," *History and Theory* 52 (2013): 81–90.

15. On this and the following, see Kradin, "Nomadic Empires in Inner Asia," 12–14; see also Khazanov, *Nomads and the Outside World;* Ernest Gellner, *State and Society in Soviet Thought: Explorations in Social Structures* (Oxford, 1988).

16. Stephen B. Dunn, *The Fall and Rise of the Asiatic Mode of Production* (London, 1982); Boris I. Vladimirtsov, *Le régime social des Mongols: Le Féodalisme nomade* (Paris, 1948).

17. Lewis H. Morgan, *Ancient Society, or Researches in the Lines of Human Progress from Savagery, through Barbarism to Civilization* (London, 1887); Friedrich Engels, *Vom Ursprung der Familie, des Privateigentums und des Staats* [1884], 13th ed. (Berlin, 1977), trans. Eleanor Leacock, *The Origin of the Family, Private Property, and the State* (New York, 1942). See also Khazanov, "'Military Democracy'"; Khazanov, *Nomads and the Outside World,* 228–31; Joachim Herrmann, "Militärische Demokratie und die Übergangsperiode zur Klassengesellschaft," *Ethnographisch-archäologische Zeitschrift* 23 (1982): 11–31. Cf. John F. Haldon, *The State and the Tributary Mode of Production* (London, 1993), 14–69.

18. Hesse, "Der Austausch als stabilisierender Faktor der politischen Herrschaft in der Geschichte der Mongolei," 152.

19. Khazanov, *Nomads and the Outside World,* 123; Anderson, *Passages from Antiquity to Feudalism,* 219.

20. On this point, cf. Ildikó Ecsedy, "Cultivators and Barbarians in Ancient China," *Acta Orient. Hung.* 28 (1974): 227–49.

21. Henri J. M. Claessen and Peter Skalník, eds., *The Early State* (The Hague, 1978).

22. Curta, *Making of the Slavs,* 325–32; for an overview of steppe society, see Kradin, "Nomadic Empires in Inner Asia," 12–15.

23. External dependence: Lattimore, *Inner Asian Frontiers*; nomadic autonomy: Lawrence Krader, *Social Organization of the Mongol-Turkic Pastoral Nomads* (The Hague, 1964); Krader, "The Origins of State among the Nomads of Asia," in Claessen and Skalník, *The Early State*, 93–107.

24. Previous important contributions include Lattimore, *Inner Asian Frontiers*; Wolfgang Eberhard, *China und seine westlichen Nachbarn* (Darmstadt, 1978).

25. Barfield, *The Perilous Frontier*, 2 and 11.

26. For a critique, see M. R. Drompp, "Imperial State Formation in Inner Asia: The Early Turkic Empires (6th to 9th Centuries)," *Acta Orient. Hung.* 58 (2005): 101–11; see also Kradin, "Nomadic Empires in Inner Asia," 24–25.

27. Di Cosmo, *Ancient China and Its Enemies*, 315. See also Di Cosmo, "China-Steppe Relations in Historical Perspective," 63–64.

28. Di Cosmo, "China-Steppe Relations in Historical Perspective," 55.

29. See also Hartog, *Le miroir d'Hérodote*.

30. Skaff, *Sui-Tang China and Its Turko-Mongol Neighbors*, esp. 288–300.

31. Skaff, *Sui-Tang China and Its Turko-Mongol Neighbors*, 288. However, see also the argument about differences between the notions of a heavenly ruler in China and among the Xiongnu and their successors in Di Cosmo, "China-Steppe Relations in Historical Perspective," 66–67; for instance, Chinese emperors got away with poor performance in office much better than steppe rulers.

32. Skaff, *Sui-Tang China and Its Turko-Mongol Neighbors*, 288–89.

33. This was emphasized as early as Wenskus, *Stammesbildung und Verfassung*, 442. Cf. also Czeglédy, "From East to West," 43. For a more recent view, see Di Cosmo, "China-Steppe Relations in Historical Perspective," 55–56.

34. Miyakawa and Kollautz, "Ein Dokument," 11; cf. Roy Andrew Miller and Te-Fen Ling-Hu, *Accounts of Western Nations in the History of the Northern Chou Dynasty* (Berkeley, 1959). Cf. sections 2.2 and 6.10.

35. Di Cosmo, "China-Steppe Relations in Historical Perspective"; Pohl, "Ethnicity and Empire."

36. Thomsen, "Alttürkische Inschriften in der Mongolei," 146–47; the Orkhon inscriptions arose after the reestablishment of the East Turkic khaganate from 700 on. An edition with English translation is found in Tekin, *A Grammar*, 231–95 (this passage at 265); for a more word-by-word translation, see Kültegin inscription, side 1, 11–13, http://bitig.org/?lang=e&mod=1&tid=1&oid=15&m=1, and very similarly, the Bilge Khagan inscription, front side, 10–12, http://bitig.org/?lang=e&mod=1&tid=1&oid=16&m=1. Quite similar processes are described in the *Secret History of the Mongols*; cf. Vladimirtsov, *Le régime social des Mongols*, 90–91; Burchard Brentjes, *Die Ahnen Dschingis Khans* (Berlin, 1988); and David Morgan, *The Mongols* (Oxford, 1986).

37. Thomsen, "Alttürkische Inschriften in der Mongolei," 145; Bilge Khagan inscription, front side, 13, http://bitig.org/?lang=e&mod=1&tid=1&oid=16&m=1.

38. On the Tonyukuk inscription, see Thomsen, "Alttürkische Inschriften in der Mongolei," 168.

39. For a classical model of the relationship between ethnic identity and forms of organization, see Wenskus, *Stammesbildung und Verfassung*. For a recent overview of the debate, see Pohl, "Von der Ethnogenese zur Identitätsforschung."

40. Theodore Syncellus 5.15, ed. and trans. Makk, 14; or trans. Pearse, 9, http://www.tertullian.org/fathers/theodore_syncellus_01_homily.htm.

41. On the Ashina dynasty, see Togan, *Ibn Fadlans Reisebericht*, 274–75; Scharlipp, *Die frühen Türken in Zentralasien*, 18; Stark, "Luxurious Necessities," 475–77; de la Vaissière, "Oncles et frères." For the Turkish wolf saga, which alternatively puts birth or suckling by a wolf bitch at the head of Turkish genealogy, see the Chinese sources translated by Liu

Mau-Tsai, *Die chinesischen Nachrichten*, 1:6 (*Zhou shu*), and 1:40–41 (*Sui shu*); see Denis Sinor, "The Legendary Origin of the Turks," in Denis Sinor, *Studies in Medieval Inner Asia*, Variorum Collected Studies (Aldershot, 1997), no. II, 223–57.

42. Theophylact Simocatta 6.11.10–18, 177–78.

43. The Bilge Khagan inscription: Thomsen, "Alttürkische Inschriften in der Mongolei," 145; front side, 7, http://bitig.org/?lang=e&mod=1&tid=1&oid=16&m=1. A very similar story is told in the Tonyukuk inscription, 3, http://bitig.org/?lang=e&mod=1&tid=1&oid=17&m=1. The Chinese sources are found in Liu Mau-Tsai, *Die chinesischen Nachrichten*, 1:47–49. On the historical background, see Ildikó Ecsedy, "Western Turks in Northern China in the Middle of the 7th Century," *Acta Antiqua Academiae Scientiarum Hungaricae* 28 (1980): 249–58.

44. As Tonyukuk, chief adviser of Bilge Khagan, put it: "For the khagan was in power, I myself was in power too, the country became the country, people became people." 55–56, http://bitig.org/?lang=e&mod=1&tid=1&oid=17&m=1. See also Thomsen, "Alttürkische Inschriften in der Mongolei," 170, and his discussion at 146–47. These are, of course, inscriptions of a khagan and his adviser.

45. Radloff, *Aus Sibirien*, 1:230.

46. Pritsak, "Tribal Names," 66–67.

47. Ildikó Ecsedy, "Tribe and Empire, Tribe and Society in the Turk Age," *Acta Orient. Hung.* 31 (1977): 7–9; Ecsedy, "Tribe and Tribal Society in the 6th Century Turk Empire," *Acta Orient. Hung.* 25 (1972): 245–47; Pritsak, "Tribal Names," 62; Hansgerd Göckenjan, "Zur Stammesstruktur und Heeresorganisation altaischer Völker: Das Dezimalsystem," in *Europa Slavica, Europa Orientalis: Festschrift für Herbert Ludat zum 70. Geburtstag*, ed. Klaus-Detlev Grothusen and Klaus Zernack (Berlin, 1980), 77; Hambly, *Zentralasien*, 21–22.

48. Göckenjan, "Zur Stammesstruktur," 51–53; Wenskus, *Stammesbildung und Verfassung*, 443–44; George Vernadsky, "Das frühe Slawentum: Das Ostslawentum bis zum Mongolensturm," in Altheim, *Historia Mundi*, 254; Herbert Franke, "Fremdherrschaften in China und ihr Einfluss auf die staatlichen Institutionen (10.–14. Jahrhundert)," *Anzeiger der Phil.-Hist. Klasse der Österreichischen Akademie der Wissenschaften* 122 (1985): 56; Czeglédy, "On the Numerical Composition"; Jaroslav Lebedinsky, *Armes et guerriers barbares au temps des grandes invasions* (Paris, 2001), 65–68.

49. Kültegin inscription, cited after Sergey A. Vasyutin, "The Model of the Political Transformation of the Da Liao as an Alternative to the Evolution of the Structures of Authority in the Early Medieval Pastoral Empires of Mongolia," in Bemmann and Schmauder, *Complexity of Interaction*, 393. Andrei N. Kononov, "Terminology of the Definition of the Cardinal Points of the Turkic People," *Acta Orient. Hung.* 31 (1977): 62–64; Robert Bleichsteiner, "Zeremonielle Trinksitten und Raumordnung bei den turko-mongolischen Nomaden," *Archiv für Völkerkunde* 6/7 (1951–52): 197–99; Michael de Ferdinandy, "Die nordeurasischen Reitervölker und der Westen bis zum Mongolensturm," in Altheim, *Historia Mundi*, 184–85; Ilse Laude-Cirtautas, *Der Gebrauch der Farbbezeichnungen in den Türkdialekten*, Ural-Altaische Bibliothek 10 (Wiesbaden, 1961); Annemarie von Gabain, "Inhalt und magische Bedeutung der alttürkischen Inschriften," *Anthropos* 48 (1953): 537–56.

50. Bleichsteiner, "Zeremonielle Trinksitten," 197.

51. *Sui shu*, in Liu Mau-Tsai, *Die chinesischen Nachrichten*, 1:41–42.

52. Omeljan Pritsak, "The Distinctive Features of the Pax Nomadica," in *Popoli delle steppe*, 2:749–80; Pritsak, "Tribal Names," 68–72; cf. Pritsak, "The Slavs and the Avars," with a rather one-sided, *Männerbund*-centered theory of the "Avar *pax*." See also Scharlipp, *Die frühen Türken in Zentralasien*, 62–67; Christian, *History of Russia, Central Asia and Mongolia*, 149–57 ("State formation in the steppes?"); Di Cosmo, *Ancient China and Its Enemies*, 167–74; Vasyutin, "Model of the Political Transformation," 393.

53. Ecsedy, "Tribe and Tribal Society," 261. The later Mongolian terminology is explicated in Vladimirtsov, *Le régime social des Mongols*, 56–59 and 73–75: state *ulus*, tribe *irgän*, and clan *oboq*; yet he understands these rather statically as a hierarchy.

54. Sneath, *The Headless State*.

55. *Strategicon* 11.2.34, 363.

56. See section 6.10.

57. On the term *aul*, see Göckenjan, "Zur Stammesstruktur," 71; de Ferdinandy, "Die nordeurasischen Reitervölker," 176. In Avar archaeology the term *aul*, which is not attested in the written sources, is sometimes applied to groups buried in smaller cemeteries; see Bóna, "Ein Vierteljahrhundert," 308–10.

58. Drompp, "Strategies of Cohesion and Control," 447.

59. Di Cosmo, "China-Steppe Relations in Historical Perspective," 68.

60. Leonid R. Kyzlasov, *The Urban Civilisation of Northern and Innermost Asia: Historical and Archaeological Research* (Bucharest, 2010), 247–382; coins: 253.

61. Golden, *Central Asia in World History*, 45.

62. Theodore Syncellus 6.26–27, ed. and trans. Makk, 16; Priscus, frag. 11.2, ed. and trans. Blockley, 269.

63. *Strategicon* 11.2, 361.

64. Karl August Wittfogel, "China und die osteurasische Kavallerie-Revolution," *UAJB* 49 (1977): 125–26.

65. Bóna, *Der Anbruch des Mittelalters*, 106.

66. Nicola Di Cosmo, ed., *Warfare in Inner Asian History (500–1800)* (Leiden, 2002); see also Christian, *History of Russia, Central Asia and Mongolia*; Golden, *Central Asia in World History*.

67. *Strategicon* 11.2, 360–69. As a result of its practical purpose, the manual on warfare is, despite some rhetorical topoi, one of the best sources for the fighting style of the Avars. Cf. Wiita, "The Ethnika in Byzantine Military Treatises"; Haldon, *Warfare and Society*, 129–30.

68. *Strategicon* 11.2, 363. For a good synthesis of Avar warcraft, see Florin Curta, "Avar Blitzkrieg: Slavic and Bulgar Raiders, and Roman Special Ops. Mobile Warriors in the 6th-Century Balkans," in Zimonyi and Karatay, *Central Eurasia in the Middle Ages*, 69–89.

69. Liu Mau-Tsai, *Die chinesischen Nachrichten*, 1:9. The *Sui shu*, cited ibid., 1:41, mentions that the bows were decorated with horn. An excellent overview of archaeological and pictorial evidence on Turkish weapons: Stark, *Die Alttürkenzeit in Mittel- und Zentralasien*, 145–69.

70. Gergely Csiky, "Armament and Society in the Mirror of the Avar Archaelogy: The Transdanubia-Phenomenon Revisited," in *Proceedings of the 1st International Conference on Interethnic Relations in Transylvania*, ed. Ioan Marian Tiplic (Sibiu, 2011), 9–34; Curta, "Avar Blitzkrieg," 74.

71. Avar exhibition, *Ausgrabungen Goldene Stiege*, exhibition catalog (Mödling, 1977), 21; Herwig Friesinger, *Die vielen Väter Österreichs: Römer—Germanen—Slawen. Eine Spurensuche* (Vienna, 1987), 94, describes the mail as a coat with overlaps. The representation does not indicate whether it was made of felt or iron. The *Strategicon* mentions both kinds of protective clothing.

72. Gyula László and Istvan Rácz, *Der Schatz von Nagyszentmiklós* (Budapest, 1977); Tibor Kovács, ed., *The Gold of the Avars: The Nagyszentmiklós Treasure*, exhibition catalog (Budapest, 2002), 17; Csanád Bálint, *Der Schatz von Nagyszentmiklós: archäologische Studien zur frühmittelalterlichen Metallgefäßkunst des Orients, Byzanz' und der Steppe* (Budapest, 2010).

73. Heinz Meyer, *Geschichte der Reiterkrieger* (Stuttgart, 1982), especially 451–53; Lebedinsky, *Armes et guerriers barbares*, 35–56.

74. Brosseder, "A Study on the Complexity and Dynamics of Interaction and Exchange," 226–29.

75. Holger Riesch, Joachim Rutschke, and Ulrich Stehli, "Nachgebaut und ausprobiert: Rekonstruktionen des Reflexbogens, der Pfeile und des Köchers aus den Žargalant Chajrchan Bergen, Chovd ajmag, Mongolei," in *Steppenkrieger: Reiternomaden des 7.–14. Jahrhunderts aus der Mongolei; Katalog der Ausstellung im LVR LandesMuseum Bonn* (Bonn, 2012), 181–98.

76. Curta, "The Earliest Avar-Age Stirrups." For an archaeological overview and methodological debate on the reflex bow, see Adam Biró, "Methodological Considerations on the Archaeology of Rigid, Reflex, Composite Bows of Eurasia in the Pre-Mongol Period," *Acta Militaria Medievalia* 9 (2013): 7–38. See also Andreas Bracher, "Der Reflexbogen als Beispiel gentiler Bewaffnung," in Wolfram and Pohl, *Typen der Ethnogenese*, 137–46.

77. The earliest figurine equipped with stirrups is dated to 322; the earliest datable example comes from a burial: Mark Edward Lewis, *China between Empires: The Northern and Southern Dynasties* (Cambridge, 2009), 60.

78. Stark, *Die Alttürkenzeit in Mittel- und Zentralasien*, 147–49.

79. Lynn T. White Jr., *Medieval Technology and Social Change* (Oxford, 1962), 14–28. In the archaeological material, the stirrup appears in Europe first among the early Avars in the late sixth century.

80. Bernard S. Bachrach, "Charles Martel, Mounted Shock Combat, the Stirrup, and Feudalism," *Studies in Medieval and Renaissance History* 7 (1970): 47–75; he minimized the role of the stirrup also among the Avars, which meant exaggerating in the other direction.

81. Curta, "The Earliest Avar-Age Stirrups," 310–11.

82. *Strategicon* 1.2, 80.

83. *Strategicon* 1.1.13–18, 76; 1.2.10–25, 79.

84. Haldon, *Warfare and Society*, 193–97; Ilkka Syvänne, *The Age of Hippotokotai: Art of War in Roman Military Revival and Disaster (491–636)* (Tampere, 2004); Curta, "Avar Blitzkrieg," 69–70.

85. *Strategicon* 1.2, 78–83. Samuel Szádeczky-Kardoss, "Der awarisch-türkische Einfluss auf die byzantinische Kriegskunst um 600 (Anmerkungen zum *Strategikon* des Maurikios)," in his *Avarica*, 205–8; Taxiarchis G. Kolias, *Byzantinische Waffen: ein Beitrag zur byzantinischen Waffenkunde von den Anfängen bis zur lateinischen Eroberung* (Vienna, 1988); Haldon, *Warfare and Society*, 130; Curta, "Avar Blitzkrieg," 87–88.

86. *Suidae Lexicon*, ed. Adler, 1:483, *s.v. Bulgaroi*.

87. Evagrius 5.11, trans. Whitby, 270.

88. *Strategicon* 11.4, 377.

89. *Strategicon* 11.2, 360. See Peter B. Golden, "War and Warfare in the Pre-Činggisid Western Steppes of Eurasia," in Di Cosmo, *Warfare in Inner Asian History*, 134–38.

90. *Strategicon* 2.1, 111; Haldon, *Warfare and Society*, 206.

91. *Strategicon* 11.2, 362.

92. *Strategicon* 4.2, 195.

93. *Strategicon* 11.2, 365.

94. Fredegar 2.57, ed. Krusch, 56–58.

95. Liudprand of Cremona, *Antapodosis* 2.15, trans. Paolo Squatriti, *The Complete Works of Liudprand of Cremona*, Medieval Texts in Translation (Washington, DC, 2007), 82–83; György Györffy, "Landnahme, Ansiedlung und Streifzüge der Ungarn," *Acta Historica Academiae Scientarum Hungaricae* 31 (1985): 242.

96. Menander, frag. 12.3, ed. and trans. Blockley, 130–32; *Miracula Demetrii* 1.2.112, 123; Theodore Syncellus 15, ed. and trans. Makk, 30.

97. Liudprand of Cremona, *Antapodosis* 2.30, trans. Squatriti, 89.

98. *Suidae Lexicon*, ed. Adler, 3:294. *s.v. lykethmós*; cf. Ludwig Steindorff, "Wölfisches Heulen: Ein Motiv in mittelalterlichen slawischen Quellen," *Byzantinoslavica* 46 (1985): 40–49.

99. *Strategicon* 11.2, 365.

100. *Strategicon* 11.2, 369.

101. Theophylact Simocatta 8.2–3, 210–13.

102. *Strategicon* 11.2, 365. On this topos, see Bohumila Zástěrová, *Les Avares et les Slaves dans la tactique de Maurice*, Rozpravy Československé Akademie 81.3 (Prague, 1971), 26; Wiita, "The Ethnika in Byzantine Military Treatises," 155–56. Similar stereotypes about the Huns: Ammianus Marcellinus 31.2.6, ed. and trans. John C. Rolfe, vol. 3, Loeb Classical Library (Cambridge, MA, 1986), 382.

103. Radloff, *Aus Sibirien*, 1:287.

104. Peter Fleming, *News from Tartary* (London, 1938); cited after D. A. Tirr, "The Attitude of the West Towards the Avars," *Acta Arch. Hung.* 28 (1976): 111.

105. *Strategicon* 11.2, 365.

106. *Strategicon* 11.2, 363; cf. Menander, frag. 15.2, ed. and trans. Blockley, 148.

107. Theophylact Simocatta 2.10, 57–58, and 2.15, 64–65.

108. Kardaras, "The Episode of Bousas"; Martin Hurbanič, "The Nomads at the Gates: Some Notes on the Use of Siege Artillery by the Avars (From the First Attack on Sirmium to the Siege of Constantinople)," in *The Cultural and Historical Heritage of Vojvodina in the Context of Classical and Medieval Studies*, ed. Djura Hardi (Novi Sad, 2015), 75–90.

109. Theophylact Simocatta 2.15, 65–66.

110. *Miracula Demetrii* 1.14, 153.

111. Paul the Deacon, *Historia Langobardorum* 4.20, ed. Waitz, 154.

112. Theophylact Simocatta 7.11, 264–65.

113. Theophylact Simocatta 7.2, 248. On the carts of the steppe peoples, see Togan, *Ibn Fadlans Reisebericht*, 120–21.

114. *Annales regni Francorum* a. 791, ed. Friedrich Kurze, MGH rer. Germ. 6 (Hanover, 1895), 58–60.

115. See the many contributions in Călin Cosma, ed., *Warriors, Weapons, and Harness from the 5th–10th Centuries in the Carpathian Basin* (Cluj-Napoca, 2015).

116. Kovrig, *Das awarenzeitliche Gräberfeld von Alattyán*, 203; Elvira Tóth, "Das Grab eines Awarenkhagans von Kunbábony," in *Awaren in Europa: Schätze eines asiatischen Reitervolkes, 6.–8. Jh.*, exhibition catalog (Frankfurt am Main, 1985), 21.

117. István Bóna, "Studien zum frühmittelalterlichen Reitergrab von Szegvár," *Acta Arch. Hung.* 32 (1980): 45, who mentions parallels from the Altai region. On Hunnic armor or protective clothing, see Maenchen-Helfen, *The World of the Huns*, 241–51.

118. Bóna, *Der Anbruch des Mittelalters*, 105–09; József Szentpéteri, "Archäologische Studien zur Schicht der Waffenträger des Awarentums im Karpatenbecken I und II," *Acta Arch. Hung.* 45 (1993): 165–216, and 46 (1994): 231–306; Péter Tomka, "Awarische Bestattungssitten: Abriß der Forschungsgeschichte bis 1963," in Daim, *Awarenforschungen*, 2:969–1023.

119. Bóna, *Der Anbruch des Mittelalters*, 105; Kovrig, "Contribution au problème," 163–65; Éva Garam, "Über die frühawarischen Gräber von Zsámbok," *Folia Archaeologica* 34 (1983): 139–41.

120. Gergely Csiky, *Avar-Age Polearms and Edged Weapons: Classification, Typology, Chronology and Technology* (Leiden, 2015).

121. Bóna, "Ein Vierteljahrhundert," 314–16; Bóna, "Studien zum frühmittelalterlichen Reitergrab," 92–93; István Bóna, "Die Awaren: Ein asiatisches Reitervolk an der mittleren Donau," in *Awaren in Europa*, exhibition catalog, 9–10.

122. Menander, frag. 5.4, ed. and trans. Blockley, 52.

123. *Capitulary of Diedenhofen (805)* 2, ed. Alfred Boretius, MGH Capit. 1 (Hanover, 1883), 44.5, 123 (805).

124. For a useful collection of source passages on the numbers of steppe armies, see Golden, "War and Warfare," 106–9.

125. *Strategicon* 9.5, 328.

126. Theophylact Simocatta 8.2–3, 211–13.

127. Menander, frag. 21, ed. and trans. Blockley, 193.

128. Theophylact Simocatta 8.3.15, 213; Theophanes, *Chronographia* 6093, 407, derived from Theophylact, has only eight hundred Slavs.

129. Theophylact Simocatta 8.3.11–12, 213.

130. Menander, frag. 10.1, ed. and trans. Blockley, 117; Theophylact Simocatta 7.8.16, 191; see section 3.5.

131. Menander, frag. 10.1, ed. and trans. Blockley, 117; frag. 12.5, 136; Theophylact Simocatta 7.4.1, 183; Zástěrová, *Les Avares et les Slaves*, 41; Göckenjan, "Zur Stammesstruktur," 51–53; Franke, "Fremdherrschaften in China," 56.

132. Wolfram, *History of the Goths*, 7.

133. Agathias 5.13, 148; see Jones, *The Later Roman Empire*, 2:679–86; Stein, *Studien zur Geschichte*, 80, n. 4; see also section 2.5.

134. *Strategicon* 11.2, 361.

135. *Strategicon* 11.2, 361; cf. 11.4, 374 on Slavic "anarchy." On the topos of nomadic despotism, see Antonio Carile, "I nomadi nelle fonti bizantine," in *Popoli delle steppe*, 1:55–88.

136. John of Plano Carpini, *Historia Mongalorum*, ed. Enrico Menestò and trans. Maria Christina Lungarotti (Spoleto, 1989); Togan, *Ibn Fadlans Reisebericht*, 285.

137. *Zhou shu* (the history of the sixth-century Northern Zhou dynasty), in Liu Mau-Tsai, *Die chinesischen Nachrichten*, 1:12. This clearly refers more to experience with Turkish warriors in the Chinese army. Theorizing about the *indiscipline fondamentale* of the steppe horsemen, cf. Deleuze and Guattari, *A Thousand Plateaus*, 358: this is perhaps the complementary topos to that of nomadic despotism.

138. René Grousset, *Die Reise nach Westen, oder wie Hsüan Tsang den Buddhismus nach China holte* (Cologne, 1986), 73.

139. Thomsen, "Alttürkische Inschriften in der Mongolei," 145; *Suidae Lexicon*, ed. Adler, 1:484, *s.v. Bulgaroi*; cf. section 8.5.

140. Veselin Beševliev, "Bulgaren als Söldner in den italienischen Kriegen Justinians I.," *Jahrbuch der Österreichischen Byzantinistik* 29 (1980): 21–26.

141. Theophylact Simocatta 8.6.1, 217; cf. section 5.9.

142. *Strategicon* 11.2, 367.

143. Theophylact Simocatta 1.14.5, 40; Moravcsik, *Byzantinoturcica*, 2:87.

144. Theophylact Simocatta 1.8, 30; cf. section 3.6.

145. Cf. sections 7.5–6.

146. On the (debated) etymology of the title and its incidence: Wilhelm Tomaschek, "Avares," in *RE* 2.2 (1896), 2264–66, explains it as Mongolian for "splitter"; also opting for Mongolian is Kurakichi Shiratori, "On the Titles Khan and Khagan," *Proceedings of the Imperial Academy of Japan* 2 (1926): 242–44; in agreement, Kollautz and Miyakawa; for a contrary view, see Herbert Franke, *Das chinesische Kaiserreich*, Fischer-Weltgeschichte 19 (Frankfurt am Main, 1968), 252–55. Cf. too Moravcsik, *Byzantinoturcica*, 2:232–34; Denis Sinor, "Qapqan," *Journal of the Royal Asiatic Society of Great Britain and Ireland*, nos. 3–4 (1954): 174–84; Josef Marquart, *Eranšahr nach der Geographie des Ps. Moses Xorenac'i* (Berlin, 1901), 53. Haussig, "Die Quellen über die zentralasiatische Herkunft," 42, explains the title as derived from Osmanli Turkic *qaban*, "wild boar," totemic animal of the Xianbei; Christian, *History of Russia, Central Asia and Mongolia*, 256.

147. Golden, *Khazar Studies*; Golden, Ben-Shammai, and Róna-Tas, *The World of the Khazars*.

148. Fredegar 4.48, ed. Krusch, 39.

149. The name of Kuvrat's son: Theophanes, *Chronographia* 6171, 498; Nicephorus 35.14, ed. and trans. Mango, 89; cf. section 6.6. It has also been transmitted with the prefixed element *bat*, from an Iranian word for "prince" or from Turkic *bäg*; cf. Haussig, "Theophylacts Exkurs," 337, and 354; Helmut Lauterbach, "Untersuchungen zur Vorgeschichte der Protobulgaren, nach einem Bericht bei Theophanes," in *Die Araber in der alten Welt*, ed. Franz Altheim and Ruth Stiehl, vol. 4, *Neue Funde* (Berlin, 1967), 590; Beševliev, *Die protobulgarische Periode*, 150–51. For another Bulgar leader called Baian: Nicephoros 79.5, ed. and trans. Mango, 153. For the Mongols, the central text is available in German translation as *Geheime Geschichte der Mongolen*, in *Dschingis Khan: Ein Weltreich zu Pferde; Das Buch vom Ursprung der Mongolen*, trans. Walther Heissig (Cologne, 1985), here at 9. A recent English version is *The Secret History of the Mongols: A Mongolian Epic Chronicle of the Thirteenth Century*, ed. Igor de Rachewiltz, 3 vols. (Leiden, 2004–13).

150. Moravcsik, *Byzantinoturcica*, 2:84 (with a review of secondary literature); Haussig, "Theophylakts Exkurs," 361. Other etymologies: András Róna-Tas, "The Problems of the East-European Scripts with Special Regards to the Newly Found Inscription of Szarvas," in *Popoli delle steppe*, 2:483–506; Karl H. Menges, "On Some Loanwords from or via Turkic in Old Russian," in *Fuad Köprülü Armagani*, ed. Osman Turan and Hasan Eren (Istanbul, 1953), 370–71 (the "singer of old tales," connected to Slavonic *boyan*/bard); similarly, Golden, *Khazar Studies*, 1:126. It is also frequently assumed that the Croatian title *ban* is derived from this term; cf. sections 7.5–7. Such honorifics and terms for high office moved from language to language (*Wanderwörter*). From philological assessments of their origins, no compelling historical conclusions can be drawn.

151. Theodore Syncellus 5.2, ed. and trans. Makk, 14; trans. Pearse, 9, http://www.tertullian.org/fathers/theodore_syncellus_01_homily.htm.

152. Paul the Deacon, *Historia Langobardorum* 4.37, ed. Waitz, 162.

153. Theophylact Simocatta 1.5, 26–27; Olajos, "La chronologie," 155. For a discussion, see section 3.5.

154. Theophylact Simocatta 7.15, 200 (seven sons die of the plague in one day); 8.3.7, 212 (Khagan's sons perish in a swamp during a battle). See sections 5.7–8.

155. For the flexible succession system and traces of tanistry among the early Turks, see Michael Drompp, "Supernumerary Sovereigns: Superfluity and Mutability in the Elite Power Structure of the Early Turks (Tu-jue)," in *Rulers from the Steppe: State Formation on the Eurasian Periphery*, ed. Gary Seaman and Daniel Marks (Los Angeles, 1991), 92–115. See, for instance, the *Sui shu*, in Liu Mau-Tsai, *Die chinesischen Nachrichten*, 1:42. On the regulation of succession among the Bulgars, see Beševliev, *Die protobulgarische Periode*, 337.

156. See section 7.6.

157. Theophylact Simocatta 8.5, 216–17.

158. For example, in Theophylact Simocatta 7.15, 200–201.

159. Menander, frag. 25.1.70–72, ed. and trans. Blockley, 220.

160. Kollautz, "Die Awaren," 134.

161. Scharlipp, *Die frühen Türken in Zentralasien*, 62–67; Christian, *History of Russia, Central Asia and Mongolia*, 252–57; Florin Curta, "Qagan, Khan, or King? Power in Early Medieval Bulgaria (Seventh to Ninth Century)," *Viator* 37 (2006): 1–31; Ziemann, *Vom Wandervolk zur Großmacht*, 306–9.

162. Bilge Khagan inscription, front side, 8–9, http://bitig.org/?lang=e&mod=1&tid=1&oid=16&m=1; see Thomsen, "Alttürkische Inschriften in der Mongolei," 145; de Ferdinandy, "Die nordeurasischen Reitervölker," 179.

163. Menander, frag. 15.1, ed. and trans. Blockley, 148; see section 3.2.

164. Menander, frag. 25.1, ed. and trans. Blockley, 224; see section 3.4.

165. Theophylact Simocatta 1.6.1–3, 28.

166. Theophylact Simocatta 6.11.6, 176.

167. Theophylact Simocatta 6.11.8, 177; see section 5.4.

168. On the "council of the *boila*" (boyars) and the Bulgar assembly, see Beševliev, *Die protobulgarische Periode*, 343–45; Ziemann, *Vom Wandervolk zur Großmacht*, 339. On the exercise of a collective will among nomadic peoples in Chinese sources, see Franke, "Fremdherrschaften in China," 62–64.

169. Cf. the description of the reception of the Avar embassy in Corippus, *In laudem Iustini* 3.230–405, ed. and trans. Cameron, 67–73; McCormick, "Analyzing Imperial Ceremonies"; cf. section 2.8.

170. Menander, frag. 5.1–2, ed. and trans. Blockley, 48–51. See section 2.1.

171. *Zhou shu*, in Liu Mau-Tsai, *Die chinesischen Nachrichten*, 1:6–7; Stark, "Luxurious Necessities," 477.

172. For generations, luxury goods had come to the barbarian elites of the Carpathian Basin from the core areas of the Roman World. For an overview of precious objects found there, see Tivadar Vida, *Late Antique Metal Vessels in the Carpathian Basin: Luxury and Power in the Early Middle Ages* (Budapest, 2016).

173. Menander, frag. 12.5, ed. and trans. Blockley, 134–36; see section 3.1.

174. Lemerle, *Les Plus Anciens Recueils*, 2:99.

175. On the "federates," see Wolfram, *History of the Goths*, 133–34. The *foideratoi* of the sixth century were already regular troops, regiments of mainly barbarian origin commanded by Roman officers. The old meaning is mostly covered by the concept of *symmachoi*; Procopius, *Bella* 3.11, ed. and trans. Dewing, 2:103; Jones, *The Later Roman Empire*, 2:654–56; Evangelos Chrysos, "Legal Concepts and Patterns for the Barbarians' Settlement on Roman Soil," in Chrysos and Schwarcz, *Das Reich und die Barbaren*, 13–24; Pohl, "The Empire and the Lombards," 75–87. Menander, frag. 8, ed. and trans. Blockley, 94, calls the contractual relationship with the Avars that ended in 565 *symmachia*.

176. See section 2.8 and Pohl, "Justinian and the Barbarian Kingdoms."

177. Menander, frag. 21, ed. and trans. Blockley, 192; see section 3.3.

178. Pohl, "Ethnicity and Empire."

179. *Sui shu*, in Liu Mau-Tsai, *Die chinesischen Nachrichten*, 1:6–7.

180. Theophylact Simocatta 1.3, 24; see section 3.5.

181. Theophylact Simocatta 7.15.14, 201; see section 5.7.

182. Theophylact Simocatta 7.10.5, 193; see sections 5.5 and 5.9.

183. 588: Menander, frag. 21, ed. and trans. Blockley, 192–94; 598: Theophylact Simocatta 7.15, 201.

184. Theophylact Simocatta 6.7, 169; 6.10, 173; 7.1, 179; 8.6–8, 218–20.

185. Theophylact Simocatta 7.3, 182–83.

186. Menander, frag. 12.6, ed. and trans. Blockley, 138.

187. Menander, frag. 5.1, ed. and trans. Blockley, 48.

188. Menander, frag. 5.2, ed. and trans. Blockley, 50.

189. Procopius, *Anecdota* 30.34, ed. and trans. Dewing, 359.

190. Agathias 5.13.5–14.2, 148–49.

191. John of Ephesus, 6.23, 245–46; 6.24, 246.

192. Gregory of Tours, *Decem libri historiarum* 4.29, ed. Krusch and Levison, 162; Fredegar 3.61, ed. Krusch, 133; see section 2.7.

193. *Sui shu*, in Liu Mau-Tsai, *Die chinesischen Nachrichten*, 1:45–46.

194. Di Cosmo, *Ancient China and Its Enemies*, 193–94; for later controversial debates about this policy, ibid., 210–15.

195. Hesse, "Der Austausch als stabilisierender Faktor der politischen Herrschaft in der Geschichte der Mongolei," 158–60; Di Cosmo, *Ancient China and Its Enemies.*

196. Franke, *Das chinesische Kaiserreich*, 210.

197. Menander, frag. 8, ed. and trans. Blockley, 94.

198. Menander, frag. 8, ed. and trans. Blockley, 94. For the terminology, see Pohl, "The Empire and the Lombards," 78–87.

199. Marcel Mauss, "Essai sur le don: Forme et raison de l'échange dans les sociétés archaïques in sociologie et anthropologie," *L'Année sociologique* 1 (1923–24): 30–186, in English as *The Gift: The Form and Reason for Exchange in Archaic Societies* (London, 2002), 95. See section 6.5.

200. Theophylact Simocatta 1.3.8–13, 24. See section 3.5.

201. Menander, frag. 25.2, ed. and trans. Blockley, 226. See section 3.4.

202. Menander, frag. 19.1, ed. and trans. Blockley, 172–74. See section 3.3.

203. Thomsen, "Alttürkische Inschriften in der Mongolei," 141; Bilge Khagan inscription, 2nd side, 5–6, http://bitig.org/?lang=e&mod=1&tid=1&oid=16&m=1.

204. Thomsen, "Alttürkische Inschriften in der Mongolei," 145.

205. Stark, "Luxurious Necessities," 488.

206. Sergey A. Yatsenko, "Images of the Early Turks in Chinese Murals and Figurines from the Recently-Discovered Tomb in Mongolia," *Silk Road Foundation Newsletter* 12 (2014): 13–24, http://www.silkroadfoundation.org/newsletter/vol12/Yatsenko_SR12_2014_pp13_24.pdf; Stark, "Luxurious Necessities," 491–92.

207. Listed in Liu Mau-Tsai, *Die chinesischen Nachrichten*, 1:410–12. With respect to the Xiongnu, see also Hesse, "Der Austausch als stabilisierender Faktor der politischen Herrschaft in der Geschichte der Mongolei."

208. *Sui shu*, in Liu Mau-Tsai, *Die chinesischen Nachrichten*, 1:43. Cf. Liu Mau-Tsai, "Kulturelle Beziehungen zwischen den Ost-Türken (= T'u-küe) und China," *Central Asiatic Journal* 3 (1957–58): 194–96.

209. Liu Mau-Tsai, "Kulturelle Beziehungen," 203–5, who also lists a series of other influences in fashions and music.

210. In the *Zhou shu*, in Liu Mau-Tsai, *Die chinesischen Nachrichten*, 1:56–57, a poem purportedly composed by her is preserved. In it she laments her life "driven by fate to the barbarian court." After the death of her husband, she fell victim to an intrigue orchestrated by the Chinese. In the West, marriages between the imperial family and barbarian dynasties were rare, and after 500 unthinkable; see Claude, "Zur Begründung familiärer Beziehungen."

211. Her brief biography is preserved in the *Zhou shu*; see in Liu Mau-Tsai, *Die chinesischen Nachrichten*, 1:19–20.

212. Nicephorus 12, ed. and trans. Mango, 57.

213. If Menander, frag. 12.6, ed. and trans. Blockley, 138, accurately reproduces the sense of his speech; see section 3.2.

214. Theodore Syncellus 6.20, ed. and trans. Makk, 16.

215. Cassiodorus, *Variae* 4.2, ed. Mommsen, 144; Paul the Deacon, *Historia Langobardorum* 1.24, ed. Waitz, 70–71. On the adoption of barbarian princes by the emperor, see Claude, "Zur Begründung familiärer Beziehungen."

216. Franke, *Das chinesische Kaiserreich*, 211.

217. Theophanes, *Chronographia* 6113, 303; Theodore Syncellus 6.14 and 34–35, ed. and trans. Makk, 16. In return, the khagan addresses Heraclius as "father."

218. *Zhou shu*, in Liu Mau-Tsai, *Die chinesischen Nachrichten*, 1:13.

219. Chavannes, *Documents sur les Tou-kiue*, 27.

220. Alexander Demandt, "Magister militum," in *RE*, Suppl., 12 (1970), 553–790, especially 753 (Attila), 788 (barbarian military aristocracy).

221. Nicephorus 9, ed. and trans. Mango, 51, and 22, 71 (the two are sometimes identified).

222. Nicephorus 42, ed. and trans. Mango 103; Beševliev, *Die protobulgarische Periode*, 193–94; Ziemann, *Vom Wandervolk zur Großmacht*, 184–87.

223. Priscus, frag. 11.1–14, ed. and trans. Blockley, 242–93.

224. Menander, frag. 27.2, ed. and trans. Blockley, 238.

225. John of Ephesus 6.49, 260; cf. section 3.5.

226. Theophylact Simocatta 7.10.4, 193.

227. The clearest reference to Sirmium is in John of Ephesus 6.49, 260, and basically says nothing more than that the Avars withdrew from Roman territory toward Sirmium, in order to protect their families and possessions; this need not have been in Sirmium itself. Theophylact Simocatta 6.4.5, 163, attests to the fact that the khagan commanded Slavs to ship the army across the Sava in the vicinity of Sirmium. Priscus's offensive of 599 would surely not have been aimed at the marshes on the lower Tisza, if the khagan's residence had been in Sirmium; cf. section 5.2.

228. Bóna, "Die Awaren," 12; Attila Kiss, "Die Goldfunde des Karpatenbeckens vom 5.–10. Jahrhundert: Angaben zu den Vergleichsmöglichkeiten der schriftlichen und archäologischen Quellen," *Acta Arch. Hung.* 38 (1986): 105–45.

229. Menander, frag. 10.3, ed. and trans. Blockley, 120; cf. Walter Pohl, "The Regia and the Hring: Barbarian Places of Power," in *Topographies of Power in the Early Middle Ages*, ed. Mayke de Jong, Frans Theuws, and Carine van Rhijn, The Transformation of the Roman World 6 (Leiden, 2001), 439–66.

230. Stark, "Luxurious Necessities," 485.

231. *Sui shu*, in Liu Mau-Tsai, *Die chinesischen Nachrichten*, 1:50.

232. Cited from Grousset, *Die Reise nach Westen*, 76 and 78.

233. Grousset, *Die Reise nach Westen*, 76, n. 1; Edouard Chavannes, "Voyage de Song-yun dans l'Udyana et le Gandhara," *Bulletin de l'Ecole Francaise d'Extrême-Orient* 3 (1903): 1–63; Samuel Beal, *Travels of Fah-Hian and Sung-Yun* (New Delhi, 1993).

234. Priscus, frag. 13, ed. and trans. Blockley, 282–89. On the role of gold and royal trasures in early medieval Europe: Matthias Hardt, *Gold und Herrschaft: Die Schätze europäischer Könige und Fürsten im ersten Jahrtausend*, Europa im Mittelalter 6 (Berlin, 2004).

235. Menander, frag. 5.1, ed. and trans. Blockley, 48.

236. Menander, frag. 8, ed. and trans. Blockley, 92.

237. John of Ephesus 6.24, 246. Similar statements had already been made of the Huns; cf. Maenchen-Helfen, *Die Welt der Hunnen*, 141.

238. Menander, frag. 12.5, ed. and trans. Blockley, 136.

239. Menander, frag. 15.6, ed. and trans. Blockley, 150 and frag. 25.2, 226. Theophylact Simocatta 1.3, ed. de Boor, 45; Whitby and Whitby, *The History of Theophylact Simocatta*, 24, translate this rather obscure passage: the Byzantines "agreed to deposit with the barbarians each year eighty thousand gold coins in the form of merchandise of silver and embroidered cloth"; similarly the German translation by Schreiner, 47, who considers the gold coins to be merely the unit of calculation. It is also possible that the barbarians quickly used a portion of the sum paid out in gold to make purchases, as Menander, frag. 4.5, ed. and trans. Blockley, 52, suggests in a scene in which the Avar envoys buy clothing with the tribute money and, to the displeasure of the emperor, also weapons. See section 3.5.

240. *Suidae Lexicon*, ed. Adler, 3:270, *s.v. lithos*.

241. Theophylact Simocatta 1.3.12, 24.

242. Theophylact Simocatta 7.13.5–6, 197.

243. *Sui shu*, in Liu Mau-Tsai, *Die chinesischen Nachrichten*, 1:64. Cf. Thomas Höllmann, *Tribes and Tributaries: Chinese Perceptions of Foreigners and Strangers* (Tempe, AZ, 2008).

244. Jones, *The Later Roman Empire*, 1:447. The information is derived from Egyptian papyri.

245. Jones, *The Later Roman Empire*, 1:397; Stein, *Studien zur Geschichte*, 154.

246. Stein, *Studien zur Geschichte*, 143. Maenchen-Helfen, *Geschichte der Hunnen*, 138, lists a series of comparative figures from the fifth century.

247. Menander, frag. 15.5, ed. and trans. Blockley, 150, and frag. 27.3, 240; Theophylact Simocatta 1.3, 24–25.

248. Theophylact Simocatta 1.6.5, 28, and 7.15.14, 201.

249. Jones, *The Later Roman Empire*, 1:192–93.

250. Liu Mau-Tsai, *Die chinesischen Nachrichten*, 1:13 and 63.

251. See the list in Liu Mau-Tsai, *Die chinesischen Nachrichten*, 1:402–5; and Stark, "Luxurious Necessities."

252. Theophanes, *Chronographia* 6096, 420; see section 7.1.

253. Nicephorus 13, ed. and trans. Mango, 59; see section 7.2.

254. See the table of tribute payments in the appendix. Kovačević, *Avarski Kaganat*, 150, reckons a total of six million solidi; Ernst Stein, "Untersuchungen zur spätbyzantinischen Verfassungs- und Wirtschaftsgeschichte," *Mitteilungen zur osmanischen Geschichte* 2 (1929): 10, assumes eight million. More cautious is the assessment by Kiss, "Die Goldfunde des Karpatenbeckens vom 5.–10. Jahrhundert," 109, taking account of the devaluation through the use of light-weight solidi, which were occasionally minted in seventh-century Byzantium for the tribute payments; cf. Howard L. Adelson, *Light Weight Solidi and Byzantine Trade during the Sixth and Seventh Centuries* (New York, 1957); Wolfgang Hahn, *Moneta Imperii Byzantini*, vol. 1, *Von Anastasius I. bis Justinianus I.* (Vienna, 1973), 148–49; Stratos, *Byzantium in the Seventh Century*, 2:167.

255. Bóna, "Die Awaren," 11; the total weight of the gold recovered up to that point from Avar graves is assessed in Kiss, "Die Goldfunde des Karpatenbeckens vom 5.–10. Jahrhundert," 130–32; Falko Daim, "Die Materialität der Macht: Drei Fallstudien zum awarischen Gold," in *Arm und Reich: Zur Ressourcenverteilung in prähistorischen Gesellschaften, 8. Mitteldeutscher Archäologentag vom 22. bis 24. Oktober 2015 in Halle (Saale) / Rich and Poor: Competing for Resources in Prehistoric Societies, 8th Archaeological Conference of Central Germany, October 22–24, 2015 in Halle (Saale)*, ed. Harald Meller et al. (Halle, 2016), 623–36.

256. Péter Somogyi, "New Remarks on the Flow of Byzantine Coins in Avaria and Walachia during the Second Half of the Seventh Century," in Curta, *The Other Europe in the Middle Ages*, 88. On coin finds in Avar graves, see Éva Garam, "Die münzdatierten Gräber der Awarenzeit," in Daim, *Awarenforschungen*, 1:135–250; Michael Winter, "Die byzantinischen Fundmünzen aus dem österreichischen Bereich der Avaria," in Daim, *Die Awaren am Rand der byzantinischen Welt*, 45–66; Somogyi, *Byzantinische Fundmünzen*; Somogyi, *Byzantinische Fundmünzen der Awarenzeit in ihrem europäischen Umfeld*.

257. Tóth, "Das Grab eines Awarenkhagans," 21; Tóth and Horváth, *Kunbábony*; Daim, "Die Materialität der Macht."

258. Bálint, *Die Archäologie der Steppe*; *L'oro degli Avari*, especially the contribution of Éva Garam, "L'oro degli Avari," 33–75. See section 7.8.

259. Joachim Werner, *Der Schatzfund von Vrap in Albanien: Beiträge zur Archäologie der Awarenzeit im mittleren Donauraum*, Studien zur Archäologie der Awaren 2, DsÖAW 184 (Vienna, 1986), 15–16 and 66, with a seventh-century dating; an eighth-century date in Éva Garam, review of *Der Schatzfund von Vrap in Albanien*, Studien zur Archäologie der Awaren 2, by Joachim Werner, *Bonner Jahrbücher* 187 (1987): 854–57; Bálint, *Die Archäologie der Steppe*, 170; Kiss, "Die Goldfunde des Karpatenbeckens vom 5.–10. Jahrhundert," 112–13; Éva Garam, "The Vrap Treasure," in *From Attila to Charlemagne: Arts of the Early Medieval Period in the Metropolitan Museum of Art* (New York, 2000), 170–79. For the

authenticity of the treasure of Erseke: Peter Stadler, "Argumente für die Echtheit des 'Avar Treasure,'" *Mitteilungen der Anthropologischen Gesellschaft in Wien* 118/19 (1988/89): 193–217.

260. *Annales regni Francorum* a. 796, ed. Kurze, 65.

261. Einhard, *Vita Karoli* 13, ed. Holder-Egger, 449.

262. "XV plauris auro argentoque palliisque olosericis pretiosis repletis, quorum quodque quatuor trahebant boves": *Annales Northumbrani*, ed. Reinhold Pauli, MGH SS 13 (Hanover, 1881), 155. See also section 8.4.

263. *Pauli Diaconi continuatio tertia*, ed. Ludwig Bethmann and Georg Waitz, MGH SS rer. Langob. (Hanover, 1878), 215.

264. *Historia Langobardorum Codicis Gothani*, ed. Waitz, 11. See also Theodulf of Orléans, *Carmina* 25 and 26, ed. Ernst Dümmler, MGH Poetae 1 (Berlin, 1881), 483–90. Victor H. Elbern, "Awarenschatz," in *Lexikon des Mittelalters*, vol. 1 (Munich, 1980), 1287.

265. Péter Prohászka and Falko Daim, "Der Kaiser auf der Mantelschließe: Zum Deckel der frühmittelalterlichen Dose von Sorpe (Provinz Lérida)," *Archäologisches Korrespondenzblatt* 45 (2015): 563–78.

266. *Sächsische Weltchronik*, ed. Ludwig Weiland, MGH Dt. Chron. 2.1 (Hanover, 1876), 148. Cf. Tirr, "The Attitude of the West," 116.

267. László and Rácz, *Der Schatz von Nagyszentmiklós*, with the outdated argument for a Hungarian origin of the hoard. Ascription to the Avars in Bóna, "Die Awaren," 18; Kiss, "Die Goldfunde des Karpatenbeckens vom 5.–10. Jahrhundert," 114 and 120; Csanád Bálint, "A Short Essay on the Nagyszentmiklós Treasure," in Kovács, *The Gold of the Avars*, 57–61; Bálint, *Der Schatz von Nagyszentmiklós*; Falko Daim et al., eds., *Der Goldschatz von Sânnicolau Mare (Nagyszentmiklós)*, RGZM Tagungen 25 (Mainz, 2015); Birgit Bühler et al., *Der Goldschatz von Sânicolau Mare (ungarisch: Nagyszentmiklós)*, RGZM Monographien 142 (Mainz, 2018).

268. Kurt Gschwantler, "The Nagyszentmiklós Treasure Catalogue 1–23," in Kovács, *The Gold of the Avars*, 15–44.

269. Gschwantler, "The Nagyszentmiklós Treasure Catalogue," 16.

270. Jugs 2 and 7: Gschwantler, "The Nagyszentmiklós Treasure Catalogue," 17 and 24; for the central Asian parallels, see Bálint, "A Short Essay," 75.

271. Bálint, "A Short Essay," 77–79; see also Viktor Freiberger and Birgit Bühler, "Der Goldschatz von Nagyszentmiklós/Sânnicolau Mare: Ergebnisse der goldschmiedetechnischen Untersuchungen und der Materialanalysen," in Daim et al., *Der Goldschatz*, 9–42, who attribute technological differences rather to differing workshop traditions than to a wide time span; Ádám Bollók, "The Visual Arts of the Sasanian Empire and the Nagyszentmiklós/Sânnicolau Mare Treasure—a Non-Specialist's View," in Daim et al., *Der Goldschatz*, 43–70.

272. Éva Garam, "The Connection of the Avar Period Princely and Common Gravegoods with the Nagyszentmiklós Treasure," in Kovács, *The Gold of the Avars*, 82–89.

273. On bowl 21, András Róna-Tas, "The Inscriptions of the Nagyszentmiklós Treasure," in Kovács, *The Gold of the Avars*, 128–29; Stefan Albrecht, "Die Inschriften des Goldschatzes von Nagyszentmiklós/Sânnicolau Mare im byzantinischen Kontext," in Daim et al., *Der Goldschatz*, 135–54. For the titles mentioned, see section 8.2. On the Greek inscriptions, see also Moravcsik, *Byzantinoturcica*, 1:163–64 and 2:30; Gabor Vékony, "Zur Lesung der griechischen Inschriften des Schatzes von Nagyszentmiklós," *Acta Arch. Hung.* 25 (1973): 293–306; Omeljan Pritsak, *Die bulgarische Fürstenliste und die Sprache der Protobulgaren*, Ural-Altaische Bibliothek (Wiesbaden, 1955), 85–89.

274. Robert Göbl and András Róna-Tas, *Die Inschriften des Schatzes von Nagy-Szentmiklós*, DsÖAW, Phil.-hist. Kl., 240 (Vienna, 1995); Róna-Tas, "The Inscriptions," 121–26. On the reading of the runiform inscriptions, see section 6.10.

275. Garam, "The Connection." Arguing for Bulgarian connections: Metodi Daskalov et al., eds., *The Nagyszentmiklós Gold Treasure* (Sofia, 2017).

276. Róna-Tas, "The Inscriptions," 126; see section 6.10.

277. Bálint, "A Short Essay"; Bálint, *Der Schatz von Nagyszentmiklós*.

278. Csanád Bálint, "Einige Fragen des Dirhem-Verkehrs in Europa," *Acta Arch. Hung.* 33 (1981): 110.

279. *Strategicon* 1.2, 79.

280. Wolfram, *History of the Goths*, 350; Hardt, *Gold und Herrschaft*.

281. *Suidae Lexicon*, ed. Adler, 1:483, *s.v. Bulgaroi*; cf. Beševliev, *Die protobulgarische Periode*, 195.

282. Rashid ad-Din 2.98–99, cited after Vladimirtsov, *Le régime social des Mongols*, 104–5; Rašīd-ad-Dīn Faḍlallāh, *Rashiduddin Fazlullah's Jami'u't-tawarikh: A Compendium of Chronicles; a History of the Mongols*, vol. 1, *Ǧāmi' al-Tawārīḫ*, trans. Wheeler M. Thackston, Sources of Oriental Languages and Literature 45 (Cambridge, MA, 1998). See also Kradin, "Nomadic Empires in Inner Asia," 26.

283. Stark, "Luxurious Necessities," 473–77; Jürgen Paul, "Perspectives nomades: État et structures militaires," *Annales: Histoire, Sciences Sociales* 59, no. 5–6 (2004): 1069–93, has distinguished between three forms of redistribution of goods in Turko-Mongol states: direct redistribution of booty (of which the khagan may have the "first pick"); the allocation of productive territories; or salaries to retainers. The second and third options are attested only rarely in the Turk khaganates, and not at all in the Avar case, but that does not exclude them.

284. Fundamental discussion from the perspective of ethnology: Mauss, *The Gift*, here 95. Critical views in Claude Lévi-Strauss, "Introduction à l'œuvre de Marcel Mauss," in Marcel Mauss, *Sociologie et anthropologie* (Paris, 1950), ix–lii. See also Maurice Godelier, *The Enigma of the Gift* (Chicago, 1999); Annette B. Weiner, *Inalienable Possessions: The Paradox of Keeping-While-Giving* (Berkeley, 1992), with a criticism of the assumption of reciprocity in a gift exchange; Gadi Algazi, Valentin Groebner, and Bernhard Jussen, eds., *Negotiating the Gift: Pre-Modern Figurations of Exchange* (Göttingen, 2003). Early medieval gift-giving: Hardt, *Gold und Herrschaft*, 35–78, with a list of the gifts that early medieval rulers gave and received; Florin Curta, "Merovingian and Carolingian Gift Giving," *Speculum* 81 (2006): 671–99; Wendy Davies and Paul Fouracre, eds., *The Languages of Gift in the Early Middle Ages* (Cambridge, 2010).

285. Mauss, *The Gift*, 96.

286. Gadi Algazi, "Introduction: Doing Things with Gifts," in Algazi, Groebner, and Jussen, *Negotiating the Gift*, 9–27.

287. Mauss, *The Gift*, 92 and 96.

288. Mario Erdheim, *Prestige und Kulturwandel: Eine Studie zum Verhältnis subjektiver und objektiver Faktoren des kulturellen Wandels zur Klassengesellschaft bei den Azteken* (Wiesbaden, 1972), 90.

289. Weiner, *Inalienable Possessions*; see also Frans Theuws and Monika Alkemade, "A Kind of Mirror for Men: Sword Depositions in Late Antique Northern Gaul," in *Rituals of Power: From Late Antiquity to the Early Middle Ages*, ed. Frans Theuws and Janet L. Nelson, The Transformation of the Roman World 8 (Leiden, 2000), 401–76.

290. A fundamental work for the more recent discussion of grave goods as markers of social differentiation is Guy Halsall, *Settlement and Social Organization: The Merovingian Region of Metz* (Cambridge, 1995); see also Effros, *Caring for Body and Soul*.

291. *Strategicon* 11.2, 361.

292. Erdheim, *Prestige und Kulturwandel*, 27.

293. Erdheim, *Prestige und Kulturwandel*, 114.

294. Stark, *Die Alttürkenzeit in Mittel- und Zentralasien*, 171.

295. Skaff, *Sui-Tang China and Its Turko-Mongol Neighbors*, 160. For the belt in the Jenisej inscriptions and elsewhere in central Asia, see Stark, *Die Alttürkenzeit in Mittel- und Zentralasien*, 170–73.

296. Skaff, *Sui-Tang China and Its Turko-Mongol Neighbors*, 155–60.

297. Bálint, "Kontakte zwischen Byzanz, Iran und der Steppe," 413.

298. Bálint, "Kontakte zwischen Byzanz, Iran und der Steppe"; Daim, "Avars and Avar Archaeology," 469–71, 492–94, 497–511.

299. Stark, "Luxurious Necessities," 490, with fig. 23; Stark, *Die Alttürkenzeit in Mittel- und Zentralasien*, 76–78.

300. Bálint, *Die Archäologie der Steppe*, 248–50 (with illustrations, also showing a cast bronze plaque with a griffin).

301. Gleb Kubarev, "Archäologische Denkmäler der Alttürken," in Bemmann, *Steppenkrieger*, 130.

302. Ursula Brosseder, "Belt Plaques as an Indicator of East–West Relations in the Eurasian Steppe at the Turn of the Millennia," in *Xiongnu Archaeology: Multidisciplinary Perspectives of the First Steppe Empire in Central Asia*, ed. Ursula Brosseder and Bryan K. Miller (Bonn, 2011), 349–424. Furnished burials contain similar types of belt plaques all over central Eurasia in the first century BCE/first century CE.

303. Overview: Daim, "Avars and Avar Archaeology," 497–511; Brosseder, "Belt Plaques," 416. See also section 8.1.

304. Daim, "Avars and Avar Archaeology," 528 (examples); Bálint, "Kontakte zwischen Byzanz, Iran und der Steppe." For a strong argument that belts with side-straps were not used in China and Iran before the seventh century or later, see Bálint, "Byzantinisches," 108–10. For the following, I am grateful to Falko Daim for information.

305. Bálint, "Byzantinisches"; Michael Schmauder, "Vielteilige Gürtelgarnituren des 6.–7. Jahrhunderts: Herkunft, Aufkommen und Trägerkreis," in Daim, *Die Awaren am Rand der byzantinischen Welt*, 35: "Without doubt, the multipartite belt did not come to Europe with the Avars." Christoph Eger, "Vielteilige Gürtel im südlichen und östlichen Mittelmeerraum," in Bollók, Csiky, and Vida, *Zwischen Byzanz und der Steppe/Between Byzantium and the Steppe*, 153–74, with further evidence from the Mediterranean area.

306. Uwe Fiedler, "Bulgars in the Lower Danube Region: A Survey of the Archaeological Evidence and the State of Current Research," in Curta, *The Other Europe in the Middle Ages*, 127.

307. Eger, "Vielteilige Gürtel."

308. *Strategicon* 12 B1, 421; the word used is *zōnaria*. The chapter about clothing and equipment of mounted warriors mentions only that in the "bow belt," *toxozōnion*, "files and awls" should be carried. There is no mention of side-straps or of any prestige value of the belt.

309. Falko Daim, "Byzantine Belt Ornaments of the 7th and 8th Centuries in Avar Contexts," in *Intelligible Beauty: Recent Research on Byzantine Jewellery*, ed. Chris Entwistle and Noël Adams (London, 2010), 61–71; Bálint, "Kontakte zwischen Byzanz, Iran und der Steppe."

310. Béla Miklós Szőke, "Veränderungen in der Struktur des awarischen Gürtels," *Antaeus* 29–30 (2008): 175–213, with new reconstructions of middle Avar belts (184–92).

311. See section 7.8.

312. Szőke, "Veränderungen," 207–9.

313. Ján Dekan, "Herkunft und Ethnizität der gegossenen Bronzeindustrie des VIII. Jahrhunderts," *Slov. Arch.* 20 (1972): 317–452.

314. Max Martin, "Die absolute Datierung der Männergürtel im merowingischen Westen und im Awarenreich," *Antaeus* 29–30 (2008), 150 and 161 (Schicht 3 according to Christlein and Martin).

315. Daim, "'Byzantinische' Gürtelgarnituren des 8. Jahrhunderts"; Daim, "Byzantine Belt Ornaments." See section 8.1.

316. Daim, "Byzantine Belts and Avar Birds"; Daim, "Byzantine Belt Ornaments."

317. On the "Hohenberg type," see Daim, "Avars and Avar Archaeology," 508. Late Avar belt fittings are sometimes found in Bulgar graves, but seem to have got there only after the end of the khaganate: Uwe Fiedler, "Die Donaubulgaren und die Mittelawarenzeit—ein Antagonismus," *Antaeus* 29–30 (2008): 132.

318. Daim, "'Byzantinische' Gürtelgarnituren des 8. Jahrhunderts"; Tang parallels for blossom décor: 132–36.

319. Daim, "'Byzantinische' Gürtelgarnituren des 8. Jahrhunderts," 185; Daim, "Avars and Avar Archaeology," 509–11; see also Schmauder, "Vielteilige Gürtelgarnituren des 6.–7. Jahrhunderts," 39 (only from the seventh century onward).

320. *Sui shu*, in Liu Mau-Tsai, *Die chinesischen Nachrichten*, 1:42; cf. Ildikó Ecsedy, "Ancient Turk (Tu-chüeh) Burial Customs," *Acta Orient. Hung.* 38 (1984): 263–87, especially 283. Cf. Christian, *History of Russia, Central Asia and Mongolia*, 144 (Scythians).

321. Falko Daim, *Das awarische Gräberfeld von Leobersdorf* (Vienna, 1988), 171.

322. Priscus, frag. 11.2, ed. and trans. Blockley, 269.

323. *Suidae Lexicon*, ed. Adler, 1:484, *s.v. Bulgaroi*.

324. See Freiberger and Bühler, "Der Goldschatz von Nagyszentmiklós/Sânnicolau Mare," with a study of different workshop traditions represented in what may be part of the khagan's treasure.

325. Thomsen, "Alttürkische Inschriften in der Mongolei," 145 and 168; cf. Pritsak, "Distinctive Features of the Pax Nomadica." In the Khazar Empire *beg* later became the title of a single prince; cf. Golden, *Khazar Studies*, 1:162, and section 8.2. Thomsen's translation "the people" represents the *qara bodun* of the original inscription. On this terminology, see Pritsak, "Tribal Names," 68–69, and the glossary in Talât Tekin, "The Tariat (Terkhin) Inscription," *Acta Orient. Hung.* 37 (1983): 62–63.

326. Published by Klyashtorny, "The Terkhin Inscription," especially 344. Cf. Klyashtorny, "The Tes Inscription of the Uighur Bögü Khagan," *Acta Orient. Hung.* 39 (1985): 137–56, especially 153; Tekin, "The Tariat (Terkhin) Inscription," 46 and the glossary, 62–63. On the interpretation, see Pritsak, "Distinctive Features of the Pax Nomadica." Klyashtorny and Tekin translate *buyruq* as "commanders," Pritsak as "retainers." In *beg* Pritsak sees a tribal chieftain, Tekin more generally "lord." For the Uyghurs, see Golden, *An Introduction*; Christian, *History of Russia, Central Asia and Mongolia*, 264–72.

327. Beševliev, *Die protobulgarische Periode*, 330–31, 352; Ziemann, *Vom Wandervolk zur Großmacht*, 306.

328. On Avar social organization, see László, *Études archéologiques*; Zástěrová, *Les Avares et les Slaves*, 27–29; Szádeczky-Kardoss, "Die Hauptzüge der Sozialordnung"; Kollautz, "Die Awaren"; Alexander Avenarius, "Struktur und Organisation der Steppenvölker," in *Popoli delle steppe*, 1:125–74; Szentpéteri, "Archäologische Studien."

329. Menander, frag. 15.1, ed. and trans. Blockley, 148.

330. Theophylact Simocatta 1.6, 51, and 6.11, 242. Avar *logades* are also mentioned by Theodore Syncellus 6.6, ed. and trans. Makk, 15.

331. Corresponding to Latin *iudices*; cf. Evangelos Chrysos, "Der Kaiser und die Könige," in Wolfram and Daim, *Die Völker an der mittleren and unteren Donau im fünften und sechsten Jahrhundert*, 146, n. 22.

332. Constantine Porphyrogenetus, *De ceremoniis aulae Byzantinae* 2.48, ed. Johann J. Reiske, 2 vols. (Bonn, 1829–30), 1:690; Beševliev, *Die protobulgarische Periode*, 336; on the use of the title *archōn* for Bulgars, see Curta, "Qagan, Khan, or King?," 10–13.

333. Maenchen-Helfen, *Die Welt der Hunnen*, 147–49.

334. Maenchen-Helfen, *Die Welt der Hunnen*, 147–49.

335. Franke, "Fremdherrschaften in China," 54–55; Vladimirtsov, *Le régime social des Mongols*, 110–12.

336. Priscus, frags. 11–14, ed. and trans. Blockley, 235–93.

337. See section 7.7.

338. Menander, frag. 5.1, ed. and trans. Blockley, 48. On the name, see Moravcsik, *Byzantinoturcica*, 2:135; Haussig, "Theophylakts Exkurs," 361. *Candac* was the name of an Alan king of the fifth century (Jordanes, *Getica*, 265–66, ed. Mommsen, 126–27) and of a *saio* or royal agent of Theodoric the Great (Cassiodorus, *Variae epistulae* 1.37, ed. A. J. Fridh, *Variarum libri XII*, Corpus Christianorum Series Latina 96 [Turnhout, 1973], 43); see Wolfram, *History of the Goths*, 241; Patrick Amory, *People and Identity in Ostrogothic Italy, 489–554* (Cambridge, 1997), 368. *Kende/kündür* was a Khazar and later a Hungarian title for a ruler: Golden, *Khazar Studies*, 1:200; *Annales Sangallenses maiores* a. 902, ed. Ildefons von Arx, MGH SS 1 (Hanover, 1826), 77; *Annales Alamannici* a. 904, ed. Georg Heinrich Pertz, MGH SS 1 (Hanover, 1826), 54; cf. Togan, *Ibn Fadlans Reisebericht*, 260; Carlile A. Macartney, *The Magyars in the Ninth Century* (Cambridge, 1930), 59 (with a reference to Kandikh). See also sections 6.10 and 8.2.

339. 565: Corippus, *In laudem Iustini*, 3.258, ed. Antès, 63; see Stache, *Flavius Cresconius Corippus*, 442–43, who prefers *Targites* over the reading *Tergazis* of earlier editions. He also has a summary of the various mentions, as does Moravcsik, *Byzantinoturcica*, 2:252. Cf. Haussig, "Theophylakts Exkurs," 361. See section 2.8.

340. Menander, frag. 12.6, ed. and trans. Blockley, 138; 12.7, 142; 25.1, 216, when he came in 579 "as usual" to cash out the subsidies.

341. Theophylact Simocatta 1.6, 52.

342. Theophylact Simocatta 1.8, 54; see section 3.6.

343. Theophylact Simocatta 6.11, 242; see section 6.3.

344. Menander, frag. 15.1, ed. and trans. Blockley, 148; see section 3.2.

345. Menander, frag. 27.3, ed. and trans. Blockley, 240.

346. Theophylact Simocatta 8.5, 292–93.

347. Viewing "Targitius" as a title of rank: Stein, *Studien zur Geschichte*, 33, n. 13; Haussig, "Theophylakts Exkurs," 358–59; Stache, *Flavius Cresconius Corippus*, 443. Of an opposing view are Zástěrová, *Les Avares et les Slaves*, 32; Deér, "Karl der Grosse," 759. A "Hunnic" military commander, Apsikh, was in the pay of the Byzantines at the same time; see Theophylact Simocatta 1.14.5, 40. On the etymology, see section 6.10.

348. Cf. section 2.5.

349. Menander, frag. 25.2, ed. and trans. Blockley, 224; Moravcsik, *Byzantinoturcica*, 2:240.

350. Theophylact Simocatta 6.4.11, 164; Moravcsik, *Byzantinoturcica*, 2:227.

351. Theophylact Simocatta 6.6.6, 167; Moravcsik, *Byzantinoturcica*, 2:153, associates this name with Turkic *kök*, "blue." With this attribute the Turks of the Orkhon inscriptions sought to enhance their prestige; cf. Thomsen, "Alttürkische Inschriften in der Mongolei," 145.

352. *Chronicon Paschale* a. 626, 178.

353. On Bookolabras, see section 6.9.

354. Menander, frag. 5.5, ed. and trans. Blockley, 50.

355. Menander, frag. 5.4, ed. and trans. Blockley, 52; see section 2.7.

356. Cf. sections 7.6 and 7.7.

357. *De Pippini regis victoria Avarica* 10, ed. Dümmler, 117; see section 8.4.

358. Bóna, "Die Awaren," 9.

359. Bóna, "Ein Vierteljahrhundert," 314–15; Szentpéteri, "Archäologische Studien."

360. Bárdos, "La necropoli avara di Zamárdi."

361. Kovrig, *Das awarenzeitliche Gräberfeld von Alattyán*, 200–202.

362. Bóna, "Ein Vierteljahrhundert," 311 (Ürbőpuszta).

363. Beševliev, *Die protobulgarische Periode*, 412–13.

364. Thus, for example, Kollautz, "Die Awaren," 129–31.

365. Eniko K. Magyari et al., "Holocene Persistence of Wooded Steppe in the Great Hungarian Plain," *Journal of Biogeography* 37 (2010): 915–35; Zsolt Molnár et al., "Past Trends, Present State and Future Prospects of Hungarian Forest-Steppe," in *Eurasian Steppes: Ecological Problems and Livelihoods in a Changing World*, ed. Marinus J. A. Werger and Marija A. van Staalduinen (Heidelberg, 2012), 209–52. See also section 8.5, with further bibliography.

366. *Strategicon* 11.2, 364, and 9.5, 328.

367. Bóna, "Ein Vierteljahrhundert," 309–11; Kovrig, *Das awarenzeitliche Gräberfeld von Alattyán*, 199–200; Daim, *Das awarische Gräberfeld von Leobersdorf.*

368. Kovrig, *Das awarenzeitliche Gräberfeld von Alattyán*, 200.

369. Maenchen-Helfen, *Geschichte der Hunnen*, 152–53; Vladimirtsov, *Le régime social des Mongols*, 73–75; Pritsak, "Distinctive Features of the Pax Nomadica." In the sources conquered peoples are often lumped together as slaves. Yet this probably describes their dependent status as a people rather than slavery in the narrower sense. The subjugated peoples were not necessarily broken up (see below).

370. Kovrig, *Das awarenzeitliche Gräberfeld von Alattyán*, 201. This at least allows a conclusion to be drawn about the low value attached to work.

371. For instance, a fine eighth-century strap end found at Klárafalva: *Awaren in Europa*, exhibition catalog, 74. On cuts of meat as grave goods, see Daim, *Das awarische Gräberfeld von Leobersdorf*, 165–66.

372. István Bóna, "Abriss der Siedlungsgeschichte Ungarns im 5.–7. Jahrhundert und die Awarensiedlung von Dunaújváros," *Archeologické rozhledy* 20 (1968): 616–18; Hajnalka Herold, "Die Awarenzeit im Burgenland: Archäologische Forschungsergebnisse zur Siedlung und zum Gräberfeld von Zillingtal," *Burgenländische Heimatblätter* 73 (2011): 134–57, http://www.zobodat.at/pdf/Burgenlaendische-Heimatblaetter_73_0134-0157.pdf.

373. Csanád Bálint, *Die awarenzeitliche Siedlung von Eperjes (Komitat Csongrád)* (Budapest, 1991); Uwe Fiedler, "Zur Datierung der Siedlungen der Awaren und der Landnahme: Ein Beitrag zur Zuordnung der Siedlung von Eperjes," *Zeitschrift für Archäologie* 28 (1994): 307–52; Daim, "Avars and Avar Archaeology," 513.

374. Fredegar 4.48, ed. Krusch, 40.

375. Theophylact Simocatta 8.3.11–12, 213.

376. Kiss, *Das awarenzeitlich-gepidische Gräberfeld*; Kiss, *Das awarenzeitliche Gräberfeld*; Attila Kiss, "Das Gräberfeld und die Siedlung der awarenzeitlichen germanischen Bevölkerung von Kölked," *Folia Archaeologica* 30 (1979): 185–91.

377. Vida, "Conflict and Coexistence," 24 and 29.

378. Cf. section 3.8.

379. Bárdos and Garam, *Das awarenzeitliche Gräberfeld*; Bárdos, "La necropoli avara di Zamárdi."

380. Vida, "Local or Foreign Romans?" See section 3.9.

381. John of Ephesus 6.45, 259; transmitted in Michael the Syrian 10.21, 362; cf. Theophylact Simocatta 1.4.1–3, 24–25, and section 3.5.

382. "One half as a tribute" has also been proposed; Vasilka Tăpkova-Zaimova, "Sur les rapports entre la population indigène des régions balkaniques et les 'barbares' aux VIe et VIIe siècles," *Byzantinobulgarica* 1 (1962): 74. If we can use the information at all, it is more likely that half of the (Roman) levy was meant, since the barbarians everywhere extracted smaller levies than the Roman bureaucracy: Marquart, *Osteuropäische und ostasiatische Streifzüge*, 482; Altheim, *Geschichte der Hunnen*, 1:89; Hauptmann, "Les rapports," 157; Szádeczky-Kardoss, "Die Hauptzüge der Sozialordnung," 222.

383. Theophylact Simocatta 6.4.1–2, 163; 7.10.1–4, 193; 7.11.7–8, 194; 8.1.11, 210. See sections 3.5 and 5.5.

384. John of Ephesus 5.32, 256.

385. *Miracula Demetrii* 2.5.285, 228.

386. Theophylact Simocatta 7.10.1, 193.

387. Theodore Syncellus 5.35–37, ed. and trans. Makk, 15; Nicephorus 10, ed. and trans. Mango, 53 (giving a number of 270,000 captives, "as was mutually confirmed by some of the prisoners who escaped"); cf. section 7.2.

388. Paul the Deacon, *Historia Langobardorum* 4.37, ed. Waitz, 162–67.

389. Altheim, *Geschichte der Hunnen*, 1:235; Mircea Eliade, *Zalmoxis, the Vanishing God: Comparative Studies in the Religions and Folklore of Dacia and Eastern Europe*, trans. Willard R. Trask (Chicago, 1972), 135–37, esp. 137; Jean-Paul Roux, "La religion des peuples des steppes," in *Popoli delle steppe*, 2:513–32, on cases of guiding animals among the steppe peoples.

390. *Miracula Demetrii* 2.5.285–93, 228–30.

391. For a skeptical reading of the *Miracula*, see Speck, "De miraculis Sancti Demetrii, qui Thessalonicam profugus venit." However, the Kuver story is not limited to biblical topoi. See also sections 6.10 and 7.7.

392. Priscus, frag. 11.2, ed. and trans. Blockley, 266–71.

393. Daim, "Byzantine Belts and Avar Birds"; Csanád Bálint, "Zur Identifizierung des Grabes von Kuvrat," *Acta Arch. Hung.* 36 (1984): 264–65; Garam, *Funde byzantinischer Herkunft*; Daim, *Die Awaren am Rand der byzantinischen Welt*; Csanád Bálint, "Avar Goldsmiths' Work from the Perspective of Cultural History," in Entwistle and Adams, *Intelligible Beauty*, 146–60; Gergely Szenthe, "Meister und ihre Kunden: Herstellung und Verbreitung gegossener Bronzegegenstände im spätawarenzeitlichen Karpatenbecken," *Archaeologiai Értesítő* 137 (2012): 57–75; Szenthe, "Antique Meaning—Avar Significance: Complex Iconographic Schemes on Early Medieval Small Objects," *Acta Arch. Hung.* 64 (2013): 139–72; Zsófia Rácz, *Die Goldschmiedgräber der Awarenzeit* (Mainz, 2014); Freiberger and Bühler, "Der Goldschatz von Nagyszentmiklós/Sânnicolau Mare."

394. Bálint, "Avar Goldsmiths' Work"; Bálint, *Der Schatz von Nagyszentmiklós*; see also Daim et al., *Der Goldschatz*.

395. Rácz, *Die Goldschmiedgräber der Awarenzeit*, 137–42 (catalog 143–200).

396. Daim, "Byzantine Belt Ornaments," 64; Daim, "Avars and Avar Archaeology," 478–80; *Awaren in Europa*, exhibition catalog, 64–65; see the catalog of finds in the goldsmiths' graves of the Avar period in Rácz, *Die Goldschmiedgräber der Awarenzeit*, 146–200.

397. A good example of this is the development of the specific early Avar zoomorphic style from Germanic and Byzantine elements; Margit Nagy, "Frühawarenzeitliche Grabfunde aus Budapest: Bemerkungen zur awarenzeitlichen Tierornamentik," in *Popoli delle steppe*, 1:373–408. In general, see Orsolya Heinrich-Tamáska, "Byzantine Goldsmithing in Avaria? Exchange and Transfer at the Edge of the Empire during the Seventh Century AD," in Bugarski et al, *GrenzÜbergänge*, 273–90.

398. Heinrich-Tamáska, "Avar-Age Metalworking Technologies," 240–48.

399. Orsolya Heinrich-Tamáska, *Die Stein- und Glasinkrustationskunst des 6. und 7. Jahrhunderts im Karpatenbecken*, Monumenta Avarorum Archaeologica 8 (Budapest, 2006).

400. John of Ephesus 6.24, 247–48; the Latin expressions are modern translations of the Syrian text. Furthermore, the passage reproduces rather what people were saying in Constantinople, and in part contradicts the more accurate account in Menander; cf. section 3.4.

401. Paul the Deacon, *Historia Langobardorum* 4.20, ed. Waitz, 154.

402. Eugippius, *Vita Severini* 8, ed. Theodor Mommsen, MGH SS rer. Germ. 26 (Berlin, 1898), 19–20.

403. *Zhou shu*, in Liu Mau-Tsai, *Die chinesischen Nachrichten*, 1:5 and 7. See Christian, *History of Russia, Central Asia and Mongolia*, 250. Targitaos: Herodotus 4.5, ed. Godley, 203–5.

404. Menander, frag. 10.3, ed. and trans. Blockley, 116.

405. Togan, *Ibn Fadlans Reisebericht*, 276. Gerhard Doerfer, *Mongolo-Tungusica* (Wiesbaden, 1985), 99, assumes that the title *tarkhan* could be derived from the meaning "smith." See also section 8.2.

406. Bálint, "Avar Goldsmiths' Work," 147: "Few scholars take into account that goldsmiths were held in relatively low esteem and belonged to the poorest groups of society." The evidence for this low rank, however, comes mostly from the West; see e.g. Claus von Carnap-Bornheim, "The Social Position of the Germanic Goldsmith in AD 0–500," in *Roman Gold and the Development of the Early Germanic Kingdoms*, ed. Bente Magnus (Stockholm, 2001), 263–78.

407. Martin Ježek, "The Disappearance of European Smiths' Burials," *Cambridge Archaeological Journal* 25, no. 1 (2015): 121–43.

408. Daim, "Avars and Avar Archaeology," 479.

409. Cf. Joachim Werner, "Zur Verbreitung frühgeschichtlicher Metallarbeiten (Werkstatt-Wanderhandwerk-Handel-Familienverbindung)," *Early Medieval Studies* 1. *Antikvarisk arkiv* 38 (1970): 65–81. Workshop analyses by Peter Wobrauschek, Wolfgang Haider, and Christina Streli in Daim, *Das awarische Gräberfeld von Leobersdorf*; Zlata Čilinská, "Anfänge des spezialisierten Handwerks und Handels bei der altslawischen Gesellschaft in der Slowakei," *Slov. Arch.* 34, no. 2 (1986): 300–301.

410. Heinrich-Tamáska, "Avar-Age Metalworking Technologies," 240–48.

411. Werner, *Der Schatzfund von Vrap in Albanien*, 45–46; Kurt Horedt, "Die Völker Südosteuropas im 6. bis 8. Jahrhundert: Probleme und Ergebnisse," in Hänsel, *Die Völker Südosteuropas vom 6.–8. Jahrhundert*, 26, assumed the use of mines in Slovakia, for which, however, there is no evidence.

412. Zlata Čilinská, "Anfänge des spezialisierten Handwerks und Handels bei der altslawischen Gesellschaft in der Slowakei," *Slov. Arch.* 34 (1986): 302.

413. Daim, *Das awarische Gräberfeld von Leobersdorf*, 166–68.

414. Bálint, *Die awarenzeitliche Siedlung von Eperjes*.

415. Zdeněk Klanica, "Vorgroßmährische Siedlung in Mikulčice und ihre Beziehungen zum Karpatenbecken," *Študijné zvesti* 16 (1968): 124–26. In the eighth-century settlement there are pits with bronze slag and traces of smithies.

416. János Gömöri, "Archaeometallurgy in Hungary: Some Results and Questions," in *The Archaeometallurgy of Iron: Recent Developments in Archaeological and Scientific Research*, ed. Jiří Hošek, Henry Cleere, and Lubomír Mihok (Prague, 2011), 65–72, 293–95.

417. Peter Donat, "Handwerk und Gewerbe," in Herrmann, *Die Slawen in Deutschland*, 103–5; on the use of bronze, see also 109.

418. Kurt Horedt, "Das Fortleben der Gepiden in der frühen Awarenzeit," *Germania* 63 (1985): 164–68.

419. *Annales Fuldenses* a. 892, ed. Friedrich Kurze and Heinrich Haefele, MGH SS rer. Germ. 7, 2nd ed. (Hanover, 1891), 121–22. Horedt, "Die Völker Südosteuropas im 6. bis 8. Jahrhundert," 25; Beševliev, *Die protobulgarische Periode*, 414; Wolfram, *Grenzen und Räume*, 269.

420. Dietrich Claude, *Der Handel im westlichen Mittelmeer während des Frühmittelalters: Untersuchungen zu Handel und Verkehr der vor- und frühgeschichtlichen Zeit im Mittel- und Nordeuropa*, Abhandlungen AW Göttingen 3, F. 144 (Göttingen, 1985), 263–64.

421. Priscus, frag. 46, ed. and trans. Blockley, 353.

422. *Sui shu*, in Liu Mau-Tsai, *Die chinesischen Nachrichten*, 1:56. On the frontier markets of the Xiongnu as an object of negotiations with the Chinese, see Hesse, "Der

Austausch als stabilisierender Faktor der politischen Herrschaft in der Geschichte der Mongolei," 165. Chinese trade with the *Liao* was also limited to the licensed border trading posts; Franke, *Das chinesische Kaiserreich*, 210.

423. See below.

424. Györffy, "Landnahme," 256.

425. Theophylact Simocatta 1.3.7, 24.

426. See section 6.4. Spices: Theophylact Simocatta 7.13.6, 197; see section 5.7.

427. Garam, *Funde byzantinischer Herkunft.*

428. Amphorae: Tivadar Vida, *Die awarenzeitliche Keramik*, vol. 1, *6.–7. Jahrhundert* (Budapest, 1999), 93 and 242–43, arguing that nothing points to regular supplies of the Avars with trade goods; Curta, "Amphorae and Seals," 307–8; Gergely Csiky and Piroska Magyar-Hársegyi, "Wine for the Avar Elite? Amphorae from Avar Period Burials in the Carpathian Basin," in *The Danubian Lands between the Black, Aegean, and Adriatic Seas (7th Century BC – 10th Century AD): Proceedings of the Fifth International Congress on Black Sea Antiquities (Belgrade, 17–21 September 2013)*, ed. Gocha R. Tsetskhladze, Alexandru Avram, and James Hargrave (Oxford, 2015), 175–82. Alcohol consumption, probably a topical remark: *Suidae Lexicon*, ed. Adler, 1:483, *s.v. Bulgaroi.*

429. See Bálint, *The Avars, Byzantium and Italy.* Cf. section 3.8.

430. *Miracula Demetrii* 2.2.214, 189.

431. Theophanes, *Chronographia* 6092, 279; Theophylact Simocatta 7.15.14, 201, knew nothing of this. It is most likely a bit of propaganda against Maurice, and it is conceivable that for this purpose the price was purposely set low. Whether these events really happened or not is uncertain; more important is that the account had an air of plausibility.

432. Jones, *The Later Roman Empire*, 1:192–93; Maenchen-Helfen, *Geschichte der Hunnen*, 140, with a series of additional examples from which it is apparent that the ransom sums were pegged to relative rank and wealth.

433. See section 7.1.

434. Paul the Deacon, *Historia Langobardorum* 4.37, ed. Waitz, 162–64. This was not particular for Avar armies; when, for instance, the Byzantines under Belisarius captured Naples in the Gothic war, the imperial troops "kept killing all whom they encountered, sparing neither old nor young, and dashing into the houses they made slaves of the women and children and secured the valuables as plunder." Procopius, *Bella* 5.10.29, ed. and trans. Dewing, 3:101.

435. Priscus, frag. 10.2, ed. and trans. Blockley, 261.

436. Menander, frag. 10.3, ed. and trans. Blockley, 120. "Those who have read the Orkhon inscriptions and the Secret History will know that the 'favourite, ideal booty' for a nomad was the female slave/concubine," asserts Pritsak, "Tribal Names," 88, which seems exaggerated. Gold, silver, and fine clothing are mentioned more frequently in the sources. In the Tonyukuk inscriptions (Thomsen, "Alttürkische Inschriften in der Mongolei," 169) gold and silver are also mentioned before the "virgins and maids" as booty.

437. Michael McCormick, *Origins of the European Economy: Communications and Commerce, A.D. 300–900* (New York, 2002), especially 243–53, 418, and 759–77.

438. Charles Verlinden, "L'origine de Sclavus=esclave," *Archivum Latinitatis Medii Aevi* 17 (1942): 97–128.

439. Joachim Henning, "Gefangenenfesseln im slawischen Siedlungsraum und der europäische Sklavenhandel im 6. bis 12. Jahrhundert," *Germania* 70 (1992): 403–26; Marek Jankowiak, "Dirhams for Slaves," project website: http://krc.orient.ox.ac.uk/dirhamsforslaves/index.php/en/news-and-events.

440. Bálint, "Einige Fragen des Dirhem-Verkehrs in Europa"; Kiss, "Die Goldfunde des Karpatenbeckens vom 5.–10. Jahrhundert," 120 and 137–38; McCormick, *Origins of the European Economy*, 829 (dirhems of 787/88 in Rečica, Slovenia) and 833 (dirhem of

777/78 in Völkermarkt, Carinthia) point to a Venetian trade route that had been established in ca. 750 (ibid., 526). See also Somogyi, *Byzantinische Fundmünzen der Awarenzeit in ihrem europäischen Umfeld*, 81.

441. Ivo Štefan, "Great Moravia, Statehood and Archaeology: The 'Decline and Fall' of One Early Medieval Polity," in *Frühgeschichtliche Zentralorte in Mitteleuropa*, ed. Jiří Macháček and Šimon Ungerman (Bonn, 2011), 342.

442. Jordanes, *Getica* 5.37, ed. Mommsen, 63.

443. Svetlana Alexandrowna Pletnewa, *Die Chasaren: Mittelalterliches Reich an Don und Wolga* (Leipzig, 1978), 108–10; the principal sources are Arabic accounts and Khagan Joseph's (still debated) letter to Hasdai ibn Shaprut (ibid., 148). Cf. Bálint, *Die Archäologie der Steppe*, 69–70.

444. Skaff, *Sui-Tang China and Its Turko-Mongol Neighbors*, 241–71. Cf. the tables in Liu Mau-Tsai, *Die chinesischen Nachrichten*, 1:410–12. On trade between the Xiongnu and China, see Hesse, "Der Austausch als stabilisierender Faktor der politischen Herrschaft in der Geschichte der Mongolei," 165.

445. Jordanes, *Getica* 5.37, ed. Mommsen, 63. On this topic, see John Smedley, "Trade in Cherson, 6th–10th Centuries," in *Actes du XVe congrès international d'études byzantines* (Athens, 1976), 4:291–97; Theodor S. Noonan, "Russia, the Near East, and the Steppe in the Early Medieval Period: An Examination of the Sasanian and Byzantine Finds from the Kama-Ural Area," *Archivum Eurasie Medii Aevi* 2 (1982): 269–302.

446. See, for example, Bálint, "Über einige östliche Beziehungen," 132–34.

447. Edith B. Thomas, "Die Romanität Pannoniens im 5. and 6. Jahrhundert," in Bott and Meier-Arendt, *Germanen, Hunnen und Awaren*, 293.

448. Edited in Marquart, *Osteuropäische und ostasiatische Streifzüge*, 205.

449. Bóna, "Studien zum frühmittelalterlichen Reitergrab," 74–76.

450. Somogyi, "New Remarks on the Flow of Byzantine Coins," 89 (twenty-six copper coins); Somogyi, *Byzantinische Fundmünzen*; Somogyi, *Byzantinische Fundmünzen der Awarenzeit in ihrem europäischen Umfeld*.

451. Wolfgang Hahn, "Die Fundmünzen des 5.–9. Jahrhunderts in Österreich und den unmittelbar angrenzenden Gebieten," in Herwig Wolfram, *Die Geburt Mitteleuropas: Geschichte Österreichs vor seiner Entstehung* (Vienna, 1987), 453–64; cf. Winter, "Die byzantinischen Fundmünzen"; Garam, "Die münzdatierten Gräber der Awarenzeit." On the circulation of coinage in Byzantium, see Morrisson, "Byzance au VIIe siècle"; Stratos, *Byzantium in the Seventh Century*, 2:167.

452. Daim, *Das awarische Gräberfeld von Leobersdorf*, 166, found clear indications for the local production of simple ornaments and utensils; see, too, Falko Daim and Andreas Lippert, *Das awarische Gräberfeld von Sommerein am Leithagebirge* (Vienna, 1984), 125.

453. Menander, frag. 21, ed. and trans. Blockley, 194; see section 3.3.

454. Györffy, "Landnahme," 258.

455. *The Russian Primary Chronicle, Povest' vremennykh let*, earlier known as the *Nestor Chronicle*. English translation, *The Russian Primary Chronicle* 17, trans. Cross and Sherbowitz-Wetzor, 59 (tribute); 19, 59 (squirrels). See also the new edition by Donald Ostrowski, *Russian Primary Chronicle (Povest' vremennykh let)* (Cambridge, MA, 2004). Cf. Pletnewa, *Die Chasaren*, 110.

456. Theophanes, *Chronographia* 6305, 681; Beševliev, *Die protobulgarische Periode*, 249–50; Ziemann, *Vom Wandervolk zur Großmacht*, 267–68.

457. *Suidae Lexicon*, ed. Adler, 1:484, *s.v. Bulgaroi*. Cf. Beševliev, *Die protobulgarische Periode*, 262. Even if the account in the *Suda Lexicon* is merely exploiting a topos on the demise of barbarian empires, as Péter Váczy, "Der fränkische Krieg und das Volk der Awaren," *Acta Antiqua Academiae Scientiarum Hungaricae* 20 (1972): 395–420, and Wolfram, *Die Geburt Mitteleuropas*, 520, n. 17 (with reference to Caesar, *De bello Gallico* 4.2)

would have it, it does at least reveal that contemporaries saw a contradiction between the steppe empires and free trade.

458. General treatment in, for example, Hans Findeisen, *Schamanentum* (Stuttgart, 1957); Mircea Eliade, *Shamanism: Archaic Techniques of Ecstasy*, trans. Willard R. Trask (Princeton, NJ, 1964); Ioan M. Lewis, *Ecstatic Religion* (London, 1971); among the Eurasian steppe peoples: Mihály Hoppál, "Shamanism: An Archaic and/or Recent System of Beliefs," *UAJB*, n.s., 5 (1985): 121–40 (with secondary literature); Vilmos Diószegi and Mihály Hoppál, *Shamanism in Siberia* (Budapest, 1978); Karl H. Menges, "Zum sibirischen Schamanismus," *Central Asiatic Journal* 25 (1981): 260–309; Walther Heissig, *The Religions of Mongolia* (London, 1981); Jean-Paul Roux, *La mort chez les peuples altaïques anciens et médiévaux d'après les documents écrits* (Paris, 1963); Jean-Paul Roux, *La religion des Turcs et des Mongols* (Paris, 1984).

459. Studies from the 1980s, still based to an extent on the old paradigms: Roux, "La religion des peuples des steppes"; János Balász, "Elementi orientali dello sciamanismo ungherese," in *Popoli delle steppe*, 2:649–76; András Róna-Tas, "Materialien zur alten Religion der Türken," in *Synkretismus in den Religionen Zentralasiens*, ed. Werner Heissig and Hans-Joachim Klimkeit (Wiesbaden, 1987), 33–45; S. G. Klyashtorny, "The Ancient Turkic Religion: Its Reconstruction and Genesis," *Information Bulletin* (1987): 44–52; Bruno Öhrig, *Bestattungsriten alttürkischer Aristokratie im Lichte der Inschriften* (Munich, 1988). Later works: Käthe Uray-Köhalmi, "Böge and Beki: Schamanentum und Ahnenkult bei den frühen Mongolen," in *Varia Eurasiatica: Festschrift für Professor András Róna-Tas* (Szeged, 1991), 229–38; Hans-Joachim Klimkeit, "Die frühe Religion der Türken im Spiegel ihrer inschriftlichen Quellen," *Zeitschrift für Religionswissenschaft* 3 (1995): 191–206; Peter B. Golden, "Religion among the Qipčaqs of Medieval Eurasia," *Central Asiatic Journal* 42 (1998): 180–237; Jean-Paul Roux, "Die alttürkische Mythologie," in *Götter und Mythen in Zentralasien und Nordasien*, ed. Egidius Schmalzriedt and Hans-Werner Haussig (Stuttgart, 1999), 173–277; S. G. Klyashtorny, "Political Background of the Old Turkic Religion," in *Roter Altai, gib dein Echo! Festschrift für Erika Taube zum 65. Geburtstag*, ed. Anett C. Oelschlägel, Ingo Nentwig, and Jakob Taube (Leipzig, 2005), 260–65. See also the volume Géza Bethlenfalvy et al., eds., *Altaic Religious Beliefs and Practices: Proceedings of the 33rd Permanent International Altaistic Conference Budapest 1990* (Budapest, 1992).

460. E.g. Peter B. Golden, "Khazaria and Judaism," *Archivum Eurasiae Medii Aevi* 3 (1983): 127–56; Golden, "The Conversion of the Khazars to Judaism," in Golden, Ben-Shammai, and Róna-Tas, *The World of the Khazars*, 123–67.

461. Menander, frag. 10.3, ed. and trans. Blockley, 118.

462. Cf. Michael Ripinsky-Naxon, *The Nature of Shamanism: Substance and Function of a Religious Metaphor* (Albany, NY, 1993).

463. Roux, "La religion des peuples des steppes," quite rightly observes that shamanism as a specific religious practice should not be mixed up with religion on the whole, comprising belief in divine beings, etc. See also Khazanov, *Nomads and the Outside World*, 11–33.

464. Theophylact Simocatta 7.8.14, 191. Cf. Scharlipp, *Die frühen Türken in Zentralasien*, 56–61.

465. "Magias artibus instructi, diversas eis fantasias ostenderunt": Gregory of Tours, *Decem libri historiarum* 4.29, ed. Krusch and Levison, 161. See section 2.7.

466. *Suidae Lexicon*, ed. Adler, 2:112, *s.v. diopteres*.

467. *Nan shi*, 79; Yu, "Doubts," 301.

468. Menander, frag. 27.3, ed. and trans. Blockley, 240.

469. Theophylact Simocatta 1.8.3, 30; see section 3.6.

470. Petkov, *Voices of Medieval Bulgaria, Seventh–Fifteenth Century*, 10 (from a ninth-century funerary inscription of a man with the title *bogotor boila kolober*). Beševliev, *Die protobulgarische Periode*, 350–51: "The function of the *kolobros* consisted in choosing the

day and hour of battle, performing magical actions, and prophesying, in order to secure the army's success"; cf. 356 and 382–85. This is, however, only a conjecture based on a passage in the *responsa* of Pope Nicholas I, *Epistola* 99, c. 35, ed. Ernst Dümmler, MGH Epp. Karolini aevi 4 (Berlin, 1925), 581: "Refertis, quod soliti fueritis, quando in proelium progrediabimini, diem et horam observare et incantationes et ioca et carmina et nonnulla auguria exercere"; there is no mention of a spiritual guide.

471. Moravcsik, *Byzantinoturcica*, 2:162; Yu, "Doubts," 301.

472. Theophylact Simocatta 7.8.15, 191.

473. Menander, frag. 25.1, ed. and trans. Blockley, 220.

474. Beševliev, *Die protobulgarische Periode*, 377, on customary Bulgarian oaths with similar content but different form.

475. Stephanus, *Vita S. Wilfridi* 28, ed. Wilhelm Levison, MGH SS rer. Merov. 6 (Hanover, 1913), 221–22; see section 7.7.

476. Nicholas I, *Epistola* 99, *Responsa*, c. 67, ed. Dümmler, 591: "Perhibetis vos consuetudinem habuisse, quotienscumque aliquem iureiurando pro qualibet re disponebatis obligare, spatham in medium afferre, et per eam iuramentum agebatur." Beševliev, *Die protobulgarische Periode*, 376; on the sword cult of the steppe peoples, see Roux, "La religion des peuples des steppes."

477. *Theophanes Continuatus, Ioannes Cameniata, Symeon Magister, Georgius Monachus*, ed. Immanuel Bekker, Corpus Scriptorum Historiae Byzantinae 48 (Bonn, 1838), 31; Beševliev, *Die protobulgarische Periode*, 377–78; Ziemann, *Vom Wandervolk zur Großmacht*, 299–300.

478. "Per canem et lupum aliasque nefandissimas et ethnicas res sacramentas et pacem egisse": *Epistula Theotmari*, in *Conversio Bagoariorum et Carantanorum und der Brief des Erzbischofs Theotmar von Salzburg*, ed. Fritz Lošek, MGH Studien und Texte 15 (Hanover, 1997), 148.

479. Denis Sinor, "Taking an Oath over a Dog Cut in Two," in Bethlenfalvy et al., *Altaic Religious Beliefs and Practices*, 301–7 (also referring to Genesis 15, where oaths are taken on other animals cut in half at the covenant between Jahwe and Abraham); Nora Berend, "Oath-Taking in Hungary: A Window on Medieval Social Interaction," in *Central and Eastern Europe in the Middle Ages: A Cultural History*, ed. Piotr Gorecki and Nancy van Deusen (London, 2005), 45; D. A. Miller, "Byzantine Treaties and Treaty-Making: 500–1025 A.D.," *Byzantinoslavica* 32 (1971): 56–76.

480. Skaff, *Sui-Tang China and Its Turko-Mongol Neighbors*, 194.

481. Radloff, *Aus Sibirien*, 2:5.

482. Jean-Paul Roux, "Tängri: Essai sur le ciel-dieu des peuples altaïques (premier article)," *Revue de l'histoire des religions*, 149, no. 1 (1956): 49–82, with sequels in 149, no. 2, 150, no. 1, and 150, no. 2 (see https://journals.openedition.org/rhr/persee-226815); Grousset, *Empire of the Steppes*, 179; de Ferdinandy, "Die nordeurasischen Reitervölker," 183–84; Heissig, "Ethnische Gruppenbildung in Zentralasien," 37; Roux, "La religion des peuples des steppes"; Golden, "Conversion of the Khazars to Judaism," 131–32.

483. Theophylact Simocatta 7.8.14–15, 191.

484. Michel Roux, "L'origine celeste de la souveraineté dans les inscriptions paleo-turques de Mongolie et de la Sibérie," in *The Sacral Kingship: Studies in the History of Religions*, ed. Giunta Centrale per gli Studi Storici (Leiden, 1959), 235–38.

485. Tonyukuk inscription, 4, http://bitig.org/?lang=e&mod=1&tid=1&oid=17&m=1.

486. Bilge Khagan inscription, front side, 1, http://bitig.org/?lang=e&mod=1&tid=1&oid=16&m=1. Thomsen, "Alttürkische Inschriften in der Mongolei," 142 and 168–70; Scharlipp, *Die frühen Türken in Zentralasien*, 59–60.

487. Kültegin inscription, 1st side, 10–11, http://bitig.org/?lang=e&mod=1&tid=1&oid=15&m=1, CE 732 (English corrected).

488. Klyashtorny, "Political Background of the Old Turkic Religion."

489. Theophylact Simocatta 7.8.14, 191.

490. Kollautz and Miyakawa, 1:282; Zoltán Kádár, "Gli animali negli oggetti ornamentali dei popoli della steppa: Unni, Avari e Magiari," in *L'uomo di fronte al mondo animale nell'alto medioevo*, SSCI 31, 2 vols. (Spoleto, 1983), 2:1373–87; Francesca Angiò, "Divinità pagane e sacrifici umani nella Vita di San Pancrazio di Taormina," *Bollettino della Badia Greca di Grottaferrata*, n.s., 52 (1998): 56–76; see also section 4.4.

491. Scharlipp, *Die frühen Türken in Zentralasien*; Christopher L. Beckwith, "A Note on the Heavenly Kings of Ancient and Medieval Central Eurasia," *Archivum Eurasiae Medii Aevi* 17 (2010): 7–10; "Heavenly Qaghan ideology": Skaff, *Sui-Tang China and Its Turko-Mongol Neighbors*, 119–22.

492. Petkov, *Voices of Medieval Bulgaria, Seventh–Fifteenth Century*, 11 (Omurtag), 12 (Malamir), 13 (Persian). Beševliev, *Die protobulgarische Periode*, 335; de Ferdinandy, "Die nordeurasischen Reitervölker," 183–84; Ziemann, *Vom Wandervolk zur Großmacht*, 307.

493. Petkov, *Voices of Medieval Bulgaria, Seventh–Fifteenth Century*, 11; for the Bulgar Tangra cult, see Fiedler, "Bulgars in the Lower Danube Region," 207–8. See also Klyashtorny, "Political Background of the Old Turkic Religion," 260.

494. Theophylact Simocatta 7.10.8, 193; 7.15, 273.

495. Beševliev, *Die protobulgarische Periode*, 379.

496. Bóna, "Ein Vierteljahrhundert," 316–17; Bálint, *Die Archäologie der Steppe*, 166 (drawing).

497. Radloff, *Aus Sibirien*, 2:7; on the tree cult of the steppe peoples, see Balász, "Elementi orientali"; Roux, "La religion des peuples des steppes."

498. Falko Daim, "Vom Umgang mit toten Awaren," in *Erinnerungskultur im Bestattungsritual: Archäologisch-Historisches Forum*, ed. Jörg Jarnut and Matthias Wemhoff with Alexandra Nusser, Mittelalter Studien 3 (Munich, 2003), 41–57. See also Ecsedy, "Ancient Turk (T'u-chüeh) Burial Customs," especially 266–67; Vasily V. Barthold and John M. Rogen, "The Burial Rites of the Turks and the Mongols," *Central Asiatic Journal* 14 (1970): 195–227.

499. Menander, frag. 19.1, ed. and trans. Blockley, 176.

500. *Sui shu*, in Liu Mau-Tsai, *Die chinesischen Nachrichten*, 1:42; and in the *Zhou Shu*, both using material from the second half of the sixth century: Stark, *Die Alttürkenzeit in Mittel- und Zentralasien*, 109–10.

501. For an overview of Avar archaeology, see sections 3.8., 7.8, and 8.1.

502. *Sui shu*, in Liu Mau-Tsai, *Die chinesischen Nachrichten*, 1:42. The relatively small number of excavated early Turkish graves—not even a hundredth of those in the Carpathian Basin from the Avar period—do not authorize a more precise determination and ethnic classification; Bálint, *Die Archäologie der Steppe*, 235–71.

503. Kovrig, *Das awarenzeitliche Gräberfeld von Alattyán*, 89–92; Daim, *Das awarische Gräberfeld von Leobersdorf*, 170; Tomka, "Die Lehre der Bestattungsbräuche."

504. Bóna, "Studien zum frühmittelalterlichen Reitergrab," 92; Daim and Lippert, *Das awarische Gräberfeld*, 127; Daim, *Das awarische Gräberfeld von Leobersdorf*, 171.

505. Kovrig, *Das awarenzeitliche Gräberfeld von Alattyán*, 73–75.

506. Kovrig, *Das awarenzeitliche Gräberfeld von Alattyán*, 63; cf. section 6.4.

507. Stark, *Die Alttürkenzeit in Mittel- und Zentralasien*, 165 and 103–5; Tomka, "Die Lehre der Bestattungsbräuche," 246–49.

508. Togan, *Ibn Fadlans Reisebericht*, 20 and 138–39; Radloff, *Aus Sibirien*, 1:380; István Fodor, *Altungarn, Bulgarotürken und Ostslawen in Südrussland (Archäologische Beiträge)*, Acta Universitatis de Attila József Nominatae, Acta Antiqua et Archaeologica 20 (Szeged, 1977), 23 and 34; Bálint, *Die Archäologie der Steppe*; Pletnewa, *Die Chasaren*, 76; István Bóna, "A Szegvár-Sápoldali lovassír," *Archaeologiai Értesítő* 106 (1979): 31, with the

assumption that for the prominent men of the first generation of Avars in the Carpathian Basin the war-horse was buried and a reserve horse consumed. Cf. Bóna, "Ein Viertel-jahrhundert," 314–16; Béla M. Szőke, "Zur Problematik des Bestattungsritus mit verstüm-melten Rinderschädel des Typs von Sopronkőhida," *Acta Arch. Hung.* 31 (1979): 51–103; Roux, *La mort chez les peuples altaïques*; Roux, "La religion des peuples des steppes"; Kollautz and Miyakawa, 2:128–30.

509. Menander, frag. 19.1, ed. and trans. Blockley, 178; Beševliev, *Die protobulgarische Periode*, 403, assembles the sources for this custom among the Bulgars. Herodotus 4.71, ed. Godley, 268–71, had recounted similar practices among the Scythians.

510. Jeannine Davis-Kimball et al., ed., *Kurgans, Ritual Sites, and Settlements: Eurasian Bronze and Iron Age*, BAR International Series 890 (Oxford, 2000).

511. Bryan K. Miller, "The Southern Xiongnu in Northern China: Navigating and Negotiating the Middle Ground," in Bemman, and Schmauder, *Complexity of Interaction*, 162–85; Brosseder and Miller, *Xiongnu Archaeology*.

512. Stark, *Die Alttürkenzeit in Mittel- und Zentralasien*, 109–41.

513. Kültegin inscription, 2nd side, 12, http://bitig.org/?lang=e&mod=1&tid=1&oid =15&m=1.

514. Petkov, *Voices of Medieval Bulgaria, Seventh–Fifteenth Century*, 3–13 ("stone annals"); Fiedler, "Bulgars in the Lower Danube Region," 203–7.

515. *Urkundenbuch des Burgenlandes, No. 1*, ed. Hans Wagner (Vienna, 1955), 1–2.

516. István Zimonyi, "Notes on the Differences between Bedouin and Inner Asian Nomadism," in *Central Asia on Display: Proceedings of the 7th Conference of the European Society for Central Asian Studies*, ed. Gabriele Rasuly-Paleczek and Julia Katschnig (Münster, 2005), 379; Golden, Ben-Shammai, and Róna-Tas, *The World of the Khazars*; Khazanov, *Nomads and the Outside World*, 11–33; in general on problems of conversion in nomadic societies, see Anatoly M. Khazanov, *Nomads, Sedentaries and Missionaries* (Cambridge, 2004).

517. "Beschreibung der Nordvölker nach dem *Kitāb al-a'lāq an-nafīsa* des Abū 'Alī ibn 'Umar ibn Rusta," trans. Göckenjan and Zimonyi, 52–53.

518. Ahmad Ibn Fadlān, *Mission to the Volga*, ed. and trans. James E. Montgomery, in *Two Arabic Travel Books*, ed. Philip F. Kennedy and Shawkat M. Toorawa (New York, 2004), 191.

519. Golden, "Khazaria and Judaism," 140; Dan D. Y. Shapira, "Iranian Sources on the Khazars," in Golden, Ben-Shammai and Róna-Tas, *The World of the Khazars*, 294–95.

520. Skaff, *Sui-Tang China and Its Turko-Mongol Neighbors*, 123–24. In general, see Heissig and Klimkeit, *Synkretismus in den Religionen Zentralasiens*.

521. Thietmar of Merseburg, *Chronicon* 8.4, ed. Robert Holtzmann, MGH SS rer. Germ. N.S. 9 (Hanover, 1935), 497.

522. Beševliev, *Die protobulgarische Periode*, 391–92; Ziemann, *Vom Wandervolk zur Großmacht*, 370–75.

523. Menander, frag. 25.1, ed. and trans. Blockley, 220.

524. "Haec autem gens bruta et irrationabilis vel certe idiotae et sine litteris": *Conventus episcoporum ad ripas Danubii*, ed. Werminghoff, 174, l. 14. In the judgment of the churchmen, this was simply due to the fact that they had not yet received the gospel. Deér, "Karl der Grosse," 726–28; Wolfram, *Grenzen und Räume*, 224. See section 8.4.

525. Jonas of Bobbio, *Life of Columbanus* 1.27, trans. O'Hara and Wood, 162. Cf. Wolfram, *Grenzen und Räume*, 103–5.

526. *Vita Amandi 1*, 16, ed. Bruno Krusch, MGH SS rer. Merov. 5 (Hanover, 1910), 440.

527. Arbeo of Freising, *Vita Haimhrammi episcopi* 4–5, ed. Bruno Krusch, SS rer. Germ. 13 (Hanover, 1920), 33 (border conflict between Avars and Bavarians at the Enns). *Vita Hrodperti* 5, ed. Wilhelm Levison, MGH SS rer. Merov. 6 (Hanover, 1913), 159 (Rupert

preaches at Lauriacum/Lorch but then turns westward again); in ca. 870, the *Conversio Bagoariorum et Carantanorum* 1, ed. Herwig Wolfram, *Conversio Bagoariorum et Carantanorum: das Weißbuch der Salzburger Kirche über die erfolgreiche Mission in Karantanien und Pannonien*, 2nd rev. ed. (Ljubljana, 2012), 58, turns that into a missionary trip to Pannonia; for a commentary, see ibid., 93.

528. Sági, "Die zweite altchristliche Basilika," 412–14; see section 3.9.

529. Thomas, "Die Romanität Pannoniens"; Vida, "Conflict and Coexistence," 31–38.

530. Gábor Kiss, "Funde der Awarenzeit aus Ungarn in Wiener Museen: I. Funde aus der Umgebung von Keszthely," *Archaeologia Austriaca* 68 (1984): 170.

531. Edith B. Thomas, "Savaria Christiana," *Savaria, A Vás Megyei Múzeumok Értesitöje* 9, no. 20 (1975–76): 128–30; Endre Tóth, "Zu den historischen Problemen der Stadt Savaria und ihrer Umgebung zwischen dem 4.–9. Jahrhundert," *Folia Archaeologica* 27 (1976): 89–120; Fülep, "Beiträge zur frühmittelalterlichen Geschichte von Pécs," 320–22.

532. Orsolya Heinrich-Tamáska, "Une époque de bouleversement? Remarques sur l'étude de l'antiquité tardive et de la paléochrétienté en Pannonie," in Bollók, Csiky, and Vida, *Zwischen Byzanz und der Steppe/Between Byzantium and the Steppe*, 294–95.

533. Florin Curta, "New Remarks on Christianity beyond the 6th and Early 7th Century Frontier of the Roman Empire," in Heinrich-Tamáska, *Keszthely-Fenékpuszta*, 313; extensive material in Arnulf Kollautz, *Denkmäler byzantinischen Christentums aus der Awarenzeit der Donauländer* (Amsterdam, 1970); Bóna, "Ein Vierteljahrhundert," 293–95.

534. Bárdos, "La necropoli avara di Zamárdi," 91–92.

535. Nicholas I, *Epistolae*, ed. Dümmler, 568–600.

536. *Conventus episcoporum ad ripas Danubii*, ed. Werminghoff, 175–76, 175, l. 39.

537. Pohl, *Die Awaren*, 215–25, with the complementary chapter "Geschichte der Nicht-Awaren," 225–36. On my approach at the time, see also Pohl, "Conceptions of Ethnicity." For history of research, see Pohl, "Von der Ethnogenese zur Identitätsforschung."

538. Fredrik Barth, *Ethnic Groups and Boundaries: The Social Organization of Culture Difference* (Oslo, 1969).

539. Pohl, "Ethnicity and Empire."

540. Timothy Reuter, "Whose Race, Whose Ethnicity? Recent Medievalists' Discussions of Identity," in Timothy Reuter, *Medieval Polities and Modern Mentalities*, ed. Janet L. Nelson (Cambridge, 2006), 102.

541. Pohl, *Die Awaren*, 219: "Reinhard Wenskus has drawn the conclusion that ethnic identity depends of the subjective sense of belonging, as long as it is accepted by the group." Wenskus, *Stammesbildung und Verfassung*, 12–13. See also Patrick J. Geary, "Ethnic Identity as a Situational Construct in the Early Middle Ages," *Mitteilungen der Anthropologischen Gesellschaft in Wien* 113 (1983): 15, who adds: "Ethnicity was not an objective phenomenon . . . but it was likewise not entirely arbitrary," 25.

542. Pohl, "Introduction. Strategies of Identification."

543. Pohl, "Introduction. Strategies of Identification."

544. Theophylact Simocatta 7.7–8, 190. See sections 2.3–4.

545. Theophylact Simocatta 7.8, 190; cf. section 3.5.

546. Theophylact Simocatta 7.7.14, 189.

547. Simon de Kéza, *The Deeds of the Hungarians* 4, ed. László Veszprémy and Frank Schaer, Central European Medieval Texts 1 (Budapest, 1999), 13–15; see also Jenő Szűcs, "Theoretical Elements in Master Simon of Kéza's Gesta Hungarorum," in *Gesta Hungarorum*, ed. László Veszprémy and Frank Schaer (Budapest, 1999), lv. A similar story was told in the *Chronica Hungarorum* of John of Thurocz from the fifteenth century, ed. Elisabeth Galántai and Gyula Kristó (Budapest, 1985), 4, 20. See István Vásáry, "Mediaeval Theories Concerning the Primordial Homeland of the Hungarians," in *Popoli delle steppe*, 1:213–42,

and Gabriel Silagi, "Die Ungarnstürme in der ungarischen Geschichtsschreibung: Anonymus und Simon von Kéza," in *Popoli delle steppe*, 1:245–68.

548. Radloff, *Aus Sibirien*, 1:230; Heissig, "Ethnische Gruppenbildung in Zentralasien," 30; Hesse, "Der Austausch als stabilisierender Faktor der politischen Herrschaft in der Geschichte der Mongolei," 156. Fundamental study of dualism: Claude Lévi-Strauss, "Do Dual Organisations Exist?," in Claude Lévi-Strauss, *Structural Anthropology*, vol. 1 (New York, 1963), 132–66.

549. "If the Avars truly were a Mongolian people, Barangar and Žuangar could have been two tribes or two military divisions of the Avars," conjectures Togan, *Ibn Fadlans Reisebericht*, 193. The similarity in the names does in fact invite speculation. Did the division into *Var* and *Chunni* originate here? Theophylact's information does not suffice to justify such far-reaching connections.

550. Rashid ad-Din, 2.28, cited from Vladimirtsov, *Le régime social des Mongols*, 56–57. Cf. *Miracula Demetrii* 25.285–86, 227–28, on the transmission of information on descent among the Greek captives of the Avars.

551. Theophylact Simocatta 1.5.11, 27; 7.7.5, 188.

552. *Strategicon*, 1.2, 79–83.

553. Theophylact Simocatta 8.3.15, 213; slightly different numbers in Theophanes, *Chronographia* 6093, 407; see below and section 5.8.

554. Cf. Pritsak, " Tribal Names," 62–63.

555. *Strategicon* 11.2, 367.

556. Menander, frag. 12.5, ed. and trans. Blockley, 136; Theophylact Simocatta 7.4.1, 183.

557. Menander, frag. 12.5, ed. and trans. Blockley, 134.

558. Alcuin, *Epistula* 110, ed. Ernst Dümmler, MGH Epp. Karolini Aevi 2 (Berlin, 1895), 157.

559. Menander, frag. 10.3, ed. and trans. Blockley, 118.

560. Cf. Erich Zöllner, "Awarisches Namensgut in Bayern und Österreich," *MIÖG* 58 (1950): 247.

561. Heissig, "Ethnische Gruppenbildung in Zentralasien," 47–50, especially 49; the quotations are from the epics *Kürel haan, Baldanteri mergen haan*, and *Erinčen mergen*.

562. Thomsen, "Alttürkische Inschriften in der Mongolei," 168–69.

563. Bilge Khagan inscription, front side, 37, http://bitig.org/?lang=e&mod=1&tid=1&oid=16&m=1.

564. The *Secret History of the Mongols* gives numerous accounts of such practices; *Geheime Geschichte der Mongolen*, trans. Heissig, 1, especially at 14–16.

565. *Miracula Demetrii* 2.5.285–86, 227. See section 7.7.

566. *Miracula Demetrii* 2.5.285–86, 227.

567. Thus also in *Miracula Demetrii* 5.2.287, 228; Lemerle here (223) translates "paiens," which the biblical allusion justifies (cf. 223, n. 2). Yet *ethnikoi* here refers to the same groups as earlier, 2.5, 285, where he translates "peuplades."

568. *Miracula Demetrii* 2.5.288, 228, states expressly that Kuver crossed the Danube "meta pantos laou" (with the entire people); shortly before he had defeated the khagan with "ton panta Rōmaiōn laon meta kai heterōn ethnikōn" (the entire Roman people and the other ethnic groups) (2.5.287, 228).

569. Koder, "Byzanz, die Griechen und die Romaiosynē."

570. *Miracula Demetrii* 2.4, 241, and 2.42, 211. At any event the Slavic names were also mentioned in sweeping fashion, *pan tōn Sklavinōn ethnos*, which, however, refers only to the *sclavinias* around Thessalonica. Similarly in *Miracula Demetrii* 2.1.179, 175.

571. Theophylact Simocatta 7.7, 256, and *Miracula Demetrii* 2.2.198 and 202, 185–86, respectively. In this same context there is mention of *panta barbara phyla*, the barbarian "clans" that the khagan ruled.

572. For this and the following, see Pohl, "Telling the Difference."

573. *Strategicon* 11.1–4, ed. Dennis and Gamillscheg, 352–89.

574. *Strategicon* 11.2, ed. Dennis and Gamillscheg, 362.

575. Theophanes, *Chronographia* 6050, 339–40.

576. Wilhelm E. Mühlmann, "Ethnogonie und Ethnogenese: Theoretisch-ethnologische und ideologiekritische Studie," in *Studien zur Ethnogenese*, 24–25.

577. Geary, "Ethnic Identity as a Situational Construct"; Timpe, "Ethnologische Begriffsbildung in der Antike." On Roman mistakes about the barbarians, see Wolfram, *The Roman Empire and Its Germanic Peoples*.

578. Daim, "Gedanken zum Ethnosbegriff," 69–71; Daim, "Archaeology, Ethnicity and the Structures of Identification"; Brather, *Ethnische Interpretationen in der frühgeschichtlichen Archäologie*; Pohl and Mehofer, *Archaeology of Identity/Archäologie der Identität*.

579. Pohl, "Ethnicity and Empire."

580. *Nan Qi shu*, 59; cited after Yu Taishan, "Doubts," 317.

581. See sections 2.3–4.

582. Karl H. Menges, inter alia, in his review of *Khazar Studies: An Historic-Philological Inquiry into the Origins of the Khazars*, by Peter B. Golden, *Central Asiatic Journal* 30 (1986): 56, evaluates as evidence the existence of words and place-names in Old Slavonic that can be explained as Mongolic but does make the reservation that most of the people who came to Europe with the Avars were in fact Turks. Cf. Karl Heinrich Menges, *Oriental Elements in the Vocabulary of the Oldest Russian Epos: The Igor Tale*, Suppl. to Word: Monographs 7 (New York, 1951). Also in favor of Mongolian categorization: Grousset, *Empire of the Steppes*, 193; Czeglédy, "From East to West," 89–91; Samolin, "Some Notes on the Avar Problem," 63; Shiratori, "On the Titles Khan and Khagan"; Kollautz and Miyakawa, 1:58; more skeptical: Togan, *Ibn Fadlans Reisebericht*, 193; cf. Barthold, *Histoire des turcs*, 19–20; Jooseppi J. Mikkola, "Avarica," *Archiv für Slavische Philologie* 42 (1929): 158–60; Bernd von Arnim, "Avarisches," *Zeitschrift für slavische Philologie* 9 (1932): 403–6.

583. Franke, *Das chinesische Kaiserreich*, 5.140; Heissig "Ethnische Gruppenbildung in Zentralasien," 29.

584. Moravcsik, *Byzantinoturcica*, 2:59–61, with secondary literature; Macartney, "On the Greek Sources," 273. More cautious is Golden, *Khazar Studies*, 1:28–29 (most Hunnic names are presumably Turkic) and 1:36 (the Avars are partly of Hunnic origin).

585. Lajos Ligeti, *A magyar nyelv török kapcsolatai a honfoglalás előtt és az Árpád-korban* (Budapest, 1986); *Popoli delle steppe*, with the contributions to the discussion by Róna-Tas, Vásáry, and Pritsak. See also Golden, "Some Notes on the Avars and Rouran," 52: the question of Avar language "is far from resolved."

586. Gerhard Doerfer, "Zur Sprache der Hunnen," *Central Asiatic Journal* 17 (1973): 1–50; his conclusion is that the Hunnic language did not belong to any known language family. Similar opinion in Paolo Daffinà, "Gli Unni e gli altri: Le fonti letterarie e le loro interpretazioni moderne," in *Popoli delle steppe*, 1:181–208.

587. Pohl, "Telling the Difference," 22–27; Oeser, "Methodologische Bemerkungen"; Mühlmann, "Ethnogonie und Ethnogenese," 15; Geary, *Myth of Nations*.

588. Walter Pohl and Bernhard Zeller, eds., *Sprache und Identität im frühen Mittelalter*, Forschungen zur Geschichte des Mittelalters 20 (Vienna, 2012).

589. Moravcsik, *Byzantinoturcica*, 2:303.

590. Cf. the detailed discussion of Hunnic names in Maenchen-Helfen, *Die Welt der Hunnen*, 255–303.

591. Also occurs as Targites or Tergazis in Menander (earliest mention in frag. 12.6, ed. and trans. Blockley, 139), Corippus (*In laudem Iustini*, 3.258, ed. Antès, 68; see Stache, *Flavius Cresconius Corippus*, 442–43, for the name form) and Theophylact Simocatta (latest occurrence in 6.11.6, 176). Targüt: Yu, "Doubts," 300.

592. Menander, frag. 5.4, ed. and trans. Blockley, 53.

593. Menander, frag. 5.1, ed. and trans. Blockley, 49; Jordanes, *Getica* 50.265–66, ed. Mommsen, 126.

594. Theophylact Simocatta 1.14.5 and 2.3.1, 40 and 46—both times explicitly called "the Hun." Of course, he could have been a dissident Avar regarded as a Hun in the Byzantine army. On the etymology of Apsikh, see Moravcsik, *Byzantinoturcica*, 2:83; Haussig, "Theophylakts Exkurs," 361 (interpreting the epithet as Turkic for "hunt-loving"); Maenchen-Helfen, *Die Welt der Hunnen*, 286, classes this as Hunnic, with the Alanic-Turkic etymology "small horse."

595. Theophylact Simocatta 6.6.6, 167; Menges, *The Turkic Languages and Peoples*, 22.

596. Theophylact Simocatta 1.8.3, 30; see sections 3.6 and 6.9. Yu, "Doubts," 301.

597. *Solakhos*: Menander, frag. 25.2, ed. and trans. Blockley, 225; *Samur*: Theophylact Simocatta 6.4.11, 164; and *Hermitzis*: *Chronicon Paschale*, 178. It is possible that *Hermitzis* is connected with the ethnonym *(K)ermichiones* (see section 2.6) and the later Bulgarian clan name *Ermi/Ermares* (see section 7.6), as Moravcsik, *Byzantinoturcica*, 2:117, and Altheim, *Geschichte der Hunnen*, 1:26–27, assume.

598. *Geheime Geschichte der Mongolen*, trans. Heissig, 2, 19; Franke, *Das chinesische Kaiserreich*, 84. A statistical analysis of 186 non-Slavic Bulgarian names up to the tenth century showed 41 percent to be Altaic (Turkic or Mongolic), 51 percent Iranian and Caucasian, and 8 percent of other origin; cf. Dimităr Ovčarov, "Die Protobulgaren und ihre Wanderungen nach Südosteuropa," in Hänsel, *Die Völker Südosteuropas vom 6.–8. Jahrhundert*, 173. Even if this investigation, like others, deals for the greater part with hypothetical etymologies, it is evident that the origin of Bulgarian names cannot be unambiguously established.

599. Menges, *The Turkic Languages and Peoples*, 20, for a Mongolian origin of the title khagan, and of the Avars. Cf. sections 2.4, 6.3, and 6.5. Later it was not infrequent that Mongolian tribes had Turkic names and Turkish tribes Mongolic names; cf. Menges's review of Golden, *Khazar Studies*, 56.

600. Skaff, *Sui-Tang China and Its Turko-Mongol Neighbors*, 119–20.

601. Cf. section 8.2.

602. Bálint, "A Short Essay"; Bálint, *Der Schatz von Nagyszentmiklós*; Daim et al., *Der Goldschatz*. On the reading of the inscriptions, see Julius Németh, "The Runiform Inscriptions from Nagyszentmiklós and the Runiform Scripts of Eastern Europe," *Acta Linguistica Hungarica* 21 (1971): 1–52; Moravcsik, *Byzantinoturcica*, 1:163–64 and 2:30; Vékony, "Zur Lesung der griechischen Inschriften"; Pritsak, *Die bulgarische Fürstenliste*, 85–89; István Vásáry, "Runiform Signs on Objects of the Avar Period (6th–8th cc. AD)," *Acta Orient. Hung.* 25 (1972): 335–47; Klaus Röhrborn and Wolfgang Veenker, eds., *Runen, Tamgas und Graffiti aus Asien und Osteuropa* (Wiesbaden, 1985); Göbl and Róna-Tas, *Die Inschriften*; Róna-Tas, "The Inscriptions."

603. Irén Juhász, *Das awarenzeitliche Gräberfeld in Szarvas-Grexa-Téglagyár*, Monumenta Avarorum Archaeologica 7 (Budapest, 2004), 91–93.

604. János Harmatta, "Turk and Avar Runic Inscriptions on Metal Belt-Plates," *Acta Antiqua Academiae Scientiarum Hungaricae* 37 (1996/97): 321–30, interpreting the Avar runes as Turkish.

605. A good summary is found in Róna-Tas, "The Problems of the East-European Scripts"; on the question of decipherment, see also the critical comments of Vásáry and Pritsak in the discussion. The Avar bone inscriptions were published by Vásáry, "Runiform Signs"; cf. Bóna, "Ein Vierteljahrhundert," 312–13; the Szarvas inscription in Irén Juhász, "Ein awarenzeitlicher Nadelbecher mit Kerbschrift aus Szarvas (Komitat Bekes)," *Acta Arch. Hung.* 35 (1983): 373–78; András Róna-Tas, "Die Inschrift des Nadelbehälters von Szarvas (Ungarn)," *UAJB*, n.s., 9 (1990): 1–30. For a Turkic interpretation, see

Harmatta, "Turk and Avar Runic Inscriptions." On eastern European runic inscriptions, see, too, the collective work Röhrborn and Veenker, *Runen Tamgas und Graffiti*; Vásáry, *Geschichte des frühen Innerasiens*, 152.

606. Róna-Tas, "The Inscriptions," 129; Albrecht, "Die Inschriften," 142–43.

607. *The Cosmography of Aethicus Ister* 113, ed. Michael W. Herren (Turnhout, 2011), 215–17; Heinz Löwe, "Aethicus Ister und das alttürkische Runenalphabet," *Deutsches Archiv für Erforschung des Mittelalters* 32 (1976): 1–22; Franz Brunhölzl, "Zur Kosmographie des Aethicus Ister," in *Festschrift für Max Spindler*, ed. Dieter Albrecht, Andreas Kraus, and Kurt Reindel (Munich, 1969), 75–90, especially at 87; Winfried Stelzer, "Ein Alt-Salzburger Fragment der Kosmographie des Aethicus Ister aus dem 8. Jahrhundert," *MIÖG* 100 (1992): 132–49; Ian N. Wood, "Aethicus Ister: An Exercise in Difference," in Pohl and Reimitz, *Grenze und Differenz*, 202–4 (interest in the Turks).

608. *Miracula Demetrii* 2.5.291, 229; Martha Grigoriou-Ionnidou, "Une remarque sur le récit des miracles de Saint Démétrius," *Publications du Comité National Grec des Études du Sud-Est Européen* 20 (1987): 3–15. Lemerle, *Les Plus Anciens Recueils*, 1:223, has a different understanding of the passage.

609. Koder, "Remarks on Linguistic Romanness," 117.

610. Priscus, frag. 13.2–3, ed. and trans. Blockley, 287–89.

611. Janós Harmatta, "Sogdian Inscriptions on Avar Objects," *Acta Orient. Hung.* 48 (1995): 61–65.

612. Cf. Horace G. Lunt, "Common Slavic, Proto-Slavic, Pan-Slavic: What Are We Talking About?," *International Journal of Slavic Linguistics and Poetics* 41 (1997): 7–67; Holzer, "Die Einheitlichkeit des Slavischen"; Curta, "The Slavic *Lingua Franca*."

613. Early evidence for the Slavicization of the Bulgar elite is the Slavic toast *zdravitsa*, which the victorious Bulgars pronounced in 811 over the skull of the emperor Nicephorus that had been made into a cup; cf. Runciman, *A History of the First Bulgarian Empire*, 57, and 70; Beševliev, *Die protobulgarische Periode*, 327. Somewhat later, Malamir is the first khan with an attested Slavic name.

614. Cf. section 2.2. On the early Bulgars, see Ziemann, *Vom Wandervolk zur Großmacht*, 24–103.

615. Petkov, *Voices of Medieval Bulgaria, Seventh–Fifteenth Century*, 2, 5, 11, and 13.

616. Cassiodorus, *Chronicon* a. 504, ed. Mommsen, 160; Ennodius, *Panegyricus dictus Theodorico* 5.19 and 12.60–69, ed. Rohr, 209 and 239–47. Ditten, "Protobulgaren und Germanen," 59 and 61–62; Hans Ditten, "Prominente Slawen und Bulgaren in byzantinischen Diensten (Ende des 7. bis zum Anfang des 10. Jahrhunderts)," in *Besonderheiten der byzantinischen Feudalentwicklung*, ed. Helga Köpstein (Berlin, 1983), 96–98; Beševliev, "Bulgaren als Söldner," 21–23; cf. also Teall, "Barbarians in Justinian's Armies."

617. Menander, frag. 12.5, ed. and trans. Blockley, 136.

618. Theophylact Simocatta 7.4, 251. See section 5.4.

619. Pritsak, "The Slavs and the Avars," 358.

620. See section 5.8. Theophylact Simocatta 8.3.14, 213; and Theophanes, *Chronographia* 6093, 407, only speak of "other barbarians."

621. *Miracula Demetrii* 2.2.198 and 202, 185–86, where they are individually named among the *ethnē*; George of Pisidia, *Bellum Avaricum* 197, ed. and trans. Pertusi, 185, where they are counted among the Huns, Scythians, Slavs, and Persians in the impressive conspiracy of peoples against Constantinople, just as in Theophanes, *Chronographia* 6117, 315; George of Pisidia, *Bellum Avaricum* 409, ed. and trans. Pertusi, 194, where they, with little concern for their status, must man the boats on the Golden Horn along with the Slavs. Neither the *Chronicon Paschale* nor Theodore Syncellus mentions the Bulgars specifically with reference to the year 626.

622. Cf. sections 7.6–7.

623. John of Biclaro, *Chronica* 19, 61–62; Menander, frag. 12.6, ed. and trans. Blockley, 138–40, frag. 12.7, 142. See sections 2.9–3.2.

624. Paul the Deacon, *Historia Langobardorum* 2.26, ed. Waitz, 103: "Unde usque hodie eorum in quibus habitant vicos Gepidos . . . appellamus."

625. Theophylact Simocatta 1.8, 53.

626. Theophylact Simocatta 6.2.3–9, 159–60; and 6.10.4–18, 174–76.

627. Theophylact Simocatta 6.8–9, 171–73.

628. Theophylact Simocatta 8.3.11–13, 213.

629. Theophylact only mentions "other barbarians" (8.3, 213), and only the Latin translation of Theophanes by Anastasius Bibliothecarius mentions 3,200 Gepids among the prisoners of war, a number added in the translation by Mango and Scott: Theophanes, *Chronographia* 6093, 407, with n. 4. This might only be Theophanes's assumption, but the fact (not the number) is plausible. See section 5.8.

630. Theophanes, *Chronographia* 6117, 446.

631. Mircea Rusu, "The Prefeudal Cemetery of Noșlac (VI–VIIc)," *Dacia* 6 (1962): 288–90; Horedt, "Das Fortleben der Gepiden," 164–66; Bóna, "Gepiden in Siebenbürgen," 41–43; Ligia Bârzu and Radu Harhoiu, "Gepiden als Nachbarn der Langobarden und das Gräberfeld von Bratei," in Bemmann and Schmauder, *Kulturwandel in Mitteleuropa*, 522–34.

632. Kiss, "Das Weiterleben der Gepiden"; see section 3.8.

633. Paul the Deacon, *Historia Langobardorum* 1.27, ed. Waitz, 81.

634. Theodulf or Orléans, *Carmen* 7, ed. Dümmler, 461, l. 32.

635. "De Gepides autem quidam adhuc ibi resident": *Conversio Bagoariorum et Carantanorum* 6, ed. Fritz Lošek, *Die Conversio Bagoariorum et Carantanorum und der Brief des Erzbischofs Theotmar von Salzburg*, MGH Studien und Texte 15 (Hanover, 1997), 110; on the date of composition, see Wolfram, *Conversio Bagoariorum*, 26.

636. Marius of Avenches, a. 569, ed. Mommsen, 238.

637. John of Ephesus, 6.45, 259; Michael the Syrian, 10.21, 361.

638. Paul the Deacon, *Historia Langobardorum* 4.37, ed. Waitz, 130–32.

639. Paul the Deacon, *Historia Langobardorum* 2.26, ed. Waitz, 103.

640. "Vigilius episcopus Scarava(n)ciensis": *Concilium Mantuanum*, ed. Werminghoff, 588. On the identification, see Endre Tóth, "Vigilius episcopus Scaravaciensis," *Acta Arch. Hung.* 26 (1974): 269–75, and Berg, "Bischöfe und Bischofssitze," 85, who adduces the relevant paleographical information. Cf. section 5.6.

641. Thomas, "Die Romanität Pannoniens," 284–86; Tóth, "Zu den historischen Problemen der Stadt Savaria," 89–91; Bierbrauer, "Die Keszthely-Kultur"; Heinrich-Tamáska, *Keszthely-Fenékpuszta*.

642. On possible Daco-Roman continuity, see Dan G. Teodor, *Continuiteta Populației Autohtone la est de Carpați în secolele VI–XI e. n.* (Iași, 1984); Mircea Rusu, "Aspects des relations entre les autochtones du bassin carpato-danubien aux VIe–IXe siècles," *Revue Roumaine d'Histoire* 19 (1980): 247–66; Horedt, "Das Awarenproblem in Rumänien"; more skeptical in Horedt, "Die Völker Südosteuropas im 6. bis 8. Jahrhundert," 22–23. In 1986 the first volume of *Erdély Története* (*History of Transylvania*) appeared in Budapest in which István Bóna, "Daciától Erdőelvéig," in *Erdély Története*, vol. 1, *A kezdetekől 1606-ig*, ed. Lázló Makkai and András Mócsy (Budapest, 1986) deals with the period from 271 to 896, skeptical about Roman survivals.

643. Johannes Kramer, "Romanen, Rumänen und Vlachen aus philologischer Sicht," in Pohl, Haubrichs, and Hartl, *Walchen, Romani und Latini*, 197–204. See also Gottfried Schramm, *Ein Damm bricht: Die römische Donaugrenze und die Invasionen des 5.–7. Jahrhunderts im Licht von Namen und Wörtern* (Munich, 1997).

644. See Pohl, Haubrichs, and Hartl, *Walchen, Romani und Latini*.

645. Pohl, "Introduction: Early Medieval Romanness."

646. E.g. Theophylact Simocatta 6.3.9–4.4, 160–63; 8.3.14–15, 213.

647. John of Ephesus 6.48, 260, who constantly confuses the Avars and Slavs; cf. section 4.5; a differing opinion in Avenarius, "Zur Problematik der awarisch-slawischen Beziehungen," 19.

648. In general, see Barford, *The Early Slavs*, 38–44.

649. Ágnes Sós was the Hungarian archaeologist specializing in Slavic finds; summarized in her "Zur Problematik der Awarenzeit in der neueren ungarischen archäologischen Forschung," in *Berichte über den 2. internationalen Kongress für slawische Archäologie* (Berlin, 1973), 2:92; see also Sós, "Archäologische Angaben zur Frage der Frühperiode des awarisch-slawischen Zusammenlebens," *Študijné zvesti* 16 (1968): 227–28, on the finds interpreted as Slavic from the cemetery at Pókaszepetk; cf. also Sós, *Die slawische Bevölkerung Westungarns im 9. Jahrhundert*, Münchner Beiträge zur Vor- und Frühgeschichte 22 (Munich, 1973). Slavs during the Avar period are assumed by Sandor Nagy, "Mečka—ein frühmittelalterliches Gräberfeld beim Dorfe Aradac," *Študijné zvesti* 16 (1968): 165–74, in Mečka near Novi Sad. Summary of early research in Bóna, "Ein Vierteljahrhundert," 303–5. See also Béla Miklós Szőke, "Das archäologische Bild der Slawen in Südwestungarn," in Bratož, *Slovenija*, 1:477–505. Even the extensive database of Peter Stadler only yields one object type that he connects tentatively with Slavs under Avar rule, spiral earrings: Stadler, *Quantitative Studien*, 131. cf. section 8.1.

650. Jozef Zábojník, "Zur Problematik der Siedlungen aus der Zeit des Awarischen Khaganats in der Slowakei," in *Kulturwandel in Mitteleuropa: Langobarden—Awaren—Slawen*, ed. Jürgen Bemmann and Michael Schmauder (Bonn, 2008), 591–600.

651. See, for instance, Zlata Čilinská, "The Development of the Slavs North of the Danube during the Avar Empire and Their Social-Cultural Contribution to Great Moravia," *Slov. Arch.* 31 (1983): 237–76. One of the discussed cemeteries was Devínska Nová Vés near Bratislava; see Ján Eisner, *Devínska Nová Vés* (Bratislava, 1952).

652. Jozef Zábojník, "On the Problems of Settlements of the Avar Khaganate Period in Slovakia," *Archeologické rozhledy* 40 (1988): 401–37; Zábojník, "Das awarische Kaganat und die Slawen an seiner nördlichen Peripherie," *Slov. Arch.* 47 (1999): 153–73; Zábojník, "The Slavs and the Avar Khaganate"; Gabriel Fusek, "Frühe Slawen im Mitteldonaugebiet," in Bemmann and Schmauder, *Kulturwandel in Mitteleuropa*, 645–56; Fusek, "Beitrag zu Problemen der Datierung"; Fusek and Zábojník, "Ausklang der Spätantike." See also Curta, "The Prague Type."

653. For earlier traces of Avar influence in Bohemia, see Nad'a Profantová, "The Middle Avar Period and the Problems of a 'Cultural Change' at the End of the Seventh Century North of the Avar Khaganate," *Antaeus* 29–30 (2008): 215–32; Profantová, "Die frühslawische Besiedlung Böhmens und archäologische Spuren der Kontakte zum früh- und mittelawarischen sowie merowingischen Kulturkreis," in Bemmann and Schmauder, *Kulturwandel in Mitteleuropa*, 619–44; Falko Daim et al., eds., *Studien zum Burgwall von Mikulčice*, vol. 1 (Brno, 1995); Lumír Poláček, "Mikulčice und Awaren: Zur Interpretation 'awarischer' Funde von Mikulčice," in Bemmann and Schmauder, *Kulturwandel in Mitteleuropa*, 579–90.

654. Eichert, *Die frühmittelalterlichen Grabfunde Kärntens*; Eichert, *Frühmittelalterliche Strukturen im Ostalpenraum*.

655. Szameit, "Zum archäologischen Bild der frühen Slawen in Österreich."

656. Curta, "The Early Slavs in the Northern and Eastern Adriatic Region."

657. Cf. section 4.5.

7. THE SEVENTH CENTURY

1. Paul the Deacon, *Historia Langobardorum* 4.26, ed. Waitz, 156.

2. Stratos, *Byzantium in the Seventh Century*, 1:66. Most (posterior) sources emphasize the favorable situation of Byzantium under Maurice in contrast to the "tyrant" Phocas:

Ralph-Johannes Lilie, "Kaiser Herakleios und die Ansiedlung der Serben: Überlegungen zum Kapitel 32 des *De administrando imperio*," *Südost-Forschungen* 44 (1985): 18–19. Still, Theophylact and Theophanes already viewed Maurice's Balkan war quite critically.

3. Sebeos, *Armenian History* 31, trans. Thomson, 57. See Curta, *Making of the Slavs*, 189.

4. Theophanes, *Chronographia* 6094, 414, similarly 6103, 429; Theophylact Simocatta 8.12.12, 230.

5. John of Nikiu, *Chronicle* 109.18, ed. and trans. R. H. Charles, *The Chronicle of John, Bishop of Nikiu: Translated from Zotenberg's Ethiopic Text* (London, 1916; repr. Merchantville, NJ, 2007), 175–76. On the work of this Coptic author, see Antonio Carile, "Giovanni di Nikiu, cronista bizantinocopto del VIIe secolo," in N. Stratos, *Byzantium*, 2:353–98; on his sources for events outside Egypt, see 362–63.

6. Isidore of Seville, *Chronicon* 5813, ed. Mommsen, 479: "Sclavi Graeciam Romanis tulerunt." On the localization, see Peter Charanis, "Graecia in Isidore of Seville," *Byzantinische Zeitschrift* 64 (1971): 22–25. Cf. Ditten, "Zur Bedeutung der Einwanderung der Slawen," 96.

7. Even in the West the Romans' defeats were later ascribed to Phocas, as in Dandolo's *Chronicle: Andrea Danduli Ducis Venetiarum Chronica*, ed. Ester Pastorello, Rerum Italicarum Scriptores, nuova edizione 12.2 (Bologna, 1938), 88: "Suoquoque tempore hinc Persae, inde Huni in Romanorum crasuntur provincias, Ierusalem capiunt."

8. Theophanes, *Chronographia* 6096, 420. Stratos, *Byzantium in the Seventh Century*, 1:61–65.

9. Stratos, *Byzantium in the Seventh Century*, 1:71–91. Lilie, "Kaiser Herakleios und die Ansiedlung der Serben," 22–23, makes Heraclius's rebellion responsible for the "definitive collapse of the Byzantine position in the Balkans." Similar judgment in Haldon, *Byzantium in the Seventh Century*, 43. Walter E. Kaegi, *Heraclius: Emperor of Byzantium* (Cambridge, 2003), 95, makes the case that Phocas knew the Balkans well, while Heraclius was ignorant of the region.

10. Theophanes, *Chronographia* 6096, 432, on the years 603–4. On Theophanes's chronology for the period after 602, cf. Ostrogorsky, "Die Chronologie des Theophanes," 1–3. On the treaty of 603–4, see Stratos, *Byzantium in the Seventh Century*, 1:66–67; Ditten "Zur Bedeutung der Einwanderung der Slawen," 95. Chosroes II attacked in the spring of 604; Phocas, with the conclusion of the treaty and the withdrawal of the army of Europe, cannot have waited long. 140,000 solidi is a plausible figure; see Kiss, "Die Goldfunde des Karpatenbeckens vom 5.–10. Jahrhundert," 109.

11. For the following, see Andrey Aladzhov, "The Final Stage in the Development of the Early Byzantine Towns on the Lower Danube," in Schwarcz, Soustal, and Tcholakova, *Der Donaulimes in der Spätantike*, 259–78.

12. Stefka Angelova and Ivan Bucharov, "Durostorum in Late Antiquity (Fourth to Seventh Centuries)," in Henning, *Post-Roman Towns*, 2:61–88. Suggesting a late destruction date: Aladzhov, "The Final Stage."

13. Alexandru Magdearu, "The End of Town-Life in Scythia Minor," *Oxford Journal of Archaeology* 20, no. 2 (2001): 207–17; Curta, *Making of the Slavs*, 155–89.

14. *Notitia ps.-Epiphanii*, ed. Heinrich Gelzer, *Ungedruckte und ungenügend veröffentlichte Texte der Notitiae Episcopatuum*, Abhandlungen der Bayerischen Akademie der Wissenschaften, phil.-hist. Kl. 21.3 (Munich, 1900), 583; Liebeschuetz, "The Lower Danube Region under Pressure," 131.

15. Stratos, *Byzantium in the Seventh Century*, 1:162 ("not a single city or large town was occupied," which is probably phrased too sweepingly); with new arguments, see Lilie, "Kaiser Herakleios und die Ansiedlung der Serben," 17–19; Curta, *Making of the Slavs*, 189.

16. Theodore Syncellus 5.2, ed. and trans. Makk, 14. See section 6.3.

17. Liu Mau-Tsai, *Die chinesischen Nachrichten*, 1:42–43; de la Vaissière, "Oncles et frères."

18. Fredegar, 4.30–31, ed. Krusch, 20; Dietrich Claude, *Geschichte der Westgoten* (Stuttgart, 1970), 75–76; Jarnut, *Geschichte der Langobarden*, 46; Ewig, *Die Merowinger und das Imperium*, 50–51; Ian Wood, *The Merovingian Kingdoms, 450–751* (London, 1994), 132; Roger Collins, *Visigothic Spain, 409–711* (Oxford, 2004), 74.

19. *Epistolae Wisigoticae* 12, ed. Walter Gundlach, MGH Epp. Karolini aevi 1 (Berlin, 1892), 678–79. The letter can be dated to 610–11, after the accession of the Gothic king, at the latest to 612, when both Gundemar and Theudebert died.

20. Paul the Deacon, *Historia Langobardorum* 4.39, ed. Waitz, 167. In Paul, the information is associated with events after the fall of Phocas. It presumably comes from the historical work of Secundus of Trento, who died in 612. Reindel, "Das Zeitalter der Agilolfinger," 143–44; Wolfram, "Ethnogenesen im frühmittelalterlichen Donau- und Ostalpenraum," 126–28; Wolfram, *Grenzen und Räume*, 79.

21. Paul the Deacon, *Historia Langobardorum* 4.37, ed. Waitz, 161–66. The dating is uncertain. With the common but imprecise phrase "circa haec tempora" Paul directly associates the incident with the fall of Phocas. Just like the battle of Aguntum, it comes before the events of chap. 40, which can be dated to 612 (the assassination of Theudebert). Most commonly accepted is a date of 610; Ewig, *Die Merowinger und das Imperium*, 51; Stefano Gasparri, *I duchi longobardi* (Rome, 1978), 66; Paschini, *Storia del Friuli*, 1:120–21; Jarnut, *Geschichte der Langobarden*, 46; more cautious is Hartmann, *Geschichte Italiens im Mittelalter*, 235, n. 9. It is often assumed that the account came from Secundus of Trento, which would mean a terminus ante quem of 612; that is, however, improbable (see Krahwinkler, *Friaul im Frühmittelalter*, 395, n. 70). Legends from Paul's native Friuli are a more likely source; the story continues with the family history of Paul the Deacon (see section 6.7). Still, the best fit for the event is in the unstable political environment around the year 611; Wolfram, *Grenzen und Räume*, 79.

22. Jarnut, *Geschichte der Langobarden*, 46, assumes Agilulf's agency behind the Avar raid; similarly, Krahwinkler, *Friaul im Frühmittelalter*, 396; Wolfram, "Ethnogenesen im frühmittelalterlichen Donau- und Ostalpenraum," 127; opposing view in Ewig, *Die Merowinger und das Imperium*, 50; Hartmann, *Geschichte Italiens im Mittelalter*, 210–11.

23. Paul the Deacon, *Historia Langobardorum* 4.40, ed. Waitz, 168.

24. Stratos, *Byzantium in the Seventh Century*, 1:103–5; Ostrogorsky, *Geschichte des byzantinischen Staates*, 56; Zakythinos, *Byzantinische Geschichte*, 60; Haldon, *Byzantium in the Seventh Century*, 42–43; Kaegi, *Heraclius*, 78–80; Walter E. Kaegi, "New Evidence on the Early Reign of Heraclius," *Byzantinische Zeitschrift* 66 (1973): 308–50, and his *Army, Society and Religion in Byzantium* (London, 1982); Mark Whittow, *The Making of Orthodox Byzantium* (Basingstoke, 1996), 75–76.

25. Stratos, *Byzantium in the Seventh Century*, 1:124–26; Kaegi, *Heraclius*, 86–91; Haldon, *Byzantium in the Seventh Century*, 191.

26. *Miracula Demetrii* 1.12.100–114, 120–22.

27. The feast day fell on a Monday so that 604 and 610 are both possible; Lemerle, *Les Plus Anciens Recueils*, 2:72–73, prefers 604. As for 610, with Heraclius deposing Phocas one could scarcely speak of a "deep peace."

28. *Miracula Demetrii* 2.1, 167–79. Lemerle, *Les Plus Anciens Recueils*, 2:91–92, establishes the date as 615 on the basis of the political situation and the information in Isidore. Although the text hardly offers any other dating criteria, this assumption is plausible. Stratos, *Byzantium in the Seventh Century*, 1:119 (616–20); Ditten, "Zur Bedeutung der Einwanderung der Slawen," 98 (ca. 610); Szádeczky-Kardoss, *Ein Versuch*, 88 (about 614); Koder, "Anmerkungen zu den Miracula Sancti Demetrii," 530 (615 give or take one year); Kaegi, *Heraclius*, 96 (614–15).

29. *Miracula Demetrii* 2.1.180, 175. Koder, "Anmerkungen zu den Miracula Sancti Demetrii," relativizes the value of the list of people, which probably already reflects the terminology of the second half of the century.

30. *Miracula Demetrii* 2.1.179, 175, names the Sagudates, Belegezites, Drogubites, to whom may be added the Strymon Slavs (after the name of the river) and the Runchines. On the names and their localization, see Lemerle, *Les Plus Anciens Recueils*, 2:89–90; Ditten, "Zur Bedeutung der Einwanderung der Slawen," 99. General discussion in Vasilka Tăpkova-Zaimova, "La ville de Salonique et son Hinterland slave (jusqu'au Xe siècle)," in her *Byzance et les Balkans à partir du VIe siècle*, 355–62.

31. An attack from the seaside is also attested in a mosaic inscription from ca. 630: Jean-Michel Spieser, "Inventaires en vue d'un recueil des inscriptions historiques de Byzance: I. Les inscriptions de Thessalonique," *Travaux et mémoires* 5 (1973): 155–56.

32. *Miracula Demetrii* 2.2.197, 185.

33. John of Nikiu, *Chronicle* 109.18, ed. and trans. Charles, 175–76; Isidore, *Chronicon* 5813, ed. Mommsen, 479.

34. Jean-Pierre Sodini, "The Transformation of Cities in Late Antiquity within the Provinces of Macedonia and Epirus," in Poulter, *The Transition to Late Antiquity*, 311–36; Liebeschuetz, "The Lower Danube Region under Pressure," 130–33; Ditten, "Zur Bedeutung der Einwanderung der Slawen," 114–16; among the fortresses that remained Byzantine were probably Philippopolis/Plovdiv, Adrianopolis/Edirne, Develtos, Mesembria, and Sozopolis. Serdica recovered at some point and was fortified again in 809: Theophanes, *Chronographia* 6301, 666; cf. Magdalina Stančeva, "Sofia au moyen âge à la lumière de nouvelles études archéologiques," *Byzantinobulgarica* 5 (1978): 211–28. On the survival of Balkan cities in the seventh and eighth centuries, see Schreiner, "Städte und Wegenetz," 65; Liebeschuetz, *Decline and Fall of the Ancient City*, 86.

35. Popović, "Les témoins archéologiques," 491 and 494–96; Lemerle, *Les Plus Anciens Recueils*, 2:100–101. On the excavations at Caričin Grad see, among others, Noël Duval and Vladislav Popović, eds., *Caričin Grad*, vol. 3, *L'acropole et ses monuments*, Collection de l'Ecole Française de Rome 75.3 (Rome, 2010).

36. John of Nikiu, *Chronicle* 109.18, ed. with French translation by Hermann Zotenberg (Paris, 1883), 430, and ed. and trans. Charles, 176, read this as 'the Illyrians' who are supposed to have devastated Christian cities together with 'the barbarians and the nations', which does not make much sense.

37. Theophylact Simocatta 6.2.12, 160.

38. *Miracula Demetrii* 2.2.196, 185; Stratos, *Byzantium in the Seventh Century*, 1:119 (possibly 623). Most other scholars prefer the date 617–18: Ditten, "Zur Bedeutung der Einwanderung der Slawen," 98; Avenarius, "Die Awaren und die Slawen," 21; Popović, "Les témoins archéologiques," 493, n. 2; Lemerle, *Les Plus Anciens Recueils*, 2:99–100; Curta, *Making of the Slavs*, 108; cf. James D. Breckenridge, "The 'Long Siege' of Thessalonika: Its Date and Iconography," *Byzantinische Zeitschrift* 48 (1955): 116–22.

39. *Miracula Demetrii* 2.2.195–215, 180–84.

40. Gregory the Great, *Registrum epistularum* 2.18, ed. Norberg, 1:104–5; 2.19, 1:105–7; 3.22, 1:167–68; 3.32, 1:178; 3.46, 1:190–91; 4.16, 1:234–35; 4.20, 1:238; 5.39, 1:314–18; 6.3, 1:371; 6.25, 1:395–97; 6.26, 1:397–98 (from the years 592–96). Cf. section 5.6.

41. *DAI* 29 and 30, 122–24 and 140–42.

42. In this sense, see Jenkins, *De administrando imperio: Commentary*, 101.

43. Nikola Jakšić, "Constantine Porphyrogenitus as the Source for the Destruction of Salona," *Disputationes Salonitanae 2: Vjesnik za Arheologiju i Historiju Dalmatinsku* 77 (1984): 315–26. In general about Constantine, see Ihor Ševčenko. "Re-reading Constantine Porphyrogenitus," in Shepard and Franklin, *Byzantine Diplomacy*, 167–201.

44. *DAI* 31, 143–44; cf. section 7.5.

45. *Corpus Inscriptionum Latinarum*, vol. 3, *Inscriptiones Asiae, provinciarum Europae Graecarum, Illyrici Latinae*, ed. Theodor Mommsen (Berlin, 1873), 9551. Radoslav Katičić, "Die Literatur des frühen kroatischen Mittelalters in ihrem slawischen und europäischen Zusammenhang," *Wiener Slavistisches Jahrbuch* 28 (1982): 29.

46. De Voinovitch, *Histoire de la Dalmatie*, 1:252–53; Stratos, *Byzantium in the Seventh Century*, 1:119; Popović, "Les témoins archéologiques," 487–88; Charanis, "Observations on the History of Greece," 19; Kollautz and Miyakawa, 1:268; Ditten, "Zur Bedeutung der Einwanderung der Slawen," 114; Szádeczky-Kardoss, *Ein Versuch*, 87.

47. Thomas Archidiaconus, *Historia Salonitana* 7, ed. Damir Karbić, Mirjana Matijević Sokol, and James Ross Sweeney, Central European Medieval Texts (Budapest, 2006), 34–43; cf. Neven Budak, "Frühes Christentum in Kroatien," in *Karantanien und der Alpen-Adria Raum im Frühmittelalter* (Vienna, 1991), 225. Occasionally even modern historians have speculated on a Gothic origin for the Croats (as in the fascist ideology of the Ustaša), e.g., Stanko Guldescu, *History of Medieval Croatia* (The Hague, 1964), 26.

48. *Le Liber pontificalis: texte, introduction et commentaire*, ed. Louis Duchesne (Rome, 1981), 1:330, and *Liber pontificalis nella recensione di Pietro Guglielmo OSB e del card. Pandolfo glossato da Pietro Bohier OSB, vescovo di Orvieto: Introduzione—Testo—Indici*, ed. Ulderico Přerovský, Studia Gratiana 22 (Rome, 1978), 2:194. At that time the bones of several Dalmatian saints from the basilica of Salona were translated to Rome (Jenkins, *De administrando imperio: Commentary*, 108). See also Ernst Dümmler, "Über die älteste Geschichte der Slawen in Dalmatien (549–928)," *Sitzungsberichte der Österreichischen Akademie der Wissenschaften* 20 (1856): 353–430. On this basis the fall of Salona was then sometimes dated to 639.

49. Popović, "Les témoins archéologiques," 488.

50. Pascale Chevalier and Jagoda Mardešić, "Le groupe épiscopal de Salone aux IVe–VIIe siècles: Urbanisme et vie quotidienne," *Les destinées de l'Illyricum méridional pendant le haut Moyen Âge. MEFRM—Moyen Âge* 120, no. 2 (2008): 227–38.

51. Franko Oreb, "Archaeological Excavations in the Eastern Part of Ancient Salona," *Disputationes Salonitanae 2: Vjesnik za Arheologiju i Historiju Dalmatinsku* 77 (1984): 25–36; Ivan Marović, "Reflexions about the Year of Destruction of Salona," *Disputationes Salonitanae 2: Vjesnik za Arheologiju i Historiju Dalmatinsku* 77 (1984): 297–99, dates the destruction to 631–39. Although urban life was disrupted, the city was still occupied in the seventh century: Ivo Goldstein, *Bizant na Jadranu od Justijana 1. do Bazilija 1* (Zagreb, 1992). Overview of the archaeology of Dark Age Dalmatia: Huw M. A. Evans, *The Early Medieval Archaeology of Croatia, 600–900* (Oxford, 1989); Curta, *Southeastern Europe in the Middle Ages*, 100–102; Dzino, *Becoming Slav, Becoming Croat*, 92–117.

52. Dzino, *Becoming Slav, Becoming Croat*.

53. On the further fate of Dalmatia, see Jadran Ferluga, *L'amministrazione bizantina in Dalmazia* (Venice, 1978); Ferluga, *Byzantium on the Balkans: Studies on the Byzantine Administration and the Southern Slavs from the VIIth to the XIIth Centuries* (Amsterdam, 1976), 97–130; Wilkes, *Dalmatia*.

54. Francesco Borri, "La Dalmazia altomedievale tra discontinuità e racconto storico (secc. VII–VIII)," *Studi Veneziani*, n.s., 58 (2009): 15–51; Borri, "Arrivano i barbari a cavallo! Foundation Myths and 'Origines gentium' in the Adriatic Arc," in Pohl and Heydemann, *Post-Roman Transitions*, 215–70.

55. Cf. section 4.2. For instance, the author of the so-called *Chronicle of Monemvasia* completed his scant knowledge from local sources with information from Theophanes, Evagrius, and others.

56. The following events are recounted in the *Chronicon Paschale*, 165; Nicephorus 10, ed. and trans. Mango, 50–53; Theophanes, *Chronographia* 6110, 433–34, who also writes of a previous Avar attack; and Theodore Syncellus 10, trans. Pearse, http://www.tertullian.org/fathers/theodore_syncellus_01_homily.htm.

57. Nicephorus 10, ed. and trans. Mango, 50–53.

58. The most extensive description of the action is given in Nicephorus 10, ed. and trans. Mango, 50–53; as the author's intention is to make the most of Heraclius's misfortunes,

some of the details may be exaggerated. But basically the account is confirmed by the *Chronicon Paschale*, 165, written within a decade of the events.

59. The *Chronicon Paschale*, 165, mentions the Church of Saints Cosmas and Damian north of Blachernai, in present-day Eyüp, and one consecrated to the archangel in the suburb of Promotos near Galata. There the Avars plundered ciboria and church treasures and broke up the altar boards.

60. The figure 270,000, given by Nicephorus 10, ed. and trans. Mango, 53, must be due to a miswriting of the seventy thousand in another source, preserved in George the Monk, ed. de Boor, 2:669, as Andreas N. Stratos, "Le guet-apens des Avars," *Jahrbuch der Österreichischen Byzantinistik* 30 (1981): 113–36, argues. Cf. Theodore Syncellus 5.35–36, ed. and trans. Makk, 15.

61. Norman H. Baynes, "The Date of the Avar Surprise: A Chronological Study," *Byzantinische Zeitschrift* 21 (1912): 111, 123–28 argued for 617 (when June 5 also fell on a Sunday), followed by Ostrogorsky, *Geschichte des byzantinischen Staates*, 56 and 61; Zakythinos, *Byzantinische Geschichte*, 60 (617); Dölger, *Regesten der Kaiserurkunden*, 171, 19. Accepting Theophanes's date 619: Szádeczky-Kardoss, *Ein Versuch*, 88; Fraňo Barišić, "Le siège de Constantinople par les Avars et les Slaves en 626," *Byzantion* 24 (1954): 391; Bury, *History of the Later Roman Empire*, 2:222; Kollautz and Miyakawa, 1:269; Lemerle, *Les Plus Anciens Recueils*, 2:101–2 (617 or 619); Martin Hurbanič, "The Eastern Roman Empire and the Avar Khaganate in the Years 622–24 AD," *Acta Antiqua Academiae Scientiarum Hungaricae* 51 (2011): 315–28. A recent narrative of the Persian campaign: James Howard-Johnston, "Heraclius' Persian Campaigns and the Revival of the East Roman Empire, 622–30," *War in History* 6, no. 1 (1999): 1–44.

62. Stratos, "Le guet-apens des Avars," 113–36; the procession is transmitted in the *typikon* of the church of Constantinople. An extensive argument in favor of the 623 date is also found in *Chronicon Paschale*, 203–5. Also for 623: Avenarius, *Die Awaren in Europa*, 113–14; Kaegi, *Heraclius*, 118–20. Heraclius could have returned from the Persian frontier in 623 and continued the offensive in 624. The description in Theodore Syncellus (6.9, ed. and trans. Makk, 16, or 11, trans. Pearse) could describe Heraclius's second departure. The emperor recommended the city to God's protection and recalled that he had also entrusted it to the faithless khagan, probably on the occasion of his first departure in 622.

63. "Huni murum longum irrumpentes et ad menia Constantinopolis peraccedentes cum predicto imperatore (i.e., Eraclio) in muro stante conlocuntur; qui acceptum precium ab eo pacis ad tempus recedunt." Isidore of Seville, *Chronica Maiora: Additamenta*, ed. Theodor Mommsen, MGH AA 11 (Berlin, 1894), 490.5.

64. Theophanes, *Chronographia* 6111, 434.

65. Theodore Syncellus 10, trans. Pearse.

66. Theodore Syncellus 5.38–40, 6.4–6, ed. and trans. Makk, 15, or 10–11, trans. Pearse.

67. Nicephorus 13, ed. and trans. Mango, 59; that this was more than forseen by the old treaty is emphasized by Theodore Syncellus 6.4–5, ed. and trans. Makk, 15, or 11, trans. Pearse. See Kaegi, *Heraclius*, 120.

68. Nicephorus 21, ed. and trans. Mango, 71, places their release in return for money after the Muslim conquest in Syria, one of the very few references to the Avars in Byzantine sources after 626 (cf. section 7.6).

69. This date, from the *Chronicon Paschale*, is to be preferred over that given in Theophanes (623), as Stratos, "Le guet-apens des Avars," 121–23, has shown in his reconstruction of the events in the East.

70. See Theophanes, *Chronographia* 6113, 435. Unfortunately, his chronology is particularly garbled for these years; he reports this Avar treaty in 618/19, but after the account of the Avar ambush in the previous year (see below).

71. Stratos, *Byzantium in the Seventh Century*, 1:125–28; the melting down of church assets and the minting of a great number of coins is first mentioned by Theophanes with reference to 621–22 (*Chronographia* 6113, 435), as a precondition for the offensive against the Persians.

72. Somogyi, "New Remarks on the Flow of Byzantine Coins," 91–92.

73. Theodore Syncellus 6.14–15 and 34–35, ed. and trans. Makk, 16; cf. section 6.9.

74. Theophanes, *Chronographia* 6113, 435.

75. Stratos, "Le guet-apens des Avars," 135, has Heraclius returning in March 623. According to Theophanes, *Chronographia* 6113, 438, he wintered in the capital after the first year of the venture.

76. Thomas Presbyter, ed. Ernest W. Brooks and Jean Baptiste Chabot, *Chronica minora*, vol. 2, CSCO (Louvain, 1907), 115; Ensslin, "Slaveneinfälle," 705.

77. Cf. section 7.4. The anonymous *Chronicle* compilation has become known under the name "Fredegar" mentioned in a late manuscript; I use this name as a shorthand term for "the author of the (fourth book of the) *Fredegar Chronicle*."

78. As argued by Stratos, "Le guet-apens des Avars," 132–33.

79. Skaff, *Sui-Tang China and Its Turko-Mongol Neighbors*, 196.

80. Nicola Di Cosmo, Clive Oppenheimer, and Ulf Büntgen, "Interplay of Environmental and Socio-political Factors in the Downfall of the Eastern Türk Empire in 630 CE," *Climatic Change* 145 (2017): 383–95, https://doi.org/10.1007/s10584-017-2111-0.

81. David A. Graff, "Strategy and Contingency in the Tang Defeat of the Eastern Turks, 629–630," in Di Cosmo, *Warfare in Inner Asian History*, 33–72.

82. Paul Lemerle, "Quelques remarques sur le règne d'Heraclius," *Studi medievali* 3, no. 1 (1960): 347–61, is of the opinion that the importance of the Avar attack of 626 has generally been exaggerated. Heraclius would have sent more than twelve thousand crack troops, if he had judged the risk to be greater.

83. Wolfram, *History of the Goths*, 278.

84. Cf. section 2.1.

85. *Epistolae Austrasicae* 10, ed. Wilhelm Gundlach, MGH Epp. Karolini aevi 1 (Berlin, 1892), 133; Stein, *Histoire du Bas-Empire*, 2:525.

86. On the events, see Barišić, "Le Siège de Constantinople," 372–77; Stratos, *Byzantium in the Seventh Century*, 1:173–96; Andreas N. Stratos, "The Avars' Attack on Constantinople in the Year 626," in *Polychordia: Festschrift Franz Dölger*, ed. Peter Wirth, Byzantinische Forschungen 2 (Amsterdam, 1967), 370–76; Michael Whitby and Mary Whitby, "The Date of Heraclius's Encounter with the Avars," Appendix 4 in *Chronicon Paschale*, trans. Whitby and Whitby, 203–5, very reasonably insisting that the dating of the contemporary *Chronicon Paschale* deserves more trust than Theophanes's chronology reconstructed two centuries later; James Howard-Johnston, "The Siege of Constantinople in 626," in *Constantinople and Its Hinterland: Papers from the Twenty-Seventh Spring Symposium of Byzantine Studies, Oxford, April 1993*, ed. Cyril Mango and Gilbert Dagron (Aldershot, 1995), 131–42; Kaegi, *Heraclius*, 132–41; Haldon, *Byzantium in the Seventh Century*, 45–46. See also the forthcoming monograph by Martin Hurbanič, *The Last Battle of Antiquity: Constantinople 626*; Czech edition: *Konstantinopol 626: Poslední bitva antiky* (Prague, 2016).

87. *Chronicon Paschale*, 169–81.

88. Theodore Syncellus, *Homily on the Siege of Constantinople in 626 AD*, a sermon probably preached on the first anniversary of the siege. I have used the English translation by Roger Pearse (2007): http://www.tertullian.org/fathers/theodore_syncellus_01_homily.htm. Two studies by Samuel Szádeczky-Kardoss, "Zur Textüberlieferung der 'Homilia de obsidione Avarica Constantinopolis auctore ut videtur Theodoro Syncello,'" and "Eine unkollationierte Handschrift der Homilie über die persisch-awarische Belagerung von Konstantinopel: Codex Athous Batopedi 84. fol. 63r–68r" are found in his *Avarica*, 173–84 and 185–95. Cf. Moravcsik, *Byzantinoturcica*, 1:330–31.

89. George of Pisidia, *Bellum Avaricum*, was edited in 1959 by Pertusi with an Italian translation. On this work, see Moravcsik, *Byzantinoturcica*, 1:455; Paul Speck, *Zufälliges zum Bellum Avaricum des Georgios Pisides*, Miscellanea Byzantina Monacensia 24 (Munich, 1980); Whitby, "Defender of the Cross," 261–62.

90. Nicephorus 13, ed. and trans. Mango, 58–61; Theophanes, *Chronographia* 6117, 446–47. "Confused and confusing": Howard-Johnston, "The Siege of Constantinople," 132 with n. 4. A series of later chroniclers, homilists, and panegyricists who referred to the events add little to our knowledge.

91. Cf. the list in Lounghis, *Les ambassades byzantines en occident*, 468–69. Unfortunately, Paul the Deacon is not very helpful for this period. Fredegar, 4.49, ed. Krusch, 41, mentions a Byzantine embassy to the Lombard king Adaloald in 623–24, which only serves as a setting for a strange legend: the king was rubbed in his bath with a magical lotion brought by the Byzantines in order to subject him to a kind of brainwashing, after which he decimated the Lombard nobility. One might assume that at least the initial Frankish support for the Bohemian Wends (see section 7.4) was orchestrated by Byzantium, even if the rebellion itself was scarcely incited by Byzantine emissaries (as Stratos, "The Avars' Attack," 370–71, assumes). The "Hun" who in about 619 was appointed *patricius* in Constantinople was probably no anti-Avar Bulgar but rather a possible ally against the Persians (see section 7.6).

92. Howard-Johnston, "Heraclius' Persian Campaigns," 19–21.

93. Theodore Syncellus 14. Efforts underlined by Howard-Johnston, "The Siege of Constantinople," 134–37.

94. Theodore Syncellus 12. This letter is also mentioned by George of Pisidia, *Bellum Avaricum* 188, ed. and trans. Pertusi, 266.

95. *Chronicon Paschale*, 172: "a muster was held and about 12,000 or more cavalry resident in the city were present." That Heraclius sent troops is mentioned by George of Pisidia, *Bellum Avaricum* 189, ed. and trans. Pertusi, 280–82; Theophanes, *Chronographia* 6117, 446. Stratos, "The Avars' Attack," 375, argues that it was not until mid-July, after the battle of Satala, that the emperor's brother Theodore set out for Constantinople and arrived there on August 7, but these seem to have been two different contingents dispatched by the emperor; see *Chronicon Paschale*, trans. Whitby and Whitby, 172 n. 461.

96. *Chronicon Paschale*, 172 and 176.

97. *Chronicon Paschale*, 171.

98. *Chronicon Paschale*, 171.

99. George of Pisidia, *Bellum Avaricum* 186, ed. and trans. Pertusi, 219. The reference has generally been taken seriously in the scholarly literature; cf. Barišić, "Le siège de Constantinople," 379; Stratos, *Byzantium in the Seventh Century*, 1:184, counts the fighters in the boats separately and comes to the figure of 120,000–150,000; Howard-Johnston, "The Siege of Constantinople," 137, observes that the numbers given in George of Pisidia and in Theodore for the vanguard and for the entire army correspond. On the Roman side, the city militias and further citizens fought alongside the twelve thousand cavalrymen. It should be borne in mind that Constantinople still had a few hundreds of thousands of inhabitants; Koder, *Der Lebensraum der Byzantiner*, 117–18. Since the rule of Justinian I the population had decreased because of the plague and other factors; Cyril Mango, *Le développement urbain de Constantinople (IVe–VIIe siècles)*, Monographies de Travaux et Mémoires du Centre de recherche d'histoire et civilisation de Byzance 2 (Paris, 1985), 54. By the iconoclast period the population had probably dropped to forty thousand residents. It should also be recalled that in the early seventh century many refugees from the Balkan provinces must have come to the city. Clearly an exaggeration is Theodore's claim (trans. Pearse, 18) that there were a hundred attackers for every defender.

100. Theodore Syncellus 11.

101. Theodore Syncellus 18; *Chronicon Paschale*, 173.

102. Speck, *Zufälliges zum Bellum Avaricum*, 27.

103. Theodore Syncellus 15.

104. Theodore Syncellus 18.

105. *Chronicon Paschale*, 19. Obviously, the majority of the khagan's troops who had encircled the city were Slavs.

106. Theodore Syncellus 20.

107. *Chronicon Paschale*, 173; George of Pisidia, *Bellum Avaricum* 186, ed. and trans. Pertusi, 220–22; Nicephorus 13, ed. and trans. Mango, 58–61; Theodore Syncellus 20; cf. also the homily of St. Germanus: Venance Grumel, "Homélie de Saint Germain sur la délivrance de Constantinople," *Revue des Études Byzantines* 16 (1958): 195.

108. *Chronicon Paschale*, 174; Nicephorus 13, ed. and trans. Mango, 59, mentions only the divine power that annihilated them.

109. *Chronicon Paschale*, 174; Theodore Syncellus 22; Nicephorus 13, ed. and trans. Mango, 59.

110. *Chronicon Paschale*, 174.

111. *Chronicon Paschale*, 175; Theodore Syncellus 20–21; George of Pisidia, *Bellum Avaricum* 191–92, ed. and trans. Pertusi, 323–24; on the khagan of the Turks, see Menander, frag. 10.3, ed. and trans. Blockley, 120–22.

112. *Chronicon Paschale*, 175 (three thousand); George of Pisidia, *Bellum Avaricum* 192, ed. and trans. Pertusi, 342 (one thousand).

113. Kaegi, *Heraclius*, 132–33 (probably July 626).

114. *Chronicon Paschale*, 175; Theodore Syncellus 21.

115. On the resettlement of Persian prisoners in Iranian towns, a practice already started after the Victory of Shapur I over Valerian in 260, see Beate Dignas and Engelbert Winter, *Rome and Persia in Late Antiquity: Neighbours and Rivals* (Cambridge, 2007), 33 and 254–63.

116. E.g. *Chronicon Paschale*, trans. Whitby and Whitby, 170 n. 175: "Their intention was throughout to remove the Romans completely from Constantinople, so that they could take over as the new imperial controller." I find it hard to grasp what they would have controlled in a metropolis without inhabitants who could operate the infrastructure of city and empire. Similarly, Howard-Johnston, "The Siege of Constantinople," 132, assumes that the empire was to be partitioned so that the Avars received the European part, including Constantinople. He does not explain what they should be doing there, but is correct in stating (n. 8): "Pohl nonetheless denies that the khagan could have conceived of incorporating Constantinople (even emptied of its inhabitants) into his realm." There is indeed no indication that Huns, Avars, or the early Magyars ever intended to occupy any city they had conquered outside their core realm permanently. In 452, Attila resided for a few weeks in the imperial palace in Milan and then took his army, laden with booty, back home again.

117. Priscus, frag. 11.1, ed. and trans. Blockley, 243, and 11.2, 249.

118. Theodore Syncellus 43.

119. *Chronicon Paschale*, 176–78; Theodore Syncellus 24.

120. *Chronicon Paschale*, 178; cf. section 6.5.

121. See Pohl, "Konfliktverlauf und Konfliktbewältigung."

122. *Chronicon Paschale*, trans. Whitby and Whitby, 178 n. 472.

123. *Chronicon Paschale*, 177–78; Theodore Syncellus 22. The Armenian historian Sebeos also speaks of this in his history of Heraclius, *Histoire d'Héraclius par l'évêque Sébéos: Traduite de l'arménien et annotée*, trans. Frederic Macler (Paris, 1904), 79. Cf. Stratos, "The Avars' Attack," 374; Barišić, "Le siège de Constantinople," 385.

124. Theodore Syncellus 24.

125. Theodore Syncellus 25.

126. George of Pisidia, *Bellum Avaricum* 193, ed. and trans. Pertusi, 366–70.

127. George of Pisidia, *Bellum Avaricum* 194, ed. and trans. Pertusi, 405. After the siege, Heraclius had the church protected by extending the wall (*Chronicon Paschale*, 181); cf. Raymond Janin, *La géographie ecclésiastique de l'empire byzantine*, vol. 1, *Le siège de Constantinople et le patriarchat oecuménique* (Paris, 1969).

128. George of Pisidia, *Bellum Avaricum* 194, ed. and trans. Pertusi, 392–93.

129. George of Pisidia, *Bellum Avaricum* 194, ed. and trans. Pertusi, 409, says that the khagan had Slavs and Bulgars enter the dugouts; Theodore Syncellus 24, usually speaks of Slavs, but also of "monoxyles filled with foreign tribes." On the question of the sea wall, see Venance Grumel, "La défence maritime de Constantinople du côté de la Corne d'Or et le siège des Avars," *Byzantinoslavica* 25 (1964): 217–33. Different view in Stratos, *Byzantium in the Seventh Century*, 1:190.

130. Nicephorus 13, ed. and trans. Mango, 61. On perceptions of fighting women in late Antiquity, see Walter Pohl, "Gender and Ethnicity in the Early Middle Ages," in *Gender in the Early Medieval World: East and West, 300–900*, ed. Leslie Brubaker and Julia M. H. Smith (Cambridge, 2004), 23–43.

131. George of Pisidia, *Bellum Avaricum* 196, ed. and trans. Pertusi, 444–45; Theodore Syncellus 24.

132. George of Pisidia, *Bellum Avaricum* 197–98, ed. and trans. Pertusi, 462–75; Theodore Syncellus 32.

133. Nicephorus 13, ed. and trans. Mango, 61.

134. *Chronicon Paschale*, 178.

135. Stratos, "The Avars' Attack," 374; Barišić, "Le siège de Constantinople," 387; Howard-Johnston, "The Siege of Constantinople," 141.

136. *Chronicon Paschale*, 178.

137. Theodore Syncellus 33.

138. Theodore Syncellus 34.

139. Theodore Syncellus 35; see also Nicephorus 13, ed. and trans. Mango, 61; *Chronicon Paschale*, 178.

140. *Chronicon Paschale*, 178–80.

141. *Chronicon Paschale*, 181; see Stratos, *Byzantium in the Seventh Century*, 1:192–93, who sees the approach of the Roman army as the reason for the rapid abandonment of the siege. Opposing view in Barišić, "Le siège de Constantinople," 392, who deems supply difficulties to have been the determining factor. Speck, *Zufälliges zum Bellum Avaricum*, 31–47, would refer the entire passage about the "departure" of the khagan (*Chronicon Paschale*, 178–80) to the events surrounding the surprise attack on the emperor (here dated to 617), which is very unlikely. In this scenario it would not have been Bonus who negotiated with the khagan, and the observation about the approaching imperial brother would not be relevant.

142. Nicephorus 21, ed. and trans. Mango, 71; see section 7.6.

143. *Chronicon Paschale*, 179–80.

144. Theodore Syncellus 34–35.

145. Theodore Syncellus, *Homily on the Siege of Constantinople in 626 AD*. For an extensive interpretation of the exegetical strategy in the sermon, see Hurbanič, *The Last Battle of Antiquity*.

146. On the role of the Virgin as protecting the city against the Avars, see Averil Cameron, "The Virgin's Robe: An Episode in the History of Early Seventh-Century Constantinople," *Byzantion* 49 (1979): 42–56.

147. Isidore of Seville, *History of the Kings of the Goths* 1 and 66, trans. Wolf, *Conquerors and Chroniclers of Early Medieval Spain*, 80–82 and 107.

148. Theodore Syncellus 44.

149. David Olster, *Roman Defeat, Christian Response, and the Literary Construction of the Jew* (Philadelphia, 1994), 73–78; Averil Cameron, "Blaming the Jews: The Seventh-Century Invasions of Palestine in Context," *Travaux et mémoires* 14 (Mélanges Gilbert Dagron) (2002): 57–78; Stefan Esders, "Herakleios, Dagobert und die 'beschnittenen Völker': Die Umwälzungen des Mittelmeerraumes im 7. Jahrhundert in der Chronik des sogenannten Fredegar," in *Jenseits der Grenzen: Studien zur spätantiken und frühmittelalterlichen Geschichtsschreibung*, ed. Andreas Goltz, Hartmut Leppin, and Heinrich Schlange-Schöningen (Berlin, 2009), 239–311; Martin Hurbanič, "Adversus Iudaeos in the Sermon Written by Theodore Syncellus on the Avar Siege of AD 626," *Studia ceranea* 6 (2016): 271–93; Hurbanič, *The Last Battle of Antiquity*.

150. Theodore Syncellus 56.

151. John Haldon, *The Empire that Would Not Die: The Paradox of Eastern Roman Survival, 640–740* (Cambridge, 2016).

152. Leena Mari Peltomaa, *The Image of the Virgin Mary in the Akatisthos Hymn*, The Medieval Mediterranean Peoples, Economies and Cultures, 400–1453, 35 (Leiden 2001). I would like to thank the author for her advice on this subject.

153. *Apocalypse of Pseudo-Methodius* 11, ed. Benjamin Garstad (Cambridge, MA, 2012), 37.

154. George of Pisidia, *Restitutio crucis*, v. 78–81, ed. Leo Sternbach, *Wiener Studien* 13 (1891): 4–8; cf. Barišić, "Le siège de Constantinople," 395; Jan W. Drijvers, "Heraclius and the Restitutio Crucis: Notes on Symbolism and Ideology," in *The Reign of Heraclius (610–641): Crisis and Confrontation*, ed. Gerrit J. Reinink and Bernard H. Stolte (Leuven, 2002), 175–90; Mary Whitby, "George of Pisidia's Presentation of the Emperor Heraclius and His Campaigns," in Reinink and Stolte, *The Reign of Heraclius*, 157–73.

155. Stratos, *Byzantium in the Seventh Century*, 1:195 and 315–17, believes that Singidunum was recovered immediately after 626; this relies on Constantine Porphyrogenitus's information that under Heraclius, a Byzantine strategos at Belegradon had helped with the settlement of the Serbs (*DAI* 32, 152; cf. Lilie, "Kaiser Herakleios und die Ansiedlung der Serben," particularly 23–26). But this is clearly a retrospective construction and has no bearing on the seventh century; see section 7.5.

156. Kaegi, *Heraclius*, 192–228.

157. Fredegar 4.47, ed. Krusch, 39. For the context, see Wood, *Merovingian Kingdoms*, 145. I am grateful to Andreas Fischer for his advice on Fredegar.

158. Fredegar 4.48, ed. Krusch, 39–40.

159. On Fredegar, see Collins, *Fredegar*; Ian N. Wood, "Fredegar's Fables," in Scharer and Scheibelreiter, *Historiographie im frühen Mittelalter*, 356–66; Reimitz, *History, Frankish Identity and the Framing of Western Ethnicity*, 166–239. Whether the Samo chapter derives from a Burgundian redaction of the 640s (with the duration of Samo's reign added later) or was composed at the court in Metz soon after 660 is difficult to determine. For the description of Avar suppression of the Wends in the beginning of the narrative, see section 4.5. See also Florin Curta, "Slavs in Fredegar: Medieval Gens or Narrative Strategy," *Acta Universitatis Szegedensis de Attila József Nominatae. Acta Historica* 103 (1996): 3–20.

160. Reimitz, *History, Frankish Identity and the Framing of Western Ethnicity*, 175 and 182.

161. Fredegar 4.48, ed. Krusch, 39: "Homo nomen Samo natione Francos de pago Senonago plures secum negutiantes adcivit, exercendum negucium in Sciavos coinomento Winedos perrexit."

162. Soignies: Charles Verlinden, "Problèmes d'histoire économique franque: I. Le franc Samo," *Revue Belge de Philologie et Histoire* 12 (1933): 1091; Sens: Gerard Labuda, *Pierwsze państwo Słowiańskie: Państwo Samona* (Posen, 1949), 112–14; Chaloupecký, "Considérations sur Samon," 224–25; Saalegau, and Samo as a Slav: Heinrich Kunstmann, "Über die

Herkunft Samos," *Die Welt der Slawen* 25 (1980): 296–98. The *Conversio Bagoariorum et Carantanorum* 4, 103 actually considered him a Slav; Wolfram, *Conversio Bagoariorum*, 115–16, shows that this goes back to a misunderstanding of the *Gesta Dagoberti* 27, ed. Bruno Krusch, MGH SS rer. Merov. 2 (Hanover, 1888), 410, which is derivative of Fredegar on this point.

163. Samo as trader: Hellmann, "Grundlagen slawischer Verfassungsgeschichte," 391; Rudolf Turek, *Böhmen im Morgengrauen der Geschichte* (Wiesbaden, 1974), 134; Kunstmann, "Über die Herkunft Samos," 311; Chaloupecký, "Considérations sur Samon," 231: "Un seigneur franc chargé de mission politique"; Preidel, *Die Anfänge der slawischen Besiedlung*, 1:83.

164. Fredegar 4.68, ed. Krusch, 56–58.

165. Fredegar 4.35, ed. Krusch, 22–23.

166. Jiří Macháček, "'Great Moravian State': A Controversy in Central European Medieval Studies," *Studia Slavica et Balcanica Petropolitana* 10, no. 1 (2012): 5–26. See also Hellmann, "Grundlagen slawischer Verfassungsgeschichte," 390–92; Heinrich Kunstmann, "Samo, Dervanus und der Slovenenfürst Wallucus," *Die Welt der Slawen* 25 (1980): 171–77.

167. Fredegar 4.49–51, ed. Krusch, 41–43.

168. Fredegar 4.48, ed. Krusch, 210.

169. Fredegar 4.68, ed. Krusch, 56–57.

170. "First Slavic state": Labuda, *Pierwsze państwo Słowiańskie*, a very influential Polish monograph that appeared in 1949, clearly in reaction to the Nazi ideology of Slavic inferiority.

171. Heinrich Kunstmann, in *Die Slaven* and in his "Samo, Dervanus und der Slovenenfürst Wallucus," has attempted to document the Slavic basis for Samo's rule through etymology. The Old Slavonic pronoun *samъ*, "self, sole," could have meant something like "lord, master" in nominal use; the title *Samo rex* would then be the equivalent of "sole ruler." Kunstmann complements this etymology with a consideration of the contemporary *duces* Dervan and Walluc, who were both subordinate to Samo's rule (Fredegar 4.68, ed. Krusch, 57 and 4.72, 61). He interprets their names as *senior dux* and *maior dux*. Yet although Dervan and Walluc attached themselves more or less closely to the successful Wendish king at some point, it may still be asked who could have imposed such a tiered terminology of office. Neither of the titles is attested elsewhere. Pritsak, "The Slavs and the Avars," 393, n. 88, considers Kunstmann's thesis "historically impossible." For a non-Slavic etymology of the name, see Jooseppi J. Mikkola, "Samo und sein Reich," *Archiv für slavische Philologie* 42 (1929): 77; Chaloupecký, "Considérations sur Samon," 225.

172. Fredegar 4.58, ed. Krusch, 48–49.

173. For the many early medieval meanings of *placitum*, see Jan F. Niermeyer, *Mediae Latinitatis Lexicon minus*, 2 vols., 2nd ed. (Leiden, 2002), s.v. *placitum*, 1044–48; this is the most likely sense in the context.

174. Fredegar 4.68, ed. Krusch, 56.

175. Chrysos, "Legal Concepts," 19: "In the international world of late Antiquity friends did not need to be equal"; similar view in Verena Epp, *Amicitia: Zur Geschichte personaler, sozialer, politischer und geistlicher Beziehungen im frühen Mittelalter*, Monographien zur Geschichte des Mittelalters 44 (Stuttgart, 1999). Differing view in Wolfgang Fritze, "Die fränkische Schwurfreundschaft der Merowingerzeit," *Zeitschrift der Savigny-Stiftung für Rechtsgeschichte: Germanistische Abteilung* 71 (1954): 113–14. In Fritze's opinion *amicitia* in the Merovingian period did not designate simply a vague relationship of friendship but was a clearly delineated legal term in a sworn friendship between peers. In this conception, Samo "would have understood the connection with Dagobert in quite different terms than Sycharius, viz., as a bond of faith that depended on mutuality and excluded both Frankish

dicio and Slavic payment of tribute," while from the Frankish point of view the Wends had the "status of a tributary state." The more recent and flexible view of the term is more adequate to the situation as described in Fredegar.

176. Fredegar 4.62, ed. Krusch, 51; Ewig, *Die Merowinger und das Imperium*, 52; Lounghis, *Les ambassades byzantines en occident*, 108.

177. Fredegar 4.68, ed. Krusch, 56–58, on the ninth year of Dagobert's reign (631–32).

178. Fredegar 4.68, ed. Krusch, 57. It is unclear whether the Lombards are counted as one of Dagobert's three *turmae*, divisions (as Kollautz and Miyakawa, 2:435, and Chaloupecký, "Considérations sur Samon," 234, assume) or operated independently, as the wording seems to imply (Krahwinkler, *Friaul im Frühmittelalter*, 401). However, no other third army is mentioned in the text. Crucially, the Bavarians are not mentioned in the text; Were they tacitly counted as the third army, or had they refused to obey? Extensive discussion in Wolfgang Fritze, *Untersuchungen zur frühslawischen und frühfränkischen Geschichte bis ins 7. Jahrhundert* (Frankfurt am Main, 1994), especially 93–95; Kahl, "Die Baiern und ihre Nachbarn," 185.

179. "Regionem quae Zellia apellatur usque ad locum qui Meclaria dicitur": Paul the Deacon, *Historia Langobardorum* 4.38, ed. Waitz, 166 (Bethmann and Waitz's MGH edition has the now superseded emendation "Medaria").

180. In favor of Maglern, inter alia, Kollautz and Miyakawa, 2:391–93; Bogo Grafenauer, *Zgodovina Slovencev* (Ljubljana, 1979), 112; Wolfram "Ethnogenesen im frühmittelalterlichen Donau- und Ostalpenraum," 127, n. 153; Klaus Bertels, "Carantania: Beobachtungen zur politisch-geographischen Terminologie und zur Geschichte des Landes und seine Bevölkerung im frühen Mittelalter," *Carinthia I* 177 (1987): 100–102; Kahl, *Der Staat der Karantanen*, 251–52; more cautious, with additional secondary literature, is Krahwinkler, *Friaul im Frühmittelalter*, 313–19.

181. Cf. section 8.5. At that time relations between the Bavarians and the Lombards were extremely tense. Liutprand (712–44) had occupied some localities in South Tyrol and, despite a marriage tie with the Agilolfings, was closely allied with the Carolingians, who intervened in Bavaria on repeated occasions. Cf. Jarnut, *Geschichte der Langobarden*, 94–95; Reindel, "Das Zeitalter der Agilolfinger," 124–25.

182. According to Paul the Deacon, *Historia Langobardorum* 4.38, ed. Waitz, 126, the patrician Gregory lured the two under false pretenses to Opitergium/Oderzo, where he had them killed. The event is mostly dated to 625; cf. Gasparri, *I duchi longobardi*, 66–67; Jörg Jarnut, *Prosopographische und sozialgeschichtliche Studien zum Langobardenreich in Italien* (Bonn, 1972), 357; Krahwinkler, *Friaul im Frühmittelalter*, 39–40; Bertels, "Carantania," 103. At the end of 625, Gregory's successor Isaac was already in office: Salvatore Cosentino, *Prosopografia dell'Italia Bizantina (493–804)*, vol. 2, *(G–O)* (Bologna, 2000), 225. Fredegar 4.69, ed. Krusch, 58, has a different version: he describes the rebellion of a Tuscan *dux* Taso against the Lombard king Charoald/Arioald (626–36), which the latter could suppress only with the help of the exarch *Hysacius*/Isaac.

183. Gerard Labuda, "Wogastis-Burg," *Slavia Antiqua* 2 (1949–50): 241–52; Chaloupecký, "Considérations sur Samon," 235; Preidel, *Die Anfänge der slawischen Besiedlung*, 1:91; Wolfram, *Conversio Bagoariorum*, 74. In favor of Burk near Forchheim in Upper Franconia: Kunstmann, *Die Slaven*, 7–10, and Hans Jakob, "War Burk das historische Wogastisburc, und wo lag das Oppidum Berleich? Eine historisch-geographische Standortanalyse," *Die Welt der Slawen* 25 (1980): 39–67. Against this localization: Hansjürgen Brachmann, "Als aber die Austrasier das castrum Wogastisburc belagerten … (Fredegar IV, 68)," *Onomastica Slavogermanica* 19 (1990): 17–33.

184. Fredegar 4.75, ed. Krusch, 63.

185. Fredegar 4.68, ed. Krusch, 57–58.

186. Fredegar 4.74–76, ed. Krusch, 62–64.

187. For a regional kingdom in Bohemia, Chaloupecký, "Considérations sur Samon," 234; Preidel, *Die Anfänge der slawischen Besiedlung*, 1:228; Kollautz and Miyakawa, 1:231–33; István Bóna, "Das erste Auftreten der Bulgaren im Karpatenbecken: Turkic-Bulgarian-Hungarian Relations (6th–11th Centuries)," *Studia Turco-Hungarica* 5 (1981): 105; Dvornik, *The Slavs*, 61; "in the Sudeten region," Wolfram, *Grenzen und Räume*, 80. For southern Moravia and northern Lower Austria: Avenarius, *Geschichte der Awaren*, 127; Friesinger, *Die vielen Väter Österreichs*, 115. Kunstmann, "Über die Herkunft Samos," 310 and 312, imagines "a smaller, probably even mobile Slavic tribal union . . . west of Bohemia . . . in eastern Francia and in the immediate vicinity of the earlier eastern Frankish frontier." For the Vienna Basin, Marchfeld, and the upper Hungarian lowlands, see Fritze, "Zur Bedeutung der Awaren," 519; with the inclusion of Slovakia, in Čilinská, "Development of the Slavs North of the Danube," 250; Peter Stadler, "Ethnische Verhältnisse im Karpatenbecken und die Beziehungen zum Westen zur Zeit des awarischen Khaganats im 6. und 7. Jahrhundert," in Bemmann and Schmauder, *Kulturwandel in Mitteleuropa*, 668–69. It is, however, hardly possible to deduce the location of Samo's ephemeral kingdom from gradual differences in the archaeological material. A strong argument against the assumption of Samo's residence on or near the Danube is that the impact of Samo's victory was felt most in the land of the Sorbs, in Thuringia and Saxony (and not in Bavaria). Furthermore, it would have been difficult to defy the Avar horsemen for such a long time in the lowlands of the Carpathian Basin.

188. Wolfram, *Grenzen und Räume*, 301–2; Avenarius, *Geschichte der Awaren*, 137. The *Conversio Bagoariorum et Carantanorum* recounts that Samo "manens in Quarantanis fuit dux gentis illius" (chap. 3.40), which, however, is due to the sources and intentions of this Salzburg pamphlet composed in about 870; see Wolfram, *Conversio Bagoariorum*, 115–17.

189. Ulf Brunnbauer, "Illyrer, Veneter, Iraner, Urserben, Makedonen, Altbulgaren . . . Autochthonistische und nichtslawische Herkunftsmythen unter den Südslawen," *Zeitschrift für Balkanologie* 42, no. 1–2 (2006): 43–48. A very valuable systematic critique of national views of Croat history is found in John V. A. Fine, *When Ethnicity Did Not Matter in the Balkans: A Study of Identity in Pre-Nationalist Croatia, Dalmatia, and Slavonia in the Medieval and Early Modern Period* (Ann Arbor, 2005). However, the book goes too far in discounting ethnicity as a divisive element, claiming that it only began to matter in modern nationalism; it does not explain why the people in the region were routinely described using ethnic names in the early medieval sources. For a more balanced critique of nationalist myths of Croatian origins, see Neven Budak, "Identities in Early Medieval Dalmatia (Seventh–Eleventh Centuries)," in *Franks, Northmen, and Slavs: Identities and State Formation in Early Medieval Europe*, ed. Ildar H. Garipzanov, Patrick J. Geary, and Przemysław Urbańczyk (Turnhout, 2008), 227–38.

190. For recent scholarly overviews of early and later Croatian history, see Ivo Goldstein, *Croatia: A History* (London, 1999); Ludwig Steindorff, *Kroatien: Vom Mittelalter bis zur Gegenwart* (Regensburg, 2001).

191. *DAI* 30 and 31. For a criticism of the text, see Lujo Margetić, "Konstantin Porfirogenet i vrijeme dolaska Hrvata," *Zbornik historijski Zavoda JAZU* 8 (1977): 14–15; Moravcsik in Jenkins, *De administrando imperio: Commentary*, 97–98; Budak, "Identities in Early Medieval Dalmatia," 225–29; Dzino, *Becoming Slav, Becoming Croat*, 197–98. Tibor Živković, *De Conversione Croatorum et Serborum: A Lost Source* (Belgrade, 2012), has attempted to identify a lost source for the chapters on Croats and Serbs, which he attributes to Anastasius Bibliothecarius in the context of the controversy about Cyrill and Method (ibid., 217). It is an interesting proposal; but in general the debate about *De administrando imperio*, its dating and its sources, is not central to the issues raised here. In any case, it was composed several centuries after the events depicted, at a time when Croats mattered in former Dalmatia.

192. *DAI* 30, 142. For the translation of *laos* as "following/followers," see Hans Ditten, "Bemerkungen zu den ersten Ansätzen zur Staatsbildung bei Kroaten und Serben im 7. Jahrhundert," in *Beiträge zur byzantinischen Geschichte im 9.–11. Jahrhundert, Kolloquium Libice 1977* (Prague, 1978), 452, who adduces *DAI* 32.41, 154 as a parallel; cf. in any case 32.124, 158.

193. *DAI* 31.1–25 and 58–60, 146–50.

194. Dümmler, "Über die älteste Geschichte der Slawen"; Bury, *History of the Later Roman Empire*, 2:275–76; additional literature in Jenkins, *De administrando imperio: Commentary*, 95–97; Dzino, *Becoming Slav, Becoming Croat*.

195. Constantine Porphyrogenitus, *De cerimoniis aulae Byzantinae*, ed. Reiske, 2:48.688; Max Vasmer, *Untersuchungen über die ältesten Wohnsitze der Slawen: Die Iranier in Südrussland* (Leipzig, 1923); Stjepan K. Sakač, "Iranische Herkunft des kroatischen Volksnamens," *Orientalia Christiana Periodica* 15 (1949): 313–40, attempted to trace the Croats back to the time of Darius; similar concerns in Vernadsky, "Das frühe Slawentum," 265–68; Dvornik, *The Making of Central and Eastern Europe*, 286–88; Dvornik, *The Slavs*, 26–27; Henri Grégoire, "L'origine et le nom des Croates et des Serbes," *Byzantion* 17 (1944–45): 88–118; see also Ditten, "Bemerkungen," 444. For an overview of older debates: John V. A. Fine, "Croats and Slavs: Theories about the Circumstances of the Croats' Appearance in the Balkans," *Byzantinische Forschungen* 26 (2000): 205–18.

196. Nada Klaić, "Problemima stare domovine, dolaska i pokrštenja dalmatinskih Hrvata," *Zgodovinski Časopis* 38 (1984): 253–70; she postulates a migration by the Croats from Carantania (which she identifies with "White Croatia") on Frankish orders at the beginning of the ninth century. In agreement are Želiko Rapanić, "La costa orientale dell'Adriatico nell'alto medioevo (Considerazioni storico-artisiche)," in *Gli slavi occidentali*, 2:839–40, and Sergij Vilfan, "Evoluzione statale degli Sloveni e Croati," in *Gli slavi occidentali*, 1:124–27; cf. the discussion of this paper in *Gli slavi occidentali*, 1:144–56, with the critique by Jadran Ferluga (149). See also Margetić, "Konstantin Porfirogenet." Skeptical is Radoslav Katičić, "Die Anfänge des kroatischen Staates," in Wolfram and Schwarcz, *Die Bayern und ihre Nachbarn*, 310, n. 49. An extensive discussion of the issue is found in Lujo Margetić, *Dolezak hrvata* (Split, 1991), 217–96. His hypothesis is that the Croats arrived as a military elite from the ephemeral Bulgar polity of Kuver in the 630s—yet another hypothesis attached to the fragmentary accounts of Kuvrat and Kuver (see section 7.7).

197. The Iranian school proposes a derivation from Iranian *haurvata*, "herdsman": Sakač, "Iranische Herkunft"; Dvornik, *The Making of Central and Eastern Europe*; further literature in Ditten, "Bemerkungen," 444. Heinrich Kunstmann, "Über den Namen der Kroaten," *Die Welt der Slawen* 27 (1982): 131–36, with an unconvincing Greek etymology on the basis of Constantine's interpretation "who possess much land." Mikkola, "Avarica," 158–60; Otto Kronsteiner, "Gab es unter der Alpenslawen eine kroatische ethnische Gruppe?," *Wiener Slavistisches Jahrbuch* 24 (1978): 155, with an explanation drawn from Turkic; contrary view in Andreas Tietze, "Kroaten ein türkisches Ethnonym?," *Wiener Slavistische Jahrbücher* 25 (1979): 140. Another possibility is the meaning "to gather" for *qubrat*, as has been suggested for the Bulgar khan Kuvrat and that already occurs in the Orkhon inscriptions; cf. Gyula Németh, "Die Herkunft der Namen Kobrat und Esperüch," *Körösö Csoma Archivum* 2, no. 6 (1932): 440–47; Dezső Pais, "A propos de l'étymologie de l'ethnique OGUR," in Ligeti, *Studia Turcica*, 369. See also Margetić, *Dolezak hrvata*, 249–51.

198. John IV: *Liber Pontificalis* 74, trans. Raymond Davis, *The Book of Pontiffs: The Ancient Biographies of the First Ninety Roman Bishops to AD 715*, Translated Texts for Historians 6 (Liverpool, 2000), 66. Agathon: *Epistula* 3, in *Patrologia cursus completus, Series Latina*, ed. J.-P. Migne, vol. 87 (Paris, 1863), cols. 1224–25; cf. Katičić, "Die Literatur des frühen kroatischen Mittelalters," 32.

199. Paul the Deacon, *Historia Langobardorum* 5.23 and 4.44, ed. Waitz, 195, 170.

200. *DAI* 29, 125.

201. Evans, *The Early Medieval Archaeology of Croatia*, 156–58; Curta, *Southeastern Europe in the Middle Ages*, 141; Dzino, *Becoming Slav, Becoming Croat*, 92–174.

202. *Annales regni Francorum* a. 821, ed. Kurze, 155 and a. 818, 149. Extensive treatment in Katičić, "Die Anfänge des kroatischen Staates," 301–3; cf. Herwig Wolfram, "Liudewit und Priwina: Ein institutioneller Vergleich," in *Interaktionen der mitteleuropäischen Slawen und anderen Ethnika im 6.–10. Jahrhundert: Symposium Nové Vozokany 3.–7. Oktober 1983*, ed. Archäologisches Institut der Slowakischen Akademie der Wissenschaften (Nitra, 1984), 293. Borna would scarcely have presented himself before the emperor Ludwig as a mere *dux Guduscanorum*, if in reality he could, as *dux Chroatorum*, derive his dukedom from a much more extensive entity.

203. The title is first attested in a charter of Trpimir's from 852, which, however, is preserved only in very late copies; Branimir's inscription from the 880s is also reconstructed from several fragments. Katičić, "Die Anfänge des kroatischen Staates," 307; Curta, *Southeastern Europe in the Middle Ages*, 139–41.

204. *The Old English Orosius*, ed. Janet Bately, Early English Text Society, Supplementary Series 8 (Oxford, 1980), 13; identified with Croats and Serbs by Dvornik, *The Making of Central and Eastern Europe*, 272–73.

205. "Beschreibung der Nordvölker nach dem *Kitāb al-aʿlāq an-nafīsa* des Abū ʿAlī ibn ʿUmar ibn Rusta," trans. Göckenjan and Zimonyi, 79. In other geographical texts the name of the city (it is clearly not supposed to be a people) is given as Hurdāb (Hudūd al-ʿĀlām, ibid., 211) or H.z.rāt (al-Marwazī, ibid., 252). See ibid., 79, n. 135, against the identification of this name with the Croats. Marquart, *Osteuropäische und ostasiatische Streifzüge*, xxxi–xxxii, 102 and 468.

206. *Nestor Chronicle* 13.96, trans. Ludolf Müller, *Die Nestorchronik: Handbuch zur Nestorchronik*, vol. 4 (Munich, 2001), 12. In the English translation, homogenized as Croats: *The Russian Primary Chronicle* 12, trans. Cross and Sherbowitz-Wetzor, 56.

207. MGH DD H IV, 390, 517 (transmitted in a falsified version).

208. Dvornik, *The Making of Central and Eastern Europe*, 277–79.

209. Mention of the *pagus Crouuati* in a diploma of Otto I: MGH DD O I, 173, 255. Cf. Wolfram, *Grenzen und Räume*, 302.

210. Herrmann, *Die Slawen in Deutschland*, 12; Vasmer, *Die Slaven in Griechenland*, at 123, 127, 175, and 319.

211. Cf. section 4.6. Heinrich Kunstmann, "Nestors Dulěbi und die Glopeani des Geographus Bavarus," *Die Welt der Slawen* 24 (1979): 44–46 (with a less than satisfactory Greek eymology); Dvornik, *The Making of Central and Eastern Europe*, 281. An early documentary source is a diploma of Louis the German from 860: MGH DD LD, 102, 148.

212. Nicephorus 24.9–12, ed. and trans. Mango, 73; see section 7.6.

213. *Miracula Demetrii* 2.5, 222–34; see section 7.7.

214. See also Haldon, *Byzantium in the Seventh Century*, 47 and 352.

215. *DAI* 32–36, 152–64. Neven Budak, "Die südslawischen Ethnogenesen an der östlichen Adriaküste im frühen Mittelalter," in Wolfram and Pohl, *Typen der Ethnogenese*, 129–36.

216. On the compilation, see Ljubomir Maksimović, "Struktura 32. glave spisa 'De administrando imperio,'" *Zbornik Radova* 21 (1982): 25–32.

217. "Sorabi, quae natio magnam Dalmatiae partem optinere dicitur": *Annales regni Francorum* a. 822, ed. Kurze, 128.

218. Konstantin Jireček, *Geschichte der Serben*, vol. 1 (Gotha, 1911), 107–8: "combinations of the tenth century on the basis of the similarity of some tribal names in the north and south"; differing opinion in Francis Dvornik's note in Jenkins, *De administrando*

imperio: Commentary, 131–32; Stratos, *Byzantium in the Seventh Century*, 1:321–22; for a critique, see Lilie, "Kaiser Herakleios und die Ansiedlung der Serben."

219. Fredegar 4.68, ed. Krusch, 155 (in the form *Surbi*).

220. The frequent occurrence of the name could also be due to its etymology: Herrmann, *Die Slawen in Deutschland*, 12, explains the name as *srb* = "of common descent"; Zbigniew Gołab, "Old Bulgarian Sěverъ (?) and Old Russian Sěverjane," *Wiener Slavistisches Jahrbücher* 30 (1984): 19–20, has "kinsmen" and interpets not only the names of the Serbs and the Sorbs but also those of the Bulgarian Severans and the Russian Severyanes in this way.

221. Chrysos, "Die Nordgrenze," 29–31; Evangelos Chrysos, "Zum Landesnamen Langobardia," in *Die Langobarden*, ed. Walter Pohl and Peter Erhart, Forschungen zur Geschichte des Mittelalters 9 (Vienna, 2005), 429–38.

222. *DAI* 30, 142; 31, 148; 32, 152; 33, 160; 35, 164; 36, 164. Each time the Avars devastate and depopulate the country, newcomers are brought by Heraclius against the Avars. The late sources for the Slavicization of Greece also make a similar distinction; cf. sections 4.2–4.

223. Budak, "Die südslawischen Ethnogenesen."

224. Dzino, *Becoming Slav, Becoming Croat*, 218.

225. Mihailo Milinkovic, "Stadt oder 'Stadt': Frühbyzantinische Siedlungsstrukturen im nördlichen Illyricum," in Henning, *Post-Roman Towns*, 2:159–92. The numbers he gives are ca. 170 early Byzantine settlements in Serbia, 500 in Macedonia (of which 400 were still used in the sixth century), and 60 in Bosnia.

226. Dzino, *Becoming Slav, Becoming Croat*, 118–54.

227. Dzino, *Becoming Slav, Becoming Croat*, 215.

228. *Annales regni Francorum* 822 (Liudewit at Siscia); *Annales regni Francorum* 818 (Borna *dux Guduscanorum et Timocianorum*).

229. Otto of Freising, *Gesta Friderici* 1.26 and 1.32, ed. Georg Waitz and Bernhard von Simson, MGH SS rer. Germ. 46 (Hanover, 1912), 41 and 49. This is the result of a name search in the online dMGH, http://www.dmgh.de.

230. *Principes Croatorum ac Narentanorum*: John the Deacon, *Istoria Veneticorum* 4.45, ed. Berto, 186; discussion of the passage: Budak, "Identities in Early Medieval Dalmatia," 234–36.

231. Cf. Pohl, "Die Gepiden und die Gentes," 252–54.

232. Jordanes, *Getica* 50.259–66, ed. Mommsen, 125–27.

233. Fredegar 4.72, ed. Krusch, 60. Kollautz and Miyakawa, 1:160 (635); Lauterbach, "Untersuchungen zur Vorgeschichte der Protobulgaren," 601 (636–39). "In this year," *eo anno*, clearly refers to Fredegar's section 4.67, the ninth year of Dagobert, while the events of the tenth year start in 4.74. The wide overview of events in the Avar lands, Italy, and Spain in sections 4.67–4.73 also contains events as late as the time of King Rothari (636–52), but the events that start off the different regional narratives after the regular phrase *eo anno* can be dated to 631/32 or close to it (for instance, the rebellion of Sisenand against the Visigothic king Suinthila, which happened in 631, in 4.73). It should also be noted that Dagobert, who gives the order to kill Bulgar refugees in 4.72, was only responsible for Austrasia until 633, when his son Sigibert became king there. For Kuvrat, see below, in this chapter.

234. Fredegar 4.72, ed. Krusch, 60.

235. Furthermore, Alciocus is later attested in Italy (see below), and the Slavs in the Eastern Alps "were the neighbors of both the Bavarians and the Lombards": Wolfram, *Conversio Bagoariorum*, 314; cf. Deér, "Karl der Grosse," 737–40.

236. Reindel, "Das Zeitalter der Agilolfinger," 154; Schlesinger, "Zur politischen Geschichte der fränkischen Ostbewegung," 40; Kahl, "Die Baiern und ihre Nachbarn," 185–86; Heinrich

Kunstmann, *Vorläufige Untersuchungen über den bairischen Bulgarenmord von 631/32* (Munich, 1982), seeks to construct an association with the emergence of the *Nibelungenlied* material. Good overview in Ziemann, *Vom Wandervolk zur Großmacht*, 130–35.

237. Paul the Deacon, *Historia Langobardorum* 5.29, ed. Waitz, 196–97: "Per haec tempora Vulgarum dux Alzeco nomine, incertum quam ob causam, a sua gente digressus, Italiam pacifice introiens, cum omni sui ducatus exercitu ad regem Grimuald venit."

238. Jarnut, *Geschichte der Langobarden*, 60; Beševliev, *Die protobulgarische Periode*, 157, with an identification of Alzeco with the unnamed fifth son of Khan Kuvrat. Against the association of Alciocus and Alzeco, see Ditten, "Protobulgaren und Germanen," 70; for it, Lauterbach, "Untersuchungen zur Vorgeschichte der Protobulgaren," 595–98, and Bertels "Carantania," 104–6.

239. Herwig Wolfram, *Intitulatio*, vol. 1, *Lateinische Königs- und Fürstentitel bis zum Ende des 8. Jahrhunderts*, MIÖG Erg. Bd. 21 (Graz, 1967), 145.

240. Transmitted in the *Chronicon Salernitanum* 20, ed. Ulla Westerbergh (Stockholm, 1956), 25. Alzeco's Bulgars were also mentioned in a brief synthesis of Lombard history in the ninth-century *Chronica Sancti Benedicti Casinensis* 2, ed. Georg Waitz, MGH SS rer. Langob. (Berlin, 1878), 469: "Alzechus Vulgar suis cum hominibus ad habitandum suscipitur."

241. Bruno Genito, "Archaeology of the Early Medieval Nomads in Southern Italy: The Horse-Burials in Molise (7th Century) South-Central Italy," in Bálint, *Kontakte zwischen Iran*, 229–48; Valeria Ceglia, "Le presenze avariche nelle necropoli altomedievali di Campochiaro," in Bemmann and Schmauder, *Kulturwandel in Mitteleuropa*, 691–703.

242. Ceglia, "Le presenze avarice," 695–98.

243. Margetić, *Dolezak hrvata*, 259–60; the succession of Raduald to the duchy of Benevento is usually dated to ca. 642, that of Grimoald to 647; see Paolo Diacono, *Storia dei Longobardi*, ed. Lidia Capo (Milan, 1992), 523–25. Alti-oq: H. W. Haussig cited for a personal comment in Beševliev, *Die protobulgarische Periode*, 520, n. 26.

244. See also Tsvetelin Stepanov, *The Bulgars and the Steppe Empire in the Early Middle Ages* (Leiden, 2010).

245. Nicephorus 22, ed. and trans. Mango, 70: "At about the same time Koubratos, the nephew of Organas and lord of the Onogundurs, rose up against the Chagan of the Avars and, after abusing the army he had from the latter, drove them out of his land. He sent an envoy to Herakleios and concluded a peace treaty which they observed until the end of their lives. (Herakleios) sent him gifts and honored him with the title of patrician." The passage comes after the account of the Islamic invasions of Syria 633–34; see Mango, "Commentary," in Nicephorus, ed. and trans. Mango, 186–88; cf. on this point, Walter E. Kaegi, *Byzantium and the Early Islamic Conquest* (Cambridge, 1992), 67.

246. John of Nikiu, *Chronicle* 120.54, ed. and trans. Charles, 196–97 (who, as the French translation by Zotenberg, 460, offers the emendation "Kubratos, chief of the Huns, the nephew of Organa"). The work of the Egyptian bishop written in Coptic or Greek is preserved in an Ethiopic recension based on an Arabic translation; cf. section 1.2. On the spelling of the names, see Josef Marquart, "Die altbulgarischen Ausdrücke in der Inschrift von Čatalar und der bulgarischen Fürstenliste," *Izvestija Russkago archaeologičeskago instituta v Konstantinople* 15 (1911): 7; Beševliev, *Die protobulgarische Periode*, 512–13 (with bibliography).

247. Theophanes, *Chronographia* 6171, 357.8–14; similarly Nicephorus 35, ed. and trans. Mango, 89. In his edition of Theophanes, de Boor prefers the reading "Krobatos," while Nicephorus has the reading "Kobratos" (in chap. 22 one manuscript has "Koubaros"). Lauterbach, "Untersuchungen zur Vorgeschichte der Protobulgaren," 555.

248. Nicephorus 9, ed. and trans. Mango, 49–51. A slightly different version is contained in *The London Manuscript of Nicephorus' "Brevarium,"* ed. Louis Orosz (Budapest, 1948), 20, 168–75.

249. In English translation: Petkov, *Voices of Medieval Bulgaria, Seventh–Fifteenth Century*, 4. Moravcsik, *Byzantinoturcica*, 2:296–97; Beševliev, *Die protobulgarische Periode*, 482; Pritsak, *Die bulgarische Fürstenliste*, 38; Charles J. Halperin, "Bulgars and Slavs in the First Bulgarian Empire: A Reconsideration of the Historiography," *Archivum Eurasiae Medii Aevi* 3 (1983): 192–93; Hans W. Haussig, "Die protobulgarische Fürstenliste," in *Die Hunnen in Osteuropa*, ed. Franz Altheim and Hans W. Haussig (Baden-Baden, 1958), 13; Ziemann, *Vom Wandervolk zur Großmacht*, 39–44.

250. Joachim Werner, *Der Grabfund von Malaja Pereščepina und Kuvrat, Kagan der Bulgaren*, Abh. Bayer. AW, n.s., 91 (Munich, 1984), 43; 44–45, on the monogram on the ring, as read by Werner Seibt (Vienna), a leading authority on Byzantine seals and monograms. A detailed discussion, with emphasis on the questions raised by the Kuvrat hypothesis, is found in Bálint, "Zur Identifizierung." Dissenting views in Hans W. Haussig, review of *Der Grabfund von Malaja Pereščepina und Kuvrat, Kagan der Bulgaren*, by Joachim Werner, *UAJB*, n.s., 5 (1985): 275–77. On the question of whether the find is from a grave or is a hoard, see Michel Kazanski and Jean-Pierre Sodini, "Byzance et l'art 'nomade': Remarques à propos de l'essai de J. Werner sur le dépôt de Malaja Pereščepina," *Revue Archéologique*, 1987, 71–83, especially at 81–83. General treatment of the archaeology of the Black Sea zone in the seventh century in Bálint, *Die Archäologie der Steppe*, 78–111.

251. Thus Moravcsik, "Zur Geschichte der Onoguren," 71–72; Runciman, *A History of the First Bulgarian Empire*, 14–15; Kollautz and Miyakawa, 1:160; Stratos, *Byzantium in the Seventh Century*, 2:163–65; Lauterbach, "Untersuchungen zur Vorgeschichte der Protobulgaren," 578–80.

252. See, for instance, Marquart, *Osteuropäische und ostasiatische Streifzüge*, 21; Beševliev, *Die protobulgarische Periode*, 519; Avenarius, *Geschichte der Awaren*, 255. Beševliev (516–19), considers John of Nikiu's account to be an interpolation and unreliable; he rather refers it to a barbarian officer in Roman service.

253. This may be concluded from Theophanes, *Chronographia* 6171, 357.11–14. The exact date is debated. During Constans's stay in the west, 663–68: Haussig, "Die protobulgarische Fürstenliste," 13; Altheim, *Geschichte der Hunnen*, 1:20; Lauterbach, "Untersuchungen zur Vorgeschichte der Protobulgaren," 581; Vasil Gjuzelev, "Chan Asparuch und die Gründung des bulgarisches Reiches," in Vasil Gjuzelev, *Forschungen zur Geschichte Bulgariens im Mittelalter*, Miscellanea Bulgarica 3 (Vienna, 1986), 13; Pritsak, *Die bulgarische Fürstenliste*, 36; Beševliev, *Die protobulgarische Periode*, 153, n. 19; Kollautz and Miyakawa, 1:159. For a date around 642: Grousset, *Empire of the Steppes*, 176; Ditten, "Zur Bedeutung der Einwanderung der Slawen," 128; Stratos, *Byzantium in the Seventh Century*, 2:165; Avenarius, *Geschichte der Awaren*, 157. Around 650: Werner, *Der Grabfund von Malaja Pereščepina*, 43; Dimităr Angelov and Dimităr Ovčarov, "Slawen, Protobulgaren und das Volk der Bulgaren," in Herrmann, *Welt der Slawen*, 64. The coins of Constans II in his grave set the date to the 640s at the earliest; otherwise, none of the hypotheses can be corroborated by the sources. If he already died in the 640s, it would be harder to bridge the gap to Asparukh's exploits in the late 670s.

254. Theophanes, *Chronographia* 6171; see the commentary in *The Chronicle of Theophanes Confessor*, trans. Mango and Scott, 500. Lauterbach, "Untersuchungen zur Vorgeschichte der Protobulgaren," 557 (identification of the *Kuphis* with the Bug). Similarly, András Róna-Tas, "Where Was Kuvrat's Bulgharia?," *Acta Orient. Hung.* 53 (2000): 1–22, places Kuvrat's realm on both sides of the Dnieper; followed by Curta, *Southeastern Europe in the Middle Ages*, 78–79, who links this localization with a number of rich seventh-century archaeological sites in the region (but archaeology has also been used to argue in favor of the Kuban, see Bálint, "Über einige östliche Beziehungen," 137). See also Ziemann, *Vom Wandervolk zur Großmacht*, 147–48. In Theophanes's account, Asparukh crossed the Dnieper and the Dniester (but not the Don) to reach the Danube. The description of the

northern coast of the Black Sea is similarly confused in *DAI* 42.49, 184, where the *Kouphis* is mentioned next to the *Bogu*/Bug; here, the Dnieper is said to flow into the Maeotis, which is then supposed to stretch as far as the *Necropyla* (thus, west of the Crimea). The Ravenna Geographer (Anonymus Ravennatis. *Cosmographia* 4.1, ed. Schnetz, 44) locates the Khazar Empire at the *Kuphis* in about 700 (and that probably meant the Kuban). Dvornik, *The Slavs*, 64, located Kuvrat's empire north of the lower Danube, which has little to recommend it.

255. Nicephorus 35, ed. and trans. Mango, 89, recounts the expansion of the Khazars directly after the story of Kuvrat. See Bálint, *Die Archäologie der Steppe*, 110.

256. Douglas M. Dunlop, *The History of the Jewish Khazars* (Princeton, NJ, 1954), 56–57; Golden, *Khazar Studies*, 1:59–60; Pletnewa, *Die Chasaren*, 64.

257. Cf. section 5.9.

258. Menander, frag. 19.1–2, ed. and trans. Blockley, 178. According to epigraphic information the city would have again fallen to Byzantium around 590; Szádeczky-Kardoss, "Über die Wandlungen," 158.

259. Theophanes, *Chronographia* 6117 and 6118, 316; Dunlop, *The History of the Jewish Khazars*, 28–30 (with a listing of further sources). On the transmission of information, see also Margit Bíró, "Georgian Sources on the Caucasian Campaign of Heracleios," *Acta Orient. Hung.* 35 (1981): 121–32; Golden, *Khazar Studies*, 1:51; Chavannes, *Documents sur les Tou-kiue*, 52.

260. This opinion was early represented by Moravcsik, "Zur Geschichte der Onoguren," 74; Pletnewa, *Die Chasaren*, 28; Avenarius, *Geschichte der Awaren*, 157.

261. Liu Mau-Tsai, *Die chinesischen Nachrichten*, 2:602; Sinor, "The Establishment and Dissolution of the Türk Empire," 308–10; de la Vaissière, "Ziebel Qaghan Identified"; Golden, *Khazar Studies*, 1:39; Moravcsik, *Byzantinoturcica*, 2:296–97.

262. Constantine Zuckerman, "The Khazars and Byzantium: The First Encounter," in Golden, Ben-Shammai, and Róna-Tas, *The World of the Khazars*, 399–432; de la Vaissière, "Ziebel Qaghan Identified," 746.

263. Bálint, "Über einige östliche Beziehungen," 132; Bálint, *Die Archäologie der Steppe*, 92–100; Igor Gavrituchin, "The Archaeological Heritage of the Avar Khaganate and the Southern Part of Eastern Europe: Periodisation, Dating and Synchronisation," *Antaeus* 29–30 (2008): 63–125; Daim, "Avars and Avar Archaeology," 481–84; Daim, "Die Materialität der Macht," 625–28.

264. Nicephorus 21, ed. and trans. Mango, 71. Accepting a date of ca. 635: Marquart, *Osteuropäische und ostasiatische Streifzüge*, 126; Josef Marquart, *Die Chronologie der alttürkischen Inschriften* (Leipzig, 1898), 75; Beševliev, *Die protobulgarische Periode*, 149; Kollautz and Miyakawa, 1:160; Stratos, *Byzantium in the Seventh Century*, 2:136. Lauterbach, "Untersuchungen zur Vorgeschichte der Protobulgaren," 576, puts the date between 630 and 634. On the hostages, see section 7.2; Stratos, *Byzantium in the Seventh Century*, 1:150.

265. Nicephorus 22, ed. and trans. Mango, 71.

266. Margetić, *Dolezak hrvata*, 265–66, assumes that the new Avar dynasty had only come into power with Kuvrat's support, and maybe in dependence from him. But that fits neither Fredegar's nor Nicephorus's account.

267. *Miracula Demetrii* 2.1.179, 175, and 2.4, 209–11 (cf. sections 4.6 and 7.1); Theophanes, *Chronographia* 6171, 359.13–14. Theophanes describes the situation of the "Seven Tribes" with the expression "being under a treaty," *hypo pakton ontes*, the meaning of which has long been debated. Does it refer to the relationship with Byzantium or with the Bulgars? Rather, this Roman legal term designates a federate relationship with Byzantium, so that the apparent paradox is easily explained; Evangelos Chrysos, "Zur Gründung des ersten bulgarischen Staates," *Cyrillomethodiana* 2 (1972–73): 7–9; Chrysos, "Die Nordgrenze," 38 (and n. 52); Hans Ditten, "Zum Verhältnis zwischen Protobulgaren und

Slawen vom Ende des 7. bis zum Anfang des 9. Jahrhunderts," in Köpstein, *Besonderheiten der byzantinischen Feudalentwicklung*, 92–95. Differing view in Beševliev, *Die protobulgarische Periode*, 179; Halperin, "Bulgars and Slavs in the First Bulgarian Empire," 185. The passage can hardly serve as a basis for an elucidation of the status of the Slavs in the Bulgar Empire.

268. Stratos, *Byzantium in the Seventh Century*, 2:163–67; Tăpkova-Zaimova, *Byzance et les Balkans à partir du VIe siècle*; Peter Charanis, "Ethnic Changes in the Byzantine Empire in the Seventh Century," *Dumbarton Oaks Papers* 13 (1959): 23–26; Haldon, *Byzantium in the Seventh Century*, 125–72; and the essays in the collective works Winkelmann et al., eds., *Byzanz im 7. Jahrhundert* and Friedhelm Winkelmann and Helga Köpstein, eds., *Studien zum 7. Jahrhundert in Byzanz: Probleme der Herausbildung des Feudalismus* (Berlin, 1976). On settlement history, see Jadran Ferluga, "Untersuchungen zur byzantinischen Ansiedlungspolitik auf dem Balkan von der Mitte des 7. bis zur Mitte des 9. Jahrhunderts," *Zbornik Radova* 23 (1984): 49–61; Koder, *Der Lebensraum der Byzantiner*, 122–24.

269. Cf. sections 7.8 and 8.1. The number of rich graves from the period indicate the continuing use of the wealth accumulated before 626. The statistics of coin finds (Somogyi, "New Remarks on the Flow of Byzantine Coins," 96–100) show a sharp drop after the 620s, a virtual standstill between 640 and 650, an increasing recovery until 680, when (after the Bulgar conquest) the influx of coins from Constantinople stops completely.

270. Paul the Deacon, *Historia Langobardorum* 5.2, ed. Waitz, 180.

271. Paul the Deacon, *Historia Langobardorum* 5.5, ed. Waitz, 185–86.

272. Stephanus, *Vita S. Wilfridi* 28, ed. Levison, 222.

273. Paul the Deacon, *Historia Langobardorum* 5.19, ed. Waitz, 193. On Constans's campaign of 663, see Stratos, *Byzantium in the Seventh Century*, 3:209–10.

274. On the Vipava, the Frigidus of Antiquity, lay the post Fluvio Frigido/Adjovščina; Krahwinkler, *Friaul im Frühmittelalter*, 42 and 403, n. 110, with a bibliography of studies on the localization of the battle and on the influence of epic prototypes in the account; Hartmann, *Geschichte Italiens im Mittelalter*, 2:253; Gasparri, *I duchi longobardi*, 68.

275. Paul the Deacon, *Historia Langobardorum* 5.20–21, ed. Waitz, 193–94.

276. Clearly, particularly during a brief period toward 670, heightened quantities of Byzantine coinage and decorative objects entered the country: Bálint, *Die Archäologie der Steppe*, 160; Somogyi, "New Remarks on the Flow of Byzantine Coins." Thus, for example, the coin hoard from Zemianský Vrbovok contained seventeen coins from the end phase of Constans II's rule (before 668), against one piece from 678; cf. Alexander Avenarius, "Die Konsolidierung des Awarenkhaganats und Byzanz im 7. Jahrhundert," in *Festschrift J. E. Karayannopoulos*, special issue, *Byzantina* 13, no. 2 (1985): 1024. These coins are hardly evidence for Avar forays against Byzantium (Avenarius) or for Onogur immigrants (Bálint); they may be associated with Constans's search for support for his Italian policy.

277. Paul the Deacon, *Historia Langobardorum* 5.22, ed. Waitz, 194; on the question of the first mention of the name of the Carantanians, see Wolfram, *Conversio Bagoariorum*, 110–11, with bibliography. Caution is called for with regard to later authors' information on earlier ethnic relationships; often enough they use the names that were familiar to them. On the other hand, this passage is the first in which Paul makes an ethnic distinction among the Slavs, something he otherwise rarely does. Cf. Bertels, "Carantania," 109; Kahl, *Der Staat der Karantanen*, 68–72.

278. Paul the Deacon, *Historia Langobardorum* 5.23, ed. Waitz, 194–95.

279. Paul the Deacon, *Historia Langobardorum* 5.29, ed. Waitz, 196–97; cf. section 7.6.

280. Theophanes, *Chronographia* 6169, 496; similarly Nicephorus 34, ed. and trans. Mango, 87.

281. Theophanes, *Chronographia* 6171, 498; Nicephorus 35, ed. and trans. Mango, 88. See section 7.6.

282. Tsvetelin Stepanov, "The System of Succession in Qubrat's 'Magna Bulgaria': A New Approach to an Old Problem," in Zimonyi and Karatay, *Central Eurasia in the Middle Ages*, 383–92.

283. Michael the Syrian 10.21, 363, where two of the brothers are called Bulgaros and Kazarig and become ancestors of the Danube Bulgars and the Khazars.

284. Theophanes, *Chronographia* 6171, 498 (who clearly states that the Onglos was on the north side of the river); Nicephorus 35, ed. and trans. Mango, 88. Beševliev, *Die protobulgarische Periode*, 174–75; Moravcsik, *Byzantinoturcica*, 2:213; Petre Diaconu, "Le problème de la localisation de l'Onglos," *Dacia*, n.s., 14 (1970): 325–34; Gjuzelev, "Chan Asparuch," 15–17. Rasho Rashev, "L'Onglos—témoignages écrites et faits archéologiques," *Bulgarian Historical Review* 10, no. 1 (1982): 68–79, opts for the Dobrudja and explains the dykes found there as Asparukh's defenses against Byzantine attacks; see also Fiedler, "Bulgars in the Lower Danube Region," 152–53. A good overview of the debate in Ziemann, *Vom Wandervolk zur Großmacht*, 163–67; Altheim, *Geschichte der Hunnen*, 1:86–88.

285. Anania Širkac'i, *Geography*, trans. Robert H. Hewsen (Wiesbaden, 1992), 6–15; see also Pseudo-Movses Chorenac'i, *Géographie*, ed. and trans. Arsene Soukry (Venice, 1881), 25; translation by Andre Maricq, "Notes sur les Slaves dans le Peloponnèse," *Byzantion* 22 (1952): 345; see also Beševliev, *Die protobulgarische Periode*, 173; Ziemann, *Vom Wandervolk zur Großmacht*, 150–51.

286. According to Michael the Syrian 10.21, 363, the Bulgars took possession of the land that the Avars had ravaged since the days of Emperor Anastasius (491–518). Marquart, *Osteuropäische und ostasiatische Streifzüge*, 479–82; Ziemann, *Vom Wandervolk zur Großmacht*, 148–50.

287. Ziemann, *Vom Wandervolk zur Großmacht*, 158–60, underlines the legendary character of the reports on Asparukh's migration, and the relative continuity of Bulgar settlement on the lower Danube before and after 680.

288. Nicephorus 36, ed. and trans. Mango 90; Theophanes, *Chronographia* 6171, 498; Haldon, *Byzantium in the Seventh Century*, 67; Jonathan Shepard, "Slavs and Bulgars," in *The New Cambridge Medieval History*, vol. 2, *c.700–c.900*, ed. Rosamond McKitterick (Cambridge, 1995), 228–48; Ziemann, *Vom Wandervolk zur Großmacht*, 161–62.

289. Fiedler, "Bulgars in the Lower Danube Region," 154–62; see also Fiedler, *Studien zu Gräberfeldern des 6.–9. Jahrhunderts.*

290. Theophanes, *Chronographia* 6171, 359; trans. Mango 499. Beševliev, *Die protobulgarische Periode*, 180. Anastasios Katsanakis, "Abaria," in *Glossar Osteuropa: Bericht einer Arbeitstagung*, Glossar zur frühmittelalterlichen Geschichte im östlichen Europa (Münster, 1982), 56, remarks that Byzantine information on the land of the Avars is "purely situational and generally names only the regions that had relevance in the framework of the Avar-Byzantine conflict," and he also stresses that the term *Abaria* is otherwise not employed in Byzantine literature. About the relationship between Bulgars and Slavs, see Ziemann, *Vom Wandervolk zur Großmacht*, 167–79.

291. Bálint, "Zur Frage der byzantinischen Beziehungen im Fundmaterial Ungarns," 210–12; Morrisson, "Byzance au VIIe siècle," 156–58; Kiss, "Die Goldfunde des Karpatenbeckens vom 5.–10. Jahrhundert"; Somogyi, "New Remarks on the Flow of Byzantine Coins"; Péter Somogyi, "Neue Überlegungen über den Zustrom byzantinischer Münzen ins Awarenland (Numismatischer Kommentar zu Csanád Bálints Betrachtungen zum Beginn der Mittelawarenzeit)," *Antaeus* 29–30 (2008): 356–57, with the caveat that solidi are also very rare in the areas now controlled by Bulgars, although Constantine IV's treaty provided for regular payments.

292. *Miraculi Demetrii* 2.5, 233–30.

293. On the events in Pannonia, see section 6.10. On the dating, see Lemerle, *Les Plus Anciens Recueils*, 2:161–62 (678–84, at the earliest 682–84); Fraňo Barišić, *Čuda Dimitrija Solunskog kao Istoriski Izvori (Les miracles de S. Démétrius de Thessalonique comme source historique)*, Akademija Nauka 219 (Belgrade, 1953), 151–52 (680–85); Avenarius, "Die Awaren und die Slawen," 26 (680s); Szádeczky-Kardoss, *Ein Versuch*, 98 (around 680); Beševliev, *Die protobulgarische Periode*, 168 (674–78); Lauterbach, "Untersuchungen zur Vorgeschichte der Protobulgaren," 598, with the now superseded assumption of 628; Ziemann, *Vom Wandervolk zur Großmacht*, 135–41 (670s or 680s). The Perbund episode can relatively surely be dated to July 677; the Kuver story in all likelihood comes afterward yet still during the rule of "our emperor" Constantine IV (†685), and certainly before Justinian II's campaign in Thessalonica (688). A date around 680 also matches with the information that more than sixty years had passed since the forced displacement of the Romans, most likely at the time of the Chatzon episode (about 616).

294. *Miracula Demetrii* 2.5.287–88, 228–29. On the localization, see Lemerle, *Les Plus Anciens Recueils*, 2:147.

295. *Miracula Demetrii* 2.5.289–91, 223–24. On Mavros's knowledge of languages, see Grigoriou-Ioannidou, "Une remarque," and section 6.10.

296. *Miracula Demetrii* 2.5.304, 233, calls the followers simply *anthropoi*, and the property, *pragmata*.

297. *Miracula Demetrii* 2.5.292, 230.

298. Theophanes, *Chronographia* 6203, 527–30. It may also have been Mavros's son. On the seal, see Georges Zacos and Alexander Veglery, *Byzantine Lead Seals* (Basel, 1972), 1.1, no. 934; Lemerle, *Les Plus Anciens Recueils*, 2:152–53; Peter Charanis, "Kouver, the Chronology of His Activities and Their Ethnic Effects on the Regions around Thessalonica," *Balkan Studies* 11 (1970): 243–44; Ziemann, *Vom Wandervolk zur Großmacht*, 140–41.

299. Theophanes, *Chronographia* 6171, 498.

300. Petkov, *Voices of Medieval Bulgaria, Seventh–Fifteenth Century*, 4; Veselin Beševliev, "Zur Deutung und Datierung der protobulgarischen Inschrift auf dem Reiterrelief von Madara, Bulgarien," *Byzantinische Zeitschrift* 47 (1954): 117–22; Beševliev, *Die protobulgarische Periode*, 170. In agreement: Lemerle, *Les Plus Anciens Recueils*, 2:145; Werner, *Der Schatzfund von Vrap in Albanien*, 19. However, Beševliev's reading of the barely decipherable fragments has not gone uncontested. A fundamentally different interpretation has been offered by Geza Féher, *Die Inschrift des Reiterreliefs von Madara* (Sofia, 1928), in which he dated this fragment, like all the other inscriptions of the relief, to the early ninth century. For a detailed overview of the debate, see Ziemann, *Vom Wandervolk zur Großmacht*, 189–98. His conclusion is that Beševliev's reading cannot bear the weight of the far-reaching interpretations attached to it.

301. Charanis, "Kouver," 242.

302. Grigoriou-Ioannidou, "Une remarque," 4, n.5; cf. Lemerle, *Les Plus Anciens Recueils*, 1:15–17.

303. The hypothesis goes back to the Byzantinist Samuel Szádeczky-Kardoss, "Kuvrat fiának, Kubernek a története és az Avar-kori régészeti leletanyag," *Antik Tanulmányok* 15 (1968): 84–87; for a recent version, see Csanád Bálint, "Der Beginn der Mittelawarenzeit und die Einwanderung Kubers," *Antaeus* 29–30 (2008): 29–62; cf. section 7.8.

304. Werner, *Der Schatzfund von Vrap in Albanien*, 19–21 and 66–67. See Garam, review of *Der Schatzfund von Vrap in Albanien*; Bálint, *Die Archäologie der Steppe*, 190; Stanislav Stanilov, *Die Metallkunst des Bulgarenkhanats an der Donau: Versuch einer empirischen Untersuchung* (Sofia, 2006).

305. *DAI* 42.77, 186.

306. Theophanes, *Chronographia* 6171, 498, with n. 13.

307. See, for instance, Grégoire, "L'origine et le nom des Croates et des Serbes."

308. In Walter Pohl, "Das Awarenreich und die 'kroatischen' Ethnogenesen," in Wolfram and Schwarcz, *Die Bayern und ihre Nachbarn*, 295–96, I have attempted an, if speculative, analysis of the mythological motifs.

309. Herwig Wolfram, "Einleitung oder Überlegungen zur *Origo gentis*," in Wolfram and Pohl, *Typen der Ethnogenese*, 19–33.

310. This was the idea behind the etymology for the name of the Croats proposed by Kronsteiner, "Gab es unter der Alpenslawen," 155. Kronsteiner's etymology does not seem to be tenable, but the idea was explored in Pohl, "Das Awarenreich," and Walter Pohl, "Die Beziehungen der Awaren zu den Slawen," in *Slowenien und die Nachbarländer zwischen Antike und karolingischer Epoche*, ed. Rajko Bratož (Ljubljana, 2000), 341–54. Margetić, *Dolezak hrvata*, 281–93, has amalgamated this approach with the theory of a Bulgar elite immigration into the Avar khaganate at the time of Kuvrat, so that the new elite troops were named after the Bulgar khan; marginalized by further political upheavals in the 680s, these "Kuvratians" remained influential in peripheral areas. However, there is no easy solution for the puzzle constituted by the three parallel narratives, and no convincing link can be established between the name Kuvrat in the seventh century and that of the Croats in the late ninth. On the other hand, it is hard to believe that the parallels come from pure coincidence. It is, of course, also possible that due to the similarity of names the Croat origin story in Constantine Porphyrogenitus was fashioned after the Kuvrat story.

311. *Annales regni Francorum* a. 818, ed. Kurze, 149; a. 821, 155.

312. For similar processes among the steppe peoples, see Haussig, "Theophylakts Exkurs," 346.

313. *DAI* 30, 143: "There are still in Croatia some who are of Avar descent, and who are recognized as Avars."

314. Somogyi, "New Remarks on the Flow of Byzantine Coins," 94. This cannot be due to a decline in minting in Byzantium—in some north Caucasian hoards, coins of Constans II issued between 642 and 652 are the most frequent (ibid., 117). See also the tables and maps in Somogyi, *Byzantinische Fundmünzen in ihrem europäischen Umfeld*, 237–61, with three known solidi from 715–75 in peripheral regions of the khaganate (241).

315. Somogyi, "New Remarks on the Flow of Byzantine Coins," 104–45, also discussing whether the solidi minted after 651 found in the Carpathian Basin could have been brought by immigrating Bulgars (possibly, but not necessarily). Solidi could also come from Italy; King Perctarit told Bishop Wilfrid that when he was in exile at the Avar court in the early 660s, Lombard envoys had arrived offering a bushel full of golden solidi for his extradition: Stephanus, *Vita S. Wilfridi* 28, ed. Levison, 222 (see section 7.7).

316. Jozef Zábojník, "Die Rolle der Münzdatierung in der Mittelawarenzeit," *Antaeus* 29–30 (2008): 301–6. See also the debate between Bálint, "Der Beginn der Mittelawarenzeit," 46–53, and Somogyi, "Neue Überlegungen"; Csanád Bálint, "Antwortschreiben an Péter Somogyi," *Antaeus* 29–30 (2008): 395–401.

317. Bóna, "Abriss der Siedlungsgeschichte Ungarns," 612–14; Bóna, "Ein Vierteljahrhundert," 292. Bóna, "Die Geschichte der Awaren," introduces a tripartite division of the early Avar period: 1.1 to 600, 1.2 from 600 to 630, and 1.3 from 630 to 670. Two phases of the early Avar period: Garam, "Der awarische Fundstoff im Karpatenbecken," 191–93; Bálint, *Die Archäologie der Steppe*, 152–59; Daim, "Avars and Avar Archaeology," 481–87. For an overview of the history of research, see Bálint, "Der Beginn der Mittelawarenzeit," 29–32.

318. Csanád Bálint, "Some Archaeological Addenda to P. Golden's *Khazar Studies*," review of *Khazar Studies: An Historic-Philological Inquiry into the Origins of the Khazars*, by Peter B. Golden, *Acta Orient. Hung.* 35 (1981): 400–401; Gavrituchin, "The Archaeological Heritage of the Avar Khaganate and the Southern Part of Eastern Europe," 76.

319. Bálint, "Der Beginn der Mittelawarenzeit," 57.

320. Daim, "Avars and Avar Archaeology," 487 (650/70); Zábojník, "Die Rolle der Münz-datierung," 306.

321. Stadler, *Quantitative Studien*, 81–84 and 128–29 (630 to 680); Gavrituchin, "The Archaeological Heritage of the Avar Khaganate and the Southern Part of Eastern Europe," 75–76 (620/40 to ca. 700); his chronology is based on a synchronization with the cultures of the Pontic steppes. Martin, "Die absolute Datierung," 167 (beginning 620/30, based on comparison with Merovingian belt-sets).

322. Bálint, "Der Beginn der Mittelawarenzeit," 29–31 and 56–59. But even he speaks of the "fact of Kuver's immigration" ("Faktum der Kuberschen Einwanderung"; ibid., 30), where we should rather be speaking of a hypothesis.

323. Kiss, "Der Wandel," 268, argues for a caesura in the Keszthely region around 630 by the destruction of the late Roman fortress. In any case, if this dating based on written evidence is correct, the conflict appears not to have damaged the region's prosperity and the dense settlement in the region, as several new cemeteries were set up around that time (see section 3.9).

324. Bóna, "Abriss der Siedlungsgeschichte Ungarns," 618.

325. Daim, "Die Materialität der Macht," 628.

326. Schmauder, "Huns, Avars, Hungarians," 678.

327. Tóth, "Das Grab eines Awarenkhagans," 20–22; Tóth and Horváth, *Kunbábony*; Falko Daim, "Kunbábony," in *RGA*, 17:490–95; Daim, "Die Materialität der Macht," 625–28. On the "drinking horn horizon" of the seventh century, see also Éva Garam, "Der Fund von Vörösmart im archäologischen Nachlass der Awarenzeit," *Folia Archaeologica* 33 (1982): 208–10.

328. Sören Stark, "Central and Inner Asian Parallels to a Find from Kunszentmiklós-Bábony (Kunbábony): Some Toughts on the Early Avar Headdress," *Ancient Civilizations from Scythia to Siberia* 15 (2009): 287–305. Since this publication, it has emerged that it was used not as a headdress but as a pectoral; I owe this information to Sören Stark.

329. An early study of the Bócsa grave and other rich finds of the seventh century (Kecel, Tépe, Kunágota, etc.) in László, *Études archéologiques*, especially 219–38; see also Garam, "L'oro degli Avari"; Daim, "Avars and Avar Archaeology," 481–83; Garam, "The Connection of the Avar Period Princely and Common Gravegoods with the Nagyszent-miklós Treasure." In Kovács, *The Gold of the Avars*, 81–112.

330. Gavrituchin, "The Archaeological Heritage of the Avar Khaganate and the Southern Part of Eastern Europe," 83.

331. Werner, *Der Grabfund von Malaja Pereščepina*; Bálint, *Die Archäologie der Steppe*, 96–100; Natalja A. Fonjakova et al., "Der Schatz von Mala Pereščepina (Malaja Pereščepina)," in Daim et al., *Hunnen + Awaren*, 209–23. Alexandru Magdearu, "The Plate of Paternus from the Malaja Pereščepina Treasure: Booty or Gift?," *Études Byzantines et Post-Byzantines* 6 (2011): 65–71. On the question of Byzantine production of golden objects in the Carpathian Basin, see Heinrich-Tamáska, "Byzantine Goldsmithing in Avaria?"

332. Daim, "Die Materialität der Macht."

333. Kovrig, *Das awarenzeitliche Gräberfeld von Alattyán*; Garam, "Der awarische Fund-stoff im Karpatenbecken," 195–97; Bálint, *Die Archäologie der Steppe*, 150 and 159–61; Daim, "Avars and Avar Archaeology," 487–97; Stadler, *Quantitative Studien*, 128–29; see also László Madaras, *Das awarenzeitliche Gräberfeld von Jászapáti*, Das awarische Corpus, Beihefte 2 (Debrecen-Budapest, 1994). A good overview of the problems connected with the definition and interpretation of the middle Avar period is found in the proceedings of a conference on its chronology, held in Budapest in 2004: "Betrachtungen zur Chronolo-gie der Awarenzeit," in *Antaeus* 29–30 (2008), 29–576.

334. Bóna, "Ein Vierteljahrhundert," 287. A coin by Constans II was found in the mouth of the deceased in a grave at Gyenesdiás: Róbert Müller, "Das Gräberfeld von Gyenesdiás,"

in Daim et al., *Hunnen + Awaren*, 411–16. On the *obolus* habit: Somogyi, *Byzantinische Fundmünzen der Awarenzeit in ihrem europäischen Umfeld*, 135–70. See also Tóth and Horváth, *Kunbábony*, 85–87 (small silver discs used in Kunbábony); Garam, "Die münzdatierten Gräber der Awarenzeit"; Winter, "Die byzantinischen Fundmünzen."

335. László, *Études archéologiques*; Gyula Fülöp, "Awarenzeitliche Fürstenfunde von Igar," *Acta Arch. Hung.* 40 (1988): 151–90; Fülöp, "New Research on Finds of Avar Chieftain-Burials at Igar, Hungary," in *From the Baltic to the Black Sea: Studies in Medieval Archaeology*, ed. David Austian and Leslie Alcock (London, 1990), 138–46; Péter Prohászka, *Az ozora-tótipusztai avar fejedelmi sírok (Die awarischen Oberschichtsgräber von Ozora-Tótipuszta)* (Budapest, 2012), German synthesis: 97–102; Madaras, *Das awarenzeitliche Gräberfeld von Jászapáti*; Bálint, "Zur Frage der byzantinischen Beziehungen im Fundmaterial Ungarns," 211; Garam, *Funde byzantinischer Herkunft*. For some stylistic parallels (for instance pseudo-buckles) in Bulgaria, see Stanilov, *Die Metallkunst des Bulgarenkhanats an der Donau*, esp. 77–81 (find of Vetren).

336. Falko Daim, Ursula Koch, and Levente Sámu, "Mit dem Bauchladen in das Awarenland," in *Festschrift für Egon Wamers* (Frankfurt, forthcoming).

337. Kovrig, *Das awarenzeitliche Gräberfeld von Alattyán*, 279; Garam, "Der awarische Fundstoff im Karpatenbecken," 197; the gradual nature of this change is emphasized in Daim, *Das awarische Gräberfeld von Leobersdorf*, 155–56. A valuable recent synthesis: Tomka, "Die Lehre der Bestattungsbräuche" (orientation: 241–45).

338. The extension of the settlement area is underlined in, for example, Bóna, "Abriss der Siedlungsgeschichte Ungarns," 613; Bálint, *Die Archäologie der Steppe*, 161; Daim, *Das awarische Gräberfeld von Leobersdorf*, 176; Michael Parczewski, "Besiedlungsgeschichte der frühmittelalterlichen Slowakei," *Acta Archaeologica Carpathica* 15 (1974): 37–40. On the Avar settlement of Transylvania, see Horedt, "Das Awarenproblem in Rumänien"; Erwin Gáll, "The Avar Conquest and What Followed: Some Ideas on the Process of 'Avarisation' of the Transylvanian Basin (6th–7th Centuries)," in *Archäologische Beiträge: Gedenkschrift zum hundertsten Geburtstag von Kurt Horedt* (Cluj-Napoca, 2014), 295–324, rather sees the change as a process of "asymmetrical" Avarization of the native population, which had been controlled by small groups of Avar warriors since the sixth century. See also Daniel-Călin Anton, "Ethnische und chronologische Verhältnisse im Gräberfeld Nr. 3 von Brateiu, Siebenbürgen," *Dacia* 59 (2015): 153–76.

339. Kovrig, *Das awarenzeitliche Gräberfeld von Alattyán*, 182; cf. Daim, *Das awarische Gräberfeld von Leobersdorf*, 157–58.

340. Theophanes, *Chronographia* 6171, 498; *Miracula Demetrii* 2.5; see sections 6.10 and 7.7.

341. Garam, "Der awarische Fundstoff im Karpatenbecken"; similar views already in Kovrig, *Das awarenzeitliche Gräberfeld von Alattyán*, 229. The chronology is often established on the basis of occupancy statistics; after 680, coin finds in graves are rare, the Byzantine material can hardly be dated precisely, and the relatively slight connections with the better datable material from the Merovingian period offers only a slim basis for drawing conclusions, despite the efforts of Frauke Stein, "Awarisch-merowingische Beziehungen, ein Beitrag zur absoluten Chronologie der awarenzeitlichen Funde," *Študijné zvesti* 16 (1968): 233–44; Martin, "Die absolute Datierung."

342. A fundamental work was István Bóna, "Avar lovassír Iváncsáról" [Grave of an Avar horseman at Iváncsa], *Archaeologiai Értesítő* 97 (1970): 243–61. Kovrig, *Das awarenzeitliche Gräberfeld von Alattyán*, 231: The differences "can be explained neither by a course of internal evolution nor by a sudden shift in styles." Research history: Bálint, "Der Beginn der Mittelawarenzeit," 29–32.

343. Gyula László, "Les problèmes soulévés par le groupe à la ceinture ornée de griffon et de rinceaux de l'époque avare finissante," *Acta Arch. Hung.* 17 (1965): 73–75;

cf. Kovrig, *Das awarenzeitliche Gräberfeld von Alattyán*, 229; Sós, "Zur Problematik der Awarenzeit," 94.

344. See section 7.7. Bóna, "Das erste Auftreten der Bulgaren im Karpatenbecken," 109–11; Szádeczky-Kardoss, "Onoguroi"; Thérèse Olajos, "Contributions à l'histoire des Onogours (installés dans le bassin des Carpathes)," *Chronica: Annual of the Institute of History, University of Szeged, Hungary* 1 (2001): 4–18. This outdated hypothesis, mainly bolstered by the fourteenth-century *Chronicum pictum* ("Viennese Chronicle"), could still be found in the "Avar Khaganate" entry at *Wikipedia* (https://en.wikipedia.org/wiki/Avar_Khaganate) on December 29, 2016.

345. Daim, *Das awarische Gräberfeld von Leobersdorf*, 158–59; Daim and Lippert, *Das awarische Gräberfeld*, 83–85; Werner, *Der Schatzfund von Vrap in Albanien*, 67; Čilinská, "The Development of the Slavs North of the Danube," 237–40. Dating the middle Avar period from 630 to 680: Stadler, "Avar Chronology Revisited"; Stadler, *Quantitative Studien*, 128–29.

346. Zlata Čilinská, "Zur Frage des 2. awarischen Khaganats," *Slov. Arch.* 15 (1967): 447–54; Ján Dekan, "Les motifs figuraux humains sur les bronzes moulés de la zone danubienne centrale à l'époque précédente l'empire de la Grande Moravie," *Studia Historica* 2 (1964): 52–102; Klanica, "Vorgroßmährische Siedlung," 132.

347. Pohl, *Die Awaren*, 280–87; see also Walter Pohl, "Das awarische Khaganat und die anderen Gentes im Karpatenbecken (6.–8. Jh.)," in Hänsel, *Die Völker Südosteuropas vom 6.–8. Jahrhundert*, 46–48. A positive echo in Attila Kiss, "Zur Frage der Kontinuität bzw. Diskontinuität des awarischen Khaganats (567–795): Wieviele Khaganate der Awaren hat es gegeben?," in Bialeková and Zábojník, *Ethnische und kulturelle Verhältnisse an der mittleren Donau*, 83–98; Somogyi, "Neue Überlegungen," 358.

348. Theophanes, *Chronographia* 6171, 498. See section 7.7.

349. Bálint, "Der Beginn der Mittelawarenzeit," 33–59.

350. Bálint, "Der Beginn der Mittelawarenzeit," 52, 55–56. For possible parallels with Kudyrge, a significant necropolis from the sphere of the Turkish khaganate, see Roman Kenk, *Früh- und hochmittelalterliche Gräber von Kudyrge am Altai* (Munich, 1982); Bálint, *Die Archäologie der Steppe*, 243–58.

351. Fiedler, "Die Donaubulgaren und die Mittelawarenzeit," 136.

352. Kovrig, *Das awarenzeitliche Gräberfeld von Alattyán*, 208 and 231; Daim and Lippert, *Das awarische Gräberfeld*, 64 and 81–83; Gavrituchin, "The Archaeological Heritage of the Avar Khaganate and the Southern Part of Eastern Europe," 63–71 (a chapter entitled "Continuity between the Early and Middle Avar Period"). Taking as an example the cemetery of Kölked-Feketekapu A: see Kiss, *Das awarenzeitlich-gepidische Gräberfeld*; Bálint, "Der Beginn der Mittelawarenzeit," 54. The cemetery at Szarvas was also in continuous use from the early to the late Avar period: Juhász, *Das awarenzeitliche Gräberfeld*. Only some cemeteries begin with the middle Avar period, for instance Jászapáti (Madaras, *Das awarenzeitliche Gräberfeld von Jászapáti*).

353. Tomka, "Die Lehre der Bestattungsbräuche," 235.

354. Bálint, *Die Archäologie der Steppe*, 159–61. See also Heinrich-Tamáska, *Die Stein- und Glasinkrustationskunst*.

355. Bóna, "Abriss der Siedlungsgeschichte Ungarns," 618; Avenarius, "Struktur und Organisation der Steppenvölker"; Hesse, "Der Austausch als stabilisierender Faktor der politischen Herrschaft in der Geschichte der Mongolei," 151, points to similar processes in Mongolia.

356. Johannes Preiser-Kapeller, "The Climate of the Khagan: Observations on Paleo-Environmental Factors in the History of the Avars (6th–9th Century AD)," in *Lebenswelten zwischen Archäologie und Geschichte: Festschrift für Falko Daim zu seinem 65. Geburtstag*, ed. Jörg Drauschke et al. (Mainz, 2018), 311–24.

357. Gavrituchin, "The Archaeological Heritage of the Avar Khaganate and the Southern Part of Eastern Europe," 87–88.

358. Kovrig, *Das awarenzeitliche Gräberfeld von Alattyán*, 203–4, calls attention to the increasing number of poor graves in the later periods of the cemetery.

359. The "gradual transformation of Avar society in the seventh century": Avenarius, "Die Konsolidierung des Awarenkhaganats," 1029.

8. THE CENTURY OF THE GRIFFIN

1. Somogyi, *Byzantinische Fundmünzen der Awarenzeit in ihrem europäischen Umfeld*, 256–57, for a map of eighth-century coin finds: only one of them was discovered in Hungary, the rest in its neighboring countries; three of them are solidi issued between 715 and 775 (241).

2. For Nagyszentmiklós, see section 6.5.

3. Gavrituchin, "The Archaeological Heritage of the Avar Khaganate and the Southern Part of Eastern Europe," 88.

4. Veselina Vachkova, "Danube Bulgaria and Khazaria as Part of the Byzantine Oikoumene," in Curta, *The Other Europe in the Middle Ages*, 351–52.

5. Fiedler, "Die Donaubulgaren und die Mittelawarenzeit," 130. See also Fiedler, "Bulgars in the Lower Danube Region."

6. Daim, "Avars and Avar Archaeology," 504: "If—as in Leobersdorf—at the end of Late Avar Period III, the 'classical' custom of grave accompaniments was given up step by step, this development may in fact have been initiated by the Avar elite two or three generations earlier."

7. For the interpretation of cemeteries as scenarios of social competition in early medieval archaeology, see Guy Halsall, *Cemeteries and Society in Merovingian Gaul: Selected Studies in History and Archaeology, 1992–2009* (Leiden, 2009); Frans C. W. J. Theuws, "Grave Goods, Ethnicity, and the Rhetoric of Burial Rites in Late Antique Northern Gaul," in *Ethnic Constructs in Antiquity: The Role of Power and Tradition*, ed. Tom Derks and Nico Roymans (Amsterdam, 2009), 283–317.

8. Daim, *Das awarische Gräberfeld von Leobersdorf*, 155–59. For some further observations on late Avar chronology, see Magdalena Maria Elisabeth Schmid, *Das Gräberfeld von Rákóczifalva in Zentralungarn und die Chronologie des spätawarenzeitlichen Fundmaterials*, Universitätsforschungen zur prähistorischen Archäologie 272 (Bonn, 2015).

9. See section 6.5. Daim, "'Byzantinische' Gürtelgarnituren des 8. Jahrhunderts"; Daim, "Byzantine Belts and Avar Birds"; see also Joszef Szentpéteri, "Gesellschaftliche Gliederung des awarenzeitlichen gemeinen Volkes von Želovce 2: Innere Gruppen der Bevölkerung (Schmuck und sonstige rangbezeichnende Beigaben)," *Acta Arch. Hung.* 38 (1986): 183.

10. Stadler, *Quantitative Studien*, 140–41.

11. Gergely Szenthe, "Crisis or Innovation? A Technology-Inspired Narrative of Social Dynamics in the Carpathian Basin during the Eighth Century," in Bollók, Csiky, and Vida, *Zwischen Byzanz und der Steppe/Between Byzantium and the Steppe*, at 351 and 354–55.

12. Bálint, *Die Archäologie der Steppe*, 53–61; Szenthe, "Crisis or Innovation?," 359; Gavrituchin, "The Archaeological Heritage of the Avar Khaganate and the Southern Part of Eastern Europe," 88.

13. Werner, *Der Schatzfund von Vrap in Albanien*; Daim, "'Byzantinische' Gürtelgarnituren des 8. Jahrhunderts," 183–84; Fiedler, "Die Donaubulgaren und die Mittelawarenzeit," 138; Szenthe, "Crisis or Innovation?," 359. See also the extensive debate about Vrap and Velino in Stanilov, *Die Metallkunst des Bulgarenkhanats an der Donau*.

14. Stanilov, *Die Metallkunst des Bulgarenkhanats an der Donau*, 91–95. However, as Fiedler, "Die Donaubulgaren und die Mittelawarenzeit," has argued, the other belt-plaques

with griffin or lattice décor found in Bulgaria are rather worn and may also have arrived there as booty or with fugitives from the Avars.

15. Heinrich-Tamáska, "Avar-Age Metalworking Technologies"; Szenthe, "Meister und ihre Kunden"; experimental archaeology casting of a bronze belt plaque: Gergely Szenthe, "Technological History, Experimental Archaeology and Bronze Casting: Research Findings and Research Perspectives in Early Medieval Studies," *Hungarian Archaeology e-Journal*, Summer 2013, http://www.hungarianarchaeology.hu/?page_id=279#post-3843.

16. For an overview of motifs, see Dekan, "Herkunft und Ethnizität." See also Garam, "Der awarische Fundstoff im Karpatenbecken," 197–99, Bálint, *Die Archäologie der Steppe*, 161–67; Daim, "Avars and Avar Archaeology," 497–516.

17. Even the Scythian zoomorphic style developed from a synthesis of barbarian, Greek, and Persian elements: see *Gold der Skythen aus der Leningrader Eremitage*, exhibition catalog (Munich, 1984), especially 144–45, 159, 162 (illustrations). Fundamental for their treatment of the Scythian zoomorphic style, even if partially superseded, are the studies of Michael Rostovzeff, e.g., *The Animal Style in South Russia and China* (Princeton, NJ, 1929). The griffin was early used in the decoration of textiles in central Asia, as shown by the finds at Noin-Ula, where a fragment of cloth with a griffin motif was discovered in kurgan 25; Kádár, "Gli animali negli oggetti ornamentali dei popoli della steppa," 1380. On the Avar griffin motif, see Falko Daim, "Der awarische Greif und die byzantinische Antike," in Friesinger and Daim, *Typen der Ethnogenese*, 273–303; he derives it mainly from Byzantine models, against the assumption of a Sassanid origin as proposed in Werner, *Der Schatzfund von Vrap in Albanien*, 58–60, and Bálint, *Die Archäologie der Steppe*, 172–74 (Iranian and central Asian origins).

18. Peter Stadler, "Die Werkstätten awarischer Riemenbeschläge mit Greifendarstellung," in Friesinger and Daim, *Typen der Ethnogenese*, 305–50; Stadler, *Quantitative Studien*, table 208.

19. Daim, *Das awarische Gräberfeld von Leobersdorf*, 167.

20. Bulgaria: Fiedler, "Bulgars in the Lower Danube Region," 218–21. East of the Carpathians: István Erdélyi, "Über die gegossenen Gürtelgarnituren der Spätawarenzeit östlich von Karpaten," in *Popoli delle steppe*, 1:351–72. Bohemia and Moravia, mainly on early Slavic hillforts (*Burgwälle*): Profantová, "The Middle Avar Period"; Jozef Zábojník, "Zum Vorkommen von Gegenständen 'awarischer' Provenienz auf den slawischen Burgwällen nördlich der Donau," in Macháček and Ungerman, *Frühgeschichtliche Zentralorte in Mitteleuropa*, 203–14.

21. Togan, *Ibn Fadlans Reisebericht*, 231; Kollautz and Miyakawa, 1:58. On the braid clasps of the late Avar period, see Szentpéteri, "Gesellschaftliche Gliederung des awarenzeitlichen gemeinen Volkes von Želovce 2," 147–49.

22. Kovrig, *Das awarenzeitliche Gräberfeld von Alattyán*, 227; Garam, "Der awarische Fundstoff im Karpatenbecken," 197–200; Zlata Čilinská, "Frauenschmuck im 7.–8. Jahrhundert im Karpatenbecken," *Slov. Arch.* 23 (1975): 63–65; Bálint, *Die Archäologie der Steppe*, 161–62; Daim, "Avars and Avar Archaeology," 497–516.

23. Ágnes Sós, "Le deuxième cimitière Avare d'Üllő," *Acta Arch. Hung.* 6 (1955): 227.

24. Eisner, *Devínska Nová Vés*; Bohuslav Chropovský, ed., *Importants sites slaves en Slovaquie* (Bratislava, 1978); Alexander Trugly, "Gräberfeld aus der Zeit des awarischen Reiches bei der Schiffswerft in Komárno I," *Slov. Arch.* 35 (1987): 251–344; Trugly, "Gräberfeld aus der Zeit des awarischen Reiches bei der Schiffswerft in Komárno II," *Slov. Arch.* 41 (1993): 191–307; Parczewski, "Besiedlungsgeschichte," 39–41; Jozef Zábojník, "Zur Problematik der Waffenvorkommen auf Gräberfeldern aus der Zeit des Awarenreiches in den nordwestlichen Teilen des Karpatenbeckens," in Archäologisches Institut der Slowakischen Akademie der Wissenschaften, *Interaktionen der mitteleuropäischen Slawen und anderen Ethnika im 6.–10. Jahrhundert*, 297–302; Zábojník, "On the Problems of Settlements of the

Avar Khaganate period in Slovakia," *Archeologické rozhledy* 40 (1988): 401–37; Zábojník, "Soziale Problematik der Gräberfelder des nördlichen und nordwestlichen Randgebietes des Awarischen Kaganats," *Slov. Arch.* 43 (1995): 205–344.

25. Christoph Lobinger, *Das awarenzeitliche Gräberfeld von Edelstal (Nemesvölgy) im Burgenland*, Universitätsforschungen zur prähistorischen Archäologie 288 (Bonn, 2016), esp. 140; the cemetery was already excavated in the 1880s, and has 256 mostly late Avar burials. Daim, *Das awarische Gräberfeld von Leobersdorf*, 99: mainly arrowheads and long knives, plus the remains of one bow and two sabers.

26. Jovan Kovačević, "Die awarische Militärgrenze in der Umgebung von Beograd im 8. Jahrhundert," *Archaeologia Iugoslavica* 14 (1973): 49–55.

27. Bálint, *Die Archäologie der Steppe*, 167; Éva Garam, *Das awarenzeitliche Gräberfeld von Tiszafüred*, Cemeteries of the Avar Period (567–829) in Hungary 3 (Budapest, 1995).

28. Eisner, *Devínska Nová Ves*, 410. In Želovce about thirty men were buried in each of three categories: with belt and weapon(s), or with only a belt *or* weapon(s). These ninety-three graves in total comprise about one tenth of the cemetery and must then represent the local elite; Joszef Szentpéteri, "Gesellschaftliche Gliederung des awarenzeitlichen gemeinen Volkes von Želovce 1: Die führende Schicht der Bevölkerung (Bewaffnete und umgegürtete Personen)." *Acta Arch. Hung.* 37 (1985): 84–85; Zlata Čilinská, *Frühmittelalterliches Gräberfeld in Želovce* (Bratislava, 1973); Zábojník, "Soziale Problematik der Gräberfelder."

29. Bóna, "Die Awaren," 16. Summarizing information on the late Avar graves of horsemen, Éva Garam, "Pferde- und Reiterbestattungen in der Spätawarenzeit (8.–9. Jahrhundert)," in *Die Bayern und ihre Nachbarn*, ed. Falko Daim and Herwig Friesinger, vol. 2, DsÖAW 179 (Vienna, 1985), 123–26.

30. Possible, albeit speculative, interpretations, influenced by Georges Dumézil's interpretation of the representational world of war bands, in Roux, "La religion des peuples des steppes."

31. Kovrig, *Das awarenzeitliche Gräberfeld von Alattyán*, 218–19; Daim, *Die Awaren in Niederösterreich*, 24; Szentpéteri, "Gesellschaftliche Gliederung des awarenzeitlichen gemeinen Volkes von Želovce 1."

32. Bálint, *Die Archäologie der Steppe*, 167; Juhász, *Das awarenzeitliche Gräberfeld*, 94.

33. Stadler, *Quantitative Studien*, 130 and 146.

34. Sós, "Le deuxième cimitière Avare d'Üllő," 226; Béla M. Szőke, "Zur awarenzeitlichen Siedlungsgeschichte des Körös-Gebietes in Südost-Ungarn," *Acta Arch. Hung.* 32 (1980): 181–83; Bóna, "Ein Vierteljahrhundert," 321–23; Stadler, *Quantitative Studien*, 158–59.

35. Daim, *Das awarische Gräberfeld von Leobersdorf*, 163–65.

36. Ibn Fadlān 71, ed. and trans. Montgomery, 239.

37. Kovrig, *Das awarenzeitliche Gräberfeld von Alattyán*, 73–75; Daim, *Die Awaren in Niederösterreich*, 24; Daim, *Das awarische Gräberfeld von Leobersdorf*, 165–67.

38. Bálint, *Die Archäologie der Steppe*, 166–67. The utilization of the cemeteries cannot, on its own, justify any compelling conclusion as to the continuous use of the associated settlements. Both transhumance between fixed sites and small-scale relocation of the settlement while retaining the cemetery are compatible with the finds.

39. Kiss, "Das Gräberfeld und die Siedlung," 190–91; Bálint, *Die awarenzeitliche Siedlung von Eperjes*; Hajnalka Herold, *Die frühmittelalterliche Siedlung von Örménykút 54*, Varia Archaeologica Hungarica 14 (Budapest, 2004); Rozália Bajkai, "The Latest Findings of the Research of Avar Age Settlements in the Region of Hajdúság," *Ziridava* 29 (2015): 227–54; Emese Szabó, "Die frühmittelalterliche Siedlung Balatonőszöd-Temetői dűlő und ihr Gräberfeld," *Antaeus* 34 (2016): 173–208. See also the contributions in Tivadar Vida, ed., *Thesaurus Avarorum: Archaeological Studies in Honour of Éva Garam* (Budapest,

2012), at 709–42. For settlements in the Banat (SW Romania): Erwin Gáll and Sándor Romát, "The Current State of Archaeological Research on the Avar Period in the Banat: Observations on the Changes in the Avar Settlement Territory in this Region and on Some Early Medieval Cultural-Sociological Phenomena," in Bollók, Csiky, and Vida, *Zwischen Byzanz und der Steppe/Between Byzantium and the Steppe*, 433–68; Slovakia: Martin Odler and Jozef Zábojník, "Sídliská z 8. storočia na juhozápadnom Slovensku: Šaľa III, Úľany nad Žitavou, Pavlová" [Settlements from the eighth century in southwestern Slovakia: Šaľa II, Úľany nad Žitavou, Pavlová], *Študijné zvesti* 50 (2011): 101–220 (mostly dealing with the pottery finds).

40. Miklós Takács, "Der Hausbau in Ungarn vom 2. bis zum 13. Jahrhundert n. Chr.: ein Zeitalter einheitlicher Grubenhäuser?," in *The Rural House from the Migration Period to the Oldest Still Standing Buildings*, ed. Ján Klápště (Prague, 2002), 272–90; Sebastian Brather, "Grubenhäuser und Haushalte: Zur Sozialstruktur frühmittelalterlicher Siedlungen in Ostmitteleuropa," in Bollók, Csiky, and Vida, *Zwischen Byzanz und der Steppe/Between Byzantium and the Steppe*, 195–208.

41. Radu Harhoiu, "Archäologische Grabungen in Schässburg—Dealul Viilor, Fundstelle 'Gräberfeld': Befund 359—ein Wohngebäude aus der Spätawarenzeit," in Bollók, Csiky, and Vida, *Zwischen Byzanz und der Steppe/Between Byzantium and the Steppe*, 393–432.

42. Daim, *Das awarische Gräberfeld von Leobersdorf*; Szőke, "Zur awarenzeitlichen Siedlungsgeschichte des Körös-Gebietes," 189–90.

43. Garam, *Das awarenzeitliche Gräberfeld von Tiszafüred*.

44. Hajnalka Herold, *Die awarenzeitliche Siedlung und die gefäßkeramischen Funde des awarenzeitlichen Gräberfeldes von Zillingtal, Burgenland*, Monographien des Römisch-Germanischen Zentralmuseums (Mainz, 2010); Herold, "Die Awarenzeit im Burgenland"; for the cemetery: Falko Daim, "Das awarische Gräberfeld von Zillingtal: Sechs Gräber mit 'westlichen' Gegenständen," *Wissenschaftliche Arbeiten aus dem Burgenland* 100 (1998): 97–135.

45. Bálint, *Die Archäologie der Steppe*, 166; Kiss, "Das Gräberfeld und die Siedlung," 189.

46. Kiss, "Das Gräberfeld und die Siedlung," 190–91; Kiss, *Das awarenzeitlich-gepidische Gräberfeld*; Kiss, *Das awarenzeitliche Gräberfeld*.

47. Kiss, "Funde der Awarenzeit aus Ungarn in Wiener Museen," 168–69; Róbert Müller, "Neue archäologische Funde der Keszthely-Kultur," in Daim, *Awarenforschungen*, 251–307; Kiss, "Der Wandel."

48. See section 6.10 and Sós, "Zur Problematik der Awarenzeit," 97; Sós, *Die slawische Bevölkerung Westungarns*; Bóna, "Ein Vierteljahrhundert," 303–5; Čilinská, "The Development of the Slavs North of the Danube," 247; Szőke, "Das archäologische Bild der Slawen in Südwestungarn"; Ágnes Cs. Sós et al., *Cemeteries of the Early Middle Ages (6th–9th Centuries A.D.) at Pókaszepetk* (Budapest, 1995).

49. Stadler, "Avar Chronology Revisited," 73–78, interprets the pottery with "comb strokes (*Kammstrich*)" present in the area from 630 onward as a Slavic feature. See also Stadler, *Quantitative Studien*, 159–60.

50. Eisner, *Devínska Nová Vés*; Čilinská, "The Development of the Slavs North of the Danube," 240–43; Parczewski, "Besiedlungsgeschichte," 39–41; Zábojník, "Das awarische Kaganat."

51. Szameit, "Zum archäologischen Bild der frühen Slawen in Österreich."

52. Daim et al., *Studien zum Burgwall*. See also Zábojník, "The Slavs and the Avar Khaganate."

53. Cf. section 6.10. See also Curta, "The Slavic *Lingua Franca*."

54. It may be methodologically more sound to use a synthetic term, such as "population of the late Avar period," in order to avoid misunderstandings. But in scholarly

discussion it should be possible speak of "Avars" as long as it is agreed that this concept does not designate a uniform *ethnos*, but only a dominant ethnic practice. Cf. section 1.3 and Pohl and Mehofer, *Archaeology of Identity/Archäologie der Identität*.

55. See sections 8.3 and 8.4.

56. Andreas Lippert, "Zur Frage der awarischen Westgrenze," *Mitteilungen der Anthropologischen Gesellschaft in Wien* 100 (1970): 165–67; Falko Daim, "Das 7. und 8. Jahrhundert in Niederösterreich," in *Germanen, Awaren, Slawen in Niederösterreich: Das erste Jahrtausend nach Christus*, Katalog der Ausstellung des Niederösterreichischen Landesmuseums (Vienna, 1977), 93; Szameit, "Zum archäologischen Bild der frühen Slawen in Österreich."

57. Kovačević, *Avarski Kaganat*.

58. Kiss, "Der Wandel," 274.

59. Curta, "The Early Slavs in the Northern and Eastern Adriatic Region."

60. On the "seemingly egalitarian nature of cast articles," see Szenthe, "Crisis or Innovation?," 362.

61. Cf. section 6.3.

62. *Zhou shu*, in Liu Mau-Tsai, *Die chinesischen Nachrichten*, 1:9.

63. Deér, "Karl der Grosse," 759–61; István Bóna, "'Cundpald fecit': Der Kelch von Petőháza und die Anfänge der bairisch-fränkischen Awarenmission in Pannonien," *Acta Arch. Hung.* 18 (1966): 322; Tomaschek, "Avares," 2265.

64. *Annales Laureshamenses*, a. 796, ed. Georg Heinrich Pertz, MGH SS 1 (Hanover, 1826), 37.

65. *Annales qui dictuntur Einhardi*, a. 782, ed. Friedrich Kurze, MGH SS rer. Germ. 6 (Hanover, 1895), 61; *Annales regni Francorum*, a. 782, ed. Kurze, 60; *Annales Fuldenses*, a. 782, ed. Kurze and Haefele, 10.

66. *Annales regni Francorum*, a. 796, ed. Kurze, 98; *Annales Fuldenses*, a. 796, ed. Kurze and Haefele, 13; *Annales Mettenses priores* a. 796, ed. Bernhard Simson, MGH SS rer. Germ. 10 (Hanover, 1905), 81.

67. *Annales regni Francorum*, a. 805, ed. Kurze, 119; *Annales Fuldenses*, a. 805, ed. Kurze and Haefele, 16.

68. *De Pippini regis victoria Avarica* 6–10, ed. Dümmler, 117–18.

69. *Annales regni Francorum*, a. 796, ed. Kurze, 98; *Annales Laureshamenses*, a. 796, ed. Pertz, 37.

70. *Annales qui dicuntur Einhardi*, a. 782, ed. Kurze, 61; *Annales Fuldenses*, a. 796, ed. Kurze and Haefele, 13.

71. Ibn Rusta, *Kitab al-Alaq an-Nafisa*, ed. Michael J. de Goeje (Leiden, 1892), 139–40; "Übersetzung von Gardīzī's Abhandlung über die Türkenstämme," trans. Göckenjan and Zimonyi, 52; Dunlop, *The History of the Jewish Khazars*, 104–5.

72. Gardīzī 11.272, trans. Göckenjan and Zimonyi, 166.

73. Ibn Fadlān 90, ed. and trans. Montgomery, 255; Togan, *Ibn Fadlans Reisebericht*, 98–100; Dunlop, *The History of the Jewish Khazars*, 111; Golden, "Conversion of the Khazars to Judaism," 142–43.

74. *DAI* 42, 182; 39, 174.

75. Al-Masudi 453, trans. Paul Lunde and Caroline Stone, *Ibn Fadlān and the Land of Darkness*, Penguin Classics (London, 2012), 135.

76. Al-Masudi 453, trans. Lunde and Stone, *Ibn Fadlān*, 135; Al-Istachri, *Kitab Masalik al-Mamalik*, ed. Michael J. de Goeje (Leiden, 1870), 222–24; Dunlop, *The History of the Jewish Khazars*, 97–98.

77. András Alföldi, "A kettős királyság a nomádknál," in *Károlyi Árpád-Emlekkönyv születese nyolcvanadik fordulojänak ünnepere* (Budapest, 1933), 28–39.

78. On bipartite forms of organization, widespread among many peoples, see Sergej G. Klyashtornyj, "The Asian Aspect of the Early Khazar History," in Klyashtornyj, *Old*

Turkic Runic Texts and History of the Eurasian Steppe, ed. Victor Spinei and Cristina Spinei (Bucharest, 2008), 330–31.

79. Togan, *Ibn Fadlans Reisebericht*, 271–73; Dunlop, *The History of the Jewish Khazars*, 208 and n. 211; Beševliev, *Die protobulgarische Periode*, 338–39; Altheim, *Geschichte der Hunnen*, 1:120; Deér, "Karl der Grosse," 760; Kollautz, "Die Awaren," 139–40 and 154; Avenarius, *Geschichte der Awaren*, 183; Bóna, "'Cundpald fecit,'" 321.

80. Dunlop, *The History of the Jewish Khazars*, 58–61, with a listing of Arabic and Armenian sources.

81. Theophanes, *Chronographia* 6196, 520–21.

82. *DAI* 42, 182.27; Pletnewa, *Die Chasaren*, especially 155.

83. Norman Golb and Omeljan Pritsak, *Khazarian Hebrew Documents of the Tenth Century* (Ithaca, NY, 1982), 106–14 (text and translation); see also Golden, *Khazar Studies*, 102–4.

84. Dunlop, *The History of the Jewish Khazars*, 159. On the letters and the question of their authenticity, see Constantine Zuckerman, "On the Date of the Khazars' Conversion to Judaism and the Chronology of the Kings of the Rus' Oleg and Igor: A Study of the Anonymous Khazar *Letter* from the Genizah of Cairo," *Revue des Études Byzantines* 53 (1995): 239–42; Golden, "Conversion of the Khazars to Judaism," 145–47.

85. Assumed by Golden, *Khazar Studies*, 1:162.

86. Turxanthos/Türk Shad was the son of Sizabulos/Sir-Yabgu; cf. Menander frag. 19.1, ed. and trans. Blockley, 176. In connection with the siege of Tiflis, Moses Dashuranc'i calls the shad the nephew of Jebu Khan/Ziebil/(Sir)Yabgu; cf. Golden, *Khazar Studies*, 1:206; Volker Rybatzki, "The Titles of Türk and Uigur Rulers in the Old Turkic Inscriptions," *Central Asiatic Journal* 44 (2000): 205–92; and section 7.4.

87. Thomsen, "Alttürkische Inschriften in der Mongolei," 145; Golden, *Khazar Studies*, 1:163. For the different meanings of *beg* in Turkish steppe empires, see Ayşe Melek Özyetgin, "The Use of the Title Beg among the Turks," *Central Asian Journal* 11 (2006): 156–70.

88. Ibn Fadlān 90A, ed. and trans. Montgomery, 255; Togan, *Ibn Fadlans Reisebericht*, 98–100; Golden, *Khazar Studies*, 1:200–201 and 191; Sergej G. Klyashtornyj, "About One Khazar Title in Ibn Fadlan," in Klyashtornyj, *Old Turkic Runic Texts*, 333–34.

89. Michail Artamonov, *Istorija Hazar* [The history of the Khazars] (Leningrad, 1962), 261–66. An opposing view in Golden, *Khazar Studies*, 1:101–2, although he too emphasizes the differences from the Turkish models.

90. Summary of the evidence in Golden, *Khazar Studies*, 1:163–64.

91. *Zhou shu (Chou-shu)*, in Liu Mau-Tsai, *Die chinesischen Nachrichten*, 1:5–6; Vásáry, *Geschichte des frühen Innerasiens*, 64–66; Golden, "Ethnogenesis in the Tribal Zone," 42–45.

92. Sinor, "The Establishment and Dissolution of the Türk Empire," 297–98, concludes that "from its very inception the Türk empire was to some extent bifocal," with the primacy in the eastern khaganate. More skeptical: Scharlipp, *Die frühen Türken in Zentralasien*, 19.

93. Sören Stark, "On Oq Bodun: The Western Turk Qağanate and the Ashina Clan," *Archivum Eurasiae Medii Aevi* 15 (2006–7): 159–72; de la Vaissière, "Oncles et frères."

94. Translated by Sinor, "The Establishment and Dissolution of the Türk Empire," 297.

95. Drompp, "Supernumerary Sovereigns." For an example, see *Zhou shu*, in Liu Mau-Tsai, *Die chinesischen Nachrichten*, 1:42–44.

96. *Zhou shu*, in Liu Mau-Tsai, *Die chinesischen Nachrichten*, 1:49.

97. Theophylact Simocatta, 7.8, 190: after Turum had proclaimed himself khagan in a revolt, he "sent an embassy to three other great khagans." See sections 2.3–4.

98. Menander, frag. 19.1, ed. and trans. Blockley, 173.

99. Sergej Klyashtornyj and Vladimir A. Livšic, "The Sogdian Inscription of Bugut Revisited," in Klyashtornyj, *Old Turkic Runic Texts*, 65–96, see esp. 70–71 and the edition

and translation, 81–82. See also Scharlipp, *Die frühen Türken in Zentralasien*, 52–54. The Mongolküre inscription, which announces the succession of Muhan's grandson Niri, omits Mahan-Tegin; he is thus also lacking from the genealogical tree in de la Vaissière, "Oncles et frères," 273.

100. Klyashtornyj and Livšic, "The Sogdian Inscription of Bugut Revisited," 81–82.

101. *Zhou shu*, in Liu Mau-Tsai, *Die chinesischen Nachrichten*, 1:8–9.

102. From then on he ate only a vegetarian diet, avoided the pagodas, and imposed other restrictions on himself, recounts the *Zhou shu*; Liu Mau-Tsai, *Die chinesischen Nachrichten*, 1:43.

103. Cf. the overview in Marquart, *Die Chronologie der alttürkischen Inschriften*, 52–53, with additional examples; Klyashtorny, "The Tes Inscription," 152–53, for the Bögü khans of the Uigurs; Klyashtorny, "The Terkhin Inscription," 12 (= repr. 174); Golden, *Khazar Studies*, 1:189–90; *Ibn Fadlan*, ed. and trans. Montgomery, 209.

104. Beševliev, *Die protobulgarische Periode*, 338–40; Haussig, "Die protobulgarische Fürstenliste," 22.

105. Beševliev, *Die protobulgarische Periode*, 341.

106. Constantine Porphyrogenitus, *De cerimoniis aulae Byzantinae* 2.47, ed. Reiske, 1:681–82; Beševliev, *Die protobulgarische Periode*, 345.

107. Bartha, *Hungarian Society*, 57; Golden, *Khazar Studies*, 1:201; Györffy, "Landnahme," 241.

108. The Bavarians had invited the kende to a banquet at the river Fischa and there killed him; *Annales Alamannici*, a. 904, ed. Pertz, 54; *Annales Sangallenses maiores*, a. 902, ed. von Arx, 77; Szabolcs de Vajay, *Der Eintritt des ungarischen Stämmesbundes in die europäische Geschichte (862–933)*, Studia Hungarica 4 (Mainz, 1968), 35. The Byzantines, a decade earlier, had already negotiated with the two "heads" of the Hungarians on the Danube; ibid., 25, with a list of sources.

109. *DAI* 40, 178.

110. Golden, *Khazar Studies*, 1:101.

111. Ibn Fadlān, 29 and 33, ed. and trans. Montgomery, 209–11.

112. Yusuf Has Hâcib, *Kutadgu Bilik*, vol. 2, *Tercüme*, ed. Reşit Rahmeti Arat (Ankara, 1959), vv. 4068–69; English translation: Yusuf Khass Hajib, *Wisdom of Royal Glory (Kutadgu Bilig): A Turko-Islamic Mirror for Princes*, trans. Robert Dankoff (Chicago, 1983). On this source, see Zeki Velidi Togan, "Zentralasiatische türkische Literaturen, II: Die islamische Zeit," in *Turkologie*, Handbuch der Orientalistik 5.1 (Leiden, 1963), 231. On the Karachanids, whose center lay on the Chu and Talas rivers, see Elena A. Davidovich, "The Karakhanids," in *History of Civilizations of Central Asia*, vol. 4, bk. 1, ed. Muhammad S. Asimov and Clifford E. Bosworth, UNESCO publications (Paris, 1988), 125–49; Peter B. Golden, "The Karakhanids and Early Islam," in Sinor, *The Cambridge History of Early Inner Asia*, 343–70; Soucek, *A History of Inner Asia*, 83–85.

113. Togan, *Ibn Fadlans Reisebericht*, 256–58; Mikkola, "Avarica," 160; Deér, "Karl der Grosse," 760.

114. Omeljan Pritsak, "Karachanidische Streitfragen 1–4," *Oriens* 3 (1950): 209–28, especially 210; Pritsak, "Die Karachaniden," *Der Islam* 31 (1954): 17–68, especially 23; Davidovich, "The Karakhanids," 133.

115. Togan, *Ibn Fadlans Reisebericht*, 258–59.

116. Mahmud Al-Kašgari, *Divan-i Lugat at-Turk (Compendium of the Turkic Dialects)*, trans. Robert Dankoff with James Kelly, 3 vols. (Cambridge, MA, 1982–85), 3:31; Togan, *Ibn Fadlans Reisebericht*, 259. Pritsak, "Die Karachaniden," considers the *yugruš* a minister.

117. Recounted, for example, by Ibn Fadlan of the Khazar khagans: Ibn Fadlān 92, ed. and trans. Montgomery, 257.

118. Davidovich, "The Karakhanids," 143–47.

119. This is evident in the Chinese accounts of the Turkish situation; cf. for example Liu Mau-Tsai, *Die chinesischen Nachrichten*, 1:42–44. Succession by a brother is also attested among the Avars; see section 6.2.

120. Lewis, *China between Empires*, 147.

121. De la Vaissière, "Oncles et frères."

122. Jack Goody, *Succession to High Office* (Cambridge, 1966), 35–36.

123. Barfield, *The Perilous Frontier*, 138.

124. Theophanes, *Chronographia* 6203, 527. *Zoilos* may be connected with the later Hungarian title *gyula*; on a seal from the same city, although three hundred years later, the title *tzoula* is found; Moravcsik, *Byzantinoturcica*, 2:14, with additional mentions (he sees a connection with *gyula*). Arguing against this connection, Golden, *Khazar Studies*, 1:178–79.

125. Examples in Chavannes, *Documents sur les Tou-kiue*, 52 and 263.

126. Such an origin for the Khazar double kingship was assumed as early as Artamonov, *Istorija Hazar*, 261–66, and, following him, Golden, *Khazar Studies*, 1:101.

127. *Annales regni Francorum*, a. 782, ed. Kurze, 60; *Annales qui dicuntur Einhardi*, a. 782, ed. Kurze, 61; *Annales Fuldenses*, a. 782, ed. Kurze and Haefele, 10.

128. *Annales regni Francorum*, a. 796, ed. Kurze, 98; *Annales Fuldenses*, a. 796, ed. Kurze and Haefele, 13.

129. *Annales Laureshamenses*, a. 796, ed. Pertz, 37.

130. Zotan: *Annales Alamannici*, a. 795, ed. Walter Lendi, *Untersuchungen zur frühalemannischen Annalistik: Die Murbacher Annalen; Mit Edition*, Scrinium Friburgense 1 (Freiburg/CH, 1971), 168–69 (on the name, cf. also 128–29); *Annales Guelferbytani*, a. 795, ed. Georg Heinrich Pertz, MGH SS 1 (Hanover, 1826), 45; *Annales Iuvavenses minores*, a. 795, and *Annales Iuvavenses maiores*, a. 796, both ed. Harry Bresslau, MGH SS 30.2 (Leipzig, 1935), 736–37. Zodan: *Annales Mettenses priores*, a. 803, ed. Simson, 90 ("Addendum"). Tudun: *Annales Mettenses priores*, a. 795 and a. 796, ed. Simson, 80–81; as *Annales qui dicuntur Einhardi*, a. 795 and a. 796, ed. Kurze, 97 and 101; *Annales regni Francorum*, a. 795, a. 796, a. 811, ed. Kurze, 96–98, 136; *Annales Fuldenses*, a. 795, ed. Kurze and Haefele, 13; Poeta Saxo, a. 795 and a. 796, ed. Paul von Winterfeld, MGH Poetae 4.1 (Berlin, 1899), 252. T(h)odanus: *Annales Laureshamenses*, a. 795, ed. Pertz, 36; *Chronicon Moissiacense*, a. 795, ed. Georg Heinrich Pertz, MGH SS 1 (Hanover, 1826), 302. There are additional variants in the various manuscripts. On the etymology, see Tomaschek, "Avares," 2265; Moravcsik, *Byzantinoturcica*, 2:267; Max Vasmer, *Russisches etymologisches Wörterbuch*, vol. 3, *Sta–Y* (Heidelberg, 1958), 143; Menges, Review of Golden, *Khazar Studies*, 68, with additional bibliography.

131. I am very grateful to Wolfgang Haubrichs for his detailed linguistic explanation (e-mail June 26, 2017).

132. *Annales qui dictuntur Einhardi*, a. 795, ed. Kurze, 97.

133. *Annales regni Francorum*, a. 795, ed. Kurze, 96; similarly *Annales Fuldenses*, a. 795, ed. Kurze and Haefele, 13.

134. *Annales Alamannici*, a. 795, ed. Lendi, 168–69.

135. *Annales Mettenses priores*, a. 803, ed. Simson, 90.

136. *Annales Laureshamenses*, a. 795, ed. Pertz, 36; *Chronicon Moissiacense*, a. 795, 302.

137. *Annales regni Francorum*, a. 795, ed. Kurze, 96.

138. *Annales regni Francorum*, a. 796, ed. Kurze, 98.

139. *Chronicon Moissiacense*, a. 795, 302.

140. *Annales regni Francorum*, a. 796, ed. Kurze, 98.

141. *Annales Mettenses priores*, a. 803, ed. Simson, 90.

142. "Pannonia and the land of the Avars were one and the same, although the latter exceeded the former Roman province." Wolfram, *Conversio Bagoariorum*, 103 (my

translation); the "ring" also lay in "Pannonia" between the Danube and the Tisza; *Annales regni Francorum*, a. 796, ed. Kurze, 98.

143. *Annales qui dicuntur Einhardi*, a. 796, ed. Kurze, 101.

144. *Annales qui dictuntur Einhardi* ("Addendum"), a. 803, ed. Kurze, 191. It is also conceivable that an earlier revolt is meant, perhaps in 797 (cf. *Annales Guelferbytani*, a. 797, ed. Pertz, 45).

145. *Annales regni Francorum*, a. 811, ed. Kurze, 135.

146. *Magnae Moraviae Fontes Historici*, ed. Dagmar Bartoňková et al., vol. 3, *Diplomata, epistolae, textus historici varii* (Brno, 1969), 255. Later also taken up by the humanist Johannes Aventinus, *Annales Boiorum* 4.4.15, ed. Dagmar Bartoňková et al., *Magnae Moraviae Fontes Historici*, vol. 1, *Annales et chronicae* (Brno, 1966), 339.

147. Ildikó Ecsedy, "Old Turkic Titles of Chinese Origin," *Acta Orient. Hung.* 18 (1965): 83–91; Marquart, *Die Chronologie der alttürkischen Inschriften*, 11; Hans W. Haussig, "Indogermanische und altaische Nomadenvölker im Grenzgebiet Irans," in Altheim, *Historia Mundi*, 246; Franke, "Fremdherrschaften in China," 51.

148. Klyashtornyj and Livšic, "The Sogdian Inscription of Bugut Revisited," 81–82 (*twdwnt* in the transcription from Sogdian). Discussion of further instances, for example in the Orkhon inscriptions, in Golden, *Khazar Studies*, 1:216. Cf. Marquart, *Die Chronologie der alttürkischen Inschriften*, 44; Grousset, *Empire of the Steppes*, 87, 119, 175; Pritsak, "Distinctive Features of the Pax Nomadica." In the *Etymologicum magnum*: Moravcsik, *Byzantinoturcica*, 2:267.

149. *Zhou shu*, Liu Mau-Tsai, *Die chinesischen Nachrichten*, 1:9; Chavannes, *Documents sur les Tou-kiue*, 21 and 24.

150. Pierre Marsone, *La steppe et l'empire: La formation de la dynastie Khitan (Liao), IVe–Xe siècle* (Paris, 2011), 54.

151. Theophanes, *Chronographia* 6203, 527–28; Nicephorus, 45, ed. and trans. Mango, 108–11. On these events, see Dunlop, *The History of the Jewish Khazars*, 174–75. On the sources, see Golden, *Khazar Studies*, 1:215. On the scarcity of the title in Khazar contexts, see Boris Zhivkov, *Khazaria in the Ninth and Tenth Centuries* (Leiden, 2015), 232.

152. On the *turun* of the fourteenth century, see Josef Marquart, "Kultur- und sprachgeschichtliche Analekten," *Ungarische Jahrbücher* 9 (1929): 80.

153. *De Pippini regis victoria Avarica* 10, ed. Dümmler, 117.

154. Togan, *Ibn Fadlans Reisebericht*, 276; de Ferdinandy, "Die nordeurasischen Reitervölker," 180; Kollautz, "Die Awaren," 155.

155. Kollautz and Miyakawa, 1:76, and 2:10; Yu, "Doubts," 300.

156. Menander, frag. 10.3, ed. and trans. Blockley, 123. On the form of the name, see Marquart, *Die Chronologie der alttürkischen Inschriften*, 43, with the reading *tamgatarkhan*, which is not substantiated in the manuscript transmission, but resembles the form *tamgan-tarkhan* of the Orkhon inscriptions (e.g. Bilge Khagan Inscription, 1st side, 15, http://bitig.org/?lang=e&mod=1&tid=1&oid=16&m=1, here transcribed as "taman qagan").

157. Klyashtornyj and Livšic, "The Sogdian Inscription of Bugut Revisited," 81.

158. *Sabra-tarkhan, Ogul-tarkhan*, etc.; cf. Marquart, *Die Chronologie der alttürkischen Inschriften*, 31–32, 49; *baga-tarqan, bilgä-tarqan* in the Terkhin inscription, see Klyashtorny, "The Terkhin Inscription," 344.

159. Thomsen, "Alttürkische Inschriften in der Mongolei," 163; Klyashtorny, "The Terkhin Inscription," 175; Pritsak, "Distinctive Features of the Pax Nomadica."

160. Altheim, *Geschichte der Hunnen*, 1:281, and 2:277–78.

161. The various mentions are assembled in Golden, *Khazar Studies*, 1:210–11; Greek instances in Moravcsik, *Byzantinoturcica*, 2:253.

162. Ibn Fadlān 33, ed. and trans. Montgomery, 211.

163. Pritsak, "Distinctive Features of the Pax Nomadica," interprets them as ministers or "civil governors" in cities, as distinct from the tudun, the military governor.

164. Golden, *Khazar Studies*, 1:212.

165. Beševliev, *Die protobulgarische Periode*, 331.

166. Petkov, *Voices of Medieval Bulgaria, Seventh–Fifteenth Century*, 10; Beševliev, *Die protobulgarische Periode*, 280 and 352–53; Veselin Beševliev, "Die zusammengesetzten Titel in den protobulgarischen Inschriften," *UAJB* 30 (1958): 98–103. Cf. Karl H. Menges, "Altaic Elements in the Proto-Bulgarian Inscriptions," *Byzantion* 21 (1951): 92 and 99; Runciman, *A History of the First Bulgarian Empire*, 285.

167. Petkov, *Voices of Medieval Bulgaria, Seventh–Fifteenth Century*, 10; Beševliev, *Die protobulgarische Periode*, 286.

168. Petkov, *Voices of Medieval Bulgaria, Seventh–Fifteenth Century*, 9–10; Beševliev, *Die protobulgarische Periode*, 353.

169. Togan, *Ibn Fadlans Reisebericht*, 141.

170. Togan, *Ibn Fadlans Reisebericht*, 221.

171. *DAI* 40, 174; cf. Julius Németh, "Türkische und ungarische Ethnonyme," *UAJB* 47 (1975): 154–60; Bartha, *Hungarian Society*, 57; Golden, *Khazar Studies*, 1:71.

172. Golden, *Khazar Studies*, 1:213.

173. László Rásonyi, "The Psychology and Categories of Name-Giving among the Turkish Peoples," in *Hungaro-Turcica: Studies in Honour of Julius Németh*, ed. Gyula Káldy-Nagy (Budapest, 1976), 212.

174. *Annales regni Francorum*, a. 805, ed. Kurze, 119; *Annales s. Emmerami maiores*, a. 805, ed. Harry Bresslau, MGH SS 30.2 (Leipzig, 1934), 737.

175. *Annales regni Francorum*, a. 805, ed. Kurze, 119–20; cf. section 8.4.

176. *Annales s. Emmerami maiores*, a. 805 (*cabuanus*), ed. Bresslau, 739; *Annales Xantenses*, a. 805, ed. Bernhard Simson, MGH SS rer. Germ. 12 (Hanover, 1909), 3 (*cappanus*); additional examples in Sigurd Abel and Bernhard Simson, *Jahrbücher des Fränkischen Reiches unter Karl dem Großen*, 2 vols., 2nd ed. (Leipzig 1883–88), 2:320–21; Deér, "Karl der Grosse," 775.

177. *Annales Mettenses priores*, a. 805, ed. Simson, 93.

178. Kollautz, "Die Awaren," 137.

179. Petkov, *Voices of Medieval Bulgaria, Seventh–Fifteenth Century*, 12; Beševliev, *Die protobulgarische Periode*, 339–40; the interpetation is based on Beševliev's reading of two rather faded inscriptions; Ziemann, *Vom Wandervolk zur Großmacht*, 236–40. On the Avar and Bulgar kapkhan, see also Moravcsik, *Byzantinoturcica*, 2:140–41.

180. Beševliev, *Die protobulgarische Periode*, 341.

181. See Tonyukuk inscription, 60–61, http://bitig.org/?lang=e&mod=1&tid=1&oid =17&m=1 (Qapaγan qaγan). For the debate, see Thomsen, "Alttürkische Inschriften in der Mongolei," 169–70; Czeglédy, "On the Numerical Composition," 275–76; Osman F. Sertkaya, "The First Line of the Tonjukuk Monument," *Central Asiatic Journal* 23 (1979): 288–91, with additional bibliography.

182. Altheim, *Geschichte der Hunnen*, 1:270–72; as an intensifier for the khan title, Sinor, "Qapqan" (which does not match up with the events of 805).

183. *Annales regni Francorum*, a. 805, ed. Kurze, 120.

184. *Annales regni Francorum*, a. 811, ed. Kurze, 135.

185. For an identification with the khagan, see Abel and Simson, *Jahrbücher*, 2:472, n. 3; Bóna, "'Cundpald fecit,'" 323. Differing view in Deér, "Karl der Grosse," 776 (with an improbable etymology from *kam*, "shaman," and *savcy*, "emissary").

186. *Annales qui dictuntur Einhardi*, a. 782, ed. Kurze, 61.

187. *Annales Fuldenses*, a. 796, ed. Kurze and Haefele, 13.

188. *Annales Lareshamenses*, a. 796, ed. Pertz, 37.

189. *Annales Mettenses priores*, a. 803, ed. Simson, 90; *Annales regni Francorum*, a. 805, ed. Kurze, 120.

190. Petkov, *Voices of Medieval Bulgaria, Seventh–Fifteenth Century*, 8–12. It is routinely used for Omurtag (ca. 815–ca. 831) and Malamir (ca. 831/32–36); it is not attested for Krum (802–14) who would be the obvious model for the Avar *canizauci*; but this is because in none of Krum's inscriptions has the beginning with the complete title been preserved. Tsvetelin Stepanov, "The Bulgar title ΚΑΝΑΣΥΒΙΤΙ: Reconstructing the Notions of Divine Kingship in Bulgaria, AD 822–836," *Early Medieval Europe* 10, 1 (2001): 1–19.

191. Beševliev, *Die protobulgarische Periode*, 334.

192. Runciman, *A History of the First Bulgarian Empire*, 284.

193. Beševliev, *Die protobulgarische Periode*, 334.

194. Beševliev, *Die protobulgarische Periode*, 336, referring to Beševliev, *Die protobulgarischen Inschriften* (Berlin, 1963), nos. 14 and 78; Moravcsik, *Byzantinoturcica*, 2:135.

195. The inscription reads: "† ΒΟΥΗΛΑ · ΖΟΑΠΑΝ · ΤΕΓΗ · ΔΥΓΕΤΟΙΓΗ · ΒΟΥΤΑΟΥΛ · ΖΩΑΠΑΝ · ΤΑΓΡΟΓΗ · ΗΤΖΙΓΗ · ΤΑΙΓΗ"; Albrecht, "Die Inschriften," 142–43, with a survey of the literature. The reading of the probably Turkish text is problematic; it has been interpeted, among others, as "Boila Zoapan had this cup made . . ." or "This is Boila Zoapan's cup, he died . . ."; Vékony, "Zur Lesung der griechischen Inschriften," especially 304; Róna-Tas, "The Inscriptions." Cf. also section 6.5.

196. For the Bulgarian *boilades*, see Petkov, *Voices of Medieval Bulgaria, Seventh–Fifteenth Century*, 12, stating that Khan Malamir "gave to the Bulgars to eat and drink many times, and to the boilas and bagains many gifts." See Beševliev, *Die protobulgarische Periode*, 343–45.

197. Bálint, "A Short Essay."

198. According to Chinese sources, one of the five leaders of the Turkic Nushibi tribes bore the title *ch'u-pan ch'i-chin* after 635; among the rival Duolu there was the *ch'u-pan cur*. Maenchen-Helfen, *Die Welt der Hunnen*, 268; Karl H. Menges, "Schwierige slawisch-orientalische Lehnbeziehungen," *UAJB* 31 (1959): 178–79.

199. Petkov, *Voices of Medieval Bulgaria, Seventh–Fifteenth Century*, 10–12; Beševliev, *Die protobulgarischen Inschriften*, no. 60, as well as an inscription on a silver bowl from Preslav; Beševliev, *Die protobulgarische Periode*, 352, assumes them to be Bulgar supervisors of the Slavic župans, which rests on the assumption that this was an originally Slavic title.

200. Petkov, *Voices of Medieval Bulgaria, Seventh–Fifteenth Century*, 8–9.

201. *DAI* 29.67, 124; 30, 145. Ludwig Steindorff, "Die Synode auf der Planities Dalmae," *MIÖG* 93 (1985): 279–324.

202. On the basis of MGH DD Kar. 1, 169, 226–28, reconstructed by Heinrich Fichtenau, "Die Urkunden Herzog Tassilos III. und der 'Stiftbrief' von Kremsmünster," in Fichtenau, *Beiträge zur Mediävistik*, vol. 2, *Urkundenforschung* (Stuttgart, 1977), 97–99; Wolfram, *Salzburg, Bayern, Österreich*, 356–79. General treatment in Ditten, "Bemerkungen," 448–50; Phaedon Malingoudis, "Die Institution des Župans als Problem der frühslawischen Geschichte," *Cyrillomethodiana* 2 (1972–73): 61–76; Matthias Hardt, "Der Supan: Ein Forschungsbericht," *Zeitschrift für Ostforschung* 39 (1990): 161–71; Peter Štih, "Structures of the Slovene Territory in the Early Middle Ages," in Štih, *The Middle Ages*, 162–64.

203. *De Pippini regis victoria Avarica* 6, ed. Dümmler, 116.

204. Barthold, *Histoire des turcs*, 29; Franke, *Das chinesische Kaiserreich*, 3:254.

205. E.g. *Wei shu*, 103 (*kehedun*): Yu, "Doubts," 300; Kollautz and Miyakawa, 1:57.

206. Klyashtorny, "The Terkhin Inscription," repr. 173; further examples in Thomsen, "Alttürkische Inschriften in der Mongolei," 149 and 167; Tekin, "The Tariat (Terkhin) Inscription," 55.

207. *Turkastank*: Pseudo-Movses Chorenac'i; cf. Marquart, *Osteuropäische und ostasiatische Streifzüge*, 58.

208. Golden, *Khazar Studies*, 1:196.

209. Dunlop, *The History of the Jewish Khazars*, 188.

210. Cf. László Rásonyi, "Der Frauenname bei den Turkvölkern," *UAJB* 34 (1962): 233. On the Mongolian *hatun*, see Vladimirtsov, *Le régime social des Mongols*, 69.

211. See section 8.4.

212. Ibn Fadlan reports twenty-five wives for the khagan of the Khazars, each of them the daughter of a neighboring ruler, plus sixty slave girls as concubines, who lived in a different building; Ibn Fadlān, 92, ed. and trans. Montgomery 257. Even the Slavic king Samo is reported to have had twelve wives; Fredegar 4.48, 40. Mavros, Kuver's right-hand man, was also polygamous; *Miracula Demetrii*, 2.5.304, 233; see section 7.7. The Avar khagans very likely were polygamous, too; this would also explain the numerous sons of the khagan around the year 600.

213. Theophylact Simocatta, 1.4.5, 25 (Whitby and Whitby translate "the khagan's harem").

214. Bóna, "Ein Vierteljahrhundert," 313.

215. See section 3.6.

216. Ibn Fadlān, 19, ed. and trans. Montgomery, 203.

217. *Zhou shu*, Liu Mau-Tsai, *Die chinesischen Nachrichten*, 1:9.

218. Gardīzī 267, trans. Göckenjan and Zimonyi, 144.

219. *Secret History of the Mongols, Geheime Geschichte der Mongolen*, trans. Heissig, 150.

220. István Erdélyi, Eszter Ojtozi, and Wladimir F. Gering, *Das Gräberfeld von Newolino: Ausgrabungen von AV Schmidt und der archäologischen Kama-Expedition*, Archaeologica Hungarica 46 (Budapest, 1969), at 93.

221. Josef Zábojník, "Zum Verhältnis zwischen Archäologie und Anthropologie am Beispiel frühmittelalterlicher Gräberfelder aus dem Mitteldonauraum (7.–10. Jahrhundert)," in *Castellum, Civitas, Urbs: Zentren und Eliten im frühmittelalterlichen Ostmitteleuropa*, ed. Orsolya Heinrich-Tamáska et al. (Rahden, 2015), 278.

222. Garam, *Das awarenzeitliche Gräberfeld von Tiszafüred*.

223. Zábojník, "Zum Verhältnis," 283–87.

224. Daim, *Das awarische Gräberfeld von Leobersdorf*, 164.

225. *Annales Laureshamenses*, a. 796, ed. Pertz, 37.

226. "The ring of the Avar people, previously long undisturbed"; *Annales regni Francorum*, a. 796, ed. Kurze, 98.

227. Poeta Saxo, a. 796, ed. von Winterfeld, 38.

228. *Annales qui dictuntur Einhardi*, a. 796, ed. Kurze, 99.

229. Notker, *Gesta Karoli Magni* 2.1, ed. Heinrich Haefele, MGH SS rer. Germ. n.s. 12 (Hanover, 1959), 49–51.

230. Pohl, "The Regia and the Hring."

231. "In campis patentibus, qui sermone barbarico 'feld' appellantur": Paul the Deacon, *Historia Langobardorum*, 1.20, ed. Waitz, 65. On the date of Paul's history: Walter Pohl, "Paolo Diacono e la costruzione dell'identità longobarda," in *Paolo Diacono—uno scrittore fra tradizione longobarda e rinnovamento carolingio*, ed. Paolo Chiesa (Udine, 2000), 413–26.

232. Petkov, *Voices of Medieval Bulgaria, Seventh–Fifteenth Century*, 11. Günter Prinzing, "Pliska in the View of the Protobulgarian Inscriptions and the Byzantine Written Sources," in Henning, *Post-Roman Towns*, 2:245–46, follows earlier Bulgarian literature in regarding *kampos* as fortified military camp, in which Omurtag built a small palace, *aulē*. Henry George Liddell and Robert Scott, *Greek-English Lexicon: With a Revised Supplement; Revised and Augmented throughout by Henry Stuart Jones with the Assistance of Roderick McKenzie and with the Cooperation of Many Scholars*, 9th ed. (Oxford, 1940), 873, do not include the Latin loanword *kampos* (only the meaning "sea-monster"). In Latin,

according to Niermeyer, *Mediae Latinitatis Lexicon minus,* "campus 5," 163, the meaning "army camp" for *campus* is only attested in the thirteenth century. See also Ziemann, *Vom Wandervolk zur Großmacht,* 331.

233. Ziemann, *Vom Wandervolk zur Großmacht,* 317–32; Paolo Squatriti, "Moving Earth and Making Difference: Dikes and Frontiers in Early Medieval Bulgaria," in Curta,*Borders, Barriers, and Ethnogenesis,* 59–90; Panos Sophoulis, *Byzantium and Bulgaria, 775–831* (Leiden, 2012), 60–65.

234. *Annales qui dicuntur Einhardi,* a. 796, ed. Kurze, 99.

235. Togan, *Ibn Fadlans Reisebericht,* 182–83. The word originally designated the royal tent.

236. Karl August Wittfogel, *China und die osteurasische Kavallerie-Revolution* (Wiesbaden, 1978), 27.

237. Vladimir Minorsky, "Tamim Ibn Bahr's Journey to the Uyghurs," *Bulletin of the School of Oriental and African Studies* 12, no. 2 (1948): 275–305, especially 284; Károly Czeglédy, "Zur Stammesorganisation der türkischen Völker," *Acta Orient. Hung.* 36 (1982): 89–93. Examples of the circular organization of nomad encampments are assembled in Pletnewa, *Die Chasaren,* 47 and 79.

238. On the Bulgar capital Pliska, see Beševliev, *Die protobulgarische Periode,* 459–67; on the Khazar capitals and on the transition from nomad camps to urban residences, see Pletnewa, *Die Chasaren,* 96–98.

239. Matthias Hardt, "Der Ring der Awaren," in Drauschke et al., *Lebenswelten zwischen Archäologie und Geschichte,* 185–92.

240. See https://hiros.hu/cimke/wilhelm-gabor (in Hungarian). I owe the information to Csanád Bálint and Tivadar Vida.

241. For the older literature, see Vilmos Balás, "Die Erdwälle der ungarischen Tiefebene," *Acta Arch. Hung.* 15 (1963): 309–36.

242. Uwe Fiedler, "Nochmals zur Datierung der Wall- und Grabenzüge an der mittleren Donau: Vorgelagerter Grenzschutz des spätrömischen Reiches oder Machtdemonstration der awarischen Herrscher?," in Bollók, Csiky, and Vida, *Zwischen Byzanz und der Steppe/Between Byzantium and the Steppe,* 335–50. See the map, ibid., 342.

243. Walter Pohl, "Frontiers and Ethnic Identities: Some Final Considerations," in Curta,*Borders, Barriers, and Ethnogenesis,* 255–65.

244. Squatriti, "Moving Earth and Making Difference."

245. Squatriti, "Moving Earth and Making Difference," 90.

246. *Annales qui dicuntur Einhardi,* a. 791, ed. Kurze, 89.

247. *Capitulary of Diedenhofen (805)* 44.7, ed. Boretius, 123; Herwig Wolfram, *Die Karolingerzeit in Niederösterreich,* Wissenschaftliche Schriftenreihe Niederösterreich 46 (St. Pölten, 1980), 15–16.

248. *Gesta Hrodberti* 5, ed. Wilhelm Levison, MGH SS rer. Merov. 6 (Hanover, 1913), 159; The *Conversio Bagoariorum et Carantanorum* 1, ed. and trans. Lošek, 91–93, turns this, for transparent reasons, into a missionary journey to Pannonia; cf. Wolfram, *Conversio Bagoariorum,* 93.

249. Arbeo of Freising, *Vita s. Haimhrammi* 5, ed. Krusch, 33. On the lives of Rupert and Emmeram, see Ian N. Wood, *The Missionary Life: Saints and Evangelisation of Europe, 400–1050* (Harlow, 2001), 145–57.

250. Gottfried Mayr, "Neuerliche Bemerkungen zur Todeszeit des heiligen Emmeram und zur Kirchenpolitik Herzog Theodos," in Wolfram and Pohl, *Typen der Ethnogenese,* 199–215 (with a dating of about 715); similarly, Wolfram, "Ethnogenesen im frühmittelalterlichen Donau- und Ostalpenraum," 131–32. For an earlier dating of about 680, see Reindel, "Das Zeitalter der Agilolfinger," 147; Deér, "Karl der Grosse," 749.

251. See section 6.9.

252. *Bede's Ecclesiastical History of the English People* 5.9, ed. Bertram Colgrave and R. A. B. Minors (Oxford, 1969), 476. Cf. Wolfgang H. Fritze, "Slawen und Avaren im angelsächsischen Missionsprogramm. III. Bedas Hunni und die Entstehung der angelsächsischen Missionsvölkerliste von 703/04," *Zeitschrift für slavische Philologie* 33 (1967/68): 358–72. The text does not say that the Huns actually became the goal of missionary activities.

253. Arbeo of Freising, *Vita Corbiniani* 15, ed. Bruno Krusch, MGH SS rer. Germ. 13 (Hanover, 1920), 202–4. "Valeria" may also have been understood as a land of the *walha*, the Romans: Katharina Winckler, *Die Alpen im Frühmittelalter: Die Geschichte eines Raumes in den Jahren 500 bis 800* (Vienna, 2012), 317–18; Herwig Wolfram, "Die frühmittelalterliche Romania im Donau- und Ostalpenraum," in Pohl, Haubrichs, and Hartl, *Walchen, Romani und Latini*, 32.

254. Edited by Oswald Holder-Egger, "Über die Heiligen Marinus und Anianus," *Neues Archiv* 13 (1888): 22–28. Cf. Reindel, "Das Zeitalter der Agilolfinger," 143; Kahl, "Die Baiern und ihre Nachbarn," 196–97. From the Carolingian period onward, the Vandals were often identified with the Wends/Slavs; see Roland Steinacher, "Wenden, Slawen, Vandalen: Eine frühmittelalterliche pseudologische Gleichsetzung und ihre Nachwirkungen," in Pohl, *Die Suche nach den Ursprüngen*, 329–53.

255. *Annales Mettenses priores*, a. 692, ed. Simson, 15; English translation of this section: *Late Merovingian France: History and Hagiography, 640–720*, ed. Paul Fouracre and Richard A. Gerberding (Manchester, 1996), 361; on the text, ibid., 330–49.

256. Paul the Deacon, *Historia Langobardorum*, 6.58, ed. Waitz, 242. The *Chronicon Benedicti Sancti Andreae* 15, ed. Georg Heinrich Pertz, MGH SS 3 (Hanover, 1839), 702, or ed. Giuseppe Zucchetti, *Il Chronicon di Sant'Andrea del Soratte e il Libellus de imperatoria potestate in urbe Roma* (Rome, 1920), 64, composed around the year 1000, which tells that Liutprand fought the Avars near Aquileia and thus attached Venetia to the Lombard kingdom, seems to be one of the rather fantastic stories that the author devised on the basis of good sources.

257. *Die Gesetze der Langobarden*, ed. Franz Beyerle (Vienna, 1947), 348. Ratchis, earlier *dux* of Friuli, knew from his own experience of the high-handed eastern policy that was pursued from Cividale; Walter Pohl, "Frontiers of Lombard Italy: The Laws of Ratchis and Aistulf," in Pohl, Wood, and Reimitz, *Transformation of Frontiers*, 117–42.

258. Renate Möhlenkamp, "Avaria," in *Glossar zur frühmittelalterlichen Geschichte im östlichen Europa, Bericht einer Arbeitstagung* (Münster, 1982), 40–41.

259. MGH DD Kar. 1, 187, 251; Diplomata of Louis the Pious 101, ed. Theo Kölzer, *Die Urkunden Ludwigs des Frommen*, 3 vols., MGH DD Karolinorum 2 (Wiesbaden, 2016), 2:245, where Aio flees "ad regnum Abarorum" and returns "de Abaria" after their defeat. For Aio's case, see section 8.4.

260. Anonymus Ravennatis, *Cosmographia* 4.14, ed. Schnetz, 53 (cf. 4.19–20, 56–58 on Pannonia).

261. *Conversio Bagoariorum et Carantanorum* 4, ed. and trans. Lošek, 104.

262. *Annales Mettenses priores*, a. 743, ed. Simson, 33–35; Wolfram, *Conversio Bagoariorum*, 119. Odilo did not return from exile until early in 741; cf. Wolfram, "Ethnogenesen im frühmittelalterlichen Donau- und Ostalpenraum," 132, n. 179.

263. *Conversio Bagoariorum et Carantanorum* 5, ed. Lošek, 105.

264. See section 8.4.

265. Herilungoburg: MGH DD LD, 9 (832), 10; Wolfram, *Die Karolingerzeit in Niederösterreich*, 12. Omundesthorf: *Annales Maximiani*, a. 791, ed. Georg Waitz, MGH SS 13 (Hanover, 1881), 22; *Annales Iuvavenses maximi*, a. 791, ed. Bresslau, 734. Deér, "Karl der Grosse," 742; Peter Csendes, "Zu den Awarenkriegen unter Karl dem Großen," *Unsere Heimat* 41 (1970): 96 (linked with St. Martin near Klosterneuburg). Cf. also Omuntesperch, named in 890 (*Annales Fuldenses*, a. 890, ed. Kurze and Haefele, 118; Wolfram, *Salzburg,*

Bayern, Österreich, 55). The place perhaps lay on the edge of the Vienna Woods but might also be sought in the vicinity of the mouth of the Enns, where Pannonia began in the ninth-century conception.

266. The Roman emissary Priscus described his route into the land of the Huns with the aid of river names; Priscus, frag. 11.3, ed. and trans. Blockley, 262. Peter Wiesinger, "Probleme der bairischen Frühzeit in Niederösterreich aus namenkundlicher Sicht," in Wolfram and Schwarcz,*Die Bayern und ihre Nachbarn*, 343, views rivers and mountains as fixed markers for the orientation of travelers, which do not necessarily imply established settlements.

267. Wolfram, *Salzburg, Bayern, Österreich*, 356–79; Wolfram, *Grenzen und Räume*, 197. The *Grunzwitigau* was only the object of a donation to Kremsmünster in 828.

268. On the erroneous equation of the founders of the Tegernsee and St. Pölten monasteries, see Johann Weissensteiner, *Tegernsee, die Bayern und Österreich: Studien zu Tegernseer Geschichtsquellen und der bayerischen Stammessage mit einer Edition der Passio secunda s. Quirini*, Archiv für Österreichische Geschichte 133 (Vienna, 1983), 63–66; Wolfram, *Die Geburt Mitteleuropas*, 254. Audaccrus: *Annales regni Francorum*, a. 788, ed. Kurze, 82–84, and section 8.4.

269. Hertha Ladenbauer-Orel, *Linz-Zizlau: Das bairische Gräberfeld an der Traunmündung* (Vienna, 1960); Stein, "Awarisch-merowingische Beziehungen," 235–36; Kurt W. Zeller, "Kulturbeziehungen im Gräberfeld Linz-Zizlau," in *Baiernzeit in Oberösterreich*, Schriftenreihe des Oberösterreich Musealvereins 10 (Linz, 1980), 75–88, especially 84; Daim, *Das awarische Gräberfeld von Leobersdorf*, 176.

270. Daim and Lippert, *Das awarische Gräberfeld*, 37–38 and 128; Falko Daim, "Archäologische Zeugnisse zur Geschichte des Wiener Raumes im Frühmittelalter," *Wiener Geschichtsblätter* 36 (1981): 194; Friesinger, *Die vielen Väter Österreichs*, 107.

271. Herwig Friesinger, "Alpenslawen und Bayern," Herrmann, *Welt der Slawen*, 110; Jochen Giesler, "Zur Archäologie des Ostalpenraumes vom 8. bis 11. Jahrhundert," *Archäologisches Korrespondezblatt* 10 (1980): 85–98; Szameit, "Slawische Körpergräber."

272. Herwig Friesinger, "Das slawische Gräberfeld von Wimm," *Archaeologia Austriaca* 68 (1984): 212.

273. Vlasta Tovornik, "Die Gräberfelder von Micheldorf-Kremsdorf, Oberösterreich," in Daim and Friesinger *Die Bayern und ihre Nachbarn*, 213–16.

274. Bóna, "Die Awaren," 20.

275. Bóna, "Die Awaren," 20; Stein, "Awarisch-merowingische Beziehungen," 238–39.

276. Remains were found in, for example, Alemannic aristocratic graves in Niederstotzingen—Peter Paulsen, *Alemannische Adelsgräber von Niederstotzingen* (Stuttgart, 1967)—and Stuttgart-Cannstatt; see Bracher, "Der Reflexbogen als Beispiel gentiler Bewaffnung."

277. See Curta, "The Earliest Avar-Age Stirrups," and section 6.2.

278. Cf. Joachim Werner, "Fernhandel und Naturalwirtschaft im östlichen Merowingerreich nach archäologischen und numismatischen Zeugnissen," in *Moneta e scambi nell'alto medioevo*, SSCI 8 (Spoleto, 1961), 557–618.

279. Einhard, *Vita Karoli* 13, ed. Holder-Egger, 16; ed. and trans. Dutton, 23.

280. Einhard, *Vita Karoli* 13, ed. Holder-Egger, 13; ed. and trans. Dutton, 24.

281. Theodulf of Orléans, *Carmen* 25, ed. Dümmler, 484.

282. Theodulf of Orléans, *Carmen* 25, ed. Dümmler, 484, ll. 39–40.

283. Paul the Deacon, *Historia Langobardorum*, 4.37, ed. Waitz, 162; above all, later authors such as Ado of Vienne (†874) underline this as a reason for war: Ado of Vienne, *Chronicon* a. 791, ed. Georg Heinrich Pertz, MGH SS 2 (Hanover, 1829), 320. Cf. Deér, "Karl der Grosse," 757 and 784.

284. Thus Heinz Löwe, *Die karolingische Reichsgründung und der Südosten: Studien zum Werden des Deutschtums und seiner Aueinandersetzung mit Rom*, Forschungen zur Kirchen- und Geistesgeschichte 13 (Stuttgart, 1937), 73. Cf. section 8.3.

285. Einhard, *Vita Karoli* 13, ed. Holder-Egger, 16; ed. and trans. Dutton, 24.

286. "Per ducentos et eo amplius annos qualescumque omnium occidentalium divitias congregantes, cum et Gothi et Wandali quietem mortalium perturbarent, orbem occiduum pene vacuum dimiserunt": thus writes, at any event two generations later, Notker in his *Gesta Karoli* 2.1, ed. Haefele, 50–51.

287. Utrecht Psalter, fol. 25r (Psalm 42), see http://psalter.library.uu.nl/page?p= 56&res=2&x=0&y=0; see also fol. 26r with Psalm 44: "Thy arrows are sharp: under thee shall people fall, into the hearts of the king's enemies." Koert van der Horst, William Noel, and Wilhelmina C. M. Wüstefeld, eds., *The Utrecht Psalter in Medieval Art: Picturing the Psalms of David* (Westrenen, 1996), 2; for the identification with the Avars, see Károly Mesterházy, "Az utrechti zsoltár avar ábrázolásai," *Alba Regia* 8–9 (1967–68): 245–48.

288. Cf. Wilhelm Störmer, *Früher Adel: Studien zur politischen Führungsschicht im fränkisch-deutschen Reich vom 8. bis 11. Jahrhundert*, 2 vols., Monographien zur Geschichte des Mittelalters 6.1 (Stuttgart, 1973), 1:202–33, especially 215–17.

289. "The advance against the Avars may also have been motivated by the intention to tie down the forces of the nobles in a military campaign and create a diversion from the difficulties of domestic politics": Karl Brunner, *Oppositionelle Gruppen in Karolingerreich*, VIÖG 25 (Vienna, 1979), 63.

290. Jarnut, *Geschichte der Langobarden*, 122–23; Stefano Gasparri, ed., *774—ipotesi su una transizione* (Turnhout, 2008).

291. MGH DD Kar. 1, 187, 251; Kollautz and Miyakawa, 2:175; Deér, "Karl der Grosse," 740; Krahwinkler, *Friaul im Frühmittelalter*, 139–41.

292. Reindel, "Das Zeitalter der Agilolfinger," 131; Wolfram, *Grenzen und Räume*, 90–91; Matthias Becher, *Eid und Herrschaft: Untersuchungen zum Herrscherethos Karls des Großen* (Sigmaringen, 1993).

293. *Annales regni Francorum*, a. 782, ed. Kurze, 69; *Annales qui dictuntur Einhardi*, a. 782, ed. Kurze, 61; *Annales Mettenses priores*, a. 782, ed. Simson, 69.

294. *Annales Iuvavenses maximi*, a. 782, ed. Bresslau, 734; *Annales s. Emmerami maiores*, a. 783, ed. Bresslau, 735.

295. Wolfram, *Die Geburt Mitteleuropas*, 187; Deér, "Karl der Grosse," 755.

296. Abel and Simson, *Jahrbücher*, 1:427–28.

297. *Annales regni Francorum*, a. 788, ed. Kurze, 80–84; Wolfram, *Grenzen und Räume*, 91–92. On Tassilo and his fall, see Stuart Airlie, "Narratives of Triumph and Rituals of Submission: Charlemagne's Mastering of Bavaria," *Transactions of the Royal Historical Society*, 6th ser., 9 (1999): 93–119; Rosamond McKitterick, *Charlemagne: The Formation of an European Identity* (Cambridge, 2008), 118–27; Herwig Wolfram, *Tassilo III.: Höchster Fürst und niedrigster Mönch* (Regensburg, 2016).

298. "Suadente . . . Liutberga . . . in adversitatem regis, et ut bellum contra Francos susciperent, Hunorum gentem concitaret": *Annales qui dictuntur Einhardi*, a. 788, ed. Kurze, 81. "Hortatu uxoris . . . iuncto foedere cum Hunnis": Einhard, *Vita Karoli* 11, ed. Holder-Egger, 14; "machinationibus, quas ipse Tassilo et coniunx illius cum omnes gentes qui in circuito Francorum erant . . . consiliati sunt contra Francos": *Annales Laureshamenses*, a. 788, ed. Pertz, 33.

299. Alcuin, *Epistula* 7, 32, ed. Dümmler, 14–15; *Annales regni Francorum*, a. 788, ed. Kurze, 56; *Annales Mettenses priores*, a. 788, ed. Simson, 77; *Annales qui dictuntur Einhardi*, a. 788, ed. Kurze, 83; *Annales Maximiani*, a. 788, ed. Waitz, 22; *Annales Sithienses*, a. 788, ed. Georg Waitz, MGH SS 13 (Hanover, 1881), 36; *Annales s. Emmerami maiores*, a. 788, ed. Bresslau, 735.

300. The charter transcribed by Onofrio Panvinio in the sixteenth century most likely was his own forgery; see Cristina La Rocca, *Pacifico di Verona: Il passato Carolingio nella*

costruzione della memoria urbana, Nuovi studi storici 31 (Rome, 1995), 27–48, with extensive study of the forged charter. Kollautz, "Awaren, Langobarden und Slawen in Noricum und Istrien," 628–29, takes the information for genuine. Damages suffered in Aquileia, of which MGH DD Kar. 1, 214, 285–87, later writes, could perhaps go back to this date; yet the charter's unspecific reference to "perfidia Gothorum et Avarorum" indicates that it talks about earlier damages, not least, by Attila's Huns.

301. *Annales regni Francorum,* a. 788, ed. Kurze, 82–84; *Annales Mettenses priores,* a. 788, ed. Simson, 77; scanter in other sources.

302. Brunner, *Oppositionelle Gruppen,* 74. On Graman, see Störmer, *Früher Adel,* 1:220.

303. A Frankish *dux* Autchar appears in 753 and 760 as an emissary in Italy; an Otachar is listed as a witness in 769 to the foundation of the Innichen monastery. Doubtless the same nobleman sided with Carloman II against Charlemagne, fled to the Lombards, and had to capitulate in Verona. In addition, there is Otkarius, who, according to the *Passio S. Quirini* 5, ed. Bruno Krusch, MGH SS rer. Merov. 3 (Hanover, 1896), 12, founded the monastery at Tegernsee with his brother Adalbert. A branch of the family in Mainz had close connections with the Fulda monastery. Michael Mitterauer, *Karolingische Markgrafen im Südosten,* Archiv für österreichische Geschichte 123 (Graz, 1963), 50–61. The Otakar family also maintained close relations with the family of the prefect of the eastern territories, Gerold, who fell in the Avar campaign in 799; cf. Brunner, *Oppositionelle Gruppen,* 138.

304. Cf. Wolfram, *Die Karolingerzeit in Niederösterreich,* 15–17.

305. Zöllner, "Awarisches Namensgut in Bayern und Österreich," 253. Cf. also Csendes, "Zu den Awarenkriegen unter Karl dem Großen," 93–94; Howorth, "The Avars," 794; Wolfram, *Die Geburt Mitteleuropas,* 187.

306. Alcuin, *Epistula* 6, ed. Dümmler, 31.

307. "Agebatur inter eos de confiniis regnorum suorum, quibus in locis esse deberent": *Annales qui dictuntur Einhardi,* a. 790, ed. Kurze, 87. See Wolfram, *Conversio Bagoariorum,* 256. On the reworking of the royal annals in ca. 800, earlier ascribed to Einhard, cf. Roger Collins, "The 'Reviser' Revised: Another Look at the Alternative Version of the *Annales regni Francorum,*" in *After Rome's Fall: Narrators and Sources of Early Medieval History. Essays Presented to Walter Goffart,* ed. Alexander C. Murray (Toronto, 1998), 191–213; McKitterick, *History and Memory,* 111–19.

308. *Annales regni Francorum,* a. 791, ed. Kurze, 86–90; *Annales Laureshamenses,* a. 791, ed. Pertz, 34; Slavs are mentioned in the Codex Turicensis of the none-too-reliable *Annales Alamannici,* a. 790, ed. Lendi, 164, which nonetheless seems plausible (on this, see Csendes, "Zu den Awarenkriegen unter Karl dem Großen," 94); Bavarians in *Annales qui dictuntur Einhardi,* a. 791, ed. Kurze, 89.

309. *Annales regni Francorum,* a. 791, ed. Kurze, 88. Cf. Abel and Simson, *Jahrbücher,* 2:23. One of Charles's charters, for the monastery of Farfa (MGH DD Kar. 1, 171, 229–30), is dated August 28; the army probably left Regensburg shortly thereafter. Abel and Simson, *Jahrbücher,* 2:17, n. 1; Csendes, "Zu den Awarenkriegen unter Karl dem Großen," 94.

310. *Annales qui dictuntur Einhardi,* a. 791, ed. Kurze, 89; *Annales Laureshamenses,* a. 791, ed. Pertz, 34. That the boats were crewed by Frisians is asserted by the *Annales Fuldenses,* a. 791, ed. Kurze and Haefele, 120. Yet this may be an error; cf. Abel and Simson, *Jahrbücher,* 2:19, n. 1. On the "propinquus regis," see Brunner, *Oppositionelle Gruppen,* 47.

311. *Die Traditionen des Hochstifts Freising,* vol. 1, ed. Theodor Bitterauf (Munich, 1905), no. 142, 146–47; no. 143a, 147–48.

312. Howorth, "The Avars," 795; Csendes, "Zu den Awarenkriegen unter Karl dem Großen," 97–100.

313. *Annales Laureshamenses,* a. 791, ed. Pertz, 34.

314. *Annales qui dictuntur Einhardi,* a. 791, ed. Kurze, 89; *Annales regni Francorum,* a. 791, ed. Kurze, 88.

315. Charlemagne, *Epistula* 20, ed. Dümmler, 528–29.

316. Einhard, *Vita Karoli* 24, ed. Holder-Egger, 28–29.

317. Michael McCormick, "The Liturgy of War," *Viator* 15 (1984): 9; McCormick, *Eternal Victory: Triumphal Rulership in Late Antiquity, Byzantium and the Early Medieval West* (Cambridge, 1986), 353–54; Walter Pohl, "Liturgie di guerra nei regni altomedievali," *Rivista di Storia del Cristianesimo* 5, no. 1 (2008): 29–31.

318. *Die Traditionen des Hochstifts Freising*, ed. Bitterauf, no. 142, 146–47. Störmer, *Früher Adel*, 1:221; Brunner, *Oppositionelle Gruppen*, 63 and 79. The charter is dated September 20; yet this need not mean that the army only left after that date. Obviously the charter was drawn up by a cleric from Freising after his return, because it also notes that the main contenders had returned to hand over the contested church. Also dated to Lorch and the year 791 is Tutilo's endowment for Freising, *Die Traditionen des Hochstifts Freising*, ed. Bitterauf, no. 143a, 147–48. Cf. also no. 141, 146, and no. 139, 145.

319. "Eo anno quo domnus rex Carolus intravit in Hunia": *Die Traditionen des Hochstifts Freising*, ed. Bitterauf, no. 139; similar formula in 141. Möhlenkamp, "Avaria," 45–46.

320. Pippin is mentioned in the *Annales Laureshamenses*, a. 792, ed. Pertz, 34; against the idea of his personal involvement, see James Bruce Ross, "Two Neglected Paladins of Charlemagne: Erich of Friuli and Gerold of Bavaria," *Speculum* 20 (1945): 216. On Duke John of Istria, who is named shortly after 800 on the occasion of the Risano *placitum* (*I placiti del Regnum Italiae*, no. 17, ed. Cesare Manaresi, Fonti per la storia d'Italia 92 [Rome, 1955], 49–56), see Krahwinkler, *Friaul im Frühmittelalter*, 151. The name is not given in the letter. It also remains an assumption that the second *dux* was that of Friuli.

321. By far the most exact account is given by Charlemagne himself in *Epistula* 20, ed. Dümmler, 528.

322. This information in Charlemagne's letter is more credible than that in the *Annales Laureshamenses*, a. 791, ed. Pertz, 34, to the effect that Pippin's army had pushed through Illyria to Pannonia and had devastated the countryside. That only a frontier fortress was captured is also stressed in Deér, "Karl der Grosse," 784; cf. Abel and Simson, *Jahrbücher*, 2:21.

323. Deér, "Karl der Grosse," 784.

324. *Annales qui dictuntur Einhardi*, a. 791, ed. Kurze, 89; *Annales regni Francorum*, a. 791, ed. Kurze, 88 (where there is mention of "in loco Camp" rather than "super Cambum fluvium"). On the localization, see Csendes, "Zu den Awarenkriegen unter Karl dem Großen," 98.

325. "Aut fossas aut aliquem firmitatem sive in montibus seu ad flumina aut in silvis factam habuerunt" (*Annales Laureshamenses*, a. 791, ed. Pertz, 34); "munitiones" (*Annales qui dictuntur Einhardi*, a. 791, ed. Kurze, 89); "firmitates" (*Annales regni Francorum*, a. 791, ed. Kurze, 60); "uualum" (Charlemagne, *Epistula* 20, ed. Dümmler, 528). The terrain was exploited for the construction of ditches and bulwarks. It is not necessary to assume that these were ad hoc fortifications realized since 788; yet the capture of these fortifications was surely not the "major objective" of the campaign, as Charles R. Bowlus, "War and Society in the Carolingian Ostmark," *Austrian History Yearbook* 14 (1978): 10–12, assumes. Even his term "castles" is surely exaggerated. The variety of names suggests that these were rather different forms of defensive structures.

326. Astronomus, *Vita Ludovici imperatoris*, 6, ed. Ernst Tremp, *Thegan, Die Taten Kaiser Ludwigs. Astronomus, Das Leben Kaiser Ludwigs*, MGH SS rer. Germ. 64 (Hanover, 1995), 301.

327. Wolfram, *Die Geburt Mitteleuropas*, 255–56.

328. *Catalogus Episcoporum Mettensium*, ed. Georg Heinrich Pertz, MGH SS 2 (Hanover, 1829), 269: "In loco qui dicitur Asnagahunc Chunisberch." On the amended reading "as haga Huni" and on the localization, see Csendes, "Zu den Awarenkriegen unter Karl dem

Großen," 96. On the question of the *Cumeoberg*, also called in some sources *Chuneberg* after the Huns, and the ancient name *Comagenis*, which was probably taken from a map or an itinerary, see Heinrich Koller, "Der 'Mons Comagenus,'" *MIÖG*71 (1963): 237–45; cf. Wolfram, "Ethnogenesen im frühmittelalterlichen Donau- und Ostalpenraum," 143.

329. Among these, Bishop Sindpert of Regensburg, who already died on September 29: *Annales s. Emmerami maiores*, a. 791, ed. Bresslau, 735; *Annales Laureshamenses*, a. 791, ed. Pertz, 34. Cf. Abel and Simson, *Jahrbücher*, 2:20.

330. *Annales Maximiani*, a. 791, ed. Waitz, 22; *Annales Iuvavenses maximi*, a. 791, ed. Bresslau, 734. Cf. section 8.3.

331. *Annales qui dicuntur Einhardi*, a. 791, ed. Kurze, 91.

332. This point has rarely been noted so far, but see Timothy Newfield, "A Great Carolingian Panzootic: The Probable Extent, Diagnosis and Impact of an Early Ninth-Century Cattle Pestilence," *Argos* 46 (2012): 200–210; Preiser-Kapeller, "The Climate of the Khagan"; I am very grateful to the author for access to his manuscript prior to publication.

333. Gábor Kiss, "Eine vergessene Episode des Awarenfeldzugs von Karl dem Großen 791: Was hat Karl der Große in Savaria gesucht und gefunden?," in Drauschke et al., *Lebenswelten zwischen Archäologie und Geschichte*, 215–22.

334. *Annales Laureshamenses*, a. 791, ed. Pertz, 34; Pippin's campaign against Odilo in 743 purportedly lasted exactly fifty-two days. Cf. *Annales Mettenses priores*, a. 743, ed. Simson, 34.

335. Astronomus, *Vita Ludovici imperatoris*, 6, ed. Tremp, 301, reports that Ludwig and his mother spent the beginning of the winter in Regensburg ("hiemem exegit imminentem") until the army returned. Bishop Angilram died on the return march, so the army had crossed the Vienna Woods by October 26 (see above).

336. Most grandiloquent are the *Annales Laureshamenses*, a. 791, ed. Pertz, 34, according to which the Franks took "spoils without measure and number, as well as captives, men, women, and children, an incalculable multitude." Similar information, albeit in very spare accounts, in most of the other annals. More laconic are the *Royal Frankish Annals* (the *Annales regni Francorum*, a. 791, ed. Kurze, 88, as well as the version in the *Annales qui dicuntur Einhardi*, a. 791, ed. Kurze, 89), which count the two armies' lack of losses as the hallmark of victory.

337. Daim, "Das 7. und 8. Jahrhundert in Niederösterreich," 94. See section 8.1.

338. *Annales Mosellani*, a. 790, ed. I. M. Lappenberg, MGH SS 16 (Hanover, 1859), 498; the text then openly admits: "not entirely subdued."

339. *Annales Guelferbytani*, a. 791, ed. Pertz, 45.

340. Evidence for his planning of the Avar war in *Annales qui dicuntur Einhardi*, a. 792 and 793, ed. Kurze, 93; Einhard, *Vita Karoli* 20, ed. Holder-Egger, 25–26.

341. Brunner, *Oppositionelle Gruppen*, 64.

342. *Annales regni Francorum*, a. 792, ed. Kurze, 60–61; *Annales qui dicuntur Einhardi*, a. 792, ed. Kurze, 93.

343. *Capitulare Aquisgranense* 10, ed. Alfred Boretius, MGH Capit. 1 (Hanover, 1883), 171.

344. *Annales qui dicuntur Einhardi*, a. 793, ed. Kurze, 93; briefer in *Annales regni Francorum*, a. 793, ed. Kurze, 92; *Chronicon Moissiacense*, a. 793, 300; *Annales Mosellani*, a. 793, ed. Lappenberg, 498. Cf. Abel and Simson, *Jahrbücher*, 2:56.

345. On the canal project and its archaeological traces, see Peter Ettel et al., *Großbaustelle 793: Das Kanalprojekt Karls des Großen zwischen Rhein und Donau* (Wiesbaden, 2014).

346. "For they thought that the Avar people must wish to take vengeance on the Christians": *Annales Laureshamenses*, a. 792, ed. Pertz, 35; *Chronicon Moissiacense*, a. 792, 299. Obviously, it was expected that the Avars—"superbissima gens"—could not take lightly the disgrace imposed by Charlemagne's offensive.

347. Abel and Simson, *Jahrbücher*, 2:36–38, with sources.

348. *Annales Laureshamenses*, a. 793, ed. Pertz, 35l; *Chronicon Moissiacense*, a. 793, 300; Abel and Simson, *Jahrbücher*, 2:57.

349. *Annales qui dictuntur Einhardi*, a. 792, ed. Kurze, 91; Einhard, *Vita Karoli* 20, ed. Holder-Egger, 25–26; Abel and Simson, *Jahrbücher*, 2:39–52.

350. *Annales regni Francorum*, a. 794 and 795, ed. Kurze, 94–97.

351. *Annales regni Francorum*, a. 796, ed. Kurze, 98: "civili bello fatigatis inter se principibus . . . chagan sive iugurro intestina clade addictis et a suis occisis"; cf. section 8.2.

352. *Annales regni Francorum*, a. 795, ed. Kurze, 96; *Annales qui dictuntur Einhardi*, a. 795, ed. Kurze, 97; *Annales Maximiani*, a. 795, ed. Waitz, 22; the *Annales Laureshamenses* already recount for the year 795 (ed. Pertz, 36) the personal appearance of the tudun, as does the *Chronicon Moissiacense*, a. 795, 302; Poeta Saxo, a. 795, ed. von Winterfeld, 252.

353. Most of the annals assign this event only to 796 and confuse it in part with the second plundering of the ring in this year. *Annales regni Francorum*, a. 796, ed. Kurze, 98; *Annales qui dictuntur Einhardi*, a. 796, ed. Kurze, 99; *Annales Laureshamenses*, a. 795, ed. Pertz, 36; Poeta Saxo, a. 796, ed. von Winterfeld, 252; *Conversio Bagoariorum et Carantanorum* 6, ed. Lošek, 110–11. The date 795 finds support in the fact that Charlemagne sent a portion of the treasure to the pope in the winter of 795–96. Also dating events to the late autumn of 795: Csendes, "Zu den Awarenkriegen unter Karl dem Großen," 100; Ross, "Two Neglected Paladins of Charlemagne," 217; Szádeczky-Kardoss, *Ein Versuch*, 108; Váczy, "Der fränkische Krieg," 407–10.

354. *Annales regni Francorum*, a. 796, ed. Kurze, 98; *Annales qui dictuntur Einhardi*, a. 796, ed. Kurze, 101; *Annales Laureshamenses*, a. 795, ed. Pertz, 36; *Chronicon Moissiacense*, a. 795, 302; *Annales Fuldenses*, a. 795, ed. Kurze and Haefele, 13; Poeta Saxo, a. 795, ed. von Winterfeld, 252, plus a series of briefer mentions. On the dating before June 796, see Johann Friedrich Böhmer and Engelbert Mühlbacher, *Die Regesten des Kaiserreichs unter den Karolingern 751–918*, vol. 1, 2nd. ed., Regesta Imperii 1 (Innsbruck, 1908) 147.

355. *Annales regni Francorum*, a. 796, ed. Kurze, 98; *Annales qui dictuntur Einhardi*, a. 796, ed. Kurze, 99; *Annales Laureshamenses*, a. 796, ed. Pertz, 37 (mentioning Bavarians and Alamans).

356. *De Pippini regis victoria Avarica*, ed. Dümmler, 116–17.

357. *Annales regni Francorum*, a. 796, ed. Kurze, 98.

358. *Annales qui dictuntur Einhardi*, a. 796, ed. Kurze, 99.

359. *Annales regni Francorum*, a. 796, ed. Kurze, 98–99.

360. *Conventus episcoporum ad ripas Danubii*, no. 20, ed. Werminghoff, 172–76. On the question of the "clerici illiterati" discussed here, see section 6.9.

361. Alcuin, *Epistula* 107, ed. Dümmler, 153–54.

362. Alcuin, *Epistulae* 110, ed. Dümmler, 157–58; 99, 143–44; 112, 162–63; 118, 173–74.

363. Alcuin, *Epistula* 99, ed. Dümmler, 143.

364. On the Avar mission, see Wolfram, *Grenzen und Räume*, 224–26; Bóna, "'Cundpald fecit,'" 307–10; Deér, "Karl der Grosse," 787.

365. Thus Váczy, "Der fränkische Krieg," 416–17; Heinrich Koller, "Die Awarenkriege Karls des Großen," *Mitteilungen der österreichischen Arbeitsgemeinschaft für Ur- und Frühgeschichte* 15 (1964): 8; Endre Tóth, "Geschichte der Oberen Wart im ersten Jahrtausend," in *Die Obere Wart* (Oberwart, 1977), 93; Bóna, "'Cundpald fecit,'" 324. Opposing view in Wolfram, *Grenzen und Räume*, 428 n. 157; Ross, "Two Neglected Paladins of Charlemagne," 218.

366. Similarly in Deér, "Karl der Grosse," 784, who states that "the fate of the Avars was not sealed in bloody battles and devastating military actions but realized in a very slow process of social and economic defeat, checked in important respects by the Frankish royal administration's tolerance for the Avar constitution."

367. *Annales Alamannici*, a. 791, ed. Lendi, 170–71, which speaks of a "proelium" with "Vandali" (Wends). Some scholars assume that the tudun's revolt already began in this year; see, for instance, Deér, "Karl der Grosse," 725; Bóna, "'Cundpald fecit,'" 310. Ross, "Two Neglected Paladins of Charlemagne," 224–25, calls the revolt of 797 an event of "minor importance."

368. *Annales regni Francorum*, a. 797, ed. Kurze, 102.

369. Alcuin, *Epistula* 146, ed. Dümmler, 236.

370. Alcuin, *Epistula* 184, ed. Dümmler, 309.

371. *Annales regni Francorum*, a. 799, ed. Kurze, 108; *Annales Guelferbytani.*, a. 799, ed. Pertz, 45; *Annales Alamannici*, a. 799, ed. Lendi 172; on Gerold, see Störmer, *Früher Adel*, 1:221. On the prefecture of the eastern territories and the "open organizational form" of Frankish Avaria, see Wolfram, *Die Karolingerzeit in Niederösterreich*, 151; Wolfram, *Grenzen und Räume*, 212–18.

372. *Annales regni Francorum*, a. 799, ed. Kurze, 108.

373. Stefan Esders, "Regionale Selbstbehauptung zwischen Byzanz und dem Frankenreich: Die inquisitio der Rechtsgewohnheiten Istriens durch die Sendboten Karls des Großen und Pippins von Italien," in *Eid und Wahrheitssuche: Studien zu rechtlichen Befragungspraktiken in Mittelalter und früher Neuzeit*, ed. Stefan Esders and Thomas Scharff (Frankfurt am Main, 1999), 49–112; Peter Štih, "Istria at the Onset of Frankish Rule, or the Impact of Global Politics on Regional and Local Conditions," in Štih, *The Middle Ages*, 216–21.

374. Wolfram, *Conversio Bagoariorum*, 262 ("a Byzantine intrigue").

375. Paulinus of Aquileia, *Versus Paulini de Herico duce*, ed. Dümmler, 131–33. An extensive analysis is offered in Krahwinkler, *Friaul im Frühmittelalter*, 156–58.

376. Einhard, *Vita Karoli* 13, ed. Holder-Egger, 16. Gerold's epitaph has the date: *Epitaphium Geroldi comitis*, ed. Ernst Dümmler, MGH Poetae 1 (Berlin, 1881), 114; cf. Abel and Simson, *Jahrbücher*, 2:189.

377. *Annales regni Francorum*, a. 799, ed. Kurze, 108. Cf. Ross, "Two Neglected Paladins of Charlemagne," 234.

378. Assumed by Deér, "Karl der Grosse," 725. In favor of this view is the fact that nothing is told of battles in Pannonia in the next two years; on the other hand, there is no mention of the successful suppression of the revolt under the year 799. In all likelihood conditions in the land of the Avars were not fully under control again until 805.

379. *Annales s. Emmerami maiores*, a. 802, ed. Bresslau, 737. These events contradict the assumptions of Ross, "Two Neglected Paladins of Charlemagne," 227, that with the exception of 803 there was little disturbance after 799. But neither can we assume that a single, unified revolt from 799 to 803 made possible a large-scale Avar restoration.

380. Wolfram, *Grenzen und Räume*, 238–39.

381. *Annales mettenses priores*, a. 803, ed. Simson, 90; *Annales regni Francorum*, a. 803, ed. Kurze, 118; Alcuin, *Epistula* 264, ed. Dümmler, 422; Abel and Simson, *Jahrbücher*, 2:297; Wolfram, *Grenzen und Räume*, 239–40.

382. *Suidae Lexicon*, ed. Adler, 1:483, *s.v. Bulgaroi*; Petkov, *Voices of Medieval Bulgaria, Seventh–Fifteenth Century*, 23–24. Cf. section 6.7.

383. Beševliev, *Die protobulgarische Periode*, 235–36; Váczy, "Der fränkische Krieg," 416–17, sees here the decisive factor in the defeat of the Avars, which is surely exaggerated. A more balanced analysis in Sós, *Die slawische Bevölkerung Westungarns*, 12–13. Vasil Gjuzelev, "Bulgarisch-fränkische Beziehungen in der ersten Hälfte des 9. Jahrhunderts," in his *Forschungen zur Geschichte Bulgariens im Mittelalter*, Miscellanea Bulgarica 3 (Vienna, 1986), 140–43, on the other hand, finds the puzzling *Suda* fragment quite insufficient to establish a Bulgar attack. Yet a campaign by Krum against the powerless remaining Avars fits the context of the times quite well. The new Bulgar khan could expect to win an

inexpensive victory and new followers. See also Andreas Schwarcz, "Pannonien im 9. Jahrhundert und die Anfänge der direkten Beziehungen zwischen dem ostfränkischen Reich und den Bulgaren," in Pohl and Reimitz, *Grenze und Differenz*, 99–104.

384. *Annales regni Francorum*, a. 805, ed. Kurze, 119.

385. *Annales regni Francorum*, a. 805, ed. Kurze, 119; *Annales s. Emmerami maiores*, a. 805, ed. Bresslau, 737; Abel and Simson, *Jahrbücher*, 2:320–22. On the title kapkhan, see section 8.2.

386. Kollautz, "Abaria," 11–12; Koller, "Die Awarenkriege Karls des Großen," 8; Herbert Mitscha-Märheim, *Dunkler Jahrhunderte goldene Spuren: Die Völkerwanderungszeit in Österreich* (Vienna, 1963), 162; Deér, "Karl der Grosse," 774–76.

387. Reimitz, "Grenzen und Grenzüberschreitungen," 151.

388. *Annales regni Francorum*, a. 805, ed. Kurze, 120. Cf. Abel and Simson, *Jahrbücher*, 2:322–23; on the difference between kapkhan and khagan, see section 8.2.

389. *Annales Iuvavenses maiores*, a. 805, ed. Bresslau, 738; *Annales s. Emmerami maiores*, a. 805, ed. Bresslau, 739.

390. *Die Traditionen des Hochstiftes Regensburg*, no. 10, ed. Josef Widemann (Munich, 1943), 8–9; Wolfram, *Salzburg, Bayern, Österreich*, 53.

391. I am grateful to Georg Holzer for his expertise and detailed explanations, which he may eventually publish.

392. Zöllner, "Awarisches Namensgut in Bayern und Österreich," 253.

393. I am grateful to Wolfgang Haubrichs for detailed etymological advice (e-mail of April 27, 2017); Fischa(ch) would have to be *Visc(h)-aha* in Old High German.

394. Herbert Mitscha-Märheim, "Nochmals: Awarische Wohnsitze und Regensburger Besitz im Burgenland," *Burgenländische Heimatblätter* 15 (1953), 46–48; Zöllner, "Awarisches Namensgut in Bayern und Österreich," 253.

395. *Antiphonae et responsoria de Haimhrammo*, ed. Bruno Krusch, MGH SS rer. Merov. 4 (Hanover, 1904), 525–26. Maximilian Diesenberger, "Repertories and Strategies in Bavaria: Hagiography," in Pohl and Heydemann, *Strategies of Identification*, 224–27. See section 8.3 for Emmeram.

396. München, Bayerisches Staatsarchiv, Clm. 22053, fol. 62r. Diesenberger, "Repertories and Strategies in Bavaria," 225.

397. Wolfram, *Die Geburt Mitteleuropas*, 265.

398. *Capitulary of Diedenhofen (805)*, c. 7, ed. Boretius, 123. Abel and Simson, *Jahrbücher*, 2:331–33. Cf. also section 6.7.

399. MGH DD Kar. 1, 212, 284; Deér, "Karl der Grosse," 743; Möhlenkamp, "Avaria," 43.

400. *Annales regni Francorum*, a. 811, ed. Kurze, 135; Abel and Simson, *Jahrbücher*, 2:472; Deér, "Karl der Grosse," 778; on the *canizauci*, cf. section 8.2.

401. *Annales regni Francorum*, a. 822, ed. Kurze, 159; on the new order of 828, see Herwig Wolfram, "Der Zeitpunkt der Einführung der Grafschaftsverfassung in Karantanien," in *Siedlung, Macht und Wirtschaft: Festschrift Fritz Posch*, ed. Gerhard Pferschy (Graz, 1981), 313–17.

402. Golden, *Central Asia in World History*, 39–44.

403. Ziemann, *Vom Wandervolk zur Großmacht*, 241–87.

404. Pál Sümegi et al., "Did an Extremely Dry Climate Lead Actually to the Collapse of the Avar Empire in the Carpathian Basin—a Fact or Fiction?," in Bollók, Csiky, and Vida, *Zwischen Byzanz und der Steppe/Between Byzantium and the Steppe*, 469–97.

405. Preiser-Kapeller, "The Climate of the Khagan."

406. Newfield, "A Great Carolingian Panzootic"; see section 8.3.

407. *The Russian Primary Chronicle* 12, trans. Cross and Sherbowitz-Wetzor, 56; see also the new edition by Ostrowski, *Russian Primary Chronicle (Povest' vremennykh let)*. On the text and its portrayal of steppe peoples, see Donald Ostrowski, "Pagan Past and

Christian Identity in the *Primary Chronicle*," in *Historical Narratives and Christian Identity on a European Periphery: Early History Writing in Northern, East-Central, and Eastern Europe (c. 1070–1200)*, ed. Ildar H. Garipzanov (Turnhout 2011), 244–47.

408. *The Russian Primary Chronicle* 11, trans. Cross and Sherbowitz-Wetzor, 55; *Nestorchronik*, Vorgeschichte 12.86, trans. Müller, 11, with n. 5; see ibid., "Zur Einführung," 14–16.

409. *The Letters of Patriarch Nikolaos Mystikos*, in *Patrologia cursus completus, Series Graeca*, ed. J.-P. Migne, vol. 111 (Paris, 1863), col. 81; Moravcsik, *Byzantinoturcica*, 1:455; Zástěrová, "Zu den Quellen," 232–33; Kollautz, "Nestors Quelle," 315.

410. Einhard, *Vita Karoli* 13, ed. Holder-Egger, 15–17.

411. *De Pippini regis victoria Avarica*, ed. Dümmler, 117.

412. Regino of Prum, *Chronicon*, a. 889, ed. Friedrich Kurze, MGH SS rer. Germ. 50 (Hanover, 1890), 131; see Györffy, "Landnahme," 232. Thietmar of Merseburg, *Chronicon* 2.2, ed. Holtzmann, 19; Godfrey of Viterbo, *Pantheon*, ed. Georg Waitz, MGH SS 22 (Hanover, 1872), 133. Cf. Vásáry, "Mediaeval Theories."

413. Dandolo, *Chronicon*, ed. Pastorello, 163.

414. Anonymus (Notary of King Béla), *The Deeds of the Hungarians* 50, ed. Martyn Rady and László Veszprémy, Central European Medieval Texts 5 (Budapest, 2010), 109; Simon de Kéza, *Deeds of the Hungarians* 1.21, ed. Veszprémy and Schaer, 71 (Székely as remnants of "Attila's peoples" or "the Huns"). This has incorrectly been taken as proof of their descent from the Avar "Huns." On the Széklers, see Hansgerd Göckenjan, *Hilfsvölker und Grenzwächter im mittelalterlichen Ungarn*, Quellen und Studien zur Geschichte des östlichen Europas 5 (Wiesbaden, 1972), 114–39, with bibliography. The more intensely debated question of the origins and composition of the Hungarians cannot be pursued here; see Nora Berend, *At the Gate of Christendom: Jews, Muslims and "Pagans" in Medieval Hungary, c. 1000–c. 1300* (Cambridge, 2001); Walter Pohl, "Huns, Avars, Hungarians: Comparative Perspectives Based on Written Evidence," in Bemmann and Schmauder *Complexity of Interaction*, 693–702.

415. *Annales regni Francorum*, a. 822, ed. Kurze, 159.

416. Szádeczky-Kardoss, *Ein Versuch*, 117–20; Wolfram, *Die Geburt Mitteleuropas*, 263–66.

417. Thus, for example, Emperor Louis II in a letter to Emperor Basileius about 871; *Chronicon Salernitanum*, 107, ed. Westerbergh, 111; a papal charter forged by Bishop Pilgrim of Passau in the late tenth century names the tudun; see section 8.2 . See Szádeczky-Kardoss, *Ein Versuch*, 118–20, for additional examples.

418. On a possible Avar survival in the Carpathian Basin, see István Bóna, "Die Verwaltung und die Bevölkerung des karolingischen Pannoniens im Spiegel der zeitgenössischen Quellen," *Miteilungen des Archäologischen Instituts der Ungarischen Akademie der Wissenschaften* 14 (1985): 156–59; Samuel Szádeczky-Kardoss, "Über etliche Quellen der awarischen Geschichte des 9. Jahrhunderts," in Szádeczky-Kardoss, *Avarica*, 146–47; Béla M. Szőke, "The Question of Continuity in the Carpathian Basin of the 9th Century A.D.," *Antaeus* 19–20 (1990–91): 145–57. See also Sós, *Die slawische Bevölkerung Westungarns*, 29–31, with a survey of earlier literature; likewise Péter Tomka, "Le Problème de la survivance des Avars dans la littérature archéologique hongroise," *Acta Orient. Hung.* 24 (1971): 217–52.

419. *Annales Fuldenses*, a. 863, ed. Kurze and Haefele, 56; *Annales Bertiniani*, a. 864, 85–86; Wolfram, *Die Geburt Mitteleuropas*, 286.

420. Regino of Prum, *Chronicon*, a. 889, ed. Kurze, 132.

421. Wolfram, "Ethnogenesen im frühmittelalterlichen Donau- und Ostalpenraum," 141–42.

422. "Populus qui remansit de Hunis et Sclavis in illis partibus": *Conversio Bagoariorum et Carantanorum* 6, ed. Lošek, 112.

423. Fights against "Bemanos, Wilzos et Avaros . . . in regione Winidum": Notker, *Gesta Karoli* 2.12, ed. Haefele, 75.

424. Sós, *Die slawische Bevölkerung Westungarns*, 80.

425. *Annales regni Francorum*, a. 822, ed. Kurze, 159.

426. On the Moravian principality, see Wolfram, *Grenzen und Räume*, 315–21; *Das Grossmährische Reich* (Prague, 1966). The attempts of Charles R. Bowlus, *Franks, Moravians, and Magyars: The Struggle for the Middle Danube, 788–907* (Philadephia, 1995), and Martin Eggers, *Das großmährische Reich: Realität oder Fiktion* (Stuttgart, 1995), to locate the kingdom of the Moravians elsewhere than in Moravia (in Serbia and along the Tisza, respectively) rest on Byzantine sources both temporally and spatially distant and offer no convincing alternative for the interpretation of the impressive archaeological evidence from ninth-century Moravia. See also Jiří Macháček, "Disputes over Great Moravia: Chiefdom or State? The Morava or the Tisza River?," *Early Medieval Europe* 17, no. 3 (2009): 248–67. "Great Moravia": *DAI* 38, 172.

427. Daim et al., *Studien zum Burgwall*; Poláček, "Mikulčice und Awaren."

428. Štefan, "Great Moravia, Statehood and Archaeology," 333–36; Lumír Poláček, "Ninth-Century Mikulčice: The 'Market of the Moravians'? The Archaeological Evidence of Trade in Great Moravia," in Henning, *Post-Roman Towns*, 1:499–524. See section 6.8. For the slave trade through Venice, see McCormick, *Origins of the European Economy*, 759–36, 77.

429. Wolfram, *Grenzen und Räume*, 248–74.

430. Čilinská, "The Development of the Slavs North of the Danube."

431. Ivo Štefan, "'Great' Moravia and the Přemyslid Bohemia from the Point of View of Archaeology," in *The Great Moravian Tradition and Memory of Great Moravia in the Medieval Central and Eastern Europe* (Opava, 2014), 9–36.

432. Wolfram, *Conversio Bagoariorum*; Maddalena Betti, *The Making of Christian Moravia (858–882): Papal Power and Political Reality* (Leiden and Boston, 2014).

433. Anonymus, *Deeds of the Hungarians*, 11.5, ed. Rady and Veszprémy, 33, and 12, 37. Gyula Moravcsik, "Der ungarische Anonymos über die Bulgaren and Griechen," *Revue des Études Sud-Est Européennes* 7 (1969): 167–74; Arnulf Kollautz, "Awaren, Franken und Slawen in Karantanien und Niederpannonien und die fränkische und byzantinische Mission," *Carinthia I* 156 (1966): 266; Beševliev, *Die protobulgarische Periode*, 236.

434. *Suidae Lexicon*, ed. Adler, 1:483–84, *s.v. Bulgaroi*; Beševliev, *Die protobulgarische Periode*, 236; Bóna, "'Cundpald fecit,'" 323–24; Schwarcz, "Pannonien im 9. Jahrhundert."

435. Einhard, *Vita Karoli* 15, ed. Holder-Egger, 17–18.

436. *Annales regni Francorum*, a. 818, ed. Kurze, 149.

437. *Annales regni Francorum*, a. 824, ed. Kurze, 165. On the Franks' Balkan policies, see Vladimir K. Ronin, "The Franks on the Balkans in the Early Ninth Century," *Études Balkaniques* 21 (1985): 39–57; Schwarcz, "Pannonien im 9. Jahrhundert."

438. *Annales regni Francorum*, a. 825, ed. Kurze, 167.

439. *Annales regni Francorum*, a. 826 and 827, ed. Kurze, 168–69 and 173.

440. For a recent balanced assessment of Bulgar presence in the Carpathian Basin, see Miklós Takács, "The Ninth-Century Carpathian Basin on the North-West Edge of the First Bulgarian State: An Overview of Some Hypotheses and Remarks and Their Evaluation," in Bollók, Csiky, and Vida, *Zwischen Byzanz und der Steppe/Between Byzantium and the Steppe*, 501–18.

441. Also arguing this line: Gjuzelev, "Bulgarisch-fränkische Beziehungen," 145–55. On the events, see Beševliev, *Die protobulgarische Periode*, 280 and 284–86.

442. *Fragmentum Vaticanum*, ed. Ivan Dujčev, "La Chronique byzantine de l'an 811," *Medioevo bizantino-slavo* 2 (1968): 435; Scriptor incertus, *Leonis Grammatici Chronographia*, ed. Immanuel Bekker (Bonn, 1842), 347. Two additional, much later attestations

in Gjuzelev, "Bulgarisch-fränkische Beziehungen," 141. See Beševliev, *Die protobulgarische Periode*, 260–61; Runciman, *A History of the First Bulgarian Empire*, 67; Ziemann, *Vom Wandervolk zur Großmacht*, 252 and 255–56 with n. 1266.

443. *Suidae Lexicon*, ed. Adler, 1:484, *s.v. Bulgaroi*. This is clearly topical and reflects Byzantine ideas about moral behavior, see Ziemann, *Vom Wandervolk zur Großmacht*, 285–87, with further bibliography. Cf. also section 6.7.

444. Garam, *Das awarenzeitliche Gräberfeld von Tiszafüred*.

445. Béla M. Szőke, "Chronologischer Grundriss der Denkmäler des 9. Jhs. im Karpatenbecken," *Mitteilungen des Archäologischen Instituts der Ungarischen Akademie der Wissenschaften* 14 (1985): 163.

446. Béla Miklós Szőke, "Westliche Beziehungen des Karpatenbeckens im 9. Jahrhundert," in *Der pannonische Raum um die Jahrtausendwende (vom 9. bis zum 12. Jahrhundert)* (Eisenstadt, 2010), 107–24; on Frankish weapons in the territories east of the Enns, see Szameit, "Slawische Körpergräber."

447. Béla Miklós Szőke, "Mosaburg/Zalavár und Pannonien in der Karolingerzeit," *Antaeus* 31–32 (2010): 9–52.

448. On the archaeology of this region, see in particular Sós, *Die slawische Bevölkerung Westungarns*, 84–86.

449. Bóna, "Ein Vierteljahrhundert," 332; Szőke, "Zur Problematik des Bestattungsritus."

450. Daim, *Das awarische Gräberfeld von Leobersdorf*, 177–78; Daim, "Das 7. und 8. Jahrhundert in Niederösterreich"; Herwig Friesinger, *Die Slawen in Niederösterreich*, Wissenschaftliche Schriftenreihe Niederösterreich 15, 2nd ed. (St. Pölten, 1978), 15; Friesinger, *Die vielen Väter Österreichs*, 116–17; Andreas Lippert, "Awaren nach 800 in Niederösterreich?," *Jahrbuch für Landeskunde von Niederösterreich*, n.s., 38 (1968–70): 145–57.

451. Samuel Szádeczky-Kardoss, "Der Awarensturm im historischen Bewusstsein der Byzantiner des 11–13. Jahrhunderts," in *Actes du XVe congrès international d'études byzantines*, 4:305–14.

452. Moravcsik, *Byzantinoturcica*, 2:302.

453. Widukind of Corvey, *Res Gestae Saxonicae* 1.17–19, ed. Paul Hirsch, MGH SS rer. Germ. 60 (Hanover, 1935), 27–29. He repeatedly calls the Hungarians Avars in the following narrative, as does, for instance, Thietmar of Merseburg, *Chronicon* 1.15, 2.7, 2.9, and passim, ed. Holtzmann, 20–21, 46, 48.

454. E.g. Lampert of Hersfeld, *Annals*, a. 791, ed. Oswald Holder-Egger, MGH SS rer. Germ. 38 (Hanover, 1894), 19.

455. *Österreichische Chronik von den 95 Herrschaften*, 66.149, ed. Josef Seemüller, MGH Dt. Chron. 6 (Hanover, 1909), 62.

456. Notker, *Gesta Karoli* 1.12, ed. Haefele, 75.

Sources

Ado of Vienne, *Chronicon*. Edited by Georg Heinrich Pertz, MGH SS 2, 317–26. Hanover, 1829.

Agathias. *Agathiae Myrinaei Historiarum libri V*. Edited by Rudolf Keydell. CFHB 2. Berlin, 1967.

Agathias. *The Histories*. Translated by Joseph D. Frendo. CFHB 2B. Berlin, 1975.

Agathon. *Epistula* 3. In *Patrologia cursus completus, Series Latina*, ed. J.-P. Migne, 87, cols. 1215–30. Paris, 1863.

Alcuin. *Epistulae*. Edited by Ernst Dümmler, MGH Epp. Karolini aevi 2, 18–481. Berlin, 1895.

Al-Istachri. *Kitab Masalik al-Mamalik*. Edited by Michael J. de Goeje. Leiden, 1870.

Al-Kašgari, Mahmud. *Divan-i Lugat at-Turk (Compendium of the Turkic Dialects)*. Translated by Robert Dankoff with James Kelly. 3 vols. Cambridge, MA, 1982–85.

Ammianus Marcellinus. Edited and translated by John C. Rolfe. Vol. 3. Loeb Classical Library. Cambridge, MA, 1986.

Anania Širkac'i. *Geography*. Translated by Robert H. Hewsen. Wiesbaden, 1992.

Annales Alamannici. Edited by Walter Lendi, *Untersuchungen zur frühalemannischen Annalistik: Die Murbacher Annalen; Mit Edition*, Scrinium Friburgense 1, 146–92. Freiburg/CH, 1971.

Annales Alamannici. Edited by Georg Heinrich Pertz, MGH SS 1, 19–60. Hanover, 1826.

Annales Fuldenses. Edited by Friedrich Kurze and Heinrich Haefele. MGH SS rer. Germ. 7. 2nd ed. Hanover, 1891.

Annales Guelferbytani. Edited by Georg Heinrich Pertz, MGH SS 1, 19–46. Hanover, 1826.

Annales Iuvavenses (maximi, maiores, minores). Edited by Harry Bresslau, MGH SS 30.2, 727–44. Leipzig, 1935.

Annales Laureshamenses. Edited by Georg Heinrich Pertz, MGH SS 1, 19–39. Hanover, 1826.

Annales Maximiani. Edited by Georg Waitz, MGH SS 13, 19–25. Hanover, 1881.

Annales Mettenses priores. Edited by Bernhard Simson, MGH SS rer. Germ. 10, 1–98. Hanover, 1905. Partially translated by Paul Fouracre and Richard A. Gerberding, *Late Merovingian France: History and Hagiography, 640–720*, 350–70. Manchester, 1996.

Annales Mosellani. Edited by I. M. Lappenberg, MGH SS 16, 491–99. Hanover, 1859.

Annales Northumbrani. Edited by Reinhold Pauli, MGH SS 13, 154–56. Hanover, 1881.

Annales regni Francorum inde ab a. 741 usque ad a. 829, qui dicuntur Laurissenses maiores et Einhardi. Edited by Friedrich Kurze, MGH SS rer. Germ. 6. Hanover, 1895.

Annales Sangallenses maiores. Edited by Ildefons von Arx, MGH SS 1, 72–85. Hanover, 1826.

Annales s. Emmerami maiores. Edited by Harry Bresslau, MGH SS 30.2, 732–44. Leipzig, 1934.

Annales Sithienses. Edited by Georg Waitz, MGH SS 13, 34–37. Hanover, 1881.

Annales Xantenses. Edited by Bernhard Simson, MGH SS rer. Germ. 12, 1–33, 34–39. Hanover, 1909.

Anonymus (Notary of King Béla). *The Deeds of the Hungarians*. Edited and translated by Martyn Rady and László Veszprémy. Central European Medieval Texts 5. Budapest, 2010.

Anonymus Ravennatis. *Cosmographia*. Edited by Joseph Schnetz, *Itineraria Romana*, vol. 2, *Ravennatis Anonymi cosmographia et Guidonos geographica*, 1–110. Leipzig, 1940.

Antiphonae et responsoria de Haimhrammo. Edited by Bruno Krusch, MGH SS rer. Merov. 4, 524–26. Hanover, 1904.

Apocalypse of Pseudo-Methodius. Edited by Benjamin Garstad. Cambridge, MA, 2012.

Arbeo of Freising. *Vita Corbiniani*. Edited by Bruno Krusch, MGH SS rer. Germ. 13, 100–234. Hanover, 1920.

Arbeo of Freising. *Vita Haimhrammi episcopi*. Edited by Bruno Krusch, MGH SS rer. Germ. 13, 26–99. Hanover, 1920.

Astronomus. *Vita Ludovici imperatoris*. Edited by Ernst Tremp, *Thegan, Die Taten Kaiser Ludwigs. Astronomus, Das Leben Kaiser Ludwigs*, MGH SS rer. Germ. 64, 279–558. Hanover, 1995.

Aventinus, Johannes. *Annales Boiorum*. Edited by Dagmar Bartoňková, Lubomír Havlík, Zdeněk Masařík, and Radoslav Večerka, *Magnae Moraviae Fontes Historici*, vol. 1, *Annales et chronicae*, 338–76. Brno, 1966.

Bede's Ecclesiastical History of the English People. Edited by Bertram Colgrave and R. A. B. Minors. Oxford, 1969.

"Beschreibung der Nordvölker nach dem *Kitāb al-a'lāq an-nafīsa* des Abū ʿAlī ibn ʿUmar ibn Rusta." German translation by Hansgerd Göckenjan and István Zimonyi, *Orientalische Berichte über die Völker Osteuropas und Zentralasiens im Mittelalter: Die Ğayhānī-Tradition (Ibn Rusta, Gardīzī, Ḥudūd al-ʿĀlam, al-Bakrī und al-Marwazī)*, Veröffentlichungen der Societas Uralo-Altaica 54, 51–94. Wiesbaden, 2001.

Die Byzantinischen Kleinchroniken, vol. 3. Vienna, 1979. Edited by Peter Schreiner.

Capitulare Aquisgranense. Edited by Alfred Boretius, MGH Capit. 1, 170–72. Hanover, 1883.

Capitulary of Diedenhofen (805). Edited by Alfred Boretius, MGH Capit. 1, 122–26. Hanover, 1883.

Carolingian Chronicles: Royal Frankish Annals, and Nithard's Histories. Translated by Bernhard Walter Scholz, with Barbara Rogers. Ann Arbor, 1970.

Cassiodorus. *Chronicon*. Edited by Theodor Mommsen, MGH AA 11, 120–61. Berlin, 1894.

Cassiodorus. *Variae epistulae*. Edited by A. J. Fridh. *Variarum libri XII*. Corpus Christianorum Series Latina 96. Turnhout, 1973.

Cassiodorus. *Variae epistulae*. Edited by Theodor Mommsen. MGH AA 12. Berlin, 1894.

Catalogus Episcoporum Mettensium. Edited by Georg Heinrich Pertz, MGH SS 2, 268–70. Hanover, 1829.

Charlemagne. *Epistulae*. Edited by Ernst Dümmler, MGH Epp. Karolini aevi 2, 494–567. Berlin, 1895.

Chronica Sancti Benedicti Casinensis. Edited by Georg Waitz, MGH SS rer. Langob., 468–89. Berlin, 1878.

Chronicon Benedicti Sancti Andreae. Edited by Georg Heinrich Pertz, MGH SS 3, 695–719. Hanover, 1839.

Chronicon Moissiacense. Edited by Georg Heinrich Pertz, MGH SS 1, 280–313. Hanover, 1826.

Il Chronicon di Sant'Andrea del Soratte e il Libellus de imperatoria potestate in urbe Roma. Edited by Giuseppe Zucchetti. Rome, 1920.

Chronicon Paschale. Edited by Ludwig Dindorf. CSHB. 2 vols. Bonn, 1832.

Chronicon Paschale, 284–628 AD. Translated by Michael Whitby and Mary Whitby. Translated Texts for Historians 7. Liverpool, 1989.

Chronicon Salernitanum. Edited by Ulla Westerbergh. Stockholm, 1956.

Concilium Mantuanum. Edited by Albert Werminghoff, MGH Concilia 2.2, 583–89. Hanover, 1908.

Concilium Universale Constantinopolitanum sub Iustiniano habitum, Acta Conciliorum Oecumenicorum. Edited by Eduard Schwartz. Berlin, 1959.

Constantine Porphyrogenitus. *De administrando imperio.* Edited by Gyula Moravcsik and translated by Romilly James Heald Jenkins. 2nd ed. Vol. 1. Budapest, 1963.

Constantine Porphyrogenitus. *De cerimoniis aulae Byzantinae.* Edited by Johann J. Reiske. 2 vols. Bonn, 1829–30.

Constantine Porphyrogenitus. *De thematibus.* Edited by Agostino Pertusi, *Costantino Porfirogenito de Thematibus: Introduzione, Testo Critico, Commento,* Biblioteca Apostolica Vaticana. Rome, 1952.

Conventus episcoporum ad ripas Danubii. Edited by Albert Werminghoff, MGH Concilia 2.1, 172–76. Hanover, 1906.

Conversio Bagoariorum et Carantanorum. Edited and translated by Fritz Lošek. In *Die Conversio Bagoariorum et Carantanorum und der Brief des Erzbischofs Theotmar von Salzburg,* MGH Studien und Texte 15, 90–135. Hanover, 1997.

Corippus, Flavius. *In laudem Iustinii Augusti Minoris libri IV.* Edited by Josef Partsch. MGH AA 3.2. Berlin, 1879.

Corippus, Flavius. *In laudem Iustinii Augusti Minoris libri IV.* Edited and translated by Averil Cameron. London, 1976.

Corippus, Flavius. *In laudem Iustini Augusti Minoris libri IV.* Edited by Serge Antès. Paris, 1981.

Corpus Inscriptionum Latinarum. Vol. 3, *Inscriptiones Asiae, provinciarum Europae Graecarum, Illyrici Latinae.* Edited by Theodor Mommsen. Berlin, 1873.

The Cosmography of Aethicus Ister. Edited by Michael W. Herren. Turnhout, 2011.

Cronaca di Monemvasia. Edited by Ivan Dujčev. Istituto Siciliano di Studi Bizantini e Neoellenici, Testi e monumenti, Testi 12. Palermo, 1976.

Andrea Danduli Ducis Venetiarum Chronica. 3 vols. Edited by Ester Pastorello. Rerum Italicarum Scriptores, nuova edizione, 12.2. Bologna, 1938.

De Pippini regis victoria Avarica. Edited by Ernst Dümmler, MGH Poetae 1, 116–17. Berlin, 1881.

Einhard. *The Life of Charlemagne.* In *Charlemagne's Courtier: The Complete Einhard,* edited and translated by Paul Edward Dutton, 15–40. Peterborough, 1998.

Einhard. *Vita Karoli Magni.* Edited by Oswald Holder-Egger. MGH SS rer. Germ. 25. Berlin, 1911.

Ennodius. *Panegyricus dictus Theoderici.* Edited by Christian Rohr, *Der Theoderich-Panegyricus des Ennodius,* MGH Studien und Texte 12. Hanover, 1995.

Epistolae Austrasicae. Edited by Wilhelm Gundlach, MGH Epp. Karolini aevi 1, 110–53. Berlin, 1892.

Epistolae Wisigoticae. Edited by Walter Gundlach, MGH Epp. Karolini aevi 1, 658–90. Berlin, 1892.

Epistula Theotmari. Edited by Fritz Lošek. In *Die Conversio Bagoariorum et Carantanorum und der Brief des Erzbischofs Theotmar von Salzburg,* MGH Studien und Texte 15, 138–57. Hanover, 1997.

Epitaphium Geroldi comitis. Edited by Ernst Dümmler, MGH Poetae 1, 114–15. Berlin, 1881.

Eugippius. *Vita Severini.* Edited by Theodor Mommsen. MGH SS rer. Germ. 26. Berlin, 1898.

Evagrius. *The Ecclesiastical History of Euagrios*. Edited by Joseph Bidez and Léon Parmentier. London, 1898; repr. Amsterdam, 1964.

Evagrius. *The Ecclesiastical History of Evagrius Scholasticus*. Translated by Michael Whitby. Translated Texts for Historians 33. Liverpool, 2000.

Fragmentum Vaticanum. Edited by Ivan Dujčev, "La Chronique byzantine de l'an 811." *Medioevo bizantino-slavo* 2 (1968): 425–89.

Fredegar. *Chronicae*. Edited by Bruno Krusch, MGH SS rer. Merov. 2, 18–193. Hanover, 1888.

Fredegar. *The Fourth Book of the Chronicles of Fredegar*. Translated by John Michael Wallace-Hadrill. London, 1960.

Gardīzī. German translation by Hansgerd Göckenjan and István Zimonyi. "Übersetzung von Gardīzī's Abhandlung über die Türkenstämme," in *Orientalische Berichte über die Völker Osteuropas und Zentralasiens im Mittelalter: Die Ğayhānī-Tradition (Ibn Rusta, Gardīzī, Ḥudūd al-ʿĀlam, al-Bakrī und al-Marwazī)*, Veröffentlichungen der Societas Uralo-Altaica 54, 95–190. Wiesbaden, 2001.

Geheime Geschichte der Mongolen. In *Dschingis Khan: Ein Weltreich zu Pferde; Das Buch vom Ursprung der Mongolen*. Translated by Walther Heissig. Cologne, 1985.

Geographi Graeci minores. Vol. 2. Edited and translated by Karl Müller. Scriptorum graecorum bibliotheca 54. Paris, 1861.

George of Pisidia. *Bellum Avaricum*. Edited and translated by Agostino Pertusi. In *Giorgio Piside, Poemi*, vol. 1, *Panegirici epici*, Studia Patristica et Byzantina 7, 176–200. Ettal, 1959.

George of Pisidia. *Restitutio crucis*. Edited by Leo Sternbach, *Wiener Studien* 13 (1891): 4–8.

George the Monk. *Chronicon*. Edited by Karl de Boor. 2 vols. Leipzig, 1904.

Die Gesetze der Langobarden. Edited by Franz Beyerle. Vienna, 1947.

Gesta Dagoberti. Edited by Bruno Krusch, MGH SS rer. Merov. 2, 396–425. Hanover, 1888.

Gesta Hrodberti. See *Vita Hrodperti*.

Godfrey of Viterbo. *Pantheon*. Edited by Georg Waitz, MGH SS 22, 107–307. Hanover, 1872.

Gregory of Tours. *Decem libri historiarum*. Edited by Bruno Krusch and Wilhelm Levison. MGH SS rer. Merov. 1.1. 1937; repr. Hanover, 1965.

Gregory of Tours. *The History of the Franks*. Translated by Lewis Thorpe. 1974; repr. London, 1986.

Gregory the Great. *Registrum epistularum*. Edited by Paul Ewald and Ludwig Hartmann. MGH Epp. 1–2. Berlin, 1891–99.

Gregory the Great. *Registrum epistolarum*. Edited by Dag Norberg. 2 vols. Corpus Christianorum Series Latina 140–140a. Turnhout, 1982.

Heraclius. *Histoire d'Héraclius par l'évêque Sébéos*. Translated by Frederic Macler. Paris, 1904.

Herodotus. *Historiae*. Edited by A. D. Godley. Loeb Classical Series. Vol. 2. Cambridge, MA, 1982.

Historia Langobardorum Codicis Gothani. Edited by Georg Waitz, MGH SS rer. Langob.. Hanover, 1878.

Ibn Fadlān, Ahmad. *Mission to the Volga*. Edited and translated by James E. Montgomery, in *Two Arabic Travel Books*, edited by Philip F. Kennedy and Shawkat M. Toorawa, 165–260. New York, 2004.

Ibn Fadlān. Translated by Paul Lunde and Caroline Stone, *Ibn Fadlān and the Land of Darkness*, Penguin Classics. London, 2012.

Ibn Rusta, *Kitab al-Alaq an-Nafisa*. Edited by Michael J. de Goeje. Leiden, 1892.

I placiti del Regnum Italiae. Edited by Cesare Manaresi. Fonti per la storia d'Italia 92. Rome, 1955.

Isidore of Seville. *Chronica*. Edited by José Carlos Martín. Corpus Christianorum Series Latina 112. Turnhout, 2003.

Isidore of Seville. *Chronica Maiora: Additamenta*. Edited by Theodor Mommsen, MGH AA 11, 489–94. Berlin 1894.

Isidore of Seville. *Chronicon*. Edited by Theodor Mommsen, MGH AA 11, 391–488. Berlin, 1894.

Isidore of Seville. *Etymologiae*. Edited by Wallace M. Lindsay. Oxford, 1911.

Isidore of Seville. *History of the Kings of the Goths*. Translated by Kenneth Baxter Wolf, *Conquerors and Chroniclers of Early Medieval Spain*, 2nd ed., Translated Texts for Historians 9, 79–109. Liverpool, 1999.

John of Antioch. *Excerpta de insidiis*. Edited by Carl de Boor, *Excerpta Historica iussu Imp. Constantini Porphyrogeniti confecta*. Vol. 1, pt. 3. Berlin, 1905.

John of Antioch. *Fragmenta ex historia chronica*. Edited by Umberto Roberto. Berlin, 2005.

John of Biclaro. *Chronica*. Edited by Theodor Mommsen, MGH AA 11, 207–20. Berlin, 1894; repr., Munich, 1981.

John of Biclaro. *Chronica*. Translated by Kenneth Baxter Wolf. In *Conquerors and Chroniclers of Early Medieval Spain*, 2nd ed., Translated Texts for Historians 9, 57–77. Liverpool, 1999.

John of Ephesus. *Historiae Ecclesiasticae pars tertia*. Edited by Ernest W. Brooks. CSCO 106, Scriptores Syri 55. Louvain, 1964.

John of Ephesus. *The Third Part of the Ecclesiastical History of John, Bishop of Ephesus*. Translated by Robert Payne-Smith. Oxford, 1860.

John of Nikiu. *Chronicle*. Edited with French translation by Hermann Zotenberg. Paris, 1883.

John of Nikiu. *Chronicle*. Edited and translated by R. H. Charles, *The Chronicle of John, Bishop of Nikiu: Translated from Zotenberg's Ethiopic Text*. London, 1916; repr. Merchantville, NJ, 2007.

John of Plano Carpini. *Historia Mongalorum*. Edited by Enrico Menestò. Translated by Maria Christina Lungarotti. Spoleto, 1989.

John of Thurocz. *Chronica Hungarorum*. Edited by Elisabeth Galántai and Gyula Kristó. Budapest, 1985.

John the Deacon. *Istoria Veneticorum*. Edited by Andrea Berto. Bologna, 1999.

John the Lydian. *De magistratibus populi Romani*. Edited by Richard Wuensch. 1903; repr. Stuttgart, 1967.

Jonas of Bobbio. *Life of Columbanus*. Translated by Alexander O'Hara and Ian Wood. Translated Texts for Historians 64. Liverpool, 2017.

Jordanes. *Getica*. Edited by Theodor Mommsen, MGH AA 5.1, 53–138. Berlin, 1882.

Jordanes. *Historia Romana*. Edited by Theodor Mommsen, MGH AA 5.1, 1–52. Berlin, 1882.

Lampert of Hersfeld. *Annals*. Edited by Oswald Holder-Egger, MGH SS rer. Germ. 38, 1–304. Hanover, 1894.

Liber pontificalis. Edited by Louis Duchesne, *Le Liber pontificalis: texte, introduction et commentaire*, vol. 1. Rome, 1981.

Liber Pontificalis. Translated by Raymond Davis, *The Book of Pontiffs: The Ancient Biographies of the First Ninety Roman Bishops to AD 715*, Translated Texts for Historians 6. Liverpool, 2000.

Liber pontificalis nella recensione di Pietro Guglielmo OSB e del card. Pandolfo glossato da Pietro Bohier OSB, vescovo di Orvieto: Introduzione—Testo—Indici. Edited by Ulderico Přerovský. Vol. 2. Studia Gratiana 22. Rome, 1978.

Liudprand of Cremona. *Antapodosis*. Translated by Paolo Squatriti, *The Complete Works of Liudprand of Cremona*, Medieval Texts in Translation, 238–81. Washington, DC, 2007.

The London Manuscript of Nicephorus' "Breviarium." Edited by Louis Orosz. Budapest, 1948.

Magnae Moraviae Fontes Historici. Edited by Dagmar Bartoňková, Lubomír Havlík, Ivan Hrbek, Jaroslav Ludvíkovský, and Radoslav Večerka. Vol. 3, *Diplomata, epistolae, textus historici varii*. Brno, 1969.

Malalas, John. *The Chronicle of John Malalas*. Translated by Elizabeth Jeffreys, Michael Jeffreys, and Roger Scott, with Brian Croke. Melbourne, 1986.

Malalas, John. *Chronographia*. Edited by Ludwig Dindorf. CSHB. Bonn, 1831.

Marcellinus Comes. *Chronicon*. Edited by Theodor Mommsen, MGH AA 11, 60–108. Berlin 1894.

Marius of Avenches. *Chronica*. Edited by Theodor Mommsen, MGH AA 11, 225–39. Berlin, 1894.

Maurice. *Strategicon*. Edited by George T. Dennis and Ernst Gamillscheg. CFHB 17. Vienna, 1981.

Maurice's Strategikon: Handbook of Byzantine Military Strategy. Translated by George T. Dennis. Philadelphia, 1984.

Menander. Edited and translated by Roger C. Blockley, *The History of Menander the Guardsman*. Liverpool, 1985.

Menander. Edited by Ludwig August Dindorf, *Historici Graeci minores*, vol. 2. Bonn, 1871.

Michael the Syrian. *Chronique de Michel le Syrien: Patriarche jacobite d'Antioche (1166–1199)*. Edited and translated by Jean Baptiste Chabot. Paris, 1899–1910; repr. Brussels, 1963.

Miracula Demetrii. Edited and translated by Paul Lemerle, *Les Plus Anciens Recueils des miracles de Saint Démétrius et la pénétration des Slaves dans les Balkans*, vol. 1. Paris, 1979.

Nestor Chronicle. Translated by Samuel Hazzard Cross and Olgerd P. Sherbowitz-Wetzor, *The Russian Primary Chronicle: Laurentian Text*. Cambridge, MA, 1953. German translation by Ludolf Müller, *Die Nestorchronik: Handbuch zur Nestorchronik*, vol. 4 (Munich, 2001).

Nestor Chronicle. Edited by Donald Ostrowski. *Russian Primary Chronicle (Povest' vremennykh let)*. Cambridge, MA, 2004.

Nicephorus. *Short History*. Edited and translated by Cyril Mango. Washington, DC, 1990.

Nicholas I. *Epistolae*. Edited by Ernst Dümmler, MGH Epp. Karolini aevi 4, 568–600. Berlin, 1925.

Nikolaos Mystikos. *The Letters of Patriarch Nikolaos Mystikos*. In *Patrologia cursus completus, Series Graeca*, ed. J.-P. Migne, 111, cols. 9–293. Paris, 1863.

Notitia ps.-Epiphanii. Edited by Heinrich Gelzer, *Ungedruckte und ungenügend veröffentlichte Texte der Notitiae Episcopatuum*, Abhandlungen der Bayerischen Akademie der Wissenschaften, phil.-hist. Kl. 21.3, 529–641. Munich, 1900.

Notker. *Gesta Karoli Magni*. Edited by Heinrich Haefele. MGH SS rer. Germ. n.s. 12. Hanover, 1959.

Orhon Yazıtları. Edited by Erhan Aydın. Konya, 2012.

The Orkhon inscriptions, http://bitig.org/?lang=e&mod=1&tid=1.

Orosius. *Seven Books of History against the Pagans*. Translated by A.T. Fear. Translated Texts for Historians 54. Liverpool, 2010.

The Old English Orosius. Edited by Janet Bately. Early English Text Society, Supplementary Series 8. Oxford, 1980.

Österreichische Chronik von den 95 Herrschaften. Edited by Josef Seemüller, MGH Dt. Chron. 6, 1–223. Hanover, 1909.

Otto of Freising. *Gesta Friderici.* Edited by Georg Waitz and Bernhard von Simson. MGH SS rer. Germ. 46. Hanover, 1912.

Passio S. Quirini. Edited by Bruno Krusch, MGH SS rer. Merov. 3, 8–20. Hanover, 1896.

Paulinus of Aquileia. *Versus Paulino de Herico duce.* Edited by Ernst Dümmler, MGH Poetae 1, 131–33. Berlin, 1881.

Pauli Diaconi continuatio tertia. Edited by Ludwig Bethmann and Georg Waitz, MGH SS rer. Langob., 203–15. Hanover, 1878.

Paul the Deacon. *Historia Langobardorum.* Edited by Georg Waitz. MGH SS rer. Germ. 48. Hanover, 1878.

Paul the Deacon. *Storia dei Longobardi.* Edited by Lidia Capo. Milan, 1992.

Poeta Saxo. Edited by Paul von Winterfeld. MGH Poetae 4.1. Berlin, 1899.

Priscus Panites. *Fragmenta.* Edited and translated by Roger C. Blockley, *The Fragmentary Classicising Historians of the Later Roman Empire,* 2:222–401. Cambridge, 1983.

Procopius. *The Anecdota or Secret History.* Edited and translated by Henry B. Dewing, *Procopius in Seven Volumes,* vol. 6. Cambridge, MA, 1935.

Procopius. *History of the Wars (Bella).* Edited and translated by Henry B. Dewing, *Procopius in Seven Volumes,* vols. 1–5. Cambridge, MA, 1914–28.

Procopius. *History of the Wars, Secret History, and Buildings.* Excerpts edited and translated by Averil Cameron. New York, 1967.

Procopius. *On Buildings (De aedificiis).* Edited and translated by Henry B. Dewing, *Procopius in Seven Volumes,* vol. 7. Cambridge, MA, 1940.

Pseudo-Caesarius. *Erotapokriseis.* Edited by Rudolf Riedinger. Munich, 1969.

Pseudo-Movses Chorenac'i. *Géographie.* Edited and translated by Arsene Soukry. Venice, 1881.

Pseudo-Zachariah Rhetor. *The Chronicle of Pseudo-Zachariah Rhetor: Church and War in Late Antiquity.* Translated by Geoffrey Greatrex, Robert R. Phenix and Cornelia B. Horn. Translated Texts for Historians 55. Liverpool, 2011.

Pseudo-Zachariah Rhetor. *Historia ecclesiastica Zachariae rhetori vulgo adscripta.* Edited by Ernest W. Brooks. CSCO 83–84/38–39. Paris, 1919–24.

Rašīd-ad-Dīn Faḍlallāh. *Rashiduddin Fazlullah's Jami'u't-tawarikh: A Compendium of Chronicles; a History of the Mongols.* Vol. 1, *Ǧāmi' al-Tawārīḫ.* Translated by Wheeler M. Thackston. Sources of Oriental Languages and Literature 45. Cambridge, MA, 1998.

Regino of Prum. *Chronicon.* Edited by Friedrich Kurze. MGH SS rer. Germ. 50. Hanover, 1890.

Russian Primary Chronicle (Povest' vremmennych let). See *Nestor Chronicle.*

Sächsische Weltchronik. Edited by Ludwig Weiland, MGH Dt. Chron. 2.1, 65–258. Hanover, 1876.

Sacrorum conciliorum nova et amplissima collectio. Edited by Joannes D. Mansi. Paris, 1901.

Scriptor incertus. Leonis Grammatici Chronographia. Edited by Immanuel Bekker. Bonn, 1842.

Sebeos. *The Armenian History attributed to Sebeos.* Translated by R. W. Thomson. Historical Commentary by J. Howard-Johnston. Translated Texts for Historians 31. 2 vols. Liverpool, 1999.

Sebeos. *Histoire d'Héraclius par l'évêque Sébéos: Traduite de l'arménien et annotée.* Translated by Frederic Macler. Paris, 1904.

The Secret History of the Mongols: A Mongolian Epic Chronicle of the Thirteenth Century. Edited by Igor de Rachewiltz. 3 vols. Leiden, 2004–13.

Simon de Kéza. *The Deeds of the Hungarians*. Edited by László Veszprémy and Frank Schaer. Central European Medieval Texts 1. Budapest, 1999.

Stephanos Byzantios. *Ethnika*. Edited by Margarethe Billerbeck and Arlette Neumann-Hartmann. Corpus Fontium Historiae Byzantinae 42. 5 vols. Berlin, 2006–17.

Stephanus. *Vita S. Wilfridi*. Edited by Wilhelm Levison, MGH SS rer. Merov. 6, 193–263. Hanover, 1913.

Suidae Lexicon. Edited by Ada Adler. 5 vols. Lexicographi Graeci 1.1–5. Leipzig, 1925–38; repr. 1967–71.

Synesius of Cyrene. *The Essays and Hymns of Synesius of Cyrene*. Edited and translated by Augustine Fitzgerald. 2 vols. London, 1930.

Testamentum Amandi. Edited by Bruno Krusch, MGH SS rer. Merov. 5, 483–85. Hanover, 1910.

Theodore Syncellus. *Homilia de Obsidione Avarica Constantinopolis*. Edited by Leo Sternbach, Analecta Avarica. Cracow, 1900. Translated by Roger Pearse as *Homily on the Siege of Constantinople in 626 AD* (Ipswich, 2007), http://www.tertullian.org/fathers/theodore_syncellus_01_homily.htm.

Theodore Syncellus. *Traduction et commentaire de l'homélie écrite probablement par Théodore le Syncelle sur le siège de Constantinople en 626*. Edited and translated by Ferenc Makk. Acta Universitatis de Attila József Nominatae, Acta Antiqua et Archaeologica 19. Szeged, 1975.

Theodulf of Orléans, *Carmina*. Edited by Ernst Dümmler, MGH Poetae 1, 437–581. Berlin, 1881.

Theophanes Byzantios. *Fragmentum*. Edited by Karl Müller. Fragmenta historicorum graecorum 4. Paris, 1885.

Theophanes Confessor. *Chronographia*. Edited by Karl de Boor. Leipzig, 1883.

Theophanes Confessor. *Chronographia*. Translated by Cyril Mango and Roger Scott, *The Chronicle of Theophanes Confessor: Byzantine and Near Eastern History AD 284–813*. Oxford, 1997.

Theophanes Continuatus: Ioannes Cameniata, Symeon Magister, Georgius Monachus. Edited by Immanuel Bekker. Corpus Scriptorum Historiae Byzantinae 48. Bonn, 1838.

Theophylact Simocatta. *Theophylacti Simocattae Historiae*. Edited by Karl de Boor. Leipzig, 1887.

Theophylact Simocatta. *The History of Theophylact Simocatta: An English Translation with Introduction and Notes*. Translated by Michael Whitby and Mary Whitby. Oxford, 1986.

Theophylaktos Simokates. *Geschichte*. Translated by Peter Schreiner. Stuttgart, 1985.

Thietmar of Merseburg, *Chronicon*. Edited by Robert Holtzmann. MGH SS rer. Germ. n.s. 9. Hanover, 1935.

Thomas Archidiaconus, *Historia Salonitana*. Edited by Damir Karbić, Mirjana Matijević Sokol, and James Ross Sweeney. Central European Medieval Texts. Budapest, 2006.

Thomas Presbyter. Edited by Ernest W. Brooks and Jean Baptiste Chabot, *Chronica minora*, vol. 2, CSCO, 77–154, 63–109. Louvain, 1907.

Die Traditionen des Hochstifts Freising. Vol 1. Edited by Theodor Bitterauf. Munich, 1905.

Die Traditionen des Hochstiftes Regensburg. Edited by Josef Widemann. Munich, 1943.

Urkundenbuch des Burgenlandes, No. 1. Edited by Hans Wagner. Vienna, 1955.

Die Urkunden Heinrichs IV. Pt. 2, *1077–1106*. Edited by Dietrich von Gladiss und Alfred Gawlik. MGH Diplomata regum et imperatorum Germaniae 6.2. Hanover, 2001.

Die Urkunden Konrad I., Heinrich I. und Otto I. Edited by Theodor Sickel. MGH Diplomata regum et imperatorum Germaniae 1. Hanover, 1879–84.

Die Urkunden Ludwigs des Deutschen, Karlmanns und Ludwigs des Jüngeren (Ludowici Germanici, Karlomanni, Ludowici Iunioris Diplomata). Edited by Paul Kehr. MGH Diplomata regum Germaniae ex stirpe Karolinorum 1. Hanover, 1932–34; repr. 1980.

Die Urkunden Ludwigs des Frommen. Edited by Theo Kölzer. 3 vols. MGH DD Kar. 2. Wiesbaden, 2016.

Die Urkunden Pippins, Karlmanns und Karls des Großen (Pippini, Carlomanni, Caroli Magni Diplomata). Edited by Engelbert Mühlbacher with the assistance of Alfons Dopsch, Johann Lechner, and Michael Tangl. MGH DD Kar. 1. Hanover, 1906.

Utrecht Psalter. The Annotated Utrecht Psalter. http://psalter.library.uu.nl/.

Versus Martini Dvmiensis episcopi in Basilica. Edited by Rudolf Peiper, MGH AA 6.2, 194–96. Berlin, 1883.

Victor of Tunnuna. *Chronica*. Edited by Antonio Placanica, *Vittore de Tunnuna, Chronica: Chiesa e imperio nell'età di Giustiniano*. Florence, 1997.

Vita Amandi 1. Edited by Bruno Krusch, MGH SS rer. Merov. 5, 428–49. Hanover, 1910.

Vita Hrodperti. Edited by Wilhelm Levison, MGH SS rer. Merov. 6, 140–62. Hanover, 1913.

Vita Willibaldi. Edited by Oswald Holder-Egger, MGH SS 15.1, 86–106. Stuttgart, 1887.

Widsith. Edited by Kemp Malone. Copenhagen, 1962.

Widukind of Corvey. *Res Gestae Saxonicae*. Edited by Paul Hirsch. MGH SS rer. Germ. 60. Hanover, 1935.

Yusuf Has Hâcib. *Kutadgu Bilik*. Vol 2, *Tercüme*. Edited by Reşit Rahmeti Arat. Ankara, 1959.

Yusuf Khass Hajib. *Wisdom of Royal Glory (Kutadgu Bilig): A Turko-Islamic Mirror for Princes*. Translated by Robert Dankoff. Chicago, 1983.

Zonaras, John. *Epitoma Historiarum*. Edited by Theodor Büttner-Wobst. Vol. 3. Corpus scriptorum historiae Byzantinae 50. Bonn, 1897.

Bibliography

Abel, Sigurd, and Bernhard Simson. *Jahrbücher des Fränkischen Reiches unter Karl dem Großen.* 2 vols. 2nd ed. Leipzig 1883–88.

Abstracts of Short Papers, the 17th International Byzantine Conference, Dumbarton Oaks/ Georgetown University, Washington, D.C., August 3–8, 1986. New York, 1986.

Actes du XVe congrès international d'études byzantines, Athènes, septembre 1976. Vol. 4, *Histoire, communications.* Athens, 1980.

Adelson, Howard L. *Light Weight Solidi and Byzantine Trade during the Sixth and Seventh Centuries.* New York, 1957.

Adler, Horst. "Die Langobarden in Niederösterreich." In *Germanen, Awaren, Slawen in Niederösterreich: Das erste Jahrtausend nach Christus,* Katalog der Ausstellung des Niederösterreichischen Landesmuseums, 73–82. Vienna, 1977.

Ahrweiler, Hélène. *Byzance et la mer.* Paris, 1966.

Airlie, Stuart. "Narratives of Triumph and Rituals of Submission: Charlemagne's Mastering of Bavaria." *Transactions of the Royal Historical Society,* 6th ser., 9 (1999): 93–119.

Aladzhov, Andrey. "The Final Stage in the Development of the Early Byzantine Towns on the Lower Danube." In Schwarcz, Soustal, and Tcholakova, *Der Donaulimes in der Spätantike,* 259–78.

Albrecht, Stefan. "Die Inschriften des Goldschatzes von Nagyszentmiklós/Sânnicolau Mare im byzantinischen Kontext." In Daim et al., *Der Goldschatz,* 135–54.

Alföldi, András. "A kettős királysag a nomádknál." In *Károlyi Árpád-Emlekkönyv születese nyolcvanadik fordulojänak ünnepere,* 28–39. Budapest, 1933.

Alföldi, Andreas. "Zur historischen Bestimmung der Awarenfunde." *Eurasia Septentrionalis Antiqua* 9 (1934): 285–307.

Algazi, Gadi. "Introduction: Doing Things with Gifts." In Algazi, Groebner, and Jussen, *Negotiating the Gift,* 9–27.

Algazi, Gadi, Valentin Groebner, and Bernhard Jussen, eds. *Negotiating the Gift: Pre-Modern Figurations of Exchange.* Göttingen, 2003.

Allen, Pauline. *Evagrius Scholasticus, the Church Historian.* Louvain, 1981.

Allen, Pauline. "A New Date for the Last Recorded Events in John of Ephesus' Historia Ecclesiastica." *Orientalia Lovanensia Periodica* 10 (1979): 251–54.

Altheim, Franz, ed. *Geschichte der Hunnen.* 5 vols. Baden-Baden, 1959–62.

Altheim, Franz, ed. *Historia Mundi: Ein Handbuch der Weltgeschichte in zehn Bänden.* Vol. 5, *Frühes Mittelalter.* Bern, 1956.

Amory, Patrick. *People and Identity in Ostrogothic Italy, 489–554.* Cambridge, 1997.

Andersen, Henning. "On SLOVĚNE and the History of Slavic Patrials." *Scando-Slavica* 63, no. 1 (2017): 3–42.

Anderson, Perry. *Passages from Antiquity to Feudalism.* London, 1975.

Angelov, Dimităr, and Dimităr Ovčarov. "Slawen, Protobulgaren und das Volk der Bulgaren." In Herrmann, *Welt der Slawen,* 57–80.

Angelova, Stefka, and Ivan Bucharov. "Durostorum in Late Antiquity (Fourth to Seventh Centuries)." In Henning, *Post-Roman Towns,* 2:61–88.

Angiò, Francesca. "Divinità pagane e sacrifici umani nella Vita di San Pancrazio di Taormina." *Bollettino della Badia Greca di Grottaferrata*, n.s., 52 (1998): 56–76.

Anton, Daniel-Călin. "Ethnische und chronologische Verhältnisse im Gräberfeld Nr. 3 von Brateiu, Siebenbürgen." *Dacia* 59 (2015): 153–76.

Archäologisches Institut der Slowakischen Akademie der Wissenschaften, ed. *Interaktionen der mitteleuropäischen Slawen und anderen Ethnika im 6.–10. Jahrhundert: Symposium Nové Vozokany 3.–7. Oktober 1983*. Nitra, 1984.

Arnim, Bernd von. "Avarisches." *Zeitschrift für slavische Philologie* 9 (1932): 403–6.

Artamonov, Michail. *Istorija Hazar* [The history of the Khazars]. Leningrad, 1962.

Askarov, Ali Asghar, Vitali Volkov, and Namsraïn Ser-Odjav. "Pastoral and Nomadic Tribes at the Beginning of the First Millennium B.C." In *History of Civilizations of Central Asia*. Vol. 1, *The Dawn of Civilisation: Earliest Times to 700 B.C.*, edited by Ahmad Hasan Dani and Vadim Mikhaïlovich Masson, 459–75. Paris, 1992.

Atwood, Christopher. "The Qai, the Khongai, and the Names of the Xiōngnú." *International Journal of Eurasian Studies* 2 (2015): 35–63.

Ausgrabungen Goldene Stiege. Mödling, 1977. Exhibition catalog.

Aussaresses, François. *L'armée byzantine à la fin du VIe siècle d'après le Strategicon de l'Empereur Maurice*. Bordeaux, 1909.

Avenarius, Alexander. *Die Awaren in Europa*. Amsterdam, 1974.

Avenarius, Alexander. "Die Awaren und die Slawen in den Miracula Sancti Demetrii." *Byzantina* 5 (1973): 11–27.

Avenarius, Alexander. "Die Konsolidierung des Awarenkhaganats und Byzanz im 7. Jahrhundert." In *Festschrift J. E. Karayannopoulos*, special issue, *Byzantina* 13, no. 2 (1985): 1021–32.

Avenarius, Alexander. "Struktur und Organisation der Steppenvölker." In *Popoli delle steppe*, 1:125–74.

Avenarius, Alexander. "Zur Problematik der awarisch-slawischen Beziehungen an der unteren Donau im 6.–7. Jh." *Studia Historica Slovaca* 7 (1974): 11–37.

Awaren in Europa: Schätze eines asiatischen Reitervolkes, 6.–8. Jh. Exhibition catalog. Frankfurt am Main, 1985.

Bachrach, Bernard S. "Charles Martel, Mounted Shock Combat, the Stirrup, and Feudalism." *Studies in Medieval and Renaissance History* 7 (1970): 47–75.

Bajkai, Rozália. "The Latest Findings of the Research of Avar Age Settlements in the Region of Hajdúság." *Ziridava* 29 (2015): 227–54.

Balás, Vilmos. "Die Erdwälle der ungarischen Tiefebene." *Acta Arch. Hung.* 15 (1963): 309–36.

Balász, János. "Elementi orientali dello sciamanismo ungherese." In *Popoli delle steppe*, 2:649–76.

Bálint, Csanád. "Antwortschreiben an Péter Somogyi." *Antaeus* 29–30 (2008): 395–401.

Bálint, Csanád. *Die Archäologie der Steppe: Steppenvölker zwischen Wolga und Donau vom 6. bis zum 9. Jahrhundert*. Vienna, 1988.

Bálint, Csanád. "Avar Goldsmiths' Work from the Perspective of Cultural History." In Entwistle and Adams, *Intelligible Beauty*, 146–60.

Bálint, Csanád. *The Avars, Byzantium and Italy*. Forthcoming.

Bálint, Csanád. *Die awarenzeitliche Siedlung von Eperjes (Komitat Csongrád)*. Budapest, 1991.

Bálint, Csanád. "Der Beginn der Mittelawarenzeit und die Einwanderung Kubers." *Antaeus* 29–30 (2008): 29–62.

Bálint, Csanád. "Byzantinisches zur Herkunftsfrage des vielteiligen Gürtels." In Bálint, *Kontakte zwischen Iran*, 99–162.

Bálint, Csanád. "A Contribution to Research on Ethnicity: A View from and on the East." In Pohl and Mehofer, *Archaeology of Identity/Archäologie der Identität*, 145–82.

Bálint, Csanád. "Einige Fragen des Dirhem-Verkehrs in Europa." *Acta Arch. Hung.* 33 (1981): 105–31.

Bálint, Csanád. "Kontakte zwischen Byzanz, Iran und der Steppe: Das Grab von Üč Tepe (Azerbaidžan) und der beschlagverzierte Gürtel im 6. und 7. Jahrhundert." In Daim, *Awarenforschungen*, 1:309–496.

Bálint, Csanád, ed. *Kontakte zwischen Iran, Byzanz und der Steppe im 6.–7. Jahrhundert.* Naples, 2000.

Bálint, Csanád. "On 'Orient Preference' in the Archaeology of the Avars, Protobulgars and Ancient Hungarians." In Henning, *Post-Roman Towns*, 1:545–67.

Bálint, Csanád. "Probleme der archäologischen Forschung zur awarischen Landnahme." In *Ausgewählte Probleme europäischer Landnahmen des Früh- und Hochmittelalter: methodische Grundlagendiskussion im Grenzbereich zwischen Archäologie und Geschichte*, edited by Michael Müller and Reinhard Schneider, 195–274. Sigmaringen, 1993.

Bálint, Csanád. *Der Schatz von Nagyszentmiklós: archäologische Studien zur frühmittelalterlichen Metallgefäßkunst des Orients, Byzanz' und der Steppe.* Budapest, 2010.

Bálint, Csanád. "A Short Essay on the Nagyszentmiklós Treasure." In Kovács, *The Gold of the Avars*, 57–80.

Bálint, Csanád. "Some Archaeological Addenda to P. Golden's *Khazar Studies*." Review of *Khazar Studies: An Historic-Philological Inquiry into the Origins of the Khazars*, by Peter B. Golden. *Acta Orient. Hung.* 35 (1981): 397–422.

Bálint, Csanád. "Über die Datierung der osteuropäischen Steppenfunde des frühen Mittelalters (Schwierigkeiten und Möglichkeiten)." *Mitteilungen des Archäologischen Instituts der Ungarischen Akademie der Wissenschaften* 14 (1985): 137–47.

Bálint, Csanád. "Über einige östliche Beziehungen der Frühawarenzeit (568–ca. 670–680)." *Mitteilungen des Archäologischen Instituts der Ungarischen Akademie der Wissenschaften* 10/11 (1980): 131–46.

Bálint, Csanád. "Zur Frage der byzantinischen Beziehungen im Fundmaterial Ungarns: Archäologische Forschungen zwischen 1970 und 1984." *Antaeus* 14 (1985): 209–23.

Bálint, Csanád. "Zur Identifizierung des Grabes von Kuvrat." *Acta Arch. Hung.* 36 (1984): 263–69.

Bárdos, Edit, and Éva Garam. *Das awarenzeitliche Gräberfeld in Zamárdi-Rétiföldek.* 2 vols. Budapest, 2009–14.

Bárdos, Elisabeth. "La necropoli avara di Zamárdi." In *L'oro degli Avari*, 76–143.

Barfield, Thomas J. *The Perilous Frontier: Nomadic Empires and China, 221 BC to AD 1757.* Cambridge, MA, 1989.

Barford, Paul M. *The Early Slavs: Culture and Society in Early Medieval Eastern Europe.* Ithaca, NY, 2001.

Barišić, Frano. *Čuda Dimitrija Solunskog kao Istoriski Izvori (Les miracles de S. Démétrius de Thessalonique comme source historique)*, Srpska Akademija Nauka 219. Belgrade, 1953.

Barišić, Frano. "Le siège de Constantinople par les Avars et les Slaves en 626." *Byzantion* 24 (1954): 371–95.

Barišić, Frano. "Visantijski Singidunum." *Zbornik Radova* 3 (1955): 1–14.

Barkóczi, László. "A 6th Century Cemetery from Keszthely-Fenékpuszta." *Acta Arch. Hung.* 20 (1968): 275–311.

Barkóczi, László, and Ágnes Salamon. "Remarks on the 6th Century History of Pannonia." *Acta Arch. Hung.* 23 (1971): 139–49.

Barth, Fredrik. *Ethnic Groups and Boundaries: The Social Organization of Culture Difference.* Oslo, 1969.

Bartha, Anthal. *Hungarian Society in the 9th and 10th Centuries.* Studia Historica Academiae Scientiarum Hungaricae 85. Budapest, 1975.

Barthold, Vasily V., and John M. Rogen. "The Burial Rites of the Turks and the Mongols." *Central Asiatic Journal* 14 (1970): 195–227.

Barthold, Wilhelm. *Histoire des turcs de l'Asie centrale.* Paris, 1945.

Barton, Peter F. *Die Frühzeit des Christentums in Österreich und Südosteuropa bis 788.* Vol. 1. Vienna, 1975.

Bârzu, Ligia, and Radu Harhoiu. "Gepiden als Nachbarn der Langobarden und das Gräberfeld von Bratei." In Bemmann and Schmauder, *Kulturwandel in Mitteleuropa,* 513–78.

Baynes, Norman H. "The Date of the Avar Surprise: A Chronological Study." *Byzantinische Zeitschrift* 21 (1912): 110–28.

Beal, Samuel. *Travels of Fah-Hian and Sung-Yun.* New Delhi, 1993.

Becher, Matthias. *Eid und Herrschaft: Untersuchungen zum Herrscherethos Karls des Großen.* Sigmaringen, 1993.

Beckwith, Christopher L. "A Note on the Heavenly Kings of Ancient and Medieval Central Eurasia." *Archivum Eurasiae Medii Aevi* 17 (2010): 7–10.

Bemmann, Jürgen. *Steppenkrieger: Reiternomaden des 7.–14. Jahrhunderts aus der Mongolei; Katalog der Ausstellung im LVR LandesMuseum Bonn.* Bonn, 2012.

Bemmann, Jürgen, and Michael Schmauder, eds. *The Complexity of Interaction along the Eurasian Steppe Zone in the First Millennium CE.* Bonn, 2015.

Bemmann, Jürgen, and Michael Schmauder, eds. *Kulturwandel in Mitteleuropa: Langobarden—Awaren—Slawen.* Bonn, 2008.

Berend, Nora. *At the Gate of Christendom: Jews, Muslims and "Pagans" in Medieval Hungary, c. 1000–c. 1300.* Cambridge, 2001.

Berend, Nora. "Oath-Taking in Hungary: A Window on Medieval Social Interaction." In *Central and Eastern Europe in the Middle Ages: A Cultural History,* edited by Piotr Gorecki and Nancy van Deusen, 42–49. London, 2005.

Berg, Heinrich. "Bischöfe und Bischofssitze im Ostalpen- und Donauraum vom 4. bis zum 8. Jahrhundert." In Wolfram and Schwarcz, *Die Bayern und ihre Nachbarn,* 61–108.

Bertels, Klaus. "Carantania: Beobachtungen zur politisch-geographischen Terminologie und zur Geschichte des Landes und seine Bevölkerung im frühen Mittelalter." *Carinthia I* 177 (1987): 87–196.

Beševliev, Veselin. "Bemerkungen über die antiken Heerstraßen in Ostteil der Balkanhalbinsel." *Klio* 51 (1969): 483–95.

Beševliev, Veselin. "Bulgaren als Söldner in den italienischen Kriegen Justinians I." *Jahrbuch der Österreichischen Byzantinistik* 29 (1980): 21–26.

Beševliev, Veselin. *Die protobulgarischen Inschriften.* Berlin, 1963.

Beševliev, Veselin. *Die protobulgarische Periode der bulgarischen Geschichte.* Amsterdam, 1981.

Beševliev, Veselin. *Zur Deutung der Kastellnamen in Prokops Werk "De aedificiis."* Amsterdam, 1970.

Beševliev, Veselin. "Zur Deutung und Datierung der protobulgarischen Inschrift auf dem Reiterrelief von Madara, Bulgarien." *Byzantinische Zeitschrift* 47 (1954): 117–22.

Beševliev, Veselin. "Die zusammengesetzten Titel in den protobulgarischen Inschriften." *UAJB* 30 (1958): 98–103.

Bethlenfalvy, Géza, Ágnes Birtalan, Alice Sárközi, and Judit Vinkovic, eds. *Altaic Religious Beliefs and Practices: Proceedings of the 33rd Permanent International Altaistic Conference Budapest 1990.* Budapest, 1992.

Betti, Maddalena. *The Making of Christian Moravia (858–882): Papal Power and Political Reality*. Leiden and Boston, 2014.

Bialeková, Darina, and Jozef Zábojník, eds. *Ethnische und kulturelle Verhältnisse an der mittleren Donau vom 6. bis zum 11. Jahrhundert: Symposium, Nitra 6. bis 10. November 1994*. Bratislava, 1996.

Bierbrauer, Volker. *Ethnos und Mobilität im 5. Jahrhundert aus archäologischer Sicht: Vom Kaukasus bis Niederösterreich*. Bayerische Akademie der Wissenschaften, phil.-hist. Kl., n.s., 131. Munich, 2008.

Bierbrauer, Volker. "Die Keszthely-Kultur und die romanische Kontinuität in Westungarn (5.–8. Jh.): Neue Überlegungen zu einem alten Problem." In *Von Sachsen nach Jerusalem: Menschen und Institutionen im Wandel der Zeit; Festschrift f. Wolfgang Giese zum 65. Geburtstag*, edited by Hubertus Seibert and Gertrud Thoma, 51–72. Munich, 2004.

Birnbaum, Henrik. "Von ethnolinguistischer Einheit zur Vielfalt: Die Slaven im Zuge der Landnahme auf der Balkanhalbinsel." *Südost-Forschungen* 51 (1992): 1–19.

Biró, Adam. "Methodological Considerations on the Archaeology of Rigid, Reflex, Composite Bows of Eurasia in the Pre-Mongol Period." *Acta Militaria Medievalia* 9 (2013): 7–38.

Bíró, Margit. "Georgian Sources on the Caucasian Campaign of Heracleios." *Acta Orient. Hung.* 35 (1981): 121–32.

Bivar, David. "Der Aufstieg des Islam." In *Zentralasien*, edited by Gavin Hambly, Fischer-Weltgeschichte 16, 73–88. Frankfurt 1966.

Blay, Adrienn, and Levente Samu. "Über die mediterranen Kontakte des frühawarenzeitlichen Karpatenbecken am Beispiel ausgewählter Fundgruppen." In Bugarski et al., *GrenzÜbergänge*, 291–310.

Bleichsteiner, Robert. "Zeremonielle Trinksitten und Raumordnung bei den turko-mongolischen Nomaden." *Archiv für Völkerkunde* 6/7 (1951–52): 181–208.

Blockley, Roger C. "Doctors as Diplomats in the Sixth Century A.D." *Florilegium* 2 (1980): 89–100.

Böhmer, Johann Friedrich, and Engelbert Mühlbacher. *Die Regesten des Kaiserreichs unter den Karolingern 751–918*. Vol. 1. 2nd. ed. Regesta Imperii 1. Innsbruck, 1908.

Bollók, Ádám, "Excavating Early Medieval Material Culture and Writing History in Late Nineteenth- and Early Twentieth-Century Hungarian Archaeology," *Hungarian Historical Review* 5, no. 2 (2016): 277–304.

Bollók, Ádám. "The Visual Arts of the Sasanian Empire and the Nagyszentmiklós/Sânnicolau Mare Treasure—a Non-Specialist's View." In Daim et al., *Der Goldschatz*, 43–70.

Bollók, Ádám, Gergely Csiky, and Tivadar Vida, eds. *Zwischen Byzanz und der Steppe: archäologische und historische Studien. Festschrift für Csanád Bálint zum 70. Geburtstag / Between Byzantium and the Steppe: Archaeological and Historical Studies in Honour of Csanád Bálint on the Occasion of His 70th Birthday*. Budapest, 2016.

Bon, Antoine. *Le Péloponnèse byzantin jusqu'en 1204*. Paris, 1951.

Bóna, István. "Abriss der Siedlungsgeschichte Ungarns im 5.–7. Jahrhundert und die Awarensiedlung von Dunaújváros." *Archeologické rozhledy* 20 (1968): 605–18.

Bóna, István. "L'agglomération avare de Dunaújváros, les différentes périodes." In *Les Questions fondamentales du peuplement du bassin des Carpathes du VIIIe au Xe siècle: Conférence internationale Szeged 1971*, 25–34. Budapest, 1972.

Bóna, István. *Der Anbruch des Mittelalters: Gepiden und Langobarden im Karpatenbecken*. Budapest, 1976.

Bóna, István. "Avar lovassír Iváncsáról" [Grave of an Avar horseman at Iváncsa]. *Archaeologiai Értesítő* 97 (1970): 243–61.

Bóna, István. "Die Awaren: Ein asiatisches Reitervolk an der mittleren Donau." In *Awaren in Europa*, exhibition catalog, 5–19.

Bóna, István. "Beiträge zu den ethnischen Verhältnissen des 6.–7. Jahrhunderts in Westungarn." *Alba Regia* 2–3 (1963): 49–68.

Bóna, István. "'Cundpald fecit': Der Kelch von Petőháza und die Anfänge der bairisch-fränkischen Awarenmission in Pannonien." *Acta Arch. Hung.* 18 (1966): 279–325.

Bóna, István. "Daciától Erdőelvéig." In *Erdély Története*, vol. 1, *A kezdetekől 1606-ig*, edited by Lázló Makkai and András Mócsy, 107–234. Budapest, 1986.

Bóna, István. *The Dawn of the Dark Ages: The Gepids and the Lombards in the Carpathian Basin*. Budapest, 1976.

Bóna, István. "Das erste Auftreten der Bulgaren im Karpatenbecken: Turkic-Bulgarian-Hungarian Relations (6th–11th Centuries)." *Studia Turco-Hungarica* 5 (1981): 79–112.

Bóna, István. "Gepiden in Siebenbürgen—Gepiden an der Theiss." *Acta Arch. Hung.* 31 (1979): 9–50.

Bóna, István, and Margit Nagy. *Gepidische Gräberfelder am Theissgebiet*. Vol. 1. Budapest, 2002.

Bóna, István. "Die Geschichte der Awaren im Lichte der archäologischen Quellen." In *Popoli delle steppe*, 2:437–64.

Bóna, István. "Studien zum frühmittelalterlichen Reitergrab von Szegvár." *Acta Arch. Hung.* 32 (1980): 31–96.

Bóna, István. "A Szegvár-Sápoldali lovassír." *Archaeologiai Értesítő* 106 (1979): 3–32.

Bóna, István. "Ungarns Völker im 5. und 6. Jahrhundert: Eine historisch-archäologische Zusammenschau." In Bott and Meier-Arendt, *Germanen, Hunnen und Awaren*, 116–29.

Bóna, István. "Die Verwaltung und die Bevölkerung des karolingischen Pannoniens im Spiegel der zeitgenössischen Quellen." *Miteilungen des Archäologischen Instituts der Ungarischen Akademie der Wissenschaften* 14 (1985): 149–60.

Bóna, István. "Ein Vierteljahrhundert Völkerwanderungszeitforschung in Ungarn." *Acta Arch. Hung.* 23 (1971): 265–336.

Bonev, Cavdar. "Les Antes et Byzance." *Études Balkaniques* 19 (1983): 108–20.

Borri, Francesco. *Alboino: Frammenti di un racconto (secoli VI–XI)*. Rome, 2017.

Borri, Francesco. "Arrivano i barbari a cavallo! Foundation Myths and 'Origines gentium' in the Adriatic Arc." In Pohl and Heydemann, *Post-Roman Transitions*, 215–70.

Borri, Francesco. "La Dalmazia altomedievale tra discontinuità e racconto storico (secc. VII–VIII)." *Studi Veneziani*, n.s., 58 (2009): 15–51.

Bosworth, C. E. "Ebn Rosta." In *Encyclopaedia Iranica*. Vol. 8, fasc. 1, 49–50. New York, 2003.

Bott, Gerhard, and Walter Meier-Arendt. *Germanen, Hunnen und Awaren: Schätze der Völkerwanderungszeit*. Nuremberg, 1987. Exhibition catalog.

Bott, Hans. "Bemerkungen zum Datierungsproblem awarenzeitlicher Funde in Pannonien, vorgelegt am Beispiel des Gräberfeldes von Környe." *Bonner Jahrbücher* 176 (1976): 201–80.

Bowlus, Charles R. *Franks, Moravians, and Magyars: The Struggle for the Middle Danube, 788–907*. Philadephia, 1995.

Bowlus, Charles R. "War and Society in the Carolingian Ostmark." *Austrian History Yearbook* 14 (1978): 3–30.

Bracher, Andreas. "Der Reflexbogen als Beispiel gentiler Bewaffnung." In Wolfram and Pohl, *Typen der Ethnogenese*, 137–46.

Brachmann, Hansjürgen. "Als aber die Austrasier das castrum Wogastisburc belagerten . . . (Fredegar IV, 68)." *Onomastica Slavogermanica* 19 (1990): 17–33.

Brachmann, Hansjürgen. "Westslawische Burgherrschaft im Übergang von der Stammes—zur Staatengesellschaft." In *Osteuropäische Geschichte in vergleichender*

Sicht, Berliner Jahrbuch für osteuropäische Geschichte 1/1996, 55–73. Berlin, 1996.

Brather, Sebastian. *Archäologie der westlichen Slawen*. Berlin, 2001.

Brather, Sebastian. "The Beginnings of Slavic Settlement East of the River Elbe." *Antiquity* 78 (2004): 314–29.

Brather, Sebastian. *Ethnische Interpretationen in der frühgeschichtlichen Archäologie: Geschichte, Grundlagen und Alternativen*, RGA Erg. Bd. 42. Berlin, 2004.

Brather, Sebastian. "Grubenhäuser und Haushalte: Zur Sozialstruktur frühmittelalterlicher Siedlungen in Ostmitteleuropa." In Bollók, Csiky, and Vida, *Zwischen Byzanz und der Steppe/Between Byzantium and the Steppe*, 195–208.

Brather, Sebastian. "Slawenbilder: 'Slawische Altertumskunde' im 19. und 20. Jahrhundert." *Archeologické rozhledy* 53 (2001): 717–51.

Brather, Sebastian, and Christine Kratzke, eds. *Auf dem Weg zum Germanica Slavica-Konzept: Perspektiven von Geschichtswissenschaft, Archäologie, Onomastik und Kunstgeschichte seit dem 19. Jahrhundert*. Leipzig, 2005.

Bratož, Rajko. "Die Auswanderung der Bevölkerung aus den pannonischen Provinzen während des 5. und 6. Jahrhunderts." In Konrad and Witschel, *Römische Legionslager in den Rhein- und Donauprovinzen*, 589–614.

Bratož, Rajko. "Das Christentum in Slowenien in der Spätantike." In *Kulturhistorische und archäologische Probleme des Südostalpenraumes in der Spätantike: Symposion Klagenfurt 1981*, edited by Herbert Grassl, 32–54. Vienna, 1985.

Bratož, Rajko. "Der Metropolitansprengel von Aquileia vom 5. bis zum frühen 7. Jahrhundert." In *Die Ausgrabungen im spätantik-frühmittelalterlichen Bischofssitz Sabiona-Säben in Südtirol*. Vol. 1, bk. 2, *Frühchristliche Kirche und Gräberfeld*, edited by Volker Bierbrauer and Hans Nothdurfter, 665–700. Munich, 2015.

Bratož, Rajko. "Il mito dei Veneti presso gil Sloveni." *Quaderni Giuliani di Storia* 26, no. 1 (2005): 17–54.

Bratož, Rajko, ed. *Slovenija in sosednje dežele med antiko in karolinško dobo: začetki slovenske etnogeneze / Slowenien und die Nachbarländer zwischen Antike und karolingischer Periode: Anfänge der slowenischen Ethnogenese*. 2 vols. Ljubljana, 2000.

Breckenridge, James D. "The 'Long Siege' of Thessalonika: Its Date and Iconography." *Byzantinische Zeitschrift* 48 (1955): 116–22.

Brentjes, Burchard. *Die Ahnen Dschingis Khans*. Berlin, 1988.

Brentjes, Burchard. "Nomadenwanderungen und Klimaschwankungen." *Central Asiatic Journal* 30 (1986): 7–21.

Brosseder, Ursula. "Belt Plaques as an Indicator of East-West Relations in the Eurasian Steppe at the Turn of the Millennia." In Brosseder and Miller, *Xiongnu Archaeology*, 349–424.

Brosseder, Ursula. "A Study on the Complexity and Dynamics of Interaction and Exchange in Late Iron Age Eurasia." In Bemmann and Schmauder, *Complexity of Interaction*, 199–332.

Brosseder, Ursula, and Bryan K. Miller, eds. *Xiongnu Archaeology: Multidisciplinary Perspectives of the First Steppe Empire in Central Asia*. Bonn, 2011.

Brozzi, Mario. "Cividale." In *RGA*, 5:3–7.

Brubaker, Leslie, and John Haldon, eds. *Byzantium in the Iconoclast Era (ca. 680–850): The Sources. An Annotated Survey*. Aldershot, 2001.

Brunhölzl, Franz. "Zur Kosmographie des Aethicus Ister." In *Festschrift für Max Spindler*, edited by Dieter Albrecht, Andreas Kraus, and Kurt Reindel, 75–90. Munich, 1969.

Brunnbauer, Ulf. "Illyrer, Veneter, Iraner, Urserben, Makedonen, Altbulgaren . . . Autochthonistische und nichtslawische Herkunftsmythen unter den Südslawen." *Zeitschrift für Balkanologie* 42, no. 1–2 (2006): 37–62.

Brunner, Karl. "Diedenhofener Kapitular." In *RGA*, 2:407–9.

Brunner, Karl. *Oppositionelle Gruppen in Karolingerreich*, VIÖG 25. Vienna, 1979.

Brunšmid, Josip. "Eine griechische Ziegelinschrift aus Sirmium." *Eranos Vindobonensis*, 1893, 331–33.

Budak, Neven. "Frühes Christentum in Kroatien." In *Karantanien und der Alpen-Adria Raum im Frühmittelalter*, 223–34. Vienna, 1991.

Budak, Neven. "Identities in Early Medieval Dalmatia (Seventh–Eleventh Centuries)." In *Franks, Northmen, and Slavs: Identities and State Formation in Early Medieval Europe*, edited by Ildar H. Garipzanov, Patrick J. Geary, and Przemysław Urbańczyk, 223–41. Turnhout, 2008.

Budak, Neven. "Die südslawischen Ethnogenesen an der östlichen Adriaküste im frühen Mittelalter." In Wolfram and Pohl, *Typen der Ethnogenese*, 129–36.

Budimir, Milan. "Antai—Antes—Anti—Anticus." *Zbornik Radova* 8 (1964): 37–45.

Bugarski, Ivan, Orsolya Heinrich-Tamáska, Vujadin Ivanišević, and Daniel Syrbe, eds. *GrenzÜbergänge: Spätrömisch, frühchristlich, frühbyzantinisch als Kategorien der historisch-archäologischen Forschung an der mittleren Donau*. Akten des 27. internationalen Symposiums der Grundprobleme der frühgeschichtlichen Entwicklung im mittleren Donauraum, Ruma, 4.–7.11.2015. Remshalden, 2016.

Bühler, Birgit, Viktor Freiberger, Falko Daim, Kurt Gschwantler, Georg Plattner, and Peter Stadler. *Der Goldschatz von Sânicolau Mare (ungarisch: Nagyszentmiklós)*. RGZM Monographien 142, Mainz, 2018.

Bury, John Bagnell. "The Chronology of Theophylaktos Simokatta." *English Historical Review* 3 (1888): 310–15.

Bury, John Bagnell. *A History of the Later Roman Empire: From Arcadius to Irene (395–800)*. 2 vols. London, 1889.

Cameron, Averil. "Blaming the Jews: The Seventh-Century Invasions of Palestine in Context." *Travaux et mémoires* 14 (Mélanges Gilbert Dagron) (2002): 57–78.

Cameron, Averil. "The Early Religious Practices of Justin II." *Church History* 13 (1976): 51–67.

Cameron, Averil. *Procopius and the Sixth Century*. Berkeley, 1985.

Cameron, Averil. "The Virgin's Robe: An Episode in the History of Early Seventh-Century Constantinople." *Byzantion* 49 (1979): 42–56.

Carile, Antonio. "Giovanni di Nikiu, cronista bizantinocopto del VIIe secolo." In N. Stratos, *Byzantium*, 2:353–98.

Carile, Antonio. "I nomadi nelle fonti bizantine." In *Popoli delle steppe*, 1:55–88.

Carnap-Bornheim, Claus von. "The Social Position of the Germanic Goldsmith in AD 0–500." In *Roman Gold and the Development of the Early Germanic Kingdoms*, edited by Bente Magnus, 263–78. Stockholm, 2001.

Carrère-d'Encausse, Hélène, and Alexandre Benningsen. "Avars." In *The Encyclopaedia of Islam*, new ed., 755–56. Leiden, 1960.

Ceglia, Valeria. "Le presenze avariche nelle necropoli altomedievali di Campochiaro." In Bemmann and Schmauder, *Kulturwandel in Mitteleuropa*, 691–703.

Chaloupecký, Vaclav. "Considérations sur Samon, le premier roi des Slaves." *Byzantinoslavica* 11 (1950): 223–39.

Charanis, Peter. "The Chronicle of Monemvasia and the Question of the Slavonic Settlements in Greece." *Dumbarton Oaks Papers* 5 (1950): 141–60.

Charanis, Peter. "Ethnic Changes in the Byzantine Empire in the Seventh Century." *Dumbarton Oaks Papers* 13 (1959): 23–44.

Charanis, Peter. "Graecia in Isidore of Seville." *Byzantinische Zeitschrift* 64 (1971): 22–25.

Charanis, Peter. "Kouver, the Chronology of His Activities and Their Ethnic Effects on the Regions around Thessalonica." *Balkan Studies* 11 (1970): 229–47.

Charanis, Peter. "Observations on the History of Greece during the Early Middle Ages." *Balkan Studies* 11 (1970): 14–34.

Charanis, Peter. "On the Capture of Corinth by the Onogurs and Its Recapture by the Byzantines." *Speculum* 27 (1952): 343–50.

Charanis, Peter. "On the Slavic Settlement in the Peloponnesus." *Byzantinische Zeitschrift* 46 (1953): 91–103.

Charanis, Peter. "The Slavs, Byzantium, and the Historical Significance of the First Bulgarian Empire." *Balkan Studies* 17 (1976): 5–24.

Charanis, Peter. *Studies in the Demography of the Byzantine Empire*. London, 1972.

Chavannes, Edouard, *Documents sur les Tou-kiue (Turcs) occidentaux*. St. Petersburg, 1907.

Chavannes, Edouard. "Voyage de Song-yun dans l'Udyana et le Gandhara." *Bulletin de l'Ecole Francaise d'Extreme-Orient* 3 (1903): 1–63.

Chazelle, Celia, and Catherine Cubitt, eds. *The Crisis of the Oikoumene: The Three Chapters and the Failed Quest for Unity in the Sixth-Century Mediterranean*, Studies in the Early Middle Ages 14. Turnhout, 2007.

Cheng Fangyi. "The Research on the Identification between Tiele (鐵勒) and the Oyuric Tribes." *Archivum Eurasiae Medii Aevi* 19 (2012): 81–113.

Chevalier, Pascale, and Jagoda Mardešić. "Le groupe épiscopal de Salone aux IVe–VIIe siècles: Urbanisme et vie quotidienne." *Les destinées de l'Illyricum méridional pendant le haut Moyen Âge. MEFRM—Moyen Âge* 120, no. 2 (2008): 227–38.

Christian, David. *A History of Russia, Central Asia and Mongolia*. Vol. 1, *Inner Eurasia from Prehistory to the Mongol Empire*. Oxford, 1998.

Christou, Konstantinos P., *Byzanz und die Langobarden: Von der Ansiedlung in Pannonien bis zur endgültigen Anerkennung 500–680*. Historical Monographs 11. Athens, 1991.

Chropovský, Bohuslav, ed. *Importants sites slaves en Slovaquie*. Bratislava, 1978.

Chrysos, Evangelos. "Der Kaiser und die Könige." In Wolfram and Daim, *Die Völker an der mittleren und unteren Donau im fünften und sechsten Jahrhundert*, 142–48.

Chrysos, Evangelos. "Legal Concepts and Patterns for the Barbarians' Settlement on Roman Soil." In Chrysos and Schwarcz, *Das Reich und die Barbaren*, 13–24.

Chrysos, Evangelos. "Die Nordgrenze des byzantinischen Reiches im 6. bis 8. Jahrhundert." In Hänsel, *Die Völker Südosteuropas vom 6.–8. Jahrhundert*, 27–40.

Chrysos, Evangelos. "Settlements of Slavs and Byzantine Sovereignty in the Balkans." In *Byzantina Mediterranea: Festschrift für Johannes Koder zum 65. Geburtstag*, edited by Klaus Belke, Ewald Kislinger, Andreas Külzer, and Maria Stassinopoulou, 123–35. Vienna, 2007.

Chrysos, Evangelos. "Zum Landesnamen Langobardia." In *Die Langobarden*, edited by Walter Pohl and Peter Erhart, Forschungen zur Geschichte des Mittelalters 9, 429–38. Vienna, 2005.

Chrysos, Evangelos. "Zur Gründung des ersten bulgarischen Staates." *Cyrillomethodiana* 2 (1972–73): 7–13.

Chrysos, Evangelos, and Andreas Schwarcz, eds. *Das Reich und die Barbaren*, VIÖG 29. Vienna, 1989.

Chuvin, Pierre. "Les ambassades byzantines auprès des premièrs souverains turcs de Sogdiane: Problèmes d'onomastique et de toponymie." *Cahiers d'Asie Centrale* 1, no. 2 (1996): 345–55.

Ciglenečki, Slavko. "Archaeological Investigations of the Decline of Antiquity in Slovenia." In Bratož, *Slovenija*, 1:119–39.

Ciglenečki, Slavko. "Castra und Höhensiedlungen vom 3. bis 6. Jahrhundert in Slowenien." In *Höhensiedlungen zwischen Antike und Mittelalter von den Ardennen bis zur Adria*, edited by Heiko Steuer and Volker Bierbrauer, 481–532. Berlin, 2008.

Ciglenečki, Slavko. "Results and Problems in the Archaeology of the Late Antiquity in Slovenia." *Arheološki vestnik* 50 (1999): 287–310.

Ciglenečki, Slavko. "Tracce di un insediamento tardo (VI–IX sec.) nei siti della tarda antichita in Slovenia." In *Il territorio tra tardoantico e altomedioevo: metodi di indagine e risultati; 3° seminario sul tardoantico e l'altomedioevo nell'area alpina e padana, Monte Barro-Galbiate (Como), 9–11 settembre 1991*, edited by Gian Pietro Brogiolo and Lanfredo Casteletti, 53–59. Florence, 1992.

Ciglenečki, Slavko. "Das Weiterleben der Spätantike bis zum Auftauchen der Slawen in Slowenien." In Hänsel, *Die Völker Südosteuropas vom 6.–8. Jahrhundert*, 265–86.

Čilinská, Zlata. "Anfänge des spezialisierten Handwerks und Handels bei der altslawischen Gesellschaft in der Slowakei." *Slov. Arch.* 34 (1986): 299–308.

Čilinská, Zlata. "The Development of the Slavs North of the Danube during the Avar Empire and Their Social-Cultural Contribution to Great Moravia." *Slov. Arch.* 31 (1983): 237–76.

Čilinská, Zlata. "Frauenschmuck im 7.–8. Jahrhundert im Karpatenbecken." *Slov. Arch.* 23 (1975): 63–96.

Čilinská, Zlata. *Frühmittelalterliches Gräberfeld in Želovce.* Bratislava, 1973.

Čilinská, Zlata. "Zur Frage des 2. awarischen Khaganats." *Slov. Arch.* 15 (1967): 447–54.

Claessen, Henri J. M., and Peter Skalník, eds. *The Early State.* The Hague, 1978.

Clastres, Pierre. *Staatsfeinde: Studien zur politischen Anthropologie.* Frankfurt am Main, 1976.

Claude, Dietrich. *Die byzantinische Stadt im 6. Jahrhundert.* Munich, 1960.

Claude, Dietrich. *Geschichte der Westgoten.* Stuttgart, 1970.

Claude, Dietrich. *Der Handel im westlichen Mittelmeer während des Frühmittelalters: Untersuchungen zu Handel und Verkehr der vor- und frühgeschichtlichen Zeit im Mittel- und Nordeuropa.* Abhandlungen AW Göttingen 3, F. 144. Göttingen, 1985.

Claude, Dietrich. "Zur Begründung familiärer Beziehungen zwischen dem Kaiser und barbarischen Herrschern." In Chrysos and Schwarcz, *Das Reich und die Barbaren*, 25–56.

Clauson, Gerard. "Turks and Wolves." *Studia Orientalia* 28 (1964): 1–22.

Clauss, Manfred. "Heerwesen (Heeresreligion)." In *Reallexikon für Antike und Christentum: Sachwörterbuch zur Auseinandersetzung des Christentums mit der antiken Welt.* Vol. 13, *Gütergemeinschaft-Heilgötter*, 1073–1113. Stuttgart, 1986.

Collins, Roger. *Fredegar.* Aldershot, 1996.

Collins, Roger. "The 'Reviser' Revised: Another Look at the Alternative Version of the *Annales regni Francorum*." In *After Rome's Fall: Narrators and Sources of Early Medieval History. Essays Presented to Walter Goffart*, edited by Alexander C. Murray, 191–213. Toronto, 1998.

Collins, Roger. *Visigothic Spain, 409–711.* Oxford, 2004.

Comşa, Maria. "La pénétration des Slaves dans le territoire de la Roumanie entre le VIe et IXe siècle à la lumière des recherches archéologiques." *Slavia Antiqua* 7 (1960): 175–88.

Conte, Francis. *Les Slaves: Aux origines des civilisations d'Europe.* Paris, 1986.

Cormack, Robin. "But Is It Art?" In Shepard and Franklin, *Byzantine Diplomacy*, 219–36.

Cosentino, Salvatore. *Prosopografia dell'Italia Bizantina (493–804).* Vol. 2, *(G–O)*. Bologna, 2000.

Cosma, Călin. "Avar Warriors in Transylvania, Sătmar and Maramureş, Crişana and Banat: Archaeological Landmarks on the Political Status of Western Romania in the Avar Khaganate." In Cosma, *Warriors, Weapons, and Harness*, 250–81.

Cosma, Călin, ed. *Warriors, Weapons, and Harness from the 5th–10th Centuries in the Carpathian Basin.* Cluj-Napoca, 2015.

Csallány, Dezső. "Der awarische Gürtel." *Acta Arch. Hung.* 14 (1962): 445–80.

Csendes, Peter. "Zu den Awarenkriegen unter Karl dem Großen." *Unsere Heimat* 41 (1970): 93–107.

Csiky, Gergely. "Armament and Society in the Mirror of the Avar Archaelogy: The Transdanubia-Phenomenon Revisited." In *Proceedings of the 1st International Conference on Interethnic Rlations in Transylvania,* edited by Ioan Marian Tiplic, 9–34. Sibiu, 2011.

Csiky, Gergely. *Avar-Age Polearms and Edged Weapons: Classification, Typology, Chronology and Technology.* Leiden, 2015.

Csiky, Gergely, and Piroska Magyar-Hársegyi. "Wine for the Avar Elite? Amphorae from Avar Period Burials in the Carpathian Basin." In *The Danubian Lands Between the Black, Aegean, and Adriatic Seas (7th Century BC – 10th Century AD): Proceedings of the Fifth International Congress on Black Sea Antiquities (Belgrade, 17–21 September 2013),* edited by Gocha R. Tsetskhladze, Alexandru Avram, and James Hargrave, 175–82. Oxford, 2015.

Curta, Florin. "Amphorae and Seals: The 'Sub-Byzantine' Avars and the Quaestura Exercitus." In Bollók, Csiky, and Vida, *Zwischen Byzanz und der Steppe/Between Byzantium and the Steppe,* 307–34.

Curta, Florin. "Avar Blitzkrieg: Slavic and Bulgar Raiders, and Roman Special Ops. Mobile Warriors in the 6th-Century Balkans." In Zimonyi and Karatay, *Central Eurasia in the Middle Ages,* 69–89.

Curta, Florin. "Barbarians in Dark-Age Greece: Slavs or Avars?" In *Civitas Divino-Humana: In honorem annorum LX Georgii Bakalov,* edited by Tsvetelin Stepanov and Veselina Vachkova, 513–50. Sofia, 2004.

Curta, Florin. "Before Cyril and Methodius: Christianity and Barbarians beyond the Sixth- and Seventh-Century Danube Frontier." In *East Central and Eastern Europe in the Middle Ages,* edited by Florin Curta, 181–219. Ann Arbor, 2005.

Curta, Florin, ed. *Borders, Barriers, and Ethnogenesis: Frontiers in Late Antiquity and the Middle Ages.* Turnhout, 2005.

Curta, Florin. "The Earliest Avar-Age Stirrups, or the 'Stirrup Controversy' Revisited." In Curta, *The Other Europe in the Middle Ages,* 297–326.

Curta, Florin. "The Early Slavs in Bohemia and Moravia: A Response to My Critics." *Archeologické rozhledy* 61 (2009): 725–54.

Curta, Florin. "The Early Slavs in the Northern and Eastern Adriatic Region: A Critical Approach." *Archeologia medievale* 37 (2010): 307–29.

Curta, Florin. "East Central Europe: The Gate to Byzantium." *Byzantinische Zeitschrift* 108 (2015): 609–52.

Curta, Florin. *The Edinburgh History of the Greeks, ca. 500 to 1050.* Edinburgh, 2011.

Curta, Florin. "Feasting with 'Kings' in an Ancient Democracy: On the Slavic Society of the Early Middle Ages (Sixth to Seventh Century A. D.)." *Essays in Medieval Studies* 15 (1997): 19–34.

Curta, Florin. "Female Dress and Slavic Bow Fibulae in Greece." *Hesperia* 74 (2005): 101–46.

Curta, Florin. "Four Questions for Those Who Still Believe in Prehistoric Slavs and Other Fairy Tales." *Starohrvatska prosvjeta* 42 (2015): 286–303.

Curta, Florin. "From Kossinna to Bromlej: Ethnogenesis in Slavic Archaeology." In Gillett, *On Barbarian Identity,* 201–18.

Curta, Florin. "Frontier Ethnogenesis in Late Antiquity: The Danube, the Tervingi, and the Slavs." In Curta, *Borders, Barriers, and Ethnogenesis,* 173–204.

Curta, Florin. "Hiding Behind a Piece of Tapestry: Jordanes and the Slavic Venethi." *Jahrbücher für Geschichte Osteuropas,* n.s., 47 (1999): 321–40.

Curta, Florin. "Horsemen in Forts or Peasants in Villages? Remarks on the Archaeology of Warfare in the 6th to 7th c. Balkans." In *War and Warfare in Late Antiquity*, edited by Alexander Sarantis and Neil Christie, 809–52. Leiden, 2013.

Curta, Florin. *The Making of the Slavs: History and Archaeology of the Lower Danube Region, c. 500–700.* Cambridge, 2001.

Curta, Florin. "The Making of the Slavs between Ethnogenesis, Invention, and Migration." *Studia Slavica et Balcanica Petropolitana* 6, no. 2 (2008): 155–72.

Curta, Florin. "Medieval Archaeology and Ethnicity: Where Are We?" *History Compass* 9, no. 7 (2011): 537–48.

Curta, Florin. "Merovingian and Carolingian Gift Giving." *Speculum* 81 (2006): 671–99.

Curta, Florin. "New Remarks on Christianity Beyond the 6th and Early 7th Century Frontier of the Roman Empire." In Heinrich-Tamáska, *Keszthely-Fenékpuszta*, 303–21.

Curta, Florin. "The North-Western Region of the Black Sea during the 6th and Early 7th Century AD." *Ancient West & East* 7 (2008): 151–87.

Curta, Florin. "Peasants as 'Makeshift Soldiers for the Occasion': Sixth-Century Settlement Patterns in the Balkans." In *Urban Centers and Rural Contexts in Late Antiquity*, edited by Thomas S. Burns and John W. Eadie, 199–217. East Lansing, 2001.

Curta, Florin. "The Prague Type: A Critical Approach to Pottery-Classification." *Archaeologia Bulgarica* 5 (2001): 73–106.

Curta, Florin. "Qagan, Khan, or King? Power in Early Medieval Bulgaria (Seventh to Ninth Century)." *Viator* 37 (2006): 1–31.

Curta, Florin. "Sklaviniai and Ethnic Adjectives: A Clarification." *Byzantion: Nea Hellás* 30 (2011): 85–98.

Curta, Florin. "'Slavic' Bow Fibulae: Twenty Years of Research." *Berichte der Römisch-Germanischen Kommission* 93 (2012): 235–342.

Curta, Florin. "The Slavic *Lingua Franca* (Linguistic Notes of an Archaeologist Turned Historian)." *East Central Europe/L'Europe du Centre-Est* 31, no. 1 (2004): 125–48.

Curta, Florin. "Slavs in Fredegar: Medieval Gens or Narrative Strategy." *Acta Universitatis Szegedensis de Attila József Nominatae. Acta Historica* 103 (1996): 3–20.

Curta, Florin. "Slavs in Fredegar and Paul the Deacon: Medieval Gens or 'Scourge of God'?" *Early Medieval Europe* 6, no. 2 (1997): 141–67.

Curta, Florin. "Some Remarks on Ethnicity in Medieval Archaeology." *Early Medieval Europe* 15, no. 2 (2007): 159–85.

Curta, Florin. *Southeastern Europe in the Middle Ages, 500–1250.* Cambridge, 2006.

Curta, Florin. "Still Waiting for the Barbarians? The Making of the Slavs in 'Dark-Age' Greece." In *Neglected Barbarians*, edited by Florin Curta, Studies in the Early Middle Ages 32, 403–78. Turnhout, 2011.

Curta, Florin. "Were There Any Slavs in Seventh-Century Macedonia?" *Istorija* 47, no. 1 (2012): 61–75.

Curta, Florin, with Roman Kovalev, eds. *The Other Europe in the Middle Ages: Avars, Bulgars, Khazars, and Cumans.* East Central and Eastern Europe in the Middle Ages, 450–1450, 2. Leiden, 2007.

Czeglédy, Károly. "From East to West: The Age of Nomadic Migrations in Eurasia." *Archivum Eurasiae Medii Aevi* 3 (1983): 25–126.

Czeglédy, Károly. "On the Numerical Composition of the Ancient Turkish Tribal Confederations." *Acta Orient. Hung.* 25 (1972): 275–81.

Czeglédy, Károly. "Pseudo-Zacharias Rhetor on the Nomads." In Ligeti, *Studia Turcica*, 133–48.

Czeglédy, Károly. "Zur Stammesorganisation der türkischen Völker." *Acta Orient. Hung.* 36 (1982): 89–93.

Daffinà, Paolo. "Gli Unni e gli altri: Le fonti letterarie e le loro interpretazioni moderne." In *Popoli delle steppe*, 1:181–208.

Daim, Falko. "Das 7. und 8. Jahrhundert in Niederösterreich." In *Germanen, Awaren, Slawen in Niederösterreich: Das erste Jahrtausend nach Christus*, Katalog der Ausstellung des Niederösterreichischen Landesmuseums, 88–94. Vienna, 1977.

Daim, Falko. "Archaeology, Ethnicity and the Structures of Identification: The Example of the Avars, Carantanians and Moravians in the Eighth Century." In Pohl and Reimitz, *Strategies of Distinction*, 71–94.

Daim, Falko. "Archäologische Zeugnisse zur Geschichte des Wiener Raumes im Frühmittelalter." *Wiener Geschichtsblätter* 36 (1981): 175–97.

Daim, Falko. "The Avars: Steppe People of Central Europe." *Archaeology* 37 (1984): 33–39.

Daim, Falko. "Avars and Avar Archaeology: An Introduction." In *Regna and Gentes: The Relationship between Late Antique and Early Medieval Peoples and Kingdoms in the Transformation of the Roman World*, edited by Hans-Werner Goetz, Jörg Jarnut, and Walter Pohl, The Transformation of the Roman World 13, 463–570. Leiden, 2003.

Daim, Falko, ed. *Awarenforschungen.* 2 vols. Vienna, 1992.

Daim, Falko, ed. *Die Awaren am Rand der byzantinischen Welt: Studien zu Diplomatie, Handel und Technologietransfer im Frühmittelalter.* Innsbruck, 2000.

Daim, Falko. *Die Awaren in Niederösterreich.* Wissenschaftliche Schriftenreihe Niederösterreichs 28. St. Pölten, 1977.

Daim, Falko. *Das awarische Gräberfeld von Leobersdorf.* Vienna, 1988.

Daim, Falko. "Das awarische Gräberfeld von Zillingtal: Sechs Gräber mit 'westlichen' Gegenständen." *Wissenschaftliche Arbeiten aus dem Burgenland* 100 (1998): 97–135.

Daim, Falko. "Der awarische Greif und die byzantinische Antike." In Friesinger and Daim, *Typen der Ethnogenese*, 273–303.

Daim, Falko. "Byzantine Belt Ornaments of the 7th and 8th Centuries in Avar Contexts." In Entwistle and Adams, *Intelligible Beauty*, 61–71.

Daim, Falko. "Byzantine Belts and Avar Birds: Diplomacy, Trade and Cultural Transfer in the Eighth Century." In Pohl, Wood, and Helut Reimitz, *The Transformation of Frontiers*, 143–88.

Daim, Falko. "'Byzantinische' Gürtelgarnituren des 8. Jahrhunderts." In Daim, *Die Awaren am Rand der byzantinischen Welt*, 77–204.

Daim, Falko. "Gedanken zum Ethnosbegriff." *Mitteilungen der Anthropologischen Gesellschaft in Wien* 112 (1982): 58–71.

Daim, Falko. "Des Kaisers ungeliebte Söhne: Die Awaren und das Byzantinische Reich." *Eurasia Antiqua* 17, 2011 (2012): 1–20.

Daim, Falko. "Keszthely." In *RGA*, 16:468–74.

Daim, Falko. "Kunbábony." In *RGA*, 17:490–95.

Daim, Falko. "Die Materialität der Macht: Drei Fallstudien zum awarischen Gold." In *Arm und Reich: Zur Ressourcenverteilung in prähistorischen Gesellschaften, 8. Mitteldeutscher Archäologentag vom 22. bis 24. Oktober 2015 in Halle (Saale) / Rich and Poor: Competing for Resources in Prehistoric Societies, 8th Archaeological Conference of Central Germany, October 22–24, 2015 in Halle (Saale)*, edited by Harald Meller, Hans Peter Hahn, Reinhard Jung, and Roberto Risch, 623–36. Halle, 2016.

Daim, Falko. "Die vielteilige Gürtelgarnitur aus Hohenberg, Steiermark." In Daim et al., *Hunnen + Awaren*, 225–27.

Daim, Falko. "Vom Umgang mit toten Awaren." In *Erinnerungskultur im Bestattungsritual: Archäologisch-Historisches Forum*, edited by Jörg Jarnut and Matthias Wemhoff with Alexandra Nusser, Mittelalter Studien 3, 41–57. Munich, 2003.

Daim, Falko, and Herwig Friesinger, eds. *Die Bayern und ihre Nachbarn.* Vol. 2, DsÖAW 179. Vienna, 1985.

Daim, Falko, Ursula Koch, and Levente Sámu. "Mit dem Bauchladen in das Awarenland." In *Festschrift für Egon Wamers.* Frankfurt, forthcoming.

Daim, Falko, and Andreas Lippert, *Das awarische Gräberfeld von Sommerein am Leithagebirge.* Vienna, 1984.

Daim, Falko, Lumír Poláček, Zdenek Štana, and Jaroslav Tejral, eds. *Studien zum Burgwall von Mikulčice.* Vol. 1. Brno, 1995.

Daim, Falko, et al., eds. *Hunnen + Awaren: Reitervölker aus dem Osten. Burgenländische Landesausstellung 1996, Schloss Halbturn, 26. April–31. Oktober 1996.* Exhibition catalog. Eisenstadt, 1996.

Daim, Falko, and Peter Stadler. "Der Goldschatz von Sînnicolaul Mare (Nagyszentmiklós)." In Daim et al., *Hunnen + Awaren*, 439–45.

Daim, Falko, Kurt Gschwantler, Georg Plattner, and Peter Stadler, eds. *Der Goldschatz von Sânnicolau Mare (Nagyszentmiklós)*, RGZM Tagungen 25. Mainz, 2015.

Darkó, Jenő. "Influences touraniennes sur l'évolution de l'art militaire des grecs, des romains et des Byzantins." *Byzantion* 12 (1937): 119–47.

Daskalov, Metodi, Snezhana Gorianova, Petya Andreeva, Georg Plattner, Karoline Zhuber-Okrog, and Galina Grozdanova, eds. *The Nagyszentmiklós Gold Treasure.* Sofia, 2017.

Dauge, Yves Albert. *Le barbare: Recherches sur la conception romaine de la barbarie et de la civilisation.* Brussels, 1981.

Davidovich, Elena A. "The Karakhanids." In *History of Civilizations of Central Asia.* Vol. 4, bk. 1, edited by Muhammad S. Asimov and Clifford E. Bosworth, UNESCO Publications, 125–49. Paris, 1988.

Davidson, Gladys R., and Tibor Horvath. "The Avar Invasion of Corinth." *Hesperia* 6 (1937): 227–34.

Davies, Wendy, and Paul Fouracre, eds. *The Languages of Gift in the Early Middle Ages.* Cambridge, 2010.

Davis-Kimball, Jeannine, Eileen M. Murphy, Ludmila Koryakova, and Leonid T. Yablonksy, eds. *Kurgans, Ritual Sites, and Settlements: Eurasian Bronze and Iron Age*, British Archaeological Reports, International Series 890. Oxford, 2000.

Deér, Josef. "Karl der Grosse und der Untergang des Awarenreiches." In *Karl der Grosse: Lebenswerk und Nachleben.* Vol. 1, *Persönlichkeit und Geschichte*, edited by Helmut Beumann, 719–91. Düsseldorf, 1967.

Dekan, Ján. "Herkunft und Ethnizität der gegossenen Bronzeindustrie des VIII. Jahrhunderts." *Slov. Arch.* 20 (1972): 317–452.

Dekan, Ján. "Les motifs figuraux humains sur les bronzes moulés de la zone danubienne centrale à l'époque précédente l'empire de la Grande Moravie." *Studia Historica* 2 (1964): 52–102.

Deleuze, Gilles, and Félix Guattari. *A Thousand Plateaus: Capitalism and Schizophrenia.* Translated by Brian Massumi. Minneapolis, 1987. Available at http://projectlamar. com/media/A-Thousand-Plateaus.pdf. Originally published as Gilles Deleuze and Félix Guattari, *Mille plateaux: Capitalisme et schizophrenie* (Paris, 1980).

Demandt, Alexander. "Magister militum." In *RE*, Suppl., 12 (1970), 553–790.

Diaconu, Petre. "Le problème de la localisation de l'Onglos." *Dacia*, n.s., 14 (1970): 325–34.

Di Cosmo, Nicola. *Ancient China and Its Enemies: The Rise of Nomadic Power in East Asia.* Cambridge, 2004.

Di Cosmo, Nicola. "China-Steppe Relations in Historical Perspective." In Bemmann and Schmauder, *Complexity of Interaction*, 49–72.

Di Cosmo, Nicola, ed. *Warfare in Inner Asian History (500–1800)*. Leiden, 2002.

Di Cosmo, Nicola, and Michael Maas, eds. *Empires and Exchanges in Eurasian Late Antiquity: Rome, China, Iran, and the Steppe, ca. 250–750*. Cambridge, 2018.

Di Cosmo, Nicola, Clive Oppenheimer, and Ulf Büntgen, "Interplay of Environmental and Socio-political Factors in the Downfall of the Eastern Türk Empire in 630 CE." *Climatic Change* 145 (2017): 383–95, https://doi.org/10.1007/s10584-017-2111-0.

Diesenberger, Maximilian. "Repertories and Strategies in Bavaria: Hagiography." In Pohl and Heydemann, *Strategies of Identification*, 209–32.

Diesenberger, Maximilian, and Herwig Wolfram. "Arn und Alkuin: Zwei Freunde und ihre Schriften." In *Erzbischof Arn von Salzburg*, edited by Meta Niederkorn-Bruck and Anton Scharer, VIÖG 40, 81–106. Vienna, 2004.

Dignas, Beate, and Engelbert Winter. *Rome and Persia in Late Antiquity: Neighbours and Rivals*. Cambridge, 2007.

Diószegi, Vilmos, and Mihály Hoppál. *Shamanism in Siberia*. Budapest, 1978.

Ditten, Hans. "Bemerkungen zu den ersten Ansätzen zur Staatsbildung bei Kroaten und Serben im 7. Jahrhundert." In *Beiträge zur byzantinischen Geschichte im 9.–11. Jahrhundert, Kolloquium Libice 1977*, 441–62. Prague, 1978.

Ditten, Hans. "Prominente Slawen und Bulgaren in byzantinischen Diensten (Ende des 7. bis zum Anfang des 10. Jahrhunderts)." In *Besonderheiten der byzantinischen Feudalentwicklung*, edited by Helga Köpstein, 95–119. Berlin, 1983.

Ditten, Hans. "Protobulgaren und Germanen im 5.–7. Jahrhundert (vor der Gründung des ersten bulgarischen Reiches)." *Bulgarian Historical Review* 8 (1980): 51–77.

Ditten, Hans. "Zum Verhältnis zwischen Protobulgaren und Slawen vom Ende des 7. bis zum Anfang des 9. Jahrhunderts." In *Besonderheiten der byzantinischen Feudalentwicklung*, edited by Helga Köpstein, 85–95. Berlin, 1983.

Ditten, Hans. "Zur Bedeutung der Einwanderung der Slawen." In Winkelmann et al., *Byzanz im 7. Jahrhundert*, 73–160.

Dittrich, Ursula-Barbara. *Die Beziehungen Roms zu den Sarmaten und Quaden im 4. Jahrhundert n. Chr. nach der Darstellung des Ammianus Marcellinus*. Bonn, 1984.

Doerfer, Gerhard. *Mongolo-Tungusica*. Wiesbaden, 1985.

Doerfer, Gerhard. "Zur Sprache der Hunnen." *Central Asiatic Journal* 17 (1973): 1–50.

Dölger, Franz. *Regesten der Kaiserurkunden des oströmischen Reiches von 565–1453*. Vol. 1. Munich, 1924.

Dolukhanov, Pavel M. *The Early Slavs: Eastern Europe from the Initial Settlement to the Kievan Rus*. New York, 1996.

Donat, Peter. "Handwerk und Gewerbe." In Herrmann, *Die Slawen in Deutschland*, 100–125.

Drauschke, Jörg, Ewald Kislinger, Karin Kühtreiber, Thomas Kühtreiber, Gabriele Scharrer-Liška, and Tivadar Vida, eds. *Lebenswelten zwischen Archäologie und Geschichte: Festschrift für Falko Daim zu seinem 65. Geburtstag*. Mainz, 2018.

Drijvers, Jan W. "Heraclius and the Restitutio Crucis: Notes on Symbolism and Ideology." In Reinink and Stolte, *The Reign of Heraclius (610–641)*, 175–90.

Drompp, Michael. "Strategies of Cohesion and Control in the Türk and Uyghur Empires." In Bemmann and Schmauder, *Complexity of Interaction*, 437–52.

Drompp, Michael. "Supernumerary Sovereigns: Superfluity and Mutability in the Elite Power Structure of the Early Turks (Tu-jue)." In *Rulers from the Steppe: State Formation on the Eurasian Periphery*, edited by Gary Seaman and Daniel Marks, 92–115. Los Angeles, 1991.

Drompp, M. R. "Imperial State Formation in Inner Asia: The Early Turkic Empires (6th to 9th Centuries)." *Acta Orient. Hung.* 58 (2005): 101–11.

Dujčev, Ivan. "Introduzione." In *Cronaca di Monemvasia*, edited by Ivan Dujčev, Istituto Siciliano di Studi Bizantini e Neoellenici, Testi e monumenti, Testi 12, vii–xlvii. Palermo, 1976.

Duket, Timothy Alan. *A Study in Byzantine Historiography: An Analysis of Theophanes' "Chronographia" and Its Relationship to Theophylact's "History."* Boston, 1980.

Dümmler, Ernst. "Über die älteste Geschichte der Slawen in Dalmatien (549–928)." *Sitzungsberichte der Österreichischen Akademie der Wissenschaften* 20 (1856): 353–430.

Dunlop, Douglas M. *The History of the Jewish Khazars*. Princeton, NJ, 1954.

Dunn, Stephen B. *The Fall and Rise of the Asiatic Mode of Production*. London, 1982.

Durkheim, Émile. *De la division du travail social*. 10th ed. Paris, 1978.

Durliat, Jean. "La peste du VIe siècle: Pour un nouvel examen des sources Byzantines." In *Hommes et richesses dans l'Empire byzantin: IVe–VIIe siècle*, edited by Cathérine Abadie-Reynal, Vassiliki Kravari, Jacques Lefort, and Cécile Morrisson, 107–25. Paris, 1989.

Duval, Noël, and Vladislav Popović, eds. *Caričin Grad*. Vol. 3, *L'acropole et ses monuments*. Collection de l'Ecole Française de Rome 75.3. Rome, 2010.

Dvornik, Francis. *The Making of Central and Eastern Europe*. London, 1949.

Dvornik, Francis. *The Slavs: Their Early History and Civilization*. Survey of Slavic Civilizations 2. Boston, 1959.

Dzino, Danijel. *Becoming Slav, Becoming Croat: Identity Transformations in Post-Roman and Early Medieval Dalmatia*. East Central and Eastern Europe in the Middle Ages, 450–1450, 12. Leiden, 2010.

Eberhard, Wolfgang. *China und seine westlichen Nachbarn*. Darmstadt, 1978.

Ecsedy, Ildikó. "Ancient Turk (Tu-chüeh) Burial Customs." *Acta Orient. Hung.* 38 (1984): 263–87.

Ecsedy, Ildikó. "Cultivators and Barbarians in Ancient China." *Acta Orient. Hung.* 28 (1974): 227–49.

Ecsedy, Ildikó. "Nomads in History and Historical Research." *Acta Orient. Hung.* 35 (1981): 201–27.

Ecsedy, Ildikó. "Old Turkic Titles of Chinese Origin." *Acta Orient. Hung.* 18 (1965): 83–91.

Ecsedy, Ildikó. "Tribe and Empire, Tribe and Society in the Turk Age." *Acta Orient. Hung.* 31 (1977): 3–15.

Ecsedy, Ildikó. "Tribe and Tribal Society in the 6th Century Turk Empire." *Acta Orient. Hung.* 25 (1972): 245–62.

Ecsedy, Ildikó. "Western Turks in Northern China in the Middle of the 7th Century." *Acta Antiqua Academiae Scientiarum Hungaricae* 28 (1980): 249–58.

Effros, Bonnie. *Caring for Body and Soul: Burial and the Afterlife in the Merovingian World*. University Park, PA, 2002.

Eger, Christoph. "Vielteilige Gürtel im südlichen und östlichen Mittelmeerraum." In Bollók, Csiky, and Vida, *Zwischen Byzanz und der Steppe/Between Byzantium and the Steppe*, 153–74.

Eggers, Martin. *Das großmährische Reich: Realität oder Fiktion*. Stuttgart, 1995.

Eichert, Stefan. *Die frühmittelalterlichen Grabfunde Kärntens: Die materielle Kultur Karantaniens anhand der Grabfunde vom Ende der Spätantike bis ins 11. Jahrhundert*. Klagenfurt, 2010.

Eichert, Stefan. *Frühmittelalterliche Strukturen im Ostalpenraum: Studien zu Geschichte und Archäologie Karantaniens*. Klagenfurt, 2012.

Eichert, Stefan. "Grabelsdorf—villa Gabrielis: Betrachtungen zur Entwicklung einer Siedlung vom 7. bis ins 11. Jahrhundert." *Carinthia I* 200 (2010): 105–32.

Eisner, Ján. *Devínska Nová Ves*. Bratislava, 1952.

Elbern, Victor H. "Awarenschatz." In *Lexikon des Mittelalters*, 1:1287. Munich, 1980.

Eliade, Mircea. *Chamanisme et les techniques de l'extase*. 2nd ed. Paris, 1968; 1st ed. translated by Willard R. Trask, *Shamanism: Archaic Techniques of Ecstasy* (Princeton, NJ, 1964).

Eliade, Mircea. *Zalmoxis, the Vanishing God: Comparative Studies in the Religions and Folklore of Dacia and Eastern Europe*. Translated by Willard R. Trask. Chicago, 1972.

Engels, Friedrich. *Vom Ursprung der Familie, des Privateigentums und des Staats* [1884]. 13th ed. Berlin, 1977. Translated by Eleanor Leacock, *The Origin of the Family, Private Property, and the State* (New York, 1942).

Ensslin, Wilhelm. "Slaveneinfälle." In *RE* 3.1 (1927), 697–706.

Entwistle, Chris, and Noël Adams, eds. *Intelligible Beauty: Recent Research on Byzantine Jewellery*. London, 2010.

Epp, Verena. *Amicitia: Zur Geschichte personaler, sozialer, politischer und geistlicher Beziehungen im frühen Mittelalter*. Monographien zur Geschichte des Mittelalters 44. Stuttgart, 1999.

Erdélyi, István. "Über die gegossenen Gürtelgarnituren der Spätawarenzeit östlich von Karpaten." In *Popoli delle steppe*, 1:351–72.

Erdélyi, István, Eszter Ojtozi, and Wladimir F. Gering. *Das Gräberfeld von Newolino: Ausgrabungen von AV Schmidt und der archäologischen Kama-Expedition*. Archaeologica Hungarica 46. Budapest, 1969.

Erdheim, Mario. *Prestige und Kulturwandel: Eine Studie zum Verhältnis subjektiver und objektiver Faktoren des kulturellen Wandels zur Klassengesellschaft bei den Azteken*. Wiesbaden, 1972.

Esders, Stefan. "Herakleios, Dagobert und die 'beschnittenen Völker': Die Umwälzungen des Mittelmeerraumes im 7. Jahrhundert in der Chronik des sogenannten Fredegar." In *Jenseits der Grenzen: Studien zur spätantiken und frühmittelalterlichen Geschichtsschreibung*, edited by Andreas Goltz, Hartmut Leppin, and Heinrich Schlange-Schöningen, 239–311. Berlin, 2009.

Esders, Stefan. "Regionale Selbstbehauptung zwischen Byzanz und dem Frankenreich: Die inquisitio der Rechtsgewohnheiten Istriens durch die Sendboten Karls des Großen und Pippins von Italien." In *Eid und Wahrheitssuche: Studien zu rechtlichen Befragungspraktiken in Mittelalter und früher Neuzeit*, edited by Stefan Esders and Thomas Scharff, 49–112. Frankfurt am Main, 1999.

Ettel, Peter, Falko Daim, Stefanie Berg-Hobohm, Lukas Werther, and Christoph Zielhofer. *Großbaustelle 793: Das Kanalprojekt Karls des Großen zwischen Rhein und Donau*. Wiesbaden, 2014.

Evans, Huw M. A. *The Early Medieval Archaeology of Croatia, 600–900*. Oxford, 1989.

Ewig, Eugen. *Die Merowinger und das Imperium*. Rhein.-westfäl. AW, Vorträge G 261. Opladen, 1983.

Faist, Thomas. *The Volume and Dynamics of International Migration and Transnational Social Spaces*. Oxford, 2000.

Fasoli, Gina. *Le incursione ungare in Europa nel secolo X*. Florence, 1945.

Féher, Geza. *Die Inschrift des Reiterreliefs von Madara*. Sofia, 1928.

Ferdinandy, Michael de. "Die nordeurasischen Reitervölker und der Westen bis zum Mongolensturm." In Altheim, *Historia Mundi*, 173–232.

Ferluga, Jadran. *L'amministrazione bizantina in Dalmazia*. Venice, 1978.

Ferluga, Jadran. *Byzantium on the Balkans: Studies on the Byzantine Administration and the Southern Slavs from the VIIth to the XIIth Centuries*. Amsterdam, 1976.

Ferluga, Jadran. "Gli Slavi del sud ed altri gruppi etnici di fronte a Bisanzio." In *Gli slavi occidentali*, 1:303–44.

Ferluga, Jadran. "Untersuchungen zur byzantinischen Ansiedlungspolitik auf dem Balkan von der Mitte des 7. bis zur Mitte des 9. Jahrhunderts." *Zbornik Radova* 23 (1984): 49–61.

Fichtenau, Heinrich. "Die Urkunden Herzog Tassilos III. und der 'Stiftbrief' von Kremsmünster." In Heinrich Fichtenau, *Beiträge zur Mediävistik*. Vol. 2, *Urkundenforschung*, 66–99. Stuttgart, 1977.

Fiedler, Uwe. "Bulgars in the Lower Danube Region: A Survey of the Archaeological Evidence and the State of Current Research." In Curta, *The Other Europe in the Middle Ages*, 151–236.

Fiedler, Uwe. "Die Donaubulgaren und die Mittelawarenzeit—ein Antagonismus." *Antaeus* 29–30 (2008): 127–41.

Fiedler, Uwe. "Nochmals zur Datierung der Wall- und Grabenzüge an der mittleren Donau: Vorgelagerter Grenzschutz des spätrömischen Reiches oder Machtdemonstration der awarischen Herrscher?" In Bollók, Csiky, and Vida, *Zwischen Byzanz und der Steppe/Between Byzantium and the Steppe*, 335–50.

Fiedler, Uwe. *Studien zu Gräberfeldern des 6.–9. Jahrhunderts an der unteren Donau.* Bonn, 1992.

Fiedler, Uwe. "Zur Datierung der Siedlungen der Awaren und der Landnahme: Ein Beitrag zur Zuordnung der Siedlung von Eperjes." *Zeitschrift für Archäologie* 28 (1994): 307–52.

Findeisen, Hans. *Schamanentum*. Stuttgart, 1957.

Fine, John V. A. "Croats and Slavs: Theories about the Circumstances of the Croats' Appearance in the Balkans." *Byzantinische Forschungen* 26 (2000): 205–18.

Fine, John V. A. *When Ethnicity Did Not Matter in the Balkans: A Study of Identity in Pre-Nationalist Croatia, Dalmatia, and Slavonia in the Medieval and Early Modern Period*. Ann Arbor, 2005.

Fleming, Peter. *News from Tartary*. London, 1938.

Fodor, István. *Altungarn, Bulgarotürken und Ostslawen in Südrussland (Archäologische Beiträge)*, Acta Universitatis de Attila József Nominatae, Acta Antiqua et Archaeologica 20. Szeged, 1977.

Fonjakova, Natalja A., Zlata A. L'vova, Boris I. Maršak, and Vera N. Zalesskaja. "Der Schatz von Mala Pereščepina (Malaja Pereščepina)." In Daim et al., *Hunnen + Awaren*, 209–23.

Franceschi, Carlo de. "Saggi e considerazioni sull'Istria nell'alto medioevo: 2. Cessensis episcopus." *Atti e Memorie della Società per la Storia dell'Istria* 18 (1970): 69–106.

Franke, Herbert. *Das chinesische Kaiserreich*. Fischer-Weltgeschichte 19. Frankfurt am Main, 1968.

Franke, Herbert. "Fremdherrschaften in China und ihr Einfluss auf die staatlichen Institutionen (10.–14. Jahrhundert)." *Anzeiger der Phil.-Hist. Klasse der Österreichischen Akademie der Wissenschaften* 122 (1985): 47–67.

Franke, Otto. *Geschichte des chinesischen Reiches*. 3 vols. Leipzig, 1936.

Freeden, Ute von. "Awarische Funde in Süddeutschland?" *Jahrbuch des Römisch-Germanischen Zentralmuseums* 38 (1991): 593–601.

Freiberger, Viktor, and Birgit Bühler. "Der Goldschatz von Nagyszentmiklós/Sânnicolau Mare: Ergebnisse der goldschmiedetechnischen Untersuchungen und der Materialanalysen." In Daim et al., *Der Goldschatz*, 9–42.

Frendo, J. D. "The Miracles of St. Demetrius and the Capture of Thessaloniki." *Byzantinoslavica* 58 (1997): 205–24.

Friesinger, Herwig. "Alpenslawen und Bayern." In Herrmann, *Welt der Slawen*, 109–22.

Friesinger, Herwig. *Die Slawen in Niederösterreich*. Wissenschaftliche Schriftenreihe Niederösterreich 15. 2nd ed. St. Pölten, 1978.

Friesinger, Herwig. "Das slawische Gräberfeld von Wimm." *Archaeologia Austriaca* 68 (1984): 203–77.

Friesinger, Herwig. *Die vielen Väter Österreichs: Römer—Germanen—Slawen. Eine Spurensuche.* Vienna, 1987.

Friesinger, Herwig, and Falko Daim, eds. *Typen der Ethnogenese unter besonderer Berücksichtigung der Bayern.* Vol. 2. DsÖAW 204. Vienna, 1990.

Fritze, Wolfgang. "Die fränkische Schwurfreundschaft der Merowingerzeit." *Zeitschrift der Savigny-Stiftung für Rechtsgeschichte: Germanistische Abteilung* 71 (1954): 74–125.

Fritze, Wolfgang. "Probleme der obodritischen Stammes- und Reichsverfassung und ihrer Entwicklung vom Stammesstaat zum Herrschaftsstaat." In *Siedlung und Verfassung der Slawen zwischen Elbe, Saale und Oder,* edited by Herbert Ludat, 141–219. Gießen, 1960.

Fritze, Wolfgang. "Slawische Altertumswissenschaft." In Wolfgang Fritze, *Frühzeit zwischen Ostsee und Donau: Ausgewählte Beiträge zum geschichtlichen Werden im östlichen Mitteleuropa,* Berliner Historische Studien 6, 17–30. Berlin, 1982.

Fritze, Wolfgang. "Universalis Gentium Confessio: Formeln, Träger und Wege universalmissionarischen Denkens im 7. Jahrhundert." *Frühmittelalterliche Studien* 2 (1959): 78–130.

Fritze, Wolfgang. *Untersuchungen zur frühslawischen und frühfränkischen Geschichte bis ins 7. Jahrhundert.* Frankfurt am Main, 1994.

Fritze, Wolfgang. "Zur Bedeutung der Awaren für die slawische Ausdehnungsbewegung im frühen Mittelalter." In Mildenberger, *Studien zur Völkerwanderungszeit im östlichen Mitteleuropa,* 498–545.

Fritze, Wolfgang H. "Slawen und Avaren im angelsächsischen Missionsprogramm. III. Bedas Hunni und die Entstehung der angelsächsischen Missionsvölkerliste von 703/04." *Zeitschrift für slavische Philologie* 33 (1967/68): 358–72.

Fülep, Ferenc. "Beiträge zur frühmittelalterlichen Geschichte von Pécs." *Acta Arch. Hung.* 25 (1973): 307–26.

Fülöp, Gyula. "Awarenzeitliche Fürstenfunde von Igar." *Acta Arch. Hung.* 40 (1988): 151–90.

Fülöp, Gyula. "New Research on Finds of Avar Chieftain-Burials at Igar, Hungary." In *From the Baltic to the Black Sea: Studies in Medieval Archaeology,* edited by David Austian and Leslie Alcock, 138–46. London, 1990.

Fusek, Gabriel. "Beitrag zu Problemen der Datierung von der Besiedlung der Westslowakei in der älteren Phase des Frühmittelalters." In *The Early Slavic Settlement of Central Europe in the Light of New Dating Evidence,* Interdisciplinary Medieval Studies 3, 139–50. Wroclaw, 2013.

Fusek, Gabriel. "Der Bestattungsritus und die materielle Kultur der Slawen im 6.–8. Jh. in der Südwestslowakei." In Bialeková and Zábojník, *Ethnische und kulturelle Verhältnisse an der mittleren Donau,* 37–50.

Fusek, Gabriel. "Formanalyse vollständiger Gefäße oder ein weiterer Versuch, frühmittelalterliche Keramikgefäße aus der Slowakei zu klassifizieren." *Spisy archeologického ústavu AV ČR Brno* 4 (1995): 15–34.

Fusek, Gabriel. "Frühe Slawen im Mitteldonaugebiet." In Bemmann and Schmauder, *Kulturwandel in Mitteleuropa,* 645–56.

Fusek, Gabriel, and Jozef Zábojník. "Ausklang der Spätantike und Anfang des Frühmittelalters in der nördlichen Peripherie des Karpatenbeckens." In *Archeologia o poczatkach Słowian: Materialy z konferencji, Kraków, 19–21 listopada 2001,* 541–66. Kraków, 2005.

Gabain, Annemarie von. "Inhalt und magische Bedeutung der alttürkischen Inschriften." *Anthropos* 48 (1953): 537–56.

Gáll, Erwin. "The Avar Conquest and What Followed: Some Ideas on the Process of 'Avarisation' of the Transylvanian Basin (6th–7th Centuries)." In *Archäologische Beiträge: Gedenkschrift zum hundertsten Geburtstag von Kurt Horedt*, 295–324. Cluj-Napoca, 2014.

Gáll, Erwin, and Sándor Romát. "The Current State of Archaeological Research on the Avar Period in the Banat: Observations on the Changes in the Avar Settlement Territory in this Region and on Some Early Medieval Cultural-Sociological Phenomena." In Bollók, Csiky, and Vida, *Zwischen Byzanz und der Steppe/Between Byzantium and the Steppe*, 433–68.

Gantner, Clemens, Cinzia Grifoni, Walter Pohl, and Marianne Pollheimer, eds. *Transformations of Romanness in the Early Middle Ages: Regions and Identities*. Berlin, 2018.

Garam, Éva. *Das awarenzeitliche Gräberfeld von Tiszafüred*. Cemeteries of the Avar Period (567–829) in Hungary 3. Budapest, 1995.

Garam, Éva. *Das awarenzeitlichen Gräberfeld von Kisköre*. Fontes Arch. Hungaricae. Budapest, 1979.

Garam, Éva. "Der awarische Fundstoff im Karpatenbecken und seine zeitliche Gliederung." In Hänsel, *Die Völker Südosteuropas vom 6.–8. Jahrhundert*, 191–202.

Garam, Éva. "Bemerkungen zum ältesten Fundmaterial der Awarenzeit." In Friesinger and Daim, *Typen der Ethnogenese*, 253–72.

Garam, Éva. "The Connection of the Avar Period Princely and Common Gravegoods with the Nagyszentmiklós Treasure." In Kovács, *The Gold of the Avars*, 81–112.

Garam, Éva. *Funde byzantinischer Herkunft in der Awarenzeit vom Ende des 6. bis zum Ende des 7. Jahrhunderts*. Budapest, 2001.

Garam, Éva. "Der Fund von Vörösmart im archäologischen Nachlass der Awarenzeit." *Folia Archaeologica* 33 (1982): 187–213.

Garam, Éva. "Kugeln—Kapseln—Taschen—Scheiben in awarenzeitlichen Gräbern." In *Festschrift für Hermann Dannheimer zum 80. Geburtstag*, edited by Rupert Gebhard, Hans-Jörg Kellner, Alois Schmid, and Ludwig Wamser, special issue, *Bayerische Vorgeschichtsblätter* 75 (2010): 147–68.

Garam, Éva. "Die münzdatierten Gräber der Awarenzeit." In Daim, *Awarenforschungen*, 1:135–250.

Garam, Éva. "L'oro degli Avari." In *L'oro degli Avari*, 33–75.

Garam, Éva. "Pferde- und Reiterbestattungen in der Spätawarenzeit (8.–9. Jahrhundert)." In Daim and Friesinger, *Die Bayern und ihre Nachbarn*, 123–26.

Garam, Éva. Review of *Der Schatzfund von Vrap in Albanien: Studien zur Archäologie der Awaren 2*, by Joachim Werner. *Bonner Jahrbücher* 187 (1987): 854–57.

Garam, Éva. "Über die frühawarischen Gräber von Zsámbok." *Folia Archaeologica* 34 (1983): 139–56.

Garam, Éva. "The Vrap Treasure." In *From Attila to Charlemagne: Arts of the Early Medieval Period in the Metropolitan Museum of Art*, 170–79. New York, 2000.

Gasparri, Stefano, ed. *774—ipotesi su una transizione*. Turnhout, 2008.

Gasparri, Stefano. *I duchi longobardi*. Rome, 1978.

Gavrituchin, Igor. "The Archaeological Heritage of the Avar Khaganate and the Southern Part of Eastern Europe: Periodisation, Dating and Synchronisation." *Antaeus* 29–30 (2008): 63–125.

Geary, Patrick J. "Ethnic Identity as a Situational Construct in the Early Middle Ages." *Mitteilungen der Anthropologischen Gesellschaft in Wien* 113 (1983): 15–26.

Geary, Patrick. J. *The Myth of Nations: The Medieval Origins of Europe*. Princeton, NJ, 2001.

Geary, Patrick J., and Krishna Veeramah. "Mapping European Population Movement through Genomic Research." *Medieval Worlds* 4 (2016): 65–78. doi: 10.1553/medievalworlds_no4_2016s65, http://www.medievalworlds.net/medieval_worlds?frames=yes

Gellner, Ernest. *State and Society in Soviet Thought: Explorations in Social Structures.* Oxford, 1988.

Genito, Bruno. "Archaeology of the Early Medieval Nomads in Southern Italy: The Horse-Burials in Molise (7th Century) South-Central Italy." In Bálint, *Kontakte zwischen Iran*, 229–48.

Gerov, Boris V. "Marcianopolis im Lichte der historischen Angaben und der archäologischen, epigraphischen und numismatischen Materialien und Forschungen." In Boris V. Gerov, *Beiträge zur Geschichte der römischen Provinzen Moesien und Thrakien: Gesammelte Aufsätze.* Vol. 1, 289–311. Amsterdam, 1980.

Ghirshman, Roman. *Les Chionites-Hephthalites.* Cairo, 1948.

Giesler, Jochen. "Zur Archäologie des Ostalpenraumes vom 8. bis 11. Jahrhundert." *Archäologisches Korrespondezblatt* 10 (1980): 85–98.

Gieysztor, Alexander. "Les antiquités slaves: Problèmes d'une historiographie bicentenaire." In *Gli slavi occidentali*, 1:15–40.

Gillett, Andrew, ed. *On Barbarian Identity: Critical Approaches to Ethnicity in the Early Middle Ages.* Studies in the Early Middle Ages 4. Turnhout, 2002.

Ginpū, Uchida. "On the Theory of Rouran-Avar Identity [in Japanese]." *Shisen* 23–24 (1962): 23–34.

Ginzel, Friedrich Karl. *Spezieller Kanon der Sonnen- und Mondfinsternisse für das Ländergebiet der klassischen Altertumswissenschaften und den Zeitraum von 900 vor Chr. bis 600 nach Chr.* Berlin, 1899.

Gjuzelev, Vasil. "Bulgarisch-fränkische Beziehungen in der ersten Hälfte des 9. Jahrhunderts." In Vasil Gjuzelev, *Forschungen zur Geschichte Bulgariens im Mittelalter*, Miscellanea Bulgarica 3, 135–59. Vienna, 1986.

Gjuzelev, Vasil. "Chan Asparuch und die Gründung des bulgarisches Reiches." In Vasil Gjuzelev, *Forschungen zur Geschichte Bulgariens im Mittelalter*, Miscellanea Bulgarica 3, 3–24. Vienna, 1986.

Glaser, Franz. *Frühes Christentum im Alpenraum.* Graz, 1997.

Glaser, Franz. "Der Untergang der Antike und ihr Nachleben in Noricum." In Bratož, *Slovenija*, 1:199–218.

Gli slavi occidentali e meridionali nell'alto medioevo. 2 vols. SSCI 30. Spoleto, 1983.

Göbl, Robert, and András Róna-Tas. *Die Inschriften des Schatzes von Nagy-Szentmiklós*, DsÖAW, Phil.-hist. Kl., 240. Vienna, 1995.

Göckenjan, Hansgerd. *Hilfsvölker und Grenzwächter im mittelalterlichen Ungarn.* Quellen und Studien zur Geschichte des östlichen Europas 5. Wiesbaden, 1972.

Göckenjan, Hansgerd. "Zur Stammesstruktur und Heeresorganisation altaischer Völker: Das Dezimalsystem." In *Europa Slavica, Europa Orientalis: Festschrift für Herbert Ludat zum 70. Geburtstag*, edited by Klaus-Detlev Grothusen and Klaus Zernack, 51–84. Berlin, 1980.

Göckenjan, Hansgerd, and István Zimonyi. *Orientalische Berichte über die Völker Osteuropas und Zentralasiens im Mittelalter: Die Ġayhānī-Tradition (Ibn Rusta, Gardīzī, Ḥudūd al-'Ālam, al-Bakrī und al-Marwazī).* Veröffentlichungen der Societas Uralo-Altaica 54. Wiesbaden, 2001.

Godelier, Maurice. *The Making of Great Men: Male Domination and Power among the New Guinea Baruya.* Cambridge, 1986.

Godelier, Maurice. *The Enigma of the Gift.* Chicago, 1999.

Godłowski, Kazimierz. "Die Frage der slawischen Einwanderung in östliche Mitteleuropa." *Zeitschrift für Ostforschung* 28 (1979): 416–47.

Godłowski, Kazimierz. "Zur Frage der Slawensitze vor der großen Slawenwanderung im 6. Jahrhundert." In *Gli slavi occidentali*, 1:257–84.

Goffart, Walter A. *The Narrators of Barbarian History (A.D. 550–800): Jordanes, Gregory of Tours, Bede, and Paul the Deacon.* Princeton, NJ, 1988.

Gojda, Martin. *The Ancient Slavs: Settlement and Society*. Edinburgh, 1991.

Gołab, Zbigniew. "Old Bulgarian Sěverъ (?) and Old Russian Sěverjane." *Wiener Slavistisches Jahrbücher* 30 (1984): 9–22.

Gołab, Zbigniew. *The Origins of the Slavs: A Linguist's View*. Columbus, 1992.

Golb, Norman, and Omeljan Pritsak. *Khazarian Hebrew Documents of the Tenth Century*. Ithaca, NY, 1982.

Gold der Skythen aus der Leningrader Eremitage. Exhibition catalog. Munich, 1984.

Golden, Peter B. *Central Asia in World History*. Oxford, 2011.

Golden, Peter B. "The Conversion of the Khazars to Judaism." In Golden, Ben-Shammai, and Róna-Tas, *The World of the Khazars*, 123–67.

Golden, Peter B. "Ethnogenesis in the Tribal Zone: The Shaping of the Turks." In Golden and Hriban, *Studies on the Peoples*, 17–64.

Golden, Peter B. *An Introduction to the History of the Turkic Peoples*. Wiesbaden, 1992.

Golden, Peter B. "The Karakhanids and Early Islam." In Sinor, *The Cambridge History of Early Inner Asia*, 343–70.

Golden, Peter B. "Khazaria and Judaism." *Archivum Eurasiae Medii Aevi* 3 (1983): 127–56.

Golden, Peter B. *Khazar Studies: An Historico-Philological Inquiry into the Origins of the Khazars*. 2 vols. Budapest, 1980.

Golden, Peter B. "The Migration of the Oguz." *Archivum Ottomanicum* 4 (1972): 41–84.

Golden, Peter B. "Nomads and Their Sedentary Neighbors in Pre-Činggisid Eurasia." *Archivum Eurasiae Medii Aevi* 7 (1987–91): 41–82.

Golden, Peter B. "Nomads of the Western Eurasian Steppes: Oγurs, Onoγurs and Khazars." In Golden and Hriban, *Studies on the Peoples*, 135–62.

Golden, Peter B. "Oq and Oğur-Oğuz." *Turkic Languages* 16 (2012): 155–99.

Golden, Peter B. "Religion among the Qipčaqs of Medieval Eurasia." *Central Asiatic Journal* 42 (1998): 180–237.

Golden, Peter B. "Some Notes on the Avars and Rouran." In *The Steppe Lands and the World Beyond Them: Studies in Honor of Victor Spinei on His 70th Birthday*, edited by Florin Curta and Bogdan-Petru Maleon, 43–66. Iaşi, 2013.

Golden, Peter B. "The Stateless Nomads of Central Eurasia." In Di Cosmo and Maas, *Empires and Exchanges in Eurasian Late Antiquity*, 317–32.

Golden, Peter B. "War and Warfare in the Pre-Činggisid Western Steppes of Eurasia." In Di Cosmo, *Warfare in Inner Asian History*, 105–72.

Golden, Peter B., Haggai Ben-Shammai, and András Róna-Tas, eds. *The World of the Khazars: New Perspectives*, Handbook of Oriental Studies 17. Leiden, 2007.

Golden, Peter B., and Catalin Hriban, eds. *Studies on the Peoples and Cultures of the Eurasian Steppes*. Bucaresti, 2011.

Goldstein, Ivo. *Bizant na Jadranu od Justijana 1. do Bazilija 1*. Zagreb, 1992.

Goldstein, Ivo. *Croatia: A History*. London, 1999.

Gömöri, János. "Archaeometallurgy in Hungary: Some Results and Questions." In *The Archaeometallurgy of Iron: Recent Developments in Archaeological and Scientific Research*, edited by Jiří Hošek, Henry Cleere, and Lubomír Mihok, 65–72, 293–95. Prague, 2011.

Goody, Jack. *Succession to High Office*. Cambridge, 1966.

Goubert, Paul. "Les Avares d'après les sources grecques du VIe siècle." In *Akten des 24. internationalen Orientalisten-Kongresses*, 214–16. Wiesbaden, 1959.

Goubert, Paul. *Byzance avant l'Islam*. Vol. 2, *Byzance et l'occident sous les successeurs de Justinien*, bk. 1, *Byzance et les Francs*. Paris, 1956.

Goubert, Paul. *Byzance avant l'Islam*. Vol. 2, *Byzance et l'occident sous les successeurs de Justinien*, bk. 2, *Rome, Byzance et Carthage*. Paris, 1965.

Goubert, Paul. "Les guerres sur le Danube à la fin du VIe siècle d'après Ménandre le Protecteur et Théophylacte Simocatta." In *Actes du XIIe Congrès des Études Byzantines*, 2:214–16. Belgrade, 1964.

Graebner, Michael D. *The Role of the Slavs Within the Byzantine Empire, 500–1018*. New Brunswick, NJ, 1975.

Grafenauer, Bogo. "Razmerje med Slovani in Obri do obleganja Carigrada (626) in njegove gospodarsko-družbene podlage." *Zgodovinski Časopis* 4 (1955): 145–53.

Grafenauer, Bogo. *Zgodovina Slovencev*. Ljubljana, 1979.

Graff, David A. "Strategy and Contingency in the Tang Defeat of the Eastern Turks, 629–630." In Di Cosmo, *Warfare in Inner Asian History*, 33–72.

Graus, František. "Deutsche und slawische Verfassungsgeschichte?" *Historische Zeitschrift* 197, no. 1 (1963): 265–317.

Graus, František. "Die Entwicklung Mitteleuropas im 8. Jahrhundert und die Vorbedingungen der Staatenentwicklung in diesem Gebiet." In *I problemi dell'occidente nel secolo VIII*, SSCI 20, 1:451–82. Spoleto, 1973.

Graus, František. *Die Nationenbildung der Westslawen im Mittelalter*. Sigmaringen, 1980.

Greatrex, Geoffrey. "Introduction." In *The Chronicle of Pseudo-Zachariah Rhetor: Church and War in Late Antiquity*, translated by Geoffrey Greatrex, Robert R. Phenix, and Cornelia B. Horn. Translated Texts for Historians 55, 1–94. Liverpool, 2011.

Greatrex, Geoffrey. "Roman Identity in the Sixth Century." In *Ethnicity and Culture in Late Antiquity*, edited by Stephen Mitchell and Geoffrey Greatrex, 267–92. Oakville, CT, 2000.

Grégoire, Henri. "L'origine et le nom des Croates et des Serbes." *Byzantion* 17 (1944–45): 88–118.

Grenet, Frantz. "Regional Interaction in Central Asia and North-West India in the Kidarite and Hephthalite Period." In *Indo-Iranian Languages and Peoples*, edited by Nicholas Sims-Williams, Proceedings of the British Academy 116, 203–34. Oxford, 2002.

Grignaschi, Mario. "La chute de l'empire hephthalite dans les sources byzantines et le problème des Avares." In Harmatta, *From Hecataeus to al-Huwarizmi*, 219–48.

Grigoriou-Ionnidou, Martha. "Une remarque sur le récit des miracles de Saint Démétrius." *Publications du Comité National Grec des Études du Sud-Est Européen* 20 (1987): 3–15.

Groh, Kurt. *Geschichte des oströmischen Kaisers Justin II*. Leipzig, 1889.

Grosse, Robert. *Römische Militärgeschichte von Gallienus bis zum Beginn der byzantinischen Themenverfassung*. Berlin, 1920.

Das Grossmährische Reich. Prague, 1966.

Grousset, René. *The Empire of the Steppes: A History of Central Asia*. Translated by Naomi Walford. New Brunswick, 1970.

Grousset, René, *Die Reise nach Westen, oder wie Hsüan Tsang den Buddhismus nach China holte*. Cologne, 1986. English translation: René Grousset, *In the Footsteps of the Buddha* (New York, 1971).

Grumel, Venance. "La défence maritime de Constantinople du côté de la Corne d'Or et le siège des Avars." *Byzantinoslavica* 25 (1964): 217–33.

Grumel, Venance. "Homélie de Saint Germain sur la délivrance de Constantinople." *Revue des Études Byzantines* 16 (1958): 183–205.

Gschwantler, Kurt. "The Nagyszentmiklós Treasure Catalogue 1–23." In Kovács, *The Gold of the Avars*, 15–44.

Gschwantler, Otto. "Die Heldensage von Alboin und Rosimund." In *Festgabe für Otto Höfler zum 75. Geburtstag*, edited by Helmut Birkhan, 214–54. Vienna, 1976.

Guignes, Joseph de. *Histoire générale des Huns, des Turcs, des Mongols et des autres Tartares occidentaux*. 4 vols. Paris, 1756–58.

Guldescu, Stanko. *History of Medieval Croatia*. The Hague, 1964.

Gutschmidt, Karl, Sebastian Kempgen, Tilman Berger, and Peter Kosta, eds. *Die slavischen Sprachen: Ein internationales Handbuch zu ihrer Struktur, ihrer Geschichte und ihrer Erforschung / The Slavic Languages: An International Handbook of Their Structure, Their History and Their Investigation*. 2 vols. Berlin, 2009–14. For a table of contents in English, see https://www.degruyter.com/viewbooktoc/product/40815.

Györffy, György. "Landnahme, Ansiedlung und Streifzüge der Ungarn." *Acta Historica Academiae Scientarum Hungaricae* 31 (1985): 231–70.

Hahn, Wolfgang. "Die Fundmünzen des 5.–9. Jahrhunderts in Österreich und den unmittelbar angrenzenden Gebieten." In Herwig Wolfram, *Die Geburt Mitteleuropas: Geschichte Österreichs vor seiner Entstehung*, 453–64. Vienna, 1987.

Hahn, Wolfgang. *Moneta Imperii Byzantini*. Vol. 1, *Von Anastasius I. bis Justinianus I.* Vienna, 1973.

Haldon, John. *Byzantium in the Seventh Century*. Cambridge, 1990.

Haldon, John. *The Empire that Would Not Die: The Paradox of Eastern Roman Survival, 640–740*. Cambridge, 2016.

Haldon, John. *Warfare and Society in the Byzantine World, 565–1204*. London, 1999.

Haldon, John F. *The State and the Tributary Mode of Production*. London, 1993.

Halperin, Charles J. "Bulgars and Slavs in the First Bulgarian Empire: A Reconsideration of the Historiography." *Archivum Eurasiae Medii Aevi* 3 (1983): 183–200.

Halsall, Guy. *Cemeteries and Society in Merovingian Gaul: Selected Studies in History and Archaeology, 1992–2009*. Leiden, 2009.

Halsall, Guy. *Settlement and Social Organization: The Merovingian Region of Metz*. Cambridge, 1995.

Hämäläinen, Pekka. "What's in a Concept? The Kinetic Empire of the Comanches." *History and Theory* 52 (2013): 81–90.

Hambly, Gavin. *Zentralasien*. Fischer-Weltgeschichte 16. Frankfurt am Main, 1966.

Hamilton, James. "Toquz-Oguz et On-Uygur." *Journal Asiatique* 250 (1962): 33–54.

Hannestad, Knud. "Les relations de Byzance avec la Transcaucasie et l'Asie centrale aux 5e et 6e siècles." *Byzantion* 25–27 (1955–57): 421–56.

Hänsel, Bernhard, ed. *Die Völker Südosteuropas vom 6.–8. Jahrhundert: Symposion Tutzing 1985*, Südosteuropäisches Jahrbuch 17. Munich, 1987.

Hansen, Valerie. *Silk Road: A New History*. Oxford, 2012.

Hardt, Matthias. *Gold und Herrschaft: Die Schätze europäischer Könige und Fürsten im ersten Jahrtausend*. Europa im Mittelalter 6. Berlin, 2004.

Hardt, Matthias. "Der Supan: Ein Forschungsbericht." *Zeitschrift für Ostforschung* 39 (1990): 161–71.

Hardt, Matthias. "Der Ring der Awaren." In Drauschke et al., *Lebenswelten zwischen Archäologie und Geschichte*, 185–92.

Harhoiu, Radu. "Archäologische Grabungen in Schässburg—Dealul Viilor, Fundstelle 'Gräberfeld': Befund 359—ein Wohngebäude aus der Spätawarenzeit." In Bollók, Csiky, and Vida, *Zwischen Byzanz und der Steppe/Between Byzantium and the Steppe*, 393–432.

Harmatta, János, ed. *From Hecateus to al-Huwarizmi: Bactrian, Pahlavi, Sogdian, Persian, Sanskrit, Syriac, Arabic, Chinese, Greek and Latin Sources for the History of Pre-Islamic Central Asia*. Collection of the Sources for the History of Pre-Islamic Asia, ser. 1, 3. Budapest, 1984.

Harmatta, János. "Sogdian Inscriptions on Avar Objects." *Acta Orient. Hung.* 48 (1995): 61–65.

Harmatta, János. "Turk and Avar Runic Inscriptions on Metal Belts." *Acta Antiqua Academiae Scientiarum Hungaricae* 37 (1996/97): 321–30.

Harrison, R. Martin. *Excavations at Sarachane in Istanbul*. Vol. 1. Princeton, NJ, 1986.

Hartmann, Ludo Moritz. *Geschichte Italiens im Mittelalter*. Vol. 2, bk. 1, *Römer und Langobarden bis zur Theilung Italiens*. Gotha, 1900.

Hartog, François. *Le miroir d'Hérodote*. Paris, 1991.

Haseloff, Günther. "Germanischer und östlicher Tierstil." In *Popoli delle steppe*, 2:681–707.

Hauptfeld, Georg. "Völker und Institutionen des Exercitus Langobardorum in Italien, 568–680." PhD diss., University of Vienna, 1982.

Hauptmann, Ludmil. "Die Frühzeit der West- und Südslawen." In Altheim, *Historia Mundi*, 301–31.

Hauptmann, Ludmil. "Politische Umwälzungen unter den Slowenen vom Ende des sechsten Jahrhunderts bis zur Mitte des neunten." *MIÖG* 36 (1915): 229–87.

Hauptmann, Ludmil. "Les rapports des Byzantins avec les Slaves et les Avares pendant la seconde moitié du VIe siècle." *Byzantion* 4 (1927–28): 137–70.

Haussig, Hans W. *Die Geschichte Zentralasiens und der Seidenstrasse in vorislamischer Zeit*. Darmstadt, 1983.

Haussig, Hans W. "Indogermanische und altaische Nomadenvölker im Grenzgebiet Irans." In Altheim, *Historia Mundi*, 233–50.

Haussig, Hans W. "Die protobulgarische Fürstenliste." In *Die Hunnen in Osteuropa*, edited by Franz Altheim and Hans W. Haussig, 9–29. Baden-Baden, 1958.

Haussig, Hans W. "Die Quellen über die zentralasiatische Herkunft der europäischen Awaren." *Central Asiatic Journal* 2 (1956): 21–43.

Haussig, Hans W. Review of *Der Grabfund von Malaja Pereščepina und Kuvrat, Kagan der Bulgaren*, by Joachim Werner. *UAJB*, n.s., 5 (1985): 275–77.

Haussig, Hans W. "Die Runen des Schatzes von Nagy-Szent-Miklós in ihrer Bedeutung für die Runeninschriften Osteuropas." In Röhrborn and Veenker, *Runen, Tamgas und Graffiti*, 17–52.

Haussig, Hans W. "Theophylakts Exkurs über die skythischen Völker." *Byzantion* 23 (1953): 275–436.

Haussig, Hans W. "Über die Bedeutung der Namen Hunnen und Awaren." *UAJB* 47 (1975): 95–103.

Haussig, Hans W. "Zur Lösung der Awarenfrage." *Byzantinoslavica* 34 (1973): 173–92.

Havlík, Lubomir E. "Die Byzantiner über die Verfassung der Slawen im 6. und 7. Jahrhundert." In *From Late Antiquity to Early Byzantium: Byzantine Symposium of the 16th Eirene Conference*, edited by Vladimir Vavřinek, 173–78. Prague, 1985.

Heather, Peter. "The Late Roman Art of Client Management: Imperial Defence in the Fourth Century West." In Pohl, Wood, and Reimitz, *The Transformation of Frontiers*, 15–68.

Heinrich-Tamáska, Orsolya. "Avar-Age Metalworking Technologies in the Carpathian Basin (Sixth to Eighth Century)." In Curta, *The Other Europe in the Middle Ages*, 237–61.

Heinrich-Tamáska, Orsolya. "Byzantine Goldsmithing in Avaria? Exchange and Transfer at the Edge of the Empire during the Seventh Century AD." In Bugarski et al., *GrenzÜbergänge*, 273–90.

Heinrich-Tamáska, Orsolya. "Une époque de bouleversement? Remarques sur l'étude de l'antiquité tardive et de la paléochrétienté en Pannonie." In Bollók, Csiky, and Vida, *Zwischen Byzanz und der Steppe/Between Byzantium and the Steppe*, 291–306.

Heinrich-Tamáska, Orsolya, ed. *Keszthely-Fenékpuszta im Kontext spätantiker Kontinuitätsforschung zwischen Noricum and Moesia*. Budapest, 2011.

Heinrich-Tamáska, Orsolya. "Sakral- oder Profanbauten? Zur Funktion und
    Datierung der Kirchen von Keszthely-Fenékpuszta (Komitat Zala, Ungarn)."
    In *Kirchenarchäologie heute: Fragestellungen—Methoden—Ergebnisse*, edited by
    Niklot Krohn, 91–112. Darmstadt, 2010.
Heinrich-Tamáska, Orsolya. "Die spätrömische Innenbefestigung von Keszthely-
    Fenékpuszta: Innere Chronologie und funktioneller Wandel." In Heinrich-
    Tamáska, *Keszthely-Fenékpuszta*, 653–702.
Heinrich-Tamáska, Orsolya. *Die Stein- und Glasinkrustationskunst des 6. und 7. Jahrhunderts
    im Karpatenbecken*. Monumenta Avarorum Archaeologica 8. Budapest, 2006.
Heinrich-Tamáska, Orsolya. "Tier- und Zahnschnittornamentik im awarenzeitlichen
    Karpatenbecken." *Berichte der Römisch-Germanischen Kommission* 87 (2006):
    507–628.
Heinrich-Tamáska, Orsolya, and Mike Schweissing. "Strontiumisotopen- und
    Radiokarbonuntersuchungen am anthropologischen Fundmaterial von Keszthely-
    Fenékpuszta: ihr Aussagepotential zu Fragen der Migration und Chronologie." In
    Heinrich-Tamáska, *Keszthely-Fenékpuszta*, 457–74.
Heinzelmann, Martin. *Gregory of Tours: History and Society in the Sixth Century*.
    Cambridge, 2001.
Heissig, Walther. "Ethnische Gruppenbildung in Zentralasien im Licht mündlicher und
    schriftlicher Überlieferung." In *Studien zur Ethnogenese*, 29–56.
Heissig, Walther. *The Religions of Mongolia*. London, 1981.
Heissig, Werner, and Hans-Joachim Klimkeit, eds. *Synkretismus in den Religionen
    Zentralasiens*. Wiesbaden, 1987.
Hellmann, Manfred. "Grundlagen slawischer Verfassungsgeschichte des frühen
    Mittelalters." *Jahrbücher für Geschichte Osteuropas*, n.s., 2 (1954): 387–404.
Hellmann, Manfred. "Problematik der slawischen Frühzeit." *Jahrbücher für Geschichte
    Osteuropas*, n.s., 7 (1959): 196–203.
Hennig, Richard. "Die Einführung der Seidenraupenzucht ins Byzantinerreich:
    eine Studie zur Aufklärung der Unklarheiten in den überlieferten Berichten."
    Byzantinische Zeitschrift 33 (1933): 295–312.
Henning, Joachim. "Gefangenenfesseln im slawischen Siedlungsraum und der
    europäische Sklavenhandel im 6. bis 12. Jahrhundert." *Germania* 70 (1992):
    403–26.
Henning, Joachim, ed. *Post-Roman Towns, Trade and Settlement in Europe and
    Byzantium*. Vol. 1, *The Heirs of the Roman West*, and Vol. 2, *Byzantium, Pliska, and
    the Balkans*, Millennium-Studies 5.1–2. Berlin, 2007.
Henning, Joachim. *Südosteuropa zwischen Antike und Mittelalter: Archäologische Beiträge
    zur Landwirtschaft des 1. Jahrtausend u. Z*. Schriften zur Ur- und Frühgeschichte
    42. Berlin, 1987.
Henning, Joachim. "Untersuchungen zur Entwicklung der Landwirtschaft in
    Südosteuropa im Übergang von der Spätantike zum frühen Mittelalter."
    Ethnographisch-archäologische Zeitschrift 25 (1984): 123–30.
Henning, Walter B. "A Farewell to the Khagan of the Aq-Aqatärän." *Bulletin of the School
    of Oriental and African Studies* 14, no. 3 (1952): 501–22.
Herold, Hajnalka. "Die Awarenzeit im Burgenland: Archäologische Forschungsergebnisse
    zur Siedlung und zum Gräberfeld von Zillingtal." *Burgenländische Heimatblätter* 73
    (2011): 134–57, http://www.zobodat.at/pdf/Burgenlaendische-Heimat
    blaetter_73_0134-0157.pdf.
Herold, Hajnalka. *Die awarenzeitliche Siedlung und die gefäßkeramischen Funde des
    awarenzeitlichen Gräberfeldes von Zillingtal, Burgenland*, Monographien des
    Römisch—Germanischen Zentralmuseums. Mainz, 2010.

Herold, Hajnalka. *Die frühmittelalterliche Siedlung von Örménykút 54*, Varia Archaeologica Hungarica 14. Budapest, 2004.

Herrmann, Erwin. *Slawisch-germanische Beziehungen im südostdeutschen Raum von der Spätantike bis zum Ungarnsturm, ein Quellenbuch mit Erläuterungen.* Veröffentlichungen des Collegium Carolinum 17. Munich, 1965.

Herrmann, Joachim. "Austausch und Handel." In Herrmann, *Die Slawen in Deutschland*, 126–52.

Herrmann, Joachim. "Byzanz und die Slawen 'am äußersten Ende des westlichen Ozeans.'" In *Les slaves et le monde mediterraneen, VIe–XIe siècles*, Symposion international de archéologie slave, 35–44. Sofia, 1973.

Herrmann, Joachim. "Germanen—Slawen—Deutsche: Neue Untersuchungen zum frühgeschichtlichen Siedlungswesen östlich der Elbe." *Prähistorische Zeitschrift* 66 (1991): 119–33.

Herrmann, Joachim. "Militärische Demokratie und die Übergangsperiode zur Klassengesellschaft." *Ethnographisch-archäologische Zeitschrift* 23 (1982): 11–31.

Herrmann, Joachim. "Die Slawen der Völkerwanderungszeit." In Herrmann, *Welt der Slawen*, 19–40.

Herrmann, Joachim, ed. *Die Slawen in Deutschland: Geschichte und Kultur der slawischen Stämme westlich von Oder und Neiße vom 6. bis 12. Jahrhundert. Ein Handbuch*, 2nd ed. Berlin, 1985.

Herrmann, Joachim. "Wanderungen und Landnahmen im westslawischen Gebiet." In *Gli slavi occidentali*, 1:75–102.

Herrmann, Joachim, ed. *Welt der Slawen: Geschichte, Gesellschaft, Kultur.* Leipzig, 1986.

Herrmann, Joachim. *Zwischen Hradschin und Vineta.* Leipzig, 1971.

Hesse, Klaus. "Der Austausch als stabilisierender Faktor der politischen Herrschaft in der Geschichte der Mongolei: Das Beispiel der Hsiung-nu." *UAJB*, n.s., 4 (1984): 150–70.

Higgins, Martin J. *The Persian War of the Emperor Maurice.* Washington, DC, 1939.

Hill, David. *An Atlas of Anglo-Saxon England.* Toronto, 1981.

Hoffmann, Hartmut. "Untersuchungen zur karolingischen Annalistik." *Bonner Historische Forschungen* 10 (1958): 42–53.

Holder-Egger, Oswald. "Über die Heiligen Marinus und Anianus." *Neues Archiv* 13 (1888): 22–28.

Höllmann, Thomas. *Tribes and Tributaries: Chinese Perceptions of Foreigners and Strangers.* Tempe, AZ, 2008.

Holthausen, Ferdinand. *Gotisches etymologisches Wörterbuch.* 2nd ed. Heidelberg, 2002.

Holzer, Georg. "Die Einheitlichkeit des Slavischen um 600 n. Chr. und ihr Zerfall." *Wiener Slavistisches Jahrbuch* 41 (1995): 55–90.

Holzer, Georg. "Gli Slavi prima del loro arrivo in Occidente." In *Lo Spazio Letterario del Medioevo*. Vol. 3, *Le Culture Slave*, edited by Mario Capaldo, 13–49. Rome, 2006.

Holzer, Georg. "Vorhistorische Periode." In Gutschmidt et al., *Die slavischen Sprachen/ The Slavic Languages*, 2:1117–31.

Honigmann, Ernest. "L'histoire ecclésiastique de Jean d'Éphèse." *Byzantion* 14 (1939): 615–24.

Hood, Sinclair F. "Isles of Refuge in the Early Byzantine Period." *Papers of the British School in Athens* 65 (1970): 37–44.

Hoppál, Mihály. "Shamanism: An Archaic and/or Recent System of Beliefs." *UAJB*, n.s., 5 (1985): 121–40.

Horedt, Kurt. "Das Awarenproblem in Rumänien." *Študijné zvesti* 16 (1968): 103–20.

Horedt, Kurt. "Ergebnisse der Frühgeschichtsforschung in Siebenbürgen während des letzten Jahrzehnts." In *Berichte über den 5. int. Kongress für Ur- und Frühgeschichte*, 407–11. Berlin, 1961.

Horedt, Kurt. "Das Fortleben der Gepiden in der frühen Awarenzeit." *Germania* 63 (1985): 164–68.

Horedt, Kurt. "Die Völker Südosteuropas im 6. bis 8. Jahrhundert: Probleme und Ergebnisse." In Hänsel, *Die Völker Südosteuropas vom 6.–8. Jahrhundert*, 11–26.

Horedt, Kurt. "Wandervölker und Romanen im 5. bis 6. Jahrhundert in Siebenbürgen." In Wolfram and Daim, *Die Völker an der mittleren und unteren Donau im fünften und sechsten Jahrhundert*, 117–22.

Hornstein, Franz. "Istros Amaxeuomenos: Zur Geschichte eines literarischen Topos." *Gymnasium* 64 (1967): 154–209.

Horst, Koert van der, William Noel, and Wilhelmina C. M. Wüstefeld, eds. *The Utrecht Psalter in Medieval Art: Picturing the Psalms of David*. Westrenen, 1996.

Howard-Johnston, James. "Heraclius' Persian Campaigns and the Revival of the East Roman Empire, 622–30." *War in History* 6, no. 1 (1999): 1–44.

Howard-Johnston, James. "The Siege of Constantinople in 626." In *Constantinople and Its Hinterland: Papers from the Twenty-Seventh Spring Symposium of Byzantine Studies, Oxford, April 1993*, edited by Cyril Mango and Gilbert Dagron, 131–42. Aldershot, 1995.

Howorth, Henry H. "The Avars." *Journal of Royal Asiatic Society of Great Britain and Ireland* 21 (1889): 721–810.

Hunger, Herbert. *Die hochsprachliche profane Literatur der Byzantiner*. 2 vols. Handbuch der Altertumswissenschaft 12.5. Munich, 1978.

Hunger, Herbert. "Der Kaiserpalast zu Konstantinopel: Seine Funktion in der byzantinischen Aussenpolitik." *Jahrbuch der Österreichischen Byzantinistik* 36 (1986): 1–11.

Hurbanič, Martin. "Adversus Iudaeos in the Sermon Written by Theodore Syncellus on the Avar Siege of AD 626." *Studia ceranea* 6 (2016): 271–93.

Hurbanič, Martin. "The Eastern Roman Empire and the Avar Khaganate in the Years 622–24 AD." *Acta Antiqua Academiae Scientiarum Hungaricae* 51 (2011): 315–28.

Hurbanič, Martin. *Konstantinopol 626: Poslední bitva antiky* [Constantinople 626: The last battle of Antiquity]. Prague, 2016. English edition, *The Last Battle of Antiquity: Constantinople 626*, forthcoming.

Hurbanič, Martin. "The Nomads at the Gates: Some Notes on the Use of Siege Artillery by the Avars (From the First Attack on Sirmium to the Siege of Constantinople)." In *The Cultural and Historical Heritage of Vojvodina in the Context of Classical and Medieval Studies*, edited by Djura Hardi, 75–90. Novi Sad, 2015.

Iatrus-Krivina: Spätantike Befestigung und frühmittelalterliche Siedlung an der unteren Donau. Vol. 1, *Ergebnisse der Ausgrabungen 1966–1973*. Berlin, 1979.

Ivison, Eric A. "Burial and Urbanism in Late Antique and Early Byzantine Corinth (c. 400–700)." In *Towns in Transition: Urban Evolution in Late Antiquity and the Early Middle Ages*, edited by Neil Christie and Simon T. Loseby, 99–125. Aldershot, 1996.

Jakob, Hans. "War Burk das historische Wogastisburc, und wo lag das Oppidum Berleich? Eine historisch-geographische Standortanalyse." *Die Welt der Slawen* 25 (1980): 39–67.

Jakšić, Nikola. "Constantine Porphyrogenitus as the Source for the Destruction of Salona." *Disputationes Salonitanae 2: Vjesnik za Arheologiju i Historiju Dalmatinsku* 77 (1984): 315–26.

Janin, Raymond. *La géographie ecclésiastique de l'empire byzantine*. Vol. 1, *Le siège de Constantinople et le patriarchat oecuménique*. Paris, 1969.

Jankowiak. Marek. "Dirhams for Slaves." Project website: http://krc.orient.ox.ac.uk/dirhamsforslaves/index.php/en/news-and-events.

Jarnut, Jörg. "Beiträge zu den fränkisch-bayerisch-langobardischen Beziehungen im 7. und 8. Jh." *Zeitschrift für bayerische Landesgeschichte* 39 (1976): 327–52.

Jarnut, Jörg. *Geschichte der Langobarden.* Stuttgart, 1982.

Jarnut, Jörg. *Prosopographische und sozialgeschichtliche Studien zum Langobardenreich in Italien.* Bonn, 1972.

Jenkins, Romilly James Heald, ed. *Constantine Porphyrogenitus, De administrando imperio,* vol. 2, *Commentary.* London, 1962.

Ježek, Martin. "The Disappearance of European Smiths' Burials." *Cambridge Archaeological Journal* 25, no. 1 (2015): 121–43.

Jilek, Sonja, and Andreas Schwarcz, eds. *Der Donaulimes in Österreich.* Vienna, 2011.

Jireček, Konstantin. *Geschichte der Serben.* Vol. 1. Gotha, 1911.

Jones, Arnold M. H. *The Later Roman Empire (284–602): A Social, Economic and Administrative Survey.* 3 vols. Oxford, 1964.

Juhász, Irén. *Das awarenzeitliche Gräberfeld in Szarvas-Grexa-Téglagyár.* Monumenta Avarorum Archaeologica 7. Budapest, 2004.

Juhász, Irén. "Ein awarenzeitlicher Nadelbecher mit Kerbschrift aus Szarvas (Komitat Bekes)." *Acta Arch. Hung.* 35 (1983): 373–78.

Kádár, Zoltán. "Gli animali negli oggetti ornamentali dei popoli della steppa: Unni, Avari e Magiari." In *L'uomo di fronte al mondo animale nell'alto medioevo,* SSCI 31, 2:1373–87. Spoleto, 1983.

Kaegi, Walter E. *Army, Society and Religion in Byzantium.* London, 1982.

Kaegi, Walter E. *Byzantium and the Early Islamic Conquest.* Cambridge, 1992.

Kaegi, Walter E. *Heraclius: Emperor of Byzantium.* Cambridge, 2003.

Kaegi, Walter E. "New Evidence on the Early Reign of Heraclius." *Byzantinische Zeitschrift* 66 (1973): 308–50.

Kahl, Hans-Dietrich. "Die Baiern und ihre Nachbarn bis zum Tode des Herzogs Theodo (717–718)." In Wolfram and Schwarcz, *Die Bayern und ihre Nachbarn,* 159–226.

Kahl, Hans-Dietrich. *Der Staat der Karantanen: Fakten, Thesen und Fragen zu einer frühen slawischen Machtbildung im Ostalpenraum (7.–9. Jh.).* Ljubljana, 2002.

Kaldellis, Anthony. *Ethnography after Antiquity: Foreign Lands and Peoples in Byzantine Literature; Empire and After.* Philadelphia, 2013.

Karayannopoulos, Johannes. "Byzance et les Slaves." In *Abstracts of Short Papers, the 17th International Byzantine Conference,* 165–66.

Karayannopoulos, Johannes. "Zur Frage der Slawenansiedlungen auf dem Peloponnes." *Revue des Études Sud-Est Européennes* 9 (1971): 443–60.

Karayannopoulos, Johannes, and Günter Weiss. *Quellenkunde zur Geschichte von Byzanz (324–1453).* 2 vols. Schriften zur Geistesgeschichte des östlichen Europa 14. Wiesbaden, 1982.

Kardaras, Georgios. "The Episode of Bousas (586/7) and the Use of Siege Engines by the Avars." *Byzantinoslavica* 63 (2005): 53–66.

Kardaras, Georgios. Το Βυζάντιο και οι Άβαροι, ΣΤ΄—Θ΄ αι. Πολιτικές, διπλωματικές και πολιτισμικές σχέσεις. ΕΙΕ/ΙΒΕ, Monographs 15. Athens, 2010. English version: *Byzantium and the Avars, 6th–9th c. A.D.: Political, Diplomatic and Cultural Relations* (Leiden, forthcoming).

Katičić, Radoslav. "Die Anfänge des kroatischen Staates." In Wolfram and Schwarcz, *Die Bayern und ihre Nachbarn.*

Katičić, Radoslav. "Die Ethnogenesen in der Avaria." In Wolfram and Pohl, *Typen der Ethnogenese,* 125–28.

Katičić, Radoslav. "Die Literatur des frühen kroatischen Mittelalters in ihrem slawischen und europäischen Zusammenhang." *Wiener Slavistisches Jahrbuch* 28 (1982): 27–52.

Katičić, Radoslav. *Literatur- und Geistesgeschichte des kroatischen Frühmittelalters.* Vienna, 1999.

Katsanakis, Anastasios. "Abaria." In *Glossar Osteuropa: Bericht einer Arbeitstagung. Glossar zur frühmittelalterlichen Geschichte im östlichen Europa,* 52–60. Münster, 1982.

Kazanski, Michel. "Les Goths et les Huns: À propos des relations entre barbares sedentaires et nomades." *Archéologie Médiévale* 22 (1992): 191–221.

Kazanski, Michel. *Les Slaves: Les origines, Ier–VIIe siècle après J.-C.* Paris, 1999.

Kazanski, Michel, and Jean-Pierre Sodini. "Byzance et l'art 'nomade': Remarques à propos de l'essai de J. Werner sur le dépôt de Malaja Pereščepina." *Revue Archéologique,* 1987, 71–83.

Kenk, Roman. *Früh- und hochmittelalterliche Gräber von Kudyrge am Altai.* Munich, 1982.

Khazanov, Anatoly. "'Military Democracy' and the Epoch of Class Formation." In *Soviet Ethnology and Anthropology Today,* edited by Julian V. Bromlej, Studies in Anthropology 1, 133–46. The Hague, 1974.

Khazanov, Anatoly M. *Nomads and the Outside World,* Studies in Social Anthropology 44. Cambridge, 1984.

Khazanov, Anatoly M. *Nomads, Sedentaries and Missionaries.* Cambridge, 2004.

Kia, Mehrdad. *The Persian Empire: A Historical Encyclopedia.* Santa Barbara, 2016.

Kislinger, Ewald. *Regionalgeschichte als Quellenproblem: Die Chronik von Monembasia und das sizilianische Demenna.* Vienna, 2001.

Kiss, Attila. *Das awarenzeitliche Gräberfeld in Kölked-Feketekapu B.* 2 vols. Budapest, 2001.

Kiss, Attila. *Das awarenzeitlich-gepidische Gräberfeld von Kölked-Feketekapu A.* Innsbruck, 1996.

Kiss, Attila. "Germanen im awarenzeitlichen Karpatenbecken." In Daim, *Awarenforschungen,* 1:35–134.

Kiss, Attila. "Die Goldfunde des Karpatenbeckens vom 5.–10. Jahrhundert: Angaben zu den Vergleichsmöglichkeiten der schriftlichen und archäologischen Quellen." *Acta Arch. Hung.* 38 (1986): 105–45.

Kiss, Attila. "Das Gräberfeld und die Siedlung der awarenzeitlichen germanischen Bevölkerung von Kölked." *Folia Archaeologica* 30 (1979): 185–91.

Kiss, Attila. "Die Stellung der Keszthely-Kultur in der Frage der Römischen Kontinuität Pannoniens." *A Janus Pannonius Múzeum Évkönyve,* 1965, 49–59.

Kiss, Attila. "Das Weiterleben der Gepiden in der Awarenzeit." In Hänsel, *Die Völker Südosteuropas vom 6.–8. Jahrhundert,* 203–18.

Kiss, Attila. "Zur Frage der Kontinuität bzw. Diskontinuität des awarischen Khaganats (567–795): Wieviele Khaganate der Awaren hat es gegeben?" In Bialeková and Zábojník, *Ethnische und kulturelle Verhältnisse an der mittleren Donau,* 83–98.

Kiss, Gábor. "Funde der Awarenzeit aus Ungarn in Wiener Museen: I. Funde aus der Umgebung von Keszthely." *Archaeologia Austriaca* 68 (1984): 161–201.

Kiss, Gábor. "Eine vergessene Episode des Awarenfeldzugs von Karl dem Großen 791: Was hat Karl der Große in Savaria gesucht und gefunden?" In Drauschke et al., *Lebenswelten zwischen Archäologie und Geschichte,* 215–22.

Kiss, Gábor. "Der Wandel im archäologischen Nachlass der Keszthely-Kultur im Laufe des 7. und 8. Jahrhunderts—Versuche zur Periodisierung." *Antaeus* 29–30 (2008): 265–77.

Klaić, Nada. "Problemima stare domovine, dolaska i pokrštenja dalmatinskih Hrvata." *Zgodovinski Časopis* 38 (1984): 253–70.

Klanica, Zdeněk. "Vorgroßmährische Siedlung in Mikulčice und ihre Beziehungen zum Karpatenbecken." *Študijné zvesti* 16 (1968): 121–34.

Klimkeit, Hans-Joachim. "Die frühe Religion der Türken im Spiegel ihrer inschriftlichen Quellen." *Zeitschrift für Religionswissenschaft* 3 (1995): 191–206.

Klyashtorny, Sergey G. "The Terkhin Inscription." *Acta Orient. Hung.* 36 (1982): 335–66.

Klyashtorny, Sergey G. "The Tes Inscription of the Uighur Bögü Khagan." *Acta Orient. Hung.* 39 (1985): 137–56.

Klyashtorny, S. G. "The Ancient Turkic Religion: Its Reconstruction and Genesis." *Information Bulletin* (1987): 44–52.

Klyashtorny, S. G. "Political Background of the Old Turkic Religion." In *Roter Altai, gib dein Echo! Festschrift für Erika Taube zum 65. Geburtstag*, edited by Anett C. Oelschlägel, Ingo Nentwig, and Jakob Taube, 260–65. Leipzig, 2005.

Klyashtornyj, Sergej G. "About One Khazar Title in Ibn Fadlan." In Klyashtornyj, *Old Turkic Runic Texts*, 333–34.

Klyashtornyj, Sergej G. "The Asian Aspect of the Early Khazar History." In Klyashtornyj, *Old Turkic Runic Texts*, 327–32.

Klyashtornyj, Sergej G. *Old Turkic Runic Texts and History of the Eurasian Steppe.* Edited by Victor Spinei and Cristina Spinei. Bucharest, 2008.

Klyashtornyj, Sergej, and Vladimir A. Livšic. "The Sogdian Inscription of Bugut Revisited." In Klyashtornyj, *Old Turkic Runic Texts*, 65–96.

Knific, Timotej. "Carniola in the Early Middle Ages." *Balcanoslavica* 5 (1976): 111–21.

Koder, Johannes. "Anmerkungen zu den Miracula Sancti Demetrii." In N. Stratos, *Byzantium*, 2:523–38.

Koder, Johannes. "Arethas von Kaisareia und die sogenannte Chronik von Monemvasia." *Jahrbuch der Österreichischen Byzantinistik* 25 (1976): 75–80.

Koder, Johannes. "Byzanz, die Griechen und die Romaiosynē—eine 'Ethnogenese' der Römer?" In Wolfram and Pohl, *Typen der Ethnogenese*, 103–12.

Koder, Johannes. *Der Lebensraum der Byzantiner: Historisch-geographischer Abriß ihres mittelalterlichen Staates im östlichen Mittelmeerraum.* Byzantinische Geschichtsschreiber Erg. Bd. 1. Graz, 1984.

Koder, Johannes. "Remarks on Linguistic Romanness in Byzantium." In Gantner et al., *Transformations of Romanness in the Early Middle Ages*, 111–22.

Koder, Johannes. "Zur Frage der slavischen Siedlungsgebiete im mittelalterlichen Griechenland." *Byzantinische Zeitschrift* 71 (1978): 315–31.

Koder, Johannes, and Friedrich Hild. *Hellas und Thessalia.* Tabula Imperii Byzantini 1. Vienna, 1976.

Kolias, Taxiarchis G. *Byzantinische Waffen: ein Beitrag zur byzantinischen Waffenkunde von den Anfängen bis zur lateinischen Eroberung.* Vienna, 1988.

Kollautz, Arnulf. "Abaria." In *Reallexikon der Byzantinistik*, 1.2:2–16.

Kollautz, Arnulf. "Die Awaren: Die Schichtung in einer Nomadenherrschaft." *Saeculum* 5 (1954): 129–78.

Kollautz, Arnulf. "Awaren, Franken und Slawen in Karantanien und Niederpannonien und die fränkische und byzantinische Mission." *Carinthia I* 156 (1966): 232–75.

Kollautz, Arnulf. "Awaren, Langobarden und Slawen in Noricum und Istrien." *Carinthia I* 155 (1965): 619–45.

Kollautz, Arnulf. *Denkmäler byzantinischen Christentums aus der Awarenzeit der Donauländer.* Amsterdam, 1970.

Kollautz, Arnulf. "Die Inschrift De Avaris von Sirmium als Dokument einer byzantinischen Gebetsanrufung." In *Studia in honorem Veselini Beševliev*, edited by Vladimir I. Georgiev, 534–62. Sofia, 1978.

Kollautz, Arnulf. "Nestors Quelle über die Unterdrückung der Duleben durch die Obri (Awaren)." *Die Welt der Slaven* 27 (1982): 307–20.

Kollautz, Arnulf. "Völkerbewegungen an der unteren und mittleren Donau im Zeitraum von 558/62 bis 582." In Mildenberger, *Studien zur Völkerwanderungszeit im östlichen Mitteleuropa*, 448–89.

Kollautz, Arnulf, and Hisayuki Miyakawa. "Abdelai." In *Reallexikon der Byzantinistik*, 1.2:88–126.

Kollautz, Arnulf, and Hisayuki Miyakawa. *Geschichte und Kultur eines völkerwanderungszeitlichen Nomadenvolkes: Die Jou-Jan der Mongolei und die Awaren in Mitteleuropa*. 2 vols. Klagenfurt, 1970.

Koller, Heinrich. "Die Awarenkriege Karls des Großen." *Mitteilungen der östereichischen Arbeitsgemeinschaft für Ur- und Frühgeschichte* 15 (1964): 1–12.

Koller, Heinrich. "Der 'Mons Comagenus.'" *MIÖG* 71 (1963): 237–45.

Koncz, István. "568—A Historical Date and Its Archaeological Consequences." *Acta Arch. Hung.* 66 (2015): 315–40.

Kononov, Andrei N. "Terminology of the Definition of the Cardinal Points of the Turkic People." *Acta Orient. Hung.* 31 (1977): 61–76.

Konrad, Michaela, and Christian Witschel, eds. *Römische Legionslager in den Rhein- und Donauprovinzen: Nuclei spätantik-frühmittelalterlichen Lebens?* Abhandlungen der Bayerischen Akademie der Wissenschaften, n.s., 138. Munich, 2011.

Köpeczi, Béla, ed. *Erdély Története három kötetben* [History of Transylvania in three volumes]. Budapest, 1986.

Kovačević, Jovan. *Avarski Kaganat*. Belgrad, 1977.

Kovačević, Jovan. "Die awarische Militärgrenze in der Umgebung von Beograd im 8. Jahrhundert." *Archaeologia Iugoslavica* 14 (1973): 49–55.

Kovács, Tibor. *The Gold of the Avars: The Nagyszentmiklós Treasure*. Exhibition catalog. Budapest, 2002.

Kovrig, Ilona. *Das awarenzeitliche Gräberfeld von Alattyán*. Archaeologica Hungarica 40. Budapest, 1963.

Kovrig, Ilona. "Contribution au problème de l'occupation de l'Hongrie par les Avares." *Acta Arch. Hung.* 6 (1955): 163–91.

Krader, Lawrence. "The Origins of State among the Nomads of Asia." In Claessen and Skalník, *The Early State*, 93–107.

Krader, Lawrence. *Peoples of Central Asia*. Bloomington, 1963.

Krader, Lawrence. *Social Organization of the Mongol-Turkic Pastoral Nomads*. The Hague, 1964.

Kradin, Nikolay N. "From Tribal Confederation to Empire: The Evolution of the Rouran Society." *Acta Orient. Hung.* 58 (2005): 149–69.

Kradin, Nikolay N. "Nomadic Empires in Inner Asia." In Bemmann and Schmauder, *Complexity of Interaction*, 11–48.

Krahwinkler, Harald. *Friaul im Frühmittelalter: Geschichte einer Region vom Ende des 5. bis zum Ende des 10. Jahrhunderts*. Vienna, 1992.

Kramer, Johannes. "Romanen, Rumänen und Vlachen aus philologischer Sicht." In Pohl, Haubrichs, and Hartl, *Walchen, Romani und Latini*, 197–204.

Kresten, Otto. "Zur Echtheit des Sigillion des Kaisers Nikephoros I. für Patras." *Römische Historische Mitteilungen* 19 (1977): 15–78.

Kronsteiner, Otto. "Gab es unter der Alpenslawen eine kroatische ethnische Gruppe?" *Wiener Slavistisches Jahrbuch* 24 (1978): 137–57.

Krumbacher, Karl. *Geschichte der byzantinischen Literatur von Justinian bis zum Ende des oströmischen Reiches (527–1453)*. 2nd ed. Munich, 1897.

Krusch, Bruno. "Die Chronicae des sog. Fredegar." *Neues Archiv* 7 (1882): 249–351, 423–516.

Kubarev, Gleb. "Archäologische Denkmäler der Alttürken." In Bemmann, *Steppenkrieger*, 127–37.

Kunstmann, Heinrich. "Kamen die west-slavischen Daleminci aus Dalmatien?" *Die Welt der Slawen* 28 (1983): 364–71.

Kunstmann, Heinrich. "Der Name der Abodriten." *Die Welt der Slawen* 26 (1981): 395–419.

Kunstmann, Heinrich. "Die Namen der altslavischen Derevljane, Polocane und Volynjane." *Die Welt der Slawen* 30 (1985): 235–59.

Kunstmann, Heinrich. "Nestors Dulěbi und die Glopeani des Geographus Bavarus." *Die Welt der Slawen* 24 (1979): 44–61.

Kunstmann, Heinrich. "Samo, Dervanus und der Slovenenfürst Wallucus." *Die Welt der Slawen* 25 (1980): 171–77.

Kunstmann, Heinrich. *Die Slaven: Ihr Name, ihre Wanderung nach Europa und die Anfänge der russischen Geschichte in historisch-onomastischer Sicht.* Stuttgart, 1996.

Kunstmann, Heinrich. "Über den Namen der Kroaten." *Die Welt der Slawen* 27 (1982): 131–36.

Kunstmann, Heinrich. "Über die Herkunft Samos." *Die Welt der Slawen* 25 (1980): 293–313.

Kunstmann, Heinrich. *Vorläufige Untersuchungen über den bairischen Bulgarenmord von 631/32.* Munich, 1982.

Kurbanov, Aydogdy. "The Hephthalites: Archaeological and Historical Analysis." PhD diss., Freie Universität Berlin, 2010. http://www.diss.fu-berlin.de/diss/servlets/ MCRFileNodeServlet/FUDISS_derivate_000000007165/01_Text.pdf.

Kurnatowska, Zofia. "Die 'Sclaveni' im Lichte der archäologischen Quellen." *Archaeologia Polona* 15 (1974): 51–56.

Kuznetsov, Vladimir A. "The Avars in the Nart Epos of the Ossets." *Acta Orient. Hung.* 38 (1984): 165–69.

Kyzlasov, Leonid R. "Northern Nomads." In Litvinsky, Guang-da, and Samghabadi, *History of Civilizations of Central Asia,* 315–26.

Kyzlasov, Leonid R. *The Urban Civilisation of Northern and Innermost Asia: Historical and Archaeological Research.* Bucharest, 2010.

Labuda, Gerard. "Chronologie des guerres de Byzance contre les Avares et les Slaves à la fin du VIe siècle." *Byzantinoslavica* 11 (1950): 167–73.

Labuda, Gerard. *Pierwsze państwo Słowiańskie: Państwo Samona.* Posen, 1949.

Labuda, Gerard. "Wogastis-Burg." *Slavia Antiqua* 2 (1949–50): 241–52.

Ladenbauer-Orel, Hertha. *Linz-Zizlau: Das bairische Gräberfeld an der Traunmündung.* Vienna, 1960.

Ladstätter, Sabine. *Die materielle Kultur der Spätantike in den Ostalpen: Eine Fallstudie am Beispiel der westlichen Doppelkirchenanlage auf dem Hemmaberg.* Mitteilungen der Prähistorischen Kommission 35. Vienna, 2000.

Ladstätter, Sabine. "Von Noricum Mediterraneum zur Provincia Sclaborum: Die Kontinuitätsfrage aus archäologischer Sicht." In Bratož, *Slovenija,* 1:219–38.

Lambropoulou, Anna. "The Presence of Slavs in the Western Peloponnese during the 7th to 8th Centuries." In Quast, *Foreigners in Early Medieval Europe,* 197–218.

La Rocca, Cristina. *Pacifico di Verona: Il passato Carolingio nella costruzione della memoria urbana.* Nuovi studi storici 31. Rome, 1995.

László, Gyula. *Das awarenzeitliche Gräberfeld in Csákberény-Orondpuszta.* Monumenta Avarorum Archaeologica 11. Budapest, 2015.

László, Gyula. *Études archéologiques sur l'histoire de la société des Avars.* Archaeologica Hungarica 24. Budapest, 1954.

László, Gyula. "Les problèmes soulévés par le groupe à la ceinture ornée de griffon et de rinceaux de l'époque avare finissante." *Acta Arch. Hung.* 17 (1965): 73–75.

László, Gyula, and Istvan Rácz. *Der Schatz von Nagyszentmiklós.* Budapest, 1977.

Lattimore, Owen. *Inner Asian Frontiers of China*. 2nd ed. New York, 1951.

Laude-Cirtautas, Ilse. *Der Gebrauch der Farbbezeichnungen in den Türkdialekten*. Ural-Altaische Bibliothek 10. Wiesbaden, 1961.

Lauterbach, Helmut. "Untersuchungen zur Vorgeschichte der Protobulgaren, nach einem Bericht bei Theophanes." In *Die Araber in der alten Welt*, edited by Franz Altheim and Ruth Stiehl, vol. 4, *Neue Funde*, 537–620. Berlin, 1967.

Lebedinsky, Jaroslav. *Armes et guerriers barbares au temps des grandes invasions*. Paris, 2001.

Lemerle Paul. "La chronique improprement dite de Monemvasie: Le contexte historique et légendaire." *Revue des Études Byzantines* 21 (1963): 5–49.

Lemerle, Paul. "La composition et la chronologie des deux premiers livres des Miracula S. Demetrii." *Byzantinische Zeitschrift* 46 (1953): 349–60.

Lemerle, Paul. "Invasions et migrations dans les Balkans depuis la fin de l'époque romaine jusqu'au VIIIe siècle." *Revue Historique* 211 (1954): 265–308.

Lemerle, Paul. *Les Plus Anciens Recueils des miracles de Saint Démétrius et la pénétration des Slaves dans les Balkans*. Vol. 2: *Commentaire*. Paris, 1981.

Lemerle, Paul. "Quelques remarques sur le règne d'Heraclius." *Studi medievali* 3, no. 1 (1960): 347–61.

Lévi-Strauss, Claude. "Do Dual Organisations Exist?" In Claude Lévi-Strauss, *Structural Anthropology*, 1:132–66. New York, 1963.

Lévi-Strauss, Claude. "Introduction à l'œuvre de Marcel Mauss." In Marcel Mauss, *Sociologie et anthropologie*, ix–lii. Paris, 1950.

Lewis, Ioan M. *Ecstatic Religion*. London, 1971.

Lewis, Mark Edward. *China between Empires: The Northern and Southern Dynasties*. Cambridge, 2009.

Liddell, Henry George, and Robert Scott. *Greek-English Lexicon: With a Revised Supplement; Revised and Augmented throughout by Henry Stuart Jones with the Assistance of Roderick McKenzie and with the Cooperation of Many Scholars*. 9th ed. Oxford, 1940.

Liebeschuetz, John H. W. G. *The Decline and Fall of the Ancient City*. Oxford, 2001.

Liebeschuetz, John H. W. G. "The Lower Danube Region under Pressure: From Valens to Heraclius." In Poulter, *The Transition to Late Antiquity*, 101–34.

Ligeti, Lajos. *A magyar nyelv török kapcsolatai a honfoglalás előtt és az Árpád-korban*. Budapest, 1986.

Ligeti, Louis, ed. *Studia Turcica*. Budapest, 1971.

Lilie, Ralph-Johannes. "Kaiser Herakleios und die Ansiedlung der Serben: Überlegungen zum Kapitel 32 des *De administrando imperio*." *Südost-Forschungen* 44 (1985): 17–43.

Lippert, Andreas. "Awaren nach 800 in Niederösterreich?" *Jahrbuch für Landeskunde von Niederösterreich*, n.s., 38 (1968–70): 145–57.

Lippert, Andreas. "Zur Frage der awarischen Westgrenze." *Mitteilungen der Anthropologischen Gesellschaft in Wien* 100 (1970): 162–72.

Lippold, Adolf. "Hephthalitai." In *RE Suppl.* 14 (1974), 137.

Lipsic, Elena E. *Byzanz und die Slawen: Beiträge zur byzantinischen Geschichte des 6.–9. Jahrhunderts*. Weimar, 1951.

Little, Lester K., ed. *Plague and the End of Antiquity: The Pandemic of 541–750*. Cambridge, 2007.

Litvinsky, Boris A. "The Hephthalite Empire." In Litvinsky, Guang-da, and Samghabadi, *History of Civilizations of Central Asia*, 135–76.

Litvinsky, Boris A., Zhang Guang-da, and Reza Shabani Samghabadi, eds. *History of Civilizations of Central Asia*. Vol. 3, *The Crossroads of Civilizations: A.D. 250 to 750*. Paris, 1996.

Liu Mau-Tsai. *Die chinesischen Nachrichten zur Geschichte der Ost-Türken (T'u-küe)*. 2 vols. Göttinger Asiatische Forschungen 10. Wiesbaden, 1958.

Liu Mau-Tsai. "Kulturelle Beziehungen zwischen den Ost-Türken (= T'u-küe) und China." *Central Asiatic Journal* 3 (1957–58): 190–205.

Lobinger, Christoph. *Das awarenzeitliche Gräberfeld von Edelstal (Nemesvölgy) im Burgenland*. Universitätsforschungen zur prähistorischen Archäologie 288. Bonn, 2016.

Lőrinczy, Gábor. "Frühawarenzeitliche Bestattungssitten im Gebiet der Grossen Ungarischen Tiefebene östlich der Theiss: Archäologische Angaben und Bemerkungen zur Geschichte der Region im 6. und 7. Jahrhundert." *Acta Arch. Hung.* 68 (2017): 137–70.

L'oro degli Avari: Popolo delle steppe in Europa. Catalogo della mostra. Milan, 2000.

Lounghis, Tēlemachos C. *Les ambassades byzantines en occident*. Athens, 1980.

Löwe, Heinz. "Aethicus Ister und das alttürkische Runenalphabet." *Deutsches Archiv für Erforschung des Mittelalters* 32 (1976): 1–22.

Löwe, Heinz. *Die karolingische Reichsgründung und der Südosten: Studien zum Werden des Deutschtums und seiner Aueinandersetzung mit Rom*. Forschungen zur Kirchen- und Geistesgeschichte 13. Stuttgart, 1937.

Löwe, Heinz. "Westliche Peregrinatio und Mission: Ihr Zusammenhang mit den länder—und völkerkundlichen Kenntnissen des früheren Mittelalters." In *Popoli e paesi nella cultura altomedievale*, SSCI 29, 1:327–572. Spoleto, 1983.

Lübke, Christian, and Andrzej Wędzki, eds. *Glossar zur frühmittelalterlichen Geschichte im östlichen Europa: Enzyklopädie zur Geschichte des östlichen Europa, 6.–13. Jahrhundert, Heft A: Aalborg–Awdańce*. Greifswald, 1998.

Lunt, Horace. "Slavs, Common Slavic and Old Church Slavonic." In *Litterae Slavicae Medii Aevi: Francisco Venceslao Mares Sexagenario Oblatae*, edited by Johannes Reinhart, 185–204. Munich, 1985.

Lunt, Horace G. "Common Slavic, Proto-Slavic, Pan-Slavic: What Are We Talking About?" *International Journal of Slavic Linguistics and Poetics* 41 (1997): 7–67.

Luo Xin. "Chinese and Inner Asian Perspectives on the History of the Northern Dynasties (386–589) in Chinese Historiography." In Di Cosmo and Maas, *Empires and Exchanges in Eurasian Late Antiquity*, 166–75.

Maas, Michael. *The Conqueror's Gift: Ethnography, Identity and Roman Imperial Power at the End of Antiquity*. Forthcoming.

Maas, Michael, and Nicola Di Cosmo, eds. *Eurasian Empires in Late Antiquity*. Forthcoming.

Macartney, Carlile A. *The Magyars in the Ninth Century*. Cambridge, 1930.

Macartney, Carlile A. *The Medieval Hungarian Historians: A Critical and Analytical Guide*. Cambridge, 1953.

Macartney, Carlile A. "On the Greek Sources for the History of the Turks." *Bulletin of the School of Oriental and African Studies* 11, no. 2 (1944): 266–75.

Macháček, Jiří. "Disputes over Great Moravia: Chiefdom or State? The Morava or the Tisza River?" *Early Medieval Europe* 17, no. 3 (2009): 248–67.

Macháček, Jiří. "'Great Moravian State': A Controversy in Central European Medieval Studies." *Studia Slavica et Balcanica Petropolitana* 10, no. 1 (2012): 5–26.

Macháček, Jiří, and Šimon Ungerman, eds. *Frühgeschichtliche Zentralorte in Mitteleuropa*. Bonn, 2011.

Madaras, László. *Das awarenzeitliche Gräberfeld von Jászapáti*. Das awarische Corpus, Beihefte 2. Debrecen-Budapest, 1994.

Maenchen-Helfen, Otto. "Akatir." *Central Asiatic Journal* 11 (1966): 275–86.

Maenchen-Helfen, Otto J. *The World of the Huns: Studies in Their History and Culture*. Berkeley, 1973.

Magdearu, Alexandru. "The End of Town-Life in Scythia Minor." *Oxford Journal of Archaeology* 20, no. 2 (2001): 207–17.

Magdearu, Alexandru. "The Plate of Paternus from the Malaja Pereščepina Treasure: Booty or Gift?" *Études Byzantines et Post-Byzantines* 6 (2011): 65–71.

Magyari, Eniko K., Jefferson C. Chapman, David G. Passmore, J. R. M. Allen, J. P. Huntley, and Brian Huntley. "Holocene Persistence of Wooded Steppe in the Great Hungarian Plain." *Journal of Biogeography* 37 (2010): 915–35.

Mair, Victor H., and Jane Hickman, eds. *Reconfiguring the Silk Road: New Research on East–West Exchange in Antiquity.* Philadelphia, 2014.

Makovski, Krzysztof A., and Frank Hadler, eds. *Approaches to Slavic Unity: Austro-Slavism, Pan-Slavism, Neo-Slavism, and Solidarity among the Slavs Today.* Poznán, 2013.

Maksimović, Ljubomir. "Chronological Notes about Slavonic Raids into Byzantine Territory at the End of the Seventies and at the Beginning of the Eighties of the 6th Century." *Zbornik Radova* 8 (1964): 263–71.

Maksimović, Ljubomir. "Struktura 32. glave spisa 'De administrando imperio.'" *Zbornik Radova* 21 (1982): 25–32.

Mal, Josip. *Probleme aus der Frühzeit der Slovenen.* Laibach, 1939.

Malingoudis, Phaedon. "Frühe slawische Elemente im Namensgut Griechenlands." *Südosteuropa-Jahrbuch* 17 (1987): 53–68.

Malingoudis, Phaedon. "Die Institution des Župans als Problem der frühslawischen Geschichte." *Cyrillomethodiana* 2 (1972–73): 61–76.

Malingoudis, Phaedon. *Studien zu den slavischen Ortsnamen Griechenlands*, vol. 1, *Slavische Flurnamen aus der messenischen Mani.* Mainz, 1981.

Mango, Cyril. "The Brevarium of the Patriarch Nikephoros." In N. Stratos, *Byzantium*, 2:539–52.

Mango, Cyril. *Le développement urbain de Constantinople (IVe–VIIe siècles).* Monographies de Travaux et Mémoires du Centre de recherche d'histoire et civilisation de Byzance 2. Paris, 1985.

Mango, Cyril, and Roger Scott. "Introduction." In *The Chronicle of Theophanes Confessor: Byzantine and Near Eastern History AD 284–813*, translated by Cyril Mango and Roger Scott, xliii–c. Oxford, 1997.

Margetić, Lujo. *Dolezak hrvata.* Split, 1991.

Margetić, Lujo. "Konstantin Porfirogenet i vrijeme dolaska Hrvata." *Zbornik historijski Zavoda JAZU* 8 (1977): 5–88.

Maricq, Andre. "Notes sur les Slaves dans le Peloponnèse." *Byzantion* 22 (1952): 337–48.

Markus, Robert A. *Gregory the Great and His World.* Cambridge, 1997.

Marović, Ivan. "Reflexions about the Year of Destruction of Salona." *Disputationes Salonitanae 2: Vjesnik za Arheologiju i Historiju Dalmatinsku* 77 (1984): 293–314.

Marquart, Josef. "Die altbulgarischen Ausdrücke in der Inschrift von Čatalar und der bulgarischen Fürstenliste." *Izvestija Russkago archaeologičeskago instituta v Konstantinople* 15 (1911): 1–30.

Marquart, Josef. *Die Chronologie der alttürkischen Inschriften.* Leipzig, 1898.

Marquart, Josef. *Eranšahr nach der Geographie des Ps. Moses Xorenac'i.* Berlin, 1901.

Marquart, Josef. "Kultur- und sprachgeschichtliche Analekten." *Ungarische Jahrbücher* 9 (1929): 68–103.

Marquart, Josef. *Osteuropäische und ostasiatische Streifzüge.* Leipzig, 1903.

Marquart, Josef. "Über das Volkstum der Komanen." *Abhandlungen der Akademie der Wissenschaften in Göttingen*, n.s., 13 (1914): 25–238.

Marsone, Pierre. *La steppe et l'empire: La formation de la dynastie Khitan (Liao), IVe–Xe siècle.* Paris, 2011.

Martin, Max. "Die absolute Datierung der Männergürtel im merowingischen Westen und im Awarenreich." *Antaeus* 29–30 (2008): 143–73.

Martindale, J. R. *The Prosopography of the Later Roman Empire*, vol. 3A–B. Cambridge, 1992.

Märtl, Claudia, and Peter Schreiner, eds. *Jakob Philipp Fallmerayer (1790–1861): Der Gelehrte und seine Aktualität im 21. Jahrhundert.* Abhandlungen der Bayerischen Akademie der Wissenschaften, phil.-hist. Klasse, n.s., 139. Munich, 2013.

Mauss, Marcel. *The Gift: The Form and Reason for Exchange in Archaic Societies.* London, 2002. Originally published as Marcel Mauss, "Essai sur le don: Forme et raison de l'échange dans les sociétés archaïques in sociologie et anthropologie." *L'Année sociologique* 1 (1923–24): 30–186.

Mayer, Theodor. "Zu Fredegars Bericht über die Slawen." In *Festschrift Oswald Redlich*, MIÖG Erg. Bd. 11, 114–20. Innsbruck, 1929.

Mayr, Gottfried. "Neuerliche Bemerkungen zur Todeszeit des heiligen Emmeram und zur Kirchenpolitik Herzog Theodos." In Wolfram and Pohl, *Typen der Ethnogenese*, 199–215.

Mayr, Gottfried. "Zur Todeszeit des hl. Emmeram und zur frühen Geschichte des Klosters Herrenchiemsee." *Zeitschrift für bayerische Landesgeschichte* 34 (1971): 358–64.

McCormick, Michael. "Analyzing Imperial Ceremonies." *Jahrbuch der Österreichischen Byzantinistik* 35 (1985): 1–20.

McCormick, Michael. "Clovis at Tours, Byzantine Public Ritual and the Origins of Medieval Ruler Symbolism." In Chrysos and Schwarcz, *Das Reich und die Barbaren*, 155–80.

McCormick, Michael. *Eternal Victory: Triumphal Rulership in Late Antiquity, Byzantium and the Early Medieval West.* Cambridge, 1986.

McCormick, Michael. "The Liturgy of War." *Viator* 15 (1984): 1–23.

McCormick, Michael. *Origins of the European Economy: Communications and Commerce, A.D. 300–900.* New York, 2002.

McKitterick, Rosamond. *Charlemagne: The Formation of an European Identity.* Cambridge, 2008.

McKitterick, Rosamond. *History and Memory in the Carolingian World.* Cambridge, 2004.

Meier, Mischa, Christine Radtki, and Fabian Schulz, eds. *Die Weltchronik des Johannes Malalas: Autor—Werk—Überlieferung.* Malalas Studien 1. Stuttgart, 2016.

Menges, Karl H. "Altaic Elements in the Proto-Bulgarian Inscriptions." *Byzantion* 21 (1951): 85–118.

Menges, Karl H. "On Some Loanwords from or via Turkic in Old Russian." In *Fuad Köprülü Armagani*, edited by Osman Turan and Hasan Eren, 369–90. Istanbul, 1953.

Menges, Karl H. Review of *Khazar Studies: An Historic-Philological Inquiry Into the Origins of the Khazars*, by Peter B. Golden. *Central Asiatic Journal* 30 (1986): 55–77.

Menges, Karl H. "Schwierige slawisch-orientalische Lehnbeziehungen." *UAJB* 31 (1959): 177–91.

Menges, Karl H. *The Turkic Languages and Peoples: An Introduction to Turkic Studies.* Wiesbaden, 1968.

Menges, Karl H. "Zum sibirischen Schamanismus." *Central Asiatic Journal* 25 (1981): 260–309.

Menges, Karl Heinrich. *Oriental Elements in the Vocabulary of the Oldest Russian Epos: The Igor Tale.* Suppl. to Word: Monographs 7. New York, 1951.

Menghin, Wilfried. *Die Langobarden: Archäologie und Geschichte.* Stuttgart, 1985.

Menke, Manfred. "Zu den Fibeln der Awarenzeit aus Keszthely." *A Wosinsky Mór Múzeum Évkönyve* 15 (1990): 187–214.

Merrills, Andrew H. *History and Geography in Late Antiquity.* Cambridge, 2005.

Mesterházy, Károly. "Az utrechti zsoltár avar ábrázolásai." *Alba Regia* 8–9 (1967–68): 245–48.

Meyer, Heinz. *Geschichte der Reiterkrieger.* Stuttgart, 1982.

Mihăescu, Haralambie. "Torna, torna, fratre." *Byzantina* 8 (1976): 21–35.

Mikkola, Jooseppi J. "Avarica." *Archiv für Slavische Philologie* 42 (1929): 158–60.

Mikkola, Jooseppi J. "Samo und sein Reich." *Archiv für Slavische Philologie* 42 (1929): 77–97.

Mildenberger, Gerhard, ed. *Studien zur Völkerwanderungszeit im östlichen Mitteleuropa.* Marburg, 1980.

Milinkovic, Mihailo. "Stadt oder 'Stadt': Frühbyzantinische Siedlungsstrukturen im nördlichen Illyricum." In Henning, *Post-Roman Towns,* 2:159–92.

Miller, Bryan K. "The Southern Xiongnu in Northern China: Navigating and Negotiating the Middle Ground." In Bemmann and Schmauder, *Complexity of Interaction,* 127–98.

Miller, D. A. "Byzantine Treaties and Treaty-Making: 500–1025 A.D." *Byzantinoslavica* 32 (1971): 56–76.

Miller, Roy Andrew, and Te-Fen Ling-Hu. *Accounts of Western Nations in the History of the Northern Chou Dynasty.* Berkeley, 1959.

Minorsky, Vladimir. "Tamim Ibn Bahr's Journey to the Uyghurs." *Bulletin of the School of Oriental and African Studies* 12, no. 2 (1948): 275–305.

Mirković, Miroslava. "Sirmium, Its History from the 1st Century AD to 582 AD." In *Sirmium,* 5–90.

Mitscha-Märheim, Herbert. *Dunkler Jahrhunderte goldene Spuren: Die Völkerwanderungszeit in Österreich.* Vienna, 1963.

Mitscha-Märheim, Herbert. "Nochmals: Awarische Wohnsitze und Regensburger Besitz im Burgenland." *Burgenländische Heimatblätter* 15 (1953), 46–48.

Mitterauer, Michael. *Karolingische Markgrafen im Südosten.* Archiv für österreichische Geschichte 123. Graz, 1963.

Miyakawa, Hisayuki, and Arnulf Kollautz. "Ein Dokument zum Fernhandel zwischen Byzanz und China zur Zeit Theophylakts." *Byzantinische Zeitschrift* 77 (1984): 6–19.

Miyakawa, Hisayuki, and Arnulf Kollautz. "Die Mongolei in der Epoche der Jou-jan (5. und 6. Jh. n. Chr.)." *Central Asiatic Journal* 12 (1968–69): 181–208.

Mócsy, Andreas. *Pannonia and Upper Moesia: A History of the Middle Danube Provinces of the Roman Empire,* The Provinces of the Roman Empire 4. London, 1974.

Mohay, András. "Priskos' Fragment über die Wanderungen der Steppenvölker." *Acta Antiqua Academiae Scientiarum Hungaricae* 24 (1976): 125–40.

Möhlenkamp, Renate. "Avaria." In *Glossar zur frühmittelalterlichen Geschichte im östlichen Europa, Bericht einer Arbeitstagung,* 39–51. Münster, 1982.

Molnár, Ádám. *Weather Magic in Inner Asia.* Bloomington, IN, 1994.

Molnár, Zsolt, Marianna Biró, Sándor Bartha, and G. Fekete. "Past Trends, Present State and Future Prospects of Hungarian Forest-Steppe." In *Eurasian Steppes: Ecological Problems and Livelihoods in a Changing World,* edited by Marinus J. A. Werger and Marija A. van Staalduinen, 209–52. Heidelberg, 2012.

Montinaro, Federico, and Marek Jankowiak, eds. *Studies in Theophanes.* Travaux et mémoires 19. Paris, 2015.

Moorhead, John. "Italian Loyalties during Justinian's Gothic War." *Byzantion* 53 (1983): 575–96.

Moravcsik, Gyula. *Byzantinoturcica*. 2nd ed. 2 vols. Berlin, 1958.

Moravcsik, Gyula. "Der ungarische Anonymos über die Bulgaren and Griechen." *Revue des Études Sud-Est Européennes* 7 (1969): 167–74.

Moravcsik, Gyula. "Zur Geschichte der Onoguren." *Ungarische Jahrbücher* 10 (1930): 53–90.

Morgan, David. *The Mongols*. Oxford, 1986.

Morgan, Lewis H. *Ancient Society, or Researches in the Lines of Human Progress from Savagery, through Barbarism to Civilization*. London, 1887.

Morrisson, Cécile. "Byzance au VIIe siècle: Le témoinage de la numismatique." In N. Stratos, *Byzantium*, 1:149–64.

Mühle, Eduard. *Die Slaven im Mittelalter*. Das mittelalterliche Jahrtausend 4. Berlin, 2016.

Mühlmann, Wilhelm E. "Ethnogonie und Ethnogenese: Theoretisch-ethnologische und ideologiekritische Studie." In *Studien zur Ethnogenese*, 9–28.

Müllenhof, Karl. *Deutsche Altertumskunde*. Vol. 2. Berlin, 1887.

Müller, Klaus E. *Geschichte der antiken Ethnographie und ethnologischen Theoriebildung*. 2 vols. Wiesbaden, 1980.

Müller, Róbert. *Die Gräberfelder von Keszthely-Fenékpuszta Ödenkirche-Flur*. Budapest, 2014.

Müller, Róbert. *Die Gräberfelder vor der Südmauer der Befestigung von Keszthely-Fenékpuszta*. Budapest, 2010.

Müller, Róbert. "Das Gräberfeld von Gyenesdiás." In Daim et al., *Hunnen + Awaren*, 411–16.

Müller, Róbert. "Neue archäologische Funde der Keszthely-Kultur." In Daim, *Awarenforschungen*, 1:251–307.

Müller, Róbert. "Spätantike Elemente in den Gräberfeldern der frühen Keszthely-Kultur." In Bollók, Csiky, and Vida, *Zwischen Byzanz und der Steppe/Between Byzantium and the Steppe*, 271–90.

Müller, Róbert. "Die spätrömische Festung Valcum am Plattensee." In Bott and Meier-Arendt, *Germanen, Hunnen und Awaren*, 270–73.

Murray, Alexander C. "Reinhard Wenskus on Ethnogenesis, Ethnicity, and the Origin of the Franks." In Gillett, *On Barbarian Identity*, 39–68.

Musset, Lucien. *Les invasions*. Vol. 2, *Le second assaut contre l'Europe chrétienne*. Nouvelle Clio 12.1. Paris, 1971.

Muthesius, Angelika. *Studies in Byzantine and Islamic Silk Weaving*. London, 1995.

Nagy, Margit. *Awarenzeitliche Gräberfelder im Stadtgebiet von Budapest*. Monumenta Avarorum Archaeologica 2. Budapest, 1998.

Nagy, Margit. "Frühawarenzeitliche Grabfunde aus Budapest: Bemerkungen zur awarenzeitlichen Tierornamentik." In *Popoli delle steppe*, 1:373–408.

Nagy, Sandor. "Mečka—ein frühmittelalterliches Gräberfeld beim Dorfe Aradac." *Studijné zvesti* 16 (1968): 165–74.

Nagy, Tibor. "Studia Avarica 1. Az avar honfoglalás útvonalának kérdéséhez (Sur l'itineraire de la conquête avare)." *Antiquitas Hungarica* 1 (1947): 56–63.

Nagy, Tibor. "Studia Avarica 2, Az avar-bizánci kapcsolatok 2 szakasának (567–82) idörend jéhez." *Antiquitas Hungarica* 2 (1948): 131–49.

Nechaeva, Ekaterina. *Embassies-Negotiations-Gifts: Systems of East Roman Diplomacy in Late Antiquity*. Stuttgart, 2014.

Németh, Gyula, *A honfoglaló magyarság kiulakalása*. Budapest, 1930.

Németh, Gyula. "Die Herkunft der Namen Kobrat und Esperüch." *Köröso Csoma Archivum* 2, no. 6 (1932): 440–47.

Németh, Julius. "The Runiform Inscriptions from Nagyszentmiklós and the Runiform Scripts of Eastern Europe." *Acta Linguistica Hungarica* 21 (1971): 1–52.

Németh, Julius. "Türkische und ungarische Ethnonyme." *UAJB* 47 (1975): 154–60.

Nestor, Jon. "La pénétration des Slaves dans la péninsule balkanique et la Grèce continentale." *Revue des Études Sud-Est Européennes* 1 (1963): 41–67.

Newfield, Timothy. "A Great Carolingian Panzootic: The Probable Extent, Diagnosis and Impact of an Early Ninth-Century Cattle Pestilence." *Argos* 46 (2012): 200–210.

Niederle, Lubomir. *Manuel d'antiquité slave.* Vol. 1, *L'histoire.* Paris, 1923.

Niederle, Lubomir. *Slovanské starožitnosti.* Vol. 1, bk. 1. Prague, 1902.

Niermeyer, Jan F. *Mediae Latinitatis Lexicon minus.* 2 vols. 2nd ed. Leiden, 2002.

Nöldeke, Theodor. *Geschichte der Perser und Araber zur Zeit der Sasaniden.* Leiden, 1879.

Noll, Rudolf. "Ein Ziegel als sprechendes Zeugnis einer historischen Katastrophe (zum Untergang Sirmiums 582 n. Chr)." *Anzeiger der Phil.-Hist. Klasse der Österreichischen Akademie der Wissenschaften* 126 (1990): 139–54.

Noonan, Theodor S. "Russia, the Near East, and the Steppe in the Early Medieval Period: An Examination of the Sasanian and Byzantine Finds from the Kama-Ural Area." *Archivum Eurasie Medii Aevi* 2 (1982): 269–302.

Nystazopoulou-Pelekidou, Maria. "Les Slaves dans l'empire byzantin." In *The 17th International Byzantine Congress: Major Papers, Dumbarton Oaks/Georgetown University, Washington, D.C., August 3–8, 1986,* 345–68. New York, 1986.

Nystazopoulou-Pelekidou, Maria. "Symbolē eis tēn chronologēsin tōn abarikōn kai slabikōn epidromōn epi Maurikiou (582–602)." *Symmeikta* 2 (1971): 145–205.

Odler, Martin, and Jozef Zábojník. "Sídliská z 8. storočia na juhozápadnom Slovensku: Šaľa III, Úľany nad Žitavou, Pavlová" [Settlements from the eighth century in southwestern Slovakia: Šaľa II, Úľany nad Žitavou, Pavlová]. *Študijné zvesti* 50 (2011): 101–220.

Oeser, Wolfgang. "Methodologische Bemerkungen." In *Entstehung von Sprachen und Völkern,* edited by Per Sture Ureland, Linguistische Arbeiten 162, 1–6. Tübingen, 1985.

Öhrig, Bruno. *Bestattungsriten alttürkischer Aristokratie im Lichte der Inschriften.* Munich, 1988.

Oikonomides, Nicolas. "Silk Trade and Production in Byzantium from the Sixth to the Ninth Century: The Seals of Kommerkiarioi." *Dumbarton Oaks Papers* 40 (1986): 33–53.

Olajos, Thérèse. "La chronologie de la dynastie avare de Baian." *Revue des Études Byzantines* 34 (1976): 151–58.

Olajos, Thérèse. "Contributions à l'histoire des Onogours (Installés dans le bassin des Carpathes)." *Chronica: Annual of the Institute of History, University of Szeged, Hungary* 1 (2001): 4–18.

Olajos, Thérèse. "Quelques remarques sur une peuplade slave en Hellade." In *Abstracts of Short Papers, the 17th International Byzantine Conference,* 243.

Olster, David. *Roman Defeat, Christian Response, and the Literary Construction of the Jew.* Philadelphia, 1994.

Oreb, Franko. "Archaeological Excavations in the Eastern Part of Ancient Salona." *Disputationes Salonitanae 2: Vjesnik za Arheologiju i Historiju Dalmatinsku* 77 (1984): 25–36.

Ostrogorsky, Georg. "Die Chronologie des Theophanes im 7. und 8. Jahrhundert." *Byzantinisch-neugriechische Jahrbücher* 7 (1928–29): 1–56.

Ostrogorsky, Georg. *Geschichte des byzantinischen Staates.* 3rd ed. Handbuch der Altertumswissenschaften 12.1.2. Munich, 1963.

Ostrogorsky, George. "Byzantine Cities in the Early Middle Ages." *Dumbarton Oaks Papers* 13 (1959): 45–66.

Ostrowski, Donald. "Pagan Past and Christian Identity in the *Primary Chronicle*." In *Historical Narratives and Christian Identity on a European Periphery: Early History Writing in Northern, East-Central, and Eastern Europe (c. 1070–1200)*, edited by Ildar H. Garipzanov, 229–53. Turnhout, 2011.

Ovčarov, Dimităr. "Die Protobulgaren und ihre Wanderungen nach Südosteuropa." In Hänsel, *Die Völker Südosteuropas vom 6.–8. Jahrhundert*, 171–90.

Özyetgin, Ayşe Melek. "The Use of the Title Beg among the Turks." *Central Asian Journal* 11 (2006): 156–70.

Pais, Dezső. "A propos de l'étymologie de l'ethnique OGUR." In Ligeti, *Studia Turcica*, 361–73.

Parczewski, Michael. "Besiedlungsgeschichte der frühmittelalterlichen Slowakei." *Acta Archaeologica Carpathica* 15 (1974): 31–50.

Parczewski, Michał. *Die Anfänge der frühslawischen Kultur in Polen*. Vienna, 1993.

Parker, Edward H. "China, the Avars and the Franks." *Asiatic Quarterly Review* 3, no. 13 (1902): 446–60.

Paschini, Pio. *Storia del Friuli*. Vol. 1, *Dalle origini al formarsi dello stato patriarcale*. 3rd ed. Udine, 1975.

Paul, Jürgen. "Perspectives nomades: État et structures militaires." *Annales: Histoire, Sciences Sociales* 59, no. 5–6 (2004): 1069–93.

Paulsen, Peter. *Alemannische Adelsgräber von Niederstotzingen*. Stuttgart, 1967.

Paxton, Frederick S. *Christianizing Death: The Creation of a Ritual Process in Early Medieval Europe*. Ithaca, NY, 1990.

Peisker, Jan. "Die älteren Beziehungen der Slaven zu Turkotataren und Germanen und ihre sozialgeschichtliche Bedeutung." *Vierteljahresschrift zur Sozial- und Wirtschaftsgeschichte* 3, no. 2–3 (Leipzig, 1905): 187–360.

Peisker, Jan. "The Expansion of the Slavs." In *Cambridge Medieval History*, vol. 2, *The Rise of the Saracens and the Foundation of the Western Empire*, 418–58. Cambridge, 1913.

Peltomaa, Leena Mari. *The Image of the Virgin Mary in the Akatisthos Hymn*. The Medieval Mediterranean Peoples, Economies and Cultures, 400–1453, 35. Leiden, 2001.

Péter, László, ed. *Historians and the History of Transylvania*. New York, 1992.

Petkov, Kiril. *The Voices of Medieval Bulgaria, Seventh–Fifteenth Century: The Records of a Bygone Culture*. Leiden, 2008.

Placanica, Antonio. "Introduzione." In *Vittore de Tunnuna, Chronica: Chiesa et imperio nell'età di Giustiniano*, edited by Antonio Placanica, i–lxiv. Florence, 1997.

Planhol, Xavier de. *Kulturgeographische Grundlagen der islamischen Geschichte*. Zurich, 1975.

Pletnewa, Svetlana Alexandrowna. *Die Chasaren: Mittelalterliches Reich an Don und Wolga*. Leipzig, 1978.

Pohl, Walter. "Alboin und der Langobardenzug nach Italien: Aufstieg und Fall eines Barbarenkönigs." In *Sie schufen Europa: Historische Portraits von Konstantin bis Karl dem Großen*, edited by Mischa Meier, 216–27. Munich, 2007.

Pohl, Walter. "Archaeology of Identity: Introduction." In Pohl and Mehofer, *Archaeology of Identity/Archäologie der Identität*, 9–24.

Pohl, Walter. "Das Awarenreich und die 'kroatischen' Ethnogenesen." In Wolfram and Schwarcz, *Die Bayern und ihre Nachbarn*, 293–98.

Pohl, Walter. "Das awarische Khaganat und die anderen Gentes im Karpatenbecken (6.–8. Jh.)." In Hänsel, *Die Völker Südosteuropas vom 6.–8. Jahrhundert*, 41–52.

Pohl, Walter. "Die Beziehungen der Awaren zu den Slawen." In *Slowenien und die Nachbarländer zwischen Antike und karolingischer Epoche*, edited by Rajko Bratož, 341–54. Ljubljana, 2000.

Pohl, Walter. "Christian and Barbarian Identities in the Early Medieval West: Introduction." In Pohl and Heydemann, *Post-Roman Transitions*, 1–46.

Pohl, Walter. "Conceptions of Ethnicity in Early Medieval Studies." *Archaeologia Polona* 29 (1991): 39–49; reprinted in *Debating the Middle Ages: Issues and Readings*, edited by Lester K. Little and Barbara Rosenwein, 15–24. Oxford, 1998.

Pohl, Walter. "The Empire and the Lombards: Treaties and Negotiations in the Sixth Century." In Pohl, *Kingdoms of the Empire*, 75–134.

Pohl, Walter. "Ethnicity and Empire in the Western Eurasian Steppes." In Maas and Di Cosmo, *Eurasian Empires in Late Antiquity*, forthcoming.

Pohl, Walter. "Ethnicity, Theory, and Tradition: A Response." In Gillett, *On Barbarian Identity*, 221–40.

Pohl, Walter. "Frontiers and Ethnic Identities: Some Final Considerations." In Curta, *Borders, Barriers, and Ethnogenesis*, 255–65.

Pohl, Walter. "Frontiers of Lombard Italy: The Laws of Ratchis and Aistulf." In Pohl, Wood, and Reimitz, *The Transformation of Frontiers*, 117–42.

Pohl, Walter. "Gender and Ethnicity in the Early Middle Ages." In *Gender in the Early Medieval World: East and West, 300–900*, edited by Leslie Brubaker and Julia M. H. Smith, 23–43. Cambridge, 2004.

Pohl, Walter. "Die Gepiden und die Gentes an der mittleren Donau nach dem Zerfall des Attilareiches." In Wolfram and Daim, *Die Völker an der mittleren und unteren Donau im fünften und sechsten Jahrhundert*, 240–305.

Pohl, Walter. *Die Germanen*. 2nd ed. Munich, 2004.

Pohl, Walter. "Der Germanenbegriff vom 3. bis 8. Jahrhundert: Identifikationen und Abgrenzungen." In *Zur Geschichte der Gleichung "germanisch-deutsch,"* edited by Heinrich Beck, Dieter Geuenich, Heiko Steuer, and Dietrich Hakelberg, RGA Erg. Bd. 34, 163–83. Berlin, 2004.

Pohl, Walter. "History in Fragments: Montecassino's Politics of Memory." *Early Medieval Europe* 10, no. 3 (2001): 343–74.

Pohl, Walter. "Huns, Avars, Hungarians: Comparative Perspectives Based on Written Evidence." In Bemmann and Schmauder, *Complexity of Interaction*, 693–702.

Pohl, Walter. "Introduction: Early Medieval Romanness—a Multiple Identity." In Gantner et al., *Transformations of Romanness in the Early Middle Ages*, 3–40.

Pohl, Walter. "Introduction: Meanings of Community and the Uses of Terminology." In *Meanings of Community across Medieval Eurasia*, edited by Walter Pohl, Christina Lutter, and Eirik Hovden, 1–20. Leiden, 2016.

Pohl, Walter. "Introduction. Strategies of Identification: A Methodological Profile." In Pohl and Heydemann, *Strategies of Identification*, 1–64.

Pohl, Walter. "Justinian and the Barbarian Kingdoms." In *The Age of Justinian*, edited by Michael Maas, 448–76. Cambridge, 2005.

Pohl, Walter, ed. *Kingdoms of the Empire: The Integration of Barbarians in Late Antiquity*. The Transformation of the Roman World 1. Leiden, 1997.

Pohl, Walter. "Konfliktverlauf und Konfliktbewältigung: Römer und Barbaren im frühen Mittelalter." *Frühmittelalterliche Studien* 26 (1992): 165–207.

Pohl, Walter. "Liturgie di guerra nei regni altomedievali." *Rivista di Storia del Cristianesimo* 5, no. 1 (2008): 29–44.

Pohl, Walter. "I longobardi e la terra." In *Expropriations et confiscations dans les royaumes barbares: Une approche régionale*, edited by Pierfrancesco Porena and Yann Rivière, 279–94. Rome, 2012.

Pohl, Walter. *Le origini etniche dell'Europa: Barbari e Romani tra antichità e medioevo*. Rome, 2000.

Pohl, Walter. "Origo gentis (Langobarden)." In *RGA*, 22:183–88.

Pohl, Walter. "Osnove Hrvatske etnogeneze: Avari i Slaveni; Grundlagen der kroatischen Ethnogenese: Awaren und Slawen." In *Etnogeneza Hrvata* [Ethnogeny of the Croats], edited by Neven Budak, 86–96, 211–23. Zagreb, 1995.

Pohl, Walter. "Paolo Diacono e la costruzione dell'identità longobarda." In *Paolo Diacono—uno scrittore fra tradizione longobarda e rinnovamento carolingio*, edited by Paolo Chiesa, 413–26. Udine, 2000.

Pohl, Walter. "Paul the Deacon—between Sacci and Marsuppia." In *Ego Trouble: Authors and Their Identities in the Early Middle Ages*, edited by Richard Corradini, Matthew Gillis, Rosamond McKitterick, and Irene van Renswoude, Forschungen zur Geschichte des Mittelalters 15, 111–24. Vienna, 2010.

Pohl, Walter. "Paulus Diaconus und die 'Historia Langobardorum': Text und Tradition." In Scharer and Scheibelreiter, *Historiographie im frühen Mittelalter*, 375–405.

Pohl, Walter. "Perceptions of Barbarian Violence." In *Violence in Late Antiquity: Perceptions and Practices*, edited by Harold A. Drake, 15–26. Aldershot, 2006.

Pohl, Walter. "The Regia and the Hring: Barbarian Places of Power." In *Topographies of Power in the Early Middle Ages*, edited by Mayke de Jong, Frans Theuws, and Carine van Rhijn, The Transformation of the Roman World 6, 439–66. Leiden, 2001.

Pohl, Walter. "Ritualized Encounters: Late Roman Diplomats and Barbarians, Fifth–Sixth Century." In *Court Ceremonies and Rituals of Power in the Medieval Mediterranean*, edited by Alexander Beihammer, Stavroula Constantinou, and Maria Parani, 67–86. Leiden, 2013.

Pohl, Walter. "The Role of Steppe Peoples in Eastern and Central Europe in the First Millennium A.D." In Urbańczyk, *Origins of Central Europe*, 65–78.

Pohl, Walter. "Steppenimperien in Mitteleuropa: Hunnen, Awaren, Ungarn." In *Gebieter über die Völker in den Filzwandzelten: Steppenimperien von Attila bis Tschinggis Khan*, edited by Johannes Gießauf and Johannes Steiner, Grazer Morgenländische Studien 7, 17–29. Graz, 2009.

Pohl, Walter, ed. *Die Suche nach den Ursprüngen: Von der Bedeutung des frühen Mittelalters*. Forschungen zur Geschichte des Mittelalters 8. Vienna, 2004.

Pohl, Walter. "Telling the Difference: Signs of Ethnic Identity." In Pohl and Reimitz, *Strategies of Distinction*, 17–69.

Pohl, Walter. "Tradition, Ethnogenese und literarische Gestaltung: eine Zwischenbilanz." In *Ethnogenese und Überlieferung: Angewandte Methoden der Frühmittelalterforschung*, edited by Karl Brunner and Brigitte Merta, VIÖG 31, 9–26. Vienna, 1994.

Pohl, Walter. "Verlaufsformen der Ethnogenese: Awaren und Bulgaren." In Wolfram and Pohl, *Typen der Ethnogenese*, 113–24.

Pohl, Walter. *Die Völkerwanderung: Eroberung und Integration*. 2nd ed. Stuttgart, 2005.

Pohl, Walter. "Von der Ethnogenese zur Identitätsforschung." In *Neue Wege der Frühmittelalterforschung*, edited by Max Diesenberger, Walter Pohl, and Bernhard Zeller. Vienna, forthcoming.

Pohl, Walter, Wolfgang Haubrichs, and Ingrid Hartl, eds. *Walchen, Romani und Latini: Variationen einer nachrömischen Gruppenbezeichnung zwischen Britannien und dem Balkan*. Forschungen zu Geschichte des Mittelalters. Vienna, 2017.

Pohl, Walter, and Gerda Heydemann, eds. *Post-Roman Transitions: Christian and Barbarian Identities in the Early Medieval West*. Turnhout, 2013.

Pohl, Walter, and Gerda Heydemann, eds. *Strategies of Identification: Ethnicity and Religion in Early Medieval Europe*. Turnhout, 2013.

Pohl, Walter, and Mathias Mehofer, eds. *Archaeology of Identity/Archäologie der Identität*. Forschungen zur Geschichte des Mittelalters 17. Vienna 2010.

Pohl, Walter, and Helmut Reimitz, eds. *Grenze und Differenz im frühen Mittelalter*. Forschungen zur Geschichte des Mittelalters 1. Vienna, 2000.

Pohl, Walter, and Bernhard Zeller, eds., *Sprache und Identität im frühen Mittelalter.* Forschungen zur Geschichte des Mittelalters 20. Vienna, 2012.

Poláček, Lumír. "Mikulčice und Awaren: Zur Interpretation 'awarischer' Funde von Mikulčice." In Bemmann and Schmauder, *Kulturwandel in Mitteleuropa*, 579–90.

Poláček, Lumír. "Ninth-Century Mikulčice: The 'Market of the Moravians'? The Archaeological Evidence of Trade in Great Moravia." In Henning, *Post-Roman Towns*, 1:499–524.

Popoli delle steppe: Unni, Avari, Ungari. 2 vols. SSCI 35. Spoleto, 1988.

Popović, Vladislav. "Aux origines de la slavisation des Balkans: La constitution des premières sklavinies macédoniennes vers la fin du VIe siècle." *Comptes rendus: Académie des Inscriptions et Belles-Lettres* 1 (1980): 230–57.

Popović, Vladislav. *Caričin Grad.* Belgrad, 1980.

Popović, Vladislav. "Le dernier évêque de Sirmium." *Revue des Études Augustiniennes* 21 (1975): 91–111.

Popović, Vladislav. "A Survey of the Topography and Urban Organization of Sirmium in the Late Empire." In *Sirmium*, 119–34.

Popović, Vladislav. "Les témoins archéologiques des invasions avaro-slaves dans l'Illyricum byzantin." *Mélanges de l'École Française de Rome* 87 (1985): 445–504.

Popowska-Taborska, Hanna. "The Slavs in the Early Middle Ages from the Viewpoint of Contemporary Linguistics." In Urbańczyk, *Origins of Central Europe*, 91–96.

Poulter, Andrew. *Nicopolis ad Istrum: A Roman, Late Roman and Early Byzantine City. Excavations 1985–1992.* Society for the Promotion of Roman Studies. London, 1995.

Poulter, Andrew, ed. *The Transition to Late Antiquity, on the Danube and Beyond.* Oxford, 2008.

Preidel, Helmut. *Die Anfänge der slawischen Besiedlung Böhmens und Mährens.* 2 vols. Gräfeling bei München, 1957.

Preiser-Kapeller, Johannes. "The Climate of the Khagan: Observations on Paleo-Environmental Factors in the History of the Avars (6th–9th Century AD)." In Drauschke et al., *Lebenswelten zwischen Archäologie und Geschichte*, 311–24.

Prinzing, Günter. "Pliska in the View of the Protobulgarian Inscriptions and the Byzantine Written Sources." In Henning, *Post-Roman Towns*, 2:241–52.

Pritsak, Omeljan. *Die bulgarische Fürstenliste und die Sprache der Protobulgaren.* Ural-Altaische Bibliothek. Wiesbaden, 1955.

Pritsak, Omeljan. "The Distinctive Features of the Pax Nomadica." In *Popoli delle steppe*, 2:749–80.

Pritsak, Omeljan. "Die Karachaniden." *Der Islam* 31 (1954): 17–68.

Pritsak, Omeljan. "Karachanidische Streitfragen 1–4." *Oriens* 3 (1950): 209–28.

Pritsak, Omeljan. "The Slavs and the Avars." In *Gli slavi occidentali*, 1:353–432.

Pritsak, Omeljan. "Tribal Names and Titles among the Altaic Peoples." In *The Turks in the Early Islamic World*, edited by C. Edmund Bosworth, 59–116. Aldershot, 2007. Original German version: "Stammesnamen und Titulaturen der altaischen Völker." *UAJB* 24 (1952): 49–104.

Profantová, Nad'a. "Die frühslawische Besiedlung Böhmens und archäologische Spuren der Kontakte zum früh- und mittelawarischen sowie merowingischen Kulturkreis." In Bemmann and Schmauder, *Kulturwandel in Mitteleuropa*, 619–44.

Profantová, Nad'a. "The Middle Avar Period and the Problems of a 'Cultural Change' at the End of the Seventh Century North of the Avar Khaganate." *Antaeus* 29–30 (2008): 215–32.

Prohászka, Péter. *Az ozora-tótipusztai avar fejedelmi sírok (Die awarischen Oberschichtsgräber von Ozora-Tótipuszta).* Budapest, 2012.

Prohászka, Péter, and Falko Daim. "Der Kaiser auf der Mantelschließe: Zum Deckel der frühmittelalterlichen Dose von Sorpe (Provinz Lérida)." *Archäologisches Korrespondenzblatt* 45 (2015): 563–78.

Pülhorn, Wolfgang. "Archäologischer Kommentar zu den 'Bauten' des Prokop." In Prokop, *Bauten*, vol. 5 of *Prokop Werke*, edited and translated by Otto Veh, 381–474. Munich, 1977.

Pulleyblank, Edwin G. "Some Remarks on the Toquz Oghuz Problem." *UAJB* 28 (1956): 35–42.

Quast, Dieter, ed. *Foreigners in Early Medieval Europe: Thirteen International Studies on Early Medieval Mobility*. Mainz, 2009.

Quast, Dieter, ed. *Das Grab des fränkischen Königs Childerich in Tournai und die Anastasis Childerici von Jean-Jacques Chifflet aus dem Jahre 1655*. Mainz, 2015.

Rácz, Zsófia. *Die Goldschmiedgräber der Awarenzeit*. Mainz, 2014.

Radloff, Wilhelm. *Aus Sibirien*. 2 vols. Leipzig, 1884.

Rapanić, Željko. "La costa orientale dell'Adriatico nell'alto medioevo (Considerazioni storico-artisiche)." In *Gli slavi occidentali*, 2:831–70.

Rashev, Rasho. "L'Onglos—témoignages écrites et faits archéologiques. " *Bulgarian Historical Review* 10, no. 1 (1982): 68–79.

Rásonyi, László. "Der Frauenname bei den Turkvölkern." *UAJB* 34 (1962): 223–39.

Rásonyi, László. "The Psychology and Categories of Name-Giving among the Turkish Peoples." In *Hungaro-Turcica: Studies in Honour of Julius Németh*, edited by Gyula Káldy-Nagy, 207–23. Budapest, 1976.

Reallexikon der Byzantinistik. Vol. 1, bk. 2. Amsterdam, 1969.

Reimitz, Helmut. "Grenzen und Grenzüberschreitungen im karolingischen Mitteleuropa." In Pohl and Reimitz, *Grenze und Differenz*, 105–66.

Reimitz, Helmut. *History, Frankish Identity and the Framing of Western Ethnicity, 550–850*. Cambridge, 2015.

Reindel, Kurt. "Das Zeitalter der Agilolfinger: Die politische Entwicklung." In *Handbuch der bayerischen Geschichte*. Vol. 1, edited by Max Spindler, 2nd ed., 99–176. Munich, 1981.

Reinink, Gerrit J., and Bernard H. Stolte, ed. *The Reign of Heraclius (610–641): Crisis and Confrontation*. Leuven, 2002.

Reisinger, Jutta and Günter Sowa. *Das Ethnikon Sclavi in den lateinischen Quellen bis zum Jahr 900*, Glossar zur frühmittelalterlichen Geschichte im östlichen Europa, Beiheft Nr. 6. Stuttgart, 1990.

Renfrew, Colin. "Introduction." In *Peer Polity Interaction and Socio-Political Change*, edited by Colin Renfrew and J. F. Cherry, 1–8. Cambridge, 1986.

Reuter, Timothy. "Whose Race, Whose Ethnicity? Recent Medievalists' Discussions of Identity." In Timothy Reuter, *Medieval Polities and Modern Mentalities*, edited by Janet L. Nelson, 100–109. Cambridge, 2006.

Riesch, Holger, Joachim Rutschke, and Ulrich Stehli. "Nachgebaut und ausprobiert: Rekonstruktionen des Reflexbogens, der Pfeile und des Köchers aus den Žargalant Chajrchan Bergen, Chovd ajmag, Mongolei." In Bemmann, *Steppenkrieger*, 181–98.

Ripinsky-Naxon, Michael. *The Nature of Shamanism: Substance and Function of a Religious Metaphor*. Albany, NY, 1993.

Rist, Josef. "Die sogenannte Kirchengeschichte des Zacharias Rhetor: Überlieferung, Inhalt und theologische Bedeutung." In *Syriaca*. Vol. 1, *Zur Geschichte, Theologie, Liturgie und Gegenwartslage der syrischen Kirchen*, ed. Martin Tamcke, Studien zur orientalischen Kirchengeschichte 17, 77–99. Münster, 2002.

Roesler, Robert. "Über den Zeitpunkt der slawischen Ansiedlung an der unteren Donau." *Sitzungsberichte der kaiserlichen Akademie der Wissenschaften* 73 (1873): 77–126.

Röhrborn, Klaus, and Wolfgang Veenker, eds. *Runen, Tamgas und Graffiti aus Asien und Osteuropa*. Wiesbaden, 1985.

Róna-Tas, András. *Hungarians and Europe in the Early Middle Ages: An Introduction to Early Hungarian History*. Budapest, 1999.

Róna-Tas, András. "Die Inschrift des Nadelbehälters von Szarvas (Ungarn)." *UAJB*, n.s., 9 (1990): 1–30.

Róna-Tas, András. "The Inscriptions of the Nagyszentmiklós Treasure." In Kovács, *The Gold of the Avars*, 120–29.

Róna-Tas, András. "The Khazars and the Magyars." In Golden, Ben-Shammai, and Róna-Tas, *The World of the Khazars*, 269–78.

Róna-Tas, András. "Materialien zur alten Religion der Türken." In Heissig and Klimkeit, *Synkretismus in den Religionen Zentralasiens*, 33–45.

Róna-Tas, András. "The Problems of the East-European Scripts with Special Regards to the Newly Found Inscription of Szarvas." In *Popoli delle steppe*, 2:483–506.

Róna-Tas, András. "Where Was Kuvrat's Bulgharia?" *Acta Orient. Hung*. 53 (2000): 1–22.

Ronin, Vladimir K. "The Franks on the Balkans in the Early Ninth Century." *Études Balkaniques* 21 (1985): 39–57.

Rosner, Gyula. *Das awarenzeitliche Gräberfeld von Szekszárd—Bogyislói Straße*. Budapest, 1999.

Ross, James Bruce. "Two Neglected Paladins of Charlemagne: Erich of Friuli and Gerold of Bavaria." *Speculum* 20 (1945): 212–35.

Rosser, John. "The Role of the Great Isthmus Corridor in the Slavonic Invasions of Greece." *Byzantinische Forschungen* 9 (1985): 245–53.

Rostovzeff, Michael. *The Animal Style in South Russia and China*. Princeton, NJ, 1929.

Roux, Jean-Paul. "Die alttürkische Mythologie." In *Götter und Mythen in Zentralasien und Nordasien*, edited by Egidius Schmalzriedt and Hans-Werner Haussig, 173–277. Stuttgart, 1999.

Roux, Jean-Paul. *La mort chez les peuples altaïques anciens et médiévaux d'après les documents écrits*. Paris, 1963.

Roux, Jean-Paul. "La religion des peuples des steppes." In *Popoli delle steppe*, 2:513–32.

Roux, Jean-Paul. *La religion des Turcs et des Mongols*. Paris, 1984.

Roux, Jean-Paul. "Tängri: Essai sur le ciel-dieu des peuples altaïques (premier article)." *Revue de l'histoire des religions* 149, no. 1 (1956): 49–82.

Roux, Michel. "L'origine celeste de la souveraineté dans les inscriptions paleo-turques de Mongolie et de la Sibérie." In *The Sacral Kingship: Studies in the History of Religions*, edited by Giunta Centrale per gli Studi Storici, 231–41. Leiden, 1959.

Runciman, Steven. *A History of the First Bulgarian Empire*. London, 1930.

Rusu, Mircea. "Aspects des relations entre les autochtones du bassin carpato-danubien aux VIe–IXe siècles." *Revue Roumaine d'Histoire* 19 (1980): 247–66.

Rusu, Mircea. "Les populations du groupe turc, les Slaves et les autochthones du bassin carpato-danubien aux VIe–IXe siècles." *Revue Roumaine d'Histoire* 19 (1980): 19–30.

Rusu, Mircea. "The Prefeudal Cemetery of Noşlac (VI–VIIc)." *Dacia* 6 (1962): 269–92.

Rybatzki, Volker. "The Titles of Türk and Uigur Rulers in the Old Turkic Inscriptions." *Central Asiatic Journal* 44 (2000): 205–92.

Šafařík, Pavel Jozef. *Slawische Altertümer*. 2 vols. Prague, 1843–44.

Sági, Károly. "Die zweite altchristliche Basilika von Fenékpuszta." *Acta Antiqua Academiae Scientiarum Hungaricae* 9 (1961): 397–459.

Sahlins, Marshall D. "Poor Man, Rich Man, Big Man, Chief: Political Types in Melanesia and Polynesia." *Comparative Studies in Society and History* 5 (1963): 283–303.

Sakać, Stjepan K. "Iranische Herkunft des kroatischen Volksnamens." *Orientalia Christiana Periodica* 15 (1949): 313–40.

Salamon, Ágnes. "Über die ethnischen und historischen Beziehungen des Gräberfeldes von Környe." *Acta Arch. Hung.* 21 (1969): 273–98.

Samolin, William. Review of Haussig, "Theophylakts Exkurs über die skythischen Völker," *Byzantion* 23 (1953): 275–436. *Central Asiatic Journal* 2 (1956): 315.

Samolin, William. "Some Notes on the Avar Problem." *Central Asiatic Journal* 3 (1957–58): 62–65.

Sarantis, Alexander. "Eastern Roman Management of Barbarian States in the Lower-Middle Danube Frontier Zones, AD 332–610." In Bugarski et al., *GrenzÜbergänge*, 41–66.

Sarantis, Alexander. *Justinian's Balkan Wars: Campaigning, Diplomacy and Development in Illyricum, Thrace and the Northern World A.D 527–65.* Prenton, 2016.

Sarkisyanz, Emanuel. *Geschichte der orientalischen Völker Russlands bis 1917.* Munich, 1961.

Šašel, Jaroslav. "Antiqui barbari: Zur Besiedlungsgeschichte Ostnoricums und Pannoniens im 5. und 6. Jahrhundert nach den Schriftquellen." In *Von der Spätantike zum frühen Mittelalter,* edited by Eugen Ewig and Joachim Werner, Vorträge und Forschungen 25, 125–39. Sigmaringen, 1979.

Scharer, Anton, and Georg Scheibelreiter, eds. *Historiographie im frühen Mittelalter.* VIÖG 32. Vienna, 1994.

Scharlipp, Wolfgang-Ekkehard. *Die frühen Türken in Zentralasien: Eine Einführung in ihre Geschichte und Kultur.* Darmstadt, 1992.

Schippmann, Klaus. *Grundzüge der Geschichte des sasanidischen Reiches.* Darmstadt, 1990.

Schmauder, Michael. *Die Hunnen: ein Reitervolk in Europa.* Darmstadt, 2009.

Schmauder, Michael. "Huns, Avars, Hungarians: Reflections on the Interactions between Steppe Empires in Southeast Europe and the Late Roman to Early Byzantine Empires." In Bemmann and Schmauder, *Complexity of Interaction,* 671–92.

Schmauder, Michael. "Vielteilige Gürtelgarnituren des 6.–7. Jahrhunderts: Herkunft, Aufkommen und Trägerkreis." In Daim, *Die Awaren am Rand der byzantinischen Welt,* 15–44.

Schmid, Magdalena Maria Elisabeth. *Das Gräberfeld von Rákóczifalva in Zentralungarn und die Chronologie des spätawarenzeitlichen Fundmaterials.* Universitätsforschungen zur prähistorischen Archäologie 272. Bonn, 2015.

Schmidt, Ludwig. *Die Ostgermanen.* 2nd ed. Munich, 1941.

Schneider, Reinhard. *Königswahl und Königserhebung im Frühmittelalter.* Stuttgart, 1972.

Schramm, Gottfried. *Ein Damm bricht: Die römische Donaugrenze und die Invasionen des 5.–7. Jahrhunderts im Licht von Namen und Wörtern.* Munich, 1997.

Schreiner, Peter. "Einleitung." In Theophylaktos Simokates, *Geschichte,* trans. Peter Schreiner, 1–25. Stuttgart, 1985.

Schreiner, Peter. "Eine merowingische Gesandtschaft in Konstantinopel (590?)." *Frühmittelalterliche Studien* 19 (1985): 195–200.

Schreiner, Peter. "Note sur la fondation de Monemvasie en 582/583." *Travaux et Mémoires* 4 (1970): 471–75. Reprinted in Schreiner, *Die byzantinischen Kleinchroniken,* vol. 1, *Einleitung und Text* (Vienna, 1975), 519–23.

Schreiner, Peter. "Städte und Wegenetz in Moesien, Dakien und Thrakien nach dem Zeugnis des Theophylaktos Simokates." In Peter Schreiner, *Studia Byzantino-Bulgarica,* Miscellanea Bulgarica 2, 59–69. Vienna, 1986.

Schuldt, Ewald. "Westslawische Brücken." In *RGA,* 3:578–80.

Schulze-Dörrlamm, Mechthild. "Awarische Einflüsse auf die Bewaffnung und Kampftechnik des ostfränkischen Heeres in der Zeit um 600?" In *Arms and Armour as Indicators of Cultural Transfer: The Steppes and the Ancient World from Hellenistic Times to the Early Middle Ages*, edited by Markus Mode and Jürgen Tubach, 485–507. Wiesbaden, 2006.

Schwarcz, Andreas. "Pannonien im 9. Jahrhundert und die Anfänge der direkten Beziehungen zwischen dem ostfränkischen Reich und den Bulgaren." In Pohl and Reimitz, *Grenze und Differenz*, 99–104.

Schwarcz, Andreas, Peter Soustal, and Antoaneta Tcholakova, eds. *Der Donaulimes in der Spätantike und im Frühmittelalter*. Miscellanea Bulgarica 22. Vienna, 2016.

Scorpan, Constantin. *Limes Scythiae: Topographical and Stratigraphical Research on the Late Roman Fortifications on the Lower Danube*. Oxford, 1985.

Scott, James C. *The Art of Not Being Governed: An Anarchist History of Upland Southeast Asia*. New Haven, CT, 2009.

Seemanova, Eva, et al. "The Slavic NBN Founder Mutation: A Role for Reproductive Fitness?" *PLoS ONE* 11 (2016), e0167984. doi: 10.1371/journal.pone.0167984, http://journals.plos.org/plosone/article?id=10.1371/journal.pone.0167984.

Sertkaya, Osman F. "The First Line of the Tonjukuk Monument." *Central Asiatic Journal* 23 (1979): 288–91.

Setton, Kenneth. "The Bulgars in the Balkans and the Occupation of Corinth in the Sixth Century." *Speculum* 25 (1950): 502–43.

Setton, Kenneth. "The Emperor Constans II. and the Capture of Corinth by the Onogur Bulgars." *Speculum* 27 (1952): 351–62.

Ševčenko, Ihor. "Re-reading Constantine Porphyrogenitus." In Shepard and Franklin, *Byzantine Diplomacy*, 167–201.

Shapira, Dan D. Y. "Iranian Sources on the Khazars." In Golden, Ben-Shammai, and Róna-Tas, *The World of the Khazars*, 291–306.

Shepard, Jonathan. "Slavs and Bulgars." In *The New Cambridge Medieval History*, vol. 2, *c.700–c.900*, edited by Rosamond McKitterick, 228–48. Cambridge, 1995.

Shepard, Jonathan, and Simon Franklin, eds. *Byzantine Diplomacy: Papers from the Twenty-fourth Spring Symposium in Byzantine Studies, Cambridge, March 1990*. Aldershot, 1992.

Shiratori, Kurakichi. "On the Titles Khan and Khagan." *Proceedings of the Imperial Academy of Japan* 2 (1926): 241–44.

Sigrist, Christian. *Regulierte Anarchie: Untersuchungen zum Fehlen und zur Entstehung politischer Herrschaft in segmentären Gesellschaften*. Freiburg, 1967.

Silagi, Gabriel. "Die Ungarnstürme in der ungarischen Geschichtsschreibung: Anonymus und Simon von Kéza." In *Popoli delle steppe*, 1:245–68.

Sinor, Denis, ed. *Cambridge History of Early Inner Asia*. Cambridge, 1990.

Sinor, Denis. "The Establishment and Dissolution of the Türk Empire." In Sinor, *The Cambridge History of Early Inner Asia*, 285–316.

Sinor, Denis. *Introduction à l'étude de l'Eurasie centrale*. Wiesbaden, 1963.

Sinor, Denis. "The Legendary Origin of the Turks." In Denis Sinor, *Studies in Medieval Inner Asia*, Variorum Collected Studies, no. II, 223–57. Aldershot, 1997.

Sinor, Denis. "Qapqan." *Journal of the Royal Asiatic Society of Great Britain and Ireland*, nos. 3–4 (1954): 174–84.

Sinor, Denis. "Taking an Oath over a Dog Cut in Two." In Bethlenflavy et al., *Altaic Religious Beliefs and Practices*, 301–7.

Sinor, Denis, and Sergei G. D. Klyashtorny. "The Türk Empire." In Litvinsky, Guang-da, and Samghabadi, *History of Civilizations of Central Asia*, 327–47.

Skaff, Jonathan. *Sui-Tang China and Its Turko-Mongol Neighbors: Culture, Power and Connections, 580–800.* Oxford, 2012.

Smedley, John. "Trade in Cherson, 6th–10th Centuries." In *Actes du XVe congrès international d'études byzantines,* 4:291–97.

Sneath, David. *The Headless State: Aristocratic Orders, Kinship Society, and Misrepresentations of Nomadic Inner Asia.* New York, 2007.

Sodini, Jean-Pierre. "The Transformation of Cities in Late Antiquity within the Provinces of Macedonia and Epirus." In Poulter, *The Transition to Late Antiquity,* 311–36.

Sokol, Vladimir. *Medieval Jewelry and Burial Assemblages in Croatia: A Study of Graves and Gravegoods, ca. 800 to ca. 1450.* Leiden, 2016.

Somogyi, Péter. *Byzantinische Fundmünzen der Awarenzeit.* Innsbruck, 1997.

Somogyi, Péter. *Byzantinische Fundmünzen der Awarenzeit in ihrem europäischen Umfeld.* Dissertationes Pannonicae Ser. IV 2. Budapest, 2014.

Somogyi, Péter. "Neue Überlegungen über den Zustrom byzantinischer Münzen ins Awarenland (Numismatischer Kommentar zu Csanád Bálints Betrachtungen zum Beginn der Mittelawarenzeit)." *Antaeus* 29–30 (2008): 347–93.

Somogyi, Péter. "New Remarks on the Flow of Byzantine Coins in Avaria and Walachia during the Second Half of the Seventh Century." In Curta, *The Other Europe in the Middle Ages,* 83–150.

Sophoulis, Panos. *Byzantium and Bulgaria, 775–831.* Leiden, 2012.

Sós, Ágnes. "Archäologische Angaben zur Frage der Frühperiode des awarisch-slawischen Zusammenlebens." *Študijné zvesti* 16 (1968): 221–31.

Sós, Ágnes. "Le deuxième cimitière Avare d'Üllő." *Acta Arch. Hung.* 6 (1955): 193–227.

Sós, Ágnes. *Die slawische Bevölkerung Westungarns im 9. Jahrhundert.* Münchner Beiträge zur Vor- und Frühgeschichte 22. Munich, 1973.

Sós, Ágnes. "Zur Problematik der Awarenzeit in der neueren ungarischen archäologischen Forschung." In *Berichte über den 2. internationalen Kongress für slawische Archäologie,* 2:85–102. Berlin, 1973.

Sós, Ágnes Cs., Ágnes Salamon, Sándor Bökönyi, and János Matolcsi. *Cemeteries of the Early Middle Ages (6th–9th Centuries A.D.) at Pókaszepetk.* Budapest, 1995.

Sotinel, Claire. "The Three Chapters and the Transformations of Italy." In Chazelle and Cubitt, *Crisis of the Oikoumene,* 85–120.

Soucek, Svat. *A History of Inner Asia.* Cambridge, 2000.

Soustal, Peter. *Nikopolis und Kephallinia.* Tabula Imperii Byzantini 3. Vienna, 1981.

Speck, Paul. "De miraculis Sancti Demetrii, qui Thessalonicam profugus venit, oder: Ketzerisches zu den Wundergeschichten des Heiligen Demetrios und zu seiner Basilika in Thessalonike." In *Varia IV,* Poikila Byzantina 12, 255–532. Bonn, 1993.

Speck, Paul. *Zufälliges zum Bellum Avaricum des Georgios Pisides.* Miscellanea Byzantina Monacensia 24. Munich, 1980.

Spieser, Jean-Michel. "Inventaires en vue d'un recueil des inscriptions historiques de Byzance: I. Les inscriptions de Thessalonique." *Travaux et mémoires* 5 (1973): 145–80.

Spieser, Jean-Michel. *Thessalonique et ses monuments du IVe au VIe siècle: Contribution à l'étude d'une ville paléochrétienne.* Athens, 1984.

Spuler, Bertold. "Geschichte Mittelasiens seit dem Auftreten der Türken." In *Geschichte Mittelasiens,* edited by Bertold Spuler, Handbuch der Orientalistik 1.5.5, 123–310. Leiden, 1966.

Squatriti, Paolo. "Moving Earth and Making Difference: Dikes and Frontiers in Early Medieval Bulgaria." In Curta, *Borders, Barriers, and Ethnogenesis,* 59–90.

Stache, Ulrich Justus. *Flavius Cresconius Corippus: In laudem Iustini Minoris. Ein Kommentar.* Berlin, 1976.

Stachowski, Stansisław. "Türkischer Einfluss auf den slavischen Wortschatz." In Gutschmidt et al., *Die slavischen Sprachen/The Slavic Languages*, 2:1198–1210.

Stadler, Peter. "Argumente für die Echtheit des 'Avar Treasure.'" *Mitteilungen der Anthropologischen Gesellschaft in Wien* 118/19 (1988/89): 193–217.

Stadler, Peter. "Avar Chronology Revisited, and the Question of Ethnicity in the Avar Quaganate." In Curta, *The Other Europe in the Middle Ages*, 47–82.

Stadler, Peter. "Ethnische Gruppen im Awarenreich." In Pohl and Mehofer, *Archaeology of Identity/Archäologie der Identität*, 111–43.

Stadler, Peter. "Ethnische Verhältnisse im Karpatenbecken und die Beziehungen zum Westen zur Zeit des awarischen Khaganats im 6. und 7. Jahrhundert." In Bemmann and Schmauder, *Kulturwandel in Mitteleuropa*, 657–78.

Stadler, Peter. *Quantitative Studien zur Archäologie der Awaren I.* With contributions fromWalter Kutschera, Walter Pohl, and Eva Maria Wild. Österreichische Akademie der Wissenschaften, Philosophisch-historische Klasse, Mitteilungen der Prähistorischen Kommission 60. Vienna, 2005.

Stadler, Peter. "Die Werkstätten awarischer Riemenbeschläge mit Greifendarstellung." In Friesinger and Daim, *Typen der Ethnogenese*, 305–50.

Stančeva, Magdalina. "Sofia au moyen âge à la lumière de nouvelles études archéologiques." *Byzantinobulgarica* 5 (1978): 211–28.

Stanilov, Stanislav. *Die Metallkunst des Bulgarenkhanats an der Donau: Versuch einer empirischen Untersuchung.* Sofia, 2006.

Stark, Sören. *Die Alttürkenzeit in Mittel- und Zentralasien: Archäologische und historische Studien.* Wiesbaden, 2008.

Stark, Sören. "Luxurious Necessities: Some Observations on Foreign Commodities and Nomadic Polities in Central Asia in the Sixth to Ninth Centuries." In Bemmann and Schmauder, *Complexity of Interaction*, 463–502.

Stark, Sören. "Nomaden und Sesshafte in Mittel- und Zentralasien: Nomadische Adaptionsstrategien am Fallbeispiel der Alttürken." In *Grenzüberschreitende Formen des Kontakts zwischen Orient und Okzident im Altertum*, edited by Monika Schuol, Udo Hartmann, and Andreas Luther, 363–404. Stuttgart, 2002.

Stark, Sören. "On Oq Bodun: The Western Turk Qağanate and the Ashina Clan." *Archivum Eurasiae Medii Aevi* 15 (2006–7): 159–72.

Stark, Sören. "Central and Inner Asian Parallels to a Find from Kunszentmiklós-Bábony (Kunbábony): Some Thoughts on the Early Avar Headdress." *Ancient Civilizations from Scythia to Siberia* 15 (2009): 287–305.

Stefan, Friedrich. *Die Münzstätte Sirmium unter den Ostgoten und Gepiden: ein Beitrag zur Geschichte des germanischen Münzwesens in der Zeit der Völkerwanderung.* Munich, 1925.

Štefan, Ivo. "'Great' Moravia and the Přemyslid Bohemia from the Point of View of Archaeology." In *The Great Moravian Tradition and Memory of Great Moravia in the Medieval Central and Eastern Europe*, 9–36. Opava, 2014.

Štefan, Ivo. "Great Moravia, Statehood and Archaeology: The 'Decline and Fall' of One Early Medieval Polity." In Macháček and Ungerman, *Frühgeschichtliche Zentralorte in Mitteleuropa*, 333–54.

Stein, Ernst. *Histoire du Bas-Empire.* 2 vols. Paris, 1949.

Stein, Ernst. *Studien zur Geschichte des byzantinischen Reiches vornehmlich unter den Kaisern Justinus II und Tiberius Constantinus.* Stuttgart, 1919.

Stein, Ernst. "Untersuchungen zur spätbyzantinischen Verfassungs- und Wirtschaftsgeschichte." *Mitteilungen zur osmanischen Geschichte* 2 (1929): 1–62.

Stein, Frauke. "Awarisch-merowingische Beziehungen, ein Beitrag zur absoluten Chronologie der awarenzeitlichen Funde." *Študijné zvesti* 16 (1968): 233–44.

Steinacher, Roland. "Wenden, Slawen, Vandalen: Eine frühmittelalterliche pseudologische Gleichsetzung und ihre Nachwirkungen." In Pohl, *Die Suche nach den Ursprüngen*, 329–53.

Steindorff, Ludwig. *Kroatien: Vom Mittelalter bis zur Gegenwart.* Regensburg, 2001.

Steindorff, Ludwig. "Die Synode auf der Planities Dalmae." *MIÖG* 93 (1985): 279–324.

Steindorff, Ludwig. "Wölfisches Heulen: Ein Motiv in mittelalterlichen slawischen Quellen." *Byzatinoslavica* 46 (1985): 40–49.

Stelzer, Winfried. "Ein Alt-Salzburger Fragment der Kosmographie des Aethicus Ister aus dem 8. Jahrhundert." *MIÖG* 100 (1992): 132–49.

Stepanov, Tsvetelin. *The Bulgars and the Steppe Empire in the Early Middle Ages.* Leiden, 2010.

Stepanov Tsvetelin. "The Bulgar title ΚΑΝΑΣΥΒΙΓΙ: Reconstructing the Notions of Divine Kingship in Bulgaria, AD 822–836." *Early Medieval Europe* 10, 1 (2001): 1–19.

Stepanov, Tsvetelin. "The System of Succession in Qubrat's 'Magna Bulgaria': A New Approach to an Old Problem." In Zimonyi and Karatay, *Central Eurasia in the Middle Ages*, 383–92.

Štih, Peter. "Istria at the Onset of Frankish Rule, or the Impact of Global Politics on Regional and Local Conditions." In Štih, *The Middle Ages*, 212–29.

Štih, Peter. *The Middle Ages between the Eastern Alps and the Northern Adriatic: Select Papers on Slovene Historiography and Medieval History.* Leiden, 2010.

Štih, Peter. "On Nationalized History, Myths and Stereotypes." In Štih, *The Middle Ages*, 9–37.

Štih, Peter. "Structures of the Slovene Territory in the Early Middle Ages." In Štih, *The Middle Ages*, 136–68.

Štih, Peter. "Wiped Out by Slavic Settlement? The Issue of Continuity between Antiquity and the Early Middle Ages in the Slovene Area." In Peter Štih, *The Middle Ages*, 87–99.

Störmer, Wilhelm. *Früher Adel: Studien zur politischen Führungsschicht im fränkisch-deutschen Reich vom 8. bis 11. Jahrhundert.* 2 vols. Monographien zur Geschichte des Mittelalters 6.1. Stuttgart, 1973.

Stratos, Andreas N. "The Avars' Attack on Constantinople in the Year 626." In *Polychordia: Festschrift Franz Dölger*, edited by Peter Wirth, Byzantinische Forschungen 2, 370–76. Amsterdam, 1967.

Stratos, Andreas N. *Byzantium in the Seventh Century.* 3 vols. Amsterdam, 1968–71.

Stratos, Andreas N. "Le guet-apens des Avars." *Jahrbuch der Österreichischen Byzantinistik* 30 (1981): 113–36.

Stratos, Nia A., ed. *Byzantium: Tribute to Andreas N. Stratos.* 2 vols. Athens, 1986.

Straw, Carole Ellen. *Gregory the Great.* Aldershot, 1996.

Studien zur Ethnogenese. Vol. 1. Abhandlungen der Rheinisch-Westfälischen AW 72. Opladen, 1985.

Struminskyj, Bohdan. "Were the Antes Eastern Slavs?" *Harvard Ukrainian Studies* 3/4 (1979–80): 786–96.

Sümegi, Pál, Katalin Náfrádi, Gusztáv Jakab, and Tünde Törőcsik. "Did an Extremely Dry Climate Lead Actually to the Collapse of the Avar Empire in the Carpathian Basin—a Fact or Fiction?" In Bollók, Csiky, and Vida, *Zwischen Byzanz und der Steppe/Between Byzantium and the Steppe*, 469–97.

Syvänne, Ilkka. *The Age of Hippotokotai: Art of War in Roman Military Revival and Disaster (491–636).* Tampere, 2004.

Szabó, Emese. "Die frühmittelalterliche Siedlung Balatonőszöd-Temetői dűlő und ihr Gräberfeld." *Antaeus* 34 (2016): 173–208.

Szádeczky-Kardoss, Samuel. *Avarica: Über die Awarengeschichte und ihre Quellen.* Acta Universitatis de Attila József Nominatae, Opuscula Byzantina 8. Szeged, 1986.

Szádeczky-Kardoss, Samuel. "Der Awarensturm im historischen Bewusstsein der Byzantiner des 11–13. Jahrhunderts." In *Actes du XVe congrès international d'études byzantines*, 4:305–14.

Szádeczky-Kardoss, Samuel. "Der awarisch-türkische Einfluss auf die byzantinische Kriegskunst um 600 (Anmerkungen zum *Strategikon* des Maurikios)." In Szádeczky-Kardoss, *Avarica*, 203–14.

Szádeczky-Kardoss, Samuel. "Die Hauptzüge der Sozialordnung des Awarenkhaganats im Zeitalter der regesten byzantinisch-awarischen Verbindungen." In Szádeczky-Kardoss, *Avarica*, 215–26.

Szádeczky-Kardoss, Samuel. "Kutriguroi." In *RE Suppl.* 12 (1970), 516–20.

Szádeczky-Kardoss, Samuel. "Kuvrat fiának, Kubernek a története és az Avar-kori régészeti leletanyag." *Antik Tanulmányok* 15 (1968): 84–87.

Szádeczky-Kardoss, Samuel. "Onoguroi." In *RE Suppl.* 12 (1970), 902–6.

Szádeczky-Kardoss, Samuel. "Scamarae." In *RE Suppl.* 11 (1968), 1239–42.

Szádeczky-Kardoss, Samuel. "Über die Wandlungen der Ostgrenze der awarischen Machtsphäre." In Szádeczky-Kardoss, *Avarica*, 153–62.

Szádeczky-Kardoss, Samuel. "Über etliche Quellen der awarischen Geschichte des 9. Jahrhunderts." In Szádeczky-Kardoss, *Avarica*, 141–52.

Szádeczky-Kardoss, Samuel. "Ugoroi." In *RE Suppl.* 14 (1974), 847–50.

Szádeczky-Kardoss, Samuel. "Eine unbeachtete Quellenstelle über die Protobulgaren am Ende des 6. Jahrhunderts." *Bulgarian Historical Review* 11, no. 2 (1983): 76–79.

Szádeczky-Kardoss, Samuel. "Eine unkollationierte Handschrift der Homilie über die persisch-awarische Belagerung von Konstantinopel: Codex Athous Batopedi 84. fol. 63r–68r." In Szádeczky-Kardoss, *Avarica*, 185–95.

Szádeczky-Kardoss, Samuel. *Ein Versuch zur Sammlung und chronologischen Anordnung der griechischen Quellen der Awarengeschichte*. Acta Universitatis de Attila József Nominatae. Acta Antiqua et Archaeologica 16, Opuscula Byzantina 1. Szeged, 1972.

Szádeczky-Kardoss, Samuel. "Zur Textüberlieferung der 'Homilia de obsidione Avarica Constantinopolis auctore ut videtur Theodoro Syncello.'" In Szádeczky-Kardoss, *Avarica*, 173–84.

Szameit, Erik. "Das frühmittelalterliche Grab von Grabelsdorf bei St. Kanzian am Klopeinersee, Kärnten: Ein Beitrag zur Datierung und Deutung awarischer Bronzen im Ostalpenraum." *Archaeologia Austriaca* 77 (1993): 213–34.

Szameit, Erik. "Slawische Körpergräber des 8. Jahrhunderts im österreichischen Donauraum und ihre Beziehungen zum spätmerowingischen Kulturkreis." In Bialeková and Zábojník, *Ethnische und kulturelle Verhältnisse an der mittleren Donau*, 215–25.

Szameit, Erik. "Zum archäologischen Bild der frühen Slawen in Österreich: Mit Fragen zur ethnischen Bestimmung karolingerzeitlicher Gräberfelder im Ostalpenraum." In Bratož, *Slovenija*, 1:507–44.

Szenthe, Gergely. "Antique Meaning—Avar Significance: Complex Iconographic Schemes on Early Medieval Small Objects." *Acta Arch. Hung.* 64 (2013): 139–72.

Szenthe, Gergely. "Crisis or Innovation? A Technology-Inspired Narrative of Social Dynamics in the Carpathian Basin during the Eighth Century." In Bollók, Csiky, and Vida, *Zwischen Byzanz und der Steppe/Between Byzantium and the Steppe*, 351–70.

Szenthe, Gergely. "Meister und ihre Kunden: Herstellung und Verbreitung gegossener Bronzegegenstände im spätawarenzeitlichen Karpatenbecken." *Archaeológiai Értesítő* 137 (2012): 57–75.

Szenthe, Gergely. "Technological History, Experimental Archaeology and Bronze Casting: Research Findings and Research Perspectives in Early Medieval Studies."

Hungarian Archaeology e-Journal, Summer 2013, http://www.hungarianar chaeology.hu/?page_id=279#post-3843.

Szentpéteri, József. "Archäologische Studien zur Schicht der Waffenträger des Awarentums im Karpatenbecken I und II." *Acta Arch. Hung.* 45 (1993): 165–216; 46 (1994): 231–306.

Szentpéteri, Joszef. "Gesellschaftliche Gliederung des awarenzeitlichen gemeinen Volkes von Želovce 1: Die führende Schicht der Bevölkerung (Bewaffnete und umgegürtete Personen)." *Acta Arch. Hung.* 37 (1985): 79–110.

Szentpéteri, Joszef. "Gesellschaftliche Gliederung des awarenzeitlichen gemeinen Volkes von Želovce 2: Innere Gruppen der Bevölkerung (Schmuck und sonstige rangbezeichnende Beigaben)." *Acta Arch. Hung.* 38 (1986): 147–84.

Szőke, Béla M. "Chronologischer Grundriss der Denkmäler des 9. Jhs. im Karpatenbecken." *Miteilungen des Archäologischen Instituts der Ungarischen Akademie der Wissenschaften* 14 (1985): 161–67.

Szőke, Béla M. "The Question of Continuity in the Carpathian Basin of the 9th Century A.D." *Antaeus* 19–20 (1990–91): 145–57.

Szőke, Béla M. "Zur awarenzeitlichen Siedlungsgeschichte des Körös-Gebietes in Südost-Ungarn." *Acta Arch. Hung.* 32 (1980): 181–203.

Szőke, Béla M. "Zur Problematik des Bestattungsritus mit verstümmelten Rinderschädel des Typs von Sopronkőhida." *Acta Arch. Hung.* 31 (1979): 51–103.

Szőke, Béla Miklós. "Das archäologische Bild der Slawen in Südwestungarn." In Bratož, *Slovenija*, 1:477–505.

Szőke, Béla Miklós. "Mosaburg/Zalavár und Pannonien in der Karolingerzeit." *Antaeus* 31–32 (2010): 9–52.

Szőke, Béla Miklós. "Veränderungen in der Struktur des awarischen Gürtels." *Antaeus* 29–30 (2008): 175–213.

Szőke, Béla Miklós. "Westliche Beziehungen des Karpatenbeckens im 9. Jahrhundert." In *Der pannonische Raum um die Jahrtausendwende (vom 9. bis zum 12. Jahrhundert)*, 107–24. Eisenstadt, 2010.

Szűcs, Jenő. "Theoretical Elements in Master Simon of Kéza's Gesta Hungarorum." In *Gesta Hungarorum*, edited by László Veszprémy and Frank Schaer, xxix–cii. Budapest, 1999.

Szydłowski, Jerzy. "Zur Anwesenheit von Westslawen an der mittleren Donau im ausgehenden 5. und 6. Jahrhundert." In Wolfram and Daim, *Die Völker an der mittleren und unteren Donau im fünften und sechsten Jahrhundert*, 233–38.

Szymánsky, Wojciech, and Elzbieta Dabrowska. *Awarzy—Węgrzy*. Warsaw, 1979.

Takacs, Miklós. "Der Hausbau in Ungarn vom 2. bis zum 13. Jahrhundert n. Chr.: ein Zeitalter einheitlicher Grubenhäuser?" In *The Rural House from the Migration Period to the Oldest Still Standing Buildings*, edited by Ján Klápště, 272–90. Prague, 2002.

Takács, Miklós. "The Ninth-Century Carpathian Basin on the North-West Edge of the First Bulgarian State: An Overview of Some Hypotheses and Remarks and Their Evaluation." In Bollók, Csiky, and Vida, *Zwischen Byzanz und der Steppe/Between Byzantium and the Steppe*, 501–18.

Tăpkova-Zaimova, Vasilka. *Byzance et les Balkans à partir du VIe siècle: Les mouvements ethniques et les états*. London, 1979.

Tăpkova-Zaimova, Vasilka. "Sur quelques aspects de la colonisation slave en Macédoine et Grèce." In Tăpkova-Zaimova, *Byzance et les Balkans à partir du VIe siècle*, 111–22.

Tăpkova-Zaimova, Vasilka. "Sur les rapports entre la population indigène des régions balkaniques et les 'barbares' aux VIe et VIIe siècles." *Byzantinobulgarica* 1 (1962): 67–77.

Tăpkova-Zaimova, Vasilka. "La ville de Salonique et son Hinterland slave (jusqu'au Xe siècle)." In Tăpkova-Zaimova, *Byzance et les Balkans à partir du VIe siècle*, 355–62.

Teall, John L. "The Barbarians in Justinian's Armies." *Speculum* 40 (1965): 294–322.

Tejral, Jaroslav. "Archäologischer Beitrag zur Kenntnis der völkerwanderungszeitlichen Ethnostrukturen nördlich der Donau." In Friesinger and Daim, *Typen der Ethnogenese*, 9–88.

Tejral, Jaroslav. "Beiträge zur Chronologie des frühmerowingischen Fundstoffes nördlich der mittleren Donau." In *Probleme der frühen Merowingerzeit im Mitteldonauraum*, edited by Jaroslav Tejral, Spisy Arch. ústavu AV ČR Brno 19, 313–58. Brno, 2002.

Tejral, Jaroslav. "Probleme der Völkerwanderungszeit nördlich der mittleren Donau." In Bott and Meier-Arendt, *Germanen, Hunnen und Awaren*, 351–60.

Tekin, Talât. *A Grammar of Orkhon Turkic*. Bloomington, 1968.

Tekin, Talât. "The Tariat (Terkhin) Inscription." *Acta Orient. Hung.* 37 (1983): 43–68.

Teodor, Dan G. *Continuiteta Populaţiei Autohtone la est de Carpaţi în secolele VI–XI e. n.* Iaşi, 1984.

Theuws, Frans, and Monika Alkemade. "A Kind of Mirror for Men: Sword Depositions in Late Antique Northern Gaul." In *Rituals of Power: From Late Antiquity to the Early Middle Ages*, edited by Frans Theuws and Janet L. Nelson, The Transformation of the Roman World 8, 401–76. Leiden, 2000.

Theuws, Frans C. W. J. "Grave Goods, Ethnicity, and the Rhetoric of Burial Rites in Late Antique Northern Gaul." In *Ethnic Constructs in Antiquity: The Role of Power and Tradition*, edited by Tom Derks and Nico Roymans, 283–317. Amsterdam, 2009.

Thomas, Edith B. "Die Romanität Pannoniens im 5. and 6. Jahrhundert." In Bott and Meier-Arendt, *Germanen, Hunnen und Awaren*, 284–94.

Thomas, Edith B. "Savaria Christiana." *Savaria: A Vás Megyei Múzeumok Értesitöje* 9, no. 20 (1975–76): 105–60.

Thompson, Margaret. *The Athenian Agora*. Vol. 2, *Coins: From the Roman through the Venetian Period*. Princeton, NJ, 1954.

Thomsen, Vilhelm. "Alttürkische Inschriften in der Mongolei." *Zeitschrift der Deutschen Morgenländischen Gesellschaft* 78 (1924–25): 121–75.

Tietze, Andreas. "Kroaten ein türkisches Ethnonym?" *Wiener Slavistisches Jahrbücher* 25 (1979): 140.

Timpe, Dieter. "Ethnologische Begriffsbildung in der Antike." In *Germanenprobleme in heutiger Sicht*, edited by Heinrich Beck, RGA Erg. Bd. 1, 22–40. Berlin, 1986.

Tirr, D. A. "The Attitude of the West Towards the Avars." *Acta Arch. Hung.* 28 (1976): 111–21.

Togan, A. Zeki Validi. *Ibn Fadlans Reisebericht*. Abhandlungen für die Kunde des Morgenlandes 24.3 Leipzig, 1939.

Togan, Zeki Velidi. "Zentralasiatische türkische Literaturen, II: Die islamische Zeit." In *Turkologie*, Handbuch der Orientalistik 5.1, 229–49. Leiden, 1963.

Tomaschek, Wilhelm. "Avares." In *RE* 2.2 (1896), 2264–66.

Tomka, Péter. "Awarische Bestattungssitten: Abriß der Forschungsgeschichte bis 1963." In Daim, *Awarenforschungen*, 2:969–1023.

Tomka, Péter. "Die Lehre der Bestattungsbräuche." *Antaeus* 29–30 (2008): 233–63.

Tomka, Péter. "Le Problème de la survivance des Avars dans la littérature archéologique hongroise." *Acta Orient. Hung.* 24 (1971): 217–52.

Tóth, Elvira. "Das Grab eines Awarenkhagans von Kunbábony." In *Awaren in Europa*, exhibition catalog, 20–23.

Tóth, Elvira H., and Attila Horváth. *Kunbábony: Das Grab eines Awarenkhagans*. Kecskémet, 1992.

Tóth, Endre. "Geschichte der Oberen Wart im ersten Jahrtausend." In *Die Obere Wart*, 77–100. Oberwart, 1977.

Tóth, Endre. "Vigilius episcopus Scaravaciensis." *Acta Arch. Hung.* 26 (1974): 269–75.

Tóth, Endre. "Zu den historischen Problemen der Stadt Savaria und ihrer Umgebung zwischen dem 4.–9. Jahrhundert." *Folia Archaeologica* 27 (1976): 89–120.

Tovornik, Vlasta. "Die Gräberfelder von Micheldorf-Kremsdorf, Oberösterreich." In Daim and Friesinger, *Die Bayern und ihre Nachbarn*, 213–16.

Treadgold, Warren. *The Early Byzantine Historians*. New York, 2010.

Trugly, Alexander. "Gräberfeld aus der Zeit des awarischen Reiches bei der Schiffswerft in Komárno I." *Slov. Arch.* 35 (1987): 251–344.

Trugly, Alexander. "Gräberfeld aus der Zeit des awarischen Reiches bei der Schiffswerft in Komárno II." *Slov. Arch.* 41 (1993): 191–307.

Turek, Rudolf. *Böhmen im Morgengrauen der Geschichte*. Wiesbaden, 1974.

Udolph, Georg. "Ethnogenese und Urheimat der Slaven." In Gutschmidt et al., *Die slavischen Sprachen/The Slavic Languages*, 2:1131–44.

Uray-Köhalmi, Käthe. "Böge and Beki: Schamanentum und Ahnenkult bei den frühen Mongolen." In *Varia Eurasiatica: Festschrift für Professor András Róna-Tas*, 229–38. Szeged, 1991.

Urbańczyk, Przemysław. "Foreign Leaders in Early Slavic Societies." In *Integration und Herrschaft: Ethnische Identitäten und kulturelle Muster im frühen Mittelalter*, edited by Walter Pohl and Max Diesenberger, Forschungen zur Geschichte des Mittelalters 3, 257–68. Vienna, 2002.

Urbańczyk, Przemysław. *Herrschaft und Politik im frühen Mittelalter: Ein historisch-anthropologischer Essay über gesellschaftlichen Wandel und Integration in Mitteleuropa*. Gesellschaften und Staaten im Epochenwandel 14. Frankfurt am Main, 2007.

Urbańczyk, Przemysław, ed. *Origins of Central Europe*. Warsaw, 1997.

Vachkova, Veselina. "Danube Bulgaria and Khazaria as Part of the Byzantine Oikoumene." In Curta, *The Other Europe in the Middle Ages*, 339–62.

Váczy, Péter. "Der fränkische Krieg und das Volk der Awaren." *Acta Antiqua Academiae Scientiarum Hungaricae* 20 (1972): 395–420.

Vaissière, Étienne de la. "Away from the Ötüken: A Geopolitical Approach to the Seventh Century Eastern Turks." In Bemmann and Schmauder, *Complexity of Interaction*, 453–62.

Vaissière, Étienne de la. "Huns et Xiongnu." *Central Asiatic Journal* 49 (2005): 3–26.

Vaissière, Étienne de la. "Is There a 'Nationality of the Hephthalites'?" *Bulletin of the Asia Institute* 17 (2007): 119–37.

Vaissière, Étienne de la. "Maurice et le qaghan: À propos de la digression de Théophylacte Simocatta sur les Turcs." *Revue des Études Byzantines* 68 (2010): 219–24.

Vaissière, Étienne de la. "Oncles et frères: Les qaghans Ashinas et le vocabulaire turc de la parenté." *Turcica* 42 (2010): 267–77.

Vaissière, Étienne de la. "The Steppe World and the Rise of the Huns." In *The Cambridge Companion to the Age of Attila*, edited by Michael Maas, 175–92. Cambridge, 2014.

Vaissière, Étienne de la. "Theophylact's Turkish Exkurs Revisited." In *De Samarcande à Istanbul: Étapes orientales. Hommages à Pierre Chuvin II*, edited by Véronique Schiltz, 91–102. Paris, 2015.

Vaissière, Étienne de la. "Ziebel Qaghan Identified." In *Constructing the Seventh Century*, edited by Constantine Zuckerman, Travaux et Mémoires 17, 741–48. Paris, 2013.

Vajay, Szabolcs de. *Der Eintritt des ungarischen Stämmesbundes in die europäische Geschichte (862–933)*. Studia Hungarica 4. Mainz, 1968.

Váňa, Zdeněk. *Die Welt der alten Slawen*. Hanau, 1996.

Vásáry, István. *Geschichte des frühen Innerasiens*. Herne, 1999.

Vásáry, István. "Mediaeval Theories Concerning the Primordial Homeland of the Hungarians." In *Popoli delle steppe*, 1:213–42.

Vásáry, István. "Runiform Signs on Objects of the Avar Period (6th–8th cc. AD)." *Acta Orient. Hung.* 25 (1972): 335–47.

Vasmer, Max. *Russisches etymologisches Wörterbuch*. Vol. 2, *L–Ssuda*. Heidelberg, 1955.

Vasmer, Max. *Russisches etymologisches Wörterbuch*. Vol. 3, *Sta–Y*. Heidelberg, 1958.

Vasmer, Max. *Die Slaven in Griechenland*. Abh. Press. AW, Ph.-H. Kl. 12. Berlin, 1941.

Vasmer, Max. *Untersuchungen über die ältesten Wohnsitze der Slawen: Die Iranier in Südrussland*. Leipzig, 1923.

Vasyutin, Sergey A. "The Model of the Political Transformation of the Da Liao as an Alternative to the Evolution of the Structures of Authority in the Early Medieval Pastoral Empires of Mongolia." In Bemmann and Schmauder, *Complexity of Interaction*, 391–436.

Vázarova, Zivka. *Slawen und Protobulgaren*. Sofia, 1976.

Vékony, Gabor. "Zur Lesung der griechischen Inschriften des Schatzes von Nagyszentmiklós." *Acta Arch. Hung.* 25 (1973): 293–306.

Velkov, Velizar. "Les campagnes et la population rurale en Thrace au IVe–VIe siècle." *Byzantinobulgarica* 1 (1962): 31–60.

Velkov, Velizar. *Cities in Thrace and Dacia in Late Antiquity*. Amsterdam, 1977.

Velkov, Velizar. "Der Donaulimes in Bulgarien und das Vordringen der Slawen." In Hänsel, *Die Völker Südosteuropas vom 6.–8. Jahrhundert*, 141–70.

Velkov, Velizar. "Zur Geschichte der Stadt Serdica/Sofia im 4.–9. Jhdt." *Études Historiques* 3 (1965): 33–36.

Verlinden, Charles. "L'origine de Sclavus=esclave." *Archivum Latinitatis Medii Aevi* 17 (1942): 97–128.

Verlinden, Charles. "Problèmes d'histoire économique franque: I. Le franc Samo." *Revue Belge de Philologie et Histoire* 12 (1933): 1090–95.

Vernadsky, George, *Ancient Russia*. New Haven, CT, 1946.

Vernadsky, George. "Das frühe Slawentum: Das Ostslawentum bis zum Mongolensturm." In Altheim, *Historia Mundi*, 251–300.

Vernadsky, George. "On the Origin of the Antae." *Journal of the American Oriental Society* 59 (1939): 56–66.

Vetters, Hermann. *Dacia Ripensis*. Schriften der Balkankommission der Österreichische Akademie der Wissenschaften 11.1. Vienna, 1950.

Vida, Tivadar. *Die awarenzeitliche Keramik*. Vol. 1, *6.–7. Jahrhundert*. Budapest, 1999.

Vida, Tivadar. "Conflict and Coexistence: The Local Population of the Carpathian Basin under Avar Rule (Sixth to Seventh Century)." In Curta, *The Other Europe in the Middle Ages*, 13–46.

Vida, Tivadar. "Das Gräberfeld neben dem Horreum in der Innenbefestingung von Keszthely-Fenékpuszta." In Heinrich-Tamáska, *Keszthely-Fenékpuszta*, 396–455.

Vida, Tivadar. "Das kulturelle Bild der Gemeinschaft von Csákberény-Orondpuszta." In László, *Das awarenzeitliche Gräberfeld*, 236–41.

Vida, Tivadar. *Late Antique Metal Vessels in the Carpathian Basin: Luxury and Power in the Early Middle Ages*. Budapest, 2016.

Vida, Tivadar. "Local or Foreign Romans? The Problem of the Late Antique Population of the 6th–7th Centuries in Pannonia." In Quast, *Foreigners in Early Medieval Europe*, 233–59.

Vida, Tivadar. "The Many Identities of the Barbarians in the Middle Danube Region in the Early Middle Ages." In *Entangled Identities and Otherness in Late Antique and Early Medieval Europe: Historical, Archaeological and Bioarchaeological Approaches*, edited by Jorge López Quiroga, Michel Kazanski, and Vujadin Ivanišević, 120–31. Oxford, 2017.

Vida, Tivadar, ed. *Thesaurus Avarorum: Archaeological Studies in Honour of Éva Garam*. Budapest, 2012.

Vida, Tivadar. "'They Asked to Be Settled in Pannonia . . .': A Study on Integration and Acculturation—the Case of the Avars." In Bollók, Csiky, and Vida, *Zwischen Byzanz und der Steppe/Between Byzantium and the Steppe*, 251–70.

Vida, Tivadar. "Die Zeit zwischen dem 4. und 6. Jahrhundert im mittleren Donauraum aus archäologischer Sicht." In Konrad and Witschel, *Römische Legionslager in den Rhein- und Donauprovinzen*, 571–88.

Vida, Tivadar, and Thomas Volling. *Das slawische Brandgräberfeld von Olympia*. Archäologie in Eurasien 9. Rahden, 2000.

Vilfan, Sergij. "Evoluzione statale degli Sloveni e Croati." In *Gli slavi occidentali*, 1:103–40.

Vinski, Zdenko. "O nalazima 6. i 7. stoljéca u Jugoslavij" [On the finds of the sixth and seventh centuries in Yugoslavia]. *Opuscula Archaeologica* 3 (1958): 13–67.

Vladimirtsov, Boris J. *Le régime social des Mongols: Le Féodalisme nomade*. Paris, 1948.

Voinovitch, Louis de. *Histoire de la Dalmatie*. 2 vols. Paris, 1934.

Vryonis, Speros. "The Evolution of Slavic Society and the Slavic Invasions in Greece: The First Major Slavic Attack on Thessaloniki, A. D. 597." *Hesperia* 50 (1981): 378–90.

Waldmüller, Lothar. *Die ersten Begegnungen der Slawen mit dem Christentum und den christlichen Völkern vom 6. bis zum 8. Jahrhundert*. Enzyclopädie der Byzantinistik 51. Amsterdam, 1976.

Wegenast. Klaus. "Zacharias Scholastikos." In *RE*, 2nd ser., 9.2 (1967), 2212–16.

Weiner, Annette B. *Inalienable Possessions: The Paradox of Keeping-While-Giving*. Berkeley, 1992.

Weissensteiner, Johann. *Tegernsee, die Bayern und Österreich: Studien zu Tegernseer Geschichtsquellen und der bayerischen Stammessage mit einer Edition der Passio secunda s. Quirini*. Archiv für Österreichische Geschichte 133. Vienna, 1983.

Weithmann, Michael. *Die slawische Bevölkerung auf der griechischen Halbinsel: Ein Beitrag zur historischen Ethnographie Südeuropas*. Munich, 1978.

Weltecke, Dorothea. *Die "Beschreibung der Zeiten" von Mōr Michael dem Großen (1126–1199): Eine Studie zu ihrem historischen und historiographiegeschichtlichen Kontext*, CSCO 594, Subsidia 110. Louvain, 2003.

Wenskus, Reinhard. *Stammesbildung und Verfassung: Das Werden der frühmittelalterlichen Gentes*. 2nd ed. Graz, 1977.

Werner, Joachim. "Fernhandel und Naturalwirtschaft im östlichen Merowingerreich nach archäologischen und numismatischen Zeugnissen." In *Moneta e scambi nell'alto medioevo*, SSCI 8, 557–618. Spoleto, 1961.

Werner, Joachim. *Der Grabfund von Malaja Pereščepina und Kuvrat, Kagan der Bulgaren*. Abh. Bayer. AW, n.s., 91. Munich, 1984.

Werner, Joachim. *Die Langobarden in Pannonien: Beiträge zur Kenntnis der langobardischen Bodenfunde vor 568*. Abhandlungen der Bayerischen Akademie der Wissenschaften, n.s., 55. Munich, 1962.

Werner, Joachim. *Der Schatzfund von Vrap in Albanien: Beiträge zur Archäologie der Awarenzeit im mittleren Donauraum*. Studien zur Archäologie der Awaren 2, DsÖAW 184. Vienna, 1986.

Werner, Joachim. "Slawische Bügelfibeln des 7. Jahrhunderts." In *Reinecke Festschrift*, 150–72. Mainz, 1950.

Werner, Joachim. "Zum Stand der Forschung über die archäologische Hinterlassenschaft der Awaren." *Beiträge zur Südosteuropaforschung*, 1966, 283–307.

Werner, Joachim. "Zur Herkunft und Ausbreitung der Anten und Sklavenen." In *Actes du VIIIe Congrés International des Sciences Préhistoriques*, 1:243–52. Belgrad, 1971.

Werner, Joachim. "Zur Verbreitung frühgeschichtlicher Metallarbeiten (Werkstatt-Wanderhandwerk-Handel-Familienverbindung)." *Early Medieval Studies 1: Antikvarisk arkiv* 38 (1970): 65–81.

Whitby, Mary. "Defender of the Cross: George of Pisidia on the Emperor Heraclius and His Deputies." In *The Propaganda of Power: The Role of Panegyric in Late Antiquity*, edited by Mary Whitby, 247–76. Leiden, 1998.

Whitby, Mary. "George of Pisidia's Presentation of the Emperor Heraclius and His Campaigns." In Reinink and Stolte, *The Reign of Heraclius (610–641)*, 157–73.

Whitby, Michael. *The Emperor Maurice and His Historian: Theophylact Simocatta on Persian and Balkan Warfare*. Oxford, 1988.

Whitby, Michael. "Theophylact's Knowledge of Languages." *Byzantion* 52 (1982): 425–28.

Whitby, Michael, and Mary Whitby. "The Date of Heraclius's Encounter with the Avars." Appendix 4 in *Chronicon Paschale, 284–628 AD*, translated by Michael Whitby and Mary Whitby, Translated Texts for Historians 7, 203–5. Liverpool, 1989.

White, Lynn T., Jr. *Medieval Technology and Social Change*. Oxford, 1962.

Whittow, Mark. "Byzantium's Eurasian Policy in the Age of the Türk Empire." In Di Cosmo and Maas, *Empires and Exchanges in Eurasian Late Antiquity*, 271–86.

Whittow, Mark. *The Making of Orthodox Byzantium*. Basingstoke, 1996.

Whittow, Mark. "Nicopolis ad Istrum: Backward and Balkan?" *Proceedings of the British Academy* 141 (2007): 375–89.

Widengren, Geo. "Xosrau Anōšurvān, les Hephthalites et les peuples turcs." *Orientalia Suecana* 1 (1952): 69–94.

Wiesinger, Peter. "Probleme der bairischen Frühzeit in Niederösterreich aus namenkundlicher Sicht." In Wolfram and Schwarcz, *Die Bayern und ihre Nachbarn*, 321–67.

Wiita, John Earl. "The Ethnika in Byzantine Military Treatises." PhD diss., University of Florida, 1977.

Wilkes, John J. *Dalmatia*. History of the Provinces of the Roman Empire. London, 1969.

Winckler, Katharina. *Die Alpen im Frühmittelalter: Die Geschichte eines Raumes in den Jahren 500 bis 800*. Vienna, 2012.

Winkelmann, Friedhelm, and Helga Köpstein, eds. *Studien zum 7. Jahrhundert in Byzanz: Probleme der Herausbildung des Feudalismus*. Berlin, 1976.

Winkelmann, Friedhelm, Helga Köpstein, Hans Ditten, and Ilse Rochow, eds. *Byzanz im 7. Jahrhundert: Untersuchungen zur Herausbildung des Feudalismus*. Berliner Byzantinische Arbeiten 48. Berlin, 1978.

Winter, Michael. "Die byzantinischen Fundmünzen aus dem österreichischen Bereich der Avaria." In Daim, *Die Awaren am Rand der byzantinischen Welt*, 45–66.

Wittfogel, Karl August. "China und die osteurasische Kavallerie-Revolution." *UAJB* 49 (1977): 121–40.

Wittfogel, Karl August. *China und die osteurasische Kavallerie-Revolution*. Wiesbaden, 1978.

Wittfogel, Karl August, and Feng Chia-Sheng. *History of Chinese Society: Liao (907–1125)*. New York, 1949.

Wolfram, Herwig, ed. and trans. *Conversio Bagoariorum et Carantanorum: das Weißbuch der Salzburger Kirche über die erfolgreiche Mission in Karantanien und Pannonien*. 2nd rev. ed. Ljubljana, 2012.

Wolfram, Herwig. "Donau §11." In *RGA*, 6:26–28.

Wolfram, Herwig. "Einleitung oder Überlegungen zur *Origo gentis*." In Wolfram and Pohl, *Typen der Ethnogenese*, 19–33.

Wolfram, Herwig. "Ethnogenesen im frühmittelalterlichen Donau- und Ostalpenraum (6. bis 10. Jahrhundert)." In *Frühmittelalterliche Ethnogenese im Alpenraum*, edited by Helmut Beumann and Werner Schröder, Nationes 5, 97–152. Sigmaringen, 1985.

Wolfram, Herwig. "Die frühmittelalterliche Romania im Donau- und Ostalpenraum." In Pohl, Haubrichs, and Hartl, *Walchen, Romani und Latini*, 27–58.

Wolfram, Herwig. *Die Geburt Mitteleuropas: Geschichte Österreichs vor seiner Entstehung.* Vienna, 1987.

Wolfram, Herwig. *Grenzen und Räume: Geschichte Österreichs vor seiner Entstehung, 378–907.* Österreichische Geschichte 1. Vienna, 1995.

Wolfram, Herwig. "Der heilige Rupert und die antikarolingische Adelsopposition." *MIÖG* 80 (1972): 4–34.

Wolfram, Herwig. *History of the Goths.* Translated by Thomas J. Dunlap. Berkeley, 1988. Originally published as Herwig Wolfram, *Die Goten: Von den Anfängen bis zur Mitte des sechsten Jahrhunderts; Versuch einer historischen Ethnographie,* 5th ed. (Munich, 2009).

Wolfram, Herwig. *Intitulatio,* vol. 1, *Lateinische Königs- und Fürstentitel bis zum Ende des 8. Jahrhunderts,* MIÖG Erg. Bd. 21. Graz, 1967.

Wolfram, Herwig. *Die Karolingerzeit in Niederösterreich.* Wissenschaftliche Schriftenreihe Niederösterreich 46. St. Pölten, 1980.

Wolfram, Herwig. "Liudewit und Priwina: Ein institutioneller Vergleich." In Archäologisches Institut der Slowakischen Akademie der Wissenschaften, *Interaktionen der mitteleuropäischen Slawen und anderen Ethnika im 6.–10. Jahrhundert,* 291–96.

Wolfram, Herwig. "Origo gentis." In *RGA,* 22:174–78.

Wolfram, Herwig. *The Roman Empire and Its Germanic Peoples.* Berkeley, 1997.

Wolfram, Herwig. *Salzburg, Bayern, Österreich: Die Conversio Bagoariorum et Carantanorum und die Quellen ihrer Zeit.* MIÖG Erg. Bd. 31. Vienna, 1995.

Wolfram, Herwig. *Tassilo III.: Höchster Fürst und niedrigster Mönch.* Regensburg, 2016.

Wolfram, Herwig. "Typen der Ethnogenese: Ein Versuch." In *Die Franken und die Alemannen bis zur "Schlacht bei Zülpich" (496/97),* edited by Dieter Geuenich, RGA Erg. Bd. 19, 608–27. Berlin, 1998.

Wolfram, Herwig. "Der Zeitpunkt der Einführung der Grafschaftsverfassung in Karantanien." In *Siedlung, Macht und Wirtschaft: Festschrift Fritz Posch,* edited by Gerhard Pferschy, 313–17. Graz, 1981.

Wolfram, Herwig, and Falko Daim, eds. *Die Völker an der mittleren und unteren Donau im fünften und sechsten Jahrhundert: Berichte des Symposions der Kommission für Frühmittelalterforschung, 24. bis 27. Oktober 1978, Stift Zwettl, Niederösterreich.* DsÖAW 145. Vienna, 1980.

Wolfram, Herwig, and Walter Pohl, eds. *Typen der Ethnogenese unter besonderer Berücksichtigung der Bayern.* Vol.1. DsÖAW 201. Vienna, 1990.

Wolfram, Herwig, and Andreas Schwarcz, eds. *Anerkennung und Integration: zu den wirtschaftlichen Grundlagen der Völkerwanderungszeit 400–600.* Vienna, 1988.

Wolfram, Herwig, and Andreas Schwarcz, eds. *Die Bayern und ihre Nachbarn.* Vol. 1. DsÖAW 179. Vienna, 1985.

Wołoszyn, Marcin. *Theophylaktos Simokates und die Slawen am Ende des westlichen Ozeans—die erste Erwähnung der Ostseeslawen?* Kraków, 2014.

Wood, Ian. *The Merovingian Kingdoms, 450–751.* London, 1994.

Wood, Ian N. "Aethicus Ister: An Exercise in Difference." In Pohl and Reimitz, *Grenze und Differenz,* 197–208.

Wood, Ian N. "Fredegar's Fables." In Scharer and Scheibelreiter, *Historiographie im frühen Mittelalter,* 356–66.

Wood, Ian N. *Gregory of Tours*. Bangor, 1994.

Wood, Ian N. *The Missionary Life: Saints and Evangelisation of Europe, 400–1050*. Harlow, 2001.

Wozniak, Frank E. "Byzantine Diplomacy and the Lombard-Gepidic Wars." *Balkan Studies* 20 (1979): 139–58.

Yarshater, Ehsan, ed. *The Cambridge History of Iran*. Vol. 3, *The Seleucid, Parthian and Sasanid Periods*, bk. 1. Cambridge, 1983.

Yatsenko, Sergey A. "Images of the Early Turks in Chinese Murals and Figurines from the Recently-Discovered Tomb in Mongolia." *Silk Road Foundation Newsletter* 12 (2014): 13–24, http://www.silkroadfoundation.org/newsletter/vol12/Yatsenko_SR12_2014_pp13_24.pdf.

Yu Taishan. "Doubts about the Theory of Rouran-Avar Identity and the Hypothesis about Avar-Yueban Identity." In Yu Taishan, *China and the Mediterranean World in Ancient Times*, edited by Victor Spinei, 297–326. Bucharest, 2014.

Zábojník, Jozef. "Das awarische Kaganat und die Slawen an seiner nördlichen Peripherie." *Slov. Arch.* 47 (1999): 153–73.

Zábojník, Jozef. "On the Problems of Settlements of the Avar Khaganate Period in Slovakia." *Archeologické rozhledy* 40 (1988): 401–37.

Zábojník, Jozef. "Die Rolle der Münzdatierung in der Mittelawarenzeit." *Antaeus* 29–30 (2008): 301–6.

Zábojník, Jozef. "The Slavs and the Avar Khaganate." In *Great Moravia and the Beginnings of Christianity*, edited by Pavel Kouřil, 35–41. Brno, 2015.

Zábojník, Jozef. "Soziale Problematik der Gräberfelder des nördlichen und nordwestlichen Randgebietes des Awarischen Kaganats." *Slov. Arch.* 43 (1995): 205–344.

Zábojník, Jozef. "Zum Verhältnis zwischen Archäologie und Anthropologie am Beispiel frühmittelalterlicher Gräberfelder aus dem Mitteldonauraum (7.–10. Jahrhundert)." In *Castellum, Civitas, Urbs: Zentren und Eliten im frühmittelalterlichen Ostmitteleuropa*, edited by Orsolya Heinrich-Tamáska, Hajnalka Herold, Péter Straub, and Tivadar Vida, 277–92. Rahden, 2015.

Zábojník, Jozef. "Zum Vorkommen von Gegenständen 'awarischer' Provenienz auf den slawischen Burgwällen nördlich der Donau." In Macháček and Ungerman, *Frühgeschichtliche Zentralorte in Mitteleuropa*, 203–14.

Zábojník, Jozef. "Zur Problematik der Siedlungen aus der Zeit des Awarischen Khaganats in der Slowakei." In Bemmann and Schmauder, *Kulturwandel in Mitteleuropa*, 591–600.

Zábojník, Jozef. "Zur Problematik der Waffenvorkommen auf Gräberfeldern aus der Zeit des Awarenreiches in den nordwestlichen Teilen des Karpatenbeckens." In Archäologisches Institut der Slowakischen Akademie der Wissenschaften, *Interaktionen der mitteleuropäischen Slawen und anderen Ethnika im 6.–10. Jahrhundert*, 297–302.

Zacos, Georges, and Alexander Veglery, *Byzantine Lead Seals*. Basel, 1972.

Zakythinos, Denis A. *Byzantinische Geschichte, 324–1071*. Vienna, 1979.

Zakythinos, Dionysios A. *Oi Slavoi en Elladhi: Simvolai is tin istorian tou mesaionikou Ellinismou*. Athens, 1945.

Zástěrová, Bohumila. *Les Avares et les Slaves dans la tactique de Maurice*. Rozpravy Československé Akademie 81.3. Prague, 1971.

Zástěrová, Bohumila. "Zu den Quellen zur Geschichte Wolhyniens und der Duleben im 6. Jahrhundert." In *Byzantinistische Beiträge*, edited by Johannes Irmscher, 231–39. Berlin, 1964.

Zeiller, Jacques. *Les origines chrétiennes dans les provinces danubiennes de l'empire romain*. Paris, 1906.

Zeller, Kurt W. "Kulturbeziehungen im Gräberfeld Linz-Zizlau." In *Baiernzeit in Oberösterreich*. Schriftenreihe des Oberösterreich Musealvereins 10, 75–88. Linz, 1980.

Zhivkov, Boris. *Khazaria in the Ninth and Tenth Centuries*. Leiden, 2015.

Ziemann, Daniel. *Vom Wandervolk zur Großmacht: die Entstehung Bulgariens im frühen Mittelalter (7.–9. Jahrhundert)*. Kölner historische Abhandlungen 43. Cologne, 2007.

Zimonyi, István. "Notes on the Differences between Bedouin and Inner Asian Nomadism." In *Central Asia on Display: Proceedings of the 7th Conference of the European Society for Central Asian Studies*, edited by Gabriele Rasuly-Paleczek and Julia Katschnig, 373–80. Münster, 2005.

Zimonyi, István, and Osman Karatay, eds. *Central Eurasia in the Middle Ages: Studies in Honour of Peter B. Golden*. Wiesbaden, 2016.

Ziółkowski, Adam. "When Did the Slavs Originate? The Case of the Antes." *Palamedes* 9–10, no. 1 (2014–15): 211–36.

Živković, Tibor. *De Conversione Croatorum et Serborum: A Lost Source*. Belgrade, 2012.

Zöllner, Erich. "Awarisches Namensgut in Bayern und Österreich." *MIÖG* 58 (1950): 244–66.

Zuckerman, Constantine. "The Khazars and Byzantium: The First Encounter." In Golden, Ben-Shammai, and Róna-Tas, *The World of the Khazars*, 399–432.

Zuckerman, Constantine. "On the Date of the Khazars' Conversion to Judaism and the Chronology of the Kings of the Rus' Oleg and Igor: A Study of the Anonymous Khazar *Letter* from the Genizah of Cairo." *Revue des Études Byzantines* 53 (1995): 237–70.

Index

Page numbers in italics refer to maps

CPSIA information can be obtained
at www.ICGtesting.com
Printed in the USA
BVHW030135071118
531826BV00001B/9/P

9 780801 442100